The Roug

Italy

written and researched by

**Ros Belford, Martin Dunford, Celia Woolfrey, Rob Andrews,
Jules Brown, Jonathan Buckley and Tim Jepson**

with additional contributions from

Natasha Foges, Joe Fullman, Charles Hebbert, Jeffrey Kennedy,
Katie Parla, Lucy Ratcliffe and Matthew Teller

ROUGH
GUIDES

www.roughguides.com

Contents

Italian food colour
section following p.168

Italian wine colour
section following p.568

Italian football colour
section following p.968

◀◀ Montalcino, Tuscany ◀ Piazza Navona, Rome

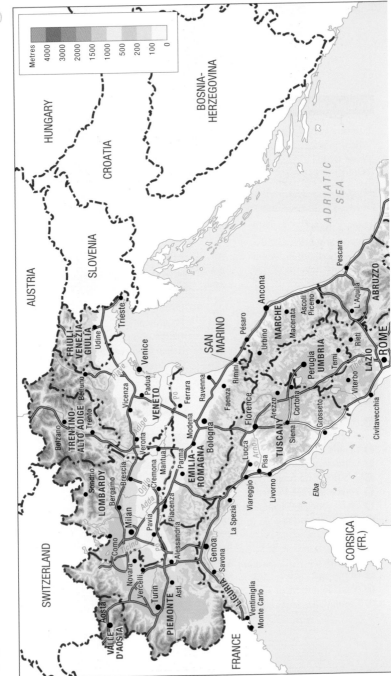

Metres
4000 3000 2000 1500 1000 500 200 100 0

HUNGARY

CROATIA

BOSNIA-
HERZEGOVINA

AUSTRIA

SLOVENIA

ADRIATIC
SEA

Trieste

FRIULI-
VENEZIA-
GIULIA

Udine

Pescara

ABRUZZO

Ancona

MARCHE

Ascoli
Piceno

L'Aquila

Venice

Piave

Pésaro

Urbino

Macerata

Rieti

ROME

Belluno

Vicenza

Padua

SAN
MARINO

Rimini

Perugia

UMBRIA

Terni

LAZIO

TRENTINO-
ALTO ADIGE

Trento

VENETO

Adige

Verona

Ferrara

Po

Ravenna

Faenza

Florence

Arezzo

Cortona

Viterbo

Civitavecchia

Bolzano

Mantua

Modena

Bologna

TUSCANY

Siena

Grosseto

Tevere

Sondrio

Brescia

Parma

Lucca

Arno

Oglio

Cremona

EMILIA-
ROMAGNA

Pisa

LOMBARDY

Bergamo

Piacenza

Viareggio

Livorno

Elba

CORSICA
(FR.)

Como

Milan

Adda

Pavia

Ticino

Po

Alessandria

La Spezia

SWITZERLAND

Novara

Genoa

Vercelli

Savona

Turin

Asti

LIGURIA

Aosta

PIEMONTE

Ventimiglia
Monte Carlo

VALLE
D'AOSTA

FRANCE

4
■

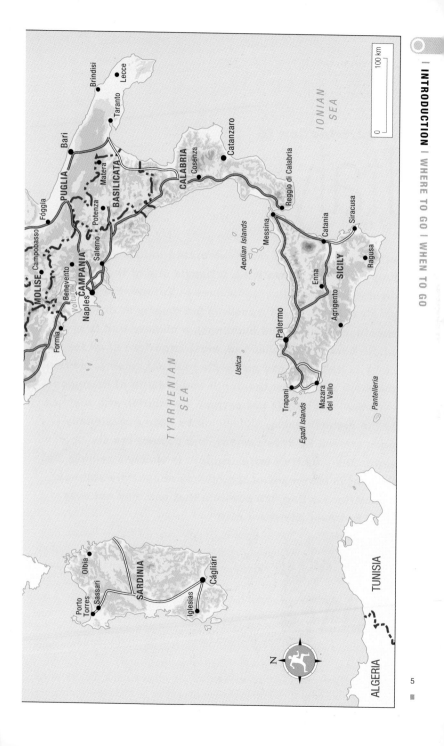

0   100 km

Introduction to
Italy

Arguably the world's most celebrated tourist destination, Italy really does have it all. It boasts one of the most diverse and beautiful landscapes in Europe, the world's greatest hoard of art treasures (on display in fittingly spectacular cities and buildings), a climate that is on the whole benign and mild, and, most important of all for many, a delicious and authentic national cuisine, made all the more alluring by the depth and breadth of its regional variation. Yet Italy is not perfect. Corruption still reaches to the highest levels, historic cities have occasionally been marred by development, and beyond the showpiece sights the country's infrastructure is visibly straining. But the fact is that many of the clichés about Italy still hold true. After visiting, it's possible that you may not ever want to travel anywhere else.

If there is a single national Italian characteristic, it's to embrace life to the full: in the hundreds of local festivals taking place across the country on any given day to celebrate a saint or the local harvest; in the importance placed on good food; in the obsession with clothes and image; and above all in the daily domestic ritual of the collective evening stroll or *passeggiata* – a sociable affair celebrated by young and old alike in every town and village across the country.

Italy only became a unified state in 1861, and, as a result, Italians often feel more loyalty to their region than to the nation as a whole – something manifest in different cuisines, dialects, landscape and often varying standards of living. There is also the country's enormous cultural legacy: Tuscany alone has more classified historical monuments than any country in the world; there are considerable remnants of the Roman Empire all over the country, notably in Rome itself; and every region retains its own relics of an artistic tradition generally acknowledged to be among the world's richest.

Yet there's no reason to be intimidated by all this. If you want to lie on a beach, there are any number of places to do so, from resorts filled with regimented rows of sun beds and umbrellas favoured by the Italians themselves, to secluded and less developed spots in the south. Mountains, too, run the country's length – from the Alps and Dolomites in the north right along

▲ Venetian window

Fact file

• Italy is a peninsula, shaped rather like a boot, jutting out into the Mediterranean Sea. It covers a **surface area** of 301,230 square km and includes the islands of Sardinia and Sicily. The distance from the tip of the country's "toe" to its northern border is about 1380km. Much of the land is mountainous, the **highest point** being Mont Blanc (4748m) in the north.

• Italy's **population** is just under 59 million, with around 4 million living in the capital, Rome. The country is divided geographically and administratively into 15 regions and 5 autonomous regions. The dominant ethnic group is Italian, with small clusters of German-, French- and Slovene-Italians in the north and Albanian- and Greek-Italians in the south. There is also a growing Muslim immigrant community.

• Italy became a **nation state** in 1861, under King Vittorio Emanuele II, and has been a **democratic republic** since 1946, when the monarchy was abolished by popular referendum. The **parliament** consists of two houses, the Senate (315 seats) and the Chamber of Deputies (630 seats); both sit for five-year terms of office and are elected by a system of proportional representation. The **president** is elected for a seven-year term by a joint session of parliament and regional representatives. Real power, however, is in the hands of the **prime minister**, who is generally the leader of the party with the biggest majority in the Chamber of Deputies.

the Apennines, which form the spine of the peninsula. Skiing and other winter sports are practised avidly, and in the national parks, protected from the national passion for hunting, wildlife of all sorts thrives.

Where to go

The north and central parts of the country constitute "discovered" Italy. The regions of **Piemonte** and **Lombardy**, in the northwest, make up the richest and most cosmopolitan part of the country, and the two main centres, Turin and Milan, are its wealthiest cities. In their southern reaches, these regions are flat and scenically dull, especially Lombardy, but in the north the presence of the Alps shapes the character of each: skiing and hiking are prime activities, and the lakes and mountains of Lombardy are time-honoured tourist territory. **Liguria**, the small coastal province to the south, has long been known as the "Italian Riviera" and is accordingly crowded with sun-seeking holiday-makers for much of the summer season. Nonetheless, it's a beautiful stretch of coast, and its capital, Genoa, is a bustling port with a long seafaring tradition.

Much of the most dramatic mountain scenery lies within the smaller northern regions. In the far northwest, the tiny bilingual region of **Valle d'Aosta** is home to some of the country's most frequented ski resorts, and is bordered by the tallest of the Alps – the Matterhorn and Mont Blanc. In the northeast, **Trentino-Alto Adige**, another bilingual region and one in which the national boundary is especially blurred, marks the beginning of the Dolomites mountain range, where Italy's largest national park, the Stelvio, lies amid some of the country's most memorable landscapes.

The Dolomites stretch into the northeastern regions of the **Veneto and Friuli-Venezia Giulia**. However, here the main focus of interest is, of course, Venice; a unique city, and every bit as beautiful as its reputation would suggest (although this means you won't be alone in appreciating it). If the crowds are too much, there's also the arc of historic towns outside the city – Verona, Padua and Vicenza, all centres of interest in their own right, although rather overshadowed by their illustrious neighbour. To the south, the region of **Emilia-Romagna** has been at

Art

Italy's artistic heritage is a huge part of its appeal. **Northern Italy** on the whole has the country's richest crop, but wherever you're travelling, even the smallest country church can boast a masterpiece or two; remote monasteries and small country towns can hold enticing museums; and the big city **galleries** – the Uffizi in Florence, Milan's Brera, too many to mention in Rome – are stacked full of beautiful paintings and sculptures. Like food, you can find different styles – and the work of different artists – in distinct regions. Of the country's ancient art, the most obvious draws are the **Roman mosaics** and murals of Pompeii and Herculaneum, and the earlier funereal sculpture and applied arts of the Etruscans of northern Lazio. Siena was home to some of the earliest **Gothic** stylists of the fourteenth century; Florence bloomed most brightly during the **Renaissance** of the fifteenth century, and Rome's most characteristic style is the later **Baroque** look of the Counter Reformation. Venice, not surprisingly, is the place to see the works of the great **Venetian** painters, Titian and Tintoretto. Your only problem will be having the time to take it all in.

Marina Piccola, Capri

Ice cream

The taste of real Italian ice cream, eaten in Italy, is absolutely unbeatable. **Gelato**, as it's known, is the country's favourite dessert, and there's no

better way to end a day, as lots of Italians do, than with a stroll through the streets sampling a *gelato* while enjoying the cool of the evening. Italian ice cream really is better than any other, and like most Italian food this is down to the local insistence on using whole milk and eggs, and adding only naturally derived flavours.

Everywhere but the tiniest village will have at least one **gelateria**, and many cafés serve ice cream as well. There will usually be at least a dozen flavours to choose from – and often many more – and you can try them either in a cone (*cono*) or tub (*coppa* or *copetta*); you can have as many scoops (*gusti*) as you want – and as many flavours too. If you want to sample the very best, look for the signs saying "*produzione artiganale*", which means that the ice cream is produced according to strictly traditional methods, and "*produzione propria*" or "*nostra produzione*" which basically means it's home-made.

the heart of Italy's postwar industrial boom and has a standard of living on a par with Piemonte and Lombardy, although it's also a traditional stronghold of the Italian Left. Its coast is popular among Italians, and Rimini is about Italy's brashest (and trendiest) seaside resort, with a high reputation on the clubbing scene. You may do better to ignore the beaches altogether, however, and concentrate on the ancient centres of Ravenna, Ferrara, Parma and the regional capital of Bologna, one of Italy's liveliest, most historic but least appreciated cities – and traditionally Italy's gastronomic and academic capital.

Central Italy represents perhaps the most commonly perceived image of the country, and **Tuscany**, with its classic rolling countryside and the art-packed towns of Florence, Pisa and Siena, to name only the three best-known centres, is one of its most visited regions. Neighbouring **Umbria** is similar in all but its tourist numbers, though it gets busier every year, as visitors flock into towns such as Perugia, Spoleto and Assisi. Further east still, the **Marche** has gone the same way, with old stone cottages being turned into foreign-owned holiday homes; the highlights of the region are the ancient towns of Urbino and Ascoli Piceno. South of the Marche, the hills begin to pucker into mountains in the twin regions of **Abruzzo** and **Molise**, one of Italy's remotest areas, centring on one of the country's highest peaks – the Gran Sasso d'Italia. Molise, particularly, is a taster of the south, as is **Lazio** to the west, in part a poor and sometimes desolate region whose often rugged landscapes, particularly south of Rome, contrast with the more manicured beauty of the other central regions. Lazio's real focal point, though, is **Rome**, Italy's capital and the one city in the country that owes allegiance neither to the north or south, its people proudly aloof from the rest of the country's squabbles. Rome is a tremendous city quite unlike any other, and in terms of historical sights outstrips everywhere else in the country by some way.

The south proper begins with the region of **Campania**, to the south of Lazio. Its capital, Naples, is a unique, unforgettable city, the spiritual heart of the Italian south, and close to some of Italy's finest ancient sites in Pompeii and Herculaneum, not to mention the country's most spectacular stretch of coast around Amalfi. **Basilicata** and **Calabria**, which make up the instep and toe of Italy's boot, are harder territory but still rewarding, the emphasis less on art, more on the landscape and quiet, relatively unspoilt coastlines. **Puglia**, the "heel" of Italy, has underrated pleasures, too, notably the landscape of its Gargano peninsula, the souk-like qualities of its capital, Bari, and the Baroque glories of Lecce in the far south, although it too is becoming more known as the years go by. As for **Sicily**, the island is really a place apart, with a wide mixture of attractions ranging from some of the finest preserved Hellenistic treasures in Europe, to a couple of Italy's most appealing beach resorts in Taormina and Cefalù, not to mention some gorgeous upland scenery. Come this far south and you're closer to Africa

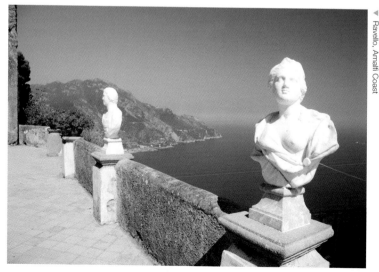

◄ Ravello, Amalfi Coast

Roman Italy: the top 10 sites

Everyone who visits Italy wants to see the sites of **ancient Rome**, and these are easy enough to find – not least in **Rome** itself, where they literally litter the city centre: the **Forum**, the heart of the city during the Republic; the adjacent **Palatine Hill**, where the city's power-brokers lived; the **columns** and **plinths** of forums commemorating various Roman emperors, as well as the iconic bulk of the **Colosseum** could keep you occupied for a couple of days on their own – and, not far from here, the Baths of Caracalla, Domus Aurea and the ruins of Via Appia Antica, for a couple of days more. A short trip outside the city, the ruins of **Ostia**, Rome's former port, are strikingly well maintained, while to the south, the ruined towns of **Pompeii** and **Herculaneum**, simultaneously destroyed and preserved by the eruption of Vesuvius in 79 AD, are remarkable.

In the north of the country, Verona's **amphitheatre** continues to serve its purpose, hosting opera performances during the summer. Several other amphitheatres around the country are in various states of repair, while a number of triumphal **arches** – in Aosta, Rimini and Benevento – testify to the emperors' warlike activities all over the peninsula.

- Colosseum, Rome
- Ostia Antica, Lazio
- Pompeii and Herculaneum, Campania
- Arch of Trajan, Benevento
- Amphitheatre, Verona
- Villa Adriana, Tivoli
- Saepinium, Abruzzo
- Cumae, Campania
- Arch of Augustus and Bridge of Tiberius, Rimini
- Piazza Armerina, Sicily

than Milan, and it shows – in the climate, the architecture and the cooking, with couscous featuring on many menus in the west of the island. **Sardinia**, too, feels far removed from the Italian mainland, especially in its relatively undiscovered interior, although you may be content to explore its fine beaches, which are among Italy's best.

When to go

taly's **climate** is one of the most hospitable in the world, with a general pattern of warm, dry summers and mild winters. There are, however, marked regional variations, ranging from the more temperate northern part of the country to the firmly Mediterranean south. Summers are hot and dry along the coastal areas, especially as you move south, cool in the major mountain areas – the Alps and Apennines. Winters are mild in the south of the country, Rome and below, but in the north they can be at least as cold as anywhere in the northern hemisphere, sometimes worse, especially across the plains of Lombardy and Emilia-Romagna, which can be very inhospitable indeed in January.

As for **when to go**, if you're planning to visit fairly popular areas, especially beach resorts, avoid July and August, when the weather can be too hot and the crowds at their most congested. The first two weeks of August are when the Italians go on holiday, so expect the crush to be especially bad in the resorts and the scene in the major historic cities – Rome, Florence, Venice

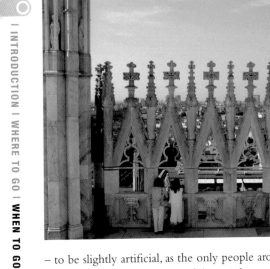

▼ Roof of Milan's Duomo

– to be slightly artificial, as the only people around are fellow tourists. The nicest time to visit, in terms of the weather and lack of crowds, is April to late June, or September and October. If you're planning to swim, however, bear in mind that only the south of the country may be warm enough outside the May to September period.

Average daily temperatures and rainfall

	Jan	Feb	Mar	Apr	May	Jun	Jul	Aug	Sep	Oct	Nov	Dec
Florence												
°C (max/min)	11/3	13/3	16/6	18/8	24/12	27/17	32/18	32/19	27/15	21/12	15/7	11/4
°F (max/min)	52/37	55/39	61/42	66/47	76/55	84/61	88/66	88/67	80/59	70/55	59/43	52/37
rainfall (mm)	51	55	74	78	76	72	44	48	82	102	80	76
Milan												
°C (max/min)	7/-3	9/-2	14/2	17/5	23/10	27/14	28/17	28/17	23/12	18/7	12/2	3/-2
°F (max/min)	45/27	48/28	57/36	63/41	73/50	81/57	82/63	82/63	73/54	64/45	54/36	37/28
rainfall (mm)	63	62	78	78	85	65	67	86	74	98	96	96
Rome												
°C (max/min)	13/4	14/4	16/6	18/8	24/13	27/16	28/18	29/18	26/17	23/13	18/8	13/5
°F (max/min)	55/39	57/39	61/42	64/46	75/55	81/61	83/64	84/64	78/63	74/55	64/46	55/41
rainfall (mm)	103	98	68	65	48	34	23	33	68	94	128	110
Venice												
°C (max/min)	7/0	8/1	13/4	17/8	23/12	25/17	27/18	27/18	24/14	17/11	12/5	7/2
°F (max/min)	45/32	46/34	55/39	63/46	73/54	77/63	81/64	81/64	75/57	63/52	54/41	45/36
rainfall (mm)	62	58	56	64	69	76	63	83	66	69	85	54

things not to miss

It's not possible to see everything that Italy has to offer in one trip – and we don't suggest you try. What follows is a selective taste, in no particular order, of the country's highlights: outstanding buildings and ancient sites, spectacular natural wonders, great food and colourful festivals. They're arranged in five colour-coded categories, which you can browse through to find the very best things to see and experience. All entries have a page reference to take you straight into the guide, where you can find out more.

01 **Sardinia's beaches** Page **987** • There are plenty of places to sun-worship in Italy, but Sardinia's coastline ranks among one of the most memorable.

02 **Matera** Page **887** • A truly unique city, sliced by a ravine containing thousands of *Sassi* – cave dwellings gouged out of the rock that were inhabited till the 1950s.

03 **Ravenna's mosaics** Page **427** • Ravenna's Byzantine mosaics – in the churches Sant'Apollinare Nuovo and San Vitale – are a stunning testimony to the city's ranking as the capital of Europe fifteen hundred years ago.

04 **Food in Emilia-Romagna** Page **391** • This region is known as Italy's gastronomic heart, home to Parma ham, parmesan cheese and balsamic vinegar all on view at Bologna's marvellous indoor food market.

05 Pompeii and Herculaneum Page 802 •

Probably the two best-preserved Roman sites in the country, destroyed and at the same time preserved by the eruption of Vesuvius in AD 79.

06 Duomo, Florence Page 456

• Florence's cathedral dome is one of the most instantly recognizable images in the world – and one of its most significant engineering feats.

07 Aeolian Islands Page 933 •

These volcanic islands off the north coast of Sicily are a relatively undiscovered gem.

09 The Italian Lakes Page **192** • If you can escape the hordes this region is probably Italy's most beguiling with stunning scenery and plenty of activities from windsurfing to walking.

08 Vatican Museums, Rome Page **706** • Put simply, this is the largest and richest collection of art and culture in the world. You'd be mad to miss it.

10 Urbino Page **613** • This so-called "ideal city" and art capital, created by Federico da Montefeltro, the ultimate Renaissance man, attracts people from miles around.

11 The Uffizi, Florence Page **460** • Italy's greatest collection of art, and – in a city not exactly short on things to see – perhaps the most essential attraction of them all.

13 Giotto's frescoes, Padua Page **328** • Giotto's frescoes in Padua's Cappella degli Scrovegni constitute one of the great works of European art.

12 Parco Nazionale d'Abruzzo Page **758** • Italy's third-largest national park, and probably its wildest, with marvellous walking and wildlife.

14 Elba Page **500** • This easily accessible, mountainous Tuscan island offers great beaches and fantastic hiking.

15 **Pizza in Naples** Page **773** ● You can eat pizza all over Italy, but nowhere is it quite as good as in its home town of Naples, served sizzling-hot straight from a wood-fired oven.

16 **Carnevale** Page **324** ● Venice's famous carnival is worth seeing for its costumes and crowds. But it's rather an exclusive affair, and events around the rest of the country – most notably in Verona or Viareggio, on the Tuscan coast – are more authentic and definitely more fun.

17 **Centro storico, Rome** Page **673** ● There's so much to see in Rome that aimlessly wandering the city's fantastic old centre can turn up a surprise at every turn – whether it's an ancient statue, a marvellous Baroque fountain or a bustling piazza.

18 **Mantua** Page **188** ● The Mantegna frescoes of Mantua's Palazzo Ducale, and the works of Guilio Romano in its Palazzo Te, make a visit to this ancient and alluring Lombard city hard to resist.

19 **Hiking in the Dolomites** Page **232** • The spiky landscape of the Dolomites is perfect hiking country and is covered in dramatic long-distance trails.

20 **Duomo, Orvieto** Page **605** • One of the country's finest – and best-sited – cathedrals, with a marvellous fresco cycle by Luca Signorelli.

21 **Tuscan hill-towns** Page **526** • The classic profile of a Tuscan hill-town is what many people think of when they think of Italy. Montepulciano, Montalcino and San Gimigniano, in particular, are some of the most beautiful.

22 Shopping Page **176** • Italy's a great place to flash the cash, and where better than in fashion's commercial home, Milan.

23 Duomo, Milan Page **161** • The world's largest and perhaps most attention-grabbing Gothic cathedral.

24 Basilica di San Francesco, Assisi Page **578** • The burial place of St Francis and one of Italy's greatest church buildings, with frescoes by Giotto, Simone Martini and others.

25 Lecce Page **972** • This exuberant city of Baroque architecture and opulent churches is one of the must-sees of the Italian south.

27 Siena Palio Page **514** • Perhaps the most fanatically followed and most violent horserace in the world – an amazing spectacle and a true slice of Sienese life.

26 The Last Supper, Milan Page **170** • Leonardo da Vinci's mural for the refectory wall of the Santa Maria delle Grazie is one of the world's most resonant images.

28 Cinque Terre Page **136** • These five fishing villages are shoehorned picturesquely into one of the most rugged parts of Liguria's coastline and linked by a highly scenic coastal walking path.

29 Staying in an agriturismo Page **41** • Farmstays and rural retreats are one of Italy's lesser-known specialities and can be among the country's most spectacular and bucolic places to stay.

30 Piazza San Marco Page **289** • Crowded or not, this is one of Europe's grandest urban spaces and home to Italy's most exotic cathedral.

31 Wine bars Page **44** • There's nothing like tasting the local wine in an enoteca (wine bar) accompanied with a plate of regional cheese and cold meats.

32 Amalfi Coast Page **823** • The views on the road that snakes along the Amalfi Coast, connecting the resorts of Positano, Amalfi and Ravello, can hardly be bettered anywhere in the world.

33 Sicily's Greek ruins Page **953** • The ancient theatres at Siracusa and Taormina are magnificent summer stages for Greek drama, while the temple complex at nearby Agrigento is one of the finest such sites outside Greece itself.

Basics

Basics

Getting there

BASICS | Getting there

The easiest way to get to Italy from the UK and Ireland is to fly. The majority of flights go to Milan and Rome, but many other cities and holiday destinations are served by scheduled flights and low-cost carriers alike. From the US and Canada there are direct flights to Milan and Rome, although you could consider flying via London or another European hub and picking up a cheap onward flight from there. There are no direct flights to Italy from Australia or New Zealand, but plenty of airlines fly to Milan and Rome via Asian or European cities.

Flights from the UK and Ireland

Of the scheduled **airlines** flying the Italian routes, British Airways (BA) and Alitalia regularly serve most of the country including Turin, Milan, Rome, Bologna, Cagliari, Bari, Pisa, Verona, Venice, Naples and Catania. The majority of the routes are from London but they also fly from Edinburgh, Manchester, Birmingham and Bristol. Aer Lingus has direct flights from Dublin to Milan, Bologna, Rome and Naples as well as Cork and Belfast to Rome. Of the **low-cost carriers**, easyJet and Ryanair fly from London and numerous smaller airports to bases throughout Italy and its islands.

Prices depend on how far in advance you book and the popularity of the destination, although season is also a factor: a ticket to anywhere between June and August will cost more than in the depths of winter (excluding Christmas and New Year). Note also that it is generally more expensive to fly at weekends. Book far enough in advance with one of the low-cost airlines and you can pick up a ticket for under £100 return, even in summer; book anything less than three weeks in advance and this could triple in price. Scheduled airline fares, booked within a month of travel, will cost around £120 out of season, and £250 in summer.

Flights from the US and Canada

Delta fly the widest choice of direct **routes** between the and Italy, with daily flights from New York, Atlanta, Chicago, Boston and Miami to Rome and Milan. American Airlines fly direct from Chicago and LA to Milan; Air One has also added several routes to its service in recent years including Baltimore and Dallas. In addition, many European carriers fly to Italy (via their capitals) from all major US and Canadian cities – for example British Airways (via London), Lufthansa (via Frankfurt), KLM (via Amsterdam), and so on.

The **direct scheduled fares** charged by each airline don't vary as much as you might think, and you'll more often than not be basing your choice around things like flight timings, routes and gateway cities, ticket restrictions, and even the airline's reputation for comfort and service. The cheapest **round-trip fares** to Rome or Milan, travelling midweek in low season, start at around US$700 from New York or Boston, rising to around US$1000 during the summer. Add another US$100–200 for flights from LA, Miami and Chicago. Note that these prices do not include taxes.

Air Canada has **direct** flights from Toronto to Rome for a low-season fare of Can$700 midweek, increasing to around Can$1000 in high season without taxes.

Flights from Australia and New Zealand

Return fares to Rome and Milan from the main cities in Australia go for A$1500–1850 in low season, and around A$2000 in high season. You are likely to get most flexibility by travelling with Malaysian, Thai, British Airways or Qantas, which offer a range of **discounted** Italian tour packages and air passes, although you can sometimes find cheaper offers with Garuda and Sri Lanka Airlines. There are no direct flights to Italy from New Zealand. Return fares to Rome from New

Six steps to a better kind of travel

At Rough Guides we are passionately committed to travel. We feel strongly that only through travelling do we truly come to understand the world we live in and the people we share it with – plus tourism has brought a great deal of benefit to developing economies around the world over the last few decades. But the extraordinary growth in tourism has also damaged some places irreparably, and of course climate change is exacerbated by most forms of transport, especially flying. This means that now more than ever it's important to travel thoughtfully and responsibly, with respect for the cultures you're visiting – not only to derive the most benefit from your trip but also in order to preserve the best bits of the planet for everyone to enjoy. At Rough Guides we feel there are six main areas in which you can make a difference:

• Consider what you're contributing to the local economy, and indeed how much the services you use do the same, whether it's through employing local workers and guides or sourcing locally grown produce and local services.

• Consider the environment on holiday as well as at home. Water is scarce in many developing destinations, and the biodiversity of local flora and fauna can be adversely affected by tourism. Patronise businesses that take account of this rather than those that trash the local environment for short-term gain.

• Give thought to how often you fly and what you can do to redress any harm that your trips create. Reduce the amount you travel by air; avoid short hops by air and more harmful night flights.

• Consider alternatives to flying, travelling instead by bus, train, boat and even by bike or on foot where possible. Take time to enjoy the journey itself as well as your final destination.

• Think about making all the trips you take "climate neutral" via a reputable carbon offset scheme. All Rough Guide flights are offset, and every year we donate money to a variety of charities devoted to combating the effects of climate change.

• Travel with a purpose, not just to tick off experiences. Consider spending longer in a place, and really getting to know it and its people – you'll find it much more rewarding than dashing from place to place.

Zealand cost from NZ$2500 depending on the season. Air New Zealand often has the best deals but KLM, British Airways, Qantas, JAL, Emirates, Malaysian and Thai can all be competitive if bought in advance.

Online booking, airlines and operators

Online booking

ⓦ www.expedia.com Discount airfares, all-airline search engine and daily deals.
ⓦ www.kayak.com Award-winning travel search engine with a clear easy-to-use format.
ⓦ www.lastminute.com Offers good last-minute holiday-package and flight-only deals.
ⓦ www.opodo.co.uk Reliable source of low airfares from the UK, run by nine major European airlines.
ⓦ www.orbitz.com Comprehensive North American web travel source, with the usual flight, car-rental and hotel deals, as well as excellent follow-up customer service.

ⓦ www.travelocity.com Destination guides plus best deals for car rental, accommodation and air fares.

Airlines

Aer Lingus UK ☏ 0870/876 5000, Ireland ☏ 0818/365 000; ⓦ www.aerlingus.com.
Air Canada ☏ 1-888/247-2262, UK ☏ 0871/220 1111, Ireland ☏ 01/679 3958, Australia ☏ 1300/655 767, NZ ☏ 0508/747 767; ⓦ www.aircanada.com.
Air New Zealand Australia ☏ 13 24 76, NZ ☏ 0800/737 000; ⓦ www.airnz.co.nz.
Air One Outside Italy ☏ 39 0648.88.0069, US ☏ 1-888/9-FLY-AIR1; ⓦ www.flyairone.it.
Alitalia US ☏ 1-800/223-5730, Canada ☏ 1-800/361-8336, UK ☏ 0870/544 8259, Ireland ☏ 01/677 5171, NZ ☏ 09/308 3357, South Africa ☏ 11/721 4500; ⓦ www.alitalia.com.
American Airlines ☏ 1-800/433-7300, UK ☏ 0845/7789 789, Ireland ☏ 01/602 0550, Australia ☏ 1300/650 747, NZ ☏ 0800/887 997; ⓦ www.aa.com.

British Airways UK ☎0844/493 0777, Ireland ☎1890/626 747, US ☎1-800/247-9297, Australia ☎1300/767 177, NZ ☎09/966 9777; ⓦwww.ba.com.

Delta US & Canada ☎1-800/231-0856, Australia ☎1300/302 849, NZ ☎011/649 977 2232; ⓦwww.delta.com.

easyJet UK ☎0905/821 0905, Ireland ☎0870/600 0000; ⓦwww.easyjet.com.

Garuda Indonesia US ☎1-212/279-0756, UK ☎020/7467 8600, Australia ☎1300/365 330 or 02/9334 9944, NZ ☎09/366 1862; ⓦwww.garuda-indonesia.com.

JAL (Japan Air Lines) US & Canada ☎1-800/525-3663, UK ☎0845/774 7700, Ireland ☎01/408 3757, Australia ☎1300/525 287, NZ ☎09/379 9906, South Africa ☎11/883 2178; ⓦwww.jal.com or www.japanair.com.

KLM (Royal Dutch Airlines) Northwest/KLM. US & Canada ☎1-800/225-2525, UK ☎0870/507 4074, Ireland ☎1850/747 400, Australia ☎1300/303 747, NZ ☎09/309 1782, South Africa ☎11/961 6727; ⓦwww.klm.com or www.nwa.com.

Lufthansa US ☎1-800/645-3880, Canada ☎1-800/563-5954, UK ☎0871/945 9747, Ireland ☎01/844 5544, Australia ☎1300/655 727, NZ ☎09/303 1529, South Africa ☎0861/842 538; ⓦwww.lufthansa.com.

Malaysia Airlines US ☎1-800/5529-264, UK ☎0870/607 9090, Ireland ☎01/6761 561, Australia ☎13 26 27, NZ ☎09/373 2741, South Africa ☎11/880 9614; ⓦwww.malaysia-airlines.com.

Qantas Airways US & Canada ☎1-800/227-4500, UK ☎0845/774 7767, Ireland ☎01/407 3278, Australia ☎13 13 13, NZ ☎0800/808 767 or 09/357 8900, South Africa ☎11/441 8550; ⓦwww.qantas.com.

Ryanair UK ☎0906/270 5656 (25p per min), Ireland ☎1530/787 787 (33c per min); ⓦwww.ryanair.com.

SriLankan Airlines US ☎1-877/915-2652, Canada ☎1-416/227-9000, UK ☎020/8538 2001, Ireland ☎1/241 8000, Australia ☎02/9244 2234, NZ ☎09/308 3353, South Africa ☎11/289 8000; ⓦwww.srilankan.aero.

Thai Airways US ☎1-212/949-8424, UK ☎0870/606 0911, Australia ☎1300/651 960, NZ ☎09/377 3886, South Africa ☎11/455 1018; ⓦwww.thaiair.com.

Trains

Travelling by **train** to Italy from the UK can be an enjoyable and environmentally friendly way of getting to the country, and you can stop off in other parts of Europe on the way. Most trains pass through Paris

and head down through France towards Milan. A standard-class return ticket from London to Milan using Eurostar for the London–Paris leg (2hr 15min) and then travelling by high-speed TGV from Paris to Milan (7hr 25min) costs from £103, but you must buy the tickets well in advance to get the best fares.

There are also two **sleeper trains** from Paris to Italy, operated by Artesia (see p.30). The "Palatino" sleeper (14hr 50min) runs from Paris to Rome via Piacenza, Parma, Bologna and Florence while the slightly faster "Stendhal" (13hr 50min) goes to Venice via Milan, Brescia, Verona, Vicenza and Padua. Each service leaves Paris in the early evening and arrives in central Rome or Venice the following morning around 9.45am. Accommodation is in four- and six-berth couchettes, and one-, two- and three-berth cabins – the more you pay, the fewer people you share with; women can opt to share with other women if they are travelling alone. Both services have a restaurant car and a steward who looks after each carriage.

Fares from Paris to both Rome and Venice start at £30 one-way, £60 return per person in a six-berth couchette, to which you should add the Eurostar fare from London to Paris, which starts at £59 per person standard class return. Advance booking is essential (and can often save you quite a lot of money); there are also discounts for children and railpass holders. Take into account also that if you travel via Paris on Eurostar you will have to change stations, so you should give yourself a good hour (more like 90min if you have to queue for metro tickets) to travel on the metro from the Gare du Nord to the Gare de Lyon (for daytime services) or the Gare de Bercy (for sleeper trains). Allow more time for the return journey across Paris, as there is a minimum thirty minute check-in for Eurostar departures. Note, there are no left-luggage lockers at Gare de Bercy.

Details on all international rail tickets and passes can be obtained by calling personally at major train stations, or from the Rail Europe Travel Centre in London's Regent Street. You can also contact the agents listed on p.30 and make ticket purchases online. A good place for timetabling information is the European rail website ⓦwww.seat61.com.

Rail passes include **InterRail** and **Eurail** which offer unlimited rail travel throughout Italy and other chosen countries, but must be bought before leaving home. See "Getting around" for details of all rail passes available, including those for use solely on the Italian rail network.

Rail contacts

Artesia ⓦ www.artesia.eu.
Eurail ⓦ www.eurail.com.
European Rail UK ☏ 020/7619 1083, ⓦ www.europeanrail.com.
Europrail International Canada ☏ 1-888/667-9734, ⓦ www.europrail.net.
Eurostar UK ☏ 0870/518 6186, ⓦ www.eurostar.com.
International Rail ☏ 0870/084 1410, ⓦ www.international-rail.com.
InterRail ⓦ www.interrailnet.com.
Rail Europe UK ☏ 0844/848 4070, ⓦ www.raileurope.co.uk; US ☏ 1-800/622-8600, Canada ☏ 1-800/361-RAIL; ⓦ www.raileurope.com/us.
Rail Plus Australia ☏ 1300/555 003 or 03/9642 8644, ⓦ www.railplus.com.au.
The Man in Seat 61 ⓦ www.seat61.com.
Trainseurope ☏ 0900/195 0101, ⓦ www.trainseurope.co.uk.

Buses

It's difficult to see why anyone would want to travel to Italy by **bus**, unless they had a phobia of flying – and of trains. National Express Eurolines (☏ 0870/580 8080, ⓦ www.nationalexpress.com/eurolines) do, however, have occasional bargain offers, and regular tickets are in any case cheap – £69 to Milan or Rome if booked a week in advance, £98 for a fully refundable and flexible ticket. The Milan service departs four times a week and takes around 20 hours; Rome adds a gruelling 10 hours to the trip.

Packages and organized tour operators

There's no shortage of **travel-plus-accommodation** deals on the market to Italy, and if you're keen to stay in one (or two) places, they can work out to be very good value. An increasing number of operators organize **specialist holidays** to Italy. These set up walking tours, art and archeology holidays, Italian food and wine jaunts, short breaks to coincide with opera festivals or even football matches; there's also a plethora of operators selling **short-break deals** to Italian cities. Finally, if you want to rent a car in Italy, it's well worth checking with tour operators (and flight agents) before you leave, as some **fly-drive** deals work out very cheaply.

Specialist tours

Abercromie and Kent UK ☏ 0845/0700 600, ⓦ www.abercromiekent.co.uk. Luxury cultural holidays.
Adventure Travel Company NZ ☏ 09/355 9135, ⓦ www.adventuretravel.co.nz. Hotels and car rental, plus walking and cycling tours in the Italian Lakes.
Alternative Travel Group UK ☏ 01865/315 678, ⓦ www.atg-oxford.co.uk. Walking and cycling holidays.
Backroads US ☏ 1-800/462-2848 or 510/527-1555, ⓦ www.backroads.com. Cooking, cycling and hiking holidays, including trips suitable for families.
Central Holidays US ☏ 1-800/539-7098, ⓦ www.centralholidays.com. Wide range of independent and escorted tours plus city breaks, including a five-day fly-drive trip to the main lakes.
CIT US & Canada ☏ 1-800/387-0711, ⓦ www.cittours-canada.com. Well-organized coach and rail tours, plus advice for independent travellers on hotels and car rental.

Martin Randall Travel UK ☎020/8742 3355, ⓦwww.martinrandall.com. Cultural tours focusing on art, architecture, music, archeology, gastronomy and history.

Mountain Travel–Sobek US ☎1-888/831-7526, ⓦwww.mtsobek.com. Hiking and special interest tours around Italy.

Walkabout Gourmet Adventures Australia ☎02/9871 5526, ⓦwww.walkaboutgourmet.com. Classy food, wine and walking tours throughout the country.

Getting around

Italy is a big country with huge regional differences and unless you opt for a one-base holiday you will probably find yourself travelling around a fair bit. Naturally, you'll have most flexibility with your own transport, allowing you to journey at your own pace and to out-of-the-way places. Roads are good in most of the country with excellent autostrada links between cities, although these often come with heavy traffic and tolls. Off the main routes, most roads are quiet and well maintained, making cycling a very pleasant – and very popular – means of getting around.

In terms of **public transport**, the easiest way of travelling around Italy is by **train**. The Italian train system is one of the least expensive in Europe, reasonably comprehensive, and, in the north of the country at least, pretty efficient. It's also far preferable over long distances to the fragmented, localized and sometimes grindingly slow **bus** service. Local buses, though, can be very efficient, and where it's actually a better idea to take a bus, we've made this clear in the text.

Internal flights are coming down in price and there are some good deals to be had on flights to the islands. **Ferries** go to all the Italian islands, and also ply routes to Greece, Albania, Croatia, Malta, Yugoslavia, Corsica and Tunisia.

We've detailed train, bus and ferry frequencies in the "Travel details" sections at the end of each chapter of the Guide; note that these refer to regular working-day schedules (Mon–Sat); services can be much reduced or even non-existent on Sundays.

By train

Italian trains are run by Ferrovie dello Stato (FS), under the brand name **Trenitalia** (☎89.20.21, ⓦwww.trenitalia.com), operating

Timetable reading

On timetables — and parking signs too — *lavorativo* or *feriale* is the word for the Monday to Saturday service, represented by two crossed hammers; and *festivo* means that a train runs only on Sundays and holidays, symbolized by a Christian cross. Some other common terms on timetables are:

escluso sabato – not including Saturdays
si effettua fino all' ... – running until
si effettua dal ... – starting from
giornalmente – daily
prenotazione obbligatoria – reservation obligatory
estivo – summer
invernale – winter

Stamp it

All stations have yellow validating machines in which passengers must stamp their ticket before embarking on their journey. Look out for them as you come onto the platform: if you fail to **validate your ticket** you'll be given a hefty on-the-spot fine.

a comprehensive network across the country with numerous types of trains. The **Eurostar Italia** (ES) runs between major cities, slightly faster and usually with newer rolling stock than the **Intercity** (IC) options. **Eurocity** (EC) and **Euronight** (EN) trains connect the major Italian cities with centres such as Paris, Vienna, Hamburg and Barcelona. Milan and Turin and Naples and Rome have recently been linked by a new high-speed service, the **Eurostar Alta Velocità**, which will eventually connect the north with the south of the country in record time. Reservations are usually required before you board the train for all of these services.

Diretto and **Interregionale** trains are the common-or-garden long-distance expresses, calling only at larger stations. Although reservations are not required for these trains, it's worth **reserving** seats if you're making a long journey, especially in summer, when they can get very crowded. Reservations can be made at any major train station or travel agent in Italy or via Italian State Railways agents (see p.30). Lastly, there are the **Regionale** services, which stop at every place with a population higher than zero.

In addition to the routes operated by FS, there are a number of **privately run** lines, using separate stations though charging similar fares. Where they're worth using, these are detailed in the text.

Timetables and fares

Timings and route information are posted up at train stations, and we give a rough idea of frequencies and journey times in the "Travel details" sections at the end of each chapter. If you're travelling extensively it would be worth investing in a copy of the twice-yearly *In Treno In Tutt'Italia* timetable (€4.50), which covers the main routes and is sold at train-station newspaper stands.

Fares are inexpensive; they are calculated by the kilometre and easy to work out for each journey. The timetables give the prices per kilometre but as a rough guide, a second-class one-way fare for the four-hour trip from Rome to Milan currently costs about €47 by Eurostar. **Sleepers** (*cuccetta*) are available on many long-distance services, and prices vary according to the length of journey and whether or not you're sharing. **Children** aged 4–12 pay half price; under 4s (not occupying a seat) travel free. Return tickets are valid within two months of the outward journey, but as two one-way tickets cost the same it's hardly worth bothering.

Rail passes and discount cards

A **rail pass** is only really worth considering if you plan to travel extensively around Italy or are visiting the country as part of a wider tour of Europe. A **Trenitalia** pass or an Italy-only InterRail pass might be worth your while if you are planning to cover a lot of Italian ground. Otherwise the Europe-wide **InterRail** passes are available to European citizens for travelling around a combination of countries in Europe; and for non-EU citizens, **Eurail** passes give unlimited travel in Europe including the Trenitalia network. With any of these passes, children from 4 to 12 years old are eligible for a 50 percent discount, youth (under-26) and group tickets are available and you'll be liable for supplements of €12 per journey on the faster trains.

Trenitalia pass

Trenitalia passes (Ⓦ www.trenitalia.it) are for non-residents In Italy and can be bought for first- or second-class travel from four to ten days in a two-month period. A second-class four-day ticket costs £174, a ten-day pass £282. It also entitles the holder to discounts on some international ferries.

InterRail pass

InterRail passes (Ⓦ www.interrail.net) are only available to those who have been resident In Europe for six months or more and are not valid in the country of residence. They come in first- and second-class over-26 and (cheaper) under-26 versions. The passes are available to a combination of countries for 5 days within a ten day period (€249 second class, €159 under-26), 10 days within a 22-day period (€359 second class, €239 under-26), 22 days consecutively (€469 second class, €309 under-26) or one month (€599 second class, €399 under-26). Italy-only passes are also available for 3 (€109 second class, €71 under-26), 4 (€139 second class, €90 under-26), 6 (€189 second class, €123 under-26) or 9 (€229 second class, €149 under-26) days.

InterRail passes do not include travel between Britain and the Continent, although InterRail passholders are eligible for discounts on rail travel in Britain and Northern Ireland and cross-Channel ferries and free travel on the Bríndisi–Patras ferry between Italy and Greece and the Villa San Giovanni Messina crossing to Sicily.

Eurail passes

A **Eurail Pass** (ⓦwww.eurail.com) is for non-European residents and comes in a variety of forms: Italy only, Italy with France, Greece or Spain, Italy with boarding countries or with 20 other European countries. The pass, which must be purchased before arrival in Europe, allows unlimited free first-class train travel in combinations from 10 days to 3 months. A one-month over-26 pass costs €810 (under-26 €527). There are numerous small-group, youth and saver versions and passes can be purchased online or from the agents listed on p.30 under "Rail contacts".

By bus

Trains don't go everywhere and sooner or later you'll probably have to use **regional buses** (*autobus*). Nearly all places are connected by some kind of bus service, but

in out-of-the-way towns and villages schedules can be sketchy and are drastically reduced – sometimes non-existent – at weekends, especially on Sundays. Bear in mind also that in rural areas schedules are often designed with the working and/or school day in mind – meaning a frighteningly early start if you want to catch that day's one bus out of town, and occasionally a complete absence of services during school holidays.

There's no national **bus company**, though a few regional ones do operate beyond their own immediate area. **Bus terminals** are often conveniently located next to the train station; wherever possible we've detailed their whereabouts in the text, but if you're not sure ask for directions to the *autostazione*. In smaller towns and villages, most buses pull in at the central piazza. **Timetables** are worth picking up from the local company's office, bus stations or on the bus. Buy **tickets** immediately before you travel from the bus station ticket office, or on the bus itself; on longer hauls you can try to buy them in advance direct from the bus company, but seat reservations are not normally possible. If you want to get off, ask *posso scendere?*; "the next stop" is *la prossima fermata*.

City buses are always cheap, usually costing a flat fare of around €1. **Tickets** are available from a variety of sources, commonly newsagents and tobacconists, but also from anywhere displaying a sticker saying tickets or *biglietti* including many campsite shops and hotel front desks. Once on board, you must register your ticket in the machine at the front or back of the bus. The whole system is based on trust, though in most cities checks for fare-dodging are regularly made, and hefty spot-fines are levied against offenders. A useful site is ⓦwww.busstation.net/main/busita.htm, which has links to websites of hundreds of Italian bus companies.

Walk/don't walk

It's worth bearing in mind that cars do not automatically stop at **pedestrian crossings** in Italy. Even on crossings with traffic lights you can be subjected to some close calls. Even when there's a green light for pedestrians to go, it will probably be green for one of the lines of traffic too.

By car

Travelling **by car** in Italy is relatively painless, though cities and their ring roads can be hard work. The roads are good, the autostrada (motorway) network very comprehensive, and the notorious Italian drivers rather less erratic than their reputation suggests. The best plan is to avoid driving in cities as much as possible; the congestion, proliferation of complex one-way systems and confusing signage can make it a nightmare.

Bear in mind that the **traffic** can be heavy on main roads (particularly over public holiday weekends and the first and last weekends of Aug) and appalling in city centres. Rush hour during the week usually runs from 7.30am to 9am and from 5pm to 9pm when roads in and around the major cities can be gridlocked.

Although Italians are by no means the world's worst drivers they don't win any **safety** prizes either. The secret is to make it very clear what you're going to do – and then do it. A particular danger for unaccustomed drivers is the large number of scooters that can appear suddenly from the blind spot or dash across junctions and red lights with alarming recklessness.

Most **petrol stations** give you the choice of self-service (*Fai da te*) or, for a few centesimi more per litre, someone will fill the tank and usually wipe down the windscreen while they're at it. Petrol stations often have the same working hours as shops, which means they'll be closed for a couple of hours at noon, shut up shop at around 7pm and are likely to be closed on Sundays. Outside these times many have a self-service facility payable into a machine between the pumps by bank note or, more rarely, credit card; these are often not well advertised so you might need to go onto the forecourt to check.

Rules of the road

Rules of the road are straightforward: drive on the right; at junctions, where there's any ambiguity, give precedence to vehicles coming from the right; observe the speed limits – 50kph in built-up areas, 110kph on dual carriage-ways and 130kph on autostradas (for camper vans, these limits are 50kph, 80kph and 100kph respectively);

and don't drink and drive. Drivers need to have their dipped headlights on while using any road outside a built-up area.

As regards **documentation**, if you're bringing your own car, as well as current insurance, you need a valid driving licence and an international driving permit if you're a non-EU licence holder. If you hold a UK pre-1991 driving licence you'll need an international driving permit or to update your licence to a photocard version. It's compulsory to carry your car documents and passport while you're driving, and you can be fined on the spot if you cannot present them when stopped by the police – not an uncommon occurrence. It's also obligatory to carry a warning triangle and a fluorescent jacket in case of breakdown. For more information consult ⓦ www.theaa.com.

Motorway driving

All **motorways** (autostrade) are toll-roads. Take a ticket as you come on and pay on exit; the amount due is flashed up on a screen in front of you. Paying by cash is the most straightforward option – booths are marked "cash/*contanti*" and colour-coded white. To pay by credit card follow the "*Viacard*" sign (colour-coded blue). Avoid the *Telepass* lane (colour-coded yellow), which is for drivers holding post-paid electronic cards. Be alert as you get into lane as traffic zigzags in and out at high speed to get pole position at the shortest-looking queue. Rates aren't especially high but they can mount up on a long journey. Since other roads can be frustratingly slow, tolls are well worth it over long distances but be prepared for queues at exits at peak times.

Parking

Parking can be a problem. Don't be surprised to see cars parked just about anywhere, notably on pavements, seemingly working tram lines and bus stops – it would be unwise to follow suit. Parking attendants are especially active in tourist areas and if you get fed up with driving around and settle for a space in a *zona di rimozione* (tow-away zone), don't expect your car to be there when you get back.

Most towns and villages have pay-and-display areas just outside the centre, but they can get very full during high season. An increasing number of towns operate a colour-coded parking scheme: **blue-zone** parking spaces (delineated by a blue line) usually have a maximum stay of one or two hours; they cost around €0.70–1.50 per hour (pay at meters, to attendants wearing authorizing badges or buy scratch-cards from local tobacconists) but are sometimes free after 8pm and on Sundays. Much coveted **white-zone** spaces (white lines) are free; **yellow-zone** areas (yellow lines) are reserved for residents. Note that walled towns that exclude cars often allow tourists to drive into the city to drop off baggage at a hotel.

Car parks, usually small, enclosed garages, are universally expensive, costing up to €20 a day in big cities; it's not unknown for hotels to state that they have parking and then direct you to the nearest paying garage. In smaller towns, it's handy to have a mini clock-like dial which you set and display in the windscreen, to indicate when you parked and that you're still within the allowed limit: rental cars generally come equipped with these, and some tourist offices have them too. Parking at night is easier than during the day, but make sure you're not parked in a street that turns into a market in the morning or on the one day of the week when it's cleaned in the small hours, otherwise you're likely to be towed.

Never leave anything visible in the car when you're not using it, including the radio. Certain cities have appalling reputations for theft – in Naples, some rental agencies won't insure a car left anywhere except in a locked garage. If you're taking your own vehicle, consider installing a detachable car-radio, and depress your aerial and tuck in your wing mirrors when you park. A patrolled car park is probably the safest option for during the night, especially if you have foreign plates.

Breakdown

If you **break down**, dial ☎116 and tell the operator where you are, the type of car you're in, and your registration number: the nearest office of the Automobile Club d'Italia (ACI) will send someone out to fix your car – however, it's not a free service and can work out very expensive if you need a tow. For this reason you might consider arranging cover with a motoring organization in your home country before you leave. Any ACI office in Italy can tell you where to get **spare parts** for your particular car.

Car rental

Car rental in Italy is pricey, especially in high season, at around €200–300 per week for a small hatchback, with unlimited mileage, if booked in advance. The major chains have offices in all the larger cities and at airports, train stations, and so on: addresses are detailed in the "Listings" sections at the end of city accounts throughout the Guide. Local firms can be less expensive and often have an office at the airport, but generally the best deals are to be had by arranging things in advance, through one of the agents listed below or with specialist tour operators when you book your flight or holiday. You need to be over 21 to rent a car in Italy and will need a credit card to act as a deposit when picking up your vehicle.

Car rental agencies

Avis UK ☎0845/818 181, Ireland ☎021/428 1111, US ☎1-800/331-1212, Canada ☎1-800/879-2847, South Africa ☎11/923 3660, Australia ☎13 63 33, NZ ☎09/526 2847; ⊛www.avis.com.

Budget UK ☎0844/581 9998, ⊛www.budget.co.uk; Ireland ☎09/0662 7711, ⊛www.budget.ie; US ☎1-800/527-0700, ⊛www.budget.com; Australia ☎1300/362 848, ⊛www.budget.com.au; NZ ☎0800/283 438, ⊛www.budget.co.nz.

Europcar UK ☎0870/607 5000, Ireland ☎01/614 2800, US & Canada ☎1-877/940 6900, Australia ☎1300/131 390; ⊛www.europcar.com; South Africa ☎11/574 4457, ⊛www.europcar.co.za.

Hertz UK ☎0870/848 8848, ⊛www.hertz.co.uk; Ireland ☎01/870 5777, ⊛www.hertz.ie; US ☎1-800/654-3001, Canada ☎1-800/263-0600; ⊛www.hertz.com; South Africa ☎0861/600 136, ⊛www.hertz.co.za; Australia ☎13 30 39, ⊛www.hertz.com.au; NZ ☎0800/654 321, ⊛www.hertz.co.nz.

National UK ☎0870/536 5365, ⊛www.nationalcar.co.uk; US ☎1-800/227-7368, ⊛www.nationalcar.com; NZ ☎0800/800 115, ⊛www.nationalcar.co.nz.

Thrifty UK ☎01494/751 500, ⊛www.thrifty.co.uk; Ireland ☎1800/515 800,

ⓦ www.thrifty.ie; US ☎ 1-800/847-4389,
ⓦ www.thrifty.com; South Africa ☎ 0861/002
111, ⓦ www.thrifty.co.za; Australia ☎ 1300/367
227, ⓦ www.thrifty.com.au; NZ ☎ 0800/73 70 70,
ⓦ www.thrifty.co.nz.

Camper van rental

Camper van or mobile home holidays are
becoming increasingly popular in Italy and
the rental market is opening up to meet the
demand. To add to the obvious convenience
of this type of holiday, facilities in campsites
are usually dependable (see p.40), and more
and more resorts have created free camper
van parking areas (*sosta camper*). The
following are just a selection of the
companies offering new (or newish) quality
vehicles for rent. Prices are usually around
€1500 for a four-berth vehicle for a week in
high season, with unlimited mileage.
Blu rent ☎ +39.0171.601.702, ⓦ www.blurent
.com. Website available in English.
Comocaravan ☎ +39.031.521.215, ⓦ www
.comocaravan.it.
Maggiore ☎ +39.840.00.8840, ⓦ www
.maggiorecamperrent.it.

By plane

In line with the rest of European airspace,
internal air fares in Italy have been revolution-
ized in the last couple of years. Small
companies have taken on the ailing state
airline and what used to be a form of business
transport has become a good-value, convenient way of getting around the country.
Budget airlines open and close every season
and there are often special deals being advertised; it pays to shop around and, as always,
book as far in advance as you can.

Airlines

Alitalia ☎ 39.199.207.080, ⓦ www.alitilia.it.
Meridiana ☎ 199.111.333 or 39.078.952.682,
ⓦ www.meridiana.it.
Myair ☎ 39.899.5000.60, ⓦ www.myair.com
Volareweb ☎ 39.899.656.545, ⓦ www.buyvolare
.com.
Windjet ☎ 39.892.020, ⓦ www.w2volawindjet.it.

By ferry and hydrofoil

Italy has a well-developed network of **ferries**
and **hydrofoils** operated by a number of
different private companies. Large car ferries

connect the major islands of Sardinia and
Sicily with the mainland ports of Genoa,
Livorno, La Spezia, Civitavecchia, Fiumicino
and Naples, while the smaller island
groupings – the Trémiti islands, the Bay of
Naples islands, the Pontine Islands – are
usually linked to a number of nearby
mainland towns. The larger lakes in the north
of the country are also well served with
regular ferries in season, although these are
drastically reduced in winter.

Fares are reasonable, and on some of the
more popular services – to Sardinia, for
example – you should book well in advance
in summer, especially if you're taking a
vehicle across. Remember, too, that sailings
are cut outside the summer months, and
some services stop altogether. You'll find a
broad guide to journey times and frequencies in the "Travel details" section at the end
of relevant chapters; for full up-to-date
schedules and prices, check the Italian
website ⓦ www.traghetti.com, which has
links to all the main ferry companies, or
contact one of the ferry agents below.

Agents for Italian ferries

SMS Travel ☎ 39.081.017.1998 from abroad or
892.123 in Italy, ⓦ www.siremar.it. Italian agents for
Siremar and Tirrenia ferries.
Viamare Travel Limited ☎ 020/8206 3420,
ⓦ www.viamare.co.uk.

By bike

Cycling is a very popular sport and mode
of transport in much of Italy. Italians in small
towns and villages are welcoming to
cyclists, and hotels and hostels will take
your bike in overnight for safekeeping. On
the islands, in the mountains, in major
resorts and larger cities, it's usually possible
to **rent** a bike, but in rural areas facilities for
this are few and far between.

Serious cyclists might consider staying at
one of a chain of hotels that cater specifically
for cycling enthusiasts. Each hotel has a
secure room for your bike, a maintenance
workshop, overnight laundry facilities,
suggested itineraries and group-tour possibilities, a doctor at hand and even dietary
consultation. Contact ☎ 39/0541.307.531,
ⓦ www.italybikehotels.it for further information and a list of hotels.

An alternative is to tour by **motorbike**, though again there are relatively few places to rent one. **Mopeds** and **scooters** are comparatively easy to find: everyone in Italy, from kids to grannies, rides one of these and although they're not really built for any kind of long-distance travel, for shooting around towns and islands they're ideal; we've detailed outlets in the chapters. Crash helmets are compulsory, though in the south at least it's a law that seems to be largely ignored.

Accommodation

Accommodation in Italy is fairly reliable and, while never especially cheap, is at least strictly regulated: hotels are star-rated and are required to post their prices clearly in each room. Most tourist offices have details of hotel rates in their town or region, and you can expect them to be broadly accurate.

In popular resorts and the major cities booking ahead is advisable, particularly during July or August, while for Venice, Rome and Florence it's pretty much essential to book ahead from Easter until late September and over Christmas and New Year. You can do this relatively painlessly with hotel booking services online or with travel and booking agents, but we've given contact details throughout the Guide in case you want to reserve direct. Make sure you get confirmation of the booking by fax, email or letter – it's far from uncommon to arrive and find all knowledge of your booking is denied. The phrases on pp.1085–1091 should help you get over the language barrier, though in many places you should be able to find someone who speaks at least some English.

Hotels

Hotels in Italy come tagged with a confusing variety of names, and, although the differences have become minimal of late, you will still find a variety of names used for what are basically private hotel facilities. A **locanda** is historically the most basic option, although these days it is often used by boutique hotels and the like to conjure up images of simple, traditional hospitality. **Pensione**, **albergo** or **hotel** are all commonly used. **Prices** vary greatly between the south and north of Italy, as well as between tourist hotspots and more rural areas. The official star system is based on facilities (TV in rooms, swimming pool, and so on) rather than character or comfort – or even price.

Accommodation price codes

Hotels in this guide have been categorized according to the **price codes** outlined below. They represent the cheapest rates for a double room in high season (July & Aug), although in places like Florence and Venice you can expect high-season rates from March to November.

① €50 and under. The cheapest kind of one-star hotels; most rooms will have shared facilities and may be quite bleak. Places in this category can be heavily booked owing to the fact that they're often used as cheap permanent accommodation. Credit cards are rarely accepted.

② €51–75. The standard one-star hotel, normally with a mixture of rooms with shared and private facilities, and in most cases comfortable enough for a short stay. In Venice, Florence and some other northern cities and resorts, you'll be extremely lucky to find one-star places at this price.

③ €76–100. Mainly two-star hotels, most with private facilities. Rooms will sometimes have a TV and telephone.

④ €101–125. In Venice and Florence there are one-stars in this category. Elsewhere, this price will get you a room in an attractive two-star, or even a three-star hotel, generally with private bath, telephone and TV.

⑤ €126–150. This should involve a room with private bath, TV and telephone pretty much everywhere in Italy, and in the south of the country and more remote places, you could be looking at something fairly swanky.

⑥ €151–200. Usually a good three-star or moderate four-star, with high standards and a range of facilities including a pool and formal restaurant.

⑦ €201–250. These should be special hotels, either by virtue of their location or facilities. Again, in Venice and Florence, you'll be paying this sort of price for rooms that would fall into one of the lower categories elsewhere.

⑧ €251–300. We have only recommended somewhere in this category if it is really special, if it enjoys a wonderful location, a superb site or building – perhaps an old convent or manor house – or if the service and food are just too good to miss.

⑨ €301 and over. The sky's-the-limit category, populated by a select few of the most celebrated hotels in Italy.

In very busy places it's not unusual to have to stay for a minimum of three nights, and many proprietors will add the price of **breakfast** to your bill whether you want it or not; try to ask for accommodation only – you can always eat more cheaply in a bar. Be warned, too, that in major resorts you will often be forced to take **half or full board** in high season. Note that people travelling alone may sometimes have to pay for the price of a double room even when they only need a single, though it can also work the other way round – if all their **single rooms** are taken, a hotelier may well put you in a double room but only charge the single rate.

Check out ⓦwww.venere.it, to access the webpages of those hotels that have them – you can also book rooms online.

Hostels

There are plenty of official **HI youth hostels** in Italy, charging around €15 per night for a dormitory bed. You can easily base a tour of the country around them, although for two people travelling together they don't always represent a massive saving on the cheapest double hotel room – especially if you take into account the bus fare you might have to fork out to reach some of them. If you're travelling on your own, on the other hand, hostels are usually more sociable and can work out a lot cheaper; many have facilities such as inexpensive restaurants and self-catering kitchens that enable you to cut costs further. In a few cases, too – notably Castroreale in Sicily and Montagnana in the Veneto – the hostels are beautifully located and in many ways preferable to any hotel.

Virtually all of the Italian hostels are members of the official International Youth Hostel Federation, and you'll need to be a member of the organization in order to use them – you can join through your home country's youth hostelling organization (see opposite) or often at the hostel on arrival. You need to reserve well ahead in the summer, most efficiently by using Hostelling Inter-national's **International Booking Network** which, for a small fee, enables you to book (including online) at hostels in selected Italian cities from your home country up to six months in advance. For more out-of-the-way hostels, you need to contact them direct at least fifteen days in advance, sending approximately a 30 percent deposit with your booking. We've listed most of the hostels in the Guide, and you can find detailed information about each one on the Ostelli Online website, ⓦwww.ostellionline.org.

In some cities, including Rome, it's also possible to stay in **student accommodation** vacated by Italian students for the summer. This is usually confined to July and August, but accommodation is generally in individual rooms and can work out a lot cheaper than a straight hotel room. Again you'll need to book in advance: we've listed possible places in the text, and you should contact them as far ahead as possible to be sure of a room.

Monasteries and convents

You will also come across accommodation operated by **religious organizations** – convents (normally for women only), welcome houses and the like, again with a mixture of dormitory and individual rooms, which can sometimes be a way of cutting costs as well as meeting like-minded people. Most operate a curfew of some sort, and you should bear in mind that they don't always work out a great deal cheaper than a bottom-line one-star hotel. Information can be found in the local tourist offices.

A new online agency, Monastery Stays (ⓦwww.monasterystays.com), offers a centralized booking service for more than two hundred and fifty convents and monasteries around the country. There are no restrictions on age, sex or faith in the establishments they cover, all rooms have private bathrooms and few places have early curfews.

Youth hostel associations

Australia ☎02/9261 1111, ⓦwww.yha.org.au.
Canada ☎613/237-7884, ⓦwww.hihostels.ca.
England and Wales ☎01629/592 700, ⓦwww.yha.org.uk.
New Zealand ☎0800/278 299, ⓦwww.yha.co.nz.
Northern Ireland ☎028/9032 4733, ⓦwww.hini.org.uk.
Ireland ☎01/830 4555, ⓦwww.irelandyha.org.
Scotland ☎0870/155 3255, ⓦwww.syha.org.uk.
US ☎301/495-1240, ⓦwww.hiayh.org.

Camping

Camping is popular in Italy and there are plenty of sites, mostly on the coast and in the mountains and generally open April to September (though winter "camping" – in caravans and camper vans – is common in ski areas). The majority are well equipped and often have bungalows, mainly with four to six beds. On the coast in high season you can expect to pay a daily rate of around €12 per person plus €10–15 per tent or caravan and €5 per vehicle. Local tourist offices have details of nearby sites, otherwise visit the Italian camping website, ⓦwww.camping.it, for information and booking facilities for campsites all over Italy.

Self-catering

Self-catering is becoming an increasingly feasible option for visitors to Italy's cities. High prices mean that renting rooms or an **apartment** can be an attractive, cost-effective choice. Usually in well-located positions in city centres, and available for anything from a couple of nights to a month or so, they come equipped with bedding and kitchen utensils and there's nothing like shopping for supplies in a local market to make you feel part of Italian daily life, even on a short break.

If you're not intending to travel around a lot it might be worth renting a **villa** or farmhouse for a week or two. Most tend to be located in the affluent northern areas of Italy, especially Tuscany and Umbria, although attractive options are also available on Sicily and Sardinia and popping up in other rural locations too. They don't come cheap, but are of a high standard and often enjoy marvellous locations.

Villa and apartment companies

Bridgewater ☏0161/787 8587, ⓦwww .bridgewater-travel.co.uk. A company with over 25 years' experience sourcing apartments, agriturismo and country hotels throughout Italy.

Carefree Italy ☏0871/700 0850, ⓦwww .carefree-italy.com. English company offering villas and apartments across the country.

Holiday Rentals ⓦwww.holiday-rentals.co.uk. This site puts you in touch directly with the owners of over 1000 Italian properties.

Ilios Travel ☏01444/880 350, ⓦwww.iliostravel .com. High-quality selection of country mansions and villas, in various parts of the country.

Italian Breaks ☏020/8666 0407, ⓦwww .italianbreaks.com. Accommodation to suit most budgets.

Italian Connection ☏01424/728 900, ⓦwww .italian-connection.co.uk. Major upmarket operator with an array of villas and smart apartments throughout the country.

Italian Homes ☏020/3178 4180, ⓦwww .Italian-homes.com. Apartments in Venice, Rome and Florence.

Livingitalia.com ☏39.06.3211.0998, ⓦwww .livingitalia.com. Offers apartments in Florence and Rome.

Owners' Syndicate ☏020/7401 1086, ⓦwww .ownerssyndicate.co.uk. More than 200 properties around Tuscany and Umbria.

Rentxpress ☏39.02.805.3151, ⓦwww .rentxpress.com. English-speaking company with apartments for rent in various cities.

Unusual villa rentals US ☏804-288-2823, ⓦwww.unusualvillarentals.com. US company offering some spectacular properties in some of the most beautiful locations in Italy.

Bed and breakfast and agriturismo

Bed and breakfast schemes are a relatively new arrival, the best ones offering a way to get a flavour of Italian home life, though they're not necessarily cheaper than an inexpensive hotel, and they rarely accept credit cards. Some places going under the name are actually little different from private rooms, with the owners not living on the premises, but you'll invariably find them clean and well maintained. In Sicily and the south of the country in general they are becoming a very popular alternative form of accommodation with attractive, good-value options becoming common. For an extensive list of Italy's B&Bs check out ⓦwww.bbitalia .it, ⓦwww.caffelletto.it or the links at ⓦwww .terranostra.it.

The **agriturismo** scheme which enables farmers to rent out converted barns and farm buildings to tourists has boomed in recent years. Usually these comprise a self-contained flat or building, though a few places just rent rooms on a bed-and-breakfast basis. While some rooms are still annexed to working farms or vineyards, many are smart, self-contained rural vacation properties; attractions may include home-grown food, swimming pools and a range of activities from walking and riding to archery and mountain biking. Many agriturismi have a minimum-stay requirement of one week in busy periods. Rates start at around €120 per night for self-contained places with two beds. Tourist offices keep lists of local properties; alternatively, you can search one of the growing number of agriturismo websites – there are hundreds of properties at ⓦwww .agriturismo.com, ⓦwww.agri-turismo.net, ⓦwww.agriitalia.it and ⓦwww.agriturist.it

Mountain refuges

If you're planning on hiking and climbing, it's worth checking out the **rifugi** network, consisting of about five hundred mountain huts, owned by the Club Alpino Italiano (**CAI** ☏02.205.7231, ⓦwww.cai.it). Non-members can use them for around €10 a night, though you should book at least ten days in advance. There are also private *rifugi* that charge around double this. Most are fairly spartan, with bunks in unheated dorms, but their settings can be magnificent and usually leave you well placed to continue your hike the next day. Bear in mind that the word *rifugio* can be used for anything from a smart chalet-hotel to a snack bar at the top of a cable-car line. We've indicated in the text where this is the case.

Food and drink

The importance Italians attach to food and drink makes any holiday in the country a treat for the taste buds. The southern Italian diet especially, with its emphasis on olive oil, fresh and plentiful fruit, vegetables and fish, is one of the healthiest in Europe, and there are few national cuisines that can boast so much variety in both ingredients and cooking methods. Italy's wines, too, are among the finest and most diverse in Europe. For more on the regional variety in cooking see the *Italian food* colour section.

Types of restaurants

Full **meals** are generally served in either a trattoria or a ristorante. Traditionally, a trattoria is a cheaper and more basic purveyor of homestyle cooking (*cucina casalinga*), while a ristorante is more upmarket, though the two are often inter-changeable. Other types of eating places include those that bill themselves as every-thing – trattoria-ristorante-pizzeria – and perform no function very well, serving mediocre food that you could get at better prices elsewhere. Look out also for *spaghet-terie*, bar-restaurants that serve basic pasta dishes and are often the hangout of the local youth. *Osterie* are common too, basically an old-fashioned restaurant or pub-like place specializing in home cooking, though some upmarket places with pretensions to estab-lished antiquity borrow the name. In all mid-range establishments, pasta dishes go for €5–10, while the main fish or meat courses will normally cost between €7 and €15.

Understanding the menu

Traditionally, lunch (*pranzo*) and dinner (*cena*) start with **antipasto** (literally "before the meal"), a course consisting of various cold cuts of meat, seafood and cold vegetable dishes, generally costing €5–10. Some places offer self-service antipasto buffets. The next course, the **primo**, involves soup, risotto or pasta dish, and is followed by the **secondo** – the meat or fish course, usually served alone, except for perhaps a wedge of lemon or tomato. Fish will often be served whole or by weight – 250g is usually plenty for one person – or ask to have a look at the fish before it's cooked. Note that by law, any ingredients that have been frozen need to be marked (usually with an asterix and "*surgelato*") on the menu. Vegetables or salads – **contorni** – are ordered and served separately, and there often won't be much choice: potatoes will usually come as fries (*patate fritte*), but you can also find boiled (*lesse*) or roast (*arrostite*) potatoes, while salads are either green (*verde*) or mixed (*mista*) and vegetables (*verdure*) usually come very well boiled. Afterwards, you nearly always get a choice of fresh local fruit (*frutta*) and a selection of **desserts** (*dolci*) – sometimes just ice cream or *macedonia* (fresh fruit salad), but often home-made items, like apple or pear cake (*torta di mela/pera*), tiramisu, or *zuppa*

No smoking

In January 2005 a law prohibiting smoking in restaurants and bars came into force across the country. Overnight, local neighbourhood bars became smoke-free zones; any establishment that wants to allow smoking has to follow very stringent rules in isolating a separate room – including doors and special air conditioning. Needless to say this is beyond the pocket of most places and so the majority remain no-smoking throughout. Don't worry, though, if you do want a puff with your coffee; the pavement outside has become a popular place.

There's a detailed **menu reader** of Italian terms on pp.1088–1091.

B

inglese (trifle). **Cheeses** (*formaggi*) are always worth a shot if you have any room left; ask to try a selection of local varieties.

You will need quite an appetite to tackle all these courses and if your stomach — or wallet — isn't up to it, it's perfectly acceptable to have less. If you're not sure of the size of the portions, start with a pasta or rice dish and ask to order the *secondo* when you've finished the first course. And, although it's not a very Italian thing to do, don't feel shy about just having an *antipasto* and a *primo*; they're probably the best way of trying local specialities anyway.

At the end of the meal ask for the bill (*il conto*); bear in mind that almost everywhere you'll pay a cover charge (*coperto*) of €1–5 a head. In many trattorias the bill amounts to little more than an illegible scrap of paper; if you want to check it, ask for a **receipt** (*ricevuta*). In more expensive places, service (*servizio*) will often be added on top of the cover charge, generally about 10 percent. If it isn't included leave what you feel Is appropriate for the service you received and the establishment – up to 10 percent. In our listings, we've indicated the regular weekly **closing day**.

Breakfast and snacks

Most Italians start their day in a bar, their **breakfast** (*prima colazione*) consisting of a coffee and a *brioche* or *cornetto* – a croissant often filled with jam, custard or chocolate, which you usually help yourself to from the counter and eat standing at the bar. It will cost between €1.30 and €1.60. Breakfast in a hotel is often a limp affair of watery coffee, bread and processed meats, often not worth the price.

Pizza, panini and picnic food

Pizza is obviously a worldwide phenomenon, but Italy remains the best place to eat it. Here pizza usually comes thin and flat, not deep-pan, and the choice of toppings is fairly limited, with none of the dubious pineapple and sweetcorn variations. For a quality pizza

opt for somewhere with a wood-fired oven (*forno a legna*) rather than a squeaky-clean electric one, so that the pizzas arrive blasted and bubbling on the surface and with a distinctive charcoal taste. This adherence to tradition means that it's unusual to find a good pizzeria open at lunchtime; it takes hours for a wood-fired oven to heat up to the necessary temperature.

Pizzerias range from a stand-up counter selling slices to a fully fledged sit-down restaurant, and on the whole they don't sell much else besides pizza, soft drinks and beer. A basic cheese and tomato *margherita* costs around €6, a fancier variety €6–10, and it's quite acceptable to cut it into slices and eat it with your fingers. Consult our food glossary (see pp.1088–1091) for the different kinds of pizza.

For a lunchtime snack **sandwiches** (*panini*) can be pretty substantial, a bread stick or roll packed with any number of fillings. A sandwich bar (*paninoteca*) in larger towns and cities, and in smaller places a grocer's shop (*alimentari*), will normally make you up whatever you want. Bars may also offer *tramezzini*, ready-made sliced white bread with mixed fillings.

Other sources of quick snacks are **markets**, where fresh, flavoursome produce is sold, often including cheese, cold meats, warm spit-roast chicken, and *arancini* (deep-fried balls of rice with meat (*rosso*) or butter and cheese (*bianco*) filling. **Bread shops** (*panetteria*) often serve slices of pizza or *focacce* (bread with oil and salt topped with rosemary, olives or tomato). **Supermarkets**, also, are an obvious stop for a picnic lunch: the major chains, Esselunga, Carrefour and Auchan, are on the outskirts of larger towns, while GS, Unes! and Sma are often in the centre.

Ice cream

Italian **ice cream** (*gelato*) is justifiably famous and a cone (*un cono*) is an indispensable accessory to the evening *passeggiata*. There's no problem locating the finest *gelateria* in town – it's the one that draws the crowds – and we've noted the really special places throughout the Guide. If in doubt, go for the places that make their own ice cream, denoted by the signs "*Produzione Propria*" outside. There's usually a veritable cornucopia of flavours ranging from those regarded as the classics – like lemon (*limone*) and pistachio (*pistacchio*) – through staples including *stracciatella* (vanilla with chocolate chips), strawberry (*fragola*) and *fiordilatte* (similar to vanilla), to house specialities that might include cinnamon (*cannella*), chocolate with chilli pepper (*cioccolato con peperoncino*) or even pumpkin (*zucca*).

Vegetarians and vegans

Although your diet will probably be based around pasta and pizza, Italy isn't a bad country to travel in if you're a vegetarian. There are numerous pasta sauces without meat, some superb vegetable antipasti and, if you eat fish and seafood, you should have no problem at all. Salads, too, are fresh and good. Outside the cities and resorts where vegetarianism can be less understood, you might be wise to check if a dish has meat in it (*C'è carne dentro?*) or ask for it "*senza carne e pesce*" to make sure it doesn't contain poultry or prosciutto.

Vegans will have a much harder time, though pizzas without cheese (*marinara* – nothing to do with fish – is a common option) are a good standby, vegetable soup (*minestrone*) is usually just that and the fruit is excellent.

Drinking

Although *un mezzo* (half-litre carafe of house wine) is a standard accompaniment to any meal, there's not a great emphasis on dedicated **drinking** in Italy. You'll rarely see drunks in public, young people don't devote their nights to getting wasted, and women especially are frowned on if they're seen to be overindulging. Nonetheless there's a wide choice of alcoholic drinks available, often at low prices; soft drinks come in multifarious hues; and, of course, there is always mineral water and crushed-ice drinks.

Where to drink

Traditional **bars** are less social centres than functional places and are all very similar to each other – brightly lit places, with a counter, a Gaggia coffee machine and a picture of the local football team on the wall. This is the place to come for a coffee in the morning, a quick beer or a cup of tea – people don't generally idle away evenings in bars. Indeed in some more rural areas it's difficult to find a bar open much after 8pm.

It's cheapest to drink standing at the counter, in which case you pay first at the cash desk (*la cassa*), present your receipt (*scontrino*) to the barperson and give your order. There's always a list of prices (*listino prezzi*) behind the bar and it's customary to leave a small coin on the counter as a tip for the barperson. If there's waiter service, just sit where you like, though bear in mind that to do this will cost up to twice as much as positioning yourself at the bar, especially if you sit outside (*fuori*) – the difference is shown on the price list as *tavola* (table) or *terrazzo* (any outside seating area). Late-night bars and pubs rarely operate on the *scontrino* system; you may be asked to pay up front, in the British manner, or be presented with a bill. If not, head for the counter when you leave – the barperson will have kept a surprisingly accurate tally.

An **osteria** can be a more congenial setting, often a traditional place where you can usually try local specialities with a glass of wine. Real enthusiasts of the grape should head for an **enoteca**, though many of these are more oriented towards selling wine by the glass than by the case. Cities offer a much greater variety of places to sit and drink in the evening, sometimes with live music or DJs. The more energetic or late-opening of these have taken to calling themselves **pubs**, a spill-over from the outrageous success of Irish pubs, at least one of which you'll find, packed to the rafters, in almost every city. Beer, particularly in its draught form, *alla spina*, has become fashionable in recent years.

Coffee and tea

Always excellent, the basic choice of **coffee** is either small and black (*espresso*, or just caffè), which costs around €1 a cup, or white and frothy (*cappuccino*, for about €1.30), but there are scores of variations. If you want your espresso watered down, ask for a *caffè lungo* or, for something more like a filter coffee, an *Americano*; with a drop of milk is *caffè macchiato*; very milky is *caffè latte* (ordering just a "*latte*" in true New York-café style will get you a glass of milk!). Coffee with a shot of alcohol – and you can ask for just about anything – is *caffè corretto*. Many places also now sell decaffeinated coffee; while in summer you might want to have your coffee on ice (*caffè freddo*).

If you're not up for a coffee, there's always **tea**. In summer you can drink this cold, too (*tè freddo*) – excellent for taking the heat off. Hot tea (*tè caldo*) comes with lemon (*con limone*) unless you ask for milk (*con latte*). A small selection of herbal teas (*infusioni*) are generally available: camomile (*camomilla*) and peppermint (*menta*) are the most common.

Soft drinks and water

There are various **soft drinks** (*analcolichi*) to choose from. Slightly fizzy, bitter drinks like San Bittèr or Crodine are common especially at *aperitvo* time. A **spremuta** is a fresh fruit juice, squeezed at the bar, usually orange, lemon or grapefruit. There are also crushed-ice **granitas**, big in Sicily and offered in several flavours, available with or without whipped cream (*panna*) on top. Otherwise there's the usual range of fizzy drinks and concentrated juices: the home-grown Italian version of Coke, Chinotto, is less sweet and good with a slice of lemon. **Tap water** (*acqua normale*) is quite drinkable, and you won't pay for a glass in a bar, though Italians prefer **mineral water** (*acqua minerale*) and drink more of it than any other country in Europe. It can be drunk either still (*senza gas* or *naturale*) or sparkling (*con gas* or *frizzante*), and costs about €1.30 a bottle.

Beer and spirits

Beer (*birra*) is always a lager-type brew which usually comes in one-third or two-third litre bottles, or on tap (*alla spina*), measure for measure more expensive than the bottled variety. A small beer is a *piccola*, (20cl or

25cl), a larger one (usually 40cl) a *media*. The cheapest and most common brands are the Italian Moretti, Peroni and Dreher, all of which are very drinkable; if this is what you want, either state the brand name or ask for *birra nazionale* or *birra chiara* – otherwise you could end up with a more expensive imported beer. You may also come across darker beers (*birra nera* or *birra rossa*), which have a sweeter, maltier taste and in appearance resemble stout or bitter.

All the usual **spirits** are on sale and known mostly by their generic names. There are also Italian brands of the main varieties: the best Italian brandies are Stock and Vecchia Romagna. A generous shot costs about €1.50, imported stuff much more.

You'll also find **fortified wines** like Martini, Cinzano and Campari; ask for a Campari-soda and you'll get a ready-mixed version from a little bottle; a slice of lemon is a *spicchio di limone*, ice is *ghiaccio*. You might also try Cynar – believe it or not, an artichoke-based sherry often drunk as an aperitif with water. There's also a daunting selection of **liqueurs**. Amaro is a bitter after-dinner drink or *digestivo*, Amaretto much sweeter with a strong taste of almond, Sambuca a sticky-sweet aniseed concoction, traditionally served with a coffee bean in it and set on fire (though, increasingly, this is something put on to impress tourists). A shot of clear grappa is a common accompaniment to a coffee and can range from a warming palate cleanser to throat-burning firewater while another sweet alternative, originally from Sorrento, is *Limoncello* or *limoncino*, a lemon-based liqueur best drunk in a frozen vase-shaped glass. *Strega* is another drink you'll see behind every bar, yellow, herb-and-saffron based stuff in tall, elongated bottles: about as sweet as it looks but not unpleasant.

Wine

From sparkling prosecco to deep-red chianti, Italy is renowned for its wines. However, it's rare to find the snobbery often associated with "serious" wine drinking. Light **reds** such as those made from the dolcetto grape are hauled out of the fridge in hot weather, while some full-bodied **whites** are drunk at near room temperature. In restaurants you'll invariably be offered red (*rosso*) or white (*bianco*) – rarely rosé (*rosato*). Don't be afraid to try the local stuff (ask for *vino sfuso*, or simply *un mezzo* – a half litre – or *un quarto* – a quarter), sometimes served straight from the barrel, particularly down south. It's often very good, and inexpensive at an average of around €5 a litre. Bottled wine is pricier but still very good value; expect to pay €9–15 a bottle depending on the restaurant, and less than half that from a shop or supermarket. In bars you can buy a decent glass of wine for about €1–2. For more background on wine see the "regional food and drink" boxes at the beginning of each chapter and the *Italian wine* colour section.

The media

Italy's decentralized press serves to emphasize the strength of regionalism in the country. Local TV is popular, too, in the light of little competition from the national channels. If you know where to look, journalistic standards can be high but you might find yourself turning to foreign TV channels or papers if you want an international outlook on events.

Newspapers

The **Italian press** is largely regionally based, with just a few newspapers available across the country. The centre-left *La Repubblica* (@www.repubblica.it) and authoritative right-slanted *Corriere della Sera* (@www.corriere .it) are the two most widely read, published nationwide with local supplements, but originating in Milan. Provincial newspapers include *La Stampa* (@www.lastampa.it), the daily of Turin, and *Il Messaggero* (@www .ilmessaggero.it) of Rome – both rather stuffy, establishment sheets. *Il Mattino* (@www.ilmattino.it) is the more readable publication of Naples and the Campania area, while other southern editions include the *Giornale di Sicilia* and *La Gazzetta del Sud* (@www.lagazzettadelsud.it). Many of the imprints you see on newsstands are the official mouthpieces for political parties: *L'Unità* (@www.unita.it) is the party organ of the former Communist Party, while *La Padania* (@www.lapadania.it) is the press of the right-wing, regionalist Lega Nord party. The traditionally radical *Il Manifesto* has always been regarded as one of the most serious and influential sources of Italian journalism. Perhaps the most avidly read newspapers of all, however, are the specialist

sports papers, most notably the *Corriere dello Sport* (@www.corrieredellosport.it) and the pink *Gazzetta dello Sport* (@www .gazzetta.it) – both essential reading if you want an insight into the Italian football scene.

English-language newspapers can be found for around three times their home cover price in all the larger cities and most resorts, usually a day late, though in Milan and Rome you can sometimes find papers on the day of publication. In remoter parts of the country it's not unusual for papers to be delayed by several days.

TV and radio

Italian **TV** is appalling, with ghastly quiz shows, mindless variety programmes and cathartic chat shows squeezed in between countless artless advertisements. Of the **three national channels**, RAI 1, 2 and 3, RAI 3 has the odd worthwhile programme, although the intelligent, satirical shows are often indecipherable to foreigners who have anything less than an encyclopedic knowledge of Italian politics from the last fifty years. **Satellite television** is fairly widely distributed, and three-star hotels and above usually offer a mix of BBC World, CNN and French-, German- and

Spanish-language news channels, as well as MTV and Eurosport.

The situation in **radio** is if anything even more anarchic, with the FM waves crowded to the extent that you continually pick up new stations whether you want to or not — Catholic Radio Maria pops up with an uncanny frequency. This means there are generally some good stations if you search hard enough, but on the whole the RAI stations are again the more professional – though even with them daytime listening is virtually undiluted Euro-pop.

Festivals

Whether for religious, traditional or cultural reasons, Italy has no shortage of festivals throughout the year, and at Christmas, Easter or during the summer months you are likely to come across at least one local festival celebrating an historic event, a patron saint's day, a town's local produce or some artistic talent.

Recently there's also been a revival of the carnival (*carnevale*), the last fling before Lent, although the anarchic fun that was enjoyed in the past has generally been replaced by elegant, self-conscious affairs, with ingenious costumes and handmade masks. The main places to head for are Venice, Viareggio in Tuscany and Acireale in Sicily, although smaller towns also often put on a parade.

Perhaps the most widespread local event in Italy is the **religious procession**, which can be a very dramatic affair. **Good Friday** is celebrated in many towns and villages – particularly in the south – by parading models of Christ through the streets accompanied by white-robed, hooded figures singing penitential hymns. Many processions have strong pagan roots, marking important dates on the calendar and only relatively recently sanctified by the Church. Superstition and a desire for good luck are very much part of these events.

Despite the dwindling number of practising Catholics in Italy, there has been a revival of **pilgrimages** over the last couple of decades. These are as much social occasions as spiritual journeys with, for example, as many as a million pilgrims travelling through the night, mostly on foot, to the **Shrine of the Madonna di Polsi** in the inhospitable Aspromonte mountains in Calabria. Sardinia's biggest festival, the **Festa di Sant'Efisio**, sees a four-day march from Cágliari to Pula and back, to commemorate the saint's martyrdom.

There are many festivals that evoke local pride in **tradition**. Medieval contests like the **Palio** horse race in Siena perpetuate allegiances to certain competing clans, while other towns put on crossbow, jousting and flag-twirling contests, with marching bands in full costume accompanying the event with enthusiastic drumming. Far from staged affairs, these festivals are highly significant to those involved, with fierce rivalry between participants.

Food-inspired *feste* are lower-key, but no less enjoyable affairs, usually celebrating the local speciality of the region to the accompaniment of dancing, music from a local brass band and noisy fireworks at the end of the evening. There are literally hundreds of food festivals, sometimes advertised as **sagre**, and every region has them – look in the local papers or ask at the tourist office during summer and autumn and you're bound to find something going on. Most are modest affairs, primarily aimed at locals and little publicized, but there are a few exceptions.

The home-town pride that sparks off many of the food festivals also expresses itself in some of the **arts festivals** spread across

Italy, particularly in the central part of the country – based in ancient amphitheatres or within medieval walls and occasionally marking the work of a native composer. Major concerts and opera are usually well advertised but also extremely popular, so you should book tickets well in advance.

One other type of festival to keep an eye out for is the summer **political** shindigs, like the *Festa de l'Unità*, advertised by posters all over the country. Begun initially to recruit members to the different political parties they have become something akin to a village fete but with a healthy Italian twist. Taking place mainly in the evenings, the food tents are a great way to try tasty local dishes washed down by a cup of wine for a couple of euro a dish. There's usually bingo going on in one corner, the sort of dancing that will make teenagers crimson with embarrassment and the odd coconut shy or the like. In larger towns these have become more sophisticated affairs with big-name national bands playing.

Festivals diary

There are literally thousands of festivals in Italy and sometimes the best ones are those that you come across unexpectedly in the smaller towns. Some of the highlights are listed below – we've detailed more throughout the Guide. Note that dates change from year to year, so it's best to contact the local tourist office for specific details.

January

Naples San Silvestro. New Year is welcomed in by bangers and fireworks on the streets and by throwing old furniture out of windows.
Milan Epifania (Jan 6). Costumed parade of the Three Kings from the Duomo to Sant'Eustorgio, the resting place of the bones of the Magi.
Rome Epifania (Jan 6). Toy and sweet fair in Piazza Navona, to celebrate the *Befana*, the good witch who brings toys and sweets to children who've been good, and coal to those who haven't.

February

Sicily Festa di Sant'Agata (Feb 3–5). Riotous religious procession in Catania.
Carnevale (weekend before Lent) Carnival festivities in Venice ⓦ www.venicecarnival.com, Viareggio ⓦ www.ilcarnevale.com, Foiano della Chiana (Arezzo), Cento (Ferrara) plus many towns throughout Italy.

Ivrea Battle of the Oranges. A messy couple of days when processions through the streets are an excuse to pelt each other with orange pulp ⓦ www .carnevalediivrea.it.
Agrigento Almond Blossom Festival (last two weeks of Feb). Colourful celebration of spring with folk music from around the world.

March

Venice Su e zo per i ponti (second Sun). A marathon "up and down the bridges".
Milan Salone Internazionale del Mobile (third week). The city becomes a showcase for the best of the world's furniture and industrial design.

April

Nocera Tirinese Rito dei Battienti (Easter Sat). Macabre parade of flagellants whipping themselves with shards of glass.
Florence Lo Scoppio del Carro (Easter Day). A symbolic firework display outside the Duomo after Mass.

May

Cocullo (L'Aquila) Festival of snakes (first week of May). One of the most ancient Italian festivals celebrating the patron saint, San Domenico Abate, in which his statue is draped with live snakes and paraded through the streets.
Gubbio Corsa dei Ceri (first Sun). Three 20ft-high wooden figures (*ceri*), representing three patron saints, are raced through the old town by *ceraioli* in medieval costume.
Camogli Fish festival of San Fortunato (second Sun). The patron saint of fishermen is celebrated with plenty of fried fish, fireworks and bonfires.
Florence Festa del Grillo (first, second and third Sun). Celebration of the cricket; contestants bring along highly ornate boxes containing crickets which are judged according to beauty and singing voice.
International Wine Day (last Sun). Wine estates all over Italy open their cellars to the public.
Siracusa Greek Drama festival (mid-May to mid-June). Classic plays performed by international companies in the spectacular ruins of the ancient Greek theatre.
Alba Truffle Festival (April 24 to May 2). Month-long opportunity to sample local delicacies as well as parades and a donkey palio.

June

Florence Calcio Storico Fiorentino (June 24). Medieval-style football match and other festivities to celebrate San Giovanni, the city's patron saint.

Verona Verona Opera season (from late June).
🕸 www.arena.it.
Positano (from late June). Amalfi Coast opera and
chamber music festival.

July

Siena Palio (July 2). Medieval bareback horse race
in the campo.
Matera Festa della Madonna della Bruna (July 2).
A statue of the town's patron saint is paraded on a
float and then burned.
Palermo Festino di Santa Rosalia (second week).
A five-day street party to celebrate the city's patron
saint.
Perugia Umbria Jazz Festival (second week)
🕸 www.umbriajazz.com.
Bologna Porretta Soul Festival (third week)
🕸 www.porrettasoul.it.
Santarcangelo di Romagna Festival
Internazionale del Teatro in Piazza (mid July)
Contemporary performance in public spaces, just
outsdie Rimini (🕸 www.santarcangelofestival.com).

August

Ferragosto (Aug 15). National holiday with local
festivals, water fights and fireworks all over Italy.
Siena (Aug 16). Second Palio horse race.
Pésaro Rossini Opera Festival (mid-month)
🕸 www.rossinioperafestival.it.
Ferrara Ferrara Buskers Festival (end of Aug).
Gathering of some of the world's best street
performers. 🕸 www.ferrarabuskers.com.
Venice (end of month). Start of the oldest
International Film Festival in the world 🕸 www
.labiennale.org.

September

Venice La Regatta di Venezia (first Sun). Gondola
race in medieval costume along the Grand Canal.
Verona (Sept 12). Street entertainment and general
partying to celebrate the birthday of the town's most
famous lover, Juliet.

Naples Festa di San Gennaro (Sept 15). Festival
for the city's patron saint with crowds gathering
in the cathedral to witness the liquefaction of San
Gennaro's blood.
San Giovanni Rotondo, Fóggia (Sept 23).
Thousands of followers commemorate the death of
Padre Pio.

October

Marino, Rome Sagra del Vino (first weekend). One
of the most famous among hundreds of wine festivals
across the country, with fountains literally flowing
with wine.
Trieste La Barcolana (second Sun). Boat race
🕸 www.barcolana.it.
Perugia Eurochocolate (third and fourth weekend).
Italy's chocolate city celebrates.
Acqualagna, Pésaro Festa del Tartufo Bianco (last
Sun). Beginning of a month-long white truffle festival.

November

Olive oil Festivals all over Italy.

December

Stiffe, L'Aquila Bethlehem in the Grotto (first
week). Life-size statues from the nativity scene
are carried into a 650-metre-deep grotto and
positioned for the month among stalagmites and a
natural waterfall.
Suvereto, Livorno Festa del Cinghiale (Dec 1–10).
A ten-day festival in honour of the wild boar.
Milan Oh Bej, Oh Bej! (Dec 7). The city's patron
saint, Sant'Ambrogio, is celebrated with a huge street
market around his church and a day off work and
school for all.
Santa Lucia (Dec 13). Milan opera season starts
with an all-star opening night at La Scala.
Orvieto Umbria Jazz Winter (end of month) 🕸 www
.umbriajazz.com.

Sports and outdoor pursuits

Spectator sports are popular in Italy, especially the hallowed calcio (football), and there is undying national passion for frenetic motor and cycle races. When it comes to participation, though, there isn't the same compulsion to hit the hell out of a squash ball or sweat your way through an aerobics class after work as there is, say, in Britain or the States. Alternatively, the country's natural advantages provide possibly the best scope for keeping trim in the most enjoyable ways possible.

For visitors to Italy, the most accessible activities are centred around the **mountains** – where you can climb, ski, paraglide, raft or simply explore on foot or cycle – and the coastal regions, with plenty of opportunities for swimming, sailing and windsurfing; Campania, Calabria and Sicily are particularly popular for scuba diving and snorkelling.

Sports

Football – or **calcio** – is the national sport, followed fanatically by millions of Italians, and if you're at all interested in the game it would be a shame to leave the country without attending a *partita* or football match. The **season** starts around the middle of August, and finishes in June. **Il campionato** (the championship) is split into four principal divisions, with the twenty teams in the Serie A being the most prestigious. Matches are normally played on Sunday afternoons, although Saturday, Sunday evening and Monday games are becoming more common. See Ⓦ www.lega-calcio.it for results, a calendar of events and English links to the official team websites. Inevitably **tickets** for Serie A matches are not cheap, starting at about €20 for "Curva" seats where the *tifosi* or hard-core fans go, rising to anything between €40 and €60 for "Tribuna" seats along the side of the pitch, and anything up to €100 for the more comfortable "Poltroncina" cushioned-seats in the centre of the *Tribuna*. Once at the football match, get into the atmosphere of the occasion by knocking back *borghetti* – little vials of cold coffee with a drop of spirit added. See the *Itallian football* colour section for more information.

Italy's chosen sport after football is **basketball**, introduced from the United States after World War II. Most cities have a team, and Italy is now ranked among the foremost in the world. The teams vying for the top spot are Montepaschi Siena, Lottomatica Virtus Roma, Premiata Monte-granaro, Armani Jeans Milan and Air Avellino. For more details on fixtures and the leagues, see Ⓦ www.eurobasket.com/ita.

In a country that has produced Ferrari, Maserati, Alfa Romeo and Fiat, it should come as no surprise that **motor racing** gives Italians such a buzz. There are grand prix tracks at Monza near Milan (home of the Italian Grand Prix) and at Ímola, where the San Marino Grand Prix is held.

The other sport popular with participants and crowds of spectators alike is **cycling**. At weekends especially, you'll often see a club group out, dressed in bright team kit, whirring along on their slender machines. The annual Giro d'Italia (Ⓦ www.ilgiroditalia.it) in the second half of May is a prestigious event that attracts scores of international participants each year, closing down roads and creating great excitement.

Outdoor pursuits

With the Alps right on the doorstep, it's easy to spend a weekend **skiing** or **snowboarding** from Milan, Turin or Venice. Some of the most popular ski resorts are Sestriere and Bardonecchia in Piemonte, Cervinia and Courmayeur in Valle d'Aosta, and the Val Gardena and Val di Fassa in the stunning Dolomite mountains of Trentino-Alto Adige and Veneto – home to one of Italy's best-known and most exclusive resorts,

Cortina d'Ampezzo. Further south you can ski at the small resorts of Abetone and Amiata in Tuscany, Monte Vettore in the Marche, Gran Sasso and Maiella in Abruzzo and on Mount Etna in Sicily. Contact the regional tourist offices for information about accommodation, ski schools and prices of lift passes.

All of these mountain resorts are equally ideal as bases for summer **hiking** and **climbing**, and most areas have detailed maps with itineraries and marked paths. For less strenuous treks, the rolling hills of Tuscany and Umbria make perfect walking and **mountain bike** country and numerous tour operators offer independent or escorted tours throughout the region. Many tourist offices also publish booklets suggesting itineraries.

If the heat of the summer lures you towards the extensive Italian coast you can expect to find all the usual seaside resort activity and plenty of opportunities for **sailing** and **windsurfing**. **Scuba diving** is popular in Sicily and off most of the smaller islands – you can either join a diving school or rent equipment from one if you're an experienced diver. You can get a guide and map suggesting **sailing itineraries** round the coast of southern Italy from the Italian State Tourist Office (see p.59).

Watersports aren't just restricted to the coast and can be found in places such as Lake Garda in the north and Trasimeno and Bolsena further south towards Rome. River **canoeing** and **rafting** are limited to the mountain areas of the north – contact the Monrosa rafting club near Turin, ⓦwww .monrosarafting.it, for details of their activities on the Sesia river.

Horseriding is becoming increasingly popular in rural areas of Italy and most tourist offices have lists of local stables (*maneggio*). Many agriturismi (see p.41) also have riding facilities and sometimes offer daily or weekly treks and night rides. Note that Italians rarely wear or provide riding hats.

Shopping

There is no shortage of temptation for shoppers and souvenir-hunters in Italy. Visitors can take advantage of Italy's traditional expertise in textiles, ceramics and leather and glassware in all price ranges; top-end Gucci garments, Murano glass or calf-skin footwear are often on sale just round the corner from somewhere offering rustic ceramics or gastronomic farm products. The regional variety of the country is reflected in the selection of goods available.

Much of Italy's manufacturing industry consists of small family-run companies. This has led to factory outlets opening across the country, particularly for clothes and other textiles but also for pottery and glass; the Guide and local tourist offices will be able to point you in the right direction. Rural areas will usually have good basketware, local terracotta or ceramic items as well a veritable banquet of locally produced wine, olive oils, cheeses, hams and salamis. It's always worth rooting out the local speciality, even in urban centres: Turin is well known for its chocolate, Milan famous for designer clothes and furniture, Venice for glassware and lace, Florence for leather goods, Sicily and Perugia for ceramics.

Every large village and town has at least one weekly **market** (detailed in the Guide), and though these are usually geared towards household goods, they can be useful for picking up cheap clothing, basketware, ceramics and picnic ingredients.

Prices are mainly in line with most of Western Europe and are always a little higher in the north of the country and urban

Clothing and shoe sizes

Women's clothing

American	4	6	8	10	12	14	16	18
British	6	8	10	12	14	16	18	20
Continental	34	36	38	40	42	44	46	48

Women's shoes

American	5	6	7	8	9	10	11
British	3	4	5	6	7	8	9
Continental	36	37	38	39	40	41	42

Men's shirts

American	14	15	15.5	16	16.5	17	17.5	18
British	14	15	15.5	16	16.5	17	17.5	18
Continental	36	38	39	41	42	43	44	45

Men's shoes

American	7	7.5	8	8.5	9.5	10	10.5	11	11.5
British	6	7	7.5	8	9	9.5	10	11	12
Continental	39	40	41	42	43	44	44	45	46

Men's suits

American	34	36	38	40	42	44	46	48
British	34	36	38	40	42	44	46	48
Continental	44	46	48	50	52	54	56	58

areas. **Credit/debit cards** are not widely used although most supermarkets and stores with pricey merchandise will accept them. **Haggling** is also uncommon in most of Italy but in more rural markets you might like to try your luck; ask for *uno sconto* (a discount) and see where it gets you. Bargaining is not practised when buying food, however, or in shops.

If you're resident outside the EU you are entitled to a rebate for the **VAT** (or *IVA*) paid on items over €180. You need to ask for a special receipt at the time of purchase and allow your goods to be checked at the airport and the receipt stamped when you leave the country. For more information, see Ⓦwww.globalrefund.com.

Travelling with children

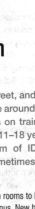

Children are adored in Italy and will be made a fuss of in the street, and welcomed and catered for in bars and restaurants. Hotels normally charge around 30 percent extra to put a bed or cot in your room, though kids pay less on trains and can generally expect discounts for museum entry: prices vary, but 11–18 year-olds are usually admitted at half price on production of some form of ID (although sometimes this applies only to EU citizens). Under 11s – or sometimes only under 6s – have free entry.

Supplies for **babies** and small children are pricey: nappies and milk formula can cost up to three times as much as in other parts of Europe. Discreet breastfeeding is widely accepted – even smiled on – but nappy changing facilities are few and far between. Branches of the children's clothes and accessories chain, Prenatal, have changing facilities and a feeding area, but otherwise you may find you have to be creative. High-chairs are unusual too, although establishments in areas that see a high-volume of foreign visitors tend to be better equipped.

Internet resources

Ⓦ**www.italyfamilyhotels.it** An organization of hotels across Italy geared up with facilities from cots and bottle warmers in rooms to baby sitters, play areas and special menus. New hotels are constantly joining.

Ⓦ**www.travelforkids.com** Advice on planning holidays with children and tips on child-friendly tourist sights and activities, region by region.

Travel With Your Children 40 Fifth Ave, New York, NY 10011 ☎212/477-5524 or 1-888/822-4388. Publishes a regular newsletter, *Family Travel Times* (Ⓦwww.familytraveltimes.com), as well as a series of books on travel with children.

Holidays With Kids Ⓦwww.holidayswithkids .com.au. The website of the popular *Holidays With Kids* magazine, this site lists kid-friendly destinations and accommodation as well as providing advice to frazzled parents. You can book tours and holidays here, too.

Work and study in Italy

All EU citizens are eligible to work and study in Italy. Work permits are pretty impossible for non-EU citizens to obtain: you must have the firm promise of a job that no Italian could do before you can even apply to the Italian embassy in your home country.

Red tape

The main bureaucratic requirements to stay legally in Italy are a *Carta di Soggiorno* and a *codigo fiscale*, respectively a card proving your right to be in the country and a tax number. Available from the *questura* (police station), a

Carta di Soggiorno requires you to produce a letter from your employer or place of study, or prove you have funds to maintain yourself. In reality, EU citizens can simply apply on the grounds of looking for work (*atessa di lavoro*) for which you'll need a passport and a photocopy, four passport photos, and a lot of patience. A **codigo fiscale** is essential for most things in Italy including buying a transport season pass, a SIM card, opening a bank account or renting a flat. It can be obtained from the local Ufficio delle Entrate although you can start the process online at ⓦwww .agenzieentrate.gov.it.

Work options

One obvious work option is to **teach English**, for which the demand has expanded enormously in recent years. You can do this in two ways: freelance private lessons, or through a language school. For the less reputable places, you can get away without any qualifications, but you'll need to show a TEFL (Teaching of English as a Foreign Language) certificate for the more professional – better paid – establishments. For the main language schools, it's best to apply in writing before you leave (look for the ads in British newspapers the *Guardian* and *Times Education Supplement*), preferably before the summer. If you're looking on the spot, sift through the phone books and do the rounds on foot but don't bother to try in August when everything is closed. The best teaching jobs of all are with a university as a *lettore*, a job requiring fewer hours than the language schools and generally providing a fuller pay-packet. Universities require English-language teachers in most faculties, and you can write to the individual faculties. Strictly speaking you could get by without any knowledge of Italian while teaching, though it obviously helps, especially when setting up private classes.

If teaching's not up your street, there's the possibility of **holiday rep work** in the summer, especially around the seaside resorts. These are good places for finding **bar or restaurant work**, too – not the most lucrative of jobs, though you should make enough to keep you over the summer. You'll have to ask around for both types of work, and some knowledge of Italian is essential. **Au pairing** is another option: sift through the ads in *The Lady* magazine to find openings.

Study programmes

One-way of spending time in Italy is to combine a visit with **learning the language**, enrolling in one of the many summer courses on Italian art and culture or joining an international work programme. There are many opportunities for studying Italian, either as part of an overseas study scheme or by applying directly to a language school when you arrive.

AFS Intercultural Programs 506 SW 6th Ave, 2nd Floor,Portland, Oregon 97204, US ☎1-800/ AFS-INFO or 212/299 9000, ⓦwww.afs.org/usa. Runs two-semester student exchange programmes.

American Institute for Foreign Study River Plaza, 9 West Broad St, Stamford, CT 06902-3788, US ☎1-800/727-2437, ⓦwww.aifs.com. Language study and cultural immersion for the summer or school year.

Australians Studying Abroad PO Box 8285, Armadale, 3143 Victoria, Australia ☎1800/645 755 or 03/9822 6899, ⓦwww.asatravinfo.com.au. Study tours focusing on art and culture.

British Council UK ☎0161/957 7755, ⓦwww .britishcouncil.org. Produces a free leaflet detailing study opportunities abroad. The Council's Central Management Direct Teaching (☎020/7389 4931) recruits TEFL teachers for posts worldwide.

Earthwatch Institute 267 Banbury Rd, Oxford OX2 7HT, UK ☎01865/318 838, ⓦwww .earthwatch.org. Exchange programme organizing research trips, which sometimes include Italy.

Elderhostel 11 Avenue de Lafayette, Boston, MA 02111, US ☎1/800-454-5768, ⓦwww.elderhostel .org. Runs activity programmes for over 60s, generally lasting a week or more and costs are in line with those of commercial tours.

International House 106 Piccadilly, London W1V 9NL, UK ☎020/7611 2400, ⓦwww.ihlondon .com. Head office for reputable English-teaching organization which offers TEFL training and recruits for teaching positions in Italy.

Italian Cultural Institute 39 Belgrave Square, London SW1X 8NX, UK ☎020/7235 1461, ⓦwww.italcultur.org.uk. The official Italian government agency for the promotion of cultural exchanges between Britain and Italy. A number of scholarships are available to British students wishing to study at Italian universities.

Socrates/Erasmus ⓦwww.ec.europa.eu. Europe-wide university-level initiative enabling students to study abroad for one year.

Travel essentials

Cost

Prices have risen considerably in Italy over the past decade, in particular accommodation costs. Generally you'll find the south much less expensive than the north. As a broad guide, expect to pay most in Venice, Milan, Florence and Bologna, less in Rome, while in Naples and Sicily prices come down quite a lot. Some **basics** are reasonably inexpensive, such as transport and, most notably, food, although drinking can be pricey unless you stick to wine. **Room rates** are in line with much of the rest of Europe, at least in the major cities and resorts. Bear in mind, too, that the **time of year** can make a big difference. During the height of summer, in July and August when the Italians take their holidays, hotel prices can escalate; outside the season, however, you can often negotiate much lower rates. There are a few **reductions** and discounts for ISIC members, under-18s and over-65s, but only in the major cities and for entry into state museums and sites.

Crime and personal safety

Despite what you hear about the Mafia, most of the **crime** you'll come across as a visitor to Italy is of the small-time variety, prevalent in the major cities and the south of the country, where pickpockets and gangs of *scippatori* or "snatchers" operate. Crowded streets or markets and packed tourist sights are the places to be wary of; *scippatori* work

on foot or on scooters, disappearing before you've had time to react. As well as handbags, they whip wallets, tear off visible jewellery and, if they're really adroit, unstrap watches. You can minimize the risk of this happening by being discreet: don't flash anything of value, keep a firm hand on your camera, and carry shoulderbags, as Italian women do, slung across your body. Never leave anything valuable in your car, and try to park in car parks on well-lit, well-used streets. On the whole it's common sense to avoid badly lit areas completely at night and deserted inner-city areas by day.

Carabinieri, with their military-style uniforms and white shoulder belts, deal with general crime, public order and drug control, while the **Vigili Urbani** are mainly concerned with directing traffic and issuing parking fines; the **Polizia Stradale** patrol the motorways. The Carabinieri tend to come from southern Italy – joining the police is one-way to escape the poverty trap – and they are posted away from home so as to be well out of the sphere of influence of their families. The **Polizia Statale**, the other general crime-fighting force, enjoy a fierce rivalry with the **Carabinieri** and are the ones you'll perhaps have most chance of coming into contact with, since **thefts** should be reported to them. You'll find the address of the **questura** or police station in the local telephone directory (in smaller places it may be just a local *commissariato*), and we've included details in the major city listings.

Emergencies

For help in an emergency, call one of the following national emergency telephone numbers:

☏ 112 for the police (Carabinieri).
☏ 113 for any emergency service, including ambulance (Soccorso Pubblico di Emergenza).
☏ 115 for the fire brigade (Vigili del Fuoco).
☏ 116 for road assistance (Soccorso Stradale).
☏ 118 for an ambulance (Ambulanza).

Electricity

The supply is 220V, though anything requiring 240V will work. Most plugs have three round pins, though you'll find the older two-pin plug in some places: a multi plug adapter is very useful.

Entry requirements

British, Irish and other EU citizens can enter Italy and stay as long as they like on production of a valid **passport**. Citizens of the United States, Canada, Australia and New Zealand need only a valid passport, too, but are limited to stays of three months. All other nationals should consult the relevant embassy about visa requirements. Legally, you're required to register with the police within three days of entering Italy, though if you're staying at a hotel this will be done for you. Although the police in some towns have become more punctilious about this, most would still be amazed at any attempt to register yourself down at the local police station while on holiday. However, if you're going to be living here for a while, you'd be advised to do it.

Italian embassies and consulates abroad

Australia Embassy: 12 Grey St, Deakin, Canberra, ACT 2600 ☎02/6273 3333, ⓦwww.ambcanberra .esteri.it. Consulates in Melbourne ☎03/9867 5744; Sydney ☎02/9392 7900; Adelaide ☎08/8337 0777; Brisbane ☎07/3229 8944.
Canada Embassy: 275 Slater St, Ottawa, ON, K1P 5H9 ☎613/232-2401, ⓦwww.ambottawa.esteri .it. Consulates in Montréal ☎514/849-8351 and Toronto ☎416/977-1566.
Ireland Embassy: 63–65 Northumberland Rd, Dublin 4 ☎01/660 1744, ⓦwww.ambdublino.esteri.it.
New Zealand Embassy: 34–38 Grant Rd, PO Box 463, Thorndon, Wellington ☎04/473-5339, ⓦwww.ambwellington.esteri.it.
South Africa Embassy: 796 George Ave, Arcadia 0083, Pretoria ☎012/423 0000, ⓦwww .ambpretoria.esteri.it.
UK Embassy: 14 Three King's Yard, London W1Y 2EH ☎020/7312 2200, ⓦwww.amblondra.esteri.it. Consulate in Manchester ☎0161/236 9024.
US Embassy: 3000 Whitehaven St NW, Washington DC 20008 ☎202/612-4400, ⓦwww .ambwashingtondc.esteri.it/. Consulates in Boston ☎617/722-9201; Chicago ☎312/467-1550; New York ☎212/737-9100; San Francisco ☎415/931-4924 and other cities nationwide.

Gay and lesbian Italy

Homosexuality is legal in Italy, and the age of consent is 16. Attitudes are most tolerant in the northern cities: Bologna is generally regarded as the gay capital, and Milan, Turin and Rome all have well-developed gay scenes; there are also a few *spiagge gay* (gay beaches) dotted along the coast: the more popular gay resorts include Taormina and Rimini. Away from the big cities and resorts, though, activity is more covert. You'll notice, in the south especially, that overt displays of affection between (all) men – linking arms during the *passeggiata*, kissing in greeting and so on – are common. The line determining what's acceptable, however, is finely drawn. The **national gay organization**, ARCI-Gay ☎051.649.3055, ⓦwww.arcigay.it, is based in Bologna but has branches in most big towns. The ⓦwww.gay.it website has a wealth of information for gays and lesbians in Italy.

Health

As a member of the European Union, Italy has free reciprocal health agreements with other member states. EU citizens are entitled to free treatment within Italy's public health-care system on production of a **European Health Insurance Card** (EHIC), which British citizens can obtain by picking up a form at the post office, calling ☎0845/606 2030, or applying online at ⓦwww.dh.gov.uk. The Australian Medicare system also has a reciprocal health-care arrangement with Italy. **Vaccinations** are not required, and Italy doesn't present any more health worries than anywhere else in Europe; the worst that's likely to happen to you is suffering from the extreme heat in summer or from an upset stomach. The **water** is perfectly safe to drink and you'll find public fountains (usually button- or tap-operated) in squares and city streets everywhere, though look out for *acqua non potabile* signs, indicating that the water is unsafe to drink. It's worth taking **insect repellent**, as even inland towns, most notoriously Milan, suffer from a persistent mosquito problem, especially in summer.

An Italian **pharmacist** (*farmacia*) is well qualified to give you advice on minor ailments and to dispense prescriptions; pharmacies are generally open all night in the bigger towns and cities. A rota system operates, and you should find the address of the one currently open on any *farmacia* door or listed in the local paper. If you need to see a **doctor** (*medico*); take your EHIC with you to enable you to get free treatment and prescriptions for medicines at the local rate – about 10 percent of the price of the medicine. If you are seriously ill or involved in an accident, go straight to the *Pronto Soccorso* (casualty) of the nearest hospital (*ospedale*), or phone ☎113 and ask for or an *ambulanza*. Throughout the Guide, you'll find listings for pharmacies, hospitals and emergency services in all the major cities. Major train stations and airports also often have first-aid stations with qualified doctors on hand.

Incidentally, try to avoid going to the **dentist** (*dentista*) while you're in Italy. These aren't covered by your EHIC or the health service, and for the smallest problem you'll pay through the teeth. Take local advice, or consult the local Yellow Pages. If you don't have a spare pair of glasses, it's worth taking a copy of your prescription so that an optician (*ottico*) can make you up a new pair should you lose or damage them.

Insurance

Even though EU health care privileges apply in Italy, you'd do well to take out an **insurance policy** before travelling to cover against theft, loss, illness or injury. A typical policy usually provides cover for the loss of baggage, tickets and – up to a certain limit – cash or cheques, as well as cancellation or curtailment of your journey. Most policies exclude so-called dangerous sports unless an extra premium is paid; in Italy this can mean scuba-diving, windsurfing and trekking. Many policies can be chopped and changed to exclude coverage you don't need – for example,

sickness and accident benefits can often be excluded or included at will. If you do take medical coverage, ascertain whether benefits will be paid as treatment proceeds or only after your return home, and whether there is a 24-hour medical emergency number. When securing baggage cover, make sure that the per-article limit – typically under £500 – will cover your most valuable possession. If you need to make a claim, you should keep receipts for medicines and medical treatment, and in the event you have anything stolen, you must obtain an official statement from the police (*polizia* or *carabinieri*).

Laundries

Coin-operated Laundromats, sometimes known as *tintorie*, are rare outside large cities, and even there, numbers are sparse; see the "Listings" sections of the main city accounts for addresses. More common is a *lavanderia*, a service-wash laundry, but this will be more expensive. Although you can usually get away with it, beware of washing clothes in your hotel room simply because the plumbing often can't cope with all the water. It's better to ask if there's somewhere you can wash your clothes.

Mail

Post office opening hours are usually Monday–Saturday 8.30am–7.30pm, though branches in smaller towns tend to close at 1pm. Note too that offices close an hour earlier on the last working day of the month. **Stamps** (*francobolli*) are sold in *tabacchi*, too, as well as in some gift shops in the tourist resorts; they will often also weigh your letter. The Italian postal system is one of the slowest in Europe so if your letter is urgent make sure you send it "*posta prioritaria*",

Rough Guides travel insurance

Rough Guides has teamed up with Columbus Direct to offer you tailor-made **travel insurance**. Products include a low-cost **backpacker** option for long stays; a **short break** option for city getaways; a typical **holiday package** option; and others. There are also annual **multi-trip** policies for those who travel regularly. Different sports and activities (trekking, skiing, etc) can usually be included.

See our website (ⓦwww.roughguides.com/website/shop) for eligibility and purchasing options. Alternatively, UK residents can call ☎0870/033 9988; Australians ☎1300/669 999 and New Zealanders ☎0800/559 911. All other nationalities should call ☎+44 870/890 2843.

which has varying rates according to weight and destination. Letters can be sent *poste restante* to any Italian post office by addressing them "*Fermo Posta*" followed by the name of the town. When picking something up take your passport, and make sure they check under middle names and initials – and every other letter when all else fails – as filing is often diabolical.

Maps

The **town plans** throughout the Guide should be fine for most purposes, and practically all tourist offices give out maps of their local area for free. The clearest and best-value large-scale commercial **road map** of Italy is the Rough Guide 1:900,000 map, which covers the whole country including Sicily and Sardinia. There are also the 1:800,000 and 1:400,000 maps produced by the Touring Club Italiano, covering north, south and central Italy, and TCI also produces excellent 1:200,000 maps of the individual regions, which are indispensable if you are touring a specific area in depth.

For **hiking** you'll need at least a scale of 1:50,000. Studio FMB and the TCI cover the major mountain areas of northern Italy to this scale, but for more detailed, down-to-scale 1:25,000 maps, both the Istituto Geografico Centrale and Kompass series cover central and northwest Italy and the Alps. The Apennines and Tuscany are covered by Multigraphic (Firenze), easiest bought in Italy, while Tabacco produces a good series detailing the Dolomites and the northeast of the country. In Italy, the Club Alpino Italiano (Ⓦwww.cai.it) is a good source of hiking maps; we've supplied details of branches throughout the Guide.

Money

Italy's currency is the **euro** (€; note that Italians pronounce it "eh-uro") which is split into 100 cents (*centesimi*). In Italy, you'll get the best rate of exchange (*cambio*) at a **bank**. **Banking hours** are normally Monday to Friday mornings from 8.30am until 1.30pm, and for an hour in the afternoon (usually 2.30–4pm). There are local variations on this and banks are usually open only in the morning on the day before a public holiday. Outside banking hours, the larger **hotels** will change money or traveller's cheques, although if you're staying in a reasonably large city the rate is invariably better at the train station **exchange bureaux** – normally open evenings and weekends. **ATMs** are common with most towns and even villages having at least one, although, as in most countries, you won't be able to withdraw more than €250 per day.

Opening hours, public holidays

Most shops and businesses open Monday to Saturday from around 8am until 1pm, and from about 4pm until 7pm, though many close on Saturday afternoons and Monday mornings, and in the south the day can begin and end an hour later. In the north some businesses work a 9-to-5 day to facilitate international dealings. Traditionally, everything except bars and restaurants closes on Sunday, though most towns have a *pasticceria* open in the mornings, while in large cities and tourist areas, Sunday shopping is becoming more common.

Churches, museums and archeological sites

Most churches open in the early morning, around 7 or 8am for Mass, and close around noon, opening up again at 4pm and closing at 7 or 8pm. In more remote places, some will only open for early morning and evening services, while others are closed at all times except Sundays and on religious holidays; if you're determined to take a look, you may have to ask around for the

Visiting churches and religious sites

The rules for visiting churches, cathedrals and religious buildings are much the same as they are all over the Mediterranean and are strictly enforced everywhere: **dress modestly**, which means no shorts (not even Bermuda-length ones) and covered shoulders for women, and try to avoid wandering around during a service.

key. Another problem is that lots of churches, monasteries, convents and oratories are **closed for restoration** (*chiuso per restauro*), though you might be able to persuade someone to show you around even if there's scaffolding everywhere.

Opening hours for state-run **museums and most private ones** are generally Tuesday to Saturday 9am until any time from 2pm until 7pm, and Sunday from 9am until 1pm. Many large museums also run late-night openings in summer (till 10pm or later Tues–Sat, or 8pm Sun). The opening times of **archeological sites** are more flexible: most sites open every day, often including Sunday, from 9am until late evening – frequently specified as one hour before sunset, and thus changing according to the time of year. In winter, times are drastically cut, principally because of the darker evenings; 4pm is a common closing time.

Public holidays

Whereas it can be fun to stumble across a local festival, it's best to know when the national holidays are as almost everything will shut down. In **August**, particularly during the weeks either side of *Ferragosto* (Aug 15), when most of the country flees to the coast and mountains, many towns are left half-deserted, with shops, bars and restaurants closed and a reduced public transport service. Local religious holidays don't necessarily close down shops and businesses, but they do mean that accommodation space may be tight. The country's official **national holidays**, on the other hand, close everything down except bars and restaurants. A recent initiative has been to open national museums and monuments on public holidays to encourage Italians to make the most of their national heritage, although it's still best to check beforehand if you are planning a trip around one particular sight.

January 1 Primo dell'anno New Year's Day
January 6 Epifania Epiphany
Pasquetta Easter Monday
April 25 Giorno della Liberazione Liberation Day
May 1 Festa dei Lavoratori Labour Day
June 2 Festa della Repubblica Republic Day
August 15 Ferragosto Assumption of the Blessed Virgin Mary

November 1 Ognissanti All Souls Day
December 8 Immacolata Immaculate Conception of the Blessed Virgin Mary
December 25 Natale Christmas
December 26 Santo Stefano St Stephen's Day

Phones

Public **telephones**, run by **Telecom Italia**, come in various forms, usually with clear instructions in English. Coin-operated machines are increasingly hard to find so you will probably have to buy a **telephone card** (*carta* or *scheda telefonica*), available from *tabacchi* and newsstands. **Telephone numbers** change with amazing frequency in Italy and codes are now an integral part of the number and always need to be dialled, regardless of whether or not you are in the zone you are telephoning. All telephone numbers listed in the Guide include the relevant code. Numbers beginning ☏800 are free, ☏170 will get you through to an English-speaking operator, ☏176 to international directory enquiries.

Phone **tariffs** are among the most expensive in Europe, especially if you're calling long-distance or internationally. You can cut costs hugely by buying a **phone card** – on sale from newspaper kiosks for upwards of €5; you don't insert it into the phone but dial a freephone central number and then a pin code given on the reverse of the card.

Time

Italy is always one hour ahead of Britain, seven hours ahead of US Eastern Standard Time and ten hours ahead of Pacific Time.

Tourist information

Before you leave home, it may be worth contacting the Italian State Tourist Office (ENIT, ⓦwww.enit.it) for a selection of maps and brochures, though you can usually pick up much the same information from tourist offices in Italy. Most towns, major train stations and airports in Italy have a **tourist office** or "APT"

Closed Mondays

Most museums, archeological sites and tourist destinations throughout the country are closed on Mondays.

Calling home from Italy

UK & Northern Ireland international access code + 44 + city code.
Ireland international access code + 353 + city code.
US & Canada international access code + 1 + area code.
Australia international access code + 61 + city code.
New Zealand international access code + 64 + city code.

(Azienda Promozione Turistica) or "IAT" (Ufficio Informazioni Accoglienza Turistica), all of which vary in degree of usefulness (and helpfulness) but usually provide at least a town plan and local listings guide. In smaller villages there is sometimes a "Pro Loco" office that has much the same kind of information, but the staff are less likely to speak English.

Opening hours vary: larger city and resort offices are likely to be open Monday to Saturday 9am to 1pm and 4 to 7pm, and sometimes for a short period on Sunday mornings; smaller offices may open weekdays only, while Pro Loco times are notoriously erratic – some open for only a couple of hours a day, even in summer.

Italian State Tourist Offices abroad

Australia Level 4, 46 Market St, Sydney, NSW 2000 ☎ 02/926-21666, ⓦ www.italiantourism.com.au.
Canada 175 Bloor St East, Suite 907, South Tower, Toronto, ON M4W 3R8 ☎ 416/925-4882, ⓦ www.italiantourism.com.
UK 1 Princes St, London W1B 2AY ☎ 0270/408 1254, ⓦ www.italiantouristboard.co.uk.
US 630 Fifth Ave, Suite 1565, New York, NY 10111 ☎ 212/245-5618; 12400 Wilshire Boulevard, Suite 550, Los Angeles, CA 90025 ☎ 310/820-1898; 500 North Michigan Ave, 506, Chicago, IL 60611 ☎ 312/644-0996; ⓦ www.italiantourism.com.

Travellers with disabilities

Facilities in Italy aren't geared towards disabled travellers, though people are helpful enough and progress is being made to make accommodation, transport and public buildings more accessible.

Public transport can be challenging, although low-level buses are gradually being introduced and some trains have disabled facilities. There will be several appropriate accommodation options in most resorts and you might want to ask the local tourist office to give you a hand with finding the most suitable. In more out-of-the-way places it's rather pot luck. Spacious, specially designed toilets are becoming increasingly common in bars and restaurants as new legislation takes force. The cobbled streets in old town and village centres can present their own problems, as can access to sights including galleries and museums. Even in the larger cities high curbs, ad hoc parking and constant building works can make life difficult for those in wheelchairs and the partially sighted.

Contacts for travellers with disabilities

Access-Able ⓦ www.access-able.com. Online resource for travellers with disabilities.
Accessible Italy Italy ☎ 378.994.1111, ⓦ www.accessibleitaly.com. Italian operation offering organized tours or tailor-made trips to foreigners.
Accessible Journeys 35 West Sellers Av, Ridley Park PA, US ☎ 800/846-4537, ⓦ www.disabilitytravel.com. Travel tips and programmes for groups or individual travellers.
Disabled Persons Assembly ☎ 04/801 9100, ⓦ www.dpa.org.nz. Resource centre with lists of travel agencies and tour operators for people with disabilities.
Holiday Care The Hawkins Suite, Enham Place, Enham Alamein, Andover SP11 6JS, UK ☎ 0845/124 9971, ⓦ www.holidaycare.org.uk. Provides free lists of accessible accommodation abroad and information on financial help for holidays.
Irish Wheelchair Association Blackheath Drive, Clontarf, Dublin 3, Ireland ☎ 01/818 6400, ⓦ www.iwa.ie. Information and listings for wheelchair users travelling abroad.
Society for the Advancement of Travellers with Handicaps (SATH) 347 5th Ave, New York, NY 10016, US ☎ 212/447-7284, ⓦ www.sath.org. Information on the accessibility of specific airlines and advice on travelling with certain conditions.
NICAN ⓦ www.ncan.com.au. Website including information about the Quantas Carers Concession card.

Guide

Guide

Piemonte and
Valle d'Aosta

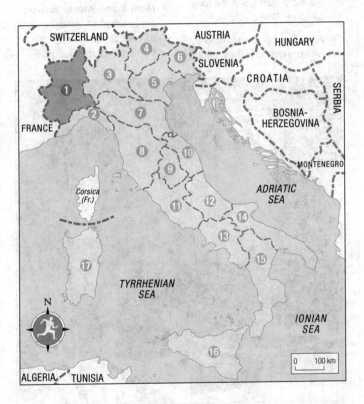

CHAPTER 1 # Highlights

* **White truffles** This very costly speciality is shaved onto pasta and washed down with the excellent local Barolo or Barbaresco wine. See p.67

* **Sacra di San Michele** The views of the surrounding valley from this fortified abbey are more than worth the long climb up. See p.82

* **Alba** This hill-town boasts a well-preserved historic centre with a fancifully decorated bubblegum-pink Gothic Duomo. See p.86

* **Parco Nazionale del Gran Paradiso** Italy's first national park preserves Alpine valleys and peaks that are home to ibex, chamois and golden eagles. See p.95

* **Mont Blanc (Monte Bianco)** Enjoy excellent views of this awe-inspiring mountain from the Testa d'Arpy. See p.99

▲ Sacra di San Michele

Piemonte and Valle d'Aosta

n the extreme northwest of Italy, fringed by the French and Swiss Alps and grooved with deep valleys, **Piemonte** and **Valle d'Aosta** are among the least "Italian" regions in the country. Piemontesi spoke French until the end of the nineteenth century and Piemontese dialects reflect Provençal influence; Valle d'Aosta is bilingual and in some valleys the locals, whose ancestors emigrated from Switzerland, still speak a dialect based on German. Piemonte (literally "at the foot of the mountains") is one of Italy's wealthiest regions, known for its fine wines and food and for being home to huge Italian corporations such as Fiat and Olivetti. Italy's longest river, the mighty Po, begins here, and the towns of its vast plain – which stretches right across northern Italy – have grown rich on both manufacturing and rice, cultivated in sweeping paddy fields.

Turin, on the main rail and road route from France to Milan, is the obvious first stop and, despite being Italy's second industrial city, retains a freshly restored Baroque core and is well placed for days out. South of Turin, **Alba** is the most enticing town, and a good base for visiting the region's wine cantinas. **Asti**, to the southeast, really comes to life during its famous medieval Palio, or horse race. For the rest of the region, winter sports and walking are the main activities; Sestriere is the main skiing centre, whilst the ascent of Monviso in the far west appeals to the climbing fraternity.

Further spectacular hikes and views are to be found in the adjoining region of **Valle d'Aosta**. Bordered by Europe's highest mountains, Mont Blanc, Monte Rosa and the Matterhorn, veined with valleys and studded with castles, the region is undeniably picturesque. The central Aosta valley cuts right across it, following the River Dora to the foot of Mont Blanc on the French border. The main valley is rather bland, and it's in the more scenic tributary valleys that you'll want to spend most of your time. **Aosta**, the regional capital, is the only town of any size and, with its attractive cobbled streets and good shopping, makes an excellent staging post on the way to the smaller mountain resorts.

Straddling the two provinces is the protected zone of Italy's oldest and largest national park, the mountainous **Gran Paradiso**. The valleys here can be busy – the mountain *rifugi* and hotels become packed in summer – but development is purposely restrained to preserve pristine conditions.

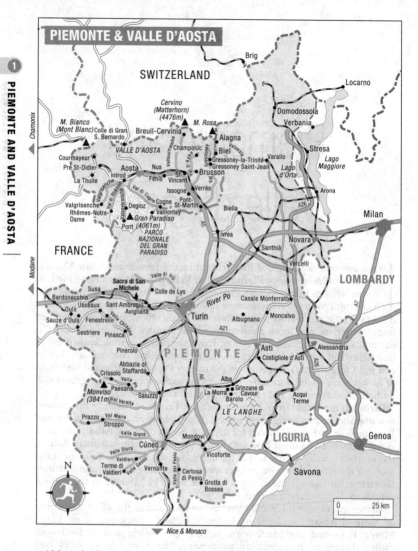

Although the western shore of **Lago Maggiore** is actually in Piemonte, we've treated all the lakes as a region and covered them in the "Lombardy and the lakes" chapter; the Maggiore account starts on p.193.

Transport

Getting around Piemonte is fairly easy. The network of trains and buses is comprehensive, and your own transport is only necessary for the out-of-the-way places. You can get to most places from Turin; Alba makes a good base for Le Langhe, Saluzzo for the western valleys.

Using public transport to explore the **Valle d'Aosta** is a bit trickier: buses run from Piemonte along the main valley past most of the castles, but services

Regional food and wine

Piemonte and Valle d'Aosta are a paradise for gastronomes and connoisseurs of vintage wines. Rich Piemontese cuisine betrays close links with France through dishes like *fonduta* (fondue) and its preference for using **butter** and **cream** in cooking. Piemonte is perhaps most famous for its **white truffles**, the most exquisite of which come from around the town of Alba and are ferociously expensive. They are most often used in the form of shavings to subtly perfume a dish of pasta or a risotto. Watch out too for porcini mushrooms, chestnuts, and **bagna caöda** – a sauce of oil, anchovies, garlic, butter and cream, also served as a fondue. *Agnolotti* (pasta filled with meat or possibly with mushrooms or other vegetables) is the best-known dish, followed by meat *buji* (boiled) or braised in wine. Cheeses to look out for are *tomini*, *robiole* and *tume*. The sweets, too, are marvellous: among the decadent delights are *spumone piemontese*, a mousse of mascarpone cheese with rum; *panna cotta*, smooth cooked cream; and light pastries like *lingue di gatto* (cat's tongues) and *baci di dama* (lady's kisses). The best known is the *bonet*, a confection of chocolate and *amaretti*. Turin is also credited as the home of *zabaglione*, an egg yolk, sugar and Marsala mixture used to fill *bignole*, or iced choux pastries.

The rolling vine-clad hills of Le Langhe and Monferrato produce traditional **wines** such as Barolo, Barbera and Nebbiolo. These fine reds need ageing, and Barolo in particular can be very expensive. More suitable for everyday drinking are wines made from the *dolcetto* grape, notably Dolcetto d'Alba, drunk young and lightly chilled. Probably the most famous is the sweet sparkling wine, Asti (wine makers dropped the "spumante" from the name in 1994 in a bid for a new image) – there has been a trend in recent years to make dry *spumante* too. Martini & Rossi and Cinzano vermouths are also produced in and around Turin, a fusion of the region's wines with at least thirteen of the wild herbs that grow on its mountains. The traditional version to drink, now a brand name, is Punt e Mes ("point and a half") – one part bitter to half-a-part sweet.

connecting the tributary valleys are infrequent, while trains are less regular and run only as far as Pré-St-Didier. For serious exploration of the quieter valleys, your own vehicle is a definite advantage. The road branches off at Aosta into Switzerland via the Grand-St-Bernard Pass and forks again some 30km further west at Pré-St-Didier: both branches run into France – the southern via the Petit-St-Bernard Pass to Chambéry, the northern to Chamonix through the Mont Blanc tunnel. As these roads link France and Italy, they are much used by long-distance lorries, which are something of an earache and eyesore. However, a tunnel between Bruzolo and St Jean de Maurienne, still in its early phases, will permit lorries to be transported by rail, and should dramatically reduce traffic and pollution by the year 2020.

Turin (Torino)

"Do you know Turin?" asked Nietzsche. "It is a city after my own heart … a princely residence of the seventeenth century, which has only one taste, giving commands to everything, the court and its nobility. Aristocratic calm is preserved in everything; there are no nasty suburbs."

Although **TURIN**'s thoroughfares are far from calm, and its suburbs are as dreary as any in Italy, the renovated city centre's gracious Baroque avenues and squares, opulent palaces, and splendid collections of Egyptian antiquities and northern European paintings are still there, as well as spanking-new

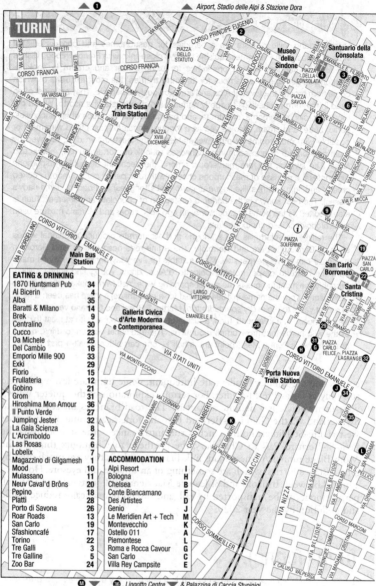

TURIN

Airport, Stadio delle Alpi & Stazione Dora

CORSO PRINCIPE EUGENIO

PIAZZA DELLO STATUTO

CORSO FRANCIA

CORSO FRANCIA

Museo della Sindone

Santuario della Consolata

PIAZZA DELLA CONSOLATA

PIAZZA SAVOIA

Porta Susa Train Station

PIAZZA XVIII DICEMBRE

Main Bus Station

PIAZZA SOLFERINO

San Carlo Borromeo

Santa Cristina

CORSO MATTEOTTI

LARGO VITTORIO

Galleria Civica d'Arte Moderna e Contemporanea

Porta Nuova Train Station

CORSO VITTORIO EMANUELE II

PIAZZA CARLO FELICE

PIAZZA LAGRANGE

PIAZZA SAN CARLO

EATING & DRINKING	
1870 Huntsman Pub	34
Al Bicerin	4
Alba	35
Baratti & Milano	14
Brek	9
Centralino	30
Cucco	23
Da Michele	25
Del Cambio	16
Emporio Mille 900	33
Exki	29
Fiorio	15
Frullateria	12
Gobino	21
Grom	31
Hiroshima Mon Amour	36
Il Punto Verde	27
Jumping Jester	32
La Gaia Scienza	8
L'Arcimboldo	2
Las Rosas	6
Lobelix	7
Magazzino di Gilgamesh	1
Mood	10
Mulassano	11
Neuv Caval'd Brôns	20
Pepino	18
Platti	28
Porto di Savona	26
Roar Roads	13
San Carlo	19
Sfashioncafé	17
Torino	22
Tre Galli	3
Tre Galline	5
Zoo Bar	24

ACCOMMODATION	
Alpi Resort	I
Bologna	H
Chelsea	B
Conte Biancamano	F
Des Artistes	D
Genio	J
Le Meridien Art + Tech	M
Montevecchio	K
Ostello 011	A
Piemontese	L
Roma e Rocca Cavour	G
San Carlo	C
Villa Rey Campsite	E

, Lingotto Centre & Palazzina di Caccia Stupinigi

pedestrian-only areas – a pleasant surprise to those who might have been expecting satanic factories and little else. Ever since the major spruce-up for the 2006 Winter Olympics, Turin's emphasis has been on promoting its historic urban charms, such as its genteel *belle époque* cafés and traditional chocolate treats – not to mention an array of walking tours that explore the city's extraordinary, vivid heritage.

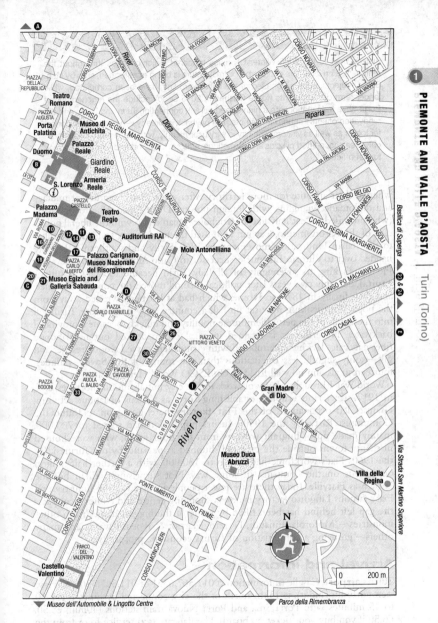

Some history

Although originally an ancient Roman settlement, it was the Savoy dynasty that left the largest impression on Turin: from 1563 the city was the seat of the **Savoy dukes**, who persecuted Piemonte's Protestants and Jews, censored the press and placed education of the nobles in the fanatical hands of the Jesuits. The Savoys gained a royal title in 1713, and a few years later acquired Sardinia, which

The transformation of Turin

Playing host to the 2006 Winter Olympics triggered major changes throughout the region. In Turin itself, the entire urban infrastructure is being transformed, step by step. Some projects, such as one leg of the new metro line, have been completed, while longer-term developments (to be finished in 2015 or so) include the regeneration of Porta Susa train station into a high-speed rail link connecting Turin and Lyon, and the renovation of some suburban districts. The payback is already very much in evidence, for locals as well as visitors. The city is very user-friendly, with many more pedestrian-only areas, face-lifted piazzas and attractions, efficient transport and friendly, informed tourist offices.

whetted their appetite for more territory. After more than a century of military and diplomatic wrangling with foreign powers, Duke Carlo Alberto di Savoia (who promised to "eat Italy like an artichoke") teamed up with the liberal politician of the Risorgimento, Cavour, who used the royal family to lend credibility to the Italian Unification movement. In 1860, Sicily and southern Italy were handed over to Vittorio Emanuele, successor to Carlo Alberto, thereby elevating Piemonte's king to sovereignty of all Italy. Turin became the new country's **capital**, but only two years later, political turmoil moved the court to Florence, and then finally in 1870, to Rome, which had at last been wrested away from the pope. With its king now set up half a country away from home, Turin fell into the hands of the petty Piemontese nobility and quickly became a provincial backwater. Nevertheless, it retained its regal centre decked out in elaborate finery: its cafés lavishly encumbered with chandeliers, carved wood, frescoes and gilt – only slightly less ostentatious than the rooms of the **Savoy palaces**, fourteen in all, and now all listed as UNESCO World Heritage sites.

World War I brought plenty of work to the city, but also food shortages, and, in 1917, street riots erupted, establishing Turin as a focus of labour activism. Gramsci led occupations of the **Fiat factory** here, going on to found the Communist Party. By the 1950s, Turin's population had soared to 700,000, mainly made up of migrant workers from the poor south, who were housed in shanty towns outside the city and shunned as peasants by the Torinesi. By the 1960s Fiat's workforce had grown to 130,000, with a further half million dependent on the company in some way. Not surprisingly, Turin became known as Fiatville. Today there are fewer people involved in the industry, and Fiat's famous Lingotto factory is now a shopping centre and conference space; the gap left behind has been filled by some of the biggest names from other industries – Motorola, Einaudi, Ferrero, Martini & Rossi, Lavazza and many others – ensuring a continuation of Turin's economic prosperity.

Arrival and information

Turin's **airport**, Caselle (information ☎011.567.6361 or 011.567.6362, ⓦwww .aeroportoditorino.it), is 15km north of the city, connected by buses every 30 to 45 minutes with Porta Susa and Porta Nuova train stations (40min; €5.50, €6.50 if you buy your ticket on board). The flat-rate **taxi** service to or from the airport costs €30. Turin's main **train station**, Porta Nuova, on Corso Vittorio Emanuele II at the southern end of Via Roma, is convenient for the city centre and hotels. Some trains also stop at Porta Susa on Corso Inghilterra (Piazza XVIII Dicembre), west of the centre and heralded as the city's primary hub in the near future (see box above). Close by, at Corso Vittorio Emanuele II, 131/H, is the main **bus station** (ⓦwww.autostazionetorino.it), the arrival and departure point for most intercity and all international buses; however, local buses to Saluzzo and Cúneo arrive at, and leave from, the top of Corso Marconi, near the junction with Via Nizza. The bus station is linked to Via Nizza (near Porta Nuova) and Porta Susa by bus #9.

The main **tourist office** is in Piazza Castello at Via Garibaldi (daily 9am–7pm; ☎011.535.181, ⓦwww.turismotorino.org). There are also branches at the Porta Nuova train station (daily 9.30am–7pm) and the airport (daily 8am–11pm); as well as a good range of information they can supply you with the very reasonable **Torino+Piemonte Card** (€18 for 48hr, €21 for 72hr or €31 for 5 days), allowing free entrance to some 180 museums and sights, plus discounts on guided tours, theatre performances, concerts, opera, parking and even car rental. It also includes free use of urban transport and a discount on the City Sightseeing bus (see below).

City transport

Most of Turin's sights are within walking distance of Porta Nuova station, although if you're pushed for time you should take advantage of the city's fast and efficient **tram and bus** network (ⓦwww.gtt.to.it). Tickets, valid for seventy minutes, must be bought before you board – they cost €1 each or €13.50 for fifteen from *tabacchi* and newsstands. Useful **routes** include tram #4, which heads north through the city from Porta Nuova along Via XX Settembre to Piazza della Repubblica; bus #1 between Porta Nuova and the Lingotto centre; tram #15 from Porta Nuova to Piazza Castello; bus #61 from Porta Nuova across the river; and bus #34 from Porta Nuova to the Sassi-Superga tramway. Alternatively, it's possible to explore the city by **City Sightseeing** (daily, circuit every hour 10am–8pm, Jan & Feb until 4pm; €15, valid 24hr), which operates a hop-on-hop-off circular route that takes in the major sights. You can pick it up at Piazza Castello and eight other points along the route. Tickets can be bought on the bus. **Taxi** ranks are found on most of the main squares in the centre of Turin, as well as at the bus and train stations and the airport, or dial ☎011.5730 or 011.5737.

Accommodation

Turin has a number of attractive **hotels** in every quarter. Demand is usually high, especially during the skiing season and trade fairs (when prices also rise), so it's a good idea to phone in advance. Be aware that virtually all of them offer special weekend packages – and that a few hotels close in August, which is low season for Turin.

Hotels

Alpi Resort Via A. Bonafous 5 ☎011.812.9677 ⓦwww.hotelalpiresort.it. An elegant entrance on a busy street near the river leads to modest but attractive soundproofed rooms. Services include parking, laundry and internet. Breakfast extra. ⑤

Bologna Corso Vittorio Emanuele II 60 ☎011.562.0191, ⓦwww.hotelbolognasrl.it. Ideally located for transport, in a period building offering 45 recently remodelled rooms. Amenities include minibars, satellite TV and parking. Breakfast included. ❸

Chelsea Via Cappel Verde 1/D ☎011.436.0100, ⓦwww.hotelchelsea.it. Newly restructured, the rooms here are well appointed and soundproof, with a/c, minibars and other quality touches. The hotel

also has its own restaurant *La Campana*, featuring Pugliese specialities. Breakfast not included. ⑤

Conte Biancamano Corso Vittorio Emanuele II 73 ☎011.562.3281, ⓦwww.hotelcontebiancamano.it. If you feel like staying in a rather grandiose setting, go for this hotel set in an old palace with panelled ceilings and large, freshly remodelled rooms. Breakfast included. ⑤

Des Artistes Via Principe Amedeo 21 ☎011.812.4416, ⓦwww.desartisteshotel.it. Not far from the main sights, this comfortable, spacious hotel has simple, smart rooms with amenities such as a/c; parking available. Breakfast included. ⑥

Genio Corso Vittorio Emanuele II 47 ☎011.650.5771, ⓦwww.hotelgenio.it. Very large, three-star Best Western, occupying a historic building just outside Porta Nuova station. Rooms are elegant and diverse, some even boasting ceiling frescoes. Impressive buffet breakfast included. ⑥

Le Meridien Art + Tech Via Nizza 230 ☎011.664.2000, @www.lemeridien-lingotto.com. For an all-out luxury treat head for this slightly out-of-the-way, five-star designer emporium set in the old Fiat works and redesigned by Renzo Piano. You can go jogging on Fiat's ex-test track on the roof – and there are some lovely views too. Sumptuous breakfast included. ⑨

Montevecchio Via Montevecchio 13 bis ☎011.562.0023, @www.hotelmontevecchio.com. That rare thing – a quiet hotel near the train station. Though rather spartan, this one also has good facilities, with TV and telephone in all rooms. Breakfast included. ❸

Piemontese Via Berthollet 21 ☎011.669.8101, @www.hotelpiemontese.it. Handy location on the colourful, commercial side of the train station. The newly refurbished rooms range from suites with Jacuzzi to comfortable singles. Buffet breakfast included (note that the afternoon aperitif and parking are extra). ⑤

Roma e Rocca Cavour Piazza Carlo Felice 60 ☎011.561.2772, @www.romarocca.it. Large,

old-style, family-run hotel in front of the Porta Nuova station, overlooking a lively square with park and fountain. All in all, good value and classically attractive, with the choice of a very substantial buffet breakfast at €8 per person. All rooms have free wi-fi. ❸

San Carlo Piazza San Carlo 197 ☎011.562.7846, @www.albergosancarlo.it. An elegant and very good-value one-star overlooking Turin's grandest piazza. No breakfast, but smart, historic cafés line the arcaded square. ❸

Hostels and campsites

Ostello 011 Corso Venezia 11 ☎011.250.535, @www.openzero11.it. This brand-new hostel although colourful, is downright spartan but comfortable enough, serving also as a youth centre. Dorm bed and breakfast rates start at €16.50, with half- and full-board also offered. Private rooms are available.

Villa Rey Strada Comunale Val San Martino Superiore 27 ☎011.819.0117, @www.campingvillarey.it. The most convenient of the city's campsites – take bus #61 from Porta Nuova, and then bus #54. Always open. From about €10 daily.

The City

The grid street-plan of Turin's Baroque centre makes it easy to find your way about. **Via Roma** is the central spine of the city, a grand affair lined with rejuvenated designer shops and ritzy cafés. It's punctuated by the city's most elegant piazzas: at one end Piazza Carlo Felice, boasting a small park; in the middle Piazza San Carlo, close to which are some of the more prestigious museums; and at the other end, Piazza Castello, with its royal palaces standing stately in a vast pedestrian-only zone. Flanking are pedestrianized shopping streets, more relaxed than Via Roma and noted for the evening *passeggiata* in summer. North is the **Piazza della Repubblica**, a huge square with the largest open-air market in Europe. To the east the porticoes of Via Po lead to Piazza Vittorio Veneto, slanting down to the **River Po**, along which a stroll southward brings you to the extensive Parco del Valentino, and some of the city's best nightlife just downriver at Murazzi. Beyond is the engaging **Museo Nazionale dell'Automobile** and the Lingotto centre, which houses the Pinacoteca Giovanni e Marella Agnelli, an art gallery displaying the Fiat magnates' superb private collection, while the hills across the river – which are peppered with the Art Nouveau villas of the richest Torinesi – are crowned by the **Basilica di Superga**. Farther south, beyond the city limits, lies the royal Stupinigi Hunting-Lodge.

Porta Nuova and around

The area along the east side of the **Porta Nuova** station was still a construction site at the time of writing and the situation has only exacerbated the usual seediness endemic to all major train stations in Italy. The western flank is uneventful, but the eastern side is a kind of no-man's-land haunt of prostitutes and petty criminals, though the potentially elegant arcades (*portici*) of Via Nizza and

Corso Vittorio Emanuele II are typical of Turin's measured symmetry – the city boasts over 40km of these colonnaded walkways.

A few blocks west of here, the **GAM** (Galleria Civica d'Arte Moderna e Contemporanea) at Via Magenta 31 (Tues–Sun 10am–6pm; €7.50; ⓦwww.gamtorino.it) features a good cross-section of twentieth-century works by artists as varied as De Chirico, Morandi, Modigliani, Picasso, Klee and Warhol. The rest of the collection is highlighted only by a fine work by the nineteenth-century French Realist painter Gustave Courbet. However, as the gallery is on the international circuit for touring exhibitions and loans, there is often more than enough to compensate.

Via Roma and Piazza San Carlo
Back at Porta Nuova, crossing the road brings you to the neat gardens of busy **Piazza Carlo Felice**, beyond which begins **Via Roma**, the stamping ground of the well heeled. Halfway down, spacious **Piazza San Carlo** is known with some justification as the parlour of Turin; it's a grand, cloister-like space fronted by Baroque facades, the porticoes of which house elegant cafés. Holding court is an equestrian statue of the Savoy duke Emanuele Filiberto raising his sword in triumph after securing Turin's independence from the French and Spanish at the battle of San Quintino in 1574. The entrance to the square is watched over by two gigantic Fascist-era reclining nudes representing Turin's two rivers, the Po and the Dora, and past them the twin Baroque churches of **San Carlo Borromeo** and **Santa Cristina**.

The Museo Egizio and Galleria Sabauda
Around the corner from Piazza San Carlo, the newly refurbished **Museo Egizio**, Via Accademia delle Scienze 6 (Tues–Sun 8.30am–7.30pm; €7.50; ⓦwww .museoegizio.it), holds a superb collection of Egyptian antiquities, begun under the aegis of Carlo Emanuele III in the mid-eighteenth century and added to over the ensuing centuries. With some thirty thousand artefacts, it's the largest collection of Egyptian antiquities outside of Cairo. The ground floor evokes a vast temple, with massive granite sphinxes, gods and pharaohs looming out of the subdued lighting. Upstairs, you'll find decorated mummy cases and an intriguing assortment of everyday objects, including castanets, sandals, a linen tunic dating from 2300 BC, and even food – eggs, pomegranates and grain, recognizable despite their shrivelled, darkened state. The collection's undoubted highlights are a **statue of Ramses II** and the **Tomb of Kha and Mirit**. The tomb, discovered in 1906 at Deir-el-Medina, is that of a 1400 BC architect, Kha, and his wife Mirit. Kha's burial chamber contains an astonishing assortment of after-life supplies, including a board game to while away the posthumous hours, as well as his own personal illustrated copy of the Egyptian Book of the Dead. And to ensure that Mirit kept up appearances, she was provided with a cosmetic case, wig, comb and tweezers.

Walking tours

Turin is very pedestrian-friendly and a fine place to take a **walking tour**, with various themes on offer. Perhaps the most intriguing tour is based on the city's age-old reputation as one of the three great European centres of the occult (along with London and Prague). To visit some of the noted esoteric sites, relating to both black and white magic, check out ⓦwww.somewhere.it for their Magic Turin evening walking tour (Thurs & Sat; 9pm at Piazza Statuto; 2hr 30min; €20). If the arcane is not your thing, they also offer at least eleven other tours, including Subterranean Turin (Fri; 8.30pm from Piazza Vittorio Veneto; 3hr; €25). Make reservations through the website.

Upstairs from the museum, the **Galleria Sabauda** (Tues, Fri, Sat & Sun 8.30am–2pm, Wed 2–7pm, Thurs 10am–7pm; closed Mon; €4, or cumulative ticket with Museo Egizio €8) was built around the Savoys' private collection and is still firmly stamped with their taste: a crowded miscellany of Italian, Dutch and Flemish paintings punctuated by some real masterpieces. Of the Italian paintings, the most arresting is perhaps Botticelli's *Venus*. She is not nearly as elaborate as her Uffizi counterpart, but every bit as alluring. The fifteenth-century *Archangel Raphael and Tobias* by Antonio and Piero Pollaiuolo is another of the gallery's signature works while the Dutch and Flemish section contains van Eyck's *Stigmatization of St Francis*, a warmly human piece and the only panel by this artist in Italy. The collections are hung in a crowded, old-fashioned manner but it's also worth seeking out Van Dyck's *The Children of Charles I of England* (a copy of which hangs in the Palazzo Reale).

Museo del Risorgimento

Via Roma continues north through the heart of Turin, passing near some of the significant monuments of the Savoys and Italian Unification. The **Museo Nazionale del Risorgimento Italiano**, Via Accademia delle Scienze 5 (closed for restoration at the time of writing but set to reopen sometime in 2010), housed in the star-flecked **Palazzo Carignano**, birthplace of Vittorio Emanuele II, is worth a visit. The first meetings of the Italian parliament were held in the palace's circular Chamber of the Subalpine Parliament, and the building was the power base of leaders like Cavour, who ousted the more radical Garibaldi to an early retirement on the island of Caprera near Sardinia. It's ironic, then, that the most interesting sections of the museum are those dedicated to Garibaldi: portraits showing him as a scruffy, long-haired revolutionary, some of his clothes – an embroidered fez, a long stripy scarf and one of the famous red shirts – adopted during his exile in South America. These shirts became the uniform of his army of a thousand volunteers who seized southern Italy and Sicily from the Bourbons.

Palazzo Reale

What Vittorio Emanuele II made of the eccentrically dressed revolutionary who secured half the kingdom for him is undocumented, but you feel sure that his residence, the sixteenth-century **Palazzo Reale** (Tues–Sun 8.30am–7.30pm; €6.50), at the head of the sprawling **Piazza Castello**, wouldn't have impressed Garibaldi. Designed by Castellamonte, this nouveau-riche palace with an unexceptional facade hides glitzy, semi-furnished rooms gilded virtually top-to-bottom and decorated with bombastic allegorical paintings. On the right-hand side of the Palazzo Reale is the **Armeria Reale** (Tues–Fri 9am–2pm; Sat, Sun & holidays 1–7pm; €4), a collection of armour and weapons spanning seven centuries and several continents started by King Carlo Alberto in 1837. Pride of place is given to his stuffed horse, which stands among cases of guns and swords. There's also an exotic, and rather chilling, collection of oriental arms, including gorgeously jewelled Turkish dagger sheaths and intimidating Japanese masks. The same building houses the **Biblioteca Reale** (Mon & Wed 8.15am–6.45pm, Tues & Thurs–Sat 8.15am–1.45pm; free, varying fees for temporary exhibitions), which occasionally displays its collection of drawings by artists including Leonardo da Vinci, Bellini, Raphael, Tiepolo and Rembrandt.

The Palazzo Madama

Across the square from the Palazzo Reale, the newly restored **Palazzo Madama** (Ⓦwww.palazzomadamatorino.it) is an altogether more appealing building, with

The Turin Shroud

During the devastating Duomo fire of 1997, a quick-thinking fireman rescued from a blazing chapel what has been called "the most remarkable forgery in history", the **Turin Shroud** – a linen sheet bearing the image of a man's body – claimed to be the shroud in which Christ was wrapped after his crucifixion. One of the most famous medieval relics, it made world headlines in 1988 after carbon-dating tests carried out by three universities each concluded it was a fake, made between 1260 and 1390. Since 1988, the Shroud has continued to be a hornet's nest of controversy amongst believers, scientists and conspiracy theorists (see Ⓦwww.shroud.com for all the froth that has been whipped up). Most recently, in 2005, an American chemist posited that all three carbon tests were mistakenly conducted on a medieval patch and that the oldest parts of the fabric were in the target age range. But even if the cloth itself was to be proven of biblical age, that's just the starting point. Unless the Vatican gives full access (unlikely) to a whole army of impartial experts to test the fragile material – including DNA tests of the supposed bloodstains – the shroud's authenticity will always remain a matter of faith.

an ornate Baroque facade by the early eighteenth-century architect Juvarra, who also redesigned the piazza and many of the streets leading off it. Inside, the originally fifteenth-century palace incorporates parts of a thirteenth-century castle and some Roman portal foundations – in effect it's an architectural cross-section of the city's history. The most noteworthy architectural pieces are Juvarra's *Great Staircase* and the archeological excavations of the Medieval Court (Tues–Fri & Sun 9am–7pm, Sat 10am–8pm; free). It's well worth visiting the **Museo Civico d'Arte Antica** (Tues–Fri & Sun 10am–6pm, Sat 10am–8pm; ticket office closes one hour before museum closing time; €7.50, free first Tues of the month) – a stunning collection of thousands of objects that includes everything from early Christian gold jewellery via a vast array of world ceramics to royal furniture such as an inlaid Gothic commode, all rearranged into chronological order complete with excellent multilingual captions.

The Duomo

Behind the Palazzo Reale – and reached through a small passage – is the fifteenth-century **Duomo** (daily 8am–noon & 3–7pm), on Via XX Settembre in Piazza San Giovanni. The only example of Renaissance architecture in Turin, it was severely damaged in a fire in 1997 but is open again to visitors and worshippers. It is most famous as the home of the **Turin Shroud** (see box above). However, the reconstruction of its fantastic Holy Shroud Chapel, designed by Guarini in 1668, will not be completed until at least 2010. Most of the time you can't see the shroud itself; it is locked away and officially only on display once every 25 years (next time April–May of 2010). However, it is sometimes brought out for special occasions (it's worth checking at the tourist office). If you don't get to see the real thing, head to the left of the nave, where there's a photographic reproduction, on which the face of a bearded man, crowned with thorns, is clearly visible, together with marks supposed to have been left by a double-thonged whip, spear wounds and bruises that could have been caused carrying a cross. For those whose interest is still not satiated, there is a museum that covers the history and science of the shroud, **Museo della Sindone** (daily 9am–noon & 3–7pm; €5.50), on Via San Domenico 28.

Relics of Turin's days as a small Roman colony are visible from outside the Duomo: the scant remains of a **theatre** and the impressive Porta Palatina – two sixteen-sided towers flanking an arched passageway. Smaller archeological finds can be seen in the **Museo di Antichita** (Tues–Sun 8.30am–7.30pm; €4; Ⓦwww.museoantichita.it), behind the Duomo, in what were the Palazzo Reale's orangeries.

Piazza della Repubblica and the Santuario della Consolata

Northwest of the Duomo, the huge **Piazza della Repubblica**, otherwise known as Porta Palazzo, hosts Europe's largest outdoor market (Mon–Fri 8.30am–1.30pm, Sun 8.30am–6.30pm), selling mainly fruit and vegetables, but also some clothes and, in the indoor market hall, cheeses, bread and *salumi*. Behind the Porta Palazzo is the Saturday-morning *Balôn*, or **flea market**, where you can find everything from pirate DVDs to fake designer gear. On the second Sunday of each month there's a Gran Balôn on the same spot, with opportunities to buy collectable items including lace, toys, secondhand furniture and books.

West of Piazza della Repubblica stands Turin's most elaborate church, the royal **Santuario della Consolata**, built to house an ancient statue of the Madonna, Maria Consolatrice, the protector of the city. Designed by Guarini, its Neoclassical facade is pink and white, while the interior has an impressive decorative altar by Juvarra. Don't miss the vast array of votive objects devout Torinesi have offered to the statue, housed in an ancient crypt below the church. Not to be missed either is the series of paintings in the church, featuring people being "saved" from such disasters as being gored by a bull, cutting overhead electricity cables with garden shears, exploding frying pans, and numerous accidents involving prams and trams. After all this, you may well want to head across the piazza to the beautiful old café, *Al Bicerin* (see p.79) for a pick-me-up. Historically, in nineteenth-century post-Unification Turin, it was the only café women could frequent without causing a scandal.

Mole Antonelliana

The porticoes of Via Po lead down to the river from Piazza Castello, ending just before the bridge in the vast arcaded Piazza Vittorio Veneto. Halfway down, a left onto Via Montebello brings you to the huge **Mole Antonelliana**, whose

▲ Inside the Mole Antonelliana

bishop's-hat dome, topped by a pagoda-like spire balancing on a mini-Greek temple, is a distinctive landmark and has been adopted as the city's emblem. Designed as a synagogue in the nineteenth century by the eccentric architect Antonelli, the building was ceded to the local council by Turin's Jewish community while still under construction because of escalating costs. The decision to house the modern **Museo Nazionale del Cinema** (Tues–Fri & Sun 9am–8pm, Sat 9am–11pm; €6.50 or €8 with lift to top of Mole; ⓦwww.museocinema.it) in this rather unusual building seems a suitable way to celebrate the sheer spectacle of the place. Turin's involvement with cinema goes back to the early years of the twentieth century, when it was one of the first Italian cities to import and experiment with the new medium. The interesting museum covers the early days of the magic lantern and experimental moving pictures, the development of the cinema as a global phenomenon, and twenty-first-century special effects.

Parco del Valentino

South along the river from Piazza Vittorio Veneto, the riverside **Parco del Valentino** borders the site of a cluster of Turin's nightclubs – known as the **Murazzi** area (see p.81). In the daytime the rambling grounds make a pleasant place to wind down after the hum of the city centre. There are two **castles** here, though only one is the genuine article. The ornate **Castello Valentino** was another Savoy residence, used mainly for wedding feasts and other extravagant parties, and is nowadays the seat of the university's faculty of architecture, while the **Borgo e Rocca Mediovale** date from an industrial exhibition held in 1884. The Borgo is a reconstructed medieval village (daily: April–Sept 9am–8pm; Oct–March 9am–7pm; free) whose houses are a synthesis of the best dwellings of medieval Piemonte and Valle d'Aosta, built with the same materials as the originals and using the same construction techniques. The centrepiece of the village (Tues–Sun: April–Sept 9am–5pm; Oct–March 9am–6pm; €5, free first Tues of each month) is a fifteenth-century castle, which, although bogus, actually conjures up a picture of life in a medieval castle far better than many of the originals, kitted out with painstaking replicas of intricately carved Gothic furniture.

Museo Nazionale dell'Automobile

Three kilometres south along the river takes you to the **Museo Nazionale dell'Automobile** at Corso Unità d'Italia 40 (closed for restoration at the time of writing; check website for re-opening date: ⓦwww.museoauto.it), Italy's only motor museum. Even if you know nothing about cars, this has some appeal – you'll discover strange vehicles from motoring's formative days and others familiar from classic films, as the museum traces the development from early cars, handcrafted for a privileged minority, to the mass-produced family version. One of the favourite luxury models is the gleaming Isotta Fraschini driven by Gloria Swanson in the film *Sunset Blvd.*, still with the initials of Norma Desmond, the character she played, on the side. The pride of the collection is the 1907 Itala, which won the Peking-to-Paris race in the same year; you can read of its adventures in Luigi Barzini's book *Peking to Paris*.

The Lingotto Centre

Walking 200m further on and turning right down Via Garessio takes you to what was the original Fiat factory, the **Lingotto Centre** at Via Nizza 250 (tram #1 or #18 from Porta Nuova). Fiat's headquarters are still here but the main part of the building, redesigned by Renzo Piano, houses a conference and exhibition space, a shopping centre, a hotel (see p.72) and the **Pinacoteca Giovanni e Marella Agnelli** at no. 230 (Tues–Sun 10am–7pm, ticket office closes at

6.15pm; €7), a very small but priceless collection of artworks donated by the head of the Fiat dynasty, Gianni Agnelli, and his wife. The paintings are housed in a glass-and-metal gallery, which overlooks the test track on top of the former Fiat car works. The collection consists of mainly nineteenth- and twentieth-century masterpieces, including a number of Matisses and a couple of Picassos, as well as Modigliani's *Nu Couché* and Manet's *La Négresse*. The eighteenth century is represented by six Canalettos and Tiepolo's *Halberdier in a Landscape*.

Parco della Rimembranza and the Basilica di Superga

Southeast of the river, Turin fades into decrepit suburbs, beyond which lie the wooded hills concealing the fancy villas of the city's industrialists. For a taste of the views enjoyed by Turin's mega-rich, take bus #70 up to the **Parco della Rimembranza**, which features ten thousand trees planted in honour of the Torinese victims of World War I and crowned with an enormous light-flashing statue of Victory. Northeast of the centre, you can take the **Sassi-Superga tram** complete with its original 1884 carriages, up to the grandiose Baroque **Basilica di Superga**, from which there are fine panoramas across the city to the Alps. Tram #15 runs Piazza Castello to Sassi station from where the Sassi-Spuperga tram runs hourly on the hour every day except Tuesday (9am–noon & 2–5pm, Sat, Sun & holidays 9am–8pm; €4 return, weekends & holidays €5.50, free with the Torino+Piemonte Card).

The **basilica** (April–Oct, Mon–Fri 9am–noon & 3–6pm, Sat & Sun 9am–12.45pm & 3–6.45pm; Nov–March, Mon–Fri 9am–noon & 3–5pm, Sat & Sun 9am–12.45 & 3–5.45pm; basilica free, €3; to climb the dome, €4 to visit the Savoy tombs and the royal apartments), a Filippo Juvarra creation, stands high on a hill above the rest of the city. In 1706 Duke Vittorio Amedeo climbed the hill in order to study the positions of the French and Spanish armies who had been besieging the city for four months, and vowed that he would erect a temple to the Madonna on this site if she were to aid him in the coming battle. Turin was spared, and the duke immediately set Juvarra to work, flattening the top of the hill and producing over the next 25 years the circular basilica you see today. The elegant dome, pierced by windows and supported on pairs of white columns, is flanked by delicately scalloped onion-domed towers and rises above a Greek temple entrance, these days defaced by graffiti. Many Torinesi come here not to pay homage to the Virgin, nor even to see the splendid tombs of the Savoys, but to visit the tomb of the 1949 Torino football team, all of whom were killed when their plane crashed into the side of the hill.

The Stupinigi Palace

A nearby attraction worth the trip is the Savoy dynasty's luxurious hunting lodge, the **Palazzina di Caccia di Stupinigi** (closed for restoration at the time of writing; opening date set for 2010). Another Juvarra design, built in the 1730s and perhaps his finest work, it's a symmetrical fantasy with a generous dash of Rococo. The exterior of the palace has been restored, while the interior is as luxurious as it ever was, also incorporating the **Museo d'Arte e Ammobiliamento**, a collection of art and furniture from other Savoy palaces. The most extravagant room, the oval Salone Centrale, is a dizzying triumph of optical illusion that merges fake features with real in a superb trompe l'oeil. Other rooms are decorated with hunting motifs: Diana, goddess of the hunt, bathes on bedroom ceilings; hunt scenes proceed across walls; and even the chapel is dedicated to St Uberto, patron saint of hunting. To get here, take bus #63 from Porta Nuova (bus stop #3492 "Porta Nuova FS" in Via Sacchi) then change at the stop after Piazza Caio Mario (bus stop #1080 "Impera") to bus #41; on the way you'll pass through the bleak Mirafiori suburbs on the west side of the city, built for workers at the nearby Fiat plant.

The Castello di Rivoli

Another rewarding trip is west to Rivoli and its **Museo d'Arte Contemporanea** housed in the baroque **Castello di Rivoli** (Piazza Mafaida di Savoia; Tues–Thurs 10am–5pm, Fri–Sun 10am–9pm; €6.50; ⓦwww.castellodirivoli.it), one-time residence of the Savoy family. It's the most important collection of postwar art in Italy, ranging from works by Jeff Koons, Carl Andre and Claes Oldenburg to Arte Povera artists such as Mario Merz and Alighiero Boetti. Take the Metro service from Stazione Porta Susa to Collegno (Metro stop Fermi) and then the shuttle to Castello di Rivoli (9am–4pm, return 11am–5.15pm; service about every 1hr 30min; total cost €1.50, free with the Torino+Piemonte Card).

Eating and drinking

It's worth taking your time over a drink, snack, pastry or ice cream in one of the fin-de-siècle **cafés** that are a Turin institution: prices are steep, but the elegant *belle époque* interiors – often with touches of Art Nouveau (known as "Liberty" style in Italy) – more than compensate. The city also has plenty of good **restaurants** in which to sample local cuisine.

Snacks, takeaways and ice cream

Brek Piazza Carlo Felice 22 and Via Santa Teresa 23 (Piazza Solferino). Part of a national chain of slick, high-quality self-service joints, with tables outside in summer. Main courses start at €5. Open daily.

Exki Via XX Settembre 12 and Via Pietro Micca 2. Natural, fresh and organic is the philosophy of this snack bar. Sandwiches, soups and drinks to eat in or take away. Closed Sun.

Frullateria Piazza Castello 44. Very central lunchtime option, with sandwiches and an array of fresh local and tropical fruits, ready for the liquidizer. Closed Sun.

Grom Piazza Paleocapa 1/D and Via Accademia delle Scienze 4. This organic gelateria has taken over the market with its vibrant all-natural flavours that are simply unforgettable. Look for the queue out into the square. Go for the unique *crema di Grom*, with cornmeal biscuit bits and dark chocolate chips, or check out the flavours of the month.

Guido Gobino Via Lagrange 1, near the Museo Egizio. Though something of a newcomer, Maestro Gobino has quickly conquered Turin with his extraordinary confections. Open Tues–Sun 10am–8pm, Mon 3–8pm. Also a boutique at Via Cagliari 15/B.

Cafés

Al Bicerin Piazza della Consolata 5. This tiny, beautiful café is the place to try a *bicerin* – a Piemontese speciality of coffee fortified with brandy, cream and chocolate. Closed Wed & Aug.

Turin's chocolate

Make sure you leave some room to sample one of Turin's signature products – **chocolate**. Best known is the hazelnut milk chocolate Gianduiotto, which dates back to the nineteenth century. Some even claim that it was the Torinesi who introduced chocolate to France when chocolate making for export began in 1678.

A good opportunity to sample it is during Turin's annual **chocolate fair** "CioccolaTò" held for three weeks in February and March (ⓦwww.cioccola-to.com). At other times, there's the opportunity to indulge with the **ChocoPass**. You can taste samples of the finest chocolate products in all of Turin's historic establishments, confectionery shops and chocolate factories: Gianduiotti, pralines, various cakes, hot chocolate, and the distinctive *bicerin*, which is a bit like a cappuccino but fortified with brandy. The ChocoPass booklets have 23 vouchers valid for three days (€15). Otherwise, the favourite Torinese place to buy chocolate is *Guido Gobino*, see above).

Baratti & Milano Piazza Castello 29. Established in 1873 and preserving its nineteenth-century interior of mirrors, chandeliers and carved wood, where genteel Torinese ladies sip teas. Great hot chocolate. Closed Mon.

Fiorio Via Po 8. Turin's most historic café, once patronized by Nietzsche, presumably for its legendary *gelato* and its signature cappuccino, €3. Closed Mon.

Mood Via Battisti 3. Books, coffee and aperitifs in the cosy Turin tradition. Not part of Turin history, like the others, but very attractive. Closed Sun.

Mulassano Piazza Castello 9. This inviting café first opened in 1900; it has marble fittings and a striking ceiling. Traditionally the favoured spot of actors and singers from the nearby Teatro Regio.

Neuv Caval'd Brôns Piazza San Carlo 155. A Torinese institution, this gustatory palace is known for its impressive help-yourself canapé selection. Closed Sat lunch & Sun.

Pepino Piazza Carignano 8. Ritzy café with summer garden, famed for its ice creams. Try the violet-flavoured *pinguino* or the outrageously rich cream-and-chocolate concoction of *pezzo duro*. Also offers an excellent Sun brunch buffet menu for about €15. Closed Mon.

Platti Corso Vittorio Emanuele II 72. Art Nouveau-furnished café dating from 1870; hosts art exhibitions and occasional live music. Good place for lunch, open daily.

San Carlo Piazza San Carlo 156. Heroes of the Risorgimento once met in this café/restaurant/ice-cream parlour, now rather grandiosely restored with gilt pilasters and an immense chandelier.

Torino Piazza San Carlo 204. A good place for a leisurely aperitif or cocktail, of which the most popular is the Torinese "Elvira", made with Martini, vodka and various secret ingredients. Illustrious regulars have included writer Cesare Pavese and Luigi Einaudi (a Torinese economist who became the second President of the Italian Republic).

Restaurants

Alba Via San Pio V 8 ☎011.669.2054. A classic trattoria, near Porta Nuova station, where everything is home-made and prices and staff are very friendly. Full meals run to about €15. Closed Fri.

Cucco Corso Casale 89 ☎011.819.5536. A big Art Nouveau place near the river, serving typical Piemontese cooking at moderate prices with a choice of around thirty antipasti. Closed Mon.

Da Michele Piazza Vittorio Veneto 4 ☎011.888.836. Offering a commanding view of the long square from under the portico, this place is locally renowned for its superb fresh pastas and strictly seasonal specialities, as well as wood-oven-fired pizzas. Full meals €20–40 per person. Closed Tues.

Del Cambio Piazza Carignano 2 ☎011.546.690. Historic, formal shrine to Piemontese food, much frequented by expense-account types. A great opportunity to feast on traditional dishes such as Cavour's favourite of *fianziera* (veal, sweetbreads and porcini, cooked with butter and wine). Prices are suitably extravagant – starting around €25 for a main – and booking is advisable. Closed Sun & three weeks in Aug.

Emporio Mille900 Via dei Mille 20 ☎011.812.8712. Lunchtime offering is a real gourmet buffet table, local dishes freshly loaded up, all you care to eat for €12. Evening set menu €30, or à la carte. Buffet brunch Sun. Closed Sat lunch & Sun dinner.

Il Punto Verde Via San Massimo 17 ☎011.885.543. Reasonably priced vegetarian restaurant with a good selection of dishes and a quiet outside terrace. Closed Sat & Sun.

L'Arcimboldo Via Santa Chiara 54 ☎011.521.1816. A simple restaurant specializing in *pasta fresca,* with a choice of a hundred sauces, all for around €8. Closed Mon.

La Gaia Scienza Via Guastalla 22 ☎011.812.3821. Old-style *osteria* serving wholesome traditional food. Expect to pay around €25 for a full meal. Closed Sun.

Porto di Savona Piazza Vittorio Veneto 2 ☎011.817.3500. Cheap and cheerful restaurant, very popular with both students and business people, attracted primarily by the formula of *piatto unico* (single option main course) and dessert for €8–10. Fried dishes a speciality. Always open.

Sfashioncafé Via Cesare Battisti 13 (Piazza Carlo Alberto) ☎011.516.0085. Enormous portions and great pizzas. Lunchtime bargains start at €8 and include a main course, a great house salad, drink and coffee or dessert. Colourful, friendly interior, plus sunny seating on the piazza.

Tre Galline Via Bellezia 37 ☎011.436.6553. The oldest restaurant in Turin, with a lovely panelled interior. The *agrodolce* (sweet-and-sour) rabbit is a house speciality. Reckon on €35 a head; booking advisable. Closed all day Sun, Mon lunchtime & Aug.

Nightlife

Turin's **nightlife** is more sedate than that of, say, Milan, but there's a reasonably varied mix of clubs and bars, with the liveliest spot down on the embankment bordered by the Parco del Valentino, known locally as the **Murazzi**. Its clubs are packed with a lively crowd at weekends so there's often a heavy police presence, and if you go, you should keep an eye on your belongings. Note that some **clubs** require membership cards, purchased when you enter (€5–10) with your first drink usually included. After that, although drink prices can be inflated measures are relatively generous. Aside from the Murazzi, a good place to wander for a drink is the more tranquil medieval area, known as the **Quadrilatero Romano**, around Piazza Emanuele Filiberto and Via Santa Chiara. Many of the old birrerias have been supplemented by new *vinerias* – wine bars – where you can also order a substantial snack (known as a *marenda sinoira*).

Bars and clubs

1870 Huntsman Pub Corso Vittorio Emanuele II 43/D. A sprawling British-style establishment offering a clubby atmosphere and a full menu. Open daily from lunchtime till the wee hours.

Centralino Via delle Rosine 16. Basement club with jazz concerts and avant-garde productions; Sun night is gay night; membership card required. Closed Mon.

Hiroshima Mon Amour Via Bossoli 83. Live music, alternative theatre and cabaret in a converted school near the Lingotto centre. Cover charge depending on the event. Closed Mon.

Jumping Jester Via Mazzini 2. Old-fashioned wooden interior with huge TV screen on which football matches are shown live. Serves a great pint of cold Caffreys or Tennants. Closed Sun.

Las Rosas Via Bellezia 15. Trendy cantina-style *taqueria*. Drinks and tacos served until 2am to the sounds of world music. Closed Sun.

Lobelix Via Corte d'Appello 15 (Piazza Savoia). Wine and cocktail bar with techno music, named for the obelisk that adorns the piazza. Closed Sun.

Magazzino di Gilgamesh Piazza Moncenisio 13/B. Birreria and coffee shop, plus an international restaurant on the third floor, with jazz, Latin, classic and rock music in the background. Closed Sun.

Roar Roads Via Carlo Alberto 3. Despite the dubious name, this is a very passable pub just off Via Po that pulls in both locals and foreigners. Closed Sun.

Tre Galli Via Sant'Agostino 25. Busy *vineria* that used to be an Agnelli (Fiat founder) hangout, with a long wine list of local and Italian wines by the bottle or glass (for the latter, ask for a *mescita a calice*) as well as plates of cheeses, ham, salami and home-made *grissini* (breadsticks). Laid-back atmosphere and tables outside on the piazza in summer. Open until 2am. Closed Sun.

Zoo Bar Corso Casale 127. Out past the Ponte Regina Margherita, this loft bar hosts live rock and pop gigs. Closed Sun.

Entertainment

Turin's cultural life is suitably comprehensive for a place of this size. The city's **opera** house, the Teatro Regio (☎011.881.5242, ⓦwww.teatroregio.torino.it), is one of the best in the country and is recognizable from its pod-like Seventies architecture, while Il Teatro Stabile (Cavallerizza Reale ☎011.517.6246, ⓦwww.teatrostabiletorino.it), one of Italy's principal publicly funded **theatre** companies, is acclaimed for its productions of major works by nineteenth- and twentieth-century European playwrights; performances are normally at the Carignano Theatre on Piazza Carignano, though it is one of at least half a dozen theatres in the city. Turin is also home of the prestigious **RAI National Symphony Orchestra**, which performs in the Arturo Toscanini Auditorium, in Piazza Rossaro. For most of September a major **festival** called MITO (☎011.442.4703, ⓦwww.mitosettembremusica.it) mixes jazz, world music, classical music and performance art at various venues in Turin and Milan. There are also four international **film** festivals held each year, including the Torino Film Festival (ⓦwww.torinofilmfest.org), a women's film festival in March, and the Torino GLBT Film Festival, "Da Sodoma a Hollywood", in April (ⓦwww.tglff.com).

For **what's on listings** and opening hours, check the pages of the Turin daily, *La Stampa*, particularly its Friday supplements. Torino Cultura in Piazza Castello at Via Garibaldi (ⓦwww.torinocultura.it) has a free **ticket reservation service**.

Listings

Bicycle rental You can rent bikes in summer at all major parks, including Parco della Colletta, Parco del Valentino, Parco della Pellerina and Parco della Mandria. Bicycle paths comprise some 40km, many along the picturesque rivers.

Books and newspapers Libreria Luxembourg, Via Cesare Battisti 7, has an excellent range of British and American paperbacks and magazines. English-language newspapers can be bought from most newsagents in the city centre, in particular the one at the Porta Nuova station.

Car parks Central city parking spots and car parks are marked with blue lines on the road and cost €1 per hr. Parking lots, more expensive, also lie under some main piazzas.

Car rental Avis, Corso Turati 37 ☏011.501.107; Europcar, Via Madama Cristina 72 ☏011.650.3603; Hertz, Via Magellano 12 ☏011.502.080. All these companies also have desks at the airport.

Closing days Some shops are closed on Mon morning, although on the other hand, expect to find a few now with Sun hours. Many establishments of every kind still follow the time-honoured Italian tradition and shut down during Aug.

Exchange Outside normal banking hours you can exchange money at Porta Nuova station (Mon–Sat 8am–8pm, Sun 10am–6pm).

Football Turin's two teams, Juventus and Torino, play on Sat and Sun afternoons at the new Stadio Olimpico, Via Filadelfia 88. You can get to the Stadio Olimpico on Line #4 from Porta Nuova station or #10 from Porta Susa. Although Juventus has been voted the most popular team in Italy, most of the locals support the underdogs, Torino.

Hospital Ospedale Molinette, Corso Bramante 88–90 ☏011.633.1633; for 24hr emergency medical attention call ☏5747, or simply ☏118 or ☏113, as throughout Italy.

Internet access Bu.Net, Via San Quintino 13 (☏011.440.7517, ⊛www.il-bu.net; 9am–1am; €0.06 per min).

Laundries Lav@sciuga, Via San Massimo 4; Via Vanchiglia 10; and Piazza della Repubblica 5. Lava e Asciuga, Via Vanchiglia 38.

Markets In addition to Porta Palazzo/Piazza della Repubblica, and the weekly Balôn and monthly Gran Balôn markets behind Porta Palazzo (see p.76), there's often heavily discounted designer fashion (the genuine thing, from end-of-line clearances) at the Crocetta market around Via Cassini and Via Marco Polo (Tues–Fri morning & all day Sat) – not exactly street market prices, but still much cheaper than in the shops.

Pharmacist Boniscontro, Corso Vittorio Emanuele II 66 (☏011.538.271), is an all-night chemist.

Police ☏113. City police station at Corso XI Febbraio 22. Dial ☏112 for Carabinieri.

Post office The central post office is at Via Alfieri 10 (Mon–Fri 8.30am–7pm, Sat 8.30am–1pm).

The Susa and Chisone valleys

The main route to France from Turin runs through the **Susa Valley**, passing nearby the region's main ski resorts. You go through long tunnels most of the way, so don't expect to see much. The one real sight to spot is the **Sacra di San Michele**, a forbidding fortified abbey anchored atop a rocky hill; it's an easy day-trip from Turin. **Susa** itself, reached by a minor branch of the rail line, was once a modest Roman town and is now a modest provincial town – a pleasant stopover but with little else to lure you.

Sacra di San Michele

The closest town to the **Sacra di San Michele** (mid-March to mid-Oct Tues–Sat 9.30am–12.30pm & 2.30–6pm, Sun 9.30am–noon & 2.40–6.30pm; July–Sept also open Mon, same hours; mid-Oct to mid-March 9.30am–12.30pm & 2.30–5pm, Sun 9.30am–noon & 2.30–5pm; weekday afternoons guided tours only; €4; ☏011.939.130, ⊛www.sacradisanmichele.com) is **SANT'AMBROGIO**, a small town at the foot of San Michele's hill. It's thirty minutes by train from Turin and connected with the abbey by a very steep one hour thirty-minute hike; with your own car, however, you can park just a ten-minute walk from the abbey. The longer walk is worth it, both for the views and for the opportunity to soak up the eerie atmosphere surrounding the glowering abbey, much of it in ruins. Climbing up to the abbey and hewn into the rock, a long flight of stairs – the *Scalone dei Morti* (Stairs of the Dead) – sets a morbid tone, for it was here that corpses used to be laid out for local peasants to come and pay their respects. The sinister ambiance is augmented by the abbey buildings proper, from the Romanesque entrance arch carved with signs of the zodiac to the Gothic-Romanesque abbey church.

Susa

Some 25km down the valley from Sant'Ambrogio, **SUSA** is a likeable, rather scruffy old town. The **tourist office** (IAT) is at Corso Inghilterra 39 (℡0122.622.447). There are a few hotels, such as the *Du Parc*, Via Rocchetta 15 (℡0122.622.273; **❷**), or the *Napoleon*, Via Mazzini 44 (℡0122.622.855, ⓦwww .hotelnapoleon.it; **❸**), which can be used as a base for exploring the area.

In ancient days when the Romans ruled most of Italy, Susa and western Piemonte remained in the hands of the Gauls. The best-known of its Gaulish leaders, Cottius, was much admired by the Romans, with whom he reached a peaceful arrangement, and a handful of Gaulish/Roman remains cluster around the town centre, notably in **Piazza San Giusto**, where there's a redoubtable defensive gate. The adjacent Romanesque **cattedrale** has a fine campanile, but its most interesting features are the external frescoes – a *Crucifixion* and an *Entry into Jerusalem*. Just above the piazza, Cottius erected the **Arco di Augusto** in honour of the Roman emperor, its top decorated with a processional frieze. Look through its broad arched opening frames for views down into a small park laid out around the remains of some **Roman baths**.

In the opposite direction, southeast, at the end of the Chisone Valley, **PINEROLO** was one of the Winter Olympics 2006 sites and is worth a short stop. It's a small town with a medieval centre that was for centuries the seat of the Acaja princedom, precursors of the House of Savoy. It's no longer possible to visit their palace, slowly deteriorating halfway up the hill, but you can visit the church of **San Maurizio**, burial place of the Acaja princes, decorated with fifteenth-century frescoes.

Piemonte's ski resorts

Close to the French border, Piemonte's three main, purpose-built ski resorts – Bardonecchia, Sestriere and Sauze d'Oulx – are well used by British tour operators and, as co-hosts of the Winter Olympics 2006, have all had their facilities recently upgraded. Moreover, Sestriere, Sauze d'Oulx, Sansicario, Cesana and Claviere now collectively constitute some 400km of interconnected runs, more than 200 in all, known as **La Vialattea** (The Milky Way; ⓦwww .vialattea.it). You can gain access from Pragelato, thanks to the new cableway Pattemouche-Anfiteatro. One daily lift pass for all five runs is €32.

SESTRIERE was the dream resort of Mussolini and the Fiat baron, Gianni Agnelli, who conceived it as an aristocratic mountain retreat, favoured by the young and the beautiful. Nowadays, the reality is a bland resort dominated by two cylindrical towers, both owned by Club Med. The mountain, however, is impeccable: the choice for World Cup and Olympic downhill races. Modern **BARDONECCHIA** – unconnected to the Milky Way – is a weekenders' haunt, with small chalet-style hotels. **SAUZE D'OULX**, a little way south, is generally known as the "Benidorm of the Alps", attracting hordes of youngsters who treat skiing as a hangover cure – though it isn't so bad that it doesn't also attract its share of families.

The Chisone Valley

Taking the parallel **Chisone Valley** to the south back towards Turin, you will encounter a much more bucolic and less developed area, dotted along the way with small towns. If you don't have your own transport, you can take one of the **buses** that regularly service almost all the towns along the way. The picturesque slate-roofed hamlet of **USSEAUX** is worth discovering, its weather-worn old walls decorated with colourful murals. For lunch, the *Trattoria La Placette*, behind the church and on the village's edge overlooking the valley, is equipped with a sunny porch on which you can partake of hearty pastas, game and mountain cheeses.

Not far away, at an altitude of nearly 2000m, the impressive **Forte di Fenestrelle** (July & Aug daily 10am–noon & 2.30–6pm; rest of year Thurs–Mon 10am–noon & 2.30–6pm; ☎0121.83.600 for reservations; €2), known as "The Great Wall of Piemonte", has been recently restored and is now a significant regional attraction. It constitutes a gigantic fortified castle and dependent buildings, along with an adjoining massive 3km rampart marching over the mountain. Built by the Savoys from 1728, it took some 122 years to complete, its purpose being to halt enemy invasions. Simply put, it's the largest defensive structure ever built in Europe. Much of the wall's length can now be visited, and the longest guided tour (€12) takes you up all of the 4000 steps and back, a strenuous seven-hour trek.

If you're tempted to spend some time in this idyllic area, note that one of the most welcoming **hotels** is the *Bella Baita*, Borgata Serre Marchetto, 1 Pinasca, nestled in a panoramic mountain forest high above the valley's villages (☎339.750.3940 or 347.984.2945, ⓦwww.bellabaita.com; ❷ including a hearty breakfast, half-board also available). The hosts are very welcoming, knowledgeable about the area, and they are trained professional chefs.

Saluzzo and the Po Valley

A flourishing medieval town, and later the seat of one of Piemonte's few Renaissance courts, **SALUZZO**, 57km south of Turin, retains much of its period appeal. Flaking ochre-washed terraces and Renaissance houses line cobbled streets that climb up to a castle, from where you can enjoy views of the town. A pleasant place to stay, the town has the added attraction of regular bus services into the Po, Varaita and Maira valleys, which cut through the foothills of the Monviso mountain towards France.

There are a few things around town worth seeing. Just below the castle, the **Torre Civica** (March–Sept Thurs–Sun 9.30am–12.30pm & 2.30–6.30pm; Oct–Feb Sat & Sun same hours as above; €1.30) gives more great views over the town and surrounding areas. On the other side of the road, the Gothic church of **San Giovanni** has a number of thirteenth- and fourteenth-century frescoes and the tomb of the leading light of Renaissance Saluzzo, Marchese Ludovico II, anachronistically depicted as a medieval knight beneath a fancily carved canopy. Close by, the Gothic **Casa Cavassa**, Via San Giovanni 5, is a fifteenth-century palace with an arcaded courtyard that doubled as a home for one of Ludovico's ministers and now houses the town's **Museo Civico** (April–Sept Tues & Wed guided tours only, at 11am & 4pm, Thurs–Sun unaccompanied visits 10am–1pm & 2–6pm; Oct–March Tues & Wed guided tours only, at 11am & 3pm, Thurs–Sun unaccompanied visits 10am–1pm & 2–5pm; €4, combined ticket with Torre Civica €5). Inside are period furniture and paintings, including the gorgeously gilded *Madonna della Misericordia*, with the Madonna sheltering Ludovico, his wife and the population of Saluzzo in the folds of her cloak.

That's about all there is to the town centre, but just to the south of Saluzzo, a five-minute bus ride from outside the train station, there's the **Castello della Manta** – a medieval fortress that was transformed into a refined residence in the fifteenth century (Tues–Sun 10am–5/6pm; €5, including audioguide). Though from the outside it's as plain and austere as Saluzzo's castle, it's worth visiting for the evocative late-Gothic frescoes in the Baronial Hall. One of these illustrates the myth of the fountain of youth, elderly people processing towards the magical waters while others impatiently rip off their clothes to plunge in. The other, *Nine Heroes and Nine Heroines*, depicts chivalrous courtiers and exquisite damsels standing beneath stylized trees with coats of arms hanging from the branches.

Practicalities

Saluzzo's **tourist office**, on Piazzetta dei Mondagli 5, at the top of Via Volta (Mon–Sat 9am–1pm & 2.30–5.30pm, Sun until 6pm; ☎0175.46.710, ⓦwww .comune.saluzzo.cn.it), can provide information on the whole of the western valleys region. Among the town's **hotels**, the cheapest is the *Persico, Vicolo Mercati* 10 (☎0175.41.213, ⓦwww.albergopersico.net; ❷), which also has a very good **restaurant** serving traditional cuisine (closed Fri); or there are a couple of three-stars, the *Astor*, Piazza Garibaldi 39 (☎0175.45.506, ⓦwww.mtrade.com /astor; ❸) and the modern *Griselda*, Corso XXVII Aprile 13 (☎0175.47.484, ⓦwww.hotelgriselda.it; ❹). If you want to **eat** in the old town, try the *Osteria dei Mondagli* (closed Wed), on Piazzetta dei Mondagli opposite the tourist office, which does a good fixed menu and has a beautiful summer terrace.

The Po Valley

West of Saluzzo, close to the French border, lies the source of the River Po, which flows right across industrial northern Italy, gathering the waste from thousands of factories before finally discharging into the Adriatic. Towards the end of the valley is the Alpine-style resort of **CRISSOLO**, served by 2–4 buses daily from Paesana, farther down the valley, which in turn is served by buses from Saluzzo. From Crissolo you can hike 5km (or take a minibus in summer) to the **Pian del Re**, a grassy plain around the source of the Po, for a view of one of the passes legend claims Hannibal and his elephants used.

Crissolo is also a good base for climbing **Monviso** (3841m), Piemonte's highest mountain; it's a long (about six hours) rocky scramble from the *Quintino Sella rifugio* (see below), two to three hours beyond the Pian del Re. Even if you don't want to scale the summit, the walk to the *rifugio* is lovely, passing a series of **mountain lakes**; or, if you prefer, it's possible to do a **circuit of the lakes**, turning off the main trail just before Lago Chiaretto, from where a path leads past Lago Superiore and back to Pian del Re.

Crissolo has a couple of average **hotels** open all year round: the *Monviso*, Piazza Umberto I 153 (☎0175.94.940; ❸) and the *Polo Nord*, Via Provinciale 22 (☎0175.94.908, ⓦwww.parks.it/alb/monviso; ❷ breakfast included). The *Quintino Sella rifugio*, near the Lago Grande del Viso, is open at Easter and from June 20 to September 20, and sometimes in winter; it's advisable to phone in advance (☎0175.94.943). The majority of **restaurants** are in the hotels, so you may find it both practical and economical to opt for half- or full-board.

Alba and Le Langhe

The town of **Alba** and the surrounding **Le Langhe** hills signify two things to the Italians: **white truffles** and **red wine**. The exquisite truffles are more delicate and aromatic than the black variety found further south, whereas most of the area's very different wines all come from the same grape, the Nebbiolo. The final taste is dependent on the soil: sandy soil produces the grapes for the light red **Nebbiolo**; calcium and mineral-rich soil for the more robust **Barolo**, the "King of Italian Reds". In the hill-villages around Alba, there are a number of wine museums and cantinas, the best being those at Barolo. Although the big cantinas all sell wine, you'll get a better deal at one of the smaller family-owned establishments scattered around the region. Buses from Alba are rather infrequent, so your own transport is best.

Alba

Whether or not you want to taste wine, **ALBA** is worth the visit for its alluring mix of red-brick medieval towers, Baroque and Renaissance palaces and cobbled streets lined with gastronomic shops. And if you come in October, you'll catch the town's hilarious annual donkey race – a skit on nearby Asti's prestigious Palio.

The town's only sight as such is its late-Gothic **Duomo**, standing confectionery pink on the central Piazza Risorgimento. But Alba is primarily a place to stroll and eat. Leading up to the centre from Piazza Savona, the main drag of **Via Vittorio Emanuele** is a fine, bustling street, with the most tempting of Alba's local produce on display – wines, truffles, cheeses, weird and wonderful mushroom varieties, and the wickedly sticky *nocciola*, a nutty, chocolatey cake. Via Cavour is a pleasant medieval street with plenty of wine shops, behind which the **donkey race** and displays of medieval pageantry attract the crowds during the festival at the beginning of October. There's also an annual **truffle festival** later in the month, when you could blow your whole budget on a knobbly truffle or a meal in one of the many swanky restaurants. At the end of April/beginning of May, the **Vinum festival** gives you the chance to taste five hundred local wines.

▲ Truffle appreciation, Alba

Practicalities

The **tourist office** (April to mid-Nov, Mon–Fri 9am–1pm & 2.30–6.30pm, Sat & Sun 9.30am–1.30pm & 2.30–6.30pm; mid-Nov to April, Mon–Fri 10am–1pm & 2–6pm; ☎0173.35.833, ⓦwww.langheroero.it) is at Piazza Risorgimento 2. They offer a free reservation service if you want to **stay**. You could try the plain but pleasant *Leon d'Oro*, with a small terrace overlooking the square; Piazza Marconi 2 (☎0173.440.536; breakfast unavailable, ❷), or the *Hotel Savona*, a modest three-star, located at Via Roma 1, with surrounding gardens and offering adjacent parking (☎0173.440.440, ⓦwww.hotelsavona.com; ❻, good deals for triples). You'll need to plan ahead to be sure of a room, especially during the October festival. The best place to sample Albese cooking is the excellent *Osteria dell'Arco*, at Piazza Savona 5 (closed Sun & Mon), which has a particularly fine selection of local cheeses. For wine by the glass as well as excellent local dishes, try 🍴 *Vincafe*, Via Vittorio Emanuele 12 (☎0173.364.603, ⓦwww.vincafe.com).

The hills of Le Langhe

A few kilometres south of Alba, in the heart of Le Langhe, **BAROLO**, a small village with peach- and ochre-washed houses set among extensive vineyards, gives its name to one of the best-known Italian wines. Geared up to the steady stream of wealthy gastronomes and wine connoisseurs who invariably come here, the **Enoteca Regionale del Barolo**, housed in a flaking turreted castle on Piazza Falletti (daily except Thurs 10am–12.30pm & 3–6.30pm; ☎0173.562.277, ⓦwww.baroloworld.it) is well worth a visit. Or indulge yourself at the *Hotel Barolo*, Via Lomondo 2 (☎0173.563.54, ⓦwww.hotelbarolo.it; ❸), featuring rooms set amidst vineyards and a renowned family-run restaurant, *Brezza* – an imperious place with a smart dress code, offering the very finest local cuisine.

Asti

Some 30km northeast of Alba, the wine continues to flow in **ASTI**, the capital of Italy's sparkling wine industry and the most famous producer of *spumante*. Each September, this small, averagely attractive town becomes the focus of attention as it gears up for its **Palio**. Though it's taken nothing like as seriously as Siena's famous pageant and race, and has been revived to some extent for tourists, you should make an effort to see it if you're near here at the right time. On the day of the race itself, the third Sunday in September, there's a thousand-strong **procession** of citizens dressed as their fourteenth-century ancestors, before the frenetic bare-backed horse race around the arena of the Campo del Palio – followed by the awarding of the *palio* (banner) to the winner and all-night feasting and boozing.

The rest of the year the Campo del Palio is a vast, bleak car park, and there's frankly not a lot to see. The arcaded Piazza Alfieri is officially the centre of town, behind which is the **Collegiata di San Secondo** (daily 8.30am–noon & 3.30–6.30pm; free), dedicated to the city's patron saint and built on the site of the saint's martyrdom in the second century. Secondo, a Roman officer of the patrician class, who converted to Christianity, was beheaded on March 29 in 119 AD, during the reign of Emperor Hadrian. The main street, Corso Alfieri, slices through the town from the Piazza Alfieri, to the east of which lies the church of **San Pietro** at Corso Alfieri 2 (Tues–Sun 10am–1pm & 3/4–6/7pm). At the other end of the Corso is the **Torre Rossa**, a medieval tower with a red-and-white chequered brick top, built on the remains of the sixteen-sided Roman tower in which San Secondo was imprisoned and tortured before his martyrdom.

Practicalities

Asti's **tourist office** is at Piazza Alfieri 29 (Mon–Sat 9am–1pm & 2.30–6.30pm, Sun 9am–1pm; ℡0141.530.357, ⓦwww.astiturismo.it). If you're intending to visit Asti on the Palio weekend, book a **room** well in advance; at other times there should be little problem. The best of the affordable options are the conveniently sited *Cavour* at Piazza Marconi 18 (℡0141.530.222, ⓦwww.hotel cavour-asti.com; ❷) and the slightly cheaper *Genova*, Corso Alessandria 26 (℡0141.593.197; ❷). Renowned for its food, Asti has a wide choice of **restaurants**, ranging from basic and cheap pizzerias like *Monna Laura*, Via Cavour 30 (closed Mon), to the excellent and rather pricey *Gener Neuv*, Lungotanaro dei Pescatori 4 (closed Sun eve & Mon), which serves delicious local cuisine. If you're into *spumante* or want to sample other wines from the region, come during the **wine festival**, the Festa della Douja d'Or, which is held from the second Friday to the third Sunday in September, with wine tastings in the piazzas from early evening until midnight. The rest of the year, you can always try the *Tre Bicchieri*, Piazza Statuto 37, an extremely well-stocked and fashionable wine bar.

Northern Piemonte

The main attraction of northern Piemonte is the mountains, especially the dramatic Alpine **Valsesia**, which winds up to the foot of Monte Rosa on the Swiss border. On the way are two of the region's most visited sanctuaries, the **Santuario di Oropa** near **Biella** and the **Sacro Monte** at **Varallo**. From here you're well poised for either Piemonte's mountains or those of Valle d'Aosta, a few kilometres west. Worth a slight detour is the magical train ride that starts at **Domodossola**, conveniently en route if you're heading for Switzerland.

Biella and Ivrea

The sizeable but bland northern-Piemonte city of Novara is a useful transport hub but otherwise not really worth a stop. In passing through, you'll note that its central basilica, **San Gaudenzio**, has a striking tower, rather resembling a 122-metre Neoclassical cucumber. On a clear day the Alps, to which this city is a gateway (along with the Italian lakes; see Chapter 3), make a stupendous backdrop. Otherwise, the area is mostly dominated by rice fields, soaking wet and heavily mosquito-infested in the warm months. A short train ride northwest from Novara brings you to the provincial capital of **BIELLA**, known for its wool industry, its periphery choked with mills and the hilltop upper town with the mansions and villas of wool barons. It's not an especially rewarding place either – apart from its small medieval quarter, reached by funicular – but it does give access to the **Santuario di Oropa** (daily 8am–noon & 2–7pm; free, €3 for the museum; ⓦwww.santuariodioropa.it), a forty-minute bus ride (#2 from the train station) about 11km northwest of Biella to the foot of Monte Mucrone. Founded in the fourth century by St Eusebio to house a black statue of the Madonna and Child, it's the most venerated of Piemonte's shrines, the main church an immense neo-Baroque concoction. It's a good starting-point for walks into the surrounding mountains, and a cable car runs regularly up Monte Mucrone from the sanctuary as far as the mountain refuge *Albergo Savoia* (℡015.849.5131; half-board ❷), which offers modest food and accommodation. A network of marked trails begins here: one of the nicest and easiest is to the **Lago Mucrone**, a small mountain lake. More energetic is the hike up to the summit of Monte Mucrone itself – a two-hour trek. If you wish, you can stay at the sanctuary, which has around 350 recently refurbished rooms – very austere unless you go for suites (℡015.2555.1200; ➊).

Biella's **tourist office** is at Piazza Vittorio Veneto 3 (Mon–Fri 8.30am–1pm & 2.30–6pm, Sat 9.30am–12.30pm & 2.30–5.30pm; May–Sept also Sun 9am–12.30pm & 2.30–5.30pm; ℡015.351.128, ⓦwww.atl.biella.it). If you need to **stay** overnight, try the clean and attractive *Bugella*, Via Cottolengo 65 (℡015.406.607, ⓦwww.hotelbugella.it; ➌). And check out *La Baracca* at Via San Eusebio 12 (closed Sat & Sun & mid-June to mid-July), a bar in a converted nineteenth-century factory building that serves authentic Piemonte meals for about €18; don't overlook the appealing antipasto buffet. Otherwise, *La Civetta*, at Piazza Cucco 10/B (eve only; closed Wed), turns out simple regional and Italian fare for €20–25.

IVREA, to the north of Turin, is well worth a visit in the week leading up to Shrove Tuesday, when there's a carnival – featuring piping, drumming, masked balls, historic processions and fireworks – that culminates in a bizarre three-day "Battle of the Oranges" when the whole town and hundreds of spectators turn out to pelt each other with oranges – you have to wear a red hat if you don't want to be a target. At the end of each day, the town is covered in a thick carpet of orange pulp, and the following morning there's a traditional handing out of polenta and cod. For a place to **stay**, try the *Aquila Nera*, Corso Nigra 56 (℡0125.641.416, ⓦwww.aquilanera.it; ➋ half- and full-board available), or head 3km northeast out of town to Chiaverano d'Ivrea for four-star *Castello San Giuseppe* (℡0125.424.370, ⓦwww.castellosangiuseppe.it; ➏), set in a converted Carmelite monastery.

Varallo and Sacro Monte

VARALLO, some 50km by train north of Novara, marks the beginning of northern Piemonte's more picturesque reaches, surrounded by steep wooded hills and filled with Art Nouveau villas and Baroque *palazzi*. It's a pretty place, enjoyable for a short visit; most people come to see the sanctuary of **Sacro Monte** (see below), just outside the town and connected by cable car (Mon–Fri 9am–6.30pm, Sat & Sun 9am–7pm; €2.50 return ticket) from the top of Via Ferrari in the centre of town.

The centre is a five-minute walk from the train station; turn right along Via Durio or Corso Roma. The **tourist office** is at Corso Roma 38 (Mon–Fri 9am–1pm & 2.30–6.30pm, Sat 9.30am–1pm & 2.30–7pm; June–Aug open Sun, same hours as Sat; ℡0163.564.404, ⓦwww.altvalsesiavercelli.it). If you want to **stay** in Varallo, head for the *Monte Rosa* at Via Regaldi 4 (℡0163.51.100, ⓦwww.albergomonterosa.it; ➋ no credit cards), a wonderful, friendly, rambling old hotel a brisk ten-minute walk away from the town centre. Or try the hostel, at Via Scarognini 37 (℡0163.51.036; €20 per person). For **food**, the restaurant *Il Tiglio*, opposite the station in Piazza Marconi 2, does good pizzas (closed Wed).

Sacro Monte

Crowning the hill above Varallo, **Sacro Monte** (in addition to regular services, Mon–Thurs 9am–12.30pm & 1–5pm; Fri 9am–noon; free; ⓦwww.sacromontevarallo.com) is a complex of 45 chapels, each housing a 3-D tableau of painted statues against frescoed scenery representing a scene from the life of Christ. Founded in the fifteenth century by a friar anxious to popularize Catholicism in a fiercely heretical region, Sacro Monte draws on sensationalism and spectacle, calculated to work on the emotions of the uneducated. The sanctuary is at its best when busy; to get a measure of its continuing popularity, you need to visit on a Sunday, when it's full of families, pensioners and nuns, all of whom picnic in the shady grounds after finishing their pilgrimage.

A bizarre spectacle, depicting the whole range of key biblical episodes from the Fall to Christ's birth, life and death, the tableaux don't pull any punches. The *Massacre of the Innocents* (#11) shows a floor littered with dead babies, while Herod's army prepares to spear, hack and slash more innocent victims. And the chapels (#30–41) that retell the events of Christ's passion indulge in flagrant emotional manipulation, with crazed flagellators, spitting soldiers and a series of liberally blood-splattered Christs. Dominating the central piazza of the sanctuary, the Baroque Basilica offers some relief, the highlight being the cupola – a nice piece of optical trickery, encrusted with figures perched on bubblegum clouds.

Valsesia

From Varallo the main road follows the River Sesia to the foot of multipeaked Monte Rosa, whose massive bulk dominates four Italian valleys and spreads north into Switzerland. **VALSESIA**, the easternmost valley, is also the most dramatic – worth going for the ride even if you don't want to launch a hiking or skiing assault on the mountains.

Flanked by dark pine-wooded slopes topped with a toothed ridge of rock, the road winds up the valley, the perspective changing at every turn.

ALAGNA, at the head of the valley, right below Monte Rosa, is the most convenient place to stay, whether you want to ski or hike. Popular and predominantly modern, it has a cluster of traditional dwellings of the age-old Swiss religious sect known as the Walsers. Some of the houses still function as farms, with hay hanging to dry on the slats and wood stacked behind, while others are holiday homes, with geraniums tumbling from window boxes. The **tourist office** (Dec–Sept Mon & Wed–Fri 9am–noon & 3–6pm, Sat & Sun 9am–1pm & 2.30–6.30pm; Oct & Nov Sat & Sun only; ☎0163.922.988, @www.turismovalsesiavercelli.it) is at Piazza Grober 1. Alagna's cheapest **hotel** is the *Genzianella*, Via Centro 33 (☎0163.923.205, @www.pensionegenzianella.com; ❸ including breakfast).

There are lots of **walks** among the foothills near Alagna, all of which are well marked. However, the toughest and most spectacular hikes are those on **Monte Rosa** itself. It's possible to save time and energy by taking the cable car up to Punta Indren (3260m), from where you can walk to one of the many *rifugi*; most of these are open from June to September and some are open all year, but check at the tourist office in Alagna before setting out. All these walks involve a good deal of scree-crossing and some sobering drops, and none is to be taken lightly – you'll need a good **map** (the IGC map of the four Monte Rosa valleys shows all paths, *rifugi* and pistes as does the Kompass Monte Rosa map) available in Alagna and Varallo, and you should monitor the weather carefully. There's also an ambitious long-distance circuit of Monte Rosa, starting at Alagna and taking in Zermatt across the Swiss border: reckon on five days if you make use of ski lifts and cable cars, and a good deal longer if you don't.

Skiing in the area is organized by Monterosa Ski (☎0125.303.111; @www.monterosa-ski.com), which has an office in Alagna, and equipment is available for rent in the village. The valleys are also popular for canoeing and rafting, and several centres organize classes and excursions – try Hidronica (☎0163.735.301, @www.hidronica.com). Check @www.alagna.it for more information on summer and winter activities in and around Alagna.

Domodossola and over the border to Locarno

At the foot of the Simplon Pass, and handily situated on the main train line between Milan and Bern, in Switzerland (15 trains daily from Novara), is the little town of **DOMODOSSOLA**. With its arcaded medieval centre and market square, it warrants a visit in its own right, but is more famous as the starting point of a scenic train ride, La Vigezzina–Centovalli, that connects Domodossola with Locarno, across the border in Switzerland, taking in the vineyards and chestnut forests of the Val Vigezzo and Centovalli along the way. The scenery is gorgeous, and, although the ride is pricier than the regular train (one-way €19.80), it's well worth it; InterRail passes are valid. The journey to Locarno takes an hour and a half, but you can get off and explore at any of the pretty flower-strewn stations en route; when you want the next train to stop, just remember to raise the red and white signal on the platform.

The road to Aosta and the eastern valleys

The tributary valleys in **eastern Valle d'Aosta** (Ⓦwww.regione.vda.it) have suffered most from the skiing industry since they are the easiest to access from Turin and Milan and therefore the most frequented. However, hiking is good here, and experienced mountaineers may be lured by the challenge of climbing Monte Rosa and the Matterhorn from **Valtournenche**. For all visitors, in the main Aosta valley you'll find one of the region's more interesting castles, **Fénis**.

Valtournenche and the Matterhorn (Cervino)

VALTOURNENCHE, headed by the **Matterhorn** (4478m) at the north end and by the town of Chatillon at the southern central valley end, should be one of the most spectacular of Italy's mountain valleys, but unfortunately the main towns are overdeveloped and hydroelectric works ruin the views on the plains. The international ski resort **Breuil-Cervinia** is a functional, modern resort, and even the **Matterhorn** is a letdown, with tribes of skiers ensuring that its glacier is grubby for much of the year. That said, these are the Alps, and if you can't manage to carry on to the other valleys further west, you will at least get a taste of chocolate-box chalets and flower-covered meadows straight out of *Heidi*.

Breuil-Cervinia and the Matterhorn

BREUIL-CERVINIA was one of Italy's first ski resorts, built in the pre-war years as part of Mussolini's drive for a healthy nation. In its heyday the ski lifts, soaring to 3500m, broke all records, and its grand hotels ensured the patronage of Europe's wealthy. Today the wealthy are cossetted in modern buildings outside the resort, leaving the tacky streets of the town for packaged hordes attracted by a large skiing area with lots of easy runs.

If you want to climb the **Matterhorn** (4478m) you should seriously consider approaching from Zermatt in Switzerland; the Italian route is strictly for experts.

Nus and the Castello di Fénis

Further up the main valley from Chatillon and overlooked by a ruined castle, the small, pretty village of **NUS** makes a good base for the **Castello di Fénis** 2km away (daily: March–June & Sept 9am–7pm; July & Aug 9am–8pm; Oct–Feb

Mon–Sat 10am–12.30pm & 1.30–5pm, Sun 10am–12.30pm & 1.30–6pm; €5, guided tours only). Backed by wooded hills and encircled by two rows of turreted walls, the castle is a fairy-tale cluster of towers decorated with scalloped arcades. These defences were primarily aesthetic, with the real job of protecting the valley being left to the less prettified fortresses of nearby Nus and Quart. Meanwhile, the Fénis branch of the Challant counts concentrated on refining their living quarters with fine Gothic frescoes; the best of these is in the courtyard, above the elaborate twin staircase that leads to the upper storeys. A courtly St George rescues a damsel in distress from the clutches of a tremendous dragon, overlooked by a tribe of protective saints brandishing moral maxims on curling scrolls.

There's a **hotel** in Fénis – *La Chatelaine* (☎0165.764.264; ❸, breakfast included), in *località* Chez Sapin, open year-round. However, as Nus has a train station and is close to the main road for buses, you may find it more convenient to sleep there: the *Florian* at Via Risorgimento 3 (☎0165.767.968; ❷, not including breakfast) has clean and comfortable doubles and is also open all year.

Aosta and around

AOSTA, the attractive mountain-valley capital of Valle d'Aosta province, is an ideal base for exploring the northwest of the region. Surrounded by the Alps, the town's key attraction is its position: with access to the lovely valleys of the **Parco Nazionale del Gran Paradiso**, the ski resorts of **Mont Blanc**, and a sprinkling of castles in between. Founded by the Romans in 25 BC Aosta was primarily an imperial military camp, vestiges of which can be seen in the extensive ruins of

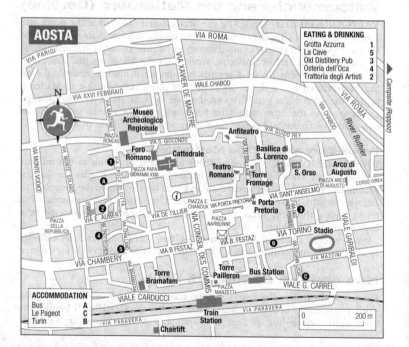

some towers and city walls. Remains of medieval Aosta predominate, its narrow cobbled streets and overhanging upper storeys giving the place a very alpine air.

Arrival and information

Aosta's **tourist office** (mid-June to Oct daily 9am–1pm & 3–8pm; Oct to mid-June Mon–Sat 9.30am–1pm & 3–6.30pm, Sun 9.30am–1pm; ☎0165.236.627, ⓦwww.regione.vda.it) is at Piazza E. Chanoux 2. You can get to most places within the region by **bus** from the bus station on Via G. Carrel, but some of the more remote valleys are served only by buses running at school times out of season (contact tourist office for seasonal timetables). The **train station** is on Piazza Manzetti, south of the centre.

Accommodation

Surprisingly, there's not much **accommodation** choice in Aosta: mostly stripped-down, modern ski-resort type structures and not a super-abundance of rooms, all told, so be sure to book early.

Hotels

Bus Via Malherbes 18/A ☎0165.43.645 ⓦwww .hotelbus.it. This bland high-rise offers solid, if unimaginative, comfort. Located on the less busy side of town, on its own quiet cul-de-sac. Parking nearby, breakfast included. ❹

Le Pageot Via G. Carrel 31 ☎0165.32.433 ⓦwww .lepageot.info. Handy for both train and bus stations, it also has easy parking and is close to all the sights. Rooms are simple, pleasant and well appointed. Breakfast included. ❺

Turin Via Torino 14 ☎0165.44.593 ⓦwww .hotelturin.it. Most centrally located, but starkly modern outside in an almost pre-fab style, and the rooms tend to be quite spartan. Nevertheless, the views of the encircling mountains can be spectacular, so ask for one on an upper floor. Breakfast included. ❸

Campsite

Milleluci Località Porossan-Roppoz 15 ☎0165.44.274, ⓦwww.campingmilleluci.com. Of the several campsites nearby, this is the nearest, just 1km from the historic centre. Set amidst mountain views and greenery, with a lodge offering meals and services. From about €8 daily.

The Town

The large, elegant **Piazza E. Chanoux** and its pavement cafés form the centre of town, from where Via Porta Pretoria and Via Sant'Anselmo lead east – the principal streets for window-shopping and people-watching. In the middle, the **Porta Pretoria** is one of the town's most impressive sights: two parallel triple-arched gateways that served as the main entrance into the Roman town. North of the gate is the **Teatro Romano** (daily: 9am–1hr before sunset; free); a section of the four-storeyed façade remains, 22m high and pierced with arched windows. Unfortunately, since 2000, scaffolding has partially obscured it, and no one will risk estimating a date for final completion of the preservation work.

A short walk east of here, outside the main town walls off Via Sant'Anselmo, the church of **Sant'Orso** (daily: March–Sept 9am–7pm; Oct–Feb 10am–12.30pm & 1.30–5pm; free) houses a number of tenth-century frescoes behind its dull facade. They're hidden up in the roof where you can examine them at close quarters from specially constructed walkways – though you'll need to find the sacristan to get up there. If you can't find him, content yourself with the fifteenth-century choir stalls, carved with a menagerie of holy men and animals, ranging from bats and monkeys to a tonsured monk. There are even better carvings on the capitals of the Romanesque **cloisters** (daily: March–June & Sept 9am–7pm; July & Aug 9am–8pm; Oct–Feb 10am–12.30pm & 1.30–5pm; free) – mostly scenes from the story of Christ.

At the far end of Via Sant'Anselmo, the **Arco di Augusto** was erected in 25 BC to honour Emperor Augustus, after whom the town was named Augusta Praetoria (Aosta is a corruption of Augusta). Though the arch loses something in being stranded in a sea of traffic and topped by a rustic eighteenth-century slate roof, it's a sturdy, dignified-looking monument. Beyond is a well-preserved **Roman bridge**, its single arch spanning the now dried-up bed of the River Buthier.

On the other side of town, the **Foro Romano** on Piazza Giovanni XXIII is the rather misleading name for another Roman relic, a vaulted passage (*cryptoporticus*) under the actual forum area, the purpose of which is not entirely clear, though it probably served as both a foundation for structures above ground and as a protected walkway. Nearby, the **Museo Archeologico Regionale** (daily 9am–7pm; free) has interesting exhibits on the settlements in and around Aosta since Neolithic times. Displays include artefacts of the Celtic Salassi tribe who ended up being sold as slaves by the Romans. The nearby **cattedrale** (April–Sept, Mon–Sat 6.30am–noon & 3–8pm, Sun 7am–noon & 3–8pm; Oct–March closes an hour earlier; free) looks unpromising from the outside, but masks a Gothic interior with more fantastically carved choir stalls, this time sporting a mermaid, lion and a snail nestled among the saints. Like Sant'Orso, too, it has some impressive tenth-century frescoes hidden in the roof, saved for posterity by the lowering of the ceiling in the fourteenth century; you can visit these on a guided tour (several daily; €7.80).

Eating and drinking

Being foremost a resort town, finding a congenial **place to eat** or drink here is no problem. There's a full range of food on offer, from snacks to Italian to French to local mountain fare, and a range of prices, as well. Via E. Aubert and Via Porta Pretoria are best for a trawl.

Grotta Azzurra Via Croce di Città 97. Pizza, pasta and good Italian side dishes keep this place filled to the brim with animated diners. Expect €15 a head. Closed Wed.

Osteria dell'Oca Via E. Aubert 15. On a quiet little square, local cuisine here includes pizzas, all choices with fresh ingredients. Closed Mon.

La Cave Via Challand 34. Good wines in a simpatico setting, this is the dining/drinking adjunct to the valley's oldest enoteca. Full meals of coldcuts or just a glass of over fifty wines on offer *alla mescita* each week, chosen from some 800 labels. Very popular in the early evening. Open daily for both lunch and dinner.

The Old Distillery Pub Via Près Fosses 7. Tucked away down a narrow side alley, this place offers a very welcoming and energetic nightlife scene, especially for, but not limited to, the Anglophone crowd. Pub food available. Open till 2am.

Trattoria degli Artisti Via Maillet 5/7 ⊕011.436.6553. Traditional Aosta fare created with imagination, includes mountain game and other meats, braised on stone. A slow-food touchstone. Starting at about €20 per person. Closed Sun & Mon lunchtime.

West from Aosta: Castello di Sarre

West from Aosta, the main valley holds a number of **castles**, the best of which is the thirteenth-century **Castello di Sarre** (July & Aug daily 9am–8pm; Sept & March–June daily 9am–7pm; Oct–Feb Tues–Sat 10am–12.30pm & 1.30–5pm, Sun till 6pm; €5), accessible by bus or train from Aosta, some 5km away. It's a ten-minute walk up a hill covered with apple orchards from the St Maurice-Sarre train station; coming by bus, walk from the bus stop up the main road and take the unmarked turning just before the tollbooth. Sarre is the former hunting lodge of **Vittorio Emanuele II**, who, the story goes, actually bought the castle by mistake. He had set his sights on the property of Aymaville opposite, but the agent sent to buy the castle was confused about the direction in which the river flowed, and ended up buying Sarre instead. The king made the best of a bad job, permanently stamping the halls of the castle with his astounding taste in interior decor, pushing the hunting-lodge motif to its limits, with horns of wild ibex lining the main gallery and thousands of white chamois skulls studding the stuccoed festoons. Pride of place is given to the first ibex slain by the king.

North from Aosta: the Colle di Gran San Bernardo

Immediately north of Aosta, the **Colle di Gran San Bernardo** (2473m) leads the way into Switzerland. Named after the famous monastery that for centuries provided shelter to travellers on the main pilgrim route from Northern Europe to Rome, it was the home of the eponymous big brown-and-white dogs that rescued Alpine travellers in distress. The history of the mountain pass is well documented in the **museum** (June–Sept daily 9am–6pm; €5) housed in the monastery-hospice, although you'll need your passport to visit as it's situated just over the border in Switzerland. The spectacular pass is open only during summer, but the border is open year-round by way of a tunnel.

The Gran Paradiso National Park

For some of Valle d'Aosta's most beautiful mountains and valleys, make for the south, down to the **Parco Nazionale del Gran Paradiso** (⑩ www.pngp.it) – Italy's first national park, spread around the valleys at the foot of 4061-metre-high Monte Gran Paradiso. The park's three valleys – **Cogne**, **Valsavarenche** and **Val di Rhêmes** – are popular, but tourist development has been cautious and well organized. The hotels are good (you get far more for your money than you would in one of the nearby towns) and the campsites not too vast – camping outside of campsites is not permitted. There are a few mountain *rifugios* and *bivacchi* (unoccupied shelters) between which run well-marked footpaths. Though it's primarily a summer resort for walkers, the cross-country skiing is also good, and every winter a 45-kilometre **Gran Paradiso** trek is organized at Cogne (contact the tourist office in Cogne for details). The starting-point for the ascent of Gran Paradiso itself is **Pont** in the Valsavarenche, while Cogne gives access to the Alta Via 2, a long, high-level mountain trail.

Park wildlife

Gran Paradiso National Park owes its foundation to King Vittorio Emanuele II, who donated his extensive hunting park to the state in 1922, ensuring that the population of **ibex** that he and his hunters had managed to reduce to near extinction, would after all survive. There are now around 3500 ibex here and about 6000 **chamois**, living most of the year above the tree line but descending to the valleys in winter and spring. The most dramatic sightings are during the mating season in November and December, when you may see pairs of males fighting it out for possession of a female. You might also spy **golden eagles** nesting, and there are a number of rare **alpine flowers**, most of which can be seen in the botanical garden in the Val di Cogne.

Regular **buses** run throughout the year from Aosta to Cogne and Valsava-renche and along the Val di Rhêmes from mid-June to mid-September (see p.100). If you're using your own transport, access to either of these valleys is easiest from the village of **Introd**, about 2km from **Villeneuve**, which is on the main bus route.

Val di Cogne

The **Val di Cogne** is the principal, most popular and most dramatic section of the park. Its lower reaches are narrow, the road running above the fast-flowing Grand Eyvia River overlooked by sheer wavy-ridged mountains. Further on, the valley broadens out around the main village, **COGNE**, which is surrounded by gentle green meadows with glacier-covered mountains rising beyond.

The **tourist office**, in the centre of town at Via Bourgeois 34 (daily 9am–12.30pm & 3–5.30/6pm; ☎0165.74.040, ⓦwww.cogne.org), has maps with descriptions in English of walks, one of which is an easy, scenic stroll that follows the river, with the glaciers in view for most of the way. Before leaving the village of Cogne, it's worth visiting the **Maison de Gerard Dayné** (July & Aug 6 tours daily 10.40am–6.30pm; at other times of the year, ask at the tourist office or call ☎0165.749.264; €3) a typical nineteenth-century Valdaostan house evocative of the traditional lifestyle.

The small village of **VALNONTEY** is 2.5km southwest of Cogne and starting-point for a steep, three-hour walk up to the *Rifugio V. Sella* (☎0165.74.310, ⓦwww.rifugiosella.com; Easter–Sept), a demanding hike that's incredibly popular on summer Sundays and in early August. The path passes a **botanical garden** (mid-June to mid-Sept daily 10am–6.30pm; €2.50), with rare Alpine flora, then zigzags up through a forest and onto exposed mountain-side before reaching the *rifugio*, set on a grassy plateau. At the mountain tarn of Lago Loson, a fifteen-minute walk from the *rifugio*, you may well spot ibex or more timid chamois, especially at sunset and sunrise, when there are fewer people around. Hardened hikers who can cope with a stretch of climbing (difficuly "E") can press on over the **Colle de Lauson** to the Val di Rhêmes.

Practicalities

Park **accommodation** is largely of the mountain lodge variety and places are regularly monitored to maintain high standards of service. Some close part of the year, and all quickly get booked solid during peak seasons. Most will require half- or full-board. There are several **campsites**, closed from about mid-September to about mid-May, so check exact dates. Many hotels here have **restaurants** open to non-guests, and Cogne has more choices, including several delicatessens that will make up sandwiches for you.

Hotels

Bellevue Rue Grand Paradis 22, Cogne ☎0165.74.825 ⓦwww.hotelbellevue.it. More alpine ambiance, but with absolute luxury as the keynote. This is a Relais & Chateau property and boasts a world-class health and beauty spa among its many amenities. Buffet breakfast included, three nights minimum, ❼. Self-contained chalets also available at about €100 per person per night for half-board. **Bouton d'Or** Viale Cavagnet 15, Cogne ☎0165.74.268 ⓦwww.hotelboutondor.it. Rustic

knotty pine inside and out, with banks of geraniums lining the porches, this choice offers a swimming pool, a sauna, a fitness room and hydro-massage. Open year-round. Half-board required. ❻ **Herbetet** Frazione Valnontey 52 ☎0165.74.180 ⓦwww.hotelherbetet.com. Swiss-chalet with rustic mountain decor, including wood-beam ceilings and cosy comforters. Menu features mostly Italian, with a mix of country game and French cuisine. Open mid-May to mid-Sept. B&B or half- or full-board available. ❹

La Barme Frazione Valnontey ℡0165.74.158 ⓦwww.hotellabarme.com. A very rustic stone complex with a small spa. Set up for both summer and winter sports, including horseriding and all sorts of skiing. Closed Oct & Nov. Restaurant offers set menus for non-guests, starting at €13. Half-board required. ❺

Paradisia Frazione Valnontey 36 ℡0165.74.158 ⓦwww.hotelparadisia.it. Converted mountain chalet offering homely comforts. Restaurant services for non-guests, featuring northern Italian and Swiss-style cookery. Open Easter to end of Sept. Breakfast included. ❸

Petit Dahu Frazione Valnontey 27 ℡0165.74.146 ⓦwww.hotelpetitdahu.com. A stone mountain retreat with glowing knotty pine interiors, Open year-round. Full range of meal choices, from B&B to full-board. ❹

Stambecco Rue des Clementines 21, Cogne ℡0165.74.068 ⓦwww.hotelstambecco.com. Alpine chalet in style, very welcoming, with rooms featuring natural wood and warm colours. Open year-round. Breakfast included. ❹

Campsites

Gran Paradiso Frazione Valnontey 59 ℡0165.749.204. 120 sites. Open mid-May to mid-Sept. Adults and sites from €5.

Lo Stambecco Frazione Valnontey 6 ℡0165.74.152 ⓦwww.campinglostambecco.com. Grassy terraced sites and pinewood groves on slopes near the village make a good departure point for mountain hikes. 130 sites. Open mid-May to mid-Sept. Adults from €7, sites from €6.

Vallée de Cogne Località Fabrique Via Cavagnet 7, Cogne ℡0165.749.279 ℻0165.749.028. Just on the northwest edge of town, prices run €5.50 per adult and €8 per site. Open year-round.

Restaurants

Brasserie du Bon Bec Rue Bourgeois 72, Cogne. Rustic mountain food served in an impressive wood-panelled "hut"; moderate prices.

Lou Ressignon Rue Mines de Cogne 22, Cogne. Hearty soups and stews plus a good wine list; full meals run €20–30. Dinner only; Sept–June open Fri & Sat; July & Aug open Wed, Fri–Sun.

Valsavarenche

Although not as spectacular as the Val di Cogne, **Valsavarenche**, the next valley west, has its own kind of beauty, attracting seasoned walkers rather than gentle amblers. The most popular route is the ascent of **Gran Paradiso**, from Pont at the end of the valley. Though reckoned to be the easiest of the higher Alps, it is nevertheless a climb rather than a hike, with no path marked beyond the *Rifugio Vittorio Emanuele II* (℡0165.95.920; mid-March to mid-Sept), two and a half hours from Pont. If you feel safer walking along footpaths, the best of the hikes are from the village of **Degioz**, a locality of Valsavarenche, up to the *Rifugio Orvielles* (2hr 30min; ℡0165.905.816) and then on to a series of high mountain lakes. This takes seven hours, but you can shorten it a bit by taking path #3a down to Pont. Less taxing is the two-hour walk from Pont towards the glacier **Grand Etret** at the head of the valley, although the first stretch is pretty boring.

Practicalities

The only **hotel** in Degioz is the *Parco Nazionale* (℡0165.905.706; Jan 1 & April–Sept; ❸, breakfast not included), while in Pont there is the *Genzianella* which may insist on half board (℡0165.95.393, ⓦwww.genzianella.aosta.it; June–Sept; ❸, breakfast not included). The area is well supplied with **campsites**, of which perhaps the nicest is *Pont Breuil* (℡0165.95.458; June–Sept), in Pont, with a well-stocked site shop (there's no other for kilometres around); ibex come down to graze on the grassy meadow around the tents. There's also a leafy campsite at località Plan de la Presse, Gran Paradiso (℡&℻0165.905.801; June–Sept). There are places to **eat** in Degioz, such as the *Pub Brasserie l'Abro de la Leunna* Frazione Degioz 93 (℡0165.905.732; closed Wed), but at Pont you'll have to cook for yourself or ask at one of the hotels.

Val di Rhêmes

The least touristed of the valleys, Val di Rhêmes, is also headed by glaciers. The best place to stay is **BRUIL**, a hamlet at the end of the valley, from where most of the walks start.

There's a fairly easy path along the river to a waterfall, the Cascata di Goletta, at its most spectacular after the spring snowmelt, and from here you can continue to the mountain lake of Goletta and the *Rifugio Gian Federico Benevolo* (T0165.936.143, Wwww.benevolo.info; March–Sept, closed first half of June) taking in some splendid views on the way. Economical hotel options in Bruil include *Chez Lidia* (T0165.936.103; ②, breakfast not included) and the *Galisia* (T&F0165.936.100; ①, breakfast not included); both are open all year.

Arvier and Valgrisenche

Valgrisenche, a few kilometres west from Val di Rhêmes, is the wildest and least accessible of Valle d'Aosta's valleys. Stunningly beautiful, it is narrow with rocky snow-dusted ridges rising above dark pine woods, although the upper reaches are defaced by the concrete dam of a reservoir. Buses into the Valgrisenche valley aren't very frequent, but buses and trains stop year-round at **ARVIER** at the mouth of the valley – one of the region's most appealing villages, with a small medieval core of twisting streets and stone houses alongside a gorge spanned by a Roman bridge. The town also produces L'Enfer d'Arvier, reckoned to be the region's best wine.

There are no **hotels** in the village of **VALGRISENCHE** itself, but the nearby hamlet of **BONNE** above the reservoir has the *Perret* (T0165.97.107; ②, not including breakfast), which boasts a restaurant, is open all year and makes a good starting point for **walks**. These include the ascent of the glaciated Testa del Rutor (3486m). There are many other walks, but none are easy – make sure you carry the Kompass *Gran Paradiso* map.

The northwest: around Mont Blanc

Dominated by the snowy peaks of **Mont Blanc** (Monte Bianco to the Italians), the northern reaches of Valle d'Aosta are spectacular and very popular. The most sensational views are from the cable cars that glide and swoop (at times, alarmingly so) across the mountain to Chamonix in France. However, the trip is expensive (€55 return, €46 one-way), even if you take a bus back to Italy through the eleven-kilometre-long Mont Blanc tunnel, and the service is often suspended because of bad weather.

If the cable car seems too pricey, you can walk up to the **Testa d'Arpy** – a natural balcony with a bird's-eye view up the valley to Mont Blanc – from the sprawling resort of **LA THUILE**, on the road to the Petit-St-Bernard Pass into France. Buses run from Pré-St-Didier at the end of the Valle d'Aosta railway line to La Thuile, from where it's just over two-hours' walk by path or road to the lodge *La Genzianella* hotel (T0165.841.689, Wwww.hotelgenzianella.net; ②) at the top of the Colle San Carlo. From here a path leads through woods to Testa d'Arpy in around ten minutes. It's well worth having a good map (IGC *Monte Bianco*), not so much to find your way as to identify the peaks and glaciers spread out before you.

La Thuile itself is a rather overdeveloped resort but it's worth popping into the **tourist office**, at Via M. Collomb 36 (daily 9am–12.30pm & 3–6pm; ☎0165.883.049, ⓦwww.lathuile.it) for maps. The best **accommodation** is up the mountain at *Du Glacier*, Petite Golette 14 (July–Sept & Nov–April; phone in advance to check that there's room, and in high season they may only take bookings for a few days; ☎0165.884.137, ⓦwww.hotelduglacier.it; minimum stays according to season ❹). Of the walks starting from the hotel the most interesting is the 45-minute hike to **Lago d'Arpy**, from where a path leads down into La Thuile.

Courmayeur and Mont Blanc

COURMAYEUR (ⓦwww.courmayeur.com) is the smartest and most popular of Valle d'Aosta's ski resorts, much used by package-tour operators. The skiing is good, though there's little to challenge experts, and the scenery is magnificent, but, predictably, what remains of the old village is enmeshed in a web of ersatz Alpine chalets and après-ski hangouts. There are two ski schools here: Monte Biano Ski and Snowboard School (ⓦwww.scuolascimontebianco.com) and the Snowboard and Ski School Courmayeur (ⓦwww.scuolascicourmayeur.it). Lift passes start at about €100 for three days, either consecutive or non-consecutive. If you've come to hike or take the cable cars across to Chamonix, the most convenient place to stay is **LA PALUD**, 5km outside Courmayeur (three buses a day).

The **cable car** runs from La Palud to Punta Helbronner all year round, but continues to Chamonix only between July and September (Punta Hellbronner-Chamonix €39, Punta Hellbronner-Chamonix and return by coach €78). There are between ten and twelve departures a day, depending on the time of year, roughly hourly starting at 8.30am – although ultimately the regularity depends on the weather. To be sure of good views, you'll need to set out early since it's usually cloudy by midday; be sure also to get there in plenty of time, especially on summer weekends, as it's much used by summer skiers. Even if it's blazing hot in the valley, the temperature plunges to near freezing at the top, so come prepared.

There are good **walks** along the two valleys at the foot of the Mont Blanc glaciers, both of which have seasonal campsites accessible by bus from Courmayeur. Val Ferret to the west is the more interesting option – you can walk back from Frebouze over Monte de la Saxe, with some incredible views of Mont Blanc en route.

If you do spend a night in Courmayeur, note that one of the cheapest of the fifty-odd **hotels** is the one-star mountain chalet *Venezia* at Via delle Villette 2 (☎&ⓕ0165.842.461; ❶); or there's the three-star *Crampon*, on the same street at no. 8 (☎0165.842.385, ⓦwww.crampon.it; Christmas–April & July to mid-Sept; ❺). Hotels in La Palud include the charming *Chalet Joli* (☎0165.869.722, ⓦwww.chaletjoli.com; ❹) and the extremely comfortable *Vallée Blanche* (☎0165.897.002, ⓦwww.hotelvalleeblanche.com; one week minimum, buffet breakfast included ❹). Most of these hotels offer special pricing arrangements with local restaurants for their guests' main meals.

Travel details

Trains

Alba to: Asti (14 daily; 40min).

Aosta to: Pré-St-Didier (11 daily; 50min); Sarre (11 daily; 6min).

Novara to: Biella (20 daily; 50min–3hr 30min); Varallo Pombia (11 daily; 25min–1hr); Varallo Sesia (22 daily; 1hr–1hr 30min).

Torino (all stations) to: Aosta (15 daily; 2–3hr); Asti (53 daily; 30min–1hr); Milano Centrale (31 daily; 2hr); Modena (11 daily; 1hr 25min–3hr 10min); Novara (37 daily; 1hr 15min–4hr 30min); Sant'Ambrogio (24 daily; 30min–1hr).

Buses

Alba to: Barolo (Mon–Sat 2 daily; 30min)

Aosta to: Cogne (6–7 daily; 50min); Courmayeur (13–16 daily; 1hr); Gran San Bernardo (2–4 daily; 55min); Pont Valsavarenche (mid-June to mid-Sept 3 daily, mid-Sept to mid-June weekdays only; 1hr 10min); Rhêmes Notre Dame (mid-June to mid-Sept 3 daily; 1hr); Valgrisenche (mid-June to mid-Sept 3 daily; mid-Sept to mid-June schooldays only; 1hr).

Biella to: Ivrea (6 daily; 2hr 25min); Santuario di Oropa (7 daily; 40min).

Chatillon to: Breuil-Cervinia (6 daily; 1hr–1hr 30min).

Cogne to: Valnontey (July & early Sept 9 daily; Aug 22 daily; 15min).

Pré-St-Didier to: Courmayeur (15 daily; 10–25min); La Thuile (11 daily; 25min).

Saluzzo to: Paesana (Valle Po; Mon–Sat 11 daily, 3 Sun; 2hr); Val Varaita (3 daily; 1hr 15min).

Torino (Corso Marconi) to: Saluzzo (10 daily; 1hr 20min).

Torino (Corso Vittorio Emanuele II 131) to: Aosta (8 daily; 2–3hr); Cervinia (1 Sun; 2hr 15min); Courmayeur (7 daily; 4hr); Ivrea (12 daily; 1hr 15min).

Liguria

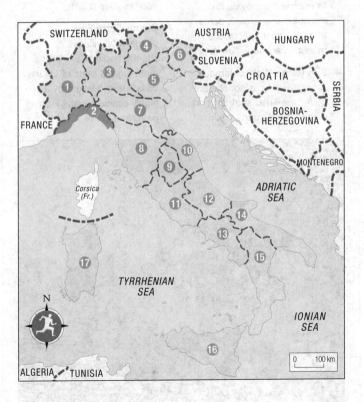

CHAPTER 2 # Highlights

* **Genoa** With its rabbit warren of medieval streets, revamped port area and clutch of first-rate museums and churches, Genoa could easily justify a week of your time. See p.106

* **The train from Genoa to Casella** An excellent way to escape the crowds on the coast and explore some of Italy's most spectacular mountain scenery. See p.122

* **San Remo** With its famous Art Nouveau casino, elegant palm-tree-lined seafront and pleasant old quarter, San Remo affords a glimpse of old-style Riviera glamour. See p.127

* **Camogli** A collection of colourful cottages surrounding an idyllic harbour, Camogli is one of the coast's prettiest fishing villages. See p.131

* **Cinque Terre** Five picturesque villages shoehorned into one of the most rugged parts of Liguria's coastline and linked by a highly scenic coastal walking path. See p.136

▲ Manarola, Cinque Terre

Liguria

heltering on the seaward side of the mountains that divide Piemonte from the coast, **Liguria** is the classic introduction to Italy for travellers journeying overland through France. There's an unexpected change as you cross the border: the **Italian Riviera** (as Liguria's commercially developed strip of coast is known) has more variety of landscape and architecture than its French counterpart, and is generally less frenetic. And if you want to escape the crowds the mountains, which in places drop sheer to the sea, can offer respite from the standard format of beach, beach and more beach.

Regional food and wine

Liguria may lie in the north of Italy, but its benign Mediterranean climate, and to some extent its cooking, belong further south. Traditionally, the recipes from this region make something out of nothing, the legacy of the hardships of life here in the past. The best-known Ligurian speciality is **pesto**. Invented by the Genoese to help their long-term sailors fight off scurvy, it's made with chopped basil, garlic, pine-nuts and grated sharp cheese (pecorino or parmesan) ground up together in olive oil – traditionally with a pestle and mortar. It's used as a sauce for pasta (often flat *trenette* noodles, or knobbly little potato-flour shapes known as **trofie**), or stirred into soup to make *minestrone alla genovese*. Otherwise, **fish** dominates – not surprising in a region where more than two-thirds of the population live on the coast. Local **anchovies** are a common antipasto, while pasta with a variety of fish and seafood sauces appears everywhere (mussels, scampi, octopus and clams are all excellent); there's also a host of specific dishes such as *ciuppin* or fish soup, *burrida di seppie* (cuttlefish stew), or fish *in carpione* (marinated in vinegar and herbs). Salt **cod** (*bacalà*) and wind-dried cod (*stoccofisso*) are big local favourites, often served fried. Other dishes to look out for are *cima alla genovese* (cold, stuffed veal) and the widely available *torta pasqualina*, a spinach-and-cheese pie with eggs. The latter is served as fast food, as are other kinds of *torta* and golden **focaccia** bread, often flavoured with olives, sage or rosemary. Chickpeas grow abundantly along the coast and crop up in **farinata**, a kind of chickpea pancake displayed in broad, round baking trays that you'll see everywhere, and in *zuppa di ceci*. Pastries, too, are excellent: Genoa is famous for its **pandolce**, a sweet cake laced with dried fruit, nuts and candied peel.

Liguria's soil and aspect aren't well suited to vine-growing, although plenty of local **wine** – mainly white – is quite drinkable. The steep, terraced slopes of the Cinque Terre are home to an eponymous white wine and the sweet, expensive dessert wine called Sciacchetrà, made from partially dried grapes. From the Riviera di Ponente, look out for the crisp whites of Pigato (from Albenga) and Vermentino (from Imperia), as well as the acclaimed Rossese di Dolceacqua, Liguria's best red.

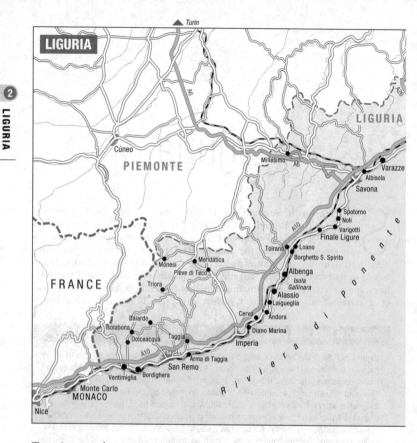

Teetering on slopes carpeted with olives and vines are isolated mountain villages that retain their own rural culture and cuisine.

The chief city of the region is **Genoa**, an ancient, sprawling port often acclaimed as the most atmospheric of all Italian cities. It has a dense and fascinating old quarter that is complemented by a vibrant social and ethnic mix and a newly energized dockside district. The city stands midway along two distinct stretches of coastline. To the west is the **Riviera di Ponente**, one long ribbon of hotels packed out in summer with Italian families. Picking your route carefully means you can avoid the worst of it. **San Remo**, the *grande-dame* of Riviera resorts, is flanked by hillsides covered with glasshouses, and is a major centre for the worldwide export of flowers; **Albenga** and **Noli** are attractive medieval centres that have also retained a good deal of character; and **Finale Ligure** is a thoroughly pleasant Mediterranean seaside town.

On Genoa's eastern side is the more rugged **Riviera di Levante**. Umbrella pines grow horizontally on the cliff-faces overlooking the water, and in the evening a glassy calm falls over the little bays and inlets. Walks on **Monte di Portofino** and through the dramatic coastal scenery of the **Cinque Terre** take you through scrubland and vineyards for memorable views over broad gulfs and jutting headlands. This mix of mountains and fishing villages, then accessible

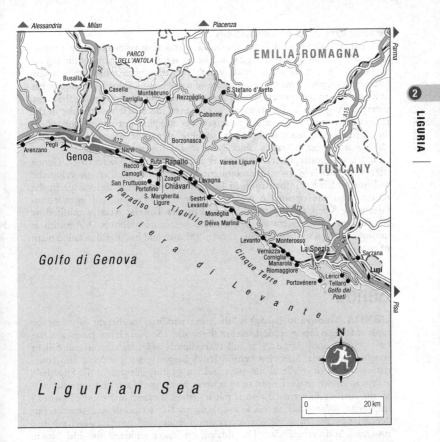

only by boat, appealed to the early nineteenth-century Romantics who "discovered" the Riviera, preparing the way for other artists and poets and the first package tourists. Now the whole area explodes into quite a ruck every July and August, with resorts like **Portofino** qualifying as among the most expensive in the country. Nearby **Santa Margherita Ligure** makes a great base for day-trips to Genoa, under an hour away, or for exploring the surrounding coastline by train or car, as does the pretty fishing village of **Camogli**. Generally the best times to visit are spring and autumn.

In the summer months, the only way to avoid the crowds is to travel inland. Minor roads and mule tracks link villages spiralling around hilltops, originally as protection against Saracen invasion. A testing long-distance footpath, the **Alta Via dei Monti Liguri**, runs from pass to mountain pass along the length of Liguria, but aside from the odd section accessible on public transport from the coast it's mainly for hardened pros. Nonetheless, high-altitude resorts such as **Santo Stefano d'Aveto** and **Torriglia** offer plenty of summer walking (and, in places, winter skiing) that can lift you a world away from the resorts down below on the sea. And the hills and mountains of the **Parco dell'Antola** (ⓦwww.parks.it/parco.antola) offer acres of protected landscape, with plenty of opportunities for walking, mountain biking and other outdoor pursuits.

Transport and information

In a **car**, the shore road is for the most part a disappointment: the coast is extremely built up, and you get a much better sense of the beauty of the region by taking the east–west autostrada which cuts through the mountains a few kilometres inland by means of a mixture of tunnels and viaducts. Fleeting bursts of daylight between tunnels give glimpses of the string of resorts along the coast, silvery olive groves and a brilliant sea. However, the easiest way to take in the region is by **train**: there are regular services stopping just about everywhere and, because the track is forced to squeeze along the narrow coastal strip, stations are almost invariably centrally located in towns and villages.

Liguria's regional **tourist office** is based at Piazza Matteotti 9, Genoa (℡010.530.8201, ⓦwww.turismoinliguria.it) – check out their encyclopedic website, which has information in English on every town and village in the region, plus the option to reserve at any hotel, campsite or agriturismo farmhouse. The excellent spiral-bound **Liguria Tourist Atlas**, published by the regional government in collaboration with cartographers DeAgostini, is invaluable if you're spending any time in the area and has useful detailed plans of town centres.

Genoa

GENOA (**Genova** in Italian) is "the most winding, incoherent of cities, the most entangled topographical ravel in the world". So said Henry James, and the city – Italy's sixth largest – is still marvellously eclectic, vibrant and full of rough-edged style. Sprawled behind Italy's biggest port is a dense and fascinating warren of medieval alleyways and *caruggi* (tiny alleyways): "La Superba", as it was known at the height of its powers, boasts more zest and intrigue than all the surrounding coastal resorts put together. It's here that most of Genoa's important *palazzi* are to be found, built in the sixteenth and seventeenth centuries by the city's wealthy mercantile families and now transformed into museums and art galleries. The tidying-up hasn't sanitized the **old town**, however; the core of the city, between the two stations and the waterfront, is still dark and slightly threatening. But despite the sleaze, the overriding impression is of a buzzing hive of activity – food shops nestled in the portals of former palaces, carpenters' workshops sandwiched between designer furniture outlets, everything surrounded by a crush of people and the squashed vowels of the impenetrable **Genoese dialect** that has, over the centuries, absorbed elements of Neapolitan, Calabrese and Portuguese. Aside from the cosmopolitan street life, you should seek out the **Cattedrale di San Lorenzo** with its fabulous treasury, small medieval churches such as **San Donato** and **Santa Maria di Castello**, and the Renaissance *palazzi* that contain Genoa's **art** collections and furniture and decor from the grandest days of the city's illustrious past.

Some history

Genoa made its money at sea, through trade, colonial exploitation and piracy. By the thirteenth century, after playing a major part in the **Crusades**, the Genoese were roaming the Mediterranean, bringing back ideas as well as goods: the city's architects were using Arab pointed arches a century before the rest of Italy. The San Giorgio banking syndicate effectively controlled the city for much of the fifteenth century, and cold-shouldered **Columbus** (who had grown up in Genoa) when he sought funding for his voyages. With Spanish

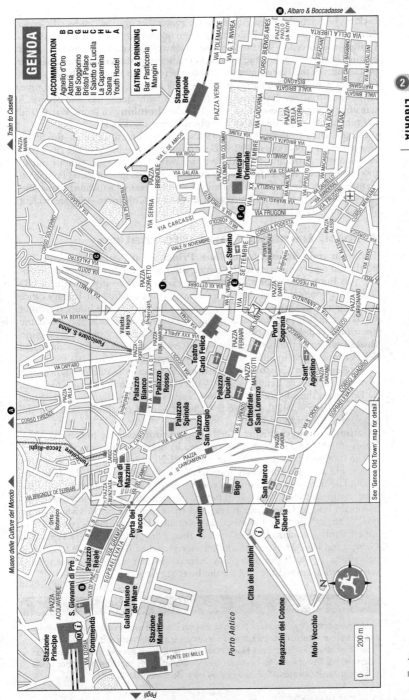

GENOA

ACCOMMODATION

Agnello d'Oro	B
Astoria	D
Bel Soggiorno	G
Bristol Palace	E
Il Salotto di Lucilla	C
La Capannina	H
Soana	F
Youth Hostel	A

EATING & DRINKING

Bar Pasticceria Mangini	1

H, Albaro & Boccadasse

Train to Casella

Museo delle Culture del Mondo

Stazione Brignole

PIAZZA VERDI

VIA TOLEMAIDE

VIA G. T. INVREA

PIAZZA PAOLO DA NOVI

VIA DELLA LIBERTA

CORSO BUENOS AIRES

VIA G. T. INVREA

PIAZZA DELLA VITTORIA

VIA CADORNA

VIA FIUME

VIA COLOMBO

PIAZZA COLOMBO

Mercato Orientale

VIA XX SETTEMBRE

VIA BRIGATA LIGURIA

VIA GRANELLO

VIA CESAREA

VIA FIASELLA

VIA MALTA

VIA APPIO D'ASTE

VIA COLOMBO

VIALE BRIGATA PARTIGIANE

VIA BRIGATA BISAGNO

VIA DIAZ

VIA DIAZ

VIA CARLO BARABINO

VIA MADDALONI

VIA MAGHELLO

VIA MARAGLIANO

VIA MACAGGI

VIA CASTELLO

VIA BANDERALI

VIA FRUGONI

VIA FRUGONI

CORSO MENTANA

VIA E. DE AMICIS

VIA RICCI

VIA GALATA

PIAZZA BRIGNOLE

VIA BRIGNOLE

VIA SERRA

VIA PESCHIERA

VIA CARCASSI

VIA S. VINCENZO

Stazione Brignole

F G

S. Stefano

VIA FOSSOLO

PIAZZA ALESSI

CORSO A. PODESTA

VIA CORSICA

PIAZZA ALESSI

VIA ALESSI

VIA BIXIO

PIAZZA MANIN

VIA ASSAROTTI

CORSO SOLFERINO

VIA PALESTRO

C

VIALE IV NOVEMBRE

PIAZZA CORVETTO

VIA GOITO

VIA MAMELI

VIA PETRARCA

PONTE MONUMENTALE

Underpass

E

VIA E. VERNAZZA

VIA XII OTTOBRE

VIA XX SETTEMBRE

1

PIAZZA DANTE

VIA FIESCHI

VIA D'ANNUNZIO

PIAZZA CARIGNANO

CORSO FIRENZE

A

VIA CAFFARO

VIA BERTANI

Villetta di Negro

Funicolare S. Anna

PIAZZA PORTELLO

Underpass

PIAZZA FONT. MAROSE

PIAZZA G. VILLA

VIA ROMA

VIA XXV APRILE

VIA GARIBALDI

VIA LUCCOLI

Palazzo Bianco

Palazzo Rosso

Teatro Carlo Felice

PIAZZA FERRARI

Porta Soprana

VIA RAVECCA

PIAZZA MATTEOTTI

Palazzo Ducale

Sant' Agostino

PIAZZA SARZANO

SOPRAELEVATA

CORSO QUADRIO

See Genoa Old Town map for detail

Funicolare Zecca–Righi

VIA BRIGNOLE DE FERRARI

Orto Botanico

PIAZZA NUNZIATA

VIA CAIROLI

LARGO ZECCA

Casa di Mazzini

Palazzo Spinola

VIA S. LUCA

Palazzo San Giorgio

VIA DEL CAMPO

PIAZZA BANCHI

VIA S. LORENZO

Cattedrale di San Lorenzo

VIA S. CROCE

PIAZZA CAVOUR

San Marco

Porta Siberia

VIA DRAMSCI

SOPRAELEVATA

Porta dei Vacca

Aquarium

PIAZZA CARICAMENTO

Bigo

Città dei Bambini

i

Porto Antico

Magazzini del Cotone

Molo Vecchio

Museo delle Culture del Mondo

Pegli

Stazione Principe

PIAZZA ACQUAVERDE

S. Giovanni di Prè

Commenda

M i

VIA DORIA

VIA DI PRE

Palazzo Reale

B

VIA BALBI

VIA GRAMSCI

Galata Museo del Mare

Stazione Marittima

PONTE DEI MILLE

N

0   200 m

backing, he opened up new Atlantic trade routes that ironically reduced *Genova La Superba* to a backwater. Following foreign invasion, in 1768 the Banco di San Giorgio was forced to sell the Genoese colony of Corsica to the French, and a century later, the city became a hotbed of radicalism: **Mazzini**, one of the main protagonists of the Risorgimento, was born here, and in 1860 **Garibaldi** set sail for Sicily with his "Thousand" from the city's harbour. Around the same time, Italy's industrial revolution began in Genoa, with steelworks and shipyards spreading along the coast. These suffered heavy **bombing** in World War II, and the subsequent economic decline hobbled Genoa for decades.

Things started to look up in the 1990s. State funding to celebrate the 500th anniversary of Columbus's 1492 voyage paid to renovate many of the city's late-Renaissance palaces and the old port area, with Genoa's most famous son of modern times, **Renzo Piano** (best known as the co-designer of Paris's Pompidou Centre), taking a leading role. The results of a twelve-year, €46-million programme, that saw Genoa becoming a **European Capital of Culture** in 2004, are evident all over the city.

Arrival, transport and information

The main **train station** is **Stazione Principe**, on Piazza Acquaverde, just north of the port and west of the centre, although a number of mainline trains also pass through **Stazione Brignole** on Piazza Verdi, to the east. Buses #33 and #37, among others, ply between the two. There's a staffed left-luggage office at Principe (daily 6am–10pm; €3.80 per piece for the first five hours, thereafter €0.60 per hour). Take care if arriving at Principe after dark, and avoid the notorious Via di Prè alley nearby, which is the core territory of Genoa's lowlife. **Buses** heading to the city outskirts – the Riviera, and inland – arrive on Piazza della Vittoria, a few minutes' walk south of Brignole.

The **Aeroporto Cristoforo Colombo** (Ⓦwww.aeroportodigenova.com) is 6km west of the city centre. Volabus #100 runs to Stazione Principe, to Piazza de Ferrari on the edge of the Old Town, and to Stazione Brignole (every hour; 25min; Ⓣ010.558.2414). Buy your €4 ticket – valid on all city buses for the whole day – from the driver.

Getting around the centre is best done **on foot**, resorting to Genoa's AMT **buses** (Ⓣ800.085.311, Ⓦwww.amt.genova.it) only for trips to outlying sights. Public transport tickets cost €2 on board, €1.20 from *tabacchi* and newspaper stands, and are valid for ninety minutes. You can also get an all-day ticket for €3.50. The tickets are valid on buses, all the city's various **funiculars** and **lifts**, local trains between Voltri and Nervi (though not on the narrow-gauge mountain line to Casella; see p.122) and the expanding metro system which now winds its way from the suburban commuter belt to the city centre. There are currently six metro stations open – Brin, Dinegro, Principe, Darsena, San Giorgio and De Ferrari – with another four, including Brignole, due to become operational by 2010 (Ⓦwww.genovametro.com). For a slightly more relaxed way of getting around the city, see the **boat** "Listings" on p.121.

Genoa addresses

Genoa is one of the handful of Italian cities with a double system of street-numbering: commercial establishments, such as bars and restaurants, have **red** numbers (*rosso*), while all other buildings have **black** numbers (*nero*) – and the two systems don't run in tandem. This means, for example, that Via Banchi 35/R might be next-door to Via Banchi 89n, but several hundred metres from Via Banchi 33/N.

The main **tourist office** is at Stazione Principe (Mon–Sun 9.30am–1pm & 2.30–6pm; ☎010.246.2633, ⊛www.turismoinliguria.it), with branches at the Porto Antico in a small booth next to the Magazzini del Coteone (daily 9am–1pm & 2.30–6.30pm), on Piazza Matteotti next to the Palazzo Ducale (daily 9.30am–1pm & 2.30–6.30pm) and at the airport (Mon–Sat 9.30am–1pm & 1.30–5pm, Sun 10am–1.30pm and 1.30–5.30pm; ☎010.601.5247).

Accommodation

There's no shortage of **accommodation** in Genoa, but many of the budget hotels – especially those around the train stations – are grimy and depressing, and you need to look hard to find the exceptions. The area just west of Stazione Brignole (Piazza Colombo and Via XX Settembre) is preferable to anything around Stazione Principe. There's a handful of quality hotels in the old quarter – though you should steer clear of the one-star places down by the port (on and around Via di Prè), some of which are the haunts of drug-dealers and prostitutes. You'll need to reserve well in advance if your visit is to coincide with the annual **Salone Nautico Internazionale** (International Boat Show; ⊛www.fiera.ge.it), usually held in early October, when many of the city's hotels are booked solid.

Hotels

Affittacamere San Lorenzo Vico Scureria La Vecchia 1 ☎010.254.3049. Two spotless rooms in a fifteenth-century building tucked away in the web of streets around the Duomo. ❷–❹

Agnello d'Oro Vico Monachette 6 ☎010.246.2084, ⊛www.hotelagnellodoro.it. Spacious, modernized rooms – some with balconies – in a seventeenth-century palace alongside the Palazzo Reale and within spitting distance of Stazione Principe. ❹

Astoria Piazza Brignole 4 ☎010.873.316, ⊛www.hotelastoria-ge.com. Large, atmospheric rooms – choose between "antique" or "restored" – and plenty of faded grandeur make this a reliable and interesting choice, a short walk from Stazione Brignole. ❹

Bel Soggiorno Via XX Settembre 19/2 ☎010.581.418, ⊛www.belsoggiornohotel.com. Run by a gregarious German woman (who speaks English), this is a welcoming place, although the standard of the rooms – both en suite and not – doesn't quite measure up to the cosiness of the lobby and breakfast room. ❷–❸

Bristol Palace Via XX Settembre 35 ☎010.592.541, ⊛www.hotelbristolpalace.com. Grand old pile near Stazione Brignole, full of antique furniture, old masters and an Edwardian sense of order and discretion. Rooms are large, attractive and a/c. Excellent last-minute weekend deals online. ❼

Cairoli Via Cairoli 14/4 ☎010.246.1454, ⊛www.hotelcairoligenova.com. A superior three-star, whose brightly furnished, modern, en-suite rooms are soundproofed. There's also a roof terrace. One of the city's best deals. ❸

Il Salotto di Lucilla Passo Palestro 3-5 ☎010.882.391 or 348.954.3277, ⊛www.ilsalottodilucilla.com. Quiet, elegant B&B with a lovely sitting room and great breakfasts. The three rooms have private bathrooms and TV. Book in advance. ❸–❺

Jolly Hotel Marina Ponte Calvi 5 ☎010.253.91, ⊛www.jollyhotels.it. Great waterfront location a few steps from the aquarium makes up for the modern but slightly characterless rooms. Big discounts to be had during Aug. Great last-minute deals online, especially at weekends. ❼

La Capannina Via Tito Speri 7 ☎010.363.205, ⊛www.lacapanninagenova.it. Down a side street off the river walkway near the charming fishing cove of Boccadasse, well east of the centre (bus #31 or #42). Well-equipped rooms (some with balconies) and a tranquil location make it well worth considering. ❸

Major Vico Spada 4 ☎010.247.4174, ℻010.246.9898. A great location in the Old Town, just off Via Luccoli, along with clean and well-furnished rooms with TV and telephone, make this a great bargain. ❷

Soana Via XX Settembre 23/8 ☎010.562.814, ⊛www.hotelsoana.it. Very friendly service, clean simple rooms and a good location right by the Porta Monumentale make this fourth-floor hotel one of the best choices in the area. ❸

Hostels and camping

Ostello di Genova Passo Costanzi 10 ☎010.242.2457, ⊛www.hihostels.com. Genoa's HI hostel is clean and well run, although its out-of-town situation means you will be heavily reliant on buses. It's up in the hills of Righi, north of the centre. From Stazione Principe take bus #35, then switch at the fifth stop onto bus #40. B&B is €16, and there are cheap meals, as well as maps and information (check-in 3.30–6pm; closed late Dec & Jan).

Villa Doria Via al Campeggio Villa Doria 15 in Pegli ☏010.696.9600, ⓦwww.camping.it/liguria /villadoria. One of the few campsites nearby, though you'd do far better to stay at one of the coastal resorts and commute into town.

The City

Genoa's atmospheric **Old Town** spreads outwards from the port in a confusion of tiny alleyways (*caruggi*), bordered by **Via Gramsci** along the waterfront and by **Via Balbi** and **Via Garibaldi** to the north. The *caruggi* are lined with high buildings, usually six or seven storeys, set very close together. Tiny grocers, textile workshops and bakeries jostle for position with boutiques, design outlets and goldsmiths amid a flurry of shouts, smells and scrawny cats.

The cramped layout of the area reflects its medieval politics. Around the thirteenth and fourteenth centuries, the city's principal families – Doria, Spinola, Grimaldi and Fieschi – marked out certain streets and squares as their territory, even extending their domains to include churches: to pray in someone else's chapel was to risk being stabbed in the back. New buildings on each family's patch had to be slotted in wherever they could, resulting in a maze of crooked alleyways that was the battleground of dynastic feuds which lasted well into the eighteenth century.

The Palazzo Ducale and around

From 1384 to 1515, except for brief periods of foreign domination, Genoa was ruled by a doge, resident at the **Palazzo Ducale** in Piazza Matteotti, right in the heart of the Old Town. The present building, with its huge vaulted atrium, was built in the sixteenth century and today makes a splendid exhibition hall (times and prices vary; ⓦwww.palazzoducale.genova.it). It also hosts shows and concerts. The **Gesù** church (daily 7am–noon & 4–5.30pm; free), across the square, was designed by Pellegrino Tibaldi at the end of the sixteenth century and contains a mass of marble and gilt stucco and some fine Baroque paintings, including Guido Reni's *Assumption* in the right aisle and two works by Rubens: *Miracles of St Ignatius* on the left and *Circumcision* on the high altar. An alley between the two leads through to **Piazza de Ferrari**, overlooked by a statue of Garibaldi in front of the grand facade of the Carlo Felice opera house.

Museum cards

If you're planning to visit a number of museums, it might be worthwhile investing in a Museum Card (*Card Musei*). There are a number of versions. The most basic costs €16 and entitles you to two days' free access to all the city's myriad museums. For €20 you get the same plus free bus travel. €35 will buy you an annual version. You can pick up the card at most of the participating museums or online at ⓦwww.museigenova.it or ⓦwww.happyticket.it.

Genoa's top five museums
Galleria Nazionale di Palazzo Spinola
Musei di Strada Nuova
Museo Nazionale dell'Antartide
Citta dei Bambini e dei Ragazzi
Acquario

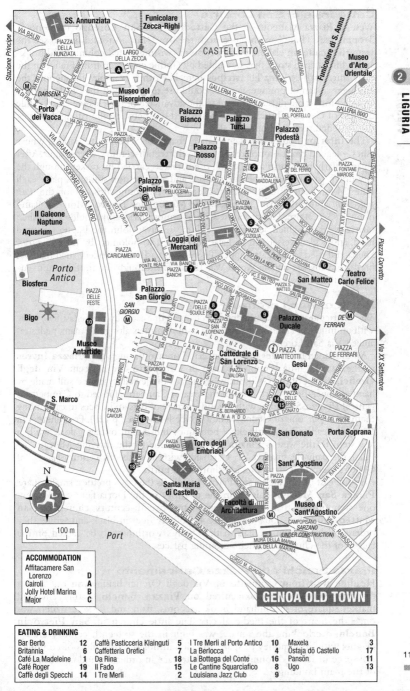

GENOA OLD TOWN

ACCOMMODATION

Affitacamere San Lorenzo	D
Cairoli	A
Jolly Hotel Marina	B
Major	C

EATING & DRINKING

Bar Berto	12	Caffè Pasticceria Klainguti	5	I Tre Merli al Porto Antico	10	Maxela	3
Britannia	6	Caffetteria Orefici	7	La Berlocca	4	Östaja dö Castello	17
Café La Madeleine	1	Da Rina	18	La Bottega del Conte	16	Pansön	11
Café Roger	19	Il Fado	15	Le Cantine Squarciafico	8	Ugo	13
Caffè degli Specchi	14	I Tre Merli	2	Louisiana Jazz Club	9		

Cattedrale di San Lorenzo

West of Piazza Matteotti, is the **Cattedrale di San Lorenzo** (9am–noon, 3–6pm; free). There's an entrance from the street, but go round first to see the western **facade**, an elaborate confection of twisting, fluted columns and black-and-white striped stone that was added by Gothic craftsmen from France in the early thirteenth century. The **stripes** here, like other examples throughout the city, were a sign of prestige: families could use them only if they had a permit, awarded for "some illustrious deed to the advantage of their native city". While the rest of Genoa's churches were portioned out between the ruling dynasties, the cathedral remained open to all.

The **interior** houses the Renaissance chapel of St John the Baptist, whose ashes – legend has it – once rested in the thirteenth-century sarcophagus. After a particularly bad storm in medieval times, priests carried his casket through the city down to the port to placate the sea, and a procession still takes place each June 24 in honour of the saint. Note the Byzantine frescoes of the *Last Judgement* above the main entrance. The **Museo del Tesoro** (Mon–Sat 9am–noon & 3–6.30pm; €5.50), housed in an atmospheric crypt, holds a polished quartz plate on which, legend says, Salome received John the Baptist's severed head, and a glass vessel said to have been given to Solomon by the Queen of Sheba and used at the Last Supper. There is also a British artillery shell that was fired from the sea during World War II and fell through the roof, but miraculously failed to explode.

North of San Lorenzo

The district around the cathedral has changed dramatically in the last few years, with an influx of art shops and trendy fashion outlets along the main, pedestrianized, Via San Lorenzo.

An unnamed lane leads north from San Lorenzo through tiny **Piazza Invrea** to the swanky little shopping square of **Campetto** and adjacent **Via degli Orefici**, "Street of the Goldsmiths". Much of the jewellery here is still made by hand at upper-floor workshops in the area of Campetto. Linked to Campetto is genteel **Piazza Soziglia**, with a good mixture of bars and places to eat, among them *Klainguti*, one of Genoa's oldest coffee houses (see p.120). From here **Via Luccoli** heads north, with glitzy boutiques and design outlets galore, while a few steps to the west is **Piazza Lavagna**, home to the thriving Mercato dei Pulci, the daily flea market. Via Garibaldi, with its sixteenth-century *palazzi* of Genoa's mercantile dynasties, is a short stroll north.

A little east of Campetto and Piazza Soziglia is the city's prettiest small square, **Piazza San Matteo**. This lay in the territory of the Doria family, who went one step further than merely striping the twelfth-century church of **San Matteo** (Mon–Sat 7.30am–noon & 4–5.30pm; free) in black and white: they ordered elaborate testimonials to the family's worthiness to be carved on the facade of the church and their adjoining palaces.

Piazza Banchi and Piazza Caricamento

Heading west from Campetto on Via degli Orefici brings you out into a thriving commercial zone centred on **Piazza Banchi**, a tiny enclosed market square of secondhand books, records, fruit and flowers which was once the heart of the medieval city. The little church of **San Pietro in Banchi**, overlooking the square, was built in the sixteenth century after a plague; with little money to spare, the city authorities sold plots of commercial space in arcades around the church terrace in order to fund construction of the main building.

▲ Via San Luca, Genoa Old Town

It's a short stroll west from Piazza Banchi out into the open spaces of Genoa's port. The sea once came up to the vaulted arcades of Via Sottoripa, which runs alongside the main **Piazza Caricamento**; these days the waterfront is blocked off by containers and fences, but there's been a market here since the twelfth century, when small boats used to come ashore from galleys at anchor. Fruit and vegetable stalls still line the arcade, interspersed with fly-pitches selling sunglasses and pirated CDs.

Towards the southern edge of the square is the **Palazzo di San Giorgio**, a brightly painted fortified palace built in 1260 from the stones of a captured Venetian fortress. After the great sea-battle of Curzola in 1298, the Genoese used the building to keep their Venetian prisoners under lock and key; among them was one **Marco Polo**, who met a Pisan writer named Rustichello inside and spun tales of adventure to him of worlds beyond the seas. After their release, Rustichello published the stories in a single volume that became *The Travels of Marco Polo*. These days, the *palazzo* is home to the harbour authorities, but you can ask the guardian on the door to let you in to see the medieval Sala dei Protettori and beautiful Sala Manica Lunga, whose decor was restored to its thirteenth-century grandeur following bomb damage in World War II.

The Galleria Nazionale di Palazzo Spinola

From Piazza Banchi, the animated medieval **Via San Luca** heads north, lined with shops selling counterfeit designer clothes and accessories. This street was in Spinola family territory, and their grand, former residence is now the excellent **Galleria Nazionale di Palazzo Spinola**, located beside Piazza

Pelliceria (Tues–Sat 8.30am–7.30pm, Sun 1.30–7.30pm; €4, joint ticket with Palazzo Reale €6.50; ⓦwww.palazzospinola.it). Exhibits include portraits by Van Dyck of Matthew, Mark, Luke and John as men of books, an intensely mournful *Ecce Homo* by the Sicilian master Antonello da Messina and the splendid *Adoration of the Magi* by Joos van Cleve, sawn into planks when stolen from the church of San Donato in the 1970s. Don't miss the little **terrace**, way up on the spine of the roof and shaded with orange and lemon trees.

The way north passes through a hectic and rather seedy neighbourhood centred on the vibrant **Via della Maddalena** alley, crowded with shops and stalls that ring with shouts in French and Arabic from the predominantly West and North African street-traders, doing business alongside Genoa's thriving red-light trade. Steep lanes rise north of Via della Maddalena, lifting you out of the melee and into the ordered calm of Via Garibaldi.

Along Via Garibaldi

When newly made fortunes encouraged Genoa's merchant bankers to move out of the cramped Old Town in the mid-sixteenth century, artisans' houses were pulled down to make way for the Strada Nuova, later named **Via Garibaldi**. To walk along the surprisingly narrow street is to stroll through a Renaissance architect's drawing pad – sculpted facades, stuccowork and medallions decorate the exterior of the three-storey *palazzi*, while the big courtyards are almost like private squares.

Three of the Via Garibaldi's finest *palazzi* – Bianco, Rosso and Tursi – have been re-branded the **Musei di Strada Nuova** and together now hold the city's finest collection of old-master paintings (€8 combined ticket). From the road's western end the first to come into view is the **Palazzo Bianco** (Tues–Fri 9am–7pm, Sat & Sun 10am–7pm; €5, Sun free; ⓦwww.museopalazzobianco.it), built between 1530 and 1540 for the important Genoese family, the Grimaldis. Its gallery houses work by the Flemish and Dutch masters (Rubens, Memling, Van Dyck) as well as the largest collection of Genoese and Ligurian painting – including work by Castiglione and Castello – on public show.

Next door stands the splendid **Palazzo Tursi**, the largest of Genoa's palaces, which boasts a glassed-in main courtyard. It's the site of the town hall and, for the past couple of years, the **Sala Paganiniana** (Tues–Fri 9am–7pm, Sat & Sun 10am–7pm; free; ⓦwww.museopalazzotursi.it), a small museum dedicated to the great Italian violinist Niccolò Paganini, who was born in Genoa in 1782, although he spent most of his professional career in Lucca. The prime exhibit, displayed with an almost religious reverence, is the *cannone*, the great man's own Guarneri violin made in 1743.

Across the road at Via Garibaldi 18 is the slightly less prestigious **Galleria di Palazzo Rosso** (Tues, Thurs & Fri 9am–1pm, Wed & Sat 9am–7pm, Sun 10am–6pm; ⓦwww.museopalazzorosso.it) where every room on the top floor has been restored to its original Baroque grandeur, bedecked with chandeliers, mirrors and an excess of gilding. Frescoes cover the ceilings, and there's a series of splendid portraits by Van Dyck of the Brignole-Sale family, who built the palace in 1671.

Along Via Balbi

A few minutes' walk west of Via Garibaldi is the house at Via Lomellini 11 where Giuseppe Mazzini, one of the most influential activists of Italian Unification, was born in 1805; it now displays documents and relics from his life as the **Museo del Risorgimento Italiano** (Tues–Fri 9am–1pm, Sat 10am–7pm; €4; ⓦwww.istitutomazziniano.it). Past traffic-heavy Piazza della Nunziata, overlooked by the giant sixteenth-century church of **Santissima Annunziata del Vastato**, which boasts one of the most exuberantly decorated interiors in the city, you'll come to the main road of **Via Balbi**, laid out a few decades after Via Garibaldi.

The Palazzo Reale

At Via Balbi 10 stands the vast **Palazzo Reale** (Tues & Wed 9am–1.30pm; Thurs–Sun 9am–7pm; €4; ⑩www.palazzorealegenova.it), built by the Balbi family in the early seventeenth century and later occupied by the Durazzo dynasty and the Savoyard royals. Entering through a huge atrium overlooking an elegant courtyard garden, you climb the grand staircase to the **ballroom**, with gilt stucco ceilings and Chinese vases. To the left are four drawing rooms, featuring a huge watercolour of the crossing of the Red Sea painted on silk. These rooms lead through to the stunning hall of mirrors, where Joseph II, Emperor of Austria, is said to have remarked in 1784 that the palace appeared more of a royal residence than his own simple pad back in Vienna. Doors lead through to the private quarters of the Duke of Genoa, with the **duke's bedchamber** featuring a sumptuous Baroque ceiling fresco and the duke's bathroom holding elegant furniture carved in England in the 1820s.

On the way back through to the east wing of the building, you pass along a **chapel gallery** behind the ballroom, covered in trompe-l'oeil frescoes by Lorenzo de Ferrari (1733). The adjacent **throne room**, its walls covered in deep red velvets and an excess of gold, is dotted with dozens of "C.A." monograms in honour of Carlo Alberto, King of Savoy. Continuing east, you come to the lavish **audience room**, with a dazzling Turkish carpet and a grand portrait of a tight-lipped Caterina Durazzo-Balbi painted by Van Dyck in 1624 during his six-year stay in Genoa. Alongside, the **king's bedchamber** has Van Dyck's first canvas of the Crucifixion, also dating from 1624. You then move into the **queen's quarters**, a series of rooms featuring a ghostly pale *Crucifixion* by the Neapolitan master Luca Giordano and a *St Lawrence* (1616) by Bernardo Strozzi. After another series of drawing rooms, one hung with Parisian tapestries, double-doors open onto the **grand terrace** giving airy views over the port.

Around Stazione Principe

Via Balbi continues west to the grandiose **Stazione Principe**. Immediately below the train station, the drab run of portfront buildings is broken by the elegant loggia of the twelfth-century **Commendà**, a former convent, hospital and lodging house for crusading knights, now a temporary exhibition space. The oddly double-apsed church of **San Giovanni di Prè**, whose landmark campanile was added in the late twelfth century, was originally reserved solely for the use of the Knights of Malta, or Knights Hospitallers, who ran the Commendà next door and who left behind them a host of Maltese crosses used as decoration on buildings all over town. From here, the busy and notoriously seedy **Via di Prè** runs parallel with the waterfront Via Gramsci and is the first real street of the Old Town. Via di Prè skirts the port as far as the twelfth-century **Porta dei Vacca**, from where alleys take you into the heart of the old quarter.

North of the station, and best reached via the lift from Via Balbi, is the **Museo delle Culture del Mondo** (Tues–Sun: April–Sept 10am–6pm; Oct–March 10am–5pm; €6; ⑩www.castellodalbertisgenova.it), or museum of world cultures. The museum is housed in the grand neo-Gothic home of the nineteenth-century adventurer Captain D'Albertis, who spent much of his later life filling its rooms with masks, musical instruments, pottery, paintings, stuffed animals and more picked up during voyages to the Americas, Africa and Oceania.

Back at the station, from Piazza Acquaverde, Via Doria runs west down to the ferry terminal, past the lavish gardens of the huge **Palazzo del Principe Doria Pamphilj** (May–July & Sept–Dec 25 Tues–Sun 10am–5pm; €7; ⓦwww .palazzodelprincipe.it) built in the early 1530s by Andrea Doria, who made his reputation and fortune attacking Turkish fleets and Barbary pirates and liberating the Genoese republic from the French and Spanish. The gardens back onto the fin-de-siècle **Stazione Marittima**, once the departure point for steamers to New York and Buenos Aires, but nowadays handling ferries to Corsica, Sardinia and Sicily (see p.121). It was from the **Ponte dei Mille** (Jetty of the Thousand) in front of the ferry terminal that **Giuseppe Garibaldi**, ex-mercenary and spaghetti salesman, persuaded his thousand Red Shirts to set off for Sicily in two clapped-out paddle steamers, armed with just a few rifles and no ammunition. Their mission, to support a Sicilian uprising and unite the island with the mainland states, greatly annoyed some northern politicians, who didn't want anything to do with the undeveloped south – an attitude which echoes in Italian politics to this day. About 1km further round the port is Genoa's restored sixteenth-century lighthouse, the **Lanterna**, as well as the **Matitone**, a postmodern polygonal tower housing municipal offices whose pointed roof has given it its sardonic nickname "The Big Pencil".

The Porto Antico

The *sopraelevata*, or elevated highway, shoots along the waterfront above Piazza Caricamento, dividing the city from the ancient port, or **Porto Antico**, pedestrianized and revitalized during the 1990s. Old warehouses have been converted into exhibition spaces, concert halls and museums, and cafés and pricey waterside bistros front the marina.

The visual centrepiece of the development is the **Bigo** – a curious multi-armed contraption, designed by Renzo Piano, intended to recall the harbourside cranes of old. It consists of a tent-roofed exhibition/concert space where waterside performances are given in summer and an ice-skating rink is set up in winter, next to which stands a circular elevator that ascends 60m in the air to let visitors see Genoa "as it is seen by the seagulls" (opening times vary, usually summer Mon 4–11pm, Tues–Sun 10am–11pm; winter 10am–5pm, but be aware that it closes when it's windy – quite a common occurrence on the seafront; €3 ⓦwww.acquariodigenova.it). East of the Bigo

Whale-watching and boat-trips

The waters off the Ligurian coast comprise a **International Whale Sanctuary**, home to twelve species of whale as well as dolphins and other marine life. It's easy to join summer boat excursions from towns along the Riviera for whale-watching in open sea (June–Sept at least once a week). All must be booked in advance and comprise a full day on board, including a light lunch and commentary from local WWF experts.

The main operator is the Consorzio Liguria Viamare, (☏010.255.975, ⓦwww .whalewatchliguria.it) – boats can be picked up from Genoa, Savona, Alassio, Varazze, Imperia and Arenzano. Prices change regularly so contact the company for current information. They also operate 45min **boat trips** around Genoa's port, departing from alongside the Aquarium (every 30min, daily 9am–5pm; €6) as well as running plenty of summer excursions west and east along the Riviera (the reasonable prices vary). Routings along the eastern coast are also operated by Golfo Paradiso, based in Camogli (☏0185.772.091, ⓦwww.golfoparadiso.it), whose boats depart from Calata Mandraccio, just south of the Bigo.

are two blocks of buildings, home to shops, restaurants, offices and, incongruously enough, the **Museo Nazionale dell' Antartide** (June–Sept Tues–Sun 10.30am–6.30pm; Oct–May Tues–Fri 9.45am–5.30pm, Sun 10am–6pm; €5.30; ⓔmna@unige.it), Europe's only Antarctic museum, which has some interesting, if not overly spectacular, displays on the wildlife, geography and explorers of the South Pole.

Just west of here is the old Porta Siberia, with the **Molo Vecchio** (Old Wharf) beyond. This was where condemned prisoners would be led to take the Last Sacrament at the little church of **San Marco** halfway along, before arriving at the gallows overlooking Piazza Cavour. Continuing west, you reach a set of restored cotton warehouses that now house a shopping-cum-entertainment centre, the **Magazzini del Cotone**, with bars, cinemas and music stores. Its main attraction is the **Città dei Bambini e dei Ragazzi** (Tues–Sun: July–Sept 11.30am–7.30pm; Oct–June 10am–6pm; adults €5, child €7; ⓦwww .cittadeibambini.net), a whiz-bang interactive children's science museum filled with gizmos and gadgets which should prove popular with its target audience. The museum is divided into separate areas: for 2- to 3-year-olds, 3- to 5-year-olds and 6- to 14-year-olds. Past the centre, you can enjoy grand sweeping views of the port from the end of the wharf.

North of the Bigo is the modern pride and joy of the city, the **Acquario di Genova** (July & Aug daily 8.30am–10pm; Sept, Oct & March–June Mon–Fri 9am–7.30pm, Sat & Sun 8.45am–8.30pm; Nov–Feb Mon–Fri 9.30am–7.30pm, Sat, Sun 9.30am–8.30pm; last entry 1hr 30min before closing; €16; joint tickets with the other museums of the Porto Antico available in many combinations; ⓦwww.acquario.ge.it). This is Europe's largest aquarium, its 70 tanks housing sea creatures from all the world's major habitats, including the world's biggest reconstruction of a Caribbean coral reef, complete with moray eels, turtles and angelfish. Although the whole affair boasts a fashionably ecology-conscious slant and excellent background information (delivered in Italian and English), the larger beasts – including grey sharks, dolphins, seals and an enclosure containing a group of Humboldt penguins – can't help but seem pathetically subdued. Alongside the aquarium are a couple of new additions to the seafront area: the futuristic-looking **Biosfera**, to the south, a steel-and-glass Renzo Piano-designed sphere housing a small tropical ecosystem, complete with trees, flowers and insects (daily 10am–5pm; €5) and, just north at the next pier opposite the *Jolly Hotel Marina*, **Il Galeone Neptune** (daily 10am–6pm; €5), a kitschy full-size replica of a seventeenth-century galleon with a huge, colourful Neptune figure head, and several decks to explore.

A couple of minutes further north, housed in a giant glass building is the wonderful **Galata, Museo del Mare** (Museum of the Sea; Tues–Sun: March–Oct 10am–7.30pm, last entry 6pm; Nov–Feb 10am–6pm, last entry 5pm; €10; ⓦwww.galatamuseodelmare.it), which details the history of Genoa and its age-old relationship with the sea, following its evolution from the late medieval period, illustrated with plenty of nautical paraphernalia and even several full-size ships.

South of San Lorenzo

The section of the Old Town south of the Cattedrale di San Lorenzo is less visited than the attraction-packed districts to the north, and more residential. Many of Genoa's students and young professionals live in the upper floors of the old buildings lining Via dei Giustiniani and Via San Bernardo, generating a lively bar culture in the surrounding alleys.

From the cathedral and Piazza Matteotti, narrow **Salita Pollaiuoli** plunges you into the gloom between high buildings down to a crossroads with **Via San**

Bernardo, built by the Romans and now one of Genoa's most characterful Old-Town streets, with grocers and bakers trading behind the portals of palaces decorated in the fifteenth and sixteenth centuries. On the south side of the crossroads is tiny **Piazza San Donato**, a quiet square overlooked by the church of San Donato, a crumbling, bare Romanesque church with a Roman architrave surviving over its door and an octagonal Byzantine-style campanile.

Piazza Sarzano and around

A shrine stuck on the side wall of San Donato faces up Stradone Sant'Agostino, laid out in the eighteenth century and now home to a quirky array of bars and workshops. At the top of the street is the long, narrow bulge of **Piazza Sarzano**, originally home to Genoa's many ropemaking workshops and, owing to its enormous length, still the scene for medieval-style jousting tournaments. The piazza is marked by the mosaic spire of the rebuilt church of **Sant'Agostino**, alongside which is the unique triangular cloister of the thirteenth-century monastery that now houses the **Museo di Sant'Agostino** (Tues–Fri 9am–7pm, Sat & Sun 10am–7pm; €4; Ⓦwww.museosantagostino.it), displaying Roman and Romanesque masonry fragments. The highlight is a fragment of the tomb of Margherita of Brabant, sculpted in 1312 by Giovanni Pisano.

Sneak down behind a remnant of the city wall at the southeastern corner of Piazza Sarzano alongside the church of San Antonio, and an alley lined with pretty houses will lead you down into the tranquil little enclosed piazza of **Campopisano**. It was here, during the wars between Genoa and Pisa, that Pisan prisoners were brought in chains, executed and buried; today, the pavement sports pretty black and white mosaics.

North from Piazza Sarzano streets connect to the **Porta Soprana**, a twin-towered stone gateway featuring impressive Gothic arches that now stands as the focus for a rather upmarket collection of bars and terrace cafés.

Modern Genoa

In the nineteenth century, Genoa began to expand beyond its old-town constraints. The newer districts begin with the large central **Piazza de Ferrari**, from where **Via XX Settembre** runs a straight course east through the commercial centre of the city towards Stazione Brignole. This grand boulevard features big department stores, shops selling designer clothes, and pavement cafés beneath its neon-lit arcades. There are prized delicatessens in the side streets around Stazione Brignole and Piazza Colombo, and a bustling covered **Mercato Orientale** partway along, in the cloisters of an old Augustinian monastery. At the eastern end of Via XX Settembre, the park outside the Stazione Brignole (hub for city buses) extends south into **Piazza della Vittoria**, a huge and dazzling white square built during the Fascist period that now serves as the long-distance bus station.

Walking north from Piazza de Ferrari takes you up to **Piazza Corvetto** – built by the Austrians in the nineteenth century and now a major confluence of traffic and people. Across the other side of the square, a thoughtful-looking statue of Giuseppe Mazzini marks the entrance to the **Villetta di Negro**, a lushly landscaped park whose artificial waterfalls and grottoes scale the hill. At the top, the **Museo d'Arte Orientale Edoardo Chiossone** (Tues–Fri 9am–1pm, Sat & Sun 10am–7pm; €4; Ⓦwww.museochiossonegenova.it) holds a collection of oriental art that includes eighteenth-century sculpture and paintings and samurai armour. Chiossone was a printer and engraver for the Italian mint, and, on the strength of his banknote-engraving skills, he was invited by the Meiji dynasty to establish the Japanese Imperial Mint. He lived in Japan from 1875 until his death in Tokyo in 1898, building up a fascinating and extensive collection.

If you're not satisfied with the view from the Villetta di Negro, you can take the Art Nouveau-style public lift from **Piazza del Portello** up to the **Castelletto**, which offers a great panorama over the port and the roofs of the Old Town; a **funicular** also leaves from the same place up to the residential **Sant'Anna** district, although the views from here aren't as good (ordinary bus tickets are valid for both). When Genoa ran out of building space, plots for houses were hewn out of the hillside behind, like the steps of an amphitheatre, and the funicular enables you to see these at close quarters, as the carriages edge past people's front windows. Another funicular runs from Largo Zecca, further west, to the suburb of **Righi**, where you can admire vistas of the city below and wander off on any of a number of paths, although locals generally come here to sit in the various panoramic restaurants for extended sessions of family dining.

The outskirts: Albaro and Boccadasse

For a spot of relaxation, head out of town to the eastern waterfront suburb of **Albaro**, at the end of Corso Italia, a broad boulevard that runs along the seafront beyond the giant Fiera exhibition area (bus #31 from Stazione Brignole). This is the place to jog, stroll, pose at one of the private lidos, or watch the sun set from a café table. From Albaro, you can walk or take bus #42 to **Boccadasse**. Once an outlying fishing port, this village is now part of the city, with boats pulled up on the pebble beach, nets hanging out to dry, some arty shops, and costly restaurants in which to sample the catch of the day.

Eating and drinking

Genoa has everything from basic **trattorias** to elegant nineteenth-century *cafés*. Piazza Caricamento is one of the best places for street food, its arcades lined with cafés serving focaccia, panini and deep-fried seafood. There are also lots of places in the Old Town selling **farinata** (see box, p.103) – try *Antica Sciamadda* at Via Ravecca 19/R (closed Mon) or *Tugnin* on Piazza Tommaseo. *Forno Patrone*, Via Ravecca 72/R (closed Wed afternoon), one of Genoa's top bakeries. Centuries of Turkish influence have produced delights such as candied fruit (best sampled at *Romanengo* in Via Soziglia) and slabs of *pandolce* as served up at *Profumo* in Via del Portello.

There are plenty of late-night **bars** along the seamy waterfront Via Gramsci, in between the strip joints and brothels, but more attractive places can be found in the Old Town around Piazza delle Erbe.

Bars and cafés

Bar Berto Piazza delle Erbe 6/R. Narrow little stand-up café-bar founded in 1904 by Signor Berto who walked some 15km west to the ceramics centre of Albisola in order to collect colourful bits of broken tile to decorate the walls. There is some seating available outside on the pedestrianized square. A trendy spot for coffee, beer or a reasonably priced light meal. Mon–Sat 8am–9pm.

Bar Pasticceria Mangini Via Roma at Piazza Corvetto. One of Genoa's most venerable *pasticcerie*, in business since the early 1800s and still top-notch today. Daily until 7.30pm.

Café La Madeleine Via della Maddalena 103/R A wonderful little café-theatre, haunt of writers, poets, musicians and story-tellers, with plenty of readings and small concerts. Closed Mon.

Café Roger Stradone di Sant'Agostino. A quirky spot designed in riotous style after the Frank Zappa song "The Dangerous Kitchen" – every shelf is wonky, fake meat-cleavers dangle overhead, plastic sharks rise out of the sink and so on. The staff, music and clientele make this a fun stop for a daytime coffee or evening beer. Open daily.

Caffè degli Specchi Salita Pollaiuoli 43/R. This has been a prime spot since 1917 for Genoese artists, writers and intellectuals to take coffee while admiring themselves in the mirrors (*specchi*) that cover the magnificent tiled interior. It also offers a small selection of dishes, such as penne with tomato sauce and mozzarella (€7.50) and *carpaccio di manzo* (€13). Closed Sun.

Caffetteria Orefici Via degli Orefici 25/R. Tiny fragrant temple to the art of coffee-making, with a range of specialist coffees and perfect results every time. Closed Sun.

Caffe Pasticceria Klainguti Piazza Soziglia 98/R. An Austrian-built *salon* dating from 1828, selling cakes, coffee and ice cream under chandeliers. They still produce the hazelnut croissant known as a *Falstaff*, much esteemed by Giuseppe Verdi, who spent forty winters in Genoa – "thanks for the Falstaff, much better than mine," he wrote to the bakers. On cold days you can warm yourself up with a bowl of their excellent *minestrone alla Genovese* (€5).

La Bottega del Conte Via delle Grazie. This cocktail bar is a dimly lit Bohemian hangout in a street behind the Porto Antico. Once a salt cod restaurant, antique culinary implements still adorn the walls. Regular live jazz.

Restaurants

Da Rina Mura delle Grazie 3/R ⓉTEL010.246.6475. It's been going for sixty years, serving simple, high-quality, Genoese cooking in unpretentious surroundings down near the waterfront. Lots of fish and classic Ligurian dishes such as *cima alla genovese*. Moderately priced. Closed Mon and Aug.

Il Fado Via San Donato 9/R ⓉTEL010.246.5171. Lots of fish and a great vegetarian menu, part of the proceeds of which go to charity. Closed Mon eve.

I Tre Merli Via dietro il coro della Maddalena 6 ⓉTEL010.247.4095. Despite its location in the heart of the red-light district, this is one of the city's very best restaurants employing an innovative approach to Ligurian cuisine – try the *pappardelle nere all' astice* for €16. There are over 300 wines on the menu, all stored in a converted fourteenth-century well. Closed Sat lunch & all Sun. Branches in Camogli and Palazzina Millo down on the seafront (*I Tre Merli al Porto Antico*, ⓉTEL010.246.4416).

La Berlocca Via del Macelli di Soziglia 45/R ⓉTEL010.247.4162. Sittiing opposite a magic shop in a narrow Old-Town alleyway, this is a cosy bistro-style establishment with an open fire in winter and a menu featuring adventurous takes on traditional Ligurian dishes, such as chestnut flour pasta with pesto. Closed Mon.

Le Cantine Squarciafico Piazza Invrea 3/R ⓉTEL010.247.0823. Atmospheric cantina in the wine-cellar of a fifteenth-century mansion just off Piazza San Lorenzo. Innovative, carefully prepared food and a great wine list complement each other perfectly. Fairly expensive. Closed second half of Aug.

Le Tre Finestre Scalinata di San Antonio 2/A ⓉTEL010.251.1750. A tiny old-time trattoria off Piazza Sarzano. There's no menu (the waitress will just rattle off the dishes of the day), and the food is cheap, plain and hearty. Join in the good old-fashioned accordion singalong on Friday nights. Closed Mon–Thurs eve & all day Sun.

Maxela Vico Inferiore del Ferro 9 ⓉTEL010.247.4209. There's been a restaurant in this building since 1790. The latest, *Maxela*, opened a few years ago and is an unashamed carnivore's delight with meat hooks hanging from the walls and a menu filled with bloody favourites, including *frattaglie* (offal), roasts and *sanguinacci* (blood sausages).Moderately priced. Closed Sun.

Östaja dö Castello Salita Santa Maria di Castello 32/R ⓉTEL010.246.8980. Great Old-Town, family-run trattoria serving good, inexpensive fish and seafood specialities, such as *polpo con patate* and *gamberi alla griglia* Closed Sun.

Pansön Piazza delle Erbe 5R ⓉTEL010.246.8903. Venerable Genoese institution, in the same family since 1790; diners sitting in this attractive, tucked-away piazza choose from a mainly fishy menu priced high to keep the riff-raff away. Highly recommended. Closed Sun eve.

Ugo Via Giustiniani 86/R. Convivial, reasonably-priced trattoria in the heart of the student quarter near San Donato, with a boisterous, friendly group of regulars who pack in at shared tables to wolf down the Genoese and Ligurian dishes – heavy on pesto and seafood. Closed Sun & Mon.

Entertainment and nightlife

If your Italian is up to it, use the best source of information on **nightlife**, which is the local daily paper *Il Secolo XIX*; in summer you can supplement this with *Genova by Night*, the tourist office's free what's-on guide. For **live music**, the *Louisiana Jazz Club* on Via Reggio Tommaso 34/R (ⓉTEL010.585.241) hosts trad jazz most nights from around 10pm, but you'll find more happening joints tucked away in the southern part of the Old Town.

The two main **theatres** in Genoa are the Teatro della Corte, Via E.F. Duca d'Aosta, and the Teatro Duse, Via Bacigalupo, who advertise their performances on the same hoardings around town and sell tickets to both venues (☎010.534.220). The Teatro Carlo Felice in Piazza de Ferrari (☎010.589.329, ⊛www.carlofelice.it) is Genoa's main **opera house**; its performances are often oversubscribed, but it's still worth an enquiry. Chamber-music concerts take place in some of Genoa's *palazzi* in summertime.

Listings

Airlines Alitalia ☎848.865.643; British Airways ☎199.712.266.

Airport ☎010.601.5410, ⊛www.aeroportodigenova.com.

Banks Various branches next to Stazione Principe in Piazza Acquaverde, on Via Balbi, and on Via XX Settembre.

Bookshops Feltrinelli (⊛www.feltrinelli.it), Via XX Settembre 233/R, has some English-language paperbacks.

Car rental Europcar, at the airport ☎010.650.4881; Hertz, Via Casaregis 78 ☎010.570.2625, airport ☎010.651.2422; Maggiore, Corso Sardegna 275 ☎010.839.2153, airport ☎010.651.2467; SIXT, Via Montevideo 111/R ☎010.315.166, airport ☎010.651.2111.

Consulate US, Via Dante 2 ☎010.584.492.

Doctor Call ☎010.354.022 for a doctor on call (nights and hols).

Ferries Any of the shipping agencies under the arcades along Piazza Caricamento can give current details of the long-distance ferries departing regularly to Bastia (Corsica), Olbia or Porto Torres (both Sardinia), Palermo (Sicily) and further afield to Barcelona. Main operators are: Moby Ferries (at the port) ☎010.254.1513, ⊛www.mobylines.it; and Tirrenia, Ponte Colombo ☎010.254.3851, ⊛www.tirrenia.it; Grandi Navi Veloci ☎010.209.4591, ⊛www.gnv.it.

Football Genoa's premier side, Sampdoria, play at the Luigi Ferraris stadium, behind Stazione Brignole. They share the stadium with the city's other major team, Genoa – founded in 1893 as the Genoa Cricket and Athletic Club, originally for British expatriates only. Bus #12 from Piazza Caricamento, and bus #37 from Stazione Principe, both pass near the stadium, or you can walk it in 15–20min from Brignole.

Hospitals Ospedale Galliera, Mura delle Cappuccine 14 (☎010.56.321), is the city's most central hospital, situated just south of Piazza Vittoria, while Ospedale Evangelico, Corso Solferino 1/A (☎010.55.221) is English-speaking. For an emergency ambulance, call ☎118.

Internet access World Communication, Via San Luca.

Parking There are a dozen or so central car parks, all of which cost around €20 per day; the largest is beneath Piazza della Vittoria (open 24hr). The old quarter is barred to traffic.

Pharmacies Ponte Monumentale, Via XX Settembre 115/R (☎010.564.430), and Farmacia Pescetto, Via Balbi 185/R (☎010.251.8777), are both open 24hr.

Police Carabinieri ☎112; Polizia ☎113; coastguard police ☎010.27.771. Genoa's police HQ is at Via Armando Diaz 2 (☎010.53.661).

Post office Via Dante 4 (Mon–Sat 8am–6.30pm; two desks with English-speaking staff). Sub-post offices are at both train stations, open same hours.

Taxis Radio Taxi Genova ☎010.5966.

Train information ☎010.247.99.09.

Around Genoa

Find time if you can to head inland to the north, especially in spring when the terraced hills are at their most verdant, the blossom in bloom, and the vines flourishing. Several small villages make good bases for scenic walking here, or you can sit back and let the train take the strain with an hour-long ride on a clanky old narrow-gauge line from Genoa up to the rustic hill-village of **Casella**.

The Genoa tourist office has the useful *Antola and its Valleys* booklet in English, complete with itinerary suggestions, a map and details of walks. AMT buses from Genoa's Piazza della Vittoria serve all the larger villages. Look out wherever you are for breads and pastas made with local chestnut flour, as well as *scarpignon*, ravioli stuffed with a meat and walnut paste.

The Narrow-guage train to Casella

Narrow-gauge FGC **trains** (T010.837.321, Wwww.ferroviagenovacasella.it), dating back to 1929, leave roughly hourly from a station in Genoa's Piazza Manin, connected to Brignole by bus #33 and Principe by bus #34. They start off climbing through the Val Bisagno and coil northwards up to **CASELLA**, in a wooded dell at the foot of Monte Maggio (55min from Genoa). Return fares to Casella are €2. Casella is the trailhead for a number of hiking routes in the picturesque **Valle Scrivia** (Wwww.altavallescrivia.it). The town has a couple of **hotels**, of which the *Magenta* at Piazza XXV Aprile 20 is the better bet if you're here in summer (T010.967.7113; ❸; June–Sept only); and there are half-a-dozen **restaurants**, including *Camugin* (closed Mon) in front of the church, known for its fresh fish, and *Chiara* (closed Mon) with a wood-fired pizza oven. You can also take a dip at the pleasant public swimming baths, **Piscina Casella**, near the station (June & Sept 11am–6pm; July & Aug 10am–7pm; €8).

The Riviera di Ponente

The towns of the **Riviera di Ponente**, the coast west of Genoa, are generally functional, unpretentious places, occasionally sporting an attractive medieval quarter but inevitably overflowing with hotels and apartment blocks. They do, however, have sandy beaches and comparatively low prices. Just about every settlement along the stretch of coast from Genoa to San Remo is a resort of some kind, most of them targeted at Italian families, so at their busiest in August. The grand old resort of **San Remo**, or the border town of **Ventimiglia**, can also make a good base for exploring sections of the Alta Via dei Monti Liguri (see box, p.126) walking route or looping through attractive and little-visited hill-towns like **Taggia** or **Dolceacqua**.

For more information on the coast, check out Wwww.inforiviera.it or call T0182.64.711. An organization of local hoteliers, Consorzio Palmhotels (T0184.66.698, Wwww.palmhotels.it), with bases in Genoa and San Remo, also details accommodation along the coast.

Savona

First impressions of **SAVONA**, 30km along the coast from Genoa, aren't impressive: it's a functional city much rebuilt after a hammering in World War II. However, its port infrastructure and ugly outskirts hide a picturesque **medieval centre**. Although you are unlikely to want to stay the night, it is worth a look, especially when it's taken over on summer Saturdays by a huge antiques and bric-a-brac market. The town's main claim to fame is as the *Città dei Papi* (City of Popes), after local boy Francesco Della Rovere who became **Pope Sixtus IV** in 1471 and his nephew Giuliano, who became **Pope Julius II** in 1503. Both men are closely linked with the Sistine Chapel in the Vatican – Sixtus IV had it built (hence the name) while Julius II commissioned Michelangelo to decorate the ceiling.

The **train station** is in the west of town, across the River Letimbro from the old quarter, which nestles in the curve of the old port and bristles with medieval towers. Via Don Minzoni, to the left of the station as you walk out, heads east across the river to the parks of Piazza del Popolo, from where the main **Via Paleocapa**, lined with Art Nouveau arcades, continues east to the port. Savona's **tourist office** is at Corso Italia 157/R (summer Mon–Sat 9.30am–1pm & 3–6.30pm, Sun 9.30am–12.30pm; winter Tues–Sat 9.30am–12.30pm & 3–6.30pm;

ⓉO19.840.2321, ⓌWww.inforiviera.it). The Dominican church of San Giovanni marks the point where Via Pia heads south into the atmospheric old quarter which is dominated by the **Duomo** and its attached **Cappella Sistina**, a Baroque extravaganza commissioned by Sixtus IV in memory of his parents.

Above the old town stands the huge **Priamàr** fortress, built in 1528 by the Genoese as a sign of their superiority over the defeated Savonese. These days it houses three museums. The **Museo d'Arte Sandro Pertini** (Sat & Sun 10am–noon), displaying modern Italian art collected by Pertini, one-time President of Italy, and the **Museo Renata Cúneo** (Mon–Sat 8.30am–12.30pm), housing contemporary sculpture by Cúneo, a Savona local, share a joint €2 admission ticket. Completing the array is the **Museo Storico-Archeologico** (winter Tues–Fri 10am–12.30pm & 3–5pm, Sat 10am–noon & 3–5pm, Sun 3–5pm; summer Tues–Sat 10am–noon & 5–7pm, Sun 5–7pm; €3; Ⓦwww.museoarcheosavona.it), which has Greek and Etruscan bits and bobs along with some Islamic and Byzantine ceramics.

Finale Ligure

Though overly tourist-oriented, busy **FINALE LIGURE**, a thirty-minute drive southwest along the coast from Savona, nevertheless manages to remain an attractive place. Most visitors are Italian families who, on summer nights, pack the outdoor restaurants, seafront fairground and open-air cinema, or take an extended *passeggiata* along the promenade and through the old alleys.

Of the town's three parts, **Finalmarina** is the main bit, with the **train station** at its western end, a good pebbly beach, a promenade lined with palms, and narrow shopping streets set back from the seafront that hold the **tourist office** at Via San Pietro 14 (Mon–Sat 9am–12.30pm & 4–7.30pm, plus Sun 9am–noon in summer; ⓉO19.681.019). The bars in the vicinity of Piazza Vittorio Emanuele II and the adjoining Piazza di Spagna, the main public space in the centre of this spread-out resort, are the points to which everyone eventually gravitates.

Finalpia is a small district five-minutes' walk to the east on the other side of the River Sciusa, focused around the twelfth-century church of Santa Maria di Pia (rebuilt in florid early eighteenth-century style) and its adjacent sixteenth-century cloistered abbey.

Finalborgo, the medieval walled quarter, sits on a slight hill 2km inland from Finalmarina, overlooked by bare rock-faces that are a favourite with free climbers who gather at *Bar Gelateria Centrale* in Finalborgo's Piazza Garibaldi at weekends. The area's wider fame comes from the **Grotte delle Arene Candide**, among Europe's most important caves for prehistoric remains; they're closed for excavation, but some finds are on display at the **Museo Civico** in Finalborgo's church of Santa Caterina (Tues–Sun: July & Aug 10am–noon & 4–7pm; Sept–June 9am–noon & 2.30–5pm; €3). The same church hosts an interesting antiques **market** on the first weekend of each month during summer.

The tourist office has information on picturesque inland **walks**, including the **Sentieri Parlanti** which zigzag across the hills past the excellent mid-priced 🅰 *Osteria La Briga* restaurant (ⓉO19.698.579; March–June & Sept–Oct weekend eve and Sun & hols lunchtimes only; July & Aug every eve, plus lunchtime Sun & hols), where you can fill up on *ortica* (nettle) and *tartufo nero* (black truffle) lasagne. **Mountain bikes** can be rented on Via Brunenghi in Finalborgo, from Raceware at no. 124, and R.C. Bike at no. 65.

Practicalities

In high season virtually all the hotels insist on full board, so the best option is the excellent 🅰 *Castello Vuillermin* HI **hostel** (one of the best in the country) which occupies an old castle high above the train station at Via Caviglia 46 and has marvellous views out to sea (℡019.690.515; €13 per person; mid-March to mid-Oct). *Eurocamping* is a well-run riverside **campsite** at Via Calvisio 37 in Finalpia (℡019.601.240, ⓦwww.eurocampingcalvisio.it; April–Sept).

The best places **to eat** need some hunting out. *Da Tonino*, Via Bolla 5, has outside seating and good pizzas. Up in Finalborgo, *Ai Torchi*, Via dell'Annunziata 12 (℡019.690.531; closed Tues except in Aug), occupies an ancient olive-oil factory and serves expensive pasta and fish dishes with care and some style.

Albenga and around

Road and railway follow the coast for another 30km to the small market town of **ALBENGA**. With the silting up of the river estuary long ago, Albenga lost its port and merits a visit these days for its business-like old quarter, still within medieval walls. The **train station** is 800m east of the old town via the twin parallel boulevards of Viale dei Mille and Viale Martiri della Libertà; the latter leads to the **tourist office** at no. 1 (Mon–Sat 9am–12.30pm & 3–6.30pm, Sun 9am–noon; ℡0182.558.444, ⓦwww.inforiviera.it), and on to **Piazza San Michele** at the heart of the old town. This small square is dominated by the elegant **cathedral**, the main part of which was built in the eleventh century and enlarged in the early fourteenth. Diagonally opposite in the Torre Comunale is the **Museo Civico Ingauno** (mid-Sept to mid-June Tues–Sun 10am–12.30pm & 2.30–6pm; mid-June to mid-Sept Tues–Sun 9.30am–noon & 3.30–7.30pm; €3; ⓦwww.iisl.it) providing access to Albenga's big draw, the **baptistry**. This ingenious building was built in the fifth century, and combines an ten-sided exterior with an octagonal interior. Inside are fragmentary mosaics showing the Apostles represented by twelve doves.

Behind the baptistry to the north, the archbishop's palace houses the diverting **Museo Diocesano** (Tues–Sun 10am–noon & 3–6pm; donation requested). Taking pride of place are the remains of the fifteenth-century frescoes that adorned what used to be a chapel and the bishop's own bedchamber. A few metres west, where Via Medaglie d'Oro crosses Via Ricci, is the thirteenth-century **Loggia dei Quattro Canti**, marking the town centre of Roman Albingaunum. Some 500m north of here, beyond Piazza Garibaldi and along Viale Pontelungo, you'll find the odd sight of the elegant, arcaded Pontelungo bridge spanning nothing much – built in the twelfth century to cross the river, which shifted course soon afterwards.

If you want a central place to stay *Sole Mare*, down on the seafront at Lungomare Colombo 15 (℡0182.51.817, ℻0182.52.752; ❹), has a range of rooms. Otherwise, in the hills less than a kilometre above town, *Villa Maria* (℡0182.559091, ⓦwww.villamaria-bb.it; ❷–❸) at Regione Miranda 25 is a fine family-run B&B with gracious rooms (though bathrooms are not en suite), gorgeous grounds, a great pool and a couple of bikes for guests. The *Lungomare* **campsite** is at the mouth of the river off Strada Vicinale Avarenna (℡0182.51.449, ℻0182.52.525; open all year). Albenga's least expensive **restaurants** are off Via Medaglie d'Oro on the alley Via Torlaro. *Da Puppo* (℡0182.98062) is a bustling little place with a wood-burning pizza oven famous for its *farinata* (closed for lunch July & Aug), while *Il Vecchio Mulino* (closed Thurs) has cheap, basic trattoria food. Pricey *Antica Osteria dei Leoni*, behind the baptistry at Vico Avarenna (℡0182.51937, closed Mon), has a good range of local dishes.

The caves of Toirano

Nurseries of artichokes and petunias, interspersed with garden centres and caravan sites, line the coast between Albenga and the town of **Borghetto**

Santo Spirito, transfer point for buses a few kilometres inland to the spectacular caves of **TOIRANO**. There are three main cave complexes (daily: July & Aug 9.30am–12.30pm & 2–5.30pm; Sept–June 9.30am–12.30pm & 2–5pm; €10; ⓦwww.toirano.it). The stalactite-adorned **Grotta della Bàsura** – dialect for "The Witch's Cave" – was the home of Stone Age inhabitants some eighty thousand years ago. These early troglodytes apparently shared their cave-dwellings with local bears: there's a mass of bear bones in the underground Bear Cemetery, and dozens of prehistoric foot- and paw-prints left in what was once mud. A path leads on to the **Grotta di Santa Lucia**, containing remarkable stalagmite and stalactite formations, with a natural spring that was dedicated in the Middle Ages to St Lucy, patron saint of eyesight, after several miraculous cures were effected here. Further on, guided tours around **Grotta del Colombo** lead you through the beautiful caverns formed in the limestone over millions of years by the action of water.

Alassio, Laigueglia and Imperia

A fifteen-minute drive from Albenga is **ALASSIO**, with a spectacular four-kilometre fine-sand beach and motorboat trips out to the Isola Gallinara island nature reserve. If you want somewhere quieter to hang out, continue to **LAIGUEGLIA**, a quiet ex-fishing port with a couple of porticoed streets to wander, and a decent beach.

A walk up the steps from the junction of Via Mimosa and the main Via Roma in Laigueglia takes you away from the coast through to the old **Roman road** near the top of the hill. From here, follow the *strada privata* into the woods and take the signposted path for about forty minutes to the ruins of the **Castello di Andora** and what is held to be one of the most important medieval monuments of the Riviera, the beautiful thirteenth-century church of Sts Giacomo and Filippo. Even if you never get to the church and castle, the walk along mule tracks between olive groves and woods is gorgeous. From the castle you can either backtrack or walk on through the outskirts of the village of **Andora** to its train station.

Some 30km west of Alassio is the provincial capital of **IMPERIA**, formed in 1923 when Mussolini linked twin townships on either side of the River Impero. Imposing **Porto Maurizio**, on the western bank, is the more attractive of the two, ascending the hillside in a series of zigzags from a marina and small beach, with its stepped old quarter dominated by a massive late-eighteenth-century cathedral and a series of Baroque churches and elegant villas. Quieter **Oneglia**, 2km east, is still very much wedded to the sea, with an active population of fisherfolk. Just behind its station at Via Garessio 13 is the **Museo dell'Olivo**, paid for by the town's leading olive-oil dynasty, the Fratelli Carli (Mon–Sat 9am–12.30pm & 3–6.30pm; free; ⓦwww.museodellolivo.com), housing modern displays devoted to the history of Liguria's green nectar. The **tourist office** is at Viale Matteotti 37 in Porto Maurizio (Mon–Sat 9am–12.30pm & 3.30–7pm; ⓣ0183.660.140), where you'll also find the comfortable **hotels** *Croce di Malta*, overlooking the old harbour at Via Scarincio 148 (ⓣ0183.667.020, ⓦwww .hotelcrocedimalta.com; ❸), and *Corallo* (ⓣ0183.666.264, ⓦwww.coralloimperia .com; ❸), where all rooms have a sea view.

The Valle Argentina

The Valle Argentina heads inland from the bustling seaside resort of **Arma di Taggia**, 6km east of San Remo. Sleepy, crumbling **TAGGIA**, 3km north, is known for its sixteen-arched **Romanesque bridge**, the *taggiasca* black olive that is famed for giving top-quality oil, and a collection of work by

Ligurian artists in the black-and-white stone convent church of **San Domenico** just outside the old walls (daily: winter 9am–noon & 2.30–5.30pm; summer 9am–noon & 3–6pm; donation requested). If you can, time a visit for the third Sunday in July, when the ancient *festa* of the Magdalene culminates in a "Dance of Death" performed by two men, traditionally from the same two families, accompanied by the local brass and woodwind band.

Some 25km further up the valley is the tiny village of **TRIORA**. The trip here from San Remo (4 services daily from the main bus station) is worth doing in its own right, the bus wending its way past small settlements with ancient bridges and farms linked to the main road across the valley by a rope and pulley system. Triora is almost within sight of Monte Pietradura, which stays snowcapped until April. In 1588, after an unexpected famine, two hundred women in this isolated community were denounced by the Inquisition as **witches**: rumour has it that thirty were tortured, fourteen were burned at the stake, and one woman committed suicide before she could be executed. Documents from the trial are preserved in the **Museo Etnografico** in the village (daily 10am–noon & 3–6pm; €2), and a commemorative plaque adorns the overgrown Cabotina just outside the village, supposed scene of the witches' gatherings. Also worth seeking out is the celebrated Sienese painter Taddeo di Bartolo's *Baptism of Christ* (1397), hung in the baptistry of the Romanesque-Gothic **Collegiata** church. The village has a single **hotel**, the peaceful *Colomba d'Oro*, Corso Italia 66 (T0184.94.051, Wwww.colombadoro.it; ❸), comfortably converted from an old monastery.

Walking the Alta Via

The **Alta Via dei Monti Liguri** is a long-distance high-level trail covering the length of Liguria, from Ventimiglia in the west all across the ridge-tops to Ceparana on the Tuscan border above La Spezia in the east, a total distance of some 440km. The mountains, which form the connection between the Alps and the Apennines, aren't high – rarely more than 1500m – meaning that the scenic route, which makes full use of the many passes between peaks, is correspondingly easy-going. The whole thing would take weeks to complete in full, but has been divided up into 43 stages of between about two and four hours each, making it easy to dip in and out. Trail support and maintenance is generally good, with *rifugi* dotted along the path and distinctive waymarks (red-white-red "AV" signs).

A sample walk starts from point 26 – **Crocetta d'Orero**, on the Genoa–Casella train line: heading east from Crocetta, an easy route covers 7.8km to point 27, **Colle di Creto** (2hr 30min, and served by Genoa buses), with a diversion along the way to a lovely flower-strewn path in and around the deserted hamlet of *Ciat*. Another sample walk, the very first stage of all, from **Ventimiglia** to La Colla, sidelining to **Dolceacqua**, is outlined on p.130. Unfortunately, access from the main coastal towns to most other parts of the Alta Via can be tricky, and requires juggling with route itineraries and bus timetables.

For information on the Alta Via, your best bet is the **Associazione Alta Via dei Monti Liguri** (Wwww.lig.camcom.it), which produces a full-colour wall-map of the route, along with detailed English descriptions and timings of all 43 stages (plus hotels and restaurants along the way). Books and an eight-pamphlet guide to the trail are on sale in bookshops. The same information is at Wwww.parks.it. **Club Alpino Italiano** offices in the major towns have information on *rifugi*, and the **Federazione Italiano Escursionismo** (FIE) publishes detailed guides to all the inland paths of Liguria.

San Remo

Set on a broad sweeping bay between twin headlands, **SAN REMO** had its heyday as a classy resort in the sixty years or so up to the outbreak of World War II, when the Empress Maria Alexandrovna headed a substantial Russian community in the town (Tchaikovsky completed *Eugene Onegin* and wrote his Fourth Symphony in San Remo in 1878). Some of the grand hotels overlooking the sea, especially those near the train station, are now grimy and crumbling, but others in the ritzier western parts of town are still in pristine condition, opening their doors to Europe's remaining aristocrats season after season. San Remo is blessed with the Italian Riviera's most famous **casino**, and remains a showy and attractive town, with a good beach and a labyrinthine old town standing guard over the palm-laden walkways below.

The town has its fair share of events too. Every January the **Festival dei Fiori** (Festival of Flowers) sees flora-bedecked floats make their way through the town, displaying products by the area's horticulturists, while July's **Campionato Mondiale di Fuochi d'Artificio**, or World Fireworks Championship, is not for the jittery.

Arrival and information

San Remo's modern – and slightly confusing – **train station** is east of the town centre on Corso Cavallotti. The **tourist office** is in a striking building at Largo Nuvoloni 1 (Mon–Sat 8am–7pm, Sun 9am–1pm; ☎0184.59.059, ⓦwww.rivieradeifiori.travel). Five-minutes' walk east from the train station along Corso Matteotti is the main **bus station** on Piazza Colombo. Local Riviera Trasporti (ⓦwww.rivieratrasporti.it) buses from here shuttle around town and up to Taggia; one-hour tickets cost €0.95. The *Diana II* (☎334.317.5504) runs **boat** trips along the coast. Advice on **hiking** can be found at the Club Alpino Italiano office, Piazza Cassini 13 (Tues & Fri 9.30am–10.30pm, Wed & Sat 6–7pm; ⓦwww.cai.it).

▲ San Remo Casino

Accommodation

Finding **accommodation** should be no problem, though most places insist on half- or full-board in high season. If you're looking for budget hotels, then the western end of the centre, on and between Corso Matteotti and Via Roma, is the area to head for. There's a **campsite**, *Villaggio dei Fiori*, west of town at Via Tiro a Volo 3 (℡0184.660.635, ⓦwww.villaggiodeifiori.it; open all year).

Al Dom Corso Mombello 13 ℡0184.501.460. Family-run hotel, with large and airy but noisy rooms. ❶–❷

Alexander Corso Garibaldi 123 ℡0184.504.591, ⓦwww.hotelalexander.info. A characterful option, near the train station, in a beautiful *Belle Époque* building set back from the road. ❷

Maristella Corso Imperatrice 77 ℡0184.667.881. Friendly place with attractive decor in a good spot, right by the sea. ❷

Paradiso Via Roccasterone 12 ℡0184.571.211, ⓦwww.paradisohotel.it. In a quiet location above the town's bustle, with a secluded garden, pool and sunny, modern rooms. ❺

Royal Hotel Corso Imperatrice 80 ℡0184.5391, ⓦwww.royalhotelsanremo.com. This expensive place scores highly for facilities and faded, old-fashioned opulence. It boasts three restaurants and a vast, heated, salt-water swimming pool set in a tropical garden. ❾

The Town

The **Palazzo di Riviera**, where the tourist office is housed, is a prime example of the kind of floral architecture that lines the palm boulevard **Corso Imperatrice** that stretches along the seafront west of the centre. Directly opposite the *palazzo* is the impressive onion-domed **Russian Orthodox church** (Tues–Sun 9.30am–12.30pm & 3–6.30pm; free) built in the 1920s and more impressive on the outside than within. About 100m further east you'll come to San Remo's landmark **Casino**, an ornate white palace with grand staircases and distinctive turrets that still stands as the epitome of the town's old-fashioned sense of monied leisure. **Corso degli Inglesi** winds around and above the casino, home to dozens of villas in varying states of repair.

From the casino, the main **Corso Matteotti**, lined with cocktail bars, *gelaterie*, cinemas and clothes stores, heads east into the commercial centre of town. Lurid neon signs on side streets point to private clubs and by-the-hour hotels, all rubbing shoulders with a handful of expensive restaurants. The cross-street **Corso Mombello** connects south to the Giardini Veneto on the seafront alongside the harbour, and north to the main central square **Piazza Eroi Sanremesi**. This huge, rambling space is partly taken up by market-stalls and terrace cafés, and a section backs onto the Gothic **Cattedrale di San Siro** (daily 7–11.15am & 3–6pm; free), which features unusual twelfth-century bas reliefs above its side doors and a processional black crucifix within. A short way east of the cathedral, at Corso Matteotti 143, is the impressive Renaissance Palazzo Borea d'Olmo housing the **Museo Civico** (Tues–Sat 9am–noon & 3–6pm; free), but its array of local finds and paintings is less memorable than the sumptuous frescoed interior. **Piazza Colombo** is just east of the museum, with Via Asquasciati heading down to the sea. If you follow the harbourside promenade east for 1km, you'll come to the marina and – on the north side of the tracks – the **Giardino Ormond** (daily 9am–7pm; free), which is filled with date palms, yuccas, olive trees, jacaranda, bougainvillea and even a grand cedar of Lebanon.

San Remo's most fascinating quarter – which stands in stark contrast to the glamour and bustle of the seafront districts – is its **old town**, accessible up steep lanes north of Piazza Eroi Sanremesi and Piazza Cassini. Known as **La Pigna** or the "Pine-Cone", its kasbah-like arched passageways and alleys leading nowhere come as a surprise after the busy, modern streets below. From the gardens at the highest peak you get excellent views across the whole of the town and surrounding countryside.

If you can drag yourself out of bed early enough, you will find that San Remo offers one of the liveliest and most engaging spectacles on the Riviera: the **wholesale flower market** at Mercato dei Fiori, Via Quinto Mansuino 12, Valle Armea, 4km east of town (℡0184.51711, Ⓦwww.sanremoflowermarket.it; visitor access Mon, Wed & Fri 4–6am). Take the Taggia or Imperia-Diano Marina bus from the centre of town for the ten-minute ride. Some eighty tonnes of flowers a day are shipped out of here, around Italy and the world. .

Eating and drinking

San Remo is well served by **restaurants**, most of which offer the local speciality of *sardenàira*, a kind of cheese-less pizza topped with tomatoes, olives, capers, garlic and fresh oregano.

Lella's Place at Corso N. Sauro 25 ℡0184.502.414. Overlooking the old port and offering a fresh menu of salads, pizza and pasta, including *spaghetti alle vongole* (€12) this is a good standby for a reasonably priced lunch. Closed Fri.

Piccolo Mondo Via Piave 7 ℡0184.509.012. This archetypally charming little trattoria in an alley off the Corso Matteotti serves delicious Ligurian dishes such as octopus and potato salad (€14), anchovies stuffed with pine nuts, mortadella and breadcrumbs (€14) and papardelle with home-made pesto, beans and zucchini (€9). The owner speaks good English. Closed Sun & Mon eve.

Solentiname Lungomare V. Emanuele 13 ℡0184.664.477. Exuberant place for a good night out, with a summer programme of live music, enjoying a wonderful waterfront setting. Try the mixed fried or grilled fish (€15) or a tagliata of Angus steak (€14) (grilled steak sliced thin). Closed Mon and Tues.

Nightlife

Nightlife revolves around San Remo's famous **Casino** (daily 2.30pm–3am; ℡0184.59.51, Ⓦwww.casinosanremo.it). Entrance is permitted only with your passport as ID; admission is free to the slot machines and from Monday to Thursday to the evocative *Belle Époque* gaming rooms (Mon–Thu free, Fri–Sun €7.50). The dress code is jacket and tie for both American and French gaming rooms, but you can get away with more casual gear in the slot-machine area.

Elsewhere around town, there's no shortage of **clubs** and **bars** – *Zoo Bizarre* on Via Gaudio is a popular place serving wine and cocktails, and with a DJ on Saturdays; while *Newport Café*, Giardini Vittorio Veneto, has salads and sandwiches at lunchtime, and great cocktails served with a variety of snacks in the evening. In summer there are open-air jazz, blues and folk **concerts** around the harbour and in the various parks.

Ventimiglia and around

Barely 6km east of the French border, **VENTIMIGLIA** is an unexceptional frontier town that enjoyed several centuries of minor prosperity thanks to constant border traffic. However, it's been experiencing hard times since the 1995 Schengen agreement permitted unchecked passage between France and Italy and rendered the town's role as customs post and refreshment point redundant. The town does make a good base for country **walks** though, especially as the **hotels** are cheaper than those in other nearby resorts. The centre is quite lively with a handful of good restaurants and delis, and the eastern side of town has a rather low-key **Area Archeologica**, where you can see some remains of a third-century Roman amphitheatre and baths. If you want to stay, the pleasant *Sea Gull*, Passeggiata Marconi 24 (℡0184.351.726,

A walk to Dolceacqua

One of the best walks around Ventimiglia comprises Stage One of the **Alta Via dei Monti Liguri** hiking trail (see box, p.126). The ten-kilometre route (an easy 3hr romp) begins from Ventimiglia tourist office, and takes you through ridge-top vineyards to the medieval village of **Dolceacqua**, known for its red wine and olive oil. **Buses** run between Dolceacqua and Ventimiglia for those who don't fancy the walk.

Ⓦwww.seagullhotel.it; ❸), has its own patch of beach below the crumbling medieval quarter, while the *XX Settembre*, Via Roma 16 (☏0184.351.222; ❷), is the pick of the low-end choices. For **food**, you could try the *Usteria d'a Porta Marina* (closed Tues eve & Wed), overlooking the river at Via Trossarelli 22.

Mórtola Inferiore

From Via Cavour in front of Ventimiglia's train station, bus #1a (every hour, on the hour, no service between 3 & 4pm) heads west for 5km to the village of **MÓRTOLA INFERIORE**, famed for the spectacular hillside **Giardini Botanici "Hanbury"** (April to mid-June daily 10am–5pm; mid-June to Sept daily 9am–6pm; Oct daily 10am–6pm; Nov–March Thurs–Tues 10am–4pm; €7.50; Ⓦwww.amicihanbury.com). The gardens were laid out in 1867 by Sir Thomas Hanbury, a London spice merchant who set up home here, and are highly atmospheric, with hidden corners and pergola-covered walks tumbling down to the sea. A thirty-minute walk further west along the coast road – or a few minutes on bus #1a – is the frontier post. A scramble down the hillside brings you to the caves of **Balzi Rossi** (Tues–Sun 9am–7pm; free; Ⓦwww.liguriaplanet.com), where remains of prehistoric civilizations dating back to the Paleolithic age were discovered; a small **Museo Preistorico** (same hours; €2) houses a collection of artefacts and crude fertility sculptures.

The Riviera di Levante

The glorious stretch of coast **east from Genoa**, dubbed the **Riviera di Levante**, is not the place to come for a get-away-from-it-all beach holiday. Ports that once eked a living from fishing and coral diving have been transformed by thirty years of tourism – the coastline is still wild and extremely beautiful, but the sense of remoteness has gone. To experience the coast at its best, visit in spring or autumn, when the hordes have gone home, the coastal path has quietened and the scenery is at its spectacular best. Even in high season, though, there are quiet spots to be discovered.

Away from the resorts, the cliffs and bays are covered with pine and olive trees, best seen from the vantage points along the footpaths crisscrossing the headland of the **Monte di Portofino**. The harbour towns of **Camogli** on the **Golfo Paradiso** and **Santa Margherita Ligure** on the Golfo Tigullio are favourite subjects for arty picture postcards, while super-chic **Portofino** on the southern tip of the headland effortlessly pulls in the international jet set. Less exclusive nightlife is found at big, feisty resorts such as **Rapallo**. Further east, the main road heads inland, bypassing the spectacular **Cinque Terre** and joining the train line at the port of **La Spezia**, which stands at the head of the idyllic Golfo dei Poeti and gives access to romantic waterside villages such as **Portovénere**. From La Spezia, there's easy access by road or rail to Pisa or Parma, and by sea to Corsica.

Camogli

CAMOGLI was the "saltiest, roughest, most piratical little place" according to Dickens when he visited the town. Though it still has the "smell of fish, and seaweed, and old rope" that the author relished, it's had its rough edges knocked off since his day, and is now one of the most attractive small resorts along this stretch of the coast, with a pretty collection of colourful cottages stacked up on a steep hillside around a small harbour.

The town's name, a contraction of *Casa Mogli* (House of Wives), comes from the days when voyages lasted for years and the women ran the port while the men were away. Camogli supported a huge fleet of 700 vessels in its day, which once saw off Napoleon. The town declined in the age of steam, but has been reborn as a classy getaway without the exaggerated prices of further round the coast.

The **train station** is just inland and uphill of the beach; turn right towards the centre for the small **tourist office**, 50m north at Via XX Settembre 33 (Mon–Sat 9am–12.30 & 3–6.30pm, Sun 9am–12.30pm; ☎0185.771.066, Ⓦwww.prolococamogli.it). From here take the steps down to the seafront. Summer **boats** shuttle over from Genoa's Porto Antico several times a day, taking an hour (€10), using the old harbour on the north side of town, separated from the pebble beach to the south by a promontory occupied by the medieval **Castello della Dragonara**. For **food**, wander along the waterfront and checkout the fish on display at the various restaurants built out over the water, or try the excellent local foccacia, on sale in most bakeries.

Accommodation

Augusta Via Piero Schiaffino 100 ☎0185.770.592, Ⓦwww.htlaugusta.com. Good-value family-run hotel with attractive a/c rooms, all en suite. ❹

Cenobio dei Dogi Via Cúneo 34 ☎0185.7241, Ⓦwww.cenobio.it. Lavish hotel, once the summer palace of Genoa's doges, with its own park, beach, pool, tennis courts and restaurants. ❻

Hotel Casmona ☎0185.770.015, Ⓦwww.casmona.com. In the centre of Camogli, this hotel is housed in a seafront nineteenth-century villa and has light, airy rooms. ❹

Portofino Kulm ☎0185.7241, Ⓦwww.portofinokulm.it. Sister hotel to the *Cenobio dei Dogi*, perched in woodland above the town in Ruta di Camogli, this has a refined secluded air, great views and provides easy access to the walks of the Portofino headland (see p.133). ❻

Villa Rosmarino Via Ficari 38 ☎0185.771580, Ⓦwww.villarosmarino.com. A hip new option, 5min walk above town. A 19th century *palazzo* with lush grounds, pool, and utterly minimalist white rooms hung with the owner's collection of contemporary art. ❼

Open or wrapped?

If you're visiting Camogli on the second Sunday in May, you won't be able to miss the **Sagra del Pesce**, preceded on the Saturday night by fireworks and a huge bonfire. This generous – and smelly – event has its origins in celebrating the munificence of the sea and retains its ancient resonance for Camogli's fisherfolk even today. Thousands of fish are plucked fresh from the waves, flipped into a giant frying-pan set up on the harbourfront and distributed free of charge to all and sundry as a demonstration of the sea's abundance (and in the hope for its continuation). In recent years the event has been beset by quibbles: bureaucrats have suggested that the frying-pan – some four metres across – is a health hazard, and there have even been allegations that frozen fish is defrosted out at sea and then passed off as fresh. For all that, local enthusiasm for the festival hasn't waned one bit.

Ferries from Camogli

Fish aside, Camogli makes its living from **ferries** operated by Golfo Paradiso, Via Scalo 3 (℡0185.772.091, Ⓦwww.golfoparadiso.it) from the little dock by the coastguard. Departures to tranquil **Punta Chiappa**, ideal for a spot of swimming and basking in the sun, and **San Fruttuoso** (see below), are most frequent (May–Sept at least hourly; Oct–April 3 weekdays, hourly at weekends; €8 to Punta Chiappa, €10 to San Fruttuoso). There are also boats east to the **Cinque Terre** (July–Sept 2–4 weekly; €22 return), which stop en route at **Portofino** and continue to **Portovénere**, as well as plenty more west to **Genoa** (€10 return). You can also take **diving** trips and courses with the B&B Diving Center, just back from the harbour (℡0185.772.751, Ⓦwww.bbdiving.it).

San Fruttuoso

The enchanting thousand-year-old abbey of **SAN FRUTTUOSO** is one of the principal draws along this stretch of the Riviera, occupying a picturesque little bay at the southern foot of Monte di Portofino. The only way to get there is **on foot** (see box opposite) or **by boat**, dozens of which shuttle backwards and forwards from practically every harbour along the coast during peak season. On summer weekends, the tiny port and church may be uncomfortably crowded, but out of season (or at twilight, courtesy of the occasional night cruise), San Fruttuoso is a peaceful, excellent place for doing very little.

The **Abbazia di San Fruttuoso** (March, April & Oct Tues–Sun 10am–4pm; May & Sept daily 10am–6pm; Dec–Feb Sat & Sun 10am–4pm; €7) was originally built to house the relics of the third-century martyr St Fructuosus, which were brought here from Spain after the Moorish invasion in 711. It was rebuilt in 984 with an unusual Byzantine-style cupola and distinctive waterside arches and later became a Benedictine abbey that exerted a sizeable degree of control over the surrounding countryside. The Doria family took over in the sixteenth century, adding the defensive **Torre dei Doria** nearby, and the small, elegant church, with its compact little cloister and half-dozen Doria tombs. Off the headland, a 1954 bronze statue known as the **Cristo degli Abissi** (Christ of the Depths) rests eight fathoms down on the sea bed, to honour the memory of divers who have lost their lives at sea and to protect those still working beneath the waves.

There are a handful of simple **restaurants** on San Fruttuoso's beach serving fish and steamed mussels, and one place **to stay** – the tiny and rather dingy *Da Giovanni* (℡0185.770.047; ➌).

Portofino and the Golfo del Tigullio

On the eastern side of Monte di Portofino headland stands the **Golfo del Tigullio**, a broad arc of a bay named after the local Tigullian tribe of pre-Roman antiquity. The gulf stretches 28km from the rocks and inlets around the millionaires' playground of **Portofino** and its friendlier neighbour **Santa Margherita Ligure** to head east along a dramatically beautiful – and densely touristed – coastline. In summer the main focus is the large resort of **Rapallo**.

The Consorzio Portofino Coast runs an **information** and hotel-booking service for the area, based at Via Lamarmora 17/6, Rapallo (℡0185.270.222, Ⓦwww.portofinocoast.it).

Portofino

There's no denying the beauty of **PORTOFINO**, tucked into a protected inlet surrounded by lush cypress- and olive-clad slopes, yet it manages to be both

Walks around Portofino

The Portofino headland – protected as the Parco Naturale Regionale di Portofino (⊛www.parks.it) and encircled by cliffs and small coves – is one of the most rewarding areas for **walking** on the Riviera coast. At 612m, **Monte di Portofino** is high enough to be interesting but not so high as to demand any specialist hiking prowess. The trails cross slopes of wild thyme, pine and holm oak, enveloped in summer in the constant whirring of cicadas. From the summit, the view over successive headlands is breathtaking. Not many people walk these marked paths, maybe because their early stages are fairly steep – but they aren't particularly strenuous, levelling off later and with plenty of places to stop.

One of the best trails skirts the whole headland, beginning in Camogli, on the western side of the promontory. The path rises gently for 1km south to **San Rocco** (221m), then follows the coast south to a viewpoint above Punta Chiappa, before swinging east to the scenic **Passo del Bacio** (200m), rising to a ridge-top and then descending gently through the olive trees and palms to **San Fruttuoso** (3hr from Camogli). It continues east over a little headland and onto the wild and beautiful clifftops above **Punta Carega**, before passing through the hamlets of Prato, Olmi and Cappelletta and down steps to **Portofino** (4hr 30min from Camogli).

There are plenty of alternative routes. About 1km south of San Rocco, an easier path forks inland up to **Portofino Vetta** and **Pietre Strette** (452m), before leading down again through the foliage to San Fruttuoso (2hr 30min from Camogli). **Ruta** is a small village 250m up on the north side of Monte di Portofino, served by buses from Camogli, Santa Margherita and Rapallo; a peaceful, little-trod trail from Ruta heads up to the summit of the mountain (2hr), or diverts partway along to take you across country to Olmi and on to Portofino (2hr 30min from Ruta).

---

attractive and off-putting at the same time. The village has been effortlessly drawing in Europe's jet set since the *dolce vita* days of Bogart and Bacall, Sophia Loren, Burton and Taylor, and Princess Grace, all of whom holidayed here, though these days there are as many B list as A list celebs booked into its hotels.

The village lies at the end of a narrow and treacherously winding road 5km south from Santa Margherita, but thanks to continuous traffic the bus journey can take longer than the boats that shuttle regularly to and from all nearby ports in summer. Once you've arrived, surveyed the expensive waterfront shops and restaurants and perhaps climbed up to Castello Brown, there's little to do other than watch the day's endless procession of tour groups do the same; bear in mind, though, that a couple of peaceful harbourside beers will leave you little change from €20.

To get a sense of Portofino's idyllic setting follow the footpath which heads south from the harbour up onto the headland. Five minutes from the village is the church of **San Giorgio**, said to contain relics of St George. A further ten minutes up is the spectacularly located **Castello Brown** (daily summer 10am–7pm, winter 10am–5pm; €4) from whose terrace there are breathtaking views of a pint-sized Portofino. The castle, which dates back to the Roman period and now frequently hosts art and photography exhibitions, is named after its former owner, British Consul Montague Yeats Brown, who bought it in 1867 and set about transforming it. In 1870 he planted two pines on the main terrace for his wedding; one for him and one for his wife, Agnes Bellingham. The sweeping pines are still a prominent feature today.

The scenic path continues south for a kilometre or so, down to the **Faro** (lighthouse) on the very tip of the promontory. The only way back is up the same path. Northwest from the village, steeply stepped paths head through vineyards and orchards to Olmi and on to San Fruttuoso. The best sandy **beach** is the sparkling cove at **Paraggi**, 3km north of Portofino on the corniche road (buses will stop on request) – not exactly remote, but less formal than Portofino, with a couple of bars set back from the water.

Practicalities

The **tourist office** is at Via Roma 35 (summer daily 10am–1pm & 2–7pm; winter Tues–Sun 10.30am–1.30pm & 2.30–4.30pm; ℡0185.269.024). **Accommodation** is absurdly expensive year-round. The *Eden* stands within its own delightful gardens in the centre at Vico Dritto 8 (℡0185.269.091, ⓦwww.hoteledenportofino.com; ❼ but a fraction of that midseason, midweek), but if money is no object, you'll want to shell out for a luxury room at the *Splendido*, Viale Baratta 16 (℡0185.269.551, ⓦwww.hotelsplendido.com; ❾), with its fabulously lush grounds and stupendous views. Doubles are from around €1300 a night (with last-minute deals running at around half that) but this is generally regarded as one of Italy's best hotels. **Eating out**, whether at the hotels or at the super-chic seafood restaurants, *Il Pitosforo* (℡0185.269.020) and *Chuflay Bar* (operated by the *Splendido*) on the harbour (℡0185.269.020; closed Mon & Tues), is best left to those who don't read their credit-card statements.

Santa Margherita Ligure

SANTA MARGHERITA LIGURE is a small, thoroughly attractive, palm-laden resort, tucked into an inlet and replete with grand hotels, garden villas and views of the glittering bay. In the daytime, trendy young Italians cruise the streets or whizz around the harbour on jetskis, while the rest of the family sunbathes or crams the *gelaterie*. Santa Margherita is far cheaper to stay in than Portofino and less crowded than Rapallo, and makes a good base both for taking boats and trains up and down the coast and for exploring the countryside on foot.

The town is famous for its **watersports** – the European Dive-In Center, Via Canevaro 2 (℡0185.293.017, ⓦwww.europeandc.com), is one outfit offering waterskiing, sailing and diving; the tourist office has a list of others and there's a handful of places on the harbourfront offering **boats for rent**. **Walking** trails cross the Monte di Portofino headland: marked paths from Santa Margherita to Pietre Strette (1hr 30min) and Olmi (1hr 40min) link in with the trails outlined in the box on p.133. The best **beaches** are out of town, accessible by bus: south towards Portofino is Paraggi (see above), while to the north the road drops down to a patch of beach in the bay of **San Michele di Pagana**. In addition

---

Boats on the Tigullio coast

During summer, dozens of **boats** serve all points on the Tigullio coast, run by companies based in Genoa (see p.116), Camogli (see p.132) and La Spezia (see p.143), along with the main local operator, Servizio Marittimo del Tigullio, Via Palestro 8/1B, Santa Margherita (℡0185.284.670, ⓦwww.traghettiportofino.it). You should **book ahead** to guarantee a place in high summer.

The most popular line shuttles to and fro between **Rapallo**, **Santa Margherita**, **Portofino** and **San Fruttuoso**, taking fifteen minutes between each (summer: hourly every day; winter: 2 on Sun). There are also lovely **night excursions** on the same route (July & Aug 2–8 weekly). The most you'll pay for a one-way fare is €15.50. Boats also connect to the **Cinque Terre** (€15). Some continue to **Portovénere** and **Lérici** (€19). The best-value round-trip cruise ticket is the **Super Cinque Terre**, which gives stops of 1hr in Riomaggiore, 3hr for lunch in Monterosso and 1hr in Vernazza (June–Sept 2 weekly; €30). Or for a whale-watching trip expect to pay €40.

to its beach bars and crystal-clear water, a *Crucifixion* by Van Dyck in the church of San Michele may prove an added incentive for a visit.

Arrival and information

The **train station** overlooks the harbour from the north; behind the waterfront Piazza Veneto 250m south is the **tourist office**, Via XXV Aprile 2/B (April–end Sept Mon–Sat 9am–12.30pm & 2.30–7pm, Sun 9.30am–12.30pm & 3–6pm; Oct–end March daily 9.30am–12.30pm & 2.30–5.30pm; ℡0185.287.485).

Accommodation

Albergo Fasce ℡0185.286.435, ⓦwww .hotelfasce.it. Good mid-price hotel nicely located on a quiet side street, with a panoramic roof terrace. ❹
Annabella Via Costasecca 10 ℡0185.286.531. Simple hotel whose attractive rooms have shared bathrooms (hence the lower prices here). ❷

Nuova Riviera, Via Belvedere 10, off Piazza Mazzini ℡0185.287.403, ⓦwww.nuovariviera.com. Welcoming place on a quiet residential street. ❸
Lido Palace, Via Doria 3 ℡0185.285.821, ⓦwww .lidopalacehotel.com. Impressive seafront hotel, with spacious modern suite-style rooms. ❼

Eating and drinking

Dei Pescatori Via Bottaro 43 ℡0185.286.747. Nice place on the waterfront in the old port for traditional fish dishes such as fish baked with potatoes, olives and pine nuts (€16). Closed Tues, except in July and Aug when it closes Mon and Tues lunchtime.
Dal Baffo 56 Via Matteotti ℡0185.288.987. Popular place serving a great range of reasonably priced pizza, pasta and fish. Closed Tues.
L'Ancora Via Maragliano 7 ℡0185.280.559 An excellent-value, mid-priced traditional fish

restaurant in the old port. Great place to try baked fish with potatoes (€15–20 depending on size of fish). Closed Tues.
Trattoria Baicin Via Algeria 5 ℡0185.286.763. A very good (and very reasonably priced) family-run seafood restaurant, just back from the waterfront park, offering great Ligurian specialities, such as swordfish with tomato sauce and olives. Closed Mon & Jan.

Rapallo

RAPALLO is a highly developed resort town with an expanse of glass-fronted restaurants and plush hotels crowding around a south-facing bay. In the early part of the twentieth century it was a backwater, and writers in particular came for the bay's extraordinary beauty, of which you now get an inkling only early in the morning or at dusk. Max Beerbohm lived in Rapallo for the second half of his life, and attracted a literary circle to the town; Ezra Pound wrote the first thirty of his *Cantos* here between 1925 and 1930, D.H. Lawrence stayed for a while and Hemingway also dropped by (but came away muttering that the sea was flat and boring). The resort's striking landmarks are the large **marina** and the **castle**, now converted into an exhibition space, stuck out at the end of a small causeway.

Arrival and information

The **tourist office** is at Via Armando Diaz 9 (Mon–Sun 9.30am–12.30pm & 2.30–7.30pm, Sun 9.30am–12.30pm, reduced hours in winter; ℡0185.230.346), and can provide details of diving outfits in the town and places to rent boats.

Accommodation

Accommodation is plentiful, but you need to pick carefully. The Rapallo **campsite** is at Via San Lazzaro 4 (℡0185.262.018, ⓦwww.campingrapallo.it; June–Sept).

Bandoni Via Marsala 24 ⓣ0185.50.423,
ⓕ0185.57.206. Housed in a fine old *palazzo* within
sight and smell of the sea, this is the best bargain
in town, if a little rough around the edges. ②
Excelsior Palace Via San Michele di Pagana 8
ⓣ0185.230.666, ⓦwww.thi.it. Rapallo's flagship
five star hotel, built right above the shore, has
splendidly lavish rooms, a state of the art spa, and
two refined, romantic restaurants. ⑨
Hotel Miramare ⓣ0185.230.261, ⓦwww
.miramare-hotel.it. Pleasant hotel overlooking the
sea with spacious, spotless rooms. ④

Riviera Lungomare Via Veneto 27 ⓣ0185.50.248,
ⓦwww.hotelrivierarapallo.com. Polished and
superior three-star overlooking the seafront.
Hemingway wrote *Cat in the Rain* while staying
here in 1923. Service is good and the owner
speaks English. ⑤
Stella Via Aurelia Ponente 6 ⓣ0185.50.367,
ⓦwww.hotelstella-riviera.com. Affordable and
welcoming place, with roof terrace, though the
busy main road outside can be noisy. ③–④

Eating and drinking

Many **restaurants** in Rapallo and along the Tigullio coast serve the local
speciality *bagnun*, a dish based on anchovies, tomato, garlic, onion and white wine.
You'll find good trattorias in the alleys behind the mediocre seafront restaurants:

🏃 **Antica Cucina Genovese** A couple of
kilometres outside the town at Santa Maria
del Campo 133, ⓣ0185.206.009. A chance not
only to sample some of the region's best vegetarian
cuisine, but to learn how to cook it as well. The
chefs here give demonstrations on cooking everything from ravioli to cheese focaccia.
Da Mario Piazza Garibaldi 23 ⓣ0185 53736.
Moderate prices, and great seafood served on tables
outside under medieval porticoes. Closed Wed.

Il Castello Lungomare Castello 6, Delightful
winebar with a waterfront terrace.
O Bansin Via Venezia 105 ⓣ0185 231119. Affordable old-town restaurant where you should try their
signature pasta dish with pesto, tomatoes and
cream. Closed Sun lunch.
Taverna Paradiso off Via Mazzini 73, Pub-like
place down a side alley, great for drinks and
snacks. Eve only.

The Cinque Terre

The stupendous folded coastline of the **Cinque Terre** (Five Lands) stretches
between the beach resort of Lévanto and the major port of La Spezia. The area
is named for five tiny villages – **Monterosso**, **Vernazza**, **Corniglia**, **Manarola**
and **Riomaggiore** – wedged into a series of coves between sheer cliffs; their
comparative remoteness, and the dramatic nature of their position on a stunning
coastline, make them the principal scenic highlight of the whole Riviera richly
deserving of their recently acquired Unesco World Heritage status. They do
inevitably get very crowded in summer and all the villages have lost some of
their character to the tide of kitschy souvenir shops and overpriced, under-
quality restaurants, but even in August you really shouldn't bypass the area – the
scenery is breathtaking and there is some lovely walking between villages.

Much of the area is now officially protected as the **Parco Nazionale delle
Cinque Terre**, the website of which, ⓦwww.cinqueterre.com, also operates a
hotel booking service. You can also book **apartments and hotels** through
Arbaspaa (ⓣ0187.760.083, ⓦwww.arbaspaa.com) based in Manarola.

The three principal ways to get to and around the villages of the Cinque
Terre are trains, boats and on foot. If you're on a fast **train**, you'll zip through
without seeing much more than a few tantalizing glimpses of turquoise water
as the train speeds from one tunnel to the next. Regular slow trains, however,
between Lévanto and La Spezia stop at every village. To make the most of
your journey, get a **Cinque Terre Card**, which gives unlimited travel
between all five villages and Lévanto, three hours mountain-bike hire, plus
access to all paths of the national park (see box opposite). It's available in

There's plenty of excellent **walking** to be done in and around the Cinque Terre. However, if you're hoping to tackle the national park's most popular route, known as the **Blue Route** (Sentiero Azzurro), or Path no. 2, from Riomaggiore to Monterosso, you'll have to purchase a Cinque Terre Card for €3, either at the entrance to the path or at any local tourist office or train station (see p.136 for details of the card's travel options). The Red Route (Sentiero Rosso), or Path no. 1, is free. The tourist offices can also provide plenty of maps and information, and can advise on good itineraries: despite its popularity we'd recommend Blue Route (11km; around 5hr), as it hugs the shoreline between all five villages, offering spectacular scenery along the way. Another highly rewarding walk is **trail no. 10**, which leads from Monterosso station up through pine woods and onto a flight of steps that emerge at the San Antonio church on the high point of the Punta Mesco headland (1hr), giving a spectacular panorama along the length of the Cinque Terre coastline.

Note that most of the paths are **unshaded** and can be blisteringly hot in summer – make sure you wear a hat and carry a water bottle for even a short stroll. Walking shoes are advisable as paths are rocky and uneven at the best of times. Also, take note of weather forecasts in spring and autumn, as rainstorms can brew up rapidly and make paths treacherously slippery.

one- (€5), two- (€8), three- (€10) or seven- (€20) day versions from the area's train stations and tourist information offices.

Boats from every company on the Riviera shuttle along this bit of coast all summer long. Make sure to confirm which of the four waterside villages you'll be stopping at (Corniglia has no harbour), and specify if you want a one-way ticket, rather than the more usual round-trip. Hopping between Cinque Terre villages by boat is easy, with between five and eight a day (April–Oct; sporadic service during winter months) going in both directions – although watch out for a lull between about noon and 2.30pm.

The most satisfactory way to get around is **on foot**: there's a network of trails (see above) linking the villages along the coast or up on the ridge-tops, which offer spectacular views. However, the coastal path in particular can get uncomfortably crowded throughout the summer months.

Trying to tour the area by **car or motorbike** truly isn't worth the effort. All five villages do now have road access, although the roads are narrow and exceptionally steep. The views are in places stupendous, but there are too many corkscrew bends to allow you to truly enjoy them. There's also very little public parking. If staying at a hotel in Monterosso's pedestrianized zone, you'll have to pay €20 for a night's parking. You'd do better to leave your vehicle in Lévanto or La Spezia.

Lévanto

Heading east out of the big resort of Sestri Levante, the train line and coastal road disappear into a series of tunnels that last almost until La Spezia. The slow bus route loops through coastal resorts and inland past red marble quarries before arriving at the unpretentious small town of **Lévanto**, last settlement before the Cinque Terre. Its sandy **beach** – the best for miles around – inexpensive hotels and good transport links make it a passable base for exploring. The only real sights in the town are architectural remnants from Lévanto's thirteenth-century heyday, including the **Loggia Comunale** on the central Piazza del Popolo, the black-and-white striped church of **Sant'Andrea** above the piazza, and the odd surviving stretch of medieval wall here and there.

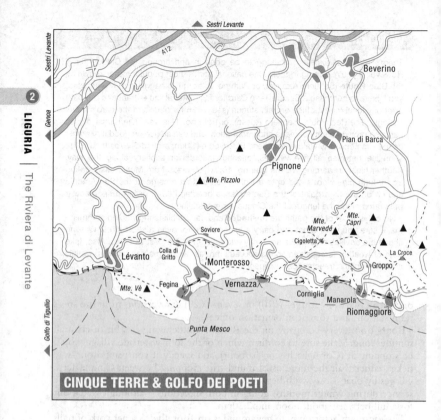

CINQUE TERRE & GOLFO DEI POETI

The **tourist office** is at the end of the main Via Roma at Piazza Mazzini 3 (Mon–Sat 9am–1pm & 3–6pm, Sun 9am–1pm; ☎0187.808.125), while the **train station** is ten-minutes' walk inland from the seafront. Of the **hotels**, some of which insist on a minimum of two nights' stay and half board in high season, the finest is *Stella Maris*, Via Marconi 4 (☎0187.808.258, ⊛www .hotelstellamaris.it; ⑤), with a handful of opulent rooms in the nineteenth-century Palazzo Vannoni, plus some others in a more modern annexe on Piazza Staglieno. The *Europa*, Via Dante Alighieri 41 (☎0187.808.126, ⊛www .europalevanto.com; ③), is a charmingly old-fashioned place with parking. There's also a clean, modern and central **youth hostel** on Via San Nicolò (☎0187.802.562, ⊛www.ospitaliadelmare.it; €21), with **internet** access. The best of a handful of **campsites** is *Acqua Dolce*, Via Semenza 5 (☎&℻0187.808.465, closed mid-Nov to mid-Dec & mid-Jan to Feb). The town's best **restaurant** is the expensive *Araldo*, Via Jacopo 24 (closed Tues except in July & Aug), featuring fresh local ingredients beneath a vaulted, painted ceiling. Don't miss the specialities *gattafin*, deep-fried vegetable ravioli, and *cotolette di acciughe*, fried, stuffed anchovies.

Monterosso

Tucked into a bay on the east side of the jutting headland of Punta Mesco, **MONTEROSSO** is the chief village of the Cinque Terre. It's the largest of

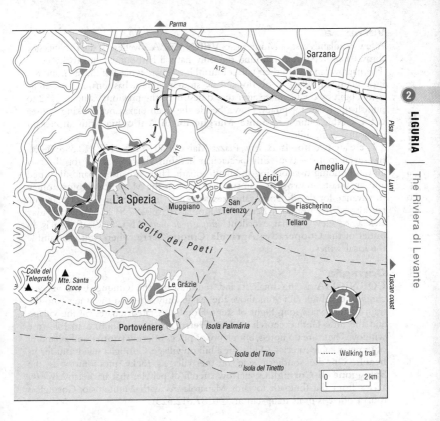

the five – population 1800 – and most developed, with the modern beach resort of **Fegina** occupying the shore just west of the old village. Beaches, both free and toll, are broad and picturesque, separated from the narrow lanes of the old quarter by a hill, atop which is the seventeenth-century **Convento dei Cappuccini**. In the centre of the old village is the striped thirteenth-century church of **San Giovanni Battista**, while a more recent claim to fame is as the home town of the Nobel Prize-winning poet Eugenio Montale; his *Ossi di Seppia* (Cuttlefish Bones) is a collection of early poems about his youth in Monterosso.

Monterosso operates the Cinque Terre's main **tourist office**, in the station (summer 8am–10pm; winter 8am–8pm; ☎0187.817.059), as well as a Pro Loco tourist association office at Via Fegina 38 (☎0187.817.506). Top **hotel** is the *Porto Roca*, Via Corone 1 (☎0187.817.502, ⓦwww.portoroca.it; March–Nov; ⑥–⑧), which sits atop the rocks at the end of a narrow lane at the southern end of town. The public areas are decorated in rather dingy style with suits of armour and huge drab pictures, but the bedrooms come with sea views, terraces and sun loungers. *Villa Adriana*, Via IV Novembre 23 (☎0187.818.109, ⓦwww .villaadriana.info; ⑤), has its own beach and even some car-parking space, while the *Amici*, at Via Buranco 36 (☎0187.817.544, ⓦwww.hotelamici.it; ⑤), is tucked away from the hubbub and has a garden with views of the sea, as well as a good restaurant.

Vernazza

A few headlands east of Monterosso, **VERNAZZA**, loveliest of the five villages, throws a protective arm around the only natural harbour on this rocky coast. The narrow lanes with their tall, colourful houses are typical of the area, and the little cramped village is overlooked by stout medieval bastions and a watch-tower, built by the Genoese after they'd destroyed the previous castle in 1182 to punish the locals for piracy. Down beside the main piazza overlooking the sea is the Gothic church of **Santa Margherita di Antiochia**, with an elegant octagonal campanile.

There are two **hotels**: *Barbara*, Piazza Marconi 30 (T&F0187.812.398; ❶–❸), has seven rooms – two with spectacular harbour views – on the top floor of an old building overlooking the main square. There are also a handful of bed and breakfasts and **rooms** – in summer – ask at the Monterosso tourist office in advance for details. Poor-value **restaurants** ring the main Piazza Marconi; try instead the *Osteria Il Baretto*, Via Roma 31 (T0187.812.381), which may lack a sea view but has excellent *antipasti di mare*. Also on Via Roma is an outlet of the **Cooperativa Agricola Cinque Terre**, where you can sample the local wines.

Corniglia

CORNIGLIA is the smallest and remotest of the Cinque Terre villages, clinging to a high cliff 90m above the sea, its only access to the water (and the train station) via a long flight of steps. Floral-decorated squares fill the village, and the little Gothic church of **San Pietro** boasts an exquisite, marble rose window. There are no hotels, but plenty of places offering **rooms**, and a handful of unremarkable eateries. Oddly for a hilltop village, Corniglia stands out for its **beach**. On the southern side of the village's rocky promontory is the **Spiaggone di Corniglia**, a narrow stretch of pebbles that has relatively easy access from the footpath towards Manarola. As with Monterosso, Corniglia's tourist office is in its train station (T0187.812.523).

Manarola

MANAROLA is almost as enchanting as Vernazza, its pastel-shaded houses crowded impossibly up the sides of a prominent headland of dark rock. The fourteenth-century church of San Lorenzo in the village has another beautiful rose window. On the road from Manarola to Corniglia above the village is the hamlet of **Groppo**, home to the **Cooperativa Agricola Cinque Terre**, which offers tastings and direct sale of the local wines (book ahead; Mon–Sat 10am–noon & 2–6pm; T0187.920.435).

Manarola's small **tourist office** is in the train station (daily: summer 7am–8pm; winter 7am–7.30pm; T0187.760.511). The town has a handful of outstanding **accommodation** options. Family-run *Ca' d'Andrean*, Via Discovolo 101 (T0187.920.040, Wwww.cadandrean.it; ❸), where breakfast is taken in the garden in summer, takes pride in its service and airy rooms (some with balcony). *Marina Piccola*, Via Birolli 120 (T0187.920.103, Wwww.hotelmarinapiccola .com; ❹; closed Nov to mid–Feb), has six elegant rooms, some with sea views. The small non-HI **hostel** *Ostello 5 Terre* is a clean, friendly place 300m up the hill from the station at Via Riccobaldi 21 (T0187.920.215, Wwww.cinqueterre .net/ostello; €23); you may need to book several weeks ahead in summer. For **eating** options, try the restaurant of the *Marina Piccola* (see above), which offers a whole raft of reasonably priced fish dishes as well as outdoor seating, or join the locals just downhill at *La Scogliera* (T0187.921.029; closed Sun), which serves some excellent Ligurian specialities.

Riomaggiore

Lively **RIOMAGGIORE** is the easternmost of the Cinque Terre, with a relatively easy road link to the outside world that makes it also the most crowded of the five. Nonetheless, its vividly multicoloured houses piling up the steep slopes above the romantic little harbour, with no two on the same

▲ Riomaggiore

level, give the place a charm untempered by the café crowds, especially the higher you climb. Aside from the requisite rose window, the church of **San Giovanni Battista** houses a striking wooden *Crucifixion* by Maragliano. Riomaggiore is also the starting-point for the twenty-minute walk on the **Via dell'Amore** (Lovers' Path) to Manarola.

As is common with several Cinque Terre towns, Riomaggiore's tourist office can be found in the train station (℡0187.760.091). The only **hotel** is the pleasantly modern *Villa Argentina*, in a lovely spot at Via De Gasperi 37 (℡0187.920.213, ⑩www.hotelvillaargentina.com; ❹). Otherwise, there are three spotless simple rooms at the B&B *Il Boma*, Via C Colombo 99, run by a couple recently returned from America (℡0187.920395, ⑩www.ilboma .com). For **food**, *La Lanterna* (closed Tues in winter) has a good, moderately priced pasta and seafood menu, and a great location at the harbour (to get there, walk under the train line from the bottom of the main street). Otherwise, *Controvelaccio* (closed Sun) on Via Colombo has various inexpensive menus and delicious fresh anchovies, and *Ripa del Sole*, Via De Gasperi 4 (℡0187.920.143; closed Sun), serves marvellous dishes such as ravioli with wild borage.

The Golfo dei Poeti

After the beauty of the Golfo Paradiso and Golfo del Tigullio, and the drama of the Cinque Terre, Liguria still has a final flourish. Hard up against the Tuscan border is the majestic Golfo di La Spezia, an impressive sweeping panorama of islands and rough headlands renamed the **Golfo dei Poeti** in 1919 by Italian playwright Sam Benelli for the succession of romantic souls who fell in love with the place. Petrarch was the first; Shelley lived and died on these shores; Byron was another regular; and D.H. Lawrence passed the pre-World War I years here. The town at the head of the gulf is workaday **La Spezia**, a major naval and shipbuilding centre with a fine art gallery. Small resorts line the fringes of the bay, linked by buses that hug the twisting roads or boats that shuttle across the glittering blue water – **Portovénere**, sitting astride a spit of land to the southwest, and **Lérici**, on the southeastern shore, are both highly picturesque stopovers.

Dozens of **boats** embark on rapid, half and all-day excursions throughout the summer – and on certain days in winter too – between just about every port along this coast. Local tourist offices have precise details of sailings. The principal operator is Consorzio Marittimo Turistico 5 Terre – Golfo dei Poeti, Via Don Minzoni 13, in La Spezia (℡0187.732.987, ⑩www .navigazionegolfodeipoeti.it); but you could also try Battellieri del Golfo, Banchina Revel (℡0187.21.010). Half- and full-day trips from La Spezia to the Cinque Terre cost €15 and €20 respectively; they are slightly cheaper from Lérici or Portovénere.

La Spezia

Up until a few years ago, most travel guides dismissed **LA SPEZIA** with a few curt comments. This ordinary working town was known mainly for its huge mercantile port and the largest naval base in the country – until the **Museo Amedeo Lia**, probably the finest collection of medieval and Renaissance art in Liguria, put it on the tourist map. Art aside, realistically priced hotels and restaurants make it a good base from which to explore both the Golfo dei Poeti and the Cinque Terre.

The **train station** is a ten-minute walk above the town centre – head left out of the station and then follow the curving Via XX Settembre all the way down until it hits the first of three long, parallel boulevards that run along the front of the port: these three are Via Chiodo, then palm-lined Viale Mazzini, and then the principal traffic street of Viale Italia. The **ferries** to Sardinia, the Cinque Terre and around the Golfo dei Poeti leave from the Porto Mercantile, on the central waterfront.

As well as a small information bureau at the station (open 8am–8pm) the main **tourist office** is just back from the port at Viale Mazzini 47 (Mon–Sat 9.30am–1pm & 3.30–7pm & Sun 9.30am–1.30pm; ℡0187.770.908, Wwww .comune.sp.it), while the **bus station** is on Piazza Chiodo, at the western end of Via Chiodo in front of the naval arsenal, where ATC buses from Tuscany and the countryside valleys arrive. Buses to Portovénere and Lérici depart either from the train station forecourt or from Piazza Cavour.

There are several **hotels** near the train station, most of which are dingy and a little seedy, though passable for a night if you have an early train to catch. *Mary*, Via Fiume 177 (℡0187.743.254, Wwww.hotelmary.it; ❸), is just by the station with bright modern rooms and a restaurant. Away from the station in the old centre is the friendly, good-value *Il Sole*, Via F. Cavalotti 31 (℡0187.735.164, Wwww.albergoilsole.com; ❷), with simple, spacious rooms and a garden. The *Jolly* is a multistorey tower overlooking the bay at Via XX Settembre 2 (℡0187.739.555, Wwww.jollyhotels.it; ❻), part of a chain and replete with all comforts.

The Town

La Spezia, sandwiched between the hills and the sea, proved an early attraction to conquerors, with its strategic importance reflected in the number of Genoese castles that stud the hills. These were the town's first fortifications, yet it took **Napoleon** to capitalize on what is one of Europe's finest natural harbours and construct a naval and military complex at La Spezia early in the nineteenth century. The naval presence made the town a prime target in World War II and most of the centre had to be rebuilt following Allied **bombing**; it's now characterized by rather drab buildings lining a regular grid of streets behind the palm-fringed harbourfront promenade of **Viale Mazzini**. At the western end are some lovely **public gardens**, a short distance from **Piazza Chiodo** and La Spezia's raison d'être – the vast naval **Arsenale**, which was rebuilt after destruction in World War II. There's no public admittance to the complex itself, but just to the left of the entrance is the engaging **Museo Tecnico Navale** (Mon–Sat 8am–6.45pm, Sun 8am–1pm; €1.55), which contains battle relics and models.

From the public gardens it's a short stroll inland on Via Prione to Piazza Beverini and the striped Duomo of **Santa Maria Assunta** housing a polychrome terracotta by Andrea della Robbia. Behind the church is the lively marketplace of **Piazza Cavour**, and some 100m east the **Museo Amedeo Lia**, Via Prione 234 (Tues–Sun 10am–6pm; €6; Wwww.castagna.it /mal). Opened in 1996, this impressive museum occupies a seventeenth-century former Franciscan convent. The entry ticket allows you unlimited access throughout the day. Highlights are Pontormo's sharp-eyed *Self-Portrait*, a supremely self-assured *Portrait of a Gentleman* by Titian, and Bellini's *Portrait of an Attorney*. Upstairs in room XI are bronzes by Giambologna and Ammanati, while room XII houses the museum's most celebrated item, the

Addolorata, a half-statue in polychrome terracotta of a sorrowful Madonna made by Benedetto da Maiano.

Eating and drinking

For **food**, La Spezia's daily covered market in Piazza Cavour is a good place to buy picnic supplies; it takes over the whole square on Saturday mornings. You can get *farinata* at *La Pia* on Via Magenta, and good pizzas at *Da Giulio*, Via San Agostino 29 (closed Wed). There's a cluster of restaurants between Via del Prione and the Arsenale – many closed in August – where prices are kept in check by the naval clientele. Down near the seafront, *Da Dino*, Via Da Passano 19 (closed Sun eve & Mon), is a down-to-earth trattoria offering good-value menus of fish and other local dishes, and *La Posta*, Via Don Minzoni 24 (closed Sat & Sun), is in much the same mould.

Portovénere

The ancient, narrow-laned village of **PORTOVÉNERE** sits astride a spit of land on the very tip of the southwestern arm of the bay, blessed with breathtaking views, a memorably tranquil atmosphere and a string of three islets just offshore, each smaller and rockier than the last. The **bus** ride from La Spezia gives fine views of the bay and the islands, though the views are just as good – and the journey more fun – on the **boats** that depart around seven times a day in season.

In the upper part of the village is the twelfth-century church of **San Lorenzo**, and higher up still the sixteenth-century **castello**, with panoramic views. Portovénere's characteristic rose- and yellow-painted tower-houses, aligned to form a defensive wall, are now transformed into a trendy waterside strip known as the Palazzata, which continues to the end of the promontory and the thirteenth-century church of **San Pietro**. The church sits over the ruins of a Roman temple to Venus, goddess of love (hence the town's name). One of the rocky coves around the base of the church is the **Grotto Arpaia**, a favoured spot of Lord Byron who swam across the bay from here to visit Shelley at San Terenzo (see below). To this day, the gulf has the nickname of the "Baía di Byron", but swimming is discouraged in favour of the **boats** that shuttle regularly to and from Lérici.

Boats from Portovénere also tour the three **islands** that lie south of the peninsula, all but the nearest of which lie in a military zone and so can only be viewed from the water. **Isola Palmária** is the largest, 500m south of Portovénere, with the Grotta Azzurra cave as its star attraction. Next is the **Isola del Tino**, a rocky islet marked with a lighthouse and the remains of a Romanesque abbey. Finally comes the even tinier **Isola del Tinetto**, also home to a monastic community in centuries gone by.

Practicalities

Portovénere's **tourist office**, at Piazza Bastreri 7 (summer daily 10am–noon & 4–8pm; winter Thu–Tues 10am–noon & 3–6pm, Sun 9am–noon; ℡0187.790.691, ⓦwww.portovenere.it), has a list of the village's various bed and breakfast options and is located alongside the least expensive hotel, two-star *Genio* (℡0187.790.611, ⓦwww.hotelgenioportovenere.com; ❹). Of the four upscale choices, the pick is the *Royal Sporting*, a short walk outside the village on the beach at Via dell'Olivo 345 (℡0187.790.326, ⓦwww.royalsporting.com; ❻). It has pleasant, cool interior courtyards, spectacular views and a huge saltwater swimming pool. In a different vein, *Locanda Lorena* offers half-a-dozen simple rooms on the Isola Palmária, at Via Cavour 4 (☎0187.792.370; ❹; April–Sept).

There's a wealth of places to **eat** in town. The atmospheric, century-old *Antica Osteria del Carrugio* (closed Thurs) is at Via Capellini 66, in the shadow of the castle; its affordable specialities are anchovies, sheep's cheese and stuffed mussels (which are cultivated on poles in Portovénere's harbour). Down on the photogenic harbourfront, Calata Doria, are a handful of pricier places, including *Le Bocche* (☎0187.900.622; closed Tues in winter) famous for its seafood salad, dressed with a kind of pesto of anchovies, capers, pistacchios and pine nuts.

Lérici and around
East of La Spezia lie several kilometres of dockyards, foundries and thriving heavy industry, eventually brought to a stop at the boundary of a protected nature reserve which covers the southern half of the gulf shore.

First of the string of small resorts here is **SAN TERENZO**, marked by its prominent castle. There's a good sandy beach and a choice of accommodation, but most insist on full or half board in high season. About 2km south of San Terenzo lies **LÉRICI**, an upwardly mobile resort of garden villas, seafront bars, trattorias and gift shops. Piazza Garibaldi, behind the marina, acts as the bus station. The **tourist office** is on the seafront north of Piazza Garibaldi, at Via Biaggini 6 (Mon–Sat 9am–1pm & 2–8pm, Sun 10am–1pm; ☎0187.9601, ⓦwww.aptcinqueterre.sp.it), and has details of the regular **boats** across to Portovénere (every hour). At the top of town, the **castle** (Tues–Sun: July & Aug 10.30am–12.30pm & 6.30pm–midnight; mid-Oct to mid-March 10.30am–12.30pm: mid-March to end June & Sept to mid-Oct 10.30am–1pm & 2.30–6pm; €5) has fabulous views across to Portovénere and the three islands and back towards La Spezia. Inside, apart from a Gothic chapel, much of the interior is given over to a museum documenting prehistoric dinosaur life in the area.

Lérici's two most pleasant **hotels** are near the tourist office: the *Shelley & Delle Palme* is at Via Biaggini 5 (☎0187.968.204, ⓦwww.hotelshelley.it; ❺) and the *Byron* at no. 19 (☎0187.965.699, ⓦwww.byronhotel.com; ❹); both have suitably poetic sea views from balconied rooms. When it comes to **eating**, the outdoor pizzerias that line Lérici's harbour provide an attractive setting as the sun goes down.

Travel details

Trains

Genoa to: Alassio (15 daily; 1hr 10min–1hr 25min); Albenga (16 daily; 1hr 10min–1hr 55min); Bologna (4 daily; 3–4hr); Camogli (every 20–30min; 30–50min); Finale Ligure (15 daily; 45min–1hr); Imperia (11 daily; 1hr 30min–2hr); La Spezia (hourly; 1hr 10min–2hr 10min); Milan (hourly; 2hr); Naples (every 2–3hr; 7–8hr); Pisa (14 daily; 2–3hr 30min); Rapallo (every 20min; 30min); Rome (every 1–2hr; 6hr); San Remo (hourly; 1hr 45min–2hr 40min); Santa Margherita (every 20min; 20min–1hr); Ventimiglia (every 30min; 2hr 55min).

Buses

Camogli to: Ruta (every 30min–1hr; 25min).
Chiávari to: Rezzoaglio (6 daily; 1hr 25min); Bologna (2 daily; 4hr).
Finale Ligure to: Borghetto Santo Spirito (every 15min; 25min).
Genoa to: Rovegno (5 daily; 1hr 50min); Torriglia (hourly; 1hr 10min).

La Spezia to: Lérici (every 10min; 20min); Portovénere (every 30min; 20min).

Rapallo to: Chiávari (hourly; 30min); Montallegro (every 2hr; 40min); Santa Margherita (every 20min; 10min).

San Remo to: Ventimiglia (every 15min; 20min).

Santa Margherita to: Portofino (every 15–20min; 15min).

Ventimiglia to: Dolceacqua (14 daily; 18min); La Mortola (9 daily; 15min).

Ferries

Genoa to: Arbatax (2 weekly; 9hr); Bastia (1 daily; 4hr 45min); Olbia (at least daily in summer; 9hr 30min); Palermo (6 weekly; 20hr); Porto Torres (1daily; 12hr); Barcelona (6 weekly in summer; 18hr).

Santa Margherita to: Portofino (8 daily; 15min).

③

Lombardy and the lakes

CHAPTER 3 # Highlights

* **Tortelli alla zucca** Tuck into a plate of delicious pumpkin ravioli topped with sage butter. **See p.152**

* **Roof of Milan's Duomo** Wander around the roof of the world's largest Gothic cathedral with the best views of the city and the mountains beyond. **See p.163**

* **The Last Supper** Leonardo da Vinci's mural for the refectory wall of Santa Maria delle Grazie is one of the world's most resonant images. **See p.170**

* **Shopping in Milan** Steel yourself for the ultimate shopping trip in the fashion and design capital of the world. **See p.176**

* **Certosa di Pavia** This Carthusian monastery is a fantastic construction rising out of the rice fields near Pavia. **See p.181**

* **Cycling round Mantua** Rent a bike and explore elegant Mantua and the surrounding waterways. **See p.185**

* **Lake Como** Explore the most romantic of the lakes by ferry. **See p.199**

* **Città Alta, Bergamo** Bergamo's medieval upper town is an enchanting spot to spend an evening. **See p.207**

▲ Villa on Lake Como

Lombardy and the lakes

ombardy, Italy's richest region, often seems to have more in common with its northern European neighbours than with the rest of Italy. Given its history, this is hardly surprising: it was ruled for almost two centuries by the French and Austrians and takes its name from the northern Lombards, who ousted the Romans. As a border region, Lombardy has always been vulnerable to invasion, just as it has always profited by being a commercial crossroads. Emperors from Charlemagne to Napoleon came to Lombardy to be crowned king – and big business continues to take Lombardy's capital, **Milan**, more seriously than Rome.

The region's people, ranging from Milanese workaholics to cosseted provincial urbanites, hardly fit the popular image of Italians – and, in truth, they have little time for most of their compatriots. This has fuelled the rise of the Lega Nord, a political party nominally demanding independence from Rome and successfully exploiting the popular sentiment that northern taxes sustain the inefficient, work-shy south.

Sadly all this economic success has taken its toll on the landscape: industry chokes the peripheries of towns, sprawls across the Po plain and even spreads its polluting tentacles into the Alpine valleys. Traffic, too, is bad, with many roads – autostradas and lakeside lanes alike – gridlocked at peak times. Nonetheless, Lombardy's towns and cities retain wanderable medieval cores boasting world-class art and architecture, and the stunning scenery of the so-called "**Italian lakes**" – notably **Lake Como** and **Lake Garda** – never fails to seduce.

Milan's lowland neighbours – **Pavia**, **Cremona**, **Mantua** – flourished during the Middle Ages and Renaissance and retain much character. To the north, Lombardy is quite different, the lakes and Prealpine valleys sheltering fewer historic towns, the cities of **Bergamo** and **Brescia** excepted. Reaching into the high Alps, lakes Como, Garda and their lesser-celebrated siblings – **Maggiore** and **Orta** – have long been popular tourist territory with both Italians and foreigners.

Although the western shore of Lake Maggiore and the northern and eastern shores of Lake Garda fall outside Lombardy (in Piemonte, Trentino and Veneto respectively), the **lakes region** and its resorts are all covered in this chapter.

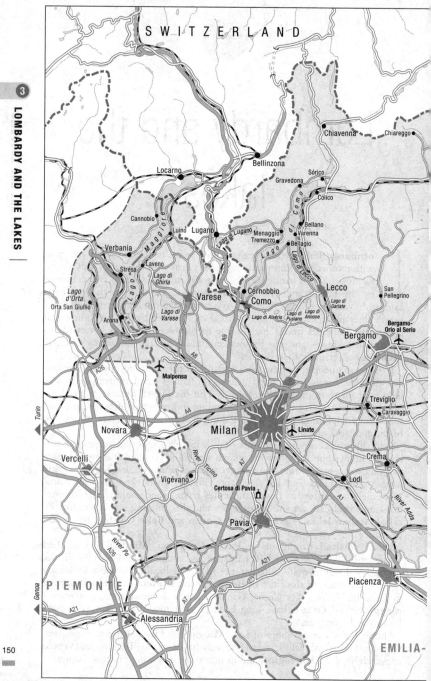

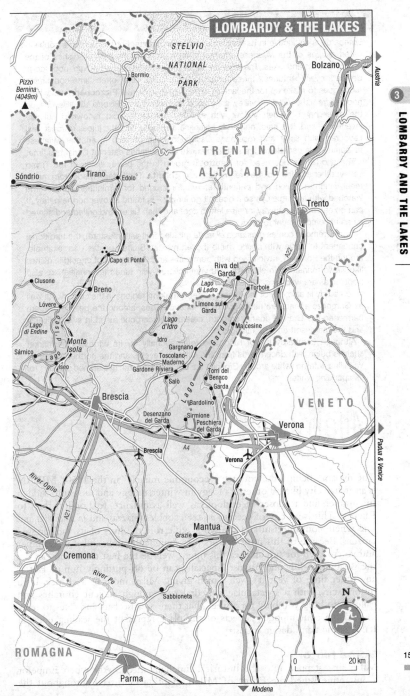

STELVIO
NATIONAL
PARK

Bolzano

Austria

Pizzo
Bernina
(4049m)

Bormio

Sóndrio   Tirano   Edolo

TRENTINO-
ALTO ADIGE

Trento

A22

Capo di Ponte

Riva del
Garda

Clusone   Breno

Lago
di Ledro

Torbole

Lóvere

Limone sul
Garda

Lago
di Endine

Lago
d'Idro

Malcesine

Sárnico   Iseo

Monte
Isola

Idro

Gargnano
Toscolano-
Maderno

Lago d'Iseo

Gardone Riviera

Torri del
Benaco

Salò

Garda

VENETO

Brescia

Bardolino

Desenzano
del Garda

Sirmione
Peschiera
del Garda

Verona

Brescia

A4   Verona   A4

River Oglio

A21

Mantua

Grazie

A22

Cremona

River Po

Sabbioneta

N

ROMAGNA

0   20 km

A1

Parma

Modena

Padua & Venice

Regional food and wine

Lombardy is distinctive in its variations in culinary habits. For example, the sophisticated recipes of the Milanese contrast sharply with the more rustic dishes of the Alpine foothills and lakes. The latter are sometimes known as *piatti poveri* (poor food): devised over centuries, these employ imagination and often time-consuming techniques to make up for the lack of expensive ingredients. **Pizzocheri**, buckwheat noodles from the Valtellina valley, are a good example of this. *Risotto alla Milanese*, on the other hand, golden yellow with saffron, is Milan's most renowned culinary invention – and, it is said, only truly Milanese if cooked with the juices of roast veal flavoured with sage and rosemary. *Ossobuco* (shin of veal) is another Milanese favourite, as is *panettone*, the soft, eggy cake with sultanas eaten at Christmas time.

The short-grain rice used for **risotto** is grown in the paddy fields of the Ticino Valley; other staples include green pasta and **polenta**. The latter – made from maize meal which is boiled and patiently stirred for around forty minutes, all the time watched with an eagle eye so it doesn't go lumpy – is found all over northern Italy. It can be eaten straightaway, or else left to cool and then sliced and grilled and served as an accompaniment to meat.

From Cremona comes *mostarda di frutta* (pickled fruit with mustard), the traditional condiment to serve with *bollito misto* (boiled meats). Stuffed pastas – for example, around the Po valley, ravioli filled with pumpkin – and veal eaten hot or cold in dishes like *vitello tonnato* (thin slices of cold veal covered with tuna mayonnaise) are also popular, as are wild *funghi* (mushrooms).

Lombardy is also one of the largest **cheese-making** regions in the country. As well as Gorgonzola there are numerous other local cheeses: among the best-known are parmesan-like Grana Padano, smooth, creamy Mascarpone (used in sweet dishes) and the tangy soft cheese Taleggio.

Although Lombardy is not renowned internationally for its **wines**, supermarket shelves bulge with decent reds from the Oltrepò Pavese, and the northern areas of Valtellina, Inferno, while around Brescia, the Franciacorta area has earned plaudits for its sparkling whites.

Milan

The dynamo behind the country's "economic miracle" in the 1950s, **MILAN** is an Italian city like no other. It's foggy in winter, muggy and mosquito-ridden in summer, and is closer in outlook, as well as distance, to London than to Palermo. This is no city of peeling *palazzi*, cobbled piazzas and *la dolce vita*, but one where consumerism and the work ethic rule the lives of its well-dressed citizens. Because of this most visitors pass straight through, and if it's summer and you're keen for sun and sea this might well be the best thing you can do; the weather, in July and August especially, can be off-puttingly humid. But at any other time of year it's well worth giving Milan more of a chance. It's a historic city, with a spectacular cathedral and enough ancient churches and galleries to keep you busy for a week, but there are also bars and cafés to relax in, and the contemporary aspects of the place represent the leading edge of Italy's fashion and design industry.

Some history

Milan first stepped into the historical limelight in 313 AD when Emperor Constantine issued the **Edict of Milan**, granting Christians throughout the

Roman Empire the freedom to worship for the first time. The city, under its charismatic bishop, **Ambrogio** (Ambrose), swiftly became a major centre of Christianity; many of today's churches stand on the sites, or even retain parts, of fourth-century predecessors.

Medieval Milan rose to prominence under the **Visconti** dynasty, who founded the florid late-Gothic **Duomo**, and built the nucleus of the **Castello** – which, under their successors, the **Sforza**, was extended to house what became one of the most luxurious courts of the Renaissance. The last Sforza, Lodovico, commissioned **Leonardo da Vinci** in 1495 to paint *The Last Supper*.

Milan fell to the French in 1499, marking the beginning of almost four centuries of foreign rule, which included the Spanish, Napoleon and the Austrian Habsburgs. **Mussolini** made his mark on the city, too: arrive by train and you emerge into the massive white Stazione Centrale, built on the dictator's orders. And it was on the insalubrious roundabout of Piazzale Loreto that the dictator's corpse was strung up for display in April 1945 as proof of his demise.

Milan's postwar development was characterized by the boom periods of the 1950s and 1980s: the city's wealth now comes from banking and its position at the top of the world's **fashion** and **design** industries. Politically, too, Milan has been key to Italy's postwar history. A bomb in Piazza Fontana in 1969 that killed sixteen people signalled the beginning of the dark and bloody period known as the **Anni di piombi**, when secret service machinations led to over a hundred deaths from bomb attacks. In the 1980s, corruption and political scandal once again focused attention on Milan, which gained the nickname **Tangentopoli** ("Bribesville"). The subsequent political reordering paved the way for Forza Italia, a political party founded by the self-promoting media magnate **Silvio Berlusconi** – Milan born and bred, he owns the football club AC Milan and has his power base in the city's media conglomerates.

Arrival

Milan has two main **airports** – Malpensa and Linate – both used by domestic and international traffic. It is also within easy reach of several smaller airports: Bergamo-Orio al Serio (see p.209) is the best connected and the most convenient, while Verona-Brescia (see p.213) is a couple of hours' drive away.

Malpensa (☎02.7485.2200, ⊛www.sea-aeroportimilano.it), 50km northwest near Lake Maggiore, is connected with Stazione Centrale, Milan's main train station, by direct **bus** (every 20min 4.25am–11.15pm; 1hr; €7), and with Milano Nord station by a fast **train**, the Malpensa Express (every 30min 4.20am–11.25pm; 50min; ☎199.151.152, ⊛www.malpensaexpress.it; early-morning and evening services are replaced by a bus from Via Leopardi, just to the left of the station as you face it; €11 if bought beforehand, more if purchased on the train). Both destinations are on the city's metro system: Stazione Centrale is termed "Centrale F.S." and Milano Nord is "Cadorna". A **taxi** from Malpensa to the centre takes about forty minutes and costs around €80 when the traffic is not too heavy.

Buses also link Malpensa's Terminal 1 to towns on nearby **Lake Maggiore**, including Stresa and Verbania (5 daily; reserve 48hr ahead ☎0323.552172, ⊛www.safduemila.com; €10.50; buy tickets at the Airport 2000 desk or on board). **Gallarate** train station, 5km from Malpensa airport by regular local buses, has trains to Stresa and Verbania, as well as Varese.

Milan's second airport, **Linate** (☎02.7485.2200, ⊛www.sea-aeroportimilano .it), is 7km east of the city centre: airport buses connect it with the Piazza Luigi di Savoia, on the east side of Stazione Centrale (every 20min 5.40am–9.30pm;

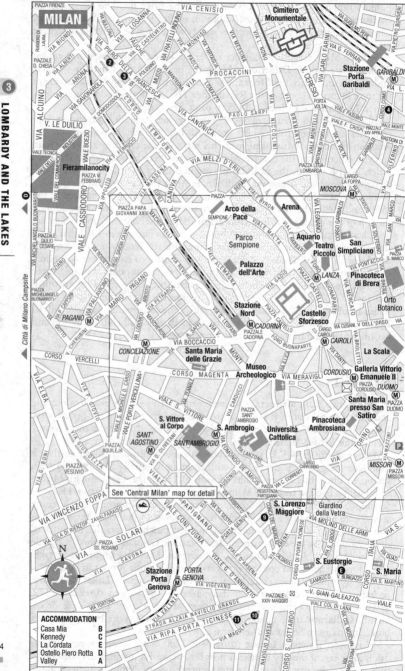

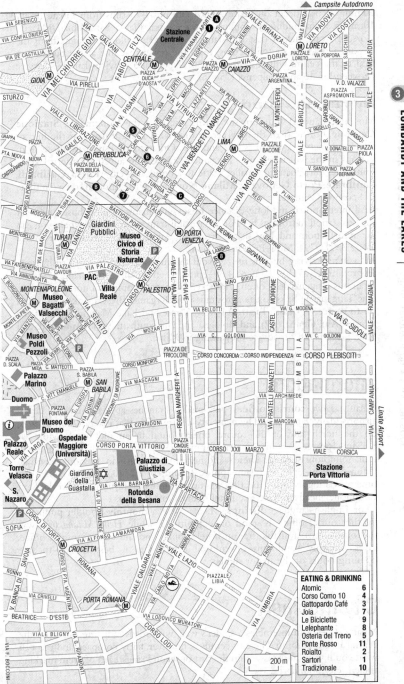

▲ Campsite Autodromo

EATING & DRINKING	
Atomic	6
Corso Como 10	4
Gattopardo Café	3
Joia	7
Le Biciclette	9
Lelephante	8
Osteria del Treno	5
Ponte Rosso	11
Roialto	2
Sartori	1
Tradizionale	10

20min; €2, buy ticket on board). ATM city bus #73 runs from Linate (every 10min 5.30am–midnight; 25min) to the central Piazza San Babila (M1) on Corso Europa; tickets cost the standard €1 and should be bought from the airport newsagent, or (with coins) from the ticket machine at the bus stop. A **taxi** to the centre will cost around €30. There's also a twice-daily bus service between Linate and Malpensa (75min).

By rail and road

Most international and domestic **trains** pull in at the monumental **Stazione Centrale**, northeast of the city centre on Piazza Duca d'Aosta, at the hub of the metro network on lines M2 and M3. Other trains, especially those from stations in the Milan region – Bergamo, Pavia, Como and the western lakes – sometimes terminate at smaller stations around the city: **Porta Garibaldi**, **Lambrate**, **Porta Genova** or **Milano Nord**, all on M2, though some continue to Stazione Centrale.

All international and long-distance **buses**, and many regional buses, arrive at the bus station in front of the Porta Garibaldi train station (M2), where you can get information and buy tickets from the Autostradale/Eurolines bus office (℡02.3391.0794; Mon–Fri 9am–6.30pm).

If you're arriving by **car**, try to avoid the morning and evening rush hours (approximately 7.30–10am & 4.30–7pm) when Milan's outer ring road, the infamous Tangenziale, is often gridlocked. Signage is copious, if not always clear. The Tangenziale links to the autostradas for Bergamo, Brescia, Lake Garda and on to Venice (A4 east), Turin (A4 west), Varese and Lake Maggiore (A8), Lake Como (A9), Genoa (A7) and Bologna and the south (the A1 "Autostrada del Sole"). See p.158 for advice on parking in Milan.

Information

Milan has two **tourist offices**, plus smaller branches at Malpensa and Linate airports (daily 9am–4pm). The main city-centre office is at Piazza Duomo 19/A, on the north side of the square, underground in an old hotel (Mon–Sat 8.45am–1pm & 2–6pm, Sun 9am–1pm & 2–5pm; ℡02.7740.4343, ❽www .milanoinfotourist.com). There's another, smaller office in Stazione Centrale (Mon–Sat 9am–6pm, Sun 9am–1pm & 2–5pm; ℡02.7740.4318), though at the time of writing its future location was unclear due to refurbishment works. Staff can phone ahead to make free hotel reservations for you.

For English-language **listings**, *Milano Mese*, a monthly booklet published by the tourist office, is good on exhibitions, while *Hello Milano* (❽www .hellomilano.it), available free in hotel lobbies and the central tourist office, gives monthly rundowns of cultural events and is best for up-to-date opening hours of the major sights.

City transport

Milan's street-plan resembles a spider's web, with roads radiating out from the central Piazza Duomo. The city centre is, however, fairly compact, and most of what you'll want to see is within the first or second rings, each of them marking ancient city boundaries.

MILAN METRO

The **metro** has four lines: **M1** (red), **M2** (green), **M3** (yellow) and *passante ferroviario* (blue). These connect at the four main hubs of Stazione Centrale, Duomo, Cadorna and Loreto (see map above). It's also worth getting to grips with the well-organized **bus and tram system**. Most stops display the route and direction, and as tickets for all three forms of transport are integrated you can hop on and off at will. Buses, trams and the metro run from around 6am to midnight, after which **nightbuses** take over, following the metro routes until 1am. For **public transport enquiries** (W www.atm-mi.it) the information offices at Duomo or Stazione Centrale metro stations have helpful, English-speaking staff.

Tickets, valid for 75 minutes, cost €1 and can be used for one metro trip and unlimited bus and tram rides. They are on sale at tobacconists, bars and at metro station newsagents; most outlets close at 8pm so it's best to buy a few tickets in advance, or a *carnet* of ten for €9.20. Some stations have automatic ticket machines, although only the newer ones give change. You can also buy a one-day (€3) or two-day pass (€5.50) at Stazione Centrale or Duomo metro stations. Remember to stamp your ticket when you enter the metro and board buses and trams, as inspections are common.

Taxis don't cruise the streets, so don't bother trying to flag one down. Either head for a taxi rank – on Piazza Duomo, Largo Cairoli, Piazza San Babila and Stazione Centrale, among others – or phone (see p.178 for numbers).

A hop-on, hop-off **bus tour** (W www.milano.city-sightseeing.it), with recorded English commentary, has two different routes departing from Piazza Castello (daily every 30min 9.30am–5.45pm; €20), while the **Gran Tour di Milano** is a coach and walking tour that includes entrance to the castle, La Scala museum and *The Last Supper* (daily 9.30am & 2.30pm; €50; W www.zaniviaggi .it); book well in advance.

Driving

Driving in the city is best avoided: the streets are congested and **parking** nigh on impossible. If you do drive, you need to know that the **Ecopass** – an initiative to cut pollution and congestion – is in force in the city centre (Mon–Fri 7am–7pm). You must buy the pass on the day of entry or up to midnight of the day afterwards; the fee is worked out on a sliding scale depending on your engine type. Payments can be made at authorized newsagents and tobacconists, through Intesa-SanPaolo ATMs, or, in English, by freephone (℡800.437.437) or online (⊕www.comune.milano.it/ecopass). If your hotel is within the Ecopass area, ask reception if they have any special provision for guests. For **parking** you're safest heading for a car park, which cost around €2.50 per hour. Central options include Autosilo Diaz, Piazza Diaz 6 (just south of Piazza Duomo); and Garage Traversi, on Via Bagutta near Piazza San Babila.

Accommodation

Much of Milan's **accommodation** is geared towards business travellers: rooms can be characterless, prices tend to be high and hotels are often booked up year-round. You'd be wise to reserve well ahead.

The area around Stazione Centrale and across to Corso Buenos Aires is home to a good proportion of the city's cheaper hotels, and although many cater to the area's considerable red-light trade, you will be fine at any of the places we recommend. As you go towards the centre, prices rise but there are still good deals to be had in some of the side streets off the city's main thoroughfares.

As many of Milan's mid-range hotels are rather dingy you may want to look into **bed-and-breakfast** accommodation. The stylish, well-run rooms at 🏃 Foresteria Monforte (℡340.237.0272, ⊕www.foresteriamonforte.it; ❹) are highly recommended, while La Casa di Leonardo is a central choice with an attractive sister option boasting a garden in La Dolce Vita (both ℡347.377.3044, ⊕www.ladolcevite.net; ❸); alternatively, if money is no object, head for the design-tastic 3 Rooms at Corso Como 10 (℡02.626.163, ⊕www.3rooms-10corsocomo.com; ❾). Look on ⊕www.bed-and-breakfast .it for further bed-and-breakfast establishments. The English-speaking outfit Rentxpress (℡02.805.3151, ⊕www.rentxpress.com) has a selection of **apartments** to rent throughout the city – these can make an economical alternative for groups or families.

Hotels

🏃 **Antica Locanda dei Mercanti** Via San Tomaso 6 ℡02.805.4080, ⊕www.locanda .it. Tucked away between the Duomo and the castle, this quietly elegant *locanda* offers individually decorated rooms; two even have their own roof terraces. Breakfast (not included) is served in the rooms. The *Alle Meraviglie* (⊕www.allemeraviglie .it), next door at no. 8, is run by the same people, with similarly bright, tasteful rooms. M Cairoli. ❻

Antica Locanda Leonardo Corso Magenta 78 ℡02.4801.4197, ⊕www.anticalocandaleonardo .com. This discreet three-star is just steps away from *The Last Supper* and has light and airy rooms, some overlooking a pretty internal garden. M Cadorna. ❺

Ariston Largo Carobbio 2 ℡02.7200.0556, ⊕www.aristonhotel.com. The best thing about this pleasant modern hotel is its position – within walking distance of the Duomo and the Navigli – and the free bicycles. Rooms are a little cramped

but all en suite and there's a decent breakfast included in the price. M Duomo, then tram #2, #3 or #14. ❺

Bulgari Via Fratelli Gabba 7/B ℡02.058.051, ⊕www.bulgarihotels.com. In a hidden corner of Brera, the city's top hotel has all the Milanese style you could wish for and none of the attitude you might expect. Staff are charming, facilities impeccable and the bar terrace and garden are an absolute treat. Rooms start at around €350 per night depending on special offers. M Montenapoleone. ❾

Casa Mia Viale Vittorio Veneto 30 ℡02.657.5249, ⊕www.casamiahotel.it. A spotless if slightly dowdy hotel with quiet en-suite rooms, just across from the Giardini Pubblici. All rooms have a/c and internet. Breakfast is included. M Repubblica. ❸

Cavour Via Fatebenefratelli 21 ℡02.620.001, ⊕www.hotelcavour.it. A business-oriented hotel in a great position between the Giardini Pubblici and the Quadrilatero d'Oro. Service is well judged and the comfortable, soundproofed rooms are good value. M Montenapoleone or Turati. ⑤

Kennedy Viale Tunisia 6, 6th floor ☏02.2940.0934, Ⓦwww.kennedyhotel.it. A well-organized, friendly one-star with bright, simple rooms, some of which are en suite. Some rooms even have their own balconies overlooking the rooftops. M Repubblica or Pta Venezia. ❷

London Via Rovello 3 ☏02.7202.0166, Ⓦwww.hotellondonmilano.com. A pleasant, family-run hotel in a good, central position. There's a choice of singles and doubles with or without en-suite shower; the decor is unexciting but all rooms have a/c. M Cairoli. ⑤

Mercure Milano Porta Venezia 1 ☏02.2940.0937, Ⓦwww.mercure.com. One of the city's several branches of this French hotel chain, offering pleasant, comfortable rooms in a convenient location right on Porta Venezia. M Pta Venezia. ⑥

Palazzo delle Stelline Corso Magenta 61 ☏02.481.8431, Ⓦwww.hotelpalazzostelline.it. Plain but pleasant rooms are set around the attractive courtyard of a renovated seventeenth-century convent opposite Santa Maria delle Grazie. The complex has an appealing garden where Leonardo da Vinci supposedly tended the vines while working on *The Last Supper*. M Cadorna. ⑤

Rovello Via Rovello 18a ☏02.8646.4654, Ⓦwww.hotel-rovello.it. Close to Castello Sforzesco, the spacious rooms at this well-located hotel are en suite and have a/c. You're paying for the location, but rates may be negotiable in summer. Breakfast included. M Cairoli. ⑤

Valley Via Soperga 19 ☏02.669.2777, Ⓦwww.hotelvalley.it. 2min walk north of the Stazione Centrale, this simple little spot is a good choice if you're catching an early train or arriving late at night. Most rooms are en suite and those at the back are pleasant and airy. M Centrale FS. ❷

Hostels and campsites

Autodromo Parco di Monza, Monza ☏039.387.771, Ⓦwww.monzanet.it. A leafy campsite in the old royal hunting grounds just north of Milan, which also house the famous Monza Formula 1 circuit. Trains run from Stazione Centrale to Monza, from where it's a short bus ride. May–Sept.

Città di Milano Via G. Airaghi 61 ☏02.4820.7017, Ⓦwww.campingmilano.it. The nearest campsite to the centre, but still a metro trip and a bus ride away. M1 to De Angeli, then bus #72. Open all year.

La Cordata Via Burigozzo 11, off Corso Italia ☏02.5831.4675, Ⓦwww.lacordata.it. Clean and basic in a very good central location, this is Milan's best hostel option by far. Bunks are in single-sex 6-, 10- or 16-bed dorms, each dorm with its own shower room. There's a large kitchen and communal room for residents' use. M Missori, or 4 stops on tram #15 from Piazza Fontana. €21 with sheets.

Ostello Piero Rotta Viale Salmoiraghi 1, corner Via Martino Bassi ☏02.3926.7095. An institutional-feeling HI hostel out in the insalubrious north-western suburbs near the San Siro football stadium. Metro line 1 to QT8, then walk 200m straight ahead and the hostel is on your right. €19 including breakfast.

The City

The obvious focal point of central Milan is Piazza Duomo, which, as well as being home to the city's iconic **Duomo**, leads on to the elegant **Galleria Vittorio Emanuele** and the Piazza della Scala, home to the world-famous **opera house**. Heading northwest along the shopping street of Via Dante takes you to the imperious **Castello Sforzesco** and the extensive **Parco Sempione** beyond. North, the well-heeled neighbourhoods of **Brera** and **Moscova** are the haunt of Milan's most style-conscious citizens. Here you'll find the fine art collection of the **Pinacoteca di Brera** and, nearby, the so-called **Quadrilatero d'Oro** (Golden Quadrangle), a concentration of top designer fashion boutiques. Slightly further north is Milan's most pleasant park, the **Giardini Pubblici**. Southwest of the Duomo, the shopping streets of Via Torino take you to the **Ticinese** district, a focal point at *aperitivo* time, and home to a couple of the city's most beautiful ancient churches. Continuing south to the **Navigli** leads to the bar and restaurant area around the city's remaining canals. West of the cathedral stands the church of **Santa Maria delle Grazie** and the adjacent refectory building, holding Leonardo da Vinci's *The Last Supper*. The

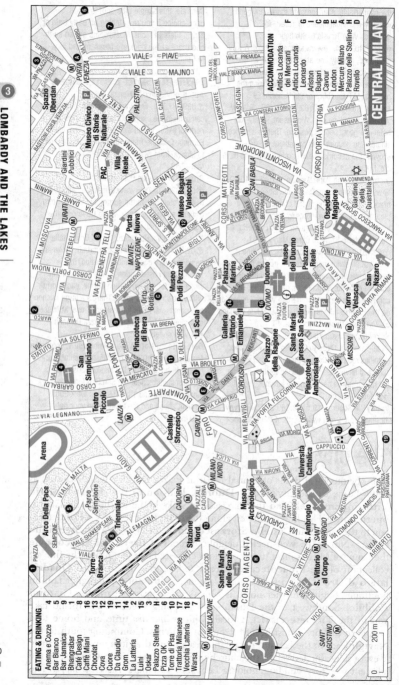

CENTRAL MILAN

ACCOMMODATION
Antica Locanda	F
Antica Locanda dei Mercanti	G
Leonardo	I
Ariston	C
Bulgari	B
Cavour	E
London	A
Mercure Milano	H
Palazzo delle Stelline	D
Rovello	

EATING & DRINKING
Anema e Cozze	4
Bar Bianco	5
Bar Jamaica	9
Bhangrabar	1
Café Design	8
Caffè Miani	16
Chocolat	13
Cova	12
Cuore	19
Da Claudio	11
Grom	14
La Latteria	2
Luini	15
Oskar	3
Palazzo Stelline	6
Pizza OK	10
Torre di Pisa	17
Trattoria Milanese	18
Vecchia Latteria	7

Museo Archeologico gives a taste of Roman Milan, while the basilica of Milan's Christian father, Sant'Ambrogio, is a couple of blocks away.

Piazza del Duomo and around

The hub of the city is **Piazza del Duomo**, a large, mostly pedestrianized square that's rarely quiet at any time of day, lorded over by the exaggerated spires of the **Duomo**, Milan's cathedral. The piazza was given its present form in 1860 when medieval buildings were demolished to allow grander, unobstructed views of the cathedral, and the **Galleria Vittorio Emanuele II** was constructed to link the piazza with the showy new opera theatre, **La Scala**. South of the piazza there are several minor gems hidden among the shops and offices in the shape of the tiny church of **Santa Maria presso San Satiro** and the seventeenth-century **Pincacoteca Ambrosiana**.

The Duomo

Milan's vast **Duomo** was begun in 1386 under the Viscontis, but not completed until the finishing touches to the facade were added in 1813. It is characterized by a hotchpotch of styles that range from Gothic to Neoclassical. From the **outside** at least it's incredible, notable as much for its strange confection of Baroque and Gothic decoration as its sheer size. The marble, chosen by the Viscontis in preference to the usual material of brick, was brought on specially built canals from the quarries of Candoglia, near Lake Maggiore, and continues to be used in renovation today.

The **interior** is striking for its dimension and atmosphere. The five aisles are separated by 52 towering piers, while an almost subterranean half-light filters through the stained-glass windows, lending the marble columns a bone-like hue that led the French writer Suarés to compare the interior to "the hollow of a colossal beast".

By the entrance, the narrow brass strip embedded in the pavement with the signs of the zodiac alongside is Europe's largest **sundial**, laid out in 1786. A beam of light still falls on it through a hole in the ceiling, though changes in the Earth's axis mean that it's no longer accurate. To the left of the entrance you'll find the remains of a fourth-century **Battistero Paleocristiano** (daily 9.30am–5.15pm; €2), where the city's patron saint, Ambrogio, baptized St Augustine in 387 AD.

At the far end of the church, the large crucifix suspended high above the chancel contains the most important of the Duomo's holy relics – **a nail from Christ's cross**, which was also crafted into the bit for the bridle of Emperor Constantine's horse. The cross is lowered once a year, on September 14, the Feast of the Cross, by a device invented by Leonardo da Vinci. Close by, beneath the presbytery, is the **Scurolo di San Carlo** (daily 9am–noon & 2.30–6pm; €1), a crypt housing the remains of San Carlo Borromeo, the zealous sixteenth-century cardinal who was canonized for his work among the poor of the city, especially during the Plague of 1630. He lies here in a glass coffin, clothed, bejewelled, masked and gloved, wearing a gold crown attributed to Cellini. Borromeo was also responsible for the large altar in the north transept, erected to close off a door that was used by locals as a shortcut to the market. Adjacent to Borromeo's resting place, the **treasury** (€3) features extravagant silverwork, Byzantine ivory carvings and heavily embroidered vestments. Here, too, is the Duomo's most surprising exhibit: British artist Mark Wallinger's haunting video installation *Via Dolorosa*. Commissioned by the diocese of Milan in a bold attempt to resurrect the role of the Church as a patron of the arts, it comprises a large screen showing the last eighteen minutes of Zeffirelli's *Jesus of Nazareth*,

③

▲ Detail of flying buttress, Milan Duomo

with 90 percent of the image blacked-out, leaving just a narrow frame visible round the sides.

To the right of the chancel, by the door to the Palazzo Reale, the sixteenth-century statue of **St Bartholomew**, with his flayed skin thrown like a toga over his shoulder, is one of the church's more gruesome statues, its veins, muscles and bones sculpted with anatomical accuracy and the draped skin retaining the form of knee, foot, toes and toenails.

Outside again, from the northwest end of the cathedral you can get to the **cathedral roof** (daily: mid-Feb to mid-Nov 9am–5.45pm; rest of year 9am–4.15pm; €5, or €7 with the lift), where you can stroll around the forest of tracery, pinnacles and statues while enjoying fine views of the city and on clear days even the Alps. The highlight is the central spire, its lacy marble crowned by a gilded statue of the Madonna – the *Madonnina*, the city's guardian – in summer looking out over the roof-top sunbathers.

Santa Maria presso San Satiro

The charming little church of **Santa Maria presso San Satiro** (daily 8–11am & 3.30–6.30pm), off the busy shopping street of Via Torino, is a study in ingenuity, commissioned from Milan's foremost Renaissance architect, Bramante, in 1478. Originally the oratory of the adjacent ninth-century church of San Satiro, it was transformed by Bramante into a long-naved basilica, by converting the long oblong oratory into the transept and adding a wonderful trompe l'oeil apse to the back wall.

Pinacoteca Ambrosiana

Five minutes west, just off Via Torino at Piazza Pio 2, the **Pinacoteca Ambrosiana** (Tues–Sun 10am–5.30pm; €8; Ⓦ www.ambrosiana.it) was founded in the early seventeenth century by Cardinal Federico Borromeo, who assembled one of the largest libraries in Europe (Mon–Fri 9.30am–5pm). The main draw though is his **art** collection, stamped with his taste for Jan Brueghel, sixteenth-century Venetians and some of the more kitsch followers of Leonardo. Among many mediocre works, there is a rare painting by Leonardo da Vinci, *Portrait of a Musician*, a cartoon by Raphael for the School of Athens, and a Caravaggio considered to be Italy's first still-life. The prize for the quirkiest exhibit is shared between a pair of white gloves that Napoleon reputedly wore at Waterloo, and a lock of Lucrezia Borgia's hair – displayed for safe-keeping in a glass phial ever since Byron (having decided that her hair was the most beautiful he had ever seen) extracted a strand as a keepsake from the library downstairs, where it used to be kept unprotected.

Galleria Vittorio Emanuele II

Leading off to the north of Piazza Duomo is the gaudily opulent **Galleria Vittorio Emanuele II**, a cruciform glass-domed gallery designed in 1865 by Giuseppe Mengoni, who was killed when he fell from the roof a few days before the inaugural ceremony. The circular mosaic beneath the glass cupola is composed of the symbols that made up the cities of the newly unified Italy: Romulus and Remus for Rome, a *fleur-de-lys* for Florence, a white shield with a red cross for Milan and a bull for Turin – it's considered good luck to spin round three times on the bull's testicles, hence the indentation in the floor.

The *galleria* was designed as a covered walkway between the Piazza del Duomo and Piazza della Scala to the north; nicknamed the "*salotto*" – or drawing room – of Milan, it used to be the focal point for the parading Milanese on their *passeggiata*. These days, visitors rather than locals are more likely to swallow the extortionate prices at the gallery's cafés, which include the historic *Zucca*, with its glorious 1920s tiled interior at one end, and the newer, stylish *Gucci Café* – the label's first foray into catering – at the other. Shops, too, are aimed at visitors to the city, with top designer labels sitting next to pricey souvenir outlets. Somehow, however, the *galleria* still manages to retain most of its original dignity, helped along by quietly elegant boutiques selling handmade leather gloves or carefully turned hats, and the handsome eighty-year-old Prada shop in the centre.

Teatro alla Scala

The main branch of Galleria Vittorio Emanuele leads through to **Piazza della Scala**, fronted by the rather plain Neoclassical facade of the world-famous Teatro alla Scala opera house, popularly known as **La Scala** (Ⓦwww.teatroallascala.org). The theatre was commissioned by Empress Maria Theresa of Austria from the architect Piermarini and opened in 1778 with the opera *Europa Riconsciuta* by Antonio Salieri. Many of the leading names in Italian opera had their major works premiered here, including Bellini, Donizetti and Rossini, but it is **Giuseppe Verdi** who is most closely associated with the opera house and whose fame was consolidated here in 1842 with the first performance of *Nabucco*, with its perfectly timed patriotic sentiments. The post-World War II period saw another breathtaking roll call of top composers and musical performers – among them Schoenberg, Lucio Berio, Rudolf Nureyev and Maria Callas – while Toscanini, perhaps the most influential conductor of all time, devoted more than fifty years to the theatre. These days, however, La Scala is a bit at sea: no quality Italian composers have emerged for over eighty years, the theatre is plagued by internal political problems and the repertoire has become a touch predictable.

To a great extent, the opera house is still the social and cultural centre of Milan's elite and although protests in the 1960s led to a more open official policy on the arts in Milan, unusually for opera-going in Italy it remains as exclusive a venue as it ever was. Every year on the opening night – December 7, the festival of Milan's patron saint, Sant'Ambrogio – when fur coats and dinner jackets are out in force, it is the target for demonstrations from political and social groups, ranging from animal rights' campaigners to local factory workers complaining about redundancies. **Tickets** can be hard to come by, but if you want to experience one of the world's most famous opera houses in action, there are numerous avenues; see p.175 for ticket information.

Tucked in one corner of the theatre, a small **museum** (daily 9am–12.30pm & 1.30–5pm; €5), features costumes, sets, composers' death masks, plaster casts of conductors' hands and a rugged statue of Puccini in a capacious overcoat. A visit to the auditorium is included in the ticket, providing there is no rehearsal taking place; times when the auditorium is empty are listed daily outside the entrance to the museum.

The Castello Sforzesco and around

Northwest out of Piazza Duomo, at the start of Via Dante, lies **Piazza dei Mercanti**, the commercial centre of medieval Milan. The square is dominated by the thirteenth-century **Palazzo della Ragione**, where council meetings and tribunals were held on the upper floor, with markets under the porticoes below. The stone relief on the facade above the arcade shows the rather forlorn-looking Oldrado di Tressano, the mayor who commissioned the building in 1228, astride his horse. Opposite, the striped black-and-white marble **Loggia degli Orsi**, built in 1316, was where council proclamations were made and sentences announced. The coats of arms of the various districts of Milan are just about visible beneath the grime left by Milanese smog.

At the far end of the pedestrianized Via Dante, the Castello Sforzesco rises imperiously from Foro Buonaparte, a road laid out by Napoleon in self-tribute. He had a vision of a grand new centre for the Italian capital, designed along Roman lines, but he only got as far as constructing an arena, a triumphal arch and these two semicircular roads before he lost Milan to the Austrians. The arena and triumphal arch still stand half forgotten behind the castle on the edges of the **Parco Sempione**, the city centre's largest patch of green and once the castle's garden and hunting grounds.

Castello Sforzesco

With its crenellated towers and fortified walls, the red-brick castle **Castello Sforzesco** (Ⓦ www.milanocastello.it) is one of Milan's most striking landmarks. The result of numerous rebuildings, it was begun by the Viscontis, destroyed by mobs rebelling against their regime in 1447, and rebuilt by their successors, the Sforzas. Under Lodovico Sforza the court became one of the most powerful, luxurious and cultured of the Renaissance, renowned for its ostentatious wealth and court artists like Leonardo and Bramante. Lodovico's days of glory came to an end when Milan was invaded by the French in 1499, and from then until the end of the nineteenth century the castle was used as a barracks by successive occupying armies. Just over a century ago it was converted into a series of museums. Ongoing restoration means that parts of the complex may be closed when you visit.

The *castello's* buildings are grouped around three courtyards: through the **Filarete Tower** (rebuilt in 1905, having been destroyed in the sixteenth century by an explosion of gunpowder) you enter the larger of the three, the dusty-looking parade ground. It's not until you're through the gateway opposite that you begin to sense a Renaissance castle: this is the Corte Ducale, which formed the centre of the residential quarters and is now the home of the castle's museums. The **Rocchetta**, to your left, was the most secure part of the fortress and is now used for temporary exhibitions. The gateway ahead leads to the Parco Sempione.

The **ticket office** (Tues–Sun 9am–5.30pm; combined ticket €3), on your right as you enter the Corte Ducale, gives access to the **Museo d'Arte Antica**, a succession of rooms containing an extensive collection of ancient artefacts saved from the city's churches and archeological excavations. More interesting than these, though, are the castle rooms themselves, especially the **Sala delle Asse**, designed by Leonardo da Vinci; his black-and-white preparatory sketches were discovered in the 1950s. After some rather dull armoury you reach the museum's star exhibit: Michelangelo's **Rondanini Pietà**, which the artist worked on for the last nine years of his life. It's an unfinished but oddly powerful work; much of the marble is unpolished and a third arm, indicating a change of position for Christ's body, hangs limply from a block of stone to his right.

Upstairs, the **Museo delle Arti Decorative** exhibits furniture and decorative arts through the ages, including fascinating early works by the great twentieth-century Milanese designer, Gio Ponte. The Torre Falconiere (the Falconry Tower) next door holds the castle's **art collection** containing numerous paintings by Lombard artists such as Foppa and Bramantino, as well as minor Venetian works, including some Canalettos. The best are all grouped together in Room XIII and include Antonello da Messina's *St Benedict*, originally part of a five-piece polyptych, of which two panels are in the Uffizi in Florence.

Across the courtyard, in the castle cellars, are the smaller **Egyptian collection**, with displays of mummies, sarcophagi and papyrus fragments from *The Book of the Dead*, and the deftly lit **prehistoric collection** – an assortment of finds from the Iron Age burial grounds of the Golasecca civilization.

Parco Sempione

The **Parco Sempione** can make a refreshing break from the city's traffic-choked roads, but it does have its sleazy side and you might feel more comfortable visiting when the locals do – at the weekend, or early evening in summer. That said, there are several sights within the park itself, the most interesting of which is the Palazzo dell'Arte or **Triennale** (Tues–Sun 10.30am–8.30pm; temporary exhibitions €8; Ⓦwww.triennale.it), on the western reaches, at Viale Emilio Alemagna 6. The soaring lines of the building and its light airy interior are reason enough for a visit, but the *palazzo* also holds good-quality temporary exhibitions of design, architecture and contemporary art, and there's the great *Café Design* (see p.173), which overflows into the park in the summer.

You might want to catch a bird's-eye view of the city from the nearby **Torre Branca** (Wed 10.30am–12.30pm & 4–6.30pm, Sat 10.30am–1pm, 3–6.30pm & 8.30pm–midnight, Sun 10.30am–2pm & 2.30–7pm; €3), designed by Gio Ponte on the occasion of the fifth Triennale in 1933, or keep children entertained at the **Aquario Civico** (Tues–Sun 9am–1pm & 2–5.30pm; free; Ⓦwww.verdeacqua .eu), a pretty Liberty building with a small collection of tanks.

Brera and Moscova

Due north of Via Manzoni, **Via Brera** sets the tone for Milan's arty quarter: small galleries nestle in the lanes surrounding the Accademia di Belle Arti and **Pinacoteca Brera**. As you'll notice from the café prices and designer styles of those who can afford to sit outside them, these cobbled streets are the terrain of the urban rich.

Across Via Fatebenefratelli, the stylish bars and traditional trattorias continue north through the neighbourhood of **Moscova**, home to the offices of the *Corriere della Sera* newspaper. A good area for shopping and browsing, Corso Garibaldi, Via Solferino and Via San Marco lead up to the bastion in Piazza XXV Aprile, which marks the beginning of **Corso Como**, a trendy street full of bars, clubs and boutiques, which in turn leads up to the train and bus station of Porto Garibaldi.

Pinacoteca di Brera

Milan's most prestigious art gallery, the **Pinacoteca di Brera**, Via Brera 28 (Tues–Sun 8.30am–7.15pm; €5; Ⓦwww.brera.beniculturali.it), was opened to the public in 1809 by Napoleon, who filled the building with works looted from the churches and aristocratic collections of French-occupied Italy. It's big: your visit will probably be more enjoyable if you're selective, dipping into the collection guided by your own personal tastes. There's a good **audioguide** available (€3.50), although it does rather gallop through the highlights.

Not surprisingly, most of the museum's paintings are Italian and predate the twentieth century. Some later works are on display, including by Modigliani, De Chirico and Carrà (Room X), but it's the Renaissance which comprises the museum's core. There's a good representation of Venetian painters – works by Bonifacio and, a century later, Paolo **Veronese**, the latter weighing in with *Supper in the House of Simon* (Room IX). The painting got him into trouble with the Inquisition, who considered the introduction of frolicking animals and unruly kids unsuitable subject matter for a religious painting. **Tintoretto**'s *Pietà* (Room IX) was more in tune with requirements of the time (the 1560s), a scene of intense concentration and grief over Christ's body. **Gentile Bellini**'s *St Mark Preaching in St Euphemia Square* (Room VIII) introduces an exotic note: the square bustles with turbaned men, veiled women, camels and even a giraffe. There are also paintings by Gentile's follower, Carpaccio – *The Presentation of the Virgin* and *The Disputation of St Stephen* (Room VI) – along with a profoundly moving *Pietà* (Room VI) by Gentile's more talented brother, **Giovanni**. Look out also for *The Dead Christ* (Room VI), a painting by Giovanni Bellini's brother-in-law, **Mantegna**: it's an ingenious composition – viewed from

Christ's wrinkled and pierced soles upwards. One of Mantegna's sons had died around the time he was working on this painting and it seems that the desolation in the women's faces and the powerful sense of bereavement emanating from the work were autobiographical.

Later rooms hold yet more quality work, of which **Piero della Francesca**'s haunting *Madonna with Angels, Saints and Federigo da Montefeltro* (Room XXIV) is the most arresting. But take a look too at **Raphael**'s *Marriage of the Virgin* (Room XXIV), whose lucid, languid Renaissance mood is in sharp contrast to the grim realism of **Caravaggio**'s *Supper at Emmaus* (Room XXIX), which is set in a dark tavern. Less well known but equally lifelike are the paintings of Lombardy's brilliant eighteenth-century realist, Ceruti – known as **Il Pitocchetto** (The Little Beggar) for his unfashionable sympathy with the poor, who stare out with reproachful dignity from his canvases (Room XXXVI). **Francesco Hayez**'s Romantic-era *The Kiss* (Room XXXVII) is one of the most reproduced of the gallery's paintings, but the artist's fine portrait of the writer Alessandro Manzoni, in the same room, is far less saccharine. The collection ends with the unfinished *Fuimaria* (Room XXXVII) by Giuseppe **Pelizza da Volpedo**, a composition revealing the artist's socialist ideals and an emerging consciousness of people-power – a theme that he returned to for *The Fourth Estate* (*Il Quarto Stato*, see p.168).

Quadrilatero d'Oro

The Roman thoroughfare **Via Manzoni** leads north from La Scala to Porta Nuova, one of the medieval entrances to the city forming one side of the **Quadrilatero d'Oro**. Comprising a few hundred square metres bordered by Via Montenapoleone, Via Sant'Andrea, Via Spiga and Via Manzoni, the quarter is home to shops of all the big international and Italian fashion names, along with design studios and contemporary art galleries. This is Milan in its element and the area is well worth a wander if only to see the city's better-heeled residents in their favourite habitat. For more on shopping in Milan, see p.176.

Museo Bagatti Valsecchi

In a house linking Via Santo Spirito with Via Gesù 5, just off Via Montenapoleone, is the **Museo Bagatti Valsecchi** (Tues–Sun 1–5.45pm; €8; Ⓦ www .museobagattivalsecchi.org). Built by the Bagatti Valsecchi brothers in the nineteenth century in homage to Renaissance style, it served as a home for their family and their collections. All the rooms are richly decorated with carved fireplaces, painted ceilings and heavy wall-hangings and paintings. The fireplace in the drawing room perfectly illustrates the brothers' eclectic approach to decoration: the main surround is sixteenth-century Venetian, the frescoes in the middle are from Cremona, while the whole ensemble is topped off with the Bagatti Valsecchi coat of arms. Modern conveniences were incorporated into the house but not allowed to ruin the harmony, so the shower in the bathroom is disguised in a niche, and the piano, which was not realized as an instrument until the eighteenth century, is incorporated within a cabinet. Look out also for touching domestic items, such as the nursery furniture for Giuseppe's children.

Museo Poldi Pezzoli

Halfway between La Scala and Porta Nuova, the eclectic **Museo Poldi Pezzoli** at Via Manzoni 12 (Tues–Sun 10am–6pm; €8; Ⓦ www.museopoldipezzoli.it) comprises pieces assembled by the nineteenth-century collector Gian Giacomo Poldi Pezzoli. Much of this is made up of rather dull rooms of clocks, watches, cutlery and jewellery, but the Salone Dorato upstairs contains a number of intriguing paintings, including a portrait of a portly San Nicola da Tolentino by Piero della Francesca, part of an altarpiece on which he worked intermittently for fifteen years. St Nicholas looks across at two works by Botticelli; one a gentle *Madonna del Libro*, among the many variations of the Madonna and Child theme which he produced at the end of the fifteenth century, and the other a mesmerizing *Deposition*, painted towards the end of his life in response to the monk Savonarola's crusade against his earlier, more humanistic canvases. Also in the room is the museum's best-known portrait, *Portrait of a Young Woman* by Pollaiuolo, whose anatomical studies are evidenced in the subtle suggestion of bone structure beneath skin.

The Giardini Pubblici

At the top of Piazza Cavour, on the northern side of Porta Nuova, lie the **Giardini Pubblici**, Milan's most attractive park. Designed by Piermarini shortly after he completed La Scala, the gardens stretch from Piazza Cavour over to Porta Venezia. Re-landscaped in the nineteenth century to give a more rustic look, the park, with its shady avenues, children's play areas and small lake, is ideal for a break from the busy streets.

Across the road, housed in Napoleon's former town residence, the **Villa Belgiojoso Bonaparte** (also called Villa Reale), is the **Museo dell'Ottocento**, Via Palestro 16 (Tues–Sun 9am–1pm & 2–5.30pm; free); skip through the unexciting collection of nineteenth-century art and sculpture to the striking canvas *Il Quarto Stato* by Giuseppe Pellizza da Volpedo, a member of the self-styled *scapigliati* ('wild-haired') movement of the late nineteenth century. Next door, the **Padiglione d'Arte Contemporanea** (PAC; Tues–Sun 9.30am–7.30pm, Thurs until 10.30pm; €6; Ⓦ www.comune.milano.it/pac) is a venue for decent, temporary exhibitions of contemporary art. Behind the art galleries, the **Giardini della Villa Reale** offer an urban oasis reserved for those with children under 13. With a small area of swings, lawns, shady trees and a little pond with ducks, turtles and giant carp, it makes a perfect bolthole.

The Ticinese district

Leading southwest away from the Duomo, past the chain stores of Via Torino, the city takes on a different, slightly more alternative air. The main thoroughfare of the **Ticinese** district, the Corso Porta Ticinese, has become a focus for fashion and is lined with small boutiques and bars. The area really comes into its own at *aperitivo* time, especially during summer when people spill on to the pedestrian streets from the numerous bars and cafés.

Towards the northern end of Corso Ticinese stands **San Lorenzo alle Colonne**, considered by Leonardo da Vinci to be the most beautiful church in Milan. It is indeed a graceful building with a quiet dignity, somewhat at odds with the skateboarding and partying that goes on in the piazza outside. One of the four churches founded by Sant'Ambrogio in the city in the fourth century, it was built with masonry salvaged from various Roman buildings. The sixteen Corinthian columns outside – the **Colonne di San Lorenzo** – were placed here as a portico to the church. To the right of the altar, the **Cappella di San Aquilino** (daily 7.30am–6pm; €2) was probably built as an imperial mausoleum. The lunettes in the Roman octagonal room hold beautiful fourth-century mosaics, which would originally have covered all the walls, while beneath the relics of St Aquilino steps lead down to what is left of the original foundations, a jigsaw of fragments of Roman architecture.

Heading south down Corso Ticinese, you come to **Sant'Eustorgio**, another fourth-century church, built to house the bones of the Magi, said to have been

Italian food

Not only does Italian food taste better on its home soil, but there's a regional variety that makes travelling from place to place a fantastic gastronomic experience. Every region thinks their way of cooking is the best, and will argue fiercely as to why. However, the one thing that every Italian you meet will agree on is that the food in Italy is the world's greatest. For more on each region's cuisine, see the box at the beginning of the Guide chapters. Buon appetito!

The north

The northern regions are home to the country's richest cuisine. **Piemonte** is famous for its meat dishes in rich, creamy sauces, as well as its white **truffles**, most celebrated in the area around Alba (which has a huge truffle festival every year in Nov), and some excellent red wines. In Lombardy you're as likely to eat risotto as pasta as a starter, and meat dishes may come with **polenta** – yellow cornmeal – instead of potatoes. In the neighbouring region, **Veneto**, the emphasis not surprisingly is on fish – manifest in fantastic risottos and black, squid-ink flavoured pasta. Fish also features strongly in the food of **Liguria**, where you should make sure to try the *stoccafisso* or fish stew and shellfish soups. But this region also gives the first taste of the kind of food you will eat further south: its valleys produce the olive oil, pine nuts and basil that go to make the ubiquitous green pasta sauce, **pesto**.

Central Italy

Emilia-Romagna is celebrated for being the Italian culinary heartland, known for its salami and cheeses, pork dishes, rich pasta sauces and fresh filled pasta, as well as **Parma ham** and **parmesan** cheese – products from the rich farmlands of the nearby Po plains. In contrast, the cuisine of **Tuscany** and to some extent neighbouring **Umbria** is simple: the trademark dish in both regions is *bistecca alla fiorentina*, chargrilled steaks from the cattle of Tuscany's Maremma plain. As in the south, **olive oil** rather than butter is used for cooking, but you're still not in pasta country, and the pasta you find tends to be fresh rather than the more common dried variety or *pasta asciutta*. **Marche** and **Abruzzo** are known for their game, and

Mercato Centrale, Florence ▲

Fresh seafood, Palermo ▼

Tuscan specialities on sale, Arezzo ▼

the cheese of choice in all these central regions is sheep's milk pecorino, which varies from the young and sweet to the sharp, salty crumble of pecorino Romano – in Rome they use it in cooking instead of Parmesan. In these central regions, you'll also find *porchetta*, or pork stuffed with herbs and roasted on a spit. Rome forms the boundary between the Italian north and south in many ways, and food is no exception. Its denizens favour pasta dishes, thick spaghetti and noodles mainly, with rough, peasant sauces. Some of the most well-known pasta sauces hail from here; *alla carbonarara* and *alla amatriciana* are Roman varieties. The city is also known for its Italian-Jewish specialities – deep-fried courgette flowers, offal dishes and *baccalà* (deep-fried cod fillets).

▲ Penne with grated pecorino

▼ Rialto market, Venice

Pasta: an a to z

Garibaldi swore that **pasta** would unite Italy, and he could have been right. There are literally hundreds of different pasta shapes, each of which are designated a number. Some, like spaghetti (number 12 in case you were wondering), you will find more or less everywhere; others are less common and usually indigenous to one particular part of the country.

▶▶ **agnolotti** literally "lambs' ears" – semicircular filled pasta pockets.

▶▶ **capelli d'angeli** very thin noodles, literally "angels' hair".

▶▶ **conchigliette** small shell-like shapes often used in soup.

▶▶ **gemelli** loose spirals of pasta.

▶▶ **manicotti** large ridged tubes, often stuffed.

▶▶ **orzo** pasta shaped like grains of rice.

▶▶ **paccheri** large tubes of pasta.

▶▶ **rotini** tight spirals of pasta.

▶▶ **strozzapreti** literally "strangled priests" – twisted flat noodles.

▶▶ **vermicelli** thin strand pasta often served in soup – literally "little worms".

▶▶ **ziti** narrow tubes.

Shopping for seafood, Venice ▲

Coffee and cannoli, Palermo ▼

The south

Southern Italy's staples include pasta, olive oil, fresh fruit and vegetables, particularly tomatoes, and fish and seafood – perhaps Italy's healthiest diet. Yet the cuisine of the south is just as complex as that of the north, and its regions as diverse. Flat breads originated here, notably focaccia, though this has spread all over the country, much like Naples' signature pasta dish of *spaghetti al pomodoro*: a simple delight of which the mayor of Naples said, "The angels in paradise eat nothing but *pasta al pomodoro*." Cheese is also the Campania region's big attraction, most notably – and deliciously – the soft white mozzarella made from the milk of the buffalo that are kept on farms south of Naples. Further south, the food reflects the influence of Arabs and Greeks, who between them brought great sweets and desserts, and a liking for spicier food. In Puglia lamb is the meat of choice. Sicily, meanwhile, has a cuisine almost of its own with ultra-sweet pastries such as ricotta-filled *cannoli* and plenty of dishes featuring couscous. Sardinia, too, has a number of unique delicacies – really pungent pecorino, and its own peculiar, wafer-thin flat bread, *carta di musica*.

Taking it slow

Created to promote the pleasures of food and drink and encouraging the use of local, high-quality ingredients, the **Slow Food movement** originated in Bra, Piemonte in 1986. It has grown from an initial 62 members in the mid-1980s to more than 80,000 in 100 different countries. Piemonte is still its main base, though, and every October Turin hosts the annual Salone del Gusto and Terra Madre conventions. See www.slowfood.com for more details.

brought here by Sant'Ambrogio. It was rebuilt in the eleventh century, and in the twelfth century was virtually destroyed by Barbarossa, who seized the Magi's bones and deposited them in Cologne's cathedral. Some of the bones were returned in 1903 and are kept in a Roman sarcophagus tucked away in the right transept. A must-see while here is the **Portinari Chapel**, accessed round to the left of the main entrance (Tues–Sun 10am–6pm; €6). The beautiful chapel consciously recalls Brunelleschi's San Lorenzo in Florence, with two domed rooms, the smaller one housing the altar. It has been credited with being Milan's first true Renaissance building because of its simple geometric design; the mixture of Lombard terracotta sculpture and Florentine monochromatic simplicity makes an enchanting stylistic fusion. It was commissioned from the Florentine architect Michelozzi in the 1460s by one Pigello Portinari, an agent of the Medici bank, to house the remains of St Peter the Martyr, an unattractive saint who was excommunicated for entertaining women in his cell, then cleared and given a job as an Inquisitor.

The Navigli

The southern end of Corso di Porta Ticinese is guarded by the nineteenth-century **Arco di Porta Ticinese**, marking the beginning of Milan's canal – or

---

Milan's canals

Improbable though it may seem, less than fifty years ago Milan was still a viable port – and less than a hundred years ago several of its main arteries – including Via Senato and Via San Marco – were busy waterways.

It was only logical for Milan's powers to want to harness the surrounding rivers for both trade and military purposes. In the twelfth century, the first **canals** linked irrigation channels and the various defensive moats of the city. Later, in 1386, the **Naviglio Grande** was opened, linking the city to the River Ticino and thus Lake Maggiore. It was Gian Galeazzo Visconti, however, who was really responsible for the development of the system, in the fourteenth century. Looking for a way to transport the building materials for the Duomo, especially marble from Lake Maggiore, he invited proposals for solving the various logistical problems involved: Leonardo da Vinci is said to have had a hand in the invention of a system of locks developed to compensate for the different water levels of the canals.

Travellers were also seen on the canals: the ruling families of the North used them to visit one another, Prospero and Miranda escaped along the Navigli in *The Tempest*, and they were still plied by the Grand Tourists in the eighteenth century; Goethe, for example, describes the hazards of journeying by canal.

A number of rivers and canals were added to the system over the centuries; the Spanish developed the **Darsena** to the south in 1603 and under Napoleon's regime the **Naviglio Pavese** was made navigable all the way to Pavia and down to the River Po, and so to the Adriatic. During the Industrial Revolution, raw materials like coal, iron and silk were brought into the city, and handmade products transported out with an efficiency that ensured Milan's commercial and economic dominance of the region. The process of covering over the canals began in the 1930s, to make way for the city's trams and trolley buses. In the 1950s, desperately needed materials were floated in for reconstructing the badly bombed city but by the mid-1970s, only a handful of canals were left uncovered; the last working boat plied the waters in 1977.

The best way to explore Milan's waterways is on a relaxing **boat trip**, which run between April and mid-September when the canals are not being dredged or cleaned; for more information ask at the tourist office or check ⓦ www.navigilombardi .it. Alternatively, grab some mosquito repellent, don a pair of walking shoes or rent a bike (see p.178) and head off down the towpaths into the paddy fields of Lombardy.

Navigli – neighbourhood, once a bustling industrial area and these days a focus for the city's nightlife. Much lauded by tourist brochures, the area is scruffy and often disappointing in the harsh light of day. The best time to visit is in the evening when the quarter's many restaurants and bars come alive, although the monthly Sunday **antiques street-market** (closed July & Aug) also brings a vivacious focus to the waterways.

South from the Darsena, the **Naviglio Grande** and the **Naviglio Pavese**, respectively the first and last of the city's canals to be completed, lead into the plains of Lombardy. This was once Milan at its grittiest. Some of the warehouses and traditional tenement blocks, or *case ringhere*, have been refurbished and become prime real estate but you'll still find plenty of unreconstructed corners. Craftsmen and artists have moved in and although the overpriced craft and antique shops won't hold your attention for long, a wander round the streets, popping into open courtyards, will give you a feel of the neighbourhood. Take a look at the prettified Vicolo dei Lavandai (Washerwomen's Alley), near the beginning of the Naviglio Grande, where washerwomen scrubbed smalls in the murky canal waters.

Five-minutes' walk west from the Naviglio Grande is **Porta Genova**, the train station for Milan's southern outskirts. It is also the name given to one of Milan's up-and-coming areas. Across the tracks from the train station, bars and restaurants have moved in and disused warehouses and factories are being reclaimed by photographers, fashion houses and designers. Giorgio Armani has an exhibition space and workshops here, as does Prada.

Santa Maria delle Grazie and around

Due west from the Duomo, on Corso Magenta, stands the attraction that brings most visitors to Milan – the beautiful terracotta-and-brick church of **Santa Maria delle Grazie**, famous for its mural of **The Last Supper** by Leonardo da Vinci. Originally built as a Gothic church by the architect Solari, it was part of the Dominican monastery that headed the Inquisition in the fifteenth and sixteenth centuries. Soon after its completion, Lodovico Sforza commissioned Bramante to rework and model the Gothic structure into a grand dynastic mausoleum. Bramante promptly tore down the existing chancel and replaced it with a massive dome supported by an airy Renaissance cube. Lodovico also intended to replace the nave and facade, but was unable to do so before Milan fell to the French, leaving an odd combination of styles – Gothic vaults, decorated in powdery blues, reds and ochre, illuminated by the light that floods through the windows of Bramante's dome. A side door leads into Bramante's cool and tranquil cloisters, from which there's a good view of the sixteen-sided drum the architect placed around his dome.

The Last Supper

Leonardo's *The Last Supper* – signposted **Cenacolo Vinciano** – is one of the world's great paintings and most resonant images. However, getting to see art of this magnitude doesn't come easy: **visits must be booked** in advance, at least a month (or more) in summer and at weekends (English-speaking reservations line Mon–Fri 9am–6pm, Sat 9am–2pm; ☎02.8942.1146, ⓦwww .cenacolovinciano.org; viewing Tues–Sun 8.15am–6.45pm; €6.50, plus €1.50 obligatory booking fee). If it's fully booked when you ring, try asking about cancellations: people don't always turn up for the early-morning viewings so it might be worth chancing your luck and going to the desk. At your allotted hour, once you've passed through a series of air-filtering systems, your fifteen-minute slot face-to-face with the masterpiece begins.

Henry James likened the painting to an "illustrious invalid" that people visited with "leave-taking sighs and almost death-bed or tip-toe precautions"; certainly it's hard, when you visit the fragile painting, not to feel that it's the last time you'll see it. A twenty-year restoration process has re-established the original colours using contemporary descriptions and copies, but that the work survived at all is something of a miracle. Leonardo's decision to use oil paint rather than the more usual faster-drying – and longer-lasting – fresco technique with watercolours led to the painting disintegrating within five years of its completion. A couple of centuries later Napoleonic troops billeted here used the wall for target practice. And, in 1943, an Allied bomb destroyed the building, amazingly leaving only *The Last Supper*'s wall standing.

A *Last Supper* was a conventional theme for refectory walls, but Leonardo's decision to capture the moment when Christ announces that one of his disciples will betray him imbues the work with an unprecedented sense of drama. Leonardo spent two years on the mural, wandering the streets of Milan searching for and sketching models. When the monks complained that the face of Judas was still unfinished, Leonardo replied that he had been searching for over a year among the city's criminals for a sufficiently evil visage, and that if he didn't find one he would use the face of the prior. Whether or not Judas is modelled on the prior is unrecorded, but Leonardo's Judas does seem, as Vasari wrote, "the very embodiment of treachery and inhumanity".

Goethe commented on how very Italian the painting was in that so much is conveyed through the expressions of the characters' hands; the group of Matthew, Thaddaeus and Simon on the far right of the mural could be discussing a football match or the latest government scandal in any bar in Italy today. The only disciple not gesticulating or protesting in some way is the recoiling Judas who has one hand clenched while a bread roll has just dropped dramatically out of the other. Christ is calmly reaching out to share his bread with him while his other hand falls open in a gesture of sacrifice.

If you feel you need any confirmation of the emotional tenor or accomplishment of the painting, take a look at the contemporary *Crucifixion* by Montorfano on the wall at other end of the refectory, not a bad fresco in itself, but destined always to pale in comparison with da Vinci's masterpiece.

Museo Archeologico and Roman remains

The **Museo Archeologico**, in the ex-Monastero Maggiore at Corso Magenta 15 (Tues–Sun 9am–1pm & 2–5.30pm; €2, free on Fri after 2pm), is worth a quick visit for a glimpse of the city's Roman heritage. The displays of glass phials, kitchen utensils and jewellery from Roman Milan are compelling, and though there's a scarcity of larger objects, you can see a colossal stone head of Jupiter, found near the castle, a carved torso of Hercules, and a smattering of mosaic pavements unearthed around the city. Perhaps the most interesting sight, though, is the 24-sided tower in the internal courtyard of the museum that was part of the Roman wall of the city.

One block east from the museum, Via Brisa runs south alongside the ruins of the imperial palace of the Roman emperor Maximian, unearthed after World War II bombing. South of here towards Via Torino, the medieval plan of the streets belies the Roman origins of the neighbourhood, where remnants of ancient mosaics and masonry are incorporated into the current buildings.

Sant'Ambrogio

A few minutes' walk southwest from Corso Magenta, the church of **Sant'Ambrogio** (Mon–Sat 7.30am–12.30pm & 2.30–9pm, Sun 7.30am–1pm & 3–8pm) was founded in the fourth century by Milan's patron saint, St Ambrose. The saint's remains still lie in the church's crypt, but there's nothing left of the original church in which his most famous convert, St Augustine, first heard him preach.

The present twelfth-century church, the blueprint for many of Lombardy's Romanesque basilicas, is, however, one of the city's loveliest, reached through a colonnaded quadrangle with column capitals carved with rearing horses, contorted dragons and an assortment of bizarre predators. Inside, to the left of the nave, a freestanding Byzantine pillar is topped with a "magic" bronze serpent, symbolizing Aaron's rod. Look, too, at the pulpit, a superb piece of Romanesque carving decorated with reliefs of wild animals and the occasional human, most of whom are intent on devouring one another. There are older relics further down the nave, notably the ciborium, reliefed with the figures of saints Gervasius and Protasius – martyred Roman soldiers whose clothed bodies flank that of St Ambrose in the crypt.

Outside (entrance to the left of the choir) is Bramante's unfinished **Cortile della Canonica**. The side that Bramante did complete, a novel concoction incorporating knobbly columns and a triumphal arch, was shattered by a World War II bomb and reconstructed from the fragments; the second side was added only in 1955. The adjacent Benedictine monastery that the Sforza family commissioned Bramante to restructure has housed the **Università Cattolica** since the 1920s.

Eating

Milan has **restaurants** and **cafés** to suit every pocket and perhaps the widest choice of cuisine in Italy. Whether you're looking for a neighbourhood trattoria, want to watch models pick at their salads or crave a bit of well-priced ethnic food, Milan has it all – usually within easy reach of wherever you're staying. If you don't fancy a sit-down meal, make the most of the Milanese custom of **aperitivo** (see box below) to curb your hunger.

Un aperitivo

An Italian custom that has been honed to a fine art in Milan is the **aperitivo**, or pre-dinner drink, usually taken between 6 and 9pm. As well as another opportunity to preen and pose, *aperitivo*-time – or "happy hour" as it is also called – is a boon for budget travellers: bar counters are often laden with hot and cold food, all of which is included in the price of your drink (somewhere between €3 and €10, depending on the establishment). Take a plate and help yourself, although if you're really planning to fill up, it'll go down better if you go back several times rather than piling your plate high. If you choose your venue wisely you won't need to spend another penny on food all night. The food in most *aperitivo* bars winds up as the evening goes on: the lights dim and the volume of the music increases and you can settle in for the night. For reviews of the city's best *aperitivo* bars see p.174.

Lunch and snack food

There are **street markets** every day, except Sunday, scattered throughout the city, selling all the cheese, salami and fruit you need for a picnic lunch; a complete list is given daily in the *Corriere della Sera* under "Mercati". Alternatively, the *mercato comunale* in Piazza Wagner sells similar fresh produce but under one large, colourful roof. For **supermarkets**, some of the handiest are Standa at Via Torino 37, near the Duomo; Esselunga at Viale Piave 38, near Porta Venezia; and the over-priced Centro Commerciale in the Stazione Centrale (daily 5.30am–midnight).

Café Design La Triennale, Viale Alemagne 6 ☎02.875.441. The chairs are all design classics in this spacious café with windows overlooking Parco Sempione. The good lunchtime menu (noon–2.30pm) features light dishes such as a trio of smoked fish or quiche and salad; Sun brunch is a relaxed, civilized affair that you'll need to book for. In good weather, head outside to sip an *aperitivo* beside sculptures by the likes of De Chirico and Toyo Ito. Closed Mon.

Da Claudio Via Ponte Vetrero 16. Mouthwateringly fresh sashimi and shellfish served at the central bar amid the bustle of this traditional fishmongers on the edge of Brera. Lunch (noon–2.30pm) and *aperitivo*-time only (5–9pm). Closed Sun & Mon.

Luini Via S. Radegonda 16. A city institution that's been serving *panzerotti* (deep-fried mini *calzone*)

round the corner from the Duomo for over 150 years. Standing places only; grab a bench in nearby Piazza San Fedele if you want to eat sitting down. Closed Sun.

Palazzo Stelline Corso Magenta 61. This sunny bar terrace overlooking the garden of the convent where Leonardo stayed while painting *The Last Supper* is a relaxing spot for a salad or toasted *panino* (daily 9am–10pm). For something more filling, head down to the cellar to the self-service restaurant *buonappetito!*, with its tempting array of hot and cold dishes. Mon–Fri noon–2.15pm.

Vecchia Latteria Via dell'Unione 6. Delicious vegetarian dishes are prepared by the owners in this tiny neighbourhood café just off Via Torino. Closed Sun.

Cafés & gelaterie

Caffè Miani Piazza Duomo 21. Opened with the *Galleria* in 1867, *Caffè Miani*, also known as *Zucca in Galleria* and *Camparino*, was where David Campari invented Milan's famous sticky red drink. These days it's both expensive and touristy, but the price of a coffee standing at the tiled bar is easier to swallow. Closed Wed.

Chocolat Via Boccaccio 9. A small, modern bar beside Milano Nord station, with comfy sofas, offering thirty different chocolate-flavoured ice creams plus some refreshing fruit ones, too; there's hot chocolate to die for in winter. Closed Sun morning.

Cova Via Montenapoleone 8. Fin-de-siècle surroundings set the scene for this elegant

tearoom dating from the Napoleonic era. Discreet service and starched linen accompany the mouthwatering chocolate delicacies, although they don't come cheap.

Grom Via Santa Margherita 16. Practically opposite *La Scala*, the central branch of this specialist ice-cream chain serves up traditional flavours using top-quality organic ingredients.

Sartori Piazza Luigi di Savoia. Legendary kiosk up against one side of the Stazione Centrale (by the airport buses), serving some of the city's best ice cream, including avocado and lychee flavours. Closed Thurs.

Restaurants

Predictably, the centre of Milan has numerous expensive, business-oriented **restaurants**, but usually, just round the corner, there is somewhere more atmospheric or better value. South of the centre, the area around the **Ticinese** and **Navigli** is full of restaurants and cafés but you should choose carefully: this is a touristy area and quality is not always a priority. We've also included a couple of bargain places around the budget hotels near **Porta Venezia**.

Anema e Cozze Via Palermo 15
☎02.8646.1646. This bright, lively
Neapolitan spot is a good choice for tasty, informal
meals. The pizzas are crispy, the seafood fresh and
the flavoursome salads make a pleasant change
from pasta; expect to pay around €30 per person.
Branches at Via Casale 7 and Via Orseolo 1 are
equally recommended.

Joia Via P. Castaldi 18 ☎02.2952.2124. Well-
established foodie haven, serving highly imaginative combinations of vegetables and fish. The
lunchtime menu is good value, but in the evenings
expect to pay around €70 per person. Closed Sat
lunch, Sun & Aug.

L'Osteria del Treno Via San Gregorio 46–48
☎02.670.0479. The welcome couldn't be friendlier
at this elegantly converted railworkers' canteen.
Many diners opt for the delicious house platters of
cold meats or cheese (€12), although the pasta
dishes are recommended, too. Closed all day Sat &
Sun evening.

La Latteria Via San Marco 24 ☎02.659.7653.
This cosy trattoria is a favourite with the designer
types of Moscova. Delicious home-made pastas
and roast meats are served up by the owner;
reckon on around €15 for a main course. Closed
Sat, Sun & Aug.

Oskar Via Palazzi 4. A popular restaurant with
plenty of local atmosphere, serving fantastic-value
pasta dishes in huge portions. Don't be put off by
the voluble owners or the Mussolini memorabilia in
the corners. Closed Sun.

Pizza OK Via Lambro 15. Very busy pizzeria that
serves some of the best – and biggest – pizzas in
town. Huge choice of toppings and good prices that
start at €4 for a margherita. Open until 12.30am.
Closed Sun lunch.

Ponte Rosso Ripa di Porta Ticinese 23
☎02.837.3132. One of the best spots in the canal
area for a tasty, relaxed meal of local flavours. A
full meal without wine costs around €35, including
one of their delicious desserts. Closed all day Sun
& Mon lunch.

Torre di Pisa Via Fiori Chiari 21 ☎02.874.877. An
authentic Tuscan restaurant offering delicious
antipasti (around €9) and great cuts of meat, in the
heart of pedestrian Brera. Closed Sun.

Tradizionale Ripa de Porta Ticinese 7
☎02.839.5133. Tasty pizzas and mouthwatering
fish dishes are on offer in the rustic atmosphere of
this popular canal-side joint. There's another
branch at Via de Amicis 26.

Trattoria Milanese Via Santa Marta 11
☎02.8645.1991. An elegant but well-priced
neighbourhood restaurant in the labyrinth of
ancient streets 10min walk west of the Duomo.
Risotto and *ossobuco* take pride of
place among all that's best of Milanese cooking.
Closed Tues.

Warsa Via Melzo 16 ☎02.201.607. An Eritrean
restaurant near Porta Venezia serving delectable
bargain food; good variety of vegetarian dishes as
well as various meat options. Around €15 for a full
meal. Closed Wed.

Drinking and nightlife

Milan's diverse **nightlife** is centred on three main areas: the chi-chi districts around
Corso Como and further south around Via Brera; Corso Sempione, which draws
people after work for an *aperitivo* and keeps them there until the small hours; and
the lively bars, restaurants and clubs of the Navigli and adjacent Ticinese quarter.

The city's **clubs** are at their hippest midweek: at weekends out-of-towners
flood in and any self-respecting Milanese heads for the coast or mountains.
Assuming you get in (this is Milan: dress to impress), you'll be given a **tessera**
or card to be punched for each drink you buy, there's usually a minimum
consumption and you settle the tab when you leave.

For an antidote to all this preening, check out Milan's healthy **alternative**
scene, which revolves around the city's many **Centri Sociali** – essentially
squats, where committees organize cheap, sometimes free, concerts, film
screenings and the like. They also contain bars and – often good – vegetarian
restaurants. Check out the flagship *Leoncavallo*, Via Watteau 7 (☎02.670.5185,
ⓦwww.leoncavallo.org), or find other *centri* listed in *Il Manifesto* newspaper.

Bars

See p.177 for details of the bars located in the fashion stores around the
Quadrilatero d'Oro.

Atomic Via Felice Casati 24. Refreshing spot just north of Porta Venezia where you can have an after-dinner drink and a dance in a cool but relaxed atmosphere – most un-Milanese. Closed Mon & Aug.

Bar Bianco Parco Sempione. Right in the heart of the park, this unassuming café kicks into action on summer nights as a late-night bar with thumping music. Closed Mon.

Bar Jamaica Via Brera 32. This bar, made famous by the Arte Povera set of the 1950s, is right in the heart of Brera. Pop in for a coffee or snack during the day or keep drinking well into the early hours.

Bhangrabar Corso Sempione 1. Opposite the Arco della Pace, this Indian-themed bar is a trendy option for *aperitivo*-time (6.30–9pm) or later, as the DJs crank up the latest electronic or world music.

Corso Como 10 Corso Como 10. The bar is the best bit of this complex of boutiques, exhibition space, restaurant and a courtyard café-bar. Prices are extortionate but the atmosphere is very chic.

Cuore Via G. Mora 3. Hidden away down a side street opposite San Lorenzo alle Colonne, this cool, friendly bar is well worth including in your night out. Good music with occasional live bands and DJs set the mixed crowd at their ease.

Gattopardo Café Via Piero della Francesca 47. This ultra-fashionable spot, located in a deconsecrated church, is decked out in homage to Visconti's film *The Leopard*. It opens at 6pm and the door policy gets stricter after 10.30pm when the extensive *aperitivo* buffet is cleared away and the DJ turns up the music. Closed Mon.

Le Biciclette Conca del Naviglio 10. Smart young things prop up the bar in this swish modern joint in a leafy street near the Navigli. The definitive *aperitivo* bar.

Lelephante Via Melzo 22. Cocktails are the speciality at this good-time bar popular with a mixed crowd. Hardly a poseur in sight.

Roialto Via Piero della Francesca 55. This huge converted garage on various levels is done out in every conceivable style from 1930s colonial to chill-out lounge. Closed Mon.

Clubs and music venues

Blue Note Via Borsieri 37 ⓦwww .bluenotemilano.com. Jazz club in the alternative neighbourhood of Isola, just north of Stazione Garibaldi. Big names and a relaxed atmosphere make this place a top venue. There's a small restaurant, as well as the bar.

Gasoline Via Bonnet 11/A ⓦwww.discogasoline.it. Small, dark, funky club near the bars of Brera and Corso Como. On Sun afternoons it hosts the popular *Bus Stop* gay club.

Hollywood Corso Como 15 ⓦwww .discotecahollywood.com. Long established as the place to go (until dawn) if you want to be surrounded by beautiful people. Very Milanese but certainly no mould-breaker.

Scimmie Via Ascanio Sforza 49 ⓦwww.scimmie.it. Ticinese club that is one of Milan's most popular venues, with a different band every night and jazz-fusion predominating. Small and fun, with a decent restaurant – and a barge on the canal in summer.

Tunnel Via Sammartini 30 ☏02.6671.1370. With its eye firmly on what's happening abroad, this large club and venue located in an old warehouse near the Stazione Centrale is as close as Milan gets to having its finger on the pulse. Closed Mon.

Opera, classical music and cinema

Milan's **La Scala**, Via dei Filodrammatici 2, is one of the world's most prestigious opera houses, staging opera from early December to July. It also puts on some classical concerts and ballet between September and November (occasionally in the less atmospheric Teatro Arcimboldi, located outside the city centre). **Tickets** cost about €60 on average – and sell out months in advance. Buy by phone or online (☏02.860.775, ⓦwww.teatroallascala.org), or in person at the Central Box Office, Galleria del Sagrato, underground in the corridors of Duomo metro station (Sept–July daily noon–6pm). Some tickets for each performance are set aside for sale on the day.

Sound and Motion Pictures (ⓦwww.spaziocinema.info; €6) shows original-language **films** at the following cinemas: Anteo, Via Milazzo 9; Arcobaleno, Viale

Tunisia 11; and Mexico, Via Savona 57. Fondazione Cineteca Italiana, at Spazio Oberdan, Viale Veneto 2 (Ⓦwww.cinetecamilano.it), has a good programme of international art-house films.

Shopping

Milan is synonymous with **shopping**. If your pockets are not deep enough to tackle the big-name design boutiques of the Galleria Vittorio Emanuele you could always rummage through last season's leftovers at the many factory outlets around town, or check out the city's wide range of medium- and budget-range clothes shops. Milan also excels in furniture and **design**, with showrooms from the world's top companies, plus a handful of shops offering a selection of brands and labels under one roof.

Most shops **open** Tuesday to Saturday (10am–12.30pm & 3.30–7pm), plus Monday afternoons, although some larger places also stay open at lunchtime and on Sunday afternoons. The summer **sale** usually lasts through July and August, the winter one around mid-January to mid-February.

Fashion

Milan's top-name fashion stores are mainly concentrated in three areas. The **Quadrilatero d'Oro** – Via Montenapoleone, Via della Spiga and around – is the place for Versace, Prada et al. **Corso di Porta Ticinese** houses funkier, more youth-oriented shops – independents as well as global names like Diesel, Carhartt and Stussy. Head to **Corso Vittorio Emanuele**, **Via Torino** or **Corso Buenos Aires** for large branches of Italian mid-range chainstores, including Max Mara, Benetton and Stefanel, plus H&M and Zara.

▲ Galleria Vittorio Emanuele II – home to Prada and Louis Vuitton

Below is just a taster of what Milan has to offer in terms of the top-label shopping experience. These days the concept of a shop is being extended further and further: in-house cafés are springing up, as are exhibition spaces, spas, barbers' and even gyms.

Dolce & Gabbana Menswear at Corso Venezia 15. Go through to the courtyard on the ground floor of this eighteenth-century *palazzo* to find a wonderful space dedicated to enhancing your shopping experience. There's an old-fashioned barber's, a small beautican's and the oh-so stylish *Bar Martini*, popular with beautiful people of all nationalities. Womenswear at Via della Spiga 26; D&G line, including D&G junior, at Corso Venezia 7.

Gianfranco Ferré Via Sant'Andrea 15. The sculptural designs of this master of couture are mirrored by the decor of his boutique with its stunning red resin wall, but it is the adjoining day-spa that makes it really special. Mon–Fri 10am–10pm, Sat 10am–9pm, Sun 11am–6pm.

Gianni Versace Via Montenapoleone 11. Unusually for Versace, this store, spread over five storeys, is remarkably understated. The clean lines provide a perfect backdrop for the luxurious ostentation of the clothes, shoes and accessories in glinting gold and swirling colours.

Giorgio Armani Via Manzoni 31. This temple to all things Giorgio is more of a mini-shopping centre than a shop. There are boutiques for all his ranges – womenswear, menswear, furnishings and homeware – accompanied by *Armani Café*, a relaxed pavement café, and *Nobu*, a pricey, high-tech Japanese restaurant with fantastically offhand service. With a book corner selling design and coffee-table books, an in-house florists and a chocolate counter offering monogrammed sugary confections, you really won't need to spend your money anywhere else in town.

Gucci Via Montenapoleone 5–7 & Galleria Vittorio Emanuele II. Every desirable fashion item imaginable is available in the warren of sleek show rooms in Montenapoleone, while the newer store in the Galleria Vittorio Emanuele II has the *Gucci Café*: revitalize in an atmosphere of elegant minimalism with a freshly squeezed fruit juice or a coffee.

Just Cavalli Boutique Via della Spiga 30. The ultimate in bling. Cavalli's leopardskin-clad clientele feel wonderfully at home in the white-cloud lift or shimmering up and down the giant central staircase. The *pièce de résistance*, however, is down in the café, *Just Cavalli Food*, where a saltwater aquarium swims with brightly coloured tropical fish.

Prada Galleria Vittorio Emanuele II. The original Prada store, dating from 1913, stands on a side corner in the centre of the galleria. Much of the elegant interior is original, including the monochrome marble floor and the polished wood display cabinets, but the best bit is the central staircase swirling down past the leather goods to the men's and women's collections in the basement. Accessories, including shoes, at Via della Spiga 18; menswear at Via Montenapoleone 6; womenswear at Via Montenapoleone 8; sportswear at Via Sant'Andrea 21.

Trussardi Via Sant'Andrea 3–7. A spacious boutique across three floors with the über-chic *Trussardi-Marino Alla Scala Café* on the ground floor and a huge video wall to keep you entertained while you sip your coffee. On the floor above the soft leather bags and crisp linens is the formal but well-priced restaurant, and one floor higher still is a contemporary gallery space. Accessories and homeware at Piazza della Scala 5.

Factory outlets

In and around Milan are **outlets** or factory shops galore, selling last season's designer-label fashions for half-price or less. Aim for the multi-label D-Magazine, Via Montenapoleone 26; the hard-to-find Basement, entered through the door to the left of no. 15 on Via Senato, with bargains from all the top labels; and DT Intrend, Galleria San Carlo 6, near the Duomo, offering discounts on the Max Mara brands. Others demand more of a hike, although the savings are higher: the *grande dame* is Il Salvagente, Via Bronzetti 16, fifteen minutes east of San Babila by bus (#54 & #61), where, with a little rummaging, you can bag a designer label for around a third of its original price.

Furniture and design

To pick up Alessi, Gio Ponte or Castiglione **designer furniture**, make for the broad streets off San Babila: Corso Europa, Via Durini, Corso Venezia and Corso Monforte are home to the furniture and lighting showrooms that made Milan the design capital of the world in the 1950s.

For a more relaxed, but very Milanese, shopping experience, try a **concept store** that sells a bit of everything: High Tech, at Pizza XXV Aprile 12, is great for getting lost among designer, imitation and ethnic knick-knacks; while 10 Corso Como sells a few perfectly chosen design and fashion objects, as well as books and music, alongside a café and art gallery.

B&B Italia Via Durini 14 ⓦ www.bebitalia.it. International name that specializes in stylish contemporary furniture with collections by big names in Italian modern design.

Cassina Via Durini 16 ⓦ www.cassina.it. The showroom of this legendary Milanese company is always worth a visit for both new designs and their range of twentieth-century design classics including Eames, De Stijl and Rennie Mackintosh chairs.

De Padova Corso Venezia 14 ⓦ www.depadova.it. Two floors of elegant own-brand furniture and houseware artfully displayed in a light, stylish showroom. Their collections are designed by big names including Vico Magestretti and Patricia Urquiola.

Driade Via Manzoni 30 ⓦ www.driade.com. A wonderful multi-brand store with their own designs, as well as work by designers like Ron Arad and Philippe Starck. The collection includes furniture, tableware, kitchen and bathroom accessories, but the real treat here is the showroom housed in an elegant nineteenth-century *palazzo*.

Listings

Airport enquiries ⓣ 02.7485.2200 (daily 7am–11pm) for both Linate and Malpensa airports.

Bicycle rental Central Milan is mainly flat and motorists show much more respect to cyclists than in London or New York. Rental outlets include AWS, Via Ponte Seveso 33 (ⓦ www.awsbici.com), and La Stazione, beside San Donato Milanese metro station (ⓦ www.piubici.org).

Consulates Australia, Via Borgogna 2 ⓣ 02.777.041; South Africa, Vicolo San Giovanni sul Muro 4 ⓣ 02.885.8581; UK, Via San Paolo 7 ⓣ 02.723.001; US, Via Principe Amadeo 2/10 ⓣ 02.290.351.

Football Inter Milan (ⓦ www.inter.it) and AC Milan (ⓦ www.acmilan.it) play on alternate Sundays at the G. Meazza (San Siro) stadium (ⓣ 02.404.2432; M Lotto, then a longish walk). The stadium has hourly guided tours (Mon–Sat 10am–5pm from Gate 21, Via Piccolomini 5; €12.50). Buy match tickets here and from New Milan Point, Piazza San Fedele (AC Milan games), or branches of Banca Popolare Milano (Inter games).

Gay and lesbian Milan Milan is one of Italy's most gay-friendly cities. The gay bookshop Libreria Babele Galleria, Via San Nicolao 10 (ⓦ www .libreriababele.it; M Cadorna), stocks the *Gay Milan* map and has details of the ArciUno Club Card, which many gay establishments require as a condition of entry. In May, a gay and lesbian film festival (ⓦ www.cinemagaylesbico.com) includes fringe events.

Medical facilities English-speaking doctors and dentists at International Health Center (ⓣ 02.7634.0720, ⓦ www.ihc.it). 24hr pharmacies include Stazione Centrale (ⓣ 02.669.0735) and Carlo Erba on Piazza Duomo (ⓣ 02.8646.4832). Ospedale Maggiore Policlinico, Via Francesco Sforza 35 (ⓣ 02.55.031), near Piazza Duomo, has 24hr casualty.

Left luggage Stazione Centrale (daily 6am–midnight; €3.80 for 5hr, then small increments up to a max of five days). Stazione Nord/Cadorna has lockers (daily 5am–11.30pm; €3.50–6.50 for 2hr 30min).

Police ⓣ 113.

Post office Via Cordusio 4, off Piazza Cordusio – not the building marked "Poste", but around the corner (Mon–Fri 8am–7pm, Sat 8.30am–noon).

Taxis To book, call ⓣ 02.6767, 02.4040 or 02.8585.

Train enquiries Ferrovie dello Stato ⓣ 848.888.088 (daily 7am–9pm; ⓦ www.trenitalia .com); Ferrovie Nord ⓣ 02.20.222 (daily 9am–6pm; ⓦ www.lenord.it).

Southern Lombardy

Apart from Milan, much of Lombardy's wealth is concentrated in the cities and towns of the broad plain of the River Po, which forms the southern belt of the region. It's a wealth that is obvious in the well-preserved medieval towns (and the industrial estates that surround them), not to mention in the well-designed clothes and new cars of its citizens.

Pavia is a pretty medieval town that makes an attractive introduction to this part of Lombardy, its cobbled streets and ancient churches taking a back seat in terms of sights to the fabulous **Certosa** monastery nearby. In the east, **Cremona**, birthplace of the violin, has a neat, well-preserved centre, but does not demand lingering attention. **Mantua**, on the eastern edge of the region, is Lombardy's most visually appealing city: the powerful Gonzaga family ruled for three hundred years from an extravagant ducal palace and later the Palazzo Te, on the outskirts of the city, which contains some of the finest (and most steamily erotic) fresco-painting of the entire Renaissance.

Pavia

PAVIA, 55km south of Milan, is close enough to be seen on a day-trip, yet retains a clear identity of its own. A comfortable provincial town with an illustrious history, it boasts one of the masterpieces of Italian architecture in the nearby Carthusian monastery, the **Certosa**.

Founded on an easily defendable stretch of land alongside the confluence of the Po and Ticino rivers, Pavia was always an important staging post en route to the Alps. Medieval Pavia was known as the city of a hundred towers, and although only a handful remain, the medieval aspect is still strong, with numerous Romanesque and Gothic churches tucked away in a wanderable web of narrow streets and cobbled squares. The town reached its zenith in the Dark Ages, when it was capital of the Kingdom of the Lombards: emperors – including Charlemagne in 774 and Frederick Barbarossa in 1155 – subsequently came to Pavia to receive the Lombards' traditional iron crown. This all came to an end in the fourteenth century when Pavia was handed over to the Viscontis and became a satellite of Milan.

Arrival, information and accommodation

Regular **trains** make the thirty-minute journey from Milan. **Buses** from Milan Famagosta metro station drop you at Pavia's bus station, round the corner from the train station, on the western edge of the centre. Buses #3 and #6 connect the train station with the centre, or it's about a ten-minute walk down Corso Cavour to Piazza della Vittoria. The **tourist office** is north off Corso Cavour, at Piazza Petrarca 4 (Mon–Sat 8.30am–12.30pm & 2–5pm; ☎0382.597.001, ⊛www.turismo.provincia.pv.it). Most of Pavia's unexciting **hotels** are near the station, including *Aurora*, Via Vittorio Emanuele 25 (☎0382.23.664, ⊛www .hotel-aurora.eu; ❸), and smarter *Moderno*, Via Vittorio Emanuele 41 (☎0382.303.401, ⊛www.hotelmoderno.it; ❻), which has a small spa and offers free use of bicycles.

The Town

Wandering is the nicest way to spend time in Pavia: pick any side street and you're almost bound to stumble on something of interest – a lofty medieval tower, a pretty Romanesque or Gothic church, or just a silent, sleepy piazza. Getting lost is difficult, as the town is still based around its Roman axes: Corso Cavour – which becomes Corso Mazzini – runs east–west along the route of the *decamanus*, while Strada Nuova runs north–south following the *cardo*.

The large, cobbled **Piazza della Vittoria**, lined with bars, *gelaterie* and restaurants, stands in the centre. At the square's southern end, the **Broletto**, medieval Pavia's town hall, abuts the rambling **Duomo**. An early Renaissance sprawl of protruding curves and jutting angles, the cathedral is best known for its huge nineteenth-century cupola, which dominates the skyline. Its facade was only added in 1933 and the building's exterior is still mainly unfinished. At the time of writing, most of the church was under restoration, due to reopen in 2010. Beside the west front of the Duomo, facing **Piazza del Duomo**, are the remnants of the eleventh-century Torre Civica, a campanile that collapsed without warning in 1989, killing four people.

Southwest of the piazza, cobbled streets lead to the charming neighbourhood church of **San Teodoro** (daily 3–7pm). The twelfth-century basilica was clumsily restored at the end of the nineteenth century, and the main reason for visiting is to see the fresco on the left-hand side of the nave near the entrance: the *View of Pavia* by Bernardino Lanazani illustrates the city in 1522 with its hundreds of civic towers built by Pavia's noble families to show their superiority over their rivals.

Also featured in the painting is the **Ponte Coperto**, the covered bridge over the River Ticino just south of the basilica. The current bridge was rebuilt slightly downriver in the 1940s after the medieval one was bombed; you can still see remnants of the original jutting out into the water. The bridge leads over to the **Borgo Ticino**, a riverside neighbourhood traditionally inhabited by fishermen and *raniere* (frog catchers); these days there are several popular local restaurants. An open park runs along the shore of both banks west of the bridge.

The best of Pavia's churches is the beautiful Romanesque **San Michele**, a five-minute walk northeast from the bridge along Via Capsoni. This is where the kings of Northern Italy were crowned: Federico I (Barbarossa) came to receive the title here in 1155. The friezes and capitals on its broad sandstone facade are carved into a menagerie of snake-tailed fish, griffins, dragons and other beasts, some locked in a struggle with people, representing the fight between good and evil. Despite restoration work in the 1960s, the sandstone is eroding and some of the figures are being lost for good.

North of here lie the attractive courtyards and sandstone buildings of the **University of Pavia**, founded in 1361 by Galeazzo II Visconti, and particularly renowned for its medicine and law faculties. Crossing Piazza Castello, you reach the **Castello Visconteo** (Tues–Sun: July, Aug & Dec–Feb 9am–1.30pm; March–June & Sept–Nov 10am–5.45pm; €6), also initiated by Galeazzo II Visconti in 1360, and added to by the Sforzas. Although it's been restored, the rooms that remain are unremarkable. The **Museo Civico** inside includes a handful of Venetian paintings, Roman artefacts and medieval architectural fragments.

Eating and drinking

Pavia's best **restaurant**, with attractive outdoor tables in summer, is in an alleyway by the church of San Michele. ✱ *Villaglori al San Michele*, Viccolo San

Michele 4 (☎0382.220.716; closed Mon & lunch Tues–Fri), offers excellently priced local wines to accompany interesting dishes like rabbit and asparagus lasagne or a mouthwatering selection of cold meats and cheeses in an elegant modern restaurant. Across Corso Strada Nuova, *Osteria della Madonna del Peo*, Via Cardano 63 (☎0382.302.833; closed Sun), is a good central option serving local specialities, such as risotto with frogs' legs, in a cosy vaulted trattoria. If you'd prefer to grab a sandwich and head down to the river, the *Punto Bar*, Strada Nuova 9, is a first-rate *paninoteca*.

Certosa di Pavia

One of the most extravagant monasteries in Europe, the **Certosa di Pavia** (Charterhouse of Pavia; Tues–Sun 9–11.30am & 2.30–5.30pm; Oct–March closes 4.30pm; free), 10km north of Pavia, was commissioned by the Duke of Milan, Gian Galeazzo Visconti, in 1396 as the family mausoleum. Visconti intended the church here to resemble Milan's late-Gothic cathedral and the same architects and craftsmen worked on the building throughout its construction. It took a century to build; by the time it was finished tastes had changed (and the Viscontis had been replaced by the Sforzas). As a work of art the monastery is one of the most important testimonies to the transformation from late-Gothic to Renaissance and Mannerist styles, but it also affords a wonderful insight into the lives and beliefs of the Carthusian monks.

The Certosa is easily reachable from both Milan and Pavia. **Buses** run hourly from Milan's Famagosta station (€3) and from Pavia's bus station, dropping you a fifteen-minute walk from the Certosa. Arriving by **train**, turn left out of the station and walk (15min) around the Certosa walls to the entrance.

The complex

The monastery lies at the end of a tree-lined avenue, part of a former Visconti hunting range that stretched all the way from Pavia's *castello*. Encircled by a high wall, the complex is entered through a central gateway bearing a motif that recurs throughout the monastery – "GRA-CAR" or "Gratiarum

▲ Certosa di Pavia monastery

Carthusiae", a reference to the fact that the Carthusian monastery is dedicated to Santa Maria delle Grazie, who appears in numerous works of art in the church. Beyond the gateway is a gracious courtyard; on the right is the seventeenth-century Palazzo Ducale, while rising up before you is the fantastical **facade** of the church, festooned with inlaid marble, twisted columns, statues and friezes – though in fact unfinished: the tympanum was never added to the top, which gives the church its stocky, truncated look. The **church** interior is no less splendid, its paintings, statues and vaults combining to create an almost ballroom glamour. Look out for the tombs of Lodovico Il Moro and Gian Galeazzo Visconti, masterpieces of the early Renaissance.

To visit the rest of the monastery you need to join a **guided tour** (free; contributions welcomed) of just under an hour, led by one of the monks released from the strict Carthusian vow of silence. Tours start from the church when a group has gathered; they are in Italian, but are well worth doing even if you don't understand a word, as they allow you to explore the best parts of the monastery complex. They move first to the **small cloister**, with fine terracotta decoration and a geometric garden around a fountain, then to the nearby **refectory**, where monks would eat together on Sundays and Holy days; the Bible was read throughout the silent meal from the pulpit (with a hidden entrance in the panelling). The dining room is divided by a blind wall, which allowed the monastery to feed lay workers and guest pilgrims without compromising the rules of their closed order. Further on, the **great cloister** is stunning for its size and tranquillity. It is surrounded on three sides by the **monks' houses**, each consisting of two rooms, a chapel, a garden and a loggia, with a bedroom above. The hatches to the side of the entrances were designed to enable food to be passed through without any communication. The final call is the Certosa **shop**, stocked with honey, chocolate, souvenirs and the famous Chartreuse liqueur.

Cremona

A cosy provincial town in the middle of the Po plain, **CREMONA** is known for its violins. Ever since Andrea Amati established the first violin workshop here in 1566, followed by his son Nicolò and pupils Guarneri and – most famously – **Antonio Stradivari** (1644–1737), Cremona has been a focus for the instrument. Today the city hosts an internationally famous school of violin-making, as well as frequent classical concerts.

Cremona has some fine Renaissance and medieval buildings, and its cobbled streets make for some pleasant wandering, but it's a modest sort of place: target it as a half-day trip from Milan, on a route towards the richer pickings of Mantua.

Arrival, information and accommodation

Cremona's **train station** is on Via Dante, ten-minutes' walk north of the main Piazza del Comune, linked to the centre by bus #1. The **tourist office** (daily 9am–12.30pm & 3–6pm, June–Aug closed Sun pm; ☎0372.23.233, ⓦwww.provincia.cremona.it) is on Piazza del Comune, opposite the Duomo. The **campsite** *Parco al Po* is at Lungo Po Europa 12 (☎0372.21.268, ⓦwww.campingcremonapo.it; April–Sept; bus #1). Of **hotels**, *Duomo*, Via Gonfalonieri 13 (☎0372.35.242; ②), is very central, offering bright, air-conditioned rooms, while *Dellearti Design Hotel*, Via Bonomelli 8 (☎0372.23.131, ⓦwww.dellearti.com; ⑤), is aimed at chi-chi urbanite guests who like their contemporary styling – rather incongruous for sleepy Cremona.

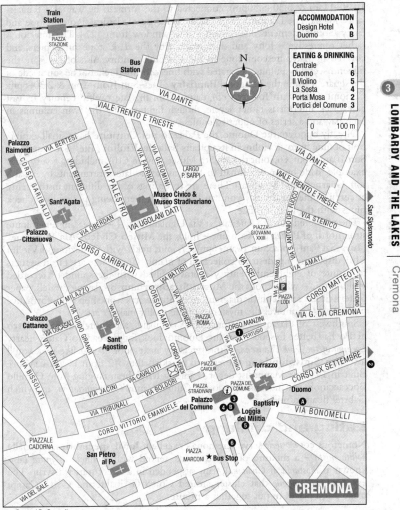

ACCOMMODATION
Design Hotel   **A**
Duomo   **B**

EATING & DRINKING
Centrale   **1**
Duomo   **6**
Il Violino   **5**
La Sosta   **4**
Porta Mosa   **2**
Portici del Comune   **3**

0   100 m

► San Sigismondo

CREMONA

▼ Parco al Po Campsite

The Town

The centre of Cremona is the splendid **Piazza del Comune**, a narrow space dominated by monumental architecture. The west side is the least dramatic, though its buildings, both thirteenth-century – the red-brick **Loggia dei Militia** (formerly headquarters of the town's soldiery) and the arched **Palazzo del Comune** – are lavish.

In the northeast corner of the square looms the gawky Romanesque **Torrazzo**, at 112m one of Italy's tallest medieval towers. Built in the mid-thirteenth century and bearing a fine Renaissance clock dating from 1583, it can be climbed for excellent views (Tues–Sun 10am–1pm & 2.30–6pm; €4, joint ticket with baptistry €5). Adjacent stands the **Duomo** (Mon–Sat 7.30am–noon & 3.30–7pm, Sun

10.30–11am & 3.30–5.30pm), connected to the Torrazzo by way of a Renaissance loggia. The Duomo's huge facade, made up of classical, Romanesque and fancy Gothic elements, focuses on a rose window from 1274. The interior is rather oppressive – lofty and dim, marked by the dark stone of its piers, and covered by naïve frescoes done in the sixteenth century. Also of note are the fifteenth-century pulpits, decorated with finely tortured reliefs. The south side of the square features the octagonal **Baptistry** (Tues–Sun 10am–1pm & 2.30–6pm; €2, joint ticket with Torrazzo €5), dating from the late twelfth century. Its vast bare-brick interior is rather severe, though lightened by the twin columns in each bay and a series of upper balconies.

Directly opposite the Duomo, the **Palazzo del Comune** has a small exhibition of nine historic violins in its upstairs **Sala dei Violini** (Tues–Sat 9am–6pm, Sun 10am–6pm; €6, joint ticket with Museo Civico €10), including a very early example made by Andrea Amati in 1566, as well as later instruments by Amati's son, Guarneri, and Stradivari. There are recordings of the different instruments; at certain times of the day you can hear one of them being played live (check times with the tourist office).

The pilastered Palazzo Affaitati, at Via Ugolani Dati 4 – a pleasant ten-minute stroll north of Piazza del Comune – holds the **Museo Civico "Ala Ponzone"** (Tues–Sat 9am–6pm, Sun 10am–6pm; €7, joint ticket with Collezione di Violini €10), displaying a pedestrian collection of mainly Cremonese art. Head upstairs to a suite of eighteenth-century rooms – filled with the sound of recorded violin music – which hold the **Museo Stradivariano**, displaying models, paper patterns, tools and acoustic diagrams from Stradivari's workshop. An informative video helps to unravel the mysteries of the violin-maker's art.

Southwest of Piazza del Comune, on Via Tibaldi, the church of **San Pietro al Po** has better frescoes than the Duomo; look for Bernadino Gatti's hearty *Feeding of the Five Thousand* in the refectory next door. If you like that, you'll love **San Sigismondo** in the eastern outskirts (bus #2 from Piazza Cavour). Built in 1441, its Mannerist decor is among Italy's best, ranging from Camillo Boccaccino's soaring apse fresco to Giulio Campi's *Annunciation*, in which Gabriel floats in mid-air.

Eating and drinking

Numerous cosy *osterie* serve Cremona's excellent **local specialities**, especially *bollito misto* – a mixture of boiled meats, served with *mostarda di frutta* (also known as *mostarda di Cremona*), fruit suspended in a sweet mustard syrup. The excellent *gastronomie* that cluster around Corso Garibaldi and Corso Campi make good places to put together a **picnic**.

Centrale Via Pertusio 4, off Via Solferino. A local institution that keeps the Cremonesi happy with well-priced traditional dishes, served with gusto. Closed Thurs.

Il Violino Via Sicardo 3 ☎0372.461.010, ⊛www .ilviolino.it. Top choice for a gastronomic experience – a quality restaurant metres from the main piazza specializing in local dishes such as *tortelli* with bass or *risotto alla zucca*, followed by a variety of excellent fish dishes. Book ahead. Closed Mon eve & Tues.

La Sosta Via Sicardo 9 ☎0372.456.656. By the main piazza, this attractive *osteria* does a great line in Cremonese specialities at reasonable prices. Closed Sun eve & Mon.

Porta Mosa Via Santa Maria Betlem 11. A simple *osteria* serving delicious local dishes, washed down by well-chosen wines. 10min walk east of Piazza del Comune. Closed Sun.

Portici del Comune Piazza del Comune 2. Nicest – and best-located – of the many pleasant pavement cafés and *gelaterie* dotted around the main squares, in a plum position under the arches directly opposite the Duomo's facade. Closed Tues.

Mantua (Mantova) and around

Aldous Huxley called it the most romantic city in the world. With a skyline of domes and towers rising above its three encircling lakes, **MANTUA** (Mantova) is undeniably evocative. This was where Romeo heard of Juliet's supposed death, and where Verdi set *Rigoletto*. Its history is one of equally operatic plots, most of them acted out by the **Gonzaga**, one of Renaissance Italy's richest and most powerful families, who ruled the town for three centuries. Its cobbled squares retain a medieval aspect, and there are two splendid palaces: the **Palazzo Ducale**, containing Mantegna's stunning fresco of the Gonzaga family and court, and **Palazzo Te**, whose frescoes by the flashy Mannerist Giulio Romano encompass steamy erotica and illusionistic fantasy. Mantua's lakes, and the flat surrounding plain, offer numerous boat cruises and cycling routes.

Arrival, information and accommodation

Mantua's **train station** – with service from Milan, Cremona and Verona – and nearby **bus station** are ten-minutes' walk west of the centre (buses from Verona drop off first in the more convenient Piazza Sordello). The city is small enough to cover on foot: even the walk south to Palazzo Te is only twenty minutes. Bus #1 follows a circular route linking the train station, the central squares and Palazzo Te. The well-organized **tourist office** is at Piazza Mantegna 6 (daily 9.30am–6.30pm; ☏0376.432.432, ⊛www.turismo .mantova.it). If you're planning more than a fleeting visit, ask the tourist office about the numerous **agriturismo** options (⊛www.agriturismomantova.it) in this part of Lombardy.

Hotels

Armellino Via Cavour 67 ☏346.314.8060, ⊛www.bebarmellino.it. Three attractively furnished double rooms in an eighteenth-century palace right in the centre of town. There's a pretty garden for drinks and breakfast is served in the period dining room. No credit cards. ❸

Broletto Via Accademia 1 ☏0376.326.784, ⊛www.hotelbroletto.com. Compact three-star family-run hotel in the historic centre. Service is

cheery and rooms are adequate (all en-suite, with air-conditioning), if a bit small. ❹

Corte San Girolamo Via San Girolamo 1, Gambarara ☏0376.391.018, ⊛www.agriturismo-sangirolamo.it. Occupying a renovated watermill 3km north of town on the cycle route from Mantua to Lake Garda, this serene agriturismo has en-suite doubles plus a four-person apartment. Bicycles available. ❸

Rechigi Via Calvi 30 ☏0376.320.781, ⊛www .rechigi.com. Top-class four-star hotel in the

---

Exploring Mantua: bikes and boats

Several companies offer **cruises** on Mantua's lakes – bulges in the course of the River Mincio – and on the river itself down to its confluence with the Po, ranging from one-hour jaunts (around €7.50) up to full-day voyages as far as Venice (around €70). All run daily but must be **booked in advance**: usually a day ahead, but sometimes an hour or so will do. The leading company is Motonavi Andes Negrini, whose ticket office is at Via San Giorgio 2 (☏0376.322.875, ⊛www.motonaviandes.it), three-minutes' walk from its jetty on Lago Inferiore. Navi Andes (☏0376.324.506, ⊛www .naviandes.com) is a separate concern, based at its jetty on Lago di Mezzo. Alternatives include the Barcaioli del Mincio (☏0376.349.292, ⊛www.fiumemincio.it), local boatmen operating small craft upstream from Mantua. Many of the boats accept bikes, so you can make a great day-trip – a morning on the boat, a picnic lunch at, say, Rivalta, then a gentle cycle-ride back in the afternoon. You can **rent bikes** (around €9 a day) from Mantua Bike, Viale Piave 22/B (☏0376.220.909).

historic centre. The lobby is a little off-putting – all gleaming marble and white sofas, with contemporary art dotted about – but the rooms are calmer: fresh and modern but decorated with taste. Excellent service. Private parking. ⑥–⑦

Hostel

Ostello del Mincio Via Porto 23, Rivalta
☎0376.653.924, ⓦwww.ostellodelmincio.org. Fine

hostel 10km west of town, in a sleepy village on the River Mincio, with canoes available for rent and boat trips. It stands 5km from Castellucchio train station (on the Cremona–Mantua line), and bus #13 (Mantua–Asola; ⓦwww.apam.it) stops outside. Dorms €16. ①

The City

The centre of Mantua is made up of four attractive squares, each connected to the next. Lively Piazza Mantegna is overlooked by the massive **Sant'Andrea** church. Beside it is the lovely Piazza Erbe, with fine arcades facing the medieval **Rotonda** church. To the north, through medieval passageways and across Piazza Broletto, the long, cobbled slope of Piazza Sordello is dominated by the **Palazzo Ducale**, the fortress and residence of the Gonzaga, packed with Renaissance art.

Mantua's other great palace stands in its own gardens 1.5km south of the historic centre – **Palazzo Te**, adorned with sensational frescoes.

Piazza Mantegna and around

Dominating **Piazza Mantegna** – a wedge-shaped open space at the end of the arcaded shopping thoroughfares of Corso Umberto and Via Roma – is the facade of Leon Battista Alberti's church of **Sant'Andrea**, an unfinished basilica that says a lot about the ego of Lodovico II Gonzaga, who commissioned it in 1470. He felt that the existing medieval church was neither impressive enough to represent the splendour of his state nor large enough to hold the droves of people who packed in every Ascension Day to see the holy relic of Christ's blood which had been found on the site. Lodovico brought in the court architect, Luca Fancelli, to oversee Alberti's plans. There was a bitchy rivalry between the two, and when, on one of his many visits, Alberti fell and hurt a testicle, Fancelli gleefully told him: "God lets men punish themselves in the place where they sin." Work started in earnest after Alberti's death in 1472, and took more than two decades to complete. The Classical facade is focused on an immense triumphal arch supported on giant pilasters. **Inside** (daily 8am–noon & 3–7pm), the vast, column-free space is roofed with one immense barrel vault, echoing the facade. The octagonal balustrade at the crossing stands above the crypt where the holy relic is kept in two vases, copies of originals designed by Cellini and stolen by the Austrians in 1846; to see them, ask the sacristan. The painter Mantegna is buried in the first chapel on the left, his tomb topped with a bust of the artist that is said to be a self-portrait. The wall-paintings in the chapel were designed by Mantegna and executed by students, one of whom was Correggio.

Beside Sant'Andrea, Piazza Mantegna gives way to atmospheric **Piazza dell'Erbe**, with a small daily market and cafés sheltering in the arcades below the thirteenth-century **Palazzo della Ragione**. Sunk below the present street level is the eleventh-century **Rotonda di San Lorenzo** (daily 10am–6pm; Mon–Fri closed 1–3pm), which was partially demolished in the sixteenth century and used as a courtyard by the surrounding houses. Rebuilt in 1908 and beautifully restored in recent years, it still contains traces of twelfth- and thirteenth-century frescoes.

At the north end of Piazza dell'Erbe, a passage leads under the red-brick **Broletto**, or medieval town hall, into the smaller **Piazza Broletto**, where you can view two reminders of how "criminals" were treated under the Gonzagas. The bridge to the right has metal rings embedded in its vault, to

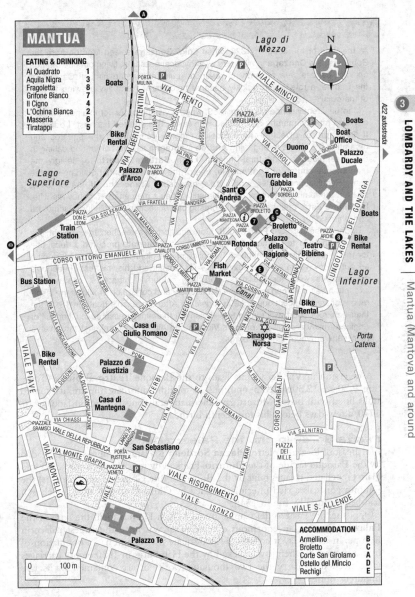

which victims were chained by the wrists, before being hauled up by a pulley and suspended in mid-air; while on your far left – actually on the corner of Piazza Sordello – the tall medieval **Torre della Gabbia** has a cage attached in which prisoners were displayed. Inside the Broletto is a small **museum** (Tues, Wed & Fri–Sun 10am–1pm & 3.30–6.30pm; March, Nov & Dec Sat & Sun only; Jan & Feb Sun only; €3) dedicated to local boy Tazio Nuvolari, Italy's most celebrated racing driver.

The Gonzaga

At the time of the coup of 1328, when **Luigi Gonzaga** seized Mantua from the Bonacolsi, the **Gonzaga** family were wealthy local peasants, living outside Mantua on vast estates with an army of retainers. Luigi nominated himself Captain of the People, a role which quickly became hereditary, eventually growing to that of marquis.

Mantua's renaissance began in 1459, when a visiting pope complained that the city was muddy, marshy and riddled with fever. This spurred his host, **Lodovico II Gonzaga**, to give the city a facelift, ranging from paving the squares and repainting the shops to engaging **Andrea Mantegna** as court artist and calling in the prestigious architectural theorist **Leon Battista Alberti** to design the monumental church of Sant'Andrea, one of the most influential buildings of the early Renaissance. Later, Lodovico's grandson, **Francesco II** (1466–1519), swelled the family coffers by hiring himself out as a mercenary – money his wife, **Isabella d'Este**, spent amassing a prestigious collection of paintings, sculpture and *objets d'art*.

Under Isabella's son, **Federico II**, Gonzaga fortunes reached their height; his marriage in 1531 to the heiress of the duchy of Monferrato procured a ducal title for the family, while he continued the policy of self-glorification by commissioning an out-of-town villa – the **Palazzo Te** – for himself and his mistress. Federico's descendants were for the most part less colourful characters, one notable exception being **Vincenzo I**, whose debauchery and corruption provided the inspiration for Verdi's licentious duke in *Rigoletto*. After Vincenzo's death in 1612, the then-bankrupt court was forced to sell many of the family treasures to Charles I of England (many are still in London's Victoria and Albert Museum), just three years before the arrival of the Habsburgs.

A diversion up Via Accademia leads to the Baroque **Teatro Bibiena** (Tues–Sun 9.30am–12.30pm & 3–6pm; €2), a splendid, intimate theatre, its curved walls lined with boxes. Mozart gave the inaugural concert here on January 16, 1770, a few days before his fourteenth birthday.

Piazza Sordello and the Palazzo Ducale

Northeast of Piazza Broletto, **Piazza Sordello** is a large, sombre square, headed by the Baroque facade of the **Duomo**. Flanked by touristy pavement cafés and grim crenellated palaces built by the Bonacolsi (the Gonzagas' predecessors) the Duomo conceals a rich interior, designed by Giulio Romano after the church had been gutted by fire in 1545.

Opposite, the Palazzo del Capitano and Magna Domus form the core of the **Palazzo Ducale**, an enormous complex that was once the largest palace in Europe. In its heyday it covered 34,000 square metres and had a population of over a thousand; when it was sacked by the Habsburgs in 1630 eighty carriages were needed to carry the two thousand works of art contained in its five hundred rooms.

Palazzo Ducale practicalities

Admission (Tues–Sun 8.45am–7.15pm, last entry 6.30pm; €6.50; @www .mantovaducale.it) is from Piazza Sordello, where you can also pick up an **audioguide** (€4, or €5.50 for two). In winter (Nov–March) you must take a guided tour (free); these start every fifteen minutes, or when twenty people have gathered, and last an hour and a half.

For conservation reasons, only 1500 people a day are allowed to visit the **Camera degli Sposi** (also called the **Camera Picta**). In the peak season for school trips (March 15–June 15 and Sept 1–Oct 15), individuals must book in advance for a timed slot for admission to this room, on ☎041.241.1897 (press 1; English-speaking operators; Mon–Fri 9am–6pm, Sat 9am–2pm). Booking costs €1 extra, payable on arrival.

Inside the Palazzo Ducale

The tour starts in the Corte Vecchia, the oldest wing of the palace. In the **Sala del Morone** (room 1) hangs a painting from 1494 by Domenico Morone showing the *Expulsion of the Bonacolsi* from Piazza Sordello, with the Duomo sporting its old, Gothic facade (replaced in the eighteenth century). In the **Sala del Pisanello** (room 3) are the fragments of a half-finished fresco by Pisanello, discovered in 1969 behind two layers of plaster.

The splendid Neoclassical **Sala dei Specchi** ("Hall of Mirrors"; room 6) was originally an open loggia, bricked up in 1773; the barrel-vaulted ceiling holds a fresco depicting teams of horses being driven from Night to Day. In the **Sala degli Arcieri** ("Hall of Archers"; room 7), a huge canvas by Rubens shows the Gonzaga family of 1604 seated comfortably in the presence of the Holy Trinity; notice Vincenzo with his handlebar moustache. The picture was originally part of a huge triptych, but Napoleonic troops carried off two-thirds of it in 1797 (one part is now in Antwerp, the other in Nancy) and chopped the remaining third into saleable chunks of portraiture; some gaps remain. Around the room is a curious frieze of horses, glimpsed behind curtains. Beyond the **Sala del Labirinto** (room 9), named for the maze on its painted and gilded wooden ceiling, the **Sala di Amore e Psiche** (room 11) is an intimate space with a wooden floor and an eighteenth-century *tondo* of Cupid and Psyche in the ceiling.

From here follow signs along corridors, down stairs and over a moat into the fourteenth-century **Castello di San Giorgio**, which contains the palace's principal treasure: Mantegna's frescoes of the Gonzaga family in the **Camera degli Sposi** (room 17). Painted between 1465–74, they're naturalistic pieces of work, giving a vivid impression of the Marquis Lodovico, his wife Barbara and their family, and of the relationships between them. In the main fresco Lodovico discusses a letter with a courtier while his wife looks on; their youngest daughter leans on her mother's lap, about to bite into an apple, while an older son and daughter look towards the door, where an ambassador from another court is being welcomed. The other fresco, divided into three sections shows Lodovico welcoming his son Francesco back from Rome. In the background are the Holy Roman Emperor Frederick III and the king of Denmark. Don't forget to look up: the ceiling features another nice piece of trompe l'oeil, in which two women, peering down from a balustrade, have balanced a tub of plants on a pole and appear to be on the verge of letting it tumble into the room.

Next comes the sixteenth-century Corte Nuova wing, designed by Giulio Romano for Federico II Gonzaga. After several formal audience rooms you come to the **Sala di Troia** (room 22), decorated with Romano's brilliantly colourful scenes from the *Iliad* and *Aeneid*. The adjacent **Galleria dei Marmi** (room 23), with delicate floral and wildlife motifs, looks out over the Cortile della Cavallerizza (Courtyard of the Riding School). Along the courtyard's long side runs the immense **Galleria della Mostra** (room 24), once hung with paintings by Titian, Caravaggio, Breughel and others, all now dispersed; in their place are 64 Roman marble busts. Push on through the smaller rooms and up more stairs to the stunning **Sala dello Zodiaco** (room 33), whose late sixteenth-century ceiling is spangled with stars and constellations. The adjoining Rococo **Sala dei Fiumi** (room 34) features an elaborate painted allegory of Mantua's six rivers, flanked by two ghastly stucco-and-mosaic fountains.

Save some wonder for rooms 35–37, beside the Sala dello Zodiaco. These comprise the **Stanze degli Arazzi**, three rooms (and a small chapel) altered in the eighteenth century to house nine sixteenth-century Flemish tapestries of exceptional virtuosity, depicting stories from the Acts of the Apostles, made from Raphael's cartoons for the Sistine Chapel (now in the V&A in London).

South of the centre

A twenty-minute walk from the centre of Mantua, at the end of the long spine of Via Principe Amedeo and Via Acerbi, the Palazzo Te is the later of the city's two Gonzaga palaces, and equally compelling.

On the way is Giulio Romano's **Fish Market**, to the left off Piazza Martiri Belfiori, a short covered bridge over the river, which is still used as a market building. Following Via Principe Amedeo south, the **Casa di Giulio Romano**, off to the right at Via Poma 18 – overshadowed by the monster-studded Palazzo di Giustizia – was meant to impress the sophisticated, who would have found the licence taken with the Classical rules of architecture witty. A five-minute walk away on busy Via Acerbi stands the austere brick **Casa del Mantegna**, now used as a contemporary art space (hours and admission vary). Across the road, the church of **San Sebastiano** (mid-March to mid-Nov Tues–Sun 10.30am–12.30pm & 3–5pm; €1.50), the work of Alberti, is famous as the first Renaissance church to be built on a central Greek cross plan, described as "curiously pagan" by Nikolaus Pevsner. Lodovico II's son was less polite: "I could not understand whether it was meant to turn out as a church, a mosque or a synagogue." The bare interior – now deconsecrated – is dedicated to Mantua's war dead.

Palazzo Te

At the southern end of Via Acerbi, set in its own grounds, the **Palazzo Te** (Mon 1–6pm, Tues–Sun 9am–6pm, last entry 5.30pm; €8) was designed by Giulio Romano in the 1520s for playboy Federico Gonzaga and his mistress, Isabella Boschetta. It's the artist's greatest work and a renowned Renaissance pleasure dome – originally an island connected to the mainland by bridge, an ideal location for an amorous retreat away from Federico's wife and the restrictions of life in the Palazzo Ducale. Although the upstairs rooms display paintings and antiquities, the main reason for visiting is to see Giulio's amazing decorative scheme on the ground floor.

A tour of the palace is like a voyage around Giulio's imagination, a sumptuous world where very little is what it seems. In the **Camera del Sole**, the sun and the moon are represented by a pair of horse-drawn chariots viewed from below, giving a fine array of human and equine bottoms on the ceiling. The **Sala dei Cavalli** holds portraits of prime specimens from the Gonzaga stud-farm (which was also on the island), standing before an illusionistic background in which simulated marble, fake pilasters and mock reliefs surround views of painted landscapes through nonexistent windows.

The function of the **Sala di Amore e Psiche**, further on, is undocumented, but the graphically erotic frescoes, and the proximity to Federico's private quarters, are powerful clues. The ceiling paintings tell the story of Cupid and Psyche with more dizzying *sotto in su* ("from the bottom up") works by Giulio, while the walls are covered with orgiastic wedding-feast scenes, at which drunken gods in various states of undress are attended by a menagerie of real and mythical beasts. On one wall, Mars and Venus are climbing out of the bath together, their cave watered by a river-god lounging above who is gushing with deliberately ambiguous liquid, flowing from his beard, a vessel he's holding and his genitals. Other scenes show Olympia about to be raped by a half-serpentine Jupiter and Pasiphae disguising herself as a cow in order to seduce a bull – all watched over by the giant Polyphemus, perched above the fireplace, clutching the pan-pipes with which he sang of his love for Galatea before murdering her lover.

Polyphemus and his fellow giants are revenged in the extraordinary **Sala dei Giganti** beyond – "the most fantastic and frightening creation of the whole Renaissance", according to the critic Frederick Hartt – showing the destruction of the giants by the gods. As if at some kind of advanced disaster movie, the destruction appears to be all around: cracking pillars, toppling brickwork and screaming giants, mangled and crushed by great chunks of architecture, appearing to crash down into the room. Stamp your feet and you'll discover another parallel to modern cinema – the sound effects that Giulio created by turning the room into an echo chamber.

Eating and drinking

Mantua has plenty of excellent, reasonably priced restaurants, many serving local **specialities** like *spezzatino di Mantova* (donkey stew), *agnoli in brodo* (pasta stuffed with cheese and sausage in broth) or the delicious *tortelli di zucca* (sweet pumpkin-filled pasta).

Al Quadrato Piazza Virgiliana 49 ☎0376.368.896. A tranquil spot away from the fray, overlooking the Piazza Virgiliana park north of the centre. Serves good pizzas (€7–8) and tasty fish dishes. Expect around €25. Closed Mon.

Aquila Nigra Vicolo Bonacolsi 4 ☎0376.327.180, Ⓦwww.aquilanigra.it. A formal restaurant housed in an elegant *palazzo* just off Piazza Sordello, serving delicious seasonal dishes complemented by an impressive wine list. The fish and, especially, seafood are highly regarded. Menus are €50-plus. Closed Sun & Mon. Closed Aug.

Fragoletta Piazza Arche 5/A ☎0376.323.300. Over towards the Lago Inferiore, this is a lively *osteria* shoehorned into a cramped little building. It's been around since 1748 and remains popular with locals for its well-priced regional cuisine. Expect to pay around €30. Closed Mon.

Grifone Bianco Piazza Erbe 6 ☎0376.365.423, Ⓦwww.grifonebianco.it. The pick of the restaurants on this square, a characterful, welcoming place serving excellent local specialities off a seasonal menu at moderate prices. Closed Tues & lunch on Wed. Closed late June.

Il Cigno (Trattoria dei Martini) Piazza d'Arco 1 ☎0376.327.101. Exceptional restaurant occupying a sixteenth-century mansion in a quiet corner away from the centre. The setting is refinement itself: a civilized, tasteful old dining room, free from music, overlooking a beautiful private garden. And the cooking is out of this world – sweet, delectable *tortelli di zucca* with amaretti, melt-in-the-mouth *luccio con salsa* (dressed pike) and the signature roast guinea-fowl, are some of the highlights from the seasonal menu. Service is spot-on – discreet, punctilious, yet welcoming and knowledgeable. There are no prices on the menu: expect well over €60 per head. Closed Mon, Tues and Aug.

L'Ochina Bianca Via Finzi 2 ☎0376.323.700. Cosy *osteria* where friendly staff serve tasty Mantuan dishes – this is a mainstay of the Italian Slow Food movement, dedicated to promoting quality and conviviality. 5min walk west from Piazza Erbe. Closed Mon.

Masseria Piazza Broletto 7 ☎0376.365.303, Ⓦwww.ristorantemasseria.it. A popular, lively place with good pizzas as well as a wide selection of other moderately priced dishes served at outside tables. Closed Wed & lunch on Thurs.

Tiratappi Piazza Alberti 30 ☎0376.322.366. Atmospheric old wine-bar on this little-visited square, down a concealed passageway beside the Sant'Andrea church. Its terrace tables are a sun-trap – perfect for sampling Mantuan vintages on a slow afternoon. The cuisine is all local as well: mid-priced specialities served with care. Closed Tues lunch & Thurs lunch.

Northern Lombardy: lakes and mountains

"One can't describe the beauty of the **Italian lakes**, nor would one try if one could." Henry James's sentiment hasn't stopped generations of writers producing reams of purple prose in the attempt. Yet, in truth, the lakes just about deserve it: their beauty is extravagant, and it's not surprising that the most romantic and melodramatic of Italy's opera composers – Verdi, Rossini and Bellini – rented villas here in which to work. British and German Romantic poets also enthused about the lakes, and in doing so planted them firmly in northern European imaginations. The result is a massive influx every summer of tourists from cooler climes, come to savour the Italian dream and to take gulps at what Keats called "the beaker of the warm south".

Garda is the largest lake, and one of the best centres in Europe for windsurfing and sailing. It is also visually stunning, especially in its mountainous northern stretches – yet **Como** matches (or, some say, betters) it, with forested slopes rising directly from the water's edge. On both lakes, the luxuriance of the water-front vegetation is equalled by the opulence of the local villas and *palazzi*; both also offer good hiking in the mountainous hinterland.

Further west, **Maggiore** is less popular yet just as beautiful, though many of its fin-de-siècle resorts are rather sedate. There are, however, some good walks, and superb formal gardens adorning Isola Bella. Nearby, the picture-postcard charms of Orta San Giulio, the main village on **Lake Orta** – with its steepled offshore islet – ensure that it is a popular spot, yet this too can be a wonderfully romantic place to hole up.

▲ Lake Garda in summer

The hilly terrain between the lakes is sliced up by **mountain valleys** – largely residential and industrial in their lower reaches though mostly untouched further up, hosting lots of modest ski resorts in winter (none worth making a special trip for). The nearby city of **Brescia** is best treated as a day-trip, though its neighbour **Bergamo** is a lovely place to stay, with an old walled hilltop quarter that ranks as one of the most alluring in Italy.

Getting around the lakes

Lakes Garda, Como and Maggiore are all well served by ferries and hydrofoils, which dock at jetties that are usually conveniently positioned on the main lakeside piazzas: travelling by water makes a lot more sense than struggling through lakeside traffic. All three also have useful **car ferry** routes that cut out the need for long road journeys around the lake perimeter.

For **timetables and fares** covering all three lakes, check Ⓦ www .navigazionelaghi.it or consult the posters displayed at every lakeside jetty (and local tourist offices). Prices aren't expensive – the two-hour voyage from Como to Bellagio is €7.90, for example, while it costs €12 to take a small car plus two people across Lake Garda – and there are good-value day passes available, with some discounts for children and EU citizens over 65.

Trains serve several points on all three lakes, and **buses** also run regularly up and down the shores. Tourist offices can advise about routes and timings, or check Ⓦ www.vcoinbus.it for transport around the western shore of Lake Maggiore (in Piemonte), Ⓦ www.aptv.it for buses along the eastern shore of Lake Garda (in Veneto), and Ⓦ www.trasporti.regione.lombardia.it for everything in between.

Lake Maggiore

For generations of overland travellers, weary of journeying over the Alps, **LAKE MAGGIORE** (*Lago Maggiore*) has been a first taste of Italy: the sight of limpid blue waters, green hills and exotic vegetation is evidence of arrival in the warm south. Unmistakebly Mediterranean in atmosphere, with palms and oleanders lining the lakeside promenades and a peaceful, serene air, Maggiore – at 66km,

---

Lago Maggiore Express

The **Lago Maggiore Express** ticket (Ⓦ www.lagomaggioreexpress.com) is one of the best round-trip excursions on the lakes. It comprises three sectors, all of them great journeys in their own right: a long **boat trip** into Switzerland, a ride on the magnificent **Centovalli** mountain railway between the lake resort of Locarno (in Switzerland) and Domodossola, and a **fast train** between Domodossola and Stresa. The schedules are flexible: you can start and end wherever you like, making your own choice of connections, and you can also do the trip in either direction. It runs in spring (mid-March to May Thurs–Sun), summer (June to mid-Sept daily) and autumn (mid-Sept to mid-Oct Sat & Sun); double-check on the website that you're consulting the right itinerary. The complete round-trip in **one day**, in either direction and from any starting-point, costs €30, while a **two-day** pass, which lets you overnight anywhere on the route and also includes free boat travel on the lake, is €36. Note that this is not a tour: you are on your own, using **public transport**. Carry your **passport** and reserve ahead for any **hydrofoil** journeys. On certain boats – marked on the time-tables – **lunch** is served (€15).

Italy's longest lake – may not be somewhere for thrill-seekers, but it is seductively relaxing. Beware that in winter (Nov–Easter) many hotels close down and attractions may be shut.

The majority of tourists head for the western shore, from where the sumptuous gardens and villas of the **Isole Borromee** are within easy reach. The area retains much of its charm: the genteel old resort of **Stresa** is still a convenient base, linked by high-speed train to Milan (1hr) and by bus and boat to all points around the lake. Across the bay, **Verbania** is also well connected by train, bus and ferry, while further north, enchanting **Cannobio** – the last stop before Switzerland – is popular with families and a good place from which to explore Maggiore's hilly hinterland. For tourism information, check ⓦwww .distrettolaghi.it.

Stresa

The Maggiore of the tourist brochures begins at **STRESA**, whose popularity as a resort began in 1906, when the Simplon Tunnel opened, the final link in a chain of railways connecting Lake Geneva to Milan, and thus northern Europe to the Mediterranean. International trains, including the *Orient Express*, were routed through Stresa, which quickly became a holiday retreat for Europe's high society. Today, it's a busy little place, but its greatest days have passed. Stroll the floral promenade, take in the lake views – which are worth coming for – then retire to the main square, lined with café tables dedicated to the mass consumption of outsize ice cream sundaes.

Separating Stresa from Lake Orta is the **Mottarone** mountain, rising to 1491m. From the top – accessed by **cable car** (*funivia*; daily every 20min 9.30am–5.30pm; €8.50 one-way, €15 return; ⓦwww.stresa-mottarone.it), rising from the Carciano ferry stop, 750m north of Stresa – the views are impressive, stretching to Monte Rosa on the Swiss border. Its wooded western slopes are a favourite destination for family outings. You can rent **mountain bikes** at the base station (€22 a day including cable-car ticket; ⓦwww.bicico.it). The easy walk up, signposted as path 1, takes four hours.

Practicalities

From Stresa's **train station**, walk right to the crossroads, then left on Via Duchessa di Genova for 200m down to the lakefront, where the **tourist office** stands beside the jetty (daily 10am–12.30pm & 3–6.30pm; Nov–Feb closed Sat & Sun; ℡0323.31.308, ⓦwww.distrettolaghi.it). Stresa's lakefront is lined with grand palace **hotels**, including the *Grand Hôtel des Îles Borromées* (which featured in Hemingway's *A Farewell to Arms*), the *Grand Hotel Bristol*, the *Regina Palace* and several more; all are opulent but old-fashioned – best appreciated over tea and cakes in the lounge rather than by paying to stay. Less pricey *Luina*, Via Garibaldi 21 (℡0323.30.285; ❷), is a friendly two-star in the centre, with compact rooms (some en suite) and a good-value restaurant serving home cooking. Nearby, the house-proud *Hotel Fiorentino*, Via A.M. Bolongaro 9 (℡0323.30.254, ⓦwww .hotelfiorentino.com; ❸), has comfortable en-suite rooms above a family-run restaurant with a sunny courtyard. *Verbano* (℡0323.30.408, ⓦwww.hotelverbano .it; ❻) – on the offshore Isola dei Pescatori – is the most atmospheric option, a small, romantic hotel with handsomely furnished rooms that make a perfect lakeside bolthole.

For eating, try the snug **restaurant** *La Botte*, Via Mazzini 6 (℡0323.30.462; closed Thurs), where the friendly host serves up Piemontese game, polenta and pasta dishes, or *Taverna del Pappagallo*, Via Principessa Margherita 46 (closed

Wed), a busy little pizzeria with an open wood fire. Simple *Osteria degli Amici*, Via A.M. Bolongaro 31 (closed Wed), serves tasty risotto and fish on an attractive vine-covered terrace.

The Borromean Islands

Lake Maggiore's leading attractions are three islands rising from the bay between Stresa and Pallanza – served by ferries from both, plus Carciano. All three are often dubbed the **Borromean Islands** (*Isole Borromee*), though strictly speaking only two are property of the Borromeo family (originally bankers, raised to nobility in the 1450s and still prominent locally). Romantics – if they can bear the crowds and the souvenir tat – will be knocked for six: the short voyage from Stresa to **Isola Bella** (mid-March to mid-Oct daily 9am–5.30pm; €11, joint ticket with Isola Madre €16.50; ⓦwww.borromeoturismo.it) is Italian lakes fantasy brought to life. In 1630, Carlo III Borromeo began a redesign of this modest rock: tons of soil were brought across from the mainland, a villa, fountains and statues were built, white peacocks imported, and terraces of orange and lemon trees, camellias, magnolias, box trees, laurels and cypresses carved out. Carlo's son Vitaliano died in 1690 with most of the work completed. As well as roaming the sumptuous Baroque gardens, complete with obelisks and classical statuary, dip into the island's opulent *palazzo*, which boasts a banqueting hall, ballroom, throne room and a three-storey domed *salone*, as well as six mirror- and shell-encrusted grottoes down at water level. It's definitely worth seeing.

Ferries move on to **Isola Madre** (same hours; €10, joint ticket €16.50), larger but less visited than Isola Bella, with a lusher, wilder garden – home to carob, hibiscus and banana plants, a colony of parrots and Europe's largest Kashmir cypress, alongside a small, tasteful *palazzo* housing a collection of eighteenth-century puppets. Boats also serve Hemingway's favourite island, **Isola dei Pescatori** (or **Isola Superiore**), which retains a certain charm, despite the sightseers and trinket shops. There are no sights as such, but it has some decent restaurants and is a good spot for a picnic.

Santa Caterina del Sasso

Aside from Isola Bella, the most popular ferry trip from Stresa is across to the hermitage of **Santa Caterina del Sasso** (April–Oct daily 8.30am–noon & 2.30–6pm; rest of year 9am–noon & 2–5pm; Nov–Feb closed Mon–Fri; free; ⓦwww.provincia .va.it/santacaterina). This beautiful little cliffside **monastery** – visible only from the water – is well worth a visit, though it can get crowded. The site dates back to 1170, when a local sailor was caught in a storm, invoked the help of St Catherine of Alexandria and survived; he withdrew to a cave, where local people began construction of a votive chapel. By 1620 fourteen monks lived here; today, it is still home to a Carmelite monk and seven oblates.

The complex is tiny: you could walk from one end to the other in three minutes. Eighty steps up from the jetty arrive at the lovely entrance gallery (1624), with arches looking out over the lake, which leads to the South Convent. Inside is the Gothic Chapterhouse, decorated with a pristine fresco from 1439 of St Eligius healing a horse. Ahead, beneath the four Gothic arches of the Small Convent (1315) is the church, with its stubby Romanesque bell tower and graceful Renaissance porch; a fresco of *God the Father*, dated 1610, adorns the Baroque vault above the high altar.

Pallanza (Verbania)

Across the bay from Stresa lies **PALLANZA** – part (along with neighbouring Suna and Intra) of the town of **VERBANIA**, whose title recalls *Lacus Verbanus*, the Roman name for verbena-fringed Lake Maggiore. The scenic lakefront is lined with manicured flower beds and dapper *gelaterie*, bars and hotels; on the hill behind there's a more down-to-earth quarter in which the souvenir shops are almost outnumbered by *alimentari*, fruit shops and *pasticcerie*. Pallanza's balmy climate prompted Captain Neil McEacharn, scion of a Scottish industrial family, to buy the lakeside **Villa Táranto** in 1931; the botanical garden he created (April–Oct daily 8.30am–6.30pm; €8.50; Ⓦwww.villataranto.it) – a thirty minute walk northeast of Pallanza; also served by regular boats – remains exceptional, taking in giant Amazonian lilies, lotus blossoms, Japanese maple and more, laid out with geometric precision.

The main **tourist office** is at Corso Zanitello 8 (April–Sept daily 9am–1pm & 3–6pm; Oct–March Mon–Fri 9am–1pm, Mon, Tues & Thurs also 3–5.30pm; Ⓣ0323.503.249), with a branch by the Pallanza landing-stage (Mon–Sat 8.30–11.30am & 2–7pm; Ⓣ0323.557.676, Ⓦwww.verbania-turismo.it). The lake's only **hostel** lies a signposted ten-minute walk uphill from the Piazza Gramsci bus terminal; it's a friendly place set in the old Villa Congreve, Via alle Rose 7 (Ⓣ0323.501.648, Ⓦwww.ostelloverbania.it; €16; March–Oct), with singles, doubles, small dorms and resourceful staff. *Il Burchiello*, Corso Zanitello 3 (Ⓦwww.ilburchiello.eu; closed Wed), is a fresh, friendly little **restaurant** with a contemporary feel, specializing in fish and seafood. From Intra, just north of Pallanza, a **car ferry** shuttles frequently over to Laveno, from where trains run direct to Milan, and roads connect to Varese and the A8 autostrada.

Cannobio

CANNOBIO, 25km north of Pallanza (and 5km from the Swiss border), is one of Lake Maggiore's most appealing places to stay, its lakefront road of pastel-washed houses giving onto a tightly tangled web of stepped alleyways and stone houses. The town's only sight is the **Santuario della Pietà**, a Bramante-inspired church beside the landing stage with a curious openwork cupola, built to house a painting of the pietà which supposedly began to bleed in 1522. Just north is a **public beach**, backed by pleasant lawns with trees and picnic tables.

The SS34 main road passes through Cannobio as Viale Vittorio Veneto; here, behind the San Vittore church, is the **tourist office** (Mon–Sat 9am–noon & 4.30–7pm, Sun 9am–noon; Ⓣ0323.71.212, Ⓦwww.procannobio.it). There are several lakeside **campsites** north of town, many with bungalows and caravans. From the tourist office, head down cobbled, pedestrianized Via Umberto I to find the serene *Hotel Pironi*, Via Marconi 35 (Ⓣ0323.70.624, Ⓦwww.pironihotel .it; March–Nov; ❺), a converted fifteenth-century convent in the old quarter; room 12 has a private, frescoed balcony. Friendly, family-run *Antica Stallera*, Via Zacchero 7 (Ⓣ0323.71.595, Ⓦwww.anticastallera.com; ❸) has a vine-shaded garden restaurant overlooked by simple, modern en-suite rooms.

Lo Scalo (Ⓣ0323.71.480, Ⓦwww.loscalo.com; closed Mon, Tues lunch), in a fourteenth-century *palazzo* on the lakefront piazza, is the best **restaurant** in town, serving classic Piemontese specialities; expect around €75 a head, with wine. Otherwise aim for *La Streccia* (closed Tues), up a narrow alley behind the lakefront, which offers good food in a rustic, low-ceilinged dining room, or the pleasant garden tables at *Antica Stallera* (see above). In summer the lakefront gelaterias are great for a coffee or light meal, while the bar below *Hotel Pironi* (see above) is a cosy hideaway.

Inland along the Val Cannobina

Extending behind Cannobio, the wooded **Val Cannobina** offers beautiful views and little-visited stone-built hamlets. Buses climb high into the valley, on one route to **Falmenta**, marooned in the jagged shadow of Monte Vadà (1836m), and on another to **Cúrsolo**, from where a scenic seven-kilometre walk heads past Finero to **Malesco** in the Val Vigezzo, a stop on the Domodossola–Locarno train line. The tourist office has details of many walks, including along the Linea Cadorna, a well-preserved World War I defence line that snaked across the peaks from the Val d'Ossola down to Cannobio.

Only 2.5km from Cannobio into the valley – also accessed by an attractive riverside cycle route (rent bikes from the shop on Viale Veneto) – a turn-off signs the **Orrido di Sant'Anna**, a spectacular rocky gorge surrounded by wooded slopes that is a popular picnic spot. Beside the Roman bridge and the chapel is a small river beach and the wonderfully sited **restaurant** *Sant'Anna* (T 0323.70.682; Sept–June closed Mon), which offers tasty and reasonably priced country-style cuisine.

The eastern shore

There is little of compelling interest on Maggiore's eastern shore, although any of the villages make feasible bases for hiking into the hills behind – and all are on a branch **rail** line out of Milan Porta Garibaldi (change at Gallarate). From **MACCAGNO**, an improbably steep track leads straight out into the hills, from where there are paths to tiny Lago Delio. Most interestingly, you can walk to the village of Curiglia, beyond which, from Ponte di Piero, a mule track climbs to the picturesque village of **Monteviasco**, 500m above. A driveable road also climbs from Maccagno through the woods to Lake Delio; the views looking back at Cannobio, 1000m below on the lake, are breathtaking. Maccagno has simple **hotels**, or aim for *Camin Hotel Colmegna* (T 0332.510.855, W www .caminhotel.com; ⑤), a friendly family-run place 4km south on the waterfront, with light, bright three-star rooms. Its tranquil lakeside gardens and swimming areas are difficult to beat.

The commercial town and rail hub of **LUINO** – with a strollable *centro storico* and frescoes by Bernardino Luini, a follower of Leonardo, at the oratory of **SS Pietro e Paolo** – is besieged every **Wednesday** by people pouring in for what is, purportedly, the largest weekly **market** in Europe; dodge the tacky handbag and novelty stalls to seek out the tasty food section, piled high with salami and cheeses from all over Italy and Switzerland, olives and fresh-baked bread. Roads are jam-packed from 7am onwards; extra boats and buses serve Luino all day long.

Roughly 25km south of Luino, **LAVENO** has car-ferries shuttling continuously across to Verbania-Intra. Laveno-Mombello station is on the train line from Luino to Milan Porta Garibaldi (change at Gallarate), while Laveno-Mombello Nord station is a terminus for trains from Milan Nord/Cadorna.

Lake Orta

The locals call **LAKE ORTA** (*Lago d'Orta*) "Cinderella", capturing perfectly the reticent beauty of this small lake, with its deep blue waters and intriguing island. Lying west of Lake Maggiore, wholly within Piemonte, it is unmissable for **Orta San Giulio**, the most captivating medieval village on this – or, perhaps, any – Italian lake, with narrow, cobbled lanes snaking between the wrought-iron balconies of tall, pastel-washed *palazzi*. The village is unforgettably romantic, but consequently popular: on summer Sundays the approach roads are jammed with traffic (though the charm returns after dark). If you can, visit midweek or out of season.

Orta San Giulio

Occupying the tip of a peninsula on the lake's eastern shore, **ORTA SAN GIULIO** is a seductive little bolthole with charm and character in spades. The pace of life is slow, with everything revolving around the main square, **Piazza Motta**, ringed around on three sides by elegant facades and open on the fourth to the lake and island. Gelaterias, terrace cafés and restaurants share space under the arcades with galleries, boutiques and fancy shops. On the north side is the **Palazzotto**, Orta's titchy town hall, decorated with faded frescoes and supported on an arcaded loggia. From here, head northwards on the main street, Via Olina – cobbled, and barely three metres wide – through the village and out for a stroll or a sunbathe on the lakeside promenade.

Motorboats do the five-minute run more or less on demand (€4 return) out to the **Isola San Giulio**, dominated by a white convent and the Romanesque tower of its basilica. According to legend, the island was the realm of dragons until 390 AD, when Julius, a Christian from Greece, crossed the lake using his staff as a rudder and his cloak as a sail, banished the monsters, founded a sanctuary and thus earned himself a sainthood. The resulting **Basilica di San Giulio** (April–Sept Mon noon–6.45pm, Tues–Sun 9.30am–6.45pm; Oct–March Mon 2–5pm, Tues–Sun 9.30am–noon & 2–5pm) has an impressively lofty interior. Much of its decoration, including the vaulting, dates from a Baroque eighteenth-century refit, but frescoes from as early as the fourteenth century survive. The fine **pulpit** was carved from local stone in the early twelfth century with symbols of the four evangelists and images of good winning over evil: note the crocodile locked in battle with the phoenix. From the church, it takes twenty minutes to walk round the island on its one cobbled lane, past a couple of shops, a restaurant and some enticingly scenic picnic spots.

Above Orta, the **Sacro Monte** – 21 chapels dedicated to St Francis of Assisi, containing awful painted terracotta statues acting out scenes from the saint's life – winds around the wooded hillsides, making up a devotional route still followed by pilgrims, though as many visitors come simply to admire the views and inhale the pine-scented air.

Arrival, information and accommodation

Three **buses** a day arrive at Orta San Giulio from Stresa. Orta-Miasino **train station** – on the Novara–Domodossola branch line – is around 3km east: turn left out of the station and walk downhill for about twenty minutes to reach Orta San Giulio. On the way, you'll pass the **tourist office** in an hut on Via Panoramica (Wed–Sun 9am–1pm & 2–6pm; ℡0322.905.163). The village (and the island of San Giulio) are both traffic-free: follow signs to the big car parks on the hillside above town. **Accommodation** is good but limited – always book in advance. For alternatives, try the **apartments** offered at ⓦwww .ortainfo.com or ⓦwww.ortalakeflats.com.

Hotels

Aracoeli Piazza Motta 34 ℡0322.905.173, ⓦwww.ortinfo.com. Eye-popping little design hotel (pronounced *ara-chaylee*) on the main square; check-in is at *Hotel Olina* down the street. There are only seven rooms, each stylishly presented with plain white walls, designer furniture, a/c and walk-in showers. Breakfast is gourmet. ❻

Contrada dei Monti Via dei Monti 10 ℡0322.905.114, ⓦwww.lacontradadeimonti.it. Comfortable, well-kept little hotel in an eighteenth-century house – better value than its neighbours. Rooms are fresh and stylish, many overlooking a little internal courtyard where breakfast is served in summer. Closed Jan. ❹

Leon d'Oro Piazza Motta 42 ⓣ 0322.911.991, ⓦ www.albergoleondoro.it. Long-standing old *albergo* directly on the waterfront behind the main square, with renovated three-star rooms offering some great lake views. ❹

Orta Piazza Motta 1 ⓣ 0322.90.253, ⓦ www .hotelorta.it. A traditional grand hotel in a perfect location on the main square, in the same family today as when it opened in 1864. Nowadays reduced to three-star status, it is still a decent

choice. The best rooms face the lake and the island. Closed Nov–March. ❸

Piccolo Hotel Olina Via Olina 40 ⓣ 0322.905.532, ⓦ www.ortainfo.com. Little hotel alongside the *Olina* restaurant in the historic centre, with twelve contemporary designed rooms of varying sizes – very clean and attractive. Also has an annexe nearby on Via Poli. Closed Nov to mid-Dec. ❸

Camping

Camping Orta Via Domodossola 28 ⓣ 0322.90.267, ⓦ www.campingorta.it. Good-quality site about 1km north of Orta, between the main road and the lake, with nice facilities and a private beach. Open year-round.

Eating and drinking

It's easy to gather **picnic** ingredients at the *gastronomie* on and off Piazza Motta. *Enoteca Il Boeuc*, Via Bersani 28, serves tasty **snacks** to accompany well-chosen wine. The *Olina* **restaurant**, Via Olina 40 (ⓣ 0322.905.656; closed Wed), serves excellent local specialities along with thoughtful extras like aperitifs on the house. *Pizzeria Annunziata*, Via Bossi 2 (closed Thurs), is a fresh, modern place with a wide range of pizzas, while the smarter *Antico Agnello*, Via Olina 18 (ⓣ 0322.90.259; closed Tues), offers tasty Lombard and Piemonte dishes, great puddings and congenial service. *Caffè Jazz*, Via Olina 13 (closed Mon), is a romantic little jazz bar also with a moderately priced menu of Piemontese specialities. On the hillside above town, the friendly *Sacro Monte* (closed Tues) offers a cosy interior and attractive alfresco tables.

Lake Como

Of all the Italian lakes, it's the forked **LAKE COMO** (*Lago di Como*) that comes most heavily praised: Wordsworth thought it "a treasure which the earth keeps to itself". Today, despite inroads caused by mass tourism, the lake is still surrounded by abundant vegetation: zigzagging slowly between shores by steamer can seem impossibly romantic. More prosaically, there is also some great walking to be done in the lake's mountainous hinterland. The principal towns – **Como** and **Lecco** – are at the southernmost tips of the lake, while of the other towns and villages, three stand out: **Varenna** and **Bellagio** for unrepentant romantics, and **Menaggio** if you want a pleasant, affordable base for walking, swimming or cycling.

Como

As the nearest resort to Milan, standing astride main routes to and from Switzerland, **COMO** is much visited. Though its outskirts are dotted with factories (which produce luxury silk items for the fashion houses of Milan, Paris and New York), Como's lakefront walled quarter is pleasant to wander. A funicular climbs wooded slopes nearby to offer wonderful views across the water.

Arrival, information and accommodation
The main **train station** is Como San Giovanni, on the fast line from Milano Centrale to Chiasso; it lies about ten-minutes' walk west of the centre. Como Lago

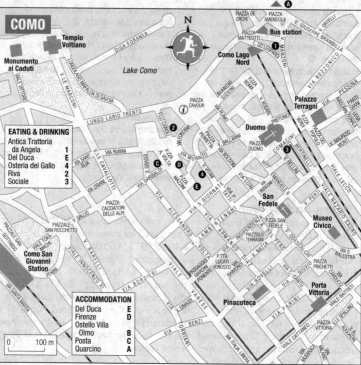

station – the terminus of a slower line from Milano Nord/Cadorna – stands on the lakefront Piazza Matteotti, alongside the old quarter and adjacent **bus station**. The **tourist office** is on Piazza Cavour (Mon–Sat 9am–1pm & 2.30–6pm; May–Sept also Sun 9.30am–12.30pm; ☎031.269.712, ⓦwww.lakecomo.org).

Hotels

Del Duca Piazza Mazzini 12 ☎031.264.859, ⓦwww.albergodelduca.it. Great little three-star hotel on a picturesque old town square, a short walk from the lake and the Duomo. Rooms are small, but windows onto the piazza – as well as nice touches like windowboxes and some two-person showers – make it special. ❹

Firenze Piazza Volta 16 ☎031.300.333, ⓦwww .albergofirenze.it. Pleasant mid-range option just back from the lakefront, with comfortable, smartly modernized rooms set mainly around a quiet internal courtyard. Some have balconies over the square. ❹

Posta Via Garibaldi 2 ☎031.266.012, ⓦwww .hotelposta.net. A dour 1930s facade belies these good budget rooms in a great central location on Piazza Volta – basic but clean and all en suite. Also some triples and a quad available. Check in at *Hotel Plinius* (Via Garibaldi 33). ❸

Quarcino Salita Quarcino 4 ☎031.303.934, ⓦwww.hotelquarcino.it. A family-run hotel on the northeast side of the old town, near the funicular, with quiet rooms, some with their own balconies overlooking the hillside. The family rooms and suites are particularly good value (€110–130) and there is parking available. ❸

Hostel

Ostello Villa Olmo (HI hostel) Via Bellinzona 2 ☎031.573.800, ⓦwww.aighostels.com. Decent hostel located within the Villa Olmo grounds; bus #1 or #6 from San Giovanni station, or take the long flight of steps in front of the station and turn left for about 1.5km along Via Borgo Vico. Serves evening meals, has laundry facilities, rents bikes and provides a discount on the funicular. Dorms €15. March–Nov.

The Town

Lakeside **Piazza Cavour** (the focus of waterfront renovation works until 2011) is bounded by modern hotels and banks. Via Plinio leads through to the Gothic **Broletto**, prettily striped in pink, white and grey, alongside the splendid **Duomo** (daily 7am–noon & 3–7pm), which was begun in the 1390s, when Gothic held sway, but wasn't completed until 1744, with the addition of a Baroque cupola. The church is reckoned to be Italy's best example of Gothic-Renaissance fusion: the fairytale pinnacles, rose windows and buffoonish gargoyles are all Gothic, while the rounded portals and statues of classical figures such as Pliny the Elder and Younger flanking the main door exemplify the Renaissance spirit. Inside, the Gothic aisles are hung with rich Renaissance tapestries, some woven with perspective scenes. In striking contrast, behind the Duomo in Piazza del Popolo stands the definitive example of Rationalist architecture by Como-born Giuseppe Terragni. Built as the headquarters for the local Fascist party in the 1930s it is now dubbed **Palazzo Terragni** and houses the Guardia di Finanza.

Northwest of Piazza Cavour, a little waterfront park is set around the **Tempio Voltiano** (Tues–Sun 10am–noon & 3–6pm; €3), dedicated to Alessandro Volta, a pioneer in electricity who gave his name to the volt. Beyond, compellingly illuminated at night, is the **Villa Olmo**, a Neoclassical pile which hosts conferences and exhibitions; whatever is on, its **gardens** are the biggest draw (Mon–Sat: summer 8am–11pm; winter 7am–7pm; free).

Stroll the lakefront northeast of Piazza Cavour to find the **funicular** (every 15–30min daily 6am–10.30pm, June–Aug until midnight; €4.25 return). It takes seven minutes to creep up the hillside past the gardens of wonderful nineteenth-century villas to **Brunate**, a small hilltop resort that has a few bars and restaurants and great views of the lake. It is also a good starting-point for hikes; the tourist office has free leaflets detailing routes.

If you're after Como silk, walk fifteen minutes south of Piazza Cavour to the **La Tessitura** outlet store, Viale Roosevelt 2a (daily 10am–10pm; Ⓦwww .latessitura.com), which sells discounted ties, scarves, blouses and home furnishings and has a stylish design café (Ⓦwww.loomcafe.com).

Eating and drinking

Antica Trattoria da Angela Via Foscolo 16. Moderately priced restaurant serving inspired regional cuisine using local ingredients. Closed Sun eve & Mon.

Del Duca Piazza Mazzini 12. Pleasant family-run restaurant with a friendly buzz, serving tasty pasta and crispy pizza.

Osteria del Gallo Via Vitani 16. Atmospheric little spot – one of several wine bars offering tasty

nibbles with a fine selection of wines. Closed Sun eve.

Riva Via Cairoli 10. Slick little restaurant just back from the waterfront, with lots of grilled meat options and an excellent range of main-course salads. Closed Mon.

Sociale Via Rodari 6. Reliable local cooking in a pleasant location just north of the Duomo. Closed Tues.

The western shore

The western lakeshore stretching north from Como is the stuff of tourist brochures: wooded mountain slopes protect the villages crammed onto the narrow shoreline from extremes of temperature, and lush gardens abound. Many of the opulent villas that line this shore are privately owned by industrialists and celebrities – George Clooney among them – and on summer weekends the lakeside road is solid with day-trippers. Further north, past the sheltered **Tremezzina** shore, **Menaggio** makes a good base for trips into the mountains behind or across to Bellagio and Varenna. Beyond Menaggio, the shore becomes rockier and less accessible until the lake peters out into the marshes that accommodate campsites around **Gravedona**.

Boats and the C10 **bus** (Ⓦwww.sptlinea.it) run northwards from Como, stopping at most villages, supplemented by **car ferries** shuttling from Cadenabbia and Menaggio across to Bellagio and Varenna.

Cernobbio and Isola Comacina

Served by frequent boats and buses from Como, **CERNOBBIO** village comprises a compact quarter of old houses, loomed over by Monte Bisbino (1325m). It is home to the palatial **Villa d'Este** hotel (Ⓣ031.3481, Ⓦwww.villadeste.it; ❾), boasting sumptuous gardens, delicate stucco-work, frescoes, marble and an atmosphere to attract the super-wealthy. An equally enticing A-list haunt is the *Gatto Nero* **restaurant**, Via Monte Santo 69 (Ⓣ031.512.042; closed Mon & Tues), a hillside trattoria serving rustic food; the terrace views are stunning, but with footballers and fashionistas as regulars, this place is just as much about who's at the next table.

A little north is **Isola Comacina**, Lake Como's only island – wild, unkempt and dotted with the ruins of nine abandoned churches. Wander at will, or book for dinner at the island's **restaurant**, *Locanda dell'Isola Comacina* (Ⓣ0344.55.083, Ⓦwww.comacina.it; June–Aug daily; March–May, Sept & Oct closed Tues; closed Nov–Feb), whose owner has made a selling-point of an elaborate "exorcism by fire" at the end of every meal, stemming from a curse supposedly laid on the island in 1169 by the Bishop of Como. It involves – essentially – flambéed liqueur coffee. Dinner is an all-in €60 (no credit cards), which covers a set menu and wine – heavily overpriced, but you're paying for the spectacle. Boat transport to and from the town of Sala Comacina adds €6.

Tremezzo and around

Sheltered by a headland, the shore above Isola Comacina, known as the **Tremezzina**, is where Como's climate is at its gentlest, the lake most tranquil and the vegetation most lush. Lined with cypresses and palms, it's lovely at any time of year, but unbeatable in spring bloom.

Access to the **Villa del Balbianello** (mid-March to mid-Nov Tues & Thurs–Sun 10am–6pm; €11, or €3 to UK National Trust cardholders; gardens only €5/free; Ⓦwww.fondoambiente.it) is chiefly by boat – small craft leave frequently from Lenno and Sala Comacina – but on Tuesdays, Saturdays and Sundays you can walk through the grounds (roughly 800m from Lenno). The house is a classic eighteenth-century set piece, but it's the **gardens** that inspire, with gravel paths between lush foliage, and stone urns framing spectacular views. George Lucas filmed parts of *Star Wars Episode II* here.

For more than 150 years, overseas visitors – particularly the British – have been holing up in **TREMEZZO** and neighbouring **CADENABBIA**; the latter's Anglican church was the first in Italy (1891). Yet the villages in the hills above retain more character: tourist offices have details of walks that pass through charming **GRIANTE**, for example – where *Casa Pini*, Via Brentano 12/F (Ⓣ0344.37.302, Ⓦwww.casapini.com; ❷), is a pleasant little B&B, serving home-cooked food – or **ROGARO**, where you'll find the family-run farmhouse restaurant *La Fagurida* (Ⓣ0344.40.676; closed Mon), specializing in home-produced *salumi*, polenta and roast rabbit.

Tremezzo is best known for **Villa Carlotta** (daily: April–Sept 9am–6pm; March & Oct 9am–noon & 2–4.30pm; €8; Ⓦwww.villacarlotta.it), located on the lakefront road but best glimpsed from the water (it has its own ferry stop).

Pink, white and exceptionally photogenic, this grand house – built in 1690 – was given by a Prussian princess to her daughter Carlotta as a wedding present. It now houses a collection of pompous eighteenth-century statuary, including Canova's romantic *Cupid & Psyche*, and boasts beautifully ordered fourteen-acre **gardens**, rich with camellias, rhododendrons and azaleas.

Menaggio

MENAGGIO, 37km north of Como, a lively and bustling village resort, is a good base for hiking and cycling in the mountains as well as sunbathing and swimming. **Ferries** dock about five-minutes' walk from the main lakefront square, Piazza Garibaldi, in and around which you'll find most of Menaggio's cafés and restaurants. The **tourist office** here (Mon–Sat 9am–12.30pm & 2.30–6pm, Sun 10am–4pm; Nov–March closed Wed & Sun; T0344.32.924, Wwww.menaggio.com) is unusually well organized, with practical information on Menaggio's numerous **hiking** possibilities, which range from a two-and-a-half hour walk to the pretty village of Codogna, to the *Sentiero delle 4 Valli*, which leads for 50km through four valleys to Lugano in Switzerland. There's a beach and vast pool at the **Lido** (late June to mid-Sept daily 9am–7pm), as well as **waterskiing** and other activities at Centro Lago Service on the waterfront.

Two historic four-star **hotels** flank Menaggio's waterfront: the *Grand Hotel Menaggio*, Via IV Novembre 69 (T0344.30.640, Wwww.grandhotelmenaggio .com; ❽; March–Oct) and *Grand Hotel Victoria*, Lungolago Castelli 9 (T0344.32.003, Wwww.grandhotelvictoria.it; ❻; March–Oct). Both are splendid, old-fashioned properties, worth a splash. Also on the lake is the stylish three-star *Bellavista*, Via IV Novembre 21 (T0344.32.136, Wwww.hotel-bellavista.org; ❹), with a terrace restaurant, pool and parking, while the *Garni Corona*, Largo Cavour 3 (T0344.32.006, Wwww.hotelgarnicorona.com; ❸; March–Nov), is a family-run lakefront two-star with plain but adequate rooms. Menaggio's excellent **HI hostel**, *Ostello La Primula*, Via IV Novembre 86 (T0344.32.356, Wwww.menaggiohostel.com; dorms €15; March–Oct), is just outside the village, with small, clean dorms and a couple of family rooms: reservations are essential. It has its own small beach, **bikes** for rent and discounts on boat rental. *Europa* **campsite** (T0344.31.187; May–Sept) is just north of town.

Menaggio's lakefront **restaurants** are trumped by those in the lanes further back. *Vecchia Menaggio*, Via al Lago 13 (closed Tues), serves simple, good-value meals for around €12, as does *Il Vapore*, Piazza Grossi 3 (closed Wed; no credit cards). The more upmarket *Corona* (aka *Il Ristorante di Paolo*), Largo Cavour 5 (T0344.32.133; closed Tues) serves well-prepared cuisine with excellent wines. With its holiday atmosphere, Menaggio can be lively after dark; *Al Paladar de la Memoria*, Via al Lago 23 (Tues–Sun 8am–2am), is a good **bar**, also serving light meals. For self-caterers, the town boasts a couple of supermarkets and some good delicatessens.

North of Menaggio

Ristorante Lauro (T348.264.6726; ❶) offers simple meals and rooms in **REZZONICO**, a sleepy hamlet of cobbled lanes woven around a thirteenth-century castle. Adjacent **PIANELLO** – served by ferries – is about as tourist-free as Lake Como gets, with local families strolling, kids playing and oldtimers soaking up the rays. Grab lunch at the village pizzeria or picnic on the shore. In **STAZZONA** – high above the next town, **Dongo** – the *Antica Trattoria Vecchia Pira* (T0344.88.277; open eves only & Sun lunch; closed Wed) is a tumbledown **restaurant** set above a rushing river, serving dishes such as smoked trout and artichoke risotto alongside local specialities (menu around €25).

GRAVEDONA, 17km north of Menaggio, is one of the few towns on the lake as old as Como, with a lazy waterfront set around a curving bay. Stroll to **Santa Maria del Tiglio**, a handsome, striped church on the lake (if it's closed, get the key from the green house on the road nearby); inside is a fine twelfth-century carving of a centaur pursuing a deer. Beyond Gravedona the terrain flattens out and there's good **sailing** and **windsurfing**: see ⓦwww.gravedona .it for details of **campsites** and modest **hotels** in the vicinity.

Bellagio

Cradled by cypress-spiked hills on the tip of the Triangolo Lariano – the triangle of mountainous land between the Como and Lecco branches of the lake – **BELLAGIO** has been called the most beautiful town in Italy. With a promenade planted with oleanders and limes, fin-de-siècle hotels painted shades of butterscotch, peach and cream, and a hilly old quarter of steep cobbled streets and alleyways – to say nothing of its spectacular mid-lake location – it's easy to see why Bellagio has become so popular. These days, the alleys are lined with upmarket souvenir shops; town life plays second fiddle to tourism but this is still a charming, attractive resort.

Arrival, information and accommodation

Boats arrive frequently from Tremezzo, Cadenábbia, Menaggio and Varenna. Passenger ships and hydrofoils dock at the main Piazza Mazzini; **car ferries** dock 150m south by the car park (you're not permitted to drive through Bellagio unless you're unloading at a hotel). **By road**, Bellagio is 30km from Como (served by **bus** C30) on a narrow, scenic road coiling along the rocky cliffs. The **tourist office**, at the dock on lakefront Piazza Mazzini (Mon–Sat 9am–12.30pm & 1–6.30pm, Sun 9.30am–12.30pm & 1–2.30pm; ☏031.950.204, ⓦwww.bellagiolakecomo.com), has information on activities including hiking, horseriding, mountain biking and watersports.

Hotels

Bellagio Salita Grandi 6 ☏031.950.424, ⓦwww .hotelbellagio.it. An appealing modern hotel in one of Bellagio's tallest buildings, with huge picture windows. Go for the rooftop vistas from the fourth floor (especially the corner rooms 401 and 404). ❹
Belvedere Via Valassina 31 ☏031.950.410, ⓦwww.belvederebellagio.com. A modern three-star hotel in its own grounds at the top of the town, with a swimming pool and wonderful views over the Lecco arm of the lake. April–Nov. ❺
Giardinetto Via Roncati 12 ☏031.950.168. Friendly one-star place at the top of Bellagio: some of the rooms have lake views and there's a garden where you can picnic. Best of the budget options. No credit cards. March–Oct. ❷
🏃 **La Pergola** Piazza del Porto 4, Pescallo ☏031.950.263, ⓦwww.lapergolabellagio.it.

Stylish, en-suite rooms with balconies overlooking the lake and the vine-covered restaurant below in this enchanting fishing hamlet. It's a good 15min walk over the hill from Bellagio, so you'll need your own transport (or taxi). April–Nov. ❹
Silvio Via Carcano 12 ☏031.950.322, ⓦwww .bellagiosilvio.com. Just out of town, this bright two-star has rooms with lake views, and an excellent restaurant serving home-made dishes featuring fish freshly caught by the friendly owner. April–Oct. ❸

Campsite

Camping Clarke ☏031.951.325, ⓦwww .bellagio-camping.com. A small, family-run campsite about 10min drive out of town on Via Valassina. May–Sept.

The Town and around

Bellagio's first hotel, the *Genazzini*, opened in 1825; its second, the *Florence*, opened in 1852. The two flank Bellagio's scenic **waterfront** to this day, and passenger boats dock midway between them (the *Genazzini* is now the *Metropole*).

The **views** from here westwards to the mountains above Cadenábbia are simply lovely; spending an afternoon watching the shadows lengthen, as the ferries parade to and fro, is pure Bellagio.

The old quarter is tiny, laid out on a grid pattern: three streets parallel to the waterfront (Piazza Mazzini at the bottom, Via Centrale in the middle, Via Garibaldi at the top) are connected by seven perpendicular stepped alleyways. At the top is the eleventh-century Romanesque church of **San Giacomo**, alongside a tower which is all that's left of Bellagio's medieval defences.

A stroll 350m north brings you to the **Punta Spartivento**, the "Point Which Divides the Winds", at the very tip of Bellagio's promontory. There's a little harbour here – nice for a cool dip – as well as a pleasant restaurant from which to enjoy the unique panorama. About ten-minutes' walk east of Bellagio on an attractive footpath through vineyards, the enchanting little harbour of **PESCALLO**, a fishing port since Roman times, offers a tremendous view of the Grigne mountains looming over the Lecco branch of the lake.

Bellagio is blessed with luxuriant flora; it's worth booking for a guided **tour** (April–Oct Tues–Sun 11am & 3.30pm; €8; buy tickets 15min in advance from the office on Piazza della Chiesa) of the gorgeous formal gardens of the **Villa Serbelloni** (now owned by the Rockefeller Foundation and maintained as a study centre), splendidly sited on a hill above the town. At the foot of the hill, the lavish *Grand Hotel Villa Serbelloni* (☎031.950.216, ⓦwww.villaserbelloni .it; ❾) is one of Lake Como's stuffiest, numbering statesmen, royalty and Hollywood stars among its guests.

South of town, the lake promenade continues for about 500m to the gardens of the **Villa Melzi** (April–Oct daily 9am–6pm; €6), a luxuriant affair crammed with azaleas, rhododendrons, ornamental lemon trees, cypresses, palms, camellias and even a sequoia. The gardens extend to the harbourside hamlet of **LÓPPIA**, a relatively quiet retreat after Bellagio.

Eating and drinking

Like everything in Bellagio, **restaurants** can be pricey – and booking is advisable. The best **ice cream** is at *Il Sorbetto* at the top of Salita Serbelloni. *BellagioPoint.com*, Salita Plinio 8, offers the intriguing combination of internet access and wine tasting.

Alle Darsene di Loppia Loppia ☎031.952.069, ⓦwww.alledarsenediloppia.com. A quiet, attractive fish restaurant on Loppia harbour, a little south of Bellagio. Closed Mon.

Du Lac Piazza Mazzini 32 ☎031.950.320. Surprisingly good for such an obvious location (beneath the arcades directly opposite the landing-stage), with carefully prepared daily specials, fair prices (€17–20), and a touch of chic atmosphere after dark.

La Grotta Salita Cernaia 14. Decent wood-fired pizza at this cosy place which serves late (until 1am). Credit cards accepted over €25. Closed Mon.

La Punta Punta Spartivento ☎031.951.888. 5min walk north of town, and serving excellent

food – especially lake fish – at good prices. Lovely views over the Punta Spartivento.

San Giacomo Salita Serbelloni ☎031.950.329. A romantic trattoria with tables on the steps, serving good local dishes off a small menu with decent wines; a meal is about €25 a head. Closed Tues.

Silvio Via Carcano 12 ☎031.950.322, ⓦwww .bellagiosilvio.com. One of Bellagio's most attractive dining spots, located just above nearby Lóppia. This is an excellent, modern restaurant attached to an old hotel; the views are beautiful, and the fish – freshly caught by Silvio himself – is superbly prepared (mains around €17). No closing day.

Varenna and the eastern shore

Gazing back at Bellagio's Punta Spartivento from the eastern shore of the lake, **VARENNA** is perhaps the loveliest spot on Lake Como. Free of through traffic, shaded by pines and planes and almost completely free of souvenir shops, the village oozes character. This is the quiet side of the lake, less visited and with fewer places to stay. North of Varenna is the attractive valley of **Valchiavenna** while to the south Lake Como forks to the southeast. This section – often dubbed "Lago di Lecco", even though it is an integral part of the whole – is austere and fjord-like, at its most atmospheric in the morning mists. At its foot is the workaday town of **Lecco** itself.

Arrival and information

Thanks to its rocky shoreline, Varenna is split into two fragments. **Boats** dock to the north, above which stands the **train station** (reached from Milano Centrale via Lecco). Some 300m south via the main road – or the *passarella*, a scenic walkway which clings to the rocks – is the main village, with the **tourist office** (April–Sept Tues–Sat 10am–12.30pm & 3–5.30pm, Sun 10am–12.30pm; Oct–March Sat 10am–5pm; ☎0341.830.367, ⓦwww.varennaitaly.com) on the central square near the D20 Lecco-Colico **bus** stop.

Accommodation

Albergo del Sole Piazza San Giorgio 21 ☎0341.815.218. Excellent three-star hotel in the village centre. Rooms are light, airy and modern – some with lake views. ❹

Albergo Milano Via XX Settembre 29 ☎0341.830.298, ⓦwww.varenna.net. One of Lake Como's friendliest, best-looking small hotels lies in the narrow lanes between the square and the waterfront. It's justifiably popular, not least for its modern design. Well run by a charming couple, it has great views and a romantic air. Closed Dec–Feb. ❺

Beretta Via per Esino 1 ☎0341.830.132, ⓦwww .hotelberetta.it. Welcoming place near the train station that is the best of the cheaper options. ❷

Olivedo Piazza Martiri 14 ☎0341.830.115, ⓦwww.olivedo.it. Eccentric, atmospheric little family-run hotel opposite the landing-stage, stuffed with old prints and knick-knacks. ❺

The village

As well as the thirteenth-century **San Giorgio** on the main piazza, Varenna also hosts one of the oldest churches on the lake, the tenth-century **San Giovanni Battista** opposite, with well-preserved, fragmentary frescoes. Varenna's other main sights are botanical: the nineteenth-century **Villa Cipressi**, on the southern fringe of the village, has terraced gardens (April–Oct daily 9am–7pm; €4) tumbling down to the lake that make a perfect spot to relax. The adjacent **Villa Monastero** gardens (April–Oct daily 9am–6pm, June–Sept until 7pm; €3) are even more lavish. The splendid house, built over a convent dissolved in 1569, is now used as a conference centre; when meetings are on, the gardens are closed. A brisk twenty-minute walk up the steep path opposite Villa Monastero leads to spectacular views from the semi-ruined **Castello di Vezio** (April–Oct daily 10am–sunset; free), allegedly founded by the Lombard Queen Theodolinda in the seventh century.

A short walk south of Varenna, **Fiumelatte** ("River of Milk") is named for the torrent which tumbles frothily through it for half the year – starting abruptly in March and running dry in October. It's the **shortest river in Italy** (and perhaps Europe), just 250m from source to outflow.

Eating and drinking

Albergo del Sole Piazza San Giorgio 21 ☎0341.815.218. Fine, inexpensive pizzeria on the main square, with an attractive summer garden. Closed Wed.

Albergo Milano Via XX Settembre 29 ☎0341.830. 298. Hide away on this beautiful little terrace for a romantic dinner of light, tasty Mediterranean cuisine. Expect around €30. Eve only. Closed Tues & Sun.

Il Cavatappi Via XX Settembre ☏ 0341.815.349, ⓦ www.ilcavatappiwine-food.it. Varenna's best place to eat – and its smallest, with just five tables. At this delightful restaurant, hidden away in the thicket of lanes off the main square, the owner/manager/chef takes the time to discuss the menu with you before turning out simple, beautifully cooked dishes with first-class ingredients. A meal is around €25 a head. Closed Wed.

Vecchia Varenna Contrada Scoscesa ☏ 0341.830.793, ⓦ www.vecchiavarenna.it. In an unbeatable location, tucked beneath the arcades on the lakeside promenade (book for a terrace table) – with food that is good, though not outstanding. Closed Mon.

North of Varenna: into the Valchiavenna

BELLANO, 4km north of Varenna, is a workaday town of silk and cotton mills. From the landing-stage follow signs for the three-minute walk to the **Orrido di Bellano** (April–Sept daily 10am–1pm & 2.30–7pm; Oct–March Sat & Sun 10am–12.30pm & 2.30–5pm; €3.50), a steep gorge with a series of walkways suspended above a roaring river. About 12km north, a minor road branches down to the tranquil Romanesque **Abbazia di Piona** (daily 9am–12.30pm & 1.30–6.30pm), perched on a headland. A shop by the gates sells bottles of the monks' fiery herb liqueur. Last stop for ferries, at the top of the lake's eastern shore, is industrial **CÓLICO**.

Trains continue north of Colico into the **Valchiavenna**, a flat-bottomed valley into which Lake Como extended as recently as Roman times. Make a beeline for the pleasant Alpine town of **CHIAVENNA**, to visit one of the many *crotti*, natural cellars in the rocks which for centuries have been used for maturing wine, salami, cured meats and cheeses. Most are now inns and restaurants; the finest is *Crotto al Prato*, Via Picchi 13 (from the station, cross the tracks and follow Via Pratogiano), where you can sit in the cosy stone interior or at terrace tables by the boules pitch with wonderful mountain views. The **tourist office** (Mon–Sat 9.30am–12.30pm & 2.30–6pm, Sun 9am–12.30pm; ☏ 0343.33.442, ⓦ www.valtellina.it), by the train station, has information on sights and practicalities.

South of Varenna: towards Lecco

Past **MANDELLO DEL LARIO**, production centre of Italy's famous **Moto Guzzi** motorbikes since 1921 – there's a museum of vintage specimens at Via Parodi 57 (guided tours Mon–Fri 3pm; free; ⓦ www.motoguzzi.it) – stands **LECCO**, 30km east of Como at the foot of this branch of the lake. It's a commercial centre with few attractions; literary types might appreciate **Villa Manzoni**, Via Guanella 7 (Tues–Sun 9.30am–5.30pm; €5), the childhood home of Alessandro Manzoni, author of the great nineteenth-century Italian novel *I Promessi Sposi* ("The Betrothed"); otherwise, pop into the lakefront **Basilica** to see its fourteenth-century Giottesque frescoes. Lecco's **tourist office** is at Via Nazario Sauro 6, off the lakefront Piazza Garibaldi (daily 9am–1pm & 2.30–6.30pm; ☏ 0341.295.720, ⓦ www.turismo.provincia.lecco.it), with information on mountain hikes in the isolated **Valsássina**.

Bergamo

Just 50km northeast of Milan, yet much closer to the mountains in look and feel, **BERGAMO** comprises two distinct parts – **Bergamo Bassa**, the modern city centre on the plain, and medieval **Bergamo Alta**, clinging to the rocky slopes 100m higher. Bergamo Bassa is a harmonious mixture of medieval cobbled quarters blending into late nineteenth- and early twentieth-century

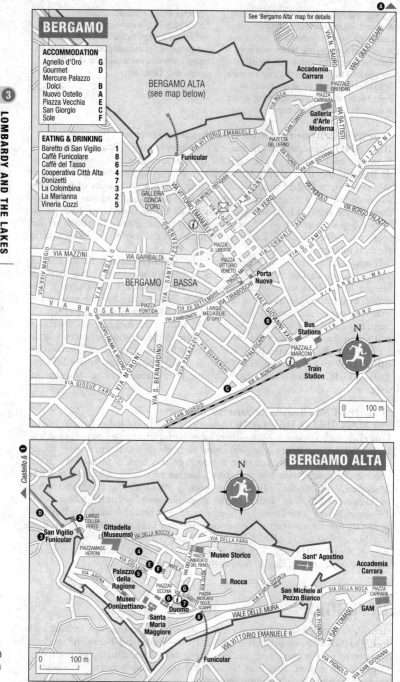

BERGAMO

ACCOMMODATION
Agnello d'Oro	G
Gourmet	D
Mercure Palazzo Dolci	B
Nuovo Ostello	A
Piazza Vecchia	E
San Giorgio	C
Sole	F

EATING & DRINKING
Baretto di San Vigilio	1
Caffè Funicolare	8
Caffè del Tasso	6
Cooperativa Città Alta	4
Donizetti	7
La Colombina	3
La Marianna	2
Vineria Cozzi	5

BERGAMO ALTA
(see map below)

Accademia Carrara

Galleria d'Arte Moderna

Funicular

GALLERIA CONCA D'ORO

BERGAMO BASSA

Porta Nuova

Bus Stations

Train Station

N

0   100 m

BERGAMO ALTA

N

Castello &

San Vigilio Funicular

LARGO COLLEO PERTO

Cittadella (Museums)

Palazzo della Ragione

Museo Donizettiano

Santa Maria Maggiore

Duomo

Museo Storico

Rocca

Sant' Agostino

Accademia Carrara

San Michele al Pozzo Bianco

GAM

VIALE DELLE MURA

Funicular

0   100 m

town planning, while Bergamo Alta is one of northern Italy's loveliest urban centres, with fresh mountain air, wanderable lanes and a lively, easygoing pace of life.

Bergamo owes much of its magic to the Venetians, who ruled the town for over 350 years, adorning facades and open spaces with the Venetian lion, symbol of the republic, and leaving a ring of gated walls. Now worn, mellow and overgrown with creepers, these kept armies out until the French invaded in 1796. Sample the best of Bergamo's atmosphere by roaming the alleyways which weave around the **Piazza Vecchia** and adjacent church of **Santa Maria Maggiore**.

Arrival and information

Bergamo's Orio al Serio **airport** (☏035.326.323, ⓦwww.orioaeroporto.it) lies 4km southeast of town. There's a well-equipped **tourist office** (daily 8am–11pm; ☏035.320.402, ⓦwww.turismo.bergamo.it) in the arrivals area, as well as kiosks selling bus tickets to Stazione Centrale in Milan (daily approx every 30min 5am–1am): Orioshuttle costs €8, while Autostradale charge €8.90 but offer three for the price of two. For Bergamo, take city bus #1 (daily every 30min 6am–midnight; €1.65, day-pass €3.50).

Bergamo **train station** is at the end of Bergamo Bassa's central avenue, Viale Papa Giovanni XXIII, which becomes Via Vittorio Emanuele II. Opposite is the **bus station**, which was being rebuilt at the time of writing. Bus #1 runs frequently between the airport, the train station, the base station of the **funicular** (from where you can make the ascent to Bergamo Alta for no extra charge as long as you show your bus ticket; otherwise €1) and on to Colle Aperto at the top of the town – though some services stop short or follow variations; check timetables carefully.

The city centre has two **tourist offices** (ⓦwww.provincia.bergamo.it /turismo) – at the train station (daily 9am–12.30pm & 2–5.30pm; Oct–May closed Sat & Sun; ☏035.210.204), and in Bergamo Alta in the Torre Gombito off Piazza Vecchia (daily 9am–12.30pm & 2–5.30pm; ☏035.242.226). A **guided walk** in English starts from Piazza Mercato delle Scarpe (April–Oct Wed & Sun 3pm; 2hr; €10).

Accommodation

Bergamo's **accommodation** is pricey and, in the centre, fairly limited: always book ahead. It's also worth checking out B&Bs (see ⓦwww.bed-and-breakfast .it, ⓦwww.bedandbergamo.it or ⓦwww.bebilmondoincasa.com) – some are located in attractive buildings in Bergamo Alta.

Agnello d'Oro Via Gombito 22 ☏035.249.883, ⓦwww.agnellodoro.it. In the heart of the upper town, this cosy two-star offers plain but comfortable en-suite rooms, some with balconies. ❸
Gourmet Via San Vigilio 1 ☏035.437.3004, ⓦwww.gourmet-bg.it. Just above Città Alta, with spacious, modern rooms boasting wonderful views. The restaurant serves local staples. ❹
Mercure Palazzo Dolci Viale Papa Giovanni XXIII 100 ☏035.227.411, ⓦwww.mercure.com. Four-star chain hotel near the station. Anonymous but stylish, convenient and excellent value, it has swish contemporary interiors and good soundproofing. ❻

Nuovo Ostello di Bergamo (HI hostel) Via Galileo Ferraris 1 ☏035.361.724, ⓦwww.ostellodibergamo .it. This award-winning hostel has bathrooms in every room, bicycles for rent and a rooftop terrace with great views. It's a fair way out: bus #3 from Piazza Mercato delle Scarpe in the Città Alta runs to the door. Dorms €17; also doubles, triples and quads. ❶
Piazza Vecchia Via Colleoni 3 ☏035.253.179, ⓦwww.hotelpiazzavecchia.it. Three-star hotel in a medieval building on Bergamo Alta's main "street" (a pedestrianized alley). The 13 arty rooms feature fresh, contemporary design – but service can be less than forthcoming. ❻

San Giorgio Via San Giorgio 10 ☏ 035.212.043, ⓦ www.sangiorgioalbergo.it. A well-run and friendly hostel-like option, 5min from the station, offering various sized rooms with or without bathrooms, all spotless. ❷

Sole Via B Colleoni 1 ☏ 035.218.238, Ⓕ 035.240.011. Just off the main square in Città Alta, this bright and breezy traditional hotel offers simple en-suite two-star rooms with little balconies looking over a back courtyard or the garden. ❸

Bergamo Alta: the upper town

With its steep, narrow streets, flanked by high facades and encircled by sixteenth-century walls, **Bergamo Alta** – the upper town – remains in appearance largely as it was in the Middle Ages. The main public spaces – **Piazza Vecchia** and adjacent **Piazza del Duomo** – combine medieval austerity with the grace of later, Renaissance design. The main street, beginning as Via Gombito and continuing as Via Colleoni, follows the line of the Roman *decumanus maximus*, topped and tailed by evidence of Bergamo's military past – the **Rocca** to the east, the **Cittadella** to the west.

Piazza Vecchia

From the upper funicular station on Piazza Mercato delle Scarpe, narrow Via Gombito leads up to Bergamo's magnificent **Piazza Vecchia**, enclosed by a harmonious miscellany of buildings, ranging from wrought-iron-balconied houses containing cafés and restaurants to the opulent Palladian-style civic library. Stendhal dubbed this "the most beautiful square on earth", and it's certainly a striking space. The most imposing presence is the medieval **Palazzo della Ragione**, a Venetian-Gothic building stretching right across the piazza opposite the library, lending a somewhat stagey atmosphere, especially at night when the wrought-iron lamps are switched on. Court cases used to be heard under the open arcades that form the ground floor. A grand covered stairway, dating from 1453, rises from alongside. The piazza was the scene of joyous celebrations in 1797, when the French formed the Republic of Bergamo: the square was carpeted with tapestries and transformed into an open-air ballroom in which – as a symbol of the new democracy – dances were led by an aristocrat partnered by a butcher.

Until 2011, while Bergamo's prestigious Accademia Carrara gallery is closed for renovation, the Palazzo della Ragione is housing around a hundred of its masterpieces (June–Sept Tues–Sun 10am–9pm, Sat until 11pm; Oct–May Tues–Fri 9.30am–5.30pm, Sat & Sun 10am–6pm; €5; ⓦ www.accademiacarrara .bergamo.it). At the time of writing the layout had not been determined; it seems likely, though, that you will be able to view **Titian**'s remarkable *Virgin and Child*, painted at the age of 27, a touchingly effeminate *St Sebastian* by the young **Raphael** and **Botticelli**'s startlingly modern *Portrait of Giuliano de' Medici* – among many other works.

To the right of the *palazzo* looms the massive **Torre Civica**, or **Campanone**, which you can ascend by lift (April–Oct Tues–Fri 9.30am–7pm, Sat & Sun 9.30am–9.30pm; Nov–March Sat & Sun 9.30am–4.30pm; €3). Its seventeenth-century bell, which narrowly escaped being melted down by the Germans during World War II, still tolls every half-hour.

Piazza del Duomo

Walk beneath the Palazzo della Ragione's arcades to enter **Piazza del Duomo** – a small, cramped space where the **Duomo** (under renovation) is of less interest than **Santa Maria Maggiore** alongside (Mon–Sat 9.30am–12.30pm & 2.30–6pm), a rambling Romanesque church with a scalloped Gothic porch. Inside, it is a perfect example of high Baroque, its ceiling marzipanned with ornament, encrusted with gilded stucco, painted vignettes and languishing statues. Look for the kitschy nineteenth-century monument to Donizetti, the Bergamo-born composer of comic opera: bas-relief putti stamp their feet and smash their lyres in misery at his death. More subtly, the intarsia biblical scenes on the choir stalls – designed by Lorenzo Lotto, and executed by a local craftsman – are remarkable not only for their intricacy but also for the incredible colour-range of the natural wood.

Even the glitziness of Santa Maria is overshadowed by the Renaissance decoration of the **Cappella Colleoni** next door (Tues–Sun 9am–12.30pm & 2–4.30pm). Commissioned by Bartolomeo Colleoni, a Bergamo mercenary in the pay of Venice, and built onto the church in the 1470s, the chapel is an extravagant confection of pastel-coloured marble carved into an abundance of miniature arcades, balustrades and twisted columns, capped with a mosque-like dome. The opulent interior, with its frescoed ceiling, shelteres Colleoni's sarcophagus, topped with a gilded equestrian statue. Note Colleoni's coat of arms on the gate as you enter; the smoothness of the decorative third "testicle" (supposedly biologically accurate) bears witness to the local tradition that rubbing it will bring you luck. Outside on the square is the free-standing **Baptistry** (kept locked), which was removed from the interior of Santa Maria Maggiore in the seventeenth century.

Around Piazza Vecchia

From the south door of Santa Maria Maggiore, **Via Arena** climbs towards the west end of the Città Alta. Partway up at number 9, a frescoed doorway opens into the grounds of the Santa Grata monastery, also home to the **Museo Donizettiano** (Tues–Fri 9.30am–1pm, Sat & Sun 9.30am–1pm & 2.30–5.30pm; €3; Ⓦwww.gaetanodonizetti.net). One of the masters of the "bel canto" opera style (along with Bellini and Rossini), Gaetano Donizetti (1797–1848), who was born and died in Bergamo, is celebrated for his melodramatic lyricism, which reached a peak in *Lucia di Lammermoor*. The museum contains portraits of the maestro, original letters and scores, as well as his fortepiano and imperial-style bed. Via San Lorenzo heads north from the Torre Gombito near Piazza Vecchia down to the **Museo Storico** (Tues–Fri 9.30am–1pm & 2–5.30pm, Sat & Sun 9am–7pm; €3). Housed on Piazza Mercato del Fieno in the ex-convent of San Francesco, with a beautiful thirteenth-century cloister, it spans the history of the city from the eighteenth century to 1945. Following Via Solata east from here leads on a short climb to the **Rocca**, rebuilt in the 1330s, from where spectacular views encompass eastern Bergamo.

Towards the Colle Aperto and San Vigilio

Leading northwest out of Piazza Vecchia, the narrow, pedestrianized **Via Colleoni** is lined with delicatessens and pastry shops selling sweet polenta cakes topped with chocolate birds. The **Teatro Sociale**, at no. 4, is occasionally open for art exhibitions; it's worth a look for its grandiose interior, designed in 1803. At the top of the street, Piazza Mascheroni lies at the entrance to the **Cittadella**, a military stronghold built by Barnabo Visconti, now housing a small theatre and two didactic (Italian only) museums of archeology and natural history. Beyond the Cittadella lies the **Colle Aperto**, a blast of modernity, with traffic and ordinary shops. From here you can either walk back through the city or follow the old **walls** – the whole circuit takes a couple of hours, with the most picturesque stretch lying between the Colle Aperto and Porta San Giacomo (from where a long flight of steps leads down into Bergamo Bassa). For the best views, head up through the Porta Sant'Alessandro, beside Colle Aperto, towards **San Vigilio**: a funicular does the short journey but the walk is pleasant, up a steep, narrow road overlooking the gardens of Bergamo's most desirable properties. At the top perches the **Castello**, alongside a sprinkling of (pricey) bars and restaurants.

Bergamo Bassa: the lower town

Bergamo Bassa spreads north from the train station in a comfortable blend of Neoclassical ostentation, Fascist severity and tree-lined elegance. At the heart of the busy, traffic-choked streets, midway along the main Viale Papa Giovanni XXIII, the mock-Doric temples of the **Porta Nuova** mark the **Sentierone**, a spacious piazza with gardens, and a favourite spot for Bergamo's citizens to meet and stroll beneath the trees. The area was laid out by Roman architect Marcello Piacentini in the 1920s with a plan focused on traditional elements – loggias, porticoes and piazzas – but had been a Bergamasque rendez-vous since the 1620s. Frowning down on the square is the **Palazzo di Giustizia**, built in the bombastic rectangular style of the Mussolini era.

From the Sentierone, Via Torquato Tasso leads east into the oldest part of the Città Bassa, formed in the Middle Ages as overspill from the upper town; narrow, gloomy **Via Pignolo** has a largely unchanged appearance, with many architectural features – balconies, mullioned windows – surviving. Follow it up to the attractive **Piazzetta del Delfino**, occupied by a dolphin fountain built here in 1526. From here, Via Pignolo continues to the Porta Sant'Agostino, at the bottom of Bergamo Alta, while Via San Tomaso, packed with galleries, antiques shops and cafés, heads right towards the Accademia Carrara – Bergamo's finest art gallery, closed for renovation until 2011 – and its neighbour, the **Galleria d'Arte Moderna e Contemporanea**, Via San Tomaso 82 (ⓦwww .gamec.it; hours and admission varies), with world-class temporary exhibits and a small permanent collection including works by Kandinsky and a moody *Still Life With Fruit* by surrealist Giorgio de Chirico.

Eating and drinking

One of the pleasures of Bergamo is its food, whether you're assembling picnics from the many *salumerie* and bakeries in the old town – most lining the main streets of Via Gombito and Via Colleoni – or can afford to graze around the city's *osterie*. The town's culinary attractions are headed by game – hunting the local wildlife is a major pastime – as well as the signature dishes of polenta and *casoncelli*, ravioli stuffed with sausage meat and served with sage butter. Always **book ahead**. You'll find the best **ice cream** under the luxuriant balconies of *La Mariana* on Largo Colle Aperto, Bergamo's oldest *pasticceria*.

Baretto di San Vigilio Via Castello 1 ☏035.253.191, ⓦwww.baretto.it. An unbeatable choice of excellent dishes on an attractive vine-covered terrace with spectacular views. Prices reflect the location – at the top station of the San Vigilio funicular – so expect to pay more than €50 per head. Closed Mon.

Caffè Funicolare In the funicular station on Piazza Mercato delle Scarpe. Good-value snacks and drinks served on a terrace with a great view over Città Bassa. Open until 2am. Closed Tues.

Caffè del Tasso Piazza Vecchia ⓦwww .caffedeltasso.it. Bergamo's oldest café and wine

bar, founded in 1476 beside the Palazzo della Ragione. With bookcases and sculptures, the barrel-vaulted interior retains its atmosphere. Tables also spill out onto the cobbles.

Cooperativa Città Alta Vicolo Sant'Agata, signposted off Via Colleoni. This cooperative venture – a cheery amalgam of café, restaurant and bar (open until 2am) – boasts good food at low prices, a happy hour on Thurs and a garden with views of the hills. Closed Wed.

Donizetti Via Gombito 17/A ☏035.242.661, ⓦwww.donizetti.it. Excellent place for a slap-up meal or a *degustazione* platter of local

3

meats and cheeses washed down with fine wine. Inside is warm and welcoming; in summer tables are laid out in the covered market space.
La Colombina Via Borgo Canale 12 ⓣ035.261.402. A wonderful little trattoria with tasty, good-value Bergamasco food and glorious views (ask for a table by the window when you book). Closed Mon & Tues.

Sole Via B. Colleoni 1 ⓣ035.218.238. A popular restaurant attached to the eponymous hotel, serving traditional local specialities and fish in an attractive garden in summer. Closed Thurs.
Vineria Cozzi Via Colleoni 22/A, ⓦwww .vineriacozzi.it. A classy wine bar with around three hundred wines to choose from and excellent local cooking. Closed Wed.

Brescia

Surrounded by vine-covered hills, the ancient settlement of **BRESCIA** is a wealthy city, boasting Roman remains, Renaissance squares and a medieval city centre juxtaposed with important twentieth-century architecture. Yet for all this, it lacks the elegance and charm of other northern Italian cities and you'd do best to visit its sights in a day and then head on your way – easy, as the town is well connected by road, rail and bus.

Arrival, information and accommodation

Verona-Brescia **airport** (ⓣ030.965.6599, ⓦwww.bresciaairport.com; also known as Gabriele D'Annunzio) is 23km southeast near Montichiari; flights are met by buses shuttling to Brescia (25min; €7.50) and Verona (45min; €11). Brescia has three exits off the A4 **autostrada** and is a principal stop for **trains** on the main line between Milan and Venice (as well as slower trains from Lecco, Bergamo and Cremona). **Buses** (ⓦwww.trasportibrescia.it) serve Verona, Mantua and Lake Garda. The **train station** – flanked by two bus stations – is a dull fifteen-minute walk from the centre; it's best to cross the road for **city bus** #1 (direction Mombello) or #2 (direction Pendolina), which both head into the centre: buy tickets (€1 valid 75min; €2.80 valid 24hr) from the driver or the shop by the bus stop. While the new metro is under construction (due to open in 2012), expect roadworks and traffic disruption. The **tourist office** is at Piazza della Loggia 6 (Mon–Sat 9.30am–6.30pm; Sun 10am–6pm; ⓣ030.240.0357, ⓦwww.bresciatourism.it).

Hotels

Ambasciatori Via Crocefissa di Rosa 90 ⓣ030.399.114, ⓦwww.ambasciatori.net. A fine, family-run four-star occupying an ugly modern building 1km north of the centre, with spacious rooms and good facilities. Free parking. Bus #1 stops outside. ❺
Antica Villa Via San Rocchino 90 ⓣ030.303.186, ⓦwww.hotelanticavilla.it. Small villa hotel north of the centre. Its fifteen en-suite rooms have character, though it is awkwardly far out. Bus #1 stops outside. ❸

Orologio Via Beccaria 17 ⓣ030.375.5411, ⓦwww.albergoorologio.it. This attractive medieval building off Piazza Paolo VI has been transformed into an a three-star boutique hotel. Rooms have been updated with a good deal of taste, matching the warm welcome and genial service. ❹
Trento Piazza Battisti 31 ⓣ030.380.768. Decent two-star on a busy square just north of the centre – best of the budget options. Take bus #7 from the train station. ❷

The City

Brescia's centre comprises a compact cluster of piazzas linked by cobbled streets. The main square, **Piazza della Loggia**, is also the prettiest, dating from 1433, when the city invited Venice to protect it from Milan's power-hungry Viscontis.

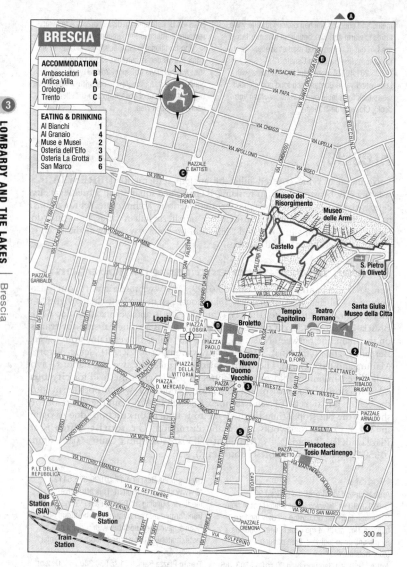

ACCOMMODATION
Ambasciatori   B
Antica Villa   A
Orologio   D
Trento   C

EATING & DRINKING
Al Bianchi   1
Al Granaio   4
Muse e Musei   2
Osteria dell'Elfo   3
Osteria La Grotta   5
San Marco   6

The Venetian influence is clearest in the fancy **Loggia**, in which both Palladio and Titian had a hand, and the **Torre dell'Orologio**, modelled on the campanile in Venice's Piazza San Marco. Below it, a monument commemorates the Fascist bombing, in 1974, of a trade-union rally here, in which eight people were killed and over a hundred injured: you can still see the blast damage on the pillar. Alongside is the **Porta Bruciata**, a defensive medieval tower-gate. Streets connect south, behind the tourist office, into the austere, Fascist-built **Piazza della Vittoria**, under the stern gaze of the monumental post office building. The south side of the square leads to **Piazza del Mercato**, a cobbled square of more interest to the stomach than the eye: as well as a supermarket, small shops selling local salamis and cheeses nestle under its dark porticoes.

Passages from Piazza della Loggia and Piazza della Vittoria lead east across galleried Via Dieci Giornate through to **Piazza Paolo VI**, one of the few squares in Italy to have two cathedrals – though, frankly, it would have been better off without the chilly **Duomo Nuovo** (Mon–Sat 7.30am–noon & 4–7pm, Sun 8am–1pm & 4–7pm), its grim Neoclassical facade concealing a tall cupola. Much more appealing is the adjacent twelfth-century **Duomo Vecchio**, or **Rotonda** (Tues–Sun: April–Oct 9am–noon & 3–7pm; Nov–March 10am–noon & 3–6pm), a unique circular church of local stone, sunk below the current level of the piazza. Inside, glass set into the transept pavement reveals the remains of Roman baths (a wall and geometrical mosaics) and the apse of an eighth-century basilica, which burned down in 1097.

From the top end of the square, Via dei Musei marks the *decumanus maximus* (east–west road) of the Roman settlement of Brixia; a short walk east brings you to **Piazza del Foro**, built over the ancient forum (which was substantially larger than the current square). Dominating the area are the tall columns of the **Tempio Capitolino** (daily 11am–4pm; free), a Roman temple built in 73 AD, now partly reconstructed with red brick. Adjacent to the east is a part-excavated Roman **theatre**.

A short walk further along Via dei Musei is Brescia's civic museum of **Santa Giulia** (Tues–Sun: June–Sept 10am–6pm; Oct–May 9.30am–5.30pm; €8; ⓦ www.bresciamusei.com), housed in an ex-Benedictine convent built over what was a Roman quarter of frescoed villas. The layers of history on show, and the well-organized layout, make this well worth an hour or two. Inside are three churches: twelfth-century San Salvatore, which includes remains of a crypt built in 762; Santa Maria in Solario, covered in frescoes painted mainly by the Renaissance artist Floriano Ferramola; and the late-sixteenth-century church of Santa Giulia, with further frescoes by Ferramola. The museum holds a collection of artefacts chronicling the city's history, including a life-sized Roman *Winged Victory* in bronze, beautifully preserved Roman mosaic floors and the eighth-century wooden cross of Desiderius, studded with more than two hundred gemstones. The complex also stages major art exhibitions (ⓦ www.lineadombra.it).

Behind the museum, Via Piamarta climbs the **Cydnean Hill**, the core of early Roman Brixia (though remains are scanty), topped by the **Castello** (daily 8am–8pm; free), begun in the fifteenth century by Luchino Visconti and added to by the Venetians, French and Austrians. The resulting confusion of towers, ramparts, halls and courtyards makes a good place for an atmospheric picnic.

A short walk south of Santa Giulia, Brescia's main art gallery, the **Pinacoteca Tosio-Martinengo**, Via Martinengo da Barco 1 (Tues–Sun: June–Sept 10.30am–6pm; Oct–May 9.30am–5pm; €5), showcases works by the Brescian Renaissance artists Romanino and Moretto, alongside major works by Lotto and others. Room 1.1 holds two masterpieces by Raphael – an *Angel* and a *Risen Christ* – while room 2.5 holds Moretto's chilling *Passion* (c.1550), depicting a reproachful Christ slouched before an angry, tearful angel.

Eating and drinking

Central Brescia has plenty of reasonably priced **places to eat**, specializing in local dishes such as *casoncei* (large meat-filled ravioli) or game. Many menus feature pasta stuffed with (or polenta smothered in) *bagòss*, a local cheese – rich, spicy and flavourful. Piazzale Arnaldo to the east of the centre has a clutch of **café–bars** that fill up quickly after work and stay buzzing into the small hours.

Al Bianchi Via Gasparo da Salò 30
℡030.292.328, ⓦwww.osteriaalbianchi.it. Historic restaurant in a quiet central location. A popular evening spot, serving a variety of tasty, moderately priced local dishes, specializing in Brescian meaty mains. Closed Tues eve & Wed.

Al Granaio Piazzale Arnaldo ℡030.375.9345. A fine *osteria* under the arcades of the old city granary. The covered terrace is an atmospheric place for lunch, and is candlelit after dark. The food is moderately priced local fare, with a broad choice of wines.

Muse e Musei Piazza T. Brusato 24 ℡030.45.048. An ideal location near the exit of the Santa Giulia museum: after all that culture, sink into a sofa or armchair for a reviving drink, or sit up for a light meal. Open until 2am. Closed Wed eve & Aug.

Osteria dell'Elfo Piazza Vescovato 1/B
℡030.377.4858. Decent little restaurant on this central square, with terrace tables catering to the pre- and post-theatre crowd – think salads and light meals of pasta and fish. Closed Tues.

Osteria La Grotta Vicolo del Prezzemolo 10
℡030.44.068, ⓦwww.osterialagrotta.it. Charming little spot with an atmospheric interior and a menu centred on its own, high-quality *salumi* and other local specialities. Expect to pay around €35. Closed Wed.

San Marco Via Spalto San Marco 15
℡030.45.541. Apparently rundown little dive on a main road south of the centre, with tired, 70s-era furnishings – but nonetheless a great place for authentic, inexpensive Brescian cooking, prepared with pride. Closed Sun, Mon eve.

Lake Garda

LAKE GARDA (*Lago di Garda*) is the largest lake in Italy (52km long by 17km wide): it's so big that it alters the local climate, which is milder and – thanks to a complex pattern of lake breezes – sunnier than might be expected. It's also the most popular of the lakes, handling around 7 percent of all tourists to Italy and acting as a bridge between the Alps and the rest of the country. The narrow north of the lake is tightly enclosed by mountains that drop sheer into the water with villages wedged into gaps in the cliffs. Further south, the lake spreads out comfortably, flanked by gentle hills and lined by placid holiday resorts.

In the south, **Desenzano** is a cheery spot with the advantage of good transport links, plus proximity to scenically impressive **Sirmione**. On the western shore are lovely **Salò** and **Gargnano**, the lake's best destination, a small village that remains largely unspoilt. In the north, **Riva del Garda** – the lake's best-known holiday spot – is a charming small town with a long history. On the eastern shore, **Malcesine** is too popular for its own good, though **Torri del Benaco** is another attractive corner that has avoided the worst of the crowds. For information on resorts and activities all round the lake, consult ⓦwww.visitgarda.com.

Note that Garda's **resorts** are packed with holiday-makers in summer, both northern Europeans (Germans and Austrians in particular taking advantage of the motorways from Munich and Innsbruck that lead over the Brenner Pass directly to Garda's eastern shore) and Italian families alike, many attracted by the variety of watersports and mountain activities on offer. Trying to move around – to say nothing of enjoying the tranquillity of the lake – is not easy on frenetic summer weekends, when you should expect some heavy traffic on the scenic lakeshore road (which has one lane in each direction, often squeezing through dimly lit tunnels). Regular **buses** ply both shores but travelling by **boat** is the most relaxing option, with at least hourly services between the main resorts. Two car ferries cross the lake (Maderno–Torri del Benaco, and Limone–Malcesine).

The southern shore

Served by the Milan–Venice autostrada and railway – and with regular buses from Brescia – **DESENZANO DEL GARDA**, the lake's largest town, is handy for stopping in to sample a taste of Garda's atmosphere. Its lakefront squares – Piazza Malvezzi and Piazza Matteotti, lined with bars and restaurants – are attractive, sitting alongside the **Roman villa** on Via Crocifisso (Tues–Sun 8.30am–7pm; Nov–Feb closes 4.30pm; €2), displaying some good mosaics, and loomed over by the **castle**, from where there are spectacular views. Boats depart from Piazza Matteotti for destinations all round the shore.

SIRMIONE, 9km east, is a beautiful village spread along a narrow promontory sticking out into the lake. It's in a striking location, though these days is suffocated with hotels, souvenir stands and holiday-makers, many of whom come to take the waters: Sirmione is one of northern Italy's top spa destinations. The ferry dock on Piazza Carducci adjoins Piazza Castello, site of the **Rocca Scaligera** (Tues–Sun 8.30am–7pm; €4), a fairytale castle with boxy towers almost entirely surrounded by water, built by the Della Scala of Verona in the thirteenth century. Press on through the crowded lanes of the village and out to the cypress-clad hills at the head of the peninsula, where stands the **Grotte di Catullo** (Tues–Sat 8.30am–7pm, Sun until 5pm; Nov–Feb closes 4.30pm; €4), the remains of a first century BC/AD Roman villa, purportedly belonging to Roman poet Catullus, though the evidence is scant. The ruins, scattered among ancient olive trees, are lovely, and offer superb views across the lake. From partway along the path, head down to water level for the **Lido delle Bionde** (May–Oct daily 8am–midnight), a beach where you can eat, drink, swim in the lake or sunbathe on the pontoon or nearby rocks. From Sirmione, boats head back to Desenzano or on to resorts such as Garda, Torri del Benaco and Salò.

The western shore

The rolling hills of the Valtenesi, overlooking the **western shore** north of Desenzano, are a good place to stock up on local produce, as much of the area is dedicated to vine and olive growing. In addition, it has plenty of lakeside campsites which make for a cheap stay. Not far from the old Venetian town of **Salò** stands the exuberant villa **Il Vittoriale**, once home to poet Gabriele D'Annunzio. Around **Gargnano** – the most attractive and unspoilt of the lake villages – the western shore is dubbed the Riviera del Limone for the citrus orchards that once flourished here. The crop, introduced by the Franciscans in the fourteenth century, was cultivated in the *limonaie*, or "lemon-houses" that

---

Garda's theme parks

If you have kids to amuse, head for one of the **theme parks** east of Sirmione, served by free shuttle buses from Peschiera train station. The biggest is **Gardaland** (March–Sept daily 10am–6pm; June–Aug until midnight; ☏045.644.9777, ⓦwww.gardaland.it; €30, children under 10 €26). You pay extra for some of the attractions, but its rides and themed entertainments are exciting and well presented. Nearby is **Canevaworld** (☏045.696.9900, ⓦwww.canevaworld.it), comprising two adjacent parks: **Movieland** (March–Sept daily 10am–6pm; July & Aug later opening), with fake movie sets and special effects shows; and **AquaParadise** (May–Sept daily 10am–6pm; July & Aug until 7pm), with slides, flumes, pools and a pirate island. Admission to either Movieland or AquaParadise is €21 (€18 for children under 1.40m); both cost €27/23.

are still in evidence, although most of the stone-pillared constructions are now abandoned. North of Gargnano the mountainous scenery is spectacular on the approach to the genteel resort of **Riva del Garda** at the head of the lake.

Salò and Gardone Riviera

SALÒ, splendidly sited on its own bay, is one of Garda's more handsome towns. Capital of the Magnifica Patria – a grouping of lake communes – for more than four hundred years until the fall of the Venetian Republic in 1797, it retains something of its old-fashioned hauteur, exemplified by the grand seventeenth-century town hall, directly on the lakefront by the ferry dock, and the unfinished Renaissance facade of the Duomo, which holds paintings by Romanino. From 1943 to 1945, Salò was the nominal capital of Italy, as the Nazis installed Mussolini here at the head of a puppet regime in a failed attempt to hold off the Allied advance. Just 2km east, **GARDONE RIVIERA** was once the most fashionable of Lake Garda's resorts; it retains its symbols of sophistication, though the elegant promenade, opulent villas and ritzy hotels now have to compete with more recent – less tasteful – tourist tack. Above the town nestles the exotic **Giardino Botanico André Heller** (March–Oct daily 9am–7pm; €9), with bamboo and banana plants laid out among artificial cliffs and streams amongst modern artworks.

Il Vittoriale

Signposted on the hillside above Gardone, **Il Vittoriale** (Tues–Sun 9.30am–7pm; Oct–March 9am–1pm & 2–5pm; €12; Ⓦ www.vittoriale.it) was the home of Italy's most notorious twentieth-century writer, Gabriele D'Annunzio. Weight of numbers means that tickets can be restricted at peak times (Sun, national holidays, some days in July & Aug), when you should arrive an hour or more before the opening time to be sure of entry. Even then, be prepared for a scrum. You can pay less to visit the **gardens** only (which means you miss out on D'Annunzio house, the **Prioria**), or an extra €4 to see the adjoining **Museo della Guerra** (War Museum; closed Wed), which isn't worth it.

D'Annunzio's personality makes itself felt from the start in the Prioria's two reception rooms – one a chilly and formal room for guests he didn't like, the other warm and inviting for those he did. Mussolini was apparently shown to the former, where the mirror has an inscription reputedly aimed at him: "Remember that you are made of glass and I of steel." Dining with D'Annunzio was never a reassuring experience: in the glitzy dining room, as a warning to

Gabriele D'Annunzio

Born in 1863, Gaetano Rapagnetta – who took the name **Gabriele D'Annunzio** (Gabriel of the Annunciation) – is often acclaimed as one of Italy's greatest poets, though he became better known as a soldier and socialite, leading his own private army and indulging in much-publicized affairs with numerous women, including the actress Eleonora Duse (when berated by his friends for treating her cruelly, he simply replied, "I gave her everything, even suffering.") He was a fervent supporter of Mussolini, providing the Fascist Party with their (meaningless) war cry *"eia! eia! alalá!"* – though Mussolini eventually found his excessive exhibitionism an embarrassment and in 1921 presented D'Annunzio with the Vittoriale villa, ostensibly to reward his patriotism, in reality to shut him up. D'Annunzio spent years expanding the villa, redesigning its interiors and acquiring neighbouring land. He died in the house in 1938, suffering a brain haemorrhage while sitting at his desk in the Zambracca room, which remains untouched.

greedy guests, pride of place was given to a gilded tortoise that had died of overeating. In fact D'Annunzio rarely ate with his guests, retreating instead to the Sala di Lebbroso, where he would lie on a bier surrounded by leopard skins and contemplate death. The rest of the house is no less bizarre: the bathroom has a bathtub hemmed in by hundreds of objects, ranging from Persian ceramic tiles and Buddhas to toy animals; and the Sala del Mappamondo, as well as the huge globe for which it is named, contains an Austrian machine gun and an oversized edition of *The Divine Comedy*. Suspended from the ceiling of the auditorium adjoining the house is the biplane that D'Annunzio used in a daring flight over Vienna in World War I.

Outside amidst the cypress trees is the prow of the battleship *Puglia* used in D'Annunzio's so-called "Fiume adventure". Fiume (now Rijeka), on the North Adriatic, had been promised to Italy before they entered World War I, but was handed to Yugoslavia instead. Incensed, D'Annunzio gathered an army, occupied Fiume and returned home a hero. Amidst the gardens above stands D'Annunzio's mausoleum, a Fascistic array of angular travertine stonework.

Practicalities

Salò's **tourist office** is behind the town hall on Piazza San Antonio (Mon–Sat 10am–12.30pm & 3–6pm, Sun 10am–1pm & 3.30–6.30pm; ☏0365.21.423, Ⓦwww.visitgarda.com). The four-star **hotel** *Bellerive*, Via Pietro da Salò 11 (☏0365.520.410, Ⓦwww.hotelbellerive.it; ❻; closed Dec & Jan), offers tasteful modern rooms with balconies and designer bathrooms; otherwise aim for *Benaco*, a decent three-star at Lungolago Zanardelli 44 (☏0365.20.308, Ⓦwww .benacohotel.com; ❹), with a fine roof terrace. *In Vino Veritas*, Via Duomo 7 (closed Mon), is a genial **restaurant** for wine-tasting and light bites, while *Osteria di Mezzo*, Via di Mezzo 10, is cosy, informal back-lane place. Atmospheric *Osteria dell'Orologio*, Via Butturini 26/A (☏0365.290.158; closed Wed), serves more upmarket fish and game specialities. In Gardone Sopra – the hillside quarter around Il Vittoriale – *La Stalla*, Via dei Colli 14 (☏0365.21.038; closed Tues), serves well-priced staples in a tranquil garden, not far from peaceful *Locanda Agli Angeli*, Piazza Garibaldi 2 (☏0365.20.832, Ⓦwww.agliangeli.com; closed Mon & Tues), a family-run restaurant serving top-quality lake fish and home-cured meats, also with a few airy, attractive rooms (❸).

San Michele

In the mountains 500m above Gardone stands the pretty village of **SAN MICHELE**. Three buses (Mon–Sat only) run from Salò and Gardone, but as the views along the road are splendid, you might want to walk the hour or so uphill; the tourist office can advise on short cuts that divert onto hillside tracks. In the village *Hotel Colombér*, Via Val di Sur 111 (☏0365.21.108, Ⓦwww .colomber.com; ❸), has comfortable en-suite rooms (some with balconies), a pool and a decent restaurant serving local specialities and well-chosen wine. It's a good base if you want to do some **walking** to the springs and waterfalls in the surrounding hills; the owners can give suggestions.

Gargnano

Some 15km north of Salò is **GARGNANO**, the prettiest village on Lake Garda. Traffic runs inland here, at a higher contour, leaving the old village itself noise-free. In addition, the narrow, difficult road north of town means tour buses don't bother trying to reach Gargnano, saving it from the worst excesses of lakes tourism. More a working village than a resort, it's the perfect spot to unwind for a day or two and wander around the abandoned olive factory or the lakefront villas with their boathouses, or just to relax in one of the waterfront cafés. D.H. Lawrence stayed here while writing *Twilight in Italy*, a work which is beautifully evocative of Lake Garda's attractions. For a weekend in early September, it hosts the **Centomiglia** sailing event, with hundreds of yachts racing from nearby Bogliaco all round the lake and back.

Apart from the harbourside ex-**Palazzo Comunale**, which has two cannon-balls wedged in the wall facing the lake – dating from the naval bombings suffered in 1866 during the war of independence from the Austrians – the main sight is the church of **San Francesco**, built in 1289; its cloister has columns carved with citrus fruits, a reference to the Franciscans' introduction of the crop to Europe. A stroll along the road which leads north from the harbour takes you for 3km through olive and lemon groves, past the exclusive luxury hotel *Villa Feltrinelli*, to the eleventh-century chapel of **San Giacomo di Calino**. On the side facing the lake, under the portico where the local fishermen keep their equipment, is a thirteenth-century fresco of St Christopher, patron saint of travellers.

Practicalities

Buses stop at Piazza Boldini on the main road, opposite the **tourist office** (Mon–Sat 9.30am–12.30pm & 5–7pm, closed Wed pm & Thurs am; ☎0365.791.243). It's a short walk down through the village to the jetty beside the old harbour, where there's another tourist office (Mon, Tues & Thurs–Sat 2.30–4.30pm). There's more information at ⓦwww.gargnanosulgarda.com. OKSurf, at Parco Fontanella (☎328.471.7777, ⓦwww.oksurf.it), runs windsurfing and kitesurfing courses, and also **rents mountain bikes** (€21 a day). The **campsite** *Rucc*, Via Rimembranza 23 (☎0365.71.805), is near the beach.

Standing out among Gargnano's **hotels**, 500m south in the hamlet of Villa, is the lovely, family-run ⚘ *Gardenia*, Via Colletta 53 (☎0365.71.195, ⓦwww .hotel-gardenia.it; closed Nov–March; ❺), rated three stars but easily worth four. The public areas feature beautifully maintained 1950s decor and fittings, while the renovated guest rooms boast antique furniture, big comfy beds, well-appointed bathrooms and airy lake views. It's outstanding value for money, aided by genial service and a great restaurant. Otherwise, aim for the same owners' *Hotel Du Lac*, Via Colletta 21 (☎0365.71.107, ⓦwww.hotel-dulac.it; closed Dec–Feb; ❹), similarly welcoming and unfussy, or one-star *Gargnano*, Piazza Feltrinelli 29 (☎0365.71.312, ⓦweb.tiscali.it/h.gar; closed Nov–March; ❷), the best of the many hotels in the village centre, directly on the old harbour and in business for over a hundred years: few budget rooms in the Italian Lakes are as nice as the corner room 9, with a sofa plus windows over the harbour and open water.

Gargnano has good **restaurants**. Various places around the harbour serve snacks and ice cream, and 1km south along the lakeside lanes, in the smaller Porto district, idyllically located *Osteria del Restauro* (closed Wed) serves good, inexpensive local cuisine at outdoor tables on the piazza. Back in the centre, *Miralago*, overlooking the lake by the jetty, offers excellent food at good prices, while just behind on Via XXIV Maggio, the cosy *La Tortuga* (☎0365.71.251; eve only; closed Mon & Tues) is a Michelin-starred restaurant offering top food in a formal atmosphere; expect €60 a head.

North of Gargnano

Through the treacherously narrow road tunnels north of Gargnano, past the mountainside turn-off to Tignale, a headland marks the **Prà de la Fam**, or Field of Hunger, so named after medieval fishermen were stranded here for several days after a storm. Nowadays serving as a marina, it's a pretty little spot for relaxing and swimming alongside the beautiful B&B *Torre degli Ulivi* (☏ 339.479.9834, ⓦ www.torredegliulivi.it; ❺), set in its own gated grounds, with five modest, airy rooms.

The last town in Lombardy, 20km from Gargnano on a tongue of land surrounded by rugged mountains, is **LIMONE SUL GARDA** (ⓦ www.visitlimonesulgarda.com). Although famous for its lemon cultivation – a commercial concern until the 1920s – the name derives from its location at what was the frontier (*limen* in Latin) of Roman control. Limone is undeniably pretty, but it is utterly overrun. A million tourists a year stay here, not counting the vast numbers who visit for the day on the boats from Riva and Malcesine; all this in a village with a settled population of just one thousand. The steep, cobbled streets are lined with stalls selling souvenirs, leather jackets and sequined T-shirts; the old stone facades are studded with plastic signs advertising restaurants and hotels; and as you elbow your way through the crowds you'll dig into more German and British ribs than Italian. It's best admired from afar.

Riva del Garda

Dramatically located beneath sheer cliffs at the northwest tip of the lake, **RIVA DEL GARDA** is the best known of the lake's resorts. It is unmistakeably a holiday town, but it has a long history and the pedestrianized old quarter is still full of character. Windsurfing (or watching others windsurf) is a major preoccupation. Cheaper than many other lake resorts, Riva is a good base for a budget holiday.

Arrival, information and accommodation

Riva's **bus station** is about 1km north of the lakefront, on Viale Trento, but all intercity buses drop off at the ferry jetty (if approaching from Limone) or Viale Carducci (if approaching from Tòrbole). The **tourist office** is on Largo Medaglie d'Oro (daily 9am–7pm; ☏ 0464.554.444, ⓦ www.gardatrentino.it), with an information kiosk at the ferry jetty (May–Sept daily 10am–1pm & 2–5.30pm; closed Wed).

Ancora Via Montanara 2 ☏ 0464.522.131, ⓦ www.rivadelgarda.com/ancora. Good-value, comfortable two-star rooms on an old-town lane. Service is friendly and there is a good terrace restaurant. ❸

Bellariva Via Franz Kafka 13 ☏ 0464.553.620, ⓦ www.hotelbellariva.com. Modest little holiday hotel away from the centre with free parking; grab a room on the uppermost floor for a bargain balcony overlooking the lake and the mountains. Closed Nov–Feb. ❹

Europa Piazza Catena 9 ☏ 0464.555.433, ⓦ www.hoteleuropariva.it. A good *Best Western* choice, occupying a tall, historic building on the main portside square. Rooms are modern, with lake-view or city-view options. Closed Nov–March. ❺

Restel de Fer Via Restel de Fer 10 ☏ 0464.553.481, ⓦ www.resteldefer.com. A real find, in the quiet backstreets away from the centre. This was once a farmhouse, out on its own in the fields; Riva has grown up around it, but the Meneghelli family are still here, 600 years on. The restaurant is outstanding and there are five guest rooms, comfortably furnished with individual touches. ❸

Ostello Benacus (HI hostel) Piazza Cavour 10 ☏ 0464.554.911, ⓦ www.ostelloriva.com. Very central hostel, well run, with renovated two-, four- and multi-bedded rooms. Closed Nov–Feb. Dorms €16. ❶

The Town

The lakefront square, **Piazza III Novembre**, is ringed by medieval facades below the rugged face of Monte Rocchetta, which towers overhead. To one side is the thirteenth-century **Torre Apponale** (March–Oct Tues–Sun

10am–6pm; June–Aug also Mon; €1), 34m high and climbable inside for sensational lake views, while behind stretches the medieval Marocco quarter alongside lively Via Fiume. Along the waterfront looms the **Rocca**, originally built in 1124 but much altered since, now housing the **Museo Civico** (March–Oct Tues–Sun 10am–12.30pm & 1.30–6pm; June–Aug also Mon; €2), with exhibits of local art and history. Just 3km north (follow Via Ardaro/Marone; 45min walk) is the **Parco Grotta Cascata Varone** (daily: May–Aug 9am–7pm; April & Sept 9am–6pm; March & Oct 9am–5pm; Nov–Feb Sun 10am–5pm; €5), where you follow catwalks into a gorge system as waterfalls thunder down from 100m above.

Eating and drinking

Binario Largo Medaglie d'Oro ☏0464.520.600, ⓦwww.restaurantcafebinario.it. Pleasant, modern café-restaurant occupying the former train station (long since disused). A perfect, airy spot for a light lunch or just coffee and pastries – the pizzas are excellent, as are salads and grills. Jazz trios play on summer weekends. Closed Tues.

Kulmbacher Am See Viale Dante 39 ☏0464.559.231. Cosy Bavarian restaurant just outside the old quarter, specializing in roast pork, goulash, bratwurst – and, of course, beer. Quality is high: with the number of Bavarian holiday-makers in Riva, it has to be. Closed Wed.

Leon d'Oro Via Fiume 28 ☏0464.552.341. Welcoming restaurant on a busy pedestrianized street, a handy place for good-quality, moderately priced pizza and fish dishes in the heart of the old quarter. No closing day.

Osteria Pane Salame Via Marocco 22 ☏0464.551.954. Tiny place on a back street – a locals' haunt, with no menu: food is cheap and uncomplicated, and there are lots of wines by the glass. Closed Mon.

The eastern shore

Overlooked by the ridges of Monte Baldo, which tops 2100m – its treeless summit poking baldly out of lushly wooded slopes – the main resorts of Lake Garda's **eastern shore** are heavily touristed and struggle to match the charm of the villages opposite. Holiday hotels and campsites line much of the lakeside

Watersports and other activities

The northern shore of Lake Garda around **Riva** – and especially **Torbole** – is a hub for sporting activity. All prices below are approximate; check details with local tourist offices. Top of the list is watersports, with a clutch of local outfits offering **windsurfing**: first-timers can get individual tuition (€70 for 3hr) or there are group lessons at various grades (€80 for 3hr). If you're already proficient, you can rent for €50 a day. **Sailing** is also popular, with beginners' courses in a dinghy or catamaran (€135 for 4hr) and rental (€70–130 per day, depending on the size of boat). Shop around: local operators include ⓦwww.pierwindsurf.it, ⓦwww.vascorenna.com, ⓦwww.sailingdulac.com, ⓦwww.surfsegnana.it, ⓦwww.surflb.com and ⓦwww.windsurfconca.com. You can **rent canoes** (€35 a day for two people) at the Sabbioni beach in Riva. With over a dozen good locations within easy reach of the lake, **canyoning** is also good bet (April–Oct only; half-day €40–60, full-day €75–110; ⓦwww.canyonadv.com & ⓦwww.wetway.it).

Several companies offer more traditional **Alpine activities** – ice-climbing, via ferrata, trekking and so on; check ⓦwww.alpinguide.com and ⓦwww.guidealpinearco.com for details. **Paragliding** – notably off Monte Baldo above Malcesine – is a spectacular way to get an eagle-eye view of the lake. Volo Libero (ⓦwww.timetofly.net) runs tandem paragliding flights for €100, as does ⓦwww.condorfly.com.

road. Aim for **Torbole** if you're a keen windsurfer or attracted by any of the other outdoor activities on offer. Just to the south, **Malcesine**'s appealing centre is swamped by holiday-makers, yet nearby **Torri del Benaco**, a lovely old village, remains popular but not ruined by tourism.

Torbole

TORBOLE, 4km east of Riva, played an important role in the fifteenth-century war between Milan and Venice, when a fleet of warships was dragged overland here and launched into the lake. Nowadays the water still dominates, since Torbole's main diversions are sailing and windsurfing, and the place has a fresh, youthful outlook. Windsurfing enthusiasts come here from all over Europe, attracted by ideal wind conditions (see box opposite). The lakefront **tourist office** (Easter–Oct Mon–Sat 9am–noon & 3–6pm; June–Aug also Sun 10am–noon & 3.30–6.30pm; Nov–Easter Mon–Fri 9am–noon & 2.30–5pm; ☎0464.505.177, ⓦwww.gardatrentino.it) has details of the dozens of **hotels**: *Lido Blu*, Via Foci del Sarca 1 (☎0464.505.180, ⓦwww.lidoblu.com; ❺), has some great beaches and cut-price deals in the low season (open year-round), while *Villa Verde*, Via Sarca Vecchio 15 (☎0464.505.274, ⓦwww.hotel -villaverde.it; ❸), has its own pool and garden.

Malcesine

Backed by the slopes of Monte Baldo and blessed with the same windsurfer-friendly winds as Torbole, **MALCESINE**, 14km south, has a pretty old quarter but tends to be inundated with British and German package tourists. The main sight is the thirteenth-century **Castello Scaligera** (daily 9.30am–8pm; Nov–March closed Mon–Fri; €5). Goethe was imprisoned here briefly in 1786, having been arrested on suspicion of being a spy: he'd been caught making sketches of the castle's towers.

For those after more active pursuits there are well-marked trails up **Monte Baldo**, or you can take the **cable car** (March–Oct daily every 30min 8am–7pm; €11 one-way, €17 return; ⓦwww.funiviamalcesine.com), which rises

▲ Torbole, Lake Garda

more than 1600m in ten minutes. Be prepared for queues. There are several special trips a day for cyclists to transport their bikes to the top; you can **rent a mountain bike** at G. Furioli in Piazza Matteotti (☎045.740.045) and make a panoramic descent down easy trails to the shore. Footpaths explore the summit ridge.

Beside Malcésine's **bus station** on the main road is a **tourist office** (Mon–Sat 9am–7pm, Sun 10am–4pm; ☎045.740.0044, ⓦwww.visitgarda .com); there's another branch near the jetty at Via Capitanato 8 (Mon–Sat 9am–1pm & 3–7pm; May–Oct also Sun 9am–1pm; ☎045.740.0837). Many **hotels** are block-booked by tour operators; *Aurora*, Piazza Matteotti 8 (☎045.740.0114, ⓦwww.aurora-malcesine.com; ❷), is a more flexible option. Most of Malcésine's **restaurants** are awful: the waterfront locations are lovely, but expect crowds, slapdash service and spag bol on the menu. *Al Corsaro*, Via Paina 17 (☎045.658.4064, ⓦwww.alcorsaro.it) breaks the mould, serving freshly caught lake fish at a beautiful location on a concealed beach under the castle walls, while the contemporary styled wine bar *Al Gremal*, on Via Scoisse above the bus station, offers a haven from the crush.

Torri del Benaco and around

Twenty kilometres south of Malcesine, **TORRI DEL BENACO** is the prettiest of the villages on this side of the lake. Its old centre – one long cobbled street, Corso Dante, crisscrossed with tunnelling alleyways – is dominated by the **Castello Scaligero** (daily: June–Sept 9.30am–1pm & 4.30–7.30pm; April, May & Oct 9.30am–12.30pm & 2.30–6pm; €3), its swallowtail battlements standing guard over the little harbour. The castle is illuminated at night to romantic effect, and with a long *limonaia*, or glasshouse, along one side to protect the lemon trees during cold weather.

The **tourist office** is on the harbour (June–Aug daily 9am–1pm & 3–7pm; otherwise restricted hours; ☎045.722.5120, ⓦwww.visitgarda.com). Budget **hotels** are led by the *Garni Onda*, Via per Albisano 28 (☎045.722.5895, ⓦwww.garnionda.com; closed Nov–Feb; ❷), 100m east of the centre. Each spotlessly clean room has its own balcony or terrace and the friendly owners provide a first-rate breakfast. The top hotel the harbourside *Gardesana*, Piazza Calderini 20 (☎045.722.5411, ⓦwww.hotel-gardesana.com; ❺), a classic old lakes hotel, first recorded in 1452. There is no sense of pomposity: service is genial and the immaculate rooms, though luxurious, are a bargain. The *Gardesana*'s **restaurant** is equally romantic, laid out along a balcony above the harbour (book for a table at the railing). Their *menù tipico del Garda* (taking in fresh-caught fish) is €45. *Trattoria Bell'Arrivo*, on Piazza Calderini, is another cosy little spot with unusually good food, priced lower. For excellent food in unbeatable surroundings, head a couple of kilometres above town towards Albisano; amid hillside olive groves, ⚞ *Trattoria agli Olivi*, Via Valmagra 7 (☎045.722.5483, ⓦwww.agliolivi.it), serves delicious local dishes at bargain prices on a splendid lake-view terrace.

Around 4km south of Torri, **PUNTA SAN VIGILIO** juts into the lake, offering a well-equipped **beach** (April–Sept €11) with sun loungers, picnic tables and children's equipment scattered on grassy slopes planted with pines and olive trees. Occupying a sixteenth-century villa in its own grounds is *Locanda San Vigilio* (☎045.725.6688, ⓦwww.locanda-sanvigilio.it; ❾), a luxury hotel worth investigating for its charming taverna, with quiet tables laid out on a tiny private harbour serving (pricey) drinks and snacks.

Garda and Bardolino

Like many of its neighbours, the ancient fishing village of **GARDA**, 7km south of Torri, has seen its narrow, winding alleys encroached on by snack bars and souvenir shops. Even the fifteenth-century **Loggia della Losa**, originally a dock for the *palazzo* behind, is now a *gelateria*. Look for the **Palazzo Fregoso**, a charming sixteenth-century house on Via Spagna with its original external staircase and a double lancet window over an arched passageway – then stroll the long, curving promenade, which offers wonderful views southwest over the lake. **Restaurants** aren't great; instead head up Via Don Gnocchi – past the **tourist office** (Mon–Sat 9am–7pm, Sun 10am–4pm; ☎045.725.5824) – for 1km to *Hostaria La Cross* (☎045.725.5795), a rumbustiously cheery local eatery, serving traditional food; book ahead – it's a popular spot, lightyears away from the tourist fare on the lake.

Some 4km south is the spruce resort of **BARDOLINO**, home of light, red Bardolino wine – at its most animated in September during the *Festa dell'Uva* (Grape Festival). A nameless bar on Via Cesare Battisti, commonly known as *Da Romaldi*, is a good place to sample local vintages, or try the delicious ice cream at lakefront *Cristallo*. A little south is the **Museo dell'Olio di Oliva** (Mon–Sat 9am–12.30pm & 2.30–7pm, Sun 9am–12.30pm; free; Ⓦ www.museum.it), centred on a shop selling local oils. On the hillside above is the **Museo del Vino** (March–Oct daily 9am–1pm & 2–6pm; free; Ⓦ www.zeni.it), part of the Zeni winery which offers free tastings.

Travel details

Full details of all public transport in Lombardy are at Ⓦ www.trasporti.regione .lombardia.it (click "orari").

Trains

Bergamo to: Brescia (hourly; 50min); Lecco (hourly; 35min); Milan (every 40min; 50min).

Brescia to: Bergamo (hourly; 50min); Cremona (approx every 2hr; 50min); Desenzano (every 30min; 20min); Milan (every 30min; 1hr); Parma (9 daily; 1hr 35min); Verona (every 30min; 45min).

Cremona to: Brescia (every 2hr; 50min); Mantua (hourly; 55min); Milan (7 daily; 1hr 40min).

Desenzano to: Brescia (every 30min; 20min); Verona (approx twice hourly; 30min).

Mantua to: Bologna (2 daily; 1hr 35min); Milan (6 daily; 2hr); Modena (every 30min; 45min); Verona (hourly; 50min).

Milan Centrale to: Bergamo (hourly; 50min); Brescia (every 45min; 1hr 15min); Certosa di Pavia (every 2hr; 30min); Como SG (hourly; 40min); Cremona (7 daily; 1hr 40min); Desenzano (every 30min; 1hr 10min); Lecco (every 2hr; 1hr); Pavia (every 30min; 25min); Peschiera (hourly; 1hr 20min); Stresa (9 daily; 1hr 10min); Varenna (every 2hr; 1hr 10min); Verona (hourly; 1hr 35min).

Milan Lambrate to: Certosa di Pavia (9 daily; 20min); Pavia (every 15min; 25min).

Milan Nord/Cadorna to: Como Lago (every 30min; 1hr).

Milan Porta Garibaldi to: Bergamo (every 40min; 55min); Luino (4 daily; 1hr 40min); Stresa (8 daily; 1hr 30min); Varese (hourly; 1hr).

Pavia to: Certosa di Pavia (14 daily; 10min).

Buses

Brescia to: Cremona (hourly; 1hr 15min); Desenzano (at least hourly; 55min); Gargnano (every 30min; 1hr 25min); Mantua (hourly; 1hr 25min); Verona (hourly; 2hr 20min).

Como to: Bellagio (hourly; 1hr 10min); Menaggio (every 20min; 1hr 10min).

Desenzano to: Riva (5 daily; 1hr 50min); Sirmione (at least hourly; 20min).

Mantua to: Brescia (hourly; 1hr 35min); Verona (6 daily; 1hr 20min).

Milan (Metro Famagosta) to: Certosa di Pavia (Mon–Sat 7 daily, 5 on Sun; 30min).

Pavia to: Certosa di Pavia (Mon–Sat every 30min, Sun hourly; 20min); Milan Famagosta (Mon–Sat every 30min, 7 on Sun; 1hr).
Riva del Garda to: Desenzano (5 daily; 1hr 50min); Malcesine (approx hourly; 25min).
Stresa to: Orta San Giulio (3 daily; 1hr).

Ferries

Following is an outline of summer services; for full information, see ⓦ www.navigazionelaghi.it.

Como to: Bellagio (6 daily; 2hr 10min); Cernobbio (every 20min; 15min); Colico (5 daily; 4hr); Menaggio (6 daily; 2hr 25min); Varenna (6 daily; 2hr 40min).
Desenzano to: Gargnano (3 daily; 2hr); Malcesine (5 daily; 3hr 15min); Riva del Garda (8 daily; 3hr 30min); Saló (5 daily; 1hr 30min); Sirmione (every 45min; 20min).
Stresa to: Isola Bella (every 30min; 10min); Pallanza (every 30min; 35min); Santa Caterina (hourly; 15min); Villa Táranto (every 30min; 45min).

Trentino-Alto Adige

CHAPTER 4 # Highlights

* **Mountain refuges** Bed, board and beer in some of Europe's most remote and scenic locations. See p.234

* **Trento's Piazza Duomo** Trento's central square, with its backdrop of mountains, is ringed by arcades, shops and cafés. See p.238

* **MART** The museum of contemporary art in Rovereto is the largest of its kind in Italy, and is strong on Futurist, avant-garde and Pop art. See p.240

* **Hiking in the Pale di San Martino** One of the most spectacular areas in the Dolomites with a great selection of high-altitude trails. See p.245

* **Ice Man** The chief exhibit in Bolzano's Museo Archeologico is the superbly preserved "Ice Man", found in the Ötzaler Alps in 1991. See p.253

* **Wine tasting along the Strada di Vino** Follow the "wine road" through the Adige valley and sample some of the region's best food and wine. See p.255

▲ Hiking in the Giuppo di Sella

Trentino-Alto Adige

"... and to dream in a vague way of those mystic mountains beyond Verona which we knew of, somewhat indefinitely, as the Dolomites."

Amelia B. Edwards (1831–92; adventurer)

taly's northernmost region, where Italy, Austria and Switzerland meet, is a major summer- and winter-holiday destination. In the past, however, it's been something of a battle zone. A string of castles along the Adige (Etsch) valley hint at the cut and thrust of medieval politics in these parts, and the area was on the front line again as recently as World War I, when Italian and Austrian troops fought a ferocious battle along the alpine ridges. These days, the invasions tend to be peaceful, as millions of holiday-makers head here to ski on sunny south-facing slopes, or take a summer break in one of the region's high-altitude resorts, in a bid to escape the sweltering cities on the plains.

As the region's name suggests, it is really two areas linked together. **Trentino**, the southern part, is 98 percent Italian-speaking and the cuisine and architecture belong predominantly to the south rather than the Alps. On the other hand, the mountainous terrain around Bolzano – known both as the **South Tyrol** and **Alto Adige** – was only incorporated into Italy at the end of the First World War (see box, p.232). Here, onion-domed churches dot the vineyards and forests, street signs are in German and Italian and the landscape is redolent of illustrations from the Brothers Grimm. Both Trentino and Alto Adige now enjoy **autonomy** from central government, along with one of the highest standards of living in Italy. In 2001, each of the two provinces gained greater political clout separately rather than jointly, although they remain linked, if only by their official name.

The main focus of a trip here is the landscape, dominated by the stark and jagged **Dolomites.** Among the most beautiful mountains in Europe, these vast massifs are steeped in legend and have been eroded over the last 200 million years into a weird and wonderful array of towers and pinnacles. Cable cars travel from the small resorts dotted around the region enabling you to go walking at 2000–3000m without needing anything beyond average fitness or expertise, and a network of trails crosses the ranges, varying in length from a day's walk to a two-week trek.

Of the towns in the area, the regional capital **Trento** is a worthwhile stopover with its atmospheric old centre, mountain views and the excellent contemporary art gallery, MART, a short train ride away. Further north, **Bolzano**, Alto Adige's chief town, has an enviable quality of life and makes a good base for seeing the rest of the region. It is worth visiting for the "Ice Man" alone, the prize exhibit at the archeological museum. Between the two towns the hillsides are planted with **vineyards** which can be visited as part of the Strada di Vino

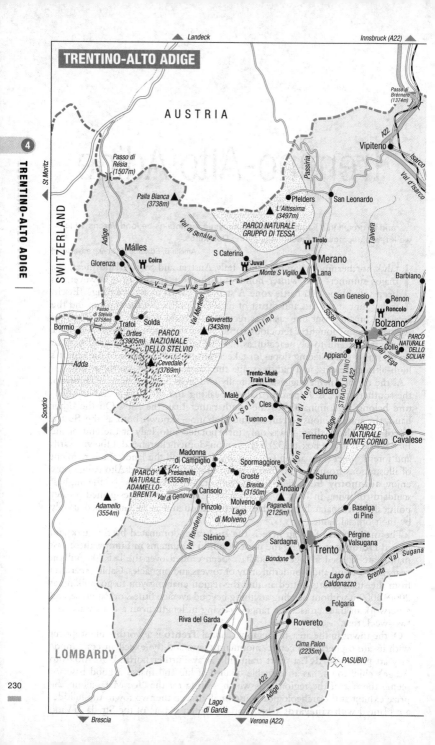

AUSTRIA

Lienz & Salzburg ▶

Gran Pilastro
(3510m) ▲

Campo Túres ▲

V a l   P u s t e r i a

Rienza

San Lorenzo

Brunico ●

Longega

Dobbiaco ●

San Cándido ●

Rienza

Fortezza ▲ Novacella

Bressanone ●

Lago
di Braies

PARCO NATURALE FANES-
SENNES-BRAIES

Val di Funes

San Vigilio
di Marebbe

Croda Rossa
(3139m) ▲

PARCO NATURALE
DOLOMITI DI SESTO

Chiusa

Ortisei ●

Pederù

Tre Cime di Lavaredo
(2999m) ▲

PARCO
NATURALE
PUEZ-ODLE

Cristallo
(3221m) ▲

Lago
di Misurina

S. Cristina Passo di Gardena
(2121m)

Val Gardena

Siusi

Corvara

Tofane
(3243m) ▲

Passo Tre
Croci (1814m)

ALPE Sella (2234m)
DI SIUSI

Sella (3151m) ▲

Passo di
Valparola

VENETO

Fié Am
Sciliar

Sasso Lungo
(3179m) ▲

Passo di
Falzarego

Cortina
d'Ampezzo ●

Rosengarten/
Catinaccio
(2981m) ▲

Sciliar (2564m) ▲

Passo
Pordoi
(2239m)

Antelao
(3263m) ▲

Calalzo ●

Vigo
di Fassa

Arabba ●

Lago
di Fedaia

Canazei ●

Val di Fassa

Marmolada
(3343m) ▲

Alleghe ●

Pelmo
(3168m) ▲

Piave

Passo di
Costalunga
(1745m)

Moena ●

Passo di San
Pellegrino (1918m)

Civetta
(3218m) ▲

FRIULI-
VENEZIA
GIULIA

Udine ▶

Predazzo ●

Panevéggio

Pale di San
Martino (3192m) ▲

Tésero ▲

V a l   d i   F i e m m e

Passo
di Rolle
(1970m)

San Martino
di Castrozza ●

PARCO
NATURALE
PANEVEGGIO

Val Canali

Passo di Cereda
(1369m)

Cima d'Asta
(2847m) ▲

Mezzano

Fiera di Primiero ●

Belluno ●

Imer

Piave

Fonzaso

Feltre ●

Vittório
Veneto ●

Trieste ▶

Brenta

Piave

N

A27

VENETO

0   10 km

231

Venice ▼

The Italianization of the Tyrol

The **South Tyrol** was Italy's prize for cooperation with the Allies in World War I. When Mussolini's fascists came to power in 1923 the region was renamed Alto Adige after the upper reaches of the Adige river. Despite the fact that German speakers outnumbered Italian speakers by about ten to one, a process of Italianization was imposed on the area. Cartographers remade maps, substituting Italian place names for German; people were forced to adopt Italian names; the teaching of German in schools was banned and stonemasons were even brought in to chip away German inscriptions from tombstones. World War II then intervened, and by 1946, Austria and Italy came to an agreement ratified under the Paris Peace Treaty that Austria would give up its claim to the region on condition that Italy took steps to redress some of the cultural damage perpetrated under Fascism.

Successive governments have channelled funds into the area allowing both more **independence** than ever before and much greater say in local law. Over the last few years, Italy has moved closer into the European Union, and its central and regional governments have had to become more tolerant of ethnic diversity and, increasingly, it is German that is the language of preference in Alto Adige.

wine-tasting route. Both Trento and Bolzano are transport hubs for the region, reachable by train via Verona and Innsbruck, and by private bus from Bergamo and other airports.

The scenic Great Dolomites Road links Bolzano with **Cortina d'Ampezzo**. Even though technically it is just across the regional border in the Veneto (and therefore served by transport links from Belluno), Cortina is very much part of the Dolomites and is probably Italy's glitziest ski resort.

Merano is another hub, serving the Val Venosta (Vischgau) and its side valleys which take you deep into the mountains of the Parco Nazionale dello **Stelvio**. More remote and less touristy than the Dolomites, this range has a different flavour of high alps topped by vast glaciers; by day you can be ascending snow-capped pasture, in the evening eating pizza in town.

Public transport and driving

It's worth noting that provincial **bus** companies stick to towns within their territory, so that some places which look as though they should be easy to get to from Bolzano, say, often are not. For example, there are more frequent buses to Canazei from Trento, and this is the case for other towns in the northern part of Trentino. If you're cycling, it's worth knowing you can stow **bikes** in the boot of buses, so helping take some of the hard work out of long ascents.

If you're **driving** outside the summer months, be aware that many passes can remain closed until well after Easter. Approach roads all have signs indicating whether the pass is open, or you can call Bolzano's information line on ✆0471.999.999. The Südtirol's official **website** Ⓦwww.south-tirol.com has some useful links and reams of information about the province, with pages devoted to individual towns and resorts.

Hiking

This region is an exhilarating area to walk, often subject to snow, ice and scorching sun in the same day. A network of refuges allow you to stay at high altitude without having to dip down to the valley for meals or accommodation. Most *rifugi* (see p.234) and cable cars are open from June 20 to September 20 which is the official **hiking** season, though there will be local variations and you'll find some also have a winter season.

There are plenty of opportunities for **day walks**: routes are well established and well signposted, and there are suggestions in this chapter for walks in some stunning scenery that are within average capabilities.

For more ambitious walking over a number of days, you might consider doing one of the longer trails, known as **alte vie** (literally "high ways"). Four of these run north–south between the Val Pusteria (Pustertal) and the Veneto; four from the Val d'Isarco (Eisacktal) south; and two from Bolzano, with plenty of mountain huts along the way for meals and overnight accommodation. Some of the initial ascents are strenuous, but once you are up on the ridges the paths level out and give superb views across the valleys and glaciers. Parts of the trails are exposed, or have snowfields across them, but other ways round these obstacles are always available.

Online, ⓦ www.dolomiti.it is a good source of information on all ten long-distance trails. Martin Collins's *Alta Via: High Level Walks in the Dolomites* (Cicerone) covers and Alte Vie 1 and 2; and if you read Italian or German, Alpina Verlag's *Dolomite Alte Vie/Dolomiten Hohenwegel 1–10* is an extremely thorough companion to each of the trails – available free from larger tourist offices.

There aren't many guides to the non-*alta via* trails in English, but the beauty of this area is that there are so many footpaths that if you invest in the Kompass 1:50,000 or Tabacco 1:25,000 maps that are on sale everywhere in the Dolomites you can plan your own routes. Paths are numbered and are easy to follow – you just look out for the red-and-white blaze on rocks and trees by the side of the path along the way. When figuring out how long hikes will take, bear in mind that an averagely fit person takes around three hours to ascend 1000m.

Vie ferrate

Vie ferrate (literally "iron ways") are a peculiarly Italian phenomenon. The easiest way to describe them is as aided rock-climbs. Consisting of fixed metal ladders, pegs and cables that climbers clip onto with karabiners, they give access to otherwise difficult routes. Many *vie ferrate* began life as far back as the late nineteenth century as mountaineering took off as a sport in Europe; Alpini troops put others in place during World War I to assist the climbs that were a matter of survival for the soldiers fighting in the mountains. In the decades since then, volunteers from local *Club Alpino Italiano* groups have created many more.

Kompass and Tabacco maps show vie ferrate as a line of little black dots or crosses, so you can easily avoid them – they are definitely not for beginners or vertigo-sufferers. To use them, you need to be confident belaying and have the proper equipment (including helmet, ropes, two self-locking karabiners and a chest- or seat-harness). Incidentally, it's not advisable to climb a *via ferrata* in a thunderstorm either; it might just become one long lightning conductor.

Of course, once you've done a few straightforward paths up in the mountains you may be inspired to tackle some *ferrate*, and there are plenty of people around who will teach you. Individual guides charge by the hour, and so become more affordable if you can get a small group together. Otherwise, enrol on a mountain skills course: both Trentino and Alto Adige provincial tourist offices keep lists of guides and mountaineering schools, but you'll need to book well in advance.

Alpinschule Südtirol Jungmannstrasse 8, Campo Túres ☎0474.690.012, ⓦwww .kammerlander.com. Courses throughout the Dolomites, from ice-climbing to *vie ferrate*. The school is run by the famous mountaineer Hans Kammerlander.

Collegio Guide Alpine Via Manci 57, Trento ☎0461.981.207, ⓦwww.guidealpine.rentino.it – central number for Alpine guides in the province

of Trentino; for Alto Adige, contact Via Grappoli 9, Bolzano ☎0471.976.357, ⓦwww.guidealpine .altoadige.it – their motto: "The mountains will always be there, the trick is to make sure you are too."

Scuola Alpinismo Orizzonti Trentini ☎0464.835.449, ⓦwww.orizzontitrentini.com. Guides based in Besenello, operate in the whole region.

Rifugi

If you're seriously into hiking or mountaineering, the most convenient places to stay once you're high up are the **rifugi** (refuges). Solidly constructed, usually two- or three-storey buildings, they provide dormitory accommodation (and often double or quad rooms if you book well ahead), meals and a bar. These days, most have hot showers. Blankets are provided, but you must bring your own sheet sleeping bag – if you don't have one, you can usually buy one at the hut for around €10. Run by enthusiastic and dedicated staff, *rifugi* are open from June until around September or October, and many also operate in the skiing season; we've given opening periods as a guide, but these are still subject to prevailing weather conditions. If you're planning a long trek that relies on *rifugi* for accommodation, you should definitely call ahead; at the same time, you can check that the place isn't likely to be packed out by a large party – nobody is ever turned away, but overflow accommodation is either on a mattress in the bar or, *in extremis*, the hen house. If you are a member of the Club Alpino Italiano (ⓦwww.cai.it) the overnight rate at CAI-run *rifugi* is around €10; if not, expect to pay around €21, but unless you want to carry food with you, count on paying €40–50 for a bunk, breakfast and dinner – good value for the hearty home cooking and local wine that are rustled up in some pretty remote locations. **Emergency calls** can be made from most *rifugi*; to call Soccorso Alpino (Alpine Rescue), dial ☎118. A directory of refuges is available on the CAI website, at ⓦwww.huts-bivouacs.com or at ⓦwww.enrosadira.it.

Skiing

Trentino–Alto Adige is home to many of Italy's top **ski resorts**. Popular with families, and with a fairly laid-back atmosphere, Skiing is often not top priority –

Mountain antidotes

For those who shudder at the idea of walking boots and rucksacks, the region is also renowned for having some of the best **spa hotels** in Italy – these are not of the stern boot-camp variety, but offer wonderful regional cuisine along with a unique array of treatments from bathing in thermal water to elaborate "dry baths" involving lying swaddled in sheep's wool or mountain hay. Trentino-Alto Adige has a burgeoning **cultural life** too with two recently opened galleries – **MART**, the museum of contemporary art in Rovereto and Bolzano's **Museion** gallery helping to counterbalance the area's touristic focus on the great outdoors. In summer there are various outdoor concerts – the best of these is the *Suoni delle Dolomiti* series of **jazz, folk and world music** concerts in stunning open-air locations – visit ⓦwww.isuonidelledolomiti.it for details. More traditionally, at **Christmas**, vast markets take over the historic centres of Trento and Bolzano, attracting visitors from miles around.

If you can never decide between schnitzel and spaghetti, this is the region for you: Alto Adige has unreservedly Germanic traditions, and Trentino mixes mountain influences with more recognizably Italian flavours. The traditional food is great for refuelling after a day of hiking or skiing and the quality of produce is often excellent, even in the simplest mountain hut.

For finer dining, adventurous chefs are reworking old recipes to make a much lighter cuisine, and it is well worth trying out some of the pricier restaurants that we list for a new take on local specialities.

A **traditional meal** starts with some kind of salami (*lucanicche* in local dialect), often paper-thin slices of salt beef, or Tyrolean *canederli* – bread dumplings flavoured with *speck* (smoked ham) often served in broth (*brodo*). You'll also see *strangolapreti* (bread and spinach gnocchi) and *schlutzkrapfen* (spinach-filled pasta) on the menu. Fresh lake and river fish, game and rabbit are popular as *secondi*, as are a rich venison goulash or boiled cured pork with sauerkraut. Desserts are often based on apples, pears or plums, readily available from the local orchards. Other sweet treats include *apfel strudel*, *sachertorte* and *kaiserschmarren*, a scrambled pancake with raisins.

A highlight of the year for food and wine-lovers is the autumn Törggelen season (see box, p.256), when everyone heads for the hills to sample the new vintage and snack on mountain ham and roast chestnuts, followed by a walk to work it all off.

Vines have been cultivated here since before Roman times, and Trentino-Alto Adige produces more **DOC wines** than any other region in Italy. Most famous are the Pinot Grigios and Chardonnays, which are bright and aromatic from being grown at high altitudes and in cool conditions. These also provide wine makers with the raw material for some outstanding traditional-method sparkling wines, often marketed under the spumante Trentino Classico label. Despite the excellence of the whites, local wine makers actually make more reds often with local varieties like Teróldego and Schiava (known as Vernatsch in German-speaking areas). Red wines made from Schiava are good when young: look out for the pale-red Kalterersee (Caldaro) and the fuller, more fruity St Magdalene (Santa Maddalena); those made from the Lagrein grape variety are more robust, such as the strong, dark Lagrein Dunkel, or the Kretzer rosé from Bolzano's vineyards at Gries. Also worth seeking out is the rare **vino santo** (not to be confused with vin santo from Tuscany) from Trentino's Valle dei Laghi – a luscious dessert wine made from local Nosiola grapes.

if you like to stop for a long lunch on a sunny terrace after a morning of piste-bashing, this is the place for you. The excellent Italian tourist offices overseas, and the regional offices in Italy, have details of *Settimane Bianche* ("White Weeks"). These are bargain package deals offering full or half board and a ski-pass, although be wary of deals very late in the season – the downside of all those south-facing slopes is that the snow deteriorates fast in the warmer spring weather. January and February are the best months to come; March can also be good although by mid-April the winter season is over. As for where to ski: **Madonna di Campiglio** is popular with wealthy Italian families as it has a good sun and snow record (it's a relatively high resort for Italy) and a lively nightlife. **Canazei** has a huge ski area particularly appealing to intermediates, who could spend a week there and barely ski the same piste twice. The resorts of the **Val Gardena** (Ortisei, S Cristina and Selva) also offer plenty of variety in terms of places to eat, stay and ski. Beginners and intermediates can cruise slopes in beautiful surroundings at the fashionable resort of **Cortina d'Ampezzo**, although the ski area is fragmented and much is only accessible by bus from the resort.

The big attraction of skiing in the eastern Dolomites is that twelve different ski areas are linked, creating long circuits including the famous "**Sella Ronda**" which takes you around **Marmolada** (3342m). You can access all areas with the **Dolomiti Superski** pass (€233 for 7 days in high season in 2009) giving use of 1220km of runs and 450 cable cars and chair lifts (see Ⓦwww .dolomitisuperski.com for details.) **Corvara** is the main resort on the Sella Ronda, and is popular with foodies and families; the slopes will appeal mainly to intermediates, but there are steeper runs at **Arabba** to challenge advanced skiers. To help decide which resort to choose, check out details of chair lifts, altitude and length of runs on the regional tourist office websites Ⓦwww .south-tirol.com and Ⓦwww.trentino.to.

Note that there's also summer skiing from June to November on glaciers accessible from the **Val Senales**, the **Stelvio Pass**, and the new, inexpensive resort at the **Passo Tonale** (which links Trentino with Lombardy), although in these days of climate change this is dependent on the state of the glaciers and there being a good dump of snow the winter before.

From December, get the latest on snow conditions in Trentino at Ⓦwww .meteotrentino.it and in Bolzano on Ⓣ0471.271.177; Bolzano's weather website, Ⓦwww.provinz.bz.it/meteo, can be useful if you speak German or Italian.

Trento

Just three hours from Venice by train, and less than an hour from Verona, **TRENTO** makes a good base for exploring the southern part of this region, not least because of its bus services into the Dolomites range. Overshadowed by Monte Bedone just 13km away, the town is beautifully situated, encircled by mountains and exuding a relaxed pace of life. The central, café-lined piazza is all fading frescoes and cobblestones, with chic fashion shops in the narrow streets off it. **MART**, Italy's largest modern art museum and **Lake Garda** (see p.216) lie 25km south.

From the tenth to the eighteenth centuries, Trento was a powerful bishopric ruled by a dynasty of princes; it was the venue of the Council of Trent in the sixteenth century, when the Catholic Church, threatened by the Reformation in northern Europe, met to plan its countermeasures – meetings that spanned a total of eighteen years. Later, throughout the nineteenth century, ownership of the city, which remained in Austrian hands, was hotly contested, and it only became properly part of Italy in 1919, after World War I.

Arrival and information

Trento's main **bus and train stations** are almost next door to each other at Piazza Dante and Via Pozzo. A secondary, combined station – **Trento-Malé**, run by a private company (Ⓣ0461.238.350) – is on Via Dogana, just beyond the train station (you don't need to leave the main station – just follow platform 1, heading north). From here you can get electric trains up to Cles in the Val di Non, Malé in the Val di Sole, and buses to the ski resorts of Madonna di Campiglio and Marilleva 900, and Lake Molveno. Visit Ⓦwww.ttspa.it for timetables for all transport in Trentino or call the information line (Ⓣ0461.821.000).

The **tourist office**, close to the main train station at Via Manci 2 (daily 9am–7pm; Ⓣ0461.216.060, Ⓦwww.apt.trento.it), stocks *Trentino Mese*, the city's monthly listings guide and sells the extremely useful **Trento Card** (€10 for 24hr, €15 for 48hr) offering many discounts. The **regional information centre** (contactable by phone/web only: Ⓣ0461.219.300, Ⓦwww.trentino.to) has details on mountain refuges, transport, hiking, skiing and agriturismo accommodation.

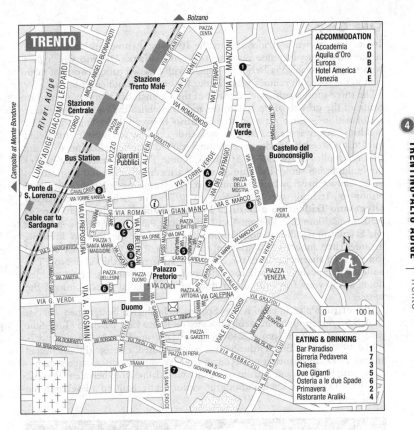

4

TRENTINO-ALTO ADIGE | Trento

Accommodation

There is a good range of **accommodation** for all budgets in and around
Trento; the busiest times are during Christmas and New Year. The nearest
campsite is the *Campeggio Malga Mezavia* Loc. Malga Mezavia (☎0461.948.178;
June–Sept & Dec–April), two-hours' trek from the top of the cable car on
Monte Bondone (see p.240). In town, good hotel options are:

Albergo Accademia Vicolo Colico 4–6
☎0461.233.600, ⓦ www.accademiahotel.it.
Family-run hotel with loads of character, friendly
service and an excellent restaurant, *Araliki*, see
p.239. ⑥
Aquila d'Oro Via Belenzani 76 ☎0461.986.282,
ⓦwww.aquiladoro.it. An old pink town house in a
central location a stone's throw from the Duomo
with clean, modern rooms. ⑥
Europa Via Torre Vanga 9, 500m to your right
beyond the station ☎0461.263.484, ⓦwww
.gayaproject.org. For visitors on a budget this
friendly hostel offers singles and doubles
(€25 per person) as well as dorm beds from
€13.50. ①

Hotel America Via Torre Verde 50
☎0461.983.010, ⓦ www.hotelamerica
.it. Affordable, close to the main station and a
short walk away from the action. There's a
friendly, efficient ambience here, with service a
strong point. Some upper-floor rooms have
wonderful views over the rooftops to the
mountains. ④
Venezia Piazza Duomo 45 ☎0461.234.559 or
234.114, ⓦwww.hotelveneziatn.it. The
cheapest hotel close to the centre. Comfortable if
a little old-fashioned, with a few rooms
overlooking the piazza and others in a thirteenth-
century tower. ②

The City

Trento was known as Tridentum to the Romans, a name celebrated by the eighteenth-century Neptune fountain in the central **Piazza Duomo**, which gives onto streets – notably Via Belanzani – lined with frescoed palaces, many of them built in the sixteenth century when Trento was an important market town.

The three most significant meetings of the Council of Trent – convened to confront the growth of Protestantism and to establish the so-called Counter Reformation – took place in the **Duomo** between 1545 and 1563. The building itself was begun in the thirteenth century, but wasn't completed until the sixteenth. Inside, an enormous carved marble baldachin over the altar is a replica of the one in St Peter's, Rome. The most interesting part of the building lies under the church, where a medieval crypt and foundations of an early Christian basilica (built over the tomb of St Vigilio, the third bishop of Trento) were discovered in 1977. The neighbouring **Museo Diocesano Tridentino e Basilica Paleocristiana** (daily: June 1 to Sept 30 9.30am–12.30pm & 2.30–6pm; Oct 1 to May 31 9.30–12.30pm & 2–5.30pm; €4; ⓦ www.museodiocesanotridentino.it), housed in the Palazzo Pretorio, includes large annotated paintings of the sessions of the Council of Trent and some carved altarpieces from the church of San Zeno in the Val di Non. The building is appealing in itself, too, with its fishtail battlements, heavy studded doors and a view from the upper floor of the frescoed palaces around the square.

Also of particular interest is the Spazio Archeologico Sotterraneo del Sas (**S.A.S.S.**) underground archaeological area on Piazza Cesare Battisti (Tues–Sun: June to Sept 9.30am–1pm & 2–6pm; Oct–May 9am–1pm & 2–5.30pm; €2). In the 1990s, when Trento's theatre was being restored, archeologists discovered around 1700 square metres of a Roman road – complete with sewage system – along with buildings and remains of the city walls dating from between 1000 BC and 400 AD. You can see it all from the visitor centre, built on a level with the existing road.

▲ Piazza Duomo, Trento

The most powerful of the Trento princes was Bernardo Clesio, who in the late fifteenth and early sixteenth centuries built up much of the city's art collection, a good proportion of which is held in the **Castello del Buonconsiglio** (Tues–Sun: Nov–May 9.30am–5pm; Jun–Oct 10am–6pm; €6; ⓦwww .buonconsiglio.it), another venue of the Council of Trent, a short walk from Piazza Duomo. It's really two castles: the thirteenth-century **Castelvecchio** and the extension built in 1530 called the **Magno Palazzo**, in which several rooms frescoed with classical subjects by the Dossi Family and Romanino lead off an inner courtyard. Upstairs is the **Museo Provinciale d'Arte**, whose highlight is the *Ciclo dei Mesi* ("Cycle of the Months"), in the Torre d'Aquila (a tour costs an extra €1 and must be booked in advance, Tues–Fri, on ☏0461.492.840). These frescoes dating from 1391 to 1407 show scenes of farming and courtly life.

Eating, drinking and nightlife

You can **eat** well in Trento and the surrounding area, feasting on unfussy local specialities. The arcades teem with shops selling local delicacies: *Macelleria Ravagni* on Piazza Duomo sells salami and cured meats while *Consorzio Produttori Latte Trento e Borgo*, via Campotrentino 9, sells cheese made on the premises, and there are also a couple of good *rosticcerie* on Via Santa Croce, near the market. From late November, hundreds of food and craft stalls fill the streets to celebrate the feast of St Lucy.

Trento doesn't resound with nightlife, but has a couple of good bars that stay open late. *Bar Paradiso*, on Largo Nazario Sauro 33 (☏0461.980.147), has a DJ on Friday nights and live music on Saturdays, and *Antica Birreria Pedavena*, Piazza Fiera 13 (☏0461.986.255, ⓦwww.birreriapedavena.com), features three kinds of beer brewed on the premises.

Restaurants

Chiesa Via San Marco ☏0461.238.766. The upmarket restaurant in this seventeenth-century *palazzo* was completely renovated in 2007 – everything's painted white and theatrical lighting has been put in, including a blue neon bar. Specializes in an *haute* version of Trentino cuisine; you can also sample local vintages in the wine bar or snack on *salumi*, cheese and antipasti in the less formal area. Closed Sun and lunch on Mon.

Due Giganti Via Simonino 14. Appealing self-service chain offering cheap and cheerful pasta dishes. Closed Sun.

🏃 **Osteria a le due Spade** Via Don Arcangelo Rizzi 11 ☏0461.234.343. Gourmands will appreciate the special four-course menus (€45–60) savoured in a cosy, low-ceilinged, wood-panelled room. This *osteria* is west of the Duomo off Via G. Verdi, and there has been an restaurant on this spot, they say, since 1545. Closed Sun & Mon lunch.

Primavera at Via Suffragio 92. Popular for inexpensive Italian standards, with outside seating under the arches. Closed Fri.

Ristorante Araliki Vicolo Collico 6, off Piazza Santa Maria Maggiore ☏0461.233.600. Enjoy local specialities such as *luganega con formai e funghi trifoladi* – local sausage with cheese and mushrooms. The restaurant is attached to the *Albergo Accademia*. Closed Mon.

Listings

Car rental Avis, 53 Via Brennero, ☏0461.420.276; SIXT, Piazza Leonardo da Vinci 3 ☏0461.263.467; Hertz, Lung'Adige Apuleio 20 ☏0461.421.555.
Doctor Servizi Guardia Medica Via Malta 4 ☏0461.915.809.Offers out-of-hours service, **Hospitals** In an emergency, call ☏118. Casualty ☏0461.903.206. San Camillo, Via Giovanelli

☏0461.216.111; Santa Chiara, Largo Medaglie d'Oro 9 ☏0461.903.111.
Internet *Call Me*, Via Belenzani 58 (daily 9am–9pm, €5 per hr). Wireless internet café: Olimpia, Via Belenzani 33 (€5 per hr).
Markets Mon–Sat mornings, food in Piazza Vittoria; Thurs mornings, weekly market in the

historic centre; second Sat of month (except Jan & Aug), flea market in Piazza Garzetti.

Pharmacies Dall'Armi, Piazza Duomo 10; Madonna, Via Manci 42; S. Chiara, Via S. Croce 57.

Police Via Fratelli Bronzetti ☎ 0461.916.111.

Post office Piazza A. Vittoria 20 ☎ 0461.984.714. Mon–Fri 8.30am–6.30pm, Sat 8am–12.30pm.

Public toilets Via Belenzani; free

Taxis Radiotaxi, Via Degasperi 27 ☎ 0461.930.002.

Around Trento

Trento's **cycle path** network is excellent, and with free bike rental if you purchase a Trento card, it's well worth exploring as an alternative to crowded buses and cable cars. The city is linked via `the grander Valle dell Adige Cycle Path to Bolzano to the north and Verona to the south, with many charming towns and villages along either route.

A cable car runs from the San Lorenzo bridge, near Trento's bus station (every 15min; €0.90), to the lower slopes of the towering Monte Bondone, from where you get a wonderful view. A five- or ten-minute walk brings you to the village of **SARDAGNA**, giving you a preview of alpine meadows and glimpses of the Dolomites in the distance.

An enjoyable half-day trip from the city (and reachable by local bus or train, or along the Adige Cycle Path) is a visit to the **ethnographic museum** (Museo degli Usi e Costumi della Gente Trentina; Tues–Sat 9am–12.30pm & 2.30–6pm; €4; ⓦ www.museosanmichele.it) at **SAN MICHELE ALL'ADIGE**, 15km northeast of Trento. One of the largest of its kind in Europe, with exhibits ranging from re-creations of village houses (complete with muddy boots drying by the stove) to displays on hunting, grazing and wine making, the museum gives a real flavour of what life in Trentino was like until the twentieth century.

Some of the bloodiest engagements of World War I took place around **Monte Pasubio**, to the southeast of Trento. A total of 460,000 lives were lost – many from the cold – and 947,000 were wounded on the Italian side alone. The recently created **Sentiero della Pace** ("Path of Peace") follows the front, from the Ortles mountains east across the ranges to Marmolada, the trail littered with old bullets and barbed wire. The Campana dei Caduti, made out of melted-down cannon, tolls every evening in memory of the dead of both sides, from the Colle di Miravalle, a hill just outside the nearby town of Rovereto.

Rovereto: MART

A trip to Italy's largest modern art museum **MART** in the centre of Rovereto, a fifteen-minute train journey south of Trento, is one of the highlights of Trentino. The striking building at Corso Bettini 43 (Tues–Sun 10am–6pm, Fri late night opening until 9pm; €10; ⓦ www.mart.trento.it) was designed by Mario Botta and opened in December 2002. A changing selection from the permanent collection of more than 9000 paintings, designs and sculptures is on show in the spacious, light-filled galleries. Particularly strong are the collections of Futurist and twentieth-century avant-garde art: Italian Futurist Fortunato Depero bequeathed his collection of 3000 works including drawings, tapestries and sculpture. Metaphysical painters including Giorgio de Chirico and Giorgio Morandi, and Arte Povera artists are well represented, and the museum has made especially important purchases of American Pop Art, including works by Lichtenstein, Rauschenberg and Warhol. An equal pleasure is discovering the work of Italian artists whom you might not have come across elsewhere – the spindly, metal sculptures of Fausto Melotti, for example, or the striking *Sale Nero* by Pier Paolo Calzolari, a frozen line made through burnt salt, chilled by a fridge motor. The gallery also runs an exciting programme of temporary exhibitions. The **Casa Museo Depero** nearby at via della Terra 53 reopened in 2009 and was laid out by Depero himself a year before his death in 1960. The space shows off his large cloth collages – the most precious items in the MART collection – to great effect.

The Dolomiti di Brenta

Northwest of Trento lies a mountain range with a separate identity from the more famous Dolomitic peaks to the east. With their sawtoothed peaks and glaciers, the **Dolomiti di Brenta** have a rougher character than, say the Catinaccio/Rosengarten range in the main Dolomites – and their trails are far less well-trodden. While they are steep, few peaks rise above 3000m, and the paths are easy to follow. It should be said, though, that the walking is strenuous. Climbers come here for the towers of Cima Tosa and Cima Brenta, accessible by *vie ferrate* – iron "ladders" knocked into the rock. Their position, clinging tenaciously to the rock walls, is sensational. If you are looking for easier strolls, head for the **Val di Genova** which has a gentler beauty, with a woodland path taking you past a number of waterfalls cascading down the mountainside.

The range is circled by a good but slow and winding road, the southern half of which passes through the quiet lake resort of **Molveno**. The Trento to Madonna di Campiglio road takes you past the frescoed churches and wooded valleys of the Valle Rendena before arriving at **Campiglio** itself, the best base for skiing in the area, and a transport hub for walkers and climbers. The northern half of the Brenta mountains is bounded by the Val di Non and the Val di Sole, both served by the private Trento-Malé railway line.

Pinzolo and the Val Genova

Buses from Trento to Madonna di Campiglio skirt Monte Bondone and wind their way past a series of patchy hills and villages, passing Lago di Toblino. From here, the road continues west, turning into the Valle Rendena at Tione di Trento, where a more remote landscape of pasture and forest begins. Two villages well worth jumping off the bus for are the ski village of **PINZOLO** and Carisolo, which lie just a couple of kilometres apart on the main road, for their well preserved sixteenth-century frescoes of the *danse macabre*.

Simone Baschenis was one of a family of itinerant artists who decorated several small churches in Trentino in the 1500s. Among them was Pinzolo's romanesque **church of San Vigilio** (Tues–Sat 9.30–11.30am & 2.30–5.30pm, Sun 2.30–5.30pm). On the south facade, a band of skeletons playing trumpets and bag-pipes accompanies a procession representing the social order of the day – from emperors, cardinals and finely dressed ladies to soldiers, beggars and even a cherubic toddler who has a mini skeleton friend to remind him of his own mortality. Inside is a fine *Annunciation* from the thirteenth century, attributed to the Tuscan school, and other works by Simone Baschenis, among them the *Life of San Vigilio*, the young Bishop of Trento.

Another good reason to pause in Pinzolo is that it makes a less expensive overnight stop than its sister ski resort of Madonna di Campiglio up the road, especially if you stay at *Salvatera*, a lovely B&B at Via Marconi 44 with a minimum stay of three days (T0465.501 171; ①). There are a couple of small **campsites** too; one of these, *Faè della Val Rendena* (T0465.507.178; June–Sept & Dec–April), is near **Sant'Antonio di Mavignola**.

The other church in these parts decorated by the same artists lies two kilometres from **Carisolo**, on the road into the beautiful **Val di Genova**. Near the start of the valley you'll see a sign pointing down a track to the church of **Santo Stefano** (Tues–Sat 10–11.30am & 3.30–5pm, Sun 3.30–5pm), which has more frescoes of the *danse macabre* by the Baschenis on an outside wall, and others inside the spare, atmospheric interior depicting the legend of Charlemagne's passage through the Val di Campiglio on the way to his coronation in Rome.

Back on the Val Genova road, your route follows a cascading river up through woods to an information point at **Ponte Verde** (4km from Carisolo) where you can rent bikes or take a footpath that passes several waterfalls, spectacular in the spring melt and after rain, or in winter when they are frozen solid and a glacial turquoise inside. Most impressive is the **Cascata di Nárdis**, a five-minute walk from Ponte Verde, where several channels spill down the granite rock walls of the mountainside. A 4.5-kilometre walk or bike ride will bring you to **Ponte Maria** (no cars are allowed beyond this point) from where a shuttle bus runs (June 28 to Aug 31, daily, every 30min) another 8.5km to **Malga Bédole** (1584m), a settlement used by shepherds in summer. A two- to three-hour hike from there along trail 212 is the *Rifugio Città di Trento* (℡0465.501.193; April & June–Sept), at 2480m, within reach of the Adamello glaciers. You don't need a car to get to Val Genova – two express bus services run from Madonna di Campiglio, and from Pinzolo and Carisolo, to Bédole once a day in the morning, returning late afternoon.

Madonna di Campiglio

The major village in the Val Rendena is **MADONNA DI CAMPIGLIO**, an upmarket ski resort 70km from Trento known as "Campiglio" for short. This is where the Austro-Hungarian aristocracy holidayed in the nineteenth century, although not much of that era remains – what you see now is a very twentieth-century resort, hotel balconies groaning under the weight of geraniums. Winter sports and a quiet summer hiking season are Campiglio's reason for existence and the climbing and walking in the Dolomiti di Brenta are superb.

A dozen buses a day run from Trento to Madonna di Campiglio's main square, while thrice-daily trains head to Malé, 23km north, from where handily timed bus connections will take you to into town. The helpful **tourist office**, not far from the main square on Via Pradalago 4 (Mon–Sat 9am–12.30pm & 2.30–6pm; ℡0465.442.000, www.campiglio.net), can provide accommodation information and detailed maps (€1) of day hikes from town. Nearby, on Piazza Brenta Alta 16, the **Alpine Guide** office (daily 10am–noon & 4–8pm; ℡0465.447.501, www.guidealpinecampiglio.it) has information on hiking trails and *vie ferrate* and offers a variety of climbing courses and mountain excursions in summer. **Internet** facilities are available at the library (Mon–Sat afternoons) upstairs at the lakeside sports centre.

As Campiglio's hotels can be pricey and often insist on a three- to seven-night minimum stay, the best option, if you're walking, is to overnight in a *rifugio* (see p.234).

The best way to approach the trailheads is by cable car from **Carlo Magno**, 3km north of the village centre, to Grostè (daily: early July to late Sept 8.30am–12.30pm & 2–5pm; middle two weeks in Aug from 8am; €10 one-way, €15 return). If you're not into hard trekking, an alternative is to take the Funivia Cinque Laghi cable car (mid-June to early Sept daily 8.30am–12.50pm & 2–5.20pm; €7 one-way, €9 return) from the centre of the village west into the Presanella group. A scenic two-and-a-half hour route will take you via **Lago Ritorto** back down to the valley.

Walking in the Brenta massif

Once you're at **GROSTÈ** (2437m) you can plan your own routes as long as you have a decent hiking map. *Rifugio Graffer* (℡0465.441.358, Ⓦwww.graffer .com; June 20–Sept 20 & Dec–April) is conveniently next to the cable-car terminus, at 2261m. You can pick up trail 316 nearby, and set out across boulder-strewn slopes towards *rifugi Sella* and *Tuckett* at 2272m (both ℡0465.441.226, Ⓔrifugiotuckett.campiglio@tin.it; June 20–Sept 20). The latter is named after the most prodigious of nineteenth-century climbers, Francis Fox Tuckett, who wrote that he "roamed amongst toppling rocks, and spires of white and brown and bronze coloured stone" when he climbed in this range, and succeeded in opening up a difficult new route called the **Bochetta di Tuckett**. As ice axes hadn't been invented, he negotiated snowfields with a ladder and alpenstock (long staff), and carried joints of meat and bottles of wine for mountaintop breakfasts.

Trail 328 (becoming 318) starts just past the *Sella* and *Tuckett* refuges, bringing you (in about four hours from Grostè) to *Rifugio Brentei* (℡0465.441.244; June 20–Sept 20), set at 2489m, midway between the Cima Brenta and Cima Tosa mountain peaks. At this point, you'll probably want to stay overnight here. Next day, if you can cope with snowfields, you can extend your walk by trekking up to the **Bocca di Brenta** and crossing over the ridge to meet trail 319 down to Molveno, or simply return to Campiglio via trails 318 and 316 (3hr 30min).

Molveno and Andalo

On the other side of the Brenta mountain range from Campiglio is the lakeside village of **MOLVENO**, and 4km away by road or beautiful wooded trail is the slightly smaller town of **ANDALO**. Both are known for the quality of their wild **mushrooms**, and many Italians come here to pick them, getting hold of a mushrooming licence (€10 per day, €24 per week) from local tourist offices. A word of warning – each year 40,000 or so Italians suffer mushroom poisoning, so obviously only pick them if you know what you are doing.

Another option is to head for the **Brown Bear Area** in Spormaggiore (mid-June to mid-Sept daily 9.30am–6.30pm; €2.50, €1.50 for under 14s, free for under 6; Ⓦwww.prolocospormaggiore.tn.it), about 14km northeast of Molveno and accessible by bus from there. The *Life Ursus* project has created a "natural habitat" for a declining bear population, with animals taken from Italian zoos to prepare them for reintroduction into the wild. The enclosed outdoor area (follow the signs for the *area orsi*) lets you observe the bears – although the stars of the show spend a lot of time sleeping. A **visitor centre** back in the village (late June to mid-Sept daily 9.30am–12.30pm & 2–6pm; mid-Sept to mid-Oct Sat & Sun only 10am–noon & 2–6pm; combined ticket with Brown Bear Area; Ⓦwww.pnab.it), tells the story of the project.

East of Trento

If you're into high mountains, a trip **east of Trento** to a group of stunning pinnacles and bare peaks called the **Pale di San Martino** is unmissable. Formed as a coral reef sixty million years ago, white shells crunch underfoot as you walk 2000m above sea level, and the pale rock reflects light, even at dawn. The Pale are part of the **Parco Naturale Panevéggio**, an area of gently rolling woods and summer pastures with many walks, trails and campsites. The nearest resort is **San Martino di Castrozzo**, the terminus for buses travelling from Trento along the **Valsugana** and the **Val di Fiemme**.

Imer, Mezzano and Fiera di Primiero

On the way from Trento to San Martino you pass through the archetypal tourist villages of **IMER** and, a couple of kilometres east, **MEZZANO**. The valley they're located in is wide, with hay meadows spreading either side, and makes a good place to walk or cycle, with cycle tracks linking the villages and easy paths running into the foothills. As far as **accommodation** goes, an alternative to the Alpine-style hotels in the villages is *Camping Calavise*, a well-signposted 1km from Imer, which has a bar and swimming pool nearby (T0439.67.468, Wwww.campingcalavise.it; €20 per tent). Or you could head for the *Rifugio Fonteghi* (T0439.67.043, Wwww.rifugiofonteghi.com; April–Oct). The 45-minute walk along the path on the south side of the Val Noana reservoir will help you build up an appetite for their home-made pasta dishes, home-grown veg and game – half pension costs €50 per person.

Around 4km from Imer, **FIERA DI PRIMIERO** is a larger resort and market town with a **tourist office** (Mon–Sat 9am–noon & 3.20–7pm, Sun 9.30am–12.30pm; T0439.62.407). It's a major crossroads in the area, from where buses run up to the beginning of the Val Canali and to Passo Cereda (1369m). The mountains around Fiera were worked for silver, iron and copper from the thirteenth century, and miner's guilds paid for the town's late-Gothic **parish church** near the fortified Palazzo delle Miniere (where the precious metals were guarded before being sent to the mint). Inside the church is a beautiful painting of *The Hunt of the Mystic Unicorn* and a fine fifteenth-century carved altar showing scenes from the Virgin Mary's life. Recent excavations have brought to light the remains of a **paleo-Christian basilica** dating from the fifth to sixth centuries. It's well worth a stroll round the village – paintings made in the sixteenth century on the outside of some of the older houses have survived the elements: in one slightly disturbing one, a Madonna della Misericordia shelters a white-cowled member of the Battuti fraternity flogging himself with a scourge.

San Martino di Castrozza

The road into **SAN MARTINO DI CASTROZZA** twists and turns, and you feel like you're in the middle of nowhere until the resort's new hotels appear around the corner. One of the smarter Dolomite resorts, tourism took off here in the nineteenth century, but as far back as the Middle Ages, travellers and pilgrims stopped here for the night, staying at the monastery, of which only traces remain. Visitors come here now for skiing and hiking – hourly buses south to Fiera di Primiero and Imer, and cable-car routes into the mountains make San Martino one of the best walking bases the area. The **tourist office**, next to the bus stop at Via Passo Rolle 165 (mid-June to Sept Mon–Sat 9am–12.30pm & 3.40–7pm, Sun 9.30–12.30pm; rest of year Mon–Sat 9am–12.30pm & 2.30–5.30pm, Sun 9.30am–12 noon; T0439.768.867, Wwww.sanmartino .com) has a detailed walking map of the area, giving information about *rifugi*, difficulty levels, approximate times and so on.

For a low-cost **place to stay**, try the *Ostello Dolomiti*, around 1km from the town centre near the Malga Ces lifts and Sass Maòr campsite on Via Laghetti 43 (T0439.769.166, Wwww.ostellodolomiti.com; €28 per person in a six-bed dorm; bedrooms for four also available). Closer to town, *Vienna* (T0439.68.078; ❸); on Via Herman Panzer 1 has a sauna, Turkish bath and spa. The alternative is to pitch a tent at the village **campsite**, *Sass Maòr* (℡0439.68.347, Ⓦwww.campingsassmaor.it) on Via Laghetti – booking ahead is essential in high season.

Parco Naturale Panevéggio

Out of San Martino, traffic files up to **Passo di Rolle**, a beautiful stretch of high moorland dotted with avalanche breaks and a few sheep. There are only two buses a day, so a car really helps here. The Passo di Rolle falls within the **Parco Naturale Panevéggio** (Ⓦwww.parcopan.org), which protects a vast area of ancient woodland as well as the high peaks of the the Pale di San Martino. Crisscrossed by nature trails and ancient paved paths called *reversi*, the park gives you a sense of rural life on the summer pastures and in the forest, and makes an atmospheric venue for some of the open-air concerts in the *Suoni delle Dolomiti* series (see p.234). Entry to the park costs €2 and the Panevéggio visitor centre offers guided half-day walks into the forest (€5).

There are three **visitor centres** in the park: **San Martino** (late June to early Sept daily 9am–12.30pm & 3–7pm; ℡0439.768.859), **Villa Welsperg** in the Val Canali (June–Sept daily 9am–12.30pm & 3–6pm, Oct to early April daily 9.30am–12.30pm & 2–5pm; mid-April to May Sun only 10am–12.30pm & 3–6pm; ℡0439.765.973) and **Paneveggio**, 7km from the pass (early June to mid-Sept daily 9am–12.30pm & 2–5.30pm; also open Christmas, New Year and Jan–March 31 same hours Tues & Fri, and from mid-April to early June same hours on Sun; ℡0462.576.283).

You can **camp** next to Lago Panevéggio: the entrance is at the end of the track marked "Area della Sosta", just past the village. Facilities are minimal and stays are limited to 24 hours. There's a proper campsite, *Bellamonte* (℡0462.576.119, Ⓦwww.campingbellamonte.it; €23 per tent), 4km down the road to Predazzo (see p.246) surrounded by meadows and hay lofts.

Hiking in the Pale di San Martino

The most dramatic part of the Panevéggio national park is the **Pale di San Martino** – a large plateau surrounded by razor-sharp peaks. Ranging from 2600m to 3200m in altitude, you should be prepared for snow, wind and rain, even in the summer, as well as scorching sunlight and the most stupendous views. There are two main entry points – the **Val Canali** (accessed from Fiera di Primiero) and the **cable car** from San Martino di Castrozza.

The **Val Canali** was described by Amelia Edwards in the nineteenth century as the most "lonely, desolate and tremendous scene to be found this side of the Andes". Things have changed since the arrival of the Alta Via 2 walking route which runs through here but the valley retains a feeling of isolation. Buses from Fiera di Primiero run to the trailheads of the valley via the Passo Cereda. You'll find the official campsite, the *Castelpietra* (℡0439.62.426, Ⓦwww.castelpietra.it; June–Oct & Nov–April; €22 per tent) opposite the National Park centre, and there are further places to camp at the head of the glen. *Rifugio Treviso* (℡0439.62.311; late June to mid-Sept) is a possible overnight stop, while the more luxurious *Cant del Gal* (℡0439.62.997; ❷), further down the valley, has ten rooms and a good restaurant – one of its specialities is local cheese *tosela* served with mushrooms and polenta.

A stiff ascent from *Rifugio Treviso* brings you onto the **Altopiano delle Pale** at Passo di Pradidali, where eagles can be seen circling above the barren plateau and the silence is broken every so often by a trickle of falling stones. Once you are at this altitude, there are many possibilities for linking up with other trails across the stark upland. *Rifugio Pedrotti alla Rosetta* (T0439.68.308, Wwww .rifugiorosetta.it; June 20–Sept 20), at 2581m, is the nearest place with accommodation (a 2hr 30min hike north; also reachable by cable car – see below); facilities include hot showers, a restaurant and bar. Run by Roberta Lott and her alpine guide husband Mariano, the *rifugio* is the base of the Orizzonti Trentini alpine guides (see p.234).

The fastest route into the Pale di San Martino is via **cable car** from San Martino. The Colverde funicular (June 14–Sept 20 daily 8am–4.45pm, closes 5.45pm at weekends and in Aug; journey up €10, down €9, return trip €16.50) from the village runs to the foot of the Pale, from where the Rosetta chair lift takes you up to to *Rifugio Pedrotti alla Rosetta*, perched on the edge of the Altopiano. From the Rosetta chair-lift terminus, you can make for *Rifugio Pradidali* at 2278m (T0439.64.180; June 20–Sept 20), a walk and descent of three hours. A more ambitious walk would be to continue on from the refuge over the **Passo di Ball**, returning from there to San Martino or descending over into Val Canali at *Rifugio Cant del Gal*. If you prefer the relative security of a guided trek, ask at the desk of the Gruppo Guide Alpine (daily 5–7pm; T0461.768.795), in the same building as the tourist office; they run graded excursions most days in July and August.

Val di Fiemme

Once you're out of the confines of the park, **PREDAZZO** is the first town you come to in the **Val di Fiemme**, which lies between two immense mountain massifs: the Latemar and the Catena di Lagorai. Predazzo has become something of a pilgrimage site for geologists, owing to the extensive collection of local rocks and fossils in the **Museo Civico di Geologia** on Piazza Santi Filippo e Giacomo (T0462.500.366; July–Sept Tues–Sat 10am–noon and 5–7pm). Surprisingly accessible to non-experts, the displays include samples of the Dolomitic calcite rock first identified by the elaborately named French mineralogist Dieudonné Sylvain Guy Tancrède de Gratet de Dolomieu.

Throughout the valley, hotel hoardings are ubiquitous, and even the tiniest villages hereabouts have a plan of the mountain ranges with chair lifts marked, but behind the modern Dolomites tourist industry, this is an ancient region that from the twelfth to the seventeenth centuries was virtually autonomous. A local parliament met at the *Banco de la reson*, a circle of stone benches surrounded by trees in **CAVALESE**, the chief town of the Val di Fiemme, and the Magnifica Comunità of Cavalese still administers communal land.

A short way beyond Cavalese's town centre, at Via Fratelli Bronzetti 60, the road to Tèsero, is a small **tourist office** (Mon–Sat 9am–noon & 3.30–7pm; July & Aug also Sun 9am–noon; T0462.241.111, info@valdifiemme.info) that can arrange visits to the medieval **Palazzo della Magnifica Comunità** in Cavalese. This was the Bishop of Trento's summer palace, and now houses a small **museum and gallery** (currently closed for renovation) containing the original valley statutes, carefully kept in wood-panelled rooms smelling of sawdust and polish, with fine wooden ceilings and painted friezes. The building's lack of fortifications indicates that Trento's bishop felt safe from the armed rebellions that had plagued him in the city, and its exterior is covered in frescoes depicting St Vigilio (Trento's patron saint).

With its cobbled streets, cake shops and ice-cream outlets, Cavalese makes a relaxing afternoon stop, but if you decide to stay, head for *Laurino*, a central **hotel** in a seventeenth-century palace that's been decorated in a beautifully pared-down Tyrolean style (T0462.340.151, Wwww.hotelgarnilaurino.com; ❸).

TÉSERO, 4km away, has a parish church frescoed with *Cristo della Domenica* (Christ of the Sabbath) who stands in the middle surrounded by more than thirty symbols depicting the things you mustn't do on a Sunday – drinking, work and commerce among them.

The Catinaccio and Gruppo di Sella

The **Catinaccio** (or **Rosengarten**) range is one of the best-known sights in the Dolomites. This immense wall of rock along the edge of the 3000m-high massif takes on a famously rosy glow at sunset, and the mountain plays a starring role in the legends of the area. Trails across this mountain are popular with mainly Italian and German walkers and, although the zig-zag paths to the peaks can be crowded in August, once you're above the cable-car line, there's plenty of wilderness to lose yourself in.

Access is simple enough from **Vigo di Fassa**, the main place to stay in the Val di Fassa, which splits off from the Val di Fiemme north of Predazzo at Moena. If you travel these roads and trails, you pass through one of the heartlands of **Ladino** culture (see box, p.248).

At the head of the Val di Fassa, **Canazei** makes a good springboard for the high plateaux of the **Gruppo di Sella**, and the gentler trail of the **Viel del Pan**, which leads down to the tiny resort of **Arabba**. On the northern side of the Sella group, **Corvara** is a much larger resort with a sizeable Ladino population.

Catinaccio

The **Catinaccio** range was described by nineteenth-century writer Theodor Christomannos as a "gigantic fortification ... the gate into the kingdom of immortal ghosts, of high-flying giants". The area's German name, **Rosengarten** (rose garden), derives from the legend of Laurin, king of the dwarves, who used to grow roses here. The king, angered when he was prevented from being with his beloved princess Similde, put a spell on the roses so that no one would see them again by day or night, but forgot to include dawn and dusk, which is when the low sun gives the rock its fiery glow.

The **trails** across the range cater for all levels of hiking ability; however, the going does get tough on the ridges, from where you can see as far as the Stubaier Alps, on the border with Austria, but if you buy a Kompass map and plan your route carefully, you can keep your walks well within your capabilities.

The most popular approach to Catinaccio is from the hamlet of **VIGO DI FASSA**. The village, served by buses on the Trento–Canazei route, has a few three-star **hotels** – try the good-value *Renato*, Strada di Solar 27 (☎0462.764.006, ⓦwww.hotelrenato.it; €80 per person, half board only) which has a spa, pool and many rooms with balconies; or the welcoming *Rifugio Roda di Vael* (☎0462.764.450, ⓦwww.rodadivael.it; June–Sept), in a spectacular position a ninety-minute walk from the village along trails 547 and 545.

The trek to **Torri del Vajolet** (2813m) from Vigo di Fassa is the classic route up onto the range. The cable car from the village to *Rifugio Ciampedie* (☎0462.764.432; mid-June to mid-Oct) covers most of the ascent, after which a well-beaten trail leads through woods to the basic *Rifugio Gardeccia* (☎0462.763.152, ⓦwww.gardeccia.it; early June to early Oct). From here it's a steep walk up to the Torri, although this doesn't put the hordes of summer weekend walkers off who form a line to make the dramatic, zigzagging climb

Ladin country

The **Ladins** (*Ladini* in Italian, *Ladinisch* in German) are a community of around 30,000 people living in the Gardena, Badia, Fassa, Livinallongo and Ampezzo valleys around the Sella massif. They're united by their ancient language – Ladin – which was once spoken over a wide area, from Austria down to the River Po (in what's now Emilia-Romagna). The Dolomitic Ladin language, preserved by the relative remoteness of the territory, is linked to Swiss Romansch (there are 40,000 speakers in the Swiss Engadine) and Friulano (more than 700,000 speakers in the Friuli region of Italy).

The history of the Ladins is recorded in their epics, which recount tales of battles, treachery and reversals of fortune. Around 400 AD, the Ladins were constantly threatened with invasion by Germanic tribes from the north and others from the Po Valley. Christianity later emerged as a major threat, but the Ladins absorbed and transformed the new religion, investing the new saints with the powers of more ancient female divinities.

The **Museo Ladin de Fascia** (June 20–Sept 10, Mon–Sat 10am–12.30pm & 3.30–7pm; other periods Tues–Sat 3–7pm; €4; Ⓦwww.istladin.net) is devoted to traditional Ladin working life and is an excellent place to find out more. The museum is situated between San Giovanni and **Vigo di Fassa**, but it has exhibits scattered throughout the territory: **Moena** is home to a restored nineteenth-century cooperage (*Botega da Pinter*) at Via Dolomiti 3; **Pera di Fassa** houses a restored watermill (*Molin de Pezol*) at Via Jumela 6; and a working, antique sawmill (*La Sia*) can be seen at Via Pian Trevisan at Penia, just outside Canazei. Tourist offices, notably the one in Corvara, have details of occasional festivals, exhibitions and events.

to *Rifugio Re Alberto* (Ⓣ0462.763.428, Ⓦwww.rifugiorealberto.com; mid-June to mid-Sept; food on Sat only), three hours from *Rifugio Ciampedie*. There's alternative accommodation nearby at the tiny *Rifugio Passo Santner* (Ⓣ0471.642.230; mid-June to Sept) or *Rifugio Vàiolet* (Ⓣ0462.763.292 or 769.045, Ⓦwww.rifugiovajolet.com; mid-June to end Sept) a welcome base for climbers since 1897 and a ninety-minute walk from Ciampedie.

The valley isn't all about hiking and skiing: for a change of pace, head to the Museo Ladin di Fascia (Mon–Thurs 9am–noon & 2–5pm, Fri 9am–noon; €3; Ⓦwww.istladin.net) for a fascinating introduction to Ladin culture. It's located in a new building between San Giovanni and Vigo di Fassa (within walking distance) and has intriguing exhibits on the language and culture of the Ladini.

Canazei

CANAZEI, a buzzing summer and winter resort at the head of the Val di Fassa (Ⓦwww.fassa.com) is a stepping stone to the stupendous high road passes between here and Cortina d'Ampezzo. You may also find yourself staying here before or after walking in the Gruppo di Sella or strolling along a much easier trail – the **Viel del Pan** opposite glacier-topped Marmolada. For a good base to **stay**, check out *La Zondra* (Ⓣ0462.601.233, Ⓦwww.lazondra.com; ❸), with balconied rooms on Via Pareda; or *Giardino delle Rose* (Ⓣ0462.602.221; ❷) on Via Dolomiti, in the village centre; *Villa Mozart* (Ⓣ0462.601.254, Ⓦwww.hotelvillamozart.com; €70 per person half board) also central, on Strada Roma, is geared up for motorbikers and offers good deals in spring and autumn.

From Canazei, it's well worth driving the **switchback road** of 27 bends that climbs for 12km towards the Passo Pordoi. Although it's often busy with

The SellaRondaBus

From early July until early September, the **SellaRondaBus** service links four mountain valleys and passes around the Sella Ronda massif which makes travel in this part of the world very much easier.

The bus does a circular route both clockwise and anti-clockwise, serving Selva Gardena, Colfosco, Corvara, Arabba and Canazei, and four mountain passes: Gardena, Campolongo, Pordoi and Sella, stopping at 30 points along the way. For timetables, go to ⓦwww.valgardena.it. You can buy tickets on the bus. See "Travel details" for more on bus frequencies throughout the region.

busloads of tourists heading for the scenic Great Dolomites Road (see p.262) and determined cyclists making the thousand-metre ascent, the view when you get there is unforgettable. Halfway along the road, the cable car at Pradel leads to **Passo di Sella** (2240m), one of the most impressive of the Dolomite passes. Paths climb from here onto the jagged peaks of the **Sasso Lungo** (Langkofel) and follow the ridges down onto the Alpe di Siusi. It takes two days to walk from the Sella pass, via *Rifugio Vicenza* (ⓣ0471.792.323, ⓦwww.rifugiovicenza .com; June–Sept), into the Val Gardena (Grödnertal), where the SellaRondaBus stops and there are services to Bolzano.

Just past Pradel the road forks. Straight ahead is the **Gruppo di Sella** – an arid lunar plateau surrounded by pink, dolomitic peaks. A right-hand turning takes you up to **Passo Pordoi** (2242m), an astonishing vantage point between the Gruppo di Sella and Marmolada. At 3246m, Marmolada is the highest Dolomite and its rounded peak is permanently shrouded by a glacier.

From here, mountains radiate in every direction, giving you a chance to identify the distinctive shapes of each of the main Dolomite ranges. In the foreground, the Sasso Lungo look like a jagged, gloved hand, flanked by two prominent peaks; the Gruppo di Sella is squat and chunky; and Sciliar (Schlern), just visible in the distance, comprises a flat rocky tabletop, culminating in two peaks. A small road winds downwards to Passo Falzárego, and ultimately Cortina d'Ampezzo. From Passo Pordoi you can join Alta Via 2, or if you simply want to stretch your legs, walk a short section of it known as the Viel del Pan (see below). Most tourist buses and plenty of bikers stop at the collection of cafés and stalls at the pass. The **hotels** here may insist on half board; try the *Pordoi* (ⓣ0462.601.115; ⓦwww.passo-pordoi.it; €60 per person, half board only). The SellaRondaBus links Passo Pordoi with four other valleys and passes (see box above).

A walk along the Viel del Pan

If you're not a great walker, there's an easy twenty-minute stroll from the Passo Pordoi that gives a terrific view of the Dolomites which is far better than the ones you get from the road. Pick up the Alta Via 2 trail just past the *Albergo Savoia*. A narrow path cut into the turf traverses the mountainside opposite the glaciers of Marmolada, which was right on the front during World War I. Entire Austrian battalions managed to overwinter inside Marmolada by blasting 8km of tunnel tens of metres deep under the ice and rock.

From the seventeenth century this path was on the grain-smuggling route called the **Viel del Pan** ("trail of bread" in Venetian dialect), and it remained busy enough in the nineteenth century for the Guardia di Finanza to set up armed patrols along it. The contrast between the glacier on Marmolada and the peaks of the Sella group – 360 degrees of mountain – is superb. When you've had enough of walking, the easiest option is to return the same way to the Passo Pordoi. Or you can keep going on the same path until you reach **Lago Fedaia**, from where there are irregular buses in summer back to Canazei.

Another possibility is to continue along the ridge, eventually heading back down to the valley to **ARABBA**, a small resort with family-run **hotels**: the *Albergo Posta* (℡0436.79.105; ❷) is basic but central and ageing gracefully, with a gorgeous terrace and an in-house pizzeria, while the *Garni Emma* (℡0436.79.116, garniemma@virgilio.it; ❷) has a family atmosphere and sits beside a small stream. From July to early September, the SellaRondaBus (see box, p.249) runs from Arabba back to Canazei. The only other bus service from here goes from Belluno to Corvara.

Corvara and around

The central town of the Ladin ethnic group, **CORVARA** is primarily a ski resort, and it also makes a good base for the excellent trails of the nearby Fánes Park (see p.260), a bus ride away, where most of the Ladin legends are based. The **tourist office** at Strada Col Alt 36 (Mon–Sat 8am–noon & 3–7pm, Sun 10am–noon & 4–6pm; ℡0471.836.176, ⓦwww.altabadia.org) has details of **hotels and rooms** in private houses. The chalet-style *Monti Pallidi*, Strada Col Alt 75 (℡0471.836.081, ⓦwww.montipallidi.net; ❸), has excellent-value, modern rooms, most with a kitchenette.

Corvara is on the SellaRondaBus route and a few buses also leave for Brunico and Belluno from outside the tourist office. Some 4.5km north of Corvara is **La Villa**, a small village with a fairy-tale sixteenth-century castle. **SAN CASSIANO**, 4km further east, towards the Paso di Valparola, is home to the luxurious *Rosa Alpina* (℡0471.849.500, ⓦwww.rosalpina.it; ❸), a spa hotel with a celebrated restaurant that's a great place to relax after a few days of walking or biking.

Bolzano (Bozen)

Situated on the junction of the rivers Talvera (Talfer) and Isarco (Eisack), **BOLZANO** (largely known by its German name, Bozen) is the capital of the autonomous province of Alto Adige. In both winter and summer, the town's 100,000 population swells with tourists although it manages to maintain a relaxed pace of life and is an excellent base from which to explore the surrounding mountains. An unmissable pleasure is the local **wine**: Bolzano is at the head of the wine road (Strada di Vino/Südtiroler Weinstrasse) which runs south to the border with Trentino.

Located in a predominantly sunny, sheltered bowl, for centuries Bolzano was a valley market town and way station whose fortunes in the Middle Ages swayed as the Counts of Tyrol and the Bishops of Trento competed for power. The town passed to the Habsburgs in the fourteenth century, then at the beginning of the nineteenth century Bavaria took control, opposed by Tyrolese patriot and military leader Andreas Hofer. His battle in 1809 to keep the Tyrol under Austrian rule was only temporarily successful, as in the same year the Austrian Emperor ceded the Tyrol to the Napoleonic kingdom of Italy. More changes followed, as Bolzano was handed back to Austria until after World War I, whereupon it passed, like the rest of the province, to Italy.

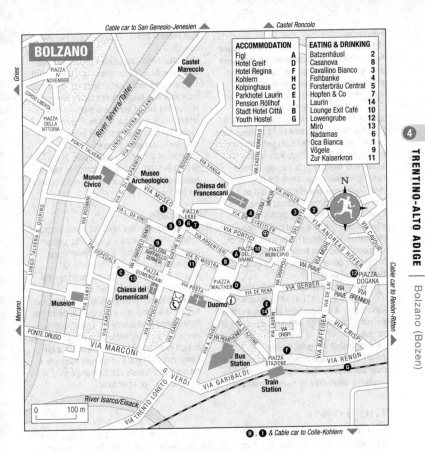

Within the map:

BOLZANO

Cable car to San Genesio-Jenesien ▲   ▲ Castel Roncolo

ACCOMMODATION	
Figl	A
Hotel Greif	D
Hotel Regina	F
Kohlern	H
Kolpinghaus	C
Parkhotel Laurin	E
Pension Röllhof	I
Stadt Hotel Città	B
Youth Hostel	G

EATING & DRINKING	
Batzenhäusl	2
Casanova	8
Cavallino Bianco	3
Fishbanke	4
Forsterbräu Central	5
Hopfen & Co	7
Laurin	14
Lounge Exil Café	10
Lowengrube	12
Mirò	13
Nadamas	6
Oca Bianca	1
Vögele	9
Zur Kaiserkron	11

Cable car to Renon-Ritten

H , **I** & Cable car to Colle-Kohlern ▼

Arrival and information

Bolzano's **bus station**, centrally placed at Via Perathoner 4, serves most of the small villages and resorts in the province; the **train station** is a few minutes' walk south of here through the park down Via Stazione. There is a city **tourist office** at Piazza Walther 8 (Mon–Fri 9am–6.30pm, Sat 9am–noon; ☎0471.307.000, Ⓦwww.bolzano-bozen.it) where you can pick up the Bolzano **museum card** (€2.50) which gives the holder discounted entry to the town's museums as well as the **Castello Róncolo** (see p.255). For regional information visit Ⓦwww.suedtirol.info.

Accommodation

Located on the historic route south from other parts of Europe, Bolzano has a long tradition of hospitality and offers some special **places to stay** that are well worth splashing out on. The best option if the budget is tight is the youth hostel (see p.255), or a *pensione* a little way out of town – the latter are listed at Ⓦwww.bolzano-bozen.it. *Moosbauer* campsite (☎0471.918.492, Ⓦwww.moosbauer.com) is on the main Bolzano–Merano road and costs €28 per tent.

Hotels

Figl Piazza del Grano 9 ℡ 0471.978.412, ⓦwww
.figl.net. Though this shuttered hotel in the square
looks old from the outside, the rooms have been
refurbished and are simple and cheerful. ❸

🏃 **Hotel Greif** Piazza Waltherplatz
℡ 0471.318.000, ⓦwww.greif.it. The
Black Griffin inn that stood on this spot for 500
years has been transformed into a boutique hotel.
Each of the 33 luxurious rooms and suites has
been designed by a contemporary artist, with
Beidermeier furniture from the original hotel
blending surprisingly well with the new hip-luxe
style. Guests have use of the park and pool at
Grief's sister hotel, the *Parkhotel Laurin*. ❻
Hotel Regina Via Renon 1 ℡ 0471.972.195,
ⓦwww.hotelreginabz.it. Great location opposite the
train station. The quietest rooms are at the back,
but specify if you want smoking or non-smoking.
Some rooms (lower rates) on the main road side
have views of the hills. ❸

🏃 **Kohlern** at the top of the Colle/Kohlern
cable car, ℡ 0471.329.978, ⓦwww
.kohlern.com. A well-run hotel with spa and small
pool, on a mountainside with bird's-eye-views of
Bolzano. ❹
Pension Röllhof Kampenn, Kohlern
℡ 0471.329.958, ⓦwww.roellhof.com. Set 930m
above sea level, this is an appealing, chalet-style
pensione a 10min drive up a steep, switchback

road from the centre of Bolzano. Open Easter–
Nov. ❷
Parkhotel Laurin Via Laurin 4 ℡ 0471.311.000,
ⓦwww.laurin.it. Popular, grand hotel built in 1910.
The rooms are restful and understated, some have
terraces, others balconies, one has its own roof
terrace. The food in the secluded open-air restaurant is excellent. The bar, with its *King Laurin*
fresco (1911) by Jugendstil artist Bruno Goldsch-
mitt, hosts jazz nights at weekends. ❻
Stadt Hotel Città Piazza Waltherplatz 21
℡ 0471.975.221, ⓦwww.hotelcitta.info. Modern,
businesslike but friendly hotel right in the centre of
the Old Town. ❻

Hostels

Kolpinghaus Via Ospedale 3, off Piazza Walther
℡ 0471.308.400, ⓦwww.kolping.it/bz. Low prices
make up for the no-frills feel of this imposing
residence with single and twin rooms. ❸
Ostello Bolzano/Jugendherberge Bozen Via
Renon 23, 200m from the train station.
℡ 0471.300.865, ⓦwww.ostello.bz. Cheerful and
modern, this hostel is one of a chain in the South
Tyrol offering good-quality, low-cost accommodation to young people and families with children. You
can get to the hostel by turning right out of the
station and you'll find it on the right-hand side of
the main road. It costs €22 for a single and €19.50
for a bed in a 3 or 4 bed room.

The Town

Central Bolzano definitely looks like a part of the German-speaking world.
Restaurants serve *speck*, *gulasch* and *knödel*, and bakers sell black bread and *sachertorte*. The centre of town is **Piazza Walther**, whose pavement cafés, around its
statue of the *minnesinger* (troubadour) Walther von der Vogelweide, are the
town's favoured meeting places. Converted into a cathedral as recently as 1964,
the **Duomo** (Dom) sits on the edge of the square; built in the fourteenth and
fifteenth centuries, and restored after being bombed in World War II, it has a
striking mosaic roof and elaborately carved spire. The fourteenth-century
Franciscan church on Via dei Francescani is also worth seeking out, embellished with a carved wooden altarpiece by Hans Klocher and with elegant,
frescoed cloisters from the same period.

A couple of streets west of Piazza Walther, on Via Cappuccini, the **Chiesa dei
Domenicani** (Dominican monastery) has frescoes of fifteenth-century courtly
life painted on the walls of the decaying cloisters, framed by a growth of stone
tracery. The **Cappella di San Giovanni**, built at the beginning of the
fourteenth century, retains frescoes by painters of the Giotto school, including
a *Triumph of Death* underneath a starry vault. Follow the street north to **Piazza
Erbe**, site of a daily fruit and vegetable market, from where the oriel windows
and eleventh-century arcades of **Via Portici** lead off to the right.

A visit to the **Museo Archeologico** (Tues–Sun 10am–6pm; also open Mon
in July, Aug and Dec; ⓦwww.archaeologiemuseum.it; €8), a ten-minute walk
west of the centre at Via Museo (Museumstrasse) 43, is a must. Its major exhibit

is the **Ice Man**, the frozen, mummified body of a man discovered in the ice of the Ötzaler Alps in 1991. At first it was thought that the body – nicknamed "Ötzi" – was that of a soldier or a mountaineer, then an investigation revealed that, amazingly, it dated from around 3300 BC. Visitors can view the mummy through a small window in a high-tech refrigeration unit while a video suggests how he may have come to his untimely end. Just as fascinating are the minutiae of the discovery: the Ice Man was around 45 years old but has no tooth decay; he carried a sophisticated fire-lighting kit of different kinds of tinder for starting a fire in extreme conditions; he wore elaborate thermal shoes, a cap and backpack, and, intriguingly, his body bears tattoos at certain neuralgic points that are thought to have relieved the pain of arthritis.

Nearby at Via Dante is Bolzano's brand-new museum of contemporary art **Museion** (daily 10am–8pm, Thurs closes 10pm; Ⓦwww.museion.it; €6). Appropriately for a bilingual area (or trilingual if you include the Ladin tongue) the theme "art and language" is central to the works in the permanent collection, with 2000 pieces in the area of art that lies between images and words. A new bridge leads from behind the huge steel-and-glass cube of the museum across the River Talvera (Talfer); a riverside walk upstream brings you to the older Ponte Talvera where Bolzano's German and Gothic quarter ends and **Piazza della Vittoria** signals the edge of the new part of town, much of it laid out by Mussolini's favourite architect, Marcello Piacentini. The epic triumphal arch (1928) on the square is something of a controversial monument, not least due to its inscription: "Here is the border of the Motherland. Set the banners down. From this point on we educated others with language, law and culture." Until a recent cleanup, it was covered with graffiti and surrounded by low railings, and was even bombed by German-speaking separatists in the late 1980s. The piazza is now the site of a big general market on Saturdays.

Eating, drinking and nightlife

If you're just after a lunchtime snack, try *wurstel* and *apfel strudel*, both available from stalls on Piazza Erbe, Piazza del Grano and Via Stazione, and the cafés of Via dei Portici. Via Museo has a good selection of **restaurants**.

There's more of a chance of finding decent **nightlife** in Bolzano than in other cities in the region, and a hard-partying *movida bolzanina* has recently been reported in the Italian press. Certainly, people travel from miles around to go clubbing in the industrial zone and new pubs have been opening up, with Friday and Saturday night crowds spilling out onto the street; for a local aperitif, ask for a *Veneziana* (Aperol, champagne or prosecco, ice and a slice).

It's worth noting that despite being a tourist destination, Bolzano practically closes down on Sunday, most supermarkets included, though on Sunday evenings, and late every night, it's possible to get **pizza** and ice cream from *Subito*, on Piazza Erbe.

Restaurants

Batzenhäusl Via A. Hofer 30 ☎0471.050.950. Old wine bar with a good food and a lively atmosphere. Live music Thurs, Fri & Sat. Closed Tues.

Cavallino Bianco (Weisses Rössel) Via dei Bottai/Bindergasse 6 ☎0471.973.267. This *bierkeller* features a menu strong on Tyrolean specialities with mains selling at €11–15. Closed Sat eve & Sun and July.

Hopfen & Co Obstplatz 17 ☎0471.300.788. On the corner of the fruit market at Piazza Erbe; highly recommended for its own beer brewed on the premises and a varied selection of dishes.

Laurin Via Laurin 4 ☎0471.311.000. Laid-back gourmet restaurant in the garden of *Parkhotel Laurin*, with dishes from top chef Egon Heiss striking a fine balance between experimental and traditional.

Lowengrube Piazza Dogana 3. A *bierlokal* serving good food and with *weissbier* on tap.

Oca Bianca Piazza Erbe 24. Home-made pasta, fish and seafood and a good choice of regional Italian wines. Closed Sun.

Vögele Goethestrasse 3 ℡ 0471.923.938. Vögele's big oak tables and wood panelling, candles and friendly staff make it a popular place to sample local wines and delicacies. If you don't want a full restaurant meal, there's a less formal café with platters to share. Closed Sun and June 20–July 10.

Zur Kaiserkron Piazza di Mostra/Musterplatz 1 ℡ 0471.303.233 Fine dining in a baroque merchant's palace, or outside on the terrace. Food from well-known South Tyrolean chef Sebastian Kaiser combines Mediterranean and local dishes. Closed Sun.

Bars and clubs

Alumix Voltastraße, 9. Some nights feature live music, others disco, but in general it's the more "alternative" venue of the South Bolzano area. Entrance is €9 (one drink included).

Casanova Erbsengasse 8 ℡ 0471.301.897. Pleasant gay-friendly pub in the historic centre open until 1am. Closed Sun.

Fishbanke, Via D. Streite 26/A ℡ 0471.971 714. Outdoor wine bar on the road running parallel with Via dei Portici, where you sip your Chardonnay and nibble on bruschetta at marble counters that once made up the city's fish market.

ForsterbräuCentral Goethestrasse 6 ℡ 0471.977.243. Good beer including the strong Sixtus ale and reasonably priced food with outside tables where you can enjoy the evening breeze.

Lounge Exil Café Piazza del Grano 2/A ℡ 0471.971.814. A young urban hangout in an industrial-style café.

Mirò Dominikanerplatz 3b. Mainly techno club in the town centre. Entry €14 includes one drink.

Nadamas Piazza Erbe 44 ℡ 0471.980.684. International-themed bar-restaurant with a huge variety of snacks and cocktails; Latin American tunes.

Rise Marie-Curie-Strasse. DJs and special guests feature at this shindig in South Bolzano. Entry €16 includes one drink.

Listings

Airport Aeroporto Bolzano Dolomiti ℡ 0471.255.255.

Car rental Hertz, airport ℡ 0471.254.266; Alamo Via Garabaldi 2 ℡ 0471.971.531.

Hospitals Ospedale Centrale di Bolzano, Via Lorenz Böhler 5 ℡ 0471.908.111. In emergency call 118.

Internet *Multikulti*, Via Doctor Streiter 9. Daily 10am–1pm.

Parking Parcheggio Piazza Walther; Central Parking, Piazza Stazione; Bolzano Centro, Via Mayr-Nusser.

Pharmacies Don Bosco, Don Bosco Platz 6/B ℡ 0471.915.239; Paris, Florenzstrasse 56 ℡ 0471.917.384; Gires, Telser Durchgang 8 ℡ 0471.285.096.

Police station Via Marconi 23 ℡ 0471.997.788 or 947.680.

Post office Piazza Parrocchia/Pfarrplatz 13 ℡ 0471.322.211. Mon–Fri 8am–6.30pm, Sat 8am–12 noon.

Taxis Radio Taxi ℡ 0471.981.111.

Around Bolzano

A trip up in any of Bolzano's three **cable cars** gives a small taste of the high peaks that surround the city. The first (open all year dawn to dusk; every 4min; journey time 10min) ascends from Via Renòn (Rittnerstrasse), a ten-minute walk from the train station, to **Soprabolzano** (Oberbozen). It's the longest cable-car journey in Europe, with the largest change in height. Alternatively the San Genesio/Jenesien cable-car ride offers stupendous views of the **Catinaccio/Rosengarten** massif – the station is at Via Sarentino (9.30am–4.30pm, every 30min), 1.5km north of the town centre along the river (bus #12 or #14 on Sun). On the high alpine pastures at the top, you'll see blond-maned Haflinger horses grazing. The third cable-car goes to **Colle/Kohlern** (7am–7pm, every 30min) from the station across the river south of the train station at Ponte Campiglio. The oldest cable-car ride in the world, it celebrated its centenary in 2008.

Bikes whizz at you from all directions in the centre of Bolzano and around 30km of **cycle paths** circle the city. You can rent bikes in summer from the stand on Viale Stazione, near Piazza Walther, or from the tourist office. Maps and signs around town point you in the direction of eight different cycle routes. A five-kilometre pedal away is the thirteenth-century **Castello Róncolo** (Schloss Runkelstein; Tues–Sun 10am–6pm; @ www.roncolo.info; €8); also reachable by free shuttle bus from the Piazza Walther (every 30min Tues–Sun, from 10am) or bus #12 (Mon–Sun) from the station. Inside the castle are probably the best secular frescoes in Europe showing people hunting and dancing, and other scenes from courtly life. Pier Paolo Pasolini filmed some his *Decameron* (1971) here (see Contexts). In the Sala del Torneo, look out for a fresco showing a fishing party: in the background a noble is offering a fish to a lady – the medieval equivalent of an indecent proposal.

Just southwest of Bolzano, high above the village of **APPIANO** (Eppan), a clutch of thirty or so fortresses and castles can be seen from the ruined battlements of **Castello Appiano** (Schloss Hocheppan), (April–June & Sept–Nov daily except Tues 9am–5pm; July daily 9am–5pm; tours 10.30am–5.30pm; ⓣ 0471.936.081, @ www.hocheppan.com). In the castle chapel, secular frescoes show women flirting at the altar and one of the earliest representations of the *knödel*, or dumpling, which still features on many a South Tyrolean menu. One of the most imposing fortresses is **Firmiano/Sigmundskron** (first Sun March to last Sun Nov, Tues–Sun 10am–6pm; ⓣ 0471.631.264, @ www .messner-mountain-museum.it; €8). Perched on an outcrop of porphyry rock it made a strategic base for the Bishop of Trento in the tenth century before falling into ruin in the sixteenth. It was rescued in 2003 by mountaineer Reinhold Messner, who turned it into the flagship of his group of mountain museums. A trail leads up and through the castle towers that contain a vast collection of paintings, sculptures – and objects such as a huge prayer wheel – celebrating the Himalayas, the Alps and the world's other high places.

The wine road

Wine enthusiasts are well catered for around Bolzano, with a **wine road** (*Strada di Vino*) that enables you to indulge in a happy combination of sightseeing and tastings. The 30km route proper begins at **Terlano** (Terlan) just north of Bolzano, but you can also join it at **Appiano** (Eppan) and wend your way through sunny vineyards to **Salerno** (Salurn) halfway between Bolzano and Trento. This is one of the oldest wine-growing areas of all German-speaking regions – some claim that the tradition goes back to the Iron Age – it's also one of the smallest in Italy. Certainly, the wine industry was well established in Roman times, with the colonists from down south finding that locally made barrels with metal hoops were much better for transporting wine back to Rome than their clay amphorae. The vines in the region are often strung on wide pergolas, the traditional method of viticulture here, which allows the *Ora* breeze blowing from Lake Garda to circulate around the grapes, giving a beneficial cooling effect. Others are on hillsides too steep for machinery, so everything still has to be done by hand.

The main village on the route is **CALDARO** (Kaltern), home to many sixteenth-century buildings in Uberetsch style, combining northern Gothic and southern Renaissance architectural details. Wines from the vineyards around this small village have won numerous awards; one of the best places to taste them is ⅍ *Punkt* (@ www.wein.kaltern.com), a wine bar/information point on the main square. Alternatively, every Wednesday at 4.30pm, the cellars of Kellerei Kaltern and Erste and Neue Kellerei Kaltern (@ www.erste-neue .it) also offer wine tasting – all of them are close to the village centre. Within walking distance, too, on the wine road on the way to Lake Caldaro, the producer Manincor (Ⓦ www.manincor.com) is well worth a visit for its combination of modern architecture and traditional estate buildings, as well as tastings of its fine vintages.

Another centre to head for is the village of **TERMENO** (Tramin), from which the varietal Gewürztraminer gets its name. Here, you could stop at the *enoteca* of Elena Walch, a star wine maker in the region.

Alpe di Siusi (Seiser Alm)

The grasslands of the **Alpe di Siusi** (Seiser Alm), to the east of Bolzano, are Europe's largest Alpine plateau, extending over sixty square kilometres above the rest of the valley bordered by **Sciliar** (Schlern), a flat-topped, sheer mountain which splits off at one end into two peaks. The lush summer pastures 2000m above sea level are superb for mountain biking and hiking, especially now that the area, protected by the **Parco Naturale dello Sciliar**, is closed to road traffic (except for guests of hotels on the Alpe) between 9am and 5pm.

A bus from Bolzano goes to **Siusi** (Seis) – you can stash mountain bikes in the luggage compartment of the bus – passing **FIÈ AM SCILIAR** (Völs am Schlern) famous for inventing the curative "haybath", presumably only beneficial if you don't suffer from hayfever. A possible detour involves changing buses at Fiè for Schloss Prösels (Presule): the simple **castle** (guided tours daily: April–Oct 11am, 2 & 3pm; €5; ☎0471.601.062, Ⓦwww.schloss-proesels.it) here was once the seat of the Lords of Völs – witch hunters, friends of Emperor Maximilian and owners of the salt mines at Hall near Innsbruck.

Alternatively, stay on the bus until Siusi, from where you can ascend to **COMPACCIO** (Compatsch) on the plateau by a connecting bus service or by cable car (May 24–Sept 28 8am–7pm; €9 one-way, €13 return; bikes are allowed). Compaccio is the starting point for many excellent day-hikes, such as the two-and-a-half-hour trek to *Tierser Alpl* or a climb of similar length to *Rifugio Bolzano al Monte Pez* (see opposite). You can get the views the easier way by taking the chair lift (€6.50 return) to *Restaurant Bullaccia/Puflatsch*, enjoying a coffee and *buchweizentorte* (buckwheat and redcurrant cake) when you get there.

A shuttle bus (free with cable-car ticket) runs to **SALTRIA** (Saltner), where a smattering of **hotels** are more or less the only buildings. Here, horses graze on the tough grass, picking their way between the bogs and streams, and the main evidence of human activity is dairy farming and some logging in the woods.

Practicalities

There's a tourist information office (Mon–Sat 9am–5pm, Sun 9am–noon; ☏0471.727.904, ⊛www.seiseralm.net) and plenty of **accommodation** in **Compaccio**. This hamlet, and Saltria, make peaceful spots to stay, especially when the day-trippers disappear back down to the valley as night draws in, and the teeth of **Sasso Lungo** (Langkofel) become blunted by cloud.

Almgasthof Tirler Saltria ☏0471.727.927, ⊛www.tirler.it. One of the better-value hotels in Saltria, with good-sized rooms and friendly service. €56 per person, half board only.
Anemone Seiseralm Compaccio ☏0471.727.963, ⊛www.anemone-seiseralm.com is a simple hotel with en-suite rooms and balconies €60 per person, half board only.
Rifugio Bolzano al Monte Pez (Schlernhaus) ☏0471.612.024, ⊛www.schlernhaus.it. One of

the original Alpine huts from the 1880s. Mid-June to early Oct.
Seiser Alm Urthaler Compaccio ☏0471.727.919, ⊛www.seiseralm.com. A beautiful hotel constructed in 2002 using sustainable building methods. €132 per person, half board only.
Tierser Alpl ☏0471.707.460 or 727.958, ⊛www.tierseralpl.com) At 2440m, this cute, red-roofed rifugio has amazing views. June to mid-Oct.

Val Gardena (Grödnertal)

Trails and chair lifts connect the Alpe di Suissi with the **Val Gardena** (Grödnertal), a valley with plenty of squeaky-clean guesthouses linked by a continuous stream of tourist buses making their way along the Great Dolomites Road to Cortina d'Ampezzo. The main village in the valley, **Ortisei** (Sankt Ulrich), has for centuries been a big producer of religious sculpture and, more recently, hand-carved wooden toys, with several families each keeping their own particular design going. Three thousand woodcarvers in the valley still make furniture and religious statues, but Ortisei, like the neighbouring villages of **Santa Cristina** (Sankt Christina) and **Selva** (Wolkenstein), is now mainly a ski resort, within easy reach of the **Sella Ronda**, a route of ski-runs and lifts encircling the Sella mountain range that takes a whole day to complete. **Buses** make the journey back to Bolzano, or you can drive in the other direction towards the Passo di Sella or Passo di Gardena.

Not in the Val Gardena itself, but across the Isarco river from Ponte Gardena, the gateway to the valley, is ⚴ *Pension Briol*, at Tre Chiese (Dreikirchen) (☏0471.650.125, ⊛www.briol.it; €70 per person, half board only; April–Oct) above the village of **Barbiano (Barbian)**. It's a rare example of Bauhaus style in the Alps – nothing much has changed since 1928, when it was designed by artist Hubert Lanzinger. Although there are few mod cons, the simplicity and unspoilt location in flower-filled meadows are unbeatable.

Northeast of Bolzano

The route northeast from Bolzano along the **Isarco** (Eisacktal) valley is one of the main routes between Italy and northern Europe, crossing the border into Austria at the Brenner Pass (1375m). Protestant reformer Martin Luther was one of many travellers to have walked over the Brenner Pass on his epic journey to Rome in 1510. A motorway and high-speed train line to Innsbruck now make light work of the distance, and the ancient towns of **Bressanone (Brixen)** and **Vipiteno (Sterzing)** are engaging places on the way to stretch the legs. Nearby is the wild protected area called the **Parco Naturale Fánes-Sénnes-Bráies** accessible via the **Val Pusteria** (Pusertal), a side valley off the

Isarco. If you are planning to walk any of the long-distance walking trails known as **alte vie** (literally "high ways") you will almost certainly visit the Val Pusteria, as most of the trails kick off from the valley. The best access by public transport is by train: the line branches off the main Bolzano–Innsbruck line at **Fortezza** (Franzenfeste) and serves the sleepy villages of the Val Pusteria, the market town of **Brunico** (Bruneck) and **Dobbiaco** (Toblach; from where there are buses to Cortina d'Ampezzo), terminating at **San Candido** (Innichen).

Bressanone (Brixen)

BRESSANONE (Brixen) in the Val d'Isarco is well worth a stop for its medieval Old Town and good selection of places to stay. The town was an independent state for a thousand years, its bishops in a constant state of rivalry with the neighbouring Counts of Tyrol based in Merano. The bishops' palace, next to the Duomo, is still the focus of the town.

Arrival, information and accommodation

Bressanone's **tourist office** (Mon–Fri 9am–12.30pm & 2–6pm, Sat 9am–12.30pm; July & Aug same hours plus Sat 2–6.30pm, ℡0472.836.401, ⓦwww .brixen.org), opposite the bus station, has information on trails around the town and further afield. There are some excellent, inexpensive **places to stay** in the Old Town.

Elephant Via Rio Bianco 4 ℡0472.832.750, ⓦwww.hotelelephant.com. One of the longest-established grand hotels in the Dolomites, furnished in elegant Tyrolean style, with a good restaurant (see opposite). ❻

Goldene Krone Via Fienili 4 ℡0472.835.154, ⓦwww.goldenekrone.com. A relatively new, upmarket hotel with an emphasis on light cuisine and wellbeing. ❺

Löwenhof Via Lago di Varna 60 ℡0472.836.216, ⓦwww.loewenhof.it. Hotel and campsite complex, with a large outdoor swimming pool, in meadow-land 5km north of Bressanone in Varna (Vahrn); several buses travel here on weekdays, fewer at weekends. Campsite closed Nov–March. €29 per tent. ❷

Mayrhofer Via Tratten 17 ℡0472.836.327, ⓦwww.mayrhofer.it. Small, family-run guesthouse in the Old Town with a secluded garden. ❸

Tallero Via Mercato Vecchio 35 ℡0472.830.577, ⓦwww.tallero.it. An excellent, inexpensive three-star hotel in the Old Town. ❸

The Town

The **Duomo** (9am–noon & 3–6pm; free) destroyed by fire in the eleventh century and rebuilt in its current Baroque style in the eighteenth, is the most imposing building in the complex: the interesting part lies to the side, in the fantastically ornate cloisters, which were frescoed in the fourteenth century. The cathedral **treasury** is now kept in the adjacent **Museo Diocesano** (mid-March to Oct & Dec 1–23, Tues–Sun 10am–5pm; Dec 2–Jan 3 daily 2–5pm; closed Nov and Feb to mid-March; €5; ⓦwww.dioezesanmuseum .bz.it). Here you can see vestments belonging to Bressanone's bishop-princes. Their strong influence in the region is evident from the present given by Emperor Henry II to Bishop Albuino: a tenth-century Byzantine silk cloak, spread with the stylized eagle that was the bishop's personal emblem. For more secular pleasures, head for the **Novacella Monastery** (Kloster Neustift), 3km away and reachable by bus (at least hourly), which produces well-regarded wine and sells direct to the public. Make time, if you can, for a guided tour around the beautiful, frescoed medieval **cloisters** (Mon–Sat: Nov–Easter 11am & 3pm; mid-July to mid-Sept additional tours noon & 1pm; Jan–March Mon by appointment only; €5,50; ℡0472.836.189, ⓦwww .kloster-neustift.it).

Just north of the Duomo lies Via Portici Maggiore, where you'll find a fascinating hotchpotch of shopping arcades and the seventeenth-century Porta de San Michele; this opens onto Via Ponte Aquila, which leads down to the river where there's a gem of a museum at no. 4/A. The **Pharmaziemuseum** (Tues–Wed 2–6pm, Sat 11am–4pm; July & Aug open Mon–Fri same hours; €3.50; ☎0472.209.112, ⊛www.pharmazie.it) is located on the second floor (follow the painted snakes) and boasts a weird and wonderful selection of antique vials and pillboxes, pharmaceutical apparatus, and sumptuously illustrated medical manuals from the late sixteenth century.

Eating and drinking

The best **restaurants** in town are *Finsterwirt* at Vicolo del Duomo 3 (☎0472.835.343; closed Sun eve & Mon), serving excellent local specialities and wine, and the restaurant and enoteca at the *Elephant* hotel (☎0472.836.579; closed Thurs mid-March to July, and all Nov & Feb) for expertly prepared regional cuisine. For picnics, try the shops in the old arcades or the Monday market on Via Brennero; alternatively grab a slice of freshly made pizza from *Pizza da Nando* on Via Fienili.

Val Pusteria (Pusertal)

The entrance to the **Val Pusteria** (Pusertal), a wide valley of maize fields and hay meadows skirting the northern edge of the Dolomites, lies 4km north of Bressanone. This is a sleepy rural area: in the side valleys dippers dart in and out of the streams and the sawing of timber cuts through the air. Higher up, you're likely to see marmots – timid creatures similar to guinea pigs – or more likely hear them, as they give out a piercing whistle as a warning before speeding off to their burrows; on the scree-covered slopes, chamois betray their presence with a tumbling of stones.

The valley is served by bus from **Brunico** (Bruneck), and by train from **Fortezza** (Franzensfeste). Many of the long-distance *alte vie* footpaths start in the Val Pusteria: Alta Via 1 starts from Lago di Bráies (Pragser Wildsee), Alta Via 3 from Villabassa (Niederdorf), Alta Via 4 from San Cándido (Innichen) and Alta Via 5 from Sesto (Sexten).

Brunico (Bruneck)

An influx of people from the surrounding villages arrives daily in the otherwise sleepy market town of **BRUNICO** (Bruneck), which is also the transport centre of the region. Brunico was the home of the painter and sculptor Michael Pacher (c.1435–98); his *Vine Madonna* is in the parish church of the village of San Lorenzo, 4km southwest of town. Pacher is probably the most famous Tyrolean painter and woodcarver, straddling German Gothic and the more spare Italian styles; there's something vaguely unsavoury about this particular Madonna and her pudgy child, gripping a bunch of black grapes, but it's refreshing to see work in its original setting rather than in a museum.

The Brunico **tourist office**, Rathausplatz 7 (July & Aug Mon–Fri 9am–7pm, Sat 9am–1pm & 3–6pm; rest of year Mon–Fri 9am–12.30pm & 3–6pm, Sat 9.30am–12.30pm; ☎0474.555.722, ⊛www.bruneck.com), has details of **places to stay**. A comfortable option is the *Andreas Hofer*, Via Campo Tures 1 (☎0474.551.469, ⊛www.andreashofer.it; ❹). The nearest **campsite** is *Camping Schiesstand*, Via Dobbiaco 4 (☎0474.401.326; May–Sept), and there's a **youth hostel** in the Val di Tùres 4.5km from Brunico called the *Holiday House Thalackerhof*, Thalackerweg 12, St Georgen (T0474.550.187, Wwww .thalackerhof.it; dorm beds €12). Further up the same small valley at **CAMPO TURES** (Sand In Taufers) is the wonderfully evocative medieval castle, **Schloss Taufers** (daily 10am–5pm; T0474.678.053; closed Nov; €5). The dungeons boast a gruesome array of torture instruments, but the most appealing aspect of the castle is its setting: stark grey walls, bristling with towers, stand in contrast to the glistening backdrop of the Zillertal glaciers.

Parco Naturale Fánes-Sénnes-Bráies

For dramatic mountain vistas and not too crowded paths - plus an insight into some of the Ladin legends – head for the **Parco Naturale Fánes-Sénnes-Bráies**, souteast of Brunico. If you have a limited amount of time to spend in the this beautiful protected area, you should aim for the upper slopes of **Alpe di Fánes**, where you pick up some of the best ridgeway paths. A regular jeep-taxi service runs between San Vigilio di Marebbe (reachable by bus from Brunico via Longega (Zwischenwasser) and *Rifugio Fánes* (T0474.501.097, Wwww.rifugiofanes.com; mid-Dec to April 30 & early June to end of Oct) at 2000m. This has rooms a cut above the usual refuge accommodation, good food and a great atmosphere.

Footpaths cross the grassy plateaus, passing the rocks of **Castel de Fánes**, home of Dolasilla, the mythical princess of the Ladini, and an area called the Marmot Parliament. The lakes are fed by underground streams, which you can sometimes hear, burbling deep beneath your feet.

Another way to see the park (although you'll come across many other hikers doing the same) is to walk the section of Alta Via 1 that runs through it, a hike which takes three to four days, with overnight stops at refuges. The trail starts at **Lago di Bráies** (Pragser Wildsee), a deep-green lake surrounded by pines, 8km off the main road through the Val Pusteria – an extraordinary place (according to legend, the lake is a gateway to an underground kingdom). Several buses go to the lake from Dobbiaco.

Also accessible from Brunico by cable car (end June to early Oct; €12 return) is the **Plan de Corones**, surrounded by jagged peaks. Here, legend has it, Dolasilla was crowned as a warrior princess at the top of the mountain with the *raiëta* – a crystal that harnessed powerful forces.

Vipiteno (Sterzing)

Situated on the busy main road leading north over the Brenner Pass to Innsbruck is **VIPITENO** (Sterzing). This close to the Austrian border, it's hardly surprising that much of Vipiteno is typically Tyrolean, with geranium-filled balconies and wood-panelled old inns. The porticoed main street, however, **Via Città Nuova** (Neustadtstrasse), is more reminiscent of places further south, lined with elegant, battlemented *palazzi* erected in Renaissance times by a locally based Florentine bank. At one end, the **Zwölferturm clocktower** divides the old town from the new: the roof was rebuilt in 1867 after fire destroyed the fifteenth-century original. The town is especially pretty on summer nights when it's lit by lanterns and there's often a a local festival, with live music and foodie specialities. The **tourist office** at Piazza Città 3 (daily 8.30am–12.30pm & 2.30–6pm; T0472.765.325, Wwww.infovipiteno.it) will tell you when these special events take place.

Cortina d'Ampezzo and around

Dubbed the "Pearl of the Dolomites", **CORTINA D'AMPEZZO** is well and truly part of the mountains of Trentino-Alto Adige, even though it officially belongs to the Veneto region next door. An upmarket, albeit slightly ageing, ski resort, Cortina certainly boasts a gorgeous setting, surrounded by a great circle of mountains, and it's had a starring role in many films, including *The Pink Panther* and *For Your Eyes Only*.

After hosting the **Winter Olympics** in 1956, Cortina swiftly became *the* resort to be seen in and in the 1960s you were as just as likely to spot Hollywood stars such as Brigitte Bardot, Sophia Loren and Clark Gable sauntering down the Corso Italia as you were people in ski boots. Nowadays, the population swells from 7000 to around 40,000 during the ski season (roughly Christmas to Easter) although many of the fur-clad crowds packing out the art galleries, designer boutiques and antiques shops are unashamedly here for the pose factor rather than the slopes around the city.

As you might guess, Cortina is a difficult place to do on a tight budget – taking a sleigh down the mountain after a meal at a glamorous restaurant, or renting a helicopter for off-piste skiing don't come cheap – but you can do your wallet a favour by avoiding the Christmas–New Year period. There is also a subdued summer hiking season, between July and September when the cable-car system operates. Extreme sports fans may enjoy a visit to the Pista Olimpica di Bob, built for the Olympics, which now plays host to the **Cortina Adrenalin Center** (☎0436.860.808, ⓦwww.adrenalincenter.it), an organization offering rafting, hydrospeeding, kayaking, mountain biking and more.

Arrival and information

Express **bus services** run from Milan, Padua and Bologna during the ski season and the tourist office offers a shuttle service from Venice airport. There are also several public buses from Dobbiaco (Toblach) each day. The **bus station** is on Via Marconi, above town. The nearest **train station** is Calalzo di Cadore, 32km east; a connecting bus runs every hour. Cortina's **tourist office** is at Piazzetta San Francisco 8 (daily 9am–12.30pm & 3.30–6.30pm; ☎0436.3231, ⓦwww.infodolomiti.it).

Several places in town rent out **bikes** – the cheapest is Cicli Cortina on Via Majon 148 (☎0436.867.215; €6 per hr, €16 for half a day). **Internet** facilites are available at *Radiofonica Piller* at Via C. Battisti 43 (☎0436.2284) or at the *Aquila* hotel opposite the pharmacy on Corso Italia.

Accommodation

Not surprisingly, **staying** in Cortina is comparatively expensive and prices climb exponentially during the peak ski season and in August. The tourist office has a list of **rooms to rent**, and in summer there's the option of **camping** at one of several well-equipped sites, all with bar and shop. Try *Olympia*, 5km north at Fiames (☎0436.5057, ⓦwww.campingolympiacortina .it; €24 per tent), which is open all year round and also has a swimming pool, or *Rochetta*, 2km south of Cortina at Campo di Sopra (☎0436.5063, ⓦwww .campingrocchetta.it; €24 per tent).

Astoria Largo della Poste 11 ⊤0436.25.25, ⓦwww.cortina.dolomiti.org/hotelastoria. A B&B with seven rooms, old-fashioned but comfortable, with an appealing lounge for guests. ❺

Hotel de La Poste Piazza Roma 14 ⊤0436.42.71, ⓦwww.delaposte.it. You're paying for location here – this hotel on the square opposite the church could not be more central. Rooms are plush but standard in style. ❾

Hotel Villa Resy Via Riva 50 ⊤0436.3303, ⓦwww.cortina.dolomiti.org/villaresy. A 20min walk from the centre along the charming, well-lit *passeggiata*, this friendly hotel has simply decorated, but characterful rooms, some with

balconies – just make sure you ask for one away from the main road – and there's a relaxing garden and a great bar and restaurant, *Smokey Joe* (see below) on site. Open July, Aug and ski season. ❻

Menardi Via Majon 110 ⊤0436.24.00, ⓦwww .hotelmenardi.it. A coaching inn in the 1800s, this family-run hotel is 2km from town. ❼

Montana Corso Italia 94 ⊤0436.860.498, ⓦwww.cortina-hotel.com. This small alpine hotel dating from 1927 is good value for its location in the pedestrianized streets right in the heart of Cortina. ❺

Eating and drinking

Eating choices vary from lively bars offering great snacks to romantic mountain restaurants; several good cafés also serve simple but tasty local dishes. *Ai due forni* at Via C. Battisti 18 is a decent pizza place with takeaway by the slice, and there's also an excellent supermarket, Cooperativa (closed Sun except in high season) on Corso Italia in the centre of town.

Bar Dolomiti Via Roma 50. A café perfect for people-watching on the main pedestrian high street.

Ciarlis Largo Delle Poste 35. A Slow Food restaurant that morphs into a disco most nights in high season and at weekends during the rest of the year.

Cinque Torri Largo Delle Poste 13. Good simple food, especially the pasta dishes, in this busy restaurant owned by Olympic skier Kristian Ghedina. Closed Thurs.

Lago Ghedina 5km west of the village ⊤0436.860.876. A restaurant in a magical setting next to a lake that reflects the Dolomite mountains, surrounded by tall firs. Among the grilled meats and fish, the fresh trout is delicious.

Leone e Anna 2km out of town on Alverà 112 ⊤0436.2768. Perfectly executed Sardinian cuisine in a great chalet atmosphere. Try *malureddus*, home-made dumplings with tomato and Sardinian salami sauce. Closed Tues.

Proscuitteria LP26 Largo delle Poste 26. A café by day and wine-bar-restaurant with a good buzz at night. As the name suggests, *proscuitto* is their speciality, with *capriolo* (roe deer) and *oca* (goose) also on the menu as well as tasty pasta dishes. Live music some nights.

Rifugio Tondi ⊤0436.5775 At the top of the Vitelli chair lift, this is a Cortina institution for lunch on the mountain, with refined cooking and a vast selection of grappas. Booking advised.

Rifugio Faloria At 2123m at the top of the Faloria cable car, this has views of the entire Cortina basin. Bask in the sun after lunch, or ski back to the valley by candlelight after dinner in winter.

Smokey Joe 5km west of the village, and part of the *Hotel Villa Resy*, this is a restaurant worth the walk for the local specialities such as *casunziei all'ampezzana*, or beetroot ravioli.

Around Cortina

Switchback roads and one high mountain pass after another make for some gripping driving into and out of Cortina. One route that presents a challenge to groups of cyclists, motorcyclists and tourist buses alike is the journey between Bolzano and Cortina which has been dubbed the **Great Dolomites Road** – the views from the high passes are unforgettable. Near Cortina is one of the most famous sights of the whole of the Dolomites: the **Tre Cime di Lavaredo**, three extraordinary mountain peaks to the northeast of the city that are the subject of many a holiday snap. Buses from the city travel there in summer, and there's also a service to the small lake at **Misurina**, another popular beauty spot.

It's not all about the great outdoors, however: fans of the painter Titian may want to head south by bus from Cortina towards Belluno in the Veneto to his home town of **PIEVE DI CADORE**, with many paintings attributed to him and his family in the local church. The one most likely to be authentic is in the third chapel on the left, check out too the altarpiece of *The Last Supper*, by his cousin Cesare. **Titian's birthplace** is represented by a stone and wood house on Via Arsenale (late June to mid-Sept Tues–Sun 10am–12.30pm & 3–7pm; €2). Although it has been equipped with furniture and a fireplace from the fifteenth century, the present structure dates from the 1800s.

Among the handful of cafés and **bars**, *Caffè Tiziano* (closed Mon), in the vaults of the old Palazzo della Magnifica Comunità Cadorina is a popular

▲ Skiers hit the slopes near Cortina d'Ampezzo

meeting point and offers snacks, great cocktails and pool on full-size tables. The **tourist office** is at Piazza Municipio 17 (daily 9am–12.30pm & 3.30–6.30pm; ℡0435.31.644).

Alleghe and Monte Civetta

Without your own vehicle, it can be difficult to reach the most interesting mountains in these parts. One place you can get to by bus (from Belluno) is the small village of **ALLEGHE**. The lake here was created after a huge rock avalanche in the eighteenth century – a common occurrence in the area. Now a peaceful summer and winter resort, Alleghe borders the northeastern edge of the lake, its aquamarine waters reflecting the pine forests around. Towering above is **Monte Civetta** (or Owl Mountain), essentially Alleghe's main attraction, and if you're lucky enough to be at Lago Coldai next to *Rifugio Coldai* (℡0437.789.160; late June to mid-Sept) on a clear evening, you get the most wonderful views of the great rock wall of Civetta glowing red in the sunset. You can walk up to the refuge from the valley (4hr & 1,156m of ascent), or take the cable car from Alleghe to Piani di Pezze, and the chair lift from there to Col dei Baldi (June 21–Sept 14 daily 8.30am–5.30pm; €9.50 return).

Hardened hikers may want to stay overnight at the refuge and start a big walk along Alta Via 1 next day. The trail crosses small snowfields, passing windows in the rock that offer dizzying glimpses of the valley and the Dolomite groups. A couple of hours from Coldai, *Rifugio Tissi* is perched improbably on an incline, on a vast slab of rock, and is cheerfully shambolic, with accommodation available (℡0437.721.644; late June to mid-Sept). From here you can continue on Alta Via 1, past *Rifugio Vazzoler* down to Listolade in the valley (5hr; hourly buses to Alleghe), or head straight down the steep trail 563 for three hours to Masare (a 20min walk from Alleghe), dipping your feet in a waterfall on the way. For refuelling in Alleghe, **places to eat** include *Enoteca Alleghe*, a great wine bar with reasonably priced local cuisine on Piazza J.F. Kennedy (closed Tues); don't miss the cakes and strudel at the *pasticceria* on the same square.

Merano and around

MERANO (Meran), an hour north by train from Bolzano, lies in a beautiful, wide part of the Adige (Etsch) valley. Neat apple orchards and vineyards cover almost every square inch of the lower slopes and valley floor, but when you look upwards the scale changes due to the two great mountain ranges – the Ortles (Ortler) and the Giogáia di Tessa (Texelgruppe) encircling the town. Closer geographically and in looks to the Swiss and Austrian Alps than the Dolomites, the grandeur of the landscape turns up a notch here – and a simple event like a summer storm becomes a drama, with the whole valley reverberating to the rumble of thunder.

A sedate **spa town**, Merano has a mild climate that attracted Central Europeans at the beginning of the last century after Empress Elizabeth of Austria – known as Sissi – chose the town for her winter cure. A resort of fin-de-siècle hotels, neat gardens and promenades evolved.

Arrival, information and accommodation

Buses arrive and depart directly outside Merano's **train station** on Piazza Stazione, ten-minutes' walk from the centre of town. The **tourist office** is at Corso Libertà 45 (Jan & Feb Mon–Fri 9am–12.30pm & 2–6.30pm; March–Sept Mon–Fri 9am–6pm, Sat 9.30am–12.30pm; Dec Mon–Fri 9am–12.30pm & 2–5pm, Sat 10am–5pm, Sun 10.30am–4pm; ☎0473.272.000, ⓦwww.meran.eu).

Hotels

🏔 **Castel Fragsburg** ☎0473.244.071, ⓦwww.fragsburg.com. Worth a splurge – this former hunting lodge perched on a mountainside above the city boasts light, modern rooms, excellent food, a spa and tremendous views – specially from the outdoor pool. ❽

Tyrol Via XXX Aprile 8 ☎0473.449.719. Quiet hotel with a garden close to the train station. ❷

Westend Speckbacherstrasse 9 ☎0473.447.654, ⓦwww.westend.it. Charming hotel set in gardens right on the river; most of the rooms have balconies. ❹

Hostel and campsite

Ostello della Gioventù Carduccistrasse 77 ☎0473.201.475, ⓦwww.jugendherberge.it. Merano's youth hostel is a 10min walk from the station. There are some en-suite rooms, a laundry and TV room, and a workshop for bicycle repairs; dorm beds are €19.50 per night, with a €2 surcharge for staying just one night.

Camping di Merano Via Piave 44 ☎0473.231.249. Large campsite with good facilities including tennis courts and a swimming pool. To reach it turn right out of the station, across the river by way of Via Resia and Via Petrarca; Via Piave is the third on the right. Open Easter–Nov.

The Town

Merano's old nucleus is **Via dei Portici**, running west from the Gothic **Duomo** and fifteenth-century castle and crisscrossed by shopping streets. On the river's south bank is Merano's impressive new **spa complex** (daily 9am–10pm; €17 for a day ticket; ⓦwww.thermemeran.it) with no less than thirteen indoor pools and a "snow room", all inside a huge steel-and-glass cube designed by architect Matteo Thun.

Within the **Trauttmansdorff botanical gardens** at Via Valentino 51 (daily: mid-March to mid-Nov 9am–6pm; mid-May to mid-Sept 9am–9pm; €9.80, €5 after 6pm; ⓦwww.trauttmansdorff.it) is the fascinating and fun **Touriseum** (museum of tourism; same hours as gardens). This delves into the relationship between political events, social change and the rise of tourism in the South Tyrol over the past couple of centuries through some really entertaining and imaginative displays.

In summer, bands perform in the gardens and twice-weekly classical concerts are held in other venues around town. If you're here on Easter Monday, head for the hippodrome to the south of the centre, where Tyrolean musicians astride huge blond-maned Haflinger horses parade around the stadium. The **grape fest** in the third week of October is another lively event.

Eating and drinking

The best place to **eat** in town is the expensive *Sissi*, at Galileistrasse 44 (☎0473.23.10.62), where renowned Italian chef Andrea Fenoglio puts a creative twist on traditional and Mediterranean dishes. Less fancy, but good nonetheless, is *Weinstube Haisrainer*, Via dei Portici 100, serving Italian and Tyrolean dishes. For information on **group hikes** visit the Club Alpino Italiano office, Via Carlo Wolff 15 (Mon–Thurs 10am–noon plus 7–8.30pm on Thurs; ☎0473.448.944, ⓦwww.caimerano.it), or Merano's Alpine association, the Alpenverein Südtirol, at Galileistraße 45 (Mon–Fri 9–11.45am; ☎0473.237.134, ⓦwww.alpenverein.it).

Around Merano

On the northern outskirts of Merano is the twelfth-century **Castel Tirolo** (mid-March to end-Nov Tues–Sun 10am–5pm and in Aug until 6pm; ℡0473.220.221, ⓦwww.schlosstirol.it; €6, guide an extra €2). Such was the infuence of its owners, the Counts of Tirol, that the whole Tyrol region takes its name from here. The castle itself is worth visiting for its museum on daily life in the Middle Ages. Below it is **Brunnenburg**, a neo-Gothic pile that's all fishtail battlements and conical towers, where American poet Ezra Pound spent the last years of his life.

Buses from Merano calling at Tirolo continue to **San Leonardo** (Sankt Leonhard), the birthplace of Andreas Hofer. Originally an innkeeper, wine merchant and cattle dealer, Hofer fought for the Tyrol's return to Austria after it had been ceded to Bavaria in 1805, becoming a hero of the people after successful uprisings against occupying Bavarian and Napoleonic troops. However, larger political forces overtook him and Hofer was arrested in 1810 and executed under Napoleon's orders in Mantua. There's a small Hofer **museum** (March–Nov Tues–Sun 10am–6pm; ⓦwww.museum.passeier.it; €5) at Passeierstr. 72 in his birthplace (now the *Sandwirt* guesthouse).

Val d'Ultimo (Ultental)

A traditional place of hiding in an area renowned for mountain warfare, the Val d'Ultimo (Ultental) stayed relatively isolated and closed to outsiders until the last century. The road into the valley begins its ascent just south of Merano at **LANA**. A fifteen-minute cable-car ride from Lana brings you to a unique spa resort of ⌘ *Vigilius* (℡0473.556.600, ⓦwww.vigilius.it; ⑨), wrapped around the mountainside of Monte San Vigilio (Vigiljoch). *Vigilius* majors on luxury, and has won awards for its energy efficiency and eco-innovations including a high-tech, biomass-fuelled heating system that provides an income for local foresters. The "parlour" restaurant called *Ida* is open to non residents.

Buses from Merano and Lana travel deep into the Val d'Ultimo, flanked by lush green pastures and ancient larches, terminating at the village of **SAN GERTRUDE** (Sankt Gertraud), from where trails (3hr) lead over rock-strewn moorland to *Rifugio Canziani* aka *Höchster Hütte* (℡0473.798.120; end June to early Sept), surrounded by the glaciers and peaks of **Gioveretto** (Zufrittspitze). If you're feeling less energetic, the valley is still a good place for some shorter walks, using the village as base. *Utnerhof*, Hauptstrasse 114 (℡0473.798.117; ②), is one of a handful of **hotels** in the village.

Parco Nazionale dello Stelvio

The **Parco Nazionale dello Stelvio** (or the Stilfser National Park) is one of Italy's major national parks: it extends north to the Swiss Engadine and southwest into Lombardy and covers the whole **Ortles** (Ortler) mountain range. The park is topped by one of Europe's largest glaciers (the Ghiacciaio dei Forni) and crossed by the **Passo dello Stelvio** (2758m), which misses being the highest pass in the Alps by just twelve metres.

Ski tourism has made its mark, and the park is as crisscrossed by lifts as anywhere in the Alps, but it's still a remarkable place. People come here for the high trails and glacier skiing in summer, or for the chance of seeing **wildlife** such as the red and roe deer, elk, chamois, golden eagles and ibex.

Arrival and information

The key point of access to the park is the **Val Venosta** (Vinschgau), served by trains from Merano, with bus services into the side valleys of **Martello**, **Trafoi** and **Solda**. It also provides the main route for traffic from the Adige valley to Switzerland. A private train service runs every thirty minutes between Merano and **Málles** (Mals) and gives access to several villages along the valley, connecting with local bus services; (note, if you're cycling, that you can take push bikes on the train for free.). For general **information** on the area visit ⓦwww.parks.it/parco.nazionale.stelvio or ⓦwww .valvenosta-vinschgau.it. The most useful **tourist offices** are in Silandro (see p.268) and Solda (see p.269).

Accommodation

As well as the smattering of mountain refuges offering **accommodation**, Trafoi and Solda make good bases to stay – both have a large range of accommodation.

Trafoi

🏃 **Hotel Bella Vista** ⓣ0473.611.716, ⓦwww .bella-vista.it. On the road up to the Stelvio Pass, this stylish hotel is the home of Olympic gold-medal-winning skiier Gustav Thöni. The hotel has large, Scandinavian-style rooms, most with balconies, as well as a sauna and Turkish bath. ❹

Tuckett ⓣ0473.611.722, ⓦwww.gasthof -tuckett.com. This chalet style *pensione* on the main road in the tiny settlement of Trafoi is a simpler alternative to the *Bella Vista*, with reasonably priced rooms with balconies. ❷

Solda

🏃 **Garni des Alpes** ⓣ0473.613.062, ⓦwww .garnidesalpes.com. A 10min walk away

from the centre, in the upper part of town, this guesthouse offers modern rooms and the services of a resident climbing/skiing guide. ❷

Paulmichl ⓣ0473.613.064, ⓦwww .pensionpaulmichl.com. A simple hotel, right next to the tourist office in Solda's lower town, which is best for restaurants and services. ❷

Ortlerhof ⓣ0473.613.052, ⓦwww .ortlerhof-sulden.com. The first hotel on the way into Solda. B&B accommodation in an en-suite room with balcony comes at an incredibly low price; May–Sept; minimum stay three days. ❶

The Val Venosta (Vinschgau)

As the main approach to the Stelvio park, the **Val Venosta** is often busy with traffic but maintains a rural feel. Every weekend during July and August, one or other of the villages celebrates summer with a **street festival**, with live music, beer gardens and fresh produce. One of the best is the *Marmor e Marillen* (Marble and Apricots) in early August in the tiny village of **Laas** which offers the chance to sample *marillenknödel* – sweet potato dumplings filled with whole apricots and rolled in sugar and breadcrumbs.

Other places of note along the main valley road are the village of **Forest** (Forst) dominated by the Forst brewery (ⓦwww.forst.it), whose delicious beers you can sample throughout the region. Also worth seeking out is the **Castello Juval** (Palm Sunday–30 June and Sept 1– first Sun in Nov, 10am–4pm; ⓦwww.messner-mountain-museum.it; €7) at Kastellbell. This is mountaineer Reinhold Messner's summer residence and has very reasonable *osteria* (ⓣ0473.668.238) serving local organic food and wines.

At the Málles (Mals) end of the valley the castle at **Coira**, more frequently known by its German name of **Churburg**, was owned by the Lords of Matsch at the beginning of the thirteenth century. Back then, it was just one

Crossing the Passo dello Stelvio

The journey across the Ortles mountains over the **Passo dello Stelvio** (*Stelvio Pass*) to Bormio in Lombardy makes for a white-knuckle drive. This amazingly convoluted route consists of 48 switchbacks and turns but is well worth it for both the thrill and the view. Motorbikers love it and cyclists view the climb as the ultimate challenge – it's often an important stage of the Girò d'Italia. Beware that this is one of the last Alpine passes to open to traffic each year, and it's not unknown for the road to stay closed until July if there's been a late fall of snow. If you're travelling by **public transport** you can access the pass on one of two afternoon buses from Málles.

The end point of the route, **Bormio**, is a rather snooty resort with a sprawl of hotels in its cobblestoned core. There's a visitor centre at Via Roma 131/B (mid-June to mid-Sept Tues–Sun 9am–1pm & 3–7pm, Aug also Mon; ☏0342.903.300, ⓦwww .bormio.info) which can advise on accommodation as well as nature trails in the southern reaches of the Stelvio national park.

castle in a whole chain stretching from Bavaria to just north of Milan and was battled over by various knights – whose suits of armour, some weighing nearly 25kg, can be seen in the **armoury** (March 20–Oct 31 Tues–Sun 10am–noon & 2–4.30pm; ☏0473.615.241, ⓦwww.churburg.com; €8).

The ancient walled village of **GLORENZA** (Glurns) is just 2.5km away. Although it has a population of less than 900, Glorenza still enjoys special privileges conferred in 1294 when it was a salt-trading centre. The tiny town is an architectural gem with porticoes and merchants' houses dating back to the sixteenth century, and well-preserved town walls. *Hotel Gasthof Grüner Baum* at Piazza Città/ Stadtplatz 7 (☏0473.831.206, ⓦwww.gasthofgruenerbaum.it; ⓸) is the place here for an overnight stop, a traditional inn that's been sensitively modernized.

The side valleys

Three main **side valleys** thread their way from the Val Venosta into the foothills of the Ortles range: the Val Martello (Martelltal), the Val di Trafoi (Trafoiertal) and the Val di Solda (Suldental).

If your ultimate destination is the Stelvio national park, a good option is to get off the Merano-Málles train at **SILANDRO** (Schlanders) and head for the **tourist office** at Kapuzinerstrasse 10 (June–Sept Mon–Fri 9am–12.30pm & 2–7pm; Sat 9am–12.30pm; July & Aug same hours plus Sat 2–7pm; Oct–May Mon–Fri 9am–12.30pm & 2–6pm; ☏0473.737.000, ⓦwww .south-tirol.com) which will provide information on *rifugi* and trails.

A bus runs from Silandro into the beautiful **VAL MARTELLO** (Martelltal), passing silver birch woods, the ruins of Castel Montani and an aviary for falcons at Morter along the way. At the head of the valley, **Paradiso del Cevedale** (2088m) is one of the busiest bases for climbers and cross-country skiers, lying close to Monte Cevedale (Zufall Spitze; 3757m); other trails lead across high passes to Val d'Ultimo and Val di Solda.

TRAFOI is a beautifully situated hamlet perched at 1543m by the side of the road towards the beginning of the main climb up to the Stelvio Pass (see box above). The uninterrupted views of the mighty **Ortles** are stupendous, and the slopes remarkably unsullied by tourism. A cable car makes the ascent from Trafoi to *Rifugio Forcola* (no accommodation) at 2250m, from where a fine path (4hr) continues up and round to the pass which until 1918 marked the frontier between Italy, Switzerland and Austria. On your way, you pass the **Pizzo Garibaldi** (Dreisprachenspitze), a spur of rock that's the symbolic meeting place for the three main languages of the area.

Just short of Trafoi, a minor road leads into an isolated tributary valley at the head of which, 8km west, lies **SOLDA** (Sulden). The hamlet has been a major climbing and skiing centre since the nineteenth century. There's a helpful **tourist office** at Via Principale 72 (Mon–Fri 8am–noon & 3–6pm, Sat 9am–noon; Aug also Sat 3–6pm; ℡0473.737.060, 🖰www.ortlergebiet.it). If you have time, it's worth checking out the tiny, eccentric **museum** (daily 9am–7pm; free) celebrating Solda's existence as a mountain resort as well as the **MMM Ortles** ice museum (2nd Sun in Dec to May 1 and 2nd Sun in June to 2nd Sun in Oct; ℡0473.613.266, 🖰www.messner-mountain -museum.it; €5), part of Reinhold Messner's network of mountain museums. As well as exhibits on the nearby glaciers of the Ortles, the highlight is the jagged skylight giving the impression you're at the bottom of a crevasse, looking up. You can warm up afterwards at Messner's **restaurant**, *Yak e Yeti*, at Suldenstrasse 55 (℡0473.613.266; closed Mon; around €30 for a three-course meal). It's one of the most celebrated in the Val Venosta, with his own yaks resident below.

Although Solda attracts fairly serious climbers and skiers, you don't have to be experienced to attempt some of the trails. There are easy paths (2hr) up to *Rifugio-Albergo Città di Milano* (*Schaubach Hütte*; ℡0473.613.002; June–Sept) at 2581m, or more difficult trails (3.5hr) to *Rifugio Payer* (℡0473.613.010; mid-June–Sept) at 3020m, a fantastic viewpoint and base for the ascent of Ortles (Ortler). At 3905m high, it was the tallest mountain of the old Austrian empire before the border changed, and was once marked on local maps as "The End of the World".

Travel details

For online train timetables, go to 🖰www .ferroviedellostato.it

Trentino transport options, visit 🖰www.ttspa.it

Transport in Alto Adige, visit 🖰www.sad.it

Buses through the Dolomites around Cortina, visit 🖰www.dolomitibus.it

Trains

Bolzano to: Bressanone (27 daily; 30min); Merano (30 daily; 40min); Trento (32 daily; 1hr or 29min express); Vipiteno (19 daily; 59min).

Brunico to: Dobbiaco (16 daily; 30min).

Fortezza to: Brunico (16 daily; 35min) then calling at Monguelfo (Welsberg), Villabassa (Niederdorf) and Dobbiaco (Toblach), terminating at S Cándido (Innichen; 16 daily; 1hr 9min).

Merano to: Silandro (every 30min; 1hr 5min); Spondigna (every 30min; 1hr 13min)

Trento to: Bologna (19 daily; 3hr 12min or 2hr 20min express); Bolzano (44 daily; 35min); Bressanone (32 daily; 1hr 6min); Malé (Trento-Malé line; 17 daily; 1hr 29min); Rovereto

(20 daily; 13min); Venice (26 daily; 3hr 39min or 2hr 21min express); Verona (32 daily; 1hr 5min).

Buses

Note that ordinary buses are significantly less frequent than the times given below on Sat, and rare on Sun and public hols and the frequencies we've given here are for during high season in summer.

Bolzano to: Caldaro (38 daily; 37min); Fiè (29 daily; 30min); Predazzo (6 daily; 1hr 45min); Ortisei (7 daily; 1hr 3min); St Christina (7 daily; 1hr 13min); Suisi (29 daily; 41min); Vigo di Fassa (6 daily; 1hr 11min).

Bressanone to: Brunico (27 daily; 1hr); Siusi (12 daily; 1hr). Ortisei (4 daily; 53min) St Christina (4 daily; 1hr 5min)

Brunico to: Bressanone (27 daily; 1hr); Campo Túres (30 daily; 28min); Corvara (12 daily; 1hr 3min); Dobbiaco (7 daily; 42min); Plan de Corones cable-car terminal (26 daily; 14min); San Vigilio di Marebbe (8 daily, change at Longega; 34min).

Cortina d'Ampezzo to: Belluno (6 daily; 2hr); Calalzo (15 daily; 1hr); Dobbiaco (1 daily; 45min); Pieve di Cadore (15 daily; 52min).

Corvara to: Longega (12 daily; 43min).

Dobbiaco to: Brunico (17 daily; 42min); Cortina d'Ampezzo (8 daily; 57min); Lago Bráies (7 daily; 28min); Villabassa (16 daily; 8min).

Fiera di Primiero to: Passo di Cereda (3 daily; 36min).

Merano to: (Katharinaberg (10 daily, may need to change at Naturns; 1hr); Lana (every 15min; 17min); Moso (13 daily; 1hr 13min); San Gertrude (12 daily; 1hr 22min); San Leonardo (8 daily; 47min); Silandro (15 daily; 1hr 8min).

San Martino di Castrozza to: Feltre, Veneto (3 daily; 1hr 30min); Fiera di Primiero (6 daily; 28min); Imer (6 daily; 40min); Milan (1 daily, via Trento, Bergamo and Brescia; 6hr 15min); Predazzo 6 daily; 1hr).

Siusi to: Ortisei (6 daily; 30min–1hr 30min).

Spondigna to: Glorenza (8 daily; 23min); Solda (4 daily; 54min); Stelvio Pass (4 daily; 1hr 14min); Trafoi (4 daily; 29min).

Trento to: Belluno (1 daily; 2hr 40min); Canazei (7 daily; 2hr 45min); Fiera di Primiero (5 daily, bus and train connection; 2hr 42min); Imer (5 daily, bus and train connection; 2hr 34min); Madonna di Campiglio (12 daily; 2hr 8min); Molveno (4 daily, change at Ponte Arche; 1hr 53min); Predazzo (7 daily; 1hr 51min); San Martino di Castrozza (5 daily, bus and train connection; 3hr 12min); San Michele Adige (6 daily; 25min); Tione (7 daily; 1hr 10min); Vigo di Fassa (7 daily; 2hr 20min).

Venice and the
Veneto

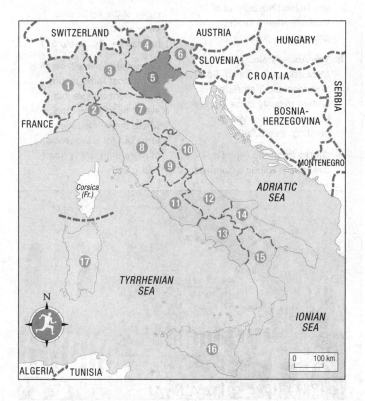

CHAPTER 5 # Highlights

* **Basilica di San Marco, Venice** San Marco is an amazing sight with its 4000 square metres of golden mosaics – all you have to work out is how to beat the queues. See p.289

* **Itinerari Segreti del Palazzo Ducale** A fascinating tour that takes you behind the scenes of Venice's superb Gothic palace. See p.295

* **The Accademia** Masterpieces by Titian, Bellini, Veronese and Tintoretto feature strongly in the world's best collection of Venetian painting. See p.299

* **Giotto frescoes** Giotto's frescoes in Padua's Cappella degli Scrovegni constitute one of the pivotal works in the history of European art. See p.331

* **Vicenza** The well-heeled city of Vicenza is renowned above all for the buildings of Palladio, perhaps the most influential architect ever. See p.336

* **Verona** Cradled in a tight curve of the Adige river, Verona is a fabulously handsome city. See p.341

* **Carnevale** Venice's carnival is the most famous, but if you want a more local event, head for Verona, where the whole town turns out for a procession of more than eighty floats. See p.350

▲ Basilica di San Marco, Venice

Venice and the Veneto

The first-time visitor to **Venice** arrives full of expectations, most of which turn out to be well founded. All the photographs you've seen of the Palazzo Ducale, of the Basilica di San Marco, of the palaces along the Canal Grande – they've simply been recording the extraordinary truth. All the bad things you've heard about the city turn out to be right as well. Economically and socially ossified, it is losing hundreds of people by the year and playing virtually no part in the life of modern Italy. It's deluged with tourists and occasionally things get so bad that entry into the city is barred to those who haven't already booked a room. And it's expensive – the price of a

Regional food and wine

Venice specializes in fish and **seafood**, together with exotic ingredients like pomegranates, pine nuts and raisins, harking back to its days as a port and merchant city. The surrounding Veneto vies with Lombardy for the risotto-making crown – the end product tending to be more liquid than those to the west, usually with a seafood base although peas (*bisi* in the local dialect) are also common, as are other seasonal vegetables including spinach, asparagus and pumpkin. The red salad leaf raddichio also has its home in the Veneto, as does the renowned Italian dessert, **tiramisù**. Polenta is eaten, too, while **pork** in all forms features strongly, together with heavy **soups** of beans, rice and root vegetables.

Pastries and **sweets** are also an area of Venetian expertise. Look out for the thin oval biscuits called *baicoli*, the ring-shaped cinnamon-flavoured *bussolai* (a speciality of the Venetian island of Burano) and *mandolato*, a cross between nougat and toffee, made with almonds.

The Veneto has been very successful at developing **wines** with French and German grape varieties, notably Merlot, Cabernet, Pinot Bianco, Pinot Grigio, Müller-Thurgau, Riesling, Chardonnay and Gewürztraminer. The quintessentially Italian Bardolino, Valpolicella and Soave are all from the Verona region and, like so many Italian wines, taste better near their region of origin. This is also true of **Prosecco**, a light champagne-like wine from the area around Conegliano. Grappa, the local firewater, is associated particularly with the upland town of Bassano di Grappa, where every *alimentari* stocks a dozen varieties. Made from grape husks, juniper berries or plums, grappa is very much an acquired taste.

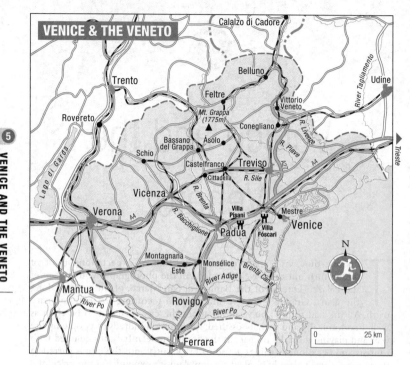

good meal almost anywhere else in Italy will get you a lousy one in Venice, and its hoteliers make the most of a situation where demand will always far outstrip supply.

As soon as you begin to explore Venice, though, every day will bring its surprises, for this is an urban landscape so rich that you can't walk for a minute without coming across something that's worth a stop. And although it's true that the city can be unbearably crowded, things aren't so bad beyond the magnetic field of San Marco and the kitsch-sellers of the vicinity, and in the off-season (Oct to Christmas and Jan to Easter, excluding Carnevale) it's possible to have even parts of the centre virtually to yourself. As for keeping your costs down, Venice has plenty of markets in addition to the celebrated Rialto, there are some good-value eating places, and you can, with planning, find a bed without spending a fortune.

Tourism is far from being the only strand to the economy of the **Veneto**, the surrounding region of which Venice is capital. The rich, flat land around the Po supports some of Italy's most productive farms and vineyards, and industrial development around the main towns rivals even the better-known areas around Milan, making the region one of the richest in Europe. At Marghera, just over the lagoon from Venice, the Veneto has the largest industrial complex in the country, albeit one that is now in decline. But tourism is important, and the region has more tourist accommodation than any other in Italy. After Venice, **Padua** and **Verona** are the main attractions, with their masterpieces by Giotto, Donatello and Mantegna and a profusion of great buildings. None of the other towns of the Veneto can match the cultural wealth of these two, but there are nonetheless plenty of places that justify a detour – the Palladian city of **Vicenza**, for instance, the fortified settlements of **Castelfranco** and **Cittadella**, and the idyllic upland town of **Ásolo**.

For outdoor types, much of the Veneto is dull, consisting of flatlands interrupted by gentle outcrops around Padua and Vicenza. The interesting terrain lies in its northern part, especially in the area above **Belluno** and **Vittorio Veneto**, where the wooded slopes of the foothills – excellent for walking – soon give way to the savage precipices of the eastern Dolomites. Because most of the high peaks of the Dolomites lie within Trentino-Alto Adige, and the mountains of the eastern Dolomites are most easily explored as part of a tour of the range as a whole, the area of the Veneto to the north of Belluno is covered in the "Trentino-Alto Adige" chapter. Similarly, the eastern shore of Lake Garda is covered as part of the lakes region in the "Lombardy and the lakes" chapter.

Venice (Venezia)

The monuments that draw the largest crowds in Venice are the **Basilica di San Marco** – the mausoleum of the city's patron saint – and the **Palazzo Ducale** – the home of the doge and all the governing councils. Certainly these are the

So much to see ...

You can spend a lifetime in Venice and still not see everything, and on a short visit nothing beats just walking and getting lost down the alleyways. However, if you want to see the main sights, you'll have to bite the bullet and join the crowds heading for the Piazza San Marco. The following suggested itineraries give you an idea of what's possible over three to five days

Three days
Day one: Basilica di San Marco early, before the queues get too long; Itinerari Segreti del Palazzo Ducale; round the corner to look at the Bridge of Sighs; after lunch, Torre dell'Orologio; Scuola di San Giorgio degli Schiavoni; tea and cake; Campo Santa Maria Formosa to see the church and at around 5pm sit in the square outside and watch and listen to the *passeggiata*.

Day two: *Traghetto* (or *vaporetto*) to the Pescheria and the Rialto market; Rialto bridge; a coffee break in the alleyways behind; the Frari; Scuola di San Rocco; after lunch, stroll down through Campo San Margherita to the Scuola Grande dei Carmini; the church of San Sebastiano; the Squero gondola workshop.

Day three: Boat to San Giorgio Maggiore for views from bell tower; boat to Záttere and stroll to the Accademia; lunch, Ca' Rezzonico; boat ride up the Canale Grande to the Ghetto; and aperitif and supper in Cannaregio

Five days
As above plus:
Day four: Boat to Murano, for churches and glass factory and shops; boat to Burano for lunch; Torcello; boat to Fondamente Nove; Madonna dell'Orto.

Day five: Miracoli; SS Giovanni e Paolo; lunch; Arsenale; Biennale gardens; boat to the Salute; the Guggenheim Collection.

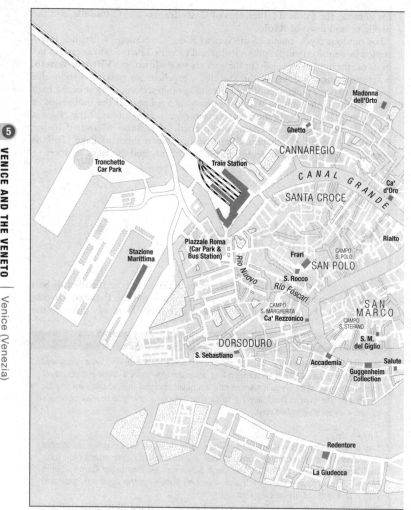

most dramatic structures in the city: the first a mosaic-clad emblem of Venice's Byzantine origins, the second perhaps the finest of all secular Gothic buildings. But every parish rewards exploration, and a roll-call of the churches worth visiting would feature over fifty names, and a list of the important paintings and sculptures they contain would be twice as long. Two of the distinctively Venetian institutions known as the **scuole** retain some of the outstanding examples of Italian Renaissance art – the **Scuola di San Rocco**, with its sequence of pictures by Tintoretto, and the **Scuola di San Giorgio degli Schiavoni**, decorated with a gorgeous sequence by Carpaccio.

Although many of the city's treasures remain in the buildings for which they were created, a sizeable number have been removed to Venice's **museums**. The

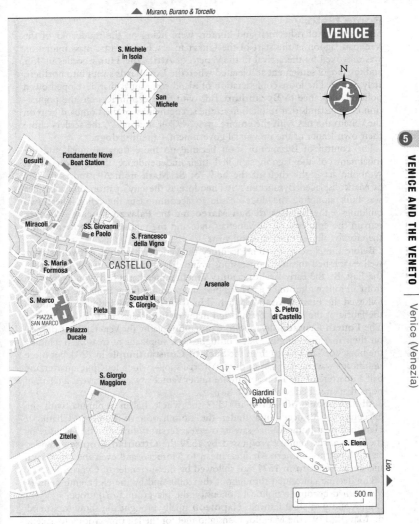

one that should not be missed is the **Accademia**, an assembly of Venetian painting that consists of virtually nothing but masterpieces; other prominent collections include the museum of eighteenth-century art in the **Ca' Rezzonico**, and the **Museo Correr**, the civic museum of Venice.

The cultural heritage preserved in the museums and churches is a source of endless fascination, but you should discard your worthy itineraries for a day and just wander – the anonymous parts of Venice reveal as much of the city's essence as the highlighted attractions. And equally indispensable for a full understanding of Venice's way of life and development are expeditions to the **islands** of the lagoon, where the incursions of the tourist industry are on the whole less obtrusive.

Some history

Small groups of fishermen and hunters were living on the mudbanks of the Venetian lagoon at the start of the Christian era, but the first mass migration was provoked by the arrival in the Veneto of **Attila the Hun**'s hordes in 453, and the rate of settlement accelerated when the **Lombards** swept into northern Italy in 568. The loose confederation of island communes that developed owed political allegiance to **Byzantium**. But with the steep increase in the population of the islands that resulted from the strengthening of the Lombard grip on the Veneto the ties with the empire grew weaker, and in 726 the settlers chose their own leader of the provincial government – the first **doge**.

The control of Byzantium soon became no more than nominal, and the inhabitants of the lagoon signalled their independence through one great symbolic act – the theft of the body of **St Mark** from Alexandria in 828. St Mark displaced Byzantium's St Theodore as the city's patron, and a basilica was built alongside the doge's castle to accommodate the relics. These two buildings – the **Basilica di San Marco** and the **Palazzo Ducale** – were to remain the emblems of the Venetian state and the repository of power within the city for almost one thousand years.

Before the close of the tenth century the Venetian **trading networks** were well established through concessions granted by Byzantium in the markets of the East. By the early twelfth century Venetian merchants had won exemption from all tolls within the eastern empire and were profiting from the chaos that followed the **First Crusade**, launched in 1095. Prosperity found expression in the fabric of the city: the basilica and many of its mosaics are from this period. The **Fourth Crusade**, diverted to Constantinople by the Venetians, set the seal on their maritime empire. They brought back shiploads of treasure (including the horses of San Marco) from the **Sack of Constantinople** in 1204, but more significant was the division of the territorial spoils, which left "one quarter and half a quarter" of the Roman Empire under Venice's sway and gave it a chain of ports that stretched to the Black Sea.

After the **Sack of Rome** in 1527 the whole Italian peninsula, with the exception of Venice, came under the domination of Emperor Charles V. Hemmed in at home, Venice saw its overseas territory further whittled away by the Turks as the century progressed: by 1529 the **Ottoman Empire** extended right along the southern Mediterranean to Morocco, and even the great naval success at **Lépanto** in **1571** was followed by the surrender of Cyprus.

The decline continued throughout the 1600s and by the eighteenth century Venice had become a political nonentity: the playground of Europe, a city of casinos and perpetual festivals. **Napoleon** finally brought the show to an end: on May 12, 1797, the Maggior Consiglio met for the last time, voting to accede to his demand that it dismantle the machinery of government. After Waterloo Venice fell to the Austrians and remained a Habsburg province until united with the Kingdom of Italy in 1866.

It was the need for a more substantial economic base that led, in the wake of World War I, to the construction of the industrial centre across the lagoon from Venice at **Marghera**. In 1933 a road link was built to carry the workforce between Venice and the expanding complex, but after World War II Marghera's growth accelerated. Its factories are essential to the economy of the province, but have caused problems too: apart from polluting the lagoon, they have siphoned many people out of Venice and into the cheaper housing of Mestre, making Mestre-Marghera today more than three times larger than the historic centre of Venice, where the population has dropped since World War II from around 170,000 to about 70,000. No city has suffered more from the tourist

industry than Venice – more than fifteen million people visit the city each year
– though without them Venice would barely survive at all.

Arrival

Arriving **by air**, you'll touch down in one of two airports: **Treviso**, 30km inland,
or at Venice's Marco Polo airport. The former is used chiefly by charter companies,
many of whom provide a bus link from the airport into Venice – the ATVO **bus**
that meets Ryanair flights, for example, costs €6 single and takes one hours ten
minutes. If such a service isn't provided, take the #6 bus from outside the terminal
building to Treviso (€1; 20min), from where there are regular bus and train
connections to Venice (buy tickets from the desk marked Public Transport to the
right in the arrivals hall). It will cost about €80 to get a **taxi** from Treviso airport
to Piazzale Roma, and under €20 to get to Treviso's train station.

Most **scheduled** flights and some charters arrive at **Marco Polo**, around 7km
north of Venice, on the edge of the lagoon. If you're on a package holiday, the
cost of transport to the city centre is likely to be covered. If not, the most
inexpensive transport is provided by the two **bus services** to the terminal at
Piazzale Roma: the ATVO (*Azienda Trasporti Veneto Orientale*) coach, which
departs every thirty minutes and takes around twenty minutes (€3), or the
ACTV (*Azienda del Consorzio Trasporti Veneziano*; ⓦ www.actv.it) bus #5 or 5D,
which is equally frequent: it's a local bus service, taking about five minutes
longer, and costs €2.30. If you'd prefer to approach the city by water, you could
take one of Alilaguna **water buses** (ⓦ www.alilaguna.it), which operate hourly
on four routes from the airport. The red (*rossa*) line goes via Murano (30min
journey time) and the Lido to San Marco (70min) and Zàttere; the blue (*blu*)
line goes via Murano, Fondamente Nove and the Lido to San Marco (80min);
and the orange (*arancio*) line goes via Murano, Guglie (50min) and then down
the Grand Canal to San Angelo (60min); and the gold (*oro*) line goes directly to
San Zaccaria and San Marco (60min). It costs €6 to Murano, €12 to most other
stops and €25 on the express gold line. A free shuttle service operates between
the terminal building and the jetty. The Public Transport ticket office – to the
left as you come out into the arrivals hall – handles all tickets, ACTV passes and
Venice Cards (see p.280) – a wise investment for almost all visitors. If the queues
are too long, there are also ticket machines by the bus stops (you'll need the
exact change) or you can buy tickets from the bus driver. Note that ACTV
passes are not valid on the Alilaguna service or on the ATVO bus.

The most luxurious way to arrive is by **water taxi**, which offers the best
views of the city – and you can't beat the thrill of arriving at the water door of
a hotel by taxi. The drivers tout for business in and around the arrivals hall and
will charge around €130 for two people. Ordinary **taxis** are ranked outside the
arrivals hall, and cost about €35 to Piazzale Roma.

By road or rail

Visitors arriving **by car** must leave their vehicle either on the mainland or in
one of the city's car parks – at Piazzale Roma or the ever-expanding Tronchetto,
Europe's largest car park. Prices at these two vary according to the time of year,
the length of stay and the size of car, but it's never cheap, and in summer the
tailbacks can be horrendous. It's better to use either the less expensive open-air
San Giuliano car park at **Mestre** (open summer, Easter and during the
Carnevale), linked by ACTV buses with central Venice, or the terminal at

Fusina, just south of Mestre (open year-round) and connected by water buses with Piazza San Marco (ACTV passes not valid).

Arriving **by train or long-distance bus**, you simply get off at the end of the line. The Piazzale Roma bus station and Santa Lucia train station are just five-minutes' walk from each other, linked by the new Ponte della Costituzione, at the top of the Canal Grande, and both are well served by *vaporetto* (water-bus) services to the core of the city.

Information

The main **tourist office** – known as the Venice Pavilion – occupies the Palazzina del Santi, on the west side of the Giardinetti Reali, within a minute of the Piazza (daily 10am–6pm; ☎041.529.8711, ⓦ www.turismovenezia.it); smaller offices operate in the corner of the Piazza at Calle dell'Ascensione 71/F (daily 9am–3.30pm; ☎041.520.8740), at the train station (daily 8am–6.30pm; ☎041.529.8727), in the airport arrivals area (Mon–Sat 9.30am–7.30pm; ☎041.541.5887), in the multistorey car park at Piazzale Roma (daily 9.30am–4.30pm; ☎041.529.8746) and on the Lido at Gran Viale S.M. Elisabetta 6 (June–Sept daily 9.30am–12.30pm & 3.30–6pm; ☎041.526.5721). The Calle dell'Ascension office is also the city's main outlet for information on the whole Veneto. These offices produce free listings of museums, exhibitions and concerts. The office at Piazzale Roma is much quieter than the others and also is a good place to buy water bus tickets, as the staff can help you in English.

The free English–Italian magazine *Un Ospite di Venezia* (ⓦ www .unospitedivenezia.it), produced fortnightly in summer and monthly in winter, has information on special events, plus extras such as *vaporetto* timetables; it is

---

The Venice Card

The **Venice Card** comes in two forms and is valid for three or seven days, with a discount for the under-30s. The **blue** card (3-day €37.50/€36.50 with discount; 7-day €58/€57) gives unlimited use of all ACTV public transport, and free access to some public toilets, most usefully those at Piazzale Roma, Campo San Bartolomeo, the Piazza (off the west side) and the Giardinetti Reali (by the tourist office). The **orange** card (3-day €62/€53.50; 7-day €85/€76) in addition gives free access to all the museums covered by the Museum Pass and the Chorus Pass (see p.292) and the Jewish Museum. For a €23 supplement you can buy a version of the blue and orange cards that's valid on Alilaguna services to and from the airport. Note that children under 6 get free museum entrance but only under-4s get free travel on public transport. You can buy Venice Cards from the tourist offices, the ACTV offices at the airport, train station and Piazzale Roma, and the Alilaguna desk at the airport. Alternatively, you can order the card a minimum of 48 hours in advance on ⓦ www .hellovenezia.com (which gives a discount of at least €4) or by calling ☎ 39.041.2424. You will be given a code number which you will need to present when you turn up to collect your ticket from any of the offices listed above.

If you're aged between 14 and 29, you are eligible for a **Rolling Venice Card**, which entitles you to discounts at some shops, restaurants, hostels, campsites, museums, concerts and exhibitions, plus a discount on the 72-hour ACTV travel pass; details are given in a leaflet that comes with the card. The card costs €4, is valid until the end of the year in which it's bought, and is excellent value – the discount on the 72-hour travel pass alone is €13. The tourist offices and ACTV offices issue it, on production of a passport or similar ID.

distributed through upmarket hotels – just ask for a copy at the reception desk. The bimonthly *Leo Bussola* publishes interesting articles (in Italian and English) on the city; both are available free from the tourist offices, but they tend to run out of stock. And the monthly *VE:News* (€2.50), which is sold at newsstands all over the city or can be picked up in hotels, has good coverage of exhibitions, cultural events, bars and restaurants, with a fair amount of text presented in English as well as Italian. For listings of nightlife and events have a look at the website ⓦ www.veneziadavivere.com.

Orientation

The 118 islands of central Venice are divided into six districts known as *sestieri*, and the houses within each *sestiere* are numbered in a sequence that makes sense solely to the functionaries of the post office – this explains how buildings facing each other across an alleyway can have numbers that are separated by hundreds.

Venice's main thoroughfare is the **Canal Grande**. Almost 4km long and between thirty and seventy metres wide (but at no point much deeper than five metres), it divides the city in half – three *sestieri* to the west and three to the east. The majority of the most important palaces in Venice stand on the Canal Grande, and the main facades of all of them are on the canalside, many properly visible only from the water.

On the east side of the Canal Grande is the *sestiere* of **San Marco**, the zone where the majority of the essential sights are clustered, and accordingly the most expensive and most crowded district of the city. To the east is **Castello**, and on the north is **Cannaregio** – both of which become more residential, and poorer and quieter, the further you get from the centre. On the other side of the Canal Grande, the largest of the *sestieri* is **Dorsoduro**, stretching from the fashionable quarter at the southern tip of the canal to the docks in the west. **Santa Croce**, named after a now-demolished church, roughly follows the curve of the Canal Grande from Piazzale Roma to a point just short of the Rialto, where it joins the smartest and commercially most active of the districts on this bank – **San Polo**.

City transport

In general, the speediest way of **getting around** is on foot – distances between major sights are extremely short and you can cross the whole city in an hour. However, you will want to get onto the water at least once during your trip, and the comprehensive water bus network makes this easy. Services are run by ACTV, which has a multilingual tourist information service, Hello Venezia (☎041.2424 daily 7.30am–8pm, or visit ⓦ www.actv.it or www.hellovenezia .it); or you can go to the ACTV information window by the ticket office at Piazzale Roma (daily 7.30am–8pm;).

Water buses

Apart from the #1 and #2 and a couple of other peak-time services that cut through the city along the Canal Grande, water buses skirt the city centre, connecting points on the periphery and the outer islands. There are two basic types of boat: the **vaporetti**, which are the lumbering workhorses used on the Canal Grande stopping service and other heavily used routes, and the

motoscafi, smaller vessels employed on routes where the volume of traffic isn't as great. The standard **fare** is €6.50 for a single journey; the ticket is valid for an hour. Should you have more than one piece of large luggage, you're supposed

Water bus routes

What follows is a run-through of the **water bus routes** that visitors are most likely to find useful; a fully comprehensive (and free) timetable can usually be picked at the major *vaporetto* stops: Piazzale Roma, Ferrovia, San Marco, San Zaccaria, Accademia, Fondamente Nove. Be warned that so many services call at San Marco, San Zaccaria, Rialto and the train station that the stops at these points are spread out over a long stretch of waterfront, so you might have to walk past several stops before finding the one you need. Note that the main San Marco stop is also known as San Marco Vallaresso, or plain Vallaresso, and that the San Zaccaria stop is as close to the basilica as is the Vallaresso stop.

#1: This is the workhorse of the system, and the one you'll use most often. It starts at the Piazzale Roma, calls at every stop on the Canal Grande except San Samuele, works its way along the San Marco waterfront to Sant'Elena, then goes to the Lido. The #1 runs between 5am and 11.45pm and 6.30am every ten minutes for most of the day.

#2: The #2 (formerly the #82) is in effect a speeded-up version of the #1, as it makes fewer stops on the Canal Grande. Its clockwise route takes it from San Zaccaria to San Giorgio Maggiore, along Giudecca, to Zàttere, Tronchetto, Piazzale Roma, the train station, then down the Canal Grande to the Rialto. Between 9.15am and 8.15pm it runs on to San Marco (Vallaresso), making fewer stops than the #1. It runs from 5.40am to 11.10pm every ten minutes for most of the day.

#3: In January 2008 a controversial move turned the #3 into a tourist-free boat on the Canal Grande for residents of the city only, but it may soon be withdrawn.

#41/42: The circular service, running right round the core of Venice, with a short detour at the northern end to San Michele and Murano. The #41 travels anticlockwise, the #42 clockwise and both run every 20min from 6.30am until around 7.30pm; after that, the #41/42 together act as a shuttle service between Murano and Fondamente Nove, running every 20min until around 11.30pm.

#51/52: Similar to the #41/42, this route also circles Venice, but heads out to the Lido (rather than Murano) at the easternmost end of the circle. The #51 runs anticlockwise, the #52 clockwise, and both run fast through the Giudecca canal, stopping only at Zàttere and Santa Marta between San Zaccaria and Piazzale Roma. Both run every 20min for most of the day. In the early morning and late evening (4.30–6am & 8.30–11pm) the boats do not run along the whole route.

#LN: For most of the day the "Laguna Nord" runs every thirty minutes from Fondamente Nove (approx hourly from 7.40pm–11.20pm), calling first at Murano-Faro before heading on to Mazzorbo, Burano (from where there is a connecting half-hourly **#T** shuttle to Torcello), Treporti, Punta Sabbioni, the Lido and San Zaccaria (the Pietà stop); it runs with the same frequency in the opposite direction.

#DM: From around 8am to 6pm the "Diretto Murano" runs from Tronchetto via Piazzale Roma and Ferrovia to Murano, where it always calls at Colonna and Museo, and often at other Murano stops too.

#N: This night service (11.30pm–4.30am) is a fusion of the #1 and #2 routes, running from the Lido to Giardini, San Zaccaria, San Marco (Vallaresso), up the Canal Grande to the train station, Piazzale Roma, Tronchetto, Sacca Fisola, San Basilio, Zàttere, along Giudecca to San Giorgio and then to San Zaccaria – and vice versa. It runs along the whole of the route in both directions roughly every 30min, and along the Rialto to Tronchetto part every 20min. Another night service, the "Notturno Laguna Nord", connects Venice with Murano and Burano, running to and from Fondamente Nove every thirty minutes between midnight and 4am.

to pay €6.50 per additional item. Children under 4 travel free. **Tickets** are available from most landing stages, from *tabacchi*, from shops displaying the ACTV sign, from the tourist offices and the ACTV office at Piazzale Roma (daily: summer 6am–11.30pm; winter 6am–8pm). Tickets can also be bought on board at the standard price, as long as you ask the attendant as soon as you get on board; if you delay, you could be liable for a spot-fine of at least €30 on top of the fare.

Unless you intend to walk all day, you'll almost certainly save money by buying some sort of **travel card** as soon as you arrive. ACTV produces a series of passes: a **12-hour** (€14), **24-hour** (€16), **36-hour** (€21), **48-hour** (€26) and **72-hour** (€31), which can be used on all ACTV services within Venice (including ACTV land buses from the airport). For seven days of unrestricted travel, you have to buy a Venice Card (see box, p.280).

If you buy one of these unrestricted travel tickets at the train station or Piazzale Roma, the train station, San Zaccaria or San Marco it will be automatically **validated** with a time-stamp unless you specifically request a non-validated one; the same goes for ordinary tickets. When using a **non-validated** ticket or pass (such as the Venice Card) you must validate it before embarking, by inserting it into one of the machines at the entrance to the *vaporetto* stop or on board the bus; the ticket is valid from that moment, and you need to validate it just once.

Traghetti

There are four bridges on the Canal Grande – at Piazzale Roma, the train station, Rialto and Accademia – so the **traghetti** (gondola ferries) that cross it can be useful time-savers. Costing just €0.50, they are also the only cheap way of getting a ride on a gondola – though it's *de rigueur* to stand in a *traghetto* rather than sit. Routes are: San Marco–Salute; Santa Maria del Giglio–Salute; San Barnaba–San Samuele; San Tomà–Santo Stefano; Riva del Carbon–Riva del Vin (near Rialto); Santa Sofia–Pescerìa; San Marcuola–Fondaco dei Turchi; train station–San Simeone. All *traghetti* run Mon–Sat from early morning to noon, while those on the routes Santa Maria del Giglio–Salute, San Tomà–Santo Stefano and Santa Sofia–Pescerìa run till around 7–9pm daily, the last two on Sundays, as well; in the winter months some *traghetti* stop running earlier, while others are suspended altogether.

Water taxis

Venice's **water taxis** are sleek and speedy vehicles that can penetrate most of the city's canals. Unfortunately they are possibly the most expensive form of taxi in western Europe: the clock starts at €13 and goes up €1.80 every minute. All sorts of additional surcharges are levied as well – €5 for each extra person if there are more than two in the party; €3 for each piece of luggage over 50cm long; €8 for a ride between 10pm and 7am. There are three ways of getting a taxi: go to one of the main stands (in front of the Piazzetta and at the airport), find one in the process of disgorging its passengers, or call one by phone (℡041.522.2303 or 041.723.112). If you use the phone, there is also a call charge of €6. Complaints to police should be made on ℡041.274.7070.

Gondolas

The famous Venetian **gondola** is no longer a form of transport but rather an adjunct of the tourist industry. That said, it can be a delightful way of relishing the sheer sense of being in Venice, and the cost isn't all that off-putting when split among a small group. To hire one costs €80 per forty minutes for up to six passengers, rising to €100 between 8pm and 8am; you pay an extra €50 for every additional 25min, or €50 from 8pm to 8am. Further hefty surcharges will be levied should you require the services of an on-board accordionist or tenor – and a surprising number of people do. Even though the tariff is set by the local authorities, it's been known for some gondoliers to try to extort even higher rates than these – if you do decide to go for a ride, establish the charge before setting off.

To minimize the chances of being ripped off, only take a boat from one of the following **official gondola stands**: west of Piazza San Marco at Calle Vallaresso, Campo San Moisè or Campo Santa Maria del Giglio; immediately north of the Piazza at Bacino Orseolo; on the Molo, in front of the Palazzo Ducale; outside the *Danieli* hotel on Riva degli Schiavoni; at the train station; at Piazzale Roma; at Campo Santa Sofia, near the Ca' d'Oro; at San Tomà; or by the Rialto Bridge on Riva Carbon.

Accommodation

Demand for holiday accommodation in Venice outstrips supply to such a degree that this city is the most expensive in western Europe, with some one-star hotels charging in excess of €150 for a double room in high season. What's more, the **high season** here is longer than anywhere else in the country – it is officially classified as running from March 15 to November 15 and then from December 21 to January 6, but many places don't recognize the existence of a low season any more. (Quite a few hotels, on the other hand, lower their prices in Aug, a month in which trade can take a bit of a dip; as every Italian knows, Venice can be hellishly hot and clogged with day-trippers during that month.)

It's never a good idea to turn up in Venice without reserving your accommodation first, and it's wisest to book your place at least three months in advance, especially if you are coming during Carnevale. If your first-choice hotel is fully booked, go to the tourist office's website (ⓦ www.turismovenezia .it), which gives details of accommodation of all types, or try the websites of the Venetian Hoteliers' Association (AVA) – ⓦ www.veneziasi.it. The AVA runs a call centre (daily 9am–11pm on ☎ 199.1733.09 within Italy or 39.041.522.2264 from abroad.)

Finally, should you bowl into town with nowhere to stay, you could call in at one of the AVA's VeneziaSi **booking offices**: at the **train station** (daily: summer 8am–9pm; winter 8am–7pm); in the multistorey car park at **Piazzale Roma** (11am–7pm); in the yellow kiosk outside the **Garage San Marco** (8am–9pm) in the southwest corner of the Piazzale; and at **Marco Polo airport** (summer 9am–7pm; winter noon–7pm). They only deal with hotels (not hostels or B&Bs) and take a deposit that's deductible from your first night's bill.

Hotels, rooms and flats

Venice has well in excess of two hundred hotels, ranging from spartan one-star joints to five-star establishments. Though there are some anomalies, the star system is a broadly reliable indicator of quality, but always bear in mind that you pay through the nose for your proximity to the **Piazza San Marco**. So if you want maximum comfort for your money, decide how much you can afford and then look for a place outside the San Marco *sestiere* – after all, it's not far to walk, wherever you're staying.

If you are looking for a small family-run establishment, a *locanda* might fit the bill: Venice's *locande* offer a standard of accommodation equivalent to three- or even four-star hotels (24hr room service is just about the only facility they don't provide), but often at a lower cost. However, some upmarket hotels use the label to give their image a more homely finish.

Breakfast is nearly always included in the room rate; if it isn't, you're best advised to take breakfast in a café, where the quality will probably be better and the price certainly lower.

If the cost of a hotel room is prohibitive it can be worth look at a **self-catering apartment**. The tourist office has a list of landlords offering apartments at Ⓦwww.turismovenezia.it, or you could look at specialized Venice flat-renting websites such as Ⓦwww.venice-rentals.com or www.visitvenice.co.uk.

San Marco

Ai Do Mori Calle Larga S. Marzo 658 ☎041.520.4817, Ⓦwww.hotelaidomori.com. Very friendly, and situated a few paces off the Piazza, this is a top recommendation for budget travellers. It has eleven rooms, singles and doubles with or without bathrooms, and no. 11 at the top has a private terrace looking over the roof of the Basilica. No lift – the rooms are on the third and fourth floors. Without bathrooms ❸, with ❺.

Al Gambero Calle dei Fabbri 4687 ☎041.522.4384, Ⓦwww.locandaalgambero.com. Twenty-six-room three-star hotel a short distance off the north side of the Piazza; many of the rooms overlook a canal that's on the standard gondola route from the Bacino Orseolo. There's a boisterous Franco–Italian bistro on the ground floor. ❽

Art Deco Calle delle Botteghe 2966 ☎041.277.0558, Ⓦwww.locandaartdeco.com. This three-star *locanda* has a seventeenth-century *palazzo* setting, but the pristinely white bedrooms have modern wrought-iron furniture. ❻

🏃 **Casa Petrarca** Calle delle Schiavini 4386 ☎041.520.0430, Ⓦwww.casapetrarca .com. A very hospitable one-star, one of the cheapest hotels near the Piazza. Just seven rooms: one is very small and five have en-suite bathrooms. All rooms on the first floor – and there is a minute lift. No credit cards. ❹

Fiorita Campiello Nuovo 3457 ☎041.523.4754, Ⓦwww.locandafiorita.com. Welcoming one-star with just ten rooms on a small square just by San Stefano church. Rooms have a/c and wi-fi access. Helpful staff. ❺

Kette Piscina S. Moisè 2053 ☎041.520.7766, Ⓦwww.hotelkette.com. A four-star favourite with the upper-bracket tour companies, mainly on account of its quiet location, in an alleyway parallel to Calle Larga XXII Marzo. In season there's nothing under €300, but out of season prices are much more reasonable. ❾

Noemi Calle dei Fabbri 909 ☎041.523.8144, Ⓦwww.hotelnoemi.com. Three-star hotel right in the thick of the action, just 1min walk north of the Piazza. The decor is eighteenth-century Venetian. ❻

🏃 **Novecento** Calle del Dose 2683 ☎041.241.3765, Ⓦwww.novecento.biz. Beautiful boutique-style three-star hotel with nine individually decorated doubles and excellent bathrooms. The eclectic style is inspired by the designer Mariano Fortuny, and there's a small courtyard for breakfast. ❼

Orseolo Corte Zorzi 1083 ☎041.520.4827, Ⓦwww .locandaorseolo.com. Family-run non-smoking *locanda*, fifty metres north of Piazza S. Marco. Rooms are spacious and light – the ones with canal views are more expensive – and breakfasts substantial. Entrance is through an iron gate in Campo S. Gallo. Has a computer terminal for internet access. ❼

Dorsoduro

Accademia Villa Maravege Fondamenta Bollani 1058 ☎041.521.0188, Ⓦwww.pensioneaccademia .it. This three-star seventeenth-century villa has a devoted following, not least on account of its garden. To be sure of a room, get your booking in at least three months ahead. The management has been known to try to palm off people with its sister hotel, a three-star in San Marco, but it lacks the charm and calm of this place. ❼

Agli Alboretti Rio Terrà Foscarini 884 ☎041.523.0058, Ⓦwww.aglialboretti.com. Friendly and comparatively inexpensive three-star with 22 rooms right next to the Accademia. Avoid murky room 19 and you can't go wrong. ❻

Antico Capon Campo S. Margherita 3004/B ☎041.528.5292, Ⓦwww.anticocapon.com.

Seven simply furnished small rooms without a/c above a pizzeria-restaurant on a lively square in the heart of the student district. Pleasant staff. ❸

Ca' Fóscari Calle della Frescada 3887/B ☎041.710.401, ⊛www.locandacafoscari.com. Quiet and well-decorated one-star, tucked away near S. Tomà. Just eleven rooms (seven en-suite with shower), so it's quickly booked out. Its hours are somewhat hostel-like, with a 1am curfew. ❸

Ca' Pisani Rio Terà Foscarini 979a ☎041.240.1411, ⊛www.capisanihotel.it. Glamorous 29-room four-star, behind the Accademia with a high-class retro look. Its 1930s style with lots of dark wood and chrome makes a refreshing break from the Renaissance and Rococo tones of many upmarket establishments. It has a steam bath and free access to a nearby gym. ❾

DD 724 Ramo da Mula 724 ☎041.277.0262, ⊛www.dd724.com. In a city awash with nostalgia, the modernist style of this new boutique hotel, right by the Guggenheim, comes as a refreshing change. It has just seven rooms, each of them impeccably cool and luxurious. ❾

🏃 **La Calcina** Záttere ai Gesuati 780 ☎041.520.6466, ⊛www.lacalcina.com. Charismatic family-run three-star hotel in the house where Ruskin wrote much of *The Stones of Venice*. From the more expensive rooms you can gaze across to the Redentore, a church that gave him apoplexy. All rooms are no-smoking and have parquet floors – unusual in Venice. ❺

Locanda San Barnaba Calle del Traghetto 2785 ☎041.241.1233, ⊛www.locanda-sanbarnaba.com. Pleasant three-star hotel right by the Ca' Rezzonico, with a delightful courtyard, 13 well-equipped rooms – some have eighteenth-century frescoes, and one has an enormous family-size bath. ❻

Messner Rio Terrà dei Catacumeni 216 ☎041.522.7443, ⊛www.hotelmessner.it. In a quiet location close to the Salute *vaporetto* stop, the friendly *Messner* has smart, modern rooms. The one-star annexe round the corner has rooms that are cheaper and more appealing than those in the two-star main building. ❺

Montin Fondamenta di Borgo 1147 ☎041.522.7151, ⊛www.locandamontin.com. The *Montin* is known principally for its upmarket restaurant; few people realize that it offers some of Venice's best budget accommodation. Only eleven rooms, three of them without private bathroom; the best rooms are spacious and balconied. Without bathroom ❹, with ❺.

Tivoli Crosera S. Pantalon 3838 ☎041.524.2460, ⊛www.hoteltivoli.it. This two-star is the biggest low–priced hotel in the immediate vicinity of the Frari and S. Rocco, and often has space – it has 22

rooms – when the rest are full. Pleasant courtyard garden. ❹

San Polo and Santa Croce

🏃 **Ca' Arco Antico** Calle del Forno, San Polo 1451 ☎041.241.1227, ⊛www .arcoanticovenice.com. An attractive mix of the traditional and the modern. With big rooms, great location – near San Polo church, down behind the *Osteria Vivaldi* – and excellent breakfast (a rarity in Venice), this offers some of the best-value accommodation in the city. ❻

Casa Peron Salizzada S. Pantalon, Santa Croce 84 ☎041.710.021, ⊛www.casaperon.com. A plain, very inexpensive and congenial one-star in the heart of the university district, very close to San Rocco and the Frari. Most of the eleven rooms have showers, but only a couple have their own toilet as well. ❸

San Cassiano-Ca' Favretto Calle della Rosa, Santa Croce 2232 ☎041.524.1768, ⊛www .sancassiano.it. Beautiful 35-room three-star, with six rooms looking across the Canal Grande towards the Ca' d'Oro. Helpful staff, a grand entrance hall and a small courtyard garden. ❽

Cannaregio

Abbazia Calle Priuli 68 ☎041.717.333, ⊛www .abbaziahotel.com. Behind the Scalzi church near the station, this is Cannaregio's most restful hotel. Occupying a former Carmelite monastery (the bar area has the old pulpit in it) the *Abbazia*'s 50 rooms provide three-star amenities without losing that air of quasi-monastic austerity. Delightful garden, too. ❻

Adua Lista di Spagna 233/a ☎041.716.184, ⊛www.aduahotel.com. Thirteen-room two-star with friendly management. One of the best hotels in this bustling area of the city. ❻

🏃 **Bernardi Semenzato** Calle dell'Oca 4366 ☎041.522.7257, ⊛www.hotelbernardi .com. Very well-priced two-star in a prime location (in an alleyway close to Campo S. Apostoli), with immensely helpful owners who speak excellent English. Has five singles for as little as €48 (with a shared bathroom). ❷

Hesperia Calle Riello 459 ☎041.715.251, ⊛www .hotelhesperiacom. Friendly 16-room two-star in a secluded alleyway a short distance up the Cannaregio canal from the Ponte delle Guglie. Rooms are small but homely, and come complete with Murano glass fittings (not the garish variety). ❻

Locanda Ai Santi Apostoli Strada Nova 4391/A ☎041.521.2612, ⊛www.locandasantiapostoli .com. On the top floor of a *palazzo* opposite the Rialto market, this eleven-room three-star is one of the pricier *locande*, but there aren't many better rooms for this price than the pair overlooking the Canal Grande. ⑤–⑥

Locanda Leon Bianco Corte Leon Bianco 5629 ℡041.523.3572, ⓦwww.leonbianco.it. Friendly and charming three-star not far from the Rialto Bridge, tucked away beside the decaying Ca' da Mosto. Only seven rooms and one apartment: three rooms overlook the Canal Grande (a €50 premium for these) and the other four are spacious and tastefully furnished in eighteenth-century style – one even has a huge fresco copied from a Tiepolo ceiling. ⑥

Palazzo Cendon Calle Cendon 533 ℡041.275.0606, ⓦwww.palazzocendon.it. Very friendly family-orientated hotel on the Cannaregio canal. It's very inconspicuous – up the alley beyond the *Al Parlamento* bar near the Tre Archi bridge. Has a lift and, like the other hotels near the station, you don't have to lug heavy bags over bridges to get here. Eighteen brightly decorated doubles, some – including two grand suites with balconies – overlooking the canal. ⑤

Villa Rosa Calle della Misericordia 389 ℡041.716.569, ⓦwww.villarosahotel.com. Clean and fairly spacious rooms at this 34-room one-star, with a/c and private bathrooms – the best even have a small balcony. Large terrace at the back for breakfast. ③

Castello

Canada Campo S. Lio 5659 ℡041.522.9912, ⓦwww.canadavenice.com. Well-kept and friendly second-floor two-star; book well in advance for the double room with a roof terrace. No lift. ⑥

Caneva Corte Rubbi 5515 ℡041.522.8118, ⓦwww.hotelcaneva.com. A well-appointed and peaceful one-star tucked away behind the church of Santa Maria della Fava, close to Campo S. Bartolomeo. Fifteen of the 23 rooms have a/c and private bathrooms; shared bathroom ②, en suite ③.

Casa Verardo Calle della Chiesa 4765 ℡041.528.6127, ⓦwww.casaverardo.it. Very fine three-star hotel just a couple of minutes from San Marco and Campo Santa Maria Formosa. Twenty two beautifully furnished rooms (one with attached terrace), a breakfast terrace downstairs and a sun lounge at the top. ⑧

Danieli Riva degli Schiavoni 4196 ℡041.522.6480, ⓦwww.starwoodhotels.com /danieli. Others might rival its prices but nowhere in Venice can compete with the glamour of the *Danieli*. This Gothic *palazzo* affords just about the most sybaritic hotel experience on the continent – provided you book a room in the old building, not the modern extension. Cheapest doubles are €810 without breakfast, while the doge's suite with a view of the lagoon will set you back €4095 a night. ⑨

🏃 **La Residenza** Campo Bandiera e Moro 3608 ℡041.528.5315, ⓦwww .veneciaresidenza.com. This fourteenth-century *palazzo* is a mid-range gem (by Venetian standards), lying on a tranquil square just off the main waterfront. The fourteen rooms are very spacious (rare at this price) and elegant, and the management extremely *simpatico*. Payment in cash preferred for short stays. ⑥

Locanda Casa Querini Campo San Giovanni Novo 4388 ℡041.241.1294, ⓦwww.locandaquerini .com. Friendly *locanda* in a quiet courtyard just behind the basilica. Six smallish but nicely furnished a/c rooms. ⑥

Scandinavia Campo S. Maria Formosa 5240 ℡041.522.3507, ⓦwww.scandinaviahotel.com. Sizeable three-star hotel on one of the city's most lively squares. Decorated mainly in eighteenth-century style (lots of Murano glass and floral motifs), its 33 rooms range from large suites to rooms with private but not en-suite bathroom. Huge reductions in the quiet months. ⑦

Bed and breakfast

The Italian tourism authorities define a **bed and breakfast** as a private dwelling in which a maximum of three bedrooms are available to paying guests, with a minimum of one shared bathroom for guests' exclusive use. The places listed below are all officially registered B&Bs whose rooms are viewable online; for full listings of Venice's B&Bs, go to ⓦwww.turismovenezia.it.

San Marco

A Le Boteghe Calle de le Botteghe 3438 ⓦwww .aleboteghe.it. ④

Casa de' Uscoli Campo Pisani San Marco 2818 ⓦwww.casadeuscoli.com. ⑦

Palazzo Duodo Gregolin Ramo Duodo 1014 ⓦwww.palazzoduodo.com. ④

Dorsoduro

Ca' Arzere Corte Maggiore 2314 ⓦwww .bbveneziarzere.com. ⑤

Ca' Turelli Fondamenta di Borgo 1162 ⓦwww .caturelli.it. ④–⑤

Corte Contarini Corte Contarini 3488r ⓦwww .cortecontarini.it. ③

Fujiyama Calle Lungo San Barnabà 2727/A
Ⓦwww.bedandbreakfast-fujiyama.it. ⑥
La Colonna Gotica Campo Angelo Raffaele 1710
Ⓦwww.veneziabedandbreakfast.it. ⑤

San Polo & Santa Croce
Al Campaniel Calle del Campaniel 2889 Ⓦwww
.alcampaniel.com. ❸
Al Campiello dei Meloni Campiello dei Meloni
1419/A Ⓦwww.ciprea.info. ❸
Corte 1321 Campiello ca' Bernardi Ⓦwww
.cabernardi.com. ❼

Cannaregio
Al Palazetto Calle delle Vele 4057 Ⓦwww
.guesthouse.it. ⑤
Al Saor Ca' d'Oro Calle Zotti 3904a Ⓦwww.alsaor
.com. ❹

At Home a Palazzo Calle Priuli 3764 Ⓦwww
.athomeapalazzo.com. ⑥

Castello
Ai Greci Calle del Magazen 3338 Ⓦwww.aigreci
.com. ⑥
Campiello Santa Giustina Calle Due Porte 6499
Ⓦwww.campiellogiustina.com. ❹
San Marco Fondamenta San Giorgio degli
Schiavoni 3385 ☎041.522.7589, Ⓦwww
.realvenice.it/smarco. ❹

La Giudecca
Casa Eden Corte Mosto 25 Ⓦwww.casaeden.it. ❹
Casa Genoveffa Calle del Forno 472 Ⓦwww
.casagenoveffa.com. ⑥

Hostels

Venice has a large HI **hostel** and a few hostel-like establishments run by religious foundations, which are generally available to tourists during the university's summer vacation – during term time they double as student accommodation. Bona-fide students looking for a room for an extended stay during the summer vacation should check out Ⓦwww.esuvenezia.it, which gives details of rooms in the various accommodation blocks of Venice's university.

Domus Ciliota Calle delle Muneghe, S. Marco
2976 ☎041.520.4888, Ⓦwww.ciliota.it.
Welcoming but expensive hostel-style accommoda-tion, close to Campo S. Stefano. Open all year.
Midnight curfew. Also has single rooms. Rooms are slightly cheaper Sun–Thurs. ❹
Domus Civica Calle Campazzo, San Polo 3082
☎041.721.103, Ⓦwww.domuscivica.com. A
student house in winter, open to visitors from mid-June to mid-Sept. A little awkward to find: it's off
Calle della Lacca, to the west of San Giovanni
Evangelista. Most rooms are doubles; showers free;
no breakfast; 11.30pm curfew. Reductions for ISIC
and Rolling Venice Card holders. ❷
Foresteria Valdese S. Maria Formosa, Castello
5170 ☎041.528.6797, Ⓦwww.foresteriavenezia.it.
Run by Waldensians, this hostel is set in a wonderful
palazzo at the end of Calle Lunga S. Maria Formosa,
with flaking frescoes in the rooms. It has several
large dorms, plus bedrooms that can accommodate
up to eight people. Dorm beds cannot be booked in
advance, except by groups. Registration 8.30am–
1pm & 4–8pm. Dorm beds €24, doubles ❸.

Ostello Santa Fosca S. Maria dei Servi,
Cannaregio 2372 ☎041.715.733, Ⓦwww
.santafosca.com. Student-run hostel in an atmos-pheric former Servite convent in a quiet part of
Cannaregio, with small dorms, double rooms and
singles, all with shared bathrooms. Check-in 5–7pm.
€20 for dorm bed, €25 per person in doubles and
singles. They take bookings one week ahead only, by
phone or email; it's essential to book in summer.
Ostello Venezia Fondamenta delle Zitelle, Giudecca
86 ☎041.523.8211, Ⓦwww.ostellovenezia.it. The
city's HI hostel occupies a superb location looking
over to San Marco, but it's run with a certain
briskness. Registration opens at 1.30pm in summer
and 4pm in winter. Curfew at 11.30pm, chucking-out
time 9.30am. Even with 270 beds it gets so busy in
summer that reservations – through the website –
must be made by April. Breakfast and sheets
included in the price – but remember to add the
expense of the boat over to Giudecca (the nearest
stop is Zitelle). No kitchen for guests, but good full
meals for around €10. From €21 per dorm bed; HI
card necessary, but you can join on the spot (€3).

Camping

If you're coming from the Marco Polo Airport and want to pitch your tent promptly, you could settle for the nearby four-star *Alba d'Oro*, Via Triestina

⑤

214/G (open all year; ☎041.541.5102, ⓦwww.ecvacanze.it; €14.40 per tent plus €8.20 per person per night, or €77 per night for a chalet), (take bus #15 to Cánoghera, the fourth stop after the airport). Plenty of sites can also be found on the outer edge of the lagoon on the **Litorale del Cavallino**, which stretches from the Punta Sabbioni to Jésolo and has a total of around sixty thousand pitches, many of them quite luxuriously appointed. *Vaporetto* #LN, from Fondamente Nove or San Zaccaria to the Punta, stops close to the two-star *Miramare*, Lungomare Dante Alighieri 29 (☎041.966.150, ⓦwww .camping-miramare.it; €15 per tent plus €7.50 per person per night; mid March to Oct); a bit further away there's the more luxurious four-star *Marina di Venezia*, Via Montello 6 (☎041.966.146, ⓦwww.marinadivenezia.it; €20 per tent plus €8.50 per person per night; May–Sept). Bear in mind, though, that it's a forty-minute boat trip into the city from here.

Alternatively, back on the mainland there's a two-star site at **Fusina**, Via Moranzani 93 (open all year; ☎041.547.0064); it has almost 1000 places, and charges €8.50 per tent plus €9 per person. A *Linea Fusina* (#16) water bus links Fusina to the Záttere in central Venice (ACTV tickets not valid), taking 25 minutes, with an hourly service from 8am till until around 10pm from late May to the end of September, and till around 6pm for the rest of the year. Alternatively, you can get a bus to Mestre and change there for the #1 water bus or a train.

The City

Venice's heart and tourist hub lies in and around Piazza San Marco and it's here, with the best-known symbols of the city's former glories, that the account below begins. The undoubted appeal of the area is matched in the quieter *sestieri*, too, where your chances of getting lost in the jumble of streets is almost guaranteed and provides one of the joys of any visit, offering the possibility of stumbling on some hidden gem of a square or tranquil side canal.

San Marco

The section of Venice enclosed by the lower loop of the Canal Grande – a rectangle smaller than 1000m by 500m – is, in essence, the Venice of the travel brochures. The plush hotels are concentrated here, in the *sestiere* of **SAN MARCO**, as are the swankier shops and the best-known cultural attractions of the city. But small though this area is, you can still lose the hordes within it.

"The finest drawing-room in Europe" was how Napoleon described its focal point, the **Piazza San Marco** – the only piazza in Venice, all other squares being *campi* or *campielli*. Less genteel phrases might seem appropriate on a suffocating summer afternoon, but the Piazza has been congested for centuries. Its parades, festivities and markets have always drawn visitors, the biggest attraction being an international trade fair known as the **Fiera della Sensa** that keeps the Piazza buzzing for the fortnight following the Ascension Day ceremony of the marriage of Venice to the sea. The coffee shops of the Piazza were a vital component of eighteenth-century high society, and the two survivors from that period – *Florian* and *Quadri* – are still the most expensive in town.

The Basilica di San Marco

The **Basilica di San Marco** (ⓦwww.basilicasanmarco.it) is the most exotic of Europe's cathedrals, and no visitor can remain dispassionate when confronted

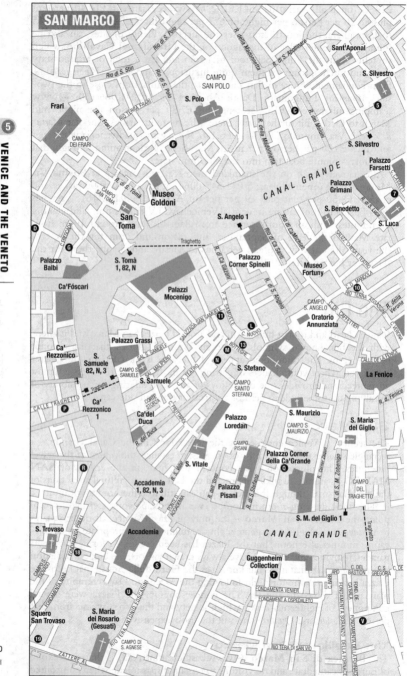

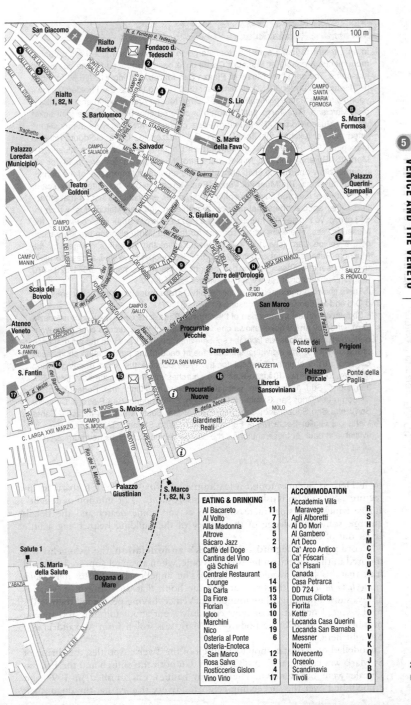

Museum and church passes

In an attempt to make sure that tourists go to see more than just the big central monuments, a couple of **Museum Cards** have been introduced for the city's civic museums. The card for **I Musei di Piazza San Marco**, costing €12 (€6.50 for ages 6–14, students under 30, EU citizens over 65 & Rolling Venice Card holders), allows you to visit the Palazzo Ducale, Museo Correr, Museo Archeologico and the Biblioteca Marciana. (The **Torre dell'Orologio** is covered only by a separate joint ticket with the Museo Correr.) The **Museum Pass**, costing €18/€12, covers the museums listed above (except the Torre), plus Ca' Rezzonico, Casa Goldoni, Palazzo Mocenigo, Ca' Pésaro (the modern art and oriental museums), the Museo del Merletto (Burano) and the Museo del Vetro (Murano). Passes are valid for six months, allow one visit to each attraction, and are available from any of the participating museums. The **Musei di Piazza San Marco** can only be visited with a card; at the other places you have the option of paying an entry charge just for that attraction. Other special offers that may be available are the San Marco Plus, which for €13 allows you to see the museums of the Piazza plus one other one covered by the Museum Pass. There are also discounts for families. Note also the orange version of the Venice Card (see box, p.280) covers all of the museums covered by the Museum Pass, and that accompanied disabled people have free access to all of these museums. These tickets can bought at the museums, on ⊤041/520.9070 (English spoken) or at ⓦ www.museicivicivveneziani.it.

There is also a combined ticket for the city's **state museums** (the Accademia, Ca' d'Oro and Museo Orientale), costing €11/€5.50.

Sixteen churches are now part of the **Chorus Pass** scheme (ⓦ www.chorusvenezia .org), whereby an €9 ticket allows one visit to each of the churches over a one-year period. All of the proceeds from the scheme are ploughed back into the maintenance of the buildings. The individual entrance fee at each of the participating churches is €3, and all the churches (except for the Frari) observe the same opening hours: Monday to Saturday 10am to 5pm. The churches involved are: the Frari (Mon–Sat 9am–6pm, Sun 1–6pm); the Gesuati; Madonna dell'Orto; the Redentore; San Giacomo dell'Orio; San Giobbe; San Giovanni Elemosinario; San Pietro di Castello; San Polo; San Sebastiano; San Stae; Sant'Alvise; Santa Maria dei Miracoli; Santa Maria del Giglio; Santa Maria Formosa; and Santo Stefano. The Chorus Pass is available at each of these churches; the orange Venice Card gives free admission to all of them.

by it. Herbert Spencer found it loathsome – "a fine sample of barbaric architecture", but to John Ruskin it was a "treasure-heap … a confusion of delight". It's certainly confusing, increasingly so as you come nearer and the details emerge; some knowledge of the history of the building helps bring a little order out of chaos.

According to the **legend of St Mark's annunciation**, the Evangelist was moored in the lagoon, on his way to Rome, when an angel appeared and told him that his body would rest there. (The angel's salute – *Pax tibi, Marce evangelista meus* – is the text cut into the book that the Lion of St Mark is always shown holding.) The founders of Venice, having persuaded themselves of the sacred ordination of their city, duly went about fulfilling the angelic prophecy, and in 828 the body of St Mark was stolen from Alexandria and brought here.

Modelled on Constantinople's Church of the Twelve Apostles, the shrine of St Mark was consecrated in 832, but in 976 both the church and the Palazzo Ducale were burnt down. The present basilica was finished in 1094 and embellished over the succeeding centuries. Every trophy that the doge stuck onto his church (this church was not the cathedral of Venice but the doge's own chapel) was proof of Venice's secular might and so of the spiritual power of St Mark.

Practicalities

The basilica is open to tourists Monday to Saturday 9.45am–5pm (4.30pm from Oct to April) and Sunday 2–4pm, though the Loggia dei Cavalli is open on Sunday morning. Entrance to the main part of the church is free, but admission fees totalling €9.50 are charged for certain parts of the church. You cannot take large bags into the church – they have to be left, free of charge, at nearby Calle San Basso 315/A. If you're visiting the basilica in summer, get there early – by midday the queues are enormous.

The exterior, narthex and Loggia dei Cavalli

Of the exterior features that can be seen easily from the ground, the **Roman-esque carvings** of the **central door** demand the closest attention – especially the middle arch's figures of the months and seasons and outer arch's series of *The Trades of Venice*. The carvings were begun around 1225 and finished in the early fourteenth century. Take a look also at the mosaic above the doorway on the far left – *The Arrival of the Body of St Mark* – which was made around 1260 (the only early mosaic left on the main facade) and includes the oldest known image of the basilica.

From the Piazza you pass into the vestibule known as the **narthex**, decorated with the first of the church's **mosaics**: Old Testament scenes on the domes and arches, together with *The Madonna with Apostles and Evangelists* in the niches of the bay in front of the main door – dating from the 1060s, the oldest mosaics in San Marco.

A steep staircase goes from the church's main door up to the **Museo di San Marco** and the Loggia dei Cavalli (daily: May–Sept 9.45am–4.45pm; Oct–April 9.45am–4pm; €4). Apart from giving you an all-round view, the loggia is also the best place from which to inspect the Gothic carvings along the apex of the facade. The **horses** outside are replicas, the genuine articles having been removed inside to the **Galleria**, along with oddments of mosaic and a fine polyptych by Paolo Veneziano. Thieved from the Hippodrome of Constantinople in 1204 during the Fourth Crusade, the horses are probably Roman works of the second century – the only such ancient group, or *quadriga*, to have survived.

The interior

With its undulating floor of twelfth-century patterned marble, its plates of eastern stone on the lower walls, and its 4000 square metres of **mosaics** covering every other inch of wall and vaulting, the interior of San Marco is the most opulent of any cathedral. One visit is not enough – there's too much to take in at one go, and the shifting light reveals and hides parts of the decoration as the day progresses; try calling in for half an hour at the beginning and end of a couple of days.

The majority of the mosaics were in position by the middle of the thirteenth century; some date from the fourteenth and fifteenth centuries, and others were created in the sixteenth to replace damaged early sections. Some of the best include the following. On the west wall, above the door – *Christ, the Virgin and St Mark*; west dome – *Pentecost*; arch between west and central domes – *Crucifixion, Resurrection*; central dome – *Ascension*; east dome – *Religion of Christ Foretold by the Prophets*.

From the south transept you can enter the **Sanctuary** (May–Sept Mon–Sat 9.45am–5pm, Sun 2–4pm; Oct–April Mon–Sat 9.45am–4pm, Sun 2–4pm; €2.50), where, behind the altar, you'll find the most precious of San Marco's treasures – the **Pala d'Oro** (Golden Altar Panel). Commissioned in 976 in Constantinople, the Pala was enlarged, enriched and rearranged by Byzantine goldsmiths in 1105, then by Venetians in 1209 (to incorporate some less cumbersome loot from the Fourth Crusade) and again (finally) in 1345. The completed screen holds 83 enamel plaques, 74 enamelled roundels, 38 chiselled figures, 300 sapphires, 300 emeralds, 400 garnets, 15 rubies, 1300 pearls and a couple of hundred other stones.

In a corner of the south transept is the door of the **Treasury** (same times as Sanctuary; €3), a small but dazzling line-up of chalices, reliquaries, candelabra and so on – many from the great Constantinople robbery of 1204.

Back in the main body of the church, there's still more to see on the lower levels of the building. Don't overlook the **rood screen**'s marble figures of The Virgin, St Mark and the Apostles, carved in 1394 by the dominant sculptors in Venice at that time, Jacobello and Pietro Paolo Dalle Masegne. The **pulpits** on each side of the screen were assembled in the early fourteenth century from miscellaneous panels (some from Constantinople); the new doge was presented to the people from the right-hand one. The tenth-century **Icon of the Madonna of Nicopeia** (in the chapel on east side of north transept) is the most revered religious image in Venice; it used to be one of the most revered in Constantinople.

The Palazzo Ducale

The **Palazzo Ducale** (daily: late March–Oct 9am–7pm; Nov–late March 9am–5pm; entrance with Museum Card – see box, p.292) was far more than the residence of the doge – it was the home of all of Venice's governing councils, many of its courts, a sizeable number of its civil servants and even its prisons. The government of Venice was administered through an intricate system of elected committees and councils – a system designed to limit the power of any individual – but for the last 500 years of the republic's existence only those families listed in the register of noble births and marriages known as the *Libro d'Oro* (Golden Book) were entitled to play a part in the system.

At the head of the network sat the **doge**, the one politician to sit on all the major councils of state and the only one elected for life; he could be immensely influential in policy and appointments, and restrictions were accordingly imposed on his actions to reduce the possibility of his abusing that power – his letters were read by censors and he wasn't permitted to receive foreign delegations alone. The privileges of the job far outweighed the inconveniences though, and men campaigned for years to increase their chances of election.

Like the basilica, the Palazzo Ducale has been rebuilt many times since its foundation in the first years of the ninth century. The principal entrance to the *palazzo* – the **Porta della Carta** – is one of the most ornate Gothic works in the city. It was commissioned in 1438 by Doge Francesco Fóscari from Bartolomeo and Giovanni Bon, but the figures of Fóscari and his lion are replicas – the originals were pulverized in 1797 as a favour to Napoleon. Fóscari's head survived the hammering, however, and is on display inside.

Tourists no longer enter the building by the Porta della Carta, but instead are herded through a doorway on the lagoon side. Once through the ticket hall you emerge in the courtyard, opposite the other end of the passageway into the Palazzo – the **Arco Fóscari**. The itinerary begins on the left side of the courtyard, where the finest of the capitals from the Palazzo's exterior arcade are displayed in the **Museo dell'Opera**. Upstairs, the route takes you through the doge's private apartments, then on to the **Anticollegio**, the room in which embassies had to wait before being admitted to the presence of the doge and his cabinet. This is one of the richest rooms in the Palazzo Ducale for paintings: four pictures by Tintoretto hang on the door walls, and facing the windows is Veronese's *Rape of Europa*.

The cycle of paintings on the ceiling of the adjoining **Sala del Collegio** is also by Veronese, and he features strongly again in the most stupendous room in the building – the **Sala del Maggior Consiglio**. Veronese's ceiling panel of *The Apotheosis of Venice* is suspended over the dais from which the doge oversaw the sessions of the city's general assembly; the backdrop is **Tintoretto**'s immense *Paradiso*, painted towards the end of his life, with the aid of his son, Domenico. At the opposite end there's a curiosity: the frieze of portraits of the first 76 doges (the series continues in the Sala dello Scrutinio – through the door at the far end) is interrupted by a painted black veil, marking the place where **Doge Marin Falier** would have been honoured had he not been beheaded for conspiring against the state in 1355

A couple of rooms later you descend to the underbelly of the Venetian state, crossing the **Ponte dei Sospiri** (Bridge of Sighs) to the prisons. Before the construction of these cells in the early seventeenth century all prisoners were kept in the Piombi (the Leads), under the roof of the Palazzo Ducale, or in the Pozzi (the Wells) in the bottom two storeys; the new block was occupied mainly by petty criminals. The route finishes with a detour through the Pozzi, but if you want to see the Piombi, and the rooms in which the day-to-day administration of Venice took place, you have to go on one of the special 'secret' tours (see box above).

The Campanile and Torre dell'Orologio

Most of the landscape of the Piazza dates from the great period of urban renewal that began at the end of the fifteenth century and went on for much of the following century. The one exception – excluding San Marco itself – is the **Campanile** (daily: April–June, Sept & Oct 9am–7.45pm; July & Aug 9am–9pm; Nov–March 9.30am–4.15pm; usually closed for 3 weeks after Christmas; €6), which began life as a lighthouse in the ninth century and was modified frequently up to the early sixteenth. The present structure is a reconstruction: the original tower collapsed on July 14, 1902 – a catastrophe that injured nobody (except a cat) and is commemorated by faked postcard photos ostensibly taken at the very instant of the disaster. The collapse reduced to rubble the **Loggetta** at the base of the campanile, but somehow it was pieced together again; built between 1537 and 1549 by Sansovino, it has served as a meeting-room for the nobility, a guardhouse and the place at which the state

Venice for kids

Venice has plenty of activities for **kids** to enjoy. Roaming around on the *vaporetti* is great fun, and you can save on the expense of a gondola by taking a *traghetto* across the Canal Grande – the boatmen won't bat an eyelid at carrying a pushchair. You can join the crowds on the Piazza feeding – or chasing – the pigeons, and if it's views you want, the campanile across the water at San Giorgio Maggiore has a lift, short queues and the best panoramas in the city. And of course there are some great ice creams to be enjoyed.

There is also a surprising number of places for children to play freely: the playground in the Parco di Cannaregio off Campo San Geremia is brilliant, while smaller **play areas** appear in several *campi* around 5pm: toys are kept at the back of the church in San Stefano, while in Campo Santa Maria Formosa they are stored in a building behind the church, and you can take them out into the square. It is useful also to note that city's network of public toilets often have nappy-changing facilities.

lottery was drawn. At 99 metres, the Campanile is the tallest structure in the city, and from the top (there is a lift) you can make out virtually every building, but not a single canal.

The other tower in the Piazza, the **Torre dell'Orologio** (Clock Tower), is ornately decorated, from the astronomical clock at the bottom up to the two figures, popularly known as the moors, who strike the large bell just before and after the hour. The tower was built between 1496 and 1506 while the clock mechanism dates from 1753. Twice a year, on 6 January and Ascension Day, crowds gather to watch the figures of the three kings parade in front of a seated Virgin and child. Now that it has finally reopened after a long – and controversial – restoration you can go on fascinating hour-long **tours**: the guide leads you up the steep narrow staircase, stopping on each of the five floors to reveal the clock's complex workings. (guided tours only, in English Mon–Wed 10am, 11am & 1pm, Thurs–Sun 2pm, 3pm & 5pm. Joint tickets with the Museo Correr are on sale at the museum, from where tours start, or see box on p.292 for booking details).

The Procuratie and Museo Correr

Away to the left of the Torre dell'Orologio stretches the **Procuratie Vecchie**; begun around 1500 by Codussi, this block housed the offices of the **Procurators of St Mark**, a committee of nine men whose responsibilities included the upkeep of the basilica and other public buildings. A century or so after taking possession, the procurators were moved to the opposite side of the Piazza, into the **Procuratie Nuove**. Napoleon converted these apartments and offices into a royal palace and then, having realized that the building lacked a ballroom, remedied the deficiency by smashing down the church of San Geminiano to connect the two Procuratie with a new wing for dancing.

Generally known as the **Ala Napoleonica**, this short side of the Piazza is partly occupied by the **Museo Correr** (daily: late March to Oct 9am–7pm; Nov–late March 9am–5pm; entrance with Museum Card – see box, p.292), an immense triple-decker museum with a vast **historical collection** of coins, weapons, regalia, prints, paintings and miscellanea. Much of this is heavy going unless you have an intense interest in Venetian history, though there's an appealing exhibition of Venetian applied arts, and one show-stopping item in the form of the original blocks and a print of Jacopo de'Barbari's astonishing aerial view of Venice, engraved in 1500. The **Quadreria** on the second floor is no rival for the Accademia's collection, but it does set out clearly the evolution of painting in Venice from the thirteenth century to around 1500, and it contains some gems – the most famous being the **Carpaccio** picture usually known as *The Courtesans*, although its subjects are really a couple of bored-looking bourgeois ladies. The section of the Correr devoted to the **Museo del Risorgimento** is largely given over to the 1848 rebellion against the Austrians, but is often *in restauro*.

Accessed from within the Correr, the **Museo Archeologico** is a somewhat scrappy museum, with cases of Roman coins and gems, fragments of sarcophagi and inscriptions, headless statues and bodiless heads interspersed with the odd Bronze Age, Egyptian or Assyrian relic. From the archeological museum you pass into the hall of the **Libreria Sansoviniana**, described by Palladio as "perhaps the richest and most ornate building to be created since the times of ancient Greece and Rome". Paintings by Veronese, Tintoretto, Andrea Schiavone and others cover the walls and ceiling, gazing down on reproductions of some of the more precious of the library's volumes; Titian's *Allegory of Wisdom* occupies the central panel of the ceiling of the anteroom, beyond which lies the intended approach to the library, a magnificent staircase encrusted with stuccowork by Vittoria.

The Piazzetta

The **Piazzetta** – the open space between San Marco and the waterfront pavement known as the Molo – was the area where the politicians used to gather before meetings. Facing the Palazzo Ducale is Sansovino's masterpiece, the **Libreria Sansoviniana** (see above), which is attached to Sansovino's first major building in Venice, the **Zecca** (Mint), built between 1537 and 1545 on the site of the thirteenth-century mint. By the beginning of the fifteenth century the city's prosperity was such that the Venetian coinage was in use in every European exchange, and the doge could with some justification call Venice "the mistress of all the gold in Christendom".

The Piazzetta's two **columns** were brought here from the Levant at the end of the twelfth century, in company with a third, which fell off the barge and still lies somewhere just off the Molo. The figures perched on top are St Theodore (the original is in the Palazzo Ducale), patron saint of Venice when it was dependent on Byzantium, and a Chimera, customized to look like the Lion of St Mark. Public executions were carried out between the columns, the techniques employed ranging from straightforward hanging to burial alive, head downwards. Superstitious Venetians avoid passing between them.

North of the Piazza

The Mercerie, a chain of streets that starts under the Torre dell'Orologio and finishes at the Campo San Bartolomeo, is the most direct route between San Marco and the Rialto Bridge and has always been the main land thoroughfare of the city and a prime site for its shopkeepers. For those immune to the charms of window-shopping there's little reason to linger until you reach the church of **San Salvador** (Mon–Sat 9am–noon & 4–6.15pm, Sun 4–6.15pm), an early sixteenth-century church cleverly planned in the form of three Greek crosses placed end to end. It has a couple of Titian paintings – an altarpiece of the *Transfiguration* (1560) and an *Annunciation* (1566), whose awkward angel is often blamed on the great man's assistants. The end of the south transept is filled by the tomb of Caterina Cornaro (see p.355).

The **Campo San Bartolomeo**, close to the foot of the Rialto Bridge, is at its best in the evening, when it's as packed as any bar in town. If the crush gets a bit too much, you can retire to the nearby **Campo San Luca**, another focus of after-work gatherings but not as much of a pressure-cooker as San Bartolomeo.

Beyond Campo San Luca is **Campo Manin**, on the south side of which is a sign for the spiral staircase known as the **Scala del Bovolo** (*bovolo* means "snail shell" in Venetian dialect), a piece of flamboyant engineering dating from around 1500 (closed at present for restoration; probable opening times April–Oct daily 10am–6pm; Nov–March Sat & Sun 10am–4pm; €3.50). The **Museo Fortuny** (daily except Tues 10am–6pm; €8) is also close at hand, similarly tucked away in a spot you'd never accidentally pass. In addition to making his famous silk dresses, which were said to be fine enough to be threaded through a wedding ring, Mariano Fortuny (1871–1949) was a painter, architect, engraver, photographer and sculptor. The *palazzo* in which the museum is housed is so fragile that only 75 people are allowed in at a time, so you may have to queue in summer, and it is also subject to unexpected closures.

West of the Piazza

Although it has its share of fashionable shops, the area to the **west of the Piazza** is less frenetic than the streets to the north. None of the premier tourist sights is here, but the walk from the Piazza to the Accademia Bridge, through a succession of *campi* each quite unlike its predecessor, isn't lacking in worthwhile diversions.

Heading west you soon reach the hypnotically dreadful **San Moisè** (daily 3.30–7pm, plus Sun 9am–noon), runaway winner of any poll for the ugliest church in Venice. The facade sculpture, featuring a species of camel unknown to zoology, was created in 1668 by Heinrich Meyring.

Halfway along the Calle Larga XXII Marzo, on the right, is the Calle del Sartor da Veste, which takes you over a canal and into the Campo San Fantin, where the Renaissance church of **San Fantin** has a graceful domed apse by Sansovino. Across the campo is Venice's largest and oldest theatre, **La Fenice**, opened in December 1792, rebuilt in 1836 after the place had been wrecked by fire, but devastated by yet another fire on the night of January 29, 1996, just as a phase of restoration was coming to a close. Tours of the grand interior with an audioguide (45min) can be booked at the box office (€7).

Back on the main road to the Accademia, another very odd church awaits – **Santa Maria del Giglio**, otherwise known as Santa Maria del Zobenigo (Mon–Sat 10am–5pm; €3 or Chorus Pass). You can stare at this all day and still not find a single Christian image. The statues are of the five Barbaro brothers who financed the rebuilding of the church in 1678; Virtue, Honour, Fame and Wisdom hover respectfully around them; and the maps in relief depict the towns the brothers graced during their military and diplomatic careers.

The tilting campanile that soon looms into view over the vapid church of San Maurizio belongs to Santo Stefano, which stands at the end of the next *campo* – the **Campo Santo Stefano**. Large enough to hold several clusters of tourists and locals plus a kids' football match or two, it's a lively place but never feels crowded. The church of **Santo Stefano** (Mon–Sat 10am–5pm) dates from the thirteenth century, but was rebuilt in the fourteenth and altered again in the first half of the fifteenth; the Gothic doorway and the ship's keel roof both belong to this last phase. The best paintings are in the sacristy (€3 or Chorus Pass) – *The Agony in the Garden*, *The Last Supper* and *The Washing of the Disciples' Feet*, all late works by Tintoretto.

Dorsoduro

Some of the finest architecture in Venice, both domestic and public, is to be found in the *sestiere* of **DORSODURO**, a situation partly attributable to the stability of its sandbanks – Dorsoduro means "hard back". Yet for all its attractions, not many visitors wander off the strip that runs between the main sights of the area – the Ca' Rezzonico, the Accademia and the Salute.

The Galleria dell'Accademia

The **Galleria dell'Accademia** (Mon 8.15am–2pm, Tues–Sun 8.15am–7.15pm; €6.50, plus €1 if you book a timed slot on ☎041.522.2247 or at ⓦwww.gallerieaccademia.org) is one of the finest specialist collections of European art, following the history of Venetian painting from the fourteenth to the eighteenth centuries. Along with the Basilica di San Marco and the Palazzo Ducale the Accademia is the third component of the triad of obligatory tourist sights in Venice. Admissions are restricted to batches of 300 people at a time although this may change with the completion of the expansion programme that's under way. For now you should expect to queue in high summer if you have not booked a ticket in advance.

The early Renaissance

The gallery is laid out in a roughly chronological succession of rooms going anticlockwise. The first room at the top of the stairs is the fifteenth-century assembly room of the Scuola della Carità, whose church and convent the gallery now occupies. This has works by the earliest known individual Venetian painters. **Paolo Veneziano** (from the first half of the fourteenth century) and his follower **Lorenzo Veneziano** are the most absorbing.

Room 2 moves on to works from the late fifteenth and early sixteenth centuries, with large altarpieces that are contemplative even when the scenes are far from calm. **Carpaccio**'s strange and gruesome *Crucifixion and Glorification of the Ten Thousand Martyrs of Mount Ararat* (painted around 1512) and his *Presentation of Jesus in the Temple* accompany works by **Giovanni Bellini** and **Cima da Conegliano**.

In the next room you can observe the emergence of the characteristically Venetian treatment of colour, but there's nothing here as exciting as the small paintings in rooms 4 and 5, a high point of the collection. Apart from an exquisite *St George* by **Mantegna** and a series of **Giovanni Bellini** Madonnas, this section contains **Giorgione**'s enigmatic *Tempest*.

The High Renaissance

Rooms 6 to 8 introduce the heavyweights of Venetian painting, Jacopo Robusti, known as **Tintoretto**, **Titian** (Tiziano Vecellio) and **Lorenzo Lotto**. Room 10 is dominated by epic productions, and an entire wall is filled by **Paolo Veronese**'s *Christ in the House of Levi*. Originally called *The Last Supper*, this picture provoked a stern reaction from the Court of the Holy Office: "Does it appear to you fitting that at our Lord's last supper you should paint buffoons, drunkards, Germans, dwarfs, and similar indecencies?" Veronese responded simply by changing the title, which made the work acceptable. The pieces by **Tintoretto** in here include three legends of St Mark: *St Mark Rescues a Slave* (1548), which was the painting that made his reputation, *The Theft of the Body of St Mark* and *St Mark Saves a Saracen* (both 1560s). All of these show Tintoretto's love of energy and drama – from the physical or psychological drama of the subject matter to the technical energy of his brush strokes, perception of colour and use of light. Opposite is an emotional late **Titian**, a pietà (1570s) intended for his own tomb in the Frari.

The eighteenth century

Room 11 contains a number of works by **Giambattista Tiepolo**, the most prominent painter of eighteenth-century Venice, including two shaped fragments rescued from the Scalzi (1743–45) and *The Translation of the Holy House of Loreto* (1743), a sketch for the same ceiling. There's also more from **Tintoretto**; the *Madonna dei Tesorieri* (1566) shows facial types still found in Venice today.

The following stretch of seventeenth- and eighteenth-century paintings isn't too enthralling – the highlights are portraits by Rosalba Carriera and interiors by Pietro Longhi in room 17.

The Vivarinis, the Bellinis and Carpaccio

Around the corner and to the right are more works from the fifteenth and early sixteenth centuries. **Alvise Vivarini**'s *Santa Chiara* is outstanding. **Giovanni Bellini** is represented by four triptychs painted, with workshop assistance, in the 1460s. The extraordinary *Blessed Lorenzo Giustinian* is by his brother, **Gentile**; one of the oldest surviving Venetian canvases, it was possibly used as a standard in processions, which would account for its state.

The magnificent cycle of pictures painted around 1500 for the Scuola di San Giovanni Evangelista, mainly illustrating the miracles of the Relic of the Cross, is displayed in room 20, off a corridor to the left. All of the paintings are replete with fascinating local details, but particularly rich are **Carpaccio**'s *Cure of a Lunatic* and **Gentile Bellini**'s *Recovery of the Relic from the Canale di San Lorenzo* and *Procession of the Relic in the Piazza*. The next room contains a complete cycle of pictures by **Carpaccio** illustrating the Story of St Ursula, painted for the Scuola di Sant'Orsola at San Zanipolo (1490–94). Restored in the mid-1980s, the paintings form one of Italy's most unforgettable groups. It tells the story of Ursula, a Breton princess, who undertook a pilgrimage with a company of 11,000 virgins that ended with a massacre by the Huns.

Finally, in room 24 (the former hostel of the Scuola), there's **Titian**'s *Presentation of the Virgin* (dating from 1539). It was painted for the place where it hangs, as was the triptych by **Antonio Vivarini** and **Giovanni d'Alemagna** (1446), another of the oldest Venetian canvases.

The Guggenheim and the Salute

Within five-minutes' walk of the Accademia, east beyond the Campo San Vio, is the unfinished Palazzo Venier dei Leoni, home of Peggy Guggenheim for thirty years until her death in 1979 and now the base for the **Guggenheim Collection** (daily except Tues 10am–6pm; June–July open Sat till 10pm; €10; ⓦwww.guggenheim-venice.it). Her private collection is a quirky choice of mainly excellent pieces from her favourite modernist movements and artists. Prime pieces include Brancusi's *Bird in Space* and *Maestra*, De Chirico's *Red Tower* and *Nostalgia of the Poet*, Max Ernst's *Robing of the Bride*, sculpture by Laurens and Lipchitz and paintings by Malevich.

Continuing along the line of the Canal Grande, you come to Santa Maria della Salute, better known simply as the **Salute** (daily 9am–noon & 3–6.30pm; closes 5.30pm in winter), built to fulfil a Senate decree of October 22, 1630, that a new church would be dedicated to Mary if the city were delivered from the plague that was ravaging it – an outbreak that killed about a third of the population. Work began in 1631 on **Baldessare Longhena**'s design and the church was consecrated in 1687. Thereafter, every November 21, the Signoria headed a procession from San Marco to the Salute, over a specially constructed pontoon bridge, to give thanks for the city's good health (*salute* meaning "health" and "salvation") – even today the festival of the Salute is a major event in the Venetian calendar.

In 1656, a hoard of **Titian** paintings from the suppressed church of Santo Spirito was moved here and is now housed in the sacristy (€1.50). The most prominent of these is the altarpiece *St Mark Enthroned with Saints Cosmas, Damian, Sebastian and Rocco* (the plague saints). The *Marriage at Cana*, with its dramatic lighting and perspective, is by **Tintoretto** (1561), and features likenesses of a number of the artist's friends.

The **Dogana di Mare** (Customs House), with its Doric facade (1676–82), occupies the spur formed by the meeting of the Canal Grande with the Giudecca canal, known as the Punta della Dogana. The gold ball, noticeable from anywhere on this busy stretch of water is a weathervane, topped by a figure representing either Justice or Fortune. Ambitious plans are turning the building into Venice's new contemporary art museum, due to open in 2009 and housing, it is rumoured, the collection of the billionaire Francois Pinault, who also owns the Palazzo Grassi.

Along the Záttere to San Sebastiano

Stretching along Dorsoduro's southern waterfront from the Punta della Dogana to the Stazione Maríttima, the **Záttere** (Rafts) was originally the place where most of the bulky goods coming into Venice were unloaded, and is now a popular place for a picnic lunch or a Sunday stroll. Its principal sight is the church of Santa Maria del Rosario, invariably known as the **Gesuati** (Mon–Sat 10am–5pm; €3, or Chorus Pass); it's worth a call for its paintings by **Giambattista Tiepolo**: three ceiling frescoes called *Scenes from the Life of St Dominic* and an altarpiece, *Madonna with three Dominican Saints*.

A diversion to the right straight after the Gesuati takes you past the **squero di San Trovaso**, one of the few gondola workshops left in Venice, and on to the church of **San Trovaso** (Mon–Sat 8–11am & 3–6pm; free). Its paintings include a fine pair by **Tintoretto** (*The Temptation of St Anthony* and *The Last Supper*), and two large scenes that were begun by Tintoretto at the very end of his life and completed by his son and other assistants: *The Adoration of the Magi* and *The Expulsion from the Temple*.

The church of **San Sebastiano** (Mon–Sat 10am–5pm; €3, or Chorus Pass), right up by the Stazione Maríttima was built between 1505 and 1545 and was the parish church of **Paolo Veronese**, who provided most of its paintings and is buried here. He was first brought in to paint the ceiling of the sacristy with a *Coronation of the Virgin* and the *Four Evangelists*, followed by the *Scenes from the Life of St Esther* on the ceiling of the church. He then painted the dome of the chancel (since destroyed), and with the help of his brother, Benedetto, moved on to the walls of the church and the nuns' choir. The paintings around the high altar and the organ came last, painted in the 1560s.

Ca' Rezzonico and Ca' Fóscari

From San Sebastiano it's a straightforward walk back towards the Canal Grande along Calle Avogaria and Calle Lunga San Barnaba, a route that deposits you in Campo San Barnaba, just yards from the **Ca' Rezzonico**, now the **Museo del Settecento Veneziano** (April–Oct 10am–6pm; Nov–March 10am–5pm; closed Tues; €6.50). Having acquired the Ca' Rezzonico in 1934, the *comune* of Venice set about furnishing and decorating it with eighteenth-century items and materials (or their closest modern equivalent), so giving the place the feel of a well-appointed house. In the collection, the plentiful and outlandish carvings by **Andrea Brustolon** are as likely to elicit revulsion as admiration. As for the paintings, the highlights are **Pietro Longhi**'s affectionate illustrations of Venice social life and pictures by **Giambattista and Giandomenico Tiepolo** – the latter's frescoes of clowns and carnival scenes are his best-known images.

Immediately north of Ca' Rezzonico, the cluster of Gothic palaces fronting the Canal Grande constitutes one of the city's architectural glories. Built in 1435, the **Ca' Fóscari**, which Ruskin thought "the noblest example in Venice" of late Gothic, was the home of Doge Francesco Fóscari. Adjoining the Ca' Fóscari are a pair of buildings of the same period – the **Palazzi Giustinian**. Wagner wrote the second act of *Tristan and Isolde* while living here.

Campo Santa Margherita and around

The nearby **Campo Santa Margherita** is the largest square on this side of the Canal Grande, but it's a modest one, with no grandiose architecture. This is the social heart of Dorsoduro, and its bars and cafés draw much of their custom from the nearby university. The **Scuola Grande dei Carmini** (daily: April–Oct 10am–5pm; Nov–March 10am–4pm; €5), in the southwest corner, is a showcase for Giambattista Tiepolo, whose ceiling paintings in the main upstairs hall from the early 1740s centre on the panel *The Virgin in Glory*.

To the north of the campo stands the church of **San Pantaleone** (Mon–Sat 4–6pm), which possesses a *Coronation of the Virgin* by Antonio Vivarini and Giovanni d'Alemagna (in the chapel to the left of the chancel) and Veronese's last painting, *San Pantaleone Healing a Boy* (second chapel on right). The church also boasts the most melodramatic ceiling in the city: *The Martyrdom and Apotheosis of San Pantaleone*, which kept Gian Antonio Fumiani busy from 1680 to 1704.

San Polo and Santa Croce

Two *sestieri* are covered in this section: **San Polo**, which extends from the Rialto market to the Frari area; and **Santa Croce**, a far less sight-heavy district which lies to the north of San Polo and reaches right across to Piazzale Roma. There are two main routes through the district – one runs between the Rialto and the Scalzi bridge, the other takes you in the opposite direction from the

▲ Gondola under the Rialto Bridge

Rialto, down towards the Accademia. Virtually all the essential sights lie around these two routes.

The Rialto Bridge

The famous **Ponte di Rialto** (Rialto Bridge) is the bustling link between San Marco and San Polo, standing at a bend in the Canal Grande, lined with shops and constantly thronged with locals and tourists. The current structure superseded a succession of wooden structures – one of Carpaccio's *Miracles of the True Cross*, in the Accademia, shows what one of the old drawbridges looked like. The decision to construct a stone bridge was taken in 1524, and the job was awarded to the aptly named **Antonio da Ponte**, whose top-heavy design was described by Edward Gibbon as "a fine bridge, spoilt by two rows of houses upon it". Until 1854, when the first Accademia Bridge was built, this was the only point at which the Canal Grande could be crossed on foot.

From the Rialto to Ca' Pésaro

West of the Rialto Bridge, the relatively stable building land drew some of the earliest lagoon settlers to the high bank (*rivo alto*) that was to develop into the **Rialto** district. While the political centre of the new city grew up around San Marco, the Rialto became the commercial zone. It was through the markets of the Rialto that Venice earned its reputation as the bazaar of Europe. Virtually anything could be bought or sold here: Italian fabrics, precious stones, silver plate and gold jewellery, and spices and dyes from the Orient. After a fire destroyed everything in the area except the church in 1514 work began on the **Fabbriche Vecchie** (the arcaded buildings along the Ruga degli Orefici and around the Campo San Giacomo); Sansovino's **Fabbriche Nuove** (running along the Canal Grande from Campo Cesare Battisti) followed about thirty years later.

Today's Rialto market may be tamer than that of Venice at its peak, but it's still one of the liveliest spots in the city, and one of the few places where it's possible to stand in a crowd and hear nothing but Italian spoken. There's a shoal of memento-sellers by the church and along the Ruga degli Orefici; the market proper lies between them and the Canal Grande – mainly fruit stalls around the

Venice in flood

Called the *acqua alta*, the **winter flooding** of Venice is caused by a combination of seasonal tides, fluctuations in atmospheric pressure in the Adriatic and persistent southeasterly winds, and has always been a feature of Venetian life. In recent years, however, it has been getting worse with sixty to a hundred floods a year. Currently most of these are not major and only last for an hour or two and are confined to the Piazza and the low-lying parts of the city. If the siren sounds, you can expect a more serious flood in three to four hours' time. A system of plank walkways is immediately set up in the low-lying parts of the city – most boat stops have maps of where those walkways run. The usual high-tide season is September to April, with the worst flooding between November and February.

A grand plan is being implemented to protect the city involving building a **tidal barrier** across the three entrances to the lagoon. Nicknamed Moisè (Moses), the cost and potential environmental impacts aroused considerable opposition. However, mounting concern about global warming gave the matter more urgency and has led to widespread acceptance of the project. More than twenty years after the first plan was submitted, work finally began on the barrier in 2003 and is due to be completed in 2012.

Campo San Giacomo, vegetable stalls and butchers' shops as you go through to the Campo Battisti, after which you come to the fish market.

A popular Venetian legend asserts that the city was founded on Friday, March 25, 421 AD at exactly midday; from the same legend derives the claim that the church of **San Giacomo di Rialto** (Mon–Sat 9.30–noon & 4–6pm) was founded in that year, and is thus the oldest church in Venice. Whether it is or not, what is not disputed is that the church was rebuilt in 1071 and that parts of the present structure date from then.

The church of **San Cassiano** (daily 9am–noon & 5–7pm) is a building you're bound to pass as you wander west from the Rialto. Don't be put off by its barn-like appearance: it contains three paintings by **Tintoretto**, *The Resurrection*, *The Descent into Limbo* and *The Crucifixion*. The last of these is one of the greatest pictures in Venice, a startling composition dominated not by the cross but by the ladder on which the executioners stand.

Nearby, and signposted from San Cassiano, is the **Ca' Pésaro**, in which you'll find both the **Galleria d'Arte Moderna** and **Museo d'Arte Orientale** (Tues–Sun: April–Oct 10am–6pm; Nov–March 10am–5pm; €5.50, or Museum Pass/Venice Card). Pieces bought from the Biennale make up the core of the modern art collection, with Italian artists predominating. The oriental galleries display a jumble of lacquer work, armour, screens and weaponry.

Campo San Polo

The largest square in Venice after the Piazza, the **Campo San Polo** used to be the city's favourite bullfighting arena as well as the site of weekly markets and occasional fairs. Nowadays it's a combination of outdoor social centre, summertime outdoor cinema and children's sports stadium.

The bleak interior of **San Polo** church (Mon–Sat 10am–5pm; €3, or Chorus Pass) should be visited for *The Last Supper* by **Tintoretto** and **Giandomenico Tiepolo**'s paintings *The Stations of the Cross*, a series painted when the artist was only twenty. The sober piety of these pictures will come as a surprise if you've been to the Ca' Rezzonico, though it often seems that his interest was less in the central drama than in the society portraits that occupy the edges of the stage.

The Frari

The Franciscans were granted a large plot of land near San Polo in about 1250, not long after the death of St Francis. Replacement of their first church by the present Santa Maria Gloriosa dei Frari – more generally known simply as the **Frari** (Mon–Sat 9am–6pm, Sun 1–6pm; €3, or Chorus Pass) – began in the mid-fourteenth century and took over a hundred years. This mountain of brick is not an immediately attractive building but its collection of paintings, sculptures and monuments make it a guaranteed highlight of anyone's visit.

Wherever you stand in the Frari, you'll be facing something that deserves your attention. Apart from the Salute and the Accademia, the Frari is the only building in Venice with more than a single significant work by **Titian**. One of these – the *Assumption*, painted in 1518 – you will see almost immediately as you look towards the altar, a swirling, dazzling piece of compositional bravura for which there was no precedent in Venetian art. The other Titian masterpiece here, the *Madonna di Ca' Pésaro*, was equally innovative in its displacement of the figure of the Virgin from the centre of the picture.

Two funerary monuments embodying the emergence in Venice of Renaissance sculptural technique flank the Titian *Assumption*: on the left the tomb of Doge Niccolò Tron, by **Antonio Rizzo** and assistants, dating from 1476; on the right, the more chaotic tomb of Doge Francesco Fóscari, carved by **Antonio and Paolo Bregno** shortly after Fóscari's death in 1457. Head through the door in the right transept for the sacristy, where on the altar stands a picture that alone would justify a visit to the Frari – the *Madonna and Child with Saints Nicholas of Bari, Peter, Mark and Benedict*, painted in 1488 by **Giovanni Bellini**. In the words of Henry James, "it is as solemn as it is gorgeous and as simple as it is deep".

Two massive tombs take up much of the nave. One is the bombastic monument to Titian, built in the mid-nineteenth century on the supposed site of his grave. Opposite is a tomb of similarly pompous dimensions but of redeeming peculiarity: the mausoleum of Canova, erected in 1827 by his pupils, following a design he had made for the tomb of Titian.

The Scuola Grande di San Rocco and San Rocco church

At the rear of the Frari is a place you should on no account miss: the **Scuola Grande di San Rocco** (daily: April–Oct 9am–5.30pm; Nov–March 10am–5pm; €5.50). St Rocco (St Roch) was attributed with the power to cure the plague and other serious illnesses, so when the saint's body was brought to Venice in 1485, this *scuola* began to profit from donations from people wishing to invoke his aid. In 1515 it commissioned this prestigious building, and soon after its completion in 1560, work began on the decorative scheme that was to put the Scuola's rivals in the shade – a cycle of more than fifty major paintings by **Tintoretto**.

The Tintoretto paintings

To appreciate the evolution of Tintoretto's art you have to begin in the smaller room on the upper storey, the **Sala dell'Albergo**. In 1564 the Scuola held a competition for the contract to paint its first picture. Tintoretto won the contest by rigging up a finished painting in the very place for which the winning picture was destined – the centre of the ceiling. The protests of his rivals, who had simply submitted sketches, were to no avail. Virtually an entire wall of the Sala is occupied by the stupendous *Crucifixion*. As Ruskin's loquacious guide to the cycle concludes: "I must leave this picture to work its will on the spectator; for it is beyond all analysis, and above all praise."

In the main upper hall, the Old Testament subjects depicted in the three large panels of the **ceiling**, with their references to the alleviation of physical suffering, are coded declarations of the Scuola's charitable activities: *Moses Striking Water from the Rock*, *The Miracle of the Brazen Serpent* and *The Miraculous Fall of Manna*. The paintings around the walls, all based on the New Testament, are an amazing feat of sustained inventiveness, in which every convention of perspective, lighting, colour and even anatomy is defied. A caricature of the irascible Tintoretto (with a jarful of paint brushes) is incorporated into the trompe-l'oeil carvings by the seventeenth-century sculptor Francesco Pianta.

Displayed on easels, either in the *sala* or main hall – they are often moved – are a handful of paintings that are easy to miss, given the competition. *Christ Carrying the Cross* is now generally thought to be an early **Titian**, though some still maintain Giorgione's authorship; Titian's *Annunciation* is similarly influenced by the earlier master. Two early **Tiepolo** paintings, also on easels, relieve the eyes with a wash of airy colour.

The paintings on the ground floor were created between 1583 and 1587, when Tintoretto was in his late 60s. The turbulent *Annunciation* is one of the most arresting images of the event ever painted, and there are few Renaissance landscapes to match those of *The Flight into Egypt* and the small paintings of *St Mary Magdalen* and *St Mary of Egypt*.

The church

Yet more paintings by Tintoretto adorn the neighbouring church of **San Rocco** (8am–12.30pm & 3–5pm). On the south wall of the nave you'll find *St Roch Taken to Prison*, and below it *The Pool of Bethesda* – though only the latter is definitely by Tintoretto. In the chancel are four large works, all of them difficult to see properly: the best are *St Roch Curing the Plague Victims* (lower right) and *St Roch in Prison* (lower left).

Cannaregio

In the northernmost section of Venice, **CANNAREGIO**, you can go from the bustle of the train station and the horrible Lista di Spagna to areas which, although no longer rural (Cannaregio comes from *canna*, meaning "reed") are still among the quietest and prettiest parts of the whole city. The district also has the dubious distinction of containing the world's original ghetto.

The station area

Walking from Piazzale Roma towards the station, you cross the **Ponte della Costituzione**, Bridge of the Constitution, a controversial construction even by Venetian standards. Critics said the fourth bridge over the Canal Grande, designed by Santiago Calatrava, was ugly, in the wrong place and, in spite of its huge cost, not even fit for disabled users – though this will soon be remedied. Such was the hostility it aroused that the bridge was opened with no fanfare in September 2008. Yet it looks graceful enough and certainly improves access from to the train station and Cannaregio.

The first building worth a look beyond the station is to the left as you come out of it – the **Scalzi** church, also called Santa Maria di Nazareth (daily 7–noon & 4–7pm; free). Built in the 1670s for the barefoot (*scalzi*) order of Carmelites, the interior, by Baldessare Longhena, is a joy for aficionados of the Baroque. There are frescoes by Giambattista Tiepolo in the first chapel on the left and the second on the right, but his major work on the ceiling was destroyed in 1915 by an Austrian bomb. A couple of fragments, now in the Accademia, were all that was salvaged.

The **Lista di Spagna**, running northeast from the train station, takes its name from the Spanish embassy, which used to be at no. 168. The street is now given over to the tourist trade, with shops and stalls, bars, restaurants and hotels all competing for the same desperate trade. If you are hunting for trinkets, food or a bed, you'll find better elsewhere. The church of **San Geremia** (Mon–Sat 8.30am–noon & 4–6.30pm, Sun 9.30am–12.15pm & 5.30–6.30pm) at the end of the street is chiefly notable for being the present home of **St Lucy**, martyred in Siracuse in 304. Lucy tore her own eyes out after an unwanted suitor kept complimenting her on their beauty, and hence became the patron saint of eyesight: the glass case on the high altar contains her desiccated body. Architecturally, the church's main point of interest is the twelfth-century campanile, one of the oldest in the city.

The ballroom of the **Palazzo Labia**, next door to the church, contains frescoes by Giambattista Tiepolo and his assistants (1745–50), illustrating the story of Antony and Cleopatra. The present owners, RAI (the state radio service), allow the public in to see them on Wednesdays, Thursdays and Fridays 3–4pm. The *palazzo*'s facade overlooks the **Canale di Cannaregio**, once the main entrance to Venice before the road and rail bridges were built. Walk along it to get to the church of **San Giobbe** (Mon–Sat 10am–5pm; €3, or Chorus Pass). Job's physical suffering in the Bible made him particularly popular with the Venetians, who regularly experienced malaria, plague and a plethora of damp-related diseases. The church was built by the Gothic architect Antonio Gambello, later assisted by Pietro Lombardo, his first work in Venice.

The Ghetto

The Venetian **Ghetto** was, in a sense, the first in the world: the word comes from the Venetian dialect *getar* (to found), or *geto* (foundry), which is what this area was until 1390. In 1516 all the city's Jews were ordered to move to the island of the Ghetto Nuovo. Distinctive badges or caps had to be worn by all Jews, and there were various economic and social restraints on the community, although oppression was lighter in Venice than in most other parts of Europe (it was one of the few states to tolerate the Jewish religion). When Jews were expelled en masse from Spain in 1492 and Portugal in 1497, many came here.

Each wave of Jewish immigrants established its own **synagogues** and four of the most significant, the ornate Scola Levantina, founded in 1538, and the Scola Spagnola together with the beautiful Scola al Canton and the Scola Italiana, can be viewed in a fascinating hourly tour of the area organized by the **Jewish Museum** in Campo Ghetto Nuovo (daily except Sat & Jewish hols: June–Sept 10am–7pm; Oct–May 10am–5.30pm; €3, or free with tour, which costs €8.50; tours in English on the half-hour; last tour June–Sept 5.30pm, Oct–May 4.30pm); the collection in the museum itself is mainly of silverware, embroidery and other liturgical objects.

The Jewish population grew to about 5000 and, even though they were allowed to spread into the **Ghetto Vecchio** (called the "old ghetto" because that's where the foundries used to be) and the **Ghetto Nuovissima**, there was gross overcrowding. As the Ghetto buildings were not allowed to be more than a third higher than the surrounding houses, the result was a stack of low-ceilinged storeys – seven is the usual number. Napoleon removed the gates of the Ghetto in 1797 but Venice's Jews didn't achieve equal rights with other Venetians until Unification with Italy in 1866. In a corner of the *campo* a series of reliefs by **Arbit Blatas** commemorate the two hundred Venetian Jews deported to the death camps during World War II – their names and ages are inscribed on a separate memorial entitled *The Last Train*. Today Venice's Jewish population of around six hundred (which includes a recent influx of young Italians and North Americans belonging to the Lubavitch sect) is spread all over the city, but the Ghetto remains the centre of the community.

Sant'Alvise and Madonna dell'Orto

A few minutes north of the Ghetto stands the church of **Sant'Alvise** (Mon–Sat 10am–5pm; €3, or Chorus Pass). Commissioned by Antonia Venier, daughter of Doge Antonio Venier, after the saint appeared to her in a vision in 1388, the church has one outstanding picture, *The Road to Calvary* by Giambattista Tiepolo, painted in 1743. His *Crown of Thorns* and *Flagellation*, slightly earlier works, are on the right-hand wall of the nave.

A circuitous stroll eastwards brings you to the Gothic church of **Madonna dell'Orto** (Mon–Sat 10am–5pm; €3, or Chorus Pass). Dedicated to St Christopher in about 1350, the church was renamed after a large stone Madonna by Giovanni de'Santi, found discarded in a local vegetable garden (*orto*), began to work miracles. Brought inside the church in 1377, the figure can still be seen (now heavily restored) in the Cappella di San Mauro through a door at the front end of the right aisle. This was Tintoretto's parish church – he's buried in the chapel to the right of the high altar – and there are a number of his paintings here, notably the colossal *Making of the Golden Calf* and *The Last Judgement*, which flank the main altar.

Ca' d'Oro and the Gesuiti

Back towards the Canal Grande the **Strada Nova** was carved through the houses in 1871–72 and is now a bustling shopping street. Nearly halfway along is the inconspicuous *calle* named after, and leading to, the **Ca' d'Oro** – a Gothic palace housing the **Galleria Giorgio Franchetti** (Mon 8.15am–2pm, Tues–Sat 8.15am–7.15pm; €5). Its main attraction is the *St Sebastian* painted by **Mantegna** shortly before his death in 1506, although the collection of sculpture has more outstanding items, notably **Tullio Lombardo**'s beautifully carved *Young Couple*, and superb portrait busts by Bernini and Alessandro Vittoria.

At the eastern end of the Strada Nova you come to the Campo dei Santi Apostoli, a general meeting-point and crossroads. Just inland from the Fondamente Nove, at the northern edge of this zone, is the **Gesuiti** church, as Santa Maria Assunta is familiarly known (daily 10am–noon & 4–6pm). The Jesuits began work on their church in 1714, and it took fifteen years to inlay the marble walls of the interior and carve its marble "curtains", with a result that is jaw-droppingly impressive even if you hate Baroque architecture. The *Martyrdom of St Lawrence* by Titian, on the first altar on the left, is a night scene made doubly obscure by the lighting arrangements.

The Miracoli

Sitting on the lip of a canal in the southeastern corner of Cannaregio you'll find the church of Santa Maria dei Miracoli – known simply as the **Miracoli** (Mon–Sat 10am–5pm; €3, or Chorus Pass) – one of the most attractive buildings in Europe. It was built in the 1480s to house a painting of the Madonna (still the altarpiece) that was believed to have performed a number of miracles, such as reviving a man who'd spent half an hour lying at the bottom of the Giudecca canal. The church is thought to have been designed by Pietro Lombardo. Typically for Renaissance architecture in Venice, richness of effect takes precedence over classical correctness – the Corinthian pilasters are set below the Ionic, so that the viewer can better appreciate the carving on the Corinthian.

The marble-lined interior contains some of the most intricate decorative sculpture to be seen in Venice. The half-length figures of two saints and the *Annunciation* on the balustrade of the raised galleries at the east end are attributed to Lombardo's son Tullio.

Castello

Bordering both San Marco and Cannaregio, and spreading right across the city to the housing estates of Sant'Elena in the east, Castello is the largest of the *sestieri*. In terms of its tourist appeal, centre stage is occupied by the huge **Santi Giovanni e Paolo**. Within a few minutes' walk of here are two other fascinating churches, **Santa Maria Formosa** and **San Zaccaria**, as well as the beguiling Carpaccio paintings in the Scuola di San Giorgio degli Schiavoni.

Much of the eastern section of the Castello *sestiere* is given over to the **Arsenale**, once the industrial hub of the city and now a large naval base. Beyond it lies a predominantly residential quarter that has little to offer of cultural significance, except when the Biennale art and architecture shows are on, though its open spaces – the **Giardini Garibaldi**, **Giardini Pubblici** and **Parco della Rimembranza** – offer a little green relief.

Campo Santi Giovanni e Paolo

After the Piazza, the Campo Santi Giovanni e Paolo – or, in its Venetian dialect form, San Zanipolo – is the most impressive open space in Venice. Dominated by the huge brick church from which it gets its name, it also has the most beautiful facade of any of the *scuole grande* and one of the finest Renaissance equestrian monuments.

The Colleoni statue and the Scuola Grande di San Marco

When the *condottiere* mercenary **Bartolomeo Colleoni** died, he left a handsome legacy to the republic on condition that a monument should be erected to him in the square before San Marco, an impossible proposition to Venice's rulers, with their cult of anonymity. They got around this dilemma by interpreting the will in a way that allowed them to raise the monument before the Scuola Grande di San Marco, rather than the basilica, and still claim the money. In 1481 the commission for the monument was won by **Andrea Verrocchio**, who was working on the piece when he died at the end of June 1488. **Alessandro Leopardi** was called in to finish the work and produce the plinth for it, which he gladly did – even adding his signature on the horse's girth and appending *del Cavallo* to his name.

A spectacular backdrop to Colleoni, the **Scuola Grande di San Marco** has provided a sumptuous facade and foyer for the Ospedale Civile since its suppression in the early nineteenth century. The facade was started by Pietro Lombardo and Giovanni Buora in 1487, and finished in 1495 by Mauro Codussi.

The church of Santi Giovanni e Paolo

The church of **Santi Giovanni e Paolo** (Mon–Sat 9am–6.30pm, Sun noon–6.30pm; €2.50) is the Dominican equivalent of the Frari, founded in 1246, rebuilt and enlarged from 1333, and finally consecrated in 1430. The sarcophagus of Doge Giacomo Tiepolo, who gave the site to the Dominicans, is on the left of the door outside.

Approximately 90 metres long, 38 metres wide at the transepts and 33 metres high in the centre, the **interior** is stunning for its sheer size, and is more spacious than it would have been up to 1682, when the wooden choir was demolished. The simplicity of the design, a nave with two aisles and gracefully soaring arches, is offset by the huge number of tombs and monuments around the walls. Contrary to the impression created, not all of the doges are buried here, just 25 of them.

In the **south aisle**, after the first altar, is the monument to the Venetian military commander Marcantonio Bragadin, to which is attached one of Venice's grisliest stories. In 1571 Bragadin was double-crossed by the Turks to whom he had been obliged to surrender Famagusta: tortured and humiliated for days by his captors, he was eventually skinned alive. Some years later the skin was brought back to Venice, and today it sits in that urn high up on the wall.

Giovanni Bellini's superb polyptych *St Vincent Ferrer, with Saints Christopher and Sebastian*, with an *Annunciation* and pietà above, occupies the next altar. At the far end of this aisle, before you turn into the transept, you'll see a small shrine with the **foot of St Catherine of Siena**: most of her body is in Rome, her head is in her house in Siena and other relics are scattered about Italy.

The **south transept** has a painting by Alvise Vivarini, *Christ Carrying the Cross* (1474), and Lorenzo Lotto's *St Antonine* (1542), painted in return for nothing more than his expenses and permission to be buried in the church. Sadly, Lotto was eventually driven from his home town by the jealousies and plots of other artists (including Titian), and died in a monastery at Loreto.

On the right of the chancel is the tomb of Doge Michele Morosini, selected by Ruskin as "the richest monument of the Gothic period in Venice". The tomb of Doge Andrea Vendramin, opposite, was singled out as its antithesis – only the half of the effigy's head that would be visible from below was completed by the artist, a short cut denounced by Ruskin as indicative of "an extreme of intellectual and moral degradation". Tullio Lombardo is thought to have been the culprit.

In 1867 a fire wrecked the **Cappella del Rosario**, at the end of the north transept, destroying paintings by Tintoretto, Palma il Giovane and others; of their replacements, the best are **Veronese**'s ceiling panels and *Adoration*. Funerary sculpture is the main attraction of the north aisle. To the left of the sacristy door is the monument to Doge Pasquale Malipiero by Pietro Lombardo, one of the earliest in Renaissance style in Venice.

Santa Maria Formosa and around

South of San Zanipolo lies Campo di Santa Maria Formosa, an atmospheric square with a modest but mouthwatering morning market. The church of **Santa Maria Formosa** (Mon–Sat 10am–5pm; €3, or Chorus Pass) was built by San Magno, Bishop of Oderzo, in the seventh century, who was inspired by a dream in which he saw a buxom (*formosa*) figure of the Madonna. The present building is another Codussi effort, dating from 1492. Palma il Vecchio's altarpiece *St Barbara*, the church's outstanding picture lying to the right of main altar, was admired by George Eliot as "an almost unique presentation of a hero-woman".

The Renaissance Palazzo Querini-Stampalia, just round the corner from Santa Maria Formosa, houses the **Pinacoteca Querini-Stampalia** (Tues–Sun 10am–8pm; €8). Unless you have a voracious appetite for seventeenth- and eighteenth-century Venetian painting, you'll get most pleasure from earlier pieces such as Palma il Vecchio's portraits *Francesco Querini* and *Paola Priuli Querini* and Giovanni Bellini's *The Presentation in the Temple*. Apart from that, the main interest is in the eighteenth-century decor of the rooms, especially the library. It's worth taking advantage of the unusual late opening times at the weekend, when you can often savour the atmosphere of the palace in peace or take in a classical concert (included in the price).

San Zaccaria and the Riva

The Campo San Zaccaria, a few yards off the waterfront, has a more torrid past than most – the convent here was notorious for its libidinous goings-on (officials were once sent to close down the nuns' parlour, only to be met with a barrage of bricks). The towering church of **San Zaccaria** (daily 10am–noon & 4–6pm), a pleasing mixture of Gothic and Renaissance, was started by Antonio Gambello and finished after his death in 1481 by Mauro Codussi, who was responsible for the facade from the first storey upwards. Inside is one of the city's most stunning altarpieces, a *Madonna and Four Saints* by Giovanni Bellini. A fee of €1 gets you into the rebuilt remnants of the old church, the Cappella di Sant'Atanasio and Cappella di San Tarasio, where you'll find an early Tintoretto, *The Birth of John the Baptist*, and three wonderful altarpieces by Antonio Vivarini and Giovanni d'Alemagna.

The principal waterfront of the area, the **Riva degli Schiavoni**, stretches right back to the Molo. It's a favourite walk, particularly as the sun goes down, and many notables have lived or stayed in houses and hotels here: Petrarch and his daughter lived at no. 4145 for a while, Henry James stayed nearby at no. 4161 when he was finishing *The Portrait of a Lady*, and the *Hotel Danieli*, at the far end, has accommodated George Sand, Charles Dickens, Proust, Wagner and the ever-present Ruskin.

Halfway along the Riva stands the **Pietà** church (or Santa Maria della Visitazione), famous as the place where Vivaldi was choirmaster – he was also violin teacher to the attached orphanage. Giorgio Massari won a competition to redesign the church in 1736, and it's possible that he consulted with Vivaldi on its acoustics; building didn't actually begin until 1745, and the facade was only finished in 1906. If concerts are resumed in the church, you might get a peep of the interior, which looks like a wedding cake turned inside out and has one of Venice's most ostentatious ceiling paintings, Giambattista Tiepolo's *The Glory of Paradise.*

The Greek quarter and the Scuola di San Giorgio degli Schiavoni

Stroll north along the flank of the Pietà and you'll enter the quarter of Venice's Greek community, identifiable by the alarmingly tilted campanile of **San Giorgio dei Greci**. The Greek presence was strong in Venice from the eleventh century, and grew stronger after Constantinople's capture by the Turks in 1453; by the close of the fifteenth century they had founded their own church, college and school here. The present *scuola*, designed (like the college) by Longhena in the seventeenth century, houses the **Museo Dipinti Sacri Bizantini** (daily 9am–5pm; €4). Although many of the most beautiful of the exhibited works (mainly fifteenth to eighteenth century) maintain the traditions of icon painting in terms of composition and use of symbolic figures rather than attempts at realism, it's fascinating to see how some of the artists absorbed Western influences. The **church** contains icons dating back to the twelfth century and a lot of work by Michael Danaskinàs, a sixteenth-century Cretan artist.

From here it's a hundred metres or so to the **Scuola di San Giorgio degli Schiavoni**, whose ground-floor hall (Mon 2.45–6pm, Tues–Sat 9.15am–1pm & 2.45–6pm, Sun 9.15am–1pm; €4) would get onto anyone's list of the ten most beautiful rooms in Europe. Venice's resident Slavs (*Schiavoni*), most of whom were traders, set up a *scuola* to look after their interests in 1451; the present building dates from the early sixteenth century, and the whole interior looks more or less as it would have then. Entering it, you step straight from the street into the superb lower hall, the walls of which are decorated with a cycle of pictures created by Vittore Carpaccio between 1502 and 1509. Outstanding among them is *The Vision of St Augustine*, depicting the moment that Augustine, while writing to St Jerome, was told in a vision of Jerome's death.

The Arsenale and Museo Storico Navale

The dockyards and factories of the **Arsenale** were the foundations on which Venice's mercantile and military supremacy rested. A corruption of the Arabic *darsin'a* (house of industry), its very name is indicative of the strength of the city's trading links with the eastern Mediterranean. Construction of the Arsenale began in the early years of the twelfth century, and by the third decade of the fifteenth century it had become the base for some 300 shipping companies, operating around 3000 vessels in excess of 200 tons.

Expansion of the Arsenale continued into the sixteenth century – Sanmicheli's covered dock for the state barge (the *Bucintoro*) was built in the 1540s, for example, and da Ponte's gigantic rope-factory (the Tana) in 1579. By then, though, the maritime strength of Venice was past its peak; militarily, too, despite the conspicuous success at Lépanto in 1571, Venice was on the wane. When

Napoleon took over the city in 1797 he burned down the wharves, sank the last *Bucintoro* and confiscated the remnant of the Venetian navy.

There's no public access to the Arsenale complex except during the Biennale, but you can get a look at part of it from the bridge connecting the Campo Arsenale and the Fondamenta dell'Arsenale. The main **gateway**, built by Antonio Gambello in 1460, was the first structure in Venice to employ the classical vocabulary of Renaissance architecture. The four **lions** to the side of the gateway must be the most photographed in the city: the two on the right were probably taken from Delos (at an unknown date); the larger pair were brought back from Piraeus in 1687 by Francesco Morosini after the reconquest of the Morea.

Nearby, on the other side of the Rio dell'Arsenale and facing the lagoon, is the **Museo Storico Navale** (Mon–Fri 8.45am–1.30pm, Sat 8.45am–1pm; €1.60). Chiefly of interest for its models of Venetian craft from the gondola to the *Bucintoro* (these models were the equivalents of blueprints), the museum gives a comprehensive picture of the working life of the Arsenale and the smaller boatyards of Venice.

San Pietro di Castello

In 1808 the greater part of the canal connecting the Bacino di San Marco to the broad inlet of the Canale di San Pietro was filled in to form what is now **Via Garibaldi**, the widest street in the city and the busiest commercial area in the eastern district. Head along the right-hand side of the street and you'll soon cross the Ponte di Quintavalle onto the island of **San Pietro**, once the ecclesiastical centre of Venice, but nowadays a slightly down-at-heel place where the chief activity is the repairing of boats. The church (Mon–Sat 10am–5pm; €3, or Chorus Pass) is basically a grandiose derivative of a plan by Palladio and has little to recommend it.

Sant'Elena

Located at the eastern limit of the city, the island of **Sant'Elena** was enlarged tenfold during the Austrian administration, partly to form exercise grounds for the troops. Much of the island used to be covered by the meadow of Sant'Elena, a favourite recreation area in the nineteenth century but since usurped by houses, leaving only a strip of park along the waterfront. Still, the walk out here is the nearest you'll get to country pleasures in Venice, and the **church of Sant'Elena** – next to the city's football stadium – is worth a visit. The spartan Gothic interior has recently been restored, as have the cloister and campanile, but the main attraction is the doorway to the church, an ensemble created in the 1470s by Antonio Rizzo. The sculptural group in the lunette – a monument to Comandante Vittore Cappello, showing him kneeling before St Helena – is the district's one major work of art.

The northern islands

The islands lying to the north of Venice – **San Michele**, **Murano**, **Burano** and **Torcello** – are the places to visit when the throng of tourists in the main part of the city becomes too oppressive, and are the source of much of the glass and lace work you see in many shops in the city.

To get to the northern islands, the main *vaporetto* stop is **Fondamente Nove** (or Nuove), as most of the island services start here or call here. For San Michele and Murano only the circular #41 and #42 vaporetti both run every twenty minutes, circling Murano before heading back towards Venice. Murano can also be reached by the #DM ("Diretto Murano"). For Murano, Burano and Torcello the #LN (Laguna Nord) leaves from Fondamente Nove (see p.282 for further details on all these routes).

San Michele

The high brick wall around the cemetery island of San Michele gives way by the landing stage to the elegant white facade of **San Michele in Isola** (daily 7.30am–12.15pm & 3–4pm), designed by Mauro Codussi in 1469. With this building, Codussi not only helped introduce Renaissance architecture to Venice, but also promoted the use of Istrian stone. Easy to carve yet resistant to water, it had been used as damp-proofing at ground level, but never before for a complete facade; it was to be used on the facades of most major buildings in Venice from the Renaissance onwards.

The main part of the island, through the cloisters, is the city **cemetery** (daily: April–Sept 7.30am–6pm; Oct–March 7.30am–4pm), established by Napoleonic decree and nowadays maintained by the Franciscans, as is the church. The majority of Venetians lie here for just ten years or so, when their bones are dug up and removed to an ossuary and the land recycled. Only those who can afford it stay longer. The cemetery is laid out in sections, the most dilapidated of which is for the Protestants (no. XV), **Ezra Pound**'s final resting place. In section XIV are the Greek and Russian Orthodox graves, including the restrained memorial stones of **Igor and Vera Stravinsky** and the more elaborate tomb of **Serge Diaghilev** – always strewn with flowers.

Even with the grave-rotation system, the island is reaching full capacity, so in 1998 a competition was held for the **redevelopment** of San Michele. The winning entry, from English architect David Chipperfield, places a sequence of formal courtyards alongside a new funerary chapel and crematorium. It promises to be an austerely beautiful place, resembling a cross between a necropolis and a philosopher's retreat.

Murano

Chiefly famed now as the home of Venice's **glass industry**, **Murano**'s main *fondamente* (canal-side streets) are full of shops catering for the tourist demand for tacky products. However, you can also find some excellent glass in bold contemporary designs – while the island itself is a pleasant small-scale version of Venice without the same press of crowds.

The glass furnaces were moved to here from Venice as a safety measure in 1291, and so jealously did the Muranese guard their industrial secrets that for a long while they had the European monopoly on glass mirror-making. The glass-blowers of Murano were accorded various privileges not allowed to other artisans, such as being able to wear swords. From 1376 the offspring of a marriage between a Venetian nobleman and the daughter of a glass-worker were allowed to be entered into the *Libro d'Oro*, unlike the children of other cross-class matches. There are numerous **furnaces** to visit, all free of charge on the assumption that you will then want to buy something. Many of the workshops are to be found along Fondamenta dei Vertrai, traditionally a glass-working centre, as the name suggests.

When the Venetian Republic fell to Napoleon in 1797, there were seventeen churches on Murano; today only two are open. The first is **San Pietro Martire** (daily 9am–noon & 3–6pm), a Dominican Gothic church begun in 1363 and largely rebuilt after a fire in 1474. Its main attraction is a pair of paintings by Giovanni Bellini hanging on the right wall: on the left is the large and elegant *Madonna and Child with Saints Mark and Augustine, and Doge Barbarigo*, and on the right an *Assumption*.

The Museo del Vetro (glass museum)

Close by, along Riva Longa, you'll find the **Museo del Vetro** (April–Oct 10am–6pm; Nov–March 10am–5pm; closed Wed; €5.50 or Museum/Venice card). Perhaps the finest single item is the dark-blue Barovier marriage cup, dating from around 1470; it's on show in room 1 on the first floor, along with some splendid Renaissance enamelled and painted glass. But every room contains some amazing creations: glass beakers that look as if they are made from veined stone; sixteenth-century platters that look like discs of crackled ice; stupendously ugly nineteenth-century decorative pieces, with fat little birds enmeshed in trellises of glass. A separate room contains a fascinating exhibition on the history of Murano glass techniques. Each room has panels in English on the history of Venetian glassmaking.

Santi Maria e Donato

Murano's finest building is the Veneto-Byzantine church of **Santi Maria e Donato**, which was founded in the seventh century and rebuilt in the twelfth (daily 7am–8pm except Jan–Feb 8am–noon, 4–5pm). Its beautiful **mosaic floor**, dated 1141 in the nave, mingles abstract patterns with images of beasts and birds – an eagle carries off a deer; two roosters carry off a fox slung from a pole. The church was originally dedicated to Mary, but in 1125 was rededicated when the relics of St Donato were brought here from the Greek Island, Kefalonia. Four splendid bones from an unfortunate dragon that was slain by the holy spit of Donato are now hanging behind the altar. Above these, in the apse, is a twelfth-century **mosaic of the Madonna** and fifteenth-century frescoes of the Evangelists.

Burano

The main route into **Burano** is a narrow street full of lace shops which soon opens out to reveal the brightly painted houses of the village itself; the colours used to be symbolic, but the meanings have become muddled over time.

This is still largely a fishing community, the lagoon's main yield being shellfish of various kinds, such as *vongole* (tiny clams) and small crabs. (The catch can be bought either here, on the Fondamenta Pescheria, or at the Rialto.) The lives of the women of Burano used to be dominated by the **lace** industry, but the production of handmade lace is no longer a large-scale enterprise, and much of the stuff sold in the shops lining the narrow street leading from the *vaporetto* stop is produced by machine.

The true skills of lacemaking are still taught at Burano's **Scuola del Merletto** (April–Oct 10am–5pm; Nov–March 10am–4pm; closed Tues; €5.50, or Museum Pass/Venice Card), on Piazza Baldassare Galuppi. Although the *scuola* has not operated as a full-time school since the late 1960s and is almost moribund, a few courses are still held here, and on weekdays you might see a few local women at work on their cylindrical cushions. Pieces produced here are displayed in the attached museum, along with specimens dating back to the sixteenth century; after even a quick tour you'll have no problems distinguishing the real thing from the machine-made and imported lace that fills the Burano shops.

Torcello

Torcello was settled as early as the fifth century, became the seat of the Bishop of Altinum from 638, and the home of about 20,000 people by the fourteenth century, before being eclipsed by Venice – by the end of the fifteenth century Torcello was largely deserted and only about thirty people remain in residence. The main reason people come here today is to visit Venice's first cathedral, **Santa Maria dell'Assunta** (daily: March–Oct 10.30am–6pm; Nov–Feb 10am–5pm; €4, joint ticket with campanile or museum €7.50, or with museum and campanile €10). An early church on the site became a cathedral after the Bishop of Altinum arrived with other emigrants from the mainland. The present Veneto-Byzantine building is on pretty much the same plan as the seventh-century one, but it was largely rebuilt in the 860s and altered again in 1008.

A stunning twelfth-century **mosaic** of the Madonna and Child, on a pure gold background, covers the semi-dome of the apse, resting on an eleventh-century mosaic frieze of the Apostles. In the centre of the frieze, below the window, is St Heliodorus, the first Bishop of Altinum, whose remains were brought here by the first settlers. It's interesting to compare this image with the gold-plated face mask given to his remains in a Roman sarcophagus in front of the original seventh-century altar. Ruskin described the view from the **campanile** as "one of the most notable scenes in this wide world", a verdict you can test for yourself as the campanile has been reopened after thirty years' service as a pigeon-loft (daily: March–Oct 10.30am–5.30pm; Nov–Feb 10am–4.30pm; €4).

The church of **Santa Fosca** (same hours as Santa Maria; free) was built in the eleventh and twelfth centuries to house the body of the eponymous saint, brought to Torcello from Libya some time before 1011 and now resting under the altar. In the square outside sits the curious **chair of Attila**. Local legend has it that if you sit in it you will be wed within a year. Behind it, in two buildings round the square, is the **Museo di Torcello** (Tues–Sun: March–Oct 10.30am–5.30pm; Nov–Feb 10am–5pm; €3), which includes nicely displayed thirteenth-century beaten gold figures, sections of mosaic heads, and jewellery.

The southern islands

The section of the lagoon to the south of the city, enclosed by the long islands of the **Lido** and **Pellestrina**, has far fewer outcrops of solid land than the northern half: once you get past **Giudecca** and **San Giorgio Maggiore** – in effect detached pieces of central Venice, served by water buses #2, and #2 plus #41 and #42 respectively – and clear of the smaller islands that dot the water off the middle section of the Lido, you could, on certain days, look in the direction of the mainland and think you were out in the open sea. The nearer islands are the more interesting: the farther-flung settlements of the southern lagoon have played a significant a role in the history of Venice but nowadays they have little going for them other than the pleasure of the trip.

San Giorgio Maggiore

The islet of **San Giorgio Maggiore** is dominated by Palladio's church of the same name (daily: May–Sept 9.30am–12.30pm & 2–5.30pm; Oct–April 9.30am–12.30pm & 2.30–5pm). Ruskin didn't much care for it: "It is impossible to conceive a design more gross, more barbarous, more childish in conception, more servile in plagiarism, more insipid in result, more contemptible under every point of rational regard." He was more taken by Tintoretto's paintings inside. Two hang in the chancel: *The Fall of Manna* and *The Last Supper*, perhaps the most famous of all his images. They were painted as a pair in 1592–94, the last years of the artist's life; another Tintoretto of the same date – a *Deposition* – hangs in the Cappella dei Morti, approached through the door on the right of the choir. On the left of the choir a corridor leads to the lift up the **campanile** (€3). Rebuilt in 1791 after the collapse of its predecessor, it's the best vantage point in the city, with the whole of Venice spread out before you.

The ex-Benedictine monastery next door to the church, now the base of the combined arts research institute, craft school and naval college known as the **Fondazione Giorgio Cini** (W www.cini.it), is one of the architectural gems of Venice, and a regular venue for exhibitions (the only time when the Fondazione is open to the public).

La Giudecca

In the earliest records of Venice, the island of **La Giudecca** was known as Spina Longa, a name clearly derived from its shape; the modern name might refer to the Jews (*Giudei*) who were based here from the late thirteenth century until their removal to the Ghetto, or to the disruptive noble families who, from the ninth century, were shoved onto this chain of islets to keep them out of mischief (*giudicati* meaning "judged"). Before the banks of the Brenta became prestigious, the Giudecca was where the wealthiest aristocrats of early Renaissance Venice built their villas, and in places you can still see traces of their gardens. Wealth is still present in the flash marinas on the southern shore and in the luxury *Cipriani* and *Hilton* hotels at either end of the island, the latter in the Mulino Stucky – the former flour mill. In between are workshops, boatyards and housing estates where everyday life goes on away from the tourist trail.

The Franciscan church of the **Redentore** (Mon–Sat 10am–5pm; €3, or Chorus Pass), designed by Palladio in 1577, is Giudecca's main monument. In 1575–76 Venice suffered an outbreak of bubonic plague that killed nearly 50,000 people – virtually a third of the city's population. The Redentore was built in thanks for Venice's deliverance, and every year the doge and his senators attended a Mass in the church on the Feast of the Redentore. The procession walked to the church over a pontoon bridge from the Záttere, a ceremony perpetuated by the people of Venice on the third Sunday in July.

The bright plasterwork of the interior manipulates the different intensities of light in the various parts of the church to draw the eye – and the mind – inward and upward. As the architect wrote, "Among all colours, none can be more suitable for temples than white because the purity of the colour is more acceptable to God." The best paintings in the church, including a *Madonna with Child and Angels* by Alvise Vivarini, are in the sacristy, which is rarely opened.

San Lazzaro degli Armeni

No foreign community has a longer pedigree in Venice than the Armenians: they were established by the end of the thirteenth century, and for around five hundred years have had a church within a few yards of the Piazza (in Calle degli Armeni). They are far less numerous now, and the most conspicuous sign of their presence is the Armenian island by the Lido, **San Lazzaro degli Armeni**, identifiable from the city by the onion-shaped top of its campanile. The Roman Catholic Armenian monastery here was founded in 1717 by Manug di Pietro (known as Mechitar, "The Consoler"), and derived its name from the island's past function as a leper colony – Lazarus being the patron saint of lepers. Visitors are received here daily from 3.25pm to 5.25pm, admission is €6 and the connecting #20 *motoscafo* leaves San Zaccaria at 3.10pm (2.45pm in summer), returning within ten minutes of the end of the guided tour.

The Lido

For about eight centuries, the **Lido** was the focus of the annual hullaballoo of Venice's "Marriage to the Sea", when the doge went out to the Porto di Lido to drop a gold ring into the brine and then disembarked for Mass at San Nicolò al Lido. It was then an unspoilt strip of land, and remained so into the nineteenth century. By the twentieth century, however, it had become the smartest bathing resort in Italy, and although it's no longer as chic as it was when Thomas Mann set *Death in Venice* here, there's less room on its beaches now than ever before. Unless you're staying at one of the flashy hotels that stand shoulder to shoulder along the seafront, or are prepared to pay a ludicrous fee to rent one of their beach huts for the day, you won't be welcomed on the prime stretch of Lido sand. The ungroomed public beaches are at the northern and southern ends of the island – though why people would want to jeopardize their health in these filthy waters is a mystery.

Eating and drinking

Not long ago the reliable judges of the Accademia della Cucina ventured that it was "a rare privilege" to eat well in Venice, and there's more than an element of truth to Venice's reputation as a place where mass tourism has produced monotonous menus, cynical service and slapdash standards in the kitchen. Venice has fewer good moderately priced **restaurants** than any other major Italian city, but things have been improving in recent years, due in part to the efforts of the Ristorante della Buona Accoglienza, an association of restaurateurs determined to present the best of genuine Venetian cuisine at sensible prices – which in the Venetian context means in the region of €35 per person.

A distinctive aspect of the Venetian social scene is the **bácaro**, which in its purest form is a bar that offers a range of snacks called **cicheti** (some times spelled *cicchetti*); the array will typically include *polpette* (small beef and garlic meatballs), *carciofini* (artichoke hearts), eggs, anchovies, *polipi* (baby octopus or squid) and tomatoes, peppers and courgettes cooked in oil. Some *bácari* also produce one or two more substantial dishes each day, such as risotto or seafood pasta. Excellent food is also served at many of Venice's **osterie** (or *ostarie*), the simplest of which are indistinguishable from *bácari*, while others have sizeable dining areas. We've classified our bars and restaurants according to which aspect of the business draws most of the customers, but if you're looking for a simple meal in a particular area of the city, be sure to check both listings.

Cafés, pasticcerie and ice cream

As in every Italian city, Venice's **cafés** are central to its social life, and you'll never be more than a couple of minutes from a decent one. In addition to their marvellous local confections, many **pasticcerie** also serve coffee, but will have at most a few bar stools. Strict budgeting is further jeopardized by Venice's terrific **gelaterie**.

▲ Musicians at the Caffè Florian

San Marco

Caffè Florian Piazza S. Marco 56–59. Opened in 1720 and decorated in a passable pastiche of that period, this has long been the café to be seen in. A simple cappuccino at a table will set you back around €8.50 and you'll have to take out a mortgage for a cocktail; if the "orchestra" is playing, you'll be taxed another €6 for the privilege. Daily 10am–midnight, closed Wed in winter.
Igloo Calle della Mandola 3651. Luscious home-made ice cream. 11am–8pm daily, closed Dec to mid-Feb; rest of year open daily.
Marchini Calle Spadaria 676. The most delicious and most expensive of Venetian *pasticcerie*, where people come on Sun morning to buy family treats. The cakes are fabulous, as is the *Marchini* chocolate. Daily 9am–8pm.

Dorsoduro

Il Caffè Campo S. Margherita 2963. Known as *Caffè Rosso* for its big red sign, this small, atmos-pheric, old-fashioned café-bar is a student favourite. Good sandwiches, and lots of seats outside in the *campo*. Mon–Sat 8am–2am.
Nico Záttere ai Gesuati 922. A high-point of a wander in the area, celebrated for an artery-clogging creation called a *gianduiotto* – ask for one *da passeggio* (to take out) and you'll be given a paper cup with a block of praline ice cream drowned in whipped cream. Closed Thurs.

San Polo and Santa Croce

Alaska Calle Larga dei Bari 1159. Friendly *gelateria*, dishing out adventurous flavours such as artichoke and fennel amid the more traditional concoctions. Open daily till 9pm or later in warm weather.
Caffè del Doge Calle dei Cinque 609. Fantastically good coffee (they supply many of the city's bars and restaurants), served in a chic minimalist set-up very close to the Rialto Bridge. Mon–Sat 7am–7pm, Sun 7am–1pm.

Cannaregio

Il Gelatone Rio Terà Maddalena 2063. The best ice creams in Cannaregio. Closed mid-Dec to mid-Jan; rest of year open daily except Wed, 11am–10pm.

Castello

La Boutique del Gelato Salizzada S. Lio 5727. Top-grade ice creams at this small outlet. Closed Jan–Dec; rest of year open daily till 11pm (8pm on Mon).
Rosa Salva Campo Santi Giovanni e Paolo 6779. With its marble-topped bar and outside tables facing Zanipolo, this is the best of the three *Rosa Salva* branches in the city. The coffee is superb. 8am–8pm, closed Wed.

Restaurants

Virtually every budget restaurant in Venice advertises a set-price **menù turistico**, which can be a cheap way of sampling Venetian specialities, but the quality and certainly the quantity won't be up to the mark of an **à la carte** meal. Value for money tends to increase with the distance from San Marco; plenty of restaurants within a short radius of the Piazza offer menus that seem to be reasonable, but you'll probably find the food unappetizing and the portions tiny. There are two notable concentrations of good-value restaurants: around San Barnaba in Dorsoduro, with several recommended places on Calle Lunga San Barnaba; and the area between the Cannaregio canal and Sant'Alvise, with the Ghetto at its centre.

We've supplied the day of the week on which each restaurant is closed (in the vast majority of cases this day is Sun or Mon), but bear in mind that many restaurateurs take their annual holiday in August, and that quite a few places close down on unscheduled days in the dead weeks of winter. In most cases, booking a table is advisable in high season, and you should also be aware that Venetians tend to eat early and that restaurateurs routinely close early if trade is slack, so if you're in town at a quiet time, don't turn up later than 8.30pm, unless you're dining at one of the city's more expensive restaurants, which tend to keep longer hours.

San Marco

Al Bacareto Calle Crosera San Samuele 3447 ☎041.528.9336. This place has been recommendable for many years, but recently has been getting smarter and more expensive. Dishes such as the excellent risottos can be eaten in the dining room or standing at the bar area (the cheaper option). You can sit outside in summer. Closed Sat evening and all day Sun.

Da Carla Sottoportego Corte Contarina 1535/A ☎041.523.7855. Tiny bar-trattoria hidden down a *sottoportego* off the west side of Frezzeria, a few paces from the Piazza. The battered old sign is misleading, as the place has undergone a makeover, but it's still packed at lunchtime with workers dropping in for sandwiches, simple pastas and salads. One of the best places for a quick bite close to the Piazza. Closed Sun.

Da Fiore Calle delle Botteghe 3461 ☎041.523.5310. Established in the mid-1990s, this popular restaurant offers genuine Venetian cuisine in a classy trattoria-style setting. The anteroom is a small bar that does very good *cicheti*. Closed Tues.

Harry's Bar Calle Vallaresso 1323 ☎041.528.5777. Often described as the most reliable of the city's gourmet restaurants (*carpaccio* – raw strips of thin beef – was first created here), though there are many who think the place's reputation has more to do with glamour. The bar itself has been fashionable since time immemorial, and is famed in equal measure for its cocktails, its sandwiches and its prices.

Osteria-Enoteca San Marco Frezzeria 1610 ☎041.528.5242. This classy modern *osteria* close to the Piazza is not cheap, but prices are not madly unreasonable for the quality of the food – and the wine list is very good. Closed Sun.

Rosticceria Gislon Calle della Bissa 5424/A. Close to the Rialto Bridge, this is a sort of glorified snack bar on the ground floor, serving pizzas and set meals from about €10 – the trick is to first grab a place at the tables along the windows, then order from the counter. Good if you need to refuel quickly and cheaply, but can't face another pizza. In the restaurant upstairs prices are considerably higher for no great increase in quality. Daily 9am–9.30pm.

Dorsoduro

Ae Oche Záttere al Ponte Lungo 1414 ☎041.520.6601. Big pizzeria with a big dining room and waterfront tables too; it does a few other basic dishes, but the huge repertoire of pizzas is what people come for. Open daily noon–3pm & 7pm–midnight.

Ai Quattro Ferri Calle Lunga S. Barnaba 2754/A ☎041.520.6978. Popular and very highly recommended *osteria* just off Campo S. Barnaba with a menu that changes daily but often consists entirely of fish and seafood, all moderately priced. Closed Sun. No credit cards. Booking essential in high season..

Casin dei Nobili Calle Lombardo 2765 ☎041.241.1841. Popular with both locals and tourists, this place serves excellent pizzas (from 7pm) plus a varied menu that includes local specialities such as eel – it is worth asking for the daily specials. *Casin* or *casino* means brothel, as you'll gather from the place mats – not to be confused with *casinò*, which means casino. Closed Mon.

Do Farai Calle Cappeller 3278 ☎041.277.0369. Tucked into an alley close to Ca' Rezzonico, this is a fine *osteria*, serving good steaks and excellent seafood and fish – the speciality is the *carpaccio* of sea bass. In summer it spreads out into the neighbouring *campo*. Closed Sun.

L'Avogaria Calle dell'Avogaria 1629 ☎041.296.0491. The ultra-refined and pricey *Avogaria* calls itself a lounge, restaurant, café and style shop, which gives you an idea of its self-image. The *orrechiette* (thick little pasta "ears") on the menu is a clue to the Puglian origins of the proprietors – this must be the only restaurant in town that marinades its prawns in grappa. Closed Tues.

🏃 **La Bitta** Calle Lunga S. Barnaba 2753/A ☎041.523.0531. Innovative fare on a menu that's remarkable for featuring no fish dishes. Debora, who serves and cajoles the guests, offers expert guidance on the impressive wine and grappa list. Delicious cheese platter, served with honey and fruit chutney. Tiny dining room (and garden), so booking is essential. Closed Sun. No credit cards.

San Polo and Santa Croce

Alla Madonna Calle della Madonna 594 ☎041.5522.3824. Roomy, loud and brightly lit seafood restaurant that's been going strong for four decades. Initial impressions are misleading – at first you might feel like tourists on the Venice conveyor belt but the service is friendly and attentive, and the menu offers well-executed Venetian staples. Closed Wed.

Al Nono Risorto Sottoportego de Siora Bettina 2338 ☎041.524.1169. Located just off Campo S. Cassiano, the "Resurrected Grandad" is a pizzeria-restaurant with a predominantly 20-something following. It often has live jazz and blues, and a pleasant small garden is a further attraction. Open noon–2pm & 7pm–midnight; closed Wed and Thurs lunch. No credit cards.

🏃 **Da Fiore** Calle del Scaleter 2202/A ☎041.721.308 🌐www.dafiore.net. Refined, elegant and super-expensive restaurant near Campo San Polo; prides itself on its seafood, regional cheeses, desserts and wine list. Among the very best in Venice, and service is faultless. You can also drop into the tiny front room bar for a quality snack. Offers a €50 lunch menu. Closed Sun & Mon.

Il Refolo Campiello del Piovan 1459 ☎041.524.0016. Run by the son of the owner of the *Da Fiore*, this canalside pizzeria fills up the tiny square that fronts the church of San Giacomo dell'Orio – its bells toll loudly over the diners' heads. The pizzas are perhaps the best in Venice and are reasonably priced (€7–12). There's also a small menu of (more expensive) restaurant dishes, featuring some terrific salads. Closed Dec–Jan; rest of year closed all Mon and Tues lunch.

Osteria al Ponte, "La Patatina" Calle dei Saoneri 2741/A ☎041.523.7238. This bustling *osteria* serves excellent *cicheti* and other Venetian specialities, alongside full-meal menus that change regularly. Open till 10pm.

Cannaregio

Ai 40 Ladroni Fondamenta della Sensa 3253 ☎041.715.736. Very busy *osteria* with high-quality *cicheti* at the bar and similarly good Venetian standards served at the tables inside and by the canal. Closed Mon.

🏃 **Alla Fontana** Fondamenta Cannaregio 1102 ☎041.715.077. Once primarily a bar, *Alla Fontana* has tranformed itself into a very good *trattoria*, offering a small menu of classic Venetian maritime dishes; tables beside the canal are an added attraction in summer. Mon–Sat 6.30–11pm, closes 10pm in winter.

Alla Vedova Calle del Pistor 3912 ☎041.528.5324. Located in an alley directly opposite the one leading to the Ca' d'Oro, this long-established little restaurant is fronted by a bar offering a great selection of *cicheti* (the *polpette* are famous) and a good range of wines. Strangely, *Alla Vedova* does not serve coffee, and the only *dolci* is sweet wine with biscuits. Closed all Thurs & Sun lunch. No credit cards.

🏃 **Anice Stellato** Fondamenta della Sensa 3272 ☎041.720.744. Hugely popular with Venetians for the superb, reasonably priced meals and unfussy atmosphere. Situated by one of the northernmost Cannaregio canals, it's rather too remote for most tourists. If you can't get a table – it's frequently booked solid – at least drop by for the excellent *cicheti* at the bar. Closed Mon & Tues (occasionally closed Wed).

Da Rioba Fondamenta della Misericordia 2553 ☎041.524.4379. This smartly austere *osteria* is often full to bursting, especially in summer, when tables are set beside the canal, but the management always keeps the atmosphere relaxed. Closed Mon.

Vini da Gigio Fondamenta S. Felice 3628/A ☎041.528.5140. Until a few years ago most customers at this family-run wine bar-trattoria were locals; it's now on the tourist map yet it retains its authenticity and is still, by Venetian standards, excellent value, even if prices have crept up. As the name suggests, the wine list is remarkable. Open till 10.30pm. Closed Mon and Tues.

Castello

Bandierette Barbaria delle Tole 6671 ☏041.522.0619. Nice seafood dishes served by nice people at nice prices – around €30 a head. It has a loyal local following, so it's best to book your table. Open till 10pm. Closed Mon eve & all Tues.

🏃 **Corte Sconta** Calle del Pestrin 3886 ☏041.522.7024. Secreted in a lane to the east of San Giovanni in Brágora, this is a candidate for the title of Venice's finest restaurant. The exceptionally pleasant staff make it difficult to resist ordering the day's specials, which could easily result in a bill of about €70 each. If expenditure is an issue, check the menu in the window before going in (often the waiters will simply recite what's on offer). It is fish only here, and they make their own pasta. Booking several days in advance essential for most of the year. Open till 9.45pm. Closed Sun & Mon.

Da Remigio Salizzada dei Greci 3416 ☏041.523.0089. Upmarket trattoria serving excellent fish dishes and home-made *gnocchi*. Be sure to book – the locals (and increasing numbers

of tourists) pack this place every night. Closed Mon eve & all Tues.

Dai Tosi Calle Secco Marina 738 ☏041.523.7102. Not to be confused with the establishment of the same name in the same street, this lively pizzeria-trattoria has a devoted local clientele – you'd be well advised to book at the weekend. There's a bar in front of the small dining room, where they mix the house aperitif, *sgropino*: vodka, peach juice, Aperol and prosecco. Closed Wed, and the kitchen often also closes Mon, Tues and/or Thurs in winter.

Burano

Al Gatto Nero Fondamenta Giudecca 88 Burano ☏041.730.120. Outstanding local trattoria, just a few minutes' walk from the busy Via Galuppi, opposite the Pescheria. Max, the owner, is a keen fisherman, and what he doesn't know about the marine delicacies of Venice isn't worth knowing. Closed Mon.

La Giudecca

🏃 **Mistrà** Giudecca 212/A ☏041.522.0743. Occupying the light-filled upper storey of a former factory right in the thick of the Giudecca boatyards, *Mistrà* caters mostly to local dockyard workers at lunchtime, when the menu is very brief, very plain and very cheap. In the evenings you'll find a more refined offering of Venetian fish and seafood, at higher but still extremely reasonable prices. Closed Mon eve & all Tues.

Bars

One of the most appealing aspects of Venetian social life is encapsulated in the phrase "*andemo a ombra*", which translates literally as an invitation to go into the shade, but is in fact an invitation for a drink – more specifically, a small glass of wine (an *ombra*), customarily downed in one. (The phrase is a vestige of the time when wines were unloaded on the Riva degli Schiavoni and then sold at a shaded kiosk at the base of the Campanile; the kiosk was shifted as the sun moved round, so as to stay in the shade.) Most bars serve some kind of **food**, their counters usually bearing trays of the characteristically Venetian fat little crustless sandwiches called *tramezzini*, which are stuffed with fillings such as eggs and mushrooms, eggs and anchovies, or Parma ham and artichokes. Many bars will have a selection of *cicheti* as well, and even two or three more substantial dishes.

Quite a few of the **bars** stay open until 2am, and squares such as Campo San Giacometto, at the San Polo end of the Rialto Bridge, and Campo San Margherita, in Dorsoduro, are heaving in the evening as punters spill out of the bars that ring them. However, Venice after dark is pretty tame, and locals tend to head to Mestre and Lido di Jesolo for clubbing.

San Marco

Al Volto Calle Cavalli 4081. This dark little bar behind San Luca church is an *enoteca* in the true

sense of the word – 600 wines from Italy and elsewhere, some cheap, many not; good snacks, too. Open till 11pm. Closed Sun.

Bácaro Jazz Salizzada Fondaco dei Tedeschi 5546. A jazz-themed bar-restaurant that's proving a big hit with Venetian kids, mainly on account of its late hours; there's food, but it's far from the best quality. Open 1pm–2am. Closed Wed.

Bar Torino Campo San Luca 4591. Lively and loud bar with live jazz on Fri and DJ sessions on Sat. Good for sandwiches and more substantial food at lunchtime. Tues–Sat 7pm–2am.

Centrale Restaurant Lounge Piscina Frezzeria 1659/B, ☎041.296.0664. The spacious *Centrale* touts itself as the best-designed and coolest bar-restaurant in town, and few would argue with this. The food is very expensive, but you might be tempted to blow a few euros for the pleasure of sinking into one of the sumptuous leather sofas, cocktail in hand, and chilling out to the music. Open 6.30pm–2am; closed Tues.

Vino Vino Ponte delle Veste 2007. Very close to the Fenice opera house, this bar stocks more than 350 wines. It also serves relatively inexpensive meals as well, and the quality has improved markedly. Daily 11.30am–11.30pm.

Dorsoduro

El Chioschetto Záttere al Ponte Lungo 1406/A. As its name suggests, this is just a canalside kiosk with outdoor tables, but an excellent place to sit with your *spritz* and a sandwich and watch the sun set over Giudecca. Has DJs or live music on Wed and Sun in summer, 7–9pm. Open from 8am till 2am in summer, until 5pm in winter. Open daily – unless the weather's bad, in which case it might not open at all.

Café Blue Calle dei Preti 3778. Lively student haunt strong on whiskies and good cocktails. Puts on photo exhibitions and hosts local jazz bands on many Fri nights. It's quieter in summer when the students are not around. Has sports on TV and free internet access. Mon–Fri 9am–2am, Sat & Sun 5pm–2am.

Café Noir Crosera San Pantalon 3805. This is another favourite student bar, with a cosmopolitan all-day crowd chatting over a *spritz* or coffee. Open Mon–Sat 7am–2am, Sun 9am–2am.

🏃 **Cantina del Vino già Schiavi** Fondamenta Nani 992. Great bar and wine shop opposite San Trovaso – do some sampling before you buy. Excellent *cicheti* and the generously filled panini too. Mon–Sat 8am–2.15pm, 3.30–8.30pm, Sun 8am–1.30pm.

Margaret DuChamp Campo S. Margherita 3019. Until *Orange* opened for business opposite, *DuChamp* was undisputedly the first-choice bar for the style-conscious, and even now it has kept its edge. Wi-fi access – €3 for 30min. Open 8am–2am. Closed Tues.

San Polo and Santa Croce

Altrove Campo San Silvestro 1105. A very slick young bar, with tables in the quiet square outside, and a decent kitchen. Mon–Sat 8.30am–12.30am.

🏃 **Bancogiro** Sottoportego del Banco Giro 122. Popular small *osteria*, in the midst of the Rialto market – it has now been joined by several other bars in the block. Come here to nurse a glass of fine wine with some fine snacks beside the Canal Grande, or for a quite pricey but well-prepared meal. Tues–Sun 9am–midnight.

🏃 **Do Mori** Calle Do Mori 429. Hidden just off Ruga Vecchia S. Giovanni, this is the most authentic old-style Venetian bar in the market area – some would say in the entire city. It's a single narrow room, with no seating, packed every evening with home-bound shopworkers, Rialto porters, and locals just out for a stroll. Delicious snacks, great range of wines and terrific atmosphere. Mon–Sat 8.30am–8pm.

Cannaregio

Al Ponte Calle Larga G. Gallina 6378. Brilliant *osteria* between the Miracoli and Santi Giovanni e Paolo: one of the best in the area for a glass of wine and a light meal or snack. Open till 8.30pm. Closed Sun.

Cantina Vecia Carbonera Rio Terrà della Maddalena 2329. Old-style *bácaro* atmosphere and a chilled-out playlist attracts a young, stylish clientele. Good wine and snacks, but now mainly table service. Open daily till 10pm.

Paradiso Perduto Fondamenta della Misericordia 2540. Lashings of simple – but not cheap – Venetian food are served at the refectory-like tables here, but essentially this is Venice's leading boho bar, run by the indefatigable trumpet-playing Maurizio. Live ethno jazz on Sun 9pm. 11am–2am. Closed Mon and Tues.

Castello

Al Portego Calle Malvasia 6015. In the middle of the day this *osteria* is crammed with customers eating *cicheti*, and in the evening there's often a queue for a place at one of the tiny tables, where some well-prepared basics (pasta, risotto) are served. No reservations are taken. Mon–Sat 10am–3pm, 6–10pm Sun 10am–3pm.

Enoteca Mascareta Calle Lunga Santa Maria Formosa 5183. Always busy wine bar with delicious snacks. Daily 7pm–2am.

Markets and shops

The parks and canalside steps make **picnicking** a pleasant alternative to a restaurant in Venice, and if you're venturing off to the outer islands it's often the only way of refuelling. Don't try to picnic in the *campi*, though – the by-laws against it are strictly enforced.

Open-air **markets** for fruit and vegetables are held in various squares every day except Sunday; check out Santa Maria Formosa, Santa Margherita, Campiello dell'Anconetta, Rio Terrà San Leonardo and the barge moored by Campo San Barnaba. The market of markets, however, is the one at the Rialto, where you can buy everything you need for an impromptu feast – it's open Monday to Saturday 8am to 1pm, with a few stalls opening again in the late afternoon.

Virtually every parish has its **alimentari** and most of them are good; one worth singling out is Aliani Gastronomia in Ruga Vecchia S. Giovanni (San Polo) – scores of cheeses, meats and salads. Alternatively, you could get everything from one of Venice's well-hidden **supermarkets**, the most central of which is *Su.Ve*, on the corner of Salizzada San Lio and Calle Mondo Nuovo (Castello). Best of the rest are as follows: *Punto Sma*, tucked between houses 3019 and 3112 on Campo Santa Margherita (Dorsoduro); and *Billa* at Záttere Ponte Lungo 1491, by the San Basilio *vaporetto* stop (Dorsoduro) and at Strada Nova 3660, near San Felice (Cannaregio). Most are open daily 8.30am–8.30pm, though some of the smaller ones close for a couple of hours in the middle of the day, and on Sunday.

Entertainment

Music in Venice, to all intents and purposes, means classical music – though the Teatro Malibran does stage concerts by Italian rock outfits from time to time. Bands rarely come nearer than Padua, and the biggest names tend to favour Verona.

La Fenice (ⓦwww.teatrolafenice.it) might be the third-ranking Italian opera house (after Milan's La Scala and Naples' San Carlo) and Venice's top music venue, yet its prices are far from exclusive: the cheapest seats (from a mere €10) give no view of the stage, but very good seats can be had for a reasonable €50–60 on most nights. You'll pay around twice as much for the opening night of a production as you would for the same seat later in the run (midweek prices are the lowest). The opera season runs from late November to the end of June, punctuated by ballet performances. Tickets can be bought at the Fenice box office, the Piazza tourist office, and the VeLa/ACTV offices at Piazzale Roma and the train station.

The city's major venues for classical music concerts are the Sale Apollinee in La Fenice, and the recently restored **Teatro Malibran**, behind the church of San Giovanni Crisostomo. Tickets for the Malibran can be bought in advance from the same outlets as tickets for the Fenice. The Malibran's own ticket office sells tickets only on the night of the concert, from around one hour before the start.

Music performances at the **Goldoni** (box office Mon–Sat 9.30am–12.30pm & 4–6pm; ⓣ041.520.5422, ⓦwww.teatrostabileveneto.it) are somewhat less frequent than at La Fenice and the Malibran; the repertoire here tends to be more populist, with a jazz series cropping up every now and then. For most of the year the Goldoni specializes in the works of the eponymous writer.

Classical concerts, with a very strong bias towards the eighteenth century (and Vivaldi in particular – hardly a week goes by without a performance of *The Four Seasons*) – are also performed at the Palazzo Prigione Vecchie, the Scuola Grande di San Giovanni Evangelista, the Scuola Grande di San Rocco, Palazzo Mocenigo (San Stae) and the churches of Santo Stefano, the Frari, San Stae, San Samuele, San Vidal, San Giacomo di Rialto, San Bartolomeo, Zitelle, San Barnaba and the Ospedaletto. The average ticket price for these concerts is around €25 (usually with a reduction for students and children).

The only **cinema** in central Venice is the small two-screen Giorgione at Rio Terrà dei Franceschi 4612/A, Cannaregio (☎041.522.6298); non-dubbed English-language films are shown on Tuesdays from October to May. From around mid-July to the end of August an open-air cinema in Campo S. Polo shows dubbed or Italian-language films. Films start each night at around 9pm, and it's worth an evening of anyone's holiday, if only for the atmosphere. For information check ⓦ www.comune.venezia.it/cinema.

Festivals and events

The *Carnevale* and the Film Festival might be the best publicized of the city's festivals, but the calendar is strewn with other special events, most of them with religious or commemorative origins. Venice also has numerous venues for temporary shows, of which **Palazzo Grassi** (ⓦ www.palazzograssi.it) maintains the highest standards.

Carnevale

Venice's **Carnevale** occupies the ten days leading up to Lent, finishing on Shrove Tuesday with a masked ball for the glitterati and dancing in the Piazza for the plebs. After falling out of fashion for many years, it was revived in 1979 and is now supported by the city authorities who organize various pageants and performances. Apart from these events, Carnevale is an endless parade where during the day people don costumes and go to the Piazza to be photographed, while business types can be seen doing their shopping in the classic white mask, black cloak and tricorn hat. In the evening some congregate in the remoter squares, while those who have spent hundreds of pounds on their costumes install themselves in the windows of *Florian* and pose for a while. Masks are on sale throughout the year in Venice, but special mask and costume shops magically appear during Carnevale, and Campo San Maurizio sprouts a marquee with mask-making demonstrations and a variety of designs for sale.

The Film Festival

The **Venice Film Festival** – the world's oldest, founded in 1932 – takes place on the Lido every year in late August and early September. The tourist office will have the festival programme a few weeks in advance. Tickets are available for the general public, but you have to go along and queue for them on the day of performance.

The Biennale

The **Venice Biennale** (ⓦ www.labiennale.org), set up in 1895 as a showpiece for international contemporary art and held from June to September of every odd-numbered year. Its permanent site in the Giardini Pubblici has pavilions for about forty countries (the largest for Italy's representatives), plus space for a thematic international exhibition. Supplementing this central part are events at venues all over the city: the salt warehouses on the Záttere, for instance, or the Corderie in the Arsenale. In even-numbered years the city hosts an architecture Biennale, a smaller-scale event which runs from the second week in September to mid-November.

La Sensa

The feast of **La Sensa** happens in May on the Sunday after Ascension Day – the latter the day on which the doge performed the wedding of Venice to the sea. The ritual has recently been revived – a distinctly feeble procession that ends with the mayor and a gang of other dignitaries getting into a present-day approximation of the *Bucintoro* (the state barge) and sailing off to the Lido. Of more interest is the **Vogalonga** (long row), held on the same day. Open to any crew in any class of rowing boat, it covers a 32-kilometre course from the Bacino di San Marco out to Burano and back; the competitors arrive at the mouth of the Canal Grande between about 11am and 3pm.

The Regata Storica

Held on the first Sunday in September, the **Regata Storica** is the annual trial of strength and skill for the city's gondoliers and other expert rowers. It starts with a procession of richly decorated historic craft along the Canal Grande course, their crews all decked out in period dress. Bystanders are expected to support contestants in the main event, and may even be issued with appropriate colours.

Religious festivals

Named after the church of the Salute (see p.300), **La Festa della Salute** is a reminder of the devastating plague of 1630–31. Every November 21 a large procession heads to the church to give thanks for good health, or to pray for the sick. It offers the only chance to see the Salute as it was designed to be seen – with its main doors open, and with hundreds of people milling up the steps and round the building. Another plague-related festival, **La Festa del Redentore** marks the end of the 1576 epidemic. Celebrated on the third Sunday in July, the day is centred on the church of the Redentore, which was built by way of thanksgiving for the city's escape. A bridge of boats is strung across the Giudecca canal to allow the faithful to walk over to the church, and on the Saturday night hundreds of people row out for a picnic on the water. The night ends with a grand fireworks display, after which it's traditional to make for the Lido to watch the sun rise.

Listings

Airport enquiries Marco Polo airport ☎041.260.9260, ⍟www.veniceairport.com; Treviso airport ☎0422.315.111, ⍟www .trevisoairport.it.

Banks Banks in Venice are concentrated on Calle Larga XXII Marzo, San Marco, west of the Piazza, and along a chain of squares and alleyways between Campo S. Bartolomeo and Campo Manin. There is not much to choose between them in terms of commission and exchange rates, and their hours are generally Mon–Fri 8.30am–1.30pm & 2.30–3.30pm.

Car rental At Marco Polo airport: Hertz ☎041.541.6075; Europcar ☎041.541.5654; Maggiore Budget ☎041.541.5040. At Piazzale Roma: Avis ☎041.523.7377; Europcar ☎041.523.8616; Hertz ☎041.528.4091.

Consulates and embassies The British consulate is on the mainland in the Palazzo Donatori di Sangue 2/5, Mestre ☎041.505.5990; this office is staffed by an honorary consul – the closest full consulate is in Milan. The nearest US consulate is also in Milan. Travellers from Ireland, Australia, New Zealand and Canada should contact their Rome embassies (see p.717).

Exchange There are clusters of exchange bureaux (*cambios*) where most tourists gather – near San Marco, the Rialto and the train station. Open late every day of the week, they can be useful in emergencies, but their rates of commission and exchange tend to be steep, with the notable exception of Travelex, which can be found at no. 142 on the Piazza, at Riva del Ferro 5126 (by the Rialto Bridge), and at the airport.

Hospital Ospedale Civile, Campo SS Giovanni e Paolo; ☏041.529.4111.

Internet access Dozens of dedicated internet points have opened in the last few years; most charge €6–8 per hr, though rates usually drop the longer you stay online. Places are opening and closing all the time, but you should find the following still in operation: **San Marco**: *Internet Point*, Campo S. Stefano 2958 (daily 10am–11pm); *Venetian Navigator*, Calle dei Stagneri 5239 (daily 10am–10pm – until 8.30pm in winter). **Dorsoduro**: *Internet Point*, Crosera S.Pantalon 3812/A (daily 10am–11pm). **San Polo**: *Venice Connection*, Calle del Campaniel (Mon–Sat 10am–10pm, Sun 11am–10pm). **Cannaregio**: *Planet Internet*, Rio Terà San Leonardo 1519 (daily 9am–11pm) by the Ponte delle Guglie. **Castello**: *Internet Corner*, Calle del Cafetier 6661/A (Mon–Sat 10am–10pm, Sun 1–9pm).

Laundries Speedy Wash, Rio Terà San Leonardo, Cannaregio 1520 (daily 8am–11pm); *Effe Erre*, Ruga Giuffa, Castello 4826 (daily 8.30am–8pm), off Campo S. Maria Formosa; Orange Laundry, Chioverette Simon 665/B Santa Croce (daily 7.30am–10.30pm); and at Fondamenta delle Zitelle 65, on Giudecca (daily 7.30am–10.30pm). You'll pay around €5 for an 8kg wash and €4 for a dryer. All over the city you'll find drycleaners, many of which will take in laundry for a service wash.

Left luggage The desk at the end of platform 14 in the train station (6am–midnight) charges €3.80 per item for 5hr, then €0.60 for each of the next 6hr, and €0.20 per hr thereafter. The office on Piazzale Roma (6am–9pm) charges €3.50 per item per 24hr.

Lost property If you lose anything on the train or at the station, call ☏041.785.531; on the buses, call ☏041.272.2838; at the airport, call ☏041.260.9222; on the *vaporetti*, call ☏041.272.2179; and anywhere in the city itself, call the town hall on ☏041.274.8225.

Police To notify police of a theft or lost passport, report to the Questura on Piazzale Roma (☏041.271.5511); in the event of an emergency, ring ☏113.

Post offices Venice's main post office is in the Fondaco dei Tedeschi, near the Rialto bridge (Mon–Sat 8.30am–6.30pm). The principal branch post offices are in Calle dell'Ascensione, at Záttere 1406, and by the Piazzale Roma *vaporetto* stops (Mon–Fri 8.30am–2pm, Sat 8.30am–1pm). Stamps can also be bought in *tabacchi*, as well as in some gift shops.

Public toilets There are toilets on or very near to most of the main squares. You'll need a €1 coin, but the toilets are usually staffed, so you can get change; note that the Venice Card (see box, p.280) gives free access twice a day to many staffed toilets. The main facilities are at the train station, at Piazzale Roma, on the west side of the Accademia bridge, by the main tourist office at the Giardinetti Reali, off the west side of the Piazza, off Campo S. Bartolomeo, on Campo Rialto Nuovo, on Campo S. Leonardo, on Campo S. Angelo and on Campo S. Margherita. Toilets are to be found in most of the city's bars as well; it's diplomatic, to say the least, to buy a drink before availing yourself.

Telephones Most of Venice's public call-boxes accept coins, and all of them take phone cards, which can be bought from *tabacchi* and some other shops (look for the *Telecom Italia* sticker).

The Veneto

Virtually every acre of the Veneto bears the imprint of Venetian rule – Venice dominated this region for centuries and is still the capital of the province today. In **Belluno**, right under the crags of the Dolomites, the style of the buildings declares the town's former allegiance, while the Lion of St Mark looks over the market square of **Verona**, on the Veneto's western edge. On the flatlands of the

Po basin (the southern border of the region) and on farming estates all over the Veneto, the elegant **villas** of the Venetian nobility are still standing.

Yet the Veneto is as diverse culturally as it is geographically. The aspects of Verona that make the city so attractive were created long before the expansion of Venice's terra firma empire, and in **Padua** – a university seat since the thirteenth century – the civilization of the Renaissance displays a character quite distinct from that which evolved in Venice. Even in **Vicenza**, which reached its present form mainly during its long period of subservience, the very appearance of the streets is proof of a fundamental independence.

Nowadays this is one of Italy's wealthiest regions. Verona, Padua, Vicenza and **Treviso**, 30km north of Venice, are all major industrial and commercial centres, while intensive dairies, fruit farms and vineyards (around Conegliano, for example) have made the Veneto a leading agricultural producer too.

The Veneto's densest concentration of industry is at **Mestre** and **Marghera**, the grim conurbation through which road and rail lines from Venice pass before spreading out over the mainland. It's less a city than an economic life-support system for Venice, and the negative impression you get on your way through is entirely valid. Some people trim their holiday expenses by staying in Mestre's cheaper hotels (Venice's tourist offices will supply addresses), but venturing further inland is a more pleasurable cost-cutting exercise.

The Brenta

The southernmost of the three main rivers that empty into the Venetian lagoon, the **Brenta** caused no end of trouble for the earliest settlers in the area, with its frequent flooding and its deposits of silt. By the sixteenth century, though, the canalization of the river had brought it under control, and it became a favoured building site for the Venetian aristocracy. Some villas were built as a combination of summer residence and farmhouse – many, however, were intended solely for the former function.

Around one hundred **villas** are left on the river between Padua and Venice: but only a handful are open to the public. Of this last category, two are outstanding – the **Villa Fóscari** and the **Villa Pisani** – both of which are accessible by bus from Venice: four ACTV buses go to the former, and the hourly buses between Padua and Venice (the ACTV bus going via Dolo, not the SITA bus that goes on the autostrada) go past both. Don't be tempted by the widely advertised boat trips along the Brenta – they cost more than €70 and stop longer for lunch than at any of the villas.

Villa Fóscari

The **Villa Fóscari** at Malcontenta (May–Oct Tues & Sat 9am–noon; €10) was designed in 1559 by Palladio (see box, p.339) and is the nearest of his villas to Venice. Most of Palladio's villas fall into two broad groups: those built on cohesive farming estates, with a central low block for living quarters and wings for storage and associated uses (the Villa Barbaro at Masèr); and the single-block villas built for landowners whose fields were dispersed or unsuitable for the construction of a major building. The Villa Fóscari is the masterpiece of this second group, evoking the architecture of ancient Rome with its rusticated exterior, massive Ionic portico and two-storey main hall.

The frescoes in the living rooms include what is said to be a portrait of a woman of the Fóscari family who was exiled here as punishment for an amorous escapade, and whose subsequent misery was the source of the name Malcontenta. The reality is more prosaic – the area has long been known by that name, either because of some local discontent over the development of the land or because of the political *malcontenti* who hid in the nearby salt marshes.

The Villa Pisani

The **VILLA PISANI** (or Nazionale) at Stra (Tues–Sun: April–Sept 9am–7pm; Oct–March 9am–4pm; €5 for house and garden, €2.50 for garden only), virtually on the outskirts of Padua (ask the bus driver where to get off), looks more like a product of the *ancien régime* than a house for the Venetian gentry. Commissioned when Alvise Pisani was elected Doge of Venice in 1735, it was the biggest such residence to be built in Venetian territory during that century. It has appealed to megalomaniacs ever since: Napoleon bought it off the Pisani in 1807 and handed it over to Eugène Beauharnais, his stepson and Viceroy of Italy; and in 1934 it was chosen for the first meeting of Mussolini and Hitler.

Most of what you see is unexciting and sparsely furnished, but stick with it for the ballroom, its ceiling covered with a dazzling fresco, *The Apotheosis of the Pisani Family*, painted by **Tiepolo** at the age of 66. And if you're trying to puzzle out what's going on – the Pisani family, accompanied by Venice, are being courted by the Arts, Sciences and Spirits of Peace, while Fame plays a fanfare in praise of the Pisani and the Madonna looks on with appropriate pride.

In the **grounds**, the long fish-pond ends in front of a stable-block which from a distance might be mistaken for another grand house. Off to the right there's an impressive maze, while the immaculate citrus garden is in stark contrast to the neglect of the house.

Padua (Padova)

Hemmed in by the sprawl that has accompanied its development as the most important economic centre of the Veneto, **PADUA** (Padova) is not immediately the most alluring city in northern Italy. It is, however, one of the most ancient, and plentiful evidence remains of its impressive lineage. A large student population creates a young, vibrant atmosphere, and yet in spite of having two big attractions – the **Giotto frescoes** and **relics of St Antony** – Padua has the feel of a town that is just getting on with its own business. And indeed, for many people Padua's main appeal is as a base from which to make day-trips to its overcrowded neighbour, Venice.

Some history

A Roman municipium from 45 BC, the city thrived until the barbarian onslaughts and the subsequent Lombard invasion at the start of the seventh century. Recovery was slow, but by the middle of the twelfth century, when it became a free commune, Padua was prosperous once again. The **university** was founded in 1221, and a decade later the city became a place of pilgrimage following the death here of St Anthony.

In 1337 the **Da Carrara** family established control. Under their domination, Padua's cultural eminence was secured – Giotto, Dante and Petrarch were among those attracted here – but Carraresi territorial ambitions led to conflict with Venice, and in 1405 the city's independence ended with its conquest by the neighbouring republic. Though politically nullified, Padua remained an artistic and intellectual centre: Donatello and Mantegna both worked here, and

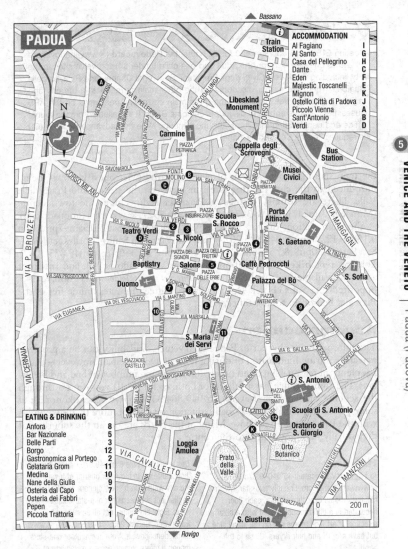

PADUA

▲ Bassano

ACCOMMODATION
Al Fagiano	I
Al Santo	G
Casa del Pellegrino	H
Dante	C
Eden	F
Majestic Toscanelli	E
Mignon	K
Ostello Città di Padova	J
Piccolo Vienna	A
Sant'Antonio	B
Verdi	D

EATING & DRINKING
Anfora	8
Bar Nazionale	5
Belle Parti	3
Borgo	12
Gastronomica al Portego	2
Gelataria Grom	11
Medina	10
Nane della Giulia	9
Osteria dal Capo	7
Osteria dei Fabbri	6
Pepen	4
Piccola Trattoria	1

0   200 m

▼ Rovigo

in the seventeenth century Galileo researched at the university, where the medical faculty was one of the most ambitious in Europe. With the fall of the Venetian Republic the city passed to Napoleon and then to the Austrians, who ruled until Padua was annexed to Italy in 1866. Bombed several times by the Allies in World War II, the city has been extensively restored.

Arrival and information

Trains arrive in the north of the town, just a few minutes' walk up Corso del Popolo from the old city walls. The main **bus station** is at Piazzale Boschetti, immediately north of the walls to the east of the Corso; however, local buses for the city and nearby towns such as Ábano and Montegrotto leave from outside

Padovacard

Costing €15 for 48 hours or €20 for 72 hours, the **Padovacard** (ⓦ www.padovacard .it) allows one free visit for one adult and one child (under 14) to twelve sites in the city, including the Musei Civici degli Eremitani, Scrovegni Chapel, and Palazzo della Ragione. There are further discounts on the other main attractions in the city and region, as well as free parking in the three main car parks, free travel on the APS buses, free bicycle rental and discounts on some B&Bs. It's available from the tourist office and participating museums and monuments. Note that advance booking (€1) is required for the Scrovegni Chapel.

the train station. A new system of electric **trams** (Metrobus) is slowly being introduced to the city; the first line runs between the station and Prato della Valle. There are **tourist offices** at Piazzetta Pedrocchi in the town centre (Mon–Sat 9am–1.30pm & 3–7pm; ☏049.876.7927, ⓦ www.turismopadova.it), at the train station, on the right as you exit (Mon–Sat 9.15am–7pm, Sun 9.15am–12.30pm; ☏049.875.2077), and on Piazza del Santo (April–Oct Mon–Sat 9am–1.30pm & 3–6pm, Sun 10am–1pm & 3–6pm; ☏049.875.3087). You can rent **bikes** at the station (discounts with Padovacard), and **internet** access is available east of the centre at *Internet Point Padova*, Via Altinate 145, opposite Santa Sofia church – or you can get fifteen minutes online free at the Piazzetta Pedrocchi tourist office.

Accommodation

Though rooms are cheaper in Padua than Venice, availability can be a problem, especially during high season or during festivals. Don't despair, however – Padua has plenty of reasonably priced hotels and a growing number of bed and breakfasts. The tourist office has a full list of both, or for B&Bs you can go through the scheme operated by *Kokonor* (☏049.864.3394, ⓦ www.bbkokonor.it); at some places you can also get a small reduction on stays of more than two nights with the Padovacard – see above. Many of the B&Bs are out in the suburbs, but they usually have good links to the centre.

Hotels

Al Fagiano Via Locatelli 45 ☏049.875.0073, ⓦ www.alfagiano.com. Friendly two-star, which has forty rooms over three floors, each floor decorated in a different colour and with a bizarre selection of art. The rooms are on the small side, but have a/c, TV and hair dryers. Close to the basilica. ❸

Al Santo Via del Santo 147 ☏049.875.2131, ⓦ www.alsanto.it. Located virtually next door to the basilica, this hotel has been recently refurbished (rather austerely, but comfortably) and upgraded to a three-star. ❸

Casa del Pellegrino Via M. Cesarotti 21 ☏049.823.9711, ⓦ www.casadelpellegrino.com. Large, inexpensive two-star popular with groups coming to pay their respects to St Antony across the road – after all, it is the "Pilgrim's House". Its 152 rooms are simply furnished and most have bathrooms. ❷

Dante Via San Polo 5 ☏049.876.0408, ⓦ www .hoteldante.eu. In a quieter quarter of town inside the city walls. The friendly signora speaks no English but she keeps her one-star establishment clean. Eight big rooms, not all en suite. ❶

Eden Via C. Battisti 255 ☏049.650.484, ⓦ www .hoteledenpadova.it. A cut above other one-stars, though it offers something of a mixed bag of rooms. All doubles have showers, but avoid the coffin-like singles. Situated in a good location near Piazza del Santo, in the university quarter. ❷

Majestic Toscanelli Via dell'Arco 2 ☏049.663.244, ⓦ www.toscanelli.com. The most appealing of the city's four-stars, probably the hotel of choice if you want to stay in style, with glitzy, nicely equipped rooms; it's located in the old Jewish quarter just south of Piazza delle Erbe, off Via SS Martino e Solferino. ❻

Mignon Via Luca Belludi 22 ☏049.661.722, ⓦ www.hotelmignonpadova.it. Lying between the

Prato della Valle and the Botanical Garden, this is a simple but comfortable two-star. It has 23 rooms with a/c and televisions. ❷

Piccolo Vienna Via Beato Pellegrino 133 ⓣ049.871.6331, ⓦwww.hotelpiccolovienna.it. One of the cheapest hotels in Padua, a 10min walk northwest from the centre. Simply furnished rooms with or without bathrooms – those at the back are quieter. ❷

Sant'Antonio Via San Fermo 118 ⓣ049.875.1393, ⓦwww.hotelsantantonio.it. Two-star with large and modern, if slightly faded, rooms; those at the back have views over the canal and the lovely Ponte Molino, and are better than the street-facing rooms. Start the day with fresh orange juice and coffee next door at the cheerful *Albabar*. ❸

Verdi Via Dondi dell'Orologio 7 ⓣ049.836.4163, ⓦwww.albergoverdipadova.it. Light and airy, this fully modernized small three-star is located a quiet street near the Teatro Verdi. ❸

Hostel and campsite

Ostello Città di Padova Via A. Aleardi 30 ⓣ049.875.2219, ⓦwww.ostellopadova.it. Padua's quiet and friendly HI hostel is a good 30min walk from the train station. Alternatively, take the tram or bus #3, #8, #12 or #18 (#32 on Sun) to Prato della Valle, from where it's a short walk northwest. Reception is closed between 9.30am and 4.30pm and there's an 11.30pm curfew. Reservations by phone or via www.hostelbookers.com or hostelsclub.com. Dorm beds cost €18.

Montegrotto Terme Via Roma 123/25 ⓣ049.793.400, ⓦwww.sportingcenter.it. This is the nearest campsite to Padua – 15km south from the city centre, but frequent trains take around 15min; a very upmarket site, it not only has a swimming pool but thermal baths too. Open March–early Nov. €15.50 per tent and €8.30 per person per night.

The City

For many people the **Giotto frescoes** in the Capella degli Scrovegni, considered to be a key work in the development of European art, are the reason for coming to Padua, but even if you're no expert the chapel exerts an extraordinary presence. However, anyone limiting their visit to Giotto would be missing out on Padua's other delights, from the fine old monuments and buildings such as the *Salone* or the Duomo baptistry, to its busy, narrow streets and bustling market squares. Padua's thirteenth-century university is the second oldest in Italy, and the city has also been a major centre of pilgrimage for almost as long.

The September 11 monument

From the train station, the Corso del Popolo and its extension Corso Garibaldi lead south passing the seventeen-metre-tall structure of glass and steel designed by the architect **Daniel Libeskind**, as a memorial to the victims of the September 11 attacks. Named "Memory and Light", it contains part of a girder salvaged from the World Trade Center. A couple of minutes' walk further on is the Cappella degli Scrovegni and Musei Civici degli Eremitani.

The Capella degli Scrovegni

The **Capella degli Scrovegni** (Scrovegni Chapel; daily 9am–10pm) was commissioned in 1303 by Enrico Scrovegni in atonement for his father's usury, which was so vicious that he was denied a Christian burial. Giotto was commissioned to cover the walls with illustrations of the life of Mary, the life of Jesus and the story of the Passion, and the finished cycle is one of the high points in the development of European art. The frescoes are a marvellous demonstration of Giotto's innovative attention to the inner nature of his subjects. In terms of sheer physical presence and the relationships between the figures and their environment, Giotto's work takes the first important strides towards realism and humanism.

The Joachim series on the top row of the north wall (facing you as you walk in) is particularly powerful – note the exchange of looks between the two shepherds in the *Arrival of Joachim*. Beneath the main pictures are shown the vices and virtues in human (usually female) form, while on the wall above the door is a *Last Judgement* – in rather poor condition and thought to be only partly by Giotto. At the bottom is a portrait of Scrovegni presenting the chapel; his tomb is at the far end, behind the altar with its statues by **Giovanni Pisano**.

Tickets (€12 reduced to €8 on Mon and after 7pm when the museum is shut; free with Padovacard,) have to be reserved at least 24 hours in advance at the ticket office, by phoning ☏049.201.0020 (Mon–Fri 9am–7pm, Sat 9am–6pm), or by booking online at Ⓦwww.cappelladegliscrovegni.it. You can book a double slot – "*doppia turno*" – for €24, or €12 after 7pm. Such is the demand, you may have to book tickets at least three days in advance, but it's still worth turning up even if you haven't reserved, as there may be space. Tickets must be picked up from the museum ticket office an hour before your timed entry; be at the chapel waiting room five minutes before your allotted time.

Groups of 25 are admitted every fifteen minutes (every 20min after 7pm), and if you miss your slot you have to book and pay again. Once inside, the air humidity of the waiting room is adjusted down to that of the chapel, while you watch a video about the frescoes. Once you are allowed into the chapel, you have a quarter of an hour to take in the frescoes. Before going in, you might want to visit the **Sala Multimediale** in the museum, which gives you a chance to look at the images in more detail.

The Musei Civici degli Eremitani

Next to the chapel, the **Musei Civici degli Eremitani** (Tues–Sun 9am–7pm; €10, free with Padovacard), formerly the monastery of the Eremitani, is a well-presented three-part museum complex. The **Museo Archeologico**, on the ground floor, has an array of pre-Roman, Roman and paleo-Christian objects. Upstairs, the vast **Museo d'Arte** houses an assembly of fourteenth- to nineteenth-century art from the Veneto and further afield. The collection is arranged in chronological order, and it's a long walk through tracts of workaday stuff, but works by names such as Titian, Tintoretto and Tiepolo leaven the mix. Highlights are the Giotto *Crucifixion* that was once in the Scrovegni chapel, and a fine *Portrait of a Young Senator* by Bellini. The Capodilista collection, an offshoot of the main gallery, has a pair of mysterious Titian and Giorgione landscapes, and some good Luca Giordano grotesques. The **Museo Bottacin**, for more specialist tastes, contains over 50,000 coins, medals and seals, making it one of the most important museums of its type in the world.

The Chiesa degli Eremitani

The neighbouring church of the **Eremitani** (Mon–Fri 8.15am–6.30pm, Sat–Sun 10am–1pm & 4.30–7pm; free), built at the turn of the fourteenth century, was wrecked by an Allied bombing raid in 1944 but has been fastidiously rebuilt. Photographs to the left of the apse show the extent of the damage, the worst aspect of which was the near-total destruction of Mantegna's frescoes of the lives of St James and St Christopher.

The central squares

Continuing down the Corso Garibaldi and turning left leads you past the **Caffè Pedrocchi**, once the city's main intellectual salon; it's no longer that, but it does have a multiplicity of functions – chic café, concert hall and conference centre. Just beyond, the **Piazza della Frutta** and **Piazza delle Erbe**, the sites of Padua's daily markets, are lined with bars, restaurants and shops. Separating them is the extraordinary **Palazzo della Ragione** or **Salone** (Tues–Sun: 9am–6pm;

€4 or €8 if there is an exhibition on in the hall, free with Padovacard), which you enter by the stairs at the eastern end of Piazza delle Erbe. When it was built in the 1210s, this vast hall was the largest room to have been built on top of another storey. Its decoration would once have been as astounding as its size, but the original frescoes by Giotto and his assistants were destroyed by fire in 1420, though some by Giusto de'Menabuoi have survived. Most of the extant frescoes are by Nicola Miretto depicting an astrological calendar distinctively medieval in its complexity. Mainly used as the city council's assembly hall, it was also a place where Padua's citizens could plead for justice – hence the appellation *della Ragione*, meaning "of reason". The large wooden horse with disproportionately gigantic gonads is modelled on Donatello's *Gattamelata*, and was made for a joust in 1466. There's a useful information screen about the frescoes and the horse in one corner of the hall.

The Duomo and baptistry

Padua's **Duomo** (Mon–Sat 7.30am–noon & 4–7.30pm, Sun 8am–1pm & 4–8.30pm; free) is an unlovely church whose architect took his design from drawings by Michelangelo. The adjacent Romanesque **baptistry**, however, is one of the unproclaimed delights of the city (daily 10am–6pm; €2.50, or free with Padovacard). Built by the Da Carraras in the thirteenth century, and still in use today, it's lined with fourteenth-century frescoes by Giusto de'Menabuoi, a cycle which makes a fascinating comparison with the Cappella degli Scrovegni. In striving for greater realism Giusto has lost Giotto's monumentality and made some of his figures unconvincing, yet many of the scenes are delightful, and the vibrancy of their colours, coupled with the relative quiet of the building, make for a memorable visit.

The university

The area just southeast of *Caffè Pedrocchi* is dominated by the main block of the **university**, the **Palazzo del Bò** ("the Ox", named after an inn that used to stand here). Established in September 1221, the University of Padua is older than any other in Italy except that of Bologna. The first permanent **anatomy theatre** was built here in 1594, a facility that doubtless greatly helped William Harvey, who went on to develop the theory of blood circulation after taking his degree here in 1602. Galileo taught physics at the university from 1592 to 1610, declaiming from a lectern that is still on show. And in 1678 Elena Lucrezia Corner Piscopia became the first woman in the world to collect a university degree – her statue is in the courtyard. The Bò is only open for guided tours (March–Oct Mon, Wed & Fri 3.15pm, 4.15pm & 5.15pm, Tues, Thurs & Sat 9.15am, 10.15am & 11.15am; Nov–Feb the 9.15am and 5.15pm tours do not run; €5); tickets (no reservations) are on sale fifteen minutes beforehand – the ticket office is by the bar in the more modern of the two courtyards and is well signposted.

The Prato della Valle and Santa Giustina

Past the *palazzo*, Via VIII Febbraio turns into Via Roma and then Via Umberto I, before opening up into the sprawling **Prato della Valle**, claimed to be the largest town square in Italy. It's a generally cheerless area, ringed by very wide roads, but the vast Saturday market and the summer funfair do a lot to make it jollier, and it's also a favourite place for the *passeggiata* on summer evenings. One side is fronted by the sixteenth-century **Basilica di Santa Giustina** (daily 7.30am–noon & 3–6.30pm; free). A pair of fifteenth-century griffins, one holding a knight and the other a lion, are the only notable adornments to the unclad brick facade; the interior has little of interest except a huge *Martyrdom of St Justina* by Paolo Veronese (in the apse), some highly proficient carving on the choir stalls, and the sarcophagus which once contained the relics of Luke the Evangelist (apse of left transept).

Il Santo

At the far end of Via Belludi on Piazza del Santo towers the Basilica di San Antonio, or **Il Santo** (daily 6.30am–7pm, Ⓦwww.basilicadelsanto.it; free). Within eighteen months of his death in 1231, St Anthony had been canonized and his tomb was attracting enough pilgrims to warrant the building of the basilica. It was not until the start of the fourteenth century that the church reached a state that enabled the saint's body to be placed in the **Cappella del Santo** (in the left transept). Plastered with such votive offerings as photographs of healed limbs and car crashes survived with the saint's intervention, the shrine has an uneasy, irresistible pull. The chapel's more formal decoration includes the most important series of relief sculpture created in sixteenth-century Italy, a sequence of nine marble panels showing scenes from the life of St Anthony. Carved between 1505 and 1577, most have the names of their sculptors incised into the base, Antonio Lombardo, Tullio Lombardo and Jacopo Sansovino being among the most famous.

Adjoining the chapel is the Cappella della Madonna Mora (named after its fourteenth-century French altar statue), which in turn gives onto the Cappella del Beato Luca, whose fourteenth-century frescoes include a lovely image of St James lifting a prison tower to free a prisoner. Back in the aisle, just outside the Cappella del Santo, is Padua's finest work by Pietro Lombardo, the monument to Antonio Roselli (1467). More impressive still are the high altar's bronze sculptures and reliefs by Donatello (1444–45), the works that introduced Renaissance classicism to Padua. Built onto the farthest point of the ambulatory, the **Cappella del Tesoro** houses the tongue and vocal chords of St Anthony, as well as a host of lesser relics. For more on St Anthony and the basilica, enter the cloisters (on the south side of the basilica) and follow the signs for the **Museo Antoniano** (daily 9am–1pm & 2.30–6pm; €2.50, €1.50 with Padovacard), which includes the fresco of St Anthony and St Bernardino by Mantegna.

In front of the basilica stands Donatello's **Monument to Gattamelata** (which translates literally as "The Honeyed Cat"), as the *condottiere* Erasmo da Narni was known. He died in 1443 and this monument was raised ten years later, the first large bronze sculpture of the Renaissance.

South of Il Santo

To the left as you leave the basilica are the **Oratorio di San Giorgio** and **Scoletta del Santo** (daily 9am–12.30pm & 2.30–7pm but closes 5pm Nov–March; €4, or €2.50 with Padovacard). The oratory was founded in 1377 as a mortuary chapel, and its frescoes by Altichiero di Zevio and Jacopo Avanzi were completed soon after. One wall is adorned by the wonderfully titled *St Lucy Remains Immovable at an Attempt to Drag Her with the Help of Oxen to a House of Ill Repute.*

The Scoletta was founded soon after Anthony's canonization, though this building only goes back as far as the early fifteenth century. The ground floor is still used for religious purposes, while upstairs is maintained to look pretty much as it would have in the sixteenth century, with its fine ceiling and paintings dating mainly from 1509–15. Four of the pictures are said to be by Titian.

Round the corner are the oldest botanic gardens in Europe, the **Orto Botanico**, on Via Donatello (April–Oct daily 9am–1pm & 3–7pm; Nov–Feb Mon–Sat 9am–1pm; €4, free with Padovacard). Planted in 1545 by the university's medical faculty as a collection of medicinal herbs, the gardens have mainly kept their original layout, and the specimens on show haven't changed too much either. Goethe came here in 1786 to see a palm tree that had been planted in 1585; the selfsame tree still stands, the oldest in the garden.

Eating and drinking

Catering for the midday stampede of ravenous students, Padua's **bars** generally produce weightier **snacks** than the routine *tramezzini* – slabs of pizza and sandwiches vast enough to satisfy a glutton are standard; you'll find several amid the food stalls underneath the Palazzo della Ragione. Several self-service **restaurants** offer good-value full menus, open for lunch and dinner, but they turn off their hotplates by 9pm. For a *passeggiata* and a place to sit and watch the world go by, the main areas to head for are Piazza dell' Erbe, Piazza Duomo, Piazza Cavour and Prato della Valle, but for the real action the studenty bars in the narrow streets around these piazzas and the university are the liveliest. For the most exquisite ice cream in the city hurry to *Gelateria Grom*, Via Roma 101 (open daily till midnight), the chain that started in Turin and is set to conquer the world.

Restaurants

Al Borgo Via L. Belludi 56. Wood-fired oven pizzeria with tables outside looking onto the Piazza del Santo; popular with locals and tourists alike. Closed Tues.

Anfora Via dei Soncin 13 ☎049.656.629. Boisterous and very reasonable bohemian restaurant that doubles up as a bar between restaurant hours (12.30–3.15pm & 8–11.30pm), with delicious snacks all day. Get there early or book in advance. Closed Sun.

Belle Parti Via Belle Parti 11 ☎049.875.1822. On a small street running between Via Verdi and Via Santa Lucia, this place has an excellent menu and a chilled elegant atmosphere. But with mains at €20–25, it is not cheap – the *degustazione* menu costs €50. Closed Mon lunch & Sun; open till 2am.

Gastronomica al Portego Via Dante 9. High-grade yet inexpensive self-service restaurant with local dishes. Closed Sun eve and all day Mon.

Medina Via S.G. Barbarigo 18 ☎049.654.597. Small, bustling pizzeria down from the Duomo, often packed with students enjoying excellent pizza and salads. Open till 2am, evenings only, closed Mon.

Nane della Giulia Via Santa Sofia 1 ☎049.660.742 An unusual mix of trendy and

unpretentious in this friendly *osteria* cum bar. Go for the reasonably priced Veneto and vegetarian specialities. Summer garden. No credit cards. Closed Mon all day and Tues lunch. Open till midnight.

Osteria dal Capo Via Obizzi 2 ☎049.663.105. In a street just off Piazza Duomo is this small restaurant renowned among the locals. Homely cuisine, regional fish dishes a speciality, and a wide range of pasta such as duck tagliatelle. Booking advised. Closed all day Sun and Mon lunchtime.

Osteria dei Fabbri Via dei Fabbri 13 ☎049.650.336. Excellent mid-range trattoria; you'll be lucky to get a seat if you haven't booked. Closed Sun.

Pepen Piazza Cavour 15. With a wonderful range of pizzas and seats on the square in the summer, this is one of Padua's best-sited pizzerias. Open till 2am, closed Sun.

Piccola Trattoria Via R Da Piazzola 21 ☎049 656.163, ⓦwww.piccolatrattoria.it. Friendly place full of locals, serving Sardinian specialities, all superbly presented, and accompanied by delicious vegetables. Its *secondi* are around €15, but it offers cheap lunchtime specials. Closed all day Sun and Mon lunch.

Nightlife and entertainment

Your best bet, as usual, is to head for the centre and follow the throng. A good place to start is around the unmarked *Bar Nazionale*, at Piazza delle Erbe 40, on the northeast corner (closed Sun). In summer it is usually open till midnight (in winter it closes around 9.30pm), after which those looking for dancing will head to out-of-town clubs. The *Anfora* (see above) also serves as a popular bar, spilling out onto the street. Padua's main theatre is the **Teatro Verdi** (closed in summer) on Corso Milano, hosting opera and big-name dramatists; details of the season's events can be obtained from the tourist office or in the bilingual information booklet *Padova Today*, distributed in some bars and most hotels. Of

the local newspapers, the most comprehensive for listings is *Il Mattino*, but for more offbeat events check out the posters up around the **city**.

Vicenza

Europe's largest producer of textiles and the focus of Italy's "Silicon Valley", **VICENZA** is a very sleek city, where it can seem that every second car is a BMW. Prosperity hasn't ruined the look of the city though, and the centre, still partly enclosed by medieval walls, is an amalgam of Gothic and Classical buildings that today looks much as it did at the close of the eighteenth century. This historic core is compact enough to be explored in a day, but the city and its environs really require a short stay to do them justice. In 1404 Vicenza was absorbed by Venice, and the city's numerous Gothic palaces reflect its status as a Venetian satellite. But in the latter half of the sixteenth century the city was transformed by the work of an architect who owed nothing to Venice and who was to influence every succeeding generation – Andrea di Pietro, alias **Palladio**.

Arrival, information and accommodation

The **train station** and **bus terminus** are a ten-minute walk southwest of the historic centre; head straight ahead through the park to reach Piazza del

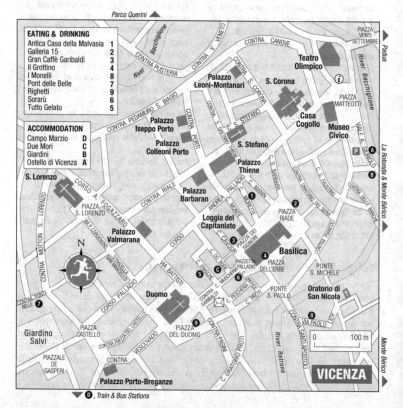

Castello. The helpful **tourist office** is at the far end of Corso Palladio, alongside the entrance to the Teatro Olimpico, at Piazza Matteotti 12 (daily 9am–1pm & 2–6pm; ☎0444.320.854, ⊛www.vicenzae.org). There's another office on Piazza Signori (daily 10am–2pm & 2.30–6.30pm). For listings look out for the local free monthly *City Lights* (Italian only). **Internet** access can be found at Vicenza.com on Piazza Signori 6 (Mon–Sat 10am–1pm 3.30–7.30pm).

Vicenza is a big conference destination, and many of its **hotels** are stuck out in characterless suburbs, so it pays to be careful where you book. Wherever you decide to stay, phone ahead in summer or early autumn – some places close in August and the main conference season is in September.

Campo Marzio Viale Roma ☎0444.545.700, ⊛www.hotelcampomarzio.com. Overlooking the large park that lies between the station and Piazza Castello, this is the only four-star in the historic centre. A modern block but with luxurious period decor. Out of season prices drop massively. ⑥

Due Mori Contrà Do Rode 26 ☎0444.321.886, ⊛www.hotelduemori.com. With some beautifully furnished and spacious rooms – especially the two rooms with disabled access – this graceful hotel offers excellent value and is within a few metres of the Piazza dei Signori. It is only a two-star, but feels better than that. ③

Giardini Via Giuriolo 10 ☎0444.326.458, ⊛www.hotelgiardini.com. A three-star modern hotel at the southern end of Piazza Matteotti which has comfortable a/c rooms – go for the quieter ones at the back. ④

Ostello Vicenza Viale Giuriolo 7 ☎0444.540.222, ⊛www.ostellovicenza.com. The only hostel in the centre of town is in a superb position just off Piazza Matteotti. Reservations by email or phone, check in 3.15–10.30pm. A dorm bed costs €18, doubles €19 per person.

The City

The main street of Vicenza, the **Corso Andrea Palladio**, cuts right through the old centre from the Piazza del Castello down to the Piazza Matteotti, and is lined with *palazzi*, all of them now occupied by shops, offices and banks. Palladio's last palace, the fragmentary **Palazzo Porto-Breganze**, stands on the southern side of Piazza Castello; no. 163 on the Corso, the **Casa Cogollo**, is confusingly known as the Casa del Palladio, though he never lived here and few people think he designed it.

The Museo Civico and Teatro Olimpico

The Corso ends with one of the architect's most imperious buildings, the Palazzo Chiericati (begun in 1550), now home of the **Museo Civico**, also known as the Pinacoteca (Tues–Sun 9am–5pm; see box, p.338, for ticket info). The core of the picture collection is made up of Vicentine artists, none of whose work will knock you flat on your back; it's left to a few more celebrated names – Memling, Tintoretto, Veronese, Tiepolo – and some fine fifteenth-century painting to make the visit memorable.

Across the Piazza Matteotti is the one building in Vicenza you shouldn't fail to go into – the **Teatro Olimpico**, the oldest indoor theatre in Europe (Tues–Sun: July & Aug 9am–7pm; Sept–June 9am–5pm). Approached in 1579 by the members of the Olympic Academy (a society dedicated to the study of the humanities) to produce a design for a permanent theatre, Palladio devised a covered amphitheatre based on his studies of Roman works. He died soon after work commenced, and the scheme was overseen by Scamozzi, who added the backstage perspective of a classical city, creating the illusion of long urban vistas by tilting the "streets" at an alarming angle. The theatre opened on March 3, 1585 and is still used for plays and concerts.

The Piazza dei Signori

At the hub of the city, the **Piazza dei Signori**, stands the most awesome of Palladio's creations – the **basilica**. Designed in the late 1540s (but not finished until almost seventy years later), this was Palladio's first public project and the one that secured his reputation. The monumental regularity of the basilica disguises the fact that the Palladian building is effectively a stupendous piece of buttressing – the Doric and Ionic colonnades enclose the fifteenth-century hall of the city council, an unstable structure that had defied all previous attempts to prop it up. The vast Gothic hall is often used for contemporary architecture exhibitions. On Tuesdays and Thursdays a vast market fills the streets between the basilica and the Duomo, though if you're shopping for picnic food, you'll save money by going down the slope and over the river, where the shops are a good bit cheaper.

A late Palladian building, the unfinished **Loggia del Capitaniato**, faces the basilica across the Piazza dei Signori. Built as accommodation for the Venetian military commander of the city, it's decorated with reliefs in celebration of the Venetian victory over the Turks at Lepanto in 1571.

The churches

Vicenza's **Duomo** was bombed flat in 1944 and, though carefully reconstructed after the war, it's a rather gloomy place. Far more interesting is **Santa Corona** (Tues–Sat 8.30am–noon & 3–6pm, Sun 3–6pm; free) on the other side of the Corso Palladio (at the Piazza Matteotti end – the entrance is up Corsa Santa Corona), a Dominican church dating from the mid-thirteenth century. Here you'll find two of the three great church paintings in Vicenza – *The Baptism of Christ*, a late work by Giovanni Bellini, and *The Adoration of the Magi*, painted in 1573 by Paolo Veronese. The cloisters house a run-of-the-mill **Museo Naturalistico-Archeologico** (Tues–Sun 9am–5pm; see box above for admission prices).

The nearby **Santo Stefano** (Mon–Fri 8.30–9.45am & 4–6pm, Sat–Sun 9am–12.30pm; free) contains third of the city's fine church paintings: Palma Vecchio's typically stolid and voluptuous *Madonna and Child with Saints George and Lucy*.

The palazzi and the parks

Santo Stefano faces a corner of the huge **Palazzo Thiene**, another of Palladio's palaces (May, June & Sept Wed & Fri 9am–noon & 3–6pm, Sat 9am–noon; Oct–April Tues & Wed 9am–noon & 3–6pm; closed July & Aug; admission free, by advance booking only, on ☏0444.542.131). It was planned to occupy the entire block down to Corso Palladio, but in the end work progressed no further than the addition of this wing to the existing fifteenth-century house. Facing Palazzo Thiene is the **Palazzo Barbarano** which houses a research institute for Palladian architecture and often has excellent exhibitions, often on classical architects.

Palladio

Born in Padua in 1508, Andrea di Pietro (or della Gondola) began his career as an apprentice stonemason in Vicenza. At 30 he became the protégé of a local nobleman, Count Giangiorgio Trissino who gave the architect his classicized name, **Palladio**. Tressino directed Palladio's training and, perhaps most crucially, took him to Rome – the first of many trips he made sketching imperial Roman remains.

Between 1540 and his death in 1580, Palladio created around a dozen palaces and public buildings in Vicenza, nearly twenty villas in the countryside of the Veneto and the churches of the Redentore and San Giorgio Maggiore in Venice. But unlike the pioneers of Renaissance Classicism – architects such as Alberti, Brunelleschi and Bramante – Palladio's reputation does not rest on a particular transformation of architectural style. Instead, his fame – and he is arguably the most influential architect in the world – rests on the way he is considered to have perfected existing values of harmony and proportion.

In particular, his lasting influence stems from I Quattro Libri dell'Architettura or "The Four Books of Architecture", a treatise he published in 1570, towards the end of his career. Other architects had written important works of theory, but Palladio's is unique in its practical applicability, serving almost as a textbook for Classical architecture. As the style spread into the rest of Europe and beyond, it was to Palladio's book that architects like Inigo Jones (and later, Thomas Jefferson) turned, finding both inspiration and guidance in his examples.

Outstanding buildings on Contrà Porti are the fourteenth-century **Palazzo Colleoni Porto** (no. 19) and Palladio's neighbouring **Palazzo Iseppo da Porto**, designed a few years after the Thiene palace. The parallel Corso A. Fogazzaro completes the itinerary of major Palladian buildings with the Palazzo Valmarana (no. 16), perhaps the most eccentric of his projects – notice the gigantic stucco figures at the sides of the facade, where you'd expect columns to be.

At the end of Contrà Santa Corona, two blocks east of Contrà Porti, the **Palazzo Leoni Montanari** (Tues–Sun 10am–6pm; €4 or Card Musei: see box opposite; Ⓦwww.palazzomontanari.com) houses a rather specialized gallery with a collection of art from the Veneto that is respectable enough, if not up to the standards of Venice, or even Padua. Eighteenth-century painting is best represented, including landscape works by Canaletto and Guardi, and there's a rather surprising collection of Russian icons.

Contrà Porti takes you towards the Pusteria Bridge and the **Parco Querini**, the biggest expanse of green in the city, enlivened by a decorative hillock populated by ducks, rabbits and peacocks.

The outskirts – Monte Bérico and the villas

In 1426 Vicenza was struck by bubonic plague, during the course of which outbreak the Virgin is said to have appeared twice at the summit of Monte Bérico – the hill on the southern edge of the city – to announce the city's deliverance. The chapel raised on the site of her appearance became a place of pilgrimage, and at the end of the seventeenth century it was replaced by the present **Basilica di Monte Bérico**. On foot it takes around thirty minutes from the centre of town. Bus #18 climbs the hill every twenty minutes at peak times from Viale Roma, the road running into the centre from the station. When it is not running you can catch a long-distance bus – #6 bound for Barbarano Vicentino – from the bus station, and get off at Monte Bérico, or even take a taxi, as it is not that far.

Pilgrims regularly arrive here by the busload, and the glossy interior of the church is immaculately maintained to receive them. Those in search of artistic fulfilment should venture into the church for Montagna's pietà (in the chapel to the right of the apse) and *The Supper of St Gregory the Great* by Veronese (in the refectory). The latter, the prototype of *The Feast in the House of Levi* in Venice's Accademia, was used for bayonet practice by Austrian troops in 1848 – the small reproduction nearby shows what a thorough job the vandals and subsequent restorers did.

Carry on towards the summit of the hill and you come to the **Museo del Risorgimento e della Resistenza**, some ten-minutes' walk beyond the basilica. The museum houses an impressive display paying particular attention to Vicenza's resistance to the Austrians in the mid-nineteenth century and to the efforts of the anti-fascist Alpine fighters a century later, but for many visitors the main attraction will be the extensive wooded parkland laid out on the slopes below the Villa Guiccioli, the main building (Tues–Sun 9am–1pm & 2.15–5pm; €3, or Card Musei: see box, p.338).

The Villa Valmarana

Ten-minutes' walk away from Monte Bérico is the **Villa Valmarana "ai Nani"** – go back down the hill, head along Via M. D'Azeglio for 100m, then turn right into the cobbled Via S. Bastiano, which ends at the villa. This is an undistinguished house made extraordinary by the decorations of Giambattista and Giandomenico Tiepolo (March 15–Nov 5 Tues–Sun 10am–noon & 3–6pm; rest of year Sat & Sun 10am–noon & 2–4pm; €8). *Nani*, by the way, means "dwarfs", the significance of which becomes clear when you see the garden wall.

There are two parts to the house: the Palazzina, containing six rooms frescoed with typical virtuosity by Giambattista (you're handed a brief guide to the paintings at the entrance); and the Foresteria, one room of which is frescoed by Giambattista and six by Giandomenico, whose predilections are a little less heroic than his father's – but his down to earth peasants have rather more appeal.

La Rotonda

From the Villa Valmarana the narrow Strada Valmarana descends the slope to one of Europe's most imitated buildings – Palladio's Villa Capra, known to most people as **La Rotonda** (grounds & villa mid-March to mid-Nov Wed 10am–noon & 3–6pm; €10; grounds Tues–Sun same weeks and hours, plus Nov–March Tues–Sun 10am–noon & 2.30–5pm; €5). La Rotonda is unique among Palladio's villas in that it was designed not as the main building of a farm but as a pavilion in which entertainments could be held and the landscape enjoyed.

Eating and drinking

Central Vicenza has a delightful buzz in the evening, as the populace gathers in the Piazza dei Signori or just saunters up and down the Corso Palladio. And there is no shortage of **bars** and **cafés** if you want to pause and watch the crowds. While there are few **restaurants** in the centre, standards are high – all of which means you'll need to book or get there early for a table. You should also remember that many places close their kitchens by 11pm – and many shut up shop altogether in August. Popular specialities include *baccalà alla Vicentina* (dried cod in milk and oil) and *sopressa*, a kind of salami from the Pasubio and Recoaro valleys, generally eaten with a slice of grilled polenta.

Cafés and restaurants

Antica Casa della Malvasia Contrà delle Morette 5. Popular budget choice; a bustling, roomy inn just off Piazza dei Signori. There's occasional live music on Wed (March–Oct) and it's open till at least 1am on Fri and Sat, though last orders from the kitchen are 11pm. Closed Mon.

Gran Caffè Garibaldi Piazza dei Signori. The largest of the cafés overlooking the basilica, with the largest terrace, this is always likely to have space. Also serves ice cream inside and heaps of food upstairs. Closed Tues.

I Monelli Contra Ponte San Paolo 13 ☏0444.540.400, ⓦ www.osteriamonelli.it. Small, atmospheric *osteria* that attracts locals for its good local food and moderate prices – its lunchtime menus are a bargain. It lies across the bridge down from Piazza delle Erbe. Open till 1am, closed Mon.

Righetti Piazza Duomo 3. There's no better place for quick, cheap food than this self-service restaurant by the Duomo – and this being Italy, self-service still means you can get great rice and pasta dishes. Open Mon–Thurs till midnight, Fri till 1am.

Sorarù Piazzetta Andrea Palladio 17. Highly recommended *pasticceria*, where the

nineteenth-century interior vies with the cakes for your attention. The location is also unbeatable: it's right in front of the basilica. The only seating is outside, when it is warm enough. Open till 8pm, closed Wed.

Ponte delle Bele Contrà Ponte delle Bele 5 ☏0444.320.647, ⓦ www.pontedellebele.it. Trattoria specializing in Trentine and South Tyrolean cuisine, but it also does Vicentine specialities in a friendly rustic atmosphere. Closed Sun & mid-Aug.

Tutto Gelato Contrà Frasche del Gambero 26 (between the basilica and the Duomo). You can find the best ice creams in town here, though the *Gran Caffè Garibaldi* runs a close second. The fruit flavours are 50 percent fruit and are made without milk.

Bars

Galleria 15 Piazza delle Biade 15. Atmospheric bar with a DJ on Frid & Sat; open till 2am.

Il Grottino Piazza delle Erbe 2. Situated under the basilica, *Il Grottino* has a good range of wines and some snacks, plenty of jazz and lounge music, and late hours. Mon–Fri 5pm–2am., Sat–Sun 4pm–2am.

Verona

With its wealth of Roman sites and streets of pink-hued medieval buildings, the easy-going city of **VERONA** has more in the way of sights than any other place in the Veneto except Venice itself. It is Shakespeare who brings most people here: the city was the setting for Romeo and Juliet, and many people come to see the scene of their great, but fictional, romance. It also hosts one of the major cultural events in the region, when the Roman Arena becomes a magical setting for an outdoor opera festival (see p.349). Unlike Venice, though, Vernona is not overwhelmed by the tourist industry and its economic success largely due to its position at the crossing of the major routes from Germany and Austria to central Italy and from the west to Venice and Trieste.

Verona's initial development as a **Roman** settlement was similarly due to its straddling the main lines of communication. A period of decline after the disintegration of the Roman Empire was followed by revival under the Ostrogoths, who in turn were succeeded by the Franks. By the twelfth century Verona had become a city-state, and in the following century approached the zenith of its independent existence with the rise of the Scaligers. The ruthless Scaligers were at the same time energetic patrons of the arts, and many of Verona's finest buildings date from their rule.

With the fall of their dynasty a time of upheaval ensued, Gian Galeazzo Visconti of Milan emerging in control of the city. Absorption into the Venetian Empire came in 1405, and Verona was governed from Venice until the arrival of Napoleon. Verona's history thereafter shadowed that of Venice.

Arrival and information

If you're flying to Verona's Valerio Catullo **airport** at Villafranca, 12km away, you can get into the city by a regular APT bus (every 20min 7am–11.30pm; €4.50) from the airport to the train and bus station. Taxis costs about €25. Flights to **Montichiari**, 52km away, also called Brescia or, more optimistically, Verona, are served by a daily shuttle bus (€11) to the station that takes an hour; by taxi you'll pay about €90. Tickets to both airports can be bought on board the bus. For more information on both airports, go to Ⓦ www .aeroportoverona.it.

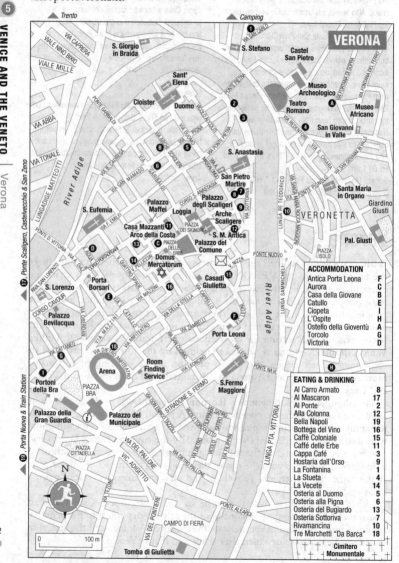

ACCOMMODATION

Antica Porta Leona	F
Aurora	C
Casa della Giovane	B
Catullo	E
Ciopeta	I
L'Ospite	H
Ostello della Gioventù	A
Torcolo	G
Victoria	D

EATING & DRINKING

Al Carro Armato	8
Al Mascaron	17
Al Ponte	2
Alla Colonna	12
Bella Napoli	19
Bottega del Vino	16
Caffè Coloniale	15
Caffé delle Erbe	11
Cappa Café	3
Hostaria dall'Orso	9
La Fontanina	1
La Stueta	4
La Vecete	14
Osteria al Duomo	5
Osteria alla Pigna	6
Osteria del Bugiardo	13
Osteria Sottoriva	7
Rivamancina	10
Tre Marchetti "Da Barca"	18

From the **train and bus station** it's a fifteen-minute walk to the centre. (Note that Verona Porta Nuova is the town's main train station, not Porta Vescovo.) Turn right outside the station (keeping to the right-hand side of the road) then left at the main junction with the broad Corso Porta Nuova, which leads straight to Piazza Bra, just inside the old city walls. If you don't fancy the walk, you can get a bus; tickets must be bought before boarding, either from the machines alongside bay A or from the *tabacchi* inside the train station ticket hall. They cost €1 and are valid for any number of journeys within an hour. If you are coming by **car** you'll find car parks well signed all round the city – eg, near the Arena or at Piazza Isolo in the Veronetta. If you are staying in a hotel in the old centre the hotel must pass your car registration number to the police.

Note that under draconian new regulations in Verona anyone dressing immodestly, littering or picnicking on the steps of public monuments can be fined.

The main **tourist office** is by the central Piazza Bra at Via degli Alpini 9, tucked into the old town walls beside the Palazzo Municipale (Mon–Sat 9am–7pm & Sun 10am–4pm; ☎045.806.8680, ⓦwww.tourism.verona.it). There are additional offices at the train station (Mon–Sat 8am–9pm, Sun 9am–3pm; ☎045.800.5681) and at the airport. The tourist offices organize daily **walking tours** of the city (€10). You can **rent bikes** from Zanchi, Corso Cavour 13/A, near the Porta Borsari (☎045.800.5681; Mon 3.30–7.30pm, Tues–Sat 9am–12.30pm & 3.30–7.30pm). For **internet** access try *Internet Train*, Via Roma 19 (Mon–Fri 10am–10pm, Sat & Sun 2–8pm), and *Internet Etc*, Via 4 Spade 3/B (Tues–Sat 10.30am–7.45pm, Sun & Mon 3.30–7.45pm).

Accommodation

Accommodation is hard to find during the opera season (late June to early Sept), so you'll need to book ahead. You could try the room-finding service, Cooperativa Albergatori Veronesi (CAV), at Via Patuzzi 5 (May to mid-Nov Mon–Sat 10am–7pm; mid-Nov to April Mon–Fri 10am–6pm; closed mid-Dec to mid-Jan; ☎045.800.9844, ⓦwww.veronabooking.com).

Hotels

Antica Porta Leona Via Corticlla Leoni 3 ☎045.595.499, ⓦwww.anticaportaleona.com. Spacious rooms in this large three-star, all with a/c, some with balconies. Has plenty of single rooms ❻

Aurora Piazzetta XIV Novembre 2 ☎045.594.717, ⓦwww.hotelaurora.biz. Upmarket two-star hotel with a welcoming atmosphere and many rooms overlooking the Piazza delle Erbe. The staff are friendly and knowledgeable, and speak good English. Excellent buffet breakfast. ❺

Catullo Via Valerio Teatro Catullo 1 ☎045.800.2786, ⓔlocandacatullo@tiscali.it. The cheapest – if not the friendliest – hotel in the centre, just off the main shopping artery of Via Mazzini. It is on the second and third floors – with no lift. The large rooms are rather shabby but have plenty of light, and some have a private bathroom. No credit cards. ❷

Ciopeta Vicolo Teatro Filarmonica 2 ☎045.800.6843, ⓦwww.ciopeta.it. This friendly, family-run one-star in an alley parallel to Via Roma should re-open after restoration in 2009. Book ahead, as it only has five rooms (all with shared bathrooms). Excellent restaurant, too, which spreads out into the alley in summer. ❷

L'Ospite Via XX Settembre 3 ☎045.803.6994, ⓦwww.lospite.com. Six apartments just across the Ponte Navi in the Veronetta run by the helpful Federica. Studio flats sleep two, one-bed flats can sleep up to four. Simply furnished but excellent value, ideal for small families. ❸

Torcolo Vicolo Listone 3 ☎045.800.7512, ⓦwww.hoteltorcolo.it. Nicely turned-out two-star hotel within 100m of the Arena, just off Piazza Bra. Extremely welcoming owners – and a favourite with the opera crowds, so book ahead. ❺

Victoria Via Adua 8 ☎045.590.566, ⓦwww.hotelvictoria.it. Housed in a complex of old buildings, this four-star has a snazzy modern foyer, well-equipped rooms and gymnasium. If you want to treat yourself, the superior doubles are gorgeous. Good deals out of season. ❼

Hostels and campsite

Casa della Giovane Via Pigna 7 ☎045.596.880, ⓦwww.casadellagiovane.com. Spartan but friendly convent-run hostel for women, with an 11pm curfew, although there is flexibility for guests with opera tickets. Reservations by phone, fax or email, max one month in advance. €18 in dorms, plus some double rooms at €20–25 per head.

Ostello della Gioventù Salita Fontana del Ferro 15 ☎045.590.360. The official HI hostel is in Villa Francescatti, up behind the Teatro Romano; as it's quite a walk from the centre, it's best to take a bus (#73, or #90 on Sun) to Piazza Isolo, then walk up

the hill. No reservations, but with over 200 beds there should be room. The 11.30pm curfew is extended for guests with opera tickets. HI membership not essential if you're staying for just one night. €18 per night; reasonably priced evening meals are available.

Campeggio Castel San Pietro Via Castel S. Pietro 2 ☎045.592.037, ⓦwww.campingcastelsanpietro .com. A pleasant site out by the old city walls, the only place to camp near the centre of Verona; take a bus to Via Marsala and then it is a steep walk up the hill. Open May–Sept.

The City

Coming from the train station, you pass Verona's south gate, the **Porta Nuova**, and come onto the long Corso Porta Nuova, which ends at the battlemented arches that precede the **Piazza Bra**. Here stands the mightiest of Verona's Roman monuments, the Arena, marking the edge of the old city that nestles in the bend of the river Adige and is crisscrossed by a neat grid of streets around the old Roman forum. Most of the sights are in this old centre, though it's worth venturing across the river to the Veronetta district for a clutch of sights, including the archeology museum.

The Arena

Dating from the first century AD, the **arena** has survived in remarkable condition, despite the twelfth-century earthquake that destroyed all but four of the arches of the outer wall. The interior (daily 8.30am–7.30pm, closes at 3.30pm during the opera season; March Mon 1.30–7.30pm, Thurs 8.30am–2pm; €4, or Verona Card – see below, free on first Sun of month) was scarcely damaged by the tremor, and where once crowds of around 20,000 packed the benches for gladiatorial contests, nowadays audiences come to watch gargantuan opera productions. Originally measuring 152m by 123m overall, and thus the third largest of all Roman amphitheatres, the arena remains an awesome sight – and offers a tremendous urban panorama from the topmost of the 44 pink marble tiers

The Casa di Giulietta and San Fermo

North of the arena, **Via Mazzini** is a narrow traffic-free street lined with generally expensive clothes, shoe and jewellery shops. A left turn at the end

---

The biglietto unico and Verona Card

A **biglietto unico**, costing €5, allows one visit each to San Zeno, San Lorenzo, the Duomo (but not the Museo Canonicale), Sant'Anastasia and San Fermo. The ticket can be bought at any of these churches, which individually charge €2.50 for admission (ⓦwww.chieseverona.it). If you're planning to be very busy, it might be worth getting the **Verona Card**, which gives access to all the sights listed above, including the Museo Canonicale, plus the arena, the Torre dei Lamberti, the Museo Lapidario, Castelvecchio, the Casa di Giulietta, the Tomba di Giulietta and the Roman Theatre, as well as free travel on city buses. A one-day Verona card costs €8, the three-day €12. You can buy it at *tabacchi* and at the museums and monuments, too, though sometimes they run out of stock. Note that many museums are closed on Monday mornings, and several are free on the first Sunday of the month.

leads to the Piazza delle Erbe, while a right takes you into **Via Cappello**, a street named after the family that Shakespeare turned into the Capulets – and on the left, at no. 23, is the **Casa di Giulietta** or Juliet's House (Mon 1.30–7.30pm; Tues–Sun 8.30am–7.30pm; €4). In fact, although the "Capulets" and the "Montagues" (Montecchi) did exist, Romeo and Juliet were entirely fictional creations. The house itself, constructed at the start of the fourteenth century, is in a fine state of preservation, but is largely empty. It's said that if you stand under the balcony and make a wish about love it will come true.

Via Cappello leads into Via Leoni with its Roman gate, the **Porta Leona**, and a segment of excavated Roman street, exposed 3m below today's street level. At the end of Via Leoni rises the red-brick **San Fermo** church (March–Oct Mon–Sat 10am–6pm, Sun 1–6pm; Nov–Feb Tues–Sat 10am–1pm & 1.30–4pm, Sun 1–5pm; €2.50 or *biglietto unico*/Verona Card – see box opposite), whose inconsistent exterior betrays the fact that it consists of two churches combined. Flooding forced the Benedictines to superimpose a second church on the one founded in the eighth century. The Romanesque lower church, entered from the left of the choir, has impressive low vaulting, sometimes obscured by exhibitions.

Piazza delle Erbe and Piazza dei Signori

Originally a major Roman crossroads and the site of the forum, **Piazza delle Erbe** is still the heart of the city. As the name suggests, the market used to sell mainly vegetables, but nowadays it has been largely taken over by ugly, semi-permanent booths selling clothes, souvenirs, antiques and fast food. The rich variety of buildings framing the square is far more attractive. Most striking are the **Domus Mercatorum** (on the left as you look from Via Cappello), which was founded in 1301 as a merchants' warehouse and exchange, the fourteenth-century **Torre del Gardello** and, to the right of the tower, the **Casa Mazzanti**, whose sixteenth-century murals are best seen after dark, under enhancing spotlights.

The neighbouring **Piazza dei Signori** used to be the chief public square of Verona. Facing you as you come into the square is the medieval **Palazzo degli Scaligeri**, residence of the Scaligers; extending from it at a right angle is the

▲ Piazza delle Erbe, Verona

fifteenth-century **Loggia del Consiglio**, the former assembly hall of the city council and Verona's outstanding early-Renaissance building. The rank of Roman notables along the roof includes Verona's most illustrious native poet, Catullus. For a dizzying view of the city, take a sharp right as soon as you come into the square, and go up the twelfth-century **Torre dei Lamberti** (Mon–Thurs 9.30am–8.30pm, Fri–Sun 8.30am–10pm; June–Sept open till midnight on Fri–Sat; €4 or Verona Card – see box p.344).

The Scaligeri tombs

5

Passing under the arch linking the Palazzo degli Scaligeri to the Palazzo del Capitano, you come to the little Romanesque church of Santa Maria Antica, in front of which are ranged the **Arche Scaligeri**, some of the most elaborate Gothic funerary monuments in Italy. Over the side entrance to the church, an equestrian statue of **Cangrande I** ("Big Dog"; died 1329) gawps down from his tomb's pyramidal roof; the statue is a copy, the original being displayed in the Castelvecchio. The canopied tombs of the rest of the clan are enclosed within a wrought-iron palisade decorated with ladder motifs, the emblem of the Scaligers. **Mastino I** ("Mastiff"; died 1277), founder of the dynasty, is buried in the simple tomb against the wall of the church; Mastino II (died 1351) is to the left of the entrance, opposite the most florid of the tombs, that of **Cansignorio** ("Top Dog"; died 1375).

Sant'Anastasia, San Pietro Martire and the Duomo

Going on past the Arche Scaligeri, and turning left along Via San Pietro, you come to **Sant'Anastasia** (March–Oct Mon–Sat 9am–6pm, Sun 1–6pm; Nov–Feb Tues–Sat 10am–1pm & 1.30–4pm, Sun 1–5pm; €2.50 or *biglietto unico*/Verona Card), Verona's largest church. Started in 1290 and completed in 1481, it's mainly Gothic in style, with undertones of the Romanesque. The fourteenth-century carvings of New Testament scenes around the doors are the most arresting feature of its bare exterior; the interior's highlight is Pisanello's delicately coloured fresco *St George and the Princess* (high above the chapel to the right of the altar), a work in which the normally martial saint appears as something of a dandy.

On one side of the little piazza fronting Sant'Anastasia stands **San Pietro Martire** (open daily, but staffed by volunteers, so its hours are irregular), deconsecrated since its ransacking by Napoleon. The highlight of the small interior is the vast lunette fresco from the sixteenth century on the east wall. Easily the strangest picture in Verona it's an allegorical account of the Virgin's Assumption, though the bizarre collection of animals appears to have little connection with a bemused-looking Madonna.

Verona's red-and-white-striped **Duomo** (March–Oct Mon–Sat 9.30am–5.30pm, Sun 1.30–5.30pm; Nov–Feb Tues–Sat 11am–1pm & 1.30–4pm, Sun 1.30–5pm; €2.50 or *biglietto unico*/Verona Card) lies just round the river's bend, past the Roman Ponte Pietra. Consecrated in 1187, it's Romanesque in its lower parts, developing into Gothic as it goes up; the two doorways are twelfth century – look for the story of Jonah and the whale on the south porch, and the statues of Roland and Oliver, two of Charlemagne's paladins, on the west. In the first chapel on the left, an *Assumption* by Titian occupies an architectural frame by Sansovino, who also designed the choir.

To the Castelvecchio

After the arena and the Teatro Romano, Verona's most impressive Roman remnant is the **Porta dei Borsari** (on the junction of Via Diaz and Corso Porta

Borsari), a structure that was as great an influence on the city's Renaissance architects as the amphitheatre. This was Verona's largest Roman gate; the inscription dates it at 265 AD, but it's almost certainly older than that.

Heading down Corso Cavour from Porta dei Borsari, past the small twelfth-century **San Lorenzo** (March–Oct Mon–Sat 10am–6pm & Sun 1–6pm; Nov–Feb Tues–Sat 10am–1pm & 1.30–4pm, Sun 1–5pm; €2.50 or *biglietto unico*/Verona Card), you come to the **Arco dei Gavi**, a first-century Roman triumphal arch that was rebuilt in 1930 after Napoleon's troops tore down the original. This is your best vantage point from which to admire the **Ponte Scaligero**, built by Cangrande II between 1355 and 1375. The retreating German army blew up the bridge in 1945, but the salvaged material was used for reconstruction.

The fortress from which the bridge springs, the **Castelvecchio** (Mon 1.30–7.30pm, Tues–Sun 8.30am–7.30pm; €4 or Verona Card, free on first Sun of month), was commissioned by Cangrande II at around the same time and became the stronghold for Verona's subsequent rulers. Opened as the city museum in 1925, it was damaged by bombing during World War II. The equestrian figure Cangrande I, removed from his tomb, is strikingly displayed on an outdoor pedestal; his expression is disconcerting at close range, the simpleton's grin being difficult to reconcile with the image of the ruthless warlord. Outstanding among paintings are two works by Jacopo Bellini, two Madonnas by Giovanni Bellini, another Madonna by Pisanello, Veronese's *Descent from the Cross*, a Tintoretto *Nativity*, a Lotto portrait and works by Giambattista and Giandomenico Tiepolo. The real joy of the museum, however, is in wandering round the medieval pieces: beautiful sculpture and frescoes by the often nameless artists of the late Middle Ages.

San Zeno Maggiore

A little over 1km northwest of the Castelvecchio is the **Basilica di San Zeno Maggiore** (March–Oct Mon–Sat 8.30am–6pm, Sun 1–6pm; Nov–Feb Tues–Sat 10am–1pm & 1.30–4pm, Sun 1–5pm; €2.50 or *biglietto unico*/Verona Card), one of the most significant Romanesque churches in northern Italy. A church was founded here, above the tomb of the city's patron saint, as early as the fifth century, but the present building and its campanile were put up in the first half of the twelfth century, with additions continuing up to the end of the fourteenth. Its large rose window, representing the Wheel of Fortune, dates from the early twelfth century, as does the magnificent portal, whose lintels bear relief sculptures representing the months – look also for St Zeno trampling the devil. Extraordinary bronze panels on the doors depict scenes from the Bible and the *Miracles of San Zeno*, their style influenced by Byzantine art; most of those on the left are from around 1100, and most of the right-hand panels date from a century or so later. Inside the lofty interior the most compulsive image is the high altar's luminous *Madonna and Saints* by Mantegna.

Across the Adige

On the other side of Ponte Garibaldi, and right along the embankments or through the public gardens, is **San Giorgio in Braida**, in terms of its works of art the richest of Verona's churches. A *Baptism* by Tintoretto hangs over the door, while the main altar, designed by Sanmicheli, incorporates a marvellous piece by Paolo **Veronese** – *The Martyrdom of St George*.

It's a short walk along the embankments, past the twelfth-century church of Santo Stefano and the Ponte Pietra, to the first-century-BC **Teatro Romano** (Mon 1.30–7.30pm, Tues–Sun 8.30am–7.30pm; €3 or Verona Card, see box p.344, free on first Sun of month); much restored, the theatre is used for concerts and plays. High above it, and reached by a rickety-looking lift, the **Museo Archeologico** (same hours & ticket) occupies the buildings of an old convent. Its well-arranged collection features a number of Greek, Roman and Etruscan finds, including a magnificent Roman bronze head; from the old frescoed chapel at the top the views are magnificent.

If you've the energy to walk up hill again, there are two sites nearby. The **Museo Africano** (Tues–Sat 9am–12.30pm, 2.30–5.30pm, Sun 2–6pm, closed Sun in July–Aug; €3 or Verona Card), off Via San Giovanni in Valle at Vicolo Pozzo 1, has a brightly lit and well-displayed collection of musical instruments and masks brought back over the years by missionaries. The leaflets on the role of spiritual healers and voodoo are very informative. Further up Via San Giovanni in Valle, just below the youth hostel, stands the small Romanesque church of **San Giovanni in Valle** (daily 9am–noon), which was founded in the eighth century and rebuilt in the twelfth after earthquake damage. Bombing in 1944 destroyed the decoration of the interior, but the crypt escaped pretty well unscathed.

Back down at river level is one of the treats of the city: the church of **Santa Maria in Organo** (daily 8am–noon & 2.30–6pm but closed Wed and Fri pm, and open from 9am at weekends; free), which possesses what Vasari praised as the finest choir stall in Italy. Dating from the 1490s, this marquetry was the work of a Benedictine monk, one Fra Giovanni, and is astonishing in its precision and use of perspective. There's more of his work in the sacristy, while in the crypt you can see reused upside-down Roman columns. Further down Via Santa Chiara you'll come to the finest formal gardens in Verona, the **Giardino Giusti** at Via Giardino Giusti 2 (daily: summer 9am–8pm; winter 9am–sunset; €5). Full of fountains and shady corners, the Giusti provides the city's most pleasant respite from the streets.

Eating and drinking

The Veronese have a reputation for liking their food – one thirteenth-century story tells of the defenders of a castle opening their gates when they heard that the besiegers were cooking *baccalà*, dried cod – although that was more likely a sign of their desperation. You can certainly eat well in the city: if the local speciality of horse meat is not to your taste you can try the local salamis, pumpkin ravioli or *bigoli*, a handmade thick version of spaghetti. The best **restaurants** in Verona tend to be packed after 9pm, so it's best to book or go out early.

As the Veneto produces more DOC **wine** than any other region in Italy, it's not surprising that Italy's main wine fair, Vinitaly, is held in Verona; it takes place in April and offers abundant sampling opportunities. For non-alcoholic pleasures, head for the best **ice cream** in the city at *Balu*, at Corso Porta Borsari 57 just inside the Roman gate (daily 1–7.30pm), or the *gelateria* at via Ponte Pietra 23, by the Roman bridge (daily 2.30–8pm). In the week before and after the arena season (July and Aug) you may find places close early or shut completely as the city takes a rest.

Restaurants

Alla Colonna Largo Pescheria Vecchia 4 ☏ 045.596.718. This place is usually packed with savvy locals – the food is simple, superb, the portions large and the prices excellent (€14 menu). Open until 2am but kitchen closes 11.30pm. Closed Sun.

Bella Napoli Via Marconi 14. Serves the best pizza – and the largest – in Verona – in a distinctly Neapolitan atmosphere. Open Sun–Thurs till 1am, Fri–Sat till 2.30am.

Bottega del Vino Vicolo Scudo di Francia 3/A ☏ 045.800.4535 ⊛ www.bottegavini.it. One of the top restaurants in Verona, with flamboyant antique decor and one of the largest selection of wines in Italy. It's not cheap – mains go up to €27 – and slightly touristy but plenty of locals drop in for a glass of wine earlier in the evening. A dish to look out for is the *risotto all'Amarone* – braised in the local wine. Open till midnight and closed Tues.

Hostaria dall'Orso Via Sottoriva 3/C
℡ 045.597.214. Friendly place under the atmospheric arches of Via Sottoriva serving good salads
and local dishes. Open till midnight Mon–Sat.
La Fontanina Piazzetta Fontanina, Veronetta
℡ 045.913.305, ⊛ www.ristorantelafontanina.com.
One of the best old-world *osterie* on the left bank.
Exclusive atmosphere (and prices to match – it has
a Michelin star), with tables hidden among crates
of wine and decorated screens. Closed all day Sun,
Mon lunch & all Aug.
La Stueta Via Redentore 4/B, Veronetta
℡ 045.803.2462. A small *osteria* next to the
Roman amphitheatre. Its well-executed seasonal
cooking includes dishes such as *garganelli con
porri e speck* (pasta in a creamy leek and bacon
sauce). Closed Tues.
Osteria alla Pigna Via Pigna 4 ℡ 045.800.4080,
⊛ www.osteriapigna.it. Elegant traditional restaurant between the Duomo and Piazza dell'Erbe that
has a well deserved reputation among locals and
tourists alike. Closed all day Sun and Mon lunch.
Osteria del Bugiardo Corso Porta Borsari 17/A
℡ 045.591.1869. Small establishment with an
excellent range of antipasti and *crostini*, as well as
some *primi* and *secondi*. Its high tables are packed
at lunchtime with locals grabbing a quick lunch.
Open till 10pm Sun–Thurs, and till midnight on
Fri–Sat, closed Mon.
Tre Marchetti "Da Barca" Vicolo Tre Marchetti
19/B ℡ 045.803.0463. A couple of steps north of
the arena, this place is perfect for a pre- or post-
opera meal of Veronese specialities, such as *bigoli*
pasta or veal braised in Amarone. It's a very elegant
family-run place – unsurprisingly pricey, given its
location. Booking essential. Closed Sun (closed Mon
only in July & Aug).

Bars and cafés

Al Carro Armato Vicolo Gatto 2/A. One of
the most atmospheric *osterie* in the city,
with a counter full of delicious antipasti for you to
choose from, such as *polpetti* (meat balls), *sfilacci*
(fine slices of horse) and beans with onions. Open
until 1am, kitchen open till 10.30pm closed Mon.
Al Ponte Via Ponte Pietra 26. Sip a glass on the
terrace here and enjoy a marvellous view of Ponte
Pietra and the Teatro Romano. Open until 3am;
closed Wed.
Caffè Coloniale Piazzetta Viviani 14/C. The best
hot chocolate in the city, and good snacks in a
mock-colonial setting, with attractive outdoor
terrace. Open 7am–midnight, closes 8pm on Mon.
Caffè delle Erbe Piazza delle Erbe 32. Known
universally as *Mazzanti*, this is the loudest,
youngest and coolest of the late-opening bars on
the square. Open until midnight. Closed Mon.
Cappa Café Piazzetta Bra Molinari 1/A. Large bar
with eastern trappings, floor cushions, riverfront
terrace and live jazz on Sun Oct–April. Open all day
till 2am daily.
Le Vecete Via Pellicciai 32. Atmospheric
osteria with a delicious selection of the
savoury tartlets known as *bocconcini*, and good
lunches. Its wine list is excellent, ranging from
cheap to very expensive. Open all afternoon, Sat
11.30am–1.30am and till 12.30am the rest of the
week – later during the opera season.
Osteria al Duomo Via Duomo 7/A. Old city bar
little changed by modern fashion and enlivened by
live music on Wed afternoons from Sept to June.
Interesting small menu, too, with local specialities
such as *bigoli* with a donkey sauce (*sugo d'asino*).
Open 4pm–midnight; closed Sun.
Osteria Sottoriva Via Sottoriva 9. Verona's
traditional *osterie* don't come much more
authentic than this: it's rumbustious, full of locals,
and serves delicious food. In summer you can sit
outside under the arches. They give out crayons to
keep the kids busy. Open 10.30am–10.30pm;
closed Wed.
Rivamancina Vicolo Quadrelli 1, Veronetta. Lively
late bar on the left bank of the Adige, with trendy
music and contemporary cocktails. Mon–Thurs
7pm–1am, Fri–Sat 7pm–2am.

Nightlife and entertainment

Music and theatre are the dominant art forms in the cultural life of Verona.
The city's **opera festival**, held in the arena during July and August, has been
a major draw since 1913, always opening with a no-expense-spared production
of *Aida*. To get the best (or last-minute) seats, call in at the office on Via Dietro
Anfiteatro 6/B; if you can't make it in person you can book by phone or
online (℡ 045.800.5151, ⊛ www.arena.it; prices €22–200). Big rock events
crop up on the arena's calendar too. A summer season of ballet and of
Shakespeare and other dramatists in Italian performed at the **Teatro Romano**.
Some events here are free; for the rest, cheapskates who don't mind inferior
acoustics can park themselves on the steps going up the hill alongside the

theatre. The box office at the Teatro Romano also sells tickets for the arena and vice versa.

The **club** scene is much livelier than in Venice, but most venues are outside the centre, such as *Alter Ego*, a couple of kilometres north of the centre across the Ponte Pietra at Via Torricelle 9 – best reached by taxi. The *Spettacoli* section of *L'Arena* (there's a copy in every bar), is a good source of information on what's happening (in Italian only).

One of the most enjoyable days in the calendar is Verona's **Carnevale**. On the Friday before Shrove Tuesday, a huge procession winds through the centre from Piazza Bra. This is a local event with none of the masks and posing of Venice – just lots of people dressing up, loud music and confetti – though mind the kids who get carried away spraying white foam everywhere. The procession is led by a large character called the Papa del Gnocco – most of the city's restaurants serve *gnocchi* on that Friday.

Treviso

One of the undiscovered gems in the Veneto is **TREVISO**, a charming, quiet town that makes an ideal jumping-off point both for Venice and the northern Veneto. Treviso was an important town long before its assimilation by Venice in 1389, and plenty of evidence of its early status survives in the form of Gothic churches, public buildings and, most dramatically of all, the paintings of **Tomaso da Modena** (1325–79), the major artist in northern Italy in the years immediately after Giotto's death. The general townscape within Treviso's sixteenth-century walls is appealing too – long porticoes and frescoed house facades give many of the streets an appearance quite distinct from those of other towns in the region.

Arrival and information

Arriving at the **train station**, head straight across the bridge, bending slightly left at the first roundabout to reach the centre. See p.279 for arriving at Treviso's **airport**. There's **internet** access at *Servicepoint*, Via Toniolo 19 (Mon–Fri 8.30am–12.30pm & 3–7pm, Sat 8.30am–12.30pm) in the centre of town. The **tourist office** is right in the centre, at Piazza Monte di Pietà 8 (Mon 9am–12.30pm, Tues–Sat 9am–12.30pm & 2–6pm, Sun 9.30am–12.30pm & 3–6pm; ☏0422.547.632, ⊛tourism.provincia.treviso.it); it dispenses useful leaflets on both Treviso and attractions throughout Treviso province.

Accommodation

The downside of the town being undiscovered is that it isn't really geared up for tourists, the main problem being that most of its **hotels** are characterless or somewhat down-at-heel "Eurobusiness" places. The tourist office can help with B&B accommodation.

Carlton Largo Porta Altinia 15 ☏0422.411.661, ⊛www.hotelcarlton.it. Large, but friendly, business-orientated four-star that's situated near the railway station. ❹

Continental Via Roma 16 ☏0422.411.216, ⊛www.hcontinental.it. Virtually next door to the

Carlton, this four-star hotel is similarly geared to business clientele. ❹

Il Focolare Piazza Ancilotto 4 ☏0422.56601, ⊛www.albergoilfocolare.net. Close to the tourist office, *Il Focolare* is a small and reasonably priced two-star hotel. ❸

The City

Treviso was pounded during both world wars and on Good Friday 1944 was half-destroyed in a single bombing raid. However, historic features are well preserved in the main street of Treviso's centre, **Calmaggiore**, where modern commerce has reached the sort of compromise with the past that the Italians seem to arrange better than anyone else.

At the bottom of Calmaggiore, on one side of the **Piazza dei Signori**, the early thirteenth-century **Palazzo dei Trecento** was one casualty of 1944. The lengthy restoration of its surviving frescoes has just been finished – check at the tourist office to see if they can be visited yet. The adjoining **Palazzo del Podestà** is a nineteenth-century concoction. Of more interest are the two churches at the back of the block: **San Vito** and **Santa Lucia** (usually open daily 9am–noon). The tiny, dark chapel of Santa Lucia has extensive frescoes by Tomaso da Modena and his followers; San Vito has even older paintings in the alcove through which you enter from Santa Lucia, though they're not in a good state.

The Duomo of Treviso, **San Pietro**, stands at the far end of Calmaggiore (Mon–Sat 7.30am–noon & 3.30–7pm, Sun 7.30am–1pm & 3.30–8pm; free). Founded in the twelfth century, San Pietro was much altered in succeeding centuries, and then rebuilt to rectify the damage of 1944. The interior is chiefly notable for the crypt – a thicket of twelfth-century columns with scraps of medieval mosaics – and the Cappella Malchiostro, with fragmentary frescoes by Pordenone and an *Annunciation* by Titian.

Just over the River Sile from the railway station is the severe Dominican church of **San Nicolò** (Mon–Fri 8am–noon & 3.30–7pm; free), which has frescoes dating from the thirteenth to the sixteenth centuries. Some of the columns are decorated with paintings by Tomaso da Modena and his school, of which the best are the *SS Jerome* and *Agnes* (by Tomaso) on the first column on your right as you enter. For a comprehensive demonstration of Tomaso da Modena's talents you have to visit the neighbouring **Seminario**, where the chapterhouse, to the left of the entrance, is decorated with forty *Portraits of Members of the Dominican Order*, painted in 1352 (Mon–Fri: summer 8am–6pm; winter 8am–12.30pm & 3–5.30pm; free – you may need to ring the bell to get in).

The Santa Caterina district

On the other side of town from San Nicolò there's another brilliant fresco cycle by Tomaso da Modena, *The Story of the Life of Saint Ursula*, in the deconsecrated church of **Santa Caterina** (Tues–Sun 9am–12.30pm, 2.30–6pm; €3) behind Piazza Giacomo Matteotti on Via Santa Caterina. Painted for the now extinct church of Santa Margherita sul Sile, the frescoes were detached from the walls in the late nineteenth century shortly before the church was destroyed, and are in a poor condition. Santa Caterina also houses some works from the old **Museo Civico**, which is closed for restoration.

The district around the church is a pleasant one, with its antiques sellers and furniture restorers and the hubbub of the stalls around the market in Piazza Matteotti on Tuesdays and Saturdays. To the south stands the **Basilica di Santa Maria Maggiore** (daily 6.30–11.45am & 3–7.30pm), which houses the most venerated image in Treviso, a fresco of the Madonna originally painted by Tomaso but subsequently retouched.

Eating, drinking and nightlife

Treviso's **restaurants** have a higher reputation that its hotels, while the **bars** and **cafés** clustered underneath and around the Palazzo dei Trecento are always buzzing. Regular features on the city menus are radicchio, the bitter red lettuce that is remarkably popular, and tiramisù, which as every local knows comes from here. Treviso's **nightlife** is very low-key, though this may change as the university population grows. Currently, if you want to dance you have to head 3km out of town to the places along the Via Fonderia, but the trendier Trevisans stay in town for a drink at *Sottoportico* (Mon–Sat till 2am) under the arcades at Sottoportico dei Buranelli 29 or *Al Tòcai* (Tues–Sun till 1am) in Piazzetta Lombardi, south of Piazza dei Signori.

Restaurants and bars

Dai Naneti Vicolo Brolo 2. Round the corner from the Palazzo Trecento, Beppe and Fabio preside over a small bar that is packed with locals sampling the wine, food and congenial atmosphere. Open till 8.30pm, closed all Sun.

Muscoli's Via Pescheria 23. The alleyway below the tourist office leads down to this marvellous bar, where the customers spill out onto the fish market island opposite when the weather permits. Excellent snacks – such as the fig and blue cheese *crostini*. Open 7am-2am, closed Sun.

Osteria al Canevon Piazza San Vito 18 ☏0422.540.208. You'll find adventurous cuisine and high standards in this friendly restaurant centrally placed on the square behind the tourist office. Specializes in fish. Open till 8.30pm, closed all day Tues and Wed lunchtime.

Osteria Arman Via Manzoni 27. An old family-run establishment behind San Francesco that sells its own Prosecco to accompany generous helpings of pasta. Open till midnight, closed Thurs all day & Sun lunchtime.

Toni del Spin Via Inferiore 7 ☏0422.543.829. A few steps from the church of San Vito, the recently refurbished *Toni del Spin*, provides superb Trevisan cuisine for around €30 per head; open till 11pm, closed all Sun & Mon lunchtime.

Castelfranco and Cittadella

CASTELFRANCO VENETO once stood on the western edge of Treviso's territory, and battlemented brick walls that the Trevisans threw round the town in 1199 to protect it against the Paduans still encircle most of the old centre (or *castello*). Of all the walled towns of the Veneto, few bear comparison with Castelfranco, and the place would merit a visit on the strength of this alone. But Castelfranco was also the birthplace of **Giorgione** and possesses a painting that single-handedly vindicates Vasari's judgement that Giorgione's place in Venetian art is equivalent to Leonardo da Vinci's in that of Florence.

Known simply as the **Castelfranco Madonna**, Giorgione's magnificent *Madonna and Child with St Francis and St Liberale* hangs in the eighteenth-century Duomo (daily 9am–noon & 3.30–6pm), in a chapel to the right of the chancel. Giorgione is the most elusive of all the great figures of the Renaissance: only six surviving paintings can indisputably be attributed to him, and so little is known about his life that legends have proliferated to fill the gaps. Next to the Duomo, the **Casa Giorgione** is a bizarre disappointment hardly worth the entry fee (Tues–Sun 10am–12.30pm, 3–6.30pm; €2.50). Its rooms are totally empty, except for a chiaroscuro frieze in one of the first-floor rooms hopefully attributed to Giorgione. The nearby **restaurant** *Alle Mura*, at Via FM Preti 69, has a bizarre interior decorated with Polynesian artefacts, but the food is faultless: the €12 lunch menu is excellent value (☏0423.498.098, closed Thurs).

When Treviso turned Castelfranco into a garrison, the Paduans promptly retaliated by reinforcing the defences of **CITTADELLA**, 15km to the west, on the train line to Vicenza. The fortified walls of Cittadella were built in the first quarter of the thirteenth century, and are even more impressive than those of its neighbour. You enter the town through one of four rugged brick gateways;

if you're coming from the train station it'll be the Porta Padova, the most daunting of the four, flanked by the **Torre di Malta**. The tower was built as a prison and torture chamber by the monstrous Ezzelino da Romano, known to those he terrorized in this region in the mid-thirteenth century as "The Son of Satan". His atrocities earned him a place in the seventh circle of Dante's *Inferno*, where he's condemned to boil eternally in a river of blood. There's not much else to Cittadella, but it's definitely worth hopping off the train for a quick circuit of the walls.

Bassano del Grappa and around

Situated on the River Brenta, **BASSANO** has expanded rapidly over the last few decades, though its historic centre remains largely unspoiled. For centuries a major producer of ceramics and wrought iron, Bassano is also renowned for its **grappa** distilleries and culinary delicacies such as porcini mushrooms, white asparagus and honey. Although it has few outstanding monuments or fine architecture, Bassano's airy situation on the edge of the mountains and the quiet charm of the old streets make it well worth the trip.

Arrival, information and accommodation

A short walk up Via Chilesotti from the **bus and train stations** brings you to Bassano's sturdy city walls. Just through the walls you'll find the **tourist office** at Largo Corona d'Italia 35 (Mon–Sat 9am–1pm & 2–6pm; ℡0424.524.351, ⓦwww.vicenzae.org).

Hotels and hostel

Al Castello Via Bonamigo 19 ℡0424.228665, ⓦwww.hotelalcastello.it. The only hotel in the old centre, this three-star is right by the castle. ➌

Brennero Via Torino 7 ℡0424.228.538, ⓦwww .hotelbrennero.com. Easy walking distance to the centre, the three-star *Brennero* lies just east of the walls. ➌

Ostelio Don Cremona Via Chini 6 ℡0424.219.137, ⓦwww.ostellobassanodelgrappa .it. For a low-budget stay, just south of the centre is

the youth hostel with 90 beds. €13 for a dorm bed, doubles €24 per person.

Villa Brocchi Colonna Contra' San Giorgio 98 ℡0424.501.580, ⓦwww .villabrocchicolonna.it. Charming converted villa 2km from the centre on the western edge of town. The welcoming mother-and-daughter team offer very comfortable rooms and the breakfast – with pancakes and a fantastic array of jams made from produce in the orchard – is delectable. ➍

The Town

All the main sights lie between the Brenta and the train station. Walking away from the station, you cross the orbital Viale delle Fosse to get to **Piazza Garibaldi**, one of the two main squares. Here, the cloister of the fourteenth-century church of San Francesco now houses the **Museo Civico** (Tues–Sat 9am–6.30pm, Sun 3.30–6.30pm; €4.50, ticket includes the Palazzo Sturm – see p.354), devoted to Roman finds and paintings by the da Ponte family (better known as the Bassano family). Jacopo Bassano is the most famous, though his works can be sentimental and derivative; his son Francesco is better represented by some brooding portraits. Don't miss the tucked-away medieval rooms concealing a couple of typically luminous Bartolomeo Vivarini works. Other rooms are devoted to a number of plaster works by Canova and to the great baritone Tito Gobbi, who was born in Bassano.

Overlooking the other side of the piazza is the **Torre Civica**, once a lookout tower for the twelfth-century inner walls, now a clock tower with spurious nineteenth-century battlements and windows (Sat–Sun 10am–noon & 2–5pm; €2). Beyond the adjacent Piazza Libertà, Piazzetta Montevecchio leads to a little jumble of streets and stairways running down to the river and the **Ponte degli Alpini**, designed by Palladio in 1568. From here, follow Via Ferracina downstream for a couple of minutes and you'll come to the eighteenth-century **Palazzo Sturm** (Tues–Sat 9am–1pm, 3–6pm Sun 3.30–6.30pm; same ticket as Museo Civico – see p.353), a showcase for the town's famed majolica ware, with a new display on the Remondini printing works, which was founded in Bassano in the seventeenth century.

Various streets and squares in Bassano commemorate the dead of the two world wars. In 1944 resistance fighters were rounded up and hanged from trees along the street now called Viale dei Martiri. The major **war memorial**, however, is out of town on **Monte Grappa**, an hour's drive away, access by car only at present – ask the tourist office if the bus has been revived. From the top (1775m) the views are astounding; on a clear day you can see Venice.

Eating and drinking

Bassano del Grappa is naturally best known for its **grappa**, the Italian firewater, and – this being Italy – where there is good alcohol you'll find good food not far behind. Bassano's central streets and squares come alive at the end of the siesta and the **bars** and **restaurants** around the main square have a real buzz by the early evening. The two big names in *grappa* can both be found by old bridge: *Poli* has a shop where you can taste the many kinds of grappa it sells, while the former *Nardini* distillery at Ponte Vecchio 2 has a period-piece bar and *grappa* shop with excellent views over the river (open till 8pm, closed Mon).

Restaurants and bars

Al Caneseo Via Vendramini 20 ☏ 0424.228.524. Both the food and the atmosphere are very good in this small restaurant, which serves dishes from Abruzzo and the Veneto. Closed Mon & all Aug.

Antica Osteria Via Matteotti 7. Old-fashioned *osteria* that has a strong local following, and serves traditional food, as well as good bar snacks. Open till 9pm, closed Mon.

Del Borgo Via Margnan 7 ☏ 0424.522.155. Classy establishment with its own garden, *Del Borgo* is very popular and comes highly recommended. It is a short walk downhill north of the old centre. Closed Wed and Sat lunch.

Al Caneva Via Matteotti 34. Cosy bar that does delicious snacks as well as more substantial dishes. Has tables out in the street when the weather permits. Open till midnight, closed Tues.

Asolo

East of Bassano, the medieval hilltop town of **ÁSOLO** presides over a tightly grouped range of nearly thirty gentle peaks in the foothills of the Dolomites. Known as *la Città dai cento orizzonti* ("the city with a hundred horizons", the town was popular with writers and artists who found the atmosphere convivial: Robert Browning's last published work – *Asolando* – was written here.

With regular **buses** from Asolo, Asolo provides a pleasant day-trip; if you want to get here from Venice, it's quickest to take a train to Treviso, from where there are buses at least hourly (some change at Montebelluna).

The bus drops you at the foot of the hill, from where a connecting minibus (€1 return) shuttles you up into the town. Memorabilia of Ásolo's celebrated residents are gathered in the **Museo Civico** in Piazza Maggiore (Sat & Sun 10am–noon, 3–7pm; €4). Especially diverting are the portraits, photos and personal effects of

Eleonora Duse. An actress in the Sarah Bernhardt mould, Duse was almost as well known for her tempestuous love life as for her roles in Shakespeare, Hugo and Ibsen, and she came to Ásolo to seek refuge from gossip.

Via Canova leads west away from the town centre past Eleonora Duse's house (no. 306), near the Porta Santa Caterina. The church of **Santa Caterina** (May–Sept daily 9am–6.30pm; Oct–April Sat & Sun only 9am–4.30pm) next to the *Carabinieri*, is deconsecrated but open to allow visitors to see its fifteenth-century frescoes. The **Rocca** above the town – which offers excellent views – was from 1489 to 1509 the home of **Caterina Cornaro**. Born into one of Venice's most powerful families, Caterina was married to Jacques II, King of Cyprus. Within a year Jacques was dead, and Caterina was pressurized into ceding Cyprus to the Republic. She was given the region of Ásolo as a sign of Venice's indebtedness. Eventually Ásolo, too, was taken away from her by the Emperor Maximilian, and she sought asylum in Venice, where she died soon after, in 1510.

Practicalities

The **tourist office** is at Piazza D'Annunzio 2 (Thurs–Sat 9.30am–12.30pm, Tues–Wed 3–6pm; ℡0423.529.046, 🌐www.asolo.it). The best **restaurant** in town is the *Ca'Derton*, Piazza D'Annunzio (℡0423.529.648, 🌐www .caderton.com; closed Sun eve & Mon, but June–Sept closed all day Sun); booking is essential. You can sample the same fine cooking more cheaply in the more informal *Enoteca di Nino e Antonietta* next door. The more basic *Cornaro*, just off Piazza Garibaldi in Via Regina Cornaro (closed Mon), has the standard *primi* and *secondi*.

The Villa Barbaro at Masèr

The **Villa Barbaro** at **MASÈR** (March–Oct Tues, Sat & Sun 3–6pm; Nov–Feb Sat–Sun 2.30–5pm; €5; 🌐www.villadimaser.it), a few kilometres northeast of Ásolo is a masterpiece of the Italian Renaissance created in unison by **Palladio** and **Paolo Veronese**, whose careers crossed here and nowhere else. The villa was commissioned in the 1550s by Daniele and Marcantonio Barbaro, Venetian abassadors and connoisseurs of the arts. Apart from its beautifully symmetrical architecture, the standout feature is the magnificent series of **frescoes** by Veronese which decorate the interior. Among the most important frescoes in Italy, they make fantastic use of trompe l'oeil effects: servants peer round painted doors, a dog sniffs along the base of a flat balustrade, a huntsman (probably Veronese himself) steps into the house through an entrance that's a solid wall. It's speculated that the woman facing the hunter at the other end was Veronese's mistress.

In the grounds in front of the villa (but now separated by a busy main road) stands Palladio's Tempietto (currently closed for restoration).

If you're reliant on **public transport**, a visit is best made by bus from Bassano via Ásolo or from Treviso – the services from Treviso to Ásolo all pass through Masèr.

Conegliano

North of Treviso, the amiable town of **CONEGLIANO** is a big attraction for wine lovers. The surrounding hills are patched with vineyards, and the production of wine (Prosecco in particular) is central to the economy of the district. Italy's first wine-growers' college was set up in Conegliano in 1876, and a couple of well-established **wine routes** meet here: the Strada dei Vini del Piave, which runs for 68km southeast to Oderzo, and the more rewarding Strada del Prosecco, the first to be established in Italy, a 42-kilometre journey west to Valdobbiádene (Ⓦwww.coneglianovaldobbiadene.it). Access to Conegliano itself is straightforward, as nearly all the regular Venice–Udine trains stop here.

The old centre of Conegliano is right in front of you as you come out of the station; just follow the road ahead and climb the steps to Via XX Settembre. This is the original main street, whose most decorative feature is the unusual facade of the **Duomo**: a fourteenth-century portico, frescoed in the sixteenth century. The interior has been much rebuilt, but retains fragments of fifteenth-century frescoes; the major adornment of the church, though, is the fine altarpiece *The Madonna and Child with Saints and Angels*, painted in 1493 by Giambattista Cima, the most famous native of Conegliano. Cima's birthplace, now the **Casa Museo di G. B. Cima** at the rear of the Duomo (Sat–Sun: April–Sept 4–7pm; Oct–March 3–5.30pm; €1), consists mainly of reproductions of his paintings and archeological finds made during the restoration of the house.

The **Museo Civico** (April–Sept Tues–Sun 10am–12.30pm & 4–7.30pm; Oct & Dec–March Tues–Sun 10am–12.30pm & 2.30–6pm; Nov Sat–Sun only; €2) is housed in the tower of the *castello* on top of the hill. On foot it's reached most quickly – though it is still a long climb – by the steep and cobbled Calle Madonna della Neve, which begins at the end of Via Accademia and follows the old city walls. The museum has some damaged frescoes by Pordenone and a small bronze horse by Giambologna, but the main reason to visit is the climb to the tower's roof from where there's a fine panorama of the vine-clad landscape.

Practicalities

Conegliano's **tourist office** is at Via XX Settembre 61 (Tues–Sun 9.30am–12.30pm and also Thurs–Sun 3–6pm; ☎0438.21.230, Ⓦturismo.provincia .treviso.it), and has details of wine-tasting tours. The three-star *Canon d'Oro* **hotel**, at Via XX Settembre 129 (☎0438.34.246, Ⓦwww.hotelcanondoro.it; ❹), is the best place to base yourself. The same street has all you'll need in the way of cafés, bars and food shops. Top recommendations for low-cost **eating** are the excellent fish menu of the *Trattoria Città di Venezia*, Via XX Settembre 77 (☎0438.23.186; closed Sun eve & Mon) – the cheaper ⚘ *Osteria La Bea Venezia* next door has similarly high standards. The main square is given over to a medieval pageant in mid-June, the **Dama Castellana**, and the streets of Conegliano host a major **wine festival** in September.

Vittorio Veneto

Thirteeen kilometres north of Conegliano, **VITTORIO VENETO** first appeared on the map in 1866 when the towns of Cèneda and Serravalle (not previously the best of friends) were knotted together and rechristened in honour of Italy's new king. A new town hall was built midway between the two, with a new train station opposite, so that the visitor steps straight from the train into a sort of no-man's-land. It's here, too, that you'll find the **tourist office** (daily 9.30am–12.30pm & Thurs–Sat 3–6pm; ☎0438.57.243) and bus station. Bus #1 runs between the two towns every fifteen minutes.

CÈNEDA is primarily worth a visit for the **Museo della Battaglia** (Tues–Sun: May–Sept 9.30am–12.30pm & 4–7pm; Oct–April 9.30am–12.30pm & 2–5pm; €3, or €5 joint ticket with the Museo del Cenedese) at Piazza G. Paolo 1, whose loggia was built by Sansovino. The museum is dedicated to the climactic Battle of Vittorio; fought in October 1918, this was the final engagement of World War I for the Italian Army and marked the end of the Austro-Hungarian Empire.

SERRAVALLE, wedged up against the mouth of a gorge, is entirely different. Most of the buildings on the stage-like Piazza Marcantonio Flaminio and the neighbouring streets date from the fifteenth and sixteenth centuries – the handsomest being the shield-encrusted Loggia Serravallese. This is now home of the **Museo del Cenedese** (see Museo della Battaglia above for times and price), a jumble of sculptural and archeological bits, detached frescoes and minor paintings. Your time will be more profitably spent in the church of **San Lorenzo dei Battuti** (same ticket and opening time as Museo del Cenedese and Museo della Battaglia), immediately inside the south gate, which is decorated with frescoes painted around 1450. Uncovered in 1953 and restored to rectify the damage done when Napoleon's soldiers used the chapel as a kitchen, this is one of the best-preserved fresco cycles in the Veneto. If it's closed, ask at the museum.

Belluno

The northernmost of the major towns of the Veneto, **BELLUNO** was once a strategically important ally of Venice, and today is the capital of a province that extends mainly over the eastern Dolomites (covered in Chapter 4). Belluno's focus of attention lies to the north – the network of the Dolomiti-Bus company radiates out from here, trains run regularly up the Piave Valley to Calalzo, and the tourist handouts are geared mostly to hikers and skiers. Just two trains a day run from Venice to Belluno directly, but it's just as quick anyway to go from Venice to Conegliano and change there; from Padua there are twelve trains daily.

Its position is Belluno's main attraction, but the old centre calls for an hour or two's exploration if you're passing through. The hub of the modern town, and where you'll find its most popular bars and cafés, is the wide **Piazza dei Martiri**, off the south side of which a road leads to the Piazza del Duomo, the kernel of the old town. The sixteenth-century **Duomo**, an amalgam of the Gothic and Classical, was designed by Tullio Lombardo. There are a couple of good paintings inside: one by Andrea Schiavone (first altar on right) and one by Jacopo Bassano (third altar on right).

Occupying one complete side of the Piazza del Duomo is the residence of the Venetian administrators of the town, the **Palazzo dei Rettori**, a frilly late-fifteenth-century building dolled up with Baroque trimmings. A relic of more independent times stands on the right – the twelfth-century **Torre Civica**, all that's left of the medieval castle. Continuing round the piazza at no. 16, along the side of the town hall, you'll find the **Museo Civico** (May–Sept Tues–Sun 10am–1pm & 4–7pm; Oct–April Mon–Sat 9am–1pm, Thurs–Fri 3–6pm; €3): the collection is strong on the work of Belluno's three best-known artists – the painters Sebastiano and Marco Ricci and the sculptor-woodcarver **Andrea Brustolon** – all of whom were born here between 1659 and 1673.

Via Duomo ends at the **Piazza del Mercato**, a tiny square hemmed in by porticoed Renaissance buildings. The principal street of the old town,

Via Mezzaterra, goes down to the medieval **Porta Rugo** (veer left along the cobbled Via Santa Croce about 50m from the end), from where the view up into the mountains is magnificent.

Practicalities

The **tourist office**, at Piazza Duomo 2 (daily 9am–12.30pm & 3.30–6.30pm, Oct to mid-June closed Sun afternoon; ℡0437.940.083, Ⓦwww.infodolomiti .it), has a good range of information on skiing and hiking in the Dolomites. The best **hotel** in the centre is the *Cappello e Cadore*, just off the main square at Via Ricci 8 (℡0437.940.246, Ⓦwww.albergocappello.com; ❸ – the more expensive rooms have Jacuzzis). Of the town's **restaurants** the *Terracotta*, near the train station at Borgo Garibaldi 61 (℡0437.942.644; closed Tues eve & Wed) is an old favourite, tending towards nouvelle cuisine; alternatively follow the locals to one of the places around Piazza del Mercato.

Travel details

Trains

Belluno to: Conegliano (8 daily; 55min); Vittorio Veneto (8 daily; 35min).

Castelfranco to: Padua (every 30min; 35min); Treviso (10 daily; 35min); Venice (every 30min; 55min).

Conegliano to: Belluno (8 daily; 55min); Udine (every 30min; 1hr 15min); Venice (every 30min; 1hr); Vittorio Veneto (15 daily; 25min).

Padua to: Bassano (hourly; 1hr 5min); Belluno (12 daily; 2hr); Milan (25 daily; 2hr 30min); Venice (every 30min; 35min); Verona (every 30min; 55min); Vicenza (every 20min; 20min).

Treviso to: Udine (hourly; 1hr 10min–1hr 30min); Venice (every 20min; 30min); Vicenza (hourly; 1hr).

Venice to: Bassano (14 daily; 1hr); Belluno (1 daily; 2hr); Conegliano (every 30min; 1hr); Milan (25 daily; 2hr 50min–3hr 50min); Padua (every 30min; 35min); Treviso (every 20min; 30min); Trieste (every 30min; 2hr 10min); Udine (every 30min; 2hr); Verona (every 30min; 1hr 30min);

Vicenza (every 30min; 55min); Vittorio Veneto (6 daily; 1–2hr).

Verona to: Milan (every 30min; 1hr 40min); Padua (every 30min; 50min); Venice (every 30min; 1hr 30min); Vicenza (every 30min; 30min).

Vicenza to: Castelfranco (hourly; 40min); Cittadella (hourly; 30min); Milan (30 daily; 1hr 40min); Padua (25 daily; 20min); Treviso (hourly; 1hr); Venice (every 30min; 55min); Verona (every 30min; 30min).

Buses

Bassano to: Ásolo (10 daily; 30min); Masèr (6 daily; 40min); Possagno (every 1–2hr; 40min).

Padua to: Bassano (every 30min; 1hr 15min).

Treviso to: Ásolo (10 daily; 1hr); Bassano (hourly; 1hr 30min); Padua (every 30min; 1hr 10min); Venice (every 20min; 55min).

Venice to: Malcontenta (hourly; 20min); Strà (every 30min; 45min).

Vicenza to: Bassano (hourly; 1hr 10min).

6

Friuli-Venezia Giulia

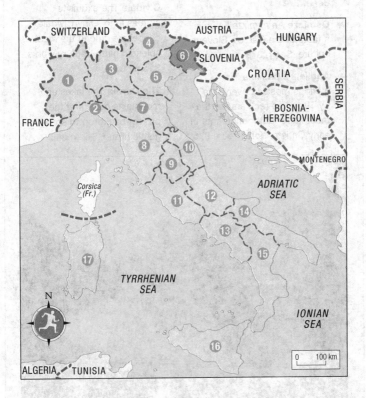

CHAPTER 6

Highlights

✳ **Trieste** From the castle atop San Giusto hill, take in a panoramic view of this elegant and inviting maritime city. See p.366

✳ **Grotta Gigante** The world's largest accessible cave. See p.372

✳ **Osmizze** An *osmizza* lunch is a taste of the Carso's Slovene culture. See p.372

✳ **Aquileia's basilica** The glorious mosaic pavements by Theodore rank among the most important monuments of early Christendom. See p.376

✳ **Udine's Piazza della Libertà** The central piazza of the region's second town is a perfect ensemble of historic Venetian buildings. See p.382

✳ **Tempietto Longobardo, Cividale** The exquisite statues in this tiny Cividale chapel are among the most splendid ninth-century works. See p.385

✳ **The Carnia** The lakes and mountains here offer the perfect backdrop to some gentle hiking. See p.386

▲ Alpine lake near Tarvisio, Carnia region

Friuli-Venezia Giulia

E stablished only in 1963 and given special status as one of Italy's five semi-autonomous regions, **Friuli–Venezia Giulia** is proudly odd, even in its name (Friuli is a corruption of the ancient name for modern-day Cividale, *Foro Iulii* "Forum of Julius" while *Venezia Giulia* "Julian Venetia" also references the area's abiding association with Caesar). Bordering Austria to the north and Slovenia to the east, it has always been a major bone of contention amongst rival powers. Today, Slavic, Germanic and Italian populations all call it home and you may hear the distinct sound of *Friulano* being spoken (a Romance language related to Swiss Romansch). The area's landscapes are equally varied with one-half alps and about one-third limestone plateaux (*carso*) and alluvial plains, with coastal shelving adorning the Adriatic.

Regional food and wine

Food in Friuli-Venezia Giulia reflects the cultural eclecticism of the place and veers towards the simple and hearty, from thick soups to warming stews, often – and unusually – combining sweet and savoury ingredients. One such dish is *cialzons*, a ravioli-type pasta filled with spinach, chocolate, raisins and nutmeg, among other dubious delights, while less challenging menu choices include polenta accompanied by *squazeto alla friulana* (lamb casserole), *jota friulana*, a thick meat, beans and cabbage stew, and *brovada*, another distinct speciality, made from wine-fermented turnips. Definitely worth seeking out is the delicious **prosciutto** from the town of San Daniele, salted and cured raw ham that melts in the mouth. Desserts head very much eastwards, with rich, Central European-influenced cakes filled with nuts and dried fruit – look out for *presnitz* and *gubana*.

If Friuli-Venezia Giulia does have something to sing about, it's the region's classy **wines**, especially its whites. The region is second only to Trentino-Alto Adige for DOC wines, with the mix of Alpine and Adriatic air creating excellent conditions, most notably in Collio Goriziano and Colli Orientali del Friuli, two areas running up against the Slovenian border. Tocai has historically been the best-known white, dry and aromatic and produced here since at least the seventeenth century. However, in 2006, the moniker finally lost a fifty-year dispute over the similarity of its name to Hungarian Tokajj, a dessert wine derived from entirely different grapes. By EU ruling, only Hungarian wines can now bear any variant of the name, so Friuli Tocai will henceforth be known as "Friulano". Meanwhile, Picolit, a sweet white hugely popular two centuries ago, is making a comeback to widespread acclaim. Reds, though not as prestigious, include Refosco and the highly drinkable Terrano.

For the full experience of specifically Friulano-Slovene country cookery, seek out one of traditional *osmizze* eateries (see box, p.372).

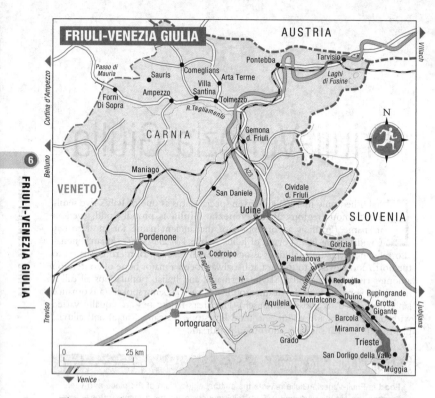

The cities and towns here are as wildly dissimilar as one might expect. **Trieste**, the capital, is an urbanely elegant Habsburg creation, instituted by Austria to showcase the empire's greatest port. In spirit and appearance it is essentially Central European, a character it shares with **Gorizia**, to the north, though the latter has an even more Slavic flavour, and in fact straddles the border with Slovenia. Both cities benefit from castles looming on a central hilltop, affording memorable views, and provide access to walkabouts in the **Carso** – the windswept, cave-riven terrain that extends from here on eastward into Slovenia – while Trieste also boasts the classy beach resorts of the **Triestine Riviera**. A bit farther along, **Udine**'s architecture and art collections evoke Venice at its grandest, while tiny and ancient **Cividale del Friuli** preserves a picturesque historic centre perched on the gorge of the Natisone River. The archeologically minded, however, head straight west to **Aquileia**, site of some of the most important Roman and most extraordinary Christian remains in Italy, and to the lagoon resort of **Grado**, which conceals a beautiful early Christian centre crowded round by beach hotels. Finally, in the far north of the region the **Carnia** is trying to develop itself to compete with the Dolomites for skiing and hiking, though in truth it has little over its neighbour other than the peace and quiet of a relative backwater.

Historically, what unites the region is its perennial role as a link between the Mediterranean and Central Europe. It has been repeatedly overrun – sometimes enriched, but often laid waste – from east and west and north, by the Romans,

Huns, Goths, Lombards, Nazis and even the Cossacks (see box, p.387). By turns, it has been lorded over by the Venetian Republic, Napoleonic France and the Austrian Empire. More recently, it witnessed some of the most savage fighting of World War I, when artillery shells splintered the limestone of the Carso into deadly shrapnel. Today the landscape is still scarred with trenches, along with war memorials and vast ossuaries. World War II saw less carnage, but Fascism was especially virulent in Trieste, site of one of Italy's two death camps.

Today, right-wing and xenophobic tendencies are still strong in the region, having peaked in the mid-1990s, when federalists demanding a separate northern Italian state or "Lega Nord" made up around 25 percent of the electorate. While most Friulani certainly want Italian nationality, the socio-political baggage of Rome and the south strike many as a drag in every way. Currently, economic anxiety and general malaise about Italy's direction have resulted in something of a conservative resurgence.

Trieste

Framed by the green and white cliffs of a limestone plateau and facing the blue Adriatic, **TRIESTE** offers an idyllic panorama from its hilltop citadel, at least when the rather endemic overcast conditions give way to sparkling sunshine. But in any weather, there's a distinct atmosphere of both grandeur and warm welcome. The city's main squares are adorned with spectacular Neoclassical buildings, and the much-photographed canal, clustered with open-air cafés, is a reminder that, just like Venice and its lagoon, this city has had its glorious seafaring history, too. Trieste on the whole is a fascinating and strange mix: an imperial creation built to play a role that no longer exists, though like so many ports in Europe, the seediness that long prevailed, still evident in some areas around the train station, is now giving way to cautious yet determined optimism.

Some history

Trieste dates back as far as the third millennium BC. Roman ruins here and there attest to its incorporation into the Roman Republic in 178 BC, when it was called Tergeste. However, with the exception of the castle and cathedral of San Giusto hill, and the tiny medieval quarter below it, the city's whole pre-nineteenth-century history seems dim and vague beside the massive Neoclassical architecture of the **Borgo Teresiano** – the name given to the modern city centre, after Empress Maria Theresa (1740–80), who initiated the development. The Austrians spared no expense on embellishing the city that would become the Habsburg Empire's premier seaport. For a time, it even eclipsed Venice, but its heyday was short-lived and drew to an ignominious close after 1918, when the city became Italian. Trieste soon discovered that despite the good intentions of all concerned, Italy really had no economic use for it. The city languished for over sixty years, but more recently things have picked up. The large container port to the south of the centre has seen an increase in seaborne trade, the labyrinthine medieval quarter has received a tasteful facelift, and the €650-million redevelopment of the Porto Vecchio in the heart of town has provided welcome leisure and business facilities.

Lying on the political and ethnic fault-line between the Latin and Slavic worlds, Trieste has long been a city of political extremes. In the nineteenth

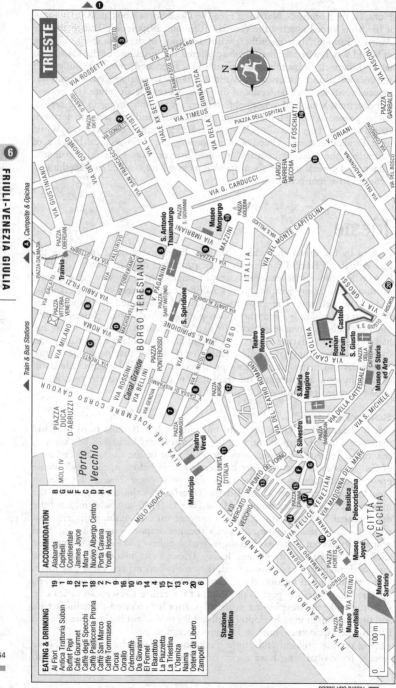

century it was a hotbed of *irredentismo* – an Italian nationalist movement to "redeem" the Austrian lands of Trieste, Istria and the Trentino. After 1918 the tensions increased, leading to a strong Fascist presence in Friuli-Venezia Giulia. Yugoslavia and the Allies fought over Trieste until 1954, when the city and a connecting strip of coast were secured for Italy, though a definitive **border settlement** was not reached until 1975. Tito kept Istria, prompting huge numbers of its fearful Italian population to abandon the peninsula: Fiume (Rijeka), for example, lost 58,000 of its 60,000 Italians. The Slovene population of the area around Trieste, previously in the majority, suddenly found itself treated as second-class citizens, with Italians dominant politically and culturally; nationalist parties built support on the back of the tensions between the two communities. Nowadays, however, Slovenes and Italians are in the phase of inevitable rapprochement, and casual visitors will notice few, if any, signs of regressive jingoism.

In fact, Trieste also has a long socialist and cosmopolitan intellectual tradition intimately embracing the city's ever-burgeoning café culture. Historically, numerous foreign writers based themselves around Trieste, most famously James Joyce (see box, p.368) and Rainer Maria Rilke, and native literati included Umberto Saba and Italo Svevo. Freud also spent some time researching in Trieste as a medical student, and the city became the first Italian centre of psychoanalytical thought under Freud's pupil Edoardo Weiss.

Arrival and information

Trieste's Piazza Libertà **bus station** is right by the central **train station**, ten-minutes' walk from the town centre. The nearest **airport** is at Ronchi dei Legionari (☎0481.773.224, ⓦwww.aeroporto.fvg.it), 31km northwest of the city, connected to the bus station by APT bus #51 (every 30min; 50min; €3 from the machine directly outside arrivals, €1 surcharge if ticket bought on bus; freephone ☎800.955.957, ⓦwww.aptgorizia.it). A **taxi** should cost about €40. The helpful main **tourist office** is on the central Piazza Unità d'Italia 4e (daily 9am–7pm; ☎040.347.8312, ⓦwww.turismofvg.it). When you arrive in town, consider buying the **FVG Card**, available at many hotels and at all tourist offices (€15 for 48hr, €20 for 72hr and €29 for a week), of advantage when exploring the entire region. Among other things, it entitles you to discounts on sport and recreation facilities, some hotels and restaurants, as well as free access to virtually all public museums, several guided tours and free use of some public transport, including the *tranvia* (see p.372) – though on the whole sightseeing on foot will prove most rewarding. Count on at least four days to do justice to the major attractions and pleasures of greater Trieste.

Accommodation

Recent years have seen an improvement in the **accommodation** available in Trieste. The cheapest decent **hotels** are all still between the train station and the town centre, but boutique hotels in the restored old quarter provide atmospheric alternatives. All the hotels listed below include breakfast in their prices.

Hotels

Alabarda Via Valdirivo 22 ☎040.630.269, ⓦwww.hotelalabarda.it. Located in the heart of the new town, the *Alabarda* is a good, inexpensive option with TVs in all its eighteen clean rooms, plus internet facilities. Double glazing keeps out most of the noise from the busy street outside. ❷

Capitelli Via Trauner 1, corner Via Capitelli ⊕ 040.305.947, ⊛ www.hotelcapitelli.it. This recently done-up hotel in the historic centre stands up towards the city's ancient Roman arch. The accommodation is fresh, light and spacious at the same time as charming, cosy and just a little rustic. ❸

Continentale Via San Nicolò 25 ⊕ 040.631.717, ⊛ www.goldengrouphotel.com. On a quiet pedestrianized street in the city centre, this is the best of Trieste's four-stars. Rooms are simple but classy, while staff are helpful and attentive. ❻

James Joyce Via dei Cavazzeni 7 ⊕ 040.302.065, ⊛ www.hoteljamesjoyce .com. In the heart of the medieval quarter, this enticing little place has retained its wood-beamed ceilings and its spiral stone staircase without compromising on comforts, such as an elevator and a/c. Guests are greeted by a life-size image of the eponymous author. ❺

Marta Via Valdirivo 11 ⊕ 040.660.242, ⊛ www .hotelmarta.it. Nicely furnished and clean rooms, all with TV; good value. Internet available. ❷

Nuovo Albergo Centro Via Roma 13 ⊕ 040.347.8790, ⊛ www.hotelcentrotrieste .it. Bright and spotlessly clean rooms in this, the most pleasant moderately priced place in town. 10 percent discount for guests showing a copy of this book. Ask for a room at the back to get away from the noise of the street. There's an equally excellent facility on the floor above, *Al Canal Grande*, run by the same family. ❸

Porta Cavana Via F. Venezian 14 ⊕ 040.301.313, ⊛ www.hotelportacavana.it. Another beautiful addition to the old quarter, warmly and richly decorated, with each room uniquely designed. ❸

Hostel and campsite

Obelisco Strada Nuova per Opicina 37 ⊕ 040.211.744, ⊛ www.campeggiobelisco.it. Campsite on an airy hill 7km away in the Carso, below Opicina; from Piazza Oberdan take either bus #4 or the *tranvia* (cable tramway), which runs upto 8pm: stop at the obelisk, cross over the tracks and you'll see a sign to the campsite which is 1min walk away. From €5 per adult and €4 per pitch; open all year.

Ostello Trieste Viale Miramare 331 ⊕ 0404.224.102, ⊛ www.ostellionline.org. Basic facilities but this HI hostel boasts stunning sea views, and is just 500m from Castello Miramare (see p.374) 5km out of the city. Take bus #51 from the airport, which lets you off about 500m away, or #36 from the station to Grignano and get off at Bivio al Miramare, from where it's a 5min walk. Beds start at €16.

The City

Today Triestine life takes place in the grid-like streets of the **Borgo Teresiano**, but the focal point of the city's pre-modern history, and its prime tourist site, is **San Giusto** hill, named after the patron saint of the city. Scattered elsewhere around the Old Town are some interesting museums and a clutch of churches and Roman remains that can easily take up a day's strolling.

San Giusto and the Old Town

At the very summit of San Giusto hill, overlooking the remnants of the Roman forum, is the **Castello** (Tues–Sun, 9am–7pm; €3.50), a fifteenth-century Venetian fortress. There's nothing much to see inside, but a walk round the ramparts offers fine views of the new town and the busy port below, while beyond the city confines the high escarpment of the Carso looms over the Adriatic. Its **museum** houses a small collection of archeological finds, including antique weaponry.

More interesting is the **Cattedrale di San Giusto** (Mon–Sat 7.30am–noon & 2.30–6.30pm, Sun 7.30am–noon & 2.30–7.30pm; free), built on the ruins of a first-century AD Roman structure. Some ancient fragments remain: the base of the campanile has been scalloped away to reveal the original pillars, the columns at the entrance were borrowed from a Roman tomb and part of the Roman floor mosaic is incorporated in the present flooring. In around 1050 an earlier Christian chapel was replaced by two churches, the Basilica di Santa Maria Assunta and the Capella di San Giusto. The site was further expanded in the early thirteenth century in an extraordinary stroke of pragmatic architectural genius: the two adjacent buildings were bridged by a high-beamed vault, forming the current cathedral nave and leaving a double aisle on each side. The complex history of the building becomes clearer if you study the arches in the interior, or look down on the apse from the castle wall behind. As it stands today, the cathedral is a typically Triestine synthesis of styles, with a serene, largely Romanesque interior marred only by an ugly modern choir. The **Cappella di Santa Maria Assunta** (north aisle) has fine Venetian-Ravennan mosaics of the Coronation of the Virgin, revealing the Byzantine roots of the style, while the **Cappella di San Giusto** (south aisle) has thirteenth-century frescoes of the life of the saint, framed between Byzantine pillars. The facade is predominantly Romanesque, but includes a Gothic rose window.

Still atop the central citadel, on the cobbled Via della Cattedrale, the **Museo Civico di Storia ed Arte** (Tues–Sun 9am–1pm; €3.50) houses a collection of cultural plunder that embraces Himalayan sculpture, Egyptian manuscripts and Roman glass. Part of the museum, the **Orto Lapidario**, is a pleasant environment in which fragments of classical statuary, pottery and inscriptions are arranged on benches and against walls, among cow-parsley and miniature palm trees. The little Corinthian temple on the upper level contains the remains of J.J. Winckelmann (1717–68), the German archeologist and theorist of Neoclassicism, who was murdered in Trieste by a man to whom he had shown off his collection of antique coins.

The tiny, now preserved remnant of the **Città Vecchia** (Old Town) lies between the castle hill and the Stazione Maritima below. It has been freshly restored – even at risk of over-restoration, as evidenced by the presence of a rather jarring design hotel (the *Urban*) inserted into its tilting medieval structures and undulating lanes. Still, the zone is delightful for a stroll, and farther down Via della Cattedrale, the tiny early Romanesque **San Silvestro** (Thurs & Sat 10am–noon; free), is worth a look as the city's oldest extant church; it's now used by adherents of the rare Helvetic-Waldensian sect. A short way below are the heavily restored remains of the Roman theatre, where performances are staged during the city's spring–autumn festival season. There's little else of monumental note in the old city, but mosaic enthusiasts may want to stop off at the remains of the **Basilica Paleocristiana** (Wed 10am–noon, or by appointment; ℡040.43.631; free) under the building at Via Madonna del Mare 11. The evocative **Arco di Riccardo**, on the nearby Piazza Barbacan, is a reassembled remnant of the Roman walls dating from 33 BC, while excavation works nearby are revealing more traces of the city's ancient imperial past and will eventually complete an archeological tourist trail from San Giusto down to Piazza Unità (see below).

The Borgo Teresiano and around

To the north of the old centre, Trieste's "new" town, the **Borgo Teresiano**, is imposingly laid out in a Neoclassical style imported from nineteenth-century Vienna, with wide boulevards and a truly vast piazza on the waterfront. The focus of the main grid of streets is the picturesque **Piazza Sant'Antonio Nuovo**, with its small yacht basin overlooked by cafés and dominated by two churches: the Neoclassical hulk of San Antonio Thaumaturgo and the smaller, more appealing Serbian Orthodox San Spiridione. The bridge here is where you'll pass a strolling James Joyce lost in literary rumination (see box, p.368). The real heart of town, however, is the grandiose **Piazza Unità d'Italia**, directly below the hill of San Giusto. Built mostly by Giuseppe Bruni in the late

Joyce in Trieste

From 1905 to 1915, and again in 1919–20, **James Joyce** and his wife Nora lived in Trieste. After staying at Piazza Ponterosso 3 for a month, they moved to the third-floor flat at Via San Nicolò 30. (In 1919 the poet Umberto Saba bought a bookshop on the ground floor at the same address. The two writers seem never to have met, though they had a common friend in the novelist Italo Svevo.) There's a plaque in Via San Nicolò, and one at Via Bramante 4, quoting the postcard that Joyce despatched in 1915 to his brother Stanislaus, whose Irredentist sympathies had landed him in an Austrian internment camp. The postcard announced that the first chapter of James's new work, *Ulysses*, was finished. For Joyce fans the tourist office publishes a leaflet listing places associated with him including the wry bronze statue of the writer, strolling bemusedly across the little canal bridge of Via Roma.

nineteenth century, the expanse of flagstones with one side open to the water is deliberately reminiscent of Venice's Piazza and Piazzetta – Trieste had commercially eclipsed the older city some years before. Projecting into the harbour nearby, the **Molo Audace**, named after the first boat of Italian soldiers to land here in 1918, is the venue for the evening *passeggiata*.

Trieste's principal museum is the **Revoltella** (Mon & Wed–Sat 9am–6pm, Sun 10am–6pm; closed July 20–Aug 31; €6, €1 more for special exhibitions; Ⓦwww.museorevoltella.it), Via Armando Diaz 27, housed in a Viennese-style *palazzo* bequeathed to the city by the financier Baron Pasquale Revoltella in 1869. Its combined display of nineteenth-century stately home furnishings and Triestine paintings is well worth a look, and the adjacent palace, redesigned by the architect Carlo Scarpa, houses an extensive collection of modern art. The nearby **Museo Sartorio**, in Largo Papa Giovanni XXIII (Tues–Sun 9am–5pm; €5), has ceramics and icons downstairs and oppressive private rooms upstairs, but its highlight, the early fourteenth-century Santa Chiara triptych, rewards a visit. The central panel contains 36 beautifully restored miniature scenes from the life of Christ. There is also an important collection of drawings by Tiepolo.

One of the ugliest episodes of recent European history is embodied by the **Risiera di San Sabba**, overlooking the southern flank of Trieste's port at Via Palatucci 5 (daily 9am–7pm; free, guided tour upon request €2.50), on the #8 and #10 bus routes. This was one of only two concentration camps in Italy and now houses a permanent exhibition that serves as a reminder of Fascist crimes in the region. Nobody knows exactly how many prisoners were burned in the Risiera crematorium before the Yugoslavs liberated the city on May 1, 1945, but a figure of five thousand is usually cited by historians. Nazism had plenty of sympathizers in this part of Italy: in 1920 Mussolini extolled the zealots of Friuli-Venezia Giulia as model Fascists, and the commander of the camp was, in fact, a local man.

Eating and drinking

Triestine **cuisine** is as mixed as its population, with goulash, potato noodles and cheese dumplings on many menus, as well as some superb fish dishes. The local *terrano*, a very sharp red wine grown only on the limestone highlands, was reputedly the favourite of the Roman Empress Livia and is supposed to be good for the blood. It's delicious in any event and should be tried, ideally as an accompaniment to the heavy Triestine food. For less stolid meals, investigate the **osmizze** (see box, p.372), impromptu eating places, traditionally in the hinterland of the Carso, which offer the simplest of local produce at rock-bottom prices. Via C. Battisti, east of Sant'Antonio, is a good street for **food shops** – cheeses, cooked meats, olives and pasta in its many guises are piled high in the windows.

Cafés and gelaterie

Coffee (see box below) and **ice cream** lovers are well catered for in Trieste with a host of places tempting you to try their products – the best area to head for is leafy, pedestrian-only Viale XX Settembre, known as the *Acquedotto* ("aqueduct"), where citizens stroll in the evening.

Caffè degli Specchi Piazza Unità. Better for its excellent position on Trieste's main square than its slightly soulless interior, the city's most famous café remains top choice for wine-sipping and people-watching.

Caffè Pasticceria Pirona Largo Barriera Vecchia. Superior cakeshop that's the place to head for a quick pastry fix – James Joyce was a regular.

Caffè San Marco Via C. Battisti. Trieste's favourite café has occupied its premises for some eighty years. It's a huge, relaxed place with a clientele of all ages chatting and playing chess in the mahogany and mirrored Art Nouveau-style interior. Closed Wed.

Caffè Tommaseo Piazza Tommaseo. Much of the historic style of the city's oldest café – a rendezvous for Italian nationalists in the nineteenth century – was lost in the latest refurbishment, but it offers a convivial setting and frequent live music.

Crèmcaffè Piazza Goldoni 10. Excellent *torre-fazione* and the city's oldest, so ignore the harsh lighting and queue up for an espresso, or make it a double with a pastry.

La Triestina Via di Cavana 2. Another great, central choice to load up on caffeine, where they skilfully roast their own select coffee beans in the great Triestine tradition.

Zampolli Viale XX Settembre. Of the many ice-cream parlours on this street, *Zampolli* is certainly the best; try the unforgettable *bacio bianco*, smooth, creamy and flavourful.

Restaurants

Trieste has a huge range of good-value **restaurants** scattered around both the new and Old Town. Especially attractive is the pedestrian-only thoroughfare Viale XX Settembre, which sports a number of lively places among its bars and cinemas. More expensive choices tend to specialize in fish, of which *branzino* and *sogliola* (sea bass and sole) are local favourites. Booking is not usually necessary.

Ai Fiori Piazza Hortis 7. Excellent, classy, gourmet trattoria on a leafy square between the Riva and the castle hill. Artful fish dishes are the focus, with a set menu including wine for €30. Closed Sun.

Antica Trattoria Suban Via Comici 2. Way out to the east of the city, this prestigious and pricey restaurant is worth the taxi ride for its superb Carso-style meat dishes, particularly the veal shank

Trieste and the roasted bean

Trieste's love affair with **coffee** dates back to the mid-eighteenth century, when importing began and when the first coffee shops opened in emulation of Vienna. Even now it's the leading coffee port in the Mediterranean – 40 percent of Italy's coffee arrives here – and Trieste's denizens imbibe twice as much on average as their fellow countrymen. One of the pleasures of walking around the city centre is the unexpected scent of roasting beans emanating from choice establishments – known as *torre-fazioni* where experts toast to order the world's most select varieties. The city's most famous brand is Illy (⬤www.illy.com), founded in 1933 and producer of a world-renowned 100 percent Arabica blend. So supreme is the coffee culture in the city that Riccardo Illy, scion of the clan, has held the offices of mayor and regional president, among numerous other posts.

▲ Caffè San Marco

steak. Set menus start at €25 including dessert but not drinks. Closed Mon at lunch, all day Tues & part of Aug.

Buffet Pepi Via Cassa di Risparmio 3. Student option that's the perfect place for snacks and lunches. Cooking emphasizes Trieste's Austrian connections with excellent sausages, gammon and bowls of steaming *jota*, beans and sauerkraut soup. Closed Sun.

Corallo Via Vidali 12. Pizzas the way the locals like them. Try the house version, loaded up with funghi, artichokes, ricotta, hard-boiled egg and *prosciutto crudo*, for under €10. Closed Thurs.

Da Giovanni Via S. Lazzaro 14. Simple buffet, with meals served at bench tables. Hams hanging from the ceiling and barrels of wine behind the bar lend a distinctly rustic air. Mixed fried fish a speciality, as well as various pork dishes, Expect €20–25 per person. Closed Sun.

El Fornel Via dei Fornelli 1. Very popular place that concentrates on the food – the freshest fish and seafood – rather than the decor, a casual nautical theme. Family-style service where you can easily spend no more than €15. Closed Sun.

Il Barattolo Piazza Sant'Antonio 2. Deservedly popular place, with friendly staff, tasty southern Italian-style food, and pleasant outdoor seating in this pretty square in the summer. Hearty Neapolitan-style pizzas for under €10. Closed Mon in winter.

L'Osmiza di Cavana Via della Torretta. Feast on products straight from the Carso countryside, including *prosciutto crudo*, olives and eggs. Closed every eight days, according to tradition. Mains €10–15.

La Piazzetta Piazza Cavana 1/B. Good value at under €20 per person (pasta dishes €7–8), including wine, with fish as a speciality in this cosy find towards the old quarter. Outdoor seating on the quiet square. Closed Mon.

Bars

Indoor-outdoor **wine bars** have now become a signature Triestine experience, and many of the city's **establishments** are as glossy as the top-notch cafés. Everywhere you turn, weather permitting, youngish and often rather sophisticated drinkers fill the outside tables along the broad sidewalks. For late drinking, Via Madonna del Mare, on the castle hill, has a number of bars whose names, managements and popularity come and go each year – it's best to follow your ears to where the crowds are.

Circus Via San Lazzaro 9. A trendy, buzzing wine bar decorated with old movie posters, and with tables outside. Drinks come with substantial snacks. Closed Sun.

Naima Via Rosetti 6. Younger and more studenty than most, this is basically a disco bar with occasional live music and dancing. Excellent for chilling on the black leather sofas but get there before midnight to claim your spot. Daily 7.30pm–3am.

Osteria da Libero Via Risorta 7. Old-fashioned establishment on the castle hill, virtually the last remaining genuine *osteria* in the city, full of quirky mementoes collected by the proprietor over the decades. Closed Sun.

Rex Café Gourmet Galleria Protti 1. Modern wine and music bar with a jazzy lounge setting and outdoor tables, too. Open early every day for breakfast, then lunch, and on till 2am, except for Sun, when it closes at 10pm.

Listings

Bus information Freephone ☏ 800.016.675. Timetables and tickets can be bought from automatic machines at main stops or from newsagents and *tabacchi*; a ten-ticket *bloquetto* saves a couple of euros and is more convenient than buying individual tickets. Town buses cost €1 for any journey of up to an hour; provincial buses cost a standard €1.20, except private APT services which depend on distance.

Car rental At Molo dei Bersaglieri 3: Avis ☏ 040.300.820; Europcar ☏ 040.322.0820; Hertz ☏ 040.322.0098. At the airport: Avis ☏ 0481.777.085; Europcar ☏ 0481.778.920; Hertz ☏ 0481.777.025.

Club Alpino Italiano Via Donota 2 ☏ 040.630.464.

Consulates UK, Via Dante Alighieri 7 (Tues 10am–noon, Fri 2.30–4.30pm; ☏ 040.347.8303); US Consular Agency, Via Roma 15 (Mon–Fri 10am–noon; ☏ 040.660.177).

Festivals and events Mid-Oct features the *Barcolana*, Italy's largest sailing regatta with countless participants of all types skimming the whitecaps of the bay; parties galore on shore. From spring to autumn, events abound, including at the Teatro Verdi (☏ 040.672.2111, ⦿ www .teatroverdi-trieste.com), offering operas and musicals throughout the year. For details, contact the tourist office or consult *Il Piccolo*, Trieste's daily paper; check for festivals in the Carso villages, too.

Hospital Ospedale Maggiore, Piazza dell'Ospedale ☏ 040.399.1111; in an emergency dial ☏ 118.

Internet access *Smilenet*, Piazza Squero Vecchio 1/C, just west of Piazza Unità (daily 10am–9pm).

Police The *Questura* is at Via Tor Bandena 6 ☏ 040.379.0111. Otherwise ring ☏ 113.

Post office The main post office is in Piazza Vittorio Veneto 1 (Mon–Fri 8.30am–7pm, Sat 8.30am–10.45pm).

Taxis Radio Taxi ☏ 040.307.730.

Travel agent Agemar, Piazza Duca degli Abruzzi 1/A ☏ 040.363.737, ⦿ www.agemar.it – for ferry tickets to Grado and Ligano, Pirano (Slovenia), Brioni and Rovigno (Croatia).

Around Trieste: the Carso

The **CARSO** is the Italian name for the terrain of limestone uplands that rise from the plain of the Veneto south of Monfalcone and eventually merge into the Istrian plateau. Although within thirty-minutes' bus ride of Trieste, it feels like an entirely different country, and is geologically, botanically and demographically distinct from anywhere else in Italy. Most of the Carso now lies within Slovenia (its Slovene name is Kras), and even the narrow strip inside Italy, though supporting a population of just 20,000, remains distinctively Slovene in culture, boasting places with names like Zagradec and Koludrovica. The dour villages of thick-walled houses seem to hunker down against the *bora*, the northeasterly wind which can blast this area at any time of year – when it's especially fierce, ropes are strung along the steeper streets in Trieste.

Like all limestone country, the environment is harsh: arid in summer and sometimes snowbound in winter. The surface of the plateau is studded with sink-holes left by streams which have slowly carved their way underground, sometimes reappearing miles away on the coast. The abundance of caves has even led to the German name for the area, *karst*, becoming the standard geographical term for this type of terrain.

The distinctive landscape and natural environment have led to proposals for creating a National Park. There is fine **walking** to be had, and several bus services run to the Carso from Trieste, including the #42 and #44. The tourist office publishes a useful map of the network of numbered footpaths in the Carso; it shouldn't be used for serious navigation but is a useful guide to what's possible – and it would be difficult to get yourself seriously lost. If the scenery isn't as grand as the Dolomites, the pace is gentler, especially if you can break your expedition at an *osmizza* (see box above).

Grotta Gigante and Rupingrande

The most picturesque way up into the Carso is to take the *tranvia* (cable tramway; 7.30am–8pm; every 20min; €1, same ticket as for buses) from Trieste's Piazza Oberdan to the village of Opicina, at the edge of the plateau. From the tram stop, cross the square and take bus #42 (which you can also take all the way from Trieste) to one of the Carso's highlights, the **Grotta Gigante** (guided visits daily: April–Sept every 30min 10am–6pm; March & Oct hourly 10am–4pm; Nov–Feb hourly 10am–noon & 2–4pm; €8.50; Ⓦwww.grottagigante.it), the world's largest accessible cave, and the second-largest natural chamber anywhere in the world (the largest is in Malaysia). As it's 107m deep by 208m broad, the dome of St Peter's would fit comfortably inside. It's a steady 11°C inside, so come prepared.

The cave is impressive in scale and, like most of the caves in the Carso, was created by the erosive action of a river, in this case the Timavo, which sank deeper and deeper underground before changing course (the cave is now dry). The stalactites and stalagmites grew later, formed by deposits of calcium carbonate and colourful metal oxides. Much more recently, ferns and moss have started to grow in what was previously a lifeless environment, thanks to photosynthesis triggered by electric lighting. The two long "pillars" in the centre of the cave are in fact wires sheathed in plastic. At the bottom end two super-accurate pendulums are suspended, used to measure seismic shifts in isolation from surface noise and air currents.

If the tour of the cave has given you an appetite, visit the nearby **trattoria** *Milic* (closed Mon), close to the bus stop, which serves tasty and reasonably priced country dishes.

Apart from the Grotta Gigante, the main sights to head for are in and around the village of **RUPINGRANDE** (aka Monrupino), just 3km northeast of the cave and also on the #42 bus route. A short walk east of the village is a fortress built in the fourteenth century to defend the area from Turkish incursions, while in Rupingrande itself the **Casa Carsica** (April–Oct Sun & hols 11am–12.30pm & 3–5pm, or by appointment; ℡040.327.122; free) exhibits old furniture and nineteenth-century peasant costumes, as well as works by local artisans. The Casa is signposted from the central crossroads in Rupingrande. Every two years (2009, 2011 and so on) the village hosts an important Slovene folk festival, the **Nozze carsiche** (Carsic wedding), on the four days leading up to the last Sunday in August.

Strada Vicentina and Val Rosandra

Two walking areas near Trieste can be particularly recommended. The **Strada Vicentina** (or Napoleonica) is some 2km long, curving along the hillside above the city, between the *Obelisco* campsite (see p.366) and the hamlet of **Borgo Nazario** (near Prosecco). It's a scenic but unstrenuous walk, partly shadowed by trees and partly cut through almost sheer limestone cliffs; on a clear day the views are superb. Access to the Strada Vicentina couldn't be simpler: *Obelisco* is a stop on the *tranvia*, and the Borgo Nazario end is near Via San Nazario, where the #42 bus stops on its way back to Trieste station.

The other area, the **Val Rosandra**, is very different. This miniature wilderness of limestone cliffs and sumac trees is the local rock-climbing headquarters and is crisscrossed with paths. Take bus #40 from Trieste's bus station to **Bagnoli Della Rosandra** and follow the road at the back of the square northeast towards the hills. After about 500m or so the tarmac gives way to a path bordered on the right by a miniature Roman aqueduct – now resembling little more than a stone-lined ditch – and on the left by a stream with pools for bathing. After thirty minutes the little sanctuary church of Santa Maria in Siaris appears, perched on a spur of rock high on the right. You can climb up to it easily enough and a steep path continues up to the top of the plateau beyond. Beyond this is a waterfall, accessible by a steep path, then the tiny hamlet of Bottazzo – the last habitation before Slovenia. At the border a sign advertises a friendship path linking communities on either side of the frontier. Don't be tempted to investigate; only locals are allowed to cross unpatrolled borders, and the military are fairly active in the area as it's a busy crossing point for illegal immigrants.

The Triestine Riviera

The thirty-odd kilometres of coastline either side of Trieste, from Múggia to the south and as far as Duino in the north, are optimistically known as the **TRIESTINE RIVIERA**. While beaches aren't as good as you'll find further down the Adriatic, or even at nearby Grado, some fine walks, historic sites and castles are worth a day-trip from Trieste. Frequent **buses** trace the coast road and, in summer, **ferries** (see p.388) call at all the coastal towns.

Múggia

Directly south across the bay from Trieste, 11km away by road, **MÚGGIA**, the last remnant of Venice's Istrian possessions, is now reduced to little more than a popular spot for lunch expeditions from Trieste, though the town comes into its own during carnival time. The ferry-trip across the bay from Trieste (summer only) can be a good enough reason in itself to visit, but there are also appealing signs of the past, particularly in the brightly painted buildings on the main square. On the east side of the piazza, the fifteenth-century **Duomo** reveals its origins in its Venetian–Gothic arches and a bas-relief of Christ Pantocrator in the lunette above the main door; the handsome **Palazzo dei Rettori**, on the north side of the square, displays the tell-tale *leone marciano*, the lion of St Mark, symbol of Venice's former hegemony here. The piazza is backed by a handful of narrow streets and tumbledown houses, many of which date back to Venetian times.

On the seaward side of the piazza, the tiny *mandracchio* is now used as a basin for pleasure boats, while the working harbour just beyond is spoilt only by the unenviable view of Trieste's industrial backside. Múggia's handful of **fish restaurants** are all within spitting distance of the water. Top recommendation, and not just for the name, is the *Trattoria Lilibontempo* (closed Tues), at Riva Nazario Sauro 10, known as the "ex-Hitler" after the former proprietor, who bore an unnerving resemblance to the Nazi dictator. Further along the harbour front and with sea views, *Trattoria Risorta* (closed Sun & Mon) does tasty fish dishes for around €15, or try the *Due Leoni* (closed Mon), opposite on the jetty, which serves similar food at slightly cheaper prices.

At Via Roma 20, in front of the **tourist office** (℡040.273.259; open Carnevale and July & Aug only), as well as from the port, you can pick up bus #20, which runs back to Trieste every 30min, but it's worth visiting **Múggia Vecchia**, on the hilltop hard against the Slovene border and less than 20km from Croatia. It's a steep twenty-minute walk past Múggia's fourteenth-century castle and town walls, but bus #50 from outside the **bus station**, 100m inland from the main road, runs every hour or so for those who don't fancy the climb.

Barcola and Miramare

BARCOLA, 2km northwest of Trieste and connected to the city by bus #36 from the bus station, is the nearest beach resort. Developed during Trieste's great days at the end of the nineteenth century, it is now really a suburb that comes to life in summer, when all Trieste seems to come here to chat, play cards, sunbathe and swim. Despite the cargo ships and tankers moored in the harbour, the water is moderately clean. Just short of the resort, perched on the slope of the limestone escarpment and offering stunning views along the coast, is the **Faro della Vittoria**, the third-tallest lighthouse in the world after New York's Statue of Liberty and the Columbus Lighthouse in Santo Domingo.

Standing at the tip of a rocky promontory 7km from Trieste, the salt-white castle of **MIRAMARE** is the area's prime tourist attraction. The Archduke Ferdinand Maximilian, Emperor Franz Josef's younger brother, was once forced ashore here by a squall, and resolved to buy the site. He built his dream castle and laid out its grounds between 1856 and 1870, but never lived to see it completed – having accepted Napoleon III's offer to make him the Emperor of Mexico, Maximilian was executed by his Mexican opponents in 1867, in the line of imperial duty. His wife Carlotta later went mad, and the legend was born that anyone who spends a night in Miramare will come to a bad end.

The park makes an excellent spot for a picnic, but the real draw is the castle's kitsch **interior** (daily 9am–6.30pm; €4), a remarkable example of regal decadence, and carved, gilded, and inlaid in every way possible. The Monarchs' Salon, for instance, is embellished with portraits of a King of Norway, the Emperor of Brazil, a Czar of Russia – anyone, no matter how fraudulent or despotic, as long as they're nominal monarchs. This softens you up for the bedroom and its images of the most important events in the history of this area, pride of place going to the construction of the castle, of course. Other rooms are panelled and furnished like a ship's quarters, reflecting Maximilian's devotion to the Austrian Navy.

There are a number of ways **to get to Miramare**, of which the simplest is to take the #36 bus from Piazza Oberdan, though the private APT service from the bus station is quicker. Trains heading west from Trieste also stop, and in summer there's a boat service from the harbour. In July and August a *son et lumière* called "Miramare's Imperial Dream" is presented beside the sea (9.30pm & 10.45pm; €7), with a regular version in English; check with Trieste's tourist office or the castle (℡040.224.143, ⓦwww.castello-miramare.it) to confirm dates and times.

Duino and Sistiana

The village of **DUINO**, 14km northwest along the coast from Trieste, is dominated by its two castles, the **Castello Vecchio**, built around the tenth century and now just a ruined eyrie above the sea, and the early fifteenth-century **Castello Nuovo**, seat of the princes of Thurn and Taxis down to the present day. The latter and its grounds opened to the public in 2003 (April–Sept Mon & Wed–Sun 9.30am–5.30pm; March & Oct Mon & Wed–Sun 9.30am–4pm; Nov–Feb Sat & Sun 9.30am–4pm; €7; ℡040.208.120, ⓦcastellodiduino .it) and visitors can now stroll through the lavishly decorated rooms, take a look at a massive doll's house given to the family by Napoleon III's widow and a history of the family's eighteenth-century pan-European postal service, and admire the fantastic coastal views from the beautiful gardens and the top of the third-century Roman tower. A small **café** in the grounds offers refreshments or, down by the harbour, a couple of **restaurants** serve more substantial food – turn left out of the castle and head downhill.

A pleasant footpath, the Sentiero Rilke – named after Rainer Maria Rilke who began the famous *Duino Elegies* while visiting the castle – runs 3km back along the coast to the **campsite** (℡040.299.264, ⓦwww.camping.it/friuli /marepinetabaiasistiana; pitch from about €30; April–Sept) at **SISTIANA**, where there's a large harbour backed by woods, and a **beach**. Bus #44 and the faster APT bus #51 run from Trieste's Piazza Oberdan and bus station to Sistiana and Duino. There are also three ferries a day to Duino harbour in summer (see p.388).

Aquileia, Grado and around

Bordered by the Tagliamento in the west and the Isonzo in the east, and drained by other rivers flowing into the sandy, shallow waters at the head of the Adriatic, the triangle of flatlands west of Trieste and south of Udine seems unpromising territory for a visitor – mile upon mile of maize fields, punctuated by telegraph poles, streams, level roads and newish villages. Yet at **Aquileia**, the dull fields of this secretive region have yielded up a wealth of Roman remains, while its glorious **Basilica** ranks among the most important monuments of early Christendom. Just to the south, tucked away amongst lagoons, the popular resort of **Grado** with its sunbed-lined beaches and crowds of holiday-makers has a completely different atmosphere, though it too preserves some beautiful early Christian remains. If you don't have your own transport, **buses** are the way to explore the region: they leave Udine for Grado at least every hour, calling at Palmanova and Aquileia on the way; from Trieste, change at **Monfalcone**, from where buses leave hourly for Aquileia and Grado or take the summer-only **ferry** from Trieste's Molo Pescheria to Grado's Molo Torpediniere (see p.388).

Aquileia

Forty-five kilometres west of Trieste, **AQUILEIA** was established as a **Roman colony** in 181 BC, its location at the eastern edge of the Venetian plain – on the bank of a navigable river a few kilometres from the sea – being ideal for defensive and trading purposes. It became the nexus for all Rome's dealings with points east and north, and by 10 BC, when the Emperor Augustus received Herod the Great here, Aquileia was the fourth most important city in Italy, after Rome, Milan and Cápua. In 314 AD the Patriarchate of Aquileia was founded, and under the first patriarch, Theodore, a great basilica was built. Sacked by Attila in 452 and again by the Lombards in 568, Aquileia lost the patriarchate to Grado, which was protected from invasion by its lagoons. Aquileia regained its primacy in the early eleventh century under Patriarch Poppo, who rebuilt the basilica and erected the campanile, a landmark for miles around. But regional power inevitably passed to Venice, and in 1751 Aquileia lost its patriarchate for the last time, to Udine. The sea has long since retreated, the River Natissa reduced to a reed-clogged stream, and Aquileia is now a quiet little town of 3500 people.

The Basilica

A UNESCO World Heritage site, Aquileia's rich history is made visible in the layers of the vast **Basilica** (summer daily 9am–7pm; winter Mon–Fri 9am–1pm & 2–5pm, Sat & Sun 9am–5pm; free), just east of the main road. The earliest part, Theodore's extraordinary **mosaic pavement**, was discovered below the nave floor at the beginning of the twentieth century and is thought to be the earliest surviving remnant of any Christian church. The mosaic undulates the full length of the nave in a riotous sequence of colours, patterns and images, many of which draw on Roman iconography. Look for the blond angel bearing the laurel wreath and palm frond – whether it represents the Pax Romana or Christian Victory, no one is sure. Beyond the red line extending across the aisle the Christian imagery begins with the story of Jonah, complete with waves, whale and fish everywhere – a motif not unconnected to the nearby Adriatic. Other mosaics from Theodore's original basilica, depicting a whole bestiary, have been discovered around the base of the campanile (access from inside the basilica). Next door, a climb up the **bell tower** (March–Oct daily 9.30am–1pm & 2.30–6pm; €1.10) gives a new perspective on the basilica as well as views stretching from the mountains to the coast.

In 1348 an earthquake destroyed much of Poppo's work, but the building is still superb, the Gothic elements of the reconstruction – all points above the capitals – harmonizing perfectly with the Romanesque below. The fine nave ceiling, like the steeple of the campanile, dates from the early sixteenth century. The ninth-century **crypt** under the chancel (€3) has very faded twelfth-century frescoes telling the story of St Hermagora, the legendary first bishop of Aquileia, including a gory beheading scene and a moving descent from the cross.

The Museo Archeologico

A couple of minutes' walk west from the basilica, on the other side of the main road, on Via Roma, is the **Museo Archeologico** (Mon 8.30am–2pm, Tues–Sun 8.30am–7.30pm; €4). Worked stone and everyday items litter the fields around Aquileia, but the finer pieces have been collected here, ranging from precise surgical needles, delicate coloured glass and precious stones to great piles of jumbled masonry. The two courtyards, in particular, resemble a junkyard of Roman stone, with hundreds of funerary monuments, including urns piled in neat pyramids; concerts are occasionally held here in summer. It's worth persevering up to the top floor of the museum where two extraordinary bronze heads are displayed side by side. One is a fantastical relief in the Hellenistic style, the other a naturalistic bust that may portray a dictator of the third century AD; the cruel expression certainly supports such speculation. On the ground floor rows of marble sculptures and busts mostly derive from the Roman tombs that once lined the roads into Aquileia.

Practicalities

The **tourist office** is at the Via Iulia Augusta bus terminal (Mon–Fri 9am–7pm, Sat & Sun 10am–1pm & 2–5pm; ☎0431.91.491, ⓦwww.turismofvg .it). The Pro Loco office beside the basilica does not provide tourist information. In the newer part of town, west of the main road past the Museo Archeologico, you'll find the cheaper of Aquileia's two three-star **hotels**, the spartan yet tidy *Aquila Nera*, Piazza Garibaldi 5 (☎0431.91.045, ⓦwww .hotelaquilanera.com; ❷), with an excellent **restaurant** attached. The more upmarket *Hotel Patriarchi* sits on the main road not far from the bus terminal (☎0431.919.595, ⓦwww.hotelpatriarchi.it; ❸). There's also a decent **HI hostel**, *Domus Augusta*, Via Roma 25 (☎043.191.024, ⓦwww.ostelloaquileia .it; €17) and a pleasant **campsite**, *Camping Aquileia* Via Gemina 10 (☎0431.91.042, ⓦwww.campingaquileia.it; mid-May to mid-Sept; pitches from €11, bungalow ❷). Of the area's **restaurants**, *Alla Basilica*, Via Della Stazione 2, serves decent pizzas, and the agriturismo *La Pergola*, in an old monastery on the main road at Località Beligna 4 (☎0431.91.561, ⓦwww .lapergolaonline.com), serves good local cookery and a full range of typical Friulani wines.

Grado

Some 11km south of Aquileia, isolated among lagoons at the end of a causeway, is the ancient island-town of **GRADO**, through which Aquileia once traded with Syria, Cyprus, Arabia and Asia Minor. But Grado is no miniature Venice, despite its parallel history and situation, the tiny historic centre being all but lost among the concrete buildings of the large, modern resort. For relaxing on the **beach**, however, this is one of the best places in the northern Adriatic, the resort extending eastwards along the length of the sandy island. The water is safe and warm as a bath, and almost as shallow – indeed, the name of the town comes from the gentle angle of its shore. The free beaches are at the eastern and western ends; if you want a locker, deckchair and shower facilities, you have to pay a few euros to one of the businesses on the Lungomare Adriatico.

It's worth seeking out the **historic centre**, however, for its three early-Christian buildings, grouped close together in the heart of a miniature network of old streets. The exteriors are of fairly rustic brick construction, though enlivened by fragments of carved Roman marble. The sixth-century **Basilica** (daily 8.30am–6.15pm; free) was heavily restored between the 1930s and 1950s, but preserves a bizarre parade of ill-matched nave pillars topped by an assortment of Corinthian capitals; it's thought that these were recycled from various Roman buildings in Aquileia. The pulpit is of similarly hybrid origins, perched on six slender Roman columns under a Venetian canopy that resembles an oriental tent. Venice's presence is also felt in the fourteenth-century silver *pala* on the high altar. The mosaic pavement, while not as impressive as Aquileia's, is beautiful, the pattern being formed by an endless knot. The adjacent octagonal **Baptistry** (erratic opening hours) also dates back to the fifth century and the arrival of the first Christians in the lagoon. The church of **Santa Maria delle Grazie** (daily 8.30am–6.15pm; free), on its far side, is from the same period and has another mongrel collection of columns and capitals. From the outside it's possible to see how the ground level has sunk over the centuries.

Practicalities

Grado's **tourist office**, at Viale Dante Alighieri 72 (April–Sept daily 8am–1pm & 3–7pm; Oct–March Mon–Thurs 8am–1pm & 2–5pm, Fri 8am–1pm; ☏0431.877.111, ⓦwww.turismofvg.it), has details of **hotels**, the majority of which are fairly expensive and sometimes insist on your taking full board. Three cheaper options are the *Villa Marin*, Via dei Provveditori 20 (☏0431.80.789, ⓔvillamarin@grado.it; ❸), overlooking the seafront wall between the two beaches; *Villa Romana Meublé*, Viale Dante Alighieri 20 (☏0431.82.604; ❷; May–Sept), just east of the historic centre and one street back from the beach; and *Al Sole Meublé*, Viale del Sole 31 (☏&ⓕ0431.80.370; ❷; April–Oct), which is near the beach, at its free, eastern end, a good ten-minute walk from the centre. The best local **campsites** are at Grado Pineta, around 3km east of the town and served by regular buses: *Camping Punta Spin* Via Monfalcone 10 (☏0431.80.732, ⓦwww.puntaspin.it; April–Sept) has a wide range of facilities including three swimming pools while *Villaggio Turistico Europa* Via Monfalcone 12 (☏0431.80.877, ⓦwww.villaggioeuropa.com; mid-April to mid-Sept) features a sizeable aquatic park.

A cluster of good **restaurants** can be found in the old streets around Santa Maria. The tiny *Santa Lucia* (closed Tues in low season), secreted in an alleyway at Campo Porta Nuova 1, serves good pizzas, while the *Enoteca In Sentina*, at 1/B, is good for wine and snacks. For Grado's fish specialities, head just west to *Trattoria de Toni*, Piazza Duca d'Aosta 37, or the *Trattoria Alla Borsa*, Via Conte di Grado 1, behind the marina.

Gorizia and around

As with other towns in this region, the tranquillity of present-day **GORIZIA** – virtually midway along the Trieste–Udine rail line – belies the turbulence of its past. The castle that dominates the old centre was the power-base of the dukes of Gorizia, who ruled the area for four centuries. After their eclipse, Venice briefly ruled the town at the start of the sixteenth century, before the Habsburgs took over. It was controlled from Vienna uninterruptedly until August 8, 1916, when the Italian army occupied it. **War cemeteries** in the area attest to the violent struggles fought over the territory. The border settlement after World War II literally split houses in Gorizia down the middle. Italy kept the town proper, but lost its eastern perimeter to what was then Yugoslavia, where the new regime resolved to build its own Gorizia: **Nova Gorica** – New Gorizia – is the result.

The town's appearance, like that of Trieste, is distinctly central European, stamped with the authority of Empress Maria Theresa. Numerous parks and gardens – thriving in the area's mild climate – further enhance the fin-de-siècle atmosphere. It's a major shopping town for Slovenes, which explains the large number of electrical, clothes and food shops, and the cafés and restaurants.

The main sight in town is the **Borgo Castello**, the quarter built round the castle by the Venetians, mostly in the sixteenth century. It's a pleasant place to wander, but the view from the castle walls is more inspiring. The graceful rooms of the **Castle** itself (Tues–Sun: April–Sept 9.30am–1pm & 3–7.30pm; Oct–March 9.30am–6pm; €3, more with exhibitions and special events) hold an unexceptional collection of musical instruments, weaponry, and paintings and models of the castle and town. One of the finest of Gorizia's Neoclassical buildings is the **Palazzo Attems** (Tues–Sun 9am–7pm; €6) in Piazza De Amicis, northwest of the castle, built by Nicolo Pacassi, Maria Theresa's favourite architect. Behind the *palazzo*, in what was once the Jewish quarter, the **Synagogue**, at Via Ascoli 19 (April–Oct Mon, Fri & Sat 4–7pm, Tues & Thurs 6–8pm, Sun 10am–1pm; Nov–March, Mon, Fri & Sat 4–7pm, Tues & Thurs 5–7pm, second Sun of month only 10am–1pm; free), is also of Neoclassical design; the serene interior resembles those in Venice's Ghetto.

Probably the strangest sight in Gorizia is the crypt in the Franciscan monastery at **Castagnavizza** – Kostanjevica, actually, because the **monastery** (Mon–Sat 9am–noon & 3–5pm, Sun 3–5pm; donation of €1.50 is expected) lies across the border in Slovenian Nova Gorica. This is the burial place of the last but one French king, Charles X. After being ousted by the bloodless revolution of July 1830 and sent into exile, the family eventually ended up in Gorizia in 1836, where the Habsburgs allowed them to stay, though Charles died of cholera just seventeen days after his arrival. The Bourbon Institute has asked for the return to France of the family's remains, but both the monks and the Slovenian government have refused, asserting that the royal relics now form part of Slovenia's history. The easiest way **to get to the monastery** is to cross the border on Via San Gabriele, in the northeast part of town (take your passport as there's usually someone checking), cross the railway line and follow the signs uphill – it's about a ten-minute walk from the border. Once there, ring the bell.

Practicalities

Gorizia's **tourist office** is at Corso Italia 9 (daily 9.30am–6.30pm; ℡0481.535.764, Ⓦ www.turismofvg.it). For **accommodation**, try the excellent and welcoming one-star *Sandro*, at Via S. Chiara 18 (℡0481.533.223; ❷, breakfast extra), not far from the central Piazza della Vittoria. If that's full, the comfortable but more expensive *Alla Transalpina*, at Via Caprin 30 (℡0481.530.291, Ⓦ www.hotel-transalpina.com; ❷, breakfast extra), is recently restructured; the restaurant is moderately priced, and it's a good 2km northeast of the centre, right on the Slovene border, but bus #1 runs every fifteen minutes from the train station through town, terminating opposite the hotel.

Gorizia is better served by **places to eat**. The *Osteria Panesale*, Corso Verdi 11 (closed Mon), on the way into the old ghetto, serves good local food in simple surroundings, as does *Alla Luna*, Via Oberdan 13 (closed Sun eve & Mon). But the best option in town is the excellent *Ai Tre Soldi Goriziana* (closed Sun eve & Mon), up an alley off Corso Italia 38. It has garden seating in summer and serves up a wide range of beautifully cooked Friulian specialities and local wines – try the *menù degustazione* for €25.

The war cemeteries

Sobering reminders of Friuli-Venezia Giulia's violent past stand close to Gorizia. Three kilometres north of the town, across the River Isonzo, is the **Sacrario di Oslavia cemetery** (Tues–Sun 8.30am–noon & 1.30–5pm; free), built in 1938 and containing the remains of around sixty thousand soldiers from World War I. To get here take bus #2 or #4 to the first stop after the river, then follow Via Bella Veduta north – it's about a ten-minute walk.

Twelve kilometres southwest of Gorizia, and accessible by train to its eponymous station, the **cemetery at Redipuglia** (daily dawn–dusk; free) is Italy's largest war memorial. A massive example of Fascist architecture, inaugurated in the same year as its counterpart in Oslavia, it holds the bones of 100,000 dead, some 60,000 of whom are unidentified. A monumental set of steps leads up to a chapel, surmounted by three bronze crosses, from where there are panoramic views of the Carso – scene of so many battles.

Udine and around

UDINE, 71km northwest of Trieste, is the second city of Friuli-Venezia Giulia. With less than half the population of the regional capital, it presents a radically different complexion. Hemmed in by sombre suburbs – to which the weather conditions are often a match – the oval-shaped historic centre comprises essentially Italian charms. In many ways Udine harks back to the Venetian Republic, of which it was also the number two city. Admittedly, its canals, called *roggie*, are little more than rivulets compared to those of Venice, but its gorgeous Piazza della Libertà could have been airlifted directly from *La Serenissima*. In addition to grand architecture, the churches and galleries here also boast scores of fine works by **Giambattista Tiepolo**, whose airy brilliance evokes the city's easygoing atmosphere on a fine day, when the watery light from the canals dances on nearby walls. Two relaxed days provide enough time to get a good taste of what Udine has to offer.

Some history

Along with Cividale (see p.385), Udine was one of the frontier towns of imperial Rome but it was not until the thirteenth century that it started to become a regional centre. Patriarch **Bertoldo di Andechs** (1218–51) can be seen as the father of Udine – he established two markets (the old market in Via Mercatovecchio, and the new one in Piazza Matteotti, still a marketplace), moved the patriarchate from Cividale to the castle of Udine and set up a city council. In 1362 the dukes of Austria acquired the place by treaty, but not for long: Venice, now hungry for territory, captured Udine in 1420, after several assaults and sieges. The city was ruled by Venetian governors for almost 400 years – until 1797, when the Venetian Republic surrendered to Napoleon. Even now, the old aristocracy of Udine speak a version of Venetian dialect, while the humbler Udinese, many of whom have migrated from the countryside, speak *Friulano*.

Arrival, information and accommodation

Udine's **train** and **bus stations** are close together in the south of the town, on Viale Europa Unità; Via Roma and its continuation Via Dante Alighieri lead from the train station into the centre. The **tourist office**, at Piazza I (primo) Maggio 7 (Mon–Sat 8.30am–6.30pm, Sun 10am–4pm; ☏0432.295.972, ⓦ www.turismofvg.it), sells the **FVG Card** (see p.365), which allows discounted entry to at least ten civic museums and exhibitions, as well as free use of local public transport. **Internet** access can be found in the centre of town, at *Internet Play*, Via San Francesco 33 (closed daily 12.45–3.30pm), near the Duomo.

Hotel options are surprisingly limited, but some attractive new options have sprung up in recent years near the centre.

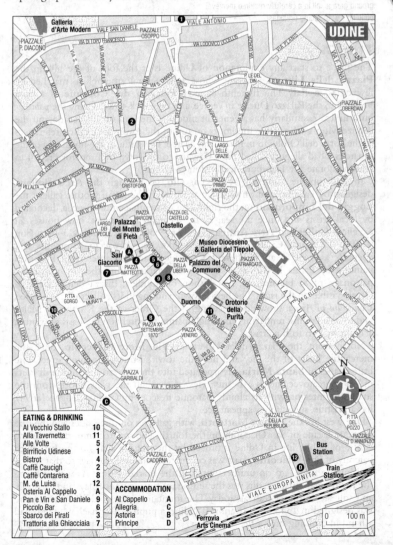

EATING & DRINKING

Al Vecchio Stallo	10
Alla Tavernetta	11
Alle Volte	5
Birrificio Udinese	1
Bistrot	4
Caffè Caucigh	2
Caffè Contarena	8
M. de Luisa	12
Osteria Al Cappello	A
Pan e Vin e San Daniele	9
Piccolo Bar	6
Sbarco dei Pirati	3
Trattoria alla Ghiacciaia	7

ACCOMMODATION

Al Cappello	A
Allegria	C
Astoria	B
Principe	D

Al Cappello Via Sarpi 5 ☎0432.299.327, ⓦwww.osteriaalcappello.it. This traditional welcoming *osteria* also offers a small *locanda* with six spacious, smartly designed rooms. The restaurant, too, is one of the most convivial and warmly attractive in town – and four-legged friends are also welcome. ❹

Allegria Vicolo Chiuso 1 ☎0432.201.116, ⓦwww.hotelallegria.it. On a quiet pedestrianized street, this is the best of the city's newest hotels. Everything is sleek, chic and state-of-the-art, including a cutting-edge car elevator to the underground garage, all in a carefully restored medieval building. ❺, including breakfast.

Astoria Piazza XX Settembre 24 ☎0432.505.091, ⓦwww.hotelastoria.udine.it. A plushly modern choice with everything you'd expect from a four-star, and weekend offers see rates fall by almost half. ❼, including breakfast.

Principe Viale Europa Unità 51 ☎0432.506.000, ⓦwww.principe-hotel.it. Ideally located for travellers by train or bus, this friendly, fresh and efficient choice is set back in its own courtyard to ensure quiet. There's free parking, too, and the choice of non-smoking rooms. ❸, including breakfast.

The City

The place to start any exploration of Udine is at the foot of the hill, in the **Piazza della Libertà**, a square whose architectural ensemble is matched by few cities in Italy. The fifteenth-century **Palazzo del Comune** is a clear homage to the Palazzo Ducale in Venice, and the clock-tower facing the *palazzo*, built in 1527, similarly has a Venetian model – the lion on the facade and the bronze Moors who strike the hours on top of the tower are explicit references to the Torre dell'Orologio in Piazza San Marco. The statue at the north end of the square is a bad allegory called *Peace*, donated to the town by Emperor Franz I to commemorate the Habsburg acquisition of Udine.

To walk up the slight hill to the **castello**, go through the **Arco Bollani**, designed by Palladio, and onwards up the graceful Venetian Gothic gallery, the **Loggia del Lippomano** on the right. The sixteenth-century *castello*, decorated by local artists and once the seat of the Friulian parliament, now houses an excellent **Galleria d'Arte Antica** (Tues–Sat 9.30am–12.30pm & 3–6pm, Sun 9.30am–12.30pm; €3.20), containing works by Carpaccio, Bronzino and Tiepolo, as well as an indifferent Caravaggio and an interesting historical painting by Palma Il Giovanni showing St Mark putting the city under the patronage of St Hermagora, first bishop of Aquileia; Piazza della Libertà is clearly visible on the right. The best-known painting in its collection is Tiepolo's *Consilium in Arena*, showing a meeting of the Order of the Knights of Malta, said to be a faithful rendering, amazingly painted entirely on the basis of written accounts given to the artist.

North from the Piazza della Libertà is **Via Mercatovecchio**, once the mercantile heart of the city and now the town's busiest shopping street. The little chapel of **Santa Maria**, incorporated into the Palazzo del Monte di Pietà in Via Mercatovecchio, is a beauty: viewed through the glass booth from the street, the interior, with its cloudy Baroque frescoes by Giulio Quaglio (1694), has a pristine, subaqueous appearance.

Due west lies the **Piazza Matteotti**, with galleries on three sides and the fine Baroque facade of San Giacomo on the fourth. The square's importance as the centre of public life in Udine is proved by the outside altar on the first-floor balcony of **San Giacomo**; mass was celebrated here on Saturdays so that selling and buying could go on uninterrupted in the market below. As well as being the town's main market, this was the setting for tournaments, plays and carnivals, and still sees summer festivals today. The fountain in the middle of the square was designed in 1543 by Giovanni da Udine, a pupil of Raphael, who also had a hand in building the castle.

▲ Piazza della Libertà, Udine

The Duomo and Galleria del Tiepolo

Off the south side of Piazza della Libertà is the **Duomo** (daily 7am–noon & 4–8pm; free), a Romanesque construction that was given a Baroque refit in the eighteenth century. Altarpieces and frescoes by Giambattista Tiepolo are the main attraction – they decorate the first two chapels on the right and the chapel of the Sacrament, a little way beyond. A series of frescoes painted by Tiepolo in collaboration with his son, Giandomenico, can be seen in the tiny **Oratorio della Purità** opposite – ask the sacristan in the Duomo to show you.

But Udine's outstanding works of art are the Giambattista Tiepolo frescoes in the nearby **Gallerie del Tiepolo** in the beautifully furnished **Palazzo Arcivescovile** (Wed–Sun 10am–noon & 3.30–6.30pm; €5, including Museo Diocesano – see p.385). Painted in the late 1720s, these luminous and consummately theatrical scenes add up to a sort of Rococo epic of the Old Testament. *Fall of the Rebel Angels* is the first work you see as you climb the staircase, while the finest room, the Gallery, is at the top, immediately on your right. Every surface is painted with either trompe-l'oeil architectural details or scenes from the story of Abraham, Isaac and Jacob. To the left is a sequence of rooms decorated in rich colours: watch for Tiepolo's *Judgement of Solomon* in the Red Room, and Bambini's wonderful *Triumph of Wisdom* in the serene Delfino library. Also inside the Palazzo Arcivescovile and arranged around the

Tiepolo galleries is the **Museo Diocesano**, with an assortment of sculpture and funerary monuments, as well as an exhibition of naive art – popular sculptures from Friuli's churches spanning the Gothic, Renaissance and Baroque periods.

Galleria d'Arte Moderna

The new **Galleria d'Arte Moderna**, Piazzale Paolo Diacono 22 (Tues–Sat 9.30am–12.30pm & 3–6pm, Sun 9.30am–12.30pm; €3.20) aims to give an overview of Italian art in the twentieth century, with a few foreign greats thrown in for good measure. Works include those by Martini, Guttuso, Fontana and de Kooning.

Eating, drinking and entertainment

Udine's thriving café society means there are scores of **cafés** and **bars** to choose from. The town can also boast dozens of **restaurants**, many of the most appealing clustered in the southwest corner of the Old Town. Most menus display a decidedly Central European bent.

In summer there's a busy programme of **cultural events** – theatre, outdoor cinema, music, dance – in and around the town: ask the tourist office for the fortnightly listings of events. Throughout the year the Ferroviario arts cinema at Via Cernaia 2 is always worth checking out for films in their original language.

Cafés and bars

Birrificio Udinese Via Caccia 5, at the top of Via Gemona and across Piazzale Osoppo. This microbrewery features regional beers – all organic – and frequent live music. Tues is jazz night.

Bistrot Piazza Matteotti 18. One of the hottest spots in this very happening square, at the centre of the city's nightlife.

Caffè Caucigh Via Gemona 36. A comfy Irish pub with occasional live music, usually on Fri.

Caffè Contarena Via Cavour 1. A visit to this elegant establishment is a classy way to start the day, with coffee and a light breakfast.

M. de Luisa Via Roma 46. A little *pasticceria* that's been turning out delicious regional treats, such as marbled *gubana* (nut-cake), for three generations.

Pan e Vin e San Daniele Piazza Lionello 12. To go with local wines, a variety of moderately priced coldcuts and cheeses are on offer, including, of course, the excellent San Daniele ham, a Friulano speciality. Closed Sun.

Piccolo Bar Via Rialto 2. This stylish option is an intimate wine bar just right for starting the evening off.

Restaurants

Alla Tavernetta Via Artico di Prampero 2. This cosy, traditional place serves hearty regional dishes, such as barley and bean soup and prosciutto of various kinds. Moderate prices. Closed Sun & Mon.

Alle Volte Via Merceria 6 & Via Mercato Vecchio 4. Atmospheric restaurant set in a fifteenth-century building – one floor is an *enoteca-osteria*, for wine-tasting and traditional snacks, the other the main restaurant. Classic dishes include swordfish and *spaghetti alle vongole* or try the fish-based tasting menu (€41 including wine). Closed Sun.

Al Vecchio Stallo Via Viola 7. An historic, slow-food *osteria* offering traditional choices such as gnocchi, salted cod dishes and *frittata* – housed, as the name reveals, in a converted old stables. Expect to pay about €35 per person with wine. Closed Wed.

Osteria Al Cappello Via Sarpi 5. The lively restaurant of the *Al Cappello* inn (see p.382) features local wines and rustic regional cookery served in a rousing atmosphere. Closed Mon.

Sbarco dei Pirati Via Bartolini 12. Enjoying a beautiful setting built over a shimmering *roggia*, this *osteria* provides a welcoming atmosphere and tempting regional dishes – try the goulash followed by *gubana* soaked in plum brandy for dessert. Closed Sun.

Trattoria alla Ghiacciaia Via Zanon 13/B. Cosy little place serving an eclectic range of good-value local dishes, including *frico*, crispy fried cheese served with polenta, most dishes running €6–8. Seating available in an attractive and tranquil canal-side garden. Closed Mon.

Cividale del Friuli

Lying only 17km east of Udine, **CIVIDALE DEL FRIULI** is a well-preserved medieval gem of a town. It's much prized by the local Friulani and is attracting increasing numbers of visitors drawn to its beautiful setting and arts treasures. It has ancient roots, founded in 50 BC by Julius Caesar at the picturesque point where the Natisone River Valley opens into the plain. In the sixth century AD it became the capital of the first Lombard duchy. In the eighth century the Patriarch of Aquileia moved here, inaugurating Cividale's most prosperous period. Cividale has been the main market town in the Natisone Valley for two hundred years, and today you'll hear Italian, *Friulano* and Slovene dialects spoken in the street.

Arrival, information and accommodation

Cividale del Friuli is connected to Udine by train (free with the FVG Card) and bus. The **tourist office**, five-minutes' walk northwest of Piazza Duomo at Piazza Diacono 9 (Mon, Fri, Sat & Sun 9.30am–noon & 3.30–6pm; ☎0432.710.460, ⓦwww.cividale.net), has details on Mittelfest, an annual summer celebration of Central European culture with concerts, theatre and dance. Most visitors are day-trippers from Udine, but for an overnight stay head for the beautiful and comfortably done-up nineteenth-century neo-Gothic castle ⚵ *Locanda al Castello*, Via del Castello 12 (☎0432.733.242, ⓦwww.alcastello.net; ❺, including breakfast), 1km southwest of town, on a hill above the road to Tarcento and Faedis. The restaurant too is recommended, especially on a sunny day when its terrace is the best place for a leisurely lunch.

The Town

Just strolling around the town, within the oval ring bisected by Via Carlo Alberto and Corso Mazzini, is a pleasure, the pace of life provincially serene. The Old Town lies between the train and coach stations and the Natisone, and the visitor need never cross the river, though a walk over the Ponte del Diavolo (Devil's Bridge, see p.386) is *de rigueur*.

The tiny **Tempietto Longobardo** (Oct–March Mon–Sat 9.30am–12.30pm & 3–5pm, Sun 9.30am–12.30pm & 2.30–6pm; April–Sept Mon–Sat 9.30am–12.30pm & 3–6.30pm, Sun 9.30am–1pm & 3–7.30pm; €2), poised above the Natisone off Piazza San Biagio, is a uniquely fine example of Lombard art. Constructed in the ninth century, largely from older fragments, much of the elaborate stuccowork inside the chapel was reduced to rubble in the terrible earthquake of 1222. The delicate interior preserves faded frescoes and carved stalls from its use as a convent chapel in the late fourteenth century, but the eye is drawn to the east wall where an exquisite stucco arch is flanked by six female figures. Whether they represent saints, queens or nuns is uncertain, but the luminous, smiling statues are among the most splendid surviving works of art from the ninth century.

Two other beautiful Lombard pieces are in the **Museo Cristiano** (April–Oct Mon–Sat 9.30am–noon & 3–6pm, Sun 3–7pm; Nov–March Mon–Sat 9.30am–noon & 3–6pm, Sun 3–6pm; free), housed in the precincts of the fifteenth-century Duomo. The Altar of Ratchis was carved for Ratchis, Duke of Cividale and King of the Lombards at Pavia, who died as a Benedictine monk at Montecassino in 759; the reliefs of *Christ in Triumph* and the *Adoration of the Magi* are delicate and haunting. The other highlight is the **Baptistry of Callisto**, named after Callisto de Treviso, the first Patriarch of Aquileia to move to Cividale. He lived here from 730 to 756 and initiated the building of the patriarchal palace, the cathedral and this octagonal baptistry, which used to stand beside the cathedral. It's constructed from older Lombard fragments, the columns and capitals dating from the fifth century.

The **Duomo** itself (Mon 9am–2pm, Tues–Sun 8.30am–7.30pm) houses a twelfth-century masterpiece of silversmithery: the *pala* (altarpiece) named after Pellegrino II, the patriarch who commissioned and donated it to the town; it depicts the Virgin seated between the archangels Michael and Gabriel, who are flanked by 25 saints and framed by more saints, prophets and the patron himself. Also in Piazza del Duomo is the **Museo Archeologico** (Mon 9am–2pm, Tues–Sun 8.30am–7.30pm; €2), which houses an excellent exhibition on the Lombards on the first floor, incorporating local finds including some beautiful gold brooches. On the ground floor is a hotchpotch of late Roman and early Christian pieces, the highlight being a second-century mosaic of a wild-eyed Neptune.

East of the piazza, on Via Monastero Maggiore, is a cellar-like cavern called the **Ipogeo Celtico** (to visit, contact the bar *All'Ipogeo* next door; donation requested). The hypogeum was probably used as a tomb for Celtic leaders between the fifth and second centuries BC, but there is still some dispute as to whether it's artificial or was merely adapted by its users. Either way, the spectral faces carved on the walls make it a most unsettling place.

Just beyond the Ipogeo, and spanning the Natisone, the **Ponte del Diavolo** (Devil's Bridge) is a reconstruction of the original fifteenth-century structure that was destroyed during World War I. Of many legends concerning the bridge's demonic name, a favourite involves the devil agreeing to aid the speedy construction of the bridge in return for the soul of the first living thing to cross it – Cividale's wily inhabitants sent a hapless dog.

Eating and drinking

Cividale del Fruili's smartest **café** is the *San Marco*, Via Gemona 31, opposite the Duomo in the loggia of the sixteenth-century town hall. Good though pricey **restaurants** include *Zorutti*, Via Borgo di Ponte 7 (closed Mon), situated just across the Natisone by the Ponte del Diavolo; and *Alla Frasca*, Stretta de Rubeis 8 (closed Mon), one block west from Piazza Duomo and boasting a vast array of truffle and mushroom dishes. A favourite with discerning locals is the excellent *Trattorie Dominissini*, at Stretta Stellini 18 (closed Mon) – take a right just short of the Ponte del Diavolo.

The Carnia

The peak district in the north of Friuli is known as the **Carnia**, a name given to it by the Celtic tribes who settled here in the fourth century BC. If you're approaching the area by road or rail from Udine, you could make a stop at pristine, mountain-backed **GEMONA** (tourist information ☎0432.981.441) a good staging post for the Carnia, offering a couple of fine and inexpensive **places to stay**. The better one is the *Agli Amici*, an *affitacamera* (guesthouse) a couple of kilometres out of the centre at Via Godo 160 (☎0432.981.013; ❶) – turn right outside the station then head along Via Piovega, following the yellow signs; the alternative is the *Si-Si* at Via Piovega 15 (☎0432.981.158, ⓦwww .hotelsisi.it; ❷). There's an excellent **trattoria** at the *Agli Amici*, while *Al Falomo*, Via Cavour 17 (closed Wed), on the main street just down from the Duomo, has pizzas and an inexpensive tourist menu.

Fighting in the Carnia

The mountainous **Carnia** region of Friuli-Venezia Giulia has frequently been the scene of fierce warfare. One of the strangest sideshows of World War II was staged in the area north of Udine: Cossack troops, led by White Russian officers, made an alliance with the Nazis and invaded the Carnia, on the promise of a **Cossack homeland** there once the Reich was secure. After the war ended, Italian partisans forced the Cossaks to flee to Austria from where, under British orders, they were handed over to the Red Army. The area also saw the invasion of **Tito** at the end of the war, with more terror and atrocities resulting in mass graves for an estimated ten thousand. No armies have invaded since, but the last border dispute between Italy and Yugoslavia was not settled until the 1970s; and when neighbouring Slovenia became independent in June 1991, Italian checkpoints were the scene of brief but fierce confrontations between Slovene and Yugoslav troops, though the fighting never spilled into Italy.

The Carnia proper begins north of Gemona, around the headwaters of the River Tagliamento, and comprises two distinct areas. To the west, hay meadows and orchards give way to the Alpine uplands and pastures of the **Alpi Carniche**, which share the culture of the eastern Dolomites. To the east, the high, sheer and often barren limestone peaks of the **Alpi Giulie** are divided by deep, forested valleys that radiate towards the borders with Austria in the north and Slovenia in the east. Both of these ranges are hardly known even within Italy, yet the area has a lot to offer the hiker and climber, including numerous **rifugi**. Linguists should get a kick out of it too, as the villagers speak strange variants of *Friulano*, German and Slovene.

To plan a Carnia **walking trip** in advance, call in at the Udine office of the *Società Alpina Friulana*, Via Odorico da Pordenone 3 (Mon–Fri 5–7.30pm plus Thurs 9–10.30pm; ℡0432.504.290, Ⓦwww.scuolecaifvg.spin.it). A useful website on the Carnia is Ⓦwww.carnia.it, providing information on mountain accommodation and other details. If you want to stay right in the heart of the mountains, your best option is the resort of **Tarvisio**, 65km northeast of Germona and just 6km from the Austrian border. A number of nature trails and longer walks radiate from the village and there's a helpful tourist office at Via Roma 10 (℡0428.2342, Ⓦwww.tarvisiano.org). The nicest place to stay is the *Albergo Valle Verde*, just outside the village at Via Priesnig 12 (℡0428.2342, Ⓦwww.hotelvalleverde.com; ❸).

Travel details

Trains

Trieste to: Gorizia (up to 27 daily; 45min); Redipuglia (up to 5 daily; 40min); Udine (up to 26 daily; 1hr 20min); Venice (up to 17 daily; 1hr 40min).

Udine to: Cividale (hourly; 20min); Gemona (14 daily; 30min); Gorizia (up to 30 daily; 30min); Redipuglia (up to 8 daily; 50min); Trieste (up to 33 daily; 1hr 30min); Venice (hourly; 1hr 45min–2hr 15min).

Buses

Gorizia to: Cividale (4 daily; 1hr).
Grado to: Gorizia (up to 22 daily; 1hr 20min).
Trieste to: Duino (hourly; 30min–1hr); Grado (14 daily; 1hr–1hr 30min); Monfalcone (for Aquileia and Grado; hourly; 45min); Udine (27 daily; 1hr 15min).
Udine to: Aquileia (16 daily; 40min); Cividale (at least 21 daily; 20min); Gemona (6 daily; 50min); Grado (12 daily; 1hr); Trieste (9 daily; 1hr).

Ferries

Trieste to: Barcola (July to mid-Sept hourly; 30min); Duino (July–Sept 3 daily via Grignano and Sistiana; 1hr 45min); Grado (mid-June to Aug 3 daily; 1hr 30min–2hr); Múggia (mid-June to Oct every 90min; 30min); Croatia: Brioni (June–Sept Tues–Sun; 4hr); Rovigno (June–Sept Tues–Sun; 3hr 10min); Slovenia: Pirano (Wed, Fri & Sun; 1 daily; 1hr 50min).

7

Emilia-Romagna

CHAPTER 7

Highlights

* **Bologna's restaurants** A meal out in the gastronomic capital of Italy is a rite of passage for any true food lover. See p.404

* **Modena's Duomo** One of the finest Romanesque buildings in Italy, with some magnificent decoration inside and out. See p.408

* **Parma and its food** Parma is inextricably linked to two great delicacies, Parma ham and Parmesan cheese, both of which can be sampled in the city or in the surrounding region. See p.412

* **Rocca Viscontea** Northern Emilia-Romagna's most magestic castle. See p.419

* **Brisighella festivals** This medieval village is known for its truffle, polenta and olive festivals in autumn. See p.420

* **Ravenna's mosaics** Unrivalled both in beauty and preservation, these mosaics are unmissable. See p.427

* **Rimini's nightlife** The hottest, loudest, wildest and fastest-changing in the country. See p.432

▲ Parmigiano Reggiano is one of the highlights of the region

7

Emilia-Romagna

Emilia-Romagna doesn't attract nearly the same volume of tourists as its neighbouring provinces of Lombardy, the Veneto and Tuscany, which is strange because it offers just as fine a distillation of the region's charms: glorious countryside, plenty of historic architecture and local cuisine renowned across the rest of Italy. It's also pretty easy to get around with

Regional food and wine

Emilia-Romagna has a just reputation for producing the richest, most lavish food in Italy, with its famous specialities of **parmesan** cheese (*parmigiano-reggiano*), egg pasta, **Parma ham** (generically known as *prosciutto di Parma*) and balsamic vinegar. Despite its current foodie connotations, **balsamic vinegar** started off as a cottage industry, with many Emilian families distilling and then redistilling local wine to form a dark liquor that is then matured in wooden barrels for at least twelve years. Bologna is regarded as the gastronomic capital of Italy, and Emilia is the only true home of **pasta** in the North: often lovingly handmade, the dough is formed into lasagne, tortellini stuffed with ricotta cheese and spinach, pumpkin or pork, and other fresh pastas served with *ragù* (meat sauce), cream sauces or simply with butter and parmesan – *alla parmigiana* usually denotes something cooked with parmesan. Modena and Parma specialize in *bollito misto* – boiled **meats**, such as flank of beef, trotters, tongue and spicy sausage – while another Modenese dish is *zampone* – stuffed pig's trotter. The region is second only to Sicily for the amount of **fish** caught in its waters.

Regional **wines** are, like the landscapes and people, quite distinct. Emilia is synonymous with **Lambrusco**, but don't despair: buy only DOC Lambrusco and be amazed by the dark, often blackberry-coloured wine that foams into the glass and cuts through the fattiness of the typically meaty Emilian meal. There are four DOC zones for Lambrusco and you get a glimpse of three of them, all around Modena, from the Via Emilia, each supporting neat rows of high-trellised vines. The fourth zone extends across the plains and foothills of the Apennines, in the province of Reggio Emilia. Other wines to try, both whites, are Trebbianino Val Trebbia and Monterosso Val D'Arda, while the lively Malvasia (also white) from the Colli di Parma goes well with the celebrated local ham.

Heading east towards the Adriatic coast, you come to the Romagna, a flatter, drier province where the wines have less exuberance but more body and are dominated by Albana and Sangiovese. The sweeter versions of **Albana** are often more successful at bringing out the peachy, toasted-almond flavours of this white. The robust red of **Sangiovese**, from the hills around Ímola and Rimini, comes in various "weights" – all around the heavy mark. Much lighter is Cagnina di Romagna, which is best drunk young (within six months of harvest).

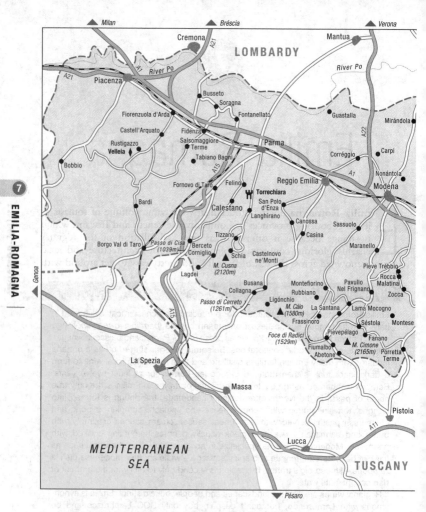

most of its main sites located along the **Via Emilia** (or more prosaically the A1 and A14 roads), the dead straight road first laid down by the Romans in 187 BC that splits the province in two along its east-west axis, dividing the Apennine mountains in the south from the flat fields of the northern plain, the Pianura Padana.

Dotted along this road are some proud, historic towns, filled with restored medieval and Renaissance *palazzi*, the legacy of a handful of feuding families – the **Este** in Ferrara and Modena, the **Farnese** in Parma, and lesser dynasties in Ravenna and Rimini – who used to control the area before the papacy took charge. The largest urban centre, and the main tourist draw, is **Bologna**, the site of Europe's first university – and today best known as the "gastronomic capital of Italy". It's generally regarded as one of the country's most beautiful cities with a mazy network of porticoed, medieval streets housing a collection of restaurants that easily live up to the town's reputation.

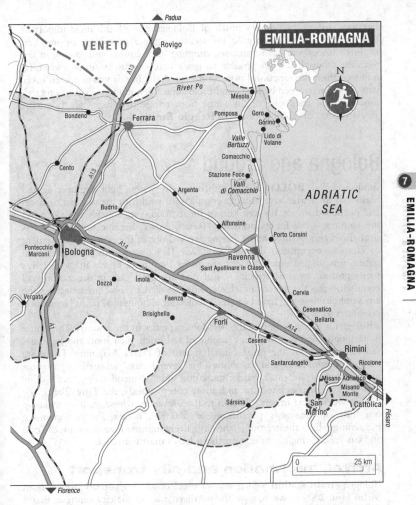

To the west are the wealthy, provincial towns of **Modena** and **Parma**, each just an hour or so away by train, and each with their own charming historic centres and gastronomic delights, while to the east lies **Ravenna**, once the capital of the Western Roman Empire and today home to the finest set of Byzantine mosaics in the world. The Adriatic coast south is an overdeveloped ribbon of settlements, although **Rimini**, at its southern end, provides a spark of interest, with its wild seaside nightlife, surprisingly historic town centre and increasingly sophisticated dining and eating options.

Away from the central artery, Emilia Romagna's **countryside** comes in two topographical varieties: flat or hilly. To the north lies one of the largest areas of flat land in Italy, a primarily agricultural region where much of the produce for the region's famed kitchens is grown. It also boasts a good deal of wildlife, particularly around the **Po Delta** on the Adriatic (a soggy expanse of marshland and lagoons that has become a prime destination for birdwatchers) and in

Ferrara, just thirty minutes north of Bologna, one of the most important Renaissance centres in Italy. To the south are the **Apennines**, an area best explored using your own transport, sampling local cuisine and joining in the festivals; although it's still possible to get a taste of this beautiful region, far removed from the functional plain to the north, by bus. If you're a keen hiker, you might be tempted by the Grand Escursione Apenninica, a 25-day-long trek following the backbone of the range from refuge to refuge, which can be accessed from the foothills south of **Reggio Emilia**.

Bologna and around

Emilia's capital, **BOLOGNA**, is a thriving city, whose light engineering and high-tech industries have brought conspicuous wealth to the old brick palaces and porticoed streets. It's well known for its food – undeniably the richest in the country – and for its **politics**. "Red Bologna" became the Italian Left's stronghold and spiritual home, having evolved out of the resistance movement to German occupation during World War II. Consequently, Bologna's train station was singled out by Fascist groups in 1980 for a bomb attack in Italy's worst postwar terrorist atrocity – a glassed-in jagged gash in the station wall commemorates the tragedy in which 84 people died. In subsequent decades, the city's political leanings have been less predictable although its "leftist" reputation continues to stick.

Bologna is certainly one of the best-looking cities in the country. The centre is startlingly medieval in plan, a jumble of red brick, tiled roofs and balconies radiating out from the great central square of Piazza Maggiore. There are enough monuments and curiosities for several days' leisured exploration, including plenty of small, quirky museums, some tremendously grand Gothic and Renaissance architecture and, most conspicuously, the **Due Torri**, the city's own "leaning towers". Thanks to the university, whose students make up one-fifth of the city's population of 500,000, there's always something happening – be it theatre, music, the city's lively summer festival, or just the café and bar scene, which is among northern Italy's most convivial.

Arrival, information and city transport

Bologna's **train station**, which will start welcoming high-speed services from Milan from 2009 onwards, is on the northern edge of the city centre at Piazza delle Medaglie d'Oro; all long-distance buses terminate at the **bus station**, next door on Piazza XX Settembre. Bus #25 outside the train station takes you to Piazza del Nettuno. Otherwise it's a ten-minute walk. Bologna's currently expanding **Marconi Airport** (☎051.647.9615, ⓦwww.bologna-airport.it) lies northwest of town, linked to the centre and the train station by the Aerobus (€5, buy tickets on board), which runs approximately every twenty minutes and takes around 25 minutes in light traffic. Taxis to the centre cost around €18. Ryanair flights land at **Forlí** (☎0543.474.921, ⓦwww.forliairport.com), 60km southeast. Special shuttle buses (E-BUS; ☎199.115.577) leave for Bologna approximately thirty minutes after the flight lands; you can buy tickets on board (€10; 1hr 25min). Otherwise a taxi will set you back around €50. If **driving**, note that the city centre is closed to private traffic between 7am and 8pm Sunday to Friday. There is **parking** on Piazza XX Settembre and Piazza VIII Agosta, adjacent to the bus station.

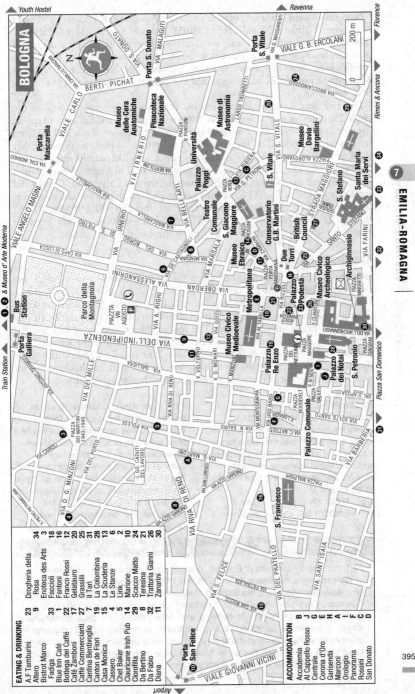

BOLOGNA

EMILIA-ROMAGNA 7

EATING & DRINKING

A.F Tamburini	23
Altero	9
Bistrot Marco	
Fadiga	33
Blue Inn Café	1
Bottega del Caffè	22
Caffè Zamboni	17
Caffè Commercianti	7
Cantina Bentivoglio	19
Canton de Fiori	15
Casa Monica	4
Cassero	5
Chet Baker	14
Clauricane Irish Pub	8
Clorofilla	29
Da Bertino	21
Da Fabio	32
Diana	11
Drogheria della	
Rosa	34
Enoteca des Arts	3
Faccioli	18
Fantoni	16
Franco Rossi	12
Gelatauro	20
Grassilli	25
Il Tari	31
La Colombina	28
La Scuderia	13
Le Stanze	15
Link	2
Marione	10
Scacco Matto	24
Teresina	21
Trattoria Gianni	26
Zanarini	30

ACCOMMODATION

Accademia	B
Al Cappello Rosso	J
Centrale	G
Corona d'Oro	E
Garisenda	H
Marconi	A
Orologio	I
Panorama	F
Rossini	C
San Donato	D

Bologna's main **tourist office**, in the Palazzo del Podestà at Piazza Maggiore 1 (daily 9.30am–7.30pm; ☎051.239.660 or 051.251.947, ⓦwww .bolognaturismo.info), has the usual array of information, plus details of gourmet tours and cookery courses. Guided sightseeing tours of the city in English leave from here every Saturday at 2pm. Other offices can be found at Marconi Airport (daily 8am–8pm) and the train station (Mon–Sat 9am–7pm, Sun 9am–3pm).

The best way to enjoy Bologna is **on foot**: strolling beneath some of the city's 25 miles of porticoes. **Buses** (ⓦwww.atc.bo.it) are fast and frequent. Tickets cost €1 each from *tabacchi*, newsstands, ticket machines and ATCittà info centres – located at the train and bus stations as well as various other locations – and are valid on as many buses as you like within one hour, or within 90 minutes during the reduced service period in August. If you plan to make frequent use of them it might be worth buying a Citypass for €6.50, valid for eight journeys. The ATCittà info points also sell tickets for the open-top, hop-on hop-off Giro Tp TramBus **tour** of the city (€10; ☎800.281.281 tollfree, ⓦwww.trambusopen.com). There are ten departures daily between 10am and 4pm from Viale Pietramellara in front of the train station.

Accommodation

Bologna's accommodation mostly caters for business travellers with only a few inexpensive **hotels**. During the trade fair peak (March to early May & Sept–Dec) prices can more than double. Many hotels prefer to take block bookings during these times and making an individual reservation can be tricky. In July and August prices are much lower. The tourist offices have hotel lists, and the Centro Servizi Per I Turisti (Tourist Service Centre), next to the tourist office desk at Piazza Maggiore 6 (Mon–Sat 10am–2pm & 3–7pm, Sun 10am–2pm; ☎051.648.7607 or 800.856.065 tollfree, ⓦwww.cst.bo.it), can book rooms for you at no charge, or you can do it yourself directly through their website.

Hotels

Accademia Via Belle Arti 6 ☎051.232.318, ⓦwww.hotelaccademia.com. In the heart of the university quarter, this large three-star hotel has modestly sized and furnished doubles (a mixture of private and shared bathrooms), some with balconies. Most rooms have a/c; those without are slightly cheaper. ❸

Al Cappello Rosso Via de' Fusari 9 ☎051.261.891, ⓦwww.alcappellorosso.it. It may be one of the city's oldest hotels, with six centuries of service behind it, but the *Cappello Rosso*, has certainly done its best to move with the times, now offering dedicated rooms for ladies, a pet-care service and a Gay-Pride package. Bedrooms are stylishly modern, but comfortable and there's a library-cum-book-swapping service. Enjoys an atmospheric location just off Piazza Maggiore. ❻

Centrale Via della Zecca 2 ☎051.225.114, ⓦwww.albergocentralebologna.it. Good-value

Castello di Galeazza

Forty minutes by car north of Bologna, near Crevalcore, stands the medieval castle of **Galeazza** (Via Provanone 8585 ☎051.985.170, ⓦwww.galeazza.com; ❶), that's now best described as a reading and cultural retreat – the brainchild of a young American, Clark Lawrence. The four frescoed rooms can accommodate up to ten guests, everyone pitches in with cleaning and cooking duties (and ideally contributes a book or two to the communal library), and there's an ongoing cultural programme of art exhibitions, classical and jazz concerts and readings. With a stimulating mix of Italians and foreigners, it makes an excellent base from which to explore Ferrara, Bologna and Modena, which are all about 40 minutes away.

two-star in the heart of the city. All of the 25 spacious rooms come with bathrooms and a/c, and there are great views from the top floor. ❸
Corona d'Oro Via Oberdan 12 ☏051.745.7611, ⓦwww.bolognarthotels.it. Four-star opulence in a refurbished *palazzo* close to the *Metropolitana* and graced with a lovely wooden portico. ❻
Garienda Galleria del Leone 15 ☏051.224.369, ⓦwww.albergogarisenda.com. The seven rooms here are pretty basic and ordinary looking – only three have bathrooms – but the location is great; above the Via Rizzoli shops right opposite the two towers. Friendly and welcoming and surprisingly quiet. ❸
Marconi Via Marconi 18 ☏051.262.832, ⓦwww.pensionemarconi.it. Although the stairway up to this friendly one-star on the first floor of a modern block is not particularly inviting, the rooms inside are clean if basic (some have private bathrooms). It's on a major road, so you might want to ask for a room at the back. No credit cards. ❷
🏃 **Orologio** Via IV Novembre 10 ☏051.745.7411, ⓦwww.bolognarthotels.it. On a side street just south of Piazza Maggiore – look for the clock sign – this elegant three-star is the most appealing of Bologna's 'art' hotels, with an air of understated luxury and well-equipped rooms. ❺
Panorama Via Livraghi 1 ☏051.221.802, ⓦwww.hotelpanoramabologna.it. Just off Via Ugo Bassi

(no sign), offering a range of accommodation, from three- and four-bedded rooms to ordinary doubles – all sharing clean and pleasant bathrooms down the corridor. Helpful owners. ❸
Rossini Via Bibiena 11 ☏051.237.716, ⓦwww.albergorossini.com. In the student quarter, just off Piazza Verdi, a small friendly two-star hotel with comfortable though basic rooms, some with bath. ❷
San Donato Via Zamboni 16 ☏051.235.395, ⓦwww.hotelsandonato.it. Now owned by Best Western, this is a very elegant four-star offering a good standard of chain hotel comfort in a great location. You can just see the two towers poking up behind the houses from the rooms overlooking the square, and there's a fantastic rooftop breakfast terrace. ❻

Hostel

San Sisto-Due Torri Via Viadagola 5 and 14 ☏051.501.810, ✉bologna@ostellionline.org. Official HI hostel 6km outside the centre of town. To get there Mon–Sat take bus #93 in the day, and from 8pm onwards bus #21b, both from Via Marconi. On Sun you'll have to rely on the less frequent #301 service from the bus station. The hostel opens at 3.30pm and there's a curfew at 11.30pm. Beds are €16 per head in a dorm, and there are also double rooms (❶). It's a busy place so book in advance.

The City

Bologna's city centre is compact with most sights within easy reach of the main ring road. Lined with shops and bars, **Via dell'Indipendenza** runs from the train station to the centre, finishing up at the linked central squares of **Piazza Maggiore** and **Piazza del Nettuno**. West of here is the commercial district, bordered by the office blocks of Via G. Marconi, while to the east lies the university quarter.

Piazza Maggiore, Piazza del Nettuno and around

At the centre of Piazza del Nettuno, the **Neptune Fountain**, one of the most celebrated symbols of the city, was created by Giambologna in the late sixteenth century. Its extravagant – and when first unveiled highly controversial – composition sees a trident-wielding Neptune sat atop a pile of *putti* and mermaids – who are themselves arranged rather indelicately astride dolphins shooting water from their breasts. Beside the fountain is a wall lined with photographs of partisans who died in World War II, near another memorial to those killed in the 1980 train station bombing. Across the square, the **Palazzo Re Enzo** takes its name from its time as the prison-home of Enzo, king of Sicily, confined here by papal supporters for two decades after the Battle of Fossalta in 1249. Next door to the Palazzo Re Enzo, **Palazzo Podestà** fills the northern side of Piazza Maggiore, built in the fifteenth century at the behest of the Bentivoglio clan. Both *palazzi* open occasionally for special exhibitions. On the piazza's western edge, the **Palazzo Comunale** gives some indication of the political shifts in power, its facade adorned by a huge statue of Pope Gregory XIII as an affirmation of papal authority. Inside are two art collections. The first, the **Museo Morandi** (Tues–Fri 9am–3pm, Sat & Sun 10am–6.30pm; Ⓦwww.museomorandi.it; free), is devoted to the life and works of one of Italy's most important twentieth-century painters. Two hundred works and a faithful reconstruction of Giorgio Morandi's studio offer a fascinating glimpse into the artist best known for his Futurist works. The other, the **Collezioni Comunali d'Arte** (Tues–Fri 9am–3pm, Sat & Sun 10am–6.30pm; free), forms one third of the city's Museo Civici d'Arte Antica, along with the Museo Davia Bargellini and the Museo Civico Medievale. Its galleries of ornate furniture and paintings include works by Vitale da Bologna, Simone dei Crocifissi and others of the Bolognese School. On the southern side of Piazza Maggiore stands the church of **San Petronio** (daily: winter 7.30am–12.30pm & 3pm–6pm; summer 7.45am–12.30pm & 3.30–6pm), one of the finest Gothic brick buildings in Italy. This enormous structure was originally intended to have been larger than St Peter's in Rome, but money and land for the side aisle were diverted by the pope's man in Bologna towards a new university and plans had to be modified. The end result looks a little strange at first glance, with the beginnings of the planned aisles on both sides of the building clearly visible. There are models of what the church was supposed to look like in the museum (Mon–Sat 9.30am–12.30pm & 2.30–5.30pm, Sun pm only; free). Note that you are not permitted to take backpacks into the church, and there are no storage facilities provided.

In the opposite direction, across Via dell'Archiginnasio from San Petronio, the **Palazzo dei Banchi** is more of a set piece than a *palazzo*, basically a facade designed by the Renaissance architect Vignola to unify a set of medieval houses that didn't really fit with the rest of the square. In the Palazzo Galvani, the **Museo Civico Archeologico** (Tues–Fri 9am–3pm, Sat & Sun 10am–6.30pm; Ⓦwww.comune.bologna.it/museoarcheologico; free) is rather stuffy but has good displays of Egyptian and Roman antiquities, and an Etruscan section that is one of the best outside Lazio, with finds drawn from the settlement of Felsina, which predated Bologna. English audioguides are available for €4.

Just north of the museum, **Via Clavature** – together with nearby Via Pescerie Vecchie and Via Draperie – is home to a grouping of **market stalls** and shops that makes for one of the city's most enticing sights. In autumn, especially, the market is a visual and aural feast, with fat porcini mushrooms, truffles in baskets of rice, thick rolls of mortadella, hanging pheasants, ducks and hares, and skinned frogs by the kilo. The church of **Santa Maria della Vita** (Mon–Sat 7.30am–6.30pm, Sun 4.30pm–7pm; free), in Via Clavature, is worth a look for its outstanding pietà by Nicola dell'Arca – seven life-sized terracotta figures that are among the most dramatic examples of Renaissance sculpture you'll see.

The Archiginnasio and around

Down the street in the other direction, Bologna's old university – the **Archiginnasio** – was founded at more or less the same time as Piazza Maggiore was laid out, predating the rest of Europe's universities, although it didn't get a special building until 1565, when Antonio Morandi was commissioned to construct the present building on the site until then reserved for San Petronio. Centralizing the university on one site was a way of maintaining control over students at a time when the Church felt particularly threatened

Bologna's porticoes

No other city has anything like the number of **porticoes** or covered walkways found in Bologna. In the city centre there are barely any stretches of pavement not topped by an ornate, arched covering. They make a vivid first impression, especially at night, while by day they provide an unofficial catwalk for Bologna's well-turned-out residents, not to mention welcome shelter from the spring rain. The first porticoes were built out of wood, some thirteenth-century examples of which still stand. They proved so popular that by the fourteenth century construction of stone or brick porticoes, high enough to accommodate people on horseback, had become compulsory on all new streets. Today, some 38km still stand, including the longest portico in the world, the 3.5-kilometre stretch leading from the city up to the Santuario di Madonna di San Luca (see p.406).

by the Reformation. You can wander freely into the main courtyard, covered with the coats of arms of its more famous graduates, and in the mornings it's also possible to visit the main upstairs **library**, and, most interestingly, the **Teatro Anatomico** (Mon–Fri 9am–1pm; ☎051.236.488; free), the original medical faculty dissection theatre. Tiers of seats surround an extraordinary professor's chair, covered with a canopy supported by figures known as *gli spellati* – "the skinned ones". Not many dissections went on, owing to prohibitions of the Church, but when they did (usually around carnival time), artists and the general public used to turn up as much for the social occasion as for studying the body.

Outside the old university, **Piazza Galvani** remembers the physicist Luigi Galvani with a statue. One of Bologna's more successful scientists, Galvani discovered electrical currents in animals, thereby lending his name to the English language in the word "galvanize". A few minutes south, down Via Garibaldi, is **Piazza San Domenico**, with its strange canopied tombs holding the bones of medieval law scholars. Bologna was instrumental in sorting out wrangles between the pope and the Holy Roman Emperor in the tenth and eleventh centuries, earning itself the title of *La Dotta* ("The Learned") and forming the basis for the university's prominent law faculties. The church of **San Domenico** was built in 1221 to house the relics of St Dominic, which were placed in the so-called *Arca di San Domenico*: a fifteenth-century work that was ostensibly the creation of Nicola Pisano – though in reality many artists contributed to it. One of Pisano's pupils was **Michelangelo** and it was his hands that sculpted the angel resting on St Dominic's tomb. While you're in the church, try also to see the **Museo di San Domenico** (Mon–Fri 9.30am–12.30pm & 3.30–6.30pm, Sat & Sun 3–5.30pm; free) displaying a very fine polychrome terracotta bust of St Dominic by Nicolò dell'Arca along with paintings, reliquaries and vestments, and, beyond, the intricately inlaid mid-sixteenth-century choir stalls.

The Due Torri and around

Bordered by Via Oberdan to the west and Strada Maggiore to the south, the eastern section of Bologna's *centro storico* preserves many of the older **university** departments, housed for the most part in large seventeenth- and eighteenth-century palaces. Bookshops, cafés and vegetarian restaurants make this atmospheric slice of studentville perfect for idling away an afternoon.

Via Rizzoli leads into the district from Piazza Maggiore, ending up at Piazza di Porta Ravegnana, where the **Torre degli Asinelli** (daily 9am–6pm; closes

▲ Medieval skyscapers – the Due Torri, Bologna

5pm in winter; €3), and the perilously leaning **Torre Garisenda** next to it, are together known as the **Due Torri**, the only two remaining of hundreds of towers that were scattered across the city in the Middle Ages. The former makes a good place from which to get an overview of the city centre and beyond.

Southeast of the Due Torri, Via Santo Stefano leads down to its medieval gateway, past a complex of four – but originally seven – churches, collectively known as **Santo Stefano**, set in a wide piazza. Three of the churches face onto the piazza, of which the striking polygonal church of **San Sepolcro** (daily 9am–noon & 3.30–6pm; free), reached through the church of **Crocifisso**, is about the most interesting. Inside, the bones of St Petronius, held in a tomb modelled on the church of the holy sepulchre in Jerusalem, provide a macabre focus typical of the relic-obsessed Middle Ages. A doorway leads from here through to **Santi Vitale e Agricola**, Bologna's oldest church, built from discarded Roman fragments in the fifth century.

From here, follow Via Gerusalemme up to Strada Maggiore and the elegant fourteenth-century **Santa Maria dei Servi**, filled with frescoes by Vitale da Bologna – it's a rare chance to see the work of the so-called "father" of Bolognese painting *in situ*. The beautiful portico holds a festive market during the Christmas season. Further north from here, Via Petroni leads through to **Piazza Verdi**, at the heart of the university district. On summer evenings it draws the crowds with its open-air bars and live music. **Via Zamboni** bisects Piazza Verdi, around and along which are many of the old palaces housing various parts of the university. The main building, the **Palazzo Poggi** at no. 33 is home to many of the university's small specialist museums on subjects as diverse as naval maps and charts, human anatomy, physics and natural history (Mon–Fri 10am–1pm & 2–4pm, Sat & Sun 10.30am–1.30pm & 2.30–5.30pm, but times frequently change so check on ☏051.209.9360, ⊛www.museopalazzopoggi.unibo.it; free). On the fourth floor, the fascinating 300-year-old **Specola**, or observatory, attracts the majority of visitors. Its small **Museo di Astronomia** (Tues–Fri 10am–1pm & 2pm–4pm, Sat 10.30am–1.30pm & 2.30pm–5.30pm; free) is home to a number of eighteenth-century instruments and a frescoed map of the constellations – painted just seventy years after Galileo was imprisoned for his heretical statements about the cosmos.

The **Museo delle Cera Anatomiche ("Luigi Cattaneo")**, a short distance north at Via Irnerio 48 (Mon–Fri 9am–5pm, after 2pm by appointment only; ☏051.244.217, ⊛www.museocereanatomiche.it; free), might seem an odd place to visit, but it would be a shame to leave Bologna without seeing its highly idiosyncratic (and beautiful) **waxworks**. These were used until the nineteenth century for medical demonstration, and are as startling as any art or sculpture in the city. Some figures, unnervingly displayed in glass cases, are modelled like classical statues, one carrying a sickle, the other a scythe.

Close by, the collection of paintings in the **Pinacoteca Nazionale** at Via delle Belle Arti 56 (Tues–Sun 9am–7pm; ⊛www.pinacotecabologna.it; €4) may provide some light relief, concentrating mainly on the work of Bolognese artists. There are canvases by the fourteenth-century painter Vitale da Bologna with later works by Francia and Tibaldi, and paintings from the city's most productive artistic period, the early seventeenth century.

Back towards the centre down Via Zamboni, in Piazza Rossini, is the church of **San Giacomo Maggiore** (daily 7am–noon & 3.30–6.30pm; free), a Romanesque structure begun in 1267 and enlarged over the centuries. The target here is the Bentivoglio Chapel, decorated with funds provided by one Annibale Bentivoglio to celebrate the family's victory in a local feud in 1488. Lorenzo Costa painted frescoes called *Apocalypse*, *Triumph of Death* and *Madonna Enthroned* as well as some of the Bentivoglio family – a deceptively pious-looking lot, captured in what was a fairly innovative picture in its time for the careful characterizations of its patrons.

Piazza Rossini is named after the nineteenth-century composer, who studied at the **Conservatorio G.B. Martini** on the square. The library here is among the most important music libraries in Europe (free entrance but visits must be arranged; ℡051.221.483) with some original manuscripts on display, along with a few paintings. On the other side of Via Zamboni at Via Valdonica 1/5 is the **Museo Ebraico** (Mon–Thurs & Sun 10am–6pm, Fri 10am–4pm; Ⓦwww .museoebraicobo.it; €4, including an English language audioguide). Situated in the old Jewish ghetto, it's the best Jewish museum in the province and presents the history of the once-thriving Jewish community in Emilia-Romagna.

The Metropolitana, Museo Civico and the Basilica di San Francesco

There's much less of interest to the north and west of Bologna's central squares. A couple of blocks north of Piazza del Nettuno, the city's cathedral, the **Metropolitana di San Pietro** (daily 8am–noon and 4–6.15pm; Ⓦwww .bologna.chiesacattolica.it), was originally a tenth-century building but has been rebuilt many times and is these days more enjoyable for its stately atmosphere than any particular features. The **Museo Civico Medievale** (Tues–Fri 9am–3pm, Sat and Sun 10am–6.30pm; Ⓦwww.commune.bologna.it/iperbole /MuseiCivici/; free), opposite, is of more interest, housed in the Renaissance Palazzo Fava at Via Manzoni 4 and decorated with frescoes by Carracci and members of the Bolognese School depicting the History of Europa, Jason's Feats and scenes from the *Aeneid*. The museum collection itself includes bits of armour, ceramics, numerous tombs and busts of various popes and other dignitaries, and a *Madonna and Saints* by Jacopo della Quercia.

West of Piazza del Nettuno, at the end of Via Ugo Bassi, the Basilica di **San Francesco** (daily 6.30am–noon & 3–7pm) is a huge Gothic brick pile supported by flying buttresses that was heavily restored in the 1920s and partly rebuilt after World War II. Inside there are a beautiful and very ornate altarpiece from 1392 and a pleasant cloister.

Museo d'Arte Moderna di Bologna

Known, inevitably perhaps, by the acronym **MAMBO**, the Museo d'Arte Moderna di Bologna (Tues–Fri 10am–6pm, Thurs till 10pm; Ⓦwww .mambo-bologna.org; free) is Bologna's answer to Bilbao's Guggenheim or New York's MOMA. Opened in 2007, it now forms the centrepiece of a spanking new cultural complex occupying a former industrial estate in the northwest of the city, around a twenty-minute bus ride from the centre (bus #35 from the railway station). Housed in a former bakery, the gallery is as stark, white and modernist looking as you'd expect and has been given the mission of providing a complete overview of Italian art in the twentieth century. It's not quite there yet. So far, it has only staged a few temporary touring exhibitions, but there are plans to unveil its permanent collection in the near future, based on the collection of the now defunct Galleria d'Arte Moderna di Bologna. Part of a self-styled *Manifattura delle Arte* (factory of arts), the museum shares the complex with a music and dance centre, **Centro di Musica e Spettacolo** (Ⓦwww.muspe .unibo.it/cimes), and an arthouse cinema and film archive, the **Cineteca** (Ⓦwww.cinetecadibologna.it), which has been constructed on the site of a former slaughterhouse, as well as various new restaurants, bars and boutiques.

Eating, drinking and entertainment

Eating is especially important to the Bolognese: the city is known as *La Grassa* ("The Fat One"), the result of a rich culinary tradition. Its restaurants are said

With its carefully preserved historic buildings and centuries of academic tradition you could be forgiven for thinking of Bologna as a rather stuffy, staid sort of a place. However, in certain regards it's one of the most forward thinking cities in the country, not least in the area of **gay and lesbian rights**. The council here was one of the first to allow gay couples to apply for municipal housing, and today the city boasts the largest openly homosexual population in Italy and is the venue for the annual Gay Pride celebrations. It's also the headquarters of the festival's organizers, the Associazione Lesbica e Gay Italiana (Italian National Gay and Lesbian Association), or Arcigay, Via Don Minzone (☏051.649.3055, ⊛www.arcigay.it). Gay-friendly hotels, clubs and bars are listed in the free *Cassero Magazine* available from the organization and the tourist office.

to be the best in Italy, and even the simplest restaurants and the many **osterie** often serve dishes of a very high standard. Handmade lasagne, tagliatelle and tortellini are excellent and regarded with great affection by Bologna's inhabitants – the first tortellini are said to have been made by a Bolognese innkeeper trying to recreate the beauty of Venus's navel.

Bologna's **bar** and **club culture** thrives thanks to its huge student population, with most drinking places centred on and around Via Zamboni. The tourist office has a free pamphlet called "2night" (⊛www.2night.it) for details of life in the city after dark.

Bologna has tried to curb the July and August exodus by mounting a summer **arts festival**, called Viva Bologna, with evening concerts and cinema screenings in the courtyards of the civic buildings. June sees the now annual Gay Pride celebrations – Bologna is the headquarters of Arcigay, the Italian National Gay Association (⊛www.bolognapride.it) – while August plays host to Ferragosto, when everyone takes to the hills for all-night revelry in one of the parks outside town. In September there's a three-day celebration of Bolognese cuisine called "Bologna – La Cita del Cibo" (⊛www.bolognalacittadelcibo.it), while in spring and autumn, classical concerts are staged under the aegis of the Bologna Festival, for which the Teatro Comunale on Piazza Verdi (⊛www.tcbo.it) is one of the main venues.

For listings there's the useful *Bologna Spettacolo* available from bookshops (⊛www.bolognaspettacolo.it). And for concerts and venues, you could try asking at the Rock Shop, Via Mazzini 146, or wading through the flyers at *La Scuderia* bar on Piazza Verdi.

Cafés, pizzerias and ice cream

🏃 **A.F Tamburini** Via Draperie 2. This fabulous, traditional delicatessen is a real gourmet's delight with its ceiling thick with hanging hams and sausages, and its counters bulging with giant cheeses. It's also got a great little café selling roasted meats and plates of filled pasta for around €3–5.

Altero Via dell'Indipendenza 33. Selling pizza by the slice till 1am – margherita €1.20, mushroom €1.40 and for the truly adventurous, a slice of white pizza topped with Nutella for €2. Not quite the gastronomy for which Bologna is famed, but still. One of three city branches.

Bottega del Caffè Via degli Orefici 6. Downstairs is a shop selling all manner of coffee paraphernalia – beans, machines and more – and chocolate, while upstairs is a quiet café.

Café Zamboni Via Zamboni 6/B. Popular student meeting spot within sight of the two towers. Its covered outdoor seating area plays host to a vibrant and ever-changing social scene throughout the day. Inside, there's a café, a gelateria and free wi-fi access.

Caffè Commercianti Strada Maggiore 23/C. Atmospheric bar that serves everything from coffee and ice cream to aperitifs. Try their *cioccolata in tazza* (hot chocolate topped with whipped cream), the perfect winter pick-me-up. Open till 8pm; closed Sun.

Canton de Fiori Via dell'Indipendenza 1. Enjoy a terribly splendid coffee and cake under the porticoes at the "corner of flowers" just off Piazza del Nettuno, served to you with all due deference by bow-tied waiters.

Il Gelatauro Via San Vitale 98/B. A 10min walk east of the centre, this is a charming little place serving organic pastries, handmade chocolates, speciality wines and, the top draw, fantastic ice cream, in all manner of flavours, including ginger, cinnamon and pumpkin.

Restaurants

Bistrot Marco Fadiga Via Rialto 23/C ☏051.220.118. Intimate venue in the heart of Bologna's theatrical quarter offering champagne and oysters pre-show and a high-end menu post. First courses are €9, while main courses start at €12 and include guinea fowl cooked in plums. Closed Sun eve & Mon.

Casa Monica Via San Rocco 15 7/A ☏051.522.522 With its bright, modern, high-ceilinged interior, this makes a welcome change from the traditional rather dark and cramped Bolognese restaurant norm. The food is modern and light, too – try the carrot, ginger and almond soup.

Clorofilla Strada Maggiore 64/C. A brightly lit, almost sterile vegetarian restaurant – just the place if the "fat of Bologna" has been weighing you down, offering over a dozen types of salad (*contadino*, *caprese*, cous cous etc), all for €6.50 Open till midnight; closed Sun.

Da Bertino Via Delle Lame 55. The place to come for no-nonsense Bolognese peasant-style cooking, including *bollito* and *arrosto* (boiled and roast meats), accompanied by traditional relishes. Open till 10.30pm; closed Sun & Sat eve in summer plus Mon in winter.

Diana Via dell' Independenza 24 ☏051.231.302. About as fancy a dining experience as Bologna offers, this large 1920s establishment – all chandeliers and bow-tied waiters – has an excellent menu, specializing in roasts. Reservations recommended. Closed Mon.

Drogheria della Rosa Via Cartoleria 10 ☏051.222.529. This converted grocery store/ pharmacy still retains many of its original features but now serves hearty prescriptions of Bolognan cuisine. It's all a bit ad hoc with a changing (and often unwritten) menu, but it's won numerous awards. Closed Sun.

Fantoni Via del Pratello 11. Family-style Bolognese restaurant (think red-and-white check tablecloths)

that's highly popular with locals – the daily menu is written in Italian only. Good value with lunchtime pasta dishes starting at €4.50 and an adventurous dinner menu with some fish specialities. Closed Sun & Mon eve.

Franco Rossi Via Goito 3 ☏051.238.818. Run by two brothers, this cosy one-room place offers light, inventive interpretations of heavy Romagnan staples, with a tourist menu (including first course, second course, side dish, dessert and wine) for €30. Closed Sun.

Grassilli Via del Luzzo 3 ☏051.222.961. Emilian dishes adapted with flair to suit modern tastes, accompanied by good service. Walls decorated with pictures of opera singers who dined here add to the glam ambience. An experience to remember, though you'll need to book and it's above averagely priced (*primi* from €12, *secondi* from €16). Closed Wed & Sun eve.

Il Tarì Via Collegio di Spagna 13. A mid-priced trattoria and pizzeria featuring fish dishes, such as delicious *spaghetti allo scoglio* – with seafood and *galletti* mushrooms. Enormous servings of everything. Open till midnight. Closed Thurs.

La Colombina Vicolo Colombina 5 ☏051.231.706. Fancy, attractive and expensive (think calf's liver in brandy for €16), but excellent value if you're looking for authentic Bolognese specialities. Expect your fellow diners to be wearing their best party frocks. Closed Tues.

La Galleria Piazza XX Settembre. This large self-service restaurant inside the bus station is a good choice if you're awaiting a connection, with a wide range of cheap quality food, including as much salad as you can pile onto your plate. Closed Sun.

Scacco Matto Via Broccaindosso 63/B ☏051.263.404. A striking dining space adorned with chess boards, this offers some of the city's most original flavours, combining Italian cuisine with Japanese influences, not to mention some of its longest dish names. It's probably best to point rather than attempting to ask for *moscardini affogati al vino rosso ed olive su zuppetta d'aglio fume* (small octopuses with red wine and olives). *Primi* €12, *secondi* €14–15. Closed Sun.

Teresina Via Oberdan 4 ☏051.228.985. A great family-run restaurant serving regional dishes as well as very good southern Italian food for around €30 a head for a full meal. Worth booking. Open till 10.30pm; closed Sun.

Trattoria Gianni Via Clavature 18 ☏051.229.434. Hidden down a narrow side alley, this is one of the top options in Bologna: try the ultra-traditional *bolliti*, a variety of meats boiled in the Emilian way, or the fantastic home-made tortellini. Moderate prices. Closed Sun eve & Mon.

Bars

Cantina Bentivoglio Via Mascarella 4/B ☎051.265.416, ⓦwww.cantinabentivoglio .it. As much an *osteria* as a bar, this place has live jazz from around 10pm in the cellars of a sixteenth-century *palazzo*, where the food (snacks to full meals) and wine are excellent. Open daily but closed Sun in summer.

Enoteca des Arts Via San Felice 9. Tiny, dark and atmospheric bar serving cheap, local wine. Organizes regular tastings, Open Mon–Sat 4.30pm–2am.

Faccioli Via Altabella 15/B. It's been described as a discreet library of a bar, with bottles, not books, lining the walls. Very pleasant place to taste wines and nibble snacks in the shadow of one of the city's towers. Open from 6pm; closed Sun & Sat in July & Aug.

Le Stanze Via Borgo di San Pietro 1/A. Elegant place to unwind and sip wine and cocktails in the airy splendour of a converted Bentivoglio *palazzo*. The sixteenth-century frescoed ceilings, romantic candles and occasional art exhibition produce an evocative atmosphere lapped up by its chic clientele.

Zanarini Piazza Galvani 1. On an elegant square, this is where the chic Bolognese gather for their *aperitivi* and to soak up the last of the sun's rays. Suitably smart and expensive – expect to pay €8 for a small *insalata di riso*.

Clubs and live music

Blue Inn Café Via Fornaciai 9 ☎051.418.0424, ⓦwww.blueinncafe.it. Large, live-music venue north of the centre, past the *tangenziale*. Blues dominates, but other styles get a look in, including swing on Tues, Funk on Frid and r'n'b on Sat, when it's open till 3am and dancing takes over from listening. Closed Mon.

Cassero Via Don Minzoni 18 ☎051.649.4416, ⓦwww.cassero.it. Housed downstairs in La Salara, one of the old city fortifications, this is the best of Bologna's gay clubs, open every day from 9pm with bar and entertainment (Thurs night is lesbian night). It also has an archive, counselling centre and meeting point (Mon–Fri 10am–1pm & 2–7pm).

Chet Baker Via Polese 7/A ☎051.223.795, ⓦwww.chetbaker.it. One of the city's most popular jazz venues attracting international names. Closed Sun.

Clauricane Irish Pub Via Zamboni 18. One of the largest bars in town, very popular with students from the university up the road, with punters spilling out onto the street on hot evenings. Open daily till 3am.

La Scuderia Piazza Verdi. Occupying a former stable block, this huge bar is aimed squarely at students. Cheap drinks, lots of flyers for gigs and seating on the square where in the evening the sound of opera wafts across from the theatre opposite.

Link Via Fioravanti ⓦwww.link.bo.it. This *centro sociale* has a bar upstairs and enormous dance floor downstairs, with avant-garde performance art and live bands early on, and ambient and techno sounds later. No entrance fee, except for gigs. Daily 10pm–5am.

Listings

Books Huge selection of English books and magazines from Feltrinelli International, Via Zamboni 7 ☎051.268.070.

Car rental Avis, Viale Pietramellara 27/D ☎051.255.024; Europcar, Via Amendola 12/F ☎051.247.101; Hertz, Via Amendola 16/A ☎051.254.830; Maggiore, Via Cairoli 4 ☎051.252.525. All the major companies also have desks at the airport.

Cinema Several including Cinema Odeon, Via Mascarella 3 ☎051.227.916; Arena Puccini, Via Serlio 25 ☎051.419.3256; and Cineteca, Via Riva di Reno 72 ☎051.219.4820 (ⓦwww.cinetecadibologna.it), an arthouse cinema and film archive in the city's northwest near the new modern art gallery.

Hospital In an emergency, dial ☎118; or go to the Pronto Soccorso (24hr casualty) at the Ospedale San Orsola Generale, Via Massarenti 9 (☎051.636.3111); bus #14 from Via Rizzoli.

Internet access There are numerous internet cafés all over Bologna. Two reasonably central options include *Liong@ate* on Via Rizzoli 9 (daily 10am–midnight) and *Happynet*, Via Oberdan 17/B (☎051.1998.4179; Mon–Fri 9am–11pm, Sat and Sun 10am–11pm), both offering access for around €2 an hr.

Laundry Laundromat, Via Petroni 38, is the most central coin-op/drop-service laundry.

Markets There are a couple of great food markets in the city centre: the large and lively Mercato delle Erbe, Via Ugo Bassi 2 (Mon–Sat 7am–1.15pm & 5–7.30pm, closed Thurs & Sat pm); and the Mercato di Mezzo on Via Pescherie Vecchie (Mon–Sat 7am–1pm & 4.15–7.30pm; closed Thurs am). For a huge range of new and secondhand clothes, handicrafts and textiles head to La Piazzola market on Piazza VIII Agosto on Fri and Sat (dawn to dusk).

Pharmacy Farmacia Comunale in Piazza Maggiore is open 24hr ☎ 051.239.690.

Police Main *questura* is at Piazza Galileo 7 ☎ 051.640.1111.

Post office The main post office is on Piazza Minghetti (Mon–Fri 8am–6.30pm, Sat 8am–12.30pm).

Shops Some of Bologna's most colourful sights are inside its many food stores, particularly those between Piazza Maggiore and the Due Torri, epitomized by Tamburini at Via Caprarie 1. The most convenient supermarket is the Co-op, at Via Montebello 2, behind the train station.

Taxis Cooperativa Taxisti Bologna ☎ 051.372.727; CAT (Consorzio Autonomo Taxista) ☎ 051.534.141.

Travel agents CTS, Largo Respighi 2/G ☎ 051.261.802; and Via C.Battisti 17 ☎ 051.296.0764.

Around Bologna

In the heat of the summer the hills that start almost as soon as you leave Bologna's gates take you high enough to catch some cooling breezes. The most obvious destination for a short trip is the eighteenth-century shrine of **Santuario di Madonna di San Luca** (7am–12.30pm and 2.30–5pm; until 7pm in summer), close on 4km southwest of the city centre but connected by way of the world's longest portico, which meanders across the hillside in a series of 666 arches – a shelter for pilgrims on the trek to the top. Bus #20 from the station drops you at the start of the route, by Porta Saragozza southwest of the centre. Further south, the N325 passes through **PONTECCHIO MARCONI**, where the physicist Guglielmo Marconi lived in the late nineteenth century, and from where, in 1895, he sent the first radio message ever – to his brother on the other side of the hill. Marconi now lies in a specially designed mausoleum in the village.

Modena and around

Though only thirty minutes northwest by train, **MODENA** has a quite distinct identity from Bologna. It proclaims itself the "spiritual capital" of Emilia and has a number of claims to fame: great car names such as Ferrari, Lamborghini and Maserati are tied to the town (celebrated in *Modena Terra di Motori* in April/May, when the piazzas are filled with classic models); the late Pavarotti was a native of Modena, his name commemorated in the recently re-branded Teatro Comunale Luciano Pavarotti; the area's balsamic vinegar has become a cult product in kitchens around the world, duly celebrated in the Balsamica festival in May; and the cathedral is considered one of the finest Romanesque buildings in Italy. Of things to see, top of most people's list are the rich collections of **paintings** and **manuscripts** built up by the Este family, who decamped here from Ferrara in 1598, after it was annexed by the Papal States, and ruled the town until the nineteenth century. But really the appeal of Modena is in wandering its labyrinthine old centre, finishing off the day with some good food.

Arrival and information

Modena's centre, marked by the main Piazza Grande, is a ten-minute walk southwest from the **train station** on Piazza Dante Alighieri, down the wide Corso Vittorio Emanuele II. Buses #7 and #11 connect the train station with the main street of Via Emilia. The **bus station** for villages on the plain or in the Apennines is on Via Fabriani, off Viale Monte Kosica, ten-minutes' walk west from the train station and northeast from the centre of town. The **tourist**

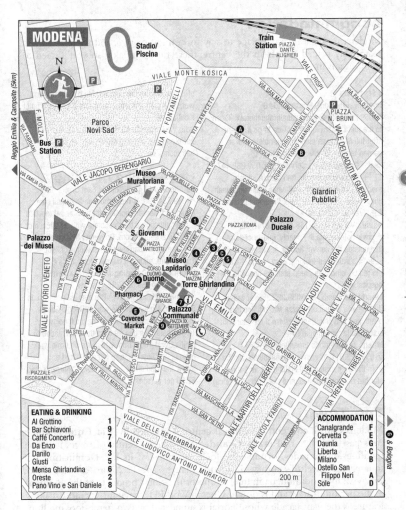

MODENA

Stadio/
Piscina

Train
Station

PIAZZA
DANTE
ALIGHIERI

Reggio Emilia & Campsite (5km)

VIALE MONTE KOSICA

VIA A. FONTANELLI

VIA GANACETO

VIA SAN MARTINO

VIA PAOLO FERRARI

PIAZZA
N. BRUNI

Parco
Novi Sad

VIA SANT'ORSOLA

CORSO VITTORIO EMANUELE II

VIALE DEI CADUTI IN GUERRA

Bus
Station

VIALE JACOPO BERENGARIO

VIA EMILIA OVEST

LARGO CORSICA

VIA R. RAMAZZINI

VIA CASTELMARALDO

VIA N. SAURO

Museo
Muratoriana

VIA CERCA BELLE ARTI

VIA POMPOSA

VIA TAGLIO

PIAZZA
SANDOMENICO

VIA FEBBRAIO

CORSO CAVOUR

Giardini
Pubblici

Palazzo
dei Musei

VIALE VITTORIO VENETO

VIA S. AGOSTINO

RUA MIRA

VIA S. EUFEMIA

VIA MALATESTA

VIA CARTERIA

VIA N. FILIPPA

PIAZZA
MATTEOTTI

VIA FARINI

VIA C. BATTISTI

PIAZZA
ROMA

VIA EMILIA

PIAZZA
GRANDE

S. Giovanni

Museo
Lapidario

Duomo

Torre Ghirlandina

Pharmacy

Palazzo
Ducale

VIA S. VICENZO

CORSO CANAL GRANDE

VIALE DEI CADUTI IN GUERRA

VIALE V. REITER

VIA G. PUCCINI

VIA E. PAPAZZONI

VIA E. CASTIGLIONE

Covered
Market

VIA STELLA

PIAZZA XX
SETTEMBRE

Palazzo
Communale

VIA UNIVERSITA

CORSO CANAL GRANDE

LARGO GARIBALDI

VIA EMILIA EST

VIA TRENTO E. TRIESTE

G & Bologna

PIAZZALE
RISORGIMENTO

RUA FRATI MINORI

VIA DEL GALLUCCI

VIA MASCHERELLA

VIALE MARTIRI DELLA LIBERTA

VIA PREMPUNI

VIALE DELLE REMEMBRANZE

VIA SAN PIETRO

VIALE LUDOVICO ANTONIO MURATORI

VIALE NICOLA FABRIZI

EATING & DRINKING	
Al Grottino	1
Bar Schiavoni	9
Caffè Concerto	7
Da Enzo	4
Danilo	3
Giusti	5
Mensa Ghirlandina	6
Oreste	2
Pano Vino e San Daniele	8

ACCOMMODATION	
Canalgrande	F
Cervetta 5	E
Daunia	G
Liberta	C
Milano	B
Ostello San Filippo Neri	A
Sole	D

0   200 m

office is just off the main Piazza Grande at Via Scudari 12 (Mon 3–6pm, Tues–Sat 9am–1pm & 3–6pm, Sun 9.30am–12.30pm; ☎059.206.660, ⓦturismo.commune.modena.it), although do note that it can be tricky to find because of a lack of clear signage. To save a bit of money, it's worth investing in Modena's **museum card**, which for just €6 enables the holder to make unlimited visits to the Museo Lapidario and the collections of the Palazzo de Musei over a two-day period. It's available at all the participating sites. You can go **online** at Piazza Grande 17 (Mon–Sat 9am–1pm & 3–7pm, closed Wed pm and Sun) for €1.5 per hour. There's **free parking** inside the stadium at Parco Novi Sad and on Piazzale N. Bruni, though most hotels in the centre either have a garage or can give you free parking permits; driving in the centre's one-way system during weekdays can be something of a nightmare though.

Accommodation

Modena makes a relaxing place to stay for a night or two, and there are a few reasonably priced **hotels** in the centre: these fill up quickly so you'll need to book in advance.

Hotels

Canalgrande Corso Canalgrande 6 ☎ 059.217.160, ⓦ www.canalgrandehotel.it. Close to the main piazza and the place to go if you're after full Modenese elegance complete with a garden terrace for chic breakfasting. ❻

🏃 **Cervetta 5** Via Cervetta 5 ☎ 059.238.447, ⓦ www.hotelcervetta5.com. A stylish, modern-looking choice – all white walls and clean lines – just off Piazza Grande. Breakfast is an extra €16. Free wi-fi access. ❸

Daunia Via del Pozzo 158 ☎ 059.371.182, ⓦ www.hoteldaunia.it. Friendly, mid-priced option just outside the centre. Rooms are large and en suite, if a little tired-looking. Easy to find – it's the big red building with green shutters opposite the hospital. ❷

Liberta Via Blasia 10 ☎ 059.222.365, ⓦ www .hotelliberta.it. Just off Piazza Mazzini lies this well positioned and chic Best Western three-star with comfortable furnishings. ❺

Milano Corso Vittorio Emanuele 68 ☎ 059.223.011, ⓦ www.modenahotel.it. Not far from the train station, this bills itself as a three-star but has the facilities (and thankfully the price) of a two. Rooms are comfortable but chintzy and worn, the staff are welcoming and it enjoys a quiet location. ❷

Sole Via Malatesta 45 ☎ 059.214.245. Rather basic one-star offering rooms with shared bathrooms. ❶

Hostels and camping

Ostello San Filippo Ner Via Sant'Orsola 52 ☎ 059.234.598, ⓔ hostelmodena@hotmail.com Clean and pleasant hostel with two- and three-bed rooms, although a touch austere with no kitchen or communal sitting room. Conveniently located for both the centre and the train station. Lockout 10am–2pm, midnight curfew. Dorm beds €16.

International Camping Modena Via Cave di Ramo 111 ☎ 059.332.252, ⓦ www .internationalcamping.org, The nearest campsite is 5km from Modena on the way to Reggio Emilia, though the nearby motorway makes it noisy. To get there take bus #9 from the train station to Emilia Ovest 1006, from where it's a 10min walk: head up Via Rosmini, turn left at the end and follow the road under the motorway approach road. €7.50 per person.

The Town

Modena's small, concentric medieval centre is bisected by **Via Emilia**, which runs past the edge of **Piazza Grande**, the nominal centre of town, its stone buildings and arcades forming the focus of much of its life. Dominating the square, the twelfth-century **Duomo** (daily 7am–12.20pm & 3.30–7pm, ⓦ www.Duomodimodena.it; free) is one of the finest products of the Romanesque period in Italy and is on the Unesco World Heritage list. Its most striking feature is the west facade whose portal is supported by two fierce-looking lions and fringed with marvellous reliefs – the work of one **Wiligelmo**, who also did the larger reliefs that run along the wall. Inside, under the choir is the plain stone coffin of St Geminianus, the patron saint of Modena – on his feast day, January 31, crowds come to visit his coffin, and a big market is held out in the main square.

Beside the main entrance to the Duomo, the **Museo Lapidario** (Tues–Sun 9.30am–12.30pm & 3.30–6.30pm; €3 or see p.407 for combined tickets) displays Roman-age marbles from the Duomo, while on the other side of the church lurches the 83-metre-high **Torre Ghirlandina**, begun at the same time as the Duomo but not completed until two hundred years later. It is currently closed for repairs, which are not due to be completed until 2010. Until then its facade and the surrounding scaffolding will be covered by a giant coloured screen designed by the artist Mimmo Paladino.

The other main focus for your wanderings is at the far, northwestern end of Via Emilia, where the **Palazzo dei Musei** houses the city museums and art galleries. Through an archway lined with Roman tombstones – nearby Piazza Matteotti was the site of a necropolis – a staircase leads off to the right up to the Biblioteca Estense, on the first floor (Mon–Sat 9am–1pm; €3) where you can see letters sent by monarchs, popes and despots, with great wax seals, old maps, and the prize treasure, Borso d'Este's Bible – the *Bibbia di Borso d'Este* – arguably the most decorated book in the world. The **Museo Civico Archeologico Etnologia** (Tues–Fri 9am–noon, Sat & Sun 10am–1pm & 3–6pm; €4), on the second floor, has a large collection of artefacts of archeological and artistic significance, while on the top floor, the **Galleria Estense** (Tues–Sun 8.30am–7.30pm; €4) is perhaps the highlight of all the exhibits. Made up of the picture collection of the Este family, it contains paintings of the local schools, from the early Renaissance through to the works of the Carraccis, Guercino and Guido Reni.

Eating and drinking

Modena is packed with places to **eat**, with a large array of restaurants in all price ranges. Try to sample some of the local pork-based specialities, like *ciccioli* – flaky pork scratchings laid out in bars in the evening – or, in a restaurant, *zampone* (pig's trotters, boned and filled with minced meat) or *cotechino* – the same thing, but stuffed inside a pig's bladder. Its **covered market** (Mon–Sat 6.30am–2pm, Sun 4pm–7pm), just south of Piazza Grande, is a must for self-caterers with a fantastic array of fresh vegetables, fruit and meat. It also stocks a good selection of balsamic vinegars (you can pick up a forty-year old vintage for around €20) and you can have blocks of parma ham and parmesan vacuum-packed to take home with you.

Al Grottino Via del Taglio 26. Dependable upper mid-priced place that gets packed out with crowds coming for the *gigante* pizzas that more than live up to their name. Big on pastas and meat with the *filete di manzo ai funghi porcini* especially recommended. Closed Wed.

Bar Schiavoni Via Albinelli 13. Good choice for a great coffee, a glass of wine and delectable and inventive panini for around €4 (open during market hours) at this tiny, busy place right by the market.

Caffé Concerto Piazza Grande. Large, elegant place that operates a buffet service during the day (a plate of your choice, water and coffee for €15) and an à la carte restaurant at night (expect to pay around €35 a head). Its main role, however, is as Modena's most celebrated meeting place and premier evening spot. Closed Tues.

Danilo Via Coltellini 51 ☏ 059.225.498. The archetypal Modena eating experience – regional specialities served in a cosy backstreet dining room. Be adventurous and try the mixed meat platter – including stuffed pig's trotters, cheek and tongue – for €16. Closed Sun.

Da Enzo Via Coltellini 17 ☏ 059.225.177. Pleasant, slightly old-fashioned place serving Modenese specialities – though not especially cheap. *Primi* €6–8, *secondi* €10–14. Closed Mon.

Giusti Via Farini 75. At the bottom end of the price scale, this place has been a delicatessen since the seventeenth century and is a good source of picnic food. Opens a small café serving a good range of pasta dishes at lunchtimes. Closed Sun & Mon.

Mensa Ghirlandina Via Leodino 9. Dedicated to feeding impoverished students, this self-service place offers reasonable quality food at low prices. Open noon–2pm. Closed Sun.

Oreste Piazza Roma 31 ☏ 059.243.324. This superb Michelin-starred affair was one of Pavarotti's favourite restaurants. Specialities include pumpkin ravioli. The decor is fusty but charming. Closed Sun.

Pano Vino e San Daniele Via del Carmine 3/5. Part of a growing regional chain, this bright modern café makes a nice spot to wind down at the end of the day, serving an excellent selection of wines, cheeses and hams. Open daily till 1am.

If you want to see Modena's famous balsamic vinegar being created, contact the **Modenatur** office next door to the tourist office at no. 8/10 Via Scudari (☏059.220.022, ⓦwww.modenatur.it) for information on trips to *aceteria* (these are free but being private establishments visits depend on owners' schedules). They also have information on tours to Lambrusco wineries, parmesan dairies and some of the region's renowned car manufacturers.

The tourist office can also advise you on "**gourmet itineraries**" in the wooded foothills of the Apennines surrounding the town. However, they're not really necessary: restaurant signs by the side of the road invite you in to try cuisine *"alla tua nonna"* – "like grandma used to make" – often involving *mortadella* (cold pork sausage, spotted with large lumps of fat and often flavoured with nutmeg, coriander and myrtle berries), salami or *crescente* (a kind of pitta bread eaten with a mixture of oil, garlic, rosemary and parmesan). Higher in the mountains you can still find *ciacci* – chestnut-flour pancakes, filled with ricotta and sugar – and walnuts that go to make *nocino* liqueur.

Around Modena

The area immediately around Modena looks rather bland and uninviting with its discount furniture and lighting stores, garages and factories. Worth a look, however, is **CARPI**, around 15km north of Modena. The town's central **Piazza dei Martiri** is an enormous and impressive open space, almost worth the trip alone, and the sixteenth-century **Castello del Pio**, a mass of ornamental turrets and towers, holds an interesting museum inside – the **Museo al Deportato** (Thurs, Sat, Sun & public hols 10am–12.30pm & 3.30–7pm; €5). Occupying German forces in World War II held prisoners awaiting deportation to concentration camps at a site in Fóssoli, 6km to the north – the camp sheds still stand, dilapidated, in a field – and the museum has sobering displays on the camps and the conditions in which the prisoners were held, putting them into context with information on political and racial exile.

The activity outside in the square provides some welcome relief with slick clothing stores running the length of its sixteenth-century red-brick **Portico Lungo**. At one end of the square is the bright ochre **Teatro Comunale**, at the other the Renaissance **Cattedrale** with a Baroque facade. There are trains and buses every hour to Modena, but if you do want to stay try the **rooms** at *Albergo da Giorgio* at Via G. Rocca 1–5 (☏059.685.365; ❸).

Also worth a detour is the **Galleria Ferrari**, at Via Dino Ferrari 43 in **MARANELLO**, around 23km south of Modena (daily 9.30am–6pm; ⓦwww.galleriaferrari.com; €12), an exhibition centre dedicated to the racing dynasty. On display are the cups and trophies won by the Ferrari team over the years, an assortment of Ferrari engines, along with vintage and contemporary examples of the cars themselves and a reconstruction of Enzo Ferrari's study. There's also a shop stocking all manner of bright red Ferrari merchandise – handbags, teddy bears, baseball caps, rocking horses etc.

Reggio Emilia and around

About 25km northwest, up the Via Emilia from Modena, is **REGGIO EMILIA**, nicknamed "the red town" – in 1960 five protestors were killed by police during demonstrations designed to prevent Fascists joining the government. You wouldn't credit such a revolutionary past wandering round this quiet, pleasant place now, more associated today with fashion house MaxMara.

The town is built around two central squares, **Piazza Prampolini** and **Piazza San Prospero**, which come alive on market days (Tues & Fri). Stalls specialize in rather tacky clothes – the shops surrounding the market are far more interesting, crammed with a mighty range of local produce such as salami and *parmigiano-reggiano*. Around the square, the buildings squeeze up so close to the church of **San Prospero** that they seem to have pushed it off-balance so that it now lurches to one side. Built in the sixteenth century, it's guarded by six lions in rose-coloured Verona marble. Via Broletto leads through into **Piazza Prampolini**, skirting the side of the **Duomo**, which displays an awkward amalgamation of styles. Underneath the marble tacked on in the sixteenth century, it's possible to see the church's Romanesque facade, with incongruously Mannerist statues of Adam and Eve lounging over the medieval portal.

At right angles to the Duomo is the sugar-pink **Palazzo del Capitano del Popolo**. The Italian tricolour of red, white and green was proclaimed here as the official national flag of Italy when Napoleon's Cispadane Republic was formed in 1797. North of here on the edge of Piazza della Vittoria are the **Musei Civici** (Tues–Fri 9am–noon, Sat, Sun & hols 10am–1pm & 4pm–7pm; free), containing an eighteenth-century private collection of archeological finds, fossils and paintings. In the corner of the square, the **Galleria Parmeggiani** (Tues–Fri 9am–noon, Sat, Sun & hols 10am–1pm & 4–7pm; free) houses an important collection of Spanish, Flemish and Italian art, including sculptures and bronzes, as well as costumes and textiles. Nearby stands the church of **Madonna della Ghiara**, built in the seventeenth century and decorated with Bolognese School frescoes of scenes from the Old Testament and a *Crucifixion* by Guercino.

Practicalities

Reggio is on the main rail line between Bologna and Milan. The **train station** is on Piazza Marconi I, just east of the old centre; the **bus station** is on the west side of the public gardens on Via Raimondo Franchetti. The **tourist office** is on the southern side of Piazza Prampolini at Via Farini 1/A (Mon–Sat 8.30am–1pm & 2.30–6pm, Sun 9am–noon; ☎0522.451.152, ⊛www .municipio.re.it/IAT/iatre.nsf), while the helpful **Club Alpino Italiano** office at Viale Mille 32 (☎0522.430.266, ⊛www.caireggioemilia.it) has information on walking in the nearby hills (Tues, Wed & Fri 6–7.30pm, Thurs & Sat 8.30–10.30pm; closed most of Aug). For **internet** access head for *Qui Qua Navigator*, Piazza Fontanesi 4 (Mon–Sat 9am–7.30pm).

If you're planning **to stay**, hotel space is often limited so book ahead. The *Ariosto* on Via San Rocco 12 (☎0522.437.320, ℉0522.452.514; ❷) is a central and reasonably priced hotel, while the four-star *Posta*, Piazza del Monte 2 (☎0522.432.944, ⊛www.hotelposta.re.it; ❺), is in the historic Palazzo del Capitano del Popolo and is the choice for anyone desiring a taste of fabulous luxury. There's an attractive **youth hostel**, *Ostello Basilica della Ghiara*, 1km from the train station at Via Guasco 6 (☎0522.452.323, but prefer reservations by fax ℉0522.454.795; no lock-out or curfew; €15 with breakfast).

Food and drink options are relatively good. *Caffè Arti E Mestieri*, Via Emilia S. Pietro 14 (☎0522.432.202, closed Sun & Mon), is a rather smart restaurant with a menu of stylishly updated classic dishes from the region (expect to pay around €35–40 for two courses with wine), while *Canossa*, at

Via Roma 37 (☎0522.454.196, closed Wed), specializes in various ham antipasti and is consistently popular with locals (€25–30 for two courses). *Sotto Broletto*, on a narrow alley by the Duomo, serves generously topped pies from €4.50.

Around Reggio

The foothills **south of Reggio** are cheese country. Signs along the roadside advertise the local *parmigiano-reggiano* and the village of **CASINA**, 27km outside Reggio on the N63 to La Spezia, holds a popular Festa del Parmigiano in August, when the vats of cheese mixture are stirred with enormous wooden paddles. Buses for here leave Reggio from the new bus station on Piazzale Europa.

With your own transport, you can take the side road leading from Casina to **CANOSSA**. This was the seat of the powerful Da Canossa family, whose most famous member, the Countess Mathilda of Tuscany (La Gran Contessa), was a big name here in the eleventh century – unusually so in a society largely controlled by warlords and the clergy. She was known for donning armour and leading troops into battle herself, and at the age of 43 scandalized the nobility by marrying a youth of 17. The remains of the **Castle** (Tues–Sun: April–Sept 9am–12.30pm & 3–7pm; Oct–March 9am–4.30pm; free) are largely thirteenth century, but it's really the location – on a rocky outcrop looking towards the mountains in one direction and over the neighbouring castle at Rossena and the towns strung out over the plain in the other – which is impressive. People from the surrounding towns are fond of coming out here at weekends to eat in the local **restaurants**, and it's a popular area for **hiking**, cross-country skiing and mushroom-collecting.

High in the surrounding hills paths lead onto the mountain *crinale*, with **Castelnovo Ne'Monti** a possible base for local walks. Further on, at **Busana**, a road forks to the left, descending through a series of hairpin bends bordered by plenty of falling rock signs, in the Secchia Valley, climbing back up the other side through Cinquecerri to **Ligonchio** – another good starting-point for walks away from cable cars and ski lifts onto nearby **Monte Cusna** (2120m). Close by here are the Prati di Sara, a windswept expanse of grassland with small tarns and the occasional tree. As you ascend, you have more of a view across the layers of ridges, often half-obscured in the mist. It's possible to stay overnight in some of the refuges that group along the **Grande Escursione Appenninica** route, a 25-day trek that weaves its way back and forth across the border between Emilia and Tuscany. The Club Alpino Italiano office in Reggio (see p.411) should have information on this route.

Parma

Generally reckoned to have one of the highest standards of living in Italy, **PARMA**, about 30km along the Via Emilia northwest of Reggio, is about as comfortable a town as you could wish for. The measured pace of its streets, the abundance of its restaurants and the general air of affluence are almost cloying, especially if you've arrived from the south. Not surprisingly, if you're travelling on a tight budget, Parma presents a few difficulties. That said, it's a friendly enough place, with plenty to see. A visit to the opera can be an experience – the audience are considered one of the toughest outside Milan's La Scala and don't pull any punches if they consider a singer to be performing

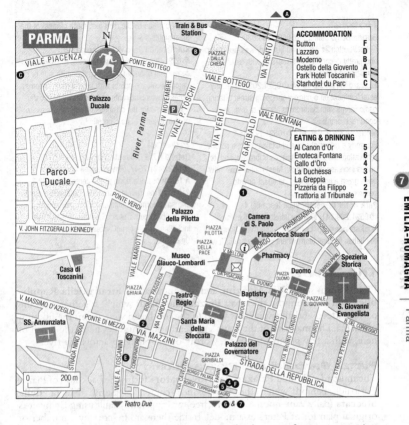

ACCOMMODATION

Button	F
Lazzaro	D
Moderno	B
Ostello della Gioventù	A
Park Hotel Toscanini	E
Starhotel du Parc	C

EATING & DRINKING

Al Canon d'Or	5
Enoteca Fontana	6
Gallo d'Oro	4
La Duchessa	3
La Greppia	1
Pizzeria da Filippo	2
Trattoria al Tribunale	7

badly – and the city's works of art include the legacy of two great artists, Correggio and Parmigianino.

Arrival and information

Parma's **train and bus stations** are fifteen-minutes' walk from the central Piazza Garibaldi, or a short ride on buses #2, #8, #9 & #13. The **tourist office** is at Via Melloni 1/A (Mon–Sat 9am–7pm, Sun 9am–1pm, closed Wed 1–3pm; ☎0521.218.889, ⍑turismo.comune.parma.it). Internet access is available at *Polidoro Web* (Mon–Sat 10am–8pm) in the Galleria Polidoro, a mall on the corner of Via Mazzini by the river. A Banco Nacionale Lavoro with an **ATM** is located on Piazza Garibaldi.

Bikes for exploring the city can be rented from Parma City Bike at Viale Mentana 8/A (Mon–Sat 9.30am–8pm; ☎0521.235,639), a few minutes' walk north of the centre, for €1 per hour.

Accommodation

If you're planning a trip during spring or the run-up to Christmas, be sure to book in advance as this is also trade-fair season in Parma. You really need to plan ahead for the town's cheaper **hotels** too, although there's a good alternative in the new HI **hostel**.

Hotels

Button Borgo Salina 7 ℡0521.208.039,
Ⓔhotelbutton@tin.it. Small but very well-appointed
and pretty decent-value three-star with air-
conditioned rooms. ❸
Lazzaro Via XX Marzo 14 ℡0521.208.944. A tiny
establishment on a narrow shopping street offering
basic rooms with bathrooms above its own, very
good restaurant. ❷
Moderno Via A. Cecchi 4 ℡0521.772.647.
Formerly a rather cheap and basic option, a recent
renovation has seen its facilities improved, and its
prices increase accordingly. Most rooms have now
been given a lick of paint and boast private
bathrooms. ❸
Park Hotel Toscanini Viale Toscanini 4
℡0521.289.141, Ⓦwww.hoteltoscanini.com
/inglese/index.asp. Lavish four-star that's home to
the Italian football team whenever they are in town.

Great position by the river just south of most of the
main sights. ❺
Starhotel du Parc Viale Piacenza 12/C
℡0521.292.929, Ⓦwww.starhotels.it. Luxurious
conversion of an old palace on the north side of the
Parco Ducale, complete with fitness room, internet
access, two restaurants and the inevitable conference rooms for the business travellers who make
up the majority of its clientele. ❾

Hostel

Ostello della Gioventu Via San Leonardo 86
℡0521.191.7547, Ⓦwww.ostelloparma.it.
A 10min bus ride north of the centre (lines #2 &
#13 from the train station), this hostel offers spick
and span dorms, double and triple rooms with
private bathrooms, plus a host of extra facilities
including wi-fi, internet access and bike rental.
Open 24hr.

The Town

Parma's main street, **Via Mazzini**, and its continuation, **Strada della Repub-blica**, run east from the river, past **Piazza Garibaldi** which, together with the narrow streets and alleyways that wind to the south and west, forms the fulcrum of Parma. The majority of the town's museums and churches lie to the north of here, with a few points of interest, worthy of a stroll, lying across the river.

Piazza Garibaldi and Piazza Duomo

The mustard-coloured **Palazzo del Governatore** forms the backdrop of Piazza Garibaldi, behind which the Renaissance church of **Santa Maria della Steccata** (daily 9am–noon & 3–6pm; free) was apparently built using Bramante's original plan for St Peter's as a model. Inside there are frescoes by a number of sixteenth-century painters, notably **Parmigianino**, who spent the last ten years of his life on this work, eventually being sacked for breach of contract by the disgruntled church authorities.

Five-minutes' walk away – turn right off Strada Cavour – the slightly gloomy **Piazza Duomo** forms part of the old *centro episcopale*, away from the shopping streets of the commercial centre. The Lombard–Romanesque **Duomo** (daily 9am–12.30pm & 3–7pm; free), dating from the eleventh century, holds earlier work by Parmigianino in its south transept, executed when the artist was a pupil of **Correggio** – who painted the fresco of the Assumption in the central cupola. Finished in 1534, this is among the most famous of Correggio's works, the Virgin Mary floating up through a sea of limbs, faces and swirling clouds, which attracted some bemused comments at the time. One contemporary compared it to a "hash of frogs' legs", while Dickens, visiting much later, thought it a sight that "no operative surgeon gone mad could imagine in his wildest delirium". Correggio was paid for the painting with a sackful of small change to annoy him, since he was known to be a great miser. The story goes that he carried the sack of coins home in the heat, caught a fever and died at the age of 40.

Just a few steps southwest of the Duomo is the beautiful twelfth-century octagonal **baptistry** (daily 9am–12.30pm & 3–6.30pm; €4), its sugary pink-and-white Verona marble rising four storeys high. Its three elaborately carved portals and frieze are the work of the architect Benedetto Antelami.

There's more work by Correggio in the cupola of the church of **San Giovanni Evangelista** behind the Duomo (daily 8am–noon & 3.30–6pm; free) – a fresco of the Vision of St John at Patmos. Next door, the **Spezieria Storica di San Giovanni Evangelista**, at Borgo Pipa 1 (daily 8.30am–1.30pm; €2), is a thirteenth-century pharmacy with a medieval interior.

Via Garibaldi and around

A short walk northwest from Piazza Duomo, the **Camera di San Paolo** in the former Benedictine Convent off Via Garibaldi on Via Melloni (daily 9am–1.45pm; €2) houses more frescoes by Correggio executed in 1519; above the fireplace, the abbess who commissioned the work is portrayed by Correggio as the goddess Diana. Just east of here, near the tourist office on Borgo del Parmigianino, is the **Pinacoteca Stuard** (Mon, Wed–Sat 9am–6.30pm, Sun 9am–6pm; €4), one of the city's newest cultural attractions. Housed in a former convent are 270 paintings from the fourteenth to the nineteenth century, including several priceless Goyas, that used to form the private collection of the nobleman Giuseppe Stuard. Upon his death in 1834, the collection was bequeathed to the congregation of San Filippo Neri, but has only gone on public display in the past few years. Around the corner on Piazza della Pace, the **Museo Glauco-Lombardi** at Via Garibaldi 15 (Tues–Sat 10am–3.30pm, Sun 9am–6pm, Sun in July–Aug 9am–1pm; €4) has a display of memorabilia relating to Marie-Louise of Austria, who reigned here after the defeat of her husband Napoleon at Waterloo. She set herself up with another suitor (much to the chagrin of her exiled spouse) and expanded the Parma violet perfume industry.

Back west, across Via Garibaldi, it's hard to miss Parma's biggest monument, the **Palazzo della Pilotta**, surrounded by vast expanses of wonderfully green lawn set off by modern fountains and some slightly incongruous-looking statues of giant saucepans and coffee pots. Begun for Alessandro Farnese – the wily Pope Paul III – in the sixteenth century, the building was reduced to a shell by World War II bombing, but has been rebuilt and now houses a number of Parma's museums, including on the second floor the main art gallery, the **Galleria Nazionale** (Tues–Sun 8.30am–1.45pm; €6, including the Teatro Farnese), a modern, high-tech display that includes work by Correggio and Parmigianino, and the remarkable *Apostles at the Sepulchre* and *Funeral of the Virgin* by Carracci – massive, overwhelming canvases, suspended either side of a gantry.

The **Teatro Farnese** (same times as gallery; €2, €6 including the Galleria Nazionale), which you pass through to get to the gallery, in the former arms room of the palace, was almost entirely destroyed by bombing in 1944. The restored theatre, still used occasionally, has an extended semicircle of seats three tiers high, made completely of wood, in a facsimile of Palladio's Teatro Olympico at Vicenza, and also houses Italy's first revolving stage. On the first floor, the **Museo Archeologico Nazionale** (daily 9am–7.30pm; €2) is a less essential stop but still worth a glance, with finds from the prehistoric lake villages around Parma, as well as the table top on which the Emperor Trajan notched up a record of his gifts to the poor.

Across the river

Behind the *palazzo*, the Ponte Verdi crosses the River Parma, bringing you to the **Parco Ducale** (daily: April–Oct 6am–midnight; Nov–March 7am–8pm; free), a set of eighteenth-century formal gardens arranged to offset the sixteenth-century **Palazzo Ducale** (Mon–Sat 9am–noon; €3) built for

Ottaviano Farnese and filled with frescoes by Carracci. Just south, the **Casa di Toscanini** on Via R. Tanzi (Tues–Sat 9am–1pm & 2–6pm, Sun 2–6pm; €2) is the birthplace of the conductor who debuted in the Teatro Regio here (see opposite), and is just one of the sights that recall Parma's strong musical heritage. Further south still, on the same side of the river, the embalmed body of the violinist Niccolo Paganini rests under a canopy in the **Cimitero della Villetta** (daily: summer 8am–12.30pm & 4–7pm; winter 8am–12.30pm & 2.30–5pm; free).

Eating and drinking

Many **restaurants** in Parma – especially the ones in the centre – can be rather pricey, though less expensive options do exist, most noticeably on Via Garibaldi and Strada Farini. Local specialities include the obvious Parma ham (*prosciutto*) and *parmigiano reggiano* – which are often served together as an antipasto – as well as *guancia di manzo*, cheek of beef. For snacks, *prosciutto* stuffed into pastries and other local delights are available for around €2 from the many bakeries, and picnic supplies can be bought at the market by the river on Piazza Ghiaia (Wed & Sat).

Al Canon d'Or Via N. Sauro 3/A. Slightly pricey place, housed in a former palace. Parmesan-flavoured specialities feature highly and there are over thirty wines on offer. Closed Wed.

Enoteca Fontana Strada Farini 24. Great authentic old bar, with long wooden tables, a huge choice of wines from all over the region and a menu that includes great sandwiches and steaming bowls of pasta – all reasonably priced. Closed Sun & Mon.

Gallo d'Oro Borgo della Salina 3 ☎0521.08.846. Reasonably priced little trattoria on a quiet side street. Excellent filled pastas are the main attraction, although the mushroom crepes are particularly good. *Primi* €7, *secondi* €7–8.50. Closed Sun.

La Duchessa Piazza Garibaldi 1. One of several restaurants with outdoor seating on the square, this offers perhaps the best food, with over thirty types of pizza, (€4.50–9.50) and great people-watching opportunities.

La Greppia Via Garibaldi 39/A ☎0521.233.686. Even by Parma's elegant, expensive standards, this is a cut above, offering dishes such as *frittata* (a type of omelette) with veal, kidneys and mushrooms. Wine buffs will be spoilt for choice with almost 600 wines available. *Primi* €11–12, *secondi* €15.50–23.50. Closed Mon & Tues.

Pizzeria da Filippo Via Mazzini 41/A. Very cheap and central option near the river. Pizzas are the main thing (€5–7) but it also serves generously filled panini (€2.80–3.30) and some local speciali-ties, including *risotto alla parmigiana*. Closed Sun.

Trattoria al Tribunale Vicolo Politi 5/B, up an alleyway off Strada Farini ☎0521.285.527. Affordable gourmet option that serves large plates of creamy pink *prosciutto* and other antipasti delights. More adventurous diners might like to try the braised veal cheek. Closed Tues.

Entertainment

For nightlife in refined Parma, **opera** and **theatre** take precedence over clubs. Fans of the former should head to the **Teatro Regio**, at Via Garibaldi 16/A (℡0521.218.678, ⊛www.teatroregioparma.org). **Teatro Due**, next to the river on Viale Basetti, is the home of one of the top theatre companies in Europe, the **Colletivo di Parma**, who perform between October and April (℡0521.230.242, ⊛www.teatrodue.org) and in the Palazzo della Pilotta in June and July – their shows draw on a tradition of comedy and political theatre. In summer the city's entertainment options become more diverse – the piazzas host live jazz bands and during July and August locals flock to the garden behind **Camera di San Paolo** for a free season on Wednesday nights of old horror movies, dubbed in Italian (⊛www.ufficiocinema.it). Tickets are €12.

South of Parma

The countryside **around Parma** is a strange mixture: some of the major roads follow bleak gorges, skirting the edge of blank rock walls for miles; others look as if they will lead precisely nowhere before emerging into meadows and orchards with rich farmland stretching into the distance.

Prime targets are any of the **medieval castles** strung out across the foothills. There are around twenty, many built by the powerful Farnese dynasty. The website ⊛www.castellidelducato.it has a useful map locating all the castles and can help you plan a tour. It's also worth buying a Castelli del Ducato card (€2) available from tourist offices or the castles themselves that will give you a €1 reduction on admission fees and is valid for a whole year. One of the best-sited castles is at **TORRECHIARA**, about 18km south of Parma and connected by hourly buses. The castle provides a superb vantage point over the surrounding area and also has frescoes by Bembo in the **Camera d'Oro** (March–Oct Tues–Sat 9am–7.30pm, Sun 10am–7pm; Nov–March Tues–Fri 9am–4.30pm, Sat & Sun 9am–5pm; €3).

One of the most famous Parma hams (*Prosciutto di Langhirano*) comes from the foothills around **LANGHIRANO**, which is a few kilometres further on and also linked by regular bus with Parma. The experts say the ham cures so successfully here because of the unique mixture of clear mountain air and sea breezes blowing over the Apennines from Liguria; it is served simply with butter, so as not to mask the fine flavour. The town itself has grown into a mass of stainless steel warehouses – there's no reason to come unless you want to carry a haunch of meat round with you for the rest of your holiday. But the countryside around, particularly near Calestano, is beautiful. Apart from the rail route, the fast way over the mountains is by **autostrada**, the A15, which snakes its way in and out of a succession of tunnels, giving glimpses of lush, hidden valleys, vines and orchards.

The slower N62 gives access to the *crinale* of the mountains: the trails are a popular attraction for walkers these days, but served a quite different purpose in the last war, when adults and children made the long journey by foot, carrying sacks of salt from the coast to trade for food. The writer Eric Newby was hidden by villagers in these mountains as an escaped prisoner of war in 1943, and the book chronicling his experiences, *Love and War in the Apennines*, captures the beauty of the region

CORNIGLIO, reached by bus from Parma, is a centre for hiking and skiing; try the atmospheric, *Ostello Corniglio.it* (℡0521.881.012, ⊛www.ostellocorniglio.it;

€13) if you want to stay. More buses squeeze themselves round the tight bends to the small villages of Monchio (16km), Trefiumi (20km) and Prato Spilla (23km from Corniglio), leaving you on the lower slopes of **Monte Malpasso** (1716m) – glistening with small lakes and tarns. Buses also run to **Lagdei** (14km), a starting point for further walks.

West of Parma

The Via Emilia continues west from Parma, with small towns mushrooming out from the edges of the road, mostly just a ribbon of shops and roadside cafés. **FIDENZA**, the first place of any size, has a Lombard-Romanesque **cathedral** with a richly decorated facade worked on by followers of the Parma master, Antelami. As Fidenza was a major staging post on the pilgrimage route to Rome, the carvings depict pilgrims as well as more domestic subjects – strings of sausages festoon one figure, while elsewhere there are hunting scenes.

The countryside **to the north** of here is the *bassa*, flat, low country (where Parmese-born Bertolucci filmed the epic *1900*) cut by drainage ditches and open fields growing wheat and corn, sugar beet and vines. In summer it's scorching hot and almost silent, with an odd, still beauty all its own, but generally it's a place to pass through on your way to somewhere else. The small towns and villages of the region are quiet and mainly undistinguished. **SORAGNA** is a good place to be at the end of April/first weekend in May for its grand agricultural *festa*, with local wine, cheese and salami tasting.

The attractive village of **FONTANELLATO**, a few kilometres northeast of Fidenza, was the site of the camp where Eric Newby was imprisoned, but is perhaps better known as a centre for the production of parmesan cheese. Its central square is dominated by the **Rocca Sanvitale** (April–Oct daily 9.30am–12.30pm & 3–6pm; Nov–March Tues–Sun 9.30am–12.30pm & 3–6pm; by tour only, in Italian, last tour an hour before closing; €3.80), a fifteenth-century moated castle that the Sanvitale family called home until the onset of World War II. Inside there are some ancient pieces of furniture and a fresco of the legend of Diana and Acteon by Parmigianino.

The Verdi trail

Five kilometres to the north, the small village of **LE RONCOLE** marks the start of **Verdi** country. By the main road on Piazza Giovannino Guareschi – named after the author of the Don Camillo books who also lived here – you can visit the humble **house** where the great composer was born (March–Oct Tues–Sun 9.30am–noon & 2.30–6pm; Nov–Feb Tues–Fri, advance booking only, Sat & Sun 9am–noon & 2–4pm; €4). Some 5km up the road is **BUSSETO**, the childhood home of Verdi and the centre of the Verdi industry that has grown up around the composer, with regular opera performances during summer. It's an appealing little battlemented town, but the main attractions are strictly for Verdi pilgrims. The **Casa Barezzi** (guided tours only Tues–Sun: April–Sept 10am–12.30pm & 3–6.30pm; Oct–March 10am–12.30pm & 2.30–6pm; €4) on the main street, Via Roma 119, now a Verdi museum, was the home of Antonio Barezzi, a wealthy merchant who spotted the young Verdi's talent and brought him in as a teacher for his daughter. Verdi lived here for a while and later married his pupil, Margherita. Now restored to its nineteenth-century state, the museum contains the piano that Verdi played on, the first portrait of the maestro and memorabilia such as the baton that Toscanini used to conduct his Verdi memorial concert in 1926. The rather unfriendly tourist office in Busseto's old *rocca* at Piazza Verdi 10 (T0524.92.487, Wwww.bussetolive.com) may give you information about the sights and about tickets for concerts in the **Verdi Theatre**. You'll need private transport to get to the last of the Verdi sights, the composer's **villa**, a couple of kilometres west of Busseto at **SANT'AGATA DI VILLANOVA**. The villa (Wwww.villaverdiorg), which contains a mock-up of the Milan hotel room where Verdi died, is open for guided tours, lasting 45 minutes (Tues–Sun: April–Oct 9–11.45am & 3–6.45pm; Oct–March 9.30–11.30am & 2.30–5pm; €6).

Castell'Arquato

A little way south of here is the beautiful **CASTELL'ARQUATO**, a nicely restored medieval town set on a hillside overlooking the Arda Valley. At the top of the town is Piazza del Municipio, lined with some stunning buildings. The thirteenth-century **Palazzo del Podestà** isn't open to the public, but you can visit the **Basilica**, a magnificently preserved Romanesque monument with an eighth-century baptismal font in the right-hand apse. The restored tower of the fourteenth-century **Rocca Viscontea** (Tues–Sun: March–Oct 10am–noon & 3–6pm; Nov–Feb 10am–noon & 3–5pm; €3) offers amazing views of the surrounding countryside.

The **tourist office** (March–Oct Tues–Sat 9.30am–12.30pm, Sun 10am–noon & 3–4.30pm; Nov–Feb Tues–Sat 9.30am–12.30pm; T0523.803.091, Wwww.comune.castellarquato.pc.it) is in a hut by the bridge over the river. **Accommodation** is thin on the ground; try the friendly, comfortable *Leon d'Oro* at Piazza Europa 6 (T0523.803.651; ❷) at the bottom of the town, which has simply furnished doubles. **Restaurants and cafés** on the other hand are plentiful: *La Falconiere* (closed Mon) serves local specialities in the atmospheric surroundings of the castle. For more humble dining there's *Osteria La Cantina*, on Vicolo Riorzo 1, which does big salads and *primi* from around €6. For snacks and pastries you can't beat the thriving bakery/café *La Casa del Pane* on Piazza Europa.

East along the Via Emilia from Bologna

East of Bologna, the Via Emilia passes through a clutch of small towns – some of them industrialized and mostly postwar, like Forlì, the unappealing administrative capital of the region, others, like **Faenza**, with medieval piazzas surrounded by towers and battlements. Both started life as Roman way-stations and were under the rule of the Papal States for much of their subsequent history. The **lowlands** to the north are farmed intensively, while on the southern side lie hilly vineyards and pastures, narrow gorges that lead up into the mountains and a couple of ski resorts around Monte Fumaiolo (1407m).

Faenza

Travelling east, cypress trees and umbrella pines, gentler hills and vineyards signal the fact that you're leaving Emilia and entering the Romagna – although strictly speaking there's no distinct boundary between the two regions. **FAENZA**, 50km from Bologna, gives its name to the faïence-ware it has been producing for the last six hundred years. This style of decorated ceramic ware reached its zenith in the fifteenth and sixteenth centuries, and the town is worth a visit for the vast **Museo Internazionale delle Ceramiche** alone (April–Oct Tues–Sun 9.30am–7pm; Nov–March Tues–Thurs 9am–1.30pm, Fri–Sun 9.30am–5.30pm; ⓦ www.micfaenza.org; €6); it's at Viale Baccarini 19. The massive collection includes early work painted in the characteristic blue and ochre, and later, more colourful work, although the highlight is perhaps the Sala Europa, featuring ceramic art by Picasso, Matisse and Chagall.

Faenza is still home to one of Italy's leading ceramics schools, teaching techniques of tin-glazing first introduced in the fourteenth century, as well as a major production centre, with small workshops down most of its side streets. Details are available from the **tourist office** in Piazza del Popolo 1 (April–Oct Mon–Sat 9.30am–12.30pm & 3.30–6.30pm, Sun 9.30am–12.30pm; Nov–March Tues–Sat 9.30am–12.30pm & 3.30–5.30pm, closed Thurs pm; ☎0546.25.231, ⓦ www.prolocofaenza.it).

The rest of Faenza is an attractive town with buildings garnished with ceramic art and an appealing medieval centre formed by the long, crenellated **Palazzo del Podestà**, the **Piazza del Popolo** and the **Piazza della Libertà**, which is the scene of much activity on market days (Tues, Thurs and Sat). **Piazza Martiri della Libertà** – through an archway from Piazza del Popolo – is where you'll find more stalls selling cheese and other local foodstuffs. In the summer local *bambini* turn entrepreneur hosting their own colourful **children's market** on Thursday afternoons in Piazza del Popolo until around 8pm, selling toys, books and bric-a-brac. Another good time to be in Faenza is for the **Palio del Niballo** (ⓦ www.racine.ra.it/niballo), which takes place on the last Sunday in June. If you want to **stay** here, you might consider a bed-and-breakfast, around half the price of a hotel – ask the tourist office for the list of *affittacamere*. The best hotel in town is the *Vittoria*, Corso Garibaldi 23 (☎0546.21.508, ⓦ www.hotel-vittoria.com; ❸), a few blocks north of Piazza del Popolo, featuring nineteenth-century decor and a dining room with a frescoed ceiling. **Eating** prospects are mainly centred around the Piazza del Popolo but the *Osteria del Mercato* in the Piazza Martiri della Libertà is a good, lively place, frequented by locals, and serving decent pizzas.

Brisighella

South of Faenza, the village of **BRISIGHELLA**, halfway up a hillside, is a real food-lover's delight, famed both for its restaurants (visited by people from as far afield as Milan) and its numerous **festivals of gastronomy**, which include the Sagra della Polenta (Oct), del Tartufo (truffle) and dell' Ulivo (both in Nov).

Of the many fine places to eat, some of the best include *La Grotta Osteria con Uso di Cucina*, which, though not cheap, does offer an affordable fixed-price menu of Romagnolo specialities for €35 (☎0546.81.829; closed Tues); the *Cantina del Bonsignore*, at Via Recuperati 4 (☎0546.81.889; open till midnight, closed Thurs), which serves an interesting, varied menu and good wine in a romantic setting; and *La Rocca*, just up the hill at Via delle Volte 10 (☎0546.81.180, ⓦ www.albergo-larocca.com; ❷), which stresses the organic, traditional nature of its cuisine – everything is locally sourced, non-intensively farmed and handmade – and also offers a few rooms in its adjoining hotel. Pick of the bunch, however, is probably the imposing *Albergo Gigiole* on the main square at Piazza Carducci 5 (☎0546.81.209, ⓦ www.gigiole.it; closed Mon; ❺), which was the town's first gourmet restaurant when it opened way back in 1957 and is still leading the way, offering a winning combination of ancient and modern recipes, plus a four-star luxury hotel.

Ferrara

Thirty-minutes' train ride north of Bologna, **FERRARA** was the residence of the Este dukes, an eccentric dynasty that ranked as a major political force throughout Renaissance times. The Este kept the main artists of the day in commissions and built a town which, despite a relatively small population, was – and still is – one of the most elegant urban creations of the period.

At the end of the sixteenth century, with no heir to inherit their lands, the Este were forced to hand over Ferrara to the papacy and leave for good. Life in the city effectively collapsed: eighteenth-century travellers found a ghost town of empty streets and clogged-up canals infested with mosquitoes. Since then Ferrara has picked itself up, dusted itself off, and is now a vibrant, provincial town that, with its grand squares, restored medieval palaces and portico-lined streets, looks a bit like a mini Bologna. It's a popular stop for tourists travelling up from Bologna to Venice, but they rarely stay, leaving the city centre enjoyably peaceful in the evenings.

Arrival and information

Ferrara's **train station** is west of the city walls, a fifteen-minute walk along Viale Cavour to the centre of town, or take bus #1, #2, #9 or #3C (#2 is the most direct). The **bus station** lies just southwest of the main square, on Corso Isonzo. **Parking** is available at the southern end of the city, by the city walls on the piazzas Kennedy and Travaglio for €2 per hour.

The main **tourist office** can be found on the north side of the *castello* courtyard (Mon–Sat 9am–1pm & 2–6pm, Sun 9.30am–1pm & 2–5.20pm; ☎0532.299.303, ⓦ www.ferraraterraeacqua.it) and has plenty of maps and general information on the town. You can check your **email** at the *Ferrara Internet Point*, Via degli Adelardi 17 (Mon–Fri 11am–1pm & Sat 3.30–5pm) for €2 per hour.

Market days are Monday and Friday with most activity taking place on Piazza Travaglio. On the first weekend of the month (except Aug) there is a large **antiques** market in the centre between the *castello* and the Duomo. One of the big annual events, held the last weekend in May, is the **Palio**,

---

Hit the streets – Ferrara by bike

Ferrara is famed as a *città della bicicletta*. Seemingly everyone in the city, from young to old, makes the majority of the journeys on two wheels. Outside of the centre, the roads are bordered by cycle lanes. No such concessions are required in the traffic-free centre, although the largely cobbled streets do pose their own set of cycling difficulties. You can **rent bicycles** at the station (to the left as you come out) from Pirani e Bagni ☎0532.772.190 or inside the city walls from Barlati Andre at Via degli Adelardi 1/3a, just by the Duomo (☎0532.206.863) for around €3 per hour. The tourist office can provide details of cycle routes both within the city and out into the Po Delta Park.

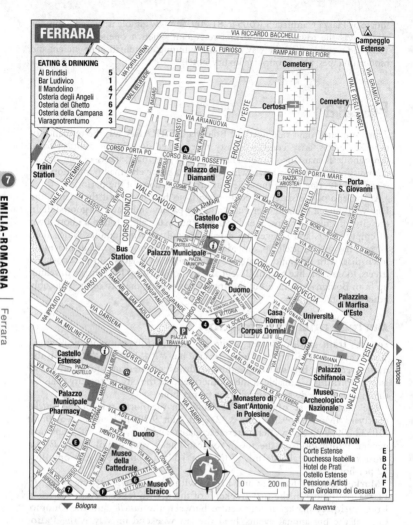

smaller than the famous Siena race, but still an exciting time to be here (Ⓦwww.paliodiferrara.it). In August, the streets of the town ring to the annual **buskers' festival** (Ⓦwww.ferrarabuskers.com), with musical offerings ranging from African drums to Dixieland bands, while the following month the skies are filled with giant blobs of colour as the **Ferrara Balloon Festival** (Ⓦwww.ferrarafestival.it), one of the largest in Europe, gets under way.

Accommodation

Ferrara has a number of affordable **hotels**, most of them handily placed in the centre, though booking is advised during the spring and autumn trade-fair season.

Hotels

Pensione Artisti Via Vittoria 66 ☎0532.761.038. Friendly, budget option in a modern block in the medieval quarter. Rooms available with or without bathrooms. ❶

Corte Estense Via Correggiari 4/A ☎0532.242.176, Ⓦwww.corteestense.it. This grand option with its elegant courtyard and spacious rooms is centrally located, close to the Duomo. ❹

🏃 **Duchessa Isabella** Via Palestro 70 ☎0532.202.121, Ⓦwww.duchessaisabella .it. This Relais & Chateaux affiliated sixteenth-century building filled with bright frescoes is the top choice for five-star luxury. The rooms come equipped with antique furniture, giant plasma screen TVs and wi-fi access. Closed Aug. ❻

Hotel de Prati Via Padiglioni 5 ☎0532.241.905, Ⓦwww.hoteldeprati.com. Close by the *castello*, this central option is draped with modern paintings and offers comfortable rooms with antique furniture and wi-fi access. ❸

San Girolamo dei Gesuati Via Madama 40/A ☎0532.207.448, Ⓦwww.sangirolamodeigesuati .com. Quiet, friendly and good-value hotel overlooking a green courtyard near the Palazzo Schifanoia with a very good restaurant. ❹

Hostel and campsite

Ostello Estense Corso Biagio Rossetti 24 ☎0532.204.227, Ⓦwww.ostelloestense.com. HI hostel situated northwest of the centre with huge, spotlessly clean rooms with grand wooden beams; reception closed 10am–3.30pm; curfew 11.30pm; dorm beds €15.

Campeggio Comunale Estense Via Gramicia 76 ☎0532.752.396, Ⓔcampeggio.estense@libero .it. Campsite on the on the northeast edge of town. Take bus #1 or #5 from the train station to Piazzale San Giovanni by the walls, from where it's a 10min walk north; open all year; €5 per person.

The Town

Ferrara's main sights are clustered together in an area that's easily explored on foot. The castle is the main focus of interest, but several other palaces and museums offer reminders of the town's more glorious past.

The Castello Estense

The bulky, moated **Castello Estense** (Tues–Sun 9.30am–5.30pm, last entry 4.30pm; Ⓦwww.castelloestense.it; €7) dominates the centre of Ferrara, built in response to a late-fourteenth-century uprising and generally held at the time to be a major feat of military engineering. Behind its impenetrable brick walls, the Este court thrived, supporting artists like Pisanello, Jacopo Bellini, Mantegna, and the poets Ariosto and Tasso. It's hard to credit all this as you walk through the castle now, most of which is used as offices and inaccessible to the public. The few rooms that you can see go some way to bringing back the days of Este magnificence, especially the *saletta* and Salone dei Giochi, or games rooms, decorated by Sebastiano Filippi with vigorous scenes of wrestling, discus-throwing, ball-tossing and chariot-racing. There's also the less-innocent poison room which was apparently mainly used as a toxic pharmacy for the Este's political enemies.

Piazza Municipio and the Duomo

Just south of here, the crenellated **Palazzo Municipale**, built in 1243 but much altered and restored since, holds statues of Nicolò III and son, Borso, on its facade – though they're actually twentieth-century reproductions. Walk through the arch into the pretty, enclosed square of **Piazza Municipio** for a view of the rest of the building. Opposite the Palazzo Municipio, the **Duomo** is a mixture of Romanesque and Gothic styles and has a monumental facade, focused on a carved central portal that was begun in the mid-twelfth century and finished a century or so later. Much of the carving depicts the Last Judgement. Inside, the main part of the church has the grandeur of a ballroom,

▲ Castello Estense, Ferrara

with sparkling chandeliers, but is much less intriguing than the exterior, and it's in the **Museo della Cattedrale**, housed in the former church of San Romano across the square (Tues–Sun 9.30am–noon & 3–6pm; €5), that the real treasures are kept. The highlight of the collection is a set of bas-reliefs illustrating the labours of the months, which formerly adorned the outside of the cathedral, and a beautiful *Madonna* by della Quercia.

The medieval quarter

The long arcaded south side of the Duomo flanks **Piazza Trento e Trieste**, whose rickety-looking rows of shops herald the arcades of the appealing **Via San Romano** that runs off the far side of the square past the museum. Beyond this lies the labyrinth of alleyways that make up Ferrara's medieval quarter; the arched **Via delle Volte**, a long street running east, parallel to Via Carlo Mayr, is one of the most characteristic. At Via Mazzini 95 a couple of **synagogues** and the **Museo Ebraico di Ferrara**, the town's small **Jewish** museum (visits by guided tour only Sun–Thurs 10am, 11am & noon; Ⓦwww.commune.fe.it /museoebraico; €4) preserve the memory of the town's small Jewish community. On the wider streets above the tangled medieval district are a number of the Renaissance palaces, most of them closed to the public. The **Casa Romei**, at Via Savonarola 30 (Tues–Sun 8.30am–7.30pm; €3), is a typical building of the time, with frescoes and graceful courtyards alongside artefacts rescued from various local churches. Just beyond is the house, at no. 19, where the monk Savonarola was born and lived for twenty years, while behind the palace, the monastery church of **Corpus Domini** at Via Pergolato 4 (Mon–Fri 9.30–11.30am & 3.30–5.30pm; free but contributions accepted) holds the tombs of Alfonso I and II d'Este and **Lucrezia Borgia**.

The southeast town centre

Two minutes southeast of Corpus Domini, the **Palazzo Schifanoia** – the "Palace of Joy" – at Via Scandiana 23 (Tues–Sun 9am–6pm; €5) is one of the grandest of Ferrara's palaces. It belonged to the Este family, and Cosimo Tura's frescoes inside transplanted their court to Arcadia. In the Salone dei Mesi (the "room of the months"), the blinds are kept closed to protect the colours, and the room seems silent and empty compared with what's happening on the walls, where three bands of frescoes depict Borso Este surrounded by friends and hunting dogs, along with groups of musicians, weavers and embroiderers with white rabbits nibbling the grass at their feet. Above, each section is topped with a sign of the zodiac and, above that, various mythological scenes.

On nearby Corso della Giovecca, at no. 170, the **Palazzina di Marfisa d'Este** (Tues–Sun 9am–1pm & 3–6pm; €3) has more frescoes, this time by Filippi, and although its gloomy interior is less impressive than the Schifanoia complex, in summer the loggia and orange grove are a welcome refuge from the heat. In the other direction, to the south, the **Museo Archeologico Nazionale**, Via XX Settembre 124 (Tues–Sun 9am–2pm; €4), holds the city's well-organized archeological collections, with finds from Spina, the Greco–Etruscan seaport and trading colony near Comacchio.

Down in the southeast corner of the town is a gem of a place: the **Monastero di Sant'Antonio in Polesine**, with exquisite frescoes (Mon–Fri 9.30–11.30am & 3–5pm, Sat 9.30–11.15am & 3–4pm; donations expected). Knock at the door of the convent and the nuns shepherd you into a chapel covered with works by the school of Giotto, including a rare *Flight from Egypt* in which Joseph carries Jesus on his shoulders.

North of the castle

There are some more impressive palaces north of the *castello*, on and around **Corso Ercole I d'Este** – named after Ercole I, who succeeded to the throne in 1441 after his father Nicolò III died, probably poisoned, and who promptly disposed of anyone likely to pose a threat. His reputation for coldness earned him nicknames such as "North Wind" and "Diamond" and his huge ambition led him to order the extension of the northern quarter of the city, the so-called "Herculean Addition", on such a grand scale that Ferrara was doubled, incorporating a planning system that was considered at the time to be boldly avant-garde. The **Palazzo dei Diamanti**, a little way down the Corso on the left, named after the 8500 pink-and-white marble ashlars in the form of pyramids (or diamonds) that stud its facade, was at the heart of Ercole's town plan and is nowadays used for temporary modern art exhibitions as well as being home to the recommended **Pinacoteca Nazionale** (Tues, Wed, Fri, Sat 9am–2pm, Thurs 9am–7pm, Sun 9am–1pm; €4), holding works from the Ferrara and Bologna schools, notably paintings by Dossi, Garofalo and Guercino, and a spirited St Christopher by "Il Bastianino" (Sebastiano Filippi).

Eating and drinking

Ferrara has a good range of **restaurants** and trattorias with prices to suit most pockets, plus a few bars in which to while away the evening with the locals. For self caterers, try *Antica Salumeria Marchetti*, a great traditional delicatessen on Via Cortevecchia 35, just south of the Palazzo Municipale, which does a particularly fine line in salamis.

Al Brindisi Via degli Adelardi 11. This unprepossessing exterior conceals Ferrara's oldest *osteria*, once frequented by the likes of Cellini and Titian. The food is reasonable and reasonably priced, with tourist menus for €13, €18 and €25, but some of the vintages in the magnificent wine collection are among Italy's finest and priced accordingly. Closed Mon.

Anima Latina Via Ragno 35 ℡0532.760.534. Down a narrow backstreet, this convivial, gay-friendly bar is a popular pre/post film stopoff for people heading to the nearby Apollo cinema, with a good selection of wines, cocktails and board games to while away the time till the main feature starts.

Bar Ludivico Piazza Ariostea 7. Welcoming café-bar set under arcades overlooking a pretty, grass-filled piazza and seemingly always filled with gossiping locals. Great inventive salads and jumbo panini take their place alongside a large drinks menu.

Il Mandolino Via del Volte ☎0532.760.080. A homey little trattoria down a narrow, atmospheric back alley (look for the flower boxes outside), offering a great range of intensely flavoured rustic dishes including a mouth-watering (and when you think about it, eye-watering) *agnello o castrato* (€8). Closed Mon eve & Tues.

Osteria degli Angeli Via delle Volte 4. A convivial place, with lots of different wines and a changing daily menu of good food. Moderately priced with *primi* €7–8, *secondi* €10–14. Open 7–10pm. Closed lunch.

Osteria della Campana Via Borgo dei Leoni 26 ☎0532.241.256. Romantic but rather pricey *osteria* down a narrow alleyway just north of the *castello*. Goose sausages with raspberries and cheese and truffle flavoured *rigatoni* are just two choices from an interesting menu. Closed Mon.

Osteria del Ghetto Via della Vittoria 26 ☎0532.764.936. On a Ghetto backstreet, set – rather incongruously – next to a modern yoga centre, this serves up a winning combination of tasty regional specialities – such as shoulder of lamb cooked in dark beer and chestnut honey (€16) – and live jazz on Fri from 9pm and on Sun lunchtimes. Closed Tues & Wed.

Ristorante Tassi Viale Repubblica 23, Bondeno ☎0532.893.030. Some 20km west of Ferrara – accessible by the "Bondeno" bus from the bus station – this place is a food lover's heaven. There's no menu; you just let Signor Tassi lead you through an amazing succession of fine dishes. It's not cheap (€30 per head without drinks) but it is unforgettable, and if you're wise, you'll book one of the comfortable large rooms upstairs (❷) so you don't have too far to stagger to bed.

The Po Delta

East of Ferrara lies the **Po Delta**, an expanse of marshland and lagoons where the River Po splits into several channels, trickling to the sea, and small fingers of land poke out into the Adriatic. Etruscan traders set up the port of Spina here between the fourth and third centuries BC, when the sea covered much of the land from Comacchio to Ravenna. Partly owing to drainage schemes, the briny waters have since retreated by 12km, and the area becomes a bit less marshy each year – an advantage for local farmers but a threat to the many varieties of sea and shore **birds** that inhabit the area. The two main lagoons of **Valli di Comacchio** and **Valle Bertuzzi** together form a major part of the Parco del Delta del Po (Ⓦwww.parcodeltapo.it), which with the surrounding wetlands now constitute one of Europe's most highly regarded birdwatching areas, providing a habitat for nesting and migrating birds, including herons, egrets, curlews, avocets and terns.

The most evocative way of seeing the delta is by **boat**. Every spring free birdwatching trips are organized by the tourist office in Comacchio as part of the annual International Po Delta Birdwatching Fair (Ⓦwww.podeltabirdfair.it). And between April and October voluntary groups run free boat tours on a typical marshland boat called a *batane* from its mooring at the fish market of Trepponti in Comacchio – call ☎0523.312.516 or 0523.312.892 for more information. Two-hour boat trips also set off from the harbour of Stazione Foce, south of Comacchio (daily April–Oct at 9am, 11am, 3pm & 5pm; ☎0348.471.0332, Ⓦwww.vallidicomacchio.it/indexe.htm; €10, accessible by car only; follow signs for "Museo delle Valli". More information is available at the tourist office in Comacchio (see opposite).

Comacchio

The region's main centre, **COMACCHIO** is a small fishing town intersected by a network of canals, with a famous local attraction in its triple-bridge or

Trepponti, built in 1634, which crosses three of the canals. Comacchio is an eel port and a good time to visit is in October when the Festival of the Eel sees wriggling masses of the creatures fished out of the canals on their way to the Sargasso Sea. Eel (*anguille*) unsurprisingly takes centre stage in many local restaurants with other regional dishes like fish risotto and *fritto misto* particularly recommended. Call in at the **tourist office** at Piazza Folegatti 28 (June–Oct Mon–Sat 9.30am–12.30pm & 4–7pm, Sun 10am–12.30pm & 4–6.30pm; ℡0533.310.111, ⑩www.comune.comacchio.fe.it) for more information.

Ravenna and around

The main reason to visit **RAVENNA**, a few kilometres inland of the Adriatic coast, is simple – it holds a set of **mosaics** generally acknowledged to be the crowning achievement of Byzantine art. No fewer than eight of Ravenna's buildings have been designated World Heritage sites by Unesco. They date from a strange interlude in the city's history during the late Roman-early Byzantine period when this otherwise unremarkable provincial centre briefly became one of the most important cities in all of Europe (see below).

Compared to places such as Florence or Venice, tourism seems almost incidental to the life of the town and for a city that has such historic monuments, the centre feels surprisingly modern – a combination of Mussolini's building programme and Allied bombing that levelled much of the city during World War II. It's a pleasant enough place to spend a couple of days and, though it has some excellent bars and restaurants, it's the churches and mosaics that will monopolize your time. Nightlife is sparse, but a number of small **coastal resorts**, known as the lido towns, a dozen or so kilometres away provide some excitement in summer. And if you're looking for a few thrills and spills, the nearby **Mirabilandia**, (℡0544.651.156, ⑩www.mirabilandia.it) a Disneyesque theme park, helps bring in the crowds during summer. You can see the park's big wheel rising above the surrounding flat countryside as you approach the city.

Some history

When Ravenna became capital of the **Western Roman Empire** sixteen hundred years ago, it was more by quirk of fate than design. The Emperor Honorius, alarmed by armies invading from the north, moved his court from Milan to this obscure town on the Romagna coast around 402; it was easy to defend, surrounded by marshland, and was situated close to the port of Classis – at the time the biggest Roman naval base on the Adriatic. After enjoying a period of great monumental adornment as chief city of the empire, Ravenna was conquered by the Goths in 476. However, the new conquerors were also Christians and continued to embellish the city lavishly, particularly the Ostrogoth Theodoric, making it one of the most sought-after towns in the Mediterranean. In the mid-sixth century Byzantine forces annexed the city to the Eastern Empire and made it into an exarchate (province), under the rule of Constantinople. The Byzantine rulers were responsible for Ravenna's most glorious era, keen to outdo rival cities with magnificent palaces, churches and art. By the end of the eighth century, however, the glory years had passed. The city was captured by the Lombards, after which the Adriatic shoreline receded – an eleven-kilometre-long canal now links Ravenna's port to the sea. Ravenna sank slowly back into obscurity, a fate which has helped preserve its artistic treasures.

Arrival and information

From the **train station** on Piazza Farini in the east of town, it's only a five-minute walk along Viale Farini and Via Armando Diaz to Ravenna's central square, **Piazza del Popolo**, which with the adjoining streets makes up the compact old centre. The **bus station** is across the tracks behind the train station, in Piazzale Aldo Moro. **Parking** is available – for around €1 per hour – on various squares around the centre, including Piazza Barracca and Piazza Mameli.

Ravenna is not simply best explored on foot; with much of the centre pedestrianized, there's a good deal that can only be explored that way unless you opt for two wheels. **Bikes** can be rented from the Coopertiva San Vitale (Mon–Sat 7am–8pm; ☏0544.370.31), the green building next to the train station, for €1 per hour or €7.75 per day; it also gives out maps and holds left luggage. The helpful **tourist office** is at Via Salara 8 (Mon–Sat 8.30am–6/7pm, Sun 10am–4pm; ☏0544.35.404, ⓦ www.turismo.ravenna.it). You can go **online** at the *Rock Café*, Via Castel San Pietro 9 – the road after Via Mazzini. There's a branch of the Banco di Romagna with an **ATM** on the Piazza del Popolo.

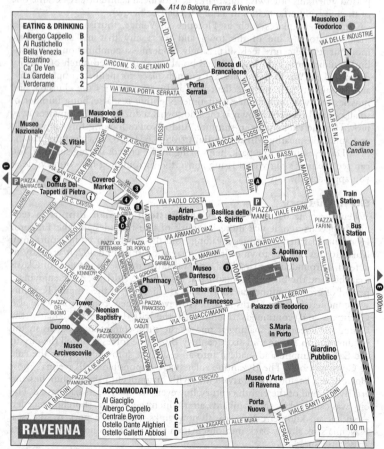

▲ A14 to Bologna, Ferrara & Venice

EATING & DRINKING

Albergo Cappello	B
Al Rustichello	1
Bella Venezia	5
Bizantino	4
Ca' De Ven	6
La Gardela	3
Verderame	2

ACCOMMODATION

Al Giaciglio	A
Albergo Cappello	B
Centrale Byron	C
Ostello Dante Alighieri	E
Ostello Galletti Abbiosi	D

RAVENNA

0   100 m

S. Apollinare in Classe & Cesena ▼

Accommodation

There isn't a great deal of affordable **accommodation** in Ravenna, but there are some decent hotels, most located just a stone's throw from the main Byzantine sites and eating options.

Hotels

Al Giaciglio Via Rocca Brancaleone 42 ☎0544.39.403, ⓦwww.albergoalgiaciglio.com. One of Ravenna's most reasonably priced hotels is this small, basic but friendly place near the station. Rooms come with or without bathrooms, but all have TVs, and there's also a decent restaurant. ❷

Cappello Via IV Novembre 41 ☎0544 219.813, ⓦwww.albergocappello.it. Old *palazzo* that's been turned into an extremely stylish small hotel with just seven chic rooms and an excellent restaurant. ❺

Centrale Byron Via IV Novembre 14 ☎0544.212.225, ⓦwww.hotelbyron.com. Comfortable place, right in the historic centre, with satellite TV in the well-appointed rooms and a/c in summer. Good value. ❸

Ostello Galletti Abbiosi Via di Roma 140 ☎0544.215.127, ⓦwww.galletti.ra.it. Stylish hotel with comfortable a/c singles and doubles. Some of the large rooms have fine painted ceilings and attractive marble floors. ❸

Hostels and campsite

Youth Hostel Dante Via Nicolodi 12 ☎0544.421.164, ⓦwww.hostelravenna.com. HI hostel, located east of the station handily opposite a large Co-op supermarket. You can get there on bus #1 and #70 or from outside the train station, or it's a 10min walk – south out of the station, east under the tracks, follow Via Candiano and then head southeast down Via T. Gulli. Lockout between 10am & 5pm; 11.30pm curfew, or you can pay €1 for your own key; €16

Camping Adriano Via dei Campeggi 7 ☎0544.437.230 ⓦwww.campingadriano.com. Campsite in the nearby coastal resort of Punta Marina Terme 8km away. To get there take bus #1 or #70 that leaves from Piazzale Farini in front of the train station.

The City

The centre of Ravenna is the **Piazza del Popolo**, an elegant open space, arcaded on two sides, that was laid out by the Venetians in the fifteenth century and is now bordered by cafés. A few blocks south of the square, across Piazza Garibaldi on Via Alighieri, the **Tomba di Dante** is a site of local pride, a small Neoclassical building which was put up in the eighteenth century to enclose the tomb of Dante. The poet had been chased out of Florence by the time he arrived in Ravenna, and he was sheltered here by the Da Polenta family – then in control of the city – while he finished his *Divine Comedy*. He died in 1321 and was laid to rest in the adjoining church of **San Francesco**, a much-restored building, elements of which date from the fourth century. File down the stairs towards the tenth-century waterlogged crypt complete with the surreal touch of swimming goldfish and remnants of a mosaic floor. The **Museo Dantesco**, situated in San Francesco's cloister on Via Alighieri is currently closed for restoration.

Ravenna's museums

Ravenna has three **museum cards**: the Ravenna Visit Card covers the basilicas of San Vitale and Sant'Apollinare Nuovo, the Neonian Baptistry, the Mausoleo di Galla Placidia and the Museo Arcivescovile – all the church-controlled sites. The card is valid for seven days, costs €8.50 (though from March to mid-June the Mausoleo costs an extra €2) and can be purchased from any participating site. For the state sites you can get a joint ticket for the Museo Nazionale and the Mausoleo di Teodorico (€6), or one that covers these two and also the Basilica di Sant'Apollinare in Classe (€8); these can be purchased at the sites.

A couple of minutes' walk west of here, a group of buildings around **Piazza del Duomo** shelters the **Duomo** itself, with its cylindrical – and slightly tipsy – tower. Originally a fifth-century building, it was completely destroyed by an earthquake in 1733 and rebuilt in unexceptional style soon after. More interesting is the **Museo Arcivescovile** in the Bishop's Palace behind, with fragments of mosaics from around the city and the palace's sixth-century Oratorio Sant'Andrea, which is adorned with mosaics of birds in a meadow above a Christ dressed in the armour, cloak and gilded leather skirt of a Roman centurion (daily: April–Sept 9am–7pm; March & Oct 9.30am–5.30pm; Nov–Feb 9.30am–4.30pm; see box, p.429 for admission details).

The **Neonian Baptistry**, on the same side of the Duomo, by the bell tower (daily: April–Sept 9am–7pm; March & Oct 9.30am–5.30pm; Nov–Feb 9.30am–4.30pm; see box, p.429 for admission) is a conversion from a Roman bathhouse. The original floor level has sunk into the marshy ground, and the remains of the previous building are now three metres below. The choice of building was a logical one as baptisms involved total immersion in those days.

Via di Roma, lined with bland, official-looking palaces, cuts right through the modern centre of Ravenna and sees much of its traffic. Halfway up on the right stands the Basilica di **Sant'Apollinare Nuovo** (daily: April–Sept 9am–7pm; Oct–March 9am–noon & 2–5pm; see box, p.429 for admission) – called Nuovo to distinguish it from the church of the same name at Classe (see p.432). Built by Theodoric in the sixth century, it contains some of Ravenna's most impressive mosaics, running the length of both sides of the nave. Each shows a line of martyrs – one side male, the other female – processing through avenues of date palms and bearing gifts for Christ and the Virgin enthroned. As a Goth, Theodoric belonged to the Arian branch of Christianity that didn't accept the absolute divinity of Christ, a heresy stamped out by Constantinople as much for political as theological reasons. When the Byzantines came along, they removed many of the mosaic figures that had been placed here under Theodoric's reign. When Theodoric built the church in the early 500s, he dedicated it to Jesus, but when the Byzantines took over it was rededicated to St Martin, who was known for his anti-heretic campaigns and is shown at the head of the line of male devotees. Still later, in the ninth century, it was rededicated yet again to the present eponymous saint.

Five-minutes' walk away up Via di Roma, next door to the Basilica dello Santo Spirito, is the **Arian Baptistry** (daily 8.30am–7.30pm; free), also built by Theodoric, with a fine mosaic ceiling showing the twelve Apostles and the baptism of Christ.

San Vitale and the Mausoleo di Galla Placidia

In terms of monuments, Ravenna's biggest draw is the area ten-minutes' walk northwest of the city centre, around the Basilica di San Vitale, which holds the finest of the mosaics and is now gathered together into one big complex, including the mausoleum of Galla Placidia and the National Museum.

San Vitale (daily: April–Sept 9.30am–6.30pm; March & Oct 9.30am–5.30pm; Nov–Feb 9.30am–4.30pm; see box, p.429 for admission), which was begun in 525 under the Roman Emperor Theodoric and finished in 548 under the Byzantine ruler Justinian, remains unique for an Italian building. Created to an Eastern-inspired arrangement of void and solid and dark and light, the design was the basis for the great church of Aghia Sofia in Istanbul, built fifteen years later.

There were definite rules about who appeared where in **mosaics** – the higher up and further to the east, the more important or holy the subject. The series in the basilica starts with Old Testament scenes spread across the semi circular lunettes of the choir; the triumphal arch shows Christ, the Apostles and sons of St Vitalis. Further in, on the semi-dome of the apse, a beardless Christ stands between two angels, presenting a model of the church to St Vitalis and Bishop Ecclesius. Of the mosaics on the side walls of the apse, the two processional panels are the best surviving portraits of the Emperor Justinian and his wife Theodora – he's on the left and she's on the right – and a rich example of Byzantine mosaic technique. The small glass *tesserae* are laid in sections, alternate rows set at slightly different angles to vary the reflection of light and give an impression of depth. Colour is used emblematically, too, with gold backgrounds denoting either holiness or high status.

Theodora looks a harsh figure under her finery, and she certainly had a reputation for calculated cruelty, arranging "disappearances" of anyone who went against her. According to the sixth-century chronicler Procopius, in his *Secret History* of the court, her rise to power was meteoric. When young she made a living as a child prostitute and circus performer with her two sisters, and later became a courtesan and an actress in bizarre sex shows. She travelled the Middle East, and when she returned brought herself to the attention of the emperor, Justinian. To the horror of the court, he rejected the well brought-up daughters of his Roman peers and lived with Theodora, giving her the rank of patrician. He was unable to marry her until his mother, the empress, was dead and the law changed; the two then embarked on a reign of staggering corruption and legalized looting.

Across the grass from the basilica is the tiny **Mausoleo di Galla Placidia** (daily: April–Sept 9.30am–6.30pm; March & Oct 9.30am–5.30pm; Nov–Feb 9.30am–4.30pm; see box, p.429 for admission) named after the half-sister of Honorius. The emperor's frequent absences left Galla in charge of the city and she was responsible for much of the grandeur of Ravenna's early days. Despite the name and the three sarcophagi inside, it's unlikely that the building ever held her bones. Galla Placidia was taken hostage when the Goths sacked Rome, and caused a scandal by marrying one of her kidnappers, Ataulf. She went into battle with him as his army forged south, and later they reigned jointly over the Gothic kingdom. When Ataulf was assassinated the Romans took her back for a ransom of corn, after which she was obliged to marry a Roman general, Constantius. Their son formally became the Emperor Valentinian III at the age of 6, and as his regent, Galla Placidia assumed control of the Western Empire.

Inside the *mausoleo*, filtered through thin alabaster windows, the light falls on mosaics that glow with a deep blue lustre, most in an earlier style than those of San Vitale, full of Roman and naturalistic motifs.

The Museo Nazionale and around

Adjacent to San Vitale on the southern side, housed in the former cloisters of the church, the **Museo Nazionale** (Tues–Sun 8.30am–7.30pm; €4) contains various items from this and later periods – fifteenth-century icons, early Byzantine glass and embroidery from Florence. Among the most eye-catching exhibits is a sixth-century statue of Hercules capturing a stag, possibly a copy of a Greek original. Just a couple of hundred metres south of San Vitale, and accessed through the small charge of Santa Eufemia, is one of the city's more recently discovered Byzantine treasures. Uncovered in the early 1990s, the **Domus dei Tappeti di Pietra** (March–Oct Mon–Fri & Sun 10am–6.30pm, Sat 10am–4.30pm; Nov–Feb Mon–Fri & Sun 10am–5.30pm, Sat 10am–4.30pm; €3.50, which translates as the "House of Stone Carpets" is the remains of a palace from the late Roman-early Byzantine period. It comprises 14 rooms, each adorned with intricately crafted floor and wall mosaics, the most striking of which shows figures representing the four seasons dancing hand in hand while another figure provides a musical accompaniment on a pan-flute.

The Mausoleo di Teodorico

Still within Ravenna, but a bit of a hike north of the train station, lies one more early sixth-century monument that's worth visiting: the **Mausoleo di Teodorico** (daily 8.30am–6.30pm; €3). This ten-sided curiosity is unique in Western architecture owing much to Syrian models of its day, and constructed of Istrian limestone. The 300-tonne cupola is a single, if cracked, chunk and no one knows exactly how it was manoeuvred into place. Inside the decagonal second storey sits an ancient porphyry bathtub, pressed into use as the royal sarcophagus.

Eating, drinking and entertainment

Central Ravenna is not exactly filled with **places to eat**, and you need to know where to go to avoid fruitless wandering. The covered market on Piazza A. Costa is open from 7am to 1.30pm and is a good source of picnic supplies.

The **Ravenna Festival** in June and July attracts big names in the classical music world (Ⓦ www.ravennafestival.org) with most performances taking place at the Teatro Dante Alighieri on Via Mariani, and the **Jazz Festival** in July and August also draws international stars.

Albergo Cappello Refined, slightly pricey, central spot offering excellent daily pasta specials, such as tagliatelle with clams and artichokes (€11), some rather unusual main courses (angler fish with bacon and asparagus (€18), plus a mouthwatering selection of appetizers at the bar. Closed Sun & Mon lunchtime.

Al Rustichello Via Maggiore 21/23 ℡0544.36.043. Consistently popular and inexpensive place where the excitable owner tells you the menu (in English too) with food that an Italian grandmother would be proud of – the *cappelletti* with asparagus is recommended. Booking advised.

Bella Venezia Via IV Novembre 16 ℡0544.212.746. Currently the city's top choice, the *Venezia* offers simple meals, expertly prepared – handmade pumpkin *cappelletti* (€10), *asparagi alla Bismarck* (asparagus topped with parmesan and an egg) etc. Eat formally inside amid the starched table cloths or informally outside watching the city pass by. Excellent service.

Bizantino Piazza A. Costa. Self-service (or 'free-flow') place, just inside the market, with excellent- value (lunch only) hot and cold dishes including some vegetarian options. Pick up three courses here for under €10.

Ca' De Ven Via C. Ricci 24. Stunning wood-panelled enoteca with painted ceilings and wine racks seemingly covering every other available space. It offers a simple changing menu of a few pizza and pasta dishes and a huge range of vintages to sample by the glass from €1 upwards. Closed Mon.

La Gardela Via Ponte Marino 3. Central place across from the Torre Civica (Ravenna's own leaning tower) with a varied menu of fish dishes and home-made pasta, all at moderate prices – *primi* €5–6, *secondi* €6.50–15. Closed Thurs.

Verderame Via Cavour 82. Behind the elegant filigree door lies a cool, dark, welcoming café. Great selection of coffees and a fine *cioccolata in tazza*. The perfect spot to rest up after a hard morning's sightseeing.

Sant'Apollinare in Classe and Ravenna's seaside resorts

About 6km south of Ravenna by train or buses #4 and #44 from the station, the remains of the old port of Classe (daily 9am–dusk; €2) are very thin indeed – the buildings have been looted for stone and the ancient harbour has now completely disappeared under the silt of the River Uniti. One building, however, does survive – the church of **Sant'Apollinare in Classe** on Via Romea Sud

(Mon–Sat 8.30am–7.30pm, Sun 1–7.30pm; €2), spared because it was the burial place of Ravenna's patron saint. It's a typical basilical church with more fine mosaics including a marvellous allegorical depiction of the Transfiguration in the apse, with Christ represented by a large cross in a star-spangled universe.

There's easy access by bus through Ravenna's heavy industry belt to the nine lido towns nearby totalling 35 kilometres of coast. **Marina di Ravenna** and **Punta Marina** are both crowded, lively places; or for something quieter head north to the beaches at **Porto Corsini**, **Casalborsetti** and **Marina Romea**. Just before Porto Corsini, you pass the **Capanno Garibaldi**, a reconstruction of the hut in which Garibaldi hid on his epic 800-kilometre march from Rome after the fall of the short-lived Roman republic in 1849. Garibaldi's life-long partner Anita, who often fought alongside him, died on the way and he was unable to stop for long enough to bury her.

Rimini

RIMINI, long the archetypal seaside resort, has been undergoing something of a makeover of late. This has been by no means comprehensive. It still makes its primary living as a traditional family resort, to which some Italians return year after year, to stay in their customary *pensione*. But there is also a newer, more upmarket side to Rimini, as represented by boutique hotels, high-end restaurants and chi-chi clubs. There's a less savoury side to the town, too. Rimini is known across Italy for its fast-living and chancy nightlife, and there's a thriving hetero- and transsexual prostitution scene alongside the town's more wholesome attractions.

Given Rimini was almost entirely destroyed in the last war, it's surprising to find that the town has a much-ignored **old centre** that is worth at least a morning of your time. But it's the beach, the crowds and the wild nights that you really come for: Rimini is still the country's best place to party.

The resort is best avoided in August, unless you have a penchant for teeming crowds. Out of season, however, it's a pleasant enough town, though bear in mind that many hotels, restaurants and shops are closed and the atmosphere along the seafront is almost eerily quiet.

Arrival, information and transport

Rimini's **train** and **bus station** is situated in the centre of town, on Piazzale Cesare Battisti, ten-minutes' walk from both the sea and the old centre. From Federico Fellini Airport (℡0541.715711, Ⓦwww.riminiairport.com), 8km south of Rimini, bus #9 goes to the train station every thirty minutes; tickets cost €1, and can be bought at the airport bar and kiosks. A taxi costs around €17. There are several places to turn for more information on Rimini including a helpful **tourist office** right outside the train station to the left (March–Oct Mon–Sat 8.30am–7pm, Sun 9.30am–12.30pm; Nov–Feb Mon–Sat 10am–4pm; ℡0541.51.331). The main tourist office is at Piazza Federico Fellini 3, just back from the seafront (April–Sept Mon–Sat 8.30am–7pm, Sun 9.30am–12.30pm; Oct–March Mon–Sat 9.30am–12.30pm & 3.30–6.30pm; ℡0541.438.211, Ⓦwww.riminiturismo.it).

Getting around is best done on foot, at least within the town centre. But if you need to use the buses, buy an orange ticket from a tobacconist or news-stand; it gives 24 hours' unlimited travel in Rimini and the surrounding area (including Santarcángelo, Riccione and Bellaria) for €3. There are also a couple of nightbus services (see "Nightlife", p.437). Alternatively, you could

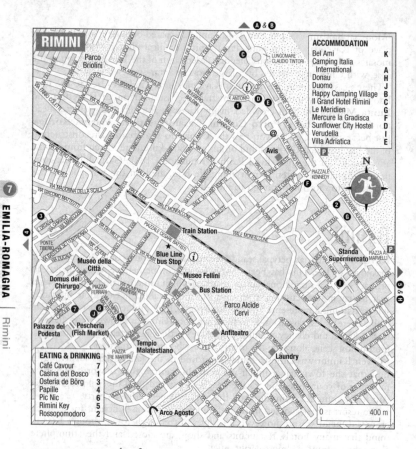

RIMINI

ACCOMMODATION
Bel Ami	K
Camping Italia International	A
Donau	H
Duomo	J
Happy Camping Village	B
Il Grand Hotel Rimini	C
Le Meridien	G
Mercure la Gradisca	F
Sunflower City Hostel	D
Verudella	I
Villa Adriatica	E

EATING & DRINKING
Café Cavour	7
Casina del Bosco	1
Osteria de Börg	3
Papille	4
Pic Nic	6
Rimini Key	5
Rossopomodoro	2

rent your own mode of transport – anything from a **bike** (€4 a day) to a quad bike (€40 a day) – from Tiraferri Aurelio on Piazzale Kennedy (℡0541.391.072). There are banks with **ATMs** right along Via Amerigo Vespucci and in the Old Town.

Accommodation

Despite its 1300 hotels, finding **accommodation** can be a problem in Rimini, and in summer especially you may have to take the expensive option of full board. Out of season those few hotels that do remain open will be mainly geared to business travellers or school groups. You can book accommodation through the tourist office or the town's hotel booking office, Rimini Reservation (June to early Sept daily 8.15am–2pm & 2.15–7.45pm; ℡0541.390.530, ℮riminibooking@iper.net) next to the tourist office by the train station.

Hotels

Bel Ami Via Metastasio 4 ℡0541.381.643. Located in a peaceful, shady side street, three blocks south of Piazzale B. Croce, this place has rather simple but comfortable rooms. ❷

Donau Viale Alfieri 12 ℡0541.381.302, ⓦ www .hoteldonau.it. On a leafy side street between Piazzale Tripoli and Piazzale B. Croce this is a welcoming, if rather basic (for the price) option. It is, however, open all year round. ❸

Duomo Via G. Bruno ☎0541242.15, ⓦwww.Duomohotel.com. A very 'new Rimini' sort of hotel – this is terribly swanky and almost self-consciously modern. The reception desk is a giant neon-adorned metal tube, the bedrooms are stark and space age (and extremely well-equipped), while the bedrooms are huge. Great breakfasts and very friendly staff. ⑧

Il Grand Hotel Rimini Parco Federico Fellini ☎0541.560.000, ⓦwww.grandhotelrimini.com. A superior slice of Fellini-esque swank at this historical hotel, right by the sea, in elegant grounds, where the rooms are decorated with Venetian and French antiques. ⑨

Le Meridien Lungomare Murri 13 ☎0541.396.600, ⓦwww.starwoodhotels.com. This recent addition to the seafront hotel scene was designed by Paolo Portoghesi and boasts every facility imaginable, including a spa, a swimming pool, a good seafood restaurant and a beach club. Rooms are either large, bright and sea-facing or rather small and dingy. Check first. ⑥

Mercure la Gradisca Viale Fiume 1 ☎0541.25.200, ⓦwww.mercure.com. Located down the main thoroughfare towards the south lies this luxurious four-star, where the decor inside and out is like the over-the-top set of a Fellini film. ⑦

Verudella Viale Tripoli 238 ☎0541.391.124, ⓔhotelverudella@libero.it. A few blocks south from the *Gradisca* this is one of the best of Rimini's affordable options. It's attractively smart and run by a friendly brother-and-sister management. Open all year round. ②

Villa Adriatica Viale Vespucci 3 ☎0541.54.599, ⓦwww.villaadriatica.it. Part of the Ambient hotel group, this is a very stylish choice close to the beach with a swimming pool. The best rooms come with wooden floors, large beds and a/c. ④

Hostels and campsites

Sunflower City Hostel on Viale Dardanelli 102 ☎0541.251.180, ⓦwww.sunflowerhotel.com. Non-HI hostel open year round and offering clean dorms, lockers, bike rental and free wi-fi access. It also operates a smaller beachside branch open from March to Oct only. €15

Camping Italia International Via Toscanelli 112 ☎0541.732.882, ⓦwww.campingitaliarimini.it. Around 3km north of the city centre, right on the seafront, this campsite boasts its own beach, plus all the facilities you'd expect. It's €10 per person high season, plus €11 for tent hire. Bus #4 from the station will drop you right outside.

Happy Camping Village Via Panzini 228, Bellaria112 ☎0541.732.882, ⓦwww .happycamping.it. Despite its name, this establishment some 12km north of Rimini seems to be moving more towards the provision of less transitory forms of accommodation, now offering a hotel, bungalows and apartments to rent. However, it still has 160 tent pitches, and guests have access to a wealth of facilities, including a private beach, a swimming pool, restaurant and supermarket. Take bus #4 from Rimni station and alight at stop 52.

The Town

Rimini's railway station divides the city into two neat parts. To the east is the main attraction, a long, clean sandy **beach**, lined along its length by largely indistinguishable three- to five-star hotels, all of whom have parcelled up their own particular stretches of beach and equipped them with beach bars, volleyball courts, watersports outfitters and other such holiday essentials. Running behind the front is Viale Amerigo Vespucci, a brash drag crammed with souvenir shops, restaurants and video arcades, while inland, past the station, sits the **Old Town**, an often unseen part of Rimini, made up of old stone buildings clustered around the twin squares of Piazza Tre Martiri and Piazza Cavour, and bordered by the port-canal and town ramparts. Unlike the tourist side of town, this quiet, refined community stays in business throughout the winter, albeit in a low-key, pottering sort of way.

Founded in 286 BC as Ariminum, Rimini was once an important Roman colony. On the southern and northern edges of the old centre respectively sit the **Arco d'Augusto** and **Ponte Tiberio**. The patched-up Arco was built at the beginning of the first century AD at the point where Via Emilia joined Via Flaminia. Rimini's other Roman remains consist of the **Anfiteatro**, of which there are sparse foundations off Via Roma, just south of the train station.

Just south of the Ponte Tiberio, **Piazza Tre Martiri** which largely follows the layout of the original Roman square, and **Piazza Cavour** are the two main squares. Piazza Cavour has a statue of Pope Paul V and the Gothic **Palazzo del Podestà**; the square was rebuilt in the 1920s, and purists argue that it was ruined, although the fishtail battlements are still impressive enough. Opposite, beyond the sixteenth-century fountain incorporating Roman reliefs, the beautiful **old fish market** often shades antiques stalls worth a browse. The **Museo della Città** at Via L. Tonini 1 (Tues–Sat 8.30am–12.30pm & 5–7pm, Sun 4–7pm; €5) has a collection of works of art dating from the fourteenth to the nineteenth centuries, the highlight of which is Giovanni Bellini's pietà. Also part of the museum, just a few metres west on Piazza Ferrari is a brand new exhibition, the **Domus del Chirurgo** (Ⓦwww.domusrimini.com). Here you can enter a glass-sided structure erected above the remains of a third-century Roman "Surgeon's House". The site has yielded numerous fascinating finds, including coins and bronze surgeon's instruments (such as forceps and pliers), which are now on display in a new archeology gallery on the ground floor of the museum. What remains here are the foundations and a set of mosaic pavements, including one showing Orpheus surrounded by animals.

Just south of here on Via IV Novembre is Rimini's best-known monument, the **Tempio Malatestiano** (Mon–Sat 8am–12.30pm & 3.30–7pm, Sun 9am–1pm & 3.30–7pm; free), which serves as the town's cathedral. Built by the Guelph family of Malatesta, it was originally a Franciscan Gothic church before being transformed in 1450 into a monument to Sigismondo Malatesta, a notorious *condottiere* whose long list of alleged crimes included rape, incest and looting. Understandably, the pope of the time, Pius II, was less than impressed and publicly consigned an ambivalent Sigismondo to hell. Sigismondo was more concerned with his great love, Isotta degli Atti, and treated the *tempio* as a private memorial chapel to her. Their initials are linked in emblems all over the building, and the Malatesta family's favourite heraldic animal – a trumpeting elephant – appears almost as often. There are a number of fine artworks, now restored, to look out for, including a *Crucifix* attributed to Giotto, friezes and reliefs by Agostino di Duccio and a fresco by Piero della Francesca of Sigismondo himself.

There's more homegrown hedonism on offer a short way south at the tiny **Museo Fellini**, Via Clementini 2 (Tues–Fri 4–7pm, Sat & Sun 10am–noon & 4–7pm; free), which celebrates the director's career with exhibits ranging from his drawings – the director began his career as a cartoon illustrator – to movie posters.

Eating and drinking

Rimini is not the best place to eat cheaply with even snack places being rather pricey. The seafront and Via Tripoli have some cheap **pizza bars** but many eating options on Rimini's seaside quarter demand formal dress and high prices. Less ritzy **restaurants** can be found in the old town and for the truly impoverished there's a large Standa supermarket handily located on Via Vespucci 133.

Caffé Cavour Piazza Cavour 13. Good choice for a quick drink, a light meal – antipasti €7–10, *insalata di mare* €10 – and an elegant recline on one of the town's finest squares.

Casina del Bosco Via Beccadelli 15. In among a row of similar establishments, this offers a large selection of generously filled (if not priced) *piadini* – tuna and carrot €4.50, roast beef, parmesan and rocket €6.20 – with seating under shady trees.

Osteria de Börg Via Forzieri 12. Relaxed and moderately priced place serving innovative regional cooking, such as *galletto al tagame* (wine-cooked chicken in a skillet, fish kebabs, fire-roasted meats and a dozen different vegetable dishes. Antipasti €8–10, *primi* €7.50–10, *secondi* €10–16). Closed Mon.

Papille Viale Tiberio 11. Friendly enoteca offering a good selection of wines (over 600 vintages) and locally sourced snacks – salami, ham, fried squid, artichokes, cheeses etc. Closed Tues & Sun eve.

Pic-Nic Via Tempio Malatestiano 30. Perennially popular place thanks to its reasonably priced pizzas (€5.50–8), calzones (€7–9) and crêpes. Vegetarian specials too. Closed Mon.

Rimini Key Piazzale B. Croce. Good-value set menus and pizzas, in a prime location for observing Rimini's evening *passeggiata* along the seafront. Closed Tues.

Rossopomodoro Via Amerigo Vespucci 50. With its rash of arcades and souvenir shops, this road is not exactly renowned for its elegant dining spaces. *Rossopomodo*, however, is an exception, with a large attractive dining space, done up in big, bold blocks of red. It also does a very good pie – €5–10.

Nightlife

Rimini's **nightlife** is mainly concentrated on the seafront and in fashionable enclave of Misano Monte above the town. Clubbing is a seasonal activity here. As full-on as things get in summer, you'll find few places open come winter. Even on a balmy July evening, things tend to start late with crowds cruising the bars from about 11pm onwards before driving to the first club at around 1am. If you haven't got a car, or are drinking, use the nightbuses called Blue Lines (ⓦ www.bluelinebus.com), which act as Rimini's club shuttles during July and August throughout the night (10.30pm–6am). There are five colour-coded lines – blue, pale blue, pink, green and yellow – with the main blue line trundling between Rimini's train station and the nearby town of Riccione every twenty minutes, stopping at over fifteen clubs en route. Nightly bus passes cost €3.50 (€14 weekly); tickets available on board.

For up-to-date information on the Rimini club scene, check the **listings** in the Italian weekly *Chiamami Città* (free in the tourist office or click on ⓦ www .chiamamicitta.com) or at ⓦ www.riminilive.com.

Byblos Piazza Castell 24 ☎ 0541.690.252, ⓦ www.byblosclub.com. Summer-only club with several different bars and dance areas as well as an outdoor courtyard with a swimming pool.

Carnaby Viale Brindisi ☎ 0541.373.204, ⓦ www .carnaby.it. Wildly popular club spread over three floors, the lowest of which is the subterranean and appropriately named, "The Cave". The music gets lighter, and less intense the higher you go. Like its namesake, it swings.

Coconuts Via Lungomare Tintori 5, ⓦ www .coconuts.it. Right on the beach, this bills itself as a "Miami-style" indoor/outdoor club, which translates as palm trees, neon, salsa and podium dancers. Attracts a slightly older crowd.

Le Cocoricò Via Chieti 44 ☎ 0541.605.183, ⓦ www.cocorico.it. One of Italy's most celebrated clubs where thousands congregate every weekend under an enormous glass pyramid to rave to the latest in Italian techno.

Nomi Via G. Bruno 28 ☎ 0541.24.215, ⓦ www .nomiclub.com. The awfully fashionable club of the *Duomo* hotel, this is a place to be seen, rather than dance too intently and risk dishevelling your carefully crafted outfit. Instead, perch yourself on one of the spring-like chairs surrounding the undulating, mirrored steel central bar and watch what happens.

Listings

Car rental Avis, Viale Trieste 16/D ☎ 0541.51.256; Europcar, Via Giovanni XXIII 126 ☎ 0541.54.746; Mondaini Massimo, Viale Tripoli 16 ☎ 0541.782.646.

Doctor ☎ 118, or Infermi hospital ☎ 0541.705.111.

Internet access The tourist office has a list of Internet cafés – two good ones are the *Email Beach* at Viale Vespucci 29/C (Mon–Sat 2–8pm) and *Cyber Pub* at Viale Mantova 70 (daily 8pm–9pm, closed Mon) in Rivazzurre, south of the centre.

Laundry Lavanderia Carla Ekoclean, 180 Via Tripoli.

Pharmacy Farmacia Comunale, Via IV Novembre 39/41 (daily except Thurs 8.30am–12.30pm & 4–8pm; ☎ 0541.24.414); when closed, details of all-night services are posted outside.

Post office Main office on Largo Giulio Cesare (Mon–Fri 8.15am–5.30pm, Sat 8.15am–1pm); smaller branch at Piazzale Tripoli 4 (Mon–Fri 8.10am–1.30pm, Sat 8.10–11.50am).

Taxis Radiotaxi Cooperative ☎ 0541.50.020; 24hr rank outside the train station. Fares are €3.62 basic, plus €0.96 per km.

San Marino

Around 25km southwest of Rimini, the **REPUBLIC OF SAN MARINO** is an unashamed, though not entirely unpleasant, tourist destination that trades on its nearly two millennia of precariously maintained autonomy. Said to have been founded around 300 AD by a monk fleeing the persecutions of Diocletian – it claims to be the world's oldest constitutional republic – it has been bumbling along ever since in a quiet, unobtrusive fashion, away from the fierce battles and intrigues of mainstream Italian politics. Essentially too small and inconsequential to be worth conquering, the republic has – save for a brief Borgia episode in the sixteenth century – been left largely to its own devices. Culturally, it is essentially Italian – there's no San Marinese language – but in legal, constitutional terms, it remains **independent**, electing its own government, passing its own laws, minting its own money, producing its own postage stamps, and even maintaining its own, largely unused, army of around a thousand.

There's not a great deal to see. The ramparts and medieval-style buildings of the citadel above Borgomaggiore, also called "San Marino", restored in the last century, are mildly interesting; there's a **waxworks museum** in Via Lapicidi Marini 17 (daily: April–Sept 8.30am–6.30pm; Oct–March 8.30am–12.30pm & 2–5.30pm; €6) as well as tacky souvenir shops and restaurants. And you can also get your passport officially stamped, for only €2.50, by the border guards or at the **information** office at Contrada del Collegio (Mon–Fri 8.30am–6.30pm, Sat & Sun 8.30am–1.30/2pm & 1.30/2–6pm; ☎0549.882.914, ⓦwww.visitsanmarino .com). All the touristy tawdriness aside, however, it's a good place just to stroll around; the walk up through town to the **rocce**, battlemented castles along the highest three ridges, is worth the effort for the all-round views. Below, in Borgomaggiore, is Giovanni Michelucci's "fearless and controversial" modernist church, built in the 1960s, with a roof that seems to cascade down in waves.

Travel details

Trains

Bologna to: Ancona (every 30min; 1hr 50min–2hr 45min); Faenza (hourly; 25–40min); Ferrara (frequent; 30–55min); Fidenza (hourly; 1hr 10min); Florence (frequent; 55min); Forlì (frequent; 35–50min); Milan (frequent; 1hr 45min–2hr); Modena (frequent; 20–40min); Parma (frequent; 55min–1hr 20min); Ravenna (hourly; 1hr 20min); Reggio Emilia (frequent; 35min–1hr; Rimini (every 20min; 55min–1hr 40min).
Faenza to: Brisighella (hourly; 10–20min).
Ferrara to: Ravenna (hourly; 1hr 15min); Rimini (frequent; 2hr–2hr 30min).
Fidenza to: Busseto (hourly; 12min); Cremona (hourly; 35min).
Modena to: Carpi (hourly; 12–20min); Mantua (hourly; 1hr–1hr 10min); Verona (11 daily; 1hr 20–2hr).
Parma to: Brescia (hourly; 1hr 45min–2hr 30min); La Spezia (11 daily; 2hr 15min).

Buses

Bologna to: Marzabotto (every 20min; 15min); Pontecchio Marconi (every 15min; 45min); Vignola (hourly; 1hr).
Ferrara to: Comacchio (10 daily; 1hr 10min).
Fidenza to: Fontanellato (3 daily; 25min); Soragna (10 daily; 20min).
Modena to: Carpi (20 daily; 40min); Maranello (hourly; 30min); Vignola (6 daily; 40min).
Parma to: Busseto/Le Roncole (5 daily; 1hr); Fontanellato (6 daily; 35min); Langhirano (hourly; 45min); Roncole Verdi (5 daily; 50min); Soragna (5 daily; 40min).
Ravenna to: Classe (every 30min; 10min); Marina di Ravenna (every 30min; 20min); Marina Romea (10 daily; 20min); Mésola (1 daily; 1hr 40min).
Reggio Emilia to: Casina (hourly; 50min).
Rimini to: Rome (2 daily in summer, 2 weekly in winter; 5hr 30min); San Marino (hourly; 30min); Santarcángelo (hourly; 30min).

Tuscany

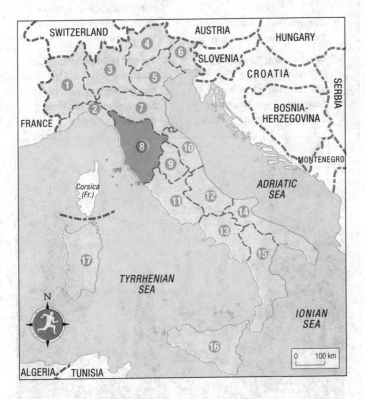

CHAPTER 8

Highlights

* **The Duomo, Florence**
  Climbing Brunelleschi's dome,
  the city's signature building, is
  a must. See p.456

* **The Uffizi** The world's
  greatest collection of Italian
  Renaissance paintings.
  See p.460

* **Chianti** The country's most
  famous vineyards. See p.482

* **The Leaning Tower, Pisa**
  Still defying gravity and
  still continuing to amaze.
  Now saved from imminent
  collapse, the tower is once

  again open to visitors.
  See p.487

* **Lucca** A stunning array of
  Romanesque churches in this
  most urbane of Tuscan towns.
  See p.491

* **The Palio** Siena's historic
  horse race, run over three
  frenetic laps of the Campo.
  See p.514

* **Tuscan hill-towns** Tuscany's
  hill-towns epitomize the
  region for many visitors, with
  San Gimignano the most
  popular. See p.526

▲ Classic Tuscan countryside near Pienza

Tuscany

The tourist brochure view of Tuscany as an idyll of olive groves, vineyards, hill-towns and frescoed churches may be distorted, but Tuscany is indeed the essence of Italy in many ways. The national language evolved from the Tuscan dialect, a supremacy ensured by Dante – who wrote the *Divine Comedy* in the vernacular of his birthplace, Florence – and Tuscan writers such as Petrarch and Boccaccio. And the era we know as the **Renaissance**, which played so large a role in forming the culture, not just of Italy but of Europe as a whole, is associated more strongly with this part of the country than with anywhere else. The very name by which we refer to this extraordinarily creative period was coined by a Tuscan, Giorgio Vasari, who wrote in the sixteenth century of the "rebirth" of the arts. **Florence** was the most active centre of the Renaissance, flourishing principally through the all-powerful patronage of the Medici dynasty. Every eminent artistic figure from Giotto onwards – Masaccio, Brunelleschi, Alberti, Donatello, Botticelli, Leonardo da Vinci, Michelangelo – is represented here, in an unrivalled gathering of churches, galleries and museums.

The problem is, of course, that the whole world knows about the attractions of Florence, with the result that the city is so busy in high season that many visitors find its commercialism offputting. **Siena** tends to provoke a less ambivalent response. This is one of the great medieval cities of Europe, almost perfectly preserved, and with superb works of art in its religious and secular buildings. Its beautiful Campo – the central, scallop-shaped market square – is the scene, too, of Tuscany's one unmissable festival, the **Palio**, which sees bareback horseriders careering around the cobbles amid an extravagant display of pageantry. Other major cities, **Pisa** and **Lucca**, provide convenient entry points to the region, either by air (via Pisa's airport) or along the coastal rail route from Genoa. **Arezzo** and **Cortona** serve as fine introductions to Tuscany if you're approaching from the south (Rome) or east (Perugia).

Tucked away to the west and south of Siena are dozens of small **hill-towns** that, for many, epitomize the region. **San Gimignano** is the best known, and is worth visiting as much for its spectacular array of frescoes as for its much-photographed bristle of medieval tower-houses, though it's now a little too popular for its own good. **Montepulciano** and **Pienza** are both superbly located and dripping with atmosphere, but the best candidates for a Tuscan hill-town escape are places such as **Volterra**, **Massa Maríttima** or **Pitigliano**, where tourism has yet to undermine local character. You may

Tuscan cooking, with its emphasis on simple dishes using fresh, quality, local ingredients, has had a seminal influence on Italian cuisine. Classic Tuscan antipasti are peasant fare: bruschetta is stale bread, toasted and dressed with oil and garlic; *crostini* is toast and pâté. **Olive oil** is the essential flavouring, used as a dressing for salads, a medium for frying and to drizzle over bread or vegetables and into soups and stews just before serving.

Soups are very popular – Tuscan menus always include either *ribollita*, a hearty stew of vegetables, beans and chunks of bread, or *zuppa di farro*, a thick soup with spelt (a barley-like grain). Fish restaurants around the region try to copy *cacciucco*, a spiced fish and seafood soup, but the best place in Italy to try it is the town of its birth, Livorno. White cannellini **beans** (*fagioli*) are another favourite, turning up in salads, with pasta (*tuoni e lampo*) or just dressed with olive oil. Tuscany is not known for its **pasta**, but many towns in the south serve *pici*, a local variety of thick spaghetti. **Meat** is kept plain, often grilled, and Florentines profess to liking nothing better than a good *bistecca alla fiorentina* (rare char-grilled steak), or the simple rustic dishes of *arista* (roast pork loin stuffed with rosemary and garlic) or *pollo alla diavola* (chicken flattened, marinated and then grilled with herbs). Hunters' fare such as *cinghiale* (wild boar) and *coniglio* (rabbit) often turns up in hill-town trattorias. Spinach is often married with ricotta and gnocchi, used as a pasta filling, and in *crespoline* (pancakes) or between two chunks of *focaccia* and eaten as a snack. Sheep's milk *pecorino* is the most widespread Tuscan **cheese** (best in Pienza), but the most famous is the oval *marzolino* from the Chianti region, which is eaten either fresh or ripened. **Dessert** menus will often include *cantuccini*, hard, almond-flavoured biscuits to be dipped in a glass of Vinsanto (sweet dessert wine); Siena is the main source of sweet treats, including almond macaroons and *panforte*, a rich and very dense cake full of nuts and fruit.

Tuscany has some of Italy's finest **wines**. Three top names, which all bear the exclusive DOCG mark (and price tags to match), are Chianti Classico, Brunello di Montalcino and Vino Nobile di Montepulciano – not the sort of thing you'd knock back at a trattoria. There are dozens of other Chianti varieties, most of them excellent, but it can be difficult to find a bargain. Both Montalcino and Montepulciano produce *rosso* varieties that are more pocket-friendly, and other names to look for include Carmignano and Rosso delle Colline Lucchesi. Two notable whites are dry Vernaccia di San Gimignano and the fresh Galestro.

find lesser-known sights even more memorable – remote monasteries like **Monte Oliveto Maggiore** and **San Galgano**, or the sulphur spa of **Bagno Vignoni**. The one area where Tuscany fails to impress is its over-developed **coast**, with horrible beach-umbrella compounds filling every last scrap of sand. **Elba**, the largest of several Tuscan islands, offers great beaches and good hiking, but is busy in summer

Tuscany's **official tourism website** – Ⓦ www.turismo.toscana.it – links all fifteen of the region's provinces and has a comprehensive accommodation database. Finding **accommodation** can be a major problem in the summer so you should definitely reserve in advance. **Agriturismo** is big business, with a plethora of family-run places dotted around the countryside offering anything from budget rooms in a farmhouse to luxury apartments in restored castles; the regional government's website (Ⓦ www.agriturismo.regione.toscana.it) has plenty of information.

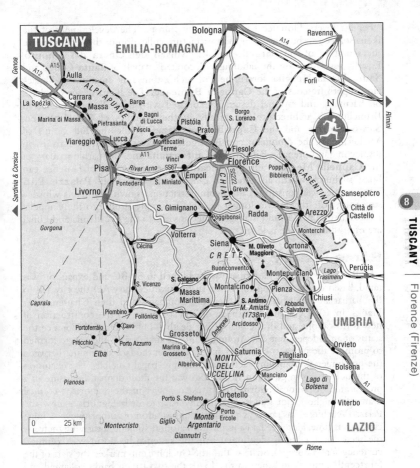

Florence (Firenze)

Since the early nineteenth century **FLORENCE** has been celebrated by many as the most beautiful city in Italy. Stendhal staggered around its streets in a perpetual stupor of delight; the Brownings sighed over its charms; and E.M. Forster's *Room with a View* portrayed it as the great southern antidote to the sterility of Anglo-Saxon life. The pinnacle of Brunelleschi's stupendous cathedral dome dominates the cityscape, and the close-up view is even more breathtaking, with the multicoloured **Duomo** rising beside the marble-clad **Baptistry**. Wander from here down towards the River Arno and the attraction still holds: beyond the broad Piazza della Signoria – site of the towering **Palazzo Vecchio** – the river is spanned by the medieval, shop-lined **Ponte Vecchio**, with the gorgeous church of **San Miniato al Monte** glistening on the hill behind it.

For art lovers, Florence has no equal in Europe. The development of the Renaissance can be plotted in the vast picture collection of the **Uffizi** and in the sculpture of the **Bargello** and the **Museo dell'Opera del Duomo**. Equally revelatory are the fabulously decorated chapels of **Santa Croce** and **Santa Maria Novella**, forerunners of such astonishing creations as Masaccio's superb frescoes in the **Cappella Brancacci**. The Renaissance emphasis on harmony and rational design is expressed with unrivalled eloquence in Brunelleschi's architecture, specifically in the churches of **San Lorenzo**, **Santo Spirito** and the **Cappella dei Pazzi**. While the full genius of Michelangelo, the dominant creative figure of sixteenth-century Italy, is on display in San Lorenzo's **Biblioteca Laurenziana** and the marble statuary of the **Cappelle Medicee** and the **Accademia**, every quarter of Florence can boast a church worth an extended call, and the enormous **Palazzo Pitti** south of the river constitutes a museum district on its own. If you're a whistle-stop tour, note that it's no longer possible to simply stroll into the Cappella Brancacci (see p.473), and that spontaneous visits to the Accademia and Uffizi are often difficult (see p.454).

Some history

The Roman colony of Florentia was established in 59 BC and expansion was rapid, based on trade along the Arno. In the sixth century AD the city fell to the barbarian hordes of Totila, then the Lombards and then Charlemagne's Franks. In 1078 Countess Mathilda of Tuscia supervised the construction of new fortifications, and in the year of her death – 1115 – granted Florence the status of an independent city. Around 1200, the first Arti (Guilds) were formed to promote the interests of traders and bankers in the face of conflict between the pro-imperial Ghibelline faction and the pro-papal Guelphs. The exclusion of the nobility from government in 1293 was the most dramatic measure in a programme of political reform that invested power in the Signoria, a council drawn from the major guilds. The mighty Palazzo della Signoria – now the Palazzo Vecchio – was raised as a visible demonstration of authority over a huge city: at this time, Florence had a population around 100,000, a thriving mercantile sector and a highly developed banking system (the florin was common currency across Europe). Strife within the Guelph camp marked the start of the fourteenth century, and then in the 1340s the two largest banks collapsed and the Black Death struck, destroying up to half the city's population.

The rise of **Cosimo de' Medici**, later dubbed Cosimo il Vecchio ("the Old"), was to some extent due to his family's sympathies with the smaller guilds. The **Medici** fortune had been made by the banking prowess of Cosimo's father, Giovanni Bicci de' Medici, and Cosimo used the power conferred by wealth to great effect. Partly through his patronage of such figures as Brunelleschi and Donatello, Florence became the centre of artistic activity in Italy.

The ascendancy continued under Cosimo's grandson **Lorenzo il Magnifico**, who in effect ruled the city at the height of its artistic prowess. Before Lorenzo's death in 1492, the Medici bank failed, and in 1494 Lorenzo's son Piero was obliged to flee. Florentine hearts and minds were seized by the charismatic Dominican monk, **Girolamo Savonarola**, who preached against the decadence and corruption of the city. Artists departed in droves as Savonarola and his cohorts, in a symbolic demonstration of the new order, gathered books, paintings, tapestries, fancy furniture and other frivolities, and piled them high in Piazza della Signoria in a **Bonfire of the Vanities**. Within a year, however, Savonarola had been found guilty of heresy and treason, and was burned alive on the same spot.

After Savonarola, the city functioned peaceably under a republican constitution headed by Piero Soderini, whose chief adviser was **Niccolò Machiavelli**. In 1512 the Medici returned, and in 1516, Giovanni de' Medici became **Pope Leo X**, granting Michelangelo and Leonardo da Vinci major commissions. After the assassination of Alessandro de' Medici in 1537, power was handed to a new Cosimo, who seized the Republic of Siena and, in 1569, took the title **Cosimo I**, Grand Duke of Tuscany.

Florence's subsequent decline was slow and painful. Each of the later Medicis was more ridiculous than the last: **Francesco** spent most of his thirteen-year reign indoors, obsessed by alchemy; **Ferdinando II** sat back as harvests failed, plagues ran riot and banking and textiles slumped to nothing; the virulently anti-Semitic **Cosimo III** spent 53 years in power cracking down on dissidents; and **Gian Gastone** spent virtually all his time drunk in bed. When Gastone died, in 1737, the Medici line died with him.

Under the terms of a treaty signed by Gian Gastone's sister, **Anna Maria Ludovica**, Florence – and the whole Grand Duchy of Tuscany – passed to Francesco of Lorraine, the future Francis I of Austria. Austrian rule lasted until the coming of the French in 1799; after a fifteen-year interval of French control, the Lorraine dynasty was brought back, remaining in residence until being overthrown in the Risorgimento upheavals of 1859. Absorbed into the united Italian state in the following year, Florence became the **capital** of the Kingdom of Italy in 1865, a position it held until 1870.

At the end of the nineteenth century, large areas of the medieval city were **demolished** by government officials and developers; buildings that had stood in the area of what is now Piazza della Repubblica since the early Middle Ages were pulled down to make way for undistinguished office blocks, and old quarters around Santa Croce and Santa Maria Novella were razed. In 1944, the retreating German army blew up all the city's bridges except the Ponte Vecchio and destroyed acres of medieval architecture. A disastrous **flood** in November 1966 drowned several people and wrecked buildings and works of art. Restoration of damage caused by the flood, and by the 1993 **car-bomb** that killed five people outside the Uffizi, is still going on. Indeed, monuments and paintings are the basis of Florence's survival in the new century, a state of affairs that gives rise to considerable discontent here. The development of new industrial parks on the northern outskirts is the latest and most ambitious attempt to break Florence's ever-increasing dependence on its tourists.

Arrival, information and transport

Pisa's Galileo Galilei airport (see p.484) is the main airport for flights into Tuscany. A small but increasing number of international air services use **Perètola** (or Amerigo Vespucci) airport (☎055.306.1300, ⓦwww.aeroporto .firenze.it), 5km northwest of the city centre; the **Volainbus** service (€4.50) provides every thirty minutes shuttles into Florence from **Perètola**.

Nearly all **trains** arrive at **Santa Maria Novella** station (**Firenze SMN**), a few blocks west of the Duomo. (A few trains – mostly in the small hours of the morning – use Campo di Marte, over in the east of the city, from where there are regular buses into the centre.) **Buses** arrive at and depart from either the main SITA bus terminal on Via di Santa Caterina da Siena, a few steps west of the station, or Largo Alinari, on the eastern side.

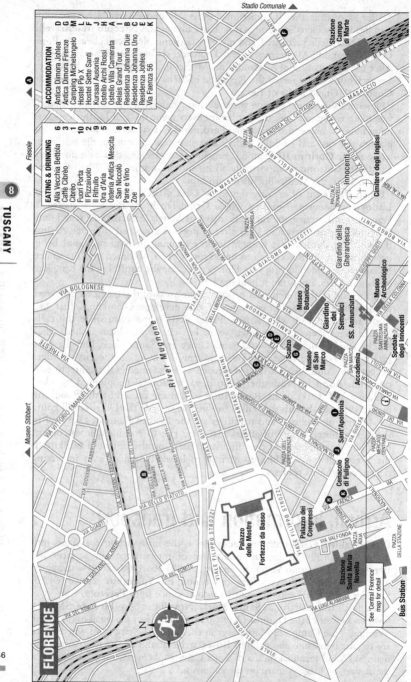

8

TUSCANY

FLORENCE

▲ Prato & Pistoia

◀ Museo Stibbert

◀ Museo Stibbert

▲ Fiesole

▲ Stadio Comunale

ACCOMMODATION

Antica Dimora Johlea	D
Antica Dimora Firenze	G
Camping Michelangelo	M
Hostel Pio X	L
Hostel Sette Santi	F
Kursaal Ausonia	J
Ostello Archi Rossi	H
Ostello Villa Camerata	A
Osteria Antica Mescita	B
Relais Grand Tour	C
Residenza Johanna Due	I
Residenza Johanna Uno	E
Residenza Johlea	K
Via Faenza 56	

EATING & DRINKING

Alla Vecchia Bettola	6
Caffè Cibrèo	3
Cibrèo	1
Fuori Porta	10
Il Pizzaiuolo	2
Il Rifrullo	9
Ora d'Aria	5
Osteria Antica Mescita San Niccolò	8
Pane e Vino	4
Zoe	7

Palazzo delle Mostre
Fortezza da Basso

Palazzo dei Congressi

Stazione Santa Maria Novella

Bus Station

See 'Central Florence' map for detail

Cenacolo di Fuligno

Sant'Apollonia

Museo di San Marco

Accademia

Scalzo

Museo Botanico

Giardino dei Semplici

SS. Annunziata

Spedale degli Innocenti

Museo Archeologico

Giardino della Gherardesca

Innocenti

Cimitero degli Inglesi

Stazione Campo di Marte

River Mugnone

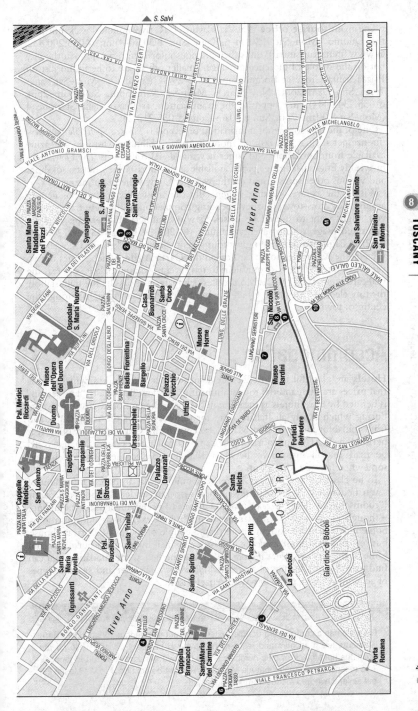

▲ S. Salvi

0   200 m

Pal. Medici
Riccardi

Cappelle
Medice

San Lorenzo

Duomo

Baptistry

Campanile

Museo
dell'Opera
del Duomo

Ospedale
S. Maria Nuova

Santa Maria
Maddalena
dei Pazzi

Synagogue

S. Ambrogio

Mercato
Sant'Ambrogio

Casa
Buonarroti

Santa Croce

Museo
Horne

Badia Fiorentina

Bargello

Orsanmichele

Palazzo
Vecchio

Uffizi

Palazzo
Davanzati

Pal.
Strozzi

Santa Trinita

Pal.
Rucellai

Santa Maria
Novella

Ognissanti

River Arno

Santo Spirito

Palazzo Pitti

La Specola

Giardino di Bóboli

Cappella
Branacacci

SantaMaria
del Carmine

Santa
Felicita

Museo
Bardini

Forte di
Belvedere

San Niccolò

River Arno

San Salvatore al Monte

San Miniato
al Monte

OLTRARNO

Porta
Romana

447

The main **tourist office** is at Via Cavour 1/R, five-minutes' walk north of the Duomo (Mon–Sat 8.30am–6.30pm, Sun 8.30am–1pm; ☎055.290.832, ⓦwww.firenzeturismo.it); this office provides information not just on the city but on the whole of Florence province. Smaller offices are to be found just off Piazza Santa Croce at Borgo Santa Croce 29/R (April–Oct Mon–Sat 9am–7pm, Sun 9am–2pm; Nov–March Mon–Sat 9am–5pm, Sun 9am–2pm; ☎055.234.0444), and opposite the train station, at Piazza della Stazione 4 (Mon–Sat 8.30am–7pm, Sun 8.30am–2pm; ☎055.212.245).

One of the best sources of information on events is *Firenze Spettacolo* (ⓦwww.firenzespettacolo.it; €1.80), a monthly, partly bilingual listings magazine available from bookshops and larger newsstands. Also useful is *The Florentine* a bi-weekly English-language paper, available at the tourist office, most bookshops and various other spots (listed on the website: ⓦwww.theflorentine.net).

Within the centre, walking is generally the most efficient way of getting around. For cross-town journeys, pending completion of the new tram system, you might want to use ATAF **buses** (ⓦwww.ataf.net). **Tickets** are valid for unlimited usage within seventy minutes (€1.20), 24 hours (€5) or 72 hours (€12). A **Biglietto Multiplo** gives four seventy-minute tickets for €4.50; better value is the ATAF electronic card called the **Carta Agile**, which comes in two versions – the €10 one is equivalent to ten seventy-minute tickets, whereas the €20 card is equivalent to 21. Most routes originate at or pass by the train station; the tiny electric buses (#A–D) are the most useful for cutting right through the centre of town.

Accommodation

Hotels are plentiful in Florence but demand is almost limitless, which means that prices are high and the tourist inundation has few slack spots: "low season" is defined by most hotels as meaning mid-July to the end of August (the weeks during which nearly all Italians head for the beaches or the mountains), and from mid-November to mid-March, except for the Christmas and New Year period. The Via Cavour tourist office can find you a hotel (for a fee), but you'd be mad to roll into town between March and October without having somewhere already sorted out.

To be classified as a hotel in Florence, a building has to have a minimum of seven bedrooms. Places with fewer rooms operate under the title *affitacamere* ("rooms for rent"), *residenze* or *residenze d'epoca* (if occupying a historic building) – though, confusingly, a *residenze d'epoca* might have as many as a dozens rooms. Some *affitacamere* are nothing more than a couple of rooms in a private house, but several – and most *residenze d'epoca* – are small hotels in all but name, and some of the city's *residenze d'epoca* are among the best accommodation you can find here. For full listings of accredited *affitacamere*, *residenze* and all other types of accommodation, go to ⓦwww.firenzeturismo.it.

Florence addresses

Florence has a complicated double system of street numbering: commercial establishments (such as bars and restaurants) have red numbers (*rosso*), while private buildings have black or blue numbers – and the two systems don't run in tandem. This means, for example, that Via Mosca 35/R might be next door to Via Mosca 89, but several hundred metres from Via Mosca 33.

Hotels

The city centre

Alessandra Borgo Santi Apostoli 17 ☎055.283.438, ⓦwww.hotelalessandra .com. One of the best and friendliest of the central two-stars, with 27 rooms occupying a sixteenth-century *palazzo* and furnished in a mixture of antique and modern styles. En-suite doubles are €150–190 – the more expensive ones overlook the river; you pay €110 for those with shared bathrooms. ❹

Cestelli Borgo SS Apostoli 25 ☎055.214.213, ⓦwww.hotelcestelli.com. Spotlessly maintained by its young Florentine-Japanese owners, this eight-roomed one-star occupies part of a house that once belonged to a minor Medici. The rooms are a good size, and most are en suite. At a mere €80–100 per double, this is an excellent deal. ❸

Helvetia & Bristol Via dei Pescioni 2 ☎055.266.51, ⓦwww.royaldemeure.com. In business since 1894 and favoured by such luminaries as Pirandello, Stravinsky and Gary Cooper, this is a superb five-star hotel. The public spaces and 67 bedrooms and suites (each unique) are faultlessly designed and fitted, mixing antique furnishings and modern facilities – such as whirlpool baths – to create a style that evokes the *Belle Époque* without being suffocatingly nostalgic. If you're going to treat yourself, this is a leading contender. Doubles start at around €400, without breakfast. ❾

Hermitage Vicolo Marzio 1/Piazza del Pesce ☎055.287.216, ⓦwww.hermitagehotel.com. Pre-booking is recommended at any time of year to secure one of the 28 rooms in this superbly located three-star hotel, right next to the Ponte Vecchio. The service is friendly, the rooms are cosy, and there are unbeatable views from some rooms, as well as from the flower-filled roof garden. Doubles (with whirlpool baths) are around €250 in high season, but only half that in low season. ❽

Torre Guelfa Borgo SS Apostoli 8 ☎055.239.6338, ⓦwww.hoteltorreguelfa.com. Twenty tastefully furnished rooms are crammed onto the third floor of this ancient tower, the tallest private building in the city. Guests can enjoy the marvellous views all over the city from the tower's small roof garden. There are also six cheaper doubles on the first floor (no TV and more noise from the road). Very charismatic (if slightly shabby in places), very popular, and quite pricey too – €210–260 for the best room, though a room on the first floor costs some €100 less. ❻

The Santa Maria Novella area

Elite Via della Scala 12 ☎055.215.395, ⓦwww.hotelelitefirenze.com. A basic ten-room two-star run by one of the most pleasant managers in town. Even in high season double rooms (most with private bathrooms) are available for less than €100. Quieter rooms are at the back. ❸

Grand Hotel Minerva Piazza Santa Maria Novella 16 ☎055.27230, ⓦwww.grandhotelminerva .com. A big four-star with big rooms, many of them overlooking the piazza. The decor is fairly bland, but the location is good, and the bar and swimming pool on the roof are major pluses. Doubles cost as little as €150, but you're more likely to pay around €200 – still a very good price in this category. ❼

Nizza Via del Giglio 5 ☎055.239.6897, ⓦwww .hotelnizza.com. A smart eighteen-room family-run two star, with helpful staff and very central location. All rooms are en suite, and are better furnished and decorated than many in this category. In high season the maximum price is €140 for an en-suite double; in low season you might get a room for half that. ❺

The station and San Lorenzo areas

Globus Via Sant'Antonino 24 ☎055.211.062, ⓦwww.hotelglobus.com. Formerly a one-star, the Globus has recently been drastically restyled (wenge furniture and natural tones throughout) and has consequently moved up two grades. The 23 a/c rooms start from as little as €70 in off-season, rising to around €170 for the best room in peak season. ❻

Kursaal Ausonia Via Nazionale 24 ☎055.496.324, ⓦwww.kursonia.com. Welcoming and recently refurbished three-star, formed in 2007 by the merger of two formerly separate hotels. If you book online, and well in advance, you might pick up a "superior" double for less than €100 in summer; the price of a "standard" room can go as low as €55 in off-season. ❸

Via Faenza 56 Several budget hotels are crammed into this address near the station. On the top floor is the *Paola* (☎055.213.682, ⓦwww.albergopaola .com; ❷), which is in effect a small hostel, with a four-bed room (with en-suite bathroom) and four six-bed mini-dorms, all painted in bright colours. You'll pay around €30 per person. On the same floor is the one-star *Merlini* (☎055.212.848, ⓦwww.hotelmerlini.it; ❷), which has ten rooms, most with private bathrooms. On the first floor you'll find the one-star *Armonia* (☎055.211.146, ⓔarmonia1962@libero.it; ❷), which has seven rooms (none with private bathroom). Also on this floor is the two-star *Azzi* (☎055.213.806,

@www.hotelazzi.com; ❹), which has fifteen bedrooms and is by far the nicest place in the building, with garden views from most of its rooms.

San Marco and Annunziata areas

Casci Via Cavour 13 ℗ 055.211.686, @www .hotelcasci.com. It would be hard to find a better two-star in central Florence than this 26-room hotel. Only two (sound-proofed) rooms face the busy street: the rest are quiet, clean and neat, and they're well-priced at around €150 for a double in high season (falling to €100 in off-season). The owners are unfailingly helpful and courteous, and the big buffet breakfast under the frescoed ceiling of the reception area is a major plus, as is free internet access. ❺

Loggiato dei Serviti Piazza Santissima Annunziata 3 ℗ 055.289.592, @www .loggiatodeiservitihotel.it. The 38 rooms of this elegant, extremely tasteful and well-priced three-star hotel have been stylishly incorporated into a structure designed in the sixteenth century to accommodate Servite priests. Their relative plainness reflects something of the building's history, but all are decorated with fine fabrics and antiques, and look out onto either the piazza or peaceful gardens to the rear. The five rooms in the annexe, at Via dei Servi 49, are similarly styled, but the building doesn't have the same charisma. Doubles in high season cost from around €200, but at other times there are special offers at around half that price. ❼

Morandi alla Crocetta Via Laura 50 ℗ 055.234.4747, @www.hotelmorandi.it. An intimate three-star gem, whose small size and friendly welcome ensure a home-from-home atmosphere. Rooms are tastefully decorated with antiques and old prints, and vivid carpets laid on parquet floors. Two rooms have balconies opening onto a modest garden; the best room – with fresco fragments and medieval nooks – was converted from a convent chapel. Doubles in high season cost around €230, but in winter there are sometimes special offers as low as €120. ❼

Oltrarno

La Scaletta Via Guicciardini 13 ℗ 055.283.028, @www.lascaletta.com. Some of the rooms in this tidy and recently refurbished sixteen-room two-star give views across to the Bóboli gardens; rooms on the Via Guicciardini side are double-glazed against the traffic. Drinks are served on the rooftop terraces, where you look across the Bóboli in one direction and the city in the other. All rooms are en suite and nicely decorated in cool milky tones. ❻

Affitacamere and residenze

San Lorenzo district

Relais Grand Tour Via Santa Reparata 21 ℗ 055.283.955 @www.florencegrandtour.com. The very hospitable owners have done a great job in turning two floors of this old *palazzo* into a superb guesthouse, with three large bedrooms on the second floor and three suites on the floor above. Each room's decor is unique – one is replete with Neapolitan majolica tiles, another has a gold-leaf wooden ceiling, and a third is loaded with mirrors ("suitable for a couple", as the website has it). ❹

Residenza Castiglioni Via del Giglio 8 ℗ 055.239.6013, @www.residenzacastiglioni.com. Run by the same team as runs the Torre Guelfa hotel, this is a discreet and hugely stylish hideaway that has just half a dozen spacious en-suite double rooms (three of them frescoed), on the second floor of a *palazzo* very close to San Lorenzo church. Doubles €80–180. ❻

San Marco and Annunziata areas

Residenza Johanna Uno Via Bonifacio Lupi 14 ℗ 055.481.896, @www.johanna.it. A genteel place that feels very much a "residence" rather than a hotel, hidden away in an unmarked apartment building in a quiet, leafy corner of the city, 5min walk north of San Marco. Rooms are cosy and well kept, there are books and magazines, and the two signore who run the place are as friendly and helpful as you could hope for. The very similar *Residenza Johanna Due* (℗ 055.473.377; same website) is located further from the main sights, at Via Cinque Giornate 12, to the north of the Fortezza da Basso. *Johanna Uno* costs in the region of €100–130 a night; *Due* is a little cheaper. ❹–❺

Residenza Johlea Via San Gallo 76 ℗ 055.463.3292, @www.johanna.it. Another venture from the people who created the nearby *Residenza Johanna* (see above), offering the same low-cost, high-comfort package, with the same level of hospitality. At nearby Via San Gallo 80 you'll find the *Antica Dimora Johlea* (℗ 055.461.185; same website), which is a somewhat plusher version of the *Residenza*, with deluxe doubles for around €125–150, and a nice roof terrace. The same team run the similarly upmarket *Antica Dimora Firenze* at Via San Gallo 72

(☎ 055.462.7296, ⓦ www.anticadimorafirenze.it), which has six very comfortable rooms (some with four-poster beds) in the same price range as the *Dimora Johlea*. ④–⑤

Oltrarno

Residenza Santo Spirito Piazza Santo Spirito 9 ☎ 055.265.8376, ⓦ www.residenzasspirito.com.

A well-presented residenza with two large double rooms (both with fantastic frescoed ceilings, and both overlooking the piazza) and a two-roomed suite. The doubles cost around €120–150; the suite about €100 more. ⑤

Hostels

Foresteria Valdese Firenze – Istituto Gould Via dei Serragli 49 ☎ 055.212.576, ⓦ www .istitutogould.it. This hostel-cum-evangelical college has 97 beds and is extremely popular, so it's wise to book in advance. Street-front rooms can be noisy (rear rooms are better – and a little more expensive), but the old courtyard, terracotta floors and stone staircases provide atmosphere throughout. Open for check-in Mon–Fri 8.45am–1pm & 3–7.30pm, Sat 9am–1.30pm & 2.30–6pm – but closed Sun. Singles €44; doubles €56–64; triples €75; quads €84–92. Nearly all rooms have private bathroom. No curfew.

Hostel Pio X Via dei Serragli 106 ☎ 055.225.044, ⓦ www.hostelpiox.it. One of the cheapest options in town, often booked up by school groups. Don't be put off by the huge picture of Pope Pius X at the top of the steps; the management is friendly and the atmosphere relaxed. Get there by 9am, as the 64 beds are quickly taken. Beds in doubles, triples, quads and quins cost around €18 per person, a few euros more with en-suite bathrooms; minimum stay two nights, maximum five. Open throughout the year; midnight curfew; no reservations by phone.

Hostel Sette Santi Viale dei Mille 11 ☎ 055.504.8452, ⓦ www.7santi.com. This new hostel occupies a converted convent on a main road just over 1km northeast of the city centre. There are 160 beds in total, some in dorms, but with 32 private rooms with bathroom, plus ten others with shower and nineteen with shared bath on the same floor. Sheets and towels are provided, as is buffet breakfast. Doubles €40–60, dorm beds around €20. Bus #17 from the station goes past the door.

Ostello Archi Rossi Via Faenza 94/R ☎ 055.290.804, ⓦ www.hostelarchirossi.com.

A 5min walk from the train station, this privately owned guesthouse/hostel is spotlessly clean and decorated with guests' wall-paintings and graffiti. It's popular – the 96 places fill up quickly – and has a pleasant garden and terrace. Single rooms around €30; dorm beds €20–25. All prices include breakfast and 30min internet time. Curfew at 2am for dorms.

Ostello Villa Camerata Viale Augusto Righi 2–4 ☎ 055.601.451, ⓦ www.ostellionline.org. An HI hostel tucked away in a beautiful park to the northeast of the city, 5km from Santa Maria Novella. This is one of Europe's most attractive hostels, a sixteenth-century house with frescoed ceilings, fronted by lemon trees in terracotta pots. Doors open at 2pm; if you'll arrive later, call ahead to make sure there's space – bookings by email or fax only. There are 322 dorm places, and a few family rooms. Breakfast and sheets are included, but there are no kitchen facilities; optional supper costs about €10. Films in English are shown every night. Dorm beds €20; two-, three- and four- bed rooms €32.50/25/22 per person. Midnight curfew. Take bus #17b from the train station – it takes about 30min.

Santa Monaca Via Santa Monaca 6 ☎ 055.268.338, ⓦ www.ostello.it. Privately owned hostel in Oltrarno, close to Santa Maria del Carmine. Has 115 beds, arranged in a dozen dorms with between four and twenty beds. Kitchen facilities (no utensils), washing machines, free hot showers and a useful noticeboard with information on lifts and onward travel. Dorm beds €17–20. Open for check-in 6am–2am. Curfew 2am, and the bedrooms have to be vacated between 10am and 2pm. It's a 15min walk from the station, or take bus #11, #36 or #37 to the second stop after the bridge.

Campsites

Camping Internazionale Firenze Via San Cristofano 2, ☎ 055.237.4704, ⓦ www.florencecamping .com. Located 5km south of Florence, in the hills a

short distance to the south of the Certosa di Galluzzo, this well-equipped three-star site offers four-berth bungalows (around €30 per person per night) in

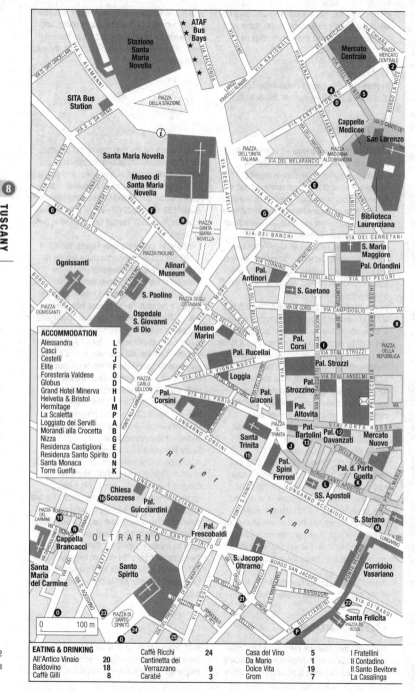

ACCOMMODATION

Alessandra	L
Casci	C
Cestelli	J
Elite	F
Foresteria Valdese	O
Globus	D
Grand Hotel Minerva	H
Helvetia & Bristol	I
Hermitage	M
La Scaletta	P
Loggiato dei Serviti	A
Morandi alla Crocetta	B
Nizza	G
Residenza Castiglioni	E
Residenza Santo Spirito	Q
Santa Monaca	N
Torre Guelfa	K

452

EATING & DRINKING

All'Antico Vinaio	20	Caffè Ricchi	24	Casa del Vino	5	I Fratellini
Baldovino	18	Cantinetta dei Verrazzano	9	Da Mario	1	Il Contadino
Caffè Gilli	8	Carabé	3	Dolce Vita	19	Il Santo Bevitore
				Grom	7	La Casalinga

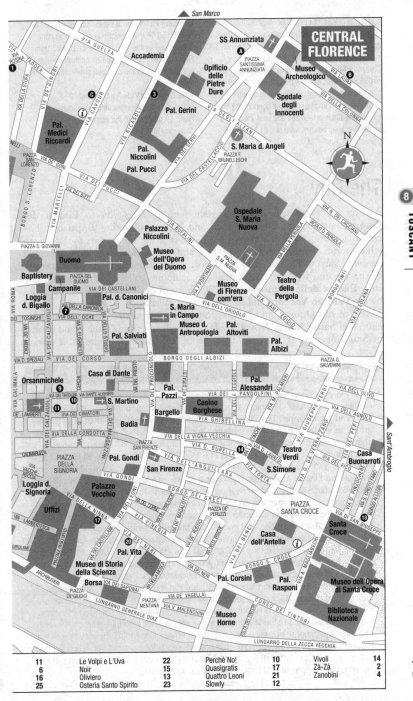

▲ San Marco

VIA ROSINA TADDEA
VIA GUELFA
VIA DELLA STUFA
VIA DE' GINORI
Accademia
SS Annunziata
PIAZZA SANTISSIMA ANNUNZIATA
Ⓐ
VIA LAURA
Ⓑ
Museo Archeologico
VIA DELLA COLONNA
Opificio delle Pietre Dure
Ⓒ
ⓘ
VIA CAVOUR
VIA RICASOLI
❸
Pal. Gerini
VIA DEGLI ALFANI
Spedale degli Innocenti
Pal. Medici Riccardi
VIA DEI SERVI
S. Maria d. Angeli
PIAZZA F. BRUNELLESCHI
NELLI
PIAZZA SAN LORENZO
VIA DE' GORI
Pal. Niccolini
Pal. Pucci
VIA DEL CASTELLACCIO
BORGO S. LORENZO
VIA MARTELLI
VIA DE' PUCCI
VIA DEI BIFFI
Palazzo Niccolini
VIA BUFALINI
Ospedale S. Maria Nuova
VIA N. DEI CACCIANI
VICOLO D. PERGOLA
VIA DELLA PERGOLA
PIAZZA S. GIOVANNI
Duomo
Museo dell'Opera del Duomo
PIAZZA S.M NUOVA
BORGO PINTI
Baptistery
PIAZZA DEL DUOMO
Campanile
Museo di Firenze com'era
Teatro della Pergola
VIA FIESOLANA
Loggia d. Bigallo
VIA DEI CASTELLANI
Pal. d. Canonici
VIA DELL'ORIUOLO
VIA SANT'EGIDIO
VIA DELLA CANONICA
❼
S. Maria in Campo
Museo d. Antropologia
Pal. Altoviti
Pal. Albizi
VIA ROMA
VIA TOSINGHI
VIA DELL'OCHE
VIA S. ELISABETTA
VIA DELLO STUDIO
Pal. Salviati
PIAZZA G. SALVEMINI
VIA CALZAIUOLI
VIA DEL CORSO
BORGO DEGLI ALBIZI
VIA DEI SPEZIALI
Orsanmichele
Casa di Dante
VIA DEL PROCONSOLO
VIA DELL'ULIVO
VIA GIRALDI
VIA CALIMALA
❾
VIA DEI TAVOLINI
VIA DANTE ALIGHIERI
⓾
Pal. Pazzi
Pal. Alessandri
VIA SEGGIOLE
VIA DEI PANDOLFINI
VIA GIUSEPPE VERDI
DE' LAMBERTI
⓫
S. Martino
VIA DEI CIMATORI
Bargello
Casino Borghese
VIA DELL'AGNOLO
VIA DEI MAGAZZINI
Badia
VIA GHIBELLINA
VIA DELLA CONDOTTA
PIAZZA SAN FIRENZE
VIA DELLA VIGNA VECCHIA
⓮
VIA DE' PEPI
Teatro Verdi
Casa Buonarroti
CALIMARUZZA
PIAZZA DELLA SIGNORIA
Pal. Gondi
VIA D. BURELLA
VIA DI LAVATO
S.Simone
VIA DEL FICO
VIA VACCHERECCIA
San Firenze
VIA DELL'ANGUILLARA
VIA TORTA
Loggia d. Signoria
VIA GONDI
BORGO DEI GRECI
PIAZZA DE' PERUZZI
PIAZZA SANTA CROCE
VIA DI SAN GIUSEPPE
⓲
Uffizi
Palazzo Vecchio
VIA DEI LEONI
VIA VINEGIA
VIA DEI BENCI
Santa Croce
⓱
VIA DELLA NINNA
VIA DEL CORNO
VIA DE' MAGALOTTI
VIA DE' RUSTICI
Casa dell'Antella
ⓘ
VIA LAMBERTESCA
⓴
Pal. Vita
VIA DEI NERI
Pal. Corsini
Pal. Rasponi
Museo dell'Opera di Santa Croce
GIROLAMI
Museo di Storia della Scienza
Borsa
VIA DE' SAPONAI
BORGO S. CROCE
VIA A. MAGLIABECHI
ARCHIBUSIERI
PIAZZA DE'GIUDICI
VIA DE' VAGELLAI
Museo Horne
CORSO DEI TINTORI
Biblioteca Nazionale
PIAZZA MENTANA
VIA V. MALENCHINI
LUNGARNO GENERALE DIAZ
LUNGARNO DELLA ZECCA VECCHIA

▲ Sant'Ambrogio

N

Ⓔ TUSCANY

addition to places for tents. Other facilties include an open-air pool, kitchen facilities, a play area for kids, and an internet point. Take bus #37 from the train station – ask for the "Bottai" stop. Open all year.
Camping Michelangiolo Viale Michelangelo 80 ☏ 055.681.1977, ⓦ www.ecvacanze.it. A 240-pitch site that's always crowded, owing to its superb hillside location in an olive grove overlooking the city centre. Kitchen facilities and well-stocked, if expensive, shop nearby. Take bus #13 from the train station. April–Oct.

Camping Panoramico Via Peramondo 1, Fiesole ☏ 055.559.069, ⓦ www.florencecamping.com. Located in Fiesole, a 15min ride on bus #7 from Florence train station, this 120-pitch three-star site has a bar, restaurant, pool and small supermarket. Open all year.
Villa Camerata Viale Augusto Righi 2–4 ☏ 055.601.451, ⓦ www.ostellionline.org. Basic 55-pitch site in the grounds of the *Villa Camerata* HI hostel.

The City

A short walk southeast from the train station brings you to **Piazza del Duomo**, site of the **Duomo** itself and the neighbouring **Baptistry**. The compact district from here south to the river is the inner core, the area into which most of the tourists are packed, and which boasts the best-preserved medieval parts of Florence and the majority of its fashionable streets. Just south of the Duomo is Florence's outstanding sculpture gallery, the **Bargello**. The large **Piazza della Signoria**, some 300m south of the Duomo, is overlooked by the **Palazzo Vecchio** and the famous art gallery of the **Uffizi**.

West of the Duomo, and backing onto the train station, is the unmissable church of **Santa Maria Novella**, while immediately north is the grand church of **San Lorenzo**, at the heart of a throng of stalls around the food market

Museums admission

All of Florence's state-run museums belong to an association called **Firenze Musei** (ⓦ www.firenzemusei.it), which sets aside a daily quota of tickets that can be **reserved in advance**. The Uffizi, the Accademia and the Bargello belong to this group, as do the Palazzo Pitti museums (including the Bóboli gardens), the Medici chapels in San Lorenzo, the archeological museum and the San Marco museum.

You can reserve tickets (booking fee of €4 for Uffizi and Accademia, €3 for the rest) by phoning ☏ 055.294.883 (Mon–Fri 8.30am–6.30pm, Sat 8.30am–12.30pm), or through the Firenze Musei website, or at the Firenze Musei booth at Orsanmichele (Mon–Sat 10am–5.30pm), or at the museums themselves, in the case of the Uffizi and Pitti. If you use the phone line, an English-speaking operator will allocate you a ticket for a specific hour, to be collected at the museum, again at a specific time, shortly before entry. That's the theory, but in reality the phone line tends to be engaged for long periods at a stretch. Generally, the under-publicized Orsanmichele booth – which is set into the wall of the church on the Via Calzaiuoli side – is the easiest option. Pre-booking is strongly recommended at any time of year for the Uffizi and the Accademia, whose allocation of reservable tickets is often sold out many days ahead.

Note that on-the-door admission to all state-run museums is free for EU citizens under 18 and over 65, on presentation of a passport; 18–25s get a 50 percent discount, as do teachers, on proof of identity. Nearly all of Florence's major museums are routinely closed on Monday, though some are open for a couple of Mondays each month. In the majority of cases, museum ticket offices close thirty minutes before the museum itself. At the Palazzo Vecchio and Museo Stibbert, however, it's one hour before, while at the Uffizi, Bargello, Museo dell'Opera del Duomo, the dome of the Duomo, the Campanile and Pitti museums it's 45 minutes.

of the **Mercato Centrale**. Clustered together just northeast of San Lorenzo are the monastery and museum of **San Marco**, with its paintings by Fra' Angelico; the **Accademia**, home of Michelangelo's *David*; and **Piazza Santissima Annunziata**, Florence's most attractive square. Heading east of the centre, the main attraction is the vast Franciscan church of **Santa Croce**.

South of the river lies the **Oltrarno** district, where the array of museums within the **Palazzo Pitti** exerts the strongest pull, along with **Santo Spirito**, the **Cappella Brancacci** and the hilltop church of **San Miniato al Monte**.

Piazza del Duomo and around

Traffic and people gravitate towards the square at the heart of Florence, **Piazza del Duomo**, beckoned by the pinnacle of Brunelleschi's extraordinary dome,

▲ Piazza del Duomo, Florence

which dominates the cityscape in a way unmatched by any architectural creation in any other Italian city. Yet even though the magnitude of the **Duomo** is apparent from a distance, the first full sight of the church and the adjacent **Baptistry** still comes as a jolt, the colours of their patterned exteriors making a startling contrast with the dun-coloured buildings around them.

The Duomo (Santa Maria del Fiore)

It was sometime in the seventh century when the seat of the Bishop of Florence was transferred from San Lorenzo to the ancient church that stood on the site of the **Duomo**. In the thirteenth century, it was decided that a new cathedral was required, to better reflect the wealth of the city and to put the Pisans and Sienese in their place. In 1294 **Arnolfo di Cambio** designed a vast basilica focused on a domed tribune; by 1418 this project was complete except for its crowning feature. The conception was magnificent: the dome was to span a distance of nearly 42m and rise from a base some 54m above the floor of the nave. It was to be the largest dome ever constructed – but nobody had yet worked out how to build it.

A committee of the masons' guild was set up to ponder the problem, and it was to them that **Filippo Brunelleschi** presented himself. Some seventeen years before, in 1401, Brunelleschi had been defeated by Ghiberti in the competition to design the Baptistry doors, and had spent the intervening time studying classical architecture and developing new theories of engineering. He won the commission on condition that he worked jointly with Ghiberti – a partnership that did not last long. The key to the dome's success was the construction of two shells: a light outer shell about one metre thick, and an inner shell four times thicker. Brunelleschi's genius was to lay the brickwork in a herringbone pattern in cantilevered rings, thus allowing the massively heavy dome to support itself as it grew, without the use of scaffolding. On March 25, 1436 – Annunciation Day, and the Florentine New Year – the completion of the dome was marked by the papal consecration of the cathedral.

The Duomo's overblown main **facade** is a nineteenth-century imitation of a Gothic front, its marble cladding quarried from the same sources as the first builders used – white stone from Carrara, red from the Maremma, green from Prato. The south side is the oldest part, but the most attractive adornment is the **Porta della Mandorla**, on the north side. This takes its name from the almond-shaped frame that contains the relief *The Assumption of the Virgin*, sculpted by Nanni di Banco around 1420.

Inside the Duomo

The Duomo's **interior** (Mon–Wed & Fri 10am–5pm, Thurs closes 3.30pm, Sat 10am–4.45pm, Sun 1.30–4.45pm, on 1st Sat of month closes 3.30pm) is a vast enclosure of bare masonry that makes a stark contrast to the fussy exterior. Initially, the most conspicuous pieces of decoration are two memorials to *condottieri* (mercenary commanders) in the north aisle – Uccello's monument to **Sir John Hawkwood**, painted in 1436, and Castagno's monument to **Niccolò da Tolentino**, created twenty years later. Just beyond, Domenico do Michelino's *Dante Explaining the Divine Comedy* makes the dome only marginally less prominent than the mountain of Purgatory. Judged by mere size, the major work of art in the Duomo is the fresco of *The Last Judgement* inside the dome; painted by Vasari and Zuccari, it merely defaces Brunelleschi's masterpiece. Below the fresco are seven stained-glass roundels designed by Uccello, Ghiberti, Castagno and Donatello; they are best inspected from the gallery immediately below them, which forms part of the route up **inside the dome** – the entrance is outside, on the north side (Mon–Fri 8.30am–7pm, Sat 8.30am–5.40pm; €6). The gallery is the queasiest part of the climb, most of which winds between the brick walls of the outer and inner shells of the dome, up to the very summit with its stunning views over the city.

In the 1960s remnants of the Duomo's predecessor, **Santa Reparata**, were uncovered beneath the west end of the **nave** (€3). A detailed model helps make sense of the jigsaw of Roman, early Christian and Romanesque remains, areas of mosaic and patches of fourteenth-century frescoes. Also down here is the **tomb of Brunelleschi**, one of the few Florentines ever honoured with burial inside the Duomo.

The Campanile

Alongside Italy's most impressive cathedral dome is perhaps its most elegant bell tower. The **Campanile** (daily 8.30am–7.30pm; €6) was begun in 1334 by **Giotto**, who was no engineer: after his death in 1337 Andrea Pisano and Francesco Talenti took over the teetering, half-built edifice, and immediately doubled the thickness of the walls to stop it collapsing. The first storey is studded with two rows of remarkable bas-reliefs; the lower, *The Creation of Man* and the *Arts and Industries*, was carved by Pisano himself, the upper by his pupils. The figures of *Prophets* and *Sibyls* in the second-storey niches were created by Donatello and others. (All the sculptures are copies – the originals are in the Museo dell'Opera del Duomo.)

The Baptistry

Generally thought to date from the sixth or seventh century, the **Baptistry** (Mon–Sat noon–7pm, Sun & first Sat of month 8.30am–2pm; €3) is the oldest building in Florence, and no building better illustrates the special relationship between Florence and the Roman world. Throughout the Middle Ages the Florentines chose to believe that the Baptistry was originally a Roman temple to Mars, a belief bolstered by the interior's inclusion of Roman granite columns. The pattern of its marble cladding, applied in the eleventh and twelfth centuries, is clearly classical in inspiration, and the Baptistry's most famous embellishments – its gilded bronze doors – mark the emergence of a self-conscious interest in the art of the ancient world.

After Andrea Pisano's success in 1336 with the **doors** that are now on the south side of the building, the merchants' guild held a competition in 1401 for the job of making a new set. The two finalists were Brunelleschi and **Lorenzo Ghiberti** – and the latter won the day. Ghiberti's **north doors** show a new naturalism and classical sense of harmony, but their innovation is timid in comparison with his sublime **east doors**. Unprecedented in the subtlety of their modelling, these Old Testament scenes are a primer of early Renaissance art, using perspective, gesture and sophisticated grouping of their subjects to convey the human drama of each scene. Ghiberti has included a self-portrait in the frame of the left-hand door – his is the fourth head from the top of the right-hand band. All the panels now set in the door are replicas, with the originals on display in the Museo dell'Opera; the original competition entries are in the Bargello.

Inside, both the mosaic floor and the magnificent mosaic ceiling – including a fearsome platoon of demons at the feet of Christ in Judgement – were created in the thirteenth century. To the right of the altar is the **tomb of John XXIII**, the schismatic pope who died in Florence in 1419. The monument, draped by an illusionistic marble canopy, is the work of Donatello and his pupil Michelozzo.

The Museo dell'Opera del Duomo

At Piazza del Duomo 9, behind the east end of the Duomo, is the **Museo dell'Opera del Duomo** (Mon–Sat 9am–7.30pm, Sun 9am–1.40pm; €6), a repository of the most precious and fragile works of art from the Duomo, Baptistry and Campanile. In the large ground-floor hall are four seated Evangelists (including **Donatello**'s fine *St John*) wrenched from the Duomo's demolished sixteenth-century facade. On the mezzanine is the highlight of the museum – **Michelangelo**'s angular and anguished pietà. This was one of his last works, carved when he was almost 80 and intended for his own tomb: Vasari records that the face of the hooded Nicodemus is a self-portrait. **Upstairs** are **Donatello**'s figures for the Campanile, the most powerful of which is the prophet *Habbakuk*, the intensity of whose gaze allegedly prompted the sculptor to seize it and yell "Speak, speak!" Donatello also created one of the ornate *cantorie* (choir-lofts) here; the other, created at the same time, is by **Luca della Robbia**. An adjacent room is dominated by Donatello's haggard wooden figure of Mary Magdalene, a wild presence amid cases full of rich vestments, jewelled reliquaries, and a huge silver-gilt **altar**. Also on this floor are the original reliefs from the Campanile and a corridor lined with equipment used in the construction of the dome – and look out for Brunelleschi's **death mask**.

You return to ground level into a covered **courtyard** where Michelangelo worked from 1501 to 1504 on his *David*. Today, it displays Ghiberti's original **bronze panels** for the Baptistry's east doors.

Piazza della Repubblica and Orsanmichele

The main route south from Piazza del Duomo is the arrow-straight **Via dei Calzaiuoli**, a catwalk for the Florentine *passeggiata*. Halfway down the street is the opening into **Piazza della Repubblica**, created in the nineteenth century by razing the old Jewish quarter and markets which once stood here in an attempt to give Florence – briefly the capital of Italy – a grand public square. It's a characterless place, notably solely for its size and upmarket cafés.

Towards the southern end of Via dei Calzaiuoli rises the block-like church of **Orsanmichele** (Tues–Sun 10am–5pm). From the ninth century, the church of San Michele ad Hortum ("at the garden") stood here, which was replaced in 1240 by a grain market and after a fire in 1304 by a merchants' loggia. In 1380 the loggia was walled in and dedicated exclusively to religious functions, while two upper storeys were added for use as emergency grain stores. Its **exterior** has some impressive sculpture, including *St Matthew*, *St Stephen* and *John the Baptist* by Ghiberti (the *Baptist* was the first life-size bronze statue of the Renaissance), and Donatello's *St George*. All these statues are replicas – nearly all of the originals are on display in the museum (Mon–Sat 10am–3pm; free), entered via the footbridge from the Palazzo dell'Arte della Lana, opposite the church entrance.

Piazza della Signoria and around

Whereas the Piazza del Duomo provides the focus for the city's religious life, the **Piazza della Signoria** – site of the mighty **Palazzo Vecchio** and forecourt to the **Uffizi** – has always been the centre of its secular existence. The most lavishly decorated rooms of the Palazzo Vecchio are now a museum, but the rest of the building is still the HQ of the city's councillors and bureaucrats, and the piazza in front of it provides the stage for major civic events and political rallies.

The piazza's array of **statuary** starts with Giambologna's equestrian statue of Cosimo I and continues with Ammannati's fatuous Neptune Fountain and copies of Donatello's *Marzocco* (the city's heraldic lion), his *Judith and Holofernes* and of Michelangelo's *David*. Conceived as a partner piece to David, Bandinelli's lumpen **Hercules and Cacus** was designed as a personal emblem of Cosimo I and a symbol of Florentine fortitude; Benvenuto Cellini described the muscle-bound Hercules as looking like "a sackful of melons. Near Ammannati's fountain is a plaque set into the pavement to mark the site of Savonarola's **Bonfire of the Vanities** and his execution. The square's **Loggia della Signoria** was built in the late fourteenth century as a dais for city officials during ceremonies; only in the late eighteenth century did it become a showcase for sculpture, the best of which are Giambologna's *Rape of the Sabine* and Cellini's superb *Perseus*.

The Palazzo Vecchio

Probably designed by Arnolfo di Cambio, Florence's fortress-like town hall, the Palazzo Vecchio (daily 9am–7pm, Thurs closes 2pm; €6), was begun as the Palazzo dei Priori in the last year of the thirteenth century, to provide premises for the highest tier of the city's republican government. Changes in the Florentine constitution over the years entailed alterations to the layout of the palace, the most radical coming in 1540, when Cosimo I moved his retinue here from the Palazzo Medici and grafted a huge extension onto the rear. The Medici remained in residence for only nine years before moving to the Palazzo Pitti; the old (*vecchio*) palace – which they left to their son, Francesco – then acquired its present name.

Giorgio Vasari, court architect from 1555 until his death in 1574, was responsible for much of the decor in the courtyard, and his limited talents were given full rein in the huge **Salone dei Cinquecento** at the top of the stairs, which was built at the end of the fifteenth century as a council assembly hall. This room might have become one of Italy's most extraordinary showcases of Renaissance art, when in 1503 Leonardo da Vinci and Michelangelo were commissioned to fresco opposite walls of the chamber. Unfortunately, Leonardo abandoned the project after his experimental fresco technique went wrong, and Michelangelo's work existed only on paper when he was summoned to Rome by Pope Julius II. A few decades later Vasari stepped in, and covered the room with drearily bombastic murals celebrating Cosimo's military prowess. Michelangelo's *Victory*, facing the entrance door, was sculpted for Julius's tomb but was donated to the Medici by the artist's nephew.

From the Salone del Cinquecento, a roped-off door allows a glimpse of the strangest room in the building, the Studiolo di Francesco I. Designed by Vasari towards the end of his career and decorated by no fewer than thirty Mannerist artists (1570–74), this windowless cell was created as a retreat for the introverted son of Cosimo and Eleanor.

Upstairs, you first enter the **Quartiere degli Elementi**, where all five salons are slavishly devoted to a different member of the Medici clan. More interesting are the private apartments of **Eleanor di Toledo**, Cosimo I's wife – especially the tiny and exquisite **chapel**, vividly decorated by Bronzino in the 1540s. Beyond the frescoed Sala dell'Udienza (originally the audience chamber of the Republic) you come to the **Sala dei Gigli**, which takes its name from the lilies (*gigli*) that adorn most of its surfaces. The room has frescoes by Domenico Ghirlandaio, but the highlight is **Donatello**'s original *Judith and Holofernes*. Commissioned by Cosimo il Vecchio, it freezes the moment at which Judith's arm begins the scything stroke that is to cut off Holofernes' head, a dramatic conception that no other sculptor of the period would have attempted.

The two small side-rooms are the Cancellaria, **Machiavelli**'s office for fifteen years and now containing a bust and portrait of the much-maligned political thinker; and the lovely **Sala delle Carte**, decorated with 57 maps painted in 1563 by the Medici court astronomer Fra' Ignazio Danti, depicting what was then the entire known world.

The Uffizi

The Galleria degli Uffizi (Tues–Sun 8.15am–6.50pm; €6.50; see box, p.454 for details of advance reservations) is, quite simply, the finest picture gallery in Italy. So many masterpieces are collected here that it's not even possible to skate over the surface in a single visit. Though you may not want to emulate Edward Gibbon, who visited the Uffizi fourteen times on a single trip to Florence, it makes sense to limit your initial tour to the first fifteen rooms, where the Florentine Renaissance works are concentrated, and to explore the rest another time.

The gallery is housed in what were once government offices (*uffizi*) built by Vasari for Cosimo I in 1560. After Vasari's death, work on the building was continued by Buontalenti, who was asked by Francesco I to glaze the upper storey so that it could house his art collection. Each of the succeeding Medici added to the family's trove of art treasures, which was preserved for public inspection by the last member of the family, Anna Maria Lodovica, whose will specified that it should be left to the people of Florence and never be allowed to leave the city. In the nineteenth century a large proportion of the statuary was transferred to the Bargello, while most of the antiquities went to the Museo Archeologico, leaving the Uffizi as essentially a gallery of paintings supplemented with some classical sculptures. The gallery is in the process of expansion, doubling the number of rooms open to the public in order to show some eight hundred pictures that have usually been kept in storage; accordingly, some paintings may not be on show precisely where they appear in the following account.

Pre-Renaissance

You can take a lift up to the galleries, but if you take the staircase instead, you'll pass the entrance to the Uffizi's prints and drawings section. The bulk of this vast collection is reserved for scholarly scrutiny but samples are often on public show.

The beginnings of the stylistic evolution of that period can be traced in the three altarpieces of the *Maestà* (Madonna Enthroned) that dominate **Room 2**: the *Madonna Rucellai*, *Maestà di Santa Trìnita* and *Madonna d'Ognissanti*, by **Duccio**, **Cimabue** and **Giotto** respectively. These great works, which dwarf everything around them, show the softening of the hieratic Byzantine style into a more tactile form of representation.

Painters from fourteenth-century Siena fill **Room 3**, with several pieces by Ambrogio and Pietro Lorenzetti and **Simone Martini**'s glorious *Annunciation*. Further on, in a room devoted to the last flowering of Gothic art, **Lorenzo Monaco** is represented by an *Adoration of the Magi* and his greatest masterpiece, *The Coronation of the Virgin* (1415). Equally arresting is the *Adoration of the Magi* (1423) by **Gentile da Fabriano**, a picture spangled with gold and crammed with incidental detail. Nearby is the *Thebaid*, a beguiling little narrative that depicts monastic life in the Egyptian desert as a sort of holy fairytale; it's generally attributed to the young Fra' Angelico.

Early Renaissance

Room 7 reveals the sheer diversity of early Renaissance painting. **Fra' Angelico**'s gorgeous *Coronation of the Virgin* takes place against a Gothic-like field of gold, but there's a very un-Gothic sensibility at work in its individualized depiction of the attendant throng. **Paolo Uccello**'s *The Battle of San Romano* once hung in Lorenzo il Magnifico's bedchamber, in company with its two companion pieces now in the Louvre and London's National Gallery. *The Madonna and Child with Sts Francis, John the Baptist, Zenobius and Lucy* is one of only twelve extant paintings by **Domenico Veneziano**, whose greatest pupil, **Piero della Francesca**, is represented in **Room 8** by the paired portraits of *Federico da Montefeltro and Battista Sforza*, the duke and duchess of Urbino. Much of this room is given over to **Fra' Filippo Lippi**, whose *Madonna and Child with Two Angels* supplies one of the gallery's most popular faces: the model was Lucrezia Buti, a convent novice who became the object of one of his more enduring sexual obsessions. Lucrezia puts in an another appearance in Lippi's crowded *Coronation of the Virgin*, where she's the young woman gazing out in the right foreground; Filippo himself, hand on chin, makes eye contact on the left side of the picture. Their liaison produced a son, the aptly named **Filippino** "Little Philip" **Lippi**, whose *Madonna degli Otto* – one of several works by him here – is typical of the more melancholic cast of the younger Lippi's art.

The Pollaiuolo brothers and Botticelli

Lippi's great pupil, Botticelli, steals some of the thunder in **Room 9** – *Fortitude*, one of the series of cardinal and theological virtues, is a very early work by him. The rest of the series is by the brothers **Piero** and **Antonio del Pollaiuolo**, whose *Sts Vincent, James and Eustace*, one of their best works, is chiefly the work of Antonio.

It's in the merged **rooms 10–14** that the finest of **Botticelli**'s productions are gathered, most notably the *Primavera* and the *Birth of Venus*. The identities of the characters in the **Primavera** are clear enough: on the right Zephyrus, god of the west wind, chases the nymph Cloris, who is then transfigured into Flora, the pregnant goddess of spring; Venus stands in the centre, to the side of the three Graces, who are targeted by Cupid; on the left Mercury wards off the clouds of winter. What this all means, however, has occupied scholars for decades, but the consensus seems to be that it shows the triumph of Venus, with the Graces as the physical embodiment of her beauty and Flora the symbol of her fruitfulness.

Botticelli's most alluring painting, the **Birth of Venus**, probably takes as its source the myth that the goddess emerged from the sea after it had been impregnated by the castration of Uranus, an allegory for the creation of beauty through the mingling of the spirit (Uranus) and the physical world.

Botticelli's devotional paintings are generally less perplexing. *The Adoration of the Magi* is traditionally thought to contain a gallery of Medici portraits: Cosimo il Vecchio as the first king, his sons Giovanni and Piero as the other two kings, Lorenzo the Magnificent on the far left, and his brother Giuliano as the black-haired young man in profile on the right. Only the identification of Cosimo is reasonably certain, along with that of Botticelli himself, on the right in the yellow robe. In later life, influenced by Savonarola's teaching, Botticelli confined himself to devotional pictures and moral fables, and his style became increasingly severe and didactic. The transformation is clear when comparing the easy grace of the *Madonna of the Magnificat* and the *Madonna of the Pomegranate* with the more rigidly composed *Pala di Sant'Ambrogio* or the angular and agitated *Calumny*.

Not quite every masterpiece in this room is by Botticelli. Set away from the walls is the *Adoration of the Shepherds* by his Flemish contemporary **Hugo van der Goes**. Brought to Florence in 1483 by Tommaso Portinari, the Medici agent in Bruges, it provided the city's artists with their first large-scale demon-stration of the realism of Northern European oil painting, and had a great influence on the way the medium was exploited here.

Leonardo to Mantegna

Works in **Room 15** trace the formative years of **Leonardo da Vinci**, whose distinctive touch appears first in the *Baptism of Christ* by his master Verrocchio: the wistful angel in profile is by the eighteen-year-old apprentice, as is the misty landscape in the background, and Leonardo also worked heavily on the figure of Christ. A similar terrain of soft-focus mountains and water occupies the far distance in Leonardo's slightly later *Annunciation*, in which a diffused light falls on a scene where everything is observed with a scientist's precision. In contrast to the poise of the *Annunciation*, the sketch of *The Adoration of the Magi* – abandoned when Leonardo left Florence for Milan in early 1482 – presents the infant Christ as the eye of a vortex of figures, all drawn into his presence by a force as irresistible as a whirlpool. Most of the rest of the room is given over to Raphael's teacher, **Perugino**.

Room 18, the octagonal **Tribuna**, now houses the most important of the Medici's collection of classical sculptures, chief among which is the *Medici Venus*. Around the walls are hung some fascinating portraits by **Bronzino**: Cosimo de' Medici, Eleonora di Toledo, Bartolomeo Panciatichi and his wife Lucrezia Panciatichi, all painted like figures of porcelain. More vital is Andrea del Sarto's flirtatious *Ritratto d'Ignota* (Portrait of a Young Woman).

The last section of this wing throws together Renaissance paintings from outside Florence. **Signorelli** and **Perugino** – with some photo-sharp portraits – are the principal artists in **Room 19**, and after them comes a room largely devoted to **Cranach** and **Dürer**. A taste of the Uffizi's remarkable collection of Venetian painting follows, with an impenetrable *Sacred Allegory* by **Giovanni Bellini**, and three works attributed to **Giorgione**. A clutch of Northern European paintings includes some superb portraits by **Holbein** (notably *Sir Richard Southwell* and a self-portrait) and Hans Memling. In the following room – called the **Correggio** room, after the trio of pictures by him on show here – there's a clutch of exquisite small paintings by **Mantegna**, including the *Madonna of the Stonecutters*, which takes its name from the minuscule figures at work in the quarry in the background.

Michelangelo, Mannerism and Titian

Beyond the stockpile of statues in the short corridor overlooking the Arno, the main attraction in **Room 25** is **Michelangelo**'s *Doni Tondo*, the only easel painting he came close to completing. The adjoining room contains **Andrea del Sarto**'s sultry *Madonna of the Harpies* and a number of compositions by **Raphael**, including his self-portrait, the lovely *Madonna of the Goldfinch* and the *Pope Leo X with Cardinals Giulio de' Medici and Luigi de' Rossi*. The Michelangelo tondo's contorted gestures and virulent colours were greatly influential on the Mannerist painters of the sixteenth century, as can be gauged from *Moses Defending the Daughters of Jethro* by **Rosso Fiorentino**, one of the seminal figures of the movement, whose works hang in **Room 27**, along with major works by Bronzino and his adoptive father, Pontormo.

Room 28 is almost entirely given over to another of the titanic figures of sixteenth-century art, **Titian**, with nine paintings on show. His *Flora* and *A Knight of Malta* are stunning, but most eyes tend to swivel towards the *Urbino Venus*, the most provocative of all Renaissance nudes, described by Mark Twain as "the foulest, the vilest, the obscenest picture the world possesses". A brief

A door on the west corridor, between rooms 25 and 34, opens onto the **Corridoio Vasariano**, a passageway built by Vasari in 1565 to link the Palazzo Vecchio to the Palazzo Pitti, via the Uffizi. Winding its way down to the river, over the Ponte Vecchio, through the church of Santa Felìcita and into the Giardino di Bóboli, it gives a fascinating series of clandestine views of the city, and is also lined with paintings, the larger portion of which comprises a gallery of **self-portraits**, featuring such greats as Andrea del Sarto, Bernini, Rubens, Velázquez, David, Delacroix and Ingres. However, the corridor is currently closed for restoration, and there are plans to move the best of the paintings into the extended Uffizi galleries. The corridor used to be open two mornings per week for small-group guided tours, and in all likelihood that will be the arrangement when the restoration is completed. For the latest situation, ask at one of the tourist offices.

diversion through the painters of the sixteenth-century Emilian school follows, centred on **Parmigianino**, whose *Madonna of the Long Neck* is one of the pivotal Mannerist creations. **Rooms 31 to 34** feature a miscellany of sixteenth-century artists (look out for the El Greco) and some top-class works from Venice and the Veneto, including **Moroni**'s *Portrait of Count Pietro Secco Suardi*, **Paolo Veronese**'s *Annunciation* and *Holy Family with St Barbara*, and a gathering of fine pieces by **Lorenzo Lotto**.

The seventeenth and eighteenth centuries

The Uffizi's collection of seventeenth-century art features strong work from **van Dyck** and **Rubens**, whose *Portrait of Isabella Brandt* is perhaps his finest painting here. The most overwhelming, however, are the huge *Henry IV at the Battle of Ivry* and *The Triumphal Entry of Henry IV into Paris* – Henry's marriage to Marie de' Medici is the connection with Florence. This pair are displayed in the majestic neo-classical Niobe Room. In this section of the gallery you'll also see some superb portraits by **Rembrandt**, **Goya** and **Chardin**.

The rooms downstairs are used at the moment for temporary exhibitions and as a showcase for Italian art of the seventeenth century. Dramatic images from Salvator Rosa, Luca Giordano and Artimisia Gentileschi make quite an impression, but the presiding genius is **Caravaggio**, with his bravura *Medusa* (painted on a shield), the smug little *Bacchus*, and the throat-grabbing *Sacrifice of Isaac*.

The Bargello

The **Museo Nazionale del Bargello** (Tues–Sat 8.15am–1.50pm, 2nd & 4th Sun of month and 1st, 3rd & 5th Mon of month same hours, longer hours and higher charge for special exhibitions; €4), which is both an outstanding museum of sculpture and a huge applied art collection, is installed in the daunting Palazzo del Bargello on Via del Proconsolo, halfway between the Duomo and the Palazzo Vecchio. The *palazzo* was built in 1255, and soon became the seat of the *Podestà*, the chief magistrate. Numerous malefactors were tried, sentenced and executed here and the building acquired its present name in the sixteenth century, after the resident *Bargello*, or police chief.

The courtyard and ground floor

From the ticket desk, you enter the beautiful Gothic **courtyard**, which is plastered with the coats of arms of the *Podestà* and contains, among many other pieces, six allegorical figures by **Ammannati**. At the foot of the courtyard steps is the **Michelangelo Room**, containing his first major sculpture, a tipsy, soft-bellied figure of Bacchus, carved at the age of 22 – a year before his great pietà in Rome. Michelangelo's style soon evolved into something less ostentatiously virtuosic, as is shown by the tender *Tondo Pitti* (1503–05), while the rugged expressivity of his late manner is exemplified by the square-jawed *Bust of Brutus* (c.1540). Works by Michelangelo's followers and contemporaries are ranged in the immediate vicinity – **Cellini**'s *Bust of Cosimo I* and **Giambologna**'s famous *Mercury* are the best of them

The upper floors

At the top of the courtyard staircase, the **loggia** has been turned into an aviary for Giambologna's bronze birds, brought here from the Medici villa at Castello. In the adjacent Salone del Consiglio Generale the dominant presence is **Donatello**. Vestiges of the sinuous Gothic manner are evident in the drapery of his marble *David*, placed against the left wall, but there's nothing antiquated in the alert, tense *St George*, carved just eight years later for the tabernacle of the armourers' guild at Orsanmichele and installed here in a replica of its original niche. In front stands Donatello's sexually ambiguous bronze *David*, cast in the early 1430s as the first freestanding nude figure since classical times. Back opposite the entrance door is Donatello's strange, jubilant figure known as *Amor Atys*, dating from the end of the 1430s, while his breathtakingly vivid bust of Niccolò da Uzzano shows that he was just as comfortable with portraiture. The less complex humanism of **Luca della Robbia** is embodied in the glazed terracotta Madonnas set round the walls, while Donatello's master, **Ghiberti**, is represented by his relief *The Sacrifice of Isaac*, his successful entry in the competition for the Baptistry doors. The treatment of the same theme submitted by **Brunelleschi** is displayed nearby. Most of the rest of this floor is occupied by a collection of **European and Islamic applied art**, of so high a standard that it would constitute an engrossing museum in its own right. Elsewhere on this floor is dazzling carved **ivory** from Byzantium and medieval France.

The sculptural display resumes on the next floor up, where you'll find superb work by the **della Robbia** family, Italy's best assembly of small Renaissance bronzes (with plentiful evidence of Giambologna's virtuosity at table-top scale) and two rooms devoted mainly to Renaissance busts, including magnificent portraits by Verrocchio, Francesco Laurana and Mino da Fiesole.

The Museo di Storia della Scienza

Long after Florence had declined from its artistic apogee, the intellectual reputation of the city was maintained by its scientists. Grand Duke Ferdinando II and his brother Leopoldo, both of whom studied with **Galileo**, founded the Accademia del Cimento (Academy of Experiment) in 1657, and the instruments made and acquired by this academy form the core of the excellent **Museo di Storia della Scienza** (Mon & Wed–Fri 9.30am–5pm, Tues & Sat 9.30am–1pm; €4), close to the river, on **Piazza dei Giudici**. The **first floor** features timepieces and measuring instruments (such as beautiful Arab astrolabes), as well as a massive armillary sphere made for Ferdinando I to prove the fallacy of Copernicus's heliocentric universe. Some of Galileo's original instruments are on show here, including the lens with which he discovered the four moons of Jupiter. On the floor above there are all kinds of exquisitely manufactured **scientific and mechanical equipment**, several of which were built to demonstrate the fundamental laws of physics. Dozens of clocks and timepieces are on show too, while the medical section is full of alarming surgical instruments and wax anatomical models for teaching obstetrics.

The western city centre

Several streets in central Florence retain their medieval character, especially in the district immediately to the west of Piazza della Signoria. Forming a gateway to this quarter is the **Mercato Nuovo** (mid-Feb to mid-Nov daily 9am–7pm; mid-Nov to mid-Feb Tues–Sat 9am–5pm), whose souvenir stalls are the busiest in the city. Usually a small group is gathered round the bronze boar known as **Il Porcellino**, trying to gain some good luck by getting a coin to fall from the animal's mouth through the grill below his head.

Palazzo Davanzati

Perhaps the most imposing exterior in this district is to be seen just to the south of the market – the thirteenth-century **Palazzo di Parte Guelfa**, financed from the confiscated property of the Ghibelline faction and later expanded by Brunelleschi. However, for a more complete re-creation of medieval Florence you should visit the fourteenth-century **Palazzo Davanzati** in Via Porta Rossa. Maintained as the **Museo della Casa Fiorentina Antica**, the house is furnished and decorated throughout in predominantly medieval style, using genuine artefacts gathered from a variety of sources. The building was closed in 1995 for major structural repairs, an operation that was at last drawing to a close as we went to press. Pending completion of this project, only a few sections of the house are open (Tues–Sat 8.15am–1.50pm, 1st, 3rd & 5th Sun of month and 2nd & 4th Mon of month same hours); there's no entrance charge, but this will change when the whole *palazzo* is once again accessible.

Santa Trinità and around

Via Porta Rossa culminates at Piazza Santa Trinità, close to the city's most stylish bridge, the **Ponte Santa Trinità**, which was rebuilt stone by stone after the retreating Nazis had blown up the original in 1944. **Santa Trinità church** (Mon–Sat 8am–noon & 4–6pm, Sun 4–6pm) was founded in the eleventh century, but piecemeal additions have lent it a pleasantly hybrid air: the largely Gothic interior contrasts with Buontalenti's Mannerist facade of 1594. The interior is notable above all for **Ghirlandaio**'s frescoes of the *Life of St Francis* in the **Cappella Sassetti** – as notable for their depiction of fifteenth-century Florence as for their ostensible subjects, they feature portraits of various Medici.

Heading north from Santa Trinità is **Via de' Tornabuoni**, home to Cartier, Versace, Armani and the famous local firms Ferragamo, Cavalli and Pucci. Conspicuous wealth is nothing new here, for looming above everything is the vast **Palazzo Strozzi**, the last, the largest and the least subtle of Florentine Renaissance palaces. Filippo Strozzi bought and demolished a dozen town houses to make space for Giuliano da Sangallo's design (1536). Part of the building is now used for exhibitions.

The church of San Pancrazio, nearby on Via della Spada, has been converted into the slick **Museo Marino Marini** (10am–5pm; closed Tues & Sun; €4), a spacious showcase for the work of one of Italy's foremost twentieth-century sculptors.

Ognissanti

In medieval times a major area of cloth production – the foundation of the Florentine economy – lay in the west of the city, in the parish of **Ognissanti** (daily 7.30am–12.30pm & 3.30–7.30pm), located on Borgo Ognissanti, five-minutes' walk west of Via de' Tornabuoni. The Baroque facade, added in the sixteenth century when Ognissanti became a Franciscan church, is not very interesting, but the interior is a different matter. The young face squeezed between the Madonna and the dark-cloaked man in **Ghirlandaio's** *Madonna della Misericordia* fresco, over the second altar on the right, is said to be that of Amerigo Vespucci – later to set sail on voyages that would give his name to America. Just beyond this, on opposite sides of the nave, are mounted **Botticelli's** *St Augustine* and Ghirlandaio's *St Jerome*, both painted in 1480. In the same year Ghirlandaio painted the bucolic *Last Supper* that covers one wall of the **refectory**, reached through the cloister entered to the left of the church (March–June Thurs–Tues 9am–5pm; rest of year Mon, Tues & Sat 9am–noon; free).

Santa Maria Novella

The focus of the western city centre is **Piazza Santa Maria Novella**, a large and formerly somewhat grubby piazza, now in the throes of a major overhaul.

The marble facade designed by Alberti for the Dominican church of **Santa Maria Novella** (Mon–Thurs 9.30am–5pm, Fri & Sun 1–5pm; €2.50) is one of the most attractive in the city, and the interior – which was designed to enable preachers to address their sermons to as large a congregation as possible – is filled with masterworks, not least **Masaccio's** extraordinary 1427 fresco of *The Trinity* (left aisle), one of the earliest works in which perspective and classical proportion were rigorously employed. Nearby, Giotto's *Crucifix*, a radically naturalistic and probably very early work (c.1288–90), hangs in what is thought to be its intended position, poised dramatically over the nave. **Filippino Lippi's** frescoes for the **Cappella di Filippo Strozzi** (immediately to the right of the chancel) are a fantasy vision of classical ruins in which the narrative often seems to take second place, and one of the first examples of an archeological interest in Roman culture. As a chronicle of fifteenth-century life in Florence, no series of frescoes is more fascinating than **Domenico Ghirlandaio's** behind the high altar; the cycle was commissioned by Giovanni Tornabuoni – which explains why certain ladies of the Tornabuoni family are present at the birth of John the Baptist and of the Virgin. **Brunelleschi's** *Crucifix*, popularly supposed to have been carved as a response to Donatello's uncouth version at Santa Croce, hangs in the Cappella Gondi, left of the chancel. At the end of the left transept is the raised **Cappella Strozzi**, whose faded frescoes by Nardo di Cione (1350s) include an entire wall of visual commentary on Dante's *Inferno*. The magnificent altarpiece by Nardo's brother Andrea (better known as **Orcagna**) is a piece of propaganda for the Dominicans – Christ is shown bestowing favour simultaneously on St Peter and St Thomas Aquinas, a figure second only to St Dominic in the order's hierarchy.

The Museo di Santa Maria Novella

More remarkable paintings are on display in the spacious Romanesque conventual buildings to the left of the church, now the **Museo di Santa Maria Novella** (Mon–Thurs & Sat 9am–5pm, Sun 9am–2pm; €2.70). The first cloister, the **Chiostro Verde**, features *Stories from Genesis* by **Paolo Uccello** and his workshop. From this cloister you enter the **Cappellone degli Spagnuoli** (Spanish Chapel), which received its new name after Eleanor of Toledo reserved it for the use of her Spanish entourage. Its fresco cycle by Andrea di Firenze, an extended depiction of the triumph of the Catholic Church, was described by Ruskin as "the most noble piece of pictorial philosophy in Italy". The left wall depicts the *Triumph of Divine Wisdom*: Thomas Aquinas is enthroned below the Virgin and Apostles amid winged Virtues and biblical notables. The more spectacular right wall depicts the *Triumph of the Church*, and includes Florence's cathedral, imagined eighty years before its actual completion.

Facing Santa Maria Novella across the piazza, the **Loggia di San Paolo** – a close imitation of Brunelleschi's Spedale degli Innocenti – is home to the new **Museo Nazionale Alinari Fotografia** (Thurs, Fri & Sun–Tues 9.30am–7.30pm, Sat 9.30am–11.30pm; €9). Part of the museum is set aside for one-off photography exhibitions, but most of the space is given over to changing displays drawn from Alinari's archive of more than four million pictures, covering everything from 1840s' daguerreotypes to the work of present-day photographers. The technology of the art is featured too, with a variety of cameras on show, plus stereoscopes and camera obscuras.

The northern city centre

The busy quarter north of the Duomo and east of the train station is focused on Florence's main food market, the vast **Mercato Centrale** (Mon–Sat 7am–2pm; winter also Sat 4–8pm). Butchers, *alimentari*, tripe sellers, greengrocers, pasta stalls and bars are all gathered under one roof, charging prices lower than you'll find elsewhere. All around is a hectic **street market** (Mon–Sat 8.30am–7pm), thronged with stalls selling leather bags, belts, clothes and shoes.

San Lorenzo

Founded in the fourth century, **San Lorenzo** (daily 10am–5.30pm; March–Oct closes Sun 1.30pm; €3.50) has a claim to be the oldest church in Florence – though the current building dates from the 1420s – and was the city's cathedral for almost three centuries. Although Michelangelo sweated to produce a scheme for San Lorenzo's facade, the bare brick of the exterior has never been clad; it's a stark, inappropriate prelude to the powerful simplicity of Brunelleschi's interior, one of the earliest Renaissance church designs. Inside are two amazing **bronze pulpits** by **Donatello**. Covered in densely populated reliefs, chiefly of scenes preceding and following the Crucifixion, these are the artist's last works and were completed by his pupils. Close by, at the foot of the altar steps, a large disc of multicoloured marble marks the grave of Cosimo il Vecchio, the artist's main patron. Further pieces by Donatello (who is buried here) adorn the beautiful **Sagrestia Vecchia**, off the left transept.

The Biblioteca Medicea-Laurenziana

A gateway to the left of the church facade leads to the Biblioteca Medicea-Laurenziana (Mon, Fri & Sat 8.30am–2pm, Tues–Thurs 8am–5pm; €3). Wishing to create a suitably grandiose home for the precious manuscripts assembled by Cosimo and Lorenzo de' Medici, Pope Clement VII – Lorenzo's nephew – asked Michelangelo to design a new library in 1524. His Ricetto, or vestibule (1559–71), is a revolutionary showpiece of Mannerist architecture, delighting in paradoxical display: brackets that support nothing, columns that sink into the walls rather than stand out from them, and a flight of steps so large that it almost fills the room. From this eccentric space, you're sometimes allowed into the tranquil reading room; here, too, almost everything is the work of Michelangelo, even the inlaid desks.

The Cappelle Medicee

Some of Michelangelo's most celebrated works are in San Lorenzo's Sagrestia Nuova, part of the **Cappelle Medicee** (Tues–Sat 8.15am–5.50pm, 1st, 3rd & 5th Sun of month and 2nd & 4th Mon of month same hours; €6). The entrance to the chapels is round the back of San Lorenzo, on Piazza Madonna degli Aldobrandini, and leads directly into the low-vaulted **crypt**, last resting place of a clutch of minor Medici. After filing through the crypt, you climb into the **Cappella dei Principi** (Chapel of the Princes), a gloomy, stone-plated octagonal hall built as a mausoleum for Cosimo I and his ancestors. Morbid and dowdy, it was the most expensive building project ever financed by the family.

A corridor leads to the **Sagrestia Nuova**, begun by Michelangelo in 1520 and intended as a tribute to, and subversion of, Brunelleschi's Sagrestia Vecchia in San Lorenzo. Architectural connoisseurs go into raptures over the complex alcoves and other such sophistications, but you might be more drawn to the fabulous **Medici tombs**, carved by Michelangelo. To the left is the **tomb of Lorenzo**, Duke of Urbino, grandson of Lorenzo il Magnifico. Opposite is the **tomb of Giuliano**, Duke of Nemours, youngest son of Lorenzo il Magnifico. Their effigies were intended to face the equally grand tombs of Lorenzo il Magnifico and his brother Giuliano, two Medici who had genuine claims to fame and honour, but the only part of the project realized by Michelangelo is the serene **Madonna and Child**, the last image of the Madonna he ever sculpted and one of the most affecting, now flanked by *Cosmas* and *Damian*, patron saints of doctors (*medici*) and thus of the dynasty.

The Palazzo Medici-Riccardi

On the northeastern edge of Piazza San Lorenzo stands the **Palazzo Medici-Riccardi** (9am–7pm; closed Wed; €5), built by Michelozzo in the 1440s for Cosimo il Vecchio and for more than a century the principal seat of the Medici. With its heavily rusticated exterior, this mighty palace was the prototype for such houses as the Palazzo Pitti and Palazzo Strozzi, but was greatly altered in the seventeenth century by its new owners, the Riccardi family, who took over after Cosimo I moved out. Of Michelozzo's original scheme, only the upstairs **chapel** remains intact, its interior covered by brilliantly colourful **frescoes** of *The Procession of the Magi*, painted around 1460 by Benozzo Gozzoli. Only fifteen people are allowed to view these paintings at any one time, so the queues can be long.

A second staircase ascends from the courtyard to the **Sala di Luca Giordano**, a gilded and mirrored gallery notable for its *Madonna and Child* by Fra' Filippo Lippi. Luca Giordano's overblown ceiling fresco, *The Apotheosis of the Medici*, shows Cosimo III with his son, Gian Gastone (d. 1737), the last male Medici.

The Accademia

Europe's first academy of drawing was founded northeast of San Lorenzo on Via Ricasoli in the mid-sixteenth century by Bronzino, Ammannati and Vasari. In 1784, Grand Duke Pietro Leopoldo opened the adjoining **Galleria dell'Accademia** (Tues–Sun 8.15am–6.50pm; €6.50), which has an impressive collection of paintings, especially of Florentine altarpieces from the fourteenth to the early sixteenth centuries. What pulls the crowds, however, is one of the most famous sculptures in the world: **Michelangelo's** *David*.

Commissioned by the Opera del Duomo in 1501, the *David* was conceived to invoke parallels with Florence's freedom from outside domination (despite the superior force of its enemies), and its recent liberation from Savonarola and the Medici. It's an incomparable show of technical bravura, all the more impressive given the difficulties posed by the marble from which it was carved. The four-metre block of stone – thin, shallow and riddled with cracks – had been quarried from Carrara forty years earlier. Several artists had already attempted to work with it, notably Agostino di Duccio, Andrea Sansovino and Leonardo da Vinci. Michelangelo succeeded where others had failed, completing the work in 1504 when he was still just 29.

When they gave Michelangelo his commission, the Opera del Duomo had in mind a large statue that would be placed high on the cathedral's facade. Perhaps because the finished *David* was even larger than had been envisaged, it was decided that it should be placed instead at ground level, in the Piazza della Signoria. The statue remained in its outdoor setting, exposed to the elements, until it was sent to the Accademia in 1873, by which time it had lost its gilded hair and the gilded band across its chest. Thoroughly cleaned in 2004, *David* now occupies a specially built alcove, protected by a glass barrier that was built in 1991, after one of its toes was cracked by a hammer-wielding artist. With its massive head and gangling arms, the *David* looks to some people like a monstrous adolescent, but its proportions would not have appeared so graceless in the setting for which it was first conceived, at a rather higher altitude and at a greater distance from the public than the position it occupies in this chapel-like space.

Michelangelo once described the process of sculpting as being the liberation of the form from within the stone, a notion that seems to be embodied by the unfinished **Slaves** that line the approach to *David*. His procedure, clearly demonstrated here, was to cut the figure as if it were a deep relief, and then to free the three-dimensional figure; often his assistants would perform the initial operation, working from the master's pencil marks, so it's possible that Michelangelo's own chisel never actually touched these stones. Carved in the 1520s and 1530s, these powerful creations were intended for the tomb of Pope Julius II, but in 1564 the artist's nephew gave them to the Medici, who installed them in the grotto of the Bòboli gardens.

The Museo di San Marco

A whole side of Piazza San Marco is taken up by the Dominican convent and church of San Marco, the first of which is now the Museo di San Marco (Tues–Thurs 8.15am–1.50pm, Fri 8.15am–6pm, Sat 8.15am–7pm; also 1st, 3rd & 5th Mon of month 8.15am–1.50pm, and 2nd & 4th Sun of month 8.15am–7pm; €4). In the 1430s, the convent was the recipient of Cosimo il Vecchio's most lavish patronage: he financed Michelozzo's enlargement of the buildings, and went on to establish a vast public library here. Ironically, the convent became the centre of resistance to the Medici later in the century – Savonarola was prior of San Marco from 1491. Meanwhile, as Michelozzo was altering and expanding the convent, its walls were being decorated by one of its friars, **Fra' Angelico**, a painter in whom a medieval simplicity of faith was allied to a Renaissance sophistication of manner. The **Ospizio dei Pellegrini** (Pilgrims' Hospice) contains around twenty paintings by Fra' Angelico, most brought here from other churches in Florence, but the most celebrated work is the glorious **Annunciation** at the summit of the main staircase. All round this upper floor are ranged 44 tiny **dormitory cells**, each frescoed either by Angelico himself or by his assistants.

The **church** of San Marco is worth a visit for two works on the second and third altars on the right: a *Madonna and Saints*, painted in 1509 by Fra' Bartolommeo (like Fra' Angelico, a friar at the convent), and an eighth-century mosaic called *The Madonna in Prayer*, brought here from Constantinople.

Piazza Santissima Annunziata

To the east of San Marco lies the handsome **Piazza Santissima Annunziata**, whose tone is set by Brunelleschi's **Spedale degli Innocenti** (Mon–Sat 8.30am–7pm, Sun 8.30am–2pm; €4), which opened in 1445 as the first found-lings' hospital in Europe and still incorporates an orphanage – Luca della

Robbia's ceramic tondi of swaddled babies advertise the building's function. The convent, centred on two beautiful cloisters, now also contains a miscellany of Florentine Renaissance art including one of Luca della Robbia's most charming Madonnas and an incident-packed *Adoration of the Magi* by Ghirlandaio.

The church of **Santissima Annunziata** (daily 7am–12.30pm & 4–6.30pm) is the mother church of the Servite order, which was founded by seven Florentine aristocrats in 1234. Its dedication took place in the fourteenth century, in recognition of a miraculous image of the Virgin which, left unfinished by the monastic artist, was purportedly completed by an angel. It attracted so many pilgrims that the Medici commissioned **Michelozzo** to rebuild the church in the second half of the fifteenth century in order to accommodate them. In the Chiostro dei Voti, the atrium that Michelozzo built onto the church, are some beautiful frescoes mainly painted in the 1510s, including a *Visitation* by **Pontormo** and a series by **Andrea del Sarto**. The adjoining Chiostro dei Morti, entered from the left transept, is worth visiting for Andrea del Sarto's *Madonna del Sacco*, painted over the door.

The Museo Archeologico

On the other side of Via della Colonna from Santissima Annunziata, the **Museo Archeologico** (Mon 2–7pm, Tues & Thurs 8.30am–7pm, Wed & Fri–Sun 8.30am–2pm; €4) houses the finest collection of its kind in northern Italy, but struggles to draw visitors for whom the Renaissance is the beginning and the end of Florence's appeal. Its special strength is its **Etruscan** collection (much of it bequeathed by the Medici), which features two outstanding bronze sculptures – the *Arringatore* (Orator) and the *Chimera*, a triple-headed monster made in the fourth century BC. The **Egyptian collection** is mostly displayed in an uninspiring manner, but a recent renovation has vastly improved the top floor, where the primary focus is on the **Greek and Roman collections**. The star piece in the huge hoard of Greek vases is the large *François Vase*, a sixth-century BC *krater* discovered in an Etruscan tomb near Chiusi in 1844. Other attention-grabbing items are the life-size bronze torso known as the *Torso di Livorno*, a large horse's head that was once a feature of the garden of the Palazzo Medici, two beautiful sixth-century BC Greek *kouroi*, and the bronze statue of a young man known as the *Idilono di Pésaro*, generally thought to be a Roman replica of a Greek figure dating from around 100 BC.

The eastern city centre

The Santa Croce district – the hub of the eastern part of central Florence – was one of Florence's more densely populated areas before November 4, 1966, when the Arno burst its banks, with catastrophic consequences for this low-lying zone, which was then packed with tenements and small workshops. Many residents moved out permanently in the following years, but now the more traditional businesses that survived the flood have been joined by a growing number of bars and restaurants. **Piazza Santa Croce**, one of the city's largest squares, has traditionally been used for ceremonies and festivities, and is still used for the **Calcio Storico**, a football tournament between the city's four *quartieri*. The contest is held in the last week of June, and is characterized by incomprehensible rules and a degree of violence so extreme that the 2006 and 2007 events were called off.

Santa Croce

Florence's two most lavish churches after the Duomo were the headquarters of the two preaching orders: the Dominicans occupied Santa Maria Novella, while the Franciscans were based at **Santa Croce** (Mon–Sat 9.30am–5.30pm, Sun 1–5.30pm; €5), which also evolved into the mausoleum of Tuscany's most eminent citizens. More than 270 monuments are to be found here, commemorating the likes of Ghiberti, Michelangelo, Alberti, Machiavelli, Galileo and **Dante** – although Dante was actually buried in Ravenna, where he died.

The tombs are not the principal attraction of Santa Croce, however. Far more remarkable are the dazzling chapels at the east end, a compendium of Florentine fourteenth-century art, showing the extent of Giotto's influence and the full diversity of his followers. The two immediately to the right of the chancel are covered with frescoes by **Giotto**: beside the chancel is the **Cappella Bardi**, featuring scenes from the life of St Francis, while next to it is the **Cappella Peruzzi** with a cycle on the lives of St John the Baptist and John the Evangelist. On the south side of the right transept is the **Cappella Baroncelli**, featuring the first night-scene in Western painting, Taddeo Gaddi's *Annunciation to the Shepherds*. On the north side of the left transept, the second **Cappella Bardi** houses a wooden *Crucifix* by **Donatello** – supposedly criticized by Brunelleschi as resembling a "peasant on the Cross".

The Pazzi chapel and Museo dell'Opera di Santa Croce

The door in the south aisle opens onto the Primo Chiostro (First Cloister), at the head of which stands Brunelleschi's **Cappella dei Pazzi**. If one building could be said to typify the spirit of the early Renaissance, this is it: geometrically perfect without seeming pedantic, it's exemplary in the way its decorative detail harmonizes with the design. The polychrome lining of the portico's shallow cupola is by **Luca della Robbia**, as is the tondo of St Andrew over the door; inside, della Robbia also produced the blue-and-white tondi of the Apostles.

Santa Croce's spacious **Secondo Chiostro** was also designed by Brunelleschi, and is perhaps the most peaceful spot in the centre of Florence. **The Museo dell'Opera di Santa Croce**, between the two cloisters, houses a damaged *Crucifixion* by **Cimabue** on the right wall, which has become the emblem of the havoc caused by the 1966 flood – six metres of filthy water surged into the church, tearing the artwork from its mounting. Also in this room are Taddeo Gaddi's fresco of the *Last Supper*, Domenico Veneziano's *Sts John and Francis*, and **Donatello**'s enormous gilded *St Louis of Toulouse*, made for Orsanmichele.

Casa Buonarroti

The **Casa Buonarroti**, located north of Santa Croce at Via Ghibellina 70 (Wed–Mon 9.30am–2pm; €6.50), occupies a site where Michelangelo probably lived intermittently between 1516 and 1525, and contains a smart but low-key museum, mostly consisting of works created in homage to the great man. The two main treasures are to be found upstairs: the *Madonna della Scala* (c.1490–92) is Michelangelo's earliest known work, a delicate relief carved when he was no older than 16; the similarly unfinished *Battle of the Centaurs* was created shortly afterwards, when the boy was living in the Medici household. In an adjacent room you'll find the artist's wooden model (1517) for the facade of San Lorenzo. Close by is the largest of all the sculptural models on display, the torso of a *River God* (1524), a work in wood and wax probably intended for the Medici chapel in San Lorenzo.

South of the river – the Oltrarno

Visitors to Florence might perceive the Arno as merely a brief interruption in the urban fabric, but Florentines talk as though a ravine divides their city. North of the river is *Arno di quà* ("over here"), while the south side is *Arno di là* ("over there"), also known as the **Oltrarno**, literally "Beyond the Arno". Traditionally an artisans' quarter, the Oltrarno is still home to plenty of small workshops (particularly furniture restorers and leather-workers), and Via Maggio remains the focus of Florence's thriving antiques trade. The ambience is distinctly less tourist-centred here than in the zone immediately across the water, which is not to say that the Oltrarno doesn't have major sights – **Palazzo Pitti**, **Santa Maria del Carmine**, **San Miniato** and **Santo Spirito** are all essential visits.

The Ponte Vecchio

The direct route from the city centre to the heart of Oltrarno crosses the river on the **Ponte Vecchio**, the only bridge not mined by the retreating Nazis in 1944. Built in 1345 to replace an ancient wooden bridge, it has always been loaded with shops. Up until the sixteenth century, butchers, fishmongers and tanners occupied the bridge, but in 1593 Ferdinando I ejected these malodorous enterprises and installed goldsmiths instead. Today, still replete with jewellery firms, the bridge is crammed with sightseers and big-spending shoppers during the day, and remains busy after the shutters come down.

The Palazzo Pitti

Although the Medici later took possession of the largest palace in Florence – the **Palazzo Pitti** – it still bears the name of the man for whom it was built. Luca Pitti was a prominent rival of Cosimo il Vecchio, and much of the impetus behind the building of his new house came from a desire to trump the Medici. No sooner was the palace completed, however, than the Pitti's fortunes began to decline and by 1549 they were forced to sell. The palace then became the Medici's family pile, growing in bulk until the seventeenth century, when it achieved its present gargantuan dimensions.

Today, the *palazzo* and the pavilions of the **Giardino di Bóboli** hold eight museums, of which the foremost is the huge art collection of the **Galleria Palatina** (Tues–Sun 8.15am–6.50pm; €8.50, including the Appartamenti Reali and Galleria d'Arte Moderna). **Andrea del Sarto** is represented by no fewer than seventeen paintings, but even more remarkable is the assembly of work by **Raphael**, including portraits of Angelo and Maddalena Doni, the celebrated *Madonna della Seggiola*, and the equally famous *Donna Velata*, for which the model was the painter's mistress, a Roman baker's daughter known to posterity as La Fornarina. An even larger contingent of supreme works by **Titian** includes a number of his most trenchant portraits – among them *Pietro Aretino*, *Cardinal Ippolito de' Medici*, and the disconcerting *Portrait of an Englishman*, a picture that makes the viewer feel as closely scrutinized as was the subject. Elsewhere in the Palatina you'll find masterpieces by **Rubens**, Fra' Filippo Lippi, Caravaggio and **Canova**, to mention but a few.

Much of the rest of this floor comprises the **Appartamenti Reali** – the Pitti's state rooms, renovated by the dukes of Lorraine in the eighteenth century, and then again by King Vittorio Emanuele when Florence became Italy's capital. On the floor above is the **Galleria d'Arte Moderna** (Tues–Sat 8.15am–6.50pm; entry with Galleria Palatina ticket). Displaying a chronological survey of primarily Tuscan art from the mid-eighteenth century to 1945, it's most rewarding in the section devoted to the Macchiaioli, the Italian division of the Impressionist movement, though the most startling pieces are the specimens of sculptural kitsch, such as Antonio Ciseri's *Pregnant Nun*. Entered from the garden courtyard, the **Museo degli Argenti** (opens daily 8.15am; March closes 5.30pm; April, May, Sept & Oct closes 6.30pm; June–Aug closes 7.30pm; Nov–Feb closes 4.30pm; closed 1st & last Mon of month; joint ticket with Museo delle Porcellane, Galleria del Costume & Giardino di Bóboli €7) is a massive collection of portable (and often hideous) luxury artefacts, including Lorenzo il Magnifico's trove of antique vases, displayed in one of the four splendidly frescoed reception rooms on the ground floor.

Visitors without a specialist interest are unlikely to be riveted by the other Pitti museums. In the Palazzina della Meridiana, the eighteenth-century southern wing of the Pitti, the **Galleria del Costume** (same hours & ticket as Museo degli Argenti) provides the opportunity to see the dress that Eleonora di Toledo is wearing in Bronzino's famous portrait of her (in the Palazzo Vecchio). The well-presented if esoteric collection of porcelain, the **Museo delle Porcellane**, is located on the other side of the Bóboli garden (same hours and ticket as Museo degli Argenti), while the **Museo delle Carrozze** (Carriage Museum) has been closed for years and will almost certainly remain so for the foreseeable future.

The Giardino di Bóboli

The delightful formal garden of the Palazzo Pitti, the **Giardino di Bóboli** (same hours and ticket as Museo degli Argenti), takes its name from the Bóboli family, erstwhile owners of much of this area, which was once a quarry. When the Medici acquired the house in 1549 they set to work transforming their back yard into an 111-acre garden. Of all the garden's Mannerist embellishments, the most celebrated is the **Grotta del Buontalenti**, beyond the turtle-back figure of Cosimo I's court dwarf (as seen on a thousand postcards). In among the fake stalactites are shepherds and sheep that look like calcified sponges, while embedded in the corners are replicas of Michelangelo's *Slaves*, replacing the originals that were here until 1908. In the deepest recesses of the cave stands Giambologna's *Venus*, leered at by attendant imps.

It's sometimes possible to leave the gardens by the gate in their southeast corner that leads to the precincts of the **Forte di Belvedere**. This star-shaped fortress was built on the orders of Ferdinando I in 1590, ostensibly for the city's protection but really to intimidate the Grand Duke's fellow Florentines. The **panorama** from here is superb and exhibitions are sometimes held in the palace in the centre of the fortress.

Santo Spirito

With its market stalls, cafés and restaurants, the lively **Piazza Santo Spirito** is the social hub of this quarter,. Don't be deterred by the vacant facade of the church of **Santo Spirito** church (Thurs–Tues 9.30am–12.30pm & 4–6pm) – the interior, one of Brunelleschi's last projects, prompted Bernini to describe it as "the most beautiful church in the world". It's so perfectly proportioned it seems artless, yet the plan is extremely sophisticated – a Latin cross with a continuous chain of 38 chapels round the outside and a line of 35 columns running in parallel right round the building. Unfortunately, a Baroque baldachin covers the high altar, but this is the sole disruption of Brunelleschi's arrangement. The best of the church's paintings is in the south transept – Filippino Lippi's **Nerli Altarpiece**.

The Cappella Brancacci

In 1771 fire wrecked the Carmelite convent and church of **Santa Maria del Carmine** some 300m west of Santo Spirito, but somehow the flames did not damage the frescoes of the church's **Cappella Brancacci**, a cycle of paintings that is one of the essential sights of Florence (Mon & Wed–Sat 10am–5pm, Sun 1–5pm; €4). The chapel is barricaded off from the rest of the Carmine, and visits are restricted to a maximum of thirty people at a time, for an inadequate fifteen minutes. At the time of writing tickets could be obtained only by reserving on ☎055.276.8224; ask the tourist office about the current situation.

The decoration of the chapel was begun in 1424 by **Masolino** and **Masaccio**, when the former was aged 41 and the latter just 22. Within a short time the elder was taking lessons from the younger, whose grasp of the texture of the real world, of the principles of perspective, and of the dramatic potential of the biblical texts they were illustrating far exceeded that of his precursors. In 1428 Masolino was called away to Rome, where he was followed by Masaccio a few months later. Neither would return to the chapel. Masaccio died the same year, aged just 27, but, in the words of Vasari, "all the most celebrated sculptors and painters since Masaccio's day have become excellent and illustrious by studying their art in this chapel."

The Brancacci frescoes are as startling as the Sistine Chapel in Rome, the brightness and delicacy of their colours and the solidity of the figures exemplifying what Bernard Berenson singled out as the tactile quality of Florentine art. The small scene on the left of the entrance arch is the quintessence of Masaccio's art. Depictions of **The Expulsion of Adam and Eve** had never before captured the desolation of the sinners so graphically – Adam presses his hands to his face in bottomless despair, Eve raises her head and screams. In contrast to the emotional charge of Masaccio's couple, Masolino's almost dainty *Adam and Eve*, opposite, pose as if to have their portraits painted.

St Peter is chief protagonist of most of the remaining scenes, some of which were left unfinished in 1428 – work did not resume until 1480, when the frescoes were completed by **Filippino Lippi**. One of the scenes finished by Lippi is the *Raising of Theophilus's Son and St Peter Enthroned*, which depicts St Peter bringing the son of the Prefect of Antioch to life and then preaching to the people of the city from a throne. The three figures to the right of the throne are thought to be portraits of Masaccio, Alberti and Brunelleschi. Masaccio originally painted himself touching Peter's robe, but Lippi considered such physical contact to be improper and painted out the offending limb – you can still see where the arm used to be.

San Miniato al Monte

The brilliant, multicoloured facade of **San Miniato al Monte** lures hordes of visitors up the hill on which it sits, and it more than fulfils the promise of its appearance from a distance: this is the finest Romanesque church in Tuscany. The church's dedicatee, St Minias, belonged to a Christian community that settled in Florence in the third century; according to legend, after his martyrdom his corpse was seen to carry his severed head over the river and up the hill to this spot, where a shrine was subsequently erected to him. Construction of the present building began in 1013 with the foundation of a Cluniac monastery. The gorgeous marble facade – alluding to the Baptistry in its geometrical patterning – was added towards the end of that century, though the external mosaic *Christ between the Virgin and St Minias* dates from the thirteenth. The **interior** (daily: summer 8am–7.30pm; winter 8am–noon & 3–6pm) is like no other in the city, with the choir raised on a platform above the large crypt; its general form has changed little since the mid-eleventh century. The main structural addition is the Cappella del Cardinale del Portogallo, a paragon of artistic collaboration: the basic design was by Antonio Manetti (a pupil of Brunelleschi), the tomb was carved by Antonio Rossellino, the terracotta decoration of the ceiling is by Luca della Robbia, and the paintings are by Alesso Baldovinetti, except for the altarpiece, which is a copy of a work by the Pollaiuolo brothers (the original is in the Uffizi). Be sure to also visit the sacristy, which is covered in *Scenes from the Life of St Benedict*, painted in the 1380s by Spinello Aretino.

Eating, drinking and entertainment

For a small city, Florence has plenty of big-city attractions: scores of cafés and restaurants, a full calendar of cultural events and a lot of chic shops to give focus to the evening *passeggiata*. The main problem is one of identity, in a city whose inhabitants are heavily outnumbered by outsiders from March to October. Restaurant standards are often patchy and many of the locals swear there's scarcely a single genuine Tuscan place left in the Tuscan capital – an exaggeration, of course, but a reflection of a general feeling that too much has been lost to tourism. Yet the situation is nowhere near as bad as some reports would have it, and if anything it's been improving in recent years, with the appearance of several stylish and good-value restaurants, alongside some superb bars. As for nightlife, the university and the influx of language students keep things lively, and seasonal events such as the Maggio Musicale maintain Florence's standing as the hub of cultural life in Tuscany.

Restaurants

Florence has scores of **restaurants**, but such is the volume of customers that in high season advance bookings are virtually compulsory – especially on Sundays, when many places are closed. And bear in mind that meals – not just snacks – are served in many Florentine bars, so if you're exploring a particular area of the city and fancy a quick bite to eat rather than a full-blown restaurant meal, take a look at the relevant section in the "Cafés and bars" listings on p.477.

West of the centre

Il Contadino Via Palazzuolo 71R. Small, popular place with simple black-and-white interior and fascinating large photos of old Florence on the walls. Fast and friendly service, shared tables (no booking), very cheap but good food. Three-course lunch and dinner menu costs a mere €10. Mon–Fri noon–9.30pm.

Snacks

Every district has its **alimentari**, which in addition to selling the choicest Tuscan produce often will make sandwiches to order. For picnic supplies an obvious place to shop is the Mercato Centrale by San Lorenzo church (Mon–Sat 7am–2pm, plus Sat 4–8pm in winter), where everything you could possibly need can be bought under one roof: bread, ham, cheese, fruit, wine, ready-made sandwiches. The Mercato Sant'Ambrogio over by Santa Croce (Mon–Fri 7am–2pm) is smaller but of comparable quality. For a hearty sit-down lunchtime snack, each of the markets has an excellent *tavola calda*, serving meatballs, pasta, stews, soups and sandwiches: *Nerbone* (Mon–Sat 7am–2pm) in the Mercato Centrale, and *Tavola Calda da Rocco* (Mon–Sat noon–2.30pm), in the Mercato di Sant'Ambrogio.

If you really want to go native, you could join the throng of office workers around the tripe stall in Piazza dei Cimatori (Mon–Fri 8.30am–8.30pm; closed four weeks July/Aug). Its speciality is the local delicacy called *lampredotto*: hot tripe served in a bun with a spicy sauce. The stall also sells wine, so you can wash the taste away should you realize you've made a horrible mistake. There's a similar operation – *Da Sergio e Pierpaolo* – parked outside the *Cibrèo* restaurant in Via de' Macci, close to the Sant'Ambrogio market (Mon–Sat 7.15am–3pm).

Oliviero Via delle Terme 51/R
℡055.240.618. *Oliviero* has a welcoming and old-fashioned feel – something like an Italian restaurant of the 1960s – and the menu, though predominantly Tuscan, includes dishes from other regions of Italy. It's not inexpensive, but neither is it overpriced for cooking of this calibre: expect to pay upwards of €50, without wine. Mon–Sat 7pm–midnight. Closed Aug.

North of the centre

Da Mario Via Rosina 2/R ℡055.218.550. For earthy Florentine cooking at very low prices, there's nowhere better then *Da Mario*, which has been in operation right by the Mercato Centrale since 1953. It's just a pity it isn't open in the evenings. Mon–Sat noon–3.30pm; closed most of Aug.

Zà-Zà Piazza del Mercato Centrale 26R ℡055.210.756. In business for more than thirty years, *Zà-Zà* is one of the best of several trattorias close to the Mercato Centrale. There's usually a set-price menu for around €15 which offers a choice of three or four pastas and main courses; otherwise you'll pay around €30 per head. Daily 11am–11pm; closed Aug.

East of the centre

Baldovino Via San Giuseppe 22/R ℡055.241.773. This superb place is renowned above all for its pizzas (made in a wood-fired oven), but the main menu (which changes monthly) is full of good Tuscan and Italian dishes, with mains around €12–17. Portions are generous. April–Oct daily 11.30am–2.30pm & 7–11.30pm; rest of year closed Mon.

Cibrèo Via de' Macci 118/R ℡055.234.1100. Fabio Picchi's *Cibrèo* is the first Florentine port-of-call for many foodies. The recipe for success is simple: superb food with a creative take on Tuscan classics, with friendly and professional service. You'll need to book days in advance for a table in the main part of the restaurant, but next door there's a small, somewhat spartan and sometimes overly busy trattoria section (*Cibreino*) where the food is virtually the same (though the menu is smaller), no bookings are taken and the prices are much lower: around €15 for the main course, as opposed to €35 in the restaurant. Both *Cibrèo* and *Cibreino* are open Tues–Sat 12.30–2.30pm & 7–11.15pm. Closed Aug.

Il Pizzaiuolo Via de' Macci 113/R ℡055.241.171. The Neapolitan pizzas here are among the best in the city. Wines and other menu items also have a Neapolitan touch, as does the atmosphere, which is friendly and high-spirited. Booking's a good idea, at least in the evening. The kitchen stays open until a little after midnight. 12.30–3pm & 7pm–1am. Closed Sun & Aug.

Ora d'Aria Via Ghibellina 3C/R ℡055.2001.699. Marco Stabile, the young boss of *Ora d'Aria*, has quickly established a high reputation with this stylish venture, which offers a high-quality mix of the traditional and the innovative, with an unusual emphasis on fish and seafood dishes. The tasting menus (from €50) are very good value; à la carte, main courses are around €30. The cool, pale and spacious dining room is one of the most relaxing in the city as well. Mon–Sat 7.30–11.30pm.

Oltrarno

Alla Vecchia Bettola Viale Lodovico Ariosto 32–34/R ℡055.224.158. Located on a major traffic intersection a couple of minutes' walk from the Carmine, this place has something of the atmosphere of an old-style drinking den, which is what it once was; nowadays it boasts a good repertoire of Tuscan meat dishes, with main courses reasonably priced from €10. Tues–Sat noon–2.30pm & 7.30–10.30pm.

Il Santo Bevitore Via Santo Spirito 64–66/R ℡055.211.264. "The Holy Drinker" is an airy and stylish gastronomic enoteca with a small but classy menu (around €30 for a meal without drinks) to complement its enticing wine list. Daily 12.30–2.30pm & 7.30–11.30pm. Closed three weeks in Aug.

La Casalinga Via del Michelozzo 9/R ℡055.218.624. This long-established family-run trattoria serves up some of the best low-cost Tuscan dishes in town (€10 for a *secondo*). Most nights it's filled with regulars and a good few outsiders – by 8pm there's invariably a queue. Mon–Sat noon–2.30pm & 7–10pm; closed three weeks in Aug.

Osteria Antica Mescita San Niccolò Via San Niccolò 60R ℡055.234.2836. This genuine old-style Oltrarno *osteria* has a small menu of robust and well-prepared Florentine staples (ribollita, lampredotto etc), at around €10 for main courses; there's also a good lunchtime buffet for a mere €10. Mon–Sat 12.30–3pm & 7pm–1am; closed Aug.

Osteria Santo Spirito Piazza di Santo Spirito 16/R Via Sant' Agostino ℡055.238.2383. This informal and modern *osteria* is serves hearty Tuscan dishes with contemporary flair, and at good prices: pasta dishes from €6, mains from €12, and there's a lunchtime set menu at a mere €12. In summer you can eat outdoors on the piazza. Daily 12.30–2.30pm & 8pm–midnight.

Pane e Vino Piazza di Cestello 3/R ℡055.247.6956. *Pane e Vino* is a stylish yet relaxed place, with a menu that's small but

consistently excellent (secondi €15–20), featuring two very enticing set menus (€35 & €45). Mon–Sat 8pm–midnight; closed two weeks in Aug.
Quattro Leoni Via dei Vellutini 1/R Piazza della Passera ☎ 055.218.562. Occupying a three-roomed medieval interior, this is a young, relaxed place with wooden beams and splashy modern paintings strung across the rough stone walls. In summer you can also eat alfresco under vast canvas umbrellas in the tiny Piazza della Passera. You can eat very well for around €40 a head. Noon–2.30pm & 7–11pm; closed Wed lunch.

Cafés, bars and gelaterie

As elsewhere in Italy, the distinction between Florentine **bars** and **cafés** can be tricky to the point of impossibility, as almost every café serves alcohol and almost every bar serves coffee. It's really just a question of degrees of emphasis: in some cafés, most of the custom comes first thing in the morning, as people on their way to work stop off for a dash of caffeine and a brioche; in others, the tables are busiest late at night, when people drop by after an evening out, to relax over a Campari or a glass of wine. There's one category of bar that's quite distinct from cafés, and that's the **enoteca**, where the enjoyment of wine is the chief point of the exercise – though in this case the complicating factor is that almost all enotecas serve food, and in some instances they've evolved into restaurants with huge wine lists.

The distinction between bars and clubs is getting vaguer too, with many of Florence's hotter bars now aiming to keep the punters on the premises all night, by serving free snacks with the *aperitivi* (usually from about 7–9/10pm) before the music kicks in – either live or (more often) courtesy of the in-house DJ. Devotees of Italian **ice cream** will find plenty of *gelaterie* in Florence to sample some wacky concoctions without straying far off the main drags.

▲ I Fratellini wine bar

Vinaii

The *vinaio* – a tiny wine bar with at most a couple of stools by the counter – was once a real Florentine institution. Customers would typically linger at these places for no more than a couple of minutes, long enough to down a glass of *rosso* and exchange a few words with the proprietor. The number of *vinaii* has declined markedly in recent years; the following are the notable survivors.

All'Antico Vinaio Via dei Neri 65/R. Located between the Uffizi and Santa Croce, this place preserves much of the rough-and-ready atmosphere that's made it one of Florence's most popular wine bars for the last hundred years. (Mon–Sat 8am–10pm; closed 3 weeks in late July & early Aug.)

I Fratellini Via dei Cimatori 38/R. This minuscule dirt-cheap bar is somehow clinging on in the immediate vicinity of the high-rent Via dei Calzaiuoli. Serves good panini and local wines. (Mid-June to Aug Mon–Fri 8am–5pm; Sept to mid-June daily 8am–8pm.)

Quasigratis Piazza del Grano 10. Little more than a window in a wall at the back of the Uffizi, and it doesn't say *Quasigratis* ("Almost free") anywhere – just "*Vini*". Serves rolls and other snacks, and wine in tiny glasses called *rasini*. (Daily 10am–11pm; closed Jan & Feb.)

City centre

Caffè Gilli Piazza della Repubblica 36–39/R. Founded in 1733, *Gilli* is the most appealing of this square's expensive cafés. The lavish *belle époque* interior is a sight in itself, but most people choose to sit on the big outdoor terrace. 8am–midnight; closed Tues.

Cantinetta dei Verrazzano Via dei Tavolini 18–20/R. Owned by a major Chianti vineyard, this wood-panelled place near Orsanmichele is part-bar, part-café and part-bakery, making its own excellent pizza, focaccia and cakes. Sept–June Mon–Sat 8am–9pm; July & Aug Mon–Sat 8am–4pm.

Grom Via del Campanile. Founded in Turin in 2003, *Grom* is a retro-styled but very slick operation, concocting fabulous *gelati* from top-quality ingredients gathered from all over Italy. Daily April–Oct 10.30am–midnight; rest of year closes 11pm.

Perchè No! Via de' Tavolini 19/R. "Why Not!" is a superb gelateria that's been in business since the 1930s. Mon & Wed–Sun 11am–11pm, Tues noon–8pm; closed Nov.

West of the centre

Noir Lungarno Corsini 12–14/R. Recently revamped in moody nocturnal tones, the bar formerly known as *Capocaccia* has been voted the Florentines' favourite night-time hangout several times, and it remains out in front. The well-designed interior is roomy and has plenty of tables and stools; there's a DJ every night. Sun brunch (12.30–3.30pm) is excellent, as is the nightly *aperitivo* buffet (7.30–10.30pm). Open daily noon–2am.

Slowly Via Porta Rossa 63. This extremely trendy bar, with its neat little banquettes and candle lanterns, tends to attract a showy, beautifully dressed young crowd. The atmosphere is pretty laid back, even when the DJ gets to work. Mon–Sat 7pm–2am.

North of the centre

Carabé Via Ricasoli 60/R. Wonderful Sicilian ice cream made with Sicilian ingredients. Also serves a variety of cakes. May–Oct daily 9am–1am; rest of year daily 9am–8pm, but closed mid-Dec to mid-Jan.

Casa del Vino Via dell'Ariento 16/R. The patrons of this atmospheric old bar are mostly Florentines, who pitch up for a drink, a chat with owner Gianni Migliorini and an assault on various panini, *crostini*, and saltless Tuscan bread and salami. Mon–Fri 9.30am–5.30pm, Sat 10am–3.30pm; closed Aug.

Zanobini Via Sant'Antonino 47/R. Like the *Casa del Vino*, its rival just around the corner, this is an authentic Florentine bar, whose feel owes much to the presence of traders from the nearby Mercato Centrale. Offers decent snacks, but most people are simply here for a chat over a glass of wine. Mon–Sat 8am–2pm & 3.30–8pm.

East of the centre

Caffè Cibrèo Via Andrea del Verrocchio 5/R. Possibly the prettiest café in Florence, *Caffè Cibrèo* opened in 1989, but the wood-panelled interior gives it the look of a place that's at least two hundred years older. Cakes and desserts are great, and the light meals bear the stamp of the *Cibrèo* restaurant kitchens opposite. Tues–Sat 8am–1am.

Vivoli Via Isola delle Stinche 7/R. Operating from deceptively unprepossessing premises in a side-street close to Santa Croce, this café has long been rated one of the best ice-cream-makers in Florence – the very best, in the opinion of many. Tues–Sun: summer 7.30am–midnight; winter closes 9pm. Closed two weeks in Aug.

Oltrarno

Caffè Ricchi Piazza di Santo Spirito 9/R. The smartest of the cafés on this square. Menus change daily, and there's a good selection of cakes, ice cream and sandwiches. Summer Mon–Sat 7am–1am; winter closes 10pm. Closed two weeks in Feb & two weeks in Aug.

Dolce Vita Piazza del Carmine 6/R. This smart and extremely popular bar-club has been going for more than a decade and has stayed ahead of the game through constant updating. Install yourself on one of the aluminium bar stools and preen with Florence's beautiful young things. Live music (often Latin or jazz) Wed & Thurs 7.30–9.30pm; *aperitivi* every night 7.30–9.30pm, then the DJ gets to work. Tues–Sun 5pm–2am.

Fuori Porta Via del Monte alle Croci 10/R ☎055.234.2483. This famous enoteca-osteria has more than four hundred wines to choose from by the bottle, and an ever-changing selection of wines by the glass. Bread, cheese, ham and salami are available, together with a selection of pasta dishes and tasty salads. Mon–Sat 12.30–3.30pm & 7pm–12.30am; closed two weeks in mid-Aug.

Il Rifrullo Via San Niccolò 53–57/R. Lying to the east of the Ponte Vecchio–Pitti Palace route, *Il Rifrullo* attracts fewer tourists than many Oltrarno café-bars. Serves delicious early evening *aperitivi* snacks (when the music gets turned up), as well as more substantial dishes, and the Sun brunch is always packed out. Has a pleasant roof terrace, too. Daily 8am–2am. Closed two weeks in Aug.

Le Volpi e L'Uva Piazza dei Rossi 1R, off Piazza di Santa Felicita. This discreet, friendly little enoteca does good business by concentrating on the wines of small producers and providing tasty cold meats and snacks to accompany them (the selection of cheeses in particular is tremendous). In summer the shady terrace is a very pleasant refuge from the heat. Mon–Sat 11am–9pm.

Zoe Via dei Renai 13. Like the neighbouring *Negroni*, *Zoe* is perennially popular for summer evening drinks, but it attracts lots of young Florentines right through the day. Does good snacks and simple meals, there's a DJ in the back room, and – like *Negroni* – it's something of an art venue too. Mon–Thurs 8am–1.30am, Fri & Sat 8am–2am, Sun 6pm–1am.

Nightlife and entertainment

Florentine **nightlife** has a reputation for catering primarily to the middle-aged and affluent, but like every university town it has its pockets of activity. Florence's **gay and lesbian** scene is small but lively, and the cultural calendar is filled out with seasons of **classical music**, **opera and dance** to rival the best in Europe.

For **information** about concerts and shows, get hold of the *Firenze Spettacolo* monthly listings magazine or drop in at the Box Office **ticket agency**, which

Gay and lesbian Florence

The leading gay bar is **Crisco**, a short distance east of the Duomo at Via Sant'Egidio 43/R (☎055.248.0580, ⊛www.crisco.it; Mon, Wed, Thurs & Sun 11pm–3am, Fri & Sat 10pm–6am), but the ambience can be a bit heavy for some tastes. **Piccolo**, Borgo Santa Croce 23/R (☎055.200.1057; daily 8pm–2.30am), has a more chilled-out atmosphere and draws a mixed gay and lesbian crowd, as does the stylish **Y.A.G. B@r**, also near Santa Croce at Via de' Macci 8/R (☎055.246.9022, ⊛www .yagbar.com; daily 8pm–3am). The key bar-club is the pioneering **Tabasco**, which has been going for more than 35 years at Piazza Santa Cecilia 3/R (☎055.213.000, ⊛www.tabascogay.it; Tues–Sun 10pm–6am). For lesbian contacts, check the noticeboard at the women's bookshop Libreria delle Donne, Via Fiesolana 2/B (Mon 3.30–7.30pm, Tues–Sat 9.30am–1pm & 3.30–7.30pm).

is to the northwest of the train station at Via Alamanni 39 (℡ 055.210.804; Mon 3–7.30pm, Tues–Sat 10am–7.30pm).

Clubs and live music venues

Auditorium FLOG Via Michele Mercati 24/B ℡ 055.490.437, ⓦ www.flog.it. One of the city's best-known mid-sized venues, and a perennial student favourite for all forms of live music (and DJs), but particularly local indie-type bands. It's usually packed, despite a position way out in the northern suburbs; to get there take bus #4, #8, #14, #20 or #28.

Central Park Via Fosso Macinante 2, Parco delle Cascine. One of the city's biggest and most commercial clubs, with several dance floors and DJs who know what they're doing – and have access to a superb sound system. A card system operates for drinks, and the first drink is included in the admission – around €20–25 after midnight, usually free before. Summer Tues–Sat 11.30pm–4.30am; winter Fri & Sat same hours..

Girasol Via del Romito 1 ℡ 055.474.948. ⓦ www.girasol.it. Florence's liveliest Latin bar, located on a minor road due north of the Fortezza da Basso, is hugely popular. As well as salsa classes, cocktails and the usual vinyl suspects, the place draws in some surprisingly good live acts, with different countries' sounds each day of the week, from Brazilian bossa nova to Cuban son. Tues–Sun 7pm–2am.

Meccanò Viale degli Olmi 1/Piazzale delle Cascine ℡ 055.331.371. People flock here for a night out from across half of Tuscany. The place is labyrinthine, with a trio of lounge and bar areas, and a huge and invariably packed dance floor playing mostly house. In summer, when the action spills out of doors, you can cool off in the gardens bordering the Cascine. The €15–20 admission includes your first drink. Summer Tues–Sat 11.30pm–4am; winter Thurs–Sat same hours; closed Nov & two weeks in Aug.

Rex Via Fiesolana 25/R ℡ 055.228.0331. One of the city's big night-time fixtures, a friendly bar-club with a varied and loyal clientele. Vast curving lights droop over the central bar, which is studded with turquoise stone and broken mirror mosaics. Big arched spaces to either side mean there's plenty of room, the cocktails and DJs are good, and the snacks excellent – the *aperitivi* session is 7–9.30pm. Mon & Wed–Sun 6pm–3am. Closed June–Aug.

Tenax Via Pratese 46 ℡ 055.632.958, ⓦ www.tenax.org. Florence's biggest club, pulling in the odd jet-setting DJ. Given its location in the northwest of town, near the airport (there's usually a shuttle bus from the train station – otherwise, take a taxi), you'll escape the hordes of *internazionalisti* in the more central clubs. With two large floors, it's a major venue for concerts as well. Admission €20–25. Thurs–Sat 10.30pm–4am. Closed mid-May to mid-Sept.

Film

In Italy the vast majority of English-language films are dubbed, but **Odeon Original Sound**, Via de' Sassetti 1 (℡ 055.214.068; closed Aug), screens films in their original language (*versione originale*) once a week, generally on Monday, for most of the year, plus Tuesday and Thursday in summer. This is the only cinema still in operation in the centre of Florence, but in summer there are often **open-air screens** at the Forte Belvedere and the Palazzo dei Congressi, near the train station.

Classical music, opera and dance

Lasting from late April to early July, the **Maggio Musicale Fiorentino** is one of Europe's leading festivals of **opera** and **classical music**. Events are staged at the Teatro Comunale, the tiny Teatro Goldoni, the Teatro della Pergola, the Palazzo dei Congressi, and occasionally in the Bóboli gardens. Information and tickets are available from the Teatro Comunale box office, Corso Italia 16 (℡ 055.213.535, ⓦ www.maggiofiorentino.com). The smaller **Estate Fiesolana** festival (mid–June to late Aug or early Sept) concentrates on chamber and symphonic music, with most events held in Fiesole's open-air Teatro Romano.

The Teatro Comunale is Florence's major concert venue, hosting a **symphony orchestra** which performs a new programme every week during the winter concert season (Jan–March), plus a prestigious **opera and ballet** season in the autumn (Oct–Dec). The Teatro della Pergola, at Via della Pergola 18 (℡055.226.4353, ⓦwww.pergola.firenze.it), which was built in 1656 and believed to be Italy's oldest surviving theatre, hosts **chamber concerts** and small-scale operas (Oct–April), while the Teatro Verdi, Via Ghibellina 99–101 (℡055.212.320, ⓦwww.teatroverdifirenze.it) is home to the Orchestra della Toscana.

Listings

Banks and exchange Florence's main bank branches are on or around Piazza della Repubblica.
Bike, scooter & moped rental Alinari, Via Guelfa 85/R ℡055.280.500, ⓦwww.alinarirental.com; Florence by Bike, Via San Zanobi 120–122/R ℡055.488.992, ⓦwww.florencebybike.it.
Car rental Avis, Borgo Ognissanti 128/R ℡055.213.629; Europcar, Borgo Ognissanti 53 ℡055.290.438; Hertz, Via Maso Finiguerra 33/R ℡055.239.8205; Italy by Car, Borgo Ognissanti 134/R ℡055.293.021; Maggiore, Via Maso Finiguerra 31/R ℡055.290.164.
Consulates UK, Lungarno Corsini 2 ℡055.284.133; US, Lungarno Amerigo Vespucci 38 ℡055.239.8276.
Doctors The Tourist Medical Service is a private service used to dealing with foreigners; they have doctors on call 24hr a day on ℡055.475.411 (ⓦwww.medicalservice.firenze.it), or you can visit their clinic at Via Lorenzo il Magnifico 59 (Mon–Fri 11am–noon & 5–6pm, Sat 11am–noon). Note that you'll need insurance cover to recoup the cost of a consultation, which will be at least €50. Florence's central hospital is on Piazza Santa Maria Nuova.
Internet Many hotels and hostels now offer free internet access, but if you need to find a computer your best bet is a branch of *Internet Train* (ⓦwww.internettrain.it), which has seven outlets in the city, including Via de Benci 36/R, Via Guelfa 54–56/R, Via Porta Rossa 38/R and Piazza Stazione 14 – they're open Mon–Sat 10am–midnight, Sun 3–11pm.
Laundry Wash & Dry has seven branches, open 8am–10pm daily: Via dei Servi 105/R, Via della

Scala 52–54/R, Via Ghibellina 143/R, Via dei Serragli 87/R, Viale Morgagni 21/R, Via Orsini 39/R and Via Nazionale 129/R.
Left luggage Santa Maria Novella station by platform 16 (daily 6am–midnight).
Lost property Lost property handed in at the city or railway police ends up at Via Circondaria 17/B (Mon–Sat 9am–noon; ℡055.367.943; take bus #23 to Viale Corsica). There's also a lost property office at Stazion Santa Maria Novella, next to the left luggage office.
Pharmacies The Farmacia Comunale, on the train station concourse, is open 24hr, as is All' Insegna del Moro, at Piazza San Giovanni 20/R, on the north side of the Baptistry, and Farmacia Molteni, at Via dei Calzaiuoli 7/R.
Police To report a theft or other crime, go to the Carabinieri at Borgo Ognissanti 48 (open 24hr), or the city police, at Via Pietrapiana 50/R (Mon–Fri 8.30am–7.30pm, Sat closes 1.30pm) – you're likelier to find an English-speaker at the latter.
Post office The main central post office is near Piazza della Repubblica at Via Pellicceria 3 (Mon–Sat 8.15am–7pm). If you're having mail sent poste restante, make sure it's marked for Via Pellicceria, otherwise it will go to Florence's biggest post office, at Via Pietrapiana 53–55 (Mon–Fri 8.15am–7pm, Sat 8.15am–12.30pm).
Toilets All locations are given on the city council website – ⓦwww.comune.fi.it – just type "bagni pubblici" into the search engine.

Around Florence

The Greater Florence area has a number of towns and attractions to entice you on a day-trip from the city or even act as a base for exploring the region. City buses run northeast to the hill-village of **Fiesole**, while inter-town services run south into the hills of **Chianti**, Italy's premier wine region.

Fiesole

A long-established Florentine retreat from the summer heat and crowds, **FIESOLE** spreads over a cluster of hilltops 8km northeast of the city. It predates Florence by several millennia: the Etruscans held out so long up here that the Romans were forced to set up permanent camp in the valley below – thus creating the beginnings of the settlement that was to become Florence. ATAF city **bus** #7 runs every twenty minutes from Florence's train station to Piazza Mino. The **tourist office** is just off the square, behind the cathedral on Via Portigiani 3 (March–Oct Mon–Sat 9am–6pm, Sun 10am–1pm, 2–6pm; Nov–Feb Mon–Sat 9am–5pm, Sun 10am–4pm; ☎055.598.720, ⓦwww.comune.fiesole.fi.it).

The slightly unkempt-looking central square, **Piazza Mino**, is named after the fifteenth-century sculptor Mino da Fiesole, who has two fine pieces in the **Duomo** (daily: summer 7.30am–noon & 3–6pm; winter 7.30am–noon & 2–5pm) that dominates the north side of the square. Nineteenth-century restoration ruined the Duomo's exterior, and the interior is something like a stripped-down version of Florence's San Miniato; the highlight is the Cappella Salutati, to the right of the choir, which contains two fine pieces by Mino – a panel of the *Madonna and Saints* and the tomb of Bishop Salutati. Behind the Duomo lie the **Museo Archeologico** (April–Sept 10am–7pm, closed Tues; Oct–March 10am–6pm, closed Tues & Wed; joint ticket, valid one day, covering all Fiesole's museums €13), containing pieces excavated from the Teatro Romano; and the **Museo Bandini** (same hours), housing a miscellany of medieval Florentine and Tuscan art. Gates give onto the Area Archeologica behind (same hours), featuring the 3000-seat **Teatro Romano**, a baths complex and an **Etruscan temple** dedicated to Minerva.

Fiesole's two other major churches are reached by the narrow Via San Francesco, which rises steeply from Piazza Mino, past the **Oratorio di San Jacopo** (Sat & Sun 10am–7pm), a little chapel containing a fifteenth-century fresco and some ecclesiastical treasures. **Sant'Alessandro** (summer Mon–Sat 9am–6pm, Sun 10am–1pm & 2–6pm; winter Mon–Sat 9am–5pm, Sun 10am–4pm) was founded in the sixth century on the site of Etruscan and Roman temples and has beautiful *marmorino cipollino* (onion marble) columns adorning its basilical interior. The Gothic church of **San Francesco** (daily: April–Sept 9am–noon & 3–7pm; Oct–March closes 6pm) occupies the site of the acropolis; across one of the tiny cloisters there's a chaotic museum of pieces brought back from Egypt and China by missionaries. For a lovely walk, head southwest from Piazza Mino for 1.5km down the narrow, winding Via Vecchia Fiesolana to the hamlet of **SAN DOMENICO**. Fra' Angelico was once prior of the Dominican **monastery** here and the church retains a 1420 *Madonna and Angels* by him (first chapel on the left), while the chapterhouse also has the Fra' Angelico fresco *The Crucifixion* (ring the bell at no. 4 for entry).

Chianti

Ask a sample of middle-class northern Europeans to define their idea of paradise and the odds are that a hefty percentage will come up with something that sounds a lot like Chianti, the territory of vineyards and hill-towns that stretches between Florence and Siena. Life in Chianti seems in perfect balance: the landscape is a softly varied terrain of hills and valleys; the climate for most of the year is sunny; and on top of all this there's the wine, the one Italian vintage that's familiar to just about everyone. Visitors from Britain and other similarly ill-favoured climes were long ago alerted to Chianti's charms, and the rate of immigration has been so rapid since the 1960s that the region is now wryly dubbed **Chiantishire**. Yet it would be an exaggeration to say that Chianti has completely lost its character: the tone of certain parts has been altered, but concessions to tourism have been more or less successfully absorbed into the rhythm of local life.

If you're relying on **buses from Florence or Siena**, the best targets are **Greve in Chianti** and **Radda in Chianti**. But the only realistic way to get to know the region is with **your own transport**, following the SS222 (or *Chiantigiana*), which snakes its way between Florence and Siena through the most beautiful parts of Chianti.

Greve in Chianti

The venue for Chianti's biggest wine fair (the Rassegna del Chianti Classico, usually held during the first week in Sept), **GREVE** is thriving mercantile town where there's wine for sale on every street. The funnel-shaped Piazza Matteotti – venue for the Saturday morning market – is focused on a statue of Giovanni da Verrazzano, the first European to see what became Manhattan; he was born in the nearby Castello di Verrazzano. Other than the piazza, Greve has just one feature that might be classified as a sight: the Museo d'Arte Sacra di San Francesco, at Via San Francesco 4 (April–Sept Thurs & Fri 10am–1pm, Sat & Sun 4–8pm; Oct–March Thurs & Fri 10am–1pm, Sat & Sun 3.30–6.30pm; €3), a minor museum where the chief exhibit is a painted terracotta Lamentation, created in the 1530s.

Greve is equipped with an efficient tourist office, tucked into a corner of Piazza Matteotti at Via delle Capanne 11 (Mon–Fri 10.30am–2pm & 3–6pm; ☏055.854.5243), which can give information on vineyards, accommodation in local farmhouses and trekking in Chianti. A couple of three-star hotels on Piazza Matteotti offer comfortable accommodation: the *Del Chianti* at no. 86 (☏055.853.763, ⊛www.albergodelchianti.it; ❸) and *Da Verrazzano* at no. 28 (☏055.853.189, ⊛www.albergoverrazzano.it; ❹). The latter is slightly more characterful and also has an extremely good restaurant (closed Mon & mid-Jan to mid-Feb). Alternatively, the *Gallo Nero*, just off the piazza at Via Cesare Batisti 6 (closed Thurs), is a perfectly acceptable bar-trattoria-pizzeria.

Radda in Chianti

A ridge 22km south of Greve is occupied by the well-heeled village of **Castellina in Chianti**, whose walls and fortress bear testimony to an embattled past on the frontline between Florence and Siena. From Castellina, the SS429 branches east, through the most beautiful Chianti landscape, to **RADDA IN CHIANTI**. The street plan of this minuscule town is centred on **Piazza Ferrucci**, where the frescoed and shield-studded Palazzo Comunale faces a church raised on a high platform.

The tourist office lurks behind the church, on the corner of Piazza del Castello (Mon–Sat 10am–1pm & 3–7pm, Sun 10.30am–12.30pm). Stylish accommodation is on offer at the three-star *Hotel Podere Le Vigne* (☏0577.738.640, ⊛www.tuscany.net/vigne; ❹), a converted farm located a kilometre outside Radda, just off the road between Radda and the hamlet of Villa a Radda; in addition to the rooms at the former farm, *Le Vigne* has some plainer (and much cheaper) but still very pleasant accommodation in the centre of Radda, and there's a good restaurant at the main site, where you'll pay around €40 each.

Pisa, Lucca and the coast

Thanks to its Leaning Tower, **Pisa** is known by name to just about every visitor to Italy, though it remains an underrated place, seen by most people on a whistle-stop day-trip that takes in nothing of the city except the tower and its immediate environs. Genteel **Lucca** nearby, its walled old town crammed with Romanesque churches, is even less explored.

Tuscany's **coast** is a mixed bag, generally too over-developed to be consistently attractive. North of Pisa, the succession of beach resorts enjoys the backdrop of the mighty Alpi Apuane, which harbour the marble quarries of Carrara. South from Pisa, past the untouristed port of **Livorno**, are a hundred scrubby strips of hotels and campsites. The Tuscan shoreline is at its best in the **Maremma** region, where you'll find the protected **Monti dell'Uccellina** reserve and the wild, wooded peninsula of **Monte Argentario**. Tuscany's main island, **Elba**, also offers a breath of fresh air.

Pisa

To too many tourists, **PISA** is known for just one thing – the **Leaning Tower**, which serves around the world as a shorthand image for Italy. It is indeed a freakishly beautiful building, a sight whose impact no amount of prior knowledge can blunt. Yet it is just a single component of Pisa's breathtaking **Campo dei Miracoli**, or Field of Miracles, where the **Duomo**, **Baptistry** and **Camposanto** complete a dazzling architectural ensemble. These amazing buildings belong to Pisa's Golden Age, from the eleventh to the thirteenth centuries, when the city was one of the maritime powers of the Mediterranean. Decline set in with defeat by the Genoese in 1284, followed by the silting-up of Pisa's harbour, and from 1406 the city was governed by Florence, whose rulers re-established the University of Pisa, one of the great intellectual establishments of the Renaissance – **Galileo** was a teacher here. Subsequent centuries saw Pisa fade into provinciality, though landmarks from its glory days now bring in hundreds of thousands of visitors a year, and the combination of tourism and a large student population give the contemporary city a lively feel.

Pisa airport

Pisa's **Aeroporto Galileo Galilei** (ⓦwww.pisa-airport.com) is just 2km south of Centrale station. Terravision buses to Florence are scheduled to synchronize with incoming budget airline flights and leave from in front of the terminal; they take seventy minutes to reach Santa Maria Novella, and tickets (€8 single) are sold in the airport concourse. Trains from the airport station are cheaper (€5.40) if often slower; there are only six direct trains daily (6.40am–10.20pm), but every thirty minutes a shuttle runs from the airport to Pisa Centrale (5min), where you can change to one of the regular services to Florence – there's rarely more than thirty minutes between trains, and the journey time is between an hour and eighty minutes. Train tickets can be bought from the office at the opposite end of the concourse from the station.

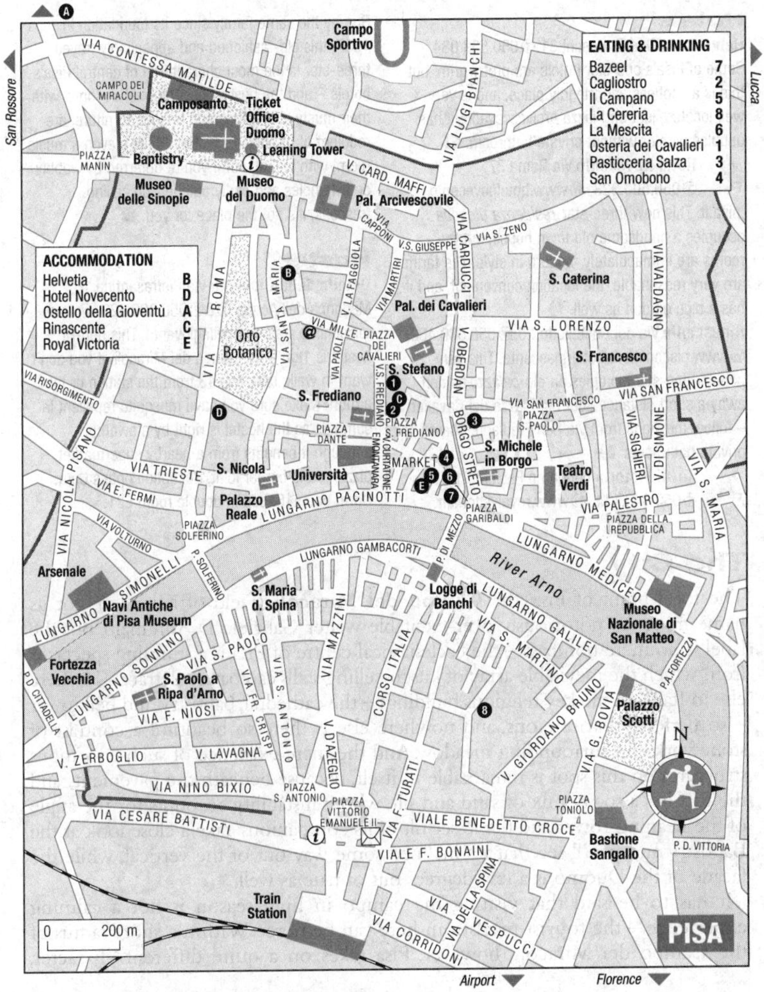
A
San Rossore
Lucca
Airport
Florence
PISA
0 200 m
EATING & DRINKING
Bazeel 7
Cagliostro 2
Il Campano 5
La Cereria 8
La Mescita 6
Osteria dei Cavalieri 1
Pasticceria Salza 3
San Omobono 4
ACCOMMODATION
Helvetia B
Hotel Novecento D
Ostello della Gioventù A
Rinascente C
Royal Victoria E
Campo Sportivo
VIA CONTESSA MATILDE
CAMPO DEI MIRACOLI
Camposanto
Ticket Office
Duomo
Leaning Tower
Baptistry
PIAZZA MANIN
Museo delle Sinopie
Museo del Duomo
VIA LUIGI BIANCHI
V. CARD. MAFFI
Pal. Arcivescovile
VIA CAPPONI
V.S. GIUSEPPE
VIA S. ZENO
VIA CARDUCCI
S. Caterina
VIA VALDAGNO
VIA ROMA
VIA SANTA MARIA
V. LA FAGGIOLA
VIA MARTIRI
Pal. dei Cavalieri
VIA S. LORENZO
Orto Botanico
VIA MILLE
PIAZZA DEI CAVALIERI
VIA PAOLI
V.S. FREDIANO
S. Stefano
V. OBERDAN
S. Francesco
VIA RISORGIMENTO
S. Frediano
VIA SAN FRANCESCO
PIAZZA S. PAOLO
PIAZZA S. FREDIANO
PIAZZA DANTE
BORGO STRETO
S. Michele in Borgo
V. CURTATONE E MONTANARA
MARKET
VIA SIGHIERI
V. DI SIMONE
VIA S. MARIA
VIA NICOLA PISANO
VIA TRIESTE
S. Nicola
Università
Teatro Verdi
VIA E. FERMI
Palazzo Reale
LUNGARNO PACINOTTI
PIAZZA GARIBALDI
VIA PALESTRO
PIAZZA DELLA REPUBBLICA
VIA VOLTURNO
PIAZZA SOLFERINO
LUNGARNO GAMBACORTI
P. DI MEZZO
LUNGARNO MEDICEO
River Arno
Arsenale
LUNGARNO SIMONELLI
P. SOLFERINO
S. Maria d. Spina
Logge di Banchi
LUNGARNO GALILEI
Navi Antiche di Pisa Museum
Museo Nazionale di San Matteo
VIA MAZZINI
CORSO ITALIA
VIA S. MARTINO
P.A. FORTEZZA
Fortezza Vecchia
LUNGARNO SONNINO
VIA S. PAOLO
S. Paolo a Ripa d'Arno
VIA FR. CRISPI
VIA S. ANTONIO
P.D. CITTADELLA
VIA F. NIOSI
V. GIORDANO BRUNO
VIA G. BOVIA
Palazzo Scotti
V. D'AZEGLIO
V. ZERBOGLIO
V. LAVAGNA
VIA NINO BIXIO
VIA F. TURATI
PIAZZA S. ANTONIO
PIAZZA VITTORIO EMANUELE II
VIA CESARE BATTISTI
VIALE BENEDETTO CROCE
PIAZZA TONIOLO
Bastione Sangallo
P. D. VITTORIA
VIALE F. BONAINI
VIA DELLA SPINA
Train Station
VIA VESPUCCI
VIA CORRIDONI
N

Arrival and information

Pisa Centrale **train station** is about 1km south of the Arno; **buses** arrive at the nearby Piazza Vittorio Emanuele II and Piazza San Antonio. From here, the Leaning Tower is about 25-minutes' walk north, or a short ride on CPT city bus #1. There are two **tourist offices**: a short way north of the train station, at Piazza Vittorio Emanuele 13 (Mon–Fri 9am–7pm, Sat 9am–1.30pm; Ⓣ050.42.291); and inside the Museo dell'Opera del Duomo (see p.489). For online information, go to Ⓦwww.pisaturismo.it.

Accommodation

Most visitors hurry through Pisa on a day-trip – which means that **accommodation** is usually not hard to find. In summer, though, it's still best to book in advance.

Hotels

Helvetia Via Don G. Boschi 31 ☏ 050.553.084. Some of Pisa's one-star hotels are pretty grim, but this is a spotless and friendly place, and is very well located, just off Piazza Arcivescovado; it has doubles with or without private bathroom. ❷

🏃 **Hotel Novecento** Via Roma 37 ☏ 050.500.323, ⓦ www.hotelnovecento .pisa.it. This new three-star *residenza d'epoca* occupies a handsome old town house, but the rooms are immaculately modern in style. The tariffs are very reasonable, the location convenient, and it has a nice garden as well. ❺

Rinascente Via del Castelletto 28 ☏ 050.580.460, ⓦ www.pisaonline.it/hotelrinascente. This very popular one-star occupies an old *palazzo* hidden away a short distance south of Piazza dei Cavalieri – follow the signs from Via San Frediano. Shared or private bathrooms. ❷

🏃 **Royal Victoria** Lungarno Pacinotti 12 ☏ 050.940.111, ⓦ www.royalvictoria.it.

Run by the same family since its foundation in 1837, this old-fashioned and appealingly frayed three-star is the most characterful of central Pisa's hotels – and the best value. The public rooms, with their musty engravings and antique furniture, are redolent of the place's history (there's even a music room, with piano), but if you're deterred by wobbly door-handles and badly patched-up ceiling frescoes, it's not the place for you. ❺

Hostel

Ostello della Gioventù Via Pietrasantina 15, Madonna dell'Acqua ☏ &ⓕ 050.890.622, ⓦ www .pisaonline.it/albergodellagioventu. This non-HI hostel is 1km from Campo dei Miracoli: if you don't want to walk, take bus #3 from the station or the airport. Make sure you have mosquito repellent in summer, as the hostel is right by a swamp, although it benefits from a nearby supermarket, pizzeria and burger joint. Reception opens 6pm. Dorm bed €16; bed in double room €21.

The City

The focal point of Pisa, the **Campo dei Miracoli** (Field of Miracles), got its name from the notoriously over-excitable writer Gabriele D'Annunzio, but the label is no mere bombast – the ecclesiastical centre of Pisa is a stunning spectacle, from which the inevitable array of kitsch-selling stalls can barely detract. Nowhere else in Italy are the key religious buildings – the cathedral, baptistry and bell tower – so perfectly harmonious, and nowhere else is there so beautiful a contrast of stonework and surrounding meadow. And the mere existence of such enormous structures on this spot is remarkable in itself, because beneath the pavements and the turf lies a soggy mix of sand and silt, whose instability accounts for the angle of the Leaning Tower and the lesser tilt of its companions: take a close look at the Baptistry and you'll see that it's inclined some way out of the vertical, while the facade of the Duomo is a few degrees out of true as well.

It has to be said that visiting the campo in high season is not a calming experience – the tourist maelstrom here can be fierce. Within a short radius of the Campo dei Miracoli, however, Pisa takes on a quite different character,

---

Tickets for the Campo dei Miracoli

Tickets for all five museums and monuments of the Campo dei Miracoli – the Duomo, Baptistry, Museo dell'Opera, Camposanto and Museo delle Sinopie – can only be bought at two ticket offices: one on the north side of the Leaning Tower (the only one that sells tickets for the tower itself), the other inside the Museo delle Sinopie. Admission to the Duomo costs €2, except from November 1 to March 1, when it's free. Single admission to the other sights costs €5. Admission to any two sights (including the Duomo) is €6, to any four is €8.50, and to all five is €10; these combined tickets are valid for the day of issue only. There's a separate ticket (€15) for the **Leaning Tower**; groups of 30 are allowed in for half an hour, and you should expect a long wait in high season. For an extra €2 you can pre-book your visit online at ⓦ www.opapisa.it, as long as you're making your reservation between 45 and 15 days in advance. Children under the age of 8 are not allowed into the tower.

because very few tourists bother to venture far from the shadow of the Leaning Tower. To the southeast of the *campo*, on the river, you'll find the **Museo Nazionale di San Matteo**, a fine collection of ecclesiastical art and sculpture, while west along the Arno stands another good museum, the **Palazzo Reale**, which faces the exquisite little Santa Maria della Spina, on the opposite bank.

The Leaning Tower

The Leaning Tower (Torre Pendente) has always tilted. Begun in 1173, it started to subside when it had reached just three of its eight storeys, but it

▲ The Leaning Tower

leaned in the opposite direction to the present one. Odd-shaped stones were inserted to correct this deficiency, whereupon the tower lurched the other way. Over the next 180 years a succession of architects continued to extend the thing upwards, each one endeavouring to compensate for the angle, the end result being that the main part of the tower is slightly bent. Around 1350, Tommaso di Andrea da Pontedera completed the magnificent stack of marble and granite arcades by crowning it with a bell chamber, set closer to the perpendicular than the storeys below it, so that it looks like a hat set at a rakish angle.

By 1990 the tower was leaning 4.5m from the upright and nearing its limits. A huge rescue operation was then launched, which involved wrapping steel bands around the lowest section of the tower, placing 900 tonnes of lead ingots at its base to counterbalance the leaning stonework, removing water and silt from beneath the tower's foundations, and finally reinforcing the foundations and walls with steel bars. Eleven years and many millions of euros later, the tower was officially reopened to the public in November 2001.

The ascent to the bellchamber takes you up a narrow spiral staircase of 294 steps, at a fairly disorientating five-degree angle. It's not for the claustrophobic or those afraid of heights, but you might think the steep admission fee is worth it for the privilege of getting inside one of the world's most famous and uncanny buildings. The opening hours are extremely complicated, but the briefest opening period is from November to February, when tours begin at 10am and finish around 4pm; for most of the summer (April–Sept) they run from 8.30am to 7.50pm, but from June 17 to September 5 the last tour departs at around 10.20pm. Tours are given in English three times daily between April and September.

The Duomo

Pisa's breathtaking **Duomo** (daily: March 10am–6pm; April–Sept Mon–Sat 10am–8pm; Oct 10am–7pm; Nov–Feb 10am–1pm & 2–5pm; no admittance to tourists before 1pm on Sun; €2, or combined ticket, free from Nov 1 to March 1) was begun in 1064 and completed around a century later. With its four levels of variegated colonnades and its subtle interplay of dark-grey marble and white stone, the building is the archetype of Pisan-Romanesque, a model often imitated in buildings across Tuscany, but never surpassed.

The vast interior is defined by the crisp black-and-white marble of the long arcades, which are suggestive of Moorish architecture. Much of the interior was redecorated, and some of the chapels remodelled, after a fire in 1595, but a notable survivor is the apse mosaic *Christ in Majesty*, completed by Cimabue in 1302. And don't miss the **pulpit**, which **Giovanni Pisano** began to sculpt in the same year. The last of the great series of three pulpits created in Tuscany by Giovanni and his father Nicola (the others are in Siena and Pistoia), it is a work of amazing virtuosity, its whole surface animated by figures almost wholly freed from the stone.

The Baptistry, the Camposanto and the museums

The **Baptistry** (daily: March 9am–6pm; April–Sept 8am–8pm; Oct 9am–7pm; Nov–Feb 10am–5pm; €5, or combined ticket), the largest such building in Italy, was begun in 1152 by a certain Diotisalvi ("God Save You"), who left his name on a column to the left of the door; it was continued in the thirteenth century by Nicola and Giovanni Pisano, and completed late in the fourteenth century. Inside you're immediately struck by the plainness of the vast interior (the acoustics are astonishing, as the guard will demonstrate), but take time to look closely at Nicola Pisano's beautiful **pulpit**, sculpted in 1260, half a century before his son's work in the cathedral.

The screen of sepulchral white marble running along the north edge of the Campo dei Miracoli is the perimeter wall of what has been called the most beautiful cemetery in the world – the **Camposanto** (same hours as Baptistry; €5, or combined ticket). According to legend, the Archbishop Ubaldo Lanfranchi had Pisan knights on the Fourth Crusade of 1203 bring a cargo of soil back to Pisa from the hill of Golgotha, in order that eminent Pisans might be buried in holy earth. The building enclosing this sanctified site was completed almost a century later and takes the form of an enormous Gothic cloister. However, when Ruskin described the Camposanto as one of the most precious buildings in Italy, it was the **frescoes** that he was praising. Paintings once covered over two thousand square metres of cloister wall, but now the brickwork is mostly bare: **incendiary bombs** dropped by Allied planes on July 27, 1944, set the roofing on fire and drenched the frescoes in molten lead. The most important survivor is the remarkable *Triumph of Death* cycle, now displayed in a room attached to the cloister.

The **Museo dell'Opera del Duomo** (same hours as Baptistry; €5, or combined ticket) is a vast array of statuary from the Duomo and Baptistry, plus ecclesiastical finery, paintings and other miscellaneous pieces. Highlights include the extraordinary bronze doors made for the Duomo by **Bonanno Pisano** (first architect of the Leaning Tower) in 1180, and Giovanni Pisano's affecting *Madonna del Colloquio* (*Madonna of the Conversation*), so called because of the intensity of the gazes exchanged by the Madonna and Child. On the south side of the Campo, the only gap in the souvenir stalls is for the **Museo delle Sinopie** (same hours as Baptistry; €5, or combined ticket). After the damage wreaked on the Camposanto, restorers removed its *sinopie* (the sketches over which frescoes are painted) and these great plates of plaster now hang from the walls of this high-tech museum.

Piazza dei Cavalieri to the Museo Nazionale

If you have time for a wider exploration of the city, head first for **Piazza dei Cavalieri**, the central civic square of medieval Pisa, which opens unexpectedly from the narrow backstreets to the southeast of the Campo. The **Palazzo dei Cavalieri**, covered in monochrome *sgraffiti* and topped with busts of the Medici, adjoins the church of **Santo Stefano**, which still houses banners captured from Turkish ships by the Knights of St Stephen – a grand title for a gang of state-sponsored pirates. On the other side of the square is the Renaissance-adapted **Palazzo dell'Orologio**, in whose tower the military leader Ugolino della Gherardesca was starved to death with his sons and grandsons in 1208, as punishment for his alleged duplicity with the Genoese enemy – the grisly episode is described in Dante's *Inferno* and Shelley's *Tower of Famine*. From here Via Dini heads east to the arcaded **Borgo Stretto**, Pisa's smartest street; Pisa's market area is to the east of here, on **Piazza Vettovaglie** and the narrow streets that surround it (Mon–Fri morning & all day Sat). The Borgo meets the river at **Piazza Garibaldi**, at the foot of the Ponte di Mezzo.

East of Piazza Garibaldi, on Lungarno Mediceo, is the **Museo Nazionale di San Matteo** (Tues–Sat 9am–7pm, Sun 9am–2pm; €5), where most of the major works of art from Pisa's churches are now gathered. Best of the paintings are polyptychs by Simone Martini and Francesco Traini, a panel of *St Paul* by Masaccio, Gentile da Fabriano's *Madonna of Humility*, and a trio of works by Gozzoli; among the sculptures, two masterpieces stand out – Donatello's reliquary bust of the introspective *St Rossore*, and Andrea and Nino Pisano's

Madonna del Latte, a touchingly crafted work showing Mary breastfeeding the baby Jesus. The museum also has a stash of fine Middle Eastern ceramics pilfered by Pisan adventurers.

The western quarters

Due south of the Camposanto you'll find the **Orto Botanico** (Mon–Sat 8am–1pm; free); founded in 1543, this is the oldest university botanical garden in the world. On the east side of the garden, Via Santa Maria crooks its way south to meet the river alongside the second of Pisa's leaning towers, the campanile of **San Nicola**, which starts off cylindrical, then becomes octagonal, and finally hexagonal.

Alongside San Nicola, fronting the Arno at Lungarno Pacinotti 46, is the **Museo Nazionale di Palazzo Reale** (Mon–Fri 9am–3pm, Sat 9am–1pm; €5), displaying artefacts that once belonged to the Medici, Lorraine and Savoy rulers of the city, who successively occupied the house. Lavish sixteenth-century Flemish tapestries share space with antique weaponry, ivory miniatures, porcelain and a largely undistinguished picture collection; the best-known painting, Bronzino's portrait of Eleanora di Toledo, is displayed alongside a dress that belonged to her.

Further along the river, on the Lungarno Simonelli, lies the Arsenale Mediceo. Built by Cosimo I, it is now being converted into a home for the sixteen Roman ships which have been excavated since 1998 from the silt at nearby San Rossore. Almost perfectly preserved in mud for two millennia, the cargo-laden fleet includes what experts believe could be the oldest Roman warship ever found. Just west of the arsenal rises the Torre Guelfa della Cittadella Vecchia, or **Fortezza Vecchia** (Jan, Feb, Nov & Dec Sat & Sun 2–5pm, plus 10am–1pm on 2nd Sun of month; rest of year Fri–Sun 3–7pm; €2). This ancient fortress, originally built in the thirteenth century, once stood guard over Pisa's harbour but now punctuates an otherwise little-explored district; the view from the tower is spectacular.

South of the river – Santa Maria della Spina

Along the **lungarni** to the west of the Ponte di Mezzo, the rather monotonous line of *palazzi* – mirroring those on the facing bank – is suddenly enlivened by the oratory of **Santa Maria della Spina** (March–Oct Tues–Fri 10am–1.30pm & 2.30–6pm, Sat & Sun 10am–1.30pm & 2.30–7pm; rest of year Tues–Sun

---

The Gioco del Ponte and other festivals

Pisa's big traditional event is the Gioco del Ponte, held on the last Sunday of June, when twelve teams from the north and south banks of the city stage a series of "push-of-war" battles, shoving a seven-tonne carriage over the Ponte di Mezzo. First recorded in 1568, the contest and attendant parades are still held in Renaissance costume. Other celebrations – concerts, regattas, art events – are held throughout June (the Giugno Pisano), a month during which the city has a distinctly festive feel. Most spectacular of the ancillary shows is the Luminara di San Ranieri (June 16), when buildings along both river banks are lit by 70,000 candles in honour of Pisa's patron saint. At 6.30pm the following evening, the various quarters of the city compete in the Palio di San Ranieri, a boat race along the Arno.

Italy's four great maritime republics (Amalfi, Pisa, Genoa and Venice) take turns to host the **Regata delle Antiche Repubbliche Marinare**, which next comes round to Pisa in late May/early June 2010. Four eight-man crews from each of the cities race against each other on the Arno, in between festivities and parades.

10am–2pm, except second Sun of month 10am–7pm; €1.50). Founded in 1230 but rebuilt in the 1320s by a merchant who had acquired one of the thorns (*spine*) of Christ's crown, this effervescent little church is the finest flourish of Pisan-Gothic. Originally built closer to the water, it was moved here for fear of floods in 1871. The single-naved interior has lost most of its furnishings, but contains a trio of statues by Andrea and Nino Pisano.

Eating and drinking

Pisa's proximity to the coast means that seafood is the staple of its **restaurant** menus, with *baccalà alla Pisana* (dried cod in tomato sauce) and *pesce spada* (swordfish) featuring prominently. Avoid the temptation to eat at one of the plethora of places in the vicinity of the Campo dei Miracoli – aimed squarely at the tourist trade, they are generally of poor quality.

Restaurants

Cagliostro Via del Castelletto 26–30 ☎050.575.413. Tucked away in an obscure alley parallel to Via San Frediano, alongside the *Rinascente* hotel, *Cagliostro* is an extremely good-restaurant-wine bar, offering a small but classy menu of classic Pisan dishes and others with an innovative twist – such as Tuscan leek soup with Stilton. The dining room is spectacular too. Expect to pay about €40 per person. Closed Sun, Mon lunchtime & Tues.

Il Campano Via Domenico Cavalca 19 ☎050.580.585. Home-made pasta and gnocchi, and local seafood, are the big things at this first-rate trattoria – though they also do meaty Tuscan classics, including a one-kilo Fiorentina steak (to share, of course). This may also be the only Pisan restaurant with ostrich on the menu. Extremely good selection of wines, too. Closed all Wed & Thurs eve.

La Cereria Via Pietro Gori 33 ☎050.20.336. Popular, unpretentious restaurant tucked away in a courtyard a short distance south of the river. Excellent seafood and pasta dishes, superb pizzas (the best in the city, some reckon) and a pleasant garden. Closed Tues.

La Mescita Via Domenico Cavalca 2 ☎050.544.294. This wine bar-restaurant, located on the edge of the Piazza Vettovaglie market, has established a good reputation with its ever-changing Tuscan menu and excellent cellar. You'll pay around €35 per person. Closed Sat & Sun eve, Mon & three weeks in Aug.

Osteria dei Cavalieri Via San Frediano 16 ☎050.580.858. Outstanding quality, good prices (about €30 per person) and a nice atmosphere. The fish is exquisite, Tuscan meat and game dishes are expertly prepared, and their vegetarian options are excellent. Closed Sat lunch & Sun, and most of Aug.

San Omobono Piazza San Omobono 6 ☎050.540.847. This city-centre trattoria serves terrific authentic Pisan home cooking, featuring dishes such as *brachette alla renaiola* – pasta in a purée of greens and smoked fish. Closed Sun & two weeks in Aug.

Cafés and bars

Bazeel Piazza Garibaldi 15. This stylish bar is currently Pisa's most favoured hangout – the interior is cool and spacious, but when the weather's good the punters prefer the outside tables, or even the parapet overlooking the river. DJs on Fri & Sat, live music Thurs & Sun. Daily 5pm–2am.

Pasticceria Salza Borgo Stretto 46. The best-known café-pasticceria in Pisa, and quite rightly so; it has a restaurant section at the back, but the coffee and cakes are the main reason to come. Tues–Sun 8am–8.30pm.

Lucca

LUCCA, 17km northeast of Pisa, is the most graceful of Tuscany's provincial capitals, set inside an imposing ring of Renaissance walls fronted by gardens and huge bastions. Charming and quiet out of season, Lucca's narrow streets become busier in summer, but never as thronged as those of Florence or Siena.

F & Pistoia ▲   ▲ **H**

▲ **I**

0 ——— 200 m

LUCCA

Porta S. Jacopo

S. Francesco

Porta Elisa

Villa Guinigi

Porta S. Maria

San Pietro Somaldi

S. Frediano

Giardino Botanico

Torre Guinigi

S. Maria Forisportam

Palazzo Pfanner

Torre delle Ore

Museo della Cattedrale

S. Agostino

S. Cristoforo

Casa di Puccini

S. Michele in Foro

Duomo

Palazzo Mansi

S. Paolino

S. Giovanni

Porta S. Pietro

Palazzo Ducale

S. Romano

Train Station

Porta S. Donato

Bus Station

Porta V. Emanuele

▲ **I** & Pisa

Viareggio ▲

ACCOMMODATION

Bernardino	H
Diana	G
La Luna	B
La Romea	C
La Torre 1, 2 & 3	A
Piccolo Hotel Puccini	D
Universo	E
Villa La Principessa	I
Villa Romantica	F

EATING & DRINKING

Buatino	1
Caffè del Mercato	9
Caffè di Simo	8
Da Giulio in Pelleria	2
Da Leo	3
Gelateria Veneta	5
Girovita	12
Locanda di Bacco	4
Osteria Machiavelli	11
Pasticceria Taddeucci	10
Puccini	7
Vineria I Santi	6

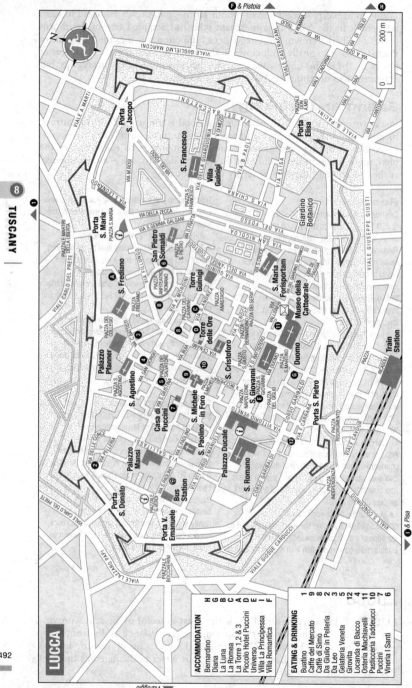

The city lies at the heart of one of Italy's richest agricultural regions, and has prospered since Roman times. Its heyday was the eleventh to fourteenth centuries, when the silk trade brought wealth and, for a time, political power. Lucca first lost its independence to Pisa in 1314, then, under Castruccio Castracani, forged an empire in the west of Tuscany. Pisa and Pistoia both fell, and, but for Castracani's untimely death in 1325, Lucca might well have taken Florence. In subsequent centuries it remained largely independent until falling into the hands of Napoleon and then the Bourbons. The city's most famous son, composer **Giacomo Puccini**, was born here in 1858. Today Lucca is among the wealthiest and most conservative cities in Tuscany, its prosperity gained largely through **silk** and high-quality **olive oil**.

Arrival and information

Lucca's **train station** (℡ 1478.88.088) is just south of the city walls. Frequent Lazzi and CLAP **buses** from Florence, and Lazzi ones from Pisa and Livorno, arrive at the western Piazzale Verdi.

Lucca's large and very helpul main **tourist office** is in the north of town, at Piazza Santa Maria 35 (daily: April–Sept 9am–7pm; Oct–March 9am–5pm; ℡ 0583.919.931, ⓦ www.luccaturismo.it). It has public toilets. Other offices are in the Cortile degli Svizzeri, behind Piazza Napoleone (same times; ℡ 0583.4171), and on Piazzale Verdi (daily: April–Sept 9am–7pm; Oct–March 9am–2pm; ℡ 0583.419.689).

Accommodation

Accommodation can be difficult at almost any time of year – the number of hotels has failed to keep pace with the town's growing popularity – so if you turn up without a booking, be prepared to move on to one of the nearby towns, or even out to Pisa or Pistoia. There are few **hotels** within the walls, although some good-value **private rooms** ease the burden (consult the tourist office).

Hotels

Bernardino Via di Tiglio 108 ℡ 0583.953.356, ⓦ www.hotelbernardino.it. A reliable 25-room three-star, 5min east of Porta Elisa, with plain but comfortable rooms, all en suite and with TV. ❸

Diana Via del Molinetto 11 ℡ 0583.492.202, ⓦ www.albergodiana.com. A block west of the Duomo, this unfussy, nine-room place has seven double rooms with private bathroom and two singles without. A nearby annexe has six smarter, more expensive rooms (❸) and a studio apartment. ❷

La Luna Corte Compagni 12 ℡ 0583.493.634, ⓦ www.hotellaluna.com. A smart and welcoming 29-room three-star within the walls, with characterful rooms ranged around an internal courtyard and free parking. Closed Jan. ❹

La Romea Vicolo delle Ventaglie 2 ℡ 0583.464.175, ⓦ www.laromea.com. Notwithstanding its imposing black gates, *La Romea*, just off Via San Andrea, is one of the friendliest and most sophisticated places in town. The five rooms are stylishly designed and an excellent home-made breakfast is served in the spacious hall. ❹

La Torre 1, 2 and 3 Reception at Piazza del Carmine 11 ℡ 0583.957.044, ⓦ www .roomslatorre.com. These three places are all close together in a quiet part of town. Service can be brusque but rooms are big and good value, especially those with shared bathrooms. ❷

Piccolo Hotel Puccini Via di Poggio 9 ℡ 0583.55.421, ⓦ www.hotelpuccini.com. Friendly three-star steps from the Casa di Puccini and San Michele. The 14 standard en-suite rooms are less stunning than the location. ❸

Universo Piazza del Giglio 1 ℡ 0583.493.678, ⓦ www.universolucca.com. A venerable and spacious old three-star, right in the centre complete with red carpet and grand, golden chairs. The varying set of rooms matches the staff for unpredictable charm. ❻

Villa La Principessa SS del Brennero 1616, Massa Pisana ℡ 0583.370.037, ⓦ www .hotelprincipessa.com. A beautifully appointed nineteenth-century country villa set in lovely grounds (with pool), 4.5km south of town. ❼

Villa Romantica Via N Barbantini 246, corner of Via Inigo Campioni ℡0583.496.872, ⓦwww .villaromantica.it. An attractive Liberty-style town house outside the city walls near the easily spotted stadium, with a swimming pool, garden and six nicely maintained rooms. ❸

Hostel

Ostello San Frediano Via della Cavallerizza 12 ℡0583.469.957, ⓦwww.ostellolucca.it. Lucca's one HI hostel, conveniently located just inside the walls. Midnight curfew; €19, double rooms ❶.

The City

Lucca is a delightful place simply to wander in randomly, with much of the centre free from traffic, although you will have to keep any eye out for the many cyclists weaving through the crowds (there are plenty of outlets that rent bikes if you wish to join them, especially near the walls). The focus of Lucca's compact *centro storico* is the vast Piazza Napoleone, but its social heart is **Piazza San Michele** just to the north. The "long thread", Via Fillungo, heads northeast to the extraordinary circular **Piazza Anfiteatro**, while farther east, beyond the Fosso ("ditch"), lies San Francesco and Lucca's major art museum, housed in the **Villa Guinigi**. Whatever else you do in town, be sure to walk – or cycle – some or all of the **walls**, which are crowned by a broad, tree-lined promenade.

San Michele and around

The historical heart of town, and once the site of the Roman forum, is now a lively square fringed with shops and cafés that plays host to a daily market (clothes, bags, sweets, tourist knick-knacks etc) that sits alongside **San Michele in Foro** (daily 7.40am–noon & 3–6pm, closes 5.30pm in winter; free), a church with one of Tuscany's most exquisite **facades**. Most of the present structure dates from the century after 1070, but the church is unfinished, as the money ran out before the body of the building could be raised to the level of the facade. The effect is wonderful, the upper loggias and the windows fronting air. Its Pisan-inspired intricacy is a triumph of poetic eccentricity: each of its myriad columns is different – some twisted, others sculpted or candy-striped. The impressive **campanile** is Lucca's tallest. It would be hard to follow this act and the **interior** barely tries; the best work of art is a beautifully framed painting called *Saints Jerome, Sebastian, Roch and Helena* by Filippino Lippi in the right-hand nave.

The composer **Giacomo Puccini** was born about a block away, on December 22, 1858, at Corte San Lorenzo 9; his father and grandfather had both been organists at San Michele. The family home, the **Casa di Puccini** (ⓦwww.puccini.it) is currently closed for renovation and no opening date has been fixed. Just west of here is the **Museo Nazionale di Palazzo Mansi**, Via Galli Tassi 43 (Tues–Sat 8.30am–7.30pm, Sun 8.30am–1.30pm; €4; joint ticket with Museo Guinigi €6.50). This seventeenth-century *palazzo* is worth seeing for its magnificent Rococo decor: from a vast, frescoed **Music Salon**, you pass through three drawing rooms hung with seventeenth-century Flemish tapestries to a gilded **bridal suite**, complete with lavish canopied bed. Rooms 11–14 in the far wing hold an indifferent **Pinacoteca**, the highlight of which is Pontormo's portrait of Alessandro de' Medici.

The Duomo and around

It needs a double-take before you realize why the **Duomo** (also known as the *Cattedrale di San Martino*) looks odd. A severely asymmetric façade fronts the building – its right-hand arch and loggias are squeezed by the bell tower, which was already in place from an earlier building. Nonetheless, little detracts from its overall grandeur, created by the repetition of tiny columns and loggias and by the stunning **atrium**, whose bas-reliefs are some of the finest sculptures in the city. The carvings over the left-hand door – a *Deposition, Annunciation, Nativity* and *Adoration of the Magi* – are by **Nicola Pisano**. Other panels display a symbolic labyrinth, a *Tree of Life* (with Adam and Eve at the bottom and Christ at the top), a bestiary of grotesques and the months of the year.

The **interior** (mid-March to Oct Mon–Fri 9.30am–5.45pm, Sat 9.30am–6.45pm, Sun 9–10.45am & noon–5pm; rest of the year closes 4.45pm Mon–Fri and 6pm Sun; free) is best known for the contribution of **Matteo Civitali** (1435–1501), who is represented here most famously by the *Tempietto*, a gilt-and-marble octagon halfway down the church. Some fanatically intense acts of devotion are performed in front of it, directed at the **Volto Santo** (Holy Face) within, a cedarwood crucifix with bulging eyes and dark brown skin popularly said to be a true effigy of Christ carved by Nicodemus, an eyewitness to the Crucifixion. Legend has it that the *Volto Santo* came to Lucca of its own volition, first journeying by boat from the Holy Land, and then brought by oxen guided by divine will. The effigy attracted pilgrims from all over Europe, including kings – William II of England used to swear by it ("*Per sanctum vultum de Lucca!*"). The **Tomb of Ilaria del Carretto** (1410) in the sacristy (Ⓦwww .museocattedralelucca.it; mid-March to Oct same hours as Duomo; rest of the year Mon–Fri 9.30am–4.45pm, Sat 9.30am–6.45pm, Sun noon–6pm; €2 or €6 with Museo della Cattedrale and church of San Giovaani) is considered the masterpiece of Sienese sculptor **Jacopo della Quercia**. It consists of a raised dais and the sculpted body of Ilaria, second wife of Paolo Guinigi, one of Lucca's medieval big shots. In a touching, almost sentimental gesture, the artist has carved the family dog at her feet. Also within the sacristy is a superb *Madonna Enthroned* by **Ghirlandaio**.

Occupying a converted twelfth-century building opposite the Duomo is the **Museo della Cattedrale** (mid-March to Oct daily 10am–6pm; Nov to mid-March Mon–Fri 10am–2pm, Sat & Sun 10am–5pm; €4, or €6 with cathedral sacristy & San Giovanni). This contains some unnerving Romanesque stone heads, human and equine, and, in room II on the upper floor, a reliquary from Limoges decorated with stories from the life of St Thomas à Becket alongside the *Croce dei Pisani*, an ornate fifteenth-century gold crucifix. West of the Duomo is the church of **San Giovanni** (same hours; €2.50, combined ticket with Tomb of Ilaria & Museo della Cattedrale €6). This was Lucca's cathedral until 715, and excavations here have unearthed a tangle of remains, from Roman mosaics to traces of a Carolingian church.

North to San Frediano

Via Cenami leads from the Duomo north to the **Torre delle Ore**, the city's clock tower since 1471. From here, **Via Fillungo** cuts through Lucca's luxury shopping district.

San Frediano, between Via Fillungo and the northwest city walls, is again Pisan-Romanesque, featuring the magnificent thirteenth-century exterior mosaic *Christ in Majesty*, with the Apostles gathered below. The **interior** (Mon–Sat 8.30am–noon & 3–5.30pm, Sun 9–11.30am & 3–5.30pm; closed during services; free) lives up to the facade's promise – a delicately lit, hall-like basilica. Facing the door is the **Fonta Lustrale**, a huge twelfth-century font executed by three unknown craftsmen. Set behind the font is an *Annunciation* by Andrea della Robbia, festooned with trailing garlands of ceramic fruit. The left-hand of the two rear chapels houses the apparently incorrupt body of **St Zita** (died 1278), a Lucchese maidservant who achieved sainthood from a white lie: she used to give bread from her household to the poor, and when challenged one day by her boss as to the contents of her apron, she replied "only roses and flowers" – into which the bread was transformed. She is commemorated on April 27 by a flower market outside the church. Lucca's best frescoes – **Amico Aspertini**'s sixteenth-century scenes of the *Arrival of the Volto Santo*, the *Life of St Augustine* and *The Miracle of St Frediano* – occupy the second chapel of the left aisle. Frediano, an Irish monk, is said to have brought Christianity to Lucca in the sixth century and is depicted here saving the city from flood.

A short distance west, at Via degli Asili 33, is the **Palazzo Pfanner** (April–Oct daily except Wed 10am–6pm; garden or palace €3, garden and palace €4.50). The *palazzo*, housing a textiles collection, is less interesting than its rear loggia and exquisite statued gardens with fountain. They can be seen to good effect from the city walls just nearby, which also yield a good overview of another fine church, **Sant'Agostino**.

East of San Frediano is the remarkable **Piazza Anfiteatro**. This ramshackle circuit of medieval buildings, built on the foundations of the Roman amphitheatre that once stood here (arches and columns of which can still be discerned), is now ringed by cafés. South past a covered market looms the **Torre Guinigi**, which once belonged to Lucca's eponymous, leading fifteenth-century family and is one of the strangest sights in town – its battlemented tower is surmounted, 44m up, by a **holm oak** whose roots have grown into the room below. You can climb the tower from Via Sant'Andrea (daily: March 9am–5pm; April 9.30am–9pm; May & Oct 10am–6pm; June–Sept 9am–midnight; Nov–Feb 9.30am–5pm; €3.50).

East to San Francesco

Running from north to south across town is a canal and Via del Fosso, across which is the church of **San Francesco** (usually open mornings only), fronted by a relatively simple facade and adjoining a crumbling brick convent. Behind the church is Lucca's key collection of painting, sculpture, furniture and applied arts, the **Museo Nazionale di Villa Guinigi**, housed in the family's much-restored mansion (Tues–Sat 8.30am–7.30pm, Sun 8.30am–1.30pm; €4, or €6.50 combined ticket with Palazzo Mansi). Its lower floor has mainly sculpture and archeological finds, with numerous Romanesque pieces and works by della Quercia and Matteo Civitali. Upstairs are lots of big sixteenth-century paintings and more impressive works by early Lucchese and Sienese masters, as well as fine Renaissance offerings from such as Fra' Bartolommeo.

Eating, drinking and entertainment

Lucca has some high-quality **restaurants**, and local specialities worth keeping an eye out for include *zuppa di farro*, a thick soup made with spelt (a type of grain), *torta di spinaci*, a sweet tart made with spinach, and *capretto*, mountain goat, often roasted. The town's **food shops** are equally good and make great places to stock up for a picnic: *Caniparoli* in Via San Paolina is a standout chocolate shop.

The **Lucchese Settembre** festival features plenty of activity throughout September, centred on a **candlelit procession** on the 13th, when the bejewelled *Volto Santo* (see p.495) is carried through the streets from San Frediano to the Duomo. Consult the tourist office for details of affiliated September events, such as **classical concerts** (including performances of a Puccini opera) at the intimate, four-tiered Teatro Comunale in Piazza del Giglio, as well as **jazz** happenings and **art** exhibitions. Another key musical event is the Summer Festival (@www.summer-festival.com) often featuring big-name international stars performing in Piazza Anfiteatro.

Cafés, bars and gelaterie

Caffè del Mercato Piazza San Michele. The most alluring of the bars around the main piazza, particularly as the church keeps it nice and shady throughout lunch.

Caffè di Simo Via Fillungo 58 ☏ 0583.496.234. Lucca's most famous café-bar was Puccini's favourite haunt and retains an appealing late nineteenth-century ambience. It serves a decent array of cakes as well as a few simple hot dishes for €6–8. Closed Mon.

Gelateria Veneta Via Vittorio Veneto 74 ☏ 0583.493.727. It's been serving some of Lucca's best ice cream since 1927 and is open conveniently late. Five scoops for €2.30. Closed mid-Jan to mid-Feb and Tues in winter.

Girovita Piazza Antelminelli 2 ☏ 0583.469.412. With tables outside in the quiet piazza opposite the cathedral, trendy *Girovita* is the place to come for an *aperitivo* or a lengthy afternoon coffee. Closed Mon.

Pasticceria Taddeucci Piazza San Michele 34 ☏ 0583.494.933. A stunning interior of wood-panelling and mosaic tiles match the selection of cakey delights and great coffee.

Vineria I Santi Via dell'Anfiteatro 29/A. ☏ 0583.496.124. Inventive, well-prepared dishes, such as goose liver paté with marmalade accompany the wine list at this bar, which has tables outside on a small piazza behind the amphitheatre. Closed Wed.

Restaurants

Buatino Borgo Giannotti 508 ☏ 0583.343.207. Outside the city walls, about 1km north of Piazzale Martiri della Libertà, but worth the walk or cycle ride. Unassuming from the outside, but tremendous food and a friendly, informal vibe with occasional live jazz. Menus change daily (reckon on €20 for a meal). They also offer three plain but inexpensive rooms with shared bath to rent above the restaurant (about €40). Closed Sun.

Da Giulio in Pelleria Via della Conce 45 ☏ 0583.55.948. A lively trattoria always packed in the evenings – the food is not exceptional, but prices are very reasonable (*primi* from €5, *secondi* €5 and up) and the atmosphere makes it worth it. Closed Sun.

Da Leo Via Tegrimi 1 ☏ 0583.492.236. Small, inexpensive locals' haunt with solid (and solidly meaty) Tuscan cooking. *Primi* €5.50, *secondi* €8–10.50. Closed Sun.

Locanda di Bacco Via San Giorgio 36 ☏ 0583.493.136. One of the city's newer restaurants, but deservedly popular, thanks to fine setting in a period building and good and thoroughly local cooking with the odd twist. Reckon on €25 for a full meal. Closed Tues and periods in Feb & Nov.

Osteria Machiavelli Via Cesare Battisti 28 ☏ 0583.467.219. Great family-run place with a jovial air of controlled chaos, fantastic food and unbeatable prices of around €15 for two courses. Closed Sun.

Puccini Corte San Lorenzo 1 ☏ 0583.316.116, ⊛ www.ristorantedipuccini.com. Opposite the composer's house, this place has a light touch and classy approach to its dishes, which include macaroni with chestnuts and mushrooms. It's not cheap (*primi* €10–12, *secondi* €17–19), but is the top choice for a lunch to remember or a romantic dinner date. Closed Tues & Wed lunch in summer, all day Tues in winter.

North of Pisa

The coast from near Pisa north to the Ligurian border is a solid strip of unattractive beach resorts. This **Riviera della Versilia** ought to be otherwise, given the dramatic backdrop of the **Alpi Apuane**, but the beaches share the coastal plain with a railway, autostrada and clogged urban roads – and, on top of this, the sea is not the cleanest in Italy. The resort of **Viareggio** provides a lively diversion on a coastal journey north to the stunning Cinque Terre. Otherwise, the only real appeal lies inland, exploring the famed marble-quarrying centre of **Carrara**.

Viareggio

VIAREGGIO, 22km northwest of Pisa, tends not to feature highly on most independent travellers' Tuscan itineraries. These days everyone wants picturesque former fishing villages and converted farmhouses but Viareggio has never been anything other than what it is – a purpose-built seaside resort. This can make visiting problematic. Many hotels insist on at least half board in summer, and most of the beach has been parcelled up into private strips controlled by the hotels – which can charge €20 or more for the use of a sun lounger and an umbrella for the day. However, to regard Viareggio as package holiday haunt to be avoided would be to do it a disservice. It's a lot better than that. The town has some very neat 1920s Art Deco buildings here unlike anything else in the province, as well as a good selection of bars and restaurants, best sampled on a night-time stroll along its three-lane-wide, several-kilometre long seafront boulevard, which, on a balmy summer evening, has a strip-like neon-lit aesthetic more American in feel than Tuscan. To see Viareggio at its liveliest, come for its famously boisterous **Carnevale** in February, when for four consecutive Sundays there's an amazing parade of floats, or *carri* – colossal, lavishly designed papier-mâché models of politicians and plenty of celebrities (ⓦwww.viareggio.ilcarnevale.com).

The **train station** is 600m back from the seafront. **Buses** (Lazzi, CAT and CLAP) stop nearer the centre; along the seafront, turn right past Piazza Mazzini, to find the **tourist office**, at Viale Carducci 10 (Mon–Sat 9am–2pm & 3–7.30pm, Sun 9am–1pm; ☏0584.962.233, ⓦwww.aptversilia.it). The town has literally hundreds of **hotels** in all price brackets; one inexpensive option is *Villa Amadei*, just west of the tourist office at Via F. Gioia 23 (☏0584.45.517, ⓦwww.hotelamadei.it; ❷). For the best **restaurant** in town head for the Michelin-starred *Romano*, Via Mazzini 120 (☏0584.31.382; closed Mon plus lunch Tues in July & Aug), for sublime fish and seafood.

Carrara

The capital of Massa-Carrara, Tuscany's northernmost province, is **Massa**, a modern town that has more or less merged with its adjacent beach resort of **Marina di Massa** in a sprawl of undistinguished holiday development. Nearby **CARRARA** sits just inside the Ligurian border, 28km north of Viareggio, and enjoys a fame that far outstrips its modest size. For the mountains here have been a principal source of **marble** since the Roman period and everyone from Michelangelo to Henry Moore has tramped up here in search of the perfect stone. Carrara is still the world's largest producer and exporter of marble, shipping out 1.5 million tonnes a year from the container port plumb in the middle of **Marina di Carrara**. But quiet Carrara itself has a pleasant, rural feel and comes as a relief after the holiday coast.

From the central **Piazza Matteotti**, the pedestrianized Via Roma heads north to the attractive Piazza Accademia, with steps down (west) to the old town and Carrara's Romanesque-Gothic **Duomo**, graced with a lovely Pisan-style marble facade. Heart of the old town is gracious **Piazza Alberica**, the focus for the town's display of contemporary marble sculpture, the biennial **Scolpire all'Aperto** (late July to early Oct), when internationally renowned artists arrive to create new works in public. For the low-down on marble, there's an impressive **Museo Civico di Marmo** on Viale XX Settembre, 2km south of town (May, June & Sept Mon–Sat 10am–6pm; July & Aug Mon–Sat 10am–8pm; Oct–April 9am–5pm; ☏0585.845.746; €4.50), served by CAT buses from Piazza Matteotti.

Any short trip into the interior brings you to the startling sight of the marble **quarries**. To get a closer view, take a bus (hourly from Via Minzoni) towards **Colonnata**, 8km northeast of Carrara, and get off before the village at the *Visita Cave* signs by the mine – if you're driving, follow the *Cava di Marmo* signs

Ferries from Livorno

Livorno is a major and mostly modern port city, 18km southwest of Pisa and of little or no interest to most casual visitors. However, there are dozens of ferry sailings running from here to **Corsica** (Bastia or Porto Vecchio), **Sardinia** (Olbia, Golfo Aranci or Cágliari), **Sicily** (Palermo) and the Tuscan Islands. Nearly all ferries to Corsica and Sardinia leave from alongside the **Stazione Marittima**, west of the centre behind the Fortezza Vecchia, although some (and boats to Sicily) depart from **Varco Galvani**, a long way west of town. Ferries to Capraia leave from the central **Porto Mediceo**. Check with the tourist office (on Piaza Municipio) and the companies themselves for times and prices; **reserve** well ahead in summer. If you're taking a car to Sardinia, note that most companies offer discount deals if you cross to Corsica and drive the 180km to the southern tip of the Island – and often the subsequent ferry to Sardinia is free. For a full list of ferries to Sardinia, see p.991 and to Elba, see p.500.

Ferry companies
Corsica Ferries/Sardinia Ferries Stazione Marittima, Calata Carrara ☎199.400.500, ⓦwww.corsicaferries.it. To Bastia (Corsica) and Golfo Aranci (Sardinia).

Corsica Marittima Stazione Marittima, Calata Carrara ☎0586.210.507. To Bastia, Porto Vecchio and Olbia (Sardinia).

Grandi Navi Veloci (Grimaldi) Varco Galvani, Calata Tripoli, Porto Nuovo ☎06.4208.3567, ⓦwww.grimaldi-ferries.it. To Palermo (Sicily).

Moby Lines Stazione Marittima, Calata Carrara ☎0586.899.950, ⓦwww.mobylines .it. To Bastia (Corsica) and Olbia (Sardinia), Porto Vecchio (Corsica) and Barcelona.

Toremar Porto Mediceo. Call centre ☎892.123 or 0586.224.511, ⓦwww.toremar.it. To Gorgona and Capraia.

from the Colonnata. You'll see a huge, blindingly white marble basin, its floor and sides perfectly squared by the enormous wire saws used to cut the blocks that litter the surroundings.

Practicalities
Carrara-Avenza train station is close to the Marina di Carrara seafront, and is served by regular **buses** that run 4km inland to drop off at Carrara's central Piazza Matteotti. The town has a **tourist office** at Via XX Settembre 46 (Mon–Sat: April & May 9am–5pm; June–Aug 9am–1pm & 4–7.30pm; Sept–March 9am–1pm & 3–5pm; ☎0585.844.403), though you'll find more information on the coast at Marina di Carrara, from where Navigazione Golfo dei Poeti runs **boats** to Portovenere and the Cinque Terre (June–Sept daily; around €20). Carrara's central **hotels** are the recently overhauled two-star *Hotel d'Ora*, on Via Apuana (☎0585.70.634, ⓦwww.hotel-dora.it; ❷), and the three-star *Michelangelo*, Corso Fratelli Rosselli 3 (☎0585.777.161, ⓦwww.rivieratoscana.com; ❸), with parking. The HI **hostel**, *Ostello Albergo Apuano per la Gioventù* (☎0585.780.034, ⓔostelloapuane@hotmail.com; mid-March to mid-Sept; curfew 11.30pm; €11), is on the seafront between Marina di Carrara and Marina di Massa at Via delle Pinete 237, alongside plenty of **campsites**. The excellent *Il Via* **restaurant**, Via Roma 17 (☎0585.779.423; closed Sun in winter), has a quality meat or fish menu at moderate prices. Elsewhere are the good-value *Roma*, Piazza Cesare Battisti 1 (☎0585.70.632; closed Sun), and *Osteria della Contrada*, Via Ulivi 2 (☎0585.776.961; closed Mon).

Elba

Mountainous **ELBA** is Italy's third-largest island – 29km long by some 19km wide – and since captivating Napoleon, has attracted visitors ever since. It has exceptionally clear water, fine white-sand beaches, and a lush, wooded interior, superb for walking, and though it's now well and truly embracing package tourism, almost everyone comes for the beach resorts – even in the height of summer, inland villages remain mostly quiet. **Portoferraio** is very much the capital, an attractive port overlooked by a warren of old alleys. Elsewhere, the most attractive towns are **Capoliveri** and **Porto Azzurro** in the southeast and little **Marciana** in the west, the last of these providing access to woodland hikes and the impressive chair lift up to **Monte Capanne** (1018m). **Biòdola** occupies an idyllic sweeping bay near Portoferraio that is largely free from the island's otherwise remorseless beach culture. You can also take a ferry from Portoferraio or Porto Azzurro to various smaller islands.

Historically, Elba has been well out of the mainstream. The principal industry from ancient times until World War II was **mining**, both of iron ore and of the extensive mineral deposits. The **Romans** wrote of "the Island of good wines" (Elban wines are still among Tuscany's finest). In later centuries control passed from Pisa to Genoa and on to the Medici, Spain, Turkey and finally France – a cosmopolitan mix that has left its legacy on both architecture and cultivation. Most people know the island as the place of exile for **Napoleon**, who, after he was banished here in May 1814, revamped education and the legal system, built roads and modernized the economy before escaping back to France in

Ferries to Elba

The main port of departure to Elba is **Piombino**, 75km south of Livorno – not a great place to stay, since it was flattened in World War II and these days makes its living from a giant steelworks. If you're arriving by train, you'll probably have to change at **Campiglia Marittima** station, from where connecting trains run through the town to Piombino Maríttima. At the port, you'll find plenty of ticket outlets for all ferry companies. Most people head to Elba's Portoferraio, to where Toremar and Moby **ferries** run every day of the year, the first around 5.50am and the last around 10.30pm (earlier and later in high summer; one-way €36 for a car and driver (plus €6.96 tax), €7.10 for additional passengers and foot passengers (€3.80 tax); summer every 30min; winter every 2hr; 1hr). If you're looking to cut costs get the cheaper ferry (€28.80 plus €6.96 tax; foot passengers €3.50 plus €3.80 tax) to Rio Marina on the island's east coast with Toremar. Port taxes add a few euros. Note that you should book your return ticket from Elba as soon in advance as possible in summer.

From Piombino Toremar also serves Rio Marina (2–3 daily) and Porto Azzurro (summer 1 daily). Toremar's **rapid ferry**, or *linea veloce*, serves Portoferraio (summer 2 daily; 40min) and Rio Marina (summer 3 daily; 30min). Toremar's **hydrofoil**, or *aliscafo*, glides to Cavo (summer 5 daily; winter 3 daily; 20min) and Portoferraio (summer 4 daily; 30min). Fares are €9.40 plus €3.80 tax per person.

Ferry company offices

Moby Nuova Stazione Marittima, Piombino ☏0565.225.211; Via Ninci 1, Portoferraio ☏0565.9361; or Viale Elba 4, Portoferraio ☏0565.914.133, ⓦwww.mobylines.it.

Toremar Nuova Stazione Marittima, Piombino ☏0565.31.100, ⓦwww.toremar.it or www.lariepalombo.com; Calata Italia 23, Portoferraio ☏0565.930.893; Calata Voltoni 20, Rio Marina ☏0565.962.073; Banchina IV Novembre 26, Porto Azzurro ☏0565.95.004; or Via Michelangelo 54, Cavo ☏0565.949.871.

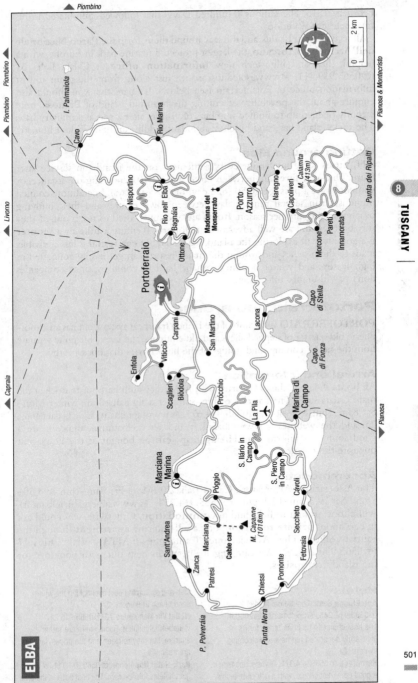

ELBA

Piombino

Piombino

Piombino

Livorno

Capraia

Bastia (Corsica)

I. Palmaiola

Cavo

Rio Marina

Nisportino

Rio nell' Elba

Bagnàia

Ottone

Madonna del Monserrato

Porto Azzurro

Naregno

Capoliveri

M. Calamita (413m)

Morcone

Pareti

Innamorata

Pianosa & Montecristo

Punta dei Ripalti

Portoferraio

Carpani

San Martino

Viticcio

Enfola

Scaglieri

Biodola

Pròcchio

La Pila

Lacona

Capo di Stella

Capo di Fonza

Marina di Campo

Pianosa

Marciana Marina

Poggio

S. Ilàrio in Campo

S. Piero in Campo

Sant'Andrea

Zanca

Marciana

Patresi

Cable car

M. Capanne (1018m)

Chiessi

Pomonte

P. Polverdia

Punta Nera

Cávoli

Seccheto

Fetovaia

N

0   2 km

February 1815. The famous "Hundred Days" that followed culminated in his final defeat at Waterloo.

All seven Tuscan Islands, and the seas around them, form the **Parco Nazionale dell'Arcipelago Toscano**, the largest protected marine park in Europe, with a helpful, slick and high-tech new **information office** at Calata Italia 31 (℡0565.919.411, ⓦwww.isoleditoscana.it), just along from the main tourist information office in Portoferraio (see below). It's here that you should also enquire about the possibility of visiting the beautiful Island of **Pianosa**, only recently opened up to limited numbers of visitors after a past as a military base. The rocky island has good beaches, abundant wildlife and no resident humans.

Getting around Elba

ATL **buses** serve just about every settlement on the island (no service after 8pm). One-way **fares** are between €0.80 and €3.10 depending on distance, or you could get a **pass** for €6.50 (one day) or €18 (six days). In addition, council minibuses run several times a day between town centres and their outlying beaches in the summer season. **Boats** are also much used to reach out-of-the-way beaches, and are well advertised at all ports. Renting a **bike** or a **scooter** is a good way of exploring the island, see p.504, but **car rental** is less advisable: roads to the beaches and around the major resorts can get nastily congested in high season, and winter bookings can be hard to come by, since companies don't pay insurance off-season.

Portoferraio and around

PORTOFERRAIO is the hub of the Island's transport system, but has an atmospheric old quarter of stepped alleys and old churches, and lives a life quite separate from the hectic comings-and-goings of the huge ferries that dock nearby.

Arrival and information

All **boats** slide past the old quarter with its Medici-built harbour to dock at the main Calata Italia. The **tourist office** (summer daily 8am–8pm; winter Mon–Sat 8am–2pm & 3–6pm; ℡0565.914.671, ⓦwww.aptelba.it) is at Calata Italia 23, and the websites ⓦwww.elbalink.it and www.elbatuttanatura.com are a good source of information. Hiking maps can be bought at the newsagent opposite the bus stop.

Accommodation

The Associazione Albergatori, Calata Italia 20 (Mon–Fri 9am–1pm & 3.30–7pm, Sat 9.30am–12.30pm; ℡0565.914.754, ⓦwww.albergatorielbani.it), will phone around to help find **accommodation**. Otherwise, you could ask in bars about **private rooms** or book a self-catering **apartment** through the tourist office. The Associazione Campeggi (FAITA), Viale Elba 7 (℡0565.930.208, ⓦwww.campingelba.net), can help out with bookings for the island's **campsites**.

Hotels

Ape Elbana Salita Cosimo dei Medici 2 ℡0565.914.245, ⓔapelbana@elba2000.it. The best choice in its price range for its pleasantly decorated rooms and welcoming owners. ❷

Hermitage ℡0565.974.811, ⓦwww.elba4star.it. A good upmarket choice, with a golf club, tennis club and swimming pool overlooking the white-sand beach at Biodola. ❾

Nobel Via Manganaro 72 ℡0565.915.217, ⓔnobel@elbalink.it. Rooms here are rather spartan, but they're clean and the prices, for Elba, are keen. ❷

Park-Hotel Napoleone ℡0565.911.111, ⓦwww .parkhotelnapoleone.com. The best hotel in the area for its sense of exclusive isolation and impeccable service. Housed in a nineteenth-century mansion beside the emperor's villa at San Martino. ❼

Villa Ombrosa Viale De Gasperi 3 ☎0565.914.363, ⓦwww.villaombrosa.it. Decent mid-range option; a modern villa with good restaurant in a panoramic position facing Le Ghiaie beach but only a few minutes' walk from the old town. ❺

Campsites

Camping le Foce ☎0565.976.456, ⓦwww .campinglafoce.com. The nicest place on the island to pitch a tent. Near Marino di Campo, with an appealing beachfront setting.

Enfola ☎0565.939.001. ⓦwww.campingenfola .it. A nicely shaded site just west of Portoferraio on the scenic coast road. April to mid-Oct.

Lacona ☎0565.964.161, ⓦwww.camping-lacona .it. Key site in Lacona, Elba's camping hotspot on the coast 7km south of Portoferraio. The site (also with apartments and bungalows) is set in pine woods a little away from the flat foreshore crowded with bars and discos.

Scaglieri ☎0565.969.940, ⓦwww .campingscaglieri.it. Lovely position the hillside above Biodola beach. Also offers bungalows and apartments for rent. April to mid-Oct.

The Town

From the quayside, head up a short flight of steps to the old quarter's "back entrance", the **Porta a Terra**. From here, steep alleys fan out on different levels; follow Via del Carmine up to the picturesque little tree-shaded **Piazza Gramsci**, perched above the old port with a café and romantic views. Via Victor Hugo (the novelist spent his boyhood in Portoferraio) continues through another tunnelled gateway up to the highest point of the old quarter and Napoleon's residence-in-exile, the **Villa dei Mulini** (Mon & Wed–Sun 9am–7pm, Sun 9am–1pm; closed Tues; €5 or €9 joint three-day ticket with Villa di San Martino). The villa was purpose-built on a well-chosen site with grand views of the bay, and is a fair-sized old building – though undoubtedly not what the emperor was used to. Inside is a gallery with Empire-style furniture, a Baroque bedroom with an absurdly over-gilded bed, a library of two thousand books sent over from Fontainebleau, and various items of memorabilia. The peaceful rear garden looks down over the rocky headland.

Stepped alleys head down from the villa through the old quarter, passing the arts centre **Pinacoteca Foresiana** (Easter–July Mon–Sat 9.30am–noon & 4–7pm; July & Aug 9.30am–12.30pm & 6pm–midnight; €4), with a small collection of paintings and Napoleonic ephemera. Nearby, the heart of the old town is **Piazza della Repubblica**, lined with cafés. Adjacent is the rather drab Piazza Cavour, from where the old Medici gate, the **Porta a Mare**, heads through to the U-shaped port. In the shadow of the Martello tower on the farthest point of the U is the fascinating **Museo Archeologico** (Tues, Wed & Fri–Sun 9am–1pm & 4–7.30pm; €2), whose best displays are the various jars and amphorae salvaged from Roman shipwrecks, still full of preserved olives and fish.

From the bus station on Viale Elba take bus #1 southwest into the hills for 5km to the **Villa di San Martino** (Tues–Fri 9am–7pm, Sat and Sun 9am–1pm; €5, or €9 joint three-day ticket with Villa dei Mulini). The arrow-straight avenue leading up to the house is designed to impress, even if the villa itself – bought by Napoleon's sister Elise just before the emperor left the island for good – is a rather chilly affair, with a drab Neoclassical facade enlivened with "N" motifs. The monograms were the idea of Prince Demidoff, husband of Napoleon's niece, and it was he who created the Napoleonic museum. The interior halls of the *palazzo* are devoted to temporary art exhibitions. Head left of the facade to the ticket office, and then up flights of stairs to the back of the site where you'll find Napoleon's modest summer retreat. Of the handful of Empire-style rooms, the best is the **Sala Egizio**, decorated with Nilotic scenes to commemorate the Egyptian campaign.

Eating and drinking

Osteria Libertaria Calata Matteotti 12. One of the key exceptions to what are often poor-value restaurants in Portoferraio. Characterful and mid-priced, with a pleasing position on the Medici harbourfront. Closed Mon.

Park-Hotel Napoleone San Martino ☎0565.918.502. Book ahead for a real treat at this hotel terrace restaurant. It's expensive but the classic Tuscan cuisine is exquisite and the service something special. Closed in winter.

Trattoria La Barca Via Guerrazzi 60 ☎0565.918.036. One street back from the waterfront and rightly considered the best restaurant in town. Closed Wed.

Listings

Bike, scooter, car and boat rental Main agencies are all near the quay: TWN, Viale Elba 32 ☎0565.914.666, ⓦwww.twn-rent.it; BW's, Via Manganaro 15 ☎0565.930.491; Rent Chiappi, Piazza Citi 5 ☎0565.913.524, ⓦwww.rentchiappi.it; and Tesi (Maggiore/Budget), Calata Italia 8 ☎0565.930.222. Cicli Brandi (Via Carducci 33 ☎0565.914.128) is a mountain-bike specialist. From any of these outlets, the per-day rate for a small car is around €40–60, a 50cc scooter €35, a mountain-bike €15, and an ordinary bike €9. A five-metre boat costs €70–100 a day (no licence needed).

Internet access Joinelba, Via Concia di Terra 40 ☎0565.919.178.

Left luggage In the bus station (daily 8am–8pm).

Markets Behind Piazza Cavour is the covered food market (Mon–Sat 7am–1pm & 4–8pm, Sun 7am–1pm) which, aside from fruit and veg, has bottles of Elba's acclaimed DOC wines, *rosso* and *bianco*. The weekly Fri market in Piazza della Repubblica focuses on clothes and bric-a-brac.

Parking The car park opposite the bus station on Viale Elba is free. Cars are banned from the old quarter during the summer.

Pharmacy Centrale, Via Cavour 20 ☎0565.914.026.

Post office Piazza della Repubblica in the old town (Mon–Fri 8.15am–7pm, Sat 8.15am–12.30pm).

Around Portoferraio

West of Portoferraio, buses head 7km to **ÉNFOLA**, a headland flanked by sandy beaches, and then wind above the coast to the village at the end of the road, **Viticcio**. From here a footpath covers ground inaccessible to vehicles for 2km south across a prominent headland to picturesque **SCAGLIERI**, fronted by a shop, a bar (which rents bikes and mopeds) and a pizzeria-restaurant. The beaches here are some of the best on the island. Just round the bay sits **Biodola** – little more than a road, a couple of hotels and a superb stretch of white sand. The main town of the area, **PROCCHIO**, lies around the next headland to the south: with its traffic, buzzing bars and shops, it's not a place to get away from it all, but the sea is welcoming and the clean white sand similarly appealing.

Eastern Elba

Eastern Elba comprises two tongues of land, each of them dominated by mountain ridges and a coastline given over entirely to beach tourism. The main road east from Portoferraio heads through **Rio nell'Elba**, once the major mining town of the east, to **RIO MARINA**. Tourism and ferry links have replaced iron ore as the town's principal source of revenue; the one **hotel** is the *Rio*, Via Palestro 31 (☎0565.924.225, ⓦwww.hotelriomarina.it; ❸), next to the public gardens overlooking the port. Some boats stop at picturesque **CAVO**, 9km north of Rio Marina; its clutch of **hotels** includes the three-star *Maristella* on the waterfront at Lungomare Kennedy 3 (☎0565.949.859, ⓦwww.hotelmaristella.com; April–Sept; ❸), and one of its best **restaurants** is mid-priced *La Scogliera* (☎0565.949.638), with tables overlooking the beach. The southeast tip of the island has some good beaches and interesting towns but is relatively developed.

Porto Azzurro and Capoliveri

The busy resort of **PORTO AZZURRO** was heavily fortified by Philip III of Spain in 1603. Today his fortress is the island's prison; a walk round the outer ramparts brings you to a shop selling crafts made by the inmates. The town's small, pretty old quarter – closed to traffic – centres on bustling **Via d'Alarcon**. Choice of the lacklustre **hotels** is *Belmare*, Banchina IV Novembre 21 (℡0564.95.012, ⊛www.elba-hotelbelmare.it; ❹). The *Arrighi* **campsite** north of town at Barbarossa (℡0565.95.568, ⊛www.campingarrighi.it; April–Nov) gives straight onto the beach. Busy town **restaurants** serve standard pasta-based nosh, including the friendly *Lo Scoglio*, Via Cavour 15 (closed Wed in winter). *All'Arco Antico* on Via d'Alarcon has snacks and pizzas from €4. Plenty of places rent **bikes**, boats and scooters, including BW's, Via Provinciale 10 (℡0565.920.196). Motorboats shuttle across the bay to the sandy beach at **Naregno**.

CAPOLIVERI, 3.5km southwest of Porto Azzurro and overlooked by Monte Calamita, is the best of the towns on Elba's eastern fringe, a prosperous inland centre whose close-knit lanes have made few concessions to tourism. Capoliveri makes an ideal base for visits south to the fine **beaches** at Morcone, Pareti and Innamorata, but **accommodation** is limited: try the comfortable two-star *Villa Miramare* in Pareti (℡0565.968.673, ⊛www.hotelvillamiramare .it; ❸). The *Sugar Reef* **bar** and music venue 1km south of Capoliveri at La Trappola (⊛www.sugar-reef.com) feeds the town's nightlife, with dance parties all summer long (daily 11pm–5am). In summer, municipal minibuses run hourly between Capoliveri and nearby beach towns until 1am.

Western Elba

The main road west from Portoferraio heads to prim **MARCIANA MARINA**, whose traffic-filled promenade of bars, restaurants and trinket shops does little to lure you into staying. However, you can **rent a bike** or scooter for a trip inland from TWN, Via Dussol 45 (℡0565.997.027), and access the **internet** at Foto Berti, Via Cavour 5 (daily 9am–1pm, 5–8pm & 9–11.30pm; ℡0565.997.053). Aquavision (℡0328.709.5470) operates sea trips on the **M/N Nautilus**, which has glass panels below the waterline.

A winding road heads south for 5km into the hills to **POGGIO**, a village renowned for its mineral water and medieval centre, with decorated doorways and a patchwork of cheerful gardens. One of Elba's leading **restaurants**, *Da Publius*, Piazza XX Settembre 13 (℡0565.99.208; closed Mon), has great views and steep prices for its classic Elban cooking (including *cacciucco* and wild boar with mushrooms).

Marciana and Monte Capanne

The high, isolated village of **MARCIANA**, up 4km of switchbacks from Poggio, is the oldest settlement and most alluring place on Elba, perfectly located between great beaches and the mountainous interior. Its steep **old quarter** is a delight of narrow alleys, arches, belvederes and stone stairs festooned with flowers and climbing plants that culminate at the twelfth-century **Fortezza Pisano** (closed to the public, but with great views from its lofty location). The best **restaurant** is the award-winning *Osteria del Noce*, high up at Via della Madonna 19 (℡0565.901.284, ⊛www.osteriadelnoce.it; daily March–Sept), with excellent mid-priced food and a terrace with spectacular views. Way up beside the Fortezza at Via del Pretorio 64 is little *Monilli*, a bar and *paninoteca* open daily until 2am, perched over a wooded hillside.

8

TUSCANY | Elba

Walks around Marciana

Various **walking** trails head out from Marciana, both up to Monte Capanne and on scenic, quiet routes down to the coast. Before setting off, you should pick up the local *Comunità Montana* **map** from the Portoferraio tourist office (see p.502).

Trail #1 is a circular route starting from the southern end of the village, which passes the fifteenth-century **Oratorio di San Cerbone** (1hr) and continues beyond the junction with trail #6 and up to the summit of the mountain (where you could take the *cabinovia* down again); you then retrace your steps and take trail #6 west across open country to La Stretta, then skirt Monte Giove back to Marciana (total 8.5km; 4hr 30min).

A different route heads uphill west of Marciana – the path begins at the *Osteria del Noce* – for about 30min to the **Santuario della Madonna del Monte**, the island's most celebrated shrine, a Renaissance church built to house a stone mysteriously painted with an image of the Virgin. From the church, trail #3 again skirts round Monte Giove to La Stretta, then continues jigging on switchbacks west and down through fragrant woodland and scrub to hit the coast at **Chiessi** (total 12km; 6hr).

The main draw of Marciana is 500m south of the village – the base-station of a **cabinovia** (cable car) that climbs 650m to the summit of **Monte Capanne** (1018m), Elba's highest point (daily: June–Sept 10am–12.15pm & 2.30–6pm; Oct–May closes 5.30pm; €12 return). Note that "cable car" is something of a misnomer: it's a series of small exposed cages, each of which is big enough for two people to stand up in, hooked onto a continually running cable: the open-air ride might give you the jitters lifting you slowly above the wooded hills and eventually above the tree line to a levelled platform with a café. From here, it's a short scramble to the summit, from where the views are suitably stupendous. Another local attraction is one of Tuscany's very few **vegetarian restaurants**, *Vegetariano alla Cabinovia* (℡0565.901.029; closed in winter), by a brook in the woods alongside the *cabinovia* base-station, which boasts an affordable menu including falafel, wholewheat pasta and organic wine.

The western coast and Marina di Campo

The spread-out village of **SANT'ANDREA**, 6km northwest of Marciana, just off the coast road, is one of Elba's trendiest retreats, with divers drawn here by the crystal-clear seas. **Hotels** are not expensive, most of them discreetly set amid near-tropical vegetation; just above the beach is the eco-friendly *Ilio* (℡0565.908.018, ⓦwww.ilio.it; ⓷), which uses all biodegradable materials and has a helpful manager and delicious breakfasts and dinners. A little west, the road hugs the coast for a lonely, scenic drive round to **CHIESSI** and **POMONTE**, each with a small stony beach, beautifully clear water and little commercialism. By **FETOVAIA** on the southwestern tip of the island you're back to beach development, but the sandy beach is superb – and a big car park prevents some of the chaos of other Elban resorts. About 2km east of Fetovaia is a stretch of **nudist** beach.

MARINA DI CAMPO was the first resort on Elba and is now the largest. The huge white **beach** and clean water are what make the place suffocatingly popular. There's also all the tourist frippery and nightlife you'd expect in any major seaside centre, as well as a **tourist office**, Piazza dei Granatieri (Mon–Wed, Fri & Sat 8am–8pm; ℡0565.977.969). Internet Planet on Via Carducci has **internet** access (daily 10am–midnight). The moderately priced **restaurant**

L'Aragosta, Via Bologna 3 (closed winter), has fresh fish served daily, while *Il Gazebo*, Piazzetta Torino, is a **bar** specializing in wholewheat panini, pizzas, *calzoni* and hot-dogs.

The Maremma

The **Maremma** is a term derived from *maríttima* and refers to the coastal strip and inland hills of the Provincia di Grosseto, Tuscany's southernmost province. This was the northern heartland of the Etruscans but was depopulated in the Middle Ages as wars disrupted the drainage schemes and allowed malarial swamps to build up behind the dunes. The area became almost synonymous with disease, and nineteenth-century guides advised strongly against a visit – even so, *butteri* cowboys roamed freely then, as now, taking care of the region's half-feral horses and its celebrated white cattle. Today, the provincial capital of **Grosseto** remains pretty uninspiring, though there are some patches of fine scenery – notably the **Monti dell'Uccellina**, protected in the **Parco Naturale della Maremma**, and the wooded peninsula of **Monte Argentario**.

Grosseto and around

Until the mid-nineteenth century, **GROSSETO** was a malaria-ridden backwater. The draining of the marshes, however, which was finally effected under Mussolini, began the transformation of the town into a provincial capital for the Maremma. Grosseto was rebuilt after the war with a rash of dreary condominiums and is deservedly undervisited, though you may well find yourself passing through.

Most mainline **trains** on the Pisa–Rome coastal line stop in Grosseto, where you can change for Siena or Orbetello. The **tourist office** is inconveniently situated out of town at Via Monterosa 206 (Mon–Sat 10am–noon & 4–6pm; ☏0564.462.611, ⒲www.lamaremma.info), though a small summer-only office usually opens on Via Gramsci near the old walls (April–Oct Mon–Sat 10am–1pm & 4–7pm; ☏0564.427.858); the former office has information on the whole province. To reach the **old town**, head up Via Roma from the station past a Fascist-era post office and piazza. The best **hotel** in the small historic centre is the four-star *Bastiani Grand Hotel*, Piazza Gioberti 64 (☏0564.20.047, ⒲www.hotelbastiani.com; ⑤).

The Monti dell'Uccellina

The hills and coastline of the **Monti dell'Uccellina**, 12km south of Grosseto, are protected as the **Parco Regionale della Maremma** (⒲www .parco-maremma.it), set to be upgraded to a Parco Nazionale – recognition for an area that, it is claimed, is the last virgin coastal landscape on the Italian peninsula. This breathtaking piece of countryside combines cliffs, coastal marsh, *macchia*, forest-covered hills, pristine beaches and some of the most beautiful stands of umbrella pines in the country. It is a microcosm of all that's best in the Maremma, devoid of the bars, marinas, hotels, roads and half-finished houses that have destroyed much of the Italian littoral. There's no public road access – all drivers should park in **ALBERESE** (scene, in August, of a *butteri* rodeo), near the visitors' centre on Via del Bersagliere 7–9 (☏0564.407.098). RAMA city **buses** #15, #16 and #17 run irregularly from Grosseto station to Alberese (Mon–Sat); otherwise, take a taxi (€18).

Admission to the park (daily: July–Sept 7.30am–dusk; Oct–June 9am–dusk; €6) secures a basic **map** and a place on an hourly bus that runs from the entrance, 10km into the hills, dropping you at the trailhead at **Pratini**. From Pratini, you're left to your own devices, or you can book ahead for a place on one of the occasional three- or five-hour **guided walks** (summer only), though frankly it's easy enough to follow the well-worn trails on your own (some trails may close in midsummer when the risk of fire is high). Most people head straight onto the *Strada degli Olivi*, which leads to the superb **beach**, an idyllic curving bay backed by cliffs and wooded hills. The circular **Trail A1** (*San Rabano*; 6km; 5hr) climbs a ridge and passes the ivy-covered eleventh-century ruined abbey of San Rabano. The last return buses from Pratini or Alberese are around 6.30pm in summer, earlier in winter. For **riding**, **canoeing** or **bike rental** in the park contact Il Rialto Centro Turismo Equestre (☎0565.407.102, ✉ilrialto@katamail.com, which is about half a kilometre north of the park centre.

Monte Argentario

The high, rocky terrain of **Monte Argentario** (⊛ www.monteargentario.it), 37km south of Grosseto, is as close to wilderness as southern Tuscany comes. The interior is mountainous, reaching 635m at its highest point, and the coast is sectioned dramatically into headlands, bays and shingle beaches. Much of the area is still uninhabited scrub and woodland, badly prone to forest fires but still excellent walking country.

Long ago, Monte Argentario was an island. Over several thousand years, inshore currents built up two narrow sand spits (*tomboli*) between the mountain and the mainland, creating a lagoon between them. The ancient town of **Orbetello** occupied a peninsula sticking out into the lagoon; then the Romans built a causeway to link Orbetello to the Argentario, forming a third spit of land and dividing the lagoon in two. Orbetello's strange location is the most exciting thing about it, and on summer weekends the roads over the northern Tombolo della Giannella sandbar and through Orbetello become bottlenecks as tourists pile into resorts such as **Porto Ercole**.

Orbetello

ORBETELLO is an unassuming place, graced with palm trees, the pastel-coloured remnants of its Spanish walls, and a lively *passeggiata* each evening along its main street, Corso Italia. It was probably Etruria's leading port, though little evidence of an ancient past remains: the sixteenth-century Spanish fortifications are the town's most conspicuous feature. The **train station** is 4km east at Orbetello Scalo. **Buses** originating in Rome or Grosseto run from Orbetello station to the bus stops near the **tourist office** at Piazza della Repubblica 1 (Mon–Sat 10am–12.30pm & 4–7pm; ☎0564.860.447, ⊛ www.proloco-orbetello.it). Best **hotel** is the simple, friendly and very central *Piccolo Parigi*, Corso Italia 169 (☎0564.867.233, ℗0564.867.211; ❷). Most of the area's thirteen **campsites** are on and around the lagoon; plump for the *Feniglia* (☎0564.831.090, ⊛ www .campingfeniglia.it; open all year), the only site on the southern Tombolo di Feniglia. One of Orbetello's best fish **restaurants** is the moderately priced *Osteria il Nocchino*, just behind Piazza della Repubblica on Via Furio Lenzi (☎0564.860.329; open weekends only Nov–Feb, lunch and dinner; rest of the year dinner only, closed Tues), otherwise there's plenty of choice on and around the main Corso Italia.

Bang on the Lazio border 20km east of Orbetello, in a landscape of dust and scrub, is one of the oddest and most engaging works of modern art in the region. The Gaudi-esque **Giardino dei Tarocchi**, or Tarot Garden, is the life-long dream of Niki de St-Phalle, wife of the late Swiss artist Jean Tinguely. Since 1978, St-Phalle has been devoting herself to constructing this physical interpretation of the tarot deck – chunky, brightly coloured cartoon figures of the **Devil**, the **Guardian Angel**, the **Hanged Man** and others loom well above the treetops, arranged around a curvaceous, arcaded **courtyard** tiled in shards of mirror and shimmering, multi-coloured plastic. The symbolism of the garden may be obscure, but kids of all ages will love it. The garden has limited **opening hours** (April to mid-Oct daily 2.30–7.30pm; €10.50; ℡0564.895.122, ⊛www.nikidesaintphalle.com). There's no public **transport**, but the sculptures are visible about 1km north of the main Livorno–Rome "Via Aurelia" highway, near the village of Pescia Fiorentina. The nearest **train station** is Chiarone, 4km south – a **taxi** from here will save on the €25 fare you're likely to run up if you come from Orbetello.

Porto Ercole

Roads from Orbetello head north and south around the base of Monte Argentario. On the south side is intimate **PORTO ERCOLE**, with an attractive old quarter and a fishing-village atmosphere. Though founded by the Romans, its chief historical monuments are two **Spanish fortresses**, facing each other across the harbour. At the entrance to the old town, a plaque on the stone gate commemorates the painter **Caravaggio**, who in 1610 keeled over with sunstroke on a beach nearby and died of a fever; he was buried in the parish church of Sant'Erasmo. From the village, you can easily **walk** across the Tombolo di Feniglia, which is barred to traffic and is a prime spot for birdwatching over the lagoon. Finest **restaurant** for fish and seafood is the classy *Gambero Rosso*, Lungomare Andrea Doria (℡0564.832.650; closed Wed).

Siena and around

SIENA is the perfect antidote to Florence, a unified, modern city at ease with its medieval aspect, ambience and traditions – indeed, exultant about them. It's a place not easily read by outsiders, and to get anything meaningful from a visit you'll need to stay at least one night; too many visitors breeze through on a day-trip.

Self-contained behind its medieval walls, Siena's great attraction is its cityscape, a majestic Gothic ensemble that could be enjoyed without venturing into a single museum. The physical and spiritual heart of the city is the great scallop-shaped piazza **Il Campo**, loveliest of all Italian squares and scene of the thrilling **Palio** bareback horserace. Siena's **Duomo** and **Palazzo Pubblico** are two of the purest examples of Italian Gothic architecture, and the best of the city's paintings – collected in the **Museo Civico** and **Pinacoteca Nazionale** – are in the same tradition; the finest example of Sienese Gothic is Duccio's *Maestà*, on show in the outstanding **Museo dell'Opera Metropolitana**. More frescoes fill the halls of **Santa Maria della Scala**, the city's hospital for over 900 years and now its premier exhibition space.

The most popular trip from Siena is northwest to the picturesque multi-towered village of **San Gimignano**. Far fewer people take the trouble to sample the ancient Etruscan town of **Volterra**, a highly rewarding stop en route west from Siena to Pisa.

Some history

Though established as a Roman colony by Augustus, it wasn't until the twelfth and thirteenth centuries that Siena, for a hundred years or so, became one of the major cities of Europe. Virtually the size of Paris, it controlled most of southern Tuscany and its wool industry, dominated the trade routes between France and Rome, and maintained Italy's richest pre-Medici banks. This era reached an apotheosis with the defeat of a much superior Florentine army at the battle of **Montaperti** in 1260. Although the result was reversed permanently nine years later, Siena embarked on an unrivalled urban development under the guidance of its mercantile governors, the **Council of Nine**. From 1287 to 1355 the city underwrote the completion of its cathedral and then the Campo and its exuberant Palazzo Pubblico. The prosperity came to an abrupt halt with the **Black Death**, which reached Siena in May 1348; by October, two-thirds of the 100,000 inhabitants had died. The city never fully recovered (the population today is 60,000) and its politics, always factional, descended into chaos. In 1557 Philip II gave up Siena to **Cosimo de' Medici** in lieu of war services, and the city subsequently became part of Cosimo's Grand Duchy of Tuscany. The lack of subsequent development explains Siena's astonishing state of preservation: little was built and still less demolished. Since World War II, Siena has again become prosperous, owing partly to **tourism** and partly to the resurgence of the **Monte dei Paschi di Siena**. This bank, founded in Siena in 1472 and currently the city's largest employer, is one of the major players in Italian finance. It today sponsors much of Siena's cultural life, coexisting, apparently easily, with one of Italy's strongest left-wing councils.

Arrival and information

Siena's **train station** is 2km northwest of town. It has a counter selling city bus tickets (Mon–Sat 5.50am–7.30pm; €0.80). To get into town, you can either walk, which takes a good 20–25 minutes, or cross the road and take just about any city **bus** heading left to Piazza Gramsci or Piazza Matteotti on the northern edge of the centre. Most **intercity buses** arrive on or near Viale Federico Tozzi, the road running alongside Piazza Gramsci-Piazza Matteotti, but note that many now avoid the centre and terminate at the train station instead. Coming from Florence or Pisa **by train**, you may need to change at Empoli (1hr 45min); **by bus**, there are hourly TRA-IN or SITA expresses (1hr 15min) plus SENA buses to and from Rome, Milan and Arezzo. The **tourist office** is at no. 56 on the Campo (daily 9am–7pm; ☎0577.280.551, ⓦwww.terresiena.it).

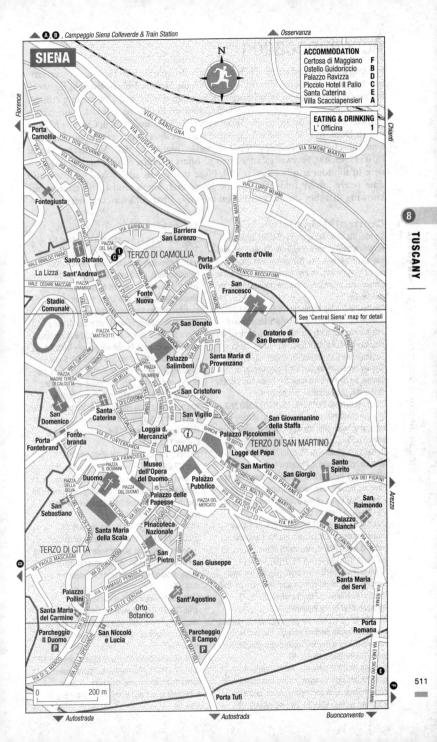

SIENA

See 'Central Siena' map for detail

ACCOMMODATION
Certosa di Maggiano | F
Ostello Guidoriccio | B
Palazzo Ravizza | D
Piccolo Hotel Il Palio | C
Santa Caterina | E
Villa Scacciapensieri | A

EATING & DRINKING
L' Officina | 1

Campeggio Siena Colleverde & Train Station

Osservanza

N

Florence

Chianti

Arezzo

Buonconvento

Autostrada

Autostrada

Porta Tufi

0   200 m

511

TERZO DI CAMOLLIA

TERZO DI SAN MARTINO

TERZO DI CITTÀ

Porta Camollia

VIALE SARDEGNA

VIA N. BIXIO

VIALE DON GIOVANNI MINZONI

VIA GIUSEPPE MAZZINI

VIA SIMONE MARTINI

VIALE LIPPO MEMMI

VIA CAMPANSI

VIA DI CAMOLLIA

VIA DEL PIGNATTELLO

Fontegiusta

VIA GARIBALDI

PIAZZA DEL SALE

Barriera San Lorenzo

Fonte d'Ovile

Porta Ovile

Santo Stefano

Sant'Andrea

La Lizza

VIALE RINALDO FRANCI

VIALE CESARE MACCARI

PIAZZA GRAMSCI

Fonte Nuova

VIA DELLA SAPIENZA SECCA

VIA DI VALLEROZZI

VIA DOMENICO BECCAFUMI

San Francesco

VIA DEL COMUNE

Stadio Comunale

PIAZZA MATTEOTTI

VIALE CURTATONE

VIALE DEI MILLE

VIA DI PIERUZZI

San Donato

VIA DEI ROSSI

VIA DEL GIGLIO

Oratorio di San Bernardino

Palazzo Salimbeni

Santa Maria di Provenzano

PIAZZA MADRE TERESA DI CALCUTTA

VIA DELLA GALLUZZA

VIA DI CAMPANSI

Santa Caterina

San Domenico

Porta Fontebranda

Fontebranda

VIA DI FONTEBRANDA

VIA FRANCIOSA

VIA DI STALLOREGGI

San Cristoforo

San Vigilio

VIA SALLUSTIO BANDINI

BANCHI DI SOPRA

Loggia d. Mercanzia

IL CAMPO

Palazzo Piccolomini

San Giovannino della Staffa

Logge del Papa

San Martino

San Giorgio

Santo Spirito

VIA DEI PISPINI

PIAZZA S. GIOVANNI

Museo dell'Opera del Duomo

Duomo

PIAZZA DELLA SELVA

PIAZZA DEL DUOMO

Palazzo delle Papesse

Palazzo Pubblico

PIAZZA DEL MERCATO

VIA DEL RIALTO

VIA S. MARTINO

VIA DEL PORRIONE

San Raimondo

Palazzo Bianchi

VIA ROMA

San Sebastiano

Pinacoteca Nazionale

Santa Maria della Scala

San Pietro

San Giuseppe

VIA GIOVANNI DUPRÈ

VIA S. PIETRO

VIA DI FONTANELLA

VIA PORTA GIUSTA

Santa Maria dei Servi

VIA PAOLO MASCAGNI

Palazzo Pollini

VIA DI S. QUIRICO

VIA TOMMASO PENDOLA

VIA DELLE CERCHIA

Sant'Agostino

Orto Botanico

VIA DI FONTANELLA

VIA DEL FOSSO DI S. ANSANO

Santa Maria del Carmine

Parcheggio Il Duomo

San Niccoló e Lucía

VIA DELLA SPERANZA

Parcheggio Il Campo

VIA REGIA ANDREA MARTINI

Porta Romana

VIA ENEA SILVIO PICCOLOMINI

VIA DI S. MARCO

Accommodation

Finding **accommodation** is barely less of a struggle than in Florence. An alternative to contacting hotels directly is to let **Siena Hotels Promotion** do the work for you – phone, fax or email bookings through them for any of the city's thirty-odd hotels are free (☎0577.288.084, ⓦwww.hotelsiena.com). If you arrive without a reservation, go to their booth on Piazza Madre Teresa di Calcutta in front of San Domenico (Mon–Sat 9am–8pm; winter closes 7pm), where you can make over-the-counter bookings for the same night for €2. **Vacanze Senesi** (☎0577.45.900, ⓦwww.vacanzesenesi.it) offers a similar service online, and has a desk in the tourist office (see p.510). Note that hotels are booked solid at **Palio** time (early July & mid-Aug). At the lower end, hotels tend to be rather plain, knowing that they can largely rely on the city's attractions for customers.

Central Siena

Bernini Via della Sapienza 15 ☎0577.289.047, ⓦwww.albergobernini.com. Friendly, well-situated one-star hotel near San Domenico, with good-value rooms – some with shared bathrooms – and a roof terrace with a fantastic view over Siena. Midnight curfew. ❷

Cannon d'Oro Via Montanini 28 ☎0577.44.321, ⓦwww.cannondoro.com. A stylish, friendly and well-maintained thirty-room hotel, tucked down an alleyway east of Piazza Matteotti. ❸

Centrale Via C. Angiolieri 26 ☎0577.280.379, ⓦwww.hotelcentralesiena.it. A block north of the Campo, up on the third floor, this place has friendly staff and a good location, but no lift. ❸

Chiusarelli Viale Curtatone 15 ☎0577.280.562, ⓦwww.chiusarelli.com. Pleasant and friendly old three-star hotel with fifty airy rooms, a garden and private parking, steps from Piazza Matteotti. ❸

Duomo Via Stalloreggi 38 ☎0577.289.088, ⓦwww.hotelDuomo.it. Pleasant hotel in a grand old building, located in a residential area. Rooms have a/c but are unremarkable, other than those with rooftop views of the Duomo. Free parking at Parcheggio Il Campo. ❹

Garibaldi Via Duprè 18 ☎0577.284.204. Seven no-nonsense rooms above a quality low-price trattoria just a few strides south of the Campo. ❸

La Perla Via delle Terme 25 ☎0577.47.144, ⓦwww.hotellaperlasiena.com. Regular one-star *pensione* with all en-suite rooms, in a very central location overlooking Piazza Indipendenza. ❶

Palazzo Bruchi Via Pantaneto 105 ☎0577.287.342, ⓦwww.palazzobruchi.it. Housed in a seventeenth century *palazzo*, this is a real bargain run by a friendly mother-and-daughter team. Lovely bright rooms. ❸

Piccolo Hotel Etruria Via delle Donzelle 3 ☎0577.288.088, ⓦwww.hoteletruria.com. Small, central place, with some poky rooms and a 12.30am curfew, but with parking nearby. ❸

Outskirts

🏃 **Certosa di Maggiano** Via Certosa 82 ☎0577.288.180, ⓦwww.certosadimaggiano.com. Surely Siena's most beautiful hotel, this former monastery in the countryside 1km southeast of the centre is absolutely stunning with large, elegant rooms surrounding the central cloister, above which peers the (still functioning) bell tower. There's also a library, a swimming pool and a fantastically swanky restaurant. Prices are equally fantastic. ❾

Ostello Guidoriccio Via Fiorentina 89, Stellino ☎0577.52.212, ⓔsiena.aighostel@virgilio.it. Non-HI 111-bed hostel, 2km northwest of the centre; take bus #3, #10 or #15 from Piazza Matteotti or, if you're coming from Florence, ask the bus driver to let you off at "Lo Stellino" (just after the Siena city sign). Dorm beds are €14.45, doubles €28.90. Curfew 11pm. ❶

Palazzo Ravizza Pian dei Mantellini 34 ☎0577.280.462, ⓦwww.palazzoravizza.it. Genteel and recently restored hotel in a pleasant backwater of town. It has a quality restaurant and charming little garden for afternoon tea. Free parking. ❻

Piccolo Hotel Il Palio Piazza del Sale 19 ☎0577.281.131, ⓦwww.piccolohotelilpalio.it. Perfectly located for bus arrivals (right near all the bus stops), but 200m north of the centre, with clean, good-sized rooms and extremely friendly staff. ❹

Santa Caterina Via E.S. Piccolomini 7 ☎0577.221.105, ⓦwww.hscsiena.it. A three-star hotel, 10min walk southeast of the campo, with the benefit of air conditioning and private parking. ❻

Villa Scacciapensieri Via di Scacciapensieri 10 ☎0577.41.441, ⓦwww.villascacciapensieri.it. Converted country villa 3km north of Siena, with great views and every luxury including a pool. ❼

The City

Everything is easily walkable from Siena's great central square, **Il Campo**, which is built at the intersection of a configuration of hills that looks, on the map, like an upside-down Y. Each arm of the Y counts as one of the city's *terzi*, or thirds, and each has its principal thoroughfare, leading out from the Campo on elevated ridges: humdrum **Banchi di Sotto** in the Terzo di San Martino on the southeast; bustling, shop-lined **Via di Città** in the Terzo di Città on the southwest; and elegant **Banchi di Sopra** in the Terzo di Camollia on the north. The central core of alleys – almost entirely medieval in plan and appearance, and closed to traffic – can get a little disorienting, and it's surprisingly easy to lose your fix on the Campo, masked as it is by high buildings. The huge **Duomo** (and attendant museums, including the unmissable **Museo dell'Opera Metropolitana** and **Santa Maria della Scala**) sits on a hill above Via di Città, looking across the deep Fontebranda valley north to the equally huge church of **San Domenico** occupying its own hill; getting from one to the other involves a lot of stairs, or a big semicircular detour in order to stay on a level.

Il Campo

Il Campo is the centre of Siena in every sense: the main streets lead into it, the Palio is held around its perimeter, and in the evenings it is the natural place to gravitate towards, for visitors and residents alike. Don't spurn the chance to soak up the atmosphere last thing at night, when the amphitheatre curve of the piazza throws the low hum of café conversation around in an invisible spiral of sound, drowned out in the daytime. Four hundred years ago, Montaigne described it as the most beautiful square in the world; it's still hard to disagree.

When the Council of Nine were planning the piazza in 1293, this old market-place, which lay at the convergence of the city quarters but was a part of none, was the only possible site. The piazza, completed in 1349, was created in nine segments in honour of the council. It was, from the start, a focus of city life, the scene of executions, bullfights, communal boxing matches, and, of course, the Palio. St Bernardino preached here, holding before him the monogram of Christ's name in Greek ("IHS"), which the council placed on the facade of the

Siena's museums

Siena has a full deck of excellent-value discounted **museum passes**, but terms and conditions tend to vary year to year They're on sale at all of the participating museums, but all permit only a single entry to each place.

Two-day passes
Museo Civico (not the tower), Santa Maria della Scala, Palazzo delle Papesse – €12. Winter Art Itinerary (Nov to mid-March): Museo Civico (not the tower), Santa Maria della Scala, Palazzo delle Papesse, Museo dell'Opera Metropolitana, Duomo and Libreria Piccolomini, Baptistry – €11.

Seven-day passes
Art Itinerary: everything included in the two-day pass, plus Chiesa di Sant'Agostino, Oratorio di San Bernardino and Museo Diocesano – €17 mid-March to Oct, €14 the rest of the year (excludes Sant'Agostino).

The **Pinacoteca Nazionale** is run by a separate body from all the above, and is not included on any of the passes.

The **Siena Palio** (ⓦpalio.comune.siena.it) is the most spectacular festival event in Italy: a twice-yearly bareback horse race around the Campo, preceded by days of preparation, medieval pageantry and chicanery. Only ten of the seventeen *contrade* can take part in any one race; these are chosen by lot, and their horses and jockeys are also assigned at random. The seven that miss out are automatically entitled to run in the following year's race. The only rule is that riders cannot interfere with each other's reins. Otherwise, anything goes: each *contrada* has a traditional rival, and ensuring that it loses is as important as winning oneself. Jockeys may be bribed to throw the race or whip a rival or a rival's horse; *contrade* have been known to drug horses and even to ambush a jockey on his way to the race. This is primarily a show for the Sienese; for visitors, in fact, the undercurrent of brutality and the bragging, days-long celebration of victory can be quite a shock.

The race has been held since at least the thirteenth century. Originally it followed a circuit through the town, but since the sixteenth century it has consisted of three laps of the **Campo**, around a track covered with sand and padded with mattresses to minimize injury to riders and horses (though this does occur, and the Palio is a passionate subject for animal-rights supporters). There are two Palios a year, with the following build-up:

June 29 and August 13: The year's horses are presented in the morning at the town hall and drawn by lot. At 7.15pm the first trial race is held in the Campo.

June 30 and August 14: Further trial races at 9am and 7.45pm.

July 1 and August 15: Two more trial races at 9am and 7.45pm, followed by a street banquet in each of the *contrade*.

July 2 and August 16: The day of the Palio opens with the *messa del Fantino* (jockeys' mass), held by the archbishop in the chapel beside the Palazzo Pubblico, before a final trial at 9am. In the early afternoon each *contrada* takes its horse to be blessed in its church (it's a good omen if the horse shits). At around 5pm the Palazzo Publico's bell begins to ring and riders and *comparse* – equerries, ensigns, pages and drummers in medieval costume – proceed to the Campo for a display of flag-twirling and other pageantry. The **race** itself begins at 7.45pm on July 2, or 7pm on August 16, and lasts little more than ninety seconds. There's no PA system to tell you what's going on. At the start (in the northwest corner of the Campo) all the horses except one are penned between two ropes; the free one charges the group from behind, when its rivals least expect it, and the race is on. It's a hectic and violent spectacle; a horse that throws its rider is still eligible to win. The jockeys don't stop at the finishing line but keep going at top speed out of the Campo, pursued by a frenzied mass of supporters. The **palio** – a silk banner – is subsequently presented to the winner.

There are viciously expensive stands for dignitaries and the rich (booked months ahead), but most spectators crowd for free into the centre of the Campo. For the **best view**, you need to have found a position on the inner rail by 2pm (ideally at the start/finish line), but be prepared to stand your ground; people keep pouring in right up until a few minutes before the race, and the swell of the crowd can be quite overwhelming. Toilets, shade and refreshments are minimal, and you won't be able to leave the Campo until at least 8.30pm. **Hotel rooms** are extremely difficult to find, and if you haven't booked, reckon on either staying up all night or travelling in from a neighbouring town. The races are shown live on national TV and repeated endlessly all evening.

The Cinema Moderno on Piazza Tolomei (May–Oct Mon–Sat) regularly screens a twenty-minute **film** explaining the history and drama of the race, dubbed into various languages.

Palazzo Pubblico, alongside the city's she-wolf symbol – a reference to Siena's legendary foundation by Senius, son of Remus.

At the highest point of the Campo the Renaissance makes a fleeting appearance with the **Fonte Gaia** (Gay Fountain), designed and carved by Jacopo della Quercia in the early fifteenth century but now replaced by a poor nineteenth-century reproduction. The badly eroded original has been restored for display in Santa Maria della Scala.

The Museo Civico

The Palazzo Pubblico (also known as Palazzo Comunale), with its 97m bell tower, the **Torre del Mangia** (see p.518) is the focus of the Campo, occupying virtually the entire south side. Its three-part windows pleased the council so much that they ordered their emulation on all other buildings on the square. The *palazzo* is still in use as Siena's town hall, but its principal rooms have been converted into the **Museo Civico** (daily: mid-March to Oct 10am–7pm; Nov & Feb to mid-March 10am–6pm; Dec & Jan 10am–5.30pm; €7.50, or €12 with Torre del Mangia) – a series of grand halls frescoed with themes integral to the secular life of the medieval city. If you have time or inclination for only one of Siena's museums, make it this one.

At the top of the stairs, you're directed through a disappointing five-room picture gallery to the **Sala del Risorgimento**, painted with nineteenth-century scenes of Vittorio Emanuele, first king of Italy. Across the corridor is a series of frescoed rooms, the **Sala di Balìa** (or dei Priori; room 10), the **Anticamera del Concistoro**, and the grand **Sala del Concistoro**. Room 13, the **Vestibolo**, holds the gilded bronze *She-Wolf Suckling Romulus and Remus* (1429), an allusion to Siena's mythical founding. Alongside is the **Anticappella**, decorated between 1407 and 1414 by Taddeo di Bartolo. Behind a majestic wrought-iron screen by Jacopo della Quercia is the **Cappella del Consiglio**, also frescoed by di Bartolo and holding an exceptional altarpiece by Sodoma and exquisite inlaid choir stalls.

All these are little more than a warm-up for room 16, the great **Sala del Mappamondo**. Taking its name from the now scarcely visible frescoed cosmology – a circular map by Lorenzetti – the room was used for several centuries as the city's law court, and contains one of the greatest of all Italian frescoes. Simone Martini's fabulous *Maestà* (Virgin in Majesty) is a painting of almost translucent colour, painted in 1315 when Martini was 30. The richly decorative style is archetypal Sienese Gothic and Martini's great innovation was the use of a canopy and a frieze of medallions to frame and organize the figures – lending a sense of space and hint of perspective that suggest a knowledge of Giotto's work. The fresco on the opposite wall, the *Equestrian Portrait of Guidoriccio da Fogliano*, is a motif for medieval chivalric Siena and was, until recently, also credited to Martini. Art historians, however, have long puzzled over the anachronistic castles, which are of a much later style than the painting's signed date of 1328. A number of historians – led by the American Gordon Moran (whom the city council accused of being a CIA agent and for a while banned from the building) – interpret the *Guidoriccio* as a sixteenth-century fake, while others maintain that it is a genuine Martini overpainted by subsequent restorers. A fresco below the portrait, of two figures in front of a castle, is meanwhile variously attributed to Martini, Duccio and Pietro Lorenzetti.

The adjacent **Sala della Pace** holds Ambrogio Lorenzetti's *Allegories of Good and Bad Government*, frescoes commissioned in 1338 to remind the councillors of their duties. This is one of Europe's most important cycles of medieval secular painting, and includes the first-known panorama in Western art. The walled city

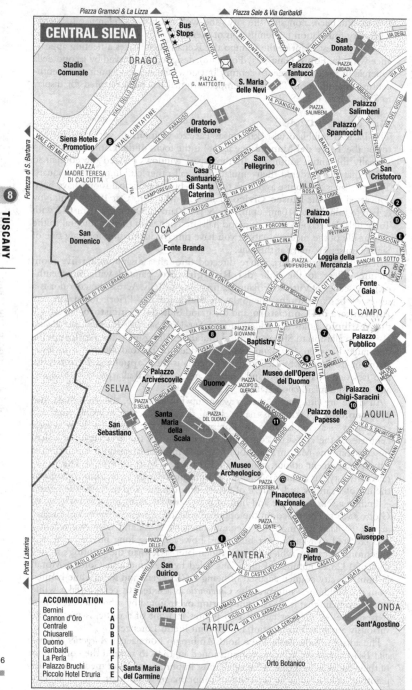

CENTRAL SIENA

Piazza Gramsci & La Lizza ▲   ▲ Piazza Sale & Via Garibaldi

DRAGO

Stadio
Comunale

Siena Hotels
Promotion **B**

San
Domenico

Fonte Branda

OCA

SELVA

San
Sebastiano

San
Quirico

Sant'Ansano

Bus
Stops

S. Maria
delle Nevi

PIAZZA
G. MATTEOTTI

Oratorio
delle Suore

Casa
Santuario
di Santa
Caterina **C**

San
Pellegrino

PIAZZA
MADRE TERESA
DI CALCUTTA

Palazzo
Tantucci **A**

San
Donato

Palazzo
Salimbeni

Palazzo
Spannocchi

San
Cristoforo

Palazzo
Tolomei

Loggia della
Mercanzia

F PIAZZA
INDIPENDENZA

Fonte
Gaia

IL CAMPO

Palazzo
Pubblico

Baptistry

PIAZZA S.
GIOVANNI

Duomo

Palazzo
Arcivescovile

Museo dell'Opera
del Duomo

Palazzo
Chigi-Saracini

AQUILA

Santa
Maria
della
Scala

Palazzo delle
Papesse

PIAZZA
DEL DUOMO

Museo
Archeologico

Pinacoteca
Nazionale

San
Giuseppe

San
Pietro

PANTERA

San
Pietro

ONDA

Sant'Agostino

TARTUCA

Santa Maria
del Carmine

Orto Botanico

ACCOMMODATION	
Bernini	C
Cannon d'Oro	A
Centrale	D
Chiusarelli	B
Duomo	I
Garibaldi	H
La Perla	F
Palazzo Bruchi	G
Piccolo Hotel Etruria	E

▼ Porta San Marco   Porta Tufi ▼

8

TUSCANY

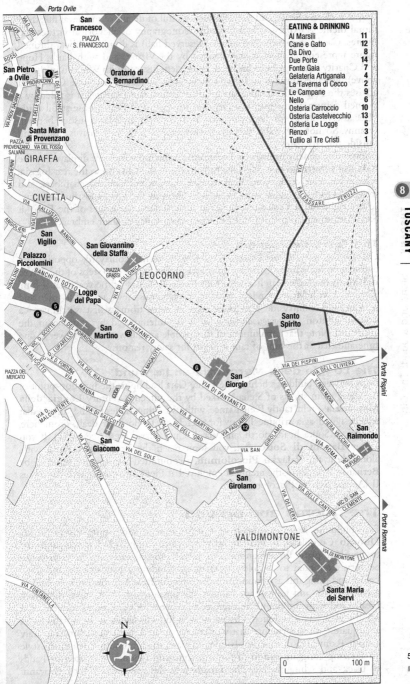

Porta Ovile

San Francesco
PIAZZA S. FRANCESCO

San Pietro a Ovile

Oratorio di S. Bernardino

Santa Maria di Provenzano
PIAZZA PROVENZANO SALVANI

GIRAFFA

CIVETTA

San Vigilio

San Giovannino della Staffa
PIAZZA GRASSI

Palazzo Piccolomini

LEOCORNO

Logge del Papa

San Martino

Santo Spirito

San Giorgio

San Raimondo

San Giacomo

San Girolamo

VALDIMONTONE

Santa Maria dei Servi

Porta Pispini

Porta Romana

EATING & DRINKING

Al Marsili	11
Cane e Gatto	12
Da Divo	8
Due Porte	14
Fonte Gaia	7
Gelateria Artiganala	4
La Taverna di Cecco	2
Le Campane	9
Nello	6
Osteria Carroccio	10
Osteria Castelvecchio	13
Osteria Le Logge	5
Renzo	3
Tullio ai Tre Cristi	1

8

TUSCANY

N

0   100 m

517

shown is clearly Siena, and the paintings are full of details of medieval life; their moral theme is expressed in a complex iconography of allegorical virtues and figures. *Good Government* (the better-preserved half) is dominated by a throned figure representing the *Comune*, flanked by the Virtues and with Faith, Hope and Charity buzzing about his head. To the left, Justice (with Wisdom in the air above) dispenses rewards and punishments, while below her throne Concordia advises the Republic's councillors on their duties. *Bad Government* is ruled by a horned demon, while over the city flies the figure of Fear, whose scroll reads: "Because he looks for his own good in the world, he places justice beneath tyranny. So nobody walks this road without Fear: robbery thrives inside and outside the city gates."

Some fine panel paintings by Lorenzetti's contemporaries are displayed in the **Sala dei Pilastri** to one side. Take time to climb the stairs up to the rear **loggia**, where you can crane your neck to see the current council chambers, also frescoed. From the loggia you can see how abruptly the town ends: buildings rise to the right and left for a few hundred metres along the ridges of the Terzo di San Martino and Terzo di Città, holding a rural valley in their embrace.

The Torre del Mangia

Off to the left of the Palazzo Pubblico's internal courtyard, opposite the entrance to the Museo Civico, a door gives access to the 503 steps of the **Torre del Mangia** (daily: March to mid-Oct 10am–7pm; rest of the year 10am–4pm; €7 or €12 with Museo Civico), which gives fabulous views across the town and surrounding countryside. The tower takes its name from its first watchman – a slothful glutton (*mangiaguadagni*) who is commemorated by a statue in the courtyard. Note that a maximum of fifty people are allowed in the tower at one time and that at the hint of rain it closes for safety reasons.

The Loggia della Mercanzia and around

Gaps between buildings behind the Fonte Gaia lead up to the junction-point of the three main streets of Siena, marked by the fifteenth-century **Loggia della Mercanzia** – reluctantly Renaissance, with its Gothic niches for the saints – that was designed as a tribune house for merchants to do their deals. From here, Banchi di Sopra heads north, and Via di Città curves west (see p.522). If you follow **Banchi di Sotto** east, you soon reach the **Logge del Papa** with, alongside it, the **Palazzo Piccolomini**, a committed Renaissance building by Bernardo Rossellino, the architect employed at Pienza by the Sienese Pope Pius II (Aeneas Sylvius Piccolomini).

The Duomo and around

Few buildings reveal so much of a city's history and aspirations as Siena's **Duomo**. Completed to virtually its present size around 1215, it was subjected to constant plans for expansion. An initial project, early in the fourteenth century, attempted to double its extent by building a baptistry on the slope below and using this as a foundation for a rebuilt nave, but the work ground to a halt as walls and joints gaped under the pressure. In 1348, came the Black Death, and with the population reduced by two thirds and funds suddenly cut off, the plan was abandoned. The part-extension still stands at the north end of the square – a vast structure that would have created the largest church in Italy outside Rome. Despite all the abandoned plans, the Duomo is a delight, its style an amazing conglomeration of Romanesque and Gothic, delineated by bands of black and white marble. The **facade** was designed in 1284 by Giovanni

Pisano, who with his workshop created much of the statuary – philosophers, patriarchs and prophets, now replaced by copies. In the next century the **Campanile** and a Gothic **rose window** were added. The mosaics in the gables, however, had to wait until the nineteenth century.

The use of black and white decoration is continued in the sgraffito marble **pavement**, which begins outside the church and takes off into a startling sequence of 56 panels adorning the **interior** (ⓦwww.operaDuomo.siena.it;

▲ Tourists relax in the Campo, Siena

March–May, Sept & Oct Mon–Sat 10.30am–5.30pm, Sun 1.30–5.30pm; June–Aug Mon–Sat 10.30am–8pm, Sun 1.30–6pm; Nov–Feb Mon–Sat 10.30am–6.30pm, Sun 1.30–5.30pm; €3, €6 during the summer uncovering of the marble pavement). They were completed between 1349 and 1547, with virtually every artist who worked in the city trying his hand on a design. However, you're unlikely to see much of the pavement, which is now protected by boarding for all but a few weeks a year in late summer. The zebra-striped interior is equally arresting above floor level, with its line of popes' heads set above the pillars, the same hollow-cheeked scowls cropping up repeatedly. The greatest individual artistic treasure is Nicola Pisano's **pulpit**, with its elaborate high-relief detail of the *Life of Jesus* and *Last Judgement*. In the north transept is a bronze statue by **Donatello**, the emaciated *St John the Baptist*, companion piece to his equally ragged *Mary Magdalene* in Florence (see p.458), and superb candelabra-carrying angels by Beccafumi flank the Renaissance High Altar.

Midway along the nave, on the left, is the entrance to the stunning **Libreria Piccolomini**. The library was commissioned by Francesco Piccolomini (who for ten days was Pius III) to house the books of his uncle Aeneas (Pius II), and to celebrate Aeneas's life in a series of crystal-sharp, brilliantly colourful frescoes by Pinturicchio. The cycle begins to the right of the window, with Aeneas attending the Council of Basel as a secretary, then, in subsequent panels around the walls, presenting himself as envoy to James II of Scotland; being crowned poet laureate by Holy Roman Emperor, Frederick II; representing Frederick on a visit to Pope Eugenius IV; and then – as Bishop of Siena – presiding over the meeting of Frederick III and his bride-to-be Eleanora outside Siena's Porta Camollia. The next panels show Aeneas being made a cardinal in 1456; being elected pope two years later; and then launching a call for a crusade against the Turks, who had just seized Constantinople. His best-remembered action was the canonization of St Catherine, shown in the penultimate panel. The last fresco shows his death at Ancona.

Santa Maria della Scala

Opposite the Duomo is **Santa Maria della Scala** (daily: mid-March to Oct 10.30am–6.30pm; Nov to mid-March 10.30am–4.30pm; €6; for information on museum passes see p.513; Ⓦwww.santamaria.comune.siena.it). For nine hundred years up until the 1980s, this vast complex served as the city's main hospital. Today its wonderful interiors are being gradually converted into a major centre for art and culture, revealing works that have been inaccessible to all but the ill and most determined of visitors for centuries.

Siena's contrade

Siena takes great pride in its division into neighbourhoods, or **contrade**, ancient self-governing wards that formed a patchwork of tribal identity within the fabric of the city and that still flourish today, helping to foster tight bonds of community and contributing to Siena's surprisingly low crime rate. Each of the seventeen *contrade* has its own church, social club and museum. Each, too, has a heraldic animal motif, displayed in a fountain-sculpture in its neighbourhood piazza. Allegiance to one's *contrada* – conferred by birth – remains a strong element of civic life, and identification with the *contrade* is integral to the competition of the Palio. You'll often see groups of *comparse* practising flag-waving and drum-playing around town.

The *contrade* **museums**, with their displays of Palio trophies, are open to visitors during the build-up to the Palio and at other times by appointment (ask the tourist office to book for you at least a week in advance).

To the left of the ticket desk is the church of **Santissima Annunziata** (also with its own door onto the piazza), blandly remodelled in the fifteenth century but with a bronze statue on the high altar of the *Risen Christ* by Vecchietta, with features so gaunt the veins show through the skin. The other way from the ticket desk leads into a vestibule, the **Cappella del Manto**, with the strikingly beautiful fresco *St Anne and St Joachim* (1512) – parents of the Virgin – by Beccafumi. Having failed to conceive during twenty years of marriage, the pair are each told by an angel to meet at Jerusalem's Golden Gate and kiss (the scene depicted in the fresco), a moment which symbolizes the Immaculate Conception of their daughter. Adjacent is a long hall, partly used as a bookshop; left off this hall is the vast **Sala del Pellegrinaio**, formerly used as the main hospital ward and entirely frescoed with scenes intended to record the hospital's history and promote the notion of charity toward the sick and orphaned. Their almost entirely secular content was extraordinary at the time they were painted (after 1440). Off to the left, in room 12, is the frescoed **Cappella del Sacro Chiodo** (also known as the Sagrestia Vecchia), which once housed a nail (*chiodo*) from the Passion.

Stairs lead down to the **Oratorio di Santa Caterina della Notte**, an oratory that belonged to one of a number of medieval confraternities that maintained places of worship in the basement vaults of the hospital. It's a dark and strangely spooky place, despite the plethora of decoration – you can easily imagine St Catherine passing nocturnal vigils down here. Also on this level is a series of rooms devoted to documenting the continuing restoration of the original **Fonte Gaia** from the Campo. Stairs lead down again to the oratory and meeting-room of the **Società di Esecutori di Pie Disposizioni** (Executors of Benevolent Legacies), oldest of the lay confraternities, which house a wooden crucifix said to be the one that inspired St Bernadino to become a monk.

The Museo dell'Opera Metropolitana

Tucked into a corner of the proposed new nave of the Duomo is the impressive **Museo dell'Opera Metropolitana** (daily March–May, Sept & Oct 9.30am–7pm; June–August 9.30am–8pm; Nov–Feb 10am–5pm; €6; Wwww.operaDuomo.siena.it). A tour starts on the top floor where room 1 houses the haunting Byzantine icon known as the **Madonna dagli Occhi Grossi** (of the Big Eyes), the Duomo's original altarpiece, as well as panels depicting St Bernardino preaching in the Campo and Piazza San Francesco. Pass through to the tiny entrance to the **Panorama dal Facciatone** – this leads to steep spiral stairs climbing the walls of the abandoned nave. The sensational view is worth the two-stage climb, but beware that the topmost walkway is narrow and scarily exposed.

Downstairs is the work that alone merits the museum admission: Duccio's vast and justly celebrated **Maestà**, which was the Duomo's altarpiece from 1311 until 1505. This is one of the superlative works of Sienese art, its iconic, Byzantine spirituality accentuated by Duccio's flowing composition, his realization of the space in which action takes place, and a new attention to narrative detail in the panels of the predella and the reverse of the altarpiece which are now displayed to its side. Downstairs again, back on ground-floor level, is the **Galleria delle Statue**, with Donatello's delicate ochre *Madonna and Child* flanked by huge, elongated, twisting figures by Giovanni Pisano. You exit the museum through the atmospheric, late-Baroque church of **San Niccolò in Sasso**, emerging onto Via del Poggio in front of a handy little café.

Along Via di Città

Via di Città, the main thoroughfare linking the Duomo with the Campo, is lined with shops and plenty of explorable side-alleys, as well as being fronted by some of Siena's finest private *palazzi*. The **Palazzo Chigi-Saracini**, at no. 82, is a Gothic beauty, with its curved facade and rear courtyard.

Via di Città continues to a small piazza from where Via San Pietro leads south to the fourteenth-century Palazzo Buonsignori, now the home of the **Pinacoteca Nazionale** (Mon 8.30am–1.30pm, Tues–Sat 8.15am–7.15pm, Sun 8.15am–1.30pm; €4). The collection is a roll of honour of Sienese Gothic painting. The first rooms – two storeys up – hold a host of gilded, thirteenth-century Madonnas; in rooms 7–8, two tiny panels recently attributed to Sassetta – *City by the Sea* and *Castle by a Lake* – are described as the first-ever landscape paintings entirely devoid of religious purpose. Down one flight are Renaissance works by such as Sodoma, whose panel of the *Deposition* (room 32) and frescoes from Sant'Agostino (room 37) show his characteristic drama and delight in costume and landscape. The gallery's topmost storey is devoted to the **Collezione Spannocchi**, a miscellany of Italian, German and Flemish works, including the only painting in the museum by a female artist – *Bernardo Campi Painting Sofonisba's Portrait* by Sofonisba Anguissola, a neat little joke in which the artist excels in her portrait of Campi, but depicts his portrait of her as a flat stereotype.

South of the Pinacoteca Nazionale is the church of **Sant'Agostino** (mid-March to Oct daily 11am–1.30pm & 2/3–5.30pm; €2.50), with outstanding paintings by Perugino (a *Crucifixion* in the second altar of the south aisle) and Sodoma (*Adoration of the Magi* in the Cappella Piccolomini). A nice walk loops southwest along Via della Cerchia into a studentish area around the church of **Santa Maria del Carmine** (which contains a hermaphrodite *St Michael and the Devil* by Beccafumi). Via del Fosso di San Ansano, north of the Carmine square, is a country lane above terraced vineyards that leads to the Selva (Rhinoceros) *contrada*'s square, from where the stepped Vicolo di San Girolamo leads up to the Duomo.

North of the Campo

Exploring only slightly beyond the touristed central alleys between the Campo and the Duomo reveals much more of the bustling everyday life of the city. North of the Campo, the main street **Banchi di Sopra** leads through the commercial heart of town to **Piazza Matteotti**, home of the main post office, north of which lies the workaday neighbourhood of the Terzi di Camollia. The church of **Santo Stefano** fronts one of the nicest *contrada* squares in the city, home of the Istrici (Porcupine), while the road emerges from the walls at the northern Porta Camollia, inscribed "Siena opens her heart to you wider than this gate." The northwest corner of the city is occupied by a stadium and the gardens of **La Lizza**, which lead up to the bastions of the **Fortezza di Santa Barbara**, rebuilt by the Medici and now housing the comprehensive wine collection of the *Enoteca Italiana* (see p.525).

San Domenico

Monasteries were essentially rural until the beginning of the thirteenth century, when the idea of an exclusively meditative retreat was displaced by the preaching orders of friars. Suddenly, in the space of a few decades, orders began to found monasteries on the periphery of the major Italian cities. In Siena the two greatest orders, the Dominicans and Franciscans, located themselves

St Catherine of Siena was born on March 25, 1347, the 24th child of Jacopo Benincasa, a dyer, and Lapa of Duccio de' Piacenti. Her path to beatification began early, with a vision aged 6 of Christ as pope, followed a year later by a vow of perpetual virginity. Her family tried to drill some sense into her by forcing her to work at household chores, but when her father discovered her at prayer one day with a dove fluttering above her head, he realized her holy destiny. Catherine took the Dominican habit aged 16, and then began charitable works in post-plague Siena before turning her hand to politics. She prevented Siena and Pisa from joining Florence in rising against Pope Urban V (then absent in Avignon), and then, in 1376, travelled herself to Avignon to persuade Pope Gregory XI to return to Rome. It was a fulfilment of the ultimate Dominican ideal – a union of the practical and mystical life. Catherine returned to Siena to a life of contemplation, retaining a political role in her attempts to reconcile the 1378 schism between the Popes and Antipopes. She died in Rome in 1380, and was the first woman ever to be **canonized** – by Pius II in 1461. Pius IX made her **co-patron of Rome** in 1866; Pius XII raised her to be **co-patron of Italy** (alongside St Francis) in 1939; and then John Paul II declared her **co-patron of Europe** in 1999.

respectively to the west and east. **San Domenico**, a vast brick church west of Piazza Matteotti (daily: April–Oct 7.30am–1pm & 3–6.30pm; Nov–March 9am–1pm & 3–6pm; free), was founded in 1125 and is closely identified with St Catherine of Siena (see box above). Inside on the right is a raised chapel with a contemporary portrait of the saint by her friend Andrea Vanni. Her own chapel, on the south side of the enormous, airy nave, has frescoes by Sodoma of her swooning (to the left of the altar) and in ecstasy (to the right), as well as a reliquary containing her head.

The **Casa Santuario di Santa Caterina** – St Catherine's family house, where she lived as a Dominican nun – is just south of the church, down the hill on Via Santa Caterina (daily: 9am–12.30pm & 3–6pm; free). The building has been much adapted, with a Renaissance loggia and a series of oratories – one on the site of her cell. At the bottom of the hill, through the Oca (Goose) *contrada*, is the **Fonte Branda**, the best-preserved of Siena's medieval fountains and, according to Sienese folklore, the haunt of werewolves, who would throw themselves into the water at dawn to return in human form.

The Oratorio di San Bernardino

St Bernardino, born in the year of St Catherine's death, began his preaching life at the chill monastic church of **San Francesco**, across the city to the east. Alongside the church is the **Oratorio di San Bernardino** (mid-March to Oct daily 10.30am–1.30pm & 3–5.30pm; closed rest of the year; €3; for museum passes see box, p.513), with a beautifully wood-panelled upper chapel frescoed by Sodoma and Beccafumi. In the lower chapel are seventeenth-century scenes from the saint's life, which was taken up by incessant travel throughout Italy, preaching against usury and denouncing political strife; his sermons in the Campo, it is said, frequently went on for the best part of a day. He was canonized in 1444, and – because of his dictum on rhetoric, "make it clear, short and to the point" – was made patron saint of advertising in the 1980s. The attached **Museo Diocesano di Arte Sacra** (same hours and ticket) contains an array of devotional art from the thirteenth to the seventeenth centuries.

Eating, drinking and nightlife

Although Siena has no shortage of places in which to **eat** well, the city feels distinctly provincial after Florence. The main action of an evening is the *passeggiata* from Piazza Matteotti along Banchi di Sopra to the Campo – and there's not much in the way of **nightlife** after that. For most visitors, though, the Campo, the city's universal gathering place, provides diversion enough, while the presence of the university ensures a bit of life in the **bars**.

Putting together a **picnic** in the Campo or elsewhere is easy: you can buy pizza by weight from many central hole-in-the-wall places. Gourmet supplies are at the extravagantly stocked food stores *Miccoli*, Via di Città 95, and nearby *Manganelli*, Via di Città 71.

Restaurants

Siena used to have a poor reputation for **restaurants** but over the last few years a range of new, imaginative *osterie* has signalled a general rise in standards. Food is often heavy so expect plenty of wild boar and rabbit. Local **specialities** include *pici* (thick, hand-rolled spaghetti with toasted breadcrumbs), *finocchiona* (minced pork flavoured with fennel), *pappa col pomodoro* (bread and tomato soup) and *fagioli all'uccelletto* (white bean and sausage stew).

Al Marsili Via del Castoro 3 ☏ 0577.47.154, ⓦwww.ristorantealmarsili.it. Elegant, upmarket restaurant serving some exellent meat dishes (including grilled lamb and steak with three-pepper sauce) and a few vegetarian choices (such as grilled vegetables with *scamorza* cheese). Attentive service. Mains from about €17. Closed Mon.

Cane e Gatto Via Pagliaresi 6 ☏ 0577.287.545. Don't be put off by the absence of a menu – this restaurant serves superb if expensive Tuscan cuisine on its seven-course *menu degustazione*. Allow around €50 per person. Eve only and closed Thurs.

Da Divo Via Franciosa 29 ☏ 0577.286.054. Book a table in the atmospheric subterranean dining room to savour hearty Tuscan food that is generally above average. Allow around €50 per person. Closed Sun in winter.

Due Porte Via di Stalloreggi 62 ☏ 0577.221.887. This place has pizza and a large Tuscan menu, lower prices than you'd expect – pizzas from €3.50, *primi* €6–7, *secondi* €5.50–12 – and an open terrace at the back on which to enjoy them. Closed Mon.

La Taverna di Cecco Via Cecco Angiolieri 19 ☏ 0577.288.518. Attentive service, moderate prices and heavenly rabbit and rocket salad. Good pasta dishes too, including tagliatelle with walnuts and cream. Open daily.

Le Campane Via delle Campane 6 ☏ 0577.284.035. High-quality Sienese cuisine at a small, formal restaurant just below the Duomo. *Primi* €8.50, *secondi* €10–13. Closed Mon.

Nello Via del Porrione 28 ☏ 0577.289.043. Sienese specialities at their best: try red chicory and smoked cheese ravioli in leek sauce, roast rabbit, or beef fillet with rocket and pecorino for around €19–23 for two courses. Closed Sun.

Osteria Carroccio Via Casato di Sotto 32 ☏ 0577.411.65. Popular little *osteria* offering good Sienese dishes (such as *pappardelle* with hare and *tagliatelle al cinghiale*, both €7) and an extensive wine list for reasonable prices – around €18–20 for two courses. The whole package let down by the slightly off-hand service. Closed Wed.

Osteria Castelvecchio Via di Castelvecchio 65 ☏ 0577.49.586. First-rate, adventurous and nicely informal *osteria* with a barrel-vaulted brick ceiling and good choices for vegetarians. Menus change daily; average price around €25 for two courses. Closed Sun.

Osteria Le Logge Via del Porrione 33 ☏ 0577.48.013. The best-looking restaurant in Siena, in an old cabinet-lined pharmacy off the Campo (avoid the less pretty dining room upstairs). Good pasta and some unusual *secondi*, but at a price – around €50 a head. Closed Sun.

Renzo Piazza Indipendenza ☏ 0577.289.296. This friendly *spaghetteria* offers light, uncomplicated meals at terrace tables on a quiet enclosed piazza off Via di Città. The large menu includes a few pizzas. Closed Fri.

Tullio ai Tre Cristi Vicolo Provenzano 1 ☏ 0577.280.608. A Sienese institution since 1830, this is the smart (and rather expensive) restaurant of the Giraffa *contrada* and is draped with heraldic banners between the frescoes and arches to accompany its traditional food – roast boar, steaks, tripe, plenty of fish and some pastas. The seasonal menu is around €60. Closed Wed.

Bars and cafés

There are pleasant **bars** all over town. *L'Officina*, north of the centre at Piazza del Sale 3/A, has around a hundred bottled beers and others on tap, and sometimes live music. Of the terrace **cafés** ringing the Campo, *Caffè Fonte Gaia* stays open later than most, but otherwise they're much of a muchness, and expensive – expect to pay €8 or more for a large beer. The garden of the *Palazzo Ravizza* hotel, Pian dei Mantellini 34, is a tranquil spot on a hot afternoon. The *Enoteca Italiana* inside the Fortezza (Mon noon–8pm, Tues–Sat noon–1am; ☎0577.228.811, ⊛www.enoteca-italiana.it) is the country's only national **wine** collection. Its cellar stocks and exhibits every single Italian wine (well over a thousand of them) and there's a **bar** where you can order by the glass or bottle.

Nightlife and entertainment

You'll spot posters for city **events** at Piazza Matteotti, and the Siena supplement of *La Nazione* newspaper has details of the day's concerts and films. **The club-bar** *Al Cambio*, Via di Pantaneto 48 (closed Sun) is more or less the sole central late-night spot, but otherwise your only chances are at the low-key **Siena Jazz** (☎0577.271.401, ⊛www.sienajazz.it) in the last week of July and miscellaneous summer events.

Siena has prestigious **classical** concerts throughout the year. The Accademia Musicale Chigiana is the driving force, staging the *Estate Musicale Chigiana* cycle all summer, and the *Settimana Musicale Senese* in late July, often featuring a major opera production. Venues vary from the Duomo and Sant'Agostino to out-of-town locations such as the atmospheric ruined abbey of San Galgano. Tickets start at €10, bookable through the tourist office or from mid-June onwards in person at the Accademia Musicale Chigiana, Via di Città 89 (daily 3–7pm; ☎0577.22.091, ⊛www.chigiana.it).

Listings

Bike rental DF Bike, some way from the centre at Via Massetana Romana 54 ☎0577.271.905, ⊛www.dfbike.it; €15 daily, €85 weekly. Perozzi Automotocicli, Via del Gazzani 16 ☎0577.223.157, ⊛www.perozzi.it.

Bus information Ticket offices beneath Piazza Gramsci have information on all routes. The Sienese bus company is called TRA-IN (☎800.905.183 or 0577.204.111, ⊛www.trainspa.it). Services run roughly every 30min to Poggibonsi, where you must change for San Gimignano (buy a through ticket),

and eight times daily to Montalcino, more to Montepulciano (though with most you have to change at Buonconvento). Note that some buses to the hill-towns south of Siena depart from the train station, not from Piazza Gramsci. TRA-IN and SITA also run regularly to Florence (take an express) and once-daily to Pisa airport (currently at 7.30am outbound, 1.30pm return).

Car rental Avis, Via Simone Martini 36 ☎0577.270.305; Hertz, Viale Sardegna 37 ☎0577.45.085.

Guided tours Walks and tours around the city and beyond can be booked through Siena Hotels Promotion, Piazza Madre Teresa di Calcutta ☎0577.288.084, ⓦwww.hotelsiena.com.

Hospital Loc. Le Scotte ☎0577.585.111.

Internet access Internet Train, Via di Città 121, and Via Pantaneto 54; MegaWeb, Via Pantaneto 132; Interfast Net, Via Casato di Sotto 1. All have long opening hours and charge around €1.50 for 15min (less for students).

Laundry Wash & Dry, Via Pantaneto 38 (daily 8am–9pm); Ondablu, Casato di Sotto 17 (daily 8am–10pm); both are self-service.

Left luggage At the TRA-IN bus information centre below Piazza Gramsci (daily 7am–7.45pm; €3.50 per piece for one per day). At the train station, there are self-service lockers on platform 1.

Lost property Comune di Siena, Casato di Sotto 23 (Mon–Fri 9am–12.30pm, Tues & Thurs also 3–5pm).

Market A huge weekly market sprawls over La Lizza (Wed 8am–1pm).

Parking The two biggest parking garages – run by the same company and clearly signposted – charge around €1.50 per hr (daily 7am–11pm) but are misleadingly named: "Parcheggio Il Campo" and "Parcheggio Il Duomo" are a long way south of either the Campo or the Duomo, just inside the Porta Tufi and Porta San Marco respectively (ⓦwww.sienaparcheggi.com). Visitors are permitted to drive through the old town alleys only in order to check in at their hotel.

Police The *Questura* is on Via del Castoro ☎0577 201.111.

Post office Piazza Matteotti 1 (Mon–Sat 8.15am–7pm).

Taxi Radio Taxi ☎0577.49.222; taxis wait on Piazza Matteotti.

Train information ☎89.20.21 or 0577.204.111, ⓦwww.trenitalia.it.

San Gimignano

SAN GIMIGNANO, 27km northwest of Siena, is perhaps the most visited small village in Italy. Its stunning hilltop skyline of towers, built in aristocratic rivalry by the feuding nobles of the twelfth and thirteenth centuries, evokes the appearance of medieval Tuscany more than any other sight. And the town is all that it's cracked up to be: quietly monumental, very well preserved, enticingly rural, and with a fine array of religious and secular frescoes. However, from Easter until October, San Gimignano has very little life of its own, with hordes of day-trippers traipsing up and down its narrow streets and filing in and out of its innumerable olive oil, wine and souvenir shops. If you want to reach beyond its facade of quaintness, try to come well out of season; if you can't, then aim to spend the night here – the town takes on a very different pace and atmosphere in the evenings.

San Gimignano was a force to be reckoned with in the early Middle Ages. It was controlled by two great families – the Ardinghelli and the Salvucci – and its 15,000 population (twice the present number) prospered on agricultural holdings and its position on the Lombardy-to-Rome pilgrim route. At its heyday, the town's walls enclosed five monasteries, four hospitals, public baths and a brothel. **Feuds**, however, had long wreaked havoc: the first Ardinghelli–Salvucci conflict erupted in 1246. Whenever the town itself was united, it picked fights with Volterra, Poggibonsi and other neighbours. These were halted only by the **Black Death**, which devastated the population and, as the pilgrim trade collapsed, the economy. Subjection to Florence broke the power of the nobles and so their tower-houses, symbolic in other towns of real control, were not torn down; today, fifteen of an original 72 survive. At the beginning of the nineteenth century, travellers spoke of San Gimignano as "miserably poor"; its postwar history, however, has been one of ever-increasing affluence, thanks to **tourism** and the production of an old-established but recently rejuvenated white **wine**, Vernaccia.

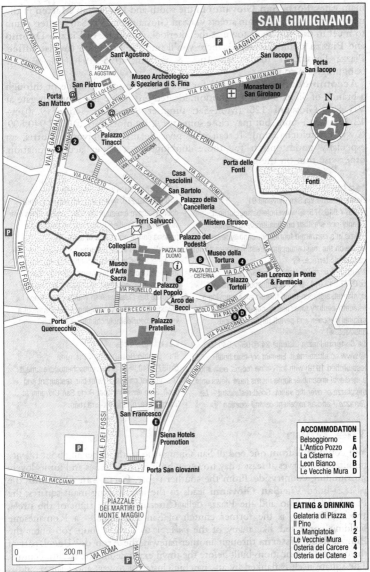

SAN GIMIGNANO

Sant'Agostino

San Iacopo

Porta
San Iacopo

PIAZZA
S. AGOSTINO

Museo Archeologico
& Spezieria di S. Fina

Monastero Di
San Girolano

San Pietro

Porta
San Matteo

VIA FOLGORE DA S. GIMIGNANO

VIA CELLOLESE

VIA SAN MARTINO

VIA XX SETTEMBRE

Palazzo
Tinacci

VIA DELLE FONTI

VIA DELLA VERGINE

VIA CAPASSI

VIA DIACCETO

VIA SAN MATTEO

Casa
Pesciolini

Porta delle
Fonti

VIA DELLE ROMITE

Fonti

San Bartolo

Palazzo della
Cancelleria

Torri Salvucci

Mistero Etrusco

Palazzo del
Podestà

Rocca

Collegiata

PIAZZA DEL
DUOMO

Museo della
Tortura

Museo
d'Arte
Sacra

PIAZZA DELLA
CISTERNA

VIA D. CASTELLO

San Lorenzo in Ponte
& Farmacia

Palazzo
del Popolo

Palazzo
Tortoli

VIA PRUNELLO

Arco dei
Becci

VIA D. QUERCECCHIO

VICOLO D. INNOCENTI

VIA PALESTRO

Porta
Quercecchio

Palazzo
Pratellesi

VIA PIANDORNELLA

VIA DI BONDA

VIA BERIGNANO

VIA S. GIOVANNI

San Francesco

Siena Hotels
Promotion

VIALE DEI FOSSI

Porta San Giovanni

STRADA DI RACCIANO

PIAZZALE
DEI MARTIRI DI
MONTE MAGGIO

0   200 m

VIA ROMA   VIA VECCHIA

VIA GHIACCIAIA

VIA BAGNAIA

VIALE GARIBALDI

VIA N. CANNICCI

VIA CEPPARELLI

Certaldo & Pontedera

VIALE GARIBALDI

VIA MAINARDI

VIA S. STEFANO

N

ACCOMMODATION

Belsoggiorno	E
L'Antico Pozzo	A
La Cisterna	C
Leon Bianco	B
Le Vecchie Mura	D

EATING & DRINKING

Gelateria di Piazza	5
Il Pino	1
La Mangiatoia	2
Le Vecchie Mura	6
Osteria del Carcere	4
Osteria del Catene	3

▼ Poggibonsi, Volterra, Siena & Campsite

Arrival, information and accommodation

Although tour buses arrive throughout the day from Siena, San Gimignano welcomes very few direct public buses from anywhere other than **Colle Val d'Elsa** and the ugly industrial town of **Poggibonsi**: you're likely to have to transfer here. There's an hourly connecting bus from Poggibonsi train station (on the Florence–Empoli–Siena line) that drops off at both of San Gimignano's main gates, **Porta San Giovanni** in the south and **Porta San Matteo** in the north. From each, the main streets Via San Giovanni and Via San Matteo climb to meet in the middle of town at the interlocking squares of **Piazza Duomo** and **Piazza della Cisterna**, where you'll find the Pro Loco **tourist office**, Piazza Duomo 1 (daily 9am–1pm & 3–7pm; ℡0577.940.008, Ⓦwww .sangimignano.com).

Accommodation is bookable for free from the tourist office or through a branch of Siena Hotels Promotion, located just inside the southern gate at Via San Giovanni 125 (Mon–Sat: summer 9am–7pm; winter 9.30am– 12.30pm & 3–6pm, but may close some weekday mornings; ℡0577.940.809, Ⓦwww.hotelsiena.com). It can also give details of **private rooms**, an especially good option for those looking for cheaper accommodation, otherwise thin on the ground.

Hotels

Belsoggiorno Via San Giovanni 91 ℡0577.940.375, Ⓦwww.hotelbelsoggiorno.it. Twenty-one smallish but beautifully appointed rooms in a converted fourteenth-century town house on the main shopping street. Restaurant with panoramic terrace. ❺

L'Antico Pozzo Via San Matteo 87 ℡0577.942.014, Ⓦwww.anticopozzo.com. An upmarket, eighteen-room three-star, occupying a fifteenth-century town house, complete with original frescoes and period furnishings and antiques. ❻

La Cisterna Piazza Cisterna 24 ℡0577.940.328, Ⓦwww.hotelcisterna.it. Elegant ivy-clad hotel (established 1919) with forty-nine rooms, built into a medieval ensemble; some rooms have views onto the piazza or over the valley. Good restaurant – *Le Terrazze* – and an excellent central location. ❸

Le Vecchie Mura Via Piandornella 13 ℡0577.940.270, Ⓦwww.vecchiemura.it. Three doubles above a restaurant with superb views over vineyards and rolling Tuscan countryside. Free parking on the other side of town. ❷

Leon Bianco Piazza Cisterna 13 ℡0577.941.294, Ⓔleonbianco@joli.it. Tasteful twenty-six room three-star hotel, in a fourteenth-century town mansion in an excellent position for sightseeing opposite the *Cisterna*. Also with a roof terrace for breakfast, drinks and lounging. Rooms without a view are considerably cheaper. ❹

Campsite

Campeggio Boschetto di Piemma ℡0577.940.352, Ⓦwww.boschettodipiemma.it. The nearest campsite (with bar, restaurant and pool), 3km downhill from Porta San Giovanni at Santa Lucia, off the Volterra road.

The Town

You could walk from one end of San Gimignano to the other in about twenty minutes. It deserves at least a day, however, both for its frescoes and for its lovely surrounding countryside. From the southern gate, **Porta San Giovanni**, the *palazzo*-lined **Via San Giovanni** leads to the interlocking main squares, the Piazza del Duomo and the Piazza della Cisterna. On the right of the street, about 100m up, is the former church of San Francesco – a Romanesque building converted, like many of the *palazzi*, to a wine shop. You enter the **Piazza della Cisterna** through another gateway, the **Arco dei Becci**, part of the original fortifications built before the town expanded in the twelfth century. The square itself is flanked by an anarchic cluster of towers and *palazzi*, and is named after the thirteenth-century public cistern, still functioning in the centre. Northwest of the square is one of the old Ardinghelli towers; a Salvucci rival rears up behind. An arch leads through to the more austere **Piazza Duomo**, with further towers and civic *palazzi*.

The Collegiata

The plain facade of the Duomo, or more properly the **Collegiata**, since San Gimignano no longer has a bishop, could hardly provide a greater contrast with its interior (April–Oct Mon–Fri 9.30am–7pm, Sat 9.30am–5pm, Sun 12.30–4.40pm; March & Nov to mid-Jan Mon–Sat 9.30am–5.10pm, Sun 12.30–5.10pm; mid-Jan to Feb open for religious celebrations only; €3.50). This is one of the most comprehensively frescoed churches in Tuscany, with cycles of paintings filling every available space, their brilliant colours set off by Pisan-Romanesque arcades of black-and-white-striped marble. Entrance is from the side courtyard, where you'll also find the small **Museo d'Arte Sacra** (April–Oct Mon–Fri 9.30am–7.10pm, Sat 9.30am–5.10pm, Sun 12.30–5.10pm; Nov–March Mon–Sat 9.30am–4.40pm, Sun 12.30–4.40pm; €3). Less spectacular than the Collegiata, it's nevertheless worth a look for its rescued religious art.

The Collegiata's three principal **fresco cycles** fill the north and south walls, plus two short side walls that protrude from the east (exit) wall of the facade. The **Old Testament** scenes on the north wall, completed by Bartolo di Fredi around 1367, are full of medieval detail in the costumes, activities and interiors. They are also quirkily naturalistic: there are few odder frescoes than the depiction of Noah exposing himself in a drunken stupor. The cycle (which reads from left to right, top to bottom) follows the story of the **Flood** with those of **Abraham and Lot** (their trip to Canaan), **Joseph** (his dream; being let down the well; having his brothers arrested, and being recognized by them), **Moses** (changing a stick into a serpent before the Pharaoh; the Red Sea; Mount Sinai) and **Job** (temptation; the devil killing his herds; thanking God; being consoled). Above, note the beautiful fresco depicting the Creation of Eve, in which Eve emerges from the rib of the sleeping Adam. The **New Testament** scenes opposite (begun 1333) have a disputed attribution – either Barna da Siena or Lippo Memmi. They impress most by the intensity of their emotional expression: in *The Kiss of Judas*, the focus of eyes is startlingly immediate. One of the most dramatic scenes is the *Resurrection of Lazarus*, in which a dumbstruck crowd witnesses the removal of a door to reveal the living Lazarus in the winding bandages of burial. An altogether different vision pervades Taddeo di Bartolo's **Last Judgement** (1410), with paradise to the left and hell to the right. This is one of the most gruesome depictions of a customarily lurid subject, with no-holds-barred illustrations of the Seven Deadly Sins.

On the north side of the Collegiata, San Gimignano's most important Renaissance artwork is the superb fresco cycle made by Domenico Ghirlandaio for the small **Cappella di Santa Fina**. The subject is a local saint, born in 1238, who was struck by a dreadful and incurable disease at the age of 10. She gave herself immediately to God, repented her sins (the worst seems to have been accepting an orange from a boy), and insisted on spending the five agonizing years until her death lying on a plank on the floor. The fresco of the right-hand lunette shows Fina experiencing a vision of St Gregory. Opposite is an even more accomplished work, the *Funeral of St Fina* – Raphael is said to have been especially impressed with it – showing the saint on her deathbed with the towers of San Gimignano in the background. Ghirlandaio left a self-portrait: he's the figure behind the bishop who is saying Mass.

The Pinacoteca

The Palazzo Popolo, the other key component of Piazza Duomo, is partly given over to council offices, but most of the building is devoted to the **Pinacoteca** and the **Torre Grossa**, the only one of San Gimignano's towers which you can climb for great views of the Val d'Elsa (both daily: March–Oct 9.30am–7pm; Nov–Feb 10am–5.30pm; €5).

The lovely courtyard was built in 1323. A loggia opens on the right, from which judicial and public decrees were occasionally proclaimed (hence the subject matter of its frescoes). Stairs lead up to a picturesque little balcony and the ticket office. The first room, frescoed with hunting scenes, is the **Sala di Dante** – the poet visited as Florence's ambassador to the town in 1299, making a plea here for Guelph unity. Most of the paintings are Sienese in origin or inspiration, and the highlight is Lippo Memmi's *Maestà* (1317). Off the Sala di Dante are busts of a winsome Santa Fina (1496) and San Gregorio by Pietro Torrigiano. Highlights upstairs include two outstanding tondi by **Filippino Lippi**. Rooms off to the right hold a triptych by **Taddeo di Bartolo**, the *Scenes from the Life of St Gimignano* (1393) – with the saint holding the eponymous town on his lap – and **Lorenzo di Niccolò**'s *Scenes from the Life of St Bartholomew* (1401), which includes a graphic depiction of the saint being flayed alive. The most enjoyable paintings are hidden away in a small room off the stairs, frescoes of wedding scenes completed in the 1320s by the Sienese painter Memmo di Filipuccio that are unique in their subject matter: they show a tournament where the wife rides on her husband's back, followed by the couple taking a shared bath and then climbing into bed – the man managing to retain the same red hat throughout.

The rest of the town

Via di Castello continues east past the Romanesque **San Lorenzo in Ponte** (with fragments of a dramatic fresco of the *Last Judgement*) to a rural lane that winds down between vineyards to the city walls; just beyond the public wellhouse or **Fonti** stretches open countryside.

A signposted lane leads from Piazza Duomo up to the **Rocca**, the old fortress, with its one surviving tower and wonderful views. It was built, at local expense, by the Florentines "in order to remove every cause of evil thinking from the inhabitants" after their union with the *Comune*. Later, its purpose presumably fulfilled, it was dismantled by Cosimo de' Medici. Nowadays it encloses an orchard-like public garden, with figs, olives and a central well.

Via San Matteo is one of the grandest and best preserved of the city streets, running north from Piazza Duomo to the main **Porta San Matteo** gate. Before the gate, Via XX Settembre heads east to the former convent of Santa Chiara, which now houses both the **Galleria d'Arte Contemporaneo**, with work by nineteenth- and twentieth-century Tuscan artists, and the interesting **Museo Archeologico** (both open daily 11am–5.30pm; closed from Jan–March & Oct–Dec; €3). In the same complex is the **Spezieria di Santa Fina**, fragrant halls filled with exhibits from the sixteenth-century spice and herb pharmacy of the town's Santa Fina hospital. In the north of the town is the large church of **Sant'Agostino** (daily 7am–noon & 3–7pm; Nov–March closes 6pm), with an outstanding fresco cycle behind the high altar by Benozzo Gozzoli, the *Life of St Augustine* (1465), which provides an amazing record of life in Renaissance Florence. Read from low down on the left, the panels depict the saint – who was born in what is now Tunisia in 354 – being taken to school and being flogged by his teacher, studying grammar at Carthage university, crossing the sea to Italy, his teaching in Rome and Milan and being received by Emperor Theodosius. Then comes the turning-point, when he hears St Ambrose preach and, while reading St Paul, hears a child's voice extolling him "*Tolle, lege*" (take and read). After this, he was baptized and returned to Africa to found a monastic community. The depiction of his death almost exactly prefigures Ghirlandaio's Collegiata fresco of the death of St Fina.

Eating and drinking

San Gimignano isn't famous for its **food** – there are too many visitors and too few locals to ensure high standards. However, the tables set out on the car-free squares and lanes, and the good local wines, make for pleasant dining. The recommended places below are all moderately priced. Good **bars** are similarly thin on the ground, though there are one or two on each of the main piazzas that are pleasant enough places from where to watch the world go by.

The little but extraordinarily popular 🏃 *Gelateria di Piazza*, Piazza della Cisterna 4 (closed mid-Nov to mid-Feb), has arguably the best **ice cream** in Tuscany. Owner Sergio has certainly won enough competitions, including the *Gelato del Mondo* in 2006. Framed plaudits cover the walls. His incomparable pistachio flavour is made from finest-quality Sicilian nuts, and his trademark *crema di Santa Fina* is perfumed with saffron, but you'd be hard-pushed on a hot afternoon to beat the trio of peach, champagne with grapefruit, and Vernaccia, the last a fragrant sorbet made from the crisp local white wine.

Restaurants

Il Pino Via San Matteo 102 ℡0577.942.225. First choice for eating, with a lovely interior, and a specialist focus on antipasti (all €12) and dishes sprinkled with truffle. Closed Thurs.

La Mangiatoia Via Mainardi 5 ℡0577.945.28. Classical music and stained glass compete for attention with some imaginative pasta dishes and wild boar stew. Mains €12–15. Closed Tues.

🏃 **Le Vecchie Mura** Via Piandornella 15 ℡0577.940.270. The restaurant is housed in an old vaulted stable and serves decent regional food (*primi* €6–9, *secondi* €10–12), but it's the terrace across the road which is the real draw offering the best views in town out across the surrounding countryside. Closed Tues & lunch.

Osteria del Carcere Via del Castello 13 ℡0577.941.905. Award-winning place run by young owners, serving Tuscan cuisine with an innovative edge. Closed Wed.

Osteria del Catene Via Mainardi 18 ℡0577.941.966. Thoroughly reliable spot for straightforward Tuscan cooking, plus an extensive wine list. Offers increasingly more elaborate set menus from €15. Closed Wed.

Volterra

The dramatic location of **VOLTERRA** – built on a high plateau enclosed by volcanic hills midway between Siena and the sea – prompted D.H. Lawrence to write that "it gets all the wind and sees all the world – a sort of inland island", and indeed, you can often find seashells embedded in the paving of streets and squares. Busy but still atmospheric, the town's walled medieval core is made from the yellow-grey stone *panchino*. **Etruscan** Volterra (Velathri) flourished through a combination of its alabaster mines and an impregnable position, attributes that ensured its survival through the Roman era and beyond. Its isolation was, however, its downfall. Under **Florentine** control from 1360, it proved unable to keep pace with changing and expanding patterns of trade, and the town itself began to subside, its walls and houses slipping away to the west over the **Balze** cliffs, which form a dramatic prospect from the Pisa road. Today, Volterra occupies less than a third of its ancient extent.

Arrival and information

Irregular **buses** run to Volterra from Larderello, Pisa and Colle Val d'Elsa. All arrive on the south side of the walls at Piazza Martiri, from where it's a two-minute walk to the central Piazza dei Priori. The **tourist office** is at Via Giusto Turazza 2 (daily: April–Oct 9am–1pm & 2–7pm; Nov–March 10am–1pm & 2–6pm;

Volterra's alabaster

Alabaster is a form of crystallized chalk that has a delicate, milky texture and lends itself to the sculpture of fine, flowing lines and close ornamental detail. In even quite large blocks, it is translucent. The Etruscans and Romans extensively mined Volterra's alabaster for sculpting and up until the 1960s, there were large alabaster factories throughout the town centre, but – not least because of the quantity of dust they threw up – large-scale production was moved to outlying areas. These days, only about a dozen artisans are permitted to maintain workshops in the centre of town, and Volterra's famous art school is the only one in Europe to train students to work alabaster.

You'll spot plenty of alabaster shops dotted around the centre – most are outlets for factories that produce machined pieces from the tasteful to the tacky. *Alab'Arte*, down the alley alongside the Museo Guarnacci at Via Orti S. Agostino 28 (☎0588.87.968), is one of the few to stick to hand production, turning out small pieces of sculpture for a few euros.

☎0588.86.150, ⓦwww.provolterra.it). There are free **car parks** on the northern side of the walls, and a pay-by-the-hour underground car park just to the south.

Volterra's most attractive **hotel** is the sixteenth-century *Villa Nencini*, in a peaceful, panoramic setting west of the centre at Borgo Santo Stefano 55 (☎0588.86.386, ⓦwww.villanencini.it; ❸). Housed in a restored fifteenth-century convent, the *Hotel San Lino*, Via San Lino 26, just inside the walls in the north of the town, has comfortable rooms and a swimming pool (☎0588.85.250, ⓦwww.hotelsanlino.com; ❸). The **campsite** *Le Balze* is 1km west of town at Via di Mandringa 15 (☎0588.87.880, ⓦwww.campinglebalze .com; April–Sept).

The Town

Dominating the almost totally medieval square of **Piazza dei Priori**, the **Palazzo dei Priori** is the oldest town hall in Tuscany, begun in 1208, which may have served as the model for Florence's Palazzo Vecchio. Upstairs inside the *palazzo* (mid-March to Oct daily 10.30am–5.30pm; Nov to mid-March Sat & Sun 11am–5pm; €1) is the **Sala del Consiglio**, used as the town's council chamber without interruption since 1257. Its end wall features a huge *Annunciation* by Orcagna.

Leaving the square west past the tourist office, you come to a crossroads overlooked by the **Torre Buomparenti**. South (left) at Via Roma 13 is the **Museo d'Arte Sacra**, a rich four-room collection (daily: mid-March to Oct 9am–1pm & 3–6pm; Nov to mid-March 9am–1pm; joint ticket with Museo Guarnacci and Pinacoteca €8), which includes a silver reliquary bust of St Ottaviano by Antonio del Pollaiuolo and a beautiful sixteenth-century alabaster ciborium. Via Roma continues into the slightly down-at-heel cathedral square, with the Pisan-Romanesque **Duomo**, consecrated in 1120 (daily 8am–12.30pm & 3–5/6pm) and **Baptistry** (late-thirteenth century). The best of the Duomo's works is a sculpture of the *Deposition* (1228) in the south transept, disarmingly repainted in its original bright colours. Behind the baptistry is an old foundling's hospital decorated by della Robbia. Via Marchesi heads south uphill to a lush area of grass, trees and shade known as the **Parco Archeologico** (daily 8.30am–dusk; free). There's not much archeology about the place – a few odd lumps of rock, said to be part of a Roman bathhouse – but it's a beautiful part of the town to walk around for a few hours. Overlooking the park to the east is the Medicean **Rocca**, with rounded bastions and a central tower; it's one of the great examples of Italian military architecture and for the last 150 years has been a prison. The first turning off Via Marchesi is Via Porta dell'Arco, which runs downhill to the **Arco Etrusco**, an Etruscan gateway, third-century BC in origin, built in cyclopean blocks of stone. The gate was narrowly saved from destruction in the last war during a ten-day battle between the partisans and Nazis.

North from the Torre Buomparenti at Via dei Sarti 1 is the beautiful Renaissance Palazzo Minucci-Solaini, now housing the **Pinacoteca e Museo Civico** (daily: mid-March to Oct 9am–7pm; Nov to mid-March 9.30am–1.30pm; €8 joint ticket with Museo Guarnacci and Museo d'Arte Sacra). The key works are Florentine: Ghirlandaio's marvellous *Christ in Glory*, Luca Signorelli's *Annunciation* and, best of all, Rosso Fiorentino's extraordinary *Deposition*. This is one of the masterpieces of Mannerism, its figures, without any central focus, creating an agitated tension from sharp lines and blocks of discordant colour. The building also contains the **Eco-Museo dell'Alabastro** (April–Oct daily 11am–5pm; Nov–March Sat & Sun 9am–1.30pm; €3), which provides an overview of alabaster working in the area from Etruscan times to the present day and has a replica sculptor's workshop.

On the same street as the Pinacoteca is **Palazzo Viti**, Via dei Sarti 41 (April–Oct daily 10am–1pm & 2.30–6.30pm; Nov–March by appointment only; €5; ☎0588.840.47), an extensively frescoed Renaissance mansion filled with alabaster, everything from two-metre-high candelabras to tiles laid in the floor of the ballroom.

The Museo Etrusco Guarnacci

The **Museo Etrusco Guarnacci**, 500m east of Piazza dei Priori at Via Don Minzoni 15 (same hours and ticket as Pinacoteca), is one of Italy's major archeological museums. On display are entirely local finds, including some six hundred Etruscan **funerary urns**. Carved in alabaster, terracotta or local sandstone or limestone, they date from the fourth to first centuries BC, and follow a standard pattern: below a reclining figure of the subject (always leaning on their left side), bas-reliefs depict domestic events, Greek myths or simply a symbolic flower – one for a young person, two for middle-aged, three for elderly. The vast collection is organized by theme, with informative notes in each room. Key highlights are **upstairs**: past a large Roman mosaic transferred here from Volterra's baths is the **Urna degli Sposi**, a rare and artistically unique clay urn lid which features a disturbing double portrait of a husband and wife, all piercing eyes and dreadful looks. The star piece is the exceptional **Ombra della Sera** ("Evening Shadow"), an elongated nude that is unique in that it has been personalized and individualized – most of the figurines in nearby cases are generic.

The Balze cliffs

To reach the eroded **Balze** cliffs, follow the Via Ricciarelli northwest from the Piazza dei Priori. As Via San Lino, this passes the church of **San Francesco**, with fifteenth-century frescoes of the *Legend of the True Cross* by Cenni di Cenni, before leaving town through the Porta San Francesco. From here, follow Borgo Santo Stefano and its continuation, Borgo San Giusto, past the Baroque church and former abbey of **San Giusto**, its striking facade framed by an avenue of cypress trees. At the Balze (almost 2km west of Piazza dei Priori) you gain a real sense of the extent of Etruscan Volterra, whose old walls drop away into the chasms. Gashes in the slopes and the natural erosion of sand and clay are made more dramatic by alabaster mines, ancient and modern. Below are buried great tracts of the Etruscan and Roman city, and landslips continue – as evidenced by the ruined eleventh-century **Badia** monastery ebbing away over the precipice.

Eating and drinking

As a renowned centre for hunting, Volterra's **restaurant** menus are dominated by wild boar (*cinghiale*), hare (*lepre*) and rabbit (*coniglio*). Most places are moderately priced, often offering fixed-price menus for around €12–€15. The vaulted gloom of *Vecchia Osteria dei Poeti*, Via Matteotti 55 (closed Thurs), is the best place to try Volterra's gamey cuisine. The brighter, airier *Don Beta*, Via Matteotti 39, serves all the main staples (pasta, pizza, steak and so forth), but with added truffles (closed Mon).

Southern Tuscany

The inland hills of **southern Tuscany** are the region at its best, an infinite gradation of trees and vineyards that encompasses the *crete* – a sparsely populated region of pale clay hillsides – before climbing into the hills around Monte Amiata. Southwest of Siena towards the sea is gentle **Massa Maríttima**, a memorable but little-visited hill-town that presides over a marshy coastal plain. Magnificent monastic architecture survives in the tranquil settings of **San Galgano** and, a short distance east, **Monte Oliveto Maggiore**, which boasts the additional attraction of some marvellous frescoes. The finest of the hill-towns to the south of Siena is **Montepulciano**, with its superb wines and an ensemble of Renaissance architecture that rivals neighbouring **Pienza**.

Further south, the tourist crush is noticeably eased in smaller towns and villages that are often overlooked by visitors gorged on Florentine art and Sienese countryside. Wild **Monte Amiata** offers scenic mountain walks, **Saturnia** has some remarkable sulphur springs, and isolated **Pitigliano** is one of the most dramatically sited medieval towns in the region, nurturing the amazing story – and scant remains – of what was once Tuscany's strongest Jewish community.

Massa Maríttima

The road south from Volterra over the mountains to **MASSA MARÍTTIMA** is scenically magnificent yet little explored: classic Tuscan countryside which is given an added surreal quality around **Larderello** by the presence of *soffioni* (hot steam geysers), huge silver pipes snaking across the fields, and sulphurous smoke rising from chimneys amid the foliage. It sees none of the crowds of San Gimignano, and even Volterra looks crowded in comparison.

Massa, like Volterra, has been a wealthy **mining** town since Etruscan times. In 1225, on the heels of a declaration of independence, it passed Europe's first-ever charter for the protection of miners; in the century afterwards, before Siena took over in 1335, its exquisite **Duomo** went up and the population doubled. The trend was reversed in the sixteenth century, and by 1737, after bouts of plague and malaria, it was a virtual ghost town. Massa gained its "Maríttima" suffix in the Middle Ages when it became the leading hill-town of this coastal region, even though the sea is 20km distant across a silty plain. Its recovery began with the draining of coastal marshes in the 1830s. Today, it's a quiet but well-off town, where the effects of mining are less evident than agriculture and low-profile tourism.

Blocks of new buildings mar the approach, but the medieval splendour of **Piazza Garibaldi**, just up from the bus stops, more than compensates. This perfect example of Tuscan town planning showcases the thirteenth-century **Duomo**, set on broad steps at a dramatically oblique angle to the square. The cathedral is dedicated to the sixth-century St Cerbone, whose claim to fame was to persuade a flock of geese to follow him when summoned to Rome on heresy charges. Its airy **interior** (irregular hours but approximately 8.30am–noon & 3–6pm; free) features eleventh-century carvings of grinning, cross-eyed faces – powerful and primitive, in dramatic contrast to the severe, polished Roman sarcophagus nearby. A modest **Museo Archeologico** occupies the Palazzo del Podestà opposite (April–Oct Tues–Sun 10am–12.30pm & 3.30–7pm; Nov–March closes 5pm; €3) – worth visiting for the town's undisputed masterpiece, a superb *Maestà* altarpiece by Ambrogio Lorenzetti, coloured in vivid pink, green and tangerine, with Cerbone and his geese lurking in the corner.

Otherwise, barring a couple of limited-interest museums devoted to mining, aim for the picturesque lane Via Moncini, which climbs steeply to the quiet Gothic **upper town**: as you emerge beneath an impressive but militarily useless arch onto **Piazza Matteotti**, facing you is the **Torre del Candeliere**, part of the thirteenth-century *Fortilizio Senese*. The tower is climbable for a stupendous panorama (April–Oct daily 10am–1pm & 3–6pm; Nov–March 11am–1pm & 2.30–4.30pm; €2.50).

Practicalities

There are three **buses** daily to Massa from Volterra (change at Larderello), one from Grosseto and three from Siena. The helpful **tourist office** is just below Piazza Garibaldi at Via Todini 3/5 (daily 9am–1pm & 3–7.30pm; April, May & Nov closed Sun pm; Dec–March closed all Sun; ☎0566.902.756, ⊛www .altamaremmaturismo.it). Massa's only central **hotel** is the comfortable *Il Sole*, Corso della Libertà 43 (☎0566.901.971, ⊜hotel@ilsolehotel.it; ❷); otherwise go for the pleasant, refurbished *Duca del Mare*, just below town at Piazza Dante Alighieri 1 (☎0566.902.284, ⊛www.ducadelmare.it; ❸). There's also a good **hostel**, *Ostello Sant'Anna*, in the higher part of town, converted from a school at Via Gramsci 3 (☎0566.901.115, ⊜leclarisse@libero.it; €15 per person; 9am–noon & 5pm–midnight).

Better **restaurants** than those lining Piazza Garibaldi include *Osteria da Tronca* at Vicolo Porte 5 (☎0566.901.991; closed lunch & Wed), offering inexpensive *osteria*-style food in a rustic stone wall setting. *Pizzeria Barbablu*, up at Piazza Matteotti 5, has excellent pizza and pasta and outside tables.

The crete

South of Siena stretches classic Tuscan countryside known as the *crete* – a sparsely populated region of pale clay hillsides dotted with sheep, cypresses and the odd monumental-looking farmhouse. These tranquil lands were one of the heartlands of medieval monasticism in Tuscany. The Vallombrosan order maintained their main house at Torri just south of Siena, the Benedictine order had theirs at Sant'Antimo near Montalcino (see p.543), while the Cistercians founded the convent and abbey of **San Galgano**; now ruined, this is one of the most alluring sights in Tuscany, complete with its hilltop chapel housing a "sword in the stone". The region's finest monastery is southeast of Siena at **Monte Oliveto Maggiore**.

San Galgano

8

The **Abbazia di San Galgano**, 26km northeast of Massa Maríttima in a peaceful rural setting, is perhaps the most evocative Gothic building in all Italy – roofless, with a grass field for a nave, nebulous patches of fresco amid the vegetation, and panoramas of the sky, clouds and hills through a rose window. In the twelfth and thirteenth centuries, local **Cistercian** monks were the leading power in Tuscany. The abbots exercised powers of arbitration in city disputes, and at Siena the monks were the city's accountants. Through them, the ideas of Gothic building were imported to Italy. The order began a hilltop **church** and monastic buildings here in 1218, but their project to build a grand abbey on the fertile land below was doomed to failure. Building work took seventy years up to 1288, but then famine struck in 1329, the Black Death in 1348, and mercenaries ran amok in subsequent decades. By 1500, all the monks had moved to the security of Siena. The buildings mouldered until 1786, when the bell tower was struck by lightning and collapsed. Three years later, the church was deconsecrated, and the complex was abandoned for good.

These days, the main appeal of the **abbey** (open all day and illuminated at night until 11.30pm) is its state of ruin, although work to halt the advance of Mother Nature is under way and there are concerts of classical music held from late July to late August.

On the hill above, the unusual round Romanesque church of **Monte Siepi** commemorates the spot where Galgano – a local twelfth-century knight – renounced his violent past by thrusting his sword into a stone. Amazingly enough, Galgano's **sword in the stone** has survived, protected under glass as an object of veneration. A side chapel preserves the decaying remains of a man's hands: local legend has it that two wolves – companions of Galgano – tore them from a robber who had broken into the saint's tomb.

There are two or three **buses** daily between Massa Maríttima and Siena that pass within sight of the abbey and you can ask to be dropped off. To one side of the abbey building, in the old vaulted scriptorium, is a small **tourist office** (April–Oct daily 10.30am–6pm; March Sat & Sun 10.30am–1pm & 2–6pm; irregular hours Nov & Dec; closed Jan & Feb; ☎0577.756.738, ⓦwww.prolocochiusdino.it).

Monte Oliveto Maggiore

Tuscany's grandest monastery, the **Abbazia di Monte Oliveto Maggiore**, is sited 26km southeast of Siena in one of the most beautiful tracts of Sienese countryside, and houses one of the most absorbing Renaissance **frescoes** you'll find anywhere. By car, you can approach from the crossroads town of Buonconvento, climbing quickly into forests of pine, oak and cypress, and then into the olive groves that enclose the monastery. One afternoon **bus** daily from Siena's train station goes to the village of Chiusure, 2km east of the abbey.

When Pius II visited in 1463, it was the overall scene that impressed him: the architecture, in honey-coloured Sienese brick, merging into the woods and gardens that the **Olivetan** or White Benedictine monks had created from the eroded hills of the *crete*. Within six years, the pope recognized the order and over the following two centuries this, their principal house, was transformed into one of the most powerful monasteries in the land. It was only in 1810, when the monastery was suppressed by Napoleon, that it fell from influence. Today it's maintained by a small group of Olivetan monks, who supplement their state income with a high-tech centre for the restoration of ancient books. At the **gatehouse**, an avenue of cypresses leads to the abbey. Signs at the bottom of the slope direct you along a walk to **Blessed Bernardo's grotto** – a chapel built on the site where the founder lived as a hermit.

The **abbey** (daily 9.15am–noon & 3.15–6pm; winter closes 5pm) is a huge complex, though much of it remains off-limits to visitors. The entrance leads to the **Chiostro Grande**, covered by a series of frescoes depicting the *Life of St Benedict*, the man traditionally regarded as the founder of Christian monasticism. The cycle begins on the east wall, just on the right of the door into the church, and was begun in 1497 by Luca Signorelli who painted nine panels in the middle of the series that start with the depiction of a collapsing house. The colourful Antonio Bazzi, known as Il Sodoma, painted the remaining 27 scenes between 1505 and 1508. He was by all accounts a lively presence, bringing with him part of his menagerie of pets, which included badgers, depicted at his feet in a self-portrait in the third panel. There's a sensuality in many of the secular figures, especially the young men – as befits the artist's nickname – but also the "evil women" (originally nudes, until protests from the abbot). The **church** (entered off the Chiostro Grande) was given a Baroque remodelling in the eighteenth century and some superb stained glass in the twentieth. Its main treasure is the choir stalls, inlaid by Giovanni di Verona and others with architectural, landscape and domestic scenes (including a nod to Sodoma's pets with a cat in a window). Stairs lead from the cloister up to the **library**, again with carving by Giovanni; sadly, it has had to be viewed from the door since the theft of sixteen of its twenty codices in 1975.

Montepulciano

The highest of the major Tuscan hill-towns, at more than 600m, **MONTEPUL-CIANO** is built on a long, narrow ridge 65km southeast of Siena, along which coils the main street, the **Corso**, flanked by a series of dark alleys that drop away to the walls, providing slivers of views between Renaissance *palazzi* out over the rolling countryside. Henry James, who compared the town to a ship, spent most of his time here drinking – a sound policy, in view of the much-celebrated **Vino Nobile**. A short distance east is the Etruscan-founded – but now rather drab – town of **Chiusi**, useful only as transport hub unless you're a devotee of Etruscan tombs and remains.

Arrival, information and accommodation

TRA-IN **buses** run roughly every hour between Buonconvento, Torrenieri (change for Montalcino), San Quírico d'Órcia, Pienza and Montepulciano – some of them begin from Siena – while LFI buses run regularly between Montepulciano, Chiusi and its **train** station.

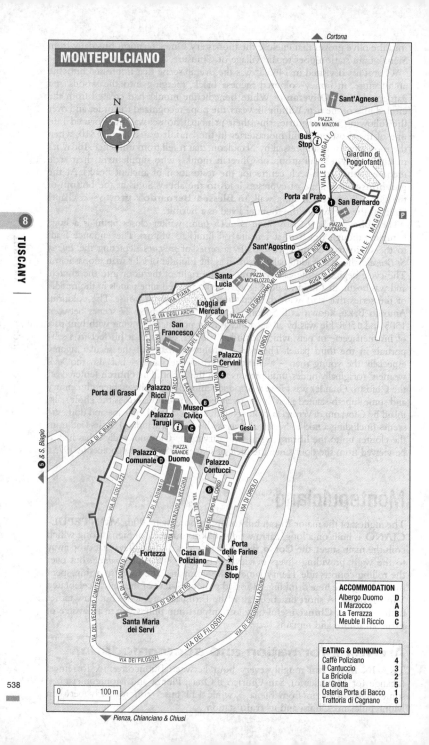

MONTEPULCIANO

Cortona

N

Sant'Agnese

PIAZZA
DON MINZONI

Bus
Stop

Giardino di
Poggiofanti

VIALE D. SANGALLO

Porta al Prato

San Bernardo

2

1

PIAZZA
SAVONAROL

VIALE I. MAGGIO

P

Sant'Agostino

3

VIA ROMA

A

RUGA DI MEZZO

Santa
Lucia

PIAZZA
MICHELOZZO

VIA DEL CORSO

RUGA DI FUORI

Loggia di
Mercato

VIA PIANA

PIAZZA
DELL'ERBE

VIA GRACCIANO NEL CORSO

San
Francesco

VIA DEGLI ARCHI

VIA DEL POGGIOLO

VIA DI VOLTAIA NEL CORSO

VIA DI OPIOLO

Palazzo
Cervini

VIA DEL PAOLINO

VIA DEL GIARDINO

VIA PIE AL SASSO

4

VIA RICCI

Porta di Grassi

Palazzo
Ricci

B

Palazzo
Tarugi

Museo
Civico

Gesù

i

C

5 & S. Biagio

VIA DI S. BIAGIO

Palazzo
Comunale

D

PIAZZA
GRANDE

Duomo

Palazzo
Contucci

VIA DI COLLAZZI

VIA DI S. DONATO

VIA FIORENZUOLA VECCHIA

VIA DEL TEATRO

6

VIA DELL'OPIO NEL CORSO

VIA DI OPIOLO

Fortezza

Casa di
Poliziano

Porta
delle Farine

Bus
Stop

VIA DEL VECCHIO CIMITERO

VIA DI S. DONATO

VIA DI SAN PIETRO

VIA DI CIRCONVALLAZIONE

Santa Maria
dei Servi

VIA DEI FILOSOFI

VIA DEI FILOSOFI

538

0   100 m

Pienza, Chianciano & Chiusi

ACCOMMODATION	
Albergo Duomo	D
Il Marzocco	A
La Terrazza	B
Meuble Il Riccio	C

EATING & DRINKING	
Caffè Poliziano	4
Il Cantuccio	3
La Briciola	2
La Grotta	5
Osteria Porta di Bacco	1
Trattoria di Cagnano	6

Montepulciano's spiralling, tortuous streets are pretty steep, and **orientation** can get confusing. The main entrance to the town – at the lowest point – is the northern gate, the **Porta al Prato**, terminus of most buses; from here, the Corso climbs south through the town (changing its name from Via di Gracciano to Via di Voltaia, then to Via dell'Opio) until it reaches the southern gate, the **Porta delle Farine**, where intercity buses also drop off. From here, the main street (Via di Poliziano, then Via di San Donato) continues its coiling path up and around to enter the main **Piazza Grande** from the south. The stiff climb on foot takes an unrelenting quarter-hour; or you could resort to the LFI town minibuses which run on a loop every 20min, starting and ending at the Porta al Prato. **Parking** is free below the eastern walls. The **tourist office** is at Piazza Don Minzoni 1 (April–Sept Mon–Sat 9am–12.30pm & 3–8pm, Sun 9am–12.30pm; Oct–March Mon–Sat 9.30am–12.30pm & 3–6pm, Sun 9.30am–12.30pm; ☎0578.757.341, ⓦwww.comune.montepulciano.si.it). It can advise on private rooms, otherwise the following hotels are your best bet.

Hotels

Albergo Duomo Via San Donato 14
☎0578.757.473, ⓔalbergoDuomo@libero.it. A short distance from Piazza Grande, the three star *Duomo* has excellent facilities and smart clean rooms. ❸

Il Marzocco Piazza Savonarola 18 ☎0578.757.262, ⓦwww.albergoilmarzocco.it. Large and elegant, the *Marzocco* occupies a sixteenth-century building. There's a restaurant and café downstairs, and relatively plain rooms upstairs. ❸

La Terrazza Via Piè al Sasso 16 ☎0578.757.440, ⓦwww.laterrazzadimontepulciano.it. Recently renovated, the friendly and well-equipped *La Terrazza* has a leafy roof terrace where breakfast is served in summer. ❸

Meuble Il Riccio Via Talosa 21 ☎&ⓕ0578.757.713, ⓦwww.ilriccio.net. Housed in a cloistered medieval building just off Piazza Grande, *Il Riccio* enjoys a central, atmospheric location. ❸

The Town

Montepulciano's unusually consistent array of Renaissance *palazzi* and churches is a reflection of its remarkable development after 1511, when, following intermittent alliance with Siena, the town finally threw in its lot with Florence. In that year the Florentines sent **Antonio Sangallo the Elder** to rebuild the town's gates and walls, which he did so impressively that the council took him on to work on the town hall and a series of churches. The local nobles meanwhile hired him, his nephew, Antonio Sangallo the Younger, and later the Modena-born **Vignola** – a founding figure of Baroque – to work on their own *palazzi*. The work of this trio is totally assured in conception and execution, and makes a fascinating comparison with Rossellino's Pienza. Sangallo's first commission was Montepulciano's main gate, the **Porta al Prato**, at the north end of town. Inside the gate at the first square, Piazza Savonarola, is a stone column bearing the heraldic lion (*marzocco*) of Florence. Just beyond is the church of **Sant'Agostino**, designed by the earlier Medici protégé, Michelozzo, who also carved the relief above the door. Within are good Sienese paintings by Lorenzo di Credi and Giovanni di Paolo.

About 100m further along is **Piazza dell'Erbe** overlooked by the Renaissance **Loggia di Mercato**, which marks a fork in the street. A right turn off the Corso brings you up steeply to a beautiful little piazza fronting the church of **Santa Lucia**, which has a fabulous *Madonna* by Signorelli in a chapel on the right. Just below Santa Lucia, Via del Poggiolo runs down to the church of San Francesco and continues – as the imposing Via Ricci – up to the Piazza Grande past the Sienese-Gothic Palazzo Neri-Orselli, home to the **Museo Civico** (April–July & Sept–Oct Tues–Sat 10am–1pm & 3–7pm; Aug daily 10am–7pm; rest of the year Tues–Sun 10am-1pm & 3–6pm; €4.13), an extensive collection of small-town Gothic and Renaissance works.

Piazza Grande, Montepulciano's theatrical flourish of a main square, is built on the highest point of the ridge, and is worth the climb. Its most distinctive building is the **Palazzo Comunale**, a thirteenth-century Gothic mansion to which Michelozzo added a tower and rustication in imitation of the Palazzo Vecchio in Florence. You can climb the **tower** (daily April–Oct 10am–6pm; €1.60) – though disappointingly not right to the top. Down below, two of the *palazzi* on the square were designed by Sangallo. The **Palazzo Tarugi**, by the lion and griffin fountain, is a highly innovative building, with a public loggia cut through one corner. Headier pleasures await at the **Palazzo Contucci**, one of many buildings scattered about the town that serve as *cantine* for the wine trade, offering free *degustazione* (tastings) and sale of the Vino Nobile. Sangallo and his contemporaries never got around to building a facade for the plain brick **Duomo** across the square (daily 9am–1pm & 3.30–7pm; free). Its interior is an elegant Renaissance design, scattered with superb sculptures by Michelozzo, while the finest of its paintings is the Sienese **Taddeo di Bartolo**'s iridescent 1401 altarpiece of the Assumption, a favourite subject among Sienese artists.

Sangallo's greatest commission came in 1518, when he was invited to design the pilgrimage church of **San Biagio** on the hillside below the town. It's a fifteen-minute walk from the centre. This was the second-largest church project of its time after St Peter's in Rome, and exercised Antonio until his death in 1534. The result is one of the most serene Renaissance creations in Italy, constructed from a porous travertine whose soft honey-coloured stone blends perfectly into its niche in the landscape. Its major architectural novelty was the use of freestanding towers to flank the facade (only one was completed). The interior is spoilt a little by Baroque trompel'oeil decoration, but remains supremely harmonious. Scarcely less perfect is the nearby **Canonica** (rectory), endowed by Sangallo with a graceful portico and double-tiered loggia.

Eating, drinking and entertainment

Montepulciano has only latterly become a stop on the visitor trail, and has relatively few restaurants, though you'll find several small **cafés** on the Corso, and plenty of places to sample the region's **Vino Nobile** wine (see box below).

Nightlife and entertainment are similarly sparse, though things liven up in July during the three-week **Cantiere Internazionale d'Arte** (℡0578.716.368, ⓦwww.cantiere.toscana.nu or www.fondazionecantiere.it), which presents exhibitions and concerts around town, and the last Sunday in August sees the **Bravìo delle Botti**, a barrel-race in medieval costume.

Wine tasting in Montepulciano

Vino Nobile di Montepulciano has been acclaimed since medieval times and today boasts a top-rated DOCG mark; something the townspeople have not been shy in exploiting. Montepulciano's streets are filled with wine shops selling gift sets, and local vineyards often offer tastings in the town (generally free, but usually requiring advance notice). Every restaurant can provide a range of vintages, the very cheapest of which will still set you back at least €20. The tourist office has a complete list of the town's wine outlets, and can organize a **wine-tasting** ramble for you. Some of the many places to check out include the venerable *Contucci*, Via San Donato 15 (℡0578.757.006, ⓦwww.contucci.it), which can trace the family line in Montepulciano back a thousand years, and the *Cantina Del Redi*, Via di Collazi 5 (℡0578.716.092, ⓦwww.cantinadelredi.com).

Cafés and restaurants

Caffè Poliziano Via di Voltaia nel Corso 27. An 1868 tearoom restored to a classic Art Nouveau design; it serves pastries and pots of tea, while its adjoining restaurant, *Il Grifin d'Oro*, serves somewhat pricey meals (at around €25), such as *pici* (fat spaghetti) with wild boar *ragù*, and offers great views from a small terrace. Daily 7am–midnight.

Il Cantuccio Via delle Cantine 1 ☏0578.757.870. A standard Tuscan menu is enlivened by items such as *bocconcini di cinghiale* (little bites of wild boar). Mains range from €8 to €15. Closed Mon.

La Briciola Via delle Cantine. Quality wood-fired pizza, as well as a range of hearty Tuscan *primi* (€8) and *secondi* (€10–12). Closed Wed.

La Grotta Via di San Biagio ☏0578.757.607. Opposite San Biagio church, about 1km outside the city walls, brick-vaulted *La Grotta* serves pricey classic Tuscan cuisine in a sixteenth-century building with its own garden. Closed Wed.

Osteria Porta di Bacco Via di Gracciano nel Corso 106 ☏0578.757.948. Just inside the Porta al Prato, this quiet, characterful old stone-arched place is one of a clutch of moderately priced options, offering a set three-course menu for €12. Closed Tues.

Trattoria di Cagnano Via dell'Opio Nel Corso 30 ☏0578.758.757. Popular and bustling, this offers a wide range of pizzas, from the simple €5 *margherita* to the €7.50 *estate* (mozzarella, tomatoes, rocket, prosciutto and parmesan), as well as outside seating. Closed Mon.

Pienza and around

PIENZA, 11km west of Montepulciano, is as complete a Renaissance creation as any in Italy, established in an act of considerable vanity by **Pope Pius II** as a Utopian "New Town". The transformation of the village of Cortignano, where Pius was born, began in 1459 under the architect **Bernardo Rossellino**. The cost was astronomical, but the cathedral, papal and bishop's palaces, and the core of a town (renamed in Pius's honour), were completed in just three years. Pius lived just two more years, and of his successors only his nephew paid Pienza any regard: the city, intended to spread across the hill, stayed village-sized. Today, despite the large number of visitors, it still has an air of emptiness and folly: a natural stage set, where Zeffirelli filmed *Romeo and Juliet*.

Traffic converges on **Piazza Dante**, just outside the main gate, Porta al Murello, and from here the **Corso** leads straight to Rossellino's centrepiece, **Piazza Pio II**, which deliberately juxtaposes civic and religious buildings – the Duomo, Palazzo Piccolomini (papal palace), Bishop's Palace and Palazzo Pubblico – to underline the balance between church and town. The square makes the usual medieval nod to Florence in its town hall, but is otherwise entirely Renaissance in conception.

The **Duomo** has one of the earliest Renaissance facades in Tuscany; the interior, on Pius's orders, took inspiration from the German hall-churches he had seen on his travels, and remains essentially Gothic. The chapels house an outstanding series of Sienese altarpieces, commissioned from the major painters of the age – Giovanni di Paolo, Matteo di Giovanni, Vecchietta and Sano di Pietro. How long the building itself will remain standing is uncertain though. Even before completion a crack appeared, and after an earthquake in the nineteenth century it has required much buttressing – the nave currently dips crazily towards the back of the church.

Pius's residence, the **Palazzo Piccolomini** (Tues–Sun: mid-March to mid-Oct 10am–6.30pm; rest of the year 10am–4pm, but closed mid-Feb to the end of Feb and mid-Nov to the end of Nov; open Mon on public hols; €7; ⓦwww .palazzopiccolominipienza.it) sits alongside the Duomo. You're free to walk into the courtyard and through to the original "hanging garden" behind to the left, with a triple-tiered loggia offering a superb view over the valley. The **apartments** above include Pius II's bedroom, library and other rooms filled with collections of weapons and medals. Further mementoes of the pope – notably his English-made embroidered cope – are across the piazza in the excellent **Museo Diocesano** (mid-March to Oct Wed–Mon 10am–1pm & 3–7pm; Nov to mid-March Sat & Sun 10am–1pm & 3–6pm; €4.10).

Practicalities

Regular **buses** between Montepulciano and Buonconvento pass through Pienza and San Quírico d'Orcia. Pienza is also a gentle day's **walk** from Montepulciano on an old cross-country route through the walled village of Monticchiello. The very helpful **tourist office** (☎0578.749.305, ⓦwww .comunepienza.it; mid-March to Oct Mon–Sat 10am–1pm & 3–6pm or later; Nov to mid-March Sat & Sun 10am–1pm, 3–5/6pm) is on the Corso in the Museo Diocesano. Pienza has pleasant rooms and self-catering apartments at *Giardino Segreto*, Via Condotti 13 (☎0578.748.539, ⓦwww.ilgiardinosegreto .toscana.nu; ❸), and the more upscale hotel *Relais Il Chiostro di Pienza*, a converted Franciscan monastery at Corso Rossellino 26 (☎0578.748.400, ⓦwww.relaisilchiostrodipienza.com; ❺). Non-guests are welcome to visit the cloisters. Its **restaurant**, *La Terrazza* (same telephone number; closed Mon), with expansive views, is the best in Pienza, but pricier than most. More afford-able eating options include *Dal Falco*, a simple trattoria in Piazza Dante with a pleasantly leafy outdoor eating area (☎0578.748.551; closed Fri), and the friendly *Latte di Luna*, (although it can get pricey if you go for the house speci-ality – *maialino arrosto*, roast suckling pig), just inside the walls at Via San Carlo 6 (☎0578.748.606; closed Tues), again with a good outside seating area. There's also plenty of **picnic food**: Pienza is centre of a region producing pecorino sheep's cheese, and has gone overboard on natural food shops: cheesy smells await around every corner.

San Quírico d'Orcia and Bagno Vignoni

SAN QUÍRICO D'ORCIA, a rambling old village, stands at a crossroads 8km west of Pienza. Despite being a major stop for TRA-IN (Siena–Montepulciano), RAMA (Siena–Arcidosso) and SIRA (Montalcino–Rome) buses, its old town is quiet and rather decayed, with an exceptionally pretty Romanesque **Collegiata** church. If you've got your own transport, you can head for the stunning *Castello Ripa d'Orcia*, an isolated castle **hotel-restaurant** 5km southwest of town down a gravel road (☎0577.897.376, ⓦwww.castelloripadorcia.com; minimum stay two nights; ❻).

Also find an hour to visit **BAGNO VIGNONI**, 6km southeast of San Quírico (also served by bus). Its central square is occupied by an arcaded Roman *piscina*, or open pool; the springs still bubble up at a steamy 51°C, and the old, flooded piazza with its backdrop of the Tuscan hills and Renaissance **loggia** – built by the Medici, who, like St Catherine of Siena, took the sulphur cure here – made a memorable scene in Tarkovsky's film *Nostalgia*. The *piscina* has been out of bounds for bathing for some years, but you can enjoy the sulphur springs at the *Piscina Val di Sole*, a modern spa complex at the charac-terful *Posta Marcucci* **hotel** (☎0577.887.112, ⓦwww.hotelpostamarcucci.it; ❻; pool free to guests, €12 per day to others). Pius II's fifteenth-century summer retreat overlooking the *piscina* is now the romantic *Albergo Le Terme* (☎0577.887.150, ⓦwww.albergoleterme.it; ❹). Best **restaurant** is the excellent *Antica Osteria del Leone*, Via dei Mulini 3 (☎0577.877.300; closed Mon).

Montalcino

MONTALCINO is another classic Tuscan hill-town, 20km west of Pienza. Set within a full circuit of walls and watched over by a *rocca*, it looks tremendous from below – and from above, the surrounding countryside strewn with vineyards, orchards and olive groves is equally impressive. Montalcino produces a top-notch DOCG **wine**, Brunello di Montalcino, reckoned by many to be the finest in Italy, and is a quiet place, affluent in an unshowy way from its tourist trade. For a time in the fifteenth century, though, the town was of great symbolic importance: it was the last of the Sienese *comune* to hold out against the Medici, the French and the Spanish after Siena itself had capitulated. This role is acknowledged at the Siena Palio, where the Montalcino contingent – under its medieval banner proclaiming "The Republic of Siena in Montalcino" – takes pride of place.

Arrival and information

Regular **buses** arrive from Buonconvento and Siena, most of which pass first through Torrenieri, from where connections head to Pienza and Montepulciano, and to Arcidosso and Abbadia San Salvatore. Montalcino's bus stop is at the north end of town in Piazza Cavour. The Pro Loco **tourist office** is in the town hall, just off the Piazza del Popolo at Costa del Municipio 8 (April–Oct Tues–Sun 10am–1pm & 2–7pm; Nov–March Tues–Sun 10am–1pm & 2–5.45pm; ℡0577.849.331, ⓦwww.prolocomontalcino.it).

Accommodation

Accommodation is severely limited and it's wise to book ahead at almost any time of year. There is only a handful of hotels, though there are some private **rooms** and numerous agriturismo rooms in the countryside immediately around town. Details are available from the tourist office.

Albergo Il Giglio Via Soccorso Saloni 5 ℡0577.848.167, ⓦwww.gigliohotel.com. A long-established hotel in a central, sixteenth-century town house that has seen better days but has been spruced up and offers pleasant, clean rooms, some with terraces. ❷

Castello di Velona Località Castello di Velona, Castelnuovo dell'Abate ℡0577.800.101, ⓦwww.castellodivelona.it. Superb twenty-room, four-star hotel, isolated in lovely open countryside on its own hill and ringed by cypress. It's close to Castelnuovo dell'Abate and Sant'Antimo, about 10km south of Montalcino. Expensive, but rates drop in low season and there are often web deals. ❾

Dei Capitani Via Lapini 6 ℡0577.847.227, ⓦwww.deicapitani.it. A good, slick three-star choice, with the bonus of a small swimming pool. The 29 rooms vary, however: some are smallish and have no view; others look out over marvellous countryside. Ask to see a selection. ❹

Vecchia Oliviera Via Landi 1 ℡0577.846.028, ⓦwww.vecchiaoliviera.com. Three-star hotel, but more expensive and not quite as central as *Dei Capitani*, its main rival. However, it has a pool, its patio has excellent views, and the eleven fine rooms form part of a well-restored former olive mill close to Porta Cerbaia and the walls. Rooms, however, can suffer from noise from the road nearby. ❺

The Town

The main street, Via Mazzini, leads from **Piazza Cavour** at the north end of town to the **Piazza del Popolo**, an odd little square set beneath the elongated tower of the town hall, based in all but its dimensions on that of Siena. An elegant double loggia occupies another side with, opposite, a wonderful and rather Germanic nineteenth-century café, the *Fiaschetteria Italiana*, which is very much the heart of town life. Steps (Scale di Via Bandi) near the café lead up to the excellent **Museo di Montalcino e Raccolta Archeologica Mediovale e Moderna** (Tues–Sun: Jan–March 10am–1pm & 2–5.30pm; April–Dec 10am–6pm; €4.50 or €6 joint ticket with the Rocca fortress). The quality of the art on show is out of all proportion to the size of the town, and takes in a wealth of Sienese painting and early sculpture. Following Via Ricasoli south brings you to the **Rocca** fortress (April–Oct daily 9am–8pm; Nov–March Tues–Sun 9am–6pm; €4 or €6 joint ticket with Museo Civico), with a plush enoteca (free). You can also get access to the ramparts from here.

Eating and drinking

Montalcino is blessed with good **restaurants**, and you'll be hard-pushed to have a bad meal in any of them. In summer it's worth booking a table at just about any of the following places.

Al Giardino Piazza Cavour 1 ☎0577.849.076, ⓦwww.ristorantealgiardino.it. Pleasant interior, with good local cooking that has won the approval of the Slow Food movement: the chef is the owner. Closed Sun.

Boccon DiVino Località Colombaio Tozzi 201 ☎0577.848.233. A kilometre east of town on the Torrenieri road, this is a great wine bar and restaurant with superb views (and a lovely summer terrace). It's housed in an old rural property, and the dining rooms have a good, rustic air. Food, though, is more refined – and expensive: reckon on €40 or so for a full meal. Closed Tues.

Enoteca Osteria Osticcio Via Matteotti 23 ☎0577.848.271, ⓦwww.osticcio.com. The smartest of Montalcino's many wine bars, but worth paying a little over the odds for your glass of Brunello and light meal simply to enjoy the spectacular views over the Tuscan countryside. Closed Sun.

Il Re di Macchia Via Soccorso Saloni 21 ☎0577.846.116. Montalcino's swankiest restaurant. While the food is usually excellent, its sometimes pretentious *cucina nuova* leanings may not be to all tastes. Closed Thurs.

Taverna Grappolo Blu Via Scale di Moglio 1 ☎0577.847.150. Located in a little alley off Via Mazzini. The old stone-walled interior is cool and appealing, and the unusual pastas are excellent.

Monte Amiata

At 1738m, the extinct volcano of **Monte Amiata** is the highest point in southern Tuscany. Rising in a succession of hills forested in chestnut and fir, it's visible for miles around. A circle of towns rings its lower slopes, but the only one worth visiting for its own sake is **Abbadia San Salvatore**; nonetheless, old castles and bucolic countryside make the area a good detour. Towns such as Abbadia are refreshingly cool for summer walking, and in winter are the nearest ski resorts to Rome. **Buses** serve Abbadia San Salvatore from Siena, Buonconvento, Chiusi and Montepulciano; those from Rome and Grosseto to Abbadia pass first through Arcidosso. Avoid the Monte Amiata **train** station – it's 45km away.

The centre of activity is **ABBADIA SAN SALVATORE**, which shelters at its heart a perfect, self-contained medieval quarter. The Benedictine **abbey**, around which the village developed, was founded under the Lombards and rebuilt in 1036. Today a mere fraction remains of the original, and most remnants date from the Middle Ages; the highlight is a large and beautiful eighth-century **crypt**, its 35 columns decorated with Lombard motifs. The town sees plenty of summer visitors, up here for the landscape, cool breezes and some good easy walks: best is the **Anello della Montagna**, a 29km path which circles the mountain between 900m and 1300m – a long day's walk, or easily manageable in sections round to Arcidosso. In July and August, buses shuttle up to the **summit**, offering a panorama that stretches to the sea. The **tourist office**, Via

Adua 25 (Mon–Sat 9am–1pm & 4–6pm, Sun 9am–1pm; ☎0577.775.811, ⓦwww.amiataturismo.it), is headquarters for the Amiata region. Best of the numerous **hotels** are the *Cesaretti*, Via Trento 37–43 (☎0577.778.198; ❶), and the central *San Marco*, Via Matteotti 19 (☎&ⓕ0577.778.089; ❷).

Pitigliano

Tuscany's deep south, on the Lazio border, is its least-touristed corner. **PITIGLIANO**, the largest town of the area, is best approached along the road from Manciano, 15km west. As you draw close, the town soars above you on a spectacular outcrop of tufa, its quarters linked by the arches of an immense aqueduct. **Etruscan** tombs honeycomb the cliffs, but the town was known for centuries for its flourishing **Jewish** community (see box, p.546). Today it has a slightly grim grandeur, owing to its mighty **fortress** and the tall and largely unaltered alleys of the old Jewish ghetto.

Immediately through the main city gate is **Piazza Garibaldi**, flanked by the fortress (1459–62) and aqueduct (1543) and with views across houses wedged against the cliffside. Within the fortress is the Renaissance **Palazzo Orsini** (Tues–Sun April–Sept 10am–1pm & 3–7pm; rest of the year closes 5/6pm; €3), its lovely interiors filled with jewellery and ecclesiastical ephemera. Opposite the fortress is the **Museo Archeologico** (same hours; €2.50), with an interesting collection of Etruscan vases and trinkets. The fortress backs onto **Piazza della Repubblica**, Pitigliano's elongated main square. Beyond lies the old town proper, a tight huddle of arches and medieval alleys. This is where you'll find the old Jewish Quarter, centred on the Via Zuccarelli, which has been turned into a sort of outdoor museum known as *La Piccolo Gerusalemme* (The Little Jerusalem), with a kosher baker, butcher, a **synagogue** and a small attached Jewish Museum, the **Mostra Ebraico** (May–Sept Mon–Fri & Sun 10am–12.30pm & 4–7pm; rest of the year 10am–12.30pm & 3–5pm; €3). Pitigliano's eighteenth-century synagogue part-collapsed in the 1960s, and lay derelict until renovation in 1995. The grand stone arch and the stairs leading up to the women's gallery are the only survivors of the old building, along with plaques commemorating visits made by grand dukes Ferdinand III in 1823 and Leopold II in 1829. Although

▲ Pitigliano

The Jews of Pitigliano

Jews began moving to Pitigliano from Rome in the thirteenth century and the community flourished until the annexation of the area by the Medici in 1608, when new laws forced the Jews to live in a **ghetto** and wear red clothing as a mark of identification. The granting of **religious freedom** throughout Tuscany by the last Medici ruler, Gian Gastone, in 1735, gave the town a new lease of life. Over the next 125 years, Jewish workshops and artisans on present-day **Via Zuccarelli** thrived, and there was even a Jewish university that attracted students from around Europe. By 1860, a third of the town, or some 2200 people, were Jewish.

It was Italian **Unification** that brought about the end. In the new Italy, individuals felt freer than before to marry across religious lines, and the removal of a Catholic Papal State in central Italy gave Jews a new freedom to travel; many headed to the southern ports to take ships bound for Palestine. By 1900, there were barely a hundred Jews left in Pitigliano. During World War II, the town's Jews were forced into **hiding**, and virtually all were protected from the Nazis by local Christian families. But by 1945 most felt unable to stay on, and departed for Rome, Livorno and Florence (all of which have large Jewish communities). Pitigliano's **synagogue** closed in the late 1950s, and today, in what was formerly one of the centres of Jewish learning in southern Europe, there are almost no Jewish residents left.

the Jewish community is virtually gone, many Italian and foreign Jews still choose to tie the knot here. Staff are happy to show you around the old ghetto, which includes a **bakery** on Via Marghera with a Star of David in its barred window. A few minutes' walk beyond, at the western end of town, you can see traces of the **Etruscan wall** below the Porta Capisotto.

Practicalities

Three RAMA **buses** daily from Manciano and Grosseto, two from Orbetello and one from Siena drop off on **Piazza Petruccioli** just outside the city gate. The helpful **tourist office** at Piazza Garibaldi 51 (Tues–Sun 10am–1pm & 3–7pm; ☎0564.617.111, ⓦwww.comune.pitigliano.gr.it) has maps of the *Vie Cave*, ancient Etruscan paths that weave between tombs (some free, some with admission) and cliffside caves all around the town. With its untouristed lanes and the drama of its cliff-edge site, Pitigliano makes a memorable overnight stop. The only **hotel** is *Guastini*, Piazza Petruccioli 16/34 (☎0564.616.065, ⓦwww .albergoguastini.it; ❸), with a good **restaurant**. Also check out the award-winning, mid-priced *Osteria Il Tufo Allegro*, carved into the cliffs at Vicolo della Costituzione 2 (☎0564.616.192; closed all Tues & Wed lunch).

Eastern Tuscany

The Valdarno (Arno valley) upstream from Florence is a heavily industrialized tract, with no compelling stop before you reach the provincial capital, **Arezzo**, which is visited by foreigners in their thousands for its Piero della Francesca frescoes, and by Italians in even greater numbers for its antiques trade. South of

Arezzo is the ancient hill-town of **Cortona**, whose picturesquely steep streets and sense of hilltop isolation make it an irresistible place for a stopover.

Arezzo and around

Piero della Francesca's frescoes – which belong in the same company as Masaccio's cycle in Florence and Michelangelo's in Rome – are what makes **AREZZO** a tourist destination, but in Italy the city is equally well known for its jewellers, its goldsmiths, and its trade in **antiques**: in the vicinity of the Piazza Grande there are shops filled with museum-quality furniture, and once a month the Fiera Antiquaria turns the piazza into a vast showroom. Arezzo has been one of Tuscany's most prosperous towns for a very long time. Occupying a site that controls the major passes of the central Apennines, it was a key settlement of the Etruscan federation, and grew to be an independent republic in the Middle Ages. In 1289, however, its Ghibelline allegiances led to a catastrophic clash with the Guelph Florentines at Campaldino; though Arezzo temporarily recovered under the leadership of the bellicose Bishop Guido Tarlati, it finally came under the control of Florence in 1384. Nowadays, while Florence's economy has become over-reliant on tourist traffic, well-heeled Arezzo goes its own way, though in recent years it has started to market itself more seriously as a place to visit.

Arrival, information and accommodation

Arezzo is a major stop for **trains** between Florence and Rome, and is also served by a branch line from Perugia; **buses** arrive opposite the train station. The main tourist office is on the edge of the train station forecourt, at Piazza

---

Arezzo festivals

Arezzo's premier folkloric event is the **Giostra del Saracino**, which was first recorded in 1535 and is nowadays held in the Piazza Grande on the first Sunday in September. The day starts off with various costumed parades; at 5pm the action switches to the jousting arena in the piazza, with a procession of some three hundred participants leading the way. Each quarter of the city is represented by a pair of knights on horseback, who do battle with a wooden effigy of a Saracen king. In one hand it holds a shield marked with point scores; in the other it has a cat-o'-three-tails which swings round when the shield is hit, necessitating nifty evasive action from the rider. A golden lance is awarded to the highest-scoring rider. In the days immediately preceding the joust you'll see rehearsals taking place, and in recent years the event has become so popular that a reduced version of the show is now held on the penultimate Saturday of June; check at the tourist office for the latest information on dates and ticket availability.

The musical tradition that began with Guido d'Arezzo (widely regarded as the inventor of modern notation) is kept alive chiefly through the international choral competition that bears his name: the **Concorso Polifonico Guido d'Arezzo**, held in the last week of August. The less ambitious **Pomeriggi Musicali** is a season of free concerts held in various churches, museums and libraries; on average there's one concert a week from mid-January to June.

The **Fiera Antiquaria** takes over the Piazza Grande on the first Sunday of each month and the preceding Saturday. The most expensive stuff is laid out by the Vasari loggia, with cheaper pieces lower down the square and in the side streets.

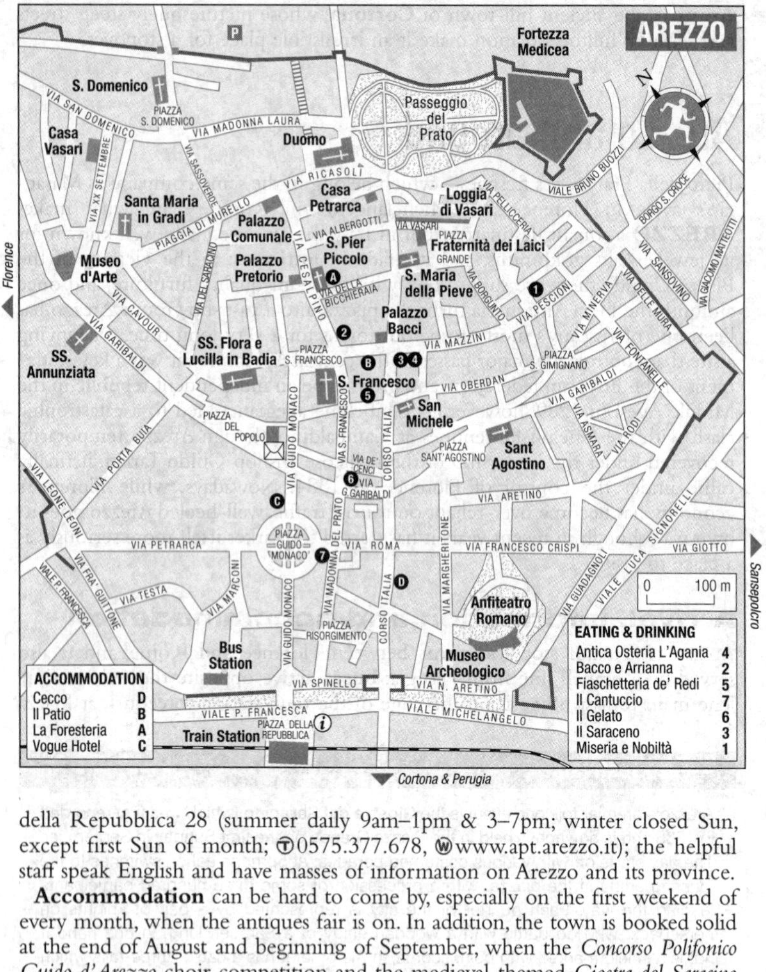

AREZZO
Fortezza Medicea
Passeggio del Prato
S. Domenico
Piazza S. Domenico
Via San Domenico
Via Madonna Laura
Casa Vasari
Duomo
Via XX Settembre
Via Sassoverde
Via Ricasoli
Casa Petrarca
Loggia di Vasari
Viale Bruno Buozzi
Borgo S. Croce
Santa Maria in Gradi
Piaggia di Murello
Palazzo Comunale
Via Albergotti
Via Vasari
Via Pellicceria
Piazza Grande
Fraternità dei Laici
S. Pier Piccolo
Via Cesalpino
Museo d'Arte
Via del Saracino
Palazzo Pretorio
Via della Bicchieraia
S. Maria della Pieve
Via Borgunto
Via Pescioni
Via Minerva
Via Sansovino
Via delle Mura
Via Giacomo Matteotti
Via Cavour
Palazzo Bacci
Via Garibaldi
Via Mazzini
SS. Annunziata
SS. Flora e Lucilla in Badia
Piazza S. Francesco
Piazza S. Gimignano
Via Fontanelle
S. Francesco
Via Oberdan
San Michele
Via Garibaldi
Piazza del Popolo
Via Guido Monaco
Via S. Francesco
Corso Italia
Via Asmara
Via Rodi
Via Porta Buia
Piazza Sant'Agostino
Sant Agostino
Via de' Cenci
Via G. Garibaldi
Via Leone Leoni
Via Aretino
Via Luca Signorelli
Piazza Guido Monaco
Via Petrarca
Via Roma
Via Francesco Crispi
Via Giotto
Via Madonna del Prato
Via Margheritone
Via Guadagnoli
Viale Luca Signorelli
0 100 m
Viale P. Francesca
Via Fra' Guittone
Via Testa
Via Marconi
Anfiteatro Romano
Piazza Risorgimento
Bus Station
Museo Archeologico
EATING & DRINKING
Antica Osteria L'Agania 4
Bacco e Arrianna 2
Fiaschetteria de' Redi 5
Il Cantuccio 7
Il Gelato 6
Il Saraceno 3
Miseria e Nobiltà 1
ACCOMMODATION
Cecco D
Il Patio B
La Foresteria A
Vogue Hotel C
Via Spinello
Via N. Aretino
Viale P. Francesca
Viale Michelangelo
Piazza della Repubblica
Train Station
Florence
Sansepolcro
Cortona & Perugia

della Repubblica 28 (summer daily 9am–1pm & 3–7pm; winter closed Sun, except first Sun of month; ⓣ0575.377.678, ⓦwww.apt.arezzo.it); the helpful staff speak English and have masses of information on Arezzo and its province.

Accommodation can be hard to come by, especially on the first weekend of every month, when the antiques fair is on. In addition, the town is booked solid at the end of August and beginning of September, when the *Concorso Polifonico Guido d'Arezzo* choir competition and the medieval-themed *Giostra del Saracino* pageant follow in quick succession. At the time of going to press, the city's youth hostel, the *Ostello Villa Severi* (some way north of the centre at Via Francesco Redi 13), was closed for rebuilding; check the tourism website for the latest situation.

Cecco Corso Italia 215 ⓣ0575.20.986, ⓦwww.hotelcecco.com. Very central 42-room two-star, above a restaurant of the same name; spacious if slightly institutional in feel. Rooms without private baths cost almost €20 less than the rest. ②

Il Patio Via Cavour 23 ⓣ0575.401.962, ⓦwww.hotelpatio.it. A small, welcoming and not overly expensive four-star, 1min stroll f rom San Francesco. The decor reflects Arezzo's love of antiques, but it's not oppressively olde-worlde. ⑦

La Foresteria Via Bicchieraia 32 ⓣ&ⓕ0575.370.474. The nicest budget accommodation in central Arezzo, *La Foresteria* comprises a dozen unfussy and well-decorated rooms in the former convent of the church of San Pier Piccolo. No credit cards. ③

Vogue Hotel Via Guido Monaco 54 ⓣ0575.24.361, ⓦwww.voguehotel.it. The new four-star *Vogue* has 26 rooms, each uniquely styled, but all with a sleekly modern look. It's a refreshing change from the retro atmosphere in the city's other higher-end hotels. ⑥

The Town

There are two distinct parts to Arezzo: the older quarter, at the top of the hill, and the businesslike lower town, much of which remains hidden from day-trippers, as it spreads behind the train station and the adjacent bus terminal. From the station forecourt, go straight ahead for Via Guido Monaco, the traffic axis between the upper and lower town. The parallel Corso Italia, now pedestrianized, is the route to walk up the hill.

The Basilica di San Francesco

In the heart of the old town, west of the main Corso Italia, stands the Basilica di **San Francesco** (summer Mon–Fri 9am–7pm, Sat 9am–6pm, Sun 1–6pm; winter closes Mon–Fri 6pm, Sat & Sun 5.30pm), home to Piero della Francesca's magnificent **fresco** cycle.

The frescoes are in the choir and can be seen from the nave, but you need to get closer to really appreciate them, and you're not allowed any closer than the altar steps unless you've bought a ticket (€6): visits are limited to 25 people at time (same hours as the church), and to thirty minutes per group. You are encouraged to book tickets in advance by phone (T0575.352.727) or online (through the tourist office website. However, you can make a reservation in person at the ticket office beside the church, and you may not have to wait long before getting in; in winter there's rarely any wait at all.

Built in 1320s, the plain basilica earned its renown in the early 1450s, when the Bacci family commissioned **Piero della Francesca** to depict **The Legend of the True Cross**, a story in which the wood of the Cross forms the link in the cycle of redemption that begins with humanity's original sin. Starting with the *Death of Adam* on the right wall, Piero painted the series in narrative sequence, working continuously until about 1457. However, the episodes are not arranged in narrative sequence, as the artist preferred to arrange them according to the precepts of symmetry: thus the two battle scenes face each other across the chapel, rather than coming where the story dictates. The literary source for the cycle, the Golden Legend by Jacopo de Voragine, is a very convoluted story, but the outline of the tale is as follows: a sprig from the Tree of Knowledge is planted in Adam's mouth; Solomon orders a bridge to be built from wood taken from the tree that grew from Adam's grave (below the *Death of Adam*, to the left); the visiting Queen of Sheba kneels, sensing the holiness of the wood, and then later (to the right) tells Solomon of her prophecy that the same wood will be used to crucify a man; Solomon then orders the beam to be buried (back wall, middle right); the Emperor Constantine (back wall, lower right) has a vision of victory under the sign of the Cross; Constantine defeats his rival Maxentius (lower right wall); under torture, Judas the Levite (back wall, middle left) reveals to St Helena, mother of Constantine, the burial places of the crosses from Golgotha, which are then excavated (middle left wall); the True Cross is recognized when it brings about a man's resurrection; and the Persian king Chosroes, who had stolen the Cross, is defeated by Emperor Heraclius (lower left wall), who returns the Cross to Jerusalem (upper left wall).

Arezzo's biglietto unico

A €12 ticket gives you a single admission to the following monuments and museums in Arezzo: the Museo Archeologico, the Museo Statale d'Arte Medievale e Moderna, the Casa Vasari and the della Francesca frescoes in San Francesco. The ticket can be bought at any of these four locations, but bear in mind that immediate admission to San Francesco may not be possible (see above).

The rest of the town

Farther up the Corso from San Francesco stands one of the finest Romanesque structures in Tuscany, the twelfth-century Pieve di Santa Maria (daily: summer 8am–1pm & 3–7pm; winter 8am–noon & 3–6pm). Its arcaded facade, elaborate yet severe, is unusual in presenting its front to a fairly narrow street rather than to the town's main square. Dating from the 1210s, the carvings of the months over the portal are an especially lively group. Known locally as "the tower of the hundred holes", the campanile was added in the fourteenth century. The oldest section of the chalky grey interior is the raised sanctuary, where the altarpiece is Pietro Lorenzetti's Madonna and Saints polyptych, painted in 1320. The unfamiliar saint on the far left, accompanying Matthew, the Baptist and John the Evangelist, is St Donatus, the second bishop of Arezzo, who was martyred in 304. His relics are in the crypt, encased in a beautiful gold and silver bust made in 1346.

The steeply sloping Piazza Grande, on the other side of the Pieve, has a diverting assortment of buildings, with the wooden balconied apartments on the east side facing the apse of the Pieve, the Baroque Palazzo dei Tribunali and the Palazzetto della Fraternità dei Laici, which has a Renaissance upper storey and a Gothic lower. The piazza's northern edge is formed by the arcades of the Loggia di Vasari, occupied by shops that in some instances still retain their original sixteenth-century stone counters. At the highest point of town looms the large and unfussy **Duomo** (daily 6.30am–12.30pm & 3–6.30pm). Inside, just beyond the organ, is the tomb of Bishop Guido Tarlati, head of the *Comune* of Arezzo during its resurgence in the early fourteenth century; the monument, plated with reliefs showing scenes from the militaristic bishop's career, was possibly designed by Giotto. The small fresco nestled against the right side of the tomb is Piero della Francesca's Magdalene, his only work in Arezzo outside San Francesco.

A short distance north of the Duomo you'll come across the church of San Domenico (daily 8am–7pm), where, above the high altar, hangs a dolorous Crucifix by Cimabue (1260), painted when the artist was about 20. Signs point the way to the nearby **Casa Vasari**, Via XX Settembre 55 (Mon & Wed–Sat 8.30am–7pm, Sun 8.30am–1pm; €2), designed and decorated luridly by the celebrated biographer-architect-painter for himself. Down the slope, at Via San Lorentino 8, the fifteenth-century Palazzo Bruni-Ciocchi houses the **Museo Statale d'Arte Medievale e Moderna** (Tues–Sun 8.30am–7pm; €4), with a collection of minor paintings by local artists and majolica work dating from the thirteenth to the eighteenth centuries.

All the principal sights are in the upper part of town, with two exceptions. The **Museo Archeologico** (daily 8.30am–7.30pm; €4), which occupies part of a monastery built into the wall of the town's Roman amphitheatre, is impressive chiefly for the marvellously coloured coralline vases produced here in the first century BC – the skill of Arezzo's glassblowers achieved a reputation throughout the Roman world. Ten-minutes' walk away, south of the city centre at the end of Viale Mecenate, stands Arezzo's most exquisite church, Santa Maria delle Grazie (daily 8am–7pm). Built at the instigation of St Bernardino, the church is fronted by a tiny pine-ringed meadow that's flanked by a pair of arcades, and is entered through a delicate portico built by Benedetto da Maiano in the 1470s. The church is essentially a single room, containing little more than a few seats and an altarpiece by Parri Spinello, painted on the instructions of St Bernardino; the beautiful marble and terracotta altar that encases it was created by Andrea della Robbia.

Eating and drinking

Arezzo's **restaurants** are of a generally high standard, and you'll find some nice **cafés** around piazzas Guido Monaco, Grande and San Francesco, and along

Corso Italia. For **ice cream**, the first choice is *Il Gelato*, off Corso Italia at Via de' Cenci 24, while for picnic provisions you can't do better than *Sbarbacipolle*, at Via Garibaldi 120.

Antica Osteria L'Agania Via Mazzini 10 ℡ 0575.25.381. A very good and informal trattoria with welcoming atmosphere and local dishes (special emphasis on truffles and mushrooms in season), at around €35 per head; it draws much of its clientele from the antiques dealers. Closed Mon & part of June.

🏃 **Bacco e Arrianna** Via Cesalpino 10. A terrific enoteca very close to San Francesco, with delicious food, too. Closed Mon & July.
Fiaschetteria de' Redi Via de' Redi 10. Busy little *osteria* with a superb range of vintages and decent simple meals. Closed Mon.
Il Cantuccio Via Madonna del Prato 76 ℡ 0575.26.830. Good-value food served in a

pleasant vaulted cellar. The home-made pasta dishes are particularly delicious. Expect to pay in the region of €30 per person. Closed Wed.
Il Saraceno Via Mazzini 6 ℡ 0575.27.644. Family-run trattoria, founded in 1946, with a good wine cellar and menus of traditional Aretine specialities (notably duck) at around €35 per head; good wood-oven pizzas too. Closed Wed & part of Jan.

🏃 **Miseria e Nobiltà** Via Piaggia di San Bartolomeo 2 ℡ 0575.21.245. With its enticing pan-Italian menu and its medieval vaulted dining room, this very stylish (but not expensive) restaurant is one of the best in town. Tues–Sun 7–11.30pm.

East of Arezzo: the Piero trail

Arezzo is the springboard for the Piero della Francesca art itinerary, which extends eastwards to Urbino and Rimini via the village of **MONTERCHI**, famous as the home of the *Madonna del Parto*, a rare depiction of the pregnant Madonna. The painting is now the focal point of a permanent exhibition (Tues–Sun 9am–1pm & 2–7pm; winter closes 6pm; €3) recounting the technical details of the fresco's restoration, and also that of the San Francesco cycle in Arezzo.

SANSEPOLCRO, 25km northeast of Arezzo (served by regular SITA **buses** and by **trains** from Perugia and Città di Castello), is where Piero della Francesca was born in the 1410s, and where he spent much of his life. Sansepolcro's **Museo Civico** (daily: June 15–Sept 15 9.30am–1.30pm & 2.30–7pm; rest of year 9.30am–1pm & 2.30–6pm; €6), houses a sizeable collection of pictures, including work by Pontormo, Signorelli and Santi di Tito, but the primary focus of attention is della Francesca's *Resurrection*. Painted for the adjoining town hall in the 1450s and moved here in the sixteenth century, it's one of the most overpowering images of the event ever created, with a muscular Christ stepping onto the edge of the tomb – banner in hand – as if it were the rampart of a conquered city. Elsewhere in the museum, an early della Francesca masterpiece, the *Madonna della Misericordia* polyptych, epitomizes the graceful solemnity of his work.

The best place to stay is the welcoming A *Fiorentino*, Via Pacioli 60 (℡ 0575.740.350, 🖰 www.albergofiorentino.com; ❷), which has been in business since 1807 and has a very good **restaurant** (closed Fri), in which you can expect to pay around €35. Another excellent restaurant in the same price range is the family-run *Da Ventura*, Via Niccolò Aggiunti 30 (℡ 0575.742.560; closed Sun eve & Mon).

Cortona

Travelling south from Arezzo you enter the **Valdichiana**, reclaimed swampland that is now prosperous farming country. From the valley floor, a 5km road winds up through terraces of vines and olives to the hill-town of CORTONA, whose heights survey a vast domain: the Valdichiana stretching westwards, with

Lago Trasimeno visible over the low hills to the south. The steep streets of Cortona are more or less untouched by modern building: limitations of space have confined almost all later development to the lower suburb of Camucia, which is where the approach road begins. Even without its monuments and art treasures, this would be a good place to rest up, with decent hotels and excellent restaurants. In recent years, though, Cortona's tourist traffic has increased markedly, in the wake of Frances Mayes' *Under the Tuscan Sun* and *Bella Tuscany*, books that continue to entice coachloads of her readers to the town. Accordingly, if you're thinking of visiting any time between Easter and late September, you'd be well advised to book your accommodation in advance.

Arrival, information and accommodation

Cortona is easily visited as a day-trip from Arezzo, but in many ways it's the more pleasant of the two in which to spend the night. There are hourly LFI buses between the two towns, and stopping trains from Arezzo call at Camucia-Cortona station, from where a shuttle (roughly every 30min) takes ten minutes to run up to the old town; buy tickets at the station bar. Florence–Rome trains stop at Teróntola, 10km south, which is also served by a shuttle roughly every hour (25min to Cortona's Piazza Garibaldi); Teróntola is the station to get off at if you are approaching from Umbria. The centre is closed to all but essential traffic, so if you're driving you should use one of the free car parks on the periphery.

The tourist office is at Via Nazionale 42 (May–Sept Mon–Sat 9am–1pm & 3–7pm, Sun 9am–1pm; Oct–April Mon–Sat 9am–1pm & 3–6pm; ☏0575.630.352, ⓦwww.cortonaweb.net).

Hotels

Sabrina Via Roma 37 ☏0575.630.397, ⓔinfo @cortonastorica.com. A cosy and inexpensive eight-room three-star; the breakfasts are excellent and it has a nice family atmosphere. ❸

San Michele Via Guelfa 15 ☏0575.604.348, ⓦwww.hotelsanmichele.net. The most expensive and luxurious in-town choice, this handsome 43-room four-star has been converted from a rambling medieval town house. The rooms are a generous size, even if the decor is rather routine. ❻

Villa Marsili Via Cesare Battisti 13 ☏0575.605.252, ⓦwww.villamarsili.net. Situated a short distance down the slope from Piazza Garibaldi, this capacious four-star – occupying an eighteenth-century villa – looks unexceptional from the outside, but the rooms are

nicely furnished with antiques (not suffocatingly so), and command a very photogenic view of the valley. Prices are very good as well – even in high season it's sometimes possible to pick up a room for a little over €100, though you're likelier to pay in the region of €150–200. ❻

Hostel

Ostello San Marco Via G. Maffei 57 ☏0575.601.392, ⓦwww.cortonahostel.com. Clean and spacious 80-bed HI hostel situated in the heart of the town in an old monastery, with fantastic views from the dormitories and friendly management. Dorm beds €14; doubles and family rooms available (€18 per person). Open mid-March to mid-Oct; reception open daily 7–10am & 3.30pm–midnight.

The Town

From **Piazza Garibaldi** Via Nazionale, the only level street in town, connects to **Piazza della Repubblica**, which is overlooked by the grandstand staircase of the squat Palazzo del Comune. Just behind is **Piazza Signorelli**, named after Luca Signorelli (1441–1523), Cortona's most famous son, and site of the Museo dell'Accademia Etrusca e della Città di Cortona – or MAEC, for short (April–Oct daily 10am–7pm; Nov–March Tues–Sun 10am–5pm; €7, or €10 combined ticket with Museo Diocesano). On the lowest floor, which charts the development of Cortona from the earliest recorded settlements to Roman times, some spectacular specimens of Etruscan gold, turquoise and crystal jewellery catch the eye. Upstairs there's a good deal more Etruscan material on show, most notably a bronze lamp from the fourth century BC, which is honoured with a room all to itself. Etruscan and later bronze figurines (none of them labelled) fill an avenue of cabinets in the middle of the main hall, surrounded by some fairly undistinguished pictures, though there's work by Pietro da Cortona, Signorelli and Pinturicchio amongst the dross.

Piazza Signorelli links with Piazza Duomo, where the **Duomo** sits hard up against the city walls. The interior is rather chilly, but there's a Pietro da Cortona Nativity on the third altar on the left, and a possible Andrea del Sarto (an *Assumption*) to the left of the high altar. Across the little piazza, a couple of churches have been knocked together to form the **Museo Diocesano** (same hours as MAEC; €5, or €10 combined ticket with MAEC), where the highlight of the small collection of Renaissance art is an exquisite *Annunciation*, painted by Fra' Angelico when he was based at Cortona's monastery of San Domenico.

In the upper town, the most engaging building is **San Nicolò**, a frail little church with a gravel forecourt, a delicate portico and a fine wooden ceiling that's sagging with age. Signorelli's high altarpiece is a standard which he painted on both sides – ring the bell and the caretaker will take you to see it. Near the summit of the town stands **Santa Margherita**, resting place of St Margaret of Cortona, the town's patron saint. Her tomb, with marble angels lifting the lid of her sarcophagus, was created in the mid-fourteenth century, and is now mounted on the wall to the left of the chancel, while her remains are on display in a glass coffin directly behind the chancel.

Eating and drinking

For a town of its size, Cortona has an abundance of good **restaurants**. Nearly all the places to eat and drink are within a very short distance of Piazza della Repubblica.

Dardano Via Dardano 24 ☎0575.601.944. An excellent, unpretentious, inexpensive and very popular trattoria – it's full to bursting most nights. Closed Wed.

Fufluns Via Ghibellina 1–3. If pizza is all you need, this spacious and bustling place is the first choice. Closed Tues.

Osteria del Teatro Via Maffei 5 ☎0575.630.556. Occupying the whole lower floor of a rambling old mansion, this is a good-naturedly busy (sometimes frantic) place, featuring delicious home-made pastas on a meat-heavy menu; portions are generous and the prices more than fair – the bill

should be around €35 per person. Closed Wed & mid-Nov to mid-Dec.

Route 66 Via Nazionale 78. This self-styled "music bar" attracts the youngest crowd in town – the soundtrack is usually loud, and it has occasional DJ nights. It does food too, but it's not the nosh that makes it popular. Open Tues–Sun till 3am.

Taverna Pane e Vino Piazza Signorelli 27. A good choice if you're after a quick lunch or a light evening meal: the menu offers various types of bruschetta, a wide selection of salamis and cheeses, plus a few more substantial dishes – and the wine list runs to some 900 different vintages. Closed Mon.

Travel details

Trains

Arezzo to: Assisi (12 daily; 1hr 35min); Bibbiena (hourly; 45min); Bolzano (3 daily; 5–7hr); Camucia-Cortona (hourly; 20min); Chiusi (hourly; 1hr); Florence (hourly; 1hr); Foligno (every 2hr; 1hr 45min); Orvieto (hourly; 50min–1hr 20min); Perugia

(8 daily; 1hr 10min); Rome (hourly; 1hr 40min); Teróntola-Cortona (hourly; 25min); Venice (5 daily; 5hr); Verona (3 daily; 3hr 30min–4hr 45min).
Empoli to: Florence (every 30min; 35min); Pisa (every 30min; 30–55min); Siena (every 30min; 55min–1hr 10min).

Florence to: Arezzo (hourly; 1hr); Assisi (8 daily; 2hr–2hr 30min); Bari (15 daily; 7hr–9hr 30min, change at Bologna or Rome); Bologna (every 30min; 1hr–1hr 40min); Bolzano (5 daily; 4hr–4hr 30min); Empoli (every 20min; 30min); Genoa (2 daily; 3hr 10min); Lecce (13 daily; 9hr 10min–15hr, change at Bologna or Rome); Livorno (12 daily; 1hr 30min); Lucca (every 30min; 1hr 15min–1hr 45min); Milan (hourly; 2hr 45min–3hr 30min); Naples (hourly; 3hr 30min–5hr); Perugia (8 daily; 1hr 35min–2hr 10min); Pisa airport (6 daily; 70–1hr 30min); Pisa central (every 30min; 60–1hr 20min); Reggio Calabria (from Campo Marte 5 direct trains daily; 9hr 15min–11hr; from Santa Maria Novella, changing at Rome 6 daily; 8hr 10min–10hr); Rimini (hourly; 2hr 20min–3hr 30min, change at Bologna); Rome (every 20min; 1hr 45min–3hr 40min); Siena (hourly; 1hr 30min–2hr); Trieste (3 daily; 4hr 40min–6hr 20min); Udine (3 daily; 4hr 20min–6hr); Venice (9 daily; 2hr 50min–3hr 45min); Verona (6 daily; 2hr 20min–2hr 45min); Viareggio (14 daily; 1hr 20min–1hr 55min).
Grosseto to: Cécina (17 daily; 45min–1hr 20min); Florence (6 daily; 3hr); Livorno (hourly; 1hr 10min–2hr); Orbetello (16 daily; 20–30min); Pisa (hourly; 1hr 20min–2hr 20min); Rome (hourly; 1hr 40min–2hr 20min); Siena (9 daily; 1hr 20min–1hr 45min).
Livorno to: Florence (12 daily; 1hr 30min); La Spezia (hourly; 1hr–1hr 30min); Pisa (every 20min; 15min); Rome (19 daily; 2hr 45min–3hr 45min).
Lucca to: Florence (every 30min; 1hr 15min–1hr 45min); Pisa (hourly; 20min); Pistoia (every 30min; 45min); Viareggio (hourly; 20min).
Pisa to: Empoli (every 30min; 30–55min); Florence (every 30min; 1hr–1hr 30min); Livorno (every 20min; 15min); Lucca (hourly; 20–30min); Viareggio (every 30min; 15–20min).
Siena to: Asciano (11 daily; 30min); Buonconvento (9 daily; 20–30min); Chiusi (hourly; 1hr 30min); Empoli (every 30min; 55min–1hr 10min); Grosseto (9 daily; 1hr 20min–1hr 45min).

Buses

Arezzo to: Città di Castello (12–15 daily; 1hr 30min); Cortona (hourly; 1hr); Sansepolcro (17 daily; 1hr); Siena (5 daily Mon–Fri; 2hr).
Chiusi to: Montepulciano (14 daily; 45min).

Cortona to: Arezzo (hourly; 50min); Chianciano (4 daily; 1hr), changing for Montepulciano.
Florence to: Bibbiena (8 daily; 2hr 15min); Castellina in Chianti (3 daily; 1hr 35min); Greve in Chianti (3 daily; 1hr 5min); Poggibonsi (10 daily; 1hr 20min); Radda in Chianti (1 daily Mon–Sat; 1hr 40min); Siena (12 express daily, plus 9 stopping services; 1hr 15min express); Volterra (6 daily; 2hr 25min). In addition to these state-owned SITA services, numerous independent bus companies operate from Florence to most Tuscan towns, including Arezzo, Grosseto, Lucca, Pisa, Sansepolcro and Viareggio.
Livorno to: Piombino (8 daily; 2hr); Pisa (every 30min; 20min).
Lucca to: Florence (30 daily; 1hr 15min); La Spezia (7 daily; 2hr 20min); Livorno (3 daily; 1hr 20min); Pisa (35 daily; 40min); Pisa Airport (3 daily; 1hr 30min); Viareggio (30 daily; 40min).
Massa Maríttima to: Piombino (2 daily; 25min); San Galgano (2 daily; 1hr); Siena (2 daily; 1hr 40min).
Montalcino to: Buonconvento (hourly; 35min); Monte Amiata (2 daily; 1hr); Siena (6 daily; 1hr).
Montepulciano to: Buonconvento (7 daily; 1hr); Chianciano (every 30min; 25min); Chiusi (every 30min; 50min); Pienza (7 daily; 20min); San Quírico (7 daily; 40min); Torrenieri (7 daily; 50min).
Pisa to: Florence (hourly; 1hr 10min); La Spezia (7 daily; 1hr 20min); Livorno (every 30min; 20min); Viareggio (hourly; 20min).
San Gimignano to: Poggibonsi (hourly; 35min).
Siena to: Abbadia San Salvatore (3 daily; 1hr 20min); Arezzo (4 daily; 2hr); Buonconvento (10 daily; 35min); Florence (30 daily; 1hr 30min–3hr); Grosseto (4 daily; 2hr); Massa Maríttima (3 daily; 1hr 20min); Montalcino (6 daily; 1hr); Montepulciano (4 daily; 1hr 20min); San Galgano (3 daily; 40min); San Gimignano (16 daily; 1hr–1hr 30min); Volterra (6 daily; 2hr).
Viareggio to: Pisa (every 30min; 35min).
Volterra to: Colle Val d'Elsa (for connections to Florence & Siena; 4 daily; 45min); Pisa (1 daily; 1hr 10min).

Ferries

Livorno to: Capraia (1–2 daily; 3hr); Portoferraio (1 daily; 4hr).
Piombino to: Portoferraio (10–18 daily; 1hr).

Umbria

CHAPTER 9

Highlights

✳ **Galleria Nazionale dell'Umbria** The region's finest and largest collection of medieval and Renaissance Umbrian paintings. See p.564

✳ **Gubbio** Best-looking of Umbria's medieval hill-towns, and without Assisi's crowds and commercialism. See p.571

✳ **Basilica di San Francesco** Burial place of St Francis and one of Italy's great buildings, with frescoes by Giotto and Simone Martini. See p.578

✳ **Valle di Spoleto** A swathe of country with four of the region's most compelling villages: Spello, Bevagna, Trevi and Montefalco. See p.583

✳ **San Francesco, Montefalco** One of Umbria's best small galleries, with a major fresco cycle by Benozzo Gozzoli. See p.585

✳ **Valnerina** A verdant, mountain-edged valley dotted with hill-villages and spectacular views. See p.594

✳ **Piano Grande** A glorious upland plain, the centrepiece of the Monti Sibillini national park. See p.596

✳ **Duomo, Orvieto** On a par with the cathedrals in Milan and Siena, Orvieto's Duomo has a glorious facade and a majestic fresco cycle by Luca Signorelli. See p.605

▲ Gubbio's medieval centre

Umbria

O
ften referred to as "the green heart of Italy", Umbria is a predominantly beautiful and – despite the many visitors – a largely unspoiled
region of rolling hills, woods, streams and valleys. Within its borders it
also contains a dozen or so classic hill-towns, each resolutely individual
and crammed with artistic and architectural treasures to rival bigger and more
famous cities. To the east, pastoral countryside gives way to more rugged
scenery, none better than the dramatic twists and turns of the Valnerina and the
high mountain landscapes of the Parco Nazionale dei Monti Sibillini.

Umbria was named by the Romans after the mysterious **Umbrii**, a tribe
cited by Pliny as the oldest in Italy, and one that controlled territory reaching
into present-day Tuscany and Marche. Although there is scant archeological
evidence about them, it seems that their influence was mainly confined to the
east of the Tiber; the darker and more sombre towns to the west – such as
Perugia and Orvieto – were founded by the **Etruscans**, whose rise forced the
Umbrii to retreat into the eastern hills. Roman domination was eventually
undermined by the so-called barbarian invasions, in the face of which the
Umbrians withdrew into fortified hill-towns, paving the way for a pattern of
bloody rivalry between independent city-states that continued through the
Middle Ages. Weakened by constant warfare, most towns eventually fell to the
papacy, entering a period of economic and cultural stagnation that continued
to the very recent past.

Historically, however, Umbria is best known as the birthplace of several saints,
St Benedict and **St Francis of Assisi** being the most famous, and for a
religious tradition that earned the region such names as *Umbra santa*, *Umbra
mistica* and *la terra dei santi* ("the land of saints"). The landscape itself has contributed much to this mystical reputation, and even on a fleeting trip it's impossible
to miss the strange quality of the Umbrian light, an oddly luminous silver haze
that hangs over the hills.

After years as an impoverished backwater, Umbria has capitalized on its
charms. Foreign acquisition of rural property is now as rapid as it was in Tuscany
thirty years ago, though outsiders have done nothing to curb the region's
renewed sense of identity and youthful enthusiasm, nor to blunt the artistic
initiatives that have turned Umbria into one of the most flourishing cultural
centres in Italy. Headline-grabbing earthquakes in 1997 briefly dented tourist
numbers, but they had a negligible long-term effect – at least as far as visitors
are concerned – as the majority of sights suffered little damage.

Most visitors head for **Perugia**, **Assisi** – the latter with its extraordinary
frescoes by Giotto in the Basilica di San Francesco – or **Orvieto**, whose

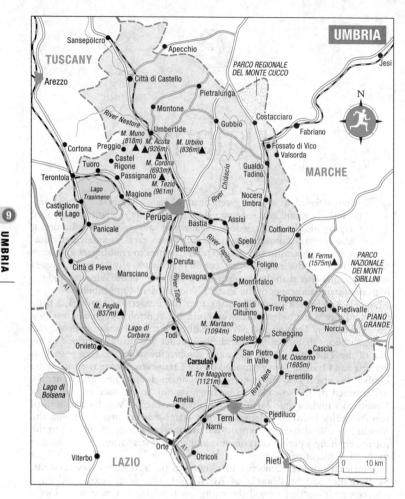

UMBRIA

TUSCANY

Sansepólcro
Apecchio
Jesi
Arezzo
Città di Castello
PARCO REGIONALE DEL MONTE CUCCO
Pietralunga
River Nestore
Montone
N
Umbertide
Gubbio
Costacciaro
M. Muno (818m) ▲ *M. Acuta (926m)* ▲
Fabriano
Cortona
Preggio
M. Urbino (836m) ▲
Fossato di Vico
Tuoro
Castel Rigone
M. Corona (693m) ▲
Gualdo Tadino
Valsorda
MARCHE
Terontola
Passignano
M. Tezio (961m) ▲
River Chiáscio
Lago Trasimeno
Magione
Nocera Umbra
Castiglione del Lago
Perugia
Bastia
Assisi
Panicale
Spello
Colfiorito
Bettona
River Topino
Foligno
M. Ferma (1575m) ▲
PARCO NAZIONALE DEI MONTI SIBILLINI
Città di Pieve
Deruta
Marsciano
Bevagna
River Tiber
Montefalco
M. Peglia (837m) ▲
Fonti di Clitunno
Triponzo
Trevi
Preci
Piedivalle
PIANO GRANDE
Lago di Corbara
M. Martano (1094m) ▲
Todi
Spoleto
Scheggino
Norcia
Orvieto
Carsulae ▼
San Pietro in Valle
M. Coscerno (1685m) ▲
Cascia
M. Tre Maggiore (1121m) ▲
River Nera
Lago di Bolsena
Ferentillo
Amelia
Piediluco
Terni
Narni
Orte
Otricoli
Rieti
Viterbo
LAZIO

0   10 km

Duomo is one of the greatest Gothic buildings in the country. For a taste of the region's more understated qualities, it's best to concentrate on lesser-known places such as **Todi**, **Gubbio**, ranked as the most perfect medieval centre in Italy, and **Spoleto**, for many people the outstanding Umbrian town. Although there are few unattractive parts of the Umbrian landscape (the factories of Terni and the Tiber Valley being the largest blots), some districts are especially enticing: principally the mountainous **Valnerina**, **Piano Grande** and **Lago Trasimeno**, the last of which is the largest lake in the Italian peninsula, with plenty of opportunities for swimming and watersports.

Getting around the region by public transport presents no problems. Distances between the main sights are short, and there are excellent rail links both within the region and to Florence and Rome. The official tourist board **website** for the area is ⓦwww.regioneumbria.eu. For travel information, visit ⓦwww.trasporti.regione.umbria.it.

Regional food and wine

The cuisine of landlocked, hilly Umbria relies heavily on rustic staples – pastas and roast meats – and in the past tended to be simple and homely. The region is also the only area outside Piemonte where **truffles** are found in any abundance, and their perfumed shavings, particularly in the east of the region, find their way onto eggs, pasta, fish and meat – but at a price that prohibits overindulgence.

Meat plays a leading role – especially **lamb** and **pork**, which is made into hams, sausage, salami and, most famously, *la porchetta*, whole suckling pig stuffed with rosemary or sage, roasted on a spit. **Game** may also crop up on some menus, most often as pigeon, pheasant or guinea fowl. The range of **fish** is restricted by the lack of a coast, but trout is pulled out of the Nera, Clitunno and Scordo rivers, while the lakes of Piediluco and Trasimeno yield eels, pike, tench and grey mullet. **Vegetable** delicacies include tiny lentils from Castelluccio, beans from Trasimeno, and celery and cardoons from around Trevi. Umbrian **olive oil**, though less hyped than Tuscan oils, has a high reputation, particularly that from around Trevi and Spoleto.

As for desserts, Perugia is renowned for its **chocolate** and pastries. **Cheeses** tend to be standard issue, although some smaller producers survive in the mountains around Norcia and Gubbio.

Umbria used to be best known outside Italy for fresh, dry white **wines**. Orvieto, once predominantly a medium-sweet wine, has been revived in a dry style, though the original *abboccato* is still available. However, the pre-eminence of Orvieto in the domestic market has been successfully challenged by Grechetto, an inexpensive and almost unfailingly good wine made by countless producers across the region. Umbria's quest for quality is also increasingly reflected in a growing number of small producers, many of which have followed the lead of Giorgio Lungarotti, one of the pioneers of Umbrian viticulture (any wine with his name on is reliable), and in some outstanding reds, notably the tiny Montefalco DOCG region close to Spoleto.

Perugia

The provincial capital, **PERUGIA** is the most obvious, if not the most picturesque, base to kick off a tour of Umbria. Although the centre of town is still medieval, it's surrounded by ugly suburbs and a considerable amount of industry. In summer, the streets become claustrophobic and exhausting, so you probably won't want to spend a lot of time here. On the other hand, there's at least a day's worth of good sightseeing, and it's not a bad place to base yourself if you want to explore the surrounding area: it has big-city amenities and trains run to all the major highlights, complemented by fast new roads and an extensive bus network.

The town's main cultural draw in summer is **Umbria Jazz**, Italy's foremost jazz event – tickets are best acquired well in advance via the website (Ⓦwww .umbriajazz.com).

Arrival and information

Arriving by **air** (Ryanair flies from the UK) you'll land at the Aeroporto Regionale Umbro Sant'Egido (Ⓣ075.592.141, Ⓦwww.airport.umbria.it), 12km east of the centre. Bus shuttles (€3.50) meet incoming flights and run to Piazza Italia. Arriving on the state train network you'll find yourself to the southwest of the centre at **Piazza Vittorio Veneto**: from here it's a fifteen-minute ride by bus (anything to Piazza Italia or Piazza Matteotti will do). City

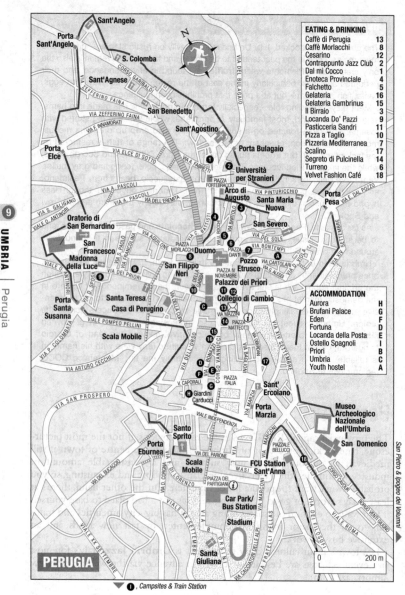

EATING & DRINKING

Caffè di Perugia	13
Caffè Morlacchi	8
Cesarino	12
Contrappunto Jazz Club	2
Dal mi Cocco	1
Enoteca Provinciale	4
Falchetto	5
Gelateria	16
Gelateria Gambrinus	15
Il Birraio	3
Locanda Do' Pazzi	9
Pasticceria Sandri	11
Pizza a Taglio	10
Pizzeria Mediterranea	7
Scalino	17
Segreto di Pulcinella	14
Turreno	6
Velvet Fashion Café	18

ACCOMMODATION

Aurora	H
Brufani Palace	G
Eden	F
Fortuna	D
Locanda della Posta	E
Ostello Spagnoli	I
Priori	B
Umbria	C
Youth hostel	A

PERUGIA

0   200 m

▼ **①**, Campsites & Train Station

bus tickets are available from the station newsagents. Avoid walking to the centre – it's a steep haul on busy roads. If you're coming on the private FCU (Ferrovie Centrale Umbra) lines from Todi or Terni to the south, or from Città di Castello or Sansepolcro to the north, you'll arrive at the more central **Stazione Sant'Anna**, near the bus terminal at **Piazza dei Partigiani**. From this large square you can jump on a *scala mobile* (escalator) as it climbs through weird subterranean streets to **Piazza Italia**.

If you're arriving by **car** all the town's approaches are up steep hills and the signposting leaves plenty to be desired. The centre is closed to traffic at peak times, and you'll do best to leave your car at the main train station and take a bus. Alternatively you could head towards one of the big peripheral car parks – Piazza dei Partigiani is the largest and most convenient. For details and a map of central **car parks**, contact Sipa (℡075.572.1938, ⓦwww .sipaonline.it).

There's a **tourist office** in the Loggia dei Linari on the east side of Piazza Matteotti at no. 18 (May–Sept Mon–Sat 8.30am–6.30pm, Sun 9am–1pm; Oct–April Mon–Sat 8.30am–1.30pm & 3.30–6.30pm, Sun 9am–1pm; ℡075.572 8937, 573.6458 or 075.577.2686, ⓦwww.umbria2000.it). Another good official site is ⓦwww.tourism.comune.perugia.it. The tourist office provides a good map, advice on city events and help in finding accommodation. There is also a private information office, the **Infotourist Point** (also known as InfoUmbria) on the northeast corner of Piazza dei Partigiani (Mon–Fri 9am–1pm & 2.30–6.30pm, Sat 9am–1pm; ℡075.5757, ⓦwww.infoumbria.com), which is a useful source of information on organized half-day and day tours.

Accommodation

Perugia has plenty of **accommodation** in all price ranges, although during term time long-stay students tend to monopolize the cheapest options. As in most of Umbria's main towns, it's a good idea to book in advance, especially during the Jazz festival in July, when room rates may well be raised.

Hotels

Aurora Viale Indipendenza 21 ℡&℻075.572.4819, ⓦwww.hotel-albergoaurora .au. Basic, clean and pleasant two-star hotel with thirteen rooms, though on a busy street. ❸

Brufani Palace Piazza Italia 12 ℡075.573.2541, ⓦwww.brufanipalace.com or www.sinahotels.it. Perugia's smartest and most luxurious option is right in the centre of town by Piazza Italia. ❾

Eden Via C. Caporali 9 ℡075.572.8102, ⓦwww .hoteleden.perugia.it. A two-star with eighteen rooms, all with private bathroom, in a quiet location close to the Corso. ❸

Fortuna Via Bonazzi 19 ℡075.572.2845, ⓦwww .umbriahotels.com. A central two-star in an historic thirteenth-century *palazzo* with frescoed ceilings in some rooms and a roof garden with good views of the old city. ❸

Locanda della Posta Corso Vannucci 97 ℡075.572.8925, ⓦwww.locandadellaposta.com. Perugia's first choice if you want an upmarket treat, not as slick as the *Brufani* but just as central and a historic building where the likes of Goethe and Hans Christian Andersen once stayed. ❻

Priori Via Vermiglioli 3 ℡075.572.3378, ⓦwww .hotelpriori.it. Perugia's first-choice mid-range three-star hotel. The 49 rooms (all with private bathroom) are tastefully fitted out and there's a terrace overlooking the rooftops. The rooms vary greatly so ask to see a selection. ❸

Umbria Via Boncambi 37 ℡075.572.1203, ⓦwww.hotel-umbria.com. Basic, centrally located two-star; all of the eighteen rooms have private bathrooms. ❸

Hostels and camping

Centro Internazionale di Accoglienza per la Gioventù Via Bontempi 13 ℡075.572.2880, ⓦwww.ostello.perugia.it. The town's original hostel is perfectly situated just 2min from the Duomo. It has 134 beds in four-, six- and eight-bed dorms; closed 9.30am–4pm & mid-Dec to mid-Jan; dorm beds €15 plus €2 sheet rental.

Ostello per la Gioventù Maria Luisa Spagnoli Via Cortonese 4, Località Pian di Massiano ℡075.501.1366, ⓦwww.umbriahostels.org, Perugia's newer hostel is down near the main station and has its own restaurant. There are 186 beds in 33 four- and six-bed dorms. €16, with breakfast; single rooms €22; open 7am to midnight year round.

Paradise d'Été Via del Mercato 29/A, Strada Fontana ℡075.517.3121, ⓦwww.wel.it /cparadis. A three-star, top-of-the-range campsite 5km out of town at Località Colle della Trinità. Take the Sulga bus marked "Colle della Trinità" from Piazza Italia or #9 bus from the station). There are also more rural sites on Lago Trasimeno (see p.567).

The Town

Once you're safely in Piazza Italia **orientation** is straightforward. The town hinges around a single street, the Corso Vannucci, one of the country's greatest people-watching streets, packed from dawn through to the early hours with a parade of tourists and Umbria's trendsetters. Named after the city's most celebrated artist, Pietro Vannucci, better known simply as Perugino, the Corso contains several of the key sights and a couple of Perugia's most atmospheric little cafés.

The Duomo and around

At the far end of the Corso Vannucci is the big and austere **Piazza IV Novembre** (once a Roman reservoir), backed by the plain-faced **Duomo**. While the Baroque interior is big on size, it's pretty small on works of art and comes as a disappointment after the fifteenth-century facade. As a change from pieces of the True Cross, the chapel almost immediately on your right as you enter, behind a heavy metal grille, contains the Virgin's "wedding ring", an unwieldy 2cm-diameter piece of agate that apparently changes colour according to the character of the person wearing it. The Perugians keep it locked up in fifteen boxes fitted into one another like Russian dolls, each opened with a key held by a different person. It's brought out for general public edification once a year on July 30. In one of the transepts there's an urn holding the ashes of Pope Martin IV, who died in the city after eating too many eels. Urban IV's remains are here too – he was reputedly poisoned with *aquetta*, an imaginative brew made by rubbing white arsenic into pork fat and distilling the unpleasantness that oozes out.

Outside in the piazza (which is the town's main hangout), the centrepiece is the **Fontana Maggiore**, designed by Fra' Bevignate, a monk, and sculpted by the father-and-son team, Nicola and Giovanni Pisano. Sculptures and bas-reliefs – depicting episodes from the Old Testament, classical myth, Aesop's fables and the twelve months of the year – on the two polygonal basins were part of a carefully conceived decorative scheme designed to illustrate the city's glory and achievements. By some canny design work they never line up directly, encouraging you to walk round the fountain chasing a point of repose that never comes.

Just east of Piazza Danti behind the cathedral at Piazza Piccinino 1 lies the entrance to the **Pozzo Etrusco** (April & Aug daily 10am–1.30pm & 2.30–6pm; May–July & Sept-Oct Tues–Sun 10am–1.30pm & 2.30–6.30pm; rest of the year Tues–Sun 11am–1.30pm & 2.30–5pm; €2.50, includes admission to San Severo & Museo delle Mura e delle Porte Urbiche), a massive and extraordinary well that does more than hint at the dazzling engineering and technical skills of its Etruscan builders.

A few minutes' walk farther east along Via del Sole brings you to the church of **San Severo** (same hours and ticket as Pozzo Etrusco) in Piazza Raffaello, known for its painting *Holy Trinity and Saints* by Raphael, who spent some five formative years in Umbria. Today it's the only **painting** by him still left in the region – Napoleon carted many of the artist's works off to France – except for

Two basic **passes** are available for all major museums and sights in Perugia. One "Card" (€7) is valid for any five sights within a four-hour period and can be purchased from any of the participating sights. The second "Card" (€12) is valid for all sights over three days. Family passes and passes with a year's validity are also usually available.

▲ Fontana Maggiore, Perugia

a painted banner in the art gallery in Città di Castello (see p.569). Perugino, his erstwhile teacher, completed the lower third of the painting, *Six Saints*, in 1521 after Raphael's death.

The Palazzo dei Priori

Just opposite the cathedral rises the gaunt mass of the **Palazzo dei Priori**, often – and rightly – described as one of the greatest public palaces in Italy. Sheer bulk aside, it's certainly impressive – with rows of trefoil windows (from which convicted criminals were once thrown to their deaths), majestic Gothic doorway, and business-like Guelph crenellations – though the overall effect is rather forbidding; its real beauty derives from the harmony set up by the medieval buildings around it. The lawyers' meeting hall, the **Sala dei Notari** (daily 9am–1pm & 3–7pm; closed Mon Oct–June; free), at the top of the fan-shaped steps, is noted for its frescoes portraying scenes from the Bible, Aesop's fables and the coats of arms of medieval civic worthies: lots of colour, fancy flags, swirls and no substance – but certainly worth a glance.

The small **Collegio della Mercanzia** (March–Oct & 20 Dec–6 Jan Tues–Sat 9am–1pm & 2.30–5.30pm, Sun 9am–1pm; rest of year Tues, Thurs & Fri 8am–2pm, Wed & Sat 8am–5pm, Sun 9am–1pm; €1.50, or €5.50 with Collegio di Cambio) lies farther down the Corso side of the palace at Corso Vannucci 15 hidden behind an innocuous door. The seat of the Merchants'

Guild, it is covered entirely in intricate and beautiful fifteenth-century panelling. A few doors down at Corso Vannucci 25, the impressive **Collegio di Cambio** (mid-March to Oct Mon–Sat 9am–12.30pm & 2.30–5.30pm, Sun 9am–1pm; rest of year closed Mon 2.30–5.30pm; €5.50, including Collegio della Mercanzia) was the town's money exchange in medieval times. The superb frescoes on the walls were executed by Perugino at the height of his powers and are considered the artist's masterpiece; in true Renaissance fashion, they attempt to fuse ancient and Christian culture. Up on the door-side wall there's a famous but unremarkable self-portrait in which the artist looks like he had a bad lunch. Giannicola di Paolo frescoed the small chapel (1519) to the right of the Collegio, the last important Umbrian painter influenced by Perugino.

The **Galleria Nazionale dell'Umbria** (Tues–Sun 8.30am–7.30pm; €6.50) is on the upper floor of the palace complex (lift or stairs), with the entrance through its opulently carved **doorway**. One of central Italy's best and most charming galleries, this takes you on a romp through the history of Umbrian painting, with masterpieces by Perugino, Pinturicchio and many others, plus one or two stunning Tuscan masterpieces (Duccio, Fra' Angelico, Piero della Francesca) thrown in for good measure. The entrance is worth every cent if you're the slightest bit interested in early and mid-Renaissance art.

North and west of Corso Vannucci

The best streets to wander around for a feel of the old city are to the east and west of the Duomo, **Via dei Priori** being the most characteristic. Just behind the Palazzo dei Priori in Via della Gabbia there once hung a large iron cage used to imprison thieves and sometimes even clergy. You can still make out long spikes on some of the lower walls, used as hooks for the heads of executed criminals. Further down, Via dei Priori passes the rarely open **Madonna della Luce** on the north side after the medieval Torre degli Scirri, little more than a chapel dominated by an impressive altarpiece by G.B. Caporali, a follower of Perugino. The church takes its name from the story that in 1513 a young barber swore so profusely on losing at cards that a Madonna in a wayside shrine closed her eyes in horror and kept them closed for four days. The miracle prompted celebrations, processions and the building of a new church. Some way beyond, as the street bears right, is a nice patch of grass perfectly placed for relaxing with the crowd from the art school next door or for admiring Agostino di Duccio's colourful **Oratorio di San Bernardino**, whose richly embellished facade (1461) is far and away the best piece of sculpture in the city. To the north is what's left of San Francesco, once a colossal church, now ruined by centuries of earthquakes, but with a curiously jumbled and striking facade still just about standing.

From here you can wander along the rather uninspiring Via A. Pascoli, under the much-photographed Acquedotto (a raised walkway from the old centre to the north of the city – well worth taking for the views) and past the hideous university buildings, to the **Università Italiana per Stranieri** (☏075.57.461, Ⓦwww.unistrapg.it) in Piazza Fortebraccio. The big patched-up gateway here is the **Arco di Augusto**, its lowest section one of the few remaining monuments of Etruscan Perugia. The Romans added the upper remnant when they captured the city in 40 BC.

About a minute's walk north on Corso Garibaldi is **Sant'Agostino**, once Romanesque, now botched Baroque and filled with wistful signs explaining what paintings used to hang in the church before they were spirited to France

Bloodlust in medieval Perugia

Medieval Perugia was evidently a hell of a place to be. "The most warlike of the people of Italy", wrote the historian Sismondi, "who always preferred Mars to the Muse." Male citizens played a game (and this was for pleasure) in which two teams, thickly padded in clothes stuffed with deer hair and wearing beaked helmets, stoned each other mercilessly until the majority of the other side were dead or wounded. Children were encouraged to join in for the first two hours to promote "application and aggression".

In 1265 Perugia was also the birthplace of the **Flagellants**, who had half of Europe whipping itself into a frenzy before the movement was declared heretical. In addition to some hearty scourging they took to the streets on moonlit nights, groaning and wailing, dancing in white sheets, singing dirges and clattering human bones together, all as expiation for sin and the wrongs of the world. Then there were the infamous **Baglioni**, the medieval family who misruled the city for several generations, their spell-binding history – full of vendetta, incest and mass-slaughter – the stuff of great medieval soap opera.

by light-fingered Napoleonic troops. The church, however, is not entirely ruined: there's a beautiful choir (probably based on a drawing by Perugino) and a couple of patches of fresco on the left-hand (north) wall, giving a tantalizing idea of what the place must once have been. Next door to the north side is the fifteenth-century **Oratorio di Sant'Agostino**, its ludicrously ornate ceiling looking as if it's about to erupt in an explosion of gilt, stucco and chubby plaster cherubs. Fifteen-minutes' walk up the street is the fifth-century church of **Sant'Angelo**, situated in a tranquil spot (with a pretty little patch of grass and trees – perfect for picnics and siestas) and based on a circular pagan temple; the 24 columns are from the earlier building. Finally, at the northern end of Corso Garibaldi is the **Museo delle Mura e delle Porta Urbiche** (April & Aug daily 10am–1pm & 2.30–6pm; May–July & Sept–Oct Tues–Sun 10am–1.30pm & 2.30–6pm; Nov–March Tues–Sun 11am–1.30pm & 2.30–5pm; same ticket as Pozzo Etrusco and San Severo – see p.562), a small museum devoted to the city's medieval defences.

Corso Cavour

The rest of Perugia's highlights are on the other side of town, grouped together on **Corso Cavour**, a busy and dustily unpleasant road in the summer. On the way over you could join the smooching couples in the small but well-kept **Giardini Carducci** (by Piazza Italia) to see why Henry James called Perugia the "little city of the infinite views". When the usual cloak of haze lifts on crisp winter mornings, half of Umbria is laid out before you, with the mountains of Tuscany in the distance.

Below the piazza stands the strange octagonal, rarely open, church of **Sant'Ercolano** – built on the site where the head of Perugia's first bishop miraculously re-attached itself to his body after the Goths chopped it off. It's worth taking a short walk past here to look into the Porta Marzia, where a subterranean road of medieval houses, **Via Baglioni Sotteranea**, leads under the ruins of the Rocca Paolina, a once-enormous papal fortress destroyed by the Perugians at Unification. This amazing underground labyrinth can also be accessed from the escalators to Piazza dei Partigiani from the west side of Piazza Italia.

Continuing on to Corso Cavour and heading south, you come to **San Domenico**, Umbria's biggest church. It has a desolate and unfinished air from the outside, but it's also appealing in a big and rather melancholy sort of way. The original Romanesque interior collapsed in the sixteenth century and the Baroque replacement is vast, cold and bare. Like Sant'Agostino, however, it's full of hints as to how beautiful it must have been – nowhere more so than in the fourth chapel on the right, where a superb **carved arch** by Agostino di Duccio is spoilt only by a doll-like Madonna. In the east transept, to the right of the altar, is the **tomb of Benedict XI** (1324), another pope who died in Perugia, this time from eating poisoned figs. It's an elegant and well-preserved piece by one of the period's three leading sculptors: Pisano, Lorenzo Maitani or Arnolfo di Cambio, no one knows which. There's also another good choir, together with some impressive **stained-glass** windows – the second biggest in Italy after those in Milan's Duomo.

Housed in the church's cloisters is the **Museo Archeologico Nazionale dell'Umbria** (Mon 10am–7.30pm, Tues–Sun 8.30am–7.30pm; €4). Before being hammered by Augustus, Perugia was a big shot in the twelve-strong Etruscan federation of cities, which is why the city has one of the most extensive Etruscan collections around. The place is definitely worth a visit, even if the Etruscans normally leave you cold, for there's far more here than the usual run of urns and funerary monuments. Particularly compelling are the Carri Etruschi di Castel San Marino, some exquisite sixth-century bronze chariots; a witty collection of eye-opening artefacts devoted to fashion and beauty in the Etruscan era; and the bewildering **Bellucci Collection**. The last is a private hoard of charms and amulets through the ages: everything from the obvious – lucky horseshoes – to strange and often sinister charms such as snakeskins and dried animals.

Farther down Corso Cavour, advertised by a rocket-shaped bell tower, is the tenth-century basilica of **San Pietro**, the most idiosyncratic of all the town's churches. Tangled up in a group of buildings belonging to the university's agriculture department, the none-too-obvious entrance is through a frescoed doorway in the far left-hand corner of the first courtyard off the road. Few churches can be so sumptuously decorated: every inch of available space is covered in gilt, paint or marble, though a guiding sense of taste seems to have prevailed, and in the candle-lit gloom it actually feels like the sacred place it's meant to be. All the woodwork is extraordinary; the **choir** has been called the best in Italy, and there is a host of works by Perugino, Fiorenzo di Lorenzo and others.

Eating and drinking

Perugia's student population ensures that there is a plethora of reasonably priced **places to eat** out, from the many snack bars around the centre of town to simple *osterie* serving traditional Umbrian cuisine. Local dishes feature wild mushrooms, truffles and game often succulently combined with home-made egg pasta. The city's liveliest **cafés** are clustered on Corso Vannucci.

Cafés

Caffè di Perugia Via Mazzini 10 ℡075.573.1863, ⓦwww.caffediperugia.it. A pleasantly smart setting with superb vaulted ceiling from the thirteenth century. All the café staples, plus a restaurant with simple meals, a pizzeria-grill and a wine bar, the last a good early evening retreat. Closed Tues.

Caffè Morlacchi Piazza Morlacchi 8 ℡075.572.1760. Smart but student-oriented bar; get to it along Via delle Volte from Piazza IV Novembre. Occasional live music. Closed Sun.

Gelateria Gambrinus Via Bonazzi 3 ℡075.573.5620. Queues from this ice cream parlour off the Corso often stretch onto the nearby

Piazza della Repubblica, especially at the height of the Sun *passeggiata*. A great choice of flavours and very generous scoops.

🏃 **Pasticceria Sandri** Corso Vannuci 32 (closed Mon). Atmospheric, old-world café in a perfect position on the main street near the Palazzo dei Priori – a high spot for the sweet-toothed.

Pizzerias and restaurants

Cesarino Piazza IV Novembre 45 ℡075.572.8974. A great central restaurant and a Perugia tradition which hasn't suffered too much from a recent interior redecoration. Meals from around €27. Booking advised. Closed Wed.

Dal mi Cocco Corso Garibaldi 12 ℡075.573.2511. Good-value traditional dishes with a variety of set menus from €14. Closed Mon.

Falchetto Via Bartolo 20, just off Piazza Danti. A reliably good and easy-going place with a medieval interior. A full meal costs around €25. Closed Mon.

Locanda Do' Pazzi Via della Sposa 1/B ℡075.572.0565. Atmospheric spot off the western end of Via dei Priori in the cellar of a former medieval church, with ancient vaults and food from across Italy. Closed Sun.

Pizza a Taglio Via dei Priori 3, corner Via della Gabbia. A little place just a few steps from Corso Vannucci for inexpensive pizza by the slice to take away. Open daily.

Pizzeria Mediterranea Piazza Piccinino 11 ℡075.572.1322. Simple and tasteful pizzeria with small wood-fired oven and a couple of brick-vaulted rooms a few steps beyond the entrance to the Pozzo Etrusco. Open daily.

🏃 **Scalino** Via Sant'Ercolano. Authentic old-fashioned pizzeria and trattoria, staffed by venerable women and patronized almost entirely by locals. Fabulous brick-vaulted dining room and very reasonable prices. Closed Fri.

Segreto di Pulcinella Via Larga 8 ℡075.573.6284. A bustling pizzeria that's very popular with students.

Turreno Piazza Danti 16 ℡075.572.1976. Superb, central *tavola calda* that offers a handful of light meals (around €10, with soft drink) and snacks daily to eat in (there are tables to the rear) or take away. Lunch only. Closed Sat.

Bars and clubs

Contrappunto Jazz Club Via Scortici 4/A (closed Mon). The best of a bunch of live music venues. Open until 2am.

Enoteca Provinciale Via Ulisse Rocchi 16–18. Close to the Duomo, this wineshop-cum-bar is the best place to indulge in the local wines; it also does excellent snacks in a room to the rear and has a vast selection of wines to buy by the bottle. Mon 4.30–8.30pm, Tues–Sat 10.30am–2.30pm & 4.30–10pm.

Il Birraio Via delle Prome 18 ℡075.572.3920. There's no mistaking the beer bias of this odd, modern place, the entrance to which is lined with the copper tanks and vats of an in-house micro-brewery. Tues–Sun 5pm–2am.

Velvet Fashion Café Viale Roma 20 ℡075.572.1321, ⊛www.velvetfashioncafe.com. Perugia's only central club. Offers smart dining, drinking and occasional live music; closed Mon & Tues.

Lago Trasimeno

The most tempting option around Perugia – whose surroundings are generally pretty bleak – is **LAGO TRASIMENO**, an ideal spot to hole up in for a few days, and particularly recommended if you want to get in some swimming, windsurfing or sailing. The lake is about 30km from Perugia and is well served by both train and bus. It's the biggest inland stretch of water on the Italian peninsula, the fourth largest in Italy overall, and, though you wouldn't think so to look at it, never deeper than 7m – hence bath-like warm water in summer.

A winning combination of tree-covered hills to the north, Umbria's subtle light, and placid lapping water produces some magical moments, but on overcast and squally days the mood can turn melancholy. Not all the reed-lined shore is uniformly pretty either; steer clear of the northern coast and head for the stretches south of Magione and Castiglione if you're after relative peace and quiet.

Passignano

Strung out along the northern shore, **PASSIGNANO**, a newish town with a medieval heart, is the lake's most accessible point, served by seven daily buses and hourly trains from Perugia and Terontola. In summer it can get a bit clogged with traffic, but in the evenings, the joint is jumping, with bars, discos and fish restaurants aplenty. There's a **tourist office** at Piazza Trento e Trieste 6 (June–Sept Mon–Sat 10.30am–12.30pm & 4–7pm, Sun 10am–12.30pm; Oct–May Fri & Sat 3–6.30pm, Sun 10am–12.30pm; ☎075.827.635), and about a dozen **hotels** – the best value of which are the twelve-room, one-star *Florida*, Via II Giugno 2 (☎075.827.228; ❷), and, for around €20 more, the larger, smarter three-star *Trasimeno*, Via Roma 16/A (☎075.829.355, ⓦwww.hoteltrasimeno.it; ❷).

Somewhere along the lakeshore towards the rambling village of Tuoro, probably at Sanguineto ("the Place of Blood") or Ossaia ("the Place of Bones"), is the spot where the Romans suffered their famous clobbering at the hands of **Hannibal** in 217 BC. Hannibal was headed for Rome, having just crossed the Alps, when he was met by a Roman force under the Consul Flaminius. Things might have gone better for Flaminius if he'd heeded the omens that piled up on the morning of battle. First he fell off his horse, next the legionary standards had to be dug out of the mud, then – and this really should have raised suspicions – the sacred chickens refused their breakfast. Poultry accompanied all Roman armies and, by some means presumably known to the legionnaire in charge of chickens, communicated the will of the gods to waiting commanders in the field. With the chickens against him Flaminius didn't stand a chance. Hannibal lured him into a masterful ambush, with the only escape a muddy retreat into the lake. Sixteen thousand Romans, including the hapless commander, were killed. A hard-to-find drive and walkway have been laid out, starting and finishing just west of Tuoro on the road to Cortona, that take in salient features of the old battlefield.

Castiglione del Lago

CASTIGLIONE DEL LAGO is the most appealing town on the lake and cuts a fine silhouette from other points around the shore, jutting out into the water on a fortified promontory. A friendly, unpretentious place, Castiglione has enough charm and action to hold anyone's interest for a couple of days – longer if all you want to do is crash out on a (albeit modest) beach. It's easy to reach by slow train either from Chiusi (heading north) or Terontola if you're coming from Arezzo or Perugia. There are also nine buses daily from Perugia.

There's a good **tourist office** at no. 10 in the main Piazza Mazzini (Mon–Fri 8.30am–1pm & 3.30–7pm, Sat 9am–1pm & 3.30–7pm, Sun 9am–1pm & 4–7pm; ☎075.965.2484 or 075.965.2738, ⓔinfo@iat.castiglione-del-lago .pg.it), with a lot of reasonable but generally characterless **rooms** on its books and apartments to rent weekly, usually a cheaper option if you can get a party together. Among the **hotels**, top dog is the three-star *Duca della Corgna*, Via B. Buozzi 143 (☎075.953.238, ⓔhotelcorgna@libero.it; ❷), with the *Trasimeno*, Via Roma 174 (☎075.965.2494, ⓕ075.952.5258; ❷), hot on its heels; more atmospheric is the *Miralago*, Piazza Mazzini 6 (☎075.951.157 or 075.953.063, ⓦwww.hotelmiralago.com; ❺), with views of the lake behind. Most of the **campsites** are off the main road some way north or south of the town. The most highly rated is the *Badiaccia*, Via Trasimeno I 91, Località Badiaccia (☎075.965.9097, ⓦwww.badiaccia.com). Aside from the summer-only

Italian wine

For years Italy was known for wines that with a few notable
exceptions were fairly easy on the pocket and the palate,
but didn't travel particularly well. In the past two decades,
however, Italian wine has come of age: there's still the same
regional variety, and plenty of high-volume, low-value plonk.
But this is now matched by high-quality vintages produced
with modern techniques and, overall, a greater pride in the
art of winemaking. For more on each region's wines see the
box at the beginning of the Guide chapters. Salute!

The north

The regional variations in Italian wine remain as strong as ever, but the areas where you can find real quality have shifted around a bit of late. In the north, Piemonte has always been known as a high-end area and it remains so; it's by no means the largest producer by volume among the Italian regions, but it's home to more DOC wines than anywhere else. The big names here are Barolo and Barbaresco, made from vines grown in the Langhe hills near Alba – full-bodied reds that are among the most complex and refined of Italian wines – along with the simpler, fruitier Dolcetto d'Alba, the white, extremely dry Gavi, and the sweet, sparkling Asti Spumante, though you may prefer to try the drier Moscato d'Asti. Neighbouring Lombardy produces some nice sparkling wines in Franciacorta in the hills around Lago d'Iseo, but the big wine region of northern Italy is the Veneto, responsible for around 25 percent of Italy's output, and well-known for a handful of Italian classics – the solid red Valpolicella and the clean, dry white Soave among them. There's also Prosecco, Italy's wonderful, light sparkling wine, from the Conegliano region in the far northeast, and of course the country's spin-off firewater, grappa, which hails from Bassano del Grappa.

Central Italy

In central Italy, the foodie region of Emilia-Romagna is best-known for much – and wrongly – maligned red and white Lambrusco, and Marche, to the south, for the light, white wine, Verdicchio. The biggest producer in central Italy, however, is Tuscany, which is at the heart of the Italian wine renaissance, producing great red wines based on the

Brunello vineyard, Tuscany ▲

Wine tasting in Florence ▼

What's in a label?

The **labelling** of Italian wine can be confusing: there is no entirely recognized system and often little geographical or varietal information to help you identify where a wine is from or what it is like. The first attempt at a labelling scheme was the **Denominazione d'Origine Controllata** (DOC) system, introduced in the 1960s with rules specifying where a certain named wine may be produced. This was added to by the **Denominazione d'Origine Controllata e Garantita** (DOCG), set up in the 1980s with wines tested by government-appointed inspectors. While it's true that the DOC and DOCG system helped lift standards, their strict laws came under fire from growers for their tendency to stifle creativity. In fact some producers have begun to disregard the DOC system and make wines that conform to a new standard, the **Indicazione Geografica Tipica** (IDT). This was introduced in 1992 to enable producers to identify their wines by geographical names and grape varieties – something that has benefited the less traditional wine makers in particular – and is well worth looking out for.

▲ Wine list at an enoteca, Venice

▼ Brunello di Montalcino on sale in its home town

▼ Oak barrels - often used to age Italian reds

indigenous sangiovese grape. The biggie here of course is Chianti, which varies from the hearty red swill of old to one of the country's most sophisticated reds. But there's also the wonderful smooth red, Brunello di Montalcino, the lesser Rosso di Montalcino and a host of fruity, drinkable and more affordable reds from the Maremma region. Conversely, neighbouring Umbria is known for just one wine – bone-dry Orvieto. Lazio, too, is a modest wine producer, but what it does, it does well, whether it's the whites of the Castelli Romani region – in particular Frascati – or the crisp, dry and wonderfully named white, Est! Est! Est!, of Montefiascone, north of Rome.

The south

In the south, the fertile volcanic soils of **Campania** have always produced decent wine, and the region is know for some very long-established whites like Fiano d'Avellino and Falanghina, as well as reds based on the rich and flavourful Aglianico grape. **Puglia**, though, is an enigma: traditionally one of the country's highest volume producers, in the last decade or so it has developed a new emphasis on quality; this shines through in big-hearted reds like Salice Salentino and others based on the **Primitivo** and **Negroamaro** grapes that thrive in the hot, dry climate down here. If there is anywhere that typifies the country's new and enlightened attitude to wine, it is Puglia, and the results are there for all to taste. Sicily, too, is beginning to produce some great wines, and there is most notably a growth of interest in its long-standing fortified sweet white, **Marsala**.

Relaxing in an enoteca, Venice ▲

Chianti grapes ready for harvest ▼

Sweet Sicilian Marsala ▼

Drinking it...

With the renaissance of Italian wine has come a resurgence in the number of places to sample it, and Italy's old wine shops, or **enotecas**, are once again thriving. Some of these places are spit-and-sawdust, classic wine shops that focus only on the wine; others – some of them with wine lists the size of diction-aries – serve classic Italian wine bar snacks to wash it down: usually a variety of locally sourced cheeses, salami and other cold meats, chosen to go with whatever you drink.

Top five enotecas

▶▶ *Do Mori*, Venice (see p.322)
▶▶ *Cantina Bentivoglio*, Bologna (see p.405)
▶▶ *Fuori Porta*, Florence (see p.479)
▶▶ *Enoteca Corsi*, Rome (see p.710)
▶▶ *Mi Manda Piccone*, Palermo (see p.927)

restaurants on the promenade, the place to eat game, fish fresh from the lake and other dishes is the mid-priced *L'Acquario*, Via Vittorio Emanuele II 69 (℡075.965.2432; closed Wed, also Tues in winter) on the old town's single main street (mains around €10). Or try the *Vinolento*, Via Vittorio Emanuele 112 (℡075.952.5262, ⓦwww.vinolento.it), a good little wine bar and *osteria*, or the long-established *Cantina* in the same street at no. 93 (℡075.965.2463; closed Mon except in summer). The best **swimming** is at the public lido on the southern side of the promontory.

Regular boats make the trip out to the **Isola Maggiore**, one of the lake's three islands, a fun ride if you don't mind the summer crowds. There's a pretty walk round the edge of the island, and one good, popular **hotel**, the three-star *Da Sauro*, Via Guglielmi 1 (℡075.826.168, ℻075.825.130; ❹), which also doubles as a fine restaurant.

The Upper Tiber

Rome's river, the **Tiber**, actually spends most of its short life in Umbria, rising in the Alpe della Luna above Sansepolcro. In its moderately pretty but rather unexciting upper reaches north of Perugia – largely given over to sheep and fields of tobacco – you're faced with the familiar problem that everything you don't want to see is easily accessible and everything you do is out of reach without your own transport. The **Ferrovia Centrale Umbra** and the fast N3 to Sansepolcro are perfect for **Città di Castello**, the area's only town of note, after which you'll probably want to strike east on the N257 across the mountains to Urbino (70km). The best reason to follow the Tiber is to stay on the trail of **Piero della Francesca's** mysterious and unsettling masterpieces at Sansepolcro, Arezzo and Monterchi.

The region's best aspect, in fact, is not the valley but the desolate countryside on either side, areas that, like the Valnerina in the east, give the lie to the notion of Umbria as some sort of pastoral idyll. With few roads and fewer villages, but thousands of hectares of natural woodland and abandoned pasture, it teems with wildlife, including many rare species of birds, deer, wild boar and even wolves, now apparently pushing farther up the Italian peninsula every year. **Pietralunga** and **Apecchio** to the north are the best exploring bases.

Città di Castello

CITTÀ DI CASTELLO is a charming and little-visited town, with a sedate and ordered medieval centre that's well worth a few hours. It's also increasingly the focus for visitors staying in the many rented villas and farmhouses in hills to the east and west. In August and early September the town becomes busier than usual during its renowned **Festival of Chamber Music** (further information ℡075.852.2823 or 075.852.4357, ⓦwww.festivalnazioni.com).

Once an important Roman centre – the grid-iron of streets is virtually the only legacy – today the plain-bound site preserves just a handful of fairly mediocre medieval monuments. The town's main attractions are a trio of museums and an art gallery, along with some quiet, pleasant medieval streets. Foremost among the museums is the **Pinacoteca** at the southern edge of town at Via della Cannoniera 22 (Tues–Sun: April–Oct 10am–1pm & 2.30–6.30pm;

Nov–March 10am–12.30pm & 3–6pm; ☎075.855.4202; €6), one of the region's best art galleries after Perugia's. The collection makes up in quality what it lacks in quantity, taking in works by **Raphael**, **Signorelli**, **Ghirlandaio** and **Lorenzetti**, plus a wondrous *Maestà* by the anonymous fourteenth-century Maestro di Città di Castello. There are also several sculptures, the most notable by Ghiberti, and a glittering reliquary of Florentine origin, dating from 1420.

The banal reworked **Duomo** in Piazza Gabriotti warrants a call for its smart and newly revamped museum, the **Museo del Duomo**, entered to the right of the church (Tues–Sun 10am–1pm & 3–6.30pm; ☎075.855.4705; €6). It contains a completely unexpected collection of big-name paintings, including major works by Rosso Fiorentino, Giulio Romano and Pinturicchio. Even better is the **treasure of** Canoscio, a precious hoard of sixth-century silver chalices dug up in 1932.

The third of the town's triumvirate of museums is the fascinating **Collezione Tessile di Tela Umbra**, just off the main square at Via Sant'Antonio 3 (Tues–Sat 10am–noon & 3.30–5.30pm, Sun 10.30am–1pm & 3–6pm; Nov–March Sun closes 5.30pm; ☎075.554.337; €3.50). The museum traces the history of textiles in the Upper Tiber valley, though in many ways the more interesting part of the concern is the original workshop, which continues to employ local women and still – almost uniquely in Italy – uses traditional hand-worked looms (workshop open museum hours Wed–Sat only; €1 in addition to museum entrance).

Just north of the Collezione Tessile is the **Palazzo Albizzini** (Tues–Sat: 9am–12.30pm & 2.30–6pm; Sun 10.30am–12.30pm & 3–6pm; ☎075.855.4649; €6) at Via degli Albizzini 1, off Piazza Garibaldi. It's home to the Collezione Burri, a medley of large sculptural works by local artist Alberto Burri. If you have come to the town from the south you'll probably have seen some distinctive and colossal buildings (on Via Pierucci) once used to dry tobacco: today they house some of Burri's larger works (same ticket and hours April–Oct; Nov–March Sat & Sun only 9am–12.30pm & 2.30–6pm). A couple of kilometres south, in the hamlet of **GARAVELLE**, is one of Umbria's best **folk museums**, the Centro delle Tradizioni Popolari (Tues–Sun: April–Oct 8.30am–12.30pm & 3–7pm; Nov–March 8.30am–12.30pm & 2–6pm; €5). Recently extended and restored, it's located in an eighteenth-century farmhouse, preserved with all the accoutrements of daily life – pots, pans, furniture and so forth, plus a range of exhibits covering rural activities such as wine making and weaving.

Practicalities

Città di Castello's **tourist office** in the Logge Bufalini just off Piazza Matteotti (Mon–Fri 9am–1pm & 3.30–6.30pm, Sat 9.30am–12.30pm & 3.30–6pm, Sun 9.30am–12.30pm; ☎075.855.4922, ✉info@iat.citta-di-castello.pg.it) deals with the whole Upper Tiber region and so is a useful stop if you're spending any time locally. Best place to stay on a budget is the excellent, modern, two-star **hotel** *Umbria*, Via dei Galanti 4, off Via Sant'Antonio (☎075.855.4925, ✉umbria@hotelumbria.net; ❷), just inside the medieval walls, in the east of the old centre. Top of the range is the central four-star *Tiferno*, Piazza Raffaello Sanzio 13 (☎075.855.0331, ⓦwww.hoteltiferno.it; ❺). There's also a pleasant, rural **campsite** at La Montesca, 1km west of town on the minor road to Monte San Marina – the *Montesca* (☎075.855.8566, ⓦwww.lamontesca.it; May–Sept). Best of several good **restaurants** is ♣ *Amici Miei*, downstairs in a medieval cellar at Via del Monte 2 (☎075.855.9904; closed Wed), off Corso Garibaldi just south of the main Piazza Matteotti: the menu changes daily and you should be able to get four courses, excluding wine, for under €25. For about the same price there's the equally good *Il Cacciatore*, Via della Braccina 10 (℡075.852.0882; closed Tues), a traditionally styled *osteria* with simple regional food. Alternatively, try *Lea*, an equally reasonable locals' favourite at Via San Florido 28 (℡075.852.1678; closed Mon), a short way south of the cathedral.

Gubbio

GUBBIO is the most thoroughly medieval of the Umbrian towns, an immediately likeable place that's hung on to its charm despite an ever-increasing influx of visitors. The streets are picture-book pretty, with houses of rosy-pink stone and seas of orange-tiled roofs; the setting is equally gorgeous with the forest-clad mountains of the Apennines rearing up behind. A broad and largely unspoilt plain stretches out in front of the town, and the whole ensemble – especially on grey, windswept days – maintains Gubbio's tough, mountain outpost atmosphere.

A powerful medieval *Comune*, and always important as the gateway to Ravenna and the Adriatic (it was a key point on the Roman Via Flaminia), these days it's a town apart, not really part of Umbria, Tuscany or Marche – one reason it's been spared the onslaught of modernity.

Arrival and accommodation

Gubbio is easiest approached by **bus** from Perugia on the intermittently pretty cross-country SS298 **road**. The nearest **train station** is at Fossato di Vico, 19km south on the Rome–Foligno–Ancona line; there are ten connecting shuttle buses to Gubbio from Monday to Saturday, six on Sundays.

You shouldn't have any problem **staying** in Gubbio, though the place does get busy, and many of the hotels and restaurants are rather smart affairs aimed at well-heeled Italians. Check for cheap **rooms** in private houses with the **tourist office**, Piazza Odersi 6 (Mon–Fri 8.30am–1.45pm & 3.30–6pm, Sat 9am–1pm & 3.30–6pm, Sun 9.30am–12.30pm; ℡075.922.0693).

Hotels

Albergo dei Consoli Via dei Consoli 59 ℡075.927.3335, ⓦwww.urbaniweb.com. Formerly a rather humble hotel that has been transformed into a four-star; has the advantage of a great position just a few steps down the hill from the Palazzo dei Consoli. ⑤

Bosone Via XX Settembre 22 ℡075.922.0688, ⓦwww.mancarelligroup.com. A long-established and traditional three-star hotel in a medieval palace with frescoed ceilings and lots of antiques. There's a good restaurant garden, too. ④

Gattapone Via G. Ansidei 6 ℡075.927.2489, ⓦwww.mancarelligroup.com. The best-priced of the town's three-star options with a peaceful garden and a central setting, but beware the bells of the nearby church if you're a light sleeper. ③

Grotta dell'Angelo Via Gioia 47 ℡075.927.1747, ⓦwww.grottadellangelo.it. A reliable two-star

option in a peaceful side street; there's also an excellent and moderately priced restaurant. ②

Le Logge Via Piccardi 7–9 ℡075.927.7574. Great rooms in the same street as the *Locanda del Duca* (see below), and a nicer proposition thanks to the pleasant owners, homely feel and pretty garden. ②

Locanda del Duca Via Piccardi 1 ℡075.927.7753. Seven decent one-star en-suite rooms in a convenient position just off the big Piazza Quaranta Martiri in a quiet side street. ②

Park Hotel ai Cappuccini Via Tifernate ℡075.9234, ⓦwww.parkhotelaicappuccini.it. A large and elegantly converted fourteenth-century monastery in parkland just outside the town, boasting a pool, gym, sauna and garden. ⑦

Relais Ducale ℡075.922.0157, ⓦwww .relaisducale.com. A classy four-star just below the cathedral and entered from one of two tiny alleys – Via Ducale or Via Galleotti (signed off the east side of

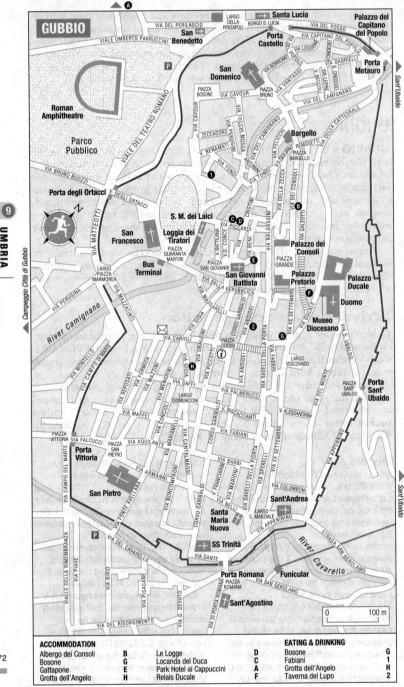

GUBBIO

Roman Amphitheatre

Parco Pubblico

VIALE UMBERTO PARRUCCINI

VIA DEL PERILASCIO

LARGO DELLA PENTAPOLI

BORGO S. LUCIA

Santa Lucia

VIA DEL FOSSO

Palazzo del Capitano del Popolo

VIA CAPITANO DEL POPOLO

San Benedetto

Porta Castello

VIA BORROMEO DEL POPOLO

VIA LOGGIA

VIA GABRIELLI

Porta Metauro

V. ONEDDEI

San Domenico

PIAZZA BOSONE

VIA CAVOUR

PIAZZA BRUNO

VIA VANTAGGI

VIA DEL CAMIGNANO

VIA DELLA CATTEDRALE

V. BECCGINI

V. LEPRE

VIA GABRIELLI

VIA DEL TEATRO ROMANO

V. CAVOUR

V. ZECCADORO

VIA PERUGINI

VIA BENAMATI

VIA TONDI

VIA TOCCHI MOSCA

VIA DEL CAMIGNANO

ANTONINI

VIA FELLUCCHI

Bargello

REMOSETTI

PIAZZA BARGELLO

V. GIULIANO

VIA DELLA ZECCA

VIA DEI CONSOLI

VIA TONDI

VIA BRUNO BUOZZI

Porta degli Ortacci

V. DEGLI ORTACCI

VIA MATTEOTTI

S. M. dei Laici

CRISTINI

PICCARDI

C **D**

VD. CONCE

VIA BALDASSINI

VIA GALEOTTI

B

San Francesco

Loggia dei Tiratori

PIAZZA QUARANTA MARTIRI

V. BATIANA

VIA BENI

E

Palazzo dei Consoli

Bus Terminal

PIAZZA SAN GIOVANNI

San Giovanni Battista

PIAZZA GRANDE

Palazzo Pretorio

F

LARGO PIAZZA MARMOREA

VIA MAZZATINTI

VIA DELLA REPUBBLICA

VIA MASSARELLI

CORSO GARIBALDI

VIA ANSIDEI

VIA XX SETTEMBRE

Duomo

Palazzo Ducale

Porta Sant'Ubaldo

VIA S. UBALDO

Museo Diocesano

G

VIA PAVIA

LARGO VESCOVADO

VIA PERUGINA

VIA MONTELLO

VIA CARIOLI

VIA UBALDINI

VIA GIOIA

PIAZZA ODESSI

H

VIA PICOTTI

VIA ANSIDEI

VIA SAVELLI DELLA PORTA

PIAZZA SANT' UBALDO

Porta Sant' Ubaldo

River Camignano

VIA CAMPO DI MARTE

VIA REPOSATI

VIA FORNICA

VIA MAZZINI

VIA MENGHINI

VIA GIOIA

VIA SAFFI

LARGO DOMENICONI

VIA PALMERUCCI

V. RISCACCIANTI

VIA DEL MONTE

VIA ALESSANDRINI

VIA MAFFEI

VIA CONCIOLI

VIA MARIANELLI

CORSO GARIBALDI

VIA FABIANI

VIA XX SETTEMBRE

VIA COLOMBONI

PIAZZA VITTORIA

VIA FALCUCCI

PIAZZA SAN PIETRO

VIA AQUILANTE

VIA CANTALMAGGI

VIA BARBI

Porta Vittoria

VIA CAMPO DEL MARTE

VIA ARMANNI

VIA BONCOMPAGNI

V. FRANCANNINI

VIA MARIONI

VIA SAVELLI DELLA PORTA

VIA SFERELLI

Sant'Andrea

San Pietro

VIA TONTE AVELLANA

CORSO GARIBALDI

VIA NELLI

Santa Maria Nuova

LARGO S. MARZIALE

VIA APPENNINO

VIA APPENNINO

River Cavarello

P

VIALE DELLA RIMEMBRANZA

VIA PIAVE

VIA BIXIO

VIA PISACANE

VIA DEL CAVARELLO

SS Trinità

VIA DANTE

VIA G. DEVITO

Porta Romana

PIAZZA ROMANA

Funicular

VIA SAN GEROLAMO

STRADA SAN GEROLAMO

VIA DI PORTA ROMANA

Sant'Agostino

VIA DEL RISORGIMENTO

0   100 m

N

Campeggio Città di Gubbio ▲

◀ Sant'Ubaldo

Sant'Ubaldo ▶

A ▲

9

UMBRIA

572

Piazza Grande). A better bet for a treat than the *Park* (above) thanks to its superior location and intimacy. ⑥

Campsite
Città di Gubbio Località Ortoguidone
ⓣ&ⓕ 075.927.2037, ⓔ info@gubbiocamping.com.

3.5km south of town just off the SS298 road, and in a pleasant setting with a swimming pool. April–Sept.

The Town

Centre-stage is the immense and austere fourteenth-century **Palazzo dei Consoli**, whose crenellated outline and 98-metre campanile immediately grab your attention. Probably designed by Matteo Gattapone, who was also responsible for Spoleto's Ponte delle Torri, the palace took a couple of hundred years to build and required the levelling of vast tracts of the medieval town, mainly to accommodate the huge and windswept Piazza Grande. The lesser **Palazzo Pretorio** opposite was built to the same plan. Deliberately dominating and humbling, it was what medieval civic pride was all about, an attempt to express power and supremacy in bricks and mortar. Behind a plain square facade (there's a small hole top right where criminals were hung in a cage called *la gogna* – from *vergogna* or "shame") is a cavernous baronial hall, the Salone dell'Arengo, where council officials and leading citizens met to discuss business. The word "harangue" derives from *arengo*, suggesting proceedings frequently boiled over.

The **Museo Civico** (daily: April–Sept 10am–1pm & 3–6pm; Oct–March 10am–1pm & 2–5pm; ⓣ 075.927.4298; €5) is also based here and includes a small archeological collection, entered from the rear of the building; this houses a typical miscellany, unremarkable except for the famous **Eugubine Tablets** (upstairs to the left), Umbria's most important archeological find. Discovered in 1444 by an illiterate shepherd, later conned into swapping his priceless treasure trove for a worthless piece of land, the seven bronze tablets are more or less the only extant record of the ancient Umbrian language, a vernacular tongue without written characters. The bastardized Etruscan and Latin of their religious texts were aimed at producing a phonetic translation of the dialect using the main languages of the day. Gubbio was close to the shrine of the so-called Apennine Jove, a major pagan deity visited by pilgrims from all over Italy, so the tablets were probably the work of Roman and Etruscan priests taking advantage of the established order to impose their religious cults in a region where their languages weren't understood. Most importantly, they suggest Romans, Etruscans and Umbrians achieved some sort of coexistence, refuting a long-held belief that succeeding civilizations wiped one another out.

Admission to the museum also gets you into the five-roomed **Pinacoteca** at the top of the palace, worth a look for works by the Gubbian School – one of central Italy's earliest, and a collection of ponderous fourteenth-century furniture. Try the door at the back for views from the palace's **loggia**. The palace also boasted 26 toilets; apparently it was the first in medieval Italy to have interior piped water.

The Duomo and Palazzo Ducale

To the north of the Piazza Grande lurks a not very inspiring thirteenth-century **Duomo**, partly redeemed by the odd fresco, twelfth-century stained glass, and some arches gracefully curved apparently to emulate the meeting of hands in prayer. There are also a pair of carved **organ lofts** that for once don't look as if they'd be more at home in a fairground. The adjoining **Museo Diocesano** (daily: April–Oct 10am–7pm; Nov–March 10am–6pm; €4; ℡075.922.0904, ⓦwww.museogubbio.it), to the right as you face the facade at the corner of Via Federico da Monefeltro, is well worth a few minutes, mainly for a florid Flemish cope, presented to the cathedral by Pope Marcellus II, who was born in Gubbio.

The plain-faced Gothic cathedral is overshadowed by the **Palazzo Ducale** in Via Federico da Montefeltro opposite (Tues–Sun 8.30am–7.30pm; ℡075.927.5872; €2), built over an earlier Lombard palace by the Dukes of Montefeltro as a scaled-down copy of their more famous palace in Urbino. The **courtyard** is particularly attractive, but the interior, stripped of most of its original furniture and other trappings, is a trifle dull, despite some fine views from the windows and the harmonious scale of the rooms.

Via dei Consoli and the Bargello

There are dozens of picturesque odds and ends around the streets, which are as wonderfully explorable as any in the region. The **Bargello** in Via dei Consoli – the main medieval street (and home to most of the ceramic shops) – the medieval police station, is worth tracking down and gives you the chance to survey the adjacent **Fontana dei Matti** (the "fountain of the mad"), undistinguished but for the tradition that anyone walking round it three times will wind up mad.

The Basilica di Sant'Ubaldo

On the hillside above the town stands the **Basilica di Sant'Ubaldo**, which has some great views (even better ones if you climb up to the **Rocca**). There's not much to see in the basilica itself, except the body of the town's patron saint, St Ubaldo, missing three fingers – they were hacked off by his manservant as a religious keepsake. You can't miss the big wooden pillars (*ceri*) featured in Gubbio's annual **Corsa dei Ceri** (see box below).

There are several ways up to the basilica, one being via the steep track that strikes off from behind the Duomo. However, it's quicker and far more fun – unless you have no head for heights – to take the **funicular** (hours vary considerably, but generally summer 8.30/9.30am–7.30pm; winter reduced hours; return €5) from Porta Romana, over on the eastern side of town; you jump on small two-person cradles, which then dangle precariously over the woods and crags below as you shudder slowly upwards. While you're waiting you could take in more of Ottaviano Nelli's paintings, tucked away in the thirteenth-century **Sant'Agostino** and **Santa Maria Nuova** nearby. The unusually lovely *Madonna del Belvedere* (1408) in the latter is a masterpiece of the detailed and highly decorative style for which he was famous. His most majestic efforts – seventeen frescoes on the life of the Virgin – are in

---

The Corsa dei Ceri

Little known outside Italy but second only to Siena's Palio in terms of exuberance and bizarre pageantry, the **Corsa dei Ceri** takes place on May 15 every year. The rules and rigmarole of the 900-year-old ceremony are mind-boggling, but they boil down to three teams racing from Piazza della Signoria to the basilica, carrying the *ceri* (each representing a different saint) on wooden stretchers. By iron-clad tradition, the *cero* of St Ubaldo always wins, the other teams having to ensure they're in the basilica before the doors are shut by the leaders.

San Francesco, the big church that dominates the Piazza dei Quaranta Martiri – the bus terminal – at the foot of the town. The piazza's named in memory of forty citizens shot by the Germans in 1944, a reprisal for partisan attacks in the surrounding hills.

Gubbio's **Porte della Morte**, the "doors of death", are as controversial as the ceri, as no-one can quite agree on their origins. Almost unique to the town (there are a few others in Assisi and southern France), these are narrow, bricked-up doorways wedged into the facades of its medieval town houses (with the best examples in Via dei Consoli). The party line is that they were used to carry a coffin out of a house, and then, having been tainted with death, were sealed up out of superstitious fear. Nice theory, and very Italian, but judging by the constricted stairways behind the doors, their purpose was probably defensive – the main door could be barricaded, leaving the more easily defended passageway as the only entrance.

Eating

Gubbio boasts a good selection of **restaurants**, with some high-quality, if rather expensive, options close to the Palazzo dei Consoli. Cheaper places for snacks, sandwiches or *pizza taglia* are found in the grid of streets to the south, and towards the northern end of Via dei Consoli.

Bosone Via XX Settembre 22 ☎075.922.0688. The restaurant of the *Bosone* hotel (see p.571) is open to non-patrons and, thanks to its garden, is the nicest place to eat outdoors in the summer. Prices are little over the average for the town, at around €12 for mains. Closed Wed except June–Sept.

Fabiani Piazza Quaranta Martiri 26A/B ☎075.927.4639, ✆www.ristorantefabiani.it. Fine, friendly place, with several dining rooms set in part of the elegant Palazzo Fabiani; attractive terrace for summer alfresco dining. Good value (meals from around €30) given the quality of the cooking. Closed Tues.

Grotta dell'Angelo Via Gioia 47 ☎075.927.3438. Annexed to the *Grotta dell'Angelo* hotel (see p.571), offering very tasty and reasonably priced basic meals in a wonderful dining room. Closed Tues.

Taverna del Lupo Via Ansidei 21 ☎075.927.4368, ✆www.mancarelligroup.com. A smart and long-established place in a medieval setting, well worth a splurge (mains around €18) for its classic Umbrian dishes and excellent truffle risotto. Closed Mon.

Parco Regionale del Monte Cucco

Some of Umbria's best upland scenery is to be found in the mountains east and north of the earthquake-battered town of Gualdo Tadino on the border with Marche, much of it protected by the **Parco Regionale del Monte Cucco**. Where this area really scores is in its organized trails and backup for outdoor activities of every kind; if you want to don walking boots without too much fuss, this is one of the areas to do it – and **access** is easy, with buses from Gualdo to Valsorda and from Perugia, Gualdo, Gubbio and Assisi to Costacciaro.

The southernmost base for exploration of the park is the resort of **VALSORDA** (1000m), 8km northeast of Gualdo on the park's southern extremity. You can tackle the straightforward trek (1hr) up **Serra Santa** (1421m) on a track of motorway proportions carved out by pilgrims over the years. From the summit you could drop into the spectacular **Valle del Fonno** gorge and follow it down to Gualdo. Paths follow the main ridge from Valsorda north and south, and it's feasible to walk all the way to Nocera Umbra (6hr). Accommodation is thin on the ground, but there's a **campsite**, the *Valsorda* (☎075.913.261; June–Sept).

To get closer to the heart of the mountains head to the unpretentious and appealing **COSTACCIARO**, centre for all the park's outdoor pursuits and access point for the **Grotta di Monte Cucco**, at 922m the fifth-deepest cave system in the world. Above, the huge, bare-sloped Monte Cucco (1566m) is the main playground for **walkers**. The best place for information is the **Centro Escursionistioo Naturalistico Speleologico**, Calcinaro 7/A; ☏&℉075.917.0400 for details of tours; ⓦwww.cens.it).

There are several places **to stay** in and around Costacciaro, the best of them being the two-star *Monte Cucco di Tobia* in the Val di Ranco (☏075.917.7194, ⓦwww.albergomontecucco.it; ❶; Easter–Oct), a fabled mountaineers' and cavers' hangout (with an inexpensive restaurant). The nearest **campsite** is the *Rio Verde* (☏075.917.0138, ⓦwww.campingrioverde.it; April–Sept) at **Fornace**, 3km north of Costacciaro. Freelance camping is prohibited within the *parco regionale*, but elsewhere you'll have few problems finding a discreet pitch for a tent.

Assisi

ASSISI is already too well known, thanks to **St Francis**, Italy's premier saint and founder of the Franciscan order, which, with its various splinter groups, forms the world's biggest religious order. Had the man not been born here in 1182 the town wouldn't be thronged with visitors and pilgrims for ten months of the year, but then neither would it have the **Basilica of St Francis**, one of the greatest monuments to thirteenth- and fourteenth-century Italian art. You'll probably feel it's worth putting up with the crowds and increasingly overwhelming commercialism, but you may not want to hang around once you've seen all there is to see – something which can easily be done in a day. That said, Assisi quietens down in the evening, and it does retain considerable medieval hill-town charm.

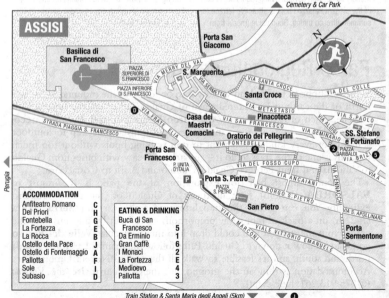

Arrival and information

Getting here is easy. **Buses** connect regularly with surrounding towns – especially Perugia – putting down and picking up in Piazza Matteotti, in the east of the town above the Duomo. In addition, one bus a day leaves for Rome and two for Florence, from Piazza Unità d'Italia. There are very frequent (at least hourly) **trains** to Foligno (via Spello) and Terontola (via Perugia), with connecting bus services between the town and the station, which is 5km away to the southwest of the centre. If you are **driving**, however, note that the centre of town is closed to traffic. Your best bet is to park either in Piazza Matteotti at the top (eastern) end of the town, or below the basilica in Piazza Unità d'Italia; either way, you will have a stiff uphill walk if you explore the whole town. The staff at the **tourist office**, at the western end of Piazza del Comune (April–Oct Mon–Sat 8am–2pm & 3–6pm, Sun 10am–1pm & 3–6pm; Nov–March Mon–Fri 8am–2pm & 2–5pm, Sat 9am–1pm & 3–6pm, Sun 9am–1pm; ☏075.812.534 or 075.813.8680, ⓔinfo @iat.assisi.pg.it), do their best to help with accommodation and provide some useful maps and pamphlets.

Accommodation

Assisi offers a wide range of **accommodation**, but the supply is often only just adequate for the number of visitors, so advance booking is highly advisable, and essential if you plan to visit over Easter or during the Festa di San Francesco (Oct 3–4) or Calendimaggio (May 21–22). The tourist office has a full list of lodgings, including over fifty **rooms** for rent and can also supply details of **pilgrim hostels**. Spello is close enough to make seeing Assisi easy. Wherever you choose to stay, try to avoid the concentration of rooms and hotels in Santa Maria degli Angeli or the grim village of Bastia, 4km out of Assisi.

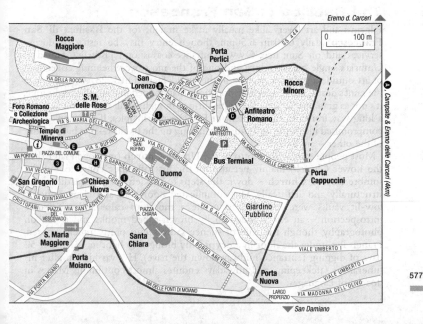

Hotels

Anfiteatro Romano Via Anfiteatro 4
℡075.813.025, ⓔhotelanfiteatro@libero.it.
A good-value one-star in a very pleasant part of
town. Choice of rooms with or without
bathrooms. ❷

Dei Priori Corso Mazzini 15 ℡075.812.237,
ⓔhpriori@tiscali.it. A three-star slightly east of
Piazza del Comune. Rooms vary greatly. ❹

Fontebella Via Fontebella 25
℡075.812.883, ⓦwww.fontebella.com.
The town's most elegant and intimate choice. Ask
for a room on one of the top floors for great
panoramas. ❾

La Fortezza Vicolo della Fortezza 19/B
℡075.812.418, ⓦwww.lafortezzahotel.com.
Friendly two-star with just seven rooms in a perfect
position next to Piazza del Comune; the co-owned
restaurant is also excellent. ❷

La Rocca Via di Porta Perlici 27
℡&ℱ075.812.284. A one-star situated at the
end of the street beyond the Duomo. Quiet
rooms, some with views, most have private
bathrooms. ❶

Pallotta Via San Rufino 6 ℡075.812.307, toll-
free in Italy 800.124.807, ⓦwww.pallottaassisi.it.
A two-star in a good location between the Duomo
and Piazza del Comune; also has a first-rate
co-owned *trattoria* just off Piazza del Comune
(see p.583). ❷

Sole Corso Mazzini 35 ℡075.812.373, ⓦwww
.assisihotelsole.com. Recently renovated but fairly
functional two-star 1min walk from the Basilica
di Santa Chiara. Good option if everywhere else is
full. ❷

Subasio Via Frate Elia 2 ℡075.821.206, ⓦwww
.hotelsubasio.com. Assisi's four-star *grande dame*,
old-world comfort with valley views and an
enviable position – right next to the porticoes of the
Basilica di San Francesco. ❽

Hostels and camping

Fontemaggio 3km east of town on Via San Rufino
Campagna ℡075.813.636 or 075.812.317,
ⓦwww.fontemaggio.it. Hostel also with a 244-
pitch campsite. The fairly rural setting is better than
the sites you may see advertised towards Baschi
on the other side of Assisi; there's also a decent
shop to save you the trek into town for supplies;
dorm beds €20.

Ostello della Pace Via di Valecchie 177 off Viale
Marconi ℡075.816.767, ⓦwww.assisihostel.com.
The larger of the two hostels this place has 66
beds. It's a a 10min downhill walk from Piazza
Unità d'Italia – follow Viale Marconi until it bends
sharp right, at which point a minor road leads off
left (ignore the minor road straight on at the same
point) and downhill, passing the *Country House*
hotel on the left after 5min and reaching the hostel
on the right shortly afterwards. Dorm beds €16.

The Basilica di San Francesco

Pilgrims and art lovers alike usually make straight for the **Basilica di San
Francesco** (daily 6.30am–6.50pm, though entry may be restricted during
services and on Sun; free; ⓦwww.sanfrancescoassisi.org) justifiably famed as
Umbria's single greatest glory, and one of the most overwhelming collections
of art outside a gallery anywhere in the world. Started in 1228, two years after
the saint's death, and financed by donations that flooded in from all over Europe,
it's not as grandiose as some religious shrines, though it still strikes you as being
a long way from the embodiment of Franciscan principles. If you don't mind
compromised ideals, the two churches making up the basilica – one built on top
of the other – are a treat.

Most people start with Giotto in the **Upper Church** (may open later than
the Lower Church) mainly because it's the first one they come to, but the
sombre **Lower Church** – down the steps to the left – comes earlier, both
structurally and artistically. The complicated floor plan and claustrophobic
low-lit vaults were intended to create a mood of calm and meditative
introspection – an effect added to by brown-robed monks and a ban on
photography, though the rule of silence sadly seems pretty much ignored.
Francis lies under the floor in a **crypt** only brought to light in 1818 after 52
days of digging (entrance midway down the nave). He was hidden after his
funeral for safekeeping, and nowadays endures almost continuous Masses in
dozens of languages.

▲ St Francis statues for sale, Assisi

Frescoes cover almost every available space and span a century of continuous artistic development. Stilted early works by anonymous painters influenced by the Byzantines sit alongside Roman painters such as Cavallini, who with Cimabue pioneered the move from mosaic to naturalism and the "new" medium of fresco. They were followed by the best of the Sienese School, **Simone Martini** and **Pietro Lorenzetti**, whose paintings are the ones to make a real point of seeing.

Martini's frescoes are in the **Cappella di San Martino** (1322–26), the first chapel on the left as you enter the nave. He was given free rein in the chapel, and every detail, right down to the floor and stained glass, follows his drawings, adding up to a unified scheme that's unique in Italy. Lorenzetti's works, dominated by a powerful *Crucifixion*, are in the transept to the left of the main altar. Vaults above the altar itself contain four magnificent frescoes, complicated but colourful allegories of the virtues on which Francis founded his order: Poverty, Chastity and Obedience. Once thought to have been the work of Giotto, they're now attributed to one of the church's army of unknown artists. The big feature in the right transept is Cimabue's over-restored *Madonna, Child and Angels with St Francis*, a painting Ruskin described as "the noblest depiction of the Virgin in Christendom." Look out for the famous portrait of Francis and for the much-reproduced fresco of St Clare on the wall to its left.

The more straightforward **Upper Church**, built to a light and airy Gothic plan – that was to be followed for countless Franciscan churches – is a completely different experience. It's less a church than an excuse to show off **Giotto**'s dazzling frescoes on the life of St Francis. *Francis Preaching to the Birds* and *Driving the Devils from Arezzo* are just two of the famous scenes reproduced worldwide on cards and posters. The cycle starts on the right-hand wall up by the main altar and continues clockwise. Giotto was still in his 20s when he accepted the commission, having been recommended for the job by Cimabue,

The most extraordinary figure that the Italian Church has produced, **St Francis** was a revolutionary figure who took Christianity back to basics. The impact that he had on the evolution of the Catholic Church stands without parallel, and everything he accomplished in his short life was achieved by nothing more persuasive than the power of preaching and personal example. Dante placed him alongside another Messianic figure, John the Baptist, and his appeal has remained undiminished – Mussolini called him "*il piu santo dei santi*" (the most saintly of the saints).

The events of his life, though doubtless embellished by myth, are well chronicled. He was born in Assisi in 1182, the son of a wealthy merchant and a Provençal woman – which is why he replaced his baptismal name, Giovanni, with Francesco (Little Frenchman). The Occitan literature of Provence, with its troubadour songs and courtly love poems, was later to be the making of Francis as a poet and speaker. One of the earliest writers in the vernacular, Francis laid the foundation of a great Franciscan literary tradition – his Fioretti and famous *Canticle to the Sun* ("brother sun … sister moon") stand comparison with the best of medieval verse.

In line with the early life of most male saints, his formative years were full of drinking and womanizing; he was, says one chronicler, "the first instigator of evil, and behind none in foolishness". Illness and imprisonment in a Perugian jail incubated the first seeds of contemplation. Abstinence and solitary wanderings soon followed. The call from God, the culmination of several visions, came in Assisi in 1209, when the crucifix in San Damiano bowed to him and told him to repair God's Church. Francis took the injunction literally, sold his father's stock of cloth and gave the money to Damiano's priest, who refused it.

Francis subsequently renounced his inheritance in the Piazza del Comune: before a large crowd and his outraged father, he stripped naked in a symbolic rejection of wealth and worldly shackles. Adopting the peasant's grey sackcloth (the brown Franciscan habit came later), he began to beg, preach and mix with lepers, a deliberate

whose own frescoes – almost ruined now by the oxidation of badly chosen pigments and further damaged in the 1997 'quake – fill large parts of the apse and transepts. In the vaults, several harsh areas of bare plaster stand as graphic monuments to the collapse of that year.

If time allows check out the **cloisters**, accessible from the rear right-hand side of the Lower Church, and the Treasury, or **Museo del Tesoro e Collezioni F.M. Perkins** (April–Oct Mon–Sat 9.30am–5pm; donation), reached via the apse of the Lower Church. The latter, often passed by, contains a rich collection of paintings – including works by Pietro Lorenzetti and Masolino da Panicale.

The rest of the Town

Via San Francesco leads back to the town centre from the basilica. Partway along the street on the left is the Palazzo Vallemani, the site of Assisi's excellent **Pinacoteca** (daily: March–May & Sept–Oct 10am–5pm; June–Aug 10am–6.30pm; Nov–Feb 10.30am–1pm & 2–5pm; €3.50, joint ticket with Foro Romano & Rocca Maggiore €5). It would be easy to ignore this after the rich artistic pickings of the basilica, but the gallery is well worth the admission, not least for the many detached frescoes rescued from churches and other buildings around Assisi, among them important works by the Gubbian artist Ottaviano Nelli. The displays are enhanced by good English commentaries.

embodiment of Christ's invocation to the Apostles "to heal the sick, and carry neither purse, nor scrip [money], nor shoes". His message was disarmingly simple: throw out the materialistic trappings of daily life and return to a love of God rooted in poverty, chastity and obedience. Furthermore, learn to see in the beauty and profusion of the natural world the all-pervasive hand of the Divine – a keystone of humanist thought and a departure from the doom-laden strictures of the Dark Ages.

In time he gathered his own twelve apostles and, after some difficulty, obtained permission from Pope Innocent III to found an order that espoused no dogma and maintained no rule. Francis himself never became a priest. In 1212 he was instrumental in the creation of a second order for women, the **Poor Clares**, and continued the vast travels that took him as far as the Holy Land with the armies of the Crusades. In Egypt he confronted the sultan, Melek el-Kamel, offering to undergo a trial by fire to prove his faith. In 1224 Francis received the stigmata on the mountaintop at La Verna. Two years later, nursing his exhausted body, he died on the mud floor of his hovel in Assisi, having scorned the offer of grander accommodation at the bishop's palace. His canonization followed swiftly, in 1228, in a service conducted by Pope Gregory.

However, a split in the Franciscan order was inevitable. Francis's message and movement had few sympathizers in the wealthy and morally bankrupt papacy of the time, and while his popularity had obliged the Vatican to applaud while he was alive, the papacy quickly moved in to quash the purist elements and encourage more "moderate" tendencies. Gradually it shaped the movement to its own designs, institutionalizing Francis's message in the process. Despite this, Francis's achievement as the first man to fracture the rigid orthodoxy of the hierarchical Church remains beyond question. Moreover, the Franciscans have not lost their ideological edge, and their views on the primacy of poverty are thought by many to be out of favour with the present Vatican administration.

A little farther down the street on the right are the remains of the fifteenth-century **Oratorio dei Pellegrini** (daily 9am–noon & 3–8pm; free), the hospice for pilgrims, frescoed inside and out by local painters Mezzastris and Matteo da Gualdo – appealing but modest offerings after the basilica (and often out of bounds because of praying nuns).

Of more limited appeal is the **Foro Romano e Collezione Archeologica** entered just off Piazza del Comune at Via Portica 2 (same hours as Pinacoteca; €3.50; joint ticket with Pinacoteca & Rocca Maggiore €5), housed in the crypt of the now defunct church of San Nicolò. The classical remains include an excavated street – probably part of the old Roman forum – buried under the Piazza del Comune. The piazza itself is dominated by the so-called **Tempio di Minerva**, an enticing and perfectly preserved classical facade from the first century, concealing a dull, if beautifully restored, seventeenth-century Baroque conversion; it was the only thing Goethe was bothered about seeing when he came to Assisi – the basilica he avoided, calling it a "Babylonian pile". Francis's birthplace lies just south of the piazza, marked by the Chiesa Nuova, a dreary church.

A short hike in the other direction up the steep Via di San Rufino brings you to the thirteenth-century **Duomo** (daily 7.30am–12.30pm & 2.30–7pm; free) with a typical and very lovely three-tiered Umbrian facade and sumptuously carved central doorway. The only point of interest in a boring interior is the font used to baptize St Francis, St Clare and – by a historical freak – the future

Emperor Frederick II, born prematurely in a field outside the town. Off the right (south) nave, there's the small **Museo Diocesano**, or **Museo della Cattedrale** (Thurs–Tues mid-March to mid-Oct 10am–1pm & 3–6pm except Aug daily 10am–6pm; rest of the year Thurs–Tues 10am–1pm & 2.30–5.30pm; €3), with a handful of good paintings, including a 1470 work by Nicolò Alunno, and an atmospheric **crypt**, the **Cripta di San Rufino** (same hours & ticket), entered outside down steps to the right of the facade. The cathedral makes a good point from which to strike off for the **Rocca Maggiore** (daily 10am–dusk; €3.50, €5 with Pinacoteca & Foro Romano), one of the bigger and better preserved in the region, with some all-embracing views the reward after a stiff climb.

Below the Duomo, on the pedestrianized Piazza Santa Chiara, stands the **Basilica di Santa Chiara** (daily 6/7am–noon & 2pm–dusk; free), burial place of St Francis's devoted early companion, who at the age of 17 founded the Order of the Poor Clares, the female wing of the Franciscans. By some peculiar and not terribly dignified quirk she's also the patron saint of television. The church was consecrated in 1265 and is a virtual facsimile of the basilica up the road, down to the simple facade and opulent rose window. The scantily decorated interior has the body of St Clare herself and the Byzantine crucifix famous for having bowed to Francis and commanded him to embark on his sacred mission to repair God's Church (see box, p.580).

You're not long off the Francis trail in Assisi. **San Damiano** (daily 10am–noon & 2–6pm, closes 4.30pm in winter; free), a peaceful spot of genuine monastic charm, is one of its highlights, and is easily reached by taking the Via Borgo Aretino beyond the basilica and following signs from the Porta Nuova, a steep downhill walk of about fifteen minutes. Original home to the Poor Clares, and one of St Francis's favourite spots (he is thought to have written his well-known *Canticle to the Sun* here), the church, cloisters and rustic setting preserve – almost uniquely in Assisi – a sense of the original Franciscan ideals of humility and simplicity often absent in the rest of the town.

From the train station you can see the town's other major attraction, the vast but uninspiring **Santa Maria degli Angeli** (daily: April–Oct 6.30am–1pm & 2.30–8pm; Nov–March 6.30am–12.30pm & 2–7.30pm; free), built in the seventeenth century and rebuilt after an earthquake in 1832. Somewhere in its Baroque bowels are the remains of the **Porzuincola**, a tiny chapel that was effectively the first Franciscan monastery. Francis lived here after founding the order in 1208, attracted by its then remote and wooded surroundings, and in time was joined by other monks and hermits who built a series of cells and mud huts in the vicinity. Today the church is crammed full of largely fourth-rate works of art and is a long way from the Franciscan ideal.

Eating and drinking

Multilingual tourist menus proliferate in the town's **restaurants**, and prices can be steep. For wonderful **ice cream** and mouthwatering **pastries**, head for the *Gran Caffè*, Corso Mazzini 16/A.

Buca di San Francesco Via Brizzi 1 ⊕075.812.204. The *Buca* has been around for ever, and is generally a reliable choice for a decent mid-price meal, though food can be variable – excellent one day, middling the next. Closed Mon. **Da Erminio** Via Montecavallo 19 ⊕075.812.506. Very good value, with full meals at around €20.

Located above the Duomo in a quiet corner. Closed Thurs, Jan, Feb & a period in July. **La Fortezza** Vicolo della Fortezza 2 ⊕075.812.418. Long-established spot just off the main Piazza del Comune; great food but slightly slow service; reservations essential in summer. Closed Feb, Thurs & lunch Mon & Wed–Fri.

Medioevo Via dell'Arco dei Priori 4/B ☎075.813.068). Just south off the Piazza del Comune, highly recommended for a splurge (mains around €20) on some eclectic cuisine that draws its inspiration from France, Germany and Austria as well as Italy. Closed Wed, Jan & a period in July.

Pallotta Via Volta Piana 2 ☎075.812.649. An unpretentious and welcoming mid-priced trattoria just south of Piazza del Comune – arrive early for a table at lunch. Closed Tues.

Spello and around

Ranged on broad terraces above the Vale of Spoleto, medieval and pink-stoned **SPELLO** is the best place for a taste of small-town Umbria if you haven't time or means to explore farther, being easy to reach by road and rail (20min from Assisi or Spoleto). Emperor Augustus gave land in the adjacent valley to faithful legionnaires who had reached the end of their careers, turning the town (Hispellum) into a sort of Roman retirement home in the process, an ambience it still rather retains.

Arrival, information and accommodation

Spello makes a reasonable base for visiting Assisi, with a good range of **accommodation**, fair restaurants and a small **tourist office** at the northern end of Piazza Matteotti at no.3 (daily 9.30am–12.30pm & 3.30–5.30pm;☎0742.301.009). If you're coming by train from the south, note that you may have to change trains at Foligno for Spello.

Hotels

Il Cacciatore Via Giulia 42 ☎0742.651.141, ⓦwww.ilcacciatorehotel.com. A reasonable-value two-star hotel, with fine views from some rooms and potentially noisier rooms looking out over the street. ⓷
La Bastiglia Via dei Molini 17 ☎0742.651.277, ⓦwww.labastiglia.com. Smart, four-star option; most of the rooms command a fine view and

there's a good if expensive Michelin-starred restaurant (reckon on about €60 for three courses. Closed Wed & Thurs lunchtimes plus a period in Jan. �7
Residence San Jacopo ☎0742.301.260, ⓦwww.residencesanjacopo.it. Above the *Pinturicchio* restaurant at the top of the main street on the left, with a warm welcome and ten excellent mini-apartments from €60 nightly, with kitchenettes for self-catering. ⓶

The Town

The walls and three gateways are the most obvious Roman remnants. Don't bother walking out to the paltry and overgrown remains of the old amphitheatre hidden away beyond the main highway to Assisi: you can see all you need to from the top of the town. By far the most distinguished sight is **Pinturicchio's fresco cycle** in the thirteenth-century church of Santa Maria Maggiore (daily: April–Oct 8.30am–12.30pm & 3–7pm; Nov–March 8.30am–12.30pm & 3–6pm; free), about a third of the way up the town's winding and steep main street on Piazza G. Matteotti. The number-two Umbrian painter after Perugino, he left other important works in Siena (the Duomo), Rome (the Sistine Chapel, Borgia apartments) and a host of churches scattered over central Italy. The frescoes themselves are fresh and glowing from restoration, with Pinturicchio's famous details and colouring brought out to stunning effect. Unfortunately they're behind glass, which also means you can't get a closer look at the chapel's praised but faded fifteenth-century **ceramic pavement**. Almost immediately to the north of the church stands an excellent little art gallery, the **Pinacoteca Civica** (Tues–Sun: April–Sept 10.30am–1pm & 3–6.30pm; Oct–March 10.30am–12.30pm & 3.30–5.30pm; €2.60). It contains a handful of masterpieces by local Umbrian painters, notably Nicolò Alunno, as well as several rare pieces of sculpture. Look out in particular for the figure of Christ with movable arms, once common, now extremely rare: during Holy Week the arms could be raised for ceremonies involving depictions of the Crucifixion and lowered for those depicting the Deposition and Resurrection. Farther up the busy, steep main street on the right stands **Sant'Andrea**, a striking Gothic church with another Pinturicchio painting in the right transept brightening up the gloomy interior. Also look out for the looming crucifix attributed to the school of Giotto.

Eating and drinking

Bar Giardino Via Cavour 12. There appears nothing special about this small bar until you take your drink out to the wonderful panoramic garden terrace at the back.

Hosteria de Dadà Via Cavour 47. A tiny place with a handful of shared tables and is good for cheap, light meals at lunch or dinner. Open daily.

Il Cacciatore Via Giulia 42 ☎ 0742.651.141, Ⓦ www.ilcacciatorehotel.com). Attached to the hotel (see p.583), with middling food and lower

prices than *La Bastiglia* but a tremendous terrace for alfresco dining. Closed Mon.

Il Molino Piazza Matteotti 6–7 ☎ 0742.651.305. Spello's most appealing restaurant, set in a vaulted medieval town house a few steps up from Santa Maria Maggiore; a fairly smart place (mains from €15) serving plenty of regional specialities – and wonderful fresh pasta – but with the unfortunate odd pretension. Closed Tues.

Bevagna

The serene, attractive backwater of **BEVAGNA** is quieter and less visited than Spello, with a windswept **central square** of stark perfection. Flanked by two of Umbria's finest Romanesque churches – both untouched and creaking with age – the Piazza S. Silvestri dates from around the thirteenth century. The only exception is the fountain, which, while blending perfectly, was installed in 1889. Look out particularly for the surreal gargoyles over the doorway of the larger church, San Michele. Also worth seeking out is the impressive **Roman mosaic** (north side of Via Porta Guelfa; same ticket and hours as Museo Civico: see below), once part of a bath complex. This fine work shows octopus, lobsters, sea-centaurs and other creatures. To get to see it you'll need to find a guide at the small **Museo Civico** to take you there (April–Sept daily 10.30am–1pm & 2.30–5.30/7pm; rest of the year closes 5pm but closed Mon; €3.50). Located at Corso Matteotti 70, the museum is devoted to the history of the village and divided into three modest sections: archeological displays, art and history, and maps, letters and other documents. The museum and mosaic joint ticket also gives access to the delightful little nineteenth-century **Torti theatre**, formerly the Palazzo Comunale, just off the main square. You can also join guided tours at the museum around the **Circuito Medievale Storie di Antichi Mestieri** (twice daily during museum opening days at 11am year-round plus 3.30pm April–May & Sept, 4.30pm June–Aug & 3pm Oct–March). This involves visits to four recreated workshops connected with medieval trades, namely paper-maker, silk-weaver, a mint and a pharmacy.

There's not a lot else to the town, other than the quaint attractiveness of the streets, but Bevagna does boast three charming **hotels**. The most central is the one-star *Il Chiostro di Bevagna*, Corso Matteotti 103 (☎ 0742.361.987,

ⓌWww.ilchiostrodibevagna,com; ❸), just off Piazza S. Silvestro, in an atmospheric renovated Dominican convent, with an original cloister. Down the same street, the three-star *Palazzo Brunamonti*, Corso Matteotti 79 (☎0742.361.932, Ⓦwww.brunamonti.com; ❸) is a sumptuous place with a period setting and trompe l'oeil decorations. *L'Orto degli Angeli* (☎0742.360.130, Ⓦwww.ortoangeli.it; ❼), just off the Corso Matteotti at the eastern end of town, is the most luxurious and historic of them all; the mansion, with porticoes, gardens and a popular gourmet restaurant, *Redibis* (closed Tues), has been in the same family since 1788. There are also a few good **restaurants** in town: try the mid-priced *Ottavio*, Via del Gonfalone 4, immediately south of Piazza S. Silvestri in the square in which the buses from Foligno and Montefalco stop; or the *Enoteca di Piazza Onofri*, just behind the Palazzo Comunale at Piazza Onofri 1 (closed Wed & a period in July or Aug), perfect for light meals or a snack and a glass of wine. Also appealing is the *Osteria del Podestà*, Corso Matteotti 67 (☎0742.361.832; closed Tues), a small, central *osteria* with full meals at around €29; main courses are traditional to Umbria, puddings a little more adventurous, and the rustic surroundings – stone walls and ceiling – a definite bonus.

Montefalco

MONTEFALCO is a pleasing and intimate medieval village that's home to a superb collection of paintings. Its name, meaning Falcon's Mount, was glorified with the appendage *la ringhiera dell'Umbria* – "the balcony of Umbria" – a tribute to its wonderful views. It was also the birthplace of eight saints, good going even by Italian standards. Nowadays the town's sleepy rather than holy, with only a stupendously ugly water tower and very slight urban sprawl to take the edge off its medieval appeal. The strong, blackberry-flavoured **local wine**, *Sagrantino Passito*, made from a grape variety found nowhere else in Europe, is well worth a try; it's available in many shops around town. Recommended producers are Adanti and Caprai, also makers of the excellent Rosso di Montefalco.

Using public transport, you can get here by **bus** from most local towns and villages, including five services daily from Bevagna and eight daily from Perugia.

The town's lofty location was a godsend to Spoleto's papal governors, left high, dry and terrified by the fourteenth-century defection of the popes to Avignon. They took refuge here, and their cowering presence accounts for some of the rich decoration of Montefalco's churches, a richness out of all proportion to the town's size. The cavernous ex-church of San Francesco, off the central Piazza del Comune at Via Ringhiera Umbra 6, is now the **Museo Civico di San Francesco** (March–May, Sept & Oct daily 10.30am–1pm & 2–6pm; June–Aug daily 10.30am–1pm & 3–7pm, Aug open until 7.30pm; Nov–Feb Tues–Sun 10.30am–1pm & 2.30–5pm; €5), housing the town's big feature, Benozzo Gozzoli's sumptuous **fresco cycle** on the life of St Francis. With Fra' Angelico, Gozzoli was one of the most prolific and influential Florentine painters to come south and show the backward Umbrians what the Renaissance was all about. Resplendent with colour and detail, the cycle copies many of the ideas and episodes from Giotto's Assisi cycle but, with two hundred years of artistic know-how to draw on, is more sophisticated and more immediately appealing.

The rest of the town is relatively low key but nice for a wander. Probably the most bizarre sight is the mummified body of **St Clare** (St Chiara), which languishes in the otherwise dismal church of the same name, five-minutes' walk from San Francesco in Via Verdi (this is a second St Clare, not to be confused with the one in Assisi). Ring the bell and, if the nuns aren't deep in prayer, they may show you round the adjoining convent: in what turns out to be a fascinating behind-the-scenes look at monastic life, you're shown the remains of the saint's heart and the scissors used to hack it out. The story goes that Christ appeared to Clare, saying the burden of carrying the cross was becoming too heavy; Clare replied she would help by carrying it in her heart. When she was opened up after her death, a cross-shaped piece of tissue was duly found on her heart. Other strange exhibits include three of her kidney stones and a tree that miraculously grew from a staff planted in the garden here by Christ, during one of his appearances to Clare; the berries are used to make rosaries and are said to have powerful medicinal qualities.

Fifty metres beyond the church, preceded by a triple-arched Renaissance porch, is the chapel of **Sant'Illuminata**, strikingly if not terribly well frescoed by local painter Melanzio and others in 1510.

Practicalities

There's no need to spend more than a morning in Montefalco, but if you do decide **to stay** – and it's a peaceful spot to rest up – try the *Hotel "Degli Affreschi"*, Via G. Mameli 45 (℡0742.379.243, ℻0742.379.643; ❷), not far from the main square. Residents have use of the swimming pool at the ugly modern sister hotel *Hotel Nuovo Mondo*, 2km outside of town on the main road. The best restaurant is the mid-priced *Coccorone*, on the corner of Largo Tempestivi and Via Fabbri (℡0742.379.535; closed Wed except in summer) – the *crespelle* (stuffed pancakes) and the *tiramisù* are especially good. Otherwise, the main square has a couple of cafés and wine bars for drinks and snacks.

If you want more **information** on the town, contact the infrequently open Pro Loco office alongside the Museo or visit the office or website of the Strada del Sagrantino (Piazza del Comune 17, ℡0742.378.490, ⓦwww .stradadelsagrantino.it), a body which promotes the wines of the region, but also has plenty of general background on places to stay, eat and visit.

Trevi

Road and rail south of Assisi and Spello run down the plain of Spoleto, past the light industrial sites that blight the whole stretch of the valley towards Terni and beyond. Not many people stop before Spoleto itself, giving **TREVI** and its towering position no more than an admiring glance. Its daunting inaccessibility is one of the reasons for its easy-going, old-fashioned charm; the feeling is of a pleasant, ordinary provincial town, unspoilt but just beginning to feel the first effects of tourism. All around it are vast expanses of olive groves, renowned for producing central Italy's finest oil.

The medieval centre, looming high on its hill, is 4km from the station, connected by bus. The main square inside the walls, Piazza Mazzini, has a small and obliging Pro Loco **tourist office** at no. 6 (daily 9am–1pm & 3–6/7pm; ℡0742.781.150, ⓦwww.protrevi.com), supplemented in a corner of the same piazza by a very helpful Tourist Co-Op (Mon–Sat 9am–1pm; ℡0742.780.066). The latter can organize all manner of accommodation locally, from rooms to villas, as well as a variety of tours and activities: despite the official afternoon closing times, there is generally someone in the office most of the day.

The key sight in town is the superb **Museo di San Francesco** (April–May & Sept Tues–Sun 10.30am–1pm & 2.30–6pm; June–July Tues–Sun 10.30am–1pm & 3.30–7pm; Aug daily 10.30am–1pm & 3–7.30pm; Oct–March Fri–Sun 10.30am–1pm & 2.30–5pm; €4) in Largo Don Bosco, in the former Convento di San Francesco, reached by taking Via di San Francesco from the northern end of Piazza Mazzini. It houses a well-presented display of coins, ceramics and Roman fragments, several paintings by Umbrian masters and one outstanding work, a *Coronation of the Virgin* (1522) by Lo Spagna. Trevi's medieval governors commissioned this last painting as a copy of a more famous work by the Florentine Ghirlandaio, mainly because they couldn't afford the real thing. In the same complex is the **Museo della Civiltà dell'Ulivo** (same hours and ticket), a smart museum devoted to history of the olive and olive oil production. It's packed with interesting information, in English as well as Italian, though the number of exhibits is small.

Practicalities

Accommodation is limited, though recent new hotels further underline the changes taking place in the town. The best central bet is the very polished *Antica Dimora alla Rocca*, Piazza della Rocca (℡0742.38.541, Ⓦwww.hotelallarocca.it; ❹), part of a historic 1650 building with frescoed ceilings and other period features, all beautifully restored. Aim to be in the main hotel, with nineteen rooms, rather than the seven-room annexe. Aternatively, try the two-star *Il Terziere* (℡0742.78.359, Ⓦwww.ilterziere.com; ❸), which has the bonus of a pleasant garden: it lies east of the vast square and car park by which you enter Trevi on its eastern side at Via Salerno 1. The tourist offices (see opposite) will be able to come up with **private rooms** to rent in and around town.

For **food** try the *Osteria La Vecchia Posta*, Piazza Mazzini 14 (closed Thurs except in July & Aug), or the more expensive, and half-hidden, *La Prepositura*, Vicolo Oscura 2/A, just below Piazza della Rocca, which has lovely medieval dining areas and full set meals, excluding wine, from €25 per person. At about the same price is *Maggiolini*, midway between the Municipio and San Francesco at Via San Francesco 20 (℡0742.381.534; closed Tues), with good Umbrian staples and housed in part of a sixteenth-century wine cellar.

Fonti di Clitunno

A short hop from Trevi on the road south are the sacred **FONTI DI CLITUNNO** (Mon–Fri: April–Sept 8.30/9am–6.30/8pm; Oct to mid-March 9am–1pm & 2–6pm; mid-March to end of March 9am–1pm & 2–6.30pm; Sat & Sun same opening and closing hours year-round but remains open all day; €2), an unexpected beauty spot given the pockmarked surroundings. There's a certain amount of commercialized fuss and bother at the entrance, but the springs, streams and willow-shaded lake beyond – painted by Corot and an inspiration to poets from Virgil to Byron – are pure, languid romanticism. The spa waters have attracted people since Roman times – the likes of Caligula and Claudius came here to party – but their major curative effect is allegedly the dubious one of completely extinguishing any appetite for alcohol. Earthquakes over the years have upset many of the underground springs, so the waters aren't as plentiful as they were, but they still flow as limpid as they did in Byron's day, the "sweetest wave of the most living crystal … the purest god of gentle waters … most serene of aspect and most clear … a mirror and a bath for Beauty's youngest daughters".

A few hundred metres north is the so-called **Tempietto di Clitunno** (Tues–Sun: April–Oct 8am–8pm; Nov–March 8am–6pm; free), looking for all the world like a miniature Greek temple but actually an eighth-century Christian church, cobbled together with a mixture of idiosyncrasy, wishful thinking and old Roman columns. It's only a small, one-off novelty, but still evocative, and with the bonus inside of some faded frescoes said to be the oldest in Umbria.

Spoleto

SPOLETO is among Umbria's most charming large towns, divided into the medieval and hill-top Upper Town, home to the Duomo and most of the key museums and galleries, and the predominantly modern Lower Town, which nonetheless preserves a handful of Romanesque churches and Roman ruins. Known these days mainly for its big **summer festival** (see box, p.591), it's also remarkable for its thorough-going medievalism, an extremely scenic setting, and several of Italy's most ancient Romanesque **churches**. Far more graceful and provincial a city than Perugia, nowadays it plays second fiddle politically to its long-time historical enemy, though for several centuries it was among the most influential of Italian towns. Two kilometres of well-preserved walls stand as testament to the one-time grandeur of Spoleto's Roman colony, though its real importance dates from the sixth century when the Lombards made it the capital of one of their three Italian dukedoms. The autonomous **Duchy of Spoleto** eventually stretched to Rome, and by 890 its rulers had become powerful enough to lay claim to the imperial throne itself, making Spoleto, for a short time at least, the capital of the entire Holy Roman Empire. Barbarossa flattened the city in a fit of pique in 1155, and in 1499 Pope Alexander VI appointed his daughter, the 19-year-old Lucrezia Borgia, governor. After that it was one long decline until about fifty years ago and the arrival of the festival.

Arrival and information

Spoleto is easily reached by **train**, with regular services on the main Rome–Ancona line and local links with Foligno, Terni, Orte and elsewhere. The train station is just northwest of the Lower Town; shuttle buses (A, B, C) to the centre (Piazza Libertà) depart from outside the station – buy tickets (€0.80) from the station newspaper stand – as do services for Norcia (see p.594); other **buses** leave from central Piazza Libertà and Piazza Garibaldi in the north of the town. The Spoleto **tourist office** is at Piazza Libertà 7 (Mon–Fri 9am–1pm & 4–7pm, Sat & Sun 10am–1pm & 4–7pm; Nov–March weekday afternoon hours 3.30–6.30pm; ☎0743.220.311, or 238.921, ✉info@iat.spoleto.pg.it).

Accommodation

Hotels

Aurora Via dell'Apollinare 3 ☎0743.220.315, ⓦwww.hotelauroraspoleto.it. The best reasonably priced hotel in town, perfectly situated three-star in an alley off Piazza Libertà. Fifteen rooms, all with private bathrooms. ❸

Clarici Piazza Garibaldi–Piazza della Vittoria 32 ☎0743.223.311, ⓦwww.hotelclarici.com. Reasonable and comfortable, but rather basic, modern three-star hotel set just outside the Upper Town walls. ❸

Clitunno Piazza Sordini 6 ☎0743.223.340, ⓦwww .hotelclitunno.com. The best of several central three-star hotels in the Upper Town just west of Piazza Libertà, but note the 35 rooms vary considerably, so ask to see a selection if possible. ❸

Gattapone Via del Ponte 6 ☎0743.223.447, ⓦwww.hotelgattapone.it. The place for a treat; lovely views from most rooms, which are spectacularly situated above the gorge and almost alongside the Ponte delle Torri. ❺

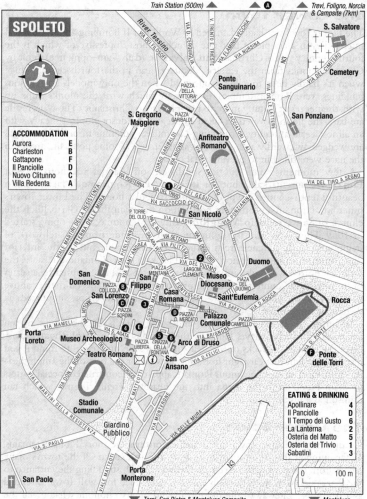

SPOLETO

N

River Tessino

VIA D. CERQUIGLIA
VIA DEI FILOSOFI
V. TRENTO E. TRIESTE
VIA FLAMINIA VECCHIA
VIA NURSINA
N3

S. Salvatore

VIA DEL CIMITERO

Cemetery

PIAZZA DELLA VITTORIA

Ponte Sanguinario

VIA DELLE LETTERE

ACCOMMODATION
Aurora	E
Charleston	B
Gattapone	F
Il Panciolle	D
Nuovo Clitunno	C
Villa Redenta	A

S. Gregorio Maggiore

PIAZZA GARIBALDI

San Ponziano

VIA CACCIATORI D. ALPI

CORSO GARIBALDI
VIA NUOVA

Anfiteatro Romano

VIA DELL'ANFITEATRO

VIA DEL TIRO A SEGNO

VIA POSTERNA

VIA DEI GESUITI

VIA DEL TRIVIO
VIA SACCOCCIO CECILI

San Nicolò

VIA PONZIANINA

P. TORRE DEL OLIO

VIA ELLADIO

VIA S. ALO
VIA SETTANO

VIALE MARTIRI DELLA RESISTENZA
VIA INTERNA DELLE MURA

VIA FILITTERIA

VIA M. DI LORI

VIA PIERLEONE

VIA FITTERIA

Duomo

VIA SANT'ANDREA
VIA SOLARA VECCHIA

VIA DEL DUOMO
LARGO D.

PIAZZA DEL DUOMO

San Domenico

PIAZZA MENTANA
VIA CLEMENTE

Museo Diocesano

San Filippo

Casa Romana

Sant'Eufemia

PIAZZA COLLICOLA

San Lorenzo

PIAZZA SORDINI

VIA D. ROCCA

Rocca

Porta Loreto

VIA MAMELI
VIA VITTORIE

VIA S. AGATA

Palazzo Comunale

PIAZZA CAMPELLO

Museo Archeologico

PIAZZA D. MERCATO

VIA BRIGNOLI

VIA D. PONTE

VIALE MATTEOTTI

PIAZZA DELLA FONTANA

Arco di Druso

VIA SAFFI

Ponte delle Torri

VIALE MARTIRI DELLA RESISTENZA

Teatro Romano

San Ansano

VIA D. FELICI

VIA DON P. BONILLI

VIA MONTERONE

VIALE DELLE MURA

EATING & DRINKING
Apollinare	4
Il Panciolle	D
Il Tempo del Gusto	6
La Lanterna	2
Osteria del Matto	5
Osteria del Trivio	1
Sabatini	3

Stadio Comunale

Giardino Pubblico

VIA S. PAOLO

San Paolo

Porta Monterone

N3

0   100 m

Il Panciolle Via del Duomo 4 ☏0743.45.677. Seven decent two-star rooms, all with private bathrooms, above the restaurant of the same name, though outdoor eating can make staying here a noisy option in summer. ❷

Villa Redenta Via di Villa Redenta 1 ☏0743.224.936, ⓔvillaredenta@hotmail.com. Inexpensive former hostel, now a simple hotel, but its Lower Town location makes this very much a second choice to Upper Town options. From the station walk the length of Viale Trento e Trieste and turn left at the end on Via Flaminia Vecchia: the simple hotel is another 7/8min walk on the left almost opposite Via delle Lettere. ❶

Campsites

Camping Monteluco ☏0743.220.358, ⓔcampeggiomonteluco@libero.it. An attractive pastoral site behind San Pietro, with only 35 places, but an uphill trek to the Upper Town. Open April–Sept.

Il Girasole ☏0743.51.335, ⓔcampingilgirasole @libero.it. In the village of Petrognano (10km northwest of Spoleto; hourly buses from the train station), this is a bigger and flashier affair than *Camping Monteluco*, with a public swimming pool nearby and tennis courts.

The Lower Town

The Lower Town was badly damaged by World War II bombing and its only real interest lies in a couple of first-rate churches, most impressive of which is the fourth-century paleo-Christian **San Salvatore** (daily 7am–5pm; free), built by Christian monks from the eastern Mediterranean in the fourth century, since when it's hardly been touched. Conceived when the only models for religious buildings were Roman temples, that's pretty much what the monks came up with, the net result leaning more to paganism than Christianity. The walls inside are bare, the floors covered in fallen stone, and the dusty gloom is heavy with an almost eerie antiquity. Crumbling Corinthian columns from different ages are wedged awkwardly alongside one another, and at some point the arches in the nave were filled in to prevent total collapse.

A few moments' walk to the southwest, off Via del Cimitero, is **San Ponziano**, unremarkable but for its distinctive Romanesque facade and a beautiful tenth-century crypt (both open irregular hours). The Lower Town's other attraction, in a prominent position on the main Piazza Garibaldi, is the church of **San Gregorio Maggiore** (daily 9am–noon & 3.30–6pm), started in 1069. The tower and intriguing portico are made from a patchwork of fragments clearly pinched from earlier Roman remains, but it's the interior that commands most attention. Stripped back to their Romanesque state, the walls are dotted with substantial patches of fresco and interrupted by a series of unusual stone confessionals. The presbytery is raised several metres above the level of the naves to allow for a masterful little crypt, supported by dozens of tiny pillars.

Tradition has it that somewhere under the church lie the bones of ten thousand Christian martyrs killed by the Romans in the **amphitheatre** close by in the military barracks on Via dell'Anfiteatro. No one seems to mind if you just walk straight in; bear right from the gateway for the best of the amphitheatre's remains. The ever-ingenious Romans apparently constructed special gutters to drain blood from the arena into the nearby Torrente Tessino, which ran crimson as a result.

The Upper Town

Cutting into the adjoining **Piazza della Fontana** are more Roman remains, all far humbler than the tourist hype leads you to expect. Of the town's many arches from the period, the **Arco di Druso** (23 AD) straddling the entrance to the Piazza del Mercato is the only one not embedded in a wall. It was intended as a triumphal gateway to the old forum, and built to honour what, given the gate's rather modest dimensions, must have been very minor campaign victories on the part of Drusus, son of Tiberius. The patched-up walls behind it are the city's oldest, built in the sixth century BC by the Umbrians. To the right of the arch is what is described as a **Roman temple**, but unless you've a vivid imagination it's difficult to see it as anything other than a ditch. Pop into the adjacent church of **San Ansano** for a look at more of the temple and the wonderful fresco-covered crypt (down the stairs to the left of the high altar), originally the home of sixth-century monks.

Nowhere do you get a better sense of Spoleto's market-town roots than in the homely **Piazza del Mercato** beyond, whose two bars on the west side offer a fine opportunity to take in some streetlife. The *alimentari* on all sides are a cornucopia of goodies, with a definite bias towards truffles and sticky liqueurs.

The Duomo and around

Leaving Piazza del Mercato to the north and turning right on Via A. Saffi brings you to the **Duomo** (daily: March–Oct 7.30am–12.30pm & 3–6pm; Nov–Feb closes 5pm; free), whose facade of restrained elegance is one of the most memorable in the region. The careful balance of Romanesque and Renaissance elements is framed by a gently sloping piazza and lovely hanging gardens, but the broad background of sky and open countryside is what sets the seal on the whole thing. The church suffered like many in Italy from the desire of rich communities to make their wealth and power conspicuous, a desire usually realized by tearing the guts out of old churches and remodelling them in the latest style. This worked well on the thirteenth-century **facade**, which has an arched portico tacked on in 1491, but less well in the interior where Pope Urban VIII's architect, Luigi Arrigucci, applied great dollops of Baroque midway through the seventeenth century. His "improvements", luckily, are eclipsed by the apse's superlative **frescoes** by the great Florentine artist Fra' Filippo Lippi, dominated by his final masterpiece, a *Coronation of the Virgin* (1469).

The artist died shortly after their completion, the rumour being that he was poisoned for seducing the daughter of a local noble family, his position as a monk having had no bearing on his sexual appetite. The Spoletans, not too perturbed by moral laxity, were delighted at having someone famous to put in their cathedral, being, as Vasari put it, "poorly provided with ornaments, above all with distinguished men", and so refused to send the dead artist back to Lorenzo de' Medici, his Florentine patron. Interred in a **tomb** designed by his son, Filippino Lippi (now in the right transept), the corpse disappeared during restoration two centuries later, the popular theory being that it was spirited away by descendants of the compromised girl – a sort of vendetta beyond the grave.

You should also make a point of seeing the **Erioli Chapels** at the beginning of the right nave, primarily for a faded *Madonna and Child* (with Lago Trasimeno in the background) by Pinturicchio (1497), and for the cruder frescoes in the adjoining chapel by the Sicilian artist Jacopo Santori. There's also a good

The Festival dei Due Mondi

Hosting Italy's leading international arts festival, the **Festival dei Due Mondi** (Festival of Two Worlds), has been a double-edged blessing for Spoleto – crowds and commercialism being the price it has had to pay for culture. Having already rejected thirty other Italian locations, the influential arts guru Giancarlo Menotti plumped for the town in 1958, attracted by its scenery, small venues and general good vibes. The ensuing jamboree is a great attraction if you're into music, dance or theatre, though the place forgoes a good part of its charm as a result. On top of the crowds, ticket prices for top companies and world-class performers can be off-putting, as can the well-heeled cut of the audiences. Be warned, too, that while the festival is in progress you can expect packed hotels, madness in the restaurants and the chance of higher prices all round. At the same time there's an Edinburgh-type fringe and plenty of fellow travellers (plus lots of films, jazz, buskers and so on). Organizers, moreover, are increasingly looking to more avant-garde shows to recover the artistic edge of the festival's early days. Check out **information** from the **tourist office** on Piazza Libertà or the festival's own **office** at Piazza del Duomo 8 (℡0743.45.028, @www.spoletofestival.it). Advance tickets can also be bought online or by phone on ℡0743.220.320 (or free phone in Italy ℡800.565.600) or in Spoleto itself at the box office at Piazza Libertà 12 (℡0743.44.700, ℻0743.46.416).

Cosmati marble floor; Umbria's earliest documented painting (a *Crucifix* of 1187, by Alberto Sotio, behind glass at the beginning of the left nave); a colourful chapel farther down the left nave containing a framed letter written by St Francis (one of only two to survive); and the inevitable **icon**, which Barbarossa gave to the town in 1185 to try to make amends for having flattened it thirty years earlier.

Palazzo Communale and around

The **Pinacoteca**, usually housed in the Palazzo Comunale, has been moved temporarily into the Rocca (see p.592). The paintings include a couple of big canvases by a follower of Perugino, Lo Spagna, one of several local Renaissance artists represented.

In a tiny side street below the Palazzo Comunale is the **Casa Romana**, Via di Visiale (daily: mid-March to mid-Oct 10am–8pm; rest of year 10am–5.30pm; €2.50), a dark and atmospheric little corner that contains the impressive remains of a Roman house. The unexciting **Galleria Civica d'Arte Moderna**, to the west across Corso Mazzini at Palazzo Collicola on Piazza Collicola (Wed to Mon mid-March to mid-Oct 10.30am–1pm & 3.30–7pm; afternoon 3–5pm the rest of the year; €4), is devoted primarily to modern Italian artists, though it contains some works by foreigners who have been connected with the Spoleto Festival over the years, among them Alexander Calder, the man responsible for the large sculpture by the railway station.

Very close to the Palazzo Comunale's back entrance is the medieval town's most celebrated **church**, the twelfth-century **Sant'Eufemia** (seen with Museo Diocesano – see below), architecturally unique in Umbria for its *matronei*, high-arched galleries above the side-naves that segregated women from the men in the main body of the church. It was built over the site of the eighth-century Lombard ducal palace and appears to have been partly constructed from the remains of this and earlier Roman monuments; one or two of the completely mismatched columns are carved with distinctive Lombard motifs. The general dank solemnity of the place clearly points to an early foundation.

Sant'Eufemia is visited in conjunction with the outstanding **Museo Diocesano**, located in the same courtyard as the church (April–July & Sept–Oct Mon–Fri 10am–1pm & 3–6pm, Sat & Sun 10am–6pm; Aug daily 10am–6pm; Nov–March Mon–Fri 10am–1pm & 3–5pm, Sat–Sun 11am–5pm; €3). The half-dozen rooms contain several surprisingly good paintings, including a *Madonna* by Fra' Filippo Lippi and an early Beccafumi, a room of old wooden statues and some wonderfully graphic votive panels offering thanks for salvation from a host of vividly illustrated mishaps.

The Rocca, Ponte delle Torri and San Pietro

If you do nothing else in Spoleto you should take the short walk out to the **Ponte delle Torri**, the town's picture-postcard favourite and an astonishing piece of medieval engineering. It's best taken in as part of a circular walk around the base of the Rocca or on the longer trek out to San Pietro (see opposite). Within a minute of leaving shady gardens in Piazza Campello you suddenly find yourself looking out over superb countryside, with a dramatic panorama across the Tessino gorge and south to the mountains of Castelmonte. There's an informal little bar, on the left before the bend, to help you enjoy the views.

The **Rocca** (Tues–Wed 9am–5pm, Thurs–Sat 9am–5.45pm, Sun 9am–7pm; longer hours Tues–Sat in summer; €6 or €7.50 with museum), everyone's idea of a cartoon castle, with towers, crenellations and sheer walls, was another in the chain of fortresses with which the tireless Cardinal Albornoz hoped to re-establish Church domination in central Italy, a primacy lost during the fourteenth-century papal exile to Avignon. It served until the early 1980s as a high-security prison – testimony to the skill of its medieval builders – and was home to, among others, Pope John Paul II's would-be assassin and leading members of the Red Brigade. After years of restoration it now houses a sleek **museum** (April–Oct Tues–Sat 9am–7.30pm, Sun 9am–1.30pm; Nov–March Tues–Wed 9am–1.30pm, Thurs–Sat 9am–7.30pm, Sun 9am–1.30pm; €6 or €7.50 for combined ticket) devoted to the Duchy of Spoleto, and with many paintings temporarily removed from the Pinacoteca during its long-term restoration. Both museum and fortress are well worth seeing, the Rocca in particular for its superb views, the imposing twin courtyards and the sheer scale of the building.

The **bridge**, too, is a genuinely impressive affair, with a 240-metre span supported by ten eighty-metre arches that have been used as a launching pad by jilted lovers for six centuries. Designed by the Gubbian architect Gattapone, who was also responsible for Gubbio's Palazzo dei Consoli, it was initially planned as an aqueduct to bring water from Monteluco, replacing an earlier Roman causeway whose design Gattapone probably borrowed and enlarged upon. In time it also became used as an escape from the Rocca when Spoleto was under siege. The remains of what used to be a covered passageway connecting the two are still visible straggling down the hillside.

It's well worth crossing the bridge and picking up the **footpath**, which zigzags up from the left-hand side of the road and then contours left into peaceful countryside within a few hundred metres, giving great views back over the gorge. Alternatively, turn right on the road and make for the church of **San Pietro**, whose facade beckons from a not-too-distant hillside. If the idea of another church doesn't appeal you can easily double back to town on the circular Via della Rocca.

Though the walk to **San Pietro** is a longish one (2km), it's pleasantly shady with some good glimpses of Spoleto, but on the country road (no pavements) beware drivers taking the bends too fast. The church would be undistinguished were it not for the splendid **sculptures** adorning its facade. Taken with Maitani's bas-reliefs in Orvieto, they are the best Romanesque carvings in Umbria, partly Lombard in their inspiration, and drawing variously on the Gospels and medieval legend for their complicated narrative and symbolic purpose. A particularly juicy scene to look out for includes the *Death of a Sinner* (left series, second from the top) where the Archangel Michael abandons the sinner to a couple of demons who bind and torture him before bringing in burning oil to finish the job. Fourth panel from the top (right series) shows a wolf disguised as a friar before a fleeing ram – a dig at dodgy monastic morals.

Eating and drinking

Apollinare Via Sant'Agata 14
☎0743.223.256, ⊛www.ristoranteapollinare
.it. Rivals *Sabatini* for the title of Spoleto's best restaurant. The blue and gold upholstery is initially off-putting, but the medieval setting is good and the welcome friendly. The *menù degustazione* is excellent value. Don't miss the sublime *caramello* starter – a cheese and truffle delight. Closed Tues.

Il Panciolle Largo Muzio Clemente–Via del Duomo 3 ☎0743.45.677. Below the hotel of the same name, this is a good choice for a reliable and reasonably priced, if never over-exciting, meal of Umbrian specialities such as *stringozzi* and fire-grilled meats. Also known for its selection of cheeses. Has a great outside terrace – though the medieval interior with open fire is cosy enough. Closed Wed.

Il Tempio del Gusto Via Arco del Druso 11 ☎0743.47.121, ⊛www.iltempiodelgusto.com. "The Temple of Taste'" was founded by Eros Patrizi, a former pupil of the legendary Vissani, patron of the eponymous restaurant near Baschi, in southern Umbria, that for years has rated as one of Italy's best. Standards – and the often recherché cooking – are similar, and you'll be paying around €70 for the works. Closed Thurs.

La Lanterna Via della Trattoria 6 ℡0743.49.815. A convivial, central place and good mid-price option on a side street left off the hill between Piazza Libertà and Piazza Fontana, with meals at about €15. Closed Wed.

Osteria del Matto Vicolo del Mercato 3 ℡0743.225.506. The best place for light meals and a glass of wine, a few steps west of Piazza del Mercato. The single room is dark and snug and the owner very welcoming. Closed Tues.

Osteria del Trivio Via del Trivio 16 ℡0743.44.349. A little away from the centre, and thus the crowds; nicely rustic, with photographs of the much-travelled owners and their family on the walls, and Spoletan classics on the menu: reckon on around €30 for a full meal. Closed Tues & a period in Jan.

Sabatini Corso Mazzini 54 ℡0743.221.831. The Upper Town's smartest spot. It has a lovely interior, with a few outside tables to the rear. Cooking is inventive, though the odd dish can be a touch precious (avoid the four-cheese risotto, for example); three courses at around €45. Closed Mon.

The Valnerina and Norcia

The **VALNERINA** is the most beautiful part of Umbria. Strictly translated as the "little valley of the Nera", it effectively refers to the whole eastern part of the region, a self-contained area of high mountains, poor communications, steep wooded valleys, upland villages and vast stretches of barren nothingness. Wolves still roam the summit ridges and the area is a genuine "forgotten corner", deserted farms everywhere bearing witness to a century of emigration.

The region is best explored with a car, as **public transport** is limited. The easiest way to get to the region without a car is by bus from Spoleto: five to seven daily run from Spoleto station to Norcia (1hr 15min). A new road tunnel links Spoleto to the valley, but for scenery stick to the old and tortuous N395 from Spoleto until you hit the "main" SS209 and the more pastoral run up the Nera Valley towards Norcia. Mountains nearby are 1500m high, with excellent walking, creeping up as you move east to about 2500m in the **Monti Sibillini**. It's difficult to explore with any sort of plan (unless you stick to the Nera), and the best approach is to follow your nose, poking into small valleys, tracing high country lanes to remote hamlets.

More deliberately, you could make for **Vallo di Nera**, the most archetypal of the **fortified villages** that pop up along the Lower Nera. Medieval **Triponzo** is a natural focus of communications, little more than a quaint staging post and fortified tower (and a better target than modernish Cerreto nearby). **Monteleone** is the only place of any size for miles, with a fine church, and popular with trippers.

Norcia

The very pleasant mountain retreat of **NORCIA** is the only place of any size or substance in the Valnerina. Noted on the one hand as the birthplace of **St Benedict** – founder of Western monasticism – and on the other as the producer of Italy's top **salami**, it has an air of charming dereliction, and its low, sturdy houses (built to be earthquake-resistant) are a world away from the pastoral, fairy-tale cities to the west. If transport allows, it could be the base for some good trips into neighbouring territory, particularly the famed Piano Grande (see p.596) and the mountains to the east and north. A big new road through the mountains into Marche has opened and brought in more visitors – good news for local employment, which is scarce, but a possible challenge to the environment. Hang-gliders and winter-sports enthusiasts have also discovered the area, another mixed blessing.

It doesn't take long to see the town, but you may want to stay on for the pleasant atmosphere and the surrounding scenery. Most of the action is in the central **Piazza San Benedetto**, site of the Roman forum and presided over by a statue of Benedict. Apart from its facade, you can largely forget about the **Duomo** – destroyed by several earthquakes (the last big one was in 1979), and patched up to look like nothing on earth. The **Castellina** is more captivating: a papal fortress full of gaunt medieval echoes, it contains a fine little **museum** (May–Sept Tues–Sun 10am–1pm & 4–7.30pm; €3) with fascinating old wooden sculptures and several surprisingly accomplished paintings. Unfortunately it keeps irregular hours, especially in winter, when it is often closed for the duration. The fortress makes a strange bedfellow for the labyrinthine church of **San Benedetto**, which supposedly was built over the saint's birthplace but was probably raised from the ruins of an earlier Roman temple. Inside there are a few paltry frescoes, nothing more, though the crypt contains the remains of a Roman-era house.

Meat-eaters would be daft not to try the deservedly famous **local pork products**. Anything that can be done to a pig, the Norcians apparently do – and supposedly better than anyone else. Even today, you still see butchers in other parts of Italy called *un nurcino*, after the town. If finances stretch, you could also indulge in the area's prized black **truffle**. The season runs from January to April (though you may come across the lesser prized summer truffles too). Plenty of shops, an attraction in themselves, are on hand to sell you all manner of local specialities, not just truffles, but also hams, the famed lentils of Castelluccio (see p.559) and lots of rare mountain cheeses.

Practicalities

There is no tourist office, but the **Casa del Parco**, an office for the Parco Nazionale dei Sibillini, at Via del Solferino 22 (Jan–June & Sept–Dec Tues–Fri 9.30am–12.30pm, Sat & Sun 9.30am–12.30pm & 3–5pm; July & Aug daily 9.30am–12.30pm & 3.30–6.30pm; ☎0743.817.090, ⓦwww.sibillini.net), has plenty of information. Norcia has always seen lots of pilgrims, in town for Benedict and trips to Assisi and Loreto in the Marche for the house of the Virgin (see p.636). But these days its **accommodation** is under pressure from growing numbers of casual visitors, so it makes sense to book rooms well in advance, especially in June and July.

Hotels

Da Benito Via Marconi 4 ☎0743.816.670, ⓦwww.hotelbenito.it. A small, central eight-room hotel; unexceptional, but an alternative to the *Grotta Azzurra* next door, if that is full. ❷

Casa Religiosa San Benedetto Via delle Vergini 13 ☎&ⓕ0743.828.208. Basic, clean and convenient. Located at the far northwest corner of the upper town, open to men and women even though it's still a working convent. ❶

Grotta Azzurra Via Alfieri 12 ☎0743.816.513, ⓕ0743.817.342. A rambling three-star with some dated rooms whose restaurant – the *Granaro del Monte* – is the best place to eat in Norcia; it's relatively inexpensive and set in large medieval banqueting halls (a former papal granary) complete with suits of armour and huge, roaring fires. ❹

Salicone Via Montedoro ☎0743.828.076, ⓦwww.bianconi.com. A comfortable modern option just outside the walls with spacious rooms, tennis courts and other sports facilities. ❻

Hostel

Ostello Norcia Via Ufente 1/B ☎0743.817.487, ⓦwww.montepatino.com. Offers beds (in two-, four-, five- and ten-bed rooms) at €15, including breakfast, but you must book in advance. It's in the northeast corner of town (take Via Anicia from behind San Benedetto and turn left at Piazza Palatina).

Around Norcia – the Piano Grande and Preci

The eerie, expansive **Piano Grande**, 20km east of Norcia, is an extraordinary prairie ringed by bare, whaleback mountains and stretching, uninterrupted by tree, hedge or habitation, for miles and miles. Five, even ten years ago, it was all-but unknown: now, in summer at least, it can be disconcertingly busy. It's much photographed – especially in spring when it's ablaze with wild flowers of every description – and was used by Zeffirelli as a setting in his Franciscan film *Brother Sun, Sister Moon*. The desperately isolated village of **CASTELLUCCIO** hangs above it at around 1400m, and although no longer the sole preserve of shepherds, it remains an unspoilt base and the ideal starting point for any number of straightforward mountain walks. To plan routes, get hold of the 1:50,000 Kompass map no. 666 or the more detailed 1:25,000 CAI maps (the latter are often available in Norcia or Castelluccio's bars). There's no public transport into the area (save for one bus in and out on a Thurs, market day in Norcia), though you might try your luck at catching lifts in high season. Rough **camping** is generally no problem, and there are a couple of two-star **hotel-restaurants** convenient for the plain and many walks: *La Sibilla*, in Castelluccio itself (booking advised, ☎0743.821.113; ❸), has an excellent restaurant.

Another worthwhile trip, if you're short of time to spend in aimless exploration, is the road north to **PRECI** and thus to Visso in the Marche. Walled and castled Preci was known throughout Europe in the sixteenth century as a school for surgeons, their main trade being removal of kidney stones. However, they had a more notorious sideline – castrating young boys who were foolish enough to show operatic potential. The town has a good place to **eat**: *Il Castoro*, Via Roma (☎0743.939.248; Oct–June closed Thurs), which offers pizza or good local food such as boar, trout or chewy *stringozzi* pasta. Full meals start at about €22. A kilometre above nearby **PIEDIVALLE** is the beautifully sited Abbey of San Eutizio, one of the cradles of the Benedictine movement. Now only a pretty – if over-restored – twelfth-century Romanesque church stands on the site, but in its day the community of monks held sway over more than a hundred castles and local churches. Above the church you can still see the caves used by the earliest hermits and by Benedict himself, who discovered his vocation while visiting the hermits from Norcia.

Terni and around

TERNI was the unlikely birthplace of one of the world's most famous saints, **St Valentine**, bishop of the town until his martyrdom in 273 and now entombed in his personal basilica at San Valentino, a village 2km to the southwest. A less romantic city, however, would be hard to imagine. Terni's important arms and steel industries made it a target for Allied bombing in 1944, and 80 percent of the town was reduced to rubble, including, sadly, the best part of its Roman and medieval heritage. Rebuilding replaced what was lost with a grey grid-iron city straight out of postwar eastern Europe; it also put the arms industry back on its feet – the gun used to assassinate Kennedy was made here – and though the town no longer lives up to its nineteenth-century nickname of "the Manchester of Italy", it's not the most enticing of prospects. The **tourist office** (Mon–Sat 9am–1pm & 4–7pm; ☎0744.423.047,

@ info@iat.terni.it), should you need it, is at Viale Battisti 7/A – take Viale della Stazione from the station, and Viale Battisti is 300m up, on the right, at the first major piazza.

Cascate delle Marmore

The best place to make for locally is the **Cascate delle Marmore** (train or bus from Terni), created by the Romans in 271 BC when they diverted the River Velino into the Nera during drainage of marshlands to the south. The highest waterfall in Europe (at 165m), it was boosted by the damming of Lago di Piediluco in the 1930s to satisfy the demands of industry for cheap hydroelectric power. Pictures of the falls in full spate adorn most Umbrian tourist offices, but what they neglect to tell you is that the water can be turned off at the flick of a switch (in favour of electric turbines), leaving a none-too-spectacular trickle. Running times vary considerably from year to year, and month to month. Summer weekends are usually a good bet, but most main tourist offices in southern Umbria carry details of current times. The observation platforms are below on the SS209 and above in the village of Marmore, with a steep path between the two (plus bus shuttle in summer when the falls are running). The green and luxuriant setting, tumbling water and expanses of gleaming polished marble add up to a spectacular show – shame about the factories round the corner, though.

The Abbazia di San Pietro in Valle

A very worthwhile excursion from Terni (or Spoleto), particularly if you're making for Norcia and the Valnerina from the south rather than Spoleto, is the **Abbazia di San Pietro in Valle** (daily 10am–noon & 2–5pm; free), 18km from Terni and signposted from Colleponte. Buses make the run up to **Triponzo**, passing the approach road to the abbey en route. Founded by the Lombard duke Faroaldo II, who retired to monastic life after being deposed by his son in 720, the abbey was among the most powerful religious houses in Umbro-Romano, controlling vast tracts of land and dominating the lives of thousands of people. It's set high on the hillside near a thickly wooded cleft, the first impression being of a dull blockhouse affair, with nothing to hint at the splendour of the Lombard and Byzantine art inside. The faded frescoes (1190) that cover the body of the main church are the first tentative attempts to create a distinctively Italian art and move away from the stylized influence of Byzantine painting, an influence that nonetheless was to prevail until the advent of Pietro Cavallini, Cimabue and Giotto a century later. The **altar**, beautifully set off by the rose-coloured stone and rich Romanesque display all around, is a rare and important example of Lombard sculpture, carved with what look like pagan, almost Celtic figures and motifs. To each side are well-preserved Roman sarcophagi, backed by a profusion of gorgeously coloured frescoes. A doorway (not always open) leads to the twelfth-century campanile, a Lombard import of a type common in Rome and Lazio and distinguished by fragments and reliefs salvaged from the eighth-century church. There's also a faultless double-tiered cloister from the twelfth century, though access to this may be restricted as the complex's private owners – only the church belongs to the state – have opened a very appealing **hotel** (T0744.780.129, W www.sanpietroinvalle.com; ④) in part of the abbey.

By following the SS209 past the walled, medieval village of **SCHEGGINO** you can pick up the Spoleto road into the Valnerina, a route covered on p.594.

If you need to **stay** locally, Scheggino's *Albergo-Trattoria del Ponte*, Via del Borgo 17 (☎0743.61.253, ✉roncamar@tiscali.it; ➌), is the best bet. Even if you're just passing through, give its excellent **restaurant** (closed Mon and periods in Sept & Nov) a try – the trout dishes with truffles, in particular, are superb.

Narni and around

It's an easy thirty-minute hop on the train from Terni to **NARNI**, which claims to be the geographical centre of Italy, with a hilltop site jutting into the Nera Valley on a majestic spur and crowned by another of Albornoz's formidable papal fortresses. Commanding one end of a steep gorge (about ten minutes of fairly spectacular train travel), it was once the gateway into Umbria, the last post before the Tiber Valley and the undefended road to Rome. However, while the town retains a fine medieval character, the views from its heights are marred by steel and chemical works around **Narni Scalo**, the new town in the valley below.

The heart of the **old town** (bus from the train station) has all the standard fittings: the medieval piazzas, the warren of streets, a modest art gallery, the usual crop of Romanesque churches, and a huge *rocca*, now open (guided tours only) after decades of restoration (Aug–Sept Fri–Sun 11am–1pm & 4.30–7.30pm; Oct–Dec Sat & Sun 11am–1pm & 3.30–5.30pm; €3), though opening times are liable to change. There's a **Roman bridge** on the outskirts, the subject of considerable local hype. Goethe arrived in Narni in the middle of the night and was peeved not to have seen it; he was only missing a solitary arch in the middle of the river – just as easily viewed from the train.

In what's an appealing but relatively low-key centre, things revolve around the narrow **Piazza dei Priori**, where pride of place goes to the fourteenth-century **Palazzo dei Priori**, now council offices, unremarkable except for a fountain and graceful **loggia** designed by the Gubbian architect Gattapone.

The bulk of the town's paintings and other works of art are housed in a new gallery, the **Museo della Città e del Territorio** (Tues–Sun: April–June & Sept 10.30am–1pm & 3.30–6pm; July & Aug 10.30am–1pm & 4.30–7.30pm; Oct–March Fri–Sun & public hols 10.30am–1pm & 3–5.30pm; €5) in the Palazzo Eroli, Via Aurelio Saffi 1. The highlight is a superlative and much-copied *Coronation of the Virgin* by Ghirlandaio, with a collection of good works by minor medieval Umbrian artists such as Mezzastris and Benozzo Gozzoli.

On the town's main street, on the other side of Piazza dei Priori, is the tiny and easily overlooked church of **Santa Maria in Pensole**, unaltered since 1175 – you can still see the date above the door – and adorned across the width of its facade with a marvellous carved frieze.

Some of Narni's most captivating sights lie beneath the streets, parts of Roman cisterns, eighth-century chapels and more, all of which can be seen on a handful of one-hour **guided tours** led by Narni Sotterranea (hours vary, but generally Sat & Sun only; €4; ☎0744.722.292, ⍟www.narnisotterranea.it), based at Via san Bernardo 12.

Practicalities

The **tourist office** is at Piazza dei Priori 3 (Easter–Oct Mon–Sat 9.30am–12.30pm & 3.30–6/7pm; Nov–Easter 10am–12.30pm & 4–7pm; Sun year-round

10am–1pm; ☎0744.747.247 or 0744.715.362, ⓦwww.comune.narni.tr.it). There's no real reason for staying overnight in Narni, but should you want to your best bet would be the cosy, central *Dei Priori*, Vicolo del Comune 4 (☎0744.726.843, ⓦwww.loggiadeipriori.it; ❷), which offers first-class meals at the lovely *La Loggia* restaurant (closed Mon & second half of July). Far cheaper is the *Casa di Accoglienza* (☎0744.715.217; €17 per person), run by the nuns of Sant'Anna at Via Gattemelata 74, close to the walls in the northeast fringe of the old town.

Amelia

AMELIA, 11km northwest of Narni and plonked on top of a sugar-loaf hilltop, is by far the most tempting local excursion. Though not big on monuments, it's charming and unvisited, noted mainly for its extraordinary cyclopean walls, claimed as some of the oldest and mightiest in Italy. Supported by their own weight and comprising vast polygonal blocks up to 7m across, they reach a height of over 20m in places and date back, according to early Roman historians, to the Umbrian settlement of the eleventh century BC.

The best of the town's archeological artefacts (and a handful of paintings) are collected in the **Museo Archeologico**, Piazza Augusto Vera 10 (April–June & Sept Tues–Sun 10.30am–1pm & 4–7pm; July & Aug Tues–Sun 10.30am–1pm & 4.30–7.30pm; Oct–March Fri–Sun 10.30am–1pm & 3–6pm; €5), most notably a superb bronze of the Roman general Germanicus, found locally in 1963. If you're in town at the weekend, be sure to explore the Roman cisterns under Piazza Matteotti (April–Sept Sat 4.30–7.30pm, Sun 10.30am–12.30pm & 4.30–7.30pm; Oct–March Sat 3–6pm, Sun 10.30am–12.30pm & 3–6pm; €2; ☎0744.978.436, ⓦwww.ameliasotterranea.it).

Most of the town's churches were ruined in the nineteenth century, and art's thin on the ground – San Giacomo's **double cloister** and a **tomb** by **Agostino di Duccio** are the only highlights – but Amelia's charm is the typically Umbrian mixture of good views, medieval streets and lovely country-side close at hand.

The **tourist office** is at Via Orvieto 1 (mid-June to mid-Sept Mon & Sun 9.30am–12.30pm, Tues–Sat 9.30am–12.30pm & 3.30–7.30pm; mid-Sept to mid-June Mon & Sat 9am–12.30pm, Tues–Fri 9am–12.30pm & 3.30–6.30pm; ☎0744.981.453, ⓔinfo@iat.amelia.tr.it). The local culinary speciality is a tooth-rotting combination of white figs, chocolate and crushed nuts (only available in winter), but for more substantial fare there are two good **restaurants**, both with **rooms** to rent but both out of the old centre: the three-star *Anita*, Via Roma 31 (☎0744.982.146, ☎0744.983.079; ❷; restaurant closed Mon); and, just 1km north of town, *Le Colonne*, Via Roma 191 (☎0744.983.529; ❷; restaurant closed Wed). In town, there is a good **hostel** at Piazza Mazzini 9 (☎0744.978.673, ⓦwww.ostellogiustiniani.it; dorm beds €16). For food, also try the more expensive *Gabelletta*, Str Tuderte Amerina 20 (☎0744.982.159; closed Mon), in an elegant villa 3.5km northeast, on the road to Montecastrilli.

The drive on to Orvieto along the back roads is a treat: plenty of oak forests and fine walks, and the chance to catch one of Umbria's Romanesque highlights, the twelfth-century church of **Santa Maria Assunata** at Lugnano in Teverina.

Todi

TODI is one of the best-known Umbrian hill-towns, at heart still a thriving and insular agricultural centre, but also a favoured trendy retreat for foreign expats and Rome's arts and media types. In the way of these things the visitors haven't been far behind, but neither fact should deter you from making a day-trip: few places beat it for sheer location – its hilltop position is stunning – and fairy-tale medievalism.

Arrival and information

Getting there by public transport and sussing out how to fit it into an itinerary are likely to be your biggest problems. Basically you come either from Terni on the hourly FCU train or from Perugia, again by FCU, or on one of the regular buses that stop below the town by the church of Santa Maria della Consolazione or higher up, just off the main square near San Fortunato. Moving on, in addition to the train, you have the option of a daily bus to Orvieto. Todi's **train stations** (there are two) are both in the middle of nowhere, and **buses** to the centre don't always connect with the trains. Ponte Rio is the station to go for; Ponte Naia, 5km distant, is marginally closer, but fewer trains stop there, bus shuttles are few and far between, and the uphill walk to town is one very, very long slog. If you want to book a **taxi**, call ☏075.894.2375, 075.894.2525 or 0347.774.8321.

The **tourist office** has shifted around town over the last four or five years, but currently is in the southeast corner of Piazza del Popolo at no. 36 (April–Oct daily 10am–1pm & 4–7pm; Nov–March Mon–Sat 10am–1pm & 3–5pm, Sun 10am–1pm; ☏075.894.5416, ⓦwww.comune.todi.pg.it).

Accommodation

Hotels are in demand, especially during the increasingly popular **Todi Festival** (first ten days of Sept; ⓦwww.todiartefestival.it), and with a couple of exceptions are characterless, modern affairs some way out of town.

Bramante Via Orvietana 48 ☏075.894.8381; ⓦwww.hotelbramante.it. The upmarket, four-star alternative to the *Fonte Cesia*. Showing its age slightly, but has a pool and tennis courts, and semi-rural setting just beyond Santa Maria della Consolazione. ⑥

Fonte Cesia, Via Lorenzo Leoni 3 ☏075.894.3737, ⓦwww.fontecesia.it. Wonderful converted medieval townhouse at the heart of the historic core. Rooms vary in size and decoration, but all have period details, rich fabrics and up-to-the-minute facilities. ⑥

Tuder Via Maestà dei Lombardi 13 ☏075.894.8571, ⓦwww.villaluisa.it. Functional three-star in an uninspiring modern, built-up district, 10min walk from Porta Romana. ④

San Lorenzo Tre Via San Lorenzo 3 ☏075.894.4555, ⓦwww.sanlorenzo3.it. Very comfortable rooms in a pleasantly and elegantly furnished townhouse in the street parallel to Via del Duomo just east of the cathedral. The breakfast, which is included, is excellent. Closed Jan & Feb. ③

The Town

The central **Piazza del Popolo** is widely held to be among the most perfect medieval piazzas in Italy. The **Duomo** (daily 8.30am–12.30pm & 2.30–6.30pm; church free, museum €1) at the far (northern) end, atop a broad flight of steps, is the main feature – a meeting point of the last of the Romanesque and the first of the Gothic forms filtering up from France in the early fourteenth century. The square, three-tiered **facade** is inspired simplicity; just a sumptuous rose window (1520) and ornately carved doorway to embellish the pinky weathered marble – the classic example of a form found all over Umbria. Inevitably the interior is less impressive. There's some delicate nineteenth-century stained glass in the arched nave on the right, and a good altarpiece by Giannicolo di Paolo (a follower of Perugino), but an appalling sixteenth-century *Last Judgement*, loosely derived from Michelangelo's, defaces the back wall. The strikingly carved **choir** (1530) – of incredible delicacy and precision – is the region's best, with panels at floor level near the front depicting the tools used to carve the piece. The crypt and small museum contains a rambling collection of ancient Roman – and possibly Etruscan – fragments and religious ephemera.

Back in the piazza, the other key buildings are the three **public palaces**, squared off near the Duomo in deliberately provocative fashion as an expression of medieval civic pride – definitely trying to put one over on the Church. The adjoining Palazzo del Capitano (1290) and adjacent Palazzo del Popolo (begun 1213) are most prominent, thanks mainly to the stone staircase that looks like the setting for a thousand B-movie sword fights.

The Palazzo del Capitano houses a superb museum, the **Museo–Pinacoteca e Museo della Città** (Tues–Sun: April–Oct 10.30am–1pm & 3–6pm; Nov–March 10am–1.30pm & 2.30–5pm; €3.50, or €6 for a combined ticket with the Cisterne Romane & Campanile di San Fortunato; see below), which brilliantly weaves an open-plan sequence of rooms into the existing medieval structure. The first section of the museum delves into Todi's history, followed by rooms devoted to archeology, coins and medallions, fabrics, ceramics and a picture gallery. In many cases the rooms are more alluring than their displays – particularly the lovely frescoed salon devoted to ceramics – but numerous individual exhibits merit a closer look, none more so than the museum's star painting: the sumptuous *Coronation of the Virgin* (1507) by Lo Spagna.

The **Palazzo dei Priori** (1293–1337) is the southernmost building in the square, with all the various crenellations, battlements and mullioned windows of the other palaces but with the difference that they've been recently restored. It's been the seat of all the town's various rulers and today is still the town hall; if you can look as if you're on council business you should be able to peep inside. The best place to enjoy the streetlife is from the **bar** down on its right-hand side, more of a locals' local than the flashy place halfway down the piazza (but which does do a good line in sandwiches). Close to this latter bar, a small side street leads off the west side of the piazza to the **Cisterne Romane** (April–Oct Tues–Sun 10.30am–1pm & 2.30–6.30pm; Nov–March Sat & Sun 10.30am–1pm & 2–4.30pm; €2, or €6 combined ticket with Museo della Città & Campanile di San Fortunato), a massive Roman cistern, which offers a graphic illustration of the Romans' prodigious engineering abilities.

San Fortunato and the rest of the town

Streets to the right of the Duomo are quiet and dozy and worth a wander, though the single most celebrated sight in town after the piazza is the church of **San Fortunato** (daily 9.30am–12.30pm & 3–6pm; free), set above some half-hearted gardens a very short stroll from the centre. It's an enormous thing given the size of the town – testimony to Todi's medieval wealth and importance. The squat, messy and clearly unfinished facade, an amalgam of Romanesque and Gothic styles, reflects the time it took to build (1292–1462) and at first glance doesn't exactly raise expectations. A florid **Gothic doorway** of arched swirls and carved craziness, however, is the first of several surprises, second of which is the enormous light, airy interior, recently highlighted by cleaning and several dazzling coats of whitewash. It marks the pinnacle of the Umbrian tradition for large vaulted churches, a style based on the smaller and basic "barn churches" common in Tuscany, which were distinguished by a single, low-pitched roof and naves and aisles of equal height. (San Domenico in Perugia, p.566, is another example.) It also marks a trend for side-chapels, a habit picked up from Catalonia and southern France in the thirteenth century and made necessary by the rising demand for daily Masses as the Franciscans became a more ministering order. There's another good **choir**, heavier and with more hints of the Baroque than the one in the Duomo, as well as a few scant patches of Sienese fresco. The fresco by **Masolino di Panicale** in the fourth chapel on the right is a good example of this rare painter's work, though a bit battered. Some lovely **cloisters** to the rear (outside and to the right) round off a distinctive and worthwhile church. Climb the **Campanile** (Tues–Sun: April–Oct 10.30am–1pm & 3–6.30pm; Nov–March 10.30am–1pm & 2.30–5pm; €1.50, or €6 combined ticket with Museo della Città & Cisterne Romane) for sweeping views over the town and surrounding countryside.

Santa Maria della Consolazione (closed daily 1–3pm), completed in 1607, is thought to have been based on an earlier Bramante draft for St Peter's in Rome; the alternating window types in the cupola are a Bramante trademark. Victorian writers called it the best Renaissance church in Italy (pretty close to saying the best in the world). It's worth a look to judge for yourself, but doesn't merit a special journey.

An ideal place for a siesta is the rambling **Giardino Pubblico**, full of shady nooks and narrow pathways, and a cut above the normal town plot. There's also a kids' playground and a very small **Rocca**, both less noteworthy than the views, which are extensive though usually hazy. The gardens are best tackled via the stony track to the right of San Fortunato, less of a sweat than the path that comes up from Piazza Oberdan.

Eating and drinking

The town's best-known **restaurant** is the *Umbria*, Via San Bonaventura (☎075.894.2737; closed Tues), beneath the museum; prices are high (€25 and up for a full meal) and service can be slapdash, but the panorama from the terrace makes it all worthwhile; in season, book to be sure of an outside table. Cheaper alternatives (reckon on €15 for a basic meal) include the unpretentious *Cavour* at Corso Cavour 21 (closed Wed) and the basic *Pizzeria Giubilei Italo*, off Corso Cavour in Piazza B. d'Alviano (closed Mon after 8pm). More recent is *Pane e Vino*, just off the main square at Via Ciuffelli 33 (☎075.894.5448; closed Wed), perfect for simple lunches and suppers (from €20 for three courses): there's a tremendous choice of antipasti.

Orvieto

Out on a limb from the rest of Umbria, **ORVIETO** is perfectly placed between Rome and Florence to serve as a historical picnic for tour operators. Visitors flood into the town in their millions, drawn by the **Duomo**, one of the greatest Gothic buildings in Italy. However, once its facade and Signorelli's frescoes have been admired, the town's not quite as exciting as guides and word of mouth make out. This is partly to do with the gloominess of the dark volcanic rock

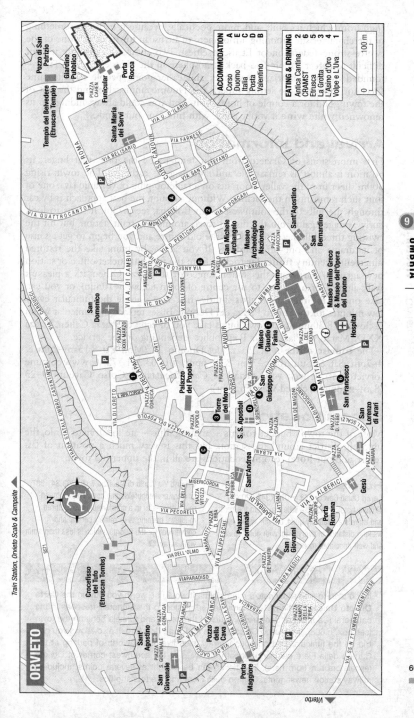

ORVIETO

- Tempio del Belvedere (Etruscan Temple)
- Pozzo di San Patrizio
- Giardino Pubblico
- Porta Rocca
- Funicular
- PIAZZA CAHEN
- Santa Maria dei Servi
- San Domenico
- San Michele Archangelo
- Museo Archeologico Nazionale
- Sant'Agostino
- San Bernardino
- Duomo
- Museo Emilio Greco & Museo dell'Opera del Duomo
- Hospital
- Museo Claudio Faina
- San Giuseppe
- Palazzo del Popolo
- Torre del Moro
- S.S. Apostoli
- San Francesco
- San Lorenzo di Arari
- Palazzo Comunale
- Sant'Andrea
- Misericordia
- San Giovanni
- Gesù
- Porta Romana
- Sant'Agostino
- San Giovenale
- Crocefisso del Tufo (Etruscan Tombs)
- Pozzo della Cava
- Porta Maggiore

Train Station, Orvieto Scalo & Campsite

Viterbo

ACCOMMODATION
- Corso — A
- Duomo — E
- Italia — C
- Posta — D
- Valentino — B

EATING & DRINKING
- Antica Cantina — 2
- CRAMST — 6
- Etrusca — 5
- La Grotta — 3
- L'Asino d'Oro — 4
- Volpe e L'Uva — 1

0 — 100 m

(*tuff*) from which it's built, and, more poetically, because it harbours something of the characteristic brooding atmosphere of Etruscan towns (it was one of the twelve-strong federation of Etruscan cities). Two thousand years on, it's not difficult to detect a more laid-back atmosphere in the cities east of the Tiber – founded by the Umbrians, a sunnier and easier-going people. All the same Orvieto is likeable, the setting superb, the Duomo unmissable, and the rest of the town good for a couple of hours' visit. And you could always indulge in its renowned white **wine** if you're stuck with time on your hands.

Arrival and information

First impressions of Orvieto from afar tend to be the ones that linger; its position is almost as remarkable and famous as its cathedral. The town, rising 300m sheer from the valley floor, sits on a tabletop plug of volcanic lava, one of four such remnants in the vicinity. Without a doubt, the best approach is by car through the hills to the southwest (from Bolsena, see p.730). It starts to look fairly average again from the dismal town around the train station, but hit the twisting three-kilometre road up to the old centre and you begin to get a sense of its drama and one-off weirdness. If you arrive by train, take the restored nineteenth-century **funicular** (tickets from the funicular ticket office or station newsagent or bar) from the station forecourt to Piazza Cahen: it's a pleasant walk along Corso Cavour to the centre of town (allow 5–10min), or you can take one of the regular minibus shuttles that stop outside the funicular every few minutes for the run to Piazza del Duomo. Buses replace the funicular when it closes at 8.30pm. Inter-town buses take you directly to Piazza Cahen, Piazza XXIX Marzo, or Piazza della Repubblica, depending on the service.

The **tourist office** is at Piazza del Duomo 24 (Mon–Fri 8.15am–2pm & 4–7pm, Sat & Sun 10am–7pm & 3–6pm; ☎0763.341.772, ⓦwww.comune .orvieto.tr.it). Check your **email** at *Caffè Montanucci*, Corso Cavour 19–23 (8am–midnight, closed Wed; €6.20hr).

Accommodation

Most of the town's budget **rooms** – and nightlife – are in Orvieto Scalo, the unlovely district around the station, but this is very much a position of last resort, and our **hotel** recommendations are all in the upper old town.

Hotels

Corso Corso Cavour 343 ☎0763.342.020, ⓦwww.hotelcorso.net. A little way from the centre, and therefore relatively quiet, but still within easy walking distance of everything, with good-value and well-appointed rooms. ❸

Duomo Via Vicolo di Maurizio 7 ☎0763.341.887, ⓦwww.orvietohotelduomo.com. This eighteen-room three-star in a comfortable restructured medieval building is extremely central and convenient for the Duomo, which is less than 1min walk away. ❹

Carta Orvieto Unica

If you plan to visit all Orvieto's main sights, it would be worth you buying the **Carta Orvieto Unica**. Costing €18, it provides admission to the Signorelli frescoes in the cathedral (Cappella di San Brizio), tours of the caves and tunnels beneath the town (see box, p.608), the Museo Claudio Faina and Torre del Moro. It also allows you one trip on the funicular and one bus journey, plus five hours' worth of parking at the Campo della Fiera car park beneath the walls at the southwest corner of Orvieto (escalators run from here). The ticket can be bought at several points, including railway station newsagents, Campo della Fiera and the tourist office.

Italia Piazza del Popolo 13 ☎ 0763.342.065, ⓦ www.grandhotelitalia.it. Unexceptional and long-established three-star; the biggest central place (48 rooms) and thus likely to have space in an emergency. ❹

Posta Via Signorelli 18 ☎ 0763.341.909, ⓦ www .orvietohotels.it. The only central hotel that can be described as a budget option; pleasantly dated, two minutes from the Duomo, and offering a wide range of single and double rooms with and without private bathrooms. ❶

Valentino Via Angelo da Orvieto 30–32 ☎ 0743.342.464, ⓔ hotelvalentino@libero.it. A reliable three-star with nineteen rooms a 5min walk from the Duomo. ❸

Campsite

Scacco Matto 10km away on the SS448 rd near Lago di Corbora ☎ 0744.950.163, ⓦ www .scaccomatto.net (bus to Baschi/Civitella). Orvieto's nearest campsite is a lowly one-star job that is open from April to October.

The Duomo

Burckhardt described Orvieto's Duomo as "the greatest and richest polychrome monument in the world", while Pope Leo XIII called it "the Golden Lily of Italian cathedrals", adding that on the Day of Judgement it would float up to heaven carried by its own beauty. According to a tradition fostered by the Church, it was built to celebrate the so-called **Miracle of Bolsena** (1263), involving a Bohemian priest who was travelling to Rome to shake off a heretical disbelief in transubstantiation – the idea that the body and blood of Christ are physically present in the Eucharist. While he celebrated Mass in a church near Lago di Bolsena, blood started to drip from the host onto the corporale, the cloth underneath the chalice on the altar. The stained linen was whisked off to Pope Urban IV, who like many a pope was in Orvieto to escape the heat and political hassle of Rome. He immediately proclaimed a miracle, and a year later Thomas Aquinas, no less, drew up a papal bull insti-gating the feast of **Corpus Domini**. The Church at the time, however, was in retreat, and the Umbrian towns were at the height of their civic expansion. It's likely that the building of an awe-inspiring cathedral in one of the region's most powerful *comuni* was less an act to commemorate a miracle than a shrewd piece of political opportunism designed to remind errant citizens of the papacy's power.

It was miraculous that the Duomo was built at all. Medieval Orvieto was so violent that at times the population thought about giving up on it altogether. Dante wrote that its family feuds were worse than those between Verona's Montagues and Capulets – the original inspiration for *Romeo and Juliet*. The building was also dogged by a committee approach to design – even the plans took thirty years to draw up. Yet though construction dragged on for three centuries and exhausted 33 architects, 152 sculptors, 68 painters and 90 mosai-cists, the final product is a surprisingly unified example of the transitional Romanesque-Gothic style. Credit for guiding the work at its most important stage goes to the Sienese architect **Lorenzo Maitani** (c.1270–1330), with the initial plans probably drawn up by Arnolfo di Cambio, architect of Florence's Palazzo Vecchio.

The facade

The facade is the star-turn, owing its undeniable impact to a decorative richness just the right side of overkill. It's a riot of columns, spires, bas-reliefs, sculptures, dazzling and almost overpowering use of colour, colossally empha-sized doorways and hundreds of capricious details just about held together by four enormous fluted columns. Stunning from the dwarfed piazza, particularly at sunset or under floodlights, it's not all superficial gloss. The **four pillars** at the base, one of the highlights of fourteenth-century Italian sculpture, are well

▲ The Duomo, Orvieto

worth a close look. The work of Maitani and his pupils, they describe episodes from the Old and New Testaments in staggering detail: lashings of plague, famine, martyrdoms, grotesque mutilation, mad and emaciated figures, the Flagellation, the Massacre of the Innocents, strange visitations, Cain slaying Abel (particularly juicy), and only the occasional touch of light relief. In its day it was there to point an accusing finger at Orvieto's moral slackers, as the none-too-cheerful final panel makes clear, with the damned packed off to fire, brimstone and eternal misery.

The interior

The inside (daily: 7.30am–12.45pm & 2.30–7.15pm; March & Oct closes 6.15pm; Nov–March closes 5.15pm; free) is a disappointment at least at first glance, as if the facade either took all the enthusiasm or all the money and the church was tacked on merely to prop everything else up. Adorned with alternating stripes of coloured marble similar to those found in the cathedrals of Siena, Florence and Pisa, it's mainly distinguished by **Luca Signorelli's** fresco cycle, *The Last Judgement* (1499–1504), in a chapel at the end of the south nave. Some claim it surpasses even Michelangelo's similar cycle in the Sistine Chapel, painted forty years later and obviously heavily influenced by Signorelli's earlier treatment. The cycle is on view again after years of restoration, and though you now have to pay for the privilege of seeing it, the admission's more than worth it (April–June Mon–Sat 9am–12.45pm & 2.30–7.15pm, Sun 2.30–5.45pm; July–Aug same hours but closes 6.45pm on Sun; Nov–Feb Mon–Sat 9am–12.45pm & 2.30–5.15pm, Sun 2.30–5.45pm; March & Oct same hours but closes 6.15pm Mon–Fri; €5, also includes Museo dell'Opera & Sant'Agostino). Tickets are not available in the cathedral, but must be bought from the tourist office.

Several painters, including Perugino and Fra' Angelico (who completed two ceiling panels), tackled the chapel before Signorelli – a free-thinking and singular artist from nearby Cortona – was commissioned to finish it off. All but the lower walls are crowded with the movement of passionate and beautifully observed muscular figures, creating an effect that's realistic and almost grotesquely fantastic at the same time. There are plenty of bizarre details to hold the narrative interest. A mass of monstrous lechery and naked writhing flesh fills the *Inferno* panel, including that of the painter's unfaithful mistress, immortalized in hell for all to see. In another an unfortunate is having his ear bitten off by a green-buttocked demon. Signorelli, suitably clad in black, has painted himself with Fra' Angelico in the lower left corner of *The Sermon of the Antichrist*, both calmly looking on as someone is garrotted at their feet.

All this overshadows the twin **Cappella del Corporale**, which contains the sacred corporale itself, locked away in a massive, jewel-encrusted casket (designed as a deliberate copy of the facade), plus some appealing frescoes by local fourteenth-century painter Ugolino di Prete, describing events connected with the Miracle of Bolsena. The entire apse is covered in more frescoes by Ugolino, many of which were partly restored by Pinturicchio, who was eventually kicked off the job for "consuming too much gold, too much azure and too much wine". Also worth a mention are an easily missed *Madonna and Child* by Gentile da Fabriano and a beautifully delicate fifteenth-century font, both near the main doors.

The rest of the town

Next to the Duomo on the right as you look at it is the **Museo dell'Opera del Duomo** (Wed–Mon: April–June & Sept–Oct 10am–6pm; July & Aug 10am–1pm & 3–7pm; Nov–March 10am–5pm; €5, includes admission to Signorelli frescoes in the Duomo & church of Sant'Agostino). Highlights are paintings by Martini and Pastura (an artist from Viterbo influenced by Perugino), several important thirteenth-century sculptures by Arnolfo di Cambio and Andrea Pisano, and a lovely font filled with Escher-like carved fishes. The **Emilio Greco** section of the museum (April–July Tues–Sun 10.30am–1pm &

Underground Orvieto

Enquire at the tourist office for details of the fascinating **Orvieto Underground** tours into the vast labyrinth of **tunnels**, caves and store rooms that riddle the soft volcanic rock on which Orvieto is built: most date back to medieval times, some to the Etruscan era. Tours leave from the tourist office daily (except Feb, when they run at weekends only) at 11am, 12.15pm, 4pm and 5.15pm (€5.50), but there is some flexibility: ask at the separate desk in the tourist office, call ☏0763.344.891 or 0339.733.2764, or visit ⓦ www.orvietounderground.it for details and bookings.

3.30–5.30pm; Aug–Sept Tues–Sun 11am–5pm; rest of the year Fri–Sun 10.30am–1pm & 2.30–4.30pm; €2.50, €5.50 for Biglietto Cumulativo, which includes Il Pozzo di San Patrizio) comprises nearly a hundred works donated to the city by the artist who created the Duomo's bronze doors in the 1960s – peek through the door beyond the ground-floor ticket office and you'll see enough of the exhibits to know if you want a closer look.

The wonderfully restored **Museo Claudio Faina** (incorporating the Museo Civico and Museo dei Ragazzi) opposite the Duomo (April–Sept daily 9.30am–6pm; Oct daily 10am–5pm; Nov–March Tues–Sun 10am–5pm; €4.50; ⓦ www.museofaina.it) has a predictable but superbly displayed collection of vases and fragments excavated from local tombs (it also offers some great **views** of the cathedral facade). These sixth-century-BC **tombs** (daily: summer 9am–7pm; winter closes 1hr before dusk; €2) are still visible just off the road which drops towards the station from Piazza Cahen and are worth tracking down for their rows of massive and sombre stone graves.

As far as the town's **churches** go, they all naturally pale beside the Duomo, though most have something worthwhile to see. The tiny Romanesque **San Lorenzo di Arari** was built in 1291 on the site of a church destroyed by monks from nearby San Francesco because the sound of its bells got on their nerves. Four recently restored **frescoes** on the left of the nave depict typically traumatic scenes from the life of St Lawrence. There's also an Etruscan sacrificial slab, which rather oddly serves as the Christian altar (*arari* meaning "altar").

From Piazzale Cacciatore there's a decent **walk** around the city's southern walls (Via Ripa Medici) with views over to a prominent outcrop of rock in the middle distance, part of the old volcanic crater. Ten minutes or so brings you to **San Giovenale**, whose rustic surroundings, on the very western tip of the *rupa*, Orvieto's volcanic plateau, are a far cry from the bustle of the Duomo. It's not much to look at from the outside, but the musty **medieval interior** is the best (and oldest) in the town. The thirteenth-century Gothic transept, with its two pointed arches, rather oddly stands a metre above the rounded Romanesque nave, making for a hybrid and distinctive church, all of it exhaustively decorated with thirteenth- and fifteenth-century **frescoes**. Check out the *Tree of Life* fresco right of the main door and the macabre *Calendar of Funeral Anniversaries* partly covered by the side entrance.

From the church back to the centre of town Via Malabranca and Via Filippeschi are the best of the **medieval streets**, all tantalizing doorways and tiled roofs, but second-rate by the standards of neighbouring hill-towns. For an overview, climb the **Torre del Moro**, a medieval tower in Corso Cavour just south of Piazza del Popolo (daily: March–April & Sept–Oct 10am–7pm; May–Aug 10am–8pm; Nov–Feb 10.30am–1pm & 2.30–5pm; €2.80).

The central **Sant'Andrea** on Piazza della Repubblica is worth a mention, more for its strange twelve-sided **campanile** than the bits and pieces of the Roman and Etruscan city in the crypt. In the Piazza del Popolo, farther up

Corso Cavour (the town's pedestrianized main drag), there's a daily fruit and veg market plus the odd craft stall – in front of the restored and impressive **Palazzo del Popolo** (closed to the public).

Il Pozzo di San Patrizio (daily: April–May & Sept 10am–5pm; June–Aug 9am–8pm; Oct–March 10am–5pm; €4.50 or €5.50 with the Emilio Greco museum), just off Piazzale Cahen, is the town's novelty act, a huge cylindrical well commissioned in 1527 by Pope Clement VII to guarantee the town's water supply during an expected siege by the Imperial Army (which never came). Water was brought to the surface by donkeys on two broad staircases, cannily designed never to intersect. It's a striking piece of engineering, 13m wide and 62m deep, named after its supposed similarity to the Irish cave where St Patrick died in 493, aged 133.

Eating and drinking

There are plenty of places to **eat** in Orvieto, though nowhere that stands out gastronomically. For a tourist town, though, many restaurants offer very good value and tasty Umbrian food. **Restaurants** are grouped together at the bottom (eastern end) of Corso Cavour. The **wine bars** around the Duomo are an expensive way of sampling the well-known Orvietan white. For great **ice cream** head for *Gelateria Pasqualetti*, an ivy-covered gelateria in the main piazza, to the north side of the Duomo; it also has an outlet at Corso Cavour 56.

Restaurants

Antica Cantina Piazza Monaldeschi 18–19 ☎0763.344.746. Popular with locals, reasonably priced (€15 will buy a good, light meal) and succeeds in reproducing the old-fashioned trattoria atmosphere and simple, but well-cooked staples. Open daily.

CRAMST Via Maitani 15 ☎0763.343.302, ⓦwww .cramst.it. Deservedly popular for its excellent value and variety; a 450-seat canteen affair, offering a choice between restaurant and self-service pizzeria. Open daily.

Etrusca Via Maitani 10 ☎0763.344.016. A traditional and relaxed trattoria that takes its cooking seriously, with classic Umbrian dishes and an attractive medieval vaulted dining room. Check out the ancient wine cellars, carved from the solid rock. Open daily.

L'Asino d'Oro Vicolo del Popolo ☎0763.344.406. Simple, hearty food served in the welcoming atmosphere of a traditional *osteria* (three courses from €25). In summer you can eat at a handful of tables on the narrow street outside. Closed Mon.

La Grotta Via Signorelli 5 ☎0763.341.348. Small, reliable trattoria just down the street from the *Posta* hotel. Reasonable value (€25 and up for a meal) for central Orvieto; friendly and has been around longer than most. Closed Tues.

Volpe e L'Uva Via Ripa Corsica 1 ☎0763.341.612. Tucked away off Via della Pace north of Piazza del Popolo, this is a wonderful trattoria offering excellent Orvietan specialities, but with the odd twist. Closed Mon & Tues.

Travel details

Trains

Assisi to: Foligno (18–24 daily; 17min); Perugia (18–24 daily; 30min); Spello (18–24 daily; 9min); Terontola (18–24 daily; connections to Chiusi, Orvieto, Arezzo, Florence and Rome; 1hr).
Città di Castello to: Perugia (hourly; 50min); Sansepolcro (hourly; 15min).
Foligno to: Ancona (13 daily; 1hr 30min–2hr); Assisi (18–24 daily; 17min); Fabriano (14 daily; 40min–1hr); Fossato di Vico (for Gubbio, 14 daily; 40min); Gualdo Tadino (8–11 daily; 40min); Narni (12–16 daily; 1hr 10min); Orte (hourly; 1hr–1hr 10min); Perugia (18–24 daily; 40min); Rome (16 daily; 1hr 55min); Spello (18–24 daily; 9min); Spoleto (12–18 daily; 20min); Terni (12–18 daily; 55min); Terontola (18–24 daily; connections for Chiusi, Orvieto, Arezzo, Florence and Rome; 1hr 15min); Trevi (12–16 daily; 7min); Tuoro sul Trasimeno (18–24 daily; 1hr 10min).

Orvieto to: Arezzo (14–20 daily; 1hr 20min); Chiusi (14–20 daily; 40min; connections to Siena, 1hr 30min); Florence (14–20 daily; 1hr 30min); Orte (14–20 daily; connections to Narni, Terni, Spoleto and Foligno; 40min); Rome (14–20 daily; 1hr 20min); Terontola (7–10 daily; connections to Perugia; 50min).

Perugia to: Assisi (18–24 daily; 30min); Città di Castello (hourly; 50min); Deruta (hourly; 30min); Florence (6 daily; 2hr 15min); Foligno (18–24 daily; 40min); Sansepolcro (hourly; 1hr 30min); Spello (18–24 daily; 30min); Terni (hourly; 1hr 40min); Terontola (18–24 daily; 35min); Todi (hourly; 50min).

Spoleto to: Arezzo (8 daily; 2hr 10min); Florence direct (8 daily; 2hr 30min); Foligno via Trevi (12–18 daily; connections for Assisi, Spello, Perugia, Terontola and Florence; 20min); Fossato di Vico (10 daily; 50min); Narni (10–17 daily; 40min); Nocera Umbra (6 daily; 35min); Perugia direct (15–20 daily; 45min); Rome (10–17 daily; 1hr 15min–1hr 45min); Terni (10–17 daily; 30min).

Terni to: Città di Castello (FCU line hourly; 2hr 30min); Foligno (18–23 daily; connections to Spello, Assisi, Gualdo Tadino, Fossato di Vico and Perugia; 40min); Narni (17 daily; 15min); Orte (12–16 daily; connections to Rome, Orvieto, Chiusi, Arezzo and Florence; 30min); Perugia (FCU line; 10–16 daily; connections at FCU Sant'Anna station in Perugia for Città di Castello and Sansepolcro, shared FCU and FS/Trenitalia station at Ponte San Giovanni for connections to Foligno and Terontola; 1hr 20min); Sansepolcro (FCU line; 10–16 daily via Perugia Sant'Anna; 3hr); Spoleto (12 daily; 20min); Todi (FCU line; 10–16 daily; 40min).

Buses

Assisi to: Bettona (1 daily; 50min); Foligno (4 daily Mon–Sat; 50min); Gualdo Tadino (1 daily; 1hr); Norcia and the Valnerina (1 daily; Mon–Sat, from Santa Maria degli Angeli); Perugia (7–10 daily; 40min); Rome (1 daily; 3hr 30min); Spello (10 daily; 40min).

Bevagna to: Foligno (5 daily Mon–Sat; 30min); Montefalco (4 daily; 40min).

Foligno to: Assisi (4 daily Mon–Sat; 50min); Bevagna (3 daily Mon–Fri; 20min); Gualdo Tadino (3 daily Mon–Sat; 50min); Montefalco (8 daily; 35min); Norcia (1 daily Mon–Sat; 1hr 35min); Perugia (4 daily; 1hr 10min); Rome (2–3 daily 1hr 35min); Spello (7 daily; 15min); Spoleto (4–8 daily; 50min); Trevi (4 daily Mon–Sat; 23min).

Gubbio to: Fossato di Vico (10 daily; 30min); Perugia (10 daily Mon–Sat, 4 daily Sun; 1hr 10min); Rome (1 daily; 2hr 40min).

Montefalco to: Bevagna (4 daily Mon–Sat; 20min).

Narni to: Amelia (4–12 daily; 15min); Orvieto (5 daily; 1hr); Otricoli (7–10 daily; 40min); Terni (4–6 daily; 30min).

Norcia to: Castelluccio (1 daily Thurs only; 50min); Perugia (1 daily Mon–Sat; 1hr 30min); Rome (2 daily Mon–Sat, 1 on Sun; 3hr); Spoleto (5–7 daily Mon–Sat, 3 on Sun; 1hr 10min); Terni (1 daily; 1hr).

Orvieto to: Amelia (5–7 daily Mon–Sat; 1hr 15min); Baschi (5–7 daily; 30min); Bolsena (2 daily Mon–Sat; 50min); Lugnano in Tevere (7 daily Mon–Sat; 1hr); Narni (5 daily Mon–Sat; 40min); Perugia (1 daily; 2hr); Terni (5 daily Mon–Sat; 2hr); Todi (1 daily Mon–Sat; 1hr 30min).

Perugia to: Áscoli Piceno (1–4 daily; 3hr); Assisi (3–12 daily; 30min); Bettona (2 daily; 40min); Castiglione del Lago (7–9 daily Mon–Sat; 1hr 15min); Chiusi (5 daily Mon–Sat; 1hr 45min); Florence (1 daily; 2hr); Foligno (4 daily; 1hr 10min); Gubbio (10 daily Mon–Sat, 4 daily Sun; 1hr 10min); Norcia (1 daily; 2hr 50min); Orvieto (1 daily; 2hr 25min); Passignano (7 daily Mon–Sat; 1hr 30min); Rome (2–6 daily; 2hr 30min); Rome Fiumicino airport (1–3 daily; 3hr); Siena (3–7 daily; 1hr 30min); Spello (5 daily Mon–Sat; 55min); Spoleto (1 direct daily Mon–Sat; 1hr 20min); Todi (via Deruta; 5–7 daily; 1hr).

Spoleto to: Cascia with connection at Serravalle (5–7 daily Mon–Sat, 3 on Sun; 1hr 5min); Foligno (Mon–Sat 4 daily; 50min); Fonti di Clitunno (7 daily; 20min); Montefalco (3–4 daily Mon–Sat; 1hr); Monteleone (via Valle di Nero and Gavelli; 1 daily in winter; 1hr 30min); Norcia via Sant'Anatolia di Narco (5–7 daily Mon–Sat, 3 on Sun; 1hr 10min); Perugia (5 daily; 1hr 20min); Rome (1 daily; 2hr 20min); Scheggino (5 daily; 1hr 10min); Terni (6 daily; 45min); Trevi (7 daily; 25min).

Terni to: Amelia (10 or more daily Mon–Sat, 1 on Sun; 50min); Cascata delle Marmore (15-plus daily Mon–Sat, 11 on Sun; 40min); Ferentillo (17 daily Mon–Sat, 12 on Sun; 40min); Orvieto (via Baschi, Guardea, Montecchio and Amelia; 5 daily Mon–Sat; 2hr); Scheggino (8 daily Mon–Sat, 5 on Sun; 50min); Todi (via Sangemini, Acquasparta or Avigliano; 3 daily Mon–Sat; 1hr); Also long-distance services to Bolsena (connection at Orvieto) and Rome.

Todi to: Deruta (3 daily Mon–Sat; 40min); Marsciano (2 daily; 30min); Orvieto (1 daily Mon–Sat; 1hr 30min); Perugia (3 daily; 1hr); Terni (3 daily Mon–Sat; 1hr).

Marche

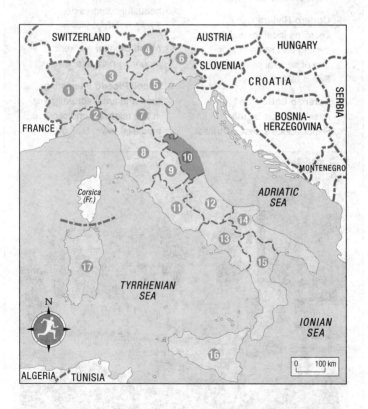

CHAPTER 10 **Highlights**

＊ **Urbino** "Ideal city" and art capital created by Federico da Montefeltro, the ultimate Renaissance man. See p.613

＊ **San Leo** This spectacular ancient town on a rocky outcrop is a landmark for miles around. See p.623

＊ **Conero Riviera** Cliffy coastline ideal for walking, cycling and swimming in one of several small bays. See p.634

＊ **Lorenzo Lotto** Don't miss paintings by the Renaissance's best portraitist at Jesi, Ancona, Recanati and particularly Loreto. See p.637

＊ **Macerata and the road to Sarnano** Catch a summer opera in this appealing old university town before driving south through some of central Italy's most beautiful countryside. See p.639 & p.643

＊ **Monti Sibillini** A hiker's mountain paradise. See p.645

＊ **Ascoli Piceno** Interesting food and architectural gems in this relatively undiscovered medieval town. See p.647

▲ Urbino

Marche

L ying between the Apennines and the Adriatic, **Marche** (sometimes anglicized as The Marches) is a varied region, and one you could spend weeks exploring. Large areas of it are unspoilt, particularly in the southwest, where stone hill-villages make atmospheric bases for hikes into the stunning **Monti Sibillini** range. Not that all of Marche is free from tourism: English and German tourists have been buying and renovating cottages in the countryside, and much of the coastline is studded with modern resorts. The area also has a fair amount of industry – in particular light engineering, shoe manufacturing and ceramics – heaviest around the port of **Ancona** and along the main road and rail route from Umbria.

Of Marche's old-fashioned and slightly forgotten seaside resorts, **Pésaro** is the largest, with a Renaissance centre maintaining its dignity behind the package-tour seafront. For more interesting sunning and swimming, head south of Ancona to the **Cónero Riviera**, a dramatic stretch of coast, with small beaches nestling beneath the craggy cliffs of Monte Conero. San Benedetto del Tronto has 6km of sand, five thousand palm trees, and numerous discos, but is not exactly a happening place compared with say Rimini. The most appealing – and best known – of Marche's sights are the small hilltop town of **Urbino**, with its spectacular Renaissance palace, and the dramatic fortress of **San Leo**, just across the border from San Marino. Further south, **Macerata** is a sleepy university town surrounded by lovely countryside, and, right on the regional border, the fascinating city of **Ascoli Piceno** is a worthy stop-off on the way into Abruzzo.

Getting around on public transport is relatively easy, though your own vehicle is useful in the more remote areas. There are two main **rail routes**: along the coast on the Milan–Bari line or across Italy on the Ancona–Rome service. The provincial capitals – Urbino, Pésaro, Macerata, Ancona and Ascoli Piceno – are all well served by public transport, and Ancona is also a major port for **ferries** to Croatia, Greece and Turkey. For hiking in the Sibillini, **Amándola** has the best bus service; if you don't mind relying on fewer buses, **Montefortino** is a prettier base.

Urbino and around

URBINO is Marche's most immediately likeable town, a walled hilltop jumble of Renaissance and medieval houses, churches and *palazzi* dominated by the tremendous Palazzo Ducale. During the second half of the fifteenth century, it was one of the most prestigious courts in Europe, ruled by the

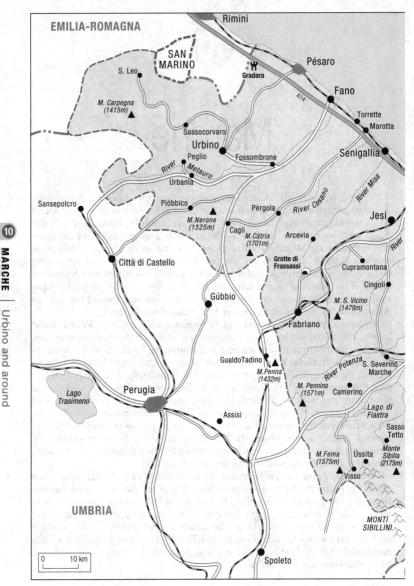

remarkable Federico da Montefeltro, who employed some of the greatest artists and architects of the time to build and decorate his palace in the town. Baldassarre Castiglione, whose sixteenth-century handbook of courtly behaviour, *Il Cortegiane* (The Courtier), is set in the palace, reckoned it to be the most beautiful in all Italy, and it does seem from contemporary accounts that fifteenth-century Urbino was an extraordinarily civilized place, a measured and urbane society in which life was lived without indulgence.

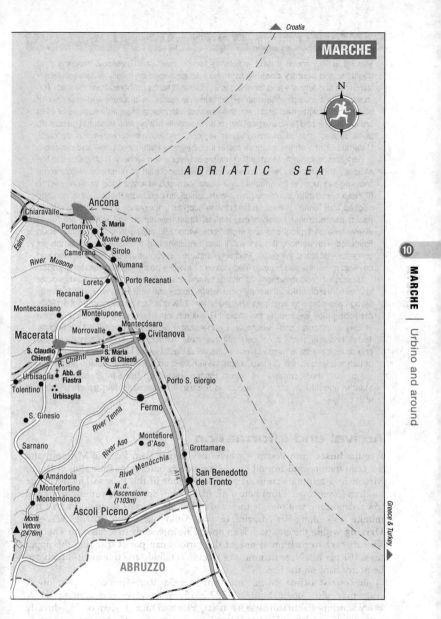

ADRIATIC SEA

Ancona
Chiaravalle
Portonovo   **S. Maria**
Monte Cónero
Camerano   Sirolo
Numana
Loreto   Porto Recanati
Recanati
Montecassiano
Montelupone
Macerata   Morrovalle   Montecósaro
Civitanova
S. Claudio
Chienti   **S. Maria**
R. Chienti   **a Piè di Chienti**
Urbisaglia   **Abb. di**
Fiastra   Porto S. Giorgio
Tolentino   **Urbisaglia**
Fermo
S. Ginesio
River Tenna
Sarnano   River Aso   Montefiore
d'Aso   Grottammare
River Menócchia
Amándola   San Benedotto
Montefortino   **M. d.**   del Tronto
Montemónaco   ▲ **Ascensione**
(1103m)
Monti
Vettore   Áscoli Piceno
(2476m)

ABRUZZO

River Musone
Esino

A14

Nowadays Urbino is saved from an existence as a museum piece by its lively university. There's a refreshing, energetic feel to the place and plenty of places to eat and drink. Its nightlife is hardly wild, but a few bars host local bands and the like. Although a new town has grown up in the valley below, it seems to have been almost wilfully designed to be as ugly as possible, so as to better highlight the glories of the walled **upper town**, which, after all, is where you'll want to spend most of your time.

615

Regional food and wine

Marche is very much a rural region, its food a mixture of **seafood** from the long coastline and **country cooking** from the interior, based on locally grown produce – tomatoes and fennel – and funghi, game, nuts and herbs gathered from the wild. The most distinctive dish, often served at summer *festas*, is a sweet-and-sour mix of olives stuffed with meat and fried, then served with *crema fritta*, little squares of fried cream. Rabbit and lamb are popular, as is *papardelle alla papara*, wide, flat pasta with duck sauce, and, as in many other regions, truffles are considered a delicacy. Unfamiliar items on the antipasti menu include *lonza* (salt-cured pork) and *ciauscolo* (a pork-based spread). Meat grilled *alla brace* (over wood embers) is ubiquitous in the Marche, and you may even come across the grand dish of *porchetta*, whole roast suckling pig, both in its original large-scale form and in a fast-food version used to fill crisp bread rolls. Don't confuse it with *coniglio in porchetta* though – this is rabbit cooked with fennel. Baked, stuffed dishes such as *vincisgrassi*, a rich layered dish of pasta, minced meat, mushrooms, giblets, brain, bechamel and truffles, are found everywhere. A typical seafood dish from Ancona is *zuppa di pesce*, a fish soup flavoured with saffron, though you'll find excellent fish broths – known simply as *brodetto* – all along the coast. Puddings include *cicercchiata*, balls of pasta fried and covered in honey, and *frappe*, fried leaves of filo-like pastry dusted with icing sugar.

Although it produces many drinkable **wines**, the Marche region is best known for just one, **Verdicchio**, a greeny-gold white, excellent with fish, which is instantly recognizable from its amphora-shaped bottle. This is in fact a hangover from a 1950s marketing ploy inspired by the ancient Greek custom of shipping wine from Ancona in clay amphorae, and, reputedly, by the shape of the actress Gina Lollobrigida. Today, however, many producers sell their best Verdicchio in standard bottles – the one to look out for is Verdicchio dei Castelli di Jesi. Lesser known **reds** include one of Italy's finest, Rosso Conero, a light wine based on the Montepulciano grape and full of fruit; more common is Rosso Piceno, based on the Sangiovese grape. A Marche aperitif now back in fashion is **mistrà**, an aniseed liqueur generally drunk with coffee.

Arrival and information

Regular **buses** from Pésaro – where they depart from Piazzale Matteotti and the train station until around 8pm – and slower buses from Fano stop in Borgo Mercatale, a terminus-cum-car park at the foot of the Palazzo Ducale in the modern lower town. From here a lift (daily 8am–8pm) takes you up to the old town, depositing you outside the Palazzo Ducale. Outside these hours it's a five minute walk along Via Mazzini, or you could take a taxi (℡0722.327.949). **Driving** within the city walls is an option available only to locals with a permit. Visitors have to park up at one of the various **car parks** that ring the upper town (€1 per hr). Note that most of Urbino is hillside and touring its streets can be pretty hard on the legs.

The **tourist office** (Mon 9am–1pm Tues–Sat 9am–1pm & 3–6pm; July & Aug may also open Sun; ℡0722.2613, ⓦwww.comune.urbino.ps.it & ⓦwww.urbinoculturaturismo.it) is at Piazza Duca Federico 35, directly opposite the Palazzo Ducale. There's an **internet café**, Netgate, at Via G. Mazzini 17 (Mon–Sat 10am–2pm & 5–11pm).

Accommodation

Urbino's **accommodation** options run from comfortable hotels and B&Bs to student halls (June–Oct only) and hostels. With your own vehicle, and especially during the oppressive heat of summer, a hotel outside the city is an option. An economical alternative if staying for a week or more is a **room in a private house** – ask the tourist office for a list and, during term time when you'll be competing for places with students, book in advance. Expect to pay about the same as for a two-star hotel (❷–❸). You could also try the **university hostel**, *Collegi Universitari* (☎0722.302.700 or 0722.302.600; ❶), which sometimes has vacancies out of term time if you book well in advance; the complex is a couple of kilometres out of town next to the main university buildings off the SS73. The nearest **campsite** is the *Pineta* (☎0722.4710, ⓔcampeggiopinetaurbino @email.it; April to mid-Sept) at Via S. Donato Ca'Mignone, in Località Fontanelle Bassa Cesana, 2km south of Urbino beyond San Bernardino; bus #4 or #7 drops you close by.

City hotels

Bed and Breakfast Il Cortegiano Via Veterani 1 ☎347.047.7214, ⓦwww.ilcortegiano.it. Two large sunny rooms just across from the Palazzo Ducale above a bar/restaurant, each with its own bathroom. ❷

Boncorte Via delle Mura 28 ☎0722.2463, ⓦwww.viphotels.it. Old-fashioned hotel just inside the city walls with views over the countryside. Breakfast is served in the tiny courtyard garden in summer. ❸

Fosca Via Raffaello 67 ☎0722.2542. Small, studenty *pensione* on the top floor of a residential *palazzo* next to the *Hotel Raffaello*, with shared bathrooms – if the owner isn't there, call ☎0722.329.622 and someone will be along. ❶

Hotel Raffaello Via Santa Margherita 38/40 ☎0722.4896, ⓦwww.albergoraffaello.com. Old town hotel with simply furnished rooms and wide views over the pantiled roofs of Urbino. It offers a pick-up facility for guests from the lower town. ❸

Italia Corso Garibaldi 32 ☎0722.2701, ⓦwww .albergo-italia-urbino.it. Renovated albergo in a porticoed street, with terracotta floors and plain but attractive rooms. Guests take breakfast in the small private garden in summer. ❸

San Domenico Piazza Rinascimento 3 ☎0722.2626, ⓦwww.viphotels.it. Located in a former religious complex across from the Palazzo Ducale, this has been sumptuously decorated, offering large rooms, big beds, polished wood floors and breakfast tables under the porticoes. ❹

San Giovanni Via Barocci 13 ☎0722.2827, ⓕ0722.329.055. This sixteenth-century Patrician house, known as Palazzo della Spillara, is cheap, neat and central. Breakfast is not included, but there is a good-value restaurant serving typical Marche dishes. Closed July. ❷

Outside the city

Balcone sul Metauro Via Manzoni 20 Peglio, near Urbania ☎0722.310.104, ⓦwww .balconesulmetauro.com A 30min drive southwest of Urbino, this modern option is a good choice. Most rooms have balconies with great views over the little town of Peglio and there's good food and an open-air swimming pool too. ❷

La Meridiana Via Urbinate 43 ☎0722.320.169, ⓦwww.la-meridiana.com. About 2km outside Urbino on the road to Pésaro, this is one of the cheapest three-star hotels in the area. The interior decoration is bland but it has a swimming pool and a restaurant, friendly staff and is useful if everything else is booked up. ❸

Nene Via Biancalana ☎0722.2996, ⓦwww .neneurbino.com. Restored stone house, 2km from Urbino, just off the "*strada rossa*" towards Fermignano, this place is visited as much for its great restaurant – with interesting vegetarian options – as for its accommodation. There's an open-air pool too. ❷

Tortorina Via Ottaviano Petrucci 4 ☎0722.327.715, ⓦwww.hotel-tortorina.it. A large apartment complex in Urbino's new town, whose soulless exteriors may come as an anticlimax after the Renaissance grandeur of the old town. Inside, the rooms are modern and facilities include a swimming pool, a fully-equipped gym and a restaurant. ❸

The Palazzo Ducale

The **Palazzo Ducale** (Mon 8.30am–2pm, Tues–Sun 8.30am–7.15pm; €8; entrance fee includes Galleria Nazionale), overlooking the surrounding countryside, is a fitting monument to Federico, the urbane ruler of fifteenth-century Urbino. An elegant combination of the aesthetic and the practical, the

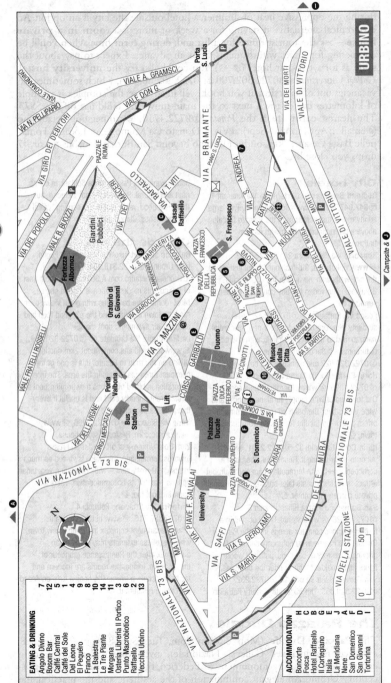

URBINO

EATING & DRINKING

Angolo Divino	7
Bosom Bar	12
Caffè Central	5
Caffè del Sole	1
Del Leone	4
El Pequeño	9
Franco	8
La Balestra	10
Le Tre Piante	14
Morgana	11
Osteria Libreria Il Portico	3
Punto Macrobiotico	6
Raffaello	2
Vecchia Urbino	13

ACCOMMODATION

Boncorte	H
Fosca	C
Hotel Raffaello	B
Il Cortegiano	G
Italia	E
La Meridiana	J
Nene	A
San Domenico	F
San Giovanni	D
Tortorina	I

facade comprises a triple-decked *loggia* in the form of a triumphal arch flanked by twin defensive towers. In contrast, the Palazzo's bare south side, forming one side of the long central Piazza Rinascimento, looks rather bleak, and it's only inside that you begin to understand its reputation as one of the finest buildings of the Renaissance. Although the Palazzo now houses the **Galleria Nazionale delle Marche**, only the few remaining original Urbino works justify much attention, and until you hit these it's the building itself that makes the biggest impression.

The courtyard and ground floor

Just inside the entrance, the **Cortile d'Onore** is your first real taste of what Urbino is about. The courtyard is not immediately striking – in fact the rest of Italy has a host of similar ones – but this is a prototype of the genre. Designed by Dalmatian-born Luciano Laurana, who was selected by Federico after he'd failed to find a suitably bold artist in Florence, it's at once elegant and restrained.

Off the Cortile is the room that housed Federico's **library**, in its day one of the most comprehensive in Europe. He spent fourteen years and over thirty thousand ducats gathering books from across the continent, and employed forty

---

Federico da Montefeltro

Federico da Motrefeltro (1422 to1482) was a formidable soldier, a shrewd and humane ruler, and a genuine intellectual – qualities that were due in part to his education at the Mantua school of the most prestigious Renaissance teacher, Vittorino da Feltre. Poor scholars and young nobles were educated together in Vittorino's classes and were taught self-discipline and frugal living as well as the more usual Latin, maths, literature and the courtly skills of riding, dancing and swordsmanship.

As the elder but illegitimate son of the Montefeltro family, Federico only became ruler of Urbino after his tyrannical half-brother Oddantonio fell victim to an assassin during a popular rebellion. Federico promptly arrived on the scene – fuelling rumours that he'd engineered the uprising himself – and was elected to office after promising not to punish those responsible for Oddantonio's death, to cut taxes, to provide an educational and medical service, and to allow the people some say in the election of magistrates.

Urbino was a small state with few natural resources and a long way from any major trading routes, so selling the military services of his army and himself was Federico's only way of keeping Urbino solvent. In high demand because of his exceptional loyalty to his employers, Federico's mercenary activities yielded a huge annual income, a substantial portion of which was used to keep taxes low, thus reducing the likelihood of social discontent during his long absences. When he was at home, he seems to have been a remarkably accessible ruler: he would leave his door open at mealtimes so that any member of his 500-strong court might speak to him between courses, and used to move around his state unarmed (unusual in a time when assassination was common), checking the welfare of his people.

Between military and political commitments, Federico also found time to indulge his interest in the arts. Though he delighted in music, his first love was architecture, which he considered to be the highest form of intellectual and aesthetic activity. He was a friend of the leading architectural theorist, Alberti, and according to his biographer, Vespasiano di Bisticci, Federico's knowledge of the art was unequalled. The Dalmatian architect Luciano Laurana was scarcely known until taken up by Federico, while his later commissions included works from the more established Francesco di Giorgio Martini and one of the greatest of all painters and theorists of architecture, Piero della Francesca.

scribes to make illuminated copies on kidskin, which were then covered in crimson and decorated with silver. They disappeared into the vaults of the Vatican after Urbino fell to the papacy in 1631, and all that's left of the room's former grandeur is one of the more outrageous representations of Federico's power – the Eagle of the Montefeltros surrounded by tongues of fire, symbolizing the artistic and spiritual gifts bestowed by Federico.

The first floor

A monumental staircase, one of the first ever built in Italy, takes you up to the first floor. Wandering through the white, airy rooms, you'll see wooden doors inlaid with everything from gyroscopes and mandolins to armour, representing the various facets of Federico's personality.

A famous portrait of Federico da Montefeltro by the Spanish artist **Pedro Berruguete** is worth seeking out. Painted, as he always was, in profile (having lost his right eye in battle), Federico is shown as warrior, ruler, scholar and dynast; wearing an ermine-fringed gown over his armour, he sits reading a book, with his pale and delicate son, Guidobaldo, standing at his feet.

The most elaborately decorated part of the *palazzo* is the suite of rooms known as the **Appartamento del Duca**. On display here are **Piero della Francesca**'s two great works: the *Madonna of Senigallia*, a haunting depiction of foreboding in which Mary, flanked by two angels, offers up her child; and the more perplexing *Flagellation*, showing Christ being almost casually beaten. Also here is Raphael's compelling portrait of a gentlewoman, *La Muta*.

Still in the Appartamento del Duca, no painting better embodies the notion of perfection held by Urbino's elite than *The Ideal City*, long attributed to Piero but now thought to be by one of his followers. Probably intended as a design for a stage set, this famous display of perspective skill depicts a perfectly symmetrical and utterly deserted cityscape, expressing the desire for a civic order that mirrors that of the heavens.

Paolo Uccello's last work, the six-panelled *Profanation of the Host*, tells the story of a woman who sold a consecrated host to a Jewish merchant. She was hanged, and the merchant and his family were burned at the stake – the angels and devils are arguing over the custody of the woman's soul. The morbid theme and fairy-tale atmosphere that pervade the work may reflect the artist's depression at getting old: shortly after completing it, he filled in his tax return with the statement, "I am old, infirm and unemployed, and my wife is ill."

It's the next three rooms of the Duke's apartment that give you the best insight into Federico's personality. A spiral staircase descends to two adjoining chapels, one dedicated to Apollo and the Muses, the other to the Christian God. This dualism typifies a strand of Renaissance thought in which mythology and Christianity were reconciled by positing a universe in which pagan deities were seen as aspects of the omnipotent Christian deity.

Back on the main floor you come to the most interesting and best-preserved of the palace's rooms, Federico's **Studiolo**, a triumph of illusory perspective created not with paint but with intarsia (inlaid wood). Shelves laden with geometrical instruments appear to protrude from the walls and cupboard doors seem to swing open to reveal lines of books, a letter lies in an apparently half-open drawer. The upper half of the room is covered with 28 portraits of great men ranging from Homer and Petrarch to Solomon and St Ambrose – another example of Federico's eclecticism.

The rest of the town

Urbino is a lively place, and its bustling streets can be a refreshing antidote to the rarefied atmosphere of the Palazzo Ducale. Next door to the palace, the town's **Duomo** is a pompous Neoclassical replacement for Francesco di Giorgio Martini's Renaissance church, destroyed in an earthquake in 1789. There's a **museum** inside (daily 9am–1pm & 2.30–6.30pm; €3), but the only reason for going in would be to see Barocci's *Last Supper*, with Christ surrounded by the chaos of washers-up, dogs and angels.

Just south, down the hill, is the **Museo della Citta** (Wed–Mon 10am–1pm & 3–6pm; free), which has displays on Urbino arranged around the central courtyard of the Renaissance Palazzo Odessi. An audioguide is available for €3 and, as the museum bills itself as a collection of ideas rather than objects, you'll probably need it to explain the thinking behind displays entitled "Desire" and "Memory". Look out for the collection of historic city signs and the scale model of Urbino.

A trek up to the gardens dominated by the sixteenth-century fortress, **Fortezza Albornoz** (9am–6pm; free), is rewarded with great views of the town and the countryside. Close by is the **Oratorio di San Giovanni** (Mon–Sat 10am–12.30pm & 3–5.30pm, Sun 10am–12.30pm; winter mornings only; €2), behind whose unfortunate modern facade is a stunning cycle of early fourteenth-century frescoes, depicting the life of St John the Baptist and the Crucifixion.

On Via Raffaello, the **Casa Natale di Raffaello**, birthplace (in 1483) of Urbino's most famous son, the painter Raphael (summer Mon–Sat 9am–1pm & 3–7pm, Sun 10am–1pm; winter Mon–Sat 9am–2pm, Sun 10am–1pm; €3), proudly displays the "stone" where Raphael and his father Giovanni Santi mixed their pigments and sizes. There's one work by Raphael, an early *Madonna and Child*, otherwise the walls are covered with reproductions and minor works by his contemporaries.

Eating, drinking and nightlife

There are plenty of reasonable places to **eat** in Urbino, with dozens of fast-food and inexpensive self-service places aimed at student budgets – the university *mensa* on Piazza San Filippo, which is open to student ID card-holders only, is the best deal. There's also more refined cooking typical of the province in a selection of more formal restaurants.

During term time when students are in town, Urbino's late-night **bars** see a brisk trade, and there are reasonable dancing and live-music options on offer too.

Restaurants

Angolo Divino Via San Andrea 14 ☎0722.327.559. Geranium-covered on the outside, and atmospheric within, this *osteria* is located in an ancient *palazzo* near the Botanical Gardens. It's well known for regional delicacies (including home-made pasta) and there are some good vegetarian choices as well. Closed Sun eve and Mon lunch.

Del Leone Via C. Battisti 5 ☎0722.329.894. This small, subterranean trattoria under the San Francesco church serves up some of the city's best food. Try the *menu di piatti tipici* featuring spinach and ricotta ravioli, whole roast big, baked potatoes, biscuits and desert wine for €20. Closed Mon.

Franco Via del Poggio 1 ☎0722.2492. Self-service place at lunchtime and a restaurant in the evening, serving *primi* such as home-made *strozzapreti* – "strangled priests" (one can only assume that its twisted shape is supposed to be resonant of a strangled neck), with vegetables, and *secondi* including rabbit cooked with fennel, all at reasonable prices. Closed Sun.

La Balestra Via Valerio 16 ☎ 0722.2942 Unpretentious restaurant with tables inside and out and serving typical local food (game and truffles) and pizzas until 3am. *Primi* €8–9, *secondi* €8–16.

Le Tre Piante Corner of Via Foro Posterula 1 and Via Voltaccia della Vecchia ☎ 0722.4863. Rather hidden away, this restaurant is worth seeking out for its small terrace overlooking the hills. Pasta dishes such as *strozzapreti* – with sausage, cream, mushrooms and peppers – and pizzas (€3.50–6.50) are excellently done, as is the *carne alla braccia*, grilled meat. Moderately priced and highly recommended. Closed Mon.

Morgana Via Nuova 3 ☎ 0722.2528. Another inexpensive choice, offering a one-course set menu for €8.50 and a two course for €9.50, Good for traditional dishes, such as *tagliatelle con erbe selvatica*, wild herbs and greens, and *tagliata di manzo con radicchio* (sliced steak with radicchio). Closed Mon.

Punto Macrobiotico Via Pozzo Nuova 6 ☎ 0722.329.790. Students pack out this 120-seater, self-service restaurant for its bargain vegetarian dishes, made from home-grown cereals and vegetables. It also operates an on-site macro-biotic shop. Closed Sun.

Raffaello Via Raffaello 41. Café-bar serving sit-down or takeaway *piadine* (flat bread with a variety of fillings, such as cheese and ham, €3–5.50) and *crescia sfogliata* (a bit like a pizza folded in half, €4). Closed Sun.

🏃 **Vecchia Urbino** Via Vasari 3/5 ☎ 0722.4447. Elegant and upmarket place with a traditional menu including *cappelletti con fegato grasso e tartufo* (pasta filled with liver and truffles, €20), marinated home-made sausage and olives as well as meat and fish grilled *alla brace* –

over a wood fire. The puddings are excellent too and the wine list is good value. *Primi* €9.50–11, *secondi* €15–20. Booking advisable. Closed Tues and for ten days in July.

Bars, clubs and live music venues

Bosom Pub Via Budassi 24 ☎ 0722.4783. Stone-vaulted, if garishly lit, pub with a well-stocked bar, including Belgian beers, and "giraffes" – tall contraptions full of several litres for a group to share. Plays mainstream latin, house, pop and rock. Decent sandwiches available too.

Caffè Central Piazza della Republica. Rather unremarkable in itself, the café's position on the city's central square has made it one of the prime local meeting spots, attracting strolling couples and jolly groups of youths throughout the evening.

🏃 **Caffe del Sole** Via Mazzini 34. Up from the bus station, on the main drag into town, this alternative café-bar is open from morning till the early hours. It has a laid-back atmosphere, comfy couches and live jazz on selected nights. Call in for details or phone ☎ 0722.2619.

El Pequéro Via San Domenico 1 ☎ 0722.327.463. Pub-restaurant that has more of an emphasis on eating than drinking, and is centrally located in a side street round the corner from the tourist office and Palazzo Ducale.

Osteria Libreria Il Portico An intriguing venue in an archway at the top of Via Mazzini that bills itself as bookshop, pizzeria, pub and *osteria*. You can browse the shelves by day – when they serve panini and snacks – or head here at night when it turns into a club open till 2am. Closed Mon.

Around Urbino

The villages north of Marche up towards San Marino are pleasant enough, although most can't compete with the crumbling hill-settlements further south. Two places, however, **Sassocorvaro** and **San Leo**, are well worth a trip and reward your efforts getting there with splendid medieval strongholds.

Sassocorvaro

Perched above a twee artificial lake some 30km northwest of Urbino by road, **SASSOCORVARO** is dominated by one of Francesco di Giorgio Martini's most ambitious **fortresses** (April–Sept daily 9.30am–12.30pm & 3.30–7pm; Oct–March Sat & Sun 9.30am–12.30pm & 2.30–6pm; €4). Built on the orders of Federico da Montefeltro for one of his *condottieri* (mercenary soldiers), Ottaviano degli Ubaldini, it was like San Leo (see opposite) designed to withstand the onslaught of cannon. Unfortunately, the site lacked San Leo's natural advantages and Francesco was forced to seek a strictly architectural solution, doing away with straight walls and building a grim fortress bulging with hourglass towers. After the functional exterior, the inside comes as something of a surprise, with an elegant Renaissance courtyard and an intimate and frescoed theatre. It's a tribute to the strength of Francesco's architecture that the fortress was selected as a safe house for some of Italy's greatest works of art during World War II, including Piero della Francesca's *Flagellation* and Giorgione's *La Tempesta*, reproductions of which are on show.

There's also a **museum** of folk life (same hours and admission ticket as the castle), with displays of traditional weaving, winemaking equipment and a mock-up of an old kitchen.

San Leo

The menacing fortress of **SAN LEO** (Nov–Feb Mon–Fri 9am–noon & 2.30–6pm; March–Oct daily 9am–6pm; €8), clamped to the summit of a dizzying precipice in the northern tip of the Marche, has staggered generations of visitors with its intimidating beauty. Machiavelli praised it, Dante modelled the terrain of his Purgatory on it, and Pietro Bembo considered it Italy's "most beautiful implement of war". In fact it's not as impregnable as it seems, and one of the few invaders to have actually been repelled was Cesare Borgia, despite his having first persuaded a weak-willed retainer to give him the key.

There's been a fortress at San Leo since the Romans founded a city on the rock. Later colonizers added to it until the fifteenth century, when Federico da Montefeltro realized that it was no match for the new gunpowder-charged weapons, and set his military architect, Francesco di Giorgio Martini, the task of creating a new one. The walls were built on a slight inward slope and backed with earth, thus reducing the impact of cannonballs. Three large squares were incorporated for the manoeuvring of heavy cannons, and every point was defended with firing posts.

From the eighteenth century San Leo was used as a prison for enemies of the Vatican, of whom the most notorious was the womanizing Count of Cagliostro, a self-proclaimed alchemist, miracle doctor and necromancer. At first the charismatic heretic was incarcerated in a regular prison, but on the insistence of his guards, who were terrified of his diabolic powers, he was moved to the so-called **Pozzetto di Cagliostro** (Cagliostro's Well), now the fortress's most memorable sight. The only entrance was through a trap door in the ceiling, so that food could be lowered to him without the warden running the risk of engaging Cagliostro's evil eye. There was one window, triple-barred and placed so that the prisoner couldn't avoid seeing San Leo's twin churches. Not that this had any effect – Cagliostro died of an apoplectic attack, unrepentant after four years of being virtually buried alive.

As well as the fortress, there's the pleasant old **village** to explore. St Leo arrived in the third century and converted the local population to Christianity, and the two village churches, though they failed to impress Cagliostro, are worth a visit. The **Pieve** was built in the ninth century, with material salvaged from a Roman temple to Jupiter, by Byzantine-influenced architects from Ravenna. Sunk into the ground behind the church is a sixth-century chapel founded by and later dedicated to St Leo, whose body lay here until 1014 when Henry II, emperor of Germany, calling in at the town on his way home from defeating the Greeks and Saracens in Rome, decided to remove it to Germany. His plans were thwarted by the horses bearing the saint's body – after a short distance they refused to go any further, so St Leo's body was left in the small village of Voghenza near Ferrara. The heavy lid of the sarcophagus remains in San Leo's twelfth-century **Duomo**, dedicated to the saint.

Getting to San Leo on public transport is a pain: you need to travel up the coast to Rimini, then catch bus #165. Once here, there's a **tourist office** at Piazza Dante 14 (daily 9am–6pm, open later in summer; ☏0541.916.306, ⓦwww.san-leo.it). There are two **hotels** in San Leo: the rambling *La Rocca*, Via G. Leopardi 16 (☏0541.916.241, ⓦwww.paginegialle.it/laroccasanleo; ❷), which has a rustic **restaurant** beneath its seven rooms, and the spick-and-span *Castello*, Piazza Dante Alighieri 11/12 (☏0541.916.214, ⓦwww.hotelristorantecastellosanleo.com; ❷), a family-run hotel, bar and restaurant on the main square. Camper vans are allowed to make overnight stops in the car park below the main square.

Pésaro and around

Most of the tourists who come to **PÉSARO** visit for a beach holiday, attracted by the string of affordable three-star hotels and the low-key family fun on offer. Germans and Brits arrive on cheap package holidays but it's a popular place with Italians, too, going through the daily ritual of beach, lunch, beach, *passeggiata* and ice cream before dinner back at the hotel. A lot of Pésaro dates from the 1920s and 1930s, and the town today is a bit of a backwater but pleasant enough nonetheless, with its long stretch of sandy **beach** and an old centre full of small craft and design shops. And with regular transport connections to lesser-known towns like Gradara and Fano, it makes a feasible base from which to explore the northern Marche.

Arrival and information

Viale Risorgimento leads from the **train station** to the town's main axis, Via Branca–Via Rossini–Viale della Repubblica, which cuts straight through the historical town to the beach. Bisecting it at Piazza del Popolo are Corso XI Settembre, scene of the evening *passeggiata*, and Via San Francesco, which leads to the **bus station** on Piazzale Matteotti. The main **tourist office** (summer Mon–Sat 8.30am–1.30pm & 3–7pm, Sun 8.30am–1pm; winter Mon–Sat 9am–1pm, Tues & Thurs 9am–1pm & 3–6pm; ☏0721.69.341, ⓦwww.turismo.pesarourbino.it) is on the seafront on Piazzale della Libertà, at the end of Viale della Repubblica.

Accommodation

There are certainly plenty of **hotels** in Pésaro, although that doesn't necessarily equate to plenty of choice. Most of the places here offer much the same level of mid-range family-orientated services and comfort. Expect to pay slightly more for a sea-facing room.

Caravelle Viale Trieste 269 ☏0721.370.450, ⓦwww.hotel-caravelle.net. Not bad, but nothing special. It's reasonably priced and conveniently situated by the beach, much like its neighbours. The rooms are light and airy and there's a swimming pool, bikes and a games room. Open May–Sept. ❷

Clipper Viale Marconi 53 ☏0721.30.915, ⓦwww.hotelclipper.it. Run by a friendly family, the *Clipper* lies a block back from the beach. The rooms are bit bland and generic, but large and well-equipped. The buffet breakfasts are served alfresco on the terrace. Open May-Sept ❷

Des Bains Viale Trieste 221 ☏0721.34.957, ⓦwww.innitalia.com. This is one of the few hotels to stay open all year. It was built in 1905, and though modernized many times since then, still has something of the "*belle époque*" about it. ❷

Napoleon Viale Fiume 118 ☏0721.31.160, ⓦwww.hotelnapoleonpesaro.it. The boxy, blue

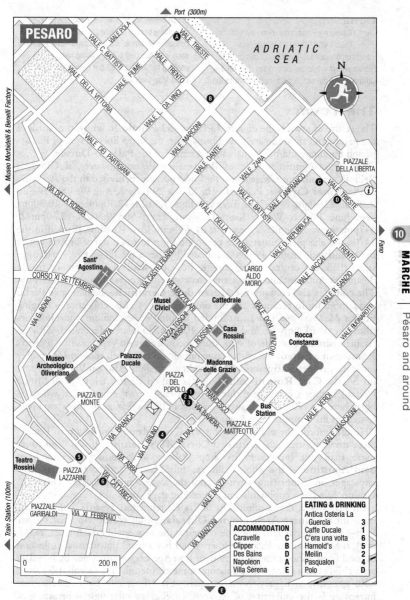

Napoleon, just across from the sea, is a summer-only hotel and geared up very much for families with mini-suites, bikes, play room, pool and waterslides. It's fairly good quality but can get very noisy. ❷

Villa Serena Via S. Nicola 6/353 ☏0721.55.211, ⓦwww.villa-serena.it. On the edge of town on the road south towards Fano,

this is a lovely, atmospheric, family-owned hotel set in a restored eighteenth-century "villa-castle" and stuffed full of antiques and heirlooms. There are just eight beautifully decorated guestrooms and a swimming pool in the rambling garden (closed Jan & Feb). ❺

Camping

Camping Panorama 7km north of Pésaro ☎ 0721.20.8145, ⓦwww .campingpanorama.it. The closest campsite to Pésaro enjoys a tranquil setting perched on a clifftop above the sea. A path leads down to the beach below. It's very well-equipped with a swimming pool, a shop, a games room and a collection of simple a/c formica-furnished chalets, each with two bedrooms, a living room and cooking facilities. It's €6 per person, €7 tent hire. Open May–Sept ②

The Town

The centre of town is the dignified **Piazza del Popolo**, in which the rituals of the pavement café scene are played out against the sharp lines of sundry Fascist-period buildings and the Renaissance restraint of the **Palazzo Ducale**.

The most significant relic of Renaissance Pésaro, however, is Giovanni Bellini's magnificent *Coronation of the Virgin* polyptych, housed in the *Pinacoteca* of the **Musei Civici** at Piazza Toschi Mosca 29 (July & Aug Wed & Fri–Sun 9.30am–12.30pm & 4–7pm, Tues & Thurs 9.30am–12.30pm & 4–10.30pm; Sept–June Tues & Wed 9.30am–12.30pm, Thurs–Sun 9.30am–12.30pm & 4–7pm; ⓦwww.museicivicipesaro.it; €4, €7 with Casa Rossini). Painted in the 1470s, the altarpiece situates the coronation not in some starry heaven but in the countryside around Pésaro, dominated by the castle of Gradara. Portraits of saints flank the central scene, ranging from the hesitant St Lawrence to the dreamy St Anthony, and below are a nativity and scenes from the saints' lives. The complex also contains the **Museo delle Ceramiche**. Renaissance Pésaro was famous for its ceramics, and the museum houses a fine collection – ranging from a *Madonna and Child* surrounded by pine cones, lemons and bilberries from the workshop of Andrea della Robbia, to plates decorated with an Arabian bandit. A couple of steps from the museum on Via Rossini is Pésaro's Romanesque **cattedrale**, with a large mosaic on two levels showing incredibly intricate geometric Byzantine and medieval designs. Also on Via Rossini, at no. 34, the **Casa Rossini** (same hours as Museo Civico; €4, €7 with Museo Civico) houses a growing shrine of memorabilia to the composer, who was born here in 1792. The Teatro Rossini on Piazza Lazzarini hosts an opera festival in his honour every August.

Heading north, the old and narrow Via Castelfidardo leads down to Pésaro's most attractive street, the porticoed **Corso XI Settembre**. If you want to do more than just browse in its shops, take a look inside the church of **Sant'Agostino** – the choir stalls are inlaid with landscapes, Renaissance cityscapes, and, displaying a wit to rival the *studiolo* in the Palazzo Ducale in Urbino, half-open cupboards and protruding stacks of books.

On Via Mazza, the continuation of Via Castelfidardo, Pésaro's archeological museum, the **Museo Archeologico Oliveriano** (July & Aug Mon–Sat 4–7pm; Sept–June Mon–Sat 9am–noon on request at the adjacent library; ☎ 0721.33344; free), is housed in the Palazzo Almerici and has a small but unusual collection of local finds. Among the relics from an Iron Age necropolis at nearby Novilara are a child's tomb filled with miniature domestic utensils and a tomb slab carved with pear-shaped figures rowing a square-sailed boat into battle. Even more intriguing is the collection of ex-votives (religious offerings) – breasts, feet, heads and even a dog – collected not from an early Catholic church but from a Roman sacred grove at San Veneranda (3km from Pésaro), consecrated in the second century BC.

A tree-lined grid of rather bland and boxy looking apartments marks Pésaro's long sandy **beachfront**, enlivened here and there by a handful of Art Deco villas, including one on Piazzale della Libertà whose eaves are supported by white plaster lobsters.

Eating and drinking

There's no shortage of places to **eat** and **drink**, although be aware that the best restaurants are all located inland in the old town. Most of the hotel restaurants along the front serve bland cuisine aimed at their multinational clientele.

Antica Osteria La Guercia Via Baviera 33 ☎0721.33.463. Next door to *Meilin*, this is one of the town's very top choices. It does amazing pasta and fish dishes at affordable prices. Try the *menu degustazione* for €20, including drinks.

Caffè Ducale Piazza del Popolo 21 ☎0721.34.279. If you feel like a sit-down and some people-watching, the square-side *Caffè Ducale* is one of the prime spots to do it. Revive yourself with one of their eponymous *caffé ducales*, a mixture of coffee, chocolate, amoretto and steamed milk.

C'era Una Volta Via Cattaneo 26 ☎0721.30.911. Long regarded as the purveyor of the best pies in town, this certainly offers plenty of choice with exactly 100 different types of pizza on the menu, from a simple cheese and tomato offering (€3) to one laden with all manner of mozzarella, sausage, ham, mushrooms, truffles and aubergines (€8). Very reasonably priced.

Harnold's Piazza Lazzarini ☎0721.65.155. Excellent filled panini that are perfect for a quick snack on the go, although you can linger longer at the tables on the square if you want. Closed Sun in winter.

Meilin Via Baviera 29 ☎0721.37.1108. If your taste buds fancy a change from the Italian norm, you could pop along to *Meilin*, just off the Piazza del Popolo, which serves Chinese food with an Italian veneer (ravioli with sweet and sour sauce etc). Takeaway service available.

Pasqualon Via G. Bruno 37 ☎0721.371.108. A fine *osteria* where you can tuck into excellent home-made pasta and a range of pizzas.

Polo Des Bains Hotel, Viale Trieste 221 ☎0721.34.957. This is one of the better restaurants along the front, although it's still not a patch on what you'll find in the old town. It offers a huge menu, including over thirty types of pizza, all cooked with uninspired efficiency.

Gradara

Inland, 15km to the north of Pésaro, is the castle of **GRADARA** (Mon 8.30am–1pm, Tues–Sun 8.30am–6.30pm; July & Aug same hours plus Thurs–Sun 9–11pm; €4), a fairy-tale confection of mellow red-brick and swallow-tail turrets but not the place to go in season if you want to avoid crowds. The castle is said to have been the scene of a thirteenth-century scandal involving Francesca da Rimini, who committed adultery with Paolo da Malatesta, her husband's brother. The lovers were killed for their transgression and later consigned to hell by Dante – he meets their spirits in Canto V of the *Inferno*, where they are caught in a ceaseless whirlwind – though Francesca's unhappy spirit is said to wander the castle when the moon is full.

Inside the castle is a room decked out as the scene of the crime, with a sumptuously refurbished four-poster bed, fake wall hangings and an open book – Francesca tells Dante in hell that it was while reading the story of Lancelot and Guinevere that she and Paolo first succumbed to their passion. Further reminders of the story are found in two nineteenth-century paintings: one showing the lovers (either dead or in a state of post-coital collapse) watched by the crippled husband; the other, less ambiguous, of the naked couple. Other rooms are furnished as a torture chamber, complete with spiked iron ball, handcuffs and lances, and as the guards' room, a strange mixture of tavern and armoury. After touring the castle, it's well worth taking a walk round the walls for the fine views over the surrounding hills.

Fano

Fifteen minutes south of Pésaro (by bus every 30min or hourly trains) lies **FANO**, no longer quite the haven it was when Robert Browning came here in 1848, seeking relief from the heat and crowds of Florence. A large swathe of the seafront is dominated by a rather ugly industrial port area, and although its beaches remain splendid, they now attract thousands of package tourists every year. Between the sandy and sheltered Lido and the long, pebbly Sassonia are good stretches where you don't have to pay, and there are further beaches at the little resorts of Torrette and Marotta to the south, both easily reached by bus. Fano is a pleasant enough place if a little humdrum, and comfortably combines its role as resort with that of small fishing port and minor historical town.

Arrival, information and accommodation

The **train station**, where buses also stop, is ten-minutes' walk from the seafront, at the end of Via Cavallotti. Fano's **tourist office**, on the front at Via C. Battisti 10 (June to mid-Sept Mon, Wed & Fri 9am–12.30pm, Tues & Thurs 9am–12.30pm & 4–7pm, Sat & Sun 9am–1pm; ☏0721.803.534, ⓦwww .turismofano.com and www.fanonline.it), is well organized, with additional offices at the nearby resorts of Torrette (Via Boscomarina 10) and Marotta (Via Viale C. Colombo 31) during July and August.

One of the most reasonably priced **hotels** is *Angela*, right on the seafront near the tourist office at Viale Adriatico 13 (☏0721.801.239; ❷), which has 37 simply furnished rooms, all with TV, and a garden. Alternatively, try the more formal *Corallo* just to the north at Via Leonardo da Vinci 3 (☏0721.804.200, ⓦwww.hotelcorallo-fano.it; ❹), on the seafront. If you have your own transport, you could stay at *Borgo della Luca* (☏0721.885.763, ⓦwww.borgodellaluca.it; ❷), a lovely **country B&B** in an old stone house around 5.5km inland from Fano towards Pésaro; it's at Strada Madonna degli Angeli, Località Sant'Andrea in Villis 95/A. Plenty of **campsites** line the coast between Pésaro and Fano: both *Norina* (☏0721.55.792; April–Sept) and *Marinella* (☏0721.55.795, ⓦwww .campingmarinella.it; April–Sept) are easily reached by bus from both towns.

The Town

If you're coming to Fano by bus, you could ask to be dropped off at the old town gate, the crenellated **Porta Maggiore**, to start your sightseeing with the remnants of the medieval defensive walls, on the southwestern side of the town centre. Behind them is a Roman gate, the **Arco di Augusto**, impressive despite having been truncated in the fifteenth century when Federico da Montefeltro blasted away its upper storey. You can see what it used to look like in a relief on the facade of the adjacent church of San Michele.

The Roman precursor of Fano, named Fanum Fortunae after its Temple of Fortune, stood at the eastern end of the Via Flaminia, which cut across the Apennines to Rome. The town is still built around a Roman crossroads plan: Via Arco di Augusto and Corso Matteotti follow the routes of the *cardus* and

---

The Guardian Angel

Not previously regarded as one of his finer works, *The Guardian Angel* by the Emilia-born Renaissance painter, **Guercino**, was quickly elevated to iconic status following a visit to Fano by the British poet, **Robert Browning**, in 1848. The picture, displayed in the Corte Malatestiana, shows a golden-haired child being shown how to pray by a rather chunky looking angel, so entranced Browning that he was inspired to write a poem of the same title. Expressing a wistful yearning to take the place of the child, the gushingly sentimental poem became incredibly popular, and Italy was flooded with reproductions of the painting for holidaying Browning fans. The keenest disciples set up a club, membership of which was gained by travelling to Fano and sending the founder a postcard.

decumanus, and their junction is marked with a copy of a Roman milestone stating its distance from the capital (195.4 Roman miles). There are few other relics of Roman Fano, although the fifteenth-century **fountain** in the main square, along Via Mazzini, is dedicated to Fortune.

Overlooking the fountain are the reconstructed thirteenth-century Palazzo della Ragione and the fifteenth-century **Corte Malatestiana**, dating from the time Fano was ruled by the Malatesta family. Its most notorious member was Sigismondo, whose disagreements with the pope led to the siege of Fano (when the Arco di Augusto lost its top) and his excommunication. After the death of his first wife – whom he was suspected of having poisoned – Sigismondo remarried in Fano in 1449, holding a three-day banquet in the Corte Malatestiana. Rumours about Sigismondo's sinister interest in his wives' diet revived when, seven years later, his second wife also died unexpectedly, leaving him free to marry his long-time mistress, Isotta degli Atti. The Corte is at its best nowadays on summer evenings, when its loggias, turrets and trefoil windows provide a backdrop for concerts. Inside there's a small **museum and art gallery** (Tues–Sat 9.30am–12.30pm & 4–7pm, Sun 10am–1pm, usually with extended hours in summer; €3), whose most striking exhibit is a mosaic of a winged figure riding a panther. The upstairs art gallery holds Guercino's *The Guardian Angel*, which, thanks to Robert Browning's literary intervention, became one of Italy's most famous paintings in the 19th century (see box opposite).

Less saccharine paintings are to be found in the Renaissance church of **Santa Maria Nuova** on Via de Pili, off the main square. The two works by Perugino, a *Madonna, Child and Saints* and an *Annunciation*, are both suffused with a calm luminosity.

Eating and drinking

As well as numerous **pizzerias** and **snack bars**, there's a pretty decent fish and seafood trattoria, *Borgo del Faro*, overlooking the harbour at Via N. Sauro 276 (closed Sun). Just around the corner from the port, don't miss one of the best budget places to eat in the province: ⅍ *Self Service Al Pesce Azzurro*, at Viale Adriatico 48 (☎0721.803.165; May–Oct closed Mon). Although it enjoys a pretty unprepossessing location, right opposite the port, the restaurant, which is run by a cooperative of fishermen's wives, offers great-value three-course set meals (lunch and dinner) of the freshest *pesce azzurro*, oily fish such as anchovies, sardines and mackerel, for just €10 a head.

Senigallia

Further down the coast, **SENIGALLIA** is an unprepossessing family resort with a good beach and most of its tourist activity packed into a short season. It makes an easy day-trip from Pésaro, which is a just a twenty-minute train ride away (roughly every 30min). The town centre focuses on the rickety **Foro Annonario**, a semicircular Neoclassical marketplace, behind which stands the imposing thirteenth-century **Rocca Roveresca** (daily 8.30am–7.30pm; €2). The *rocca*, or castle, was built for Federico da Montefeltro's son-in-law by Luciano Laurana, architect of the Palazzo Ducale in Urbino. Below the elegant Renaissance halls lies an underground warren of vaulted storage rooms and dungeons. Upstairs, the fireplaces and beautiful spiral staircase show little sign of use. The cells, however, are a different matter. Converted from cannon positions when the region fell to the pope, they have tiny air holes designed to inflict a slow and agonizing suffocation on their occupants. Fine views are to be had from the towers, built in the fifteenth century when the Adriatic coast was plagued by Turkish bandits.

Ancona and around

Severely damaged by war and earthquakes, workaday **ANCONA** has few historical monuments embedded in its tangle of commercial buildings. The modern centre is a grid of broad avenues and palm-shaded piazzas, while the station area, with its heavy trucks travelling noisily to and from the port, will probably make you want to take the next train out. However, as one of the Adriatic's largest ports it's a convenient departure point, and you may well pass through in order to catch one of the regular ferries to Croatia, Greece and Turkey. These days the city is even more of a gateway to the Marche region with Ryanair's direct flights from the UK to Falconara airport, 10km away.

Arrival and information

Via Marconi and its continuation, Via XXIX Settembre, run along the coast from the train station to the port and the centre of town. Via XXIX Settembre ends in the adjacent piazzas of Kennedy and Repubblica, from which the modern centre's three parallel avenues – Corso Stamira, Corso Garibaldi and Corso Mazzini – slice up to Piazza Cavour, while Via della Loggia runs up above the port to the alleyways of the old town. The main **bus terminus** is Piazza Cavour. From here, buses operated by Comero (℡071.280.2092, ⓦwww.cormerobus.it), link up with the **train station** on Piazza Rosselli, and the **Stazione Marittima**, where the ferries dock. Buses also connect the **airport** with the train station, taking around thirty minutes. Buy your ticket (€1) before boarding from any bar or newspaper kiosk. They run roughly hourly from 6.30am to 7.30pm. A taxi will cost a steep €35 (℡071.43.321). **Driving** Ancona's fiercely congested streets is not recommended, particularly as there is extremely limited parking.

The main **tourist office** for Ancona and the Marche region recently moved to Largo XXIV Maggio 1 (℡071.2221, ⓦwww.comune.ancona.it). There's also a seasonal office at the Stazione Marittima, open July and August only (ⓔiat.ancona@regione.marche.it).

Accommodation

If you want to **stay** the night in Ancona you will find no shortage of cheap and cheerful places opposite the train station. The town's **youth hostel** is 100m from the station at Via Lamaticci 7 (℡071.42.257, ⓔancona@ostellionline.org; €17 without bathroom, €25 with bathroom); note that there's a lock-out between 11am and 4.30pm.

Grand Hotel Passetto Via Thaon de Revel 1 ℡071.31.307, ⓦwww.hotelpassetto.it. Perched on a hill in a quiet part of town, this luxurious establishment offers excellent service, as well as a pool, a cocktail bar, health club and great views out over the Adriatic. ❻

Jolly Hotel Ancona Rupi di Via XXIX Settembre 14, ℡071.201.171, ⓦwww.jollyhotels.com. Handily situated if you're catching the ferry, albeit a bit of a trek up the hill, this provides reliable chain comfort and a restaurant with sea views. ❸

Milano Via Montebello 1 ℡071.201.147. Clean, appealing and centrally located bargain of a place. It's very popular so book ahead. ❶

Roma e Pace Via G. Leopardi 1 ℡071.202.007, ⓦwww.hotelromaepace.it. Right in the centre of town, this is the most interesting of the mid-range hotels and abounds with original fittings and faded 1930s elegance – entering this place is like stepping into an Agatha Christie novel. ❸

The Town

Regular buses run along the seafront from the train station to the port, passing the pentagonal **Lazzaretto**, built within the harbour in the eighteenth century as a quarantine station for immigrants. The port itself is headed by a well-preserved Roman arch, the **Arco di Traiano**, raised in honour of Emperor Trajan, under whose rule Ancona first became a major port. Behind it is the **Arco Clementino**, a piece of architectural self-congratulation by Pope Clement XII, who made Ancona a free port in the eighteenth century.

On a steep hill overlooking the port rises the town's Romanesque Duomo, while what survives of old Ancona is spread out below. At the foot of the hill is Piazza della Repubblica, from which Via della Loggia leads past the **Loggia dei Mercanti**, whose Gothic splendours include figures of medieval dignitaries and horsemen below its elaborately carved windows. Walk along the narrow road into Piazza del Plebiscito and you come to the **Museo della Città** (mid-June to mid-Sept Mon 4.30am–noon, Tues–Fri 6–10pm, Sat & Sun 10am–1pm & 6–10pm; rest of year Tues & Wed 10am–1pm, Thurs–Sun 10am–1pm & 4–7.30pm; €4), with models, paintings, sculptures and original documents showing key events in Ancona from 2000 BC to 2000 AD. Backtracking to Piazza della Repubblica, take a left into Corso Mazzini, where there's a long sixteenth-century **fountain** with thirteen spouting heads, all with interesting expressions, attributed to the sixteenth-century sculptor Pellegrino Tibaldi.

Equally appealing, a short walk away on Piazzetta S. Maria (walk straight ahead until you hit the train line, then turn right), is the decrepit Romanesque church

> ### Onwards to Croatia, Albania, Greece and Turkey
>
> Ferries leave from the Stazione Marittima, a couple of kilometres north of the train station (bus #1 or #4), close to the centre of town. For the best at-a-glance idea of timetables and routes, visit ⓦwww.doricaportservices.it. Each of the main ferry lines has a ticket office (closed 1–3pm) and you can also buy tickets from the agencies all around the port, or alternatively, book online.
>
> Among the main **ferry companies**, Superfast (ⓣ071.202.033 or 071.202.034, ⓦwww.superfast.com) sail to Igoumenitsa (15hr 30min) and Patras (21hr) in Greece. Minoan (ⓣ071.201.708, ⓦwww.minoan.it) and Anek (ⓦwww.ferries.gr) also operate along this route. Jadrolinija (ⓣ071.204.305, ⓦwww.jadrolinija.hr) sails to Croatia and the Dalmatian Islands (8–9hr), and Marmara Lines (ⓣ071.207.6165, ⓦwww.marmaralines.com) sails to Çesme in southwest Turkey (2 days), as do Amatori (ⓣ071.562.16, ⓦwww.amatori.com) who also operate services to the Croatian Islands and Split.
>
> **Ticket prices** depend on the speed of the crossing, with one-way fares starting at around €60 per person to Croatia; if you're taking a car add another €60. For the 21-hour overnight journey to Patras in July and August, reckon on paying €75 for deck class (cabins are available at additional cost), with an extra €120 for a car. For the mammoth crossing to Turkey (43hr 15min to 55hr) with Marmaris Lines, you can expect to pay €150 for a Pullman seat plus €165 for a car one-way in high season. Most of the shipping lines offer some good five-adult/one-car deals. There are no discounts for holders of InterRail and Eurail passes, but outside high season prices drop by 15–20 percent. There are also 20 percent discounts on return journeys, and some lines will give a discount if you have a student card. Check whether boarding taxes are included in your ticket; sometimes an additional fuel tax is payable to the port agency at the time of embarkation for a car. You should book in advance, and you should always aim to arrive at the Stazione Marittima two hours before your ferry is due to depart (3hr if you're taking a camper van).

of **Santa Maria della Piazza**, its facade a fantasia of blind loggias and its portal carved with chunky figures and elegant birds. Behind the church, on Via Pizzecolli, is the town's **Pinacoteca Comunale Francesco Podesti** (Mon 9am–1pm, Tues–Fri 9am–7pm, Sat 8.30am–6pm, Sun 3–7pm; €4). The highlight here is Titian's *Apparition of the Virgin*, a sombre yet impassioned work, with the Virgin appearing to a rotund and fluffy-bearded bishop in a stormy sunset sky. There's also a glorious *Holy Conversation* by Lotto, and an exquisite yet chilling *Madonna and Child* by Carlo Crivelli, with a mean-looking Mary pinching the toe of a rather pained Christ.

Beyond the gallery is the church of **San Francesco delle Scale**, named for the steps leading up to it. Titian's *Apparition* was painted for this church, but today its most remarkable work is an almost orgasmic *Assumption* by Lotto. Further up the hill, still on Via Pizzecolli, the **Museo Archeologico** is not a bad place to spend an hour (Tues–Sun 8.30am–7.30pm; closed Tues July–Sept; €4), its wacky moulded ceilings vaulting over a collection of finds ranging from red- and black-figure Greek craters to a stunning Celtic gold crown.

From here, passing the remains of the Roman amphitheatre, you can climb up to the pink-and-white **Duomo**, San Ciriaco. Though mostly built in a restrained Romanesque style, there's an outburst of Gothic exuberance in the doorway's cluster of slender columns, some plain, others twisted and carved. The most memorable feature, however, is a screen along the edge of the raised right transept, one section of which is carved with eagles, fantastic birds and storks entwined in a tree, the other with saints.

Eating and drinking

You can eat well in Ancona, particularly in the family-run fish restaurants scattered around town. Afterwards, Piazza Roma is the place to hang out – there are plenty of cafés with tables outside in the pedestrianized cobbled square.

Clarice Via del Traffico 6 ☎071.20.29.26. An old-style, family place in a cobbled alleyway off Corso Garibaldi (on the right as you walk up from the sea). It serves traditional, very reasonably priced food, with many local dishes such as *seppie e piselli* (cuttlefish and peas). Closed Sat eve and Sun.

La Cantineta Via Gramsci 1/C ☎071.201.107. This place, just off Piazza del Plebiscito, may look unprepossessing but their speciality, *stoccafisso all'Anconetana*, a traditional recipe involving salt cod, is well worth sampling. Closed Mon eve.

La Luna al Passetto ☎338.853.5005. Take the bus to the beach, Spiaggia di Passetto, at the end of Viale della Vittoria for excellent seafood, including a fishy, fixed-price *degustazione* menu for €35 that will probably be more than you can eat.

Open May–Aug; from Sept–April they move to Via Trieste 5 and call themselves *La Luna d'Inverno*.

Osteria del Pozzo Via Bonda 2/C ☎071.207.3996. A small, traditional restaurant on a narrow lane off Piazza del Plebiscito, where you can tuck into seafood and pasta dishes. If you call in advance, they'll make you a *brodetto*, fish soup, or oven-baked *baccala*. Closed Sun.

Roma e Pace Via G. Leopardi 1. A popular restaurant from the same era as the hotel of the same name (see p.630), with white linen tablecloths and pizzas cooked in a wood-fired oven.

Ristorante Giardino Via Filzi Fabio ☎071.20.29.26. Great seafood specials, such as clams and langoustines, plus oven-fired pizzas at this local favourite.

Inland: the Esino Valley

West of Ancona and cutting right across the Marche, the **Esino Valley** is broad and bland in the east, but narrows to a dramatic limestone gorge – the Gola di Rossa – just before the town of **FABRIANO** and the border with Umbria. Famous for two things – paper-making and Gentile da Fabriano, the best of the International Gothic artists – Fabriano is now heavily industrialized and a pretty dismal town – one you're likely to pass straight through on your way to Umbria and Rome. Although Fabriano and **Jesi** are built up, most of the valley is given over to agriculture and is best known for **Verdicchio**, a dry white wine produced in the hilltop villages around Jesi. What most visitors come for, however, are the vast **Frasassi caves**.

Jesi

Though its industrial development has led to **JESI** (served by frequent buses from Ancona) being known as "the little Milan of the Marche", the historic centre of the town is well preserved. Clinging to a long ridge, it's fringed by medieval walls and retains a scattering of Renaissance and Baroque palaces. One of the most majestic of these, the Palazzo Pianetti, is home to the **Pinacoteca Civica** (mid-June to Sept Tues–Sun 10am–8pm; Oct to mid-June Tues–Sat 9am–1pm & 4–7pm, Sun 10am–1pm & 5–8pm; €5.50). The highlight of its opulent interior is the magnificent 72-metre-long stuccoed, gilded and frescoed gallery – a Rococo fantasy of shells, flowers and festoons framing cloud-backed allegorical figures. The collection of paintings is best known for some late works by **Lorenzo Lotto**, including *The Annunciation* and *The Visitation* (both circa 1520). Lotto, unlike his contemporaries Titian

▲ The Visitation by Lorenzo Lotto, Pinacoteca Civica, Jesi

and Giorgione, chose to be an outsider from the Venetian artworld. As a result his work was long-neglected, though his use of colour and the expressive intensity of his portraits is exceptional.

A stroll around town takes you past the **Teatro Pergolesi**, a vast eighteenth-century opera house in Piazza della Repubblica, named after local-born composer Giovanni Battista Pergolesi. Encircling the town are the massive **ramparts**, restructured in the fourteenth century and built on top of the foundations of Roman walls – an escalator takes you through the ramparts, several metres thick, from the lower town to the upper town (with steps back down again).

The village of **CUPRAMONTANA** in the hills above Jesi is known as the capital of Verdicchio country. The best time to visit (there are daily buses from Jesi) is on the first Sunday in October, when there's a parade and dancing, and the village streets are lined with stalls of wine and food for the **grape festival**. Theoretically, this marks the eve of the harvest but, owing to hangovers, it's usually a couple of days before anyone feels fit enough to start work. A *cantina aperta* ("open cellar") day at the end of May gives you the chance to sample the fruits of the winemakers' labours – if you're interested in knowing more about producers and vineyards, contact the local wine association, Assivip (℡0731.703.844, ⓦwww.assivip.it). The regional enoteca at Via Federico Conti 5 (daily: April–Oct 11am–1pm & 5.30–9.30pm; Nov–March 5–9pm; ℡0731.213.386) in Jesi's historic centre (near the top of the escalator), holds tasting sessions of local wines every Monday.

The Grotte di Frasassi

Further up the Esino Valley, just after the Gola di Rossa, a road leads up from Genga train station to the Frasassi gorge, carved by the River Sentino, which was also responsible for creating the 18km of caves beneath it. The largest of the **Grotte di Frasassi**, or Frasassi caves, (guided tours only, March–Oct daily 10am, 11am, noon, 1pm, 3pm, 4pm, 5pm & 6pm; Nov–Feb Mon–Fri 11am & 4pm, Sat & hols 11am, 12.30pm, 3pm & 4.30; €15; ⓦwww.frasassi.com) was discovered only in 1971, and just over a kilometre of its caverns and tunnels is now open to the public on tours that last seventy minutes – note that the average temperature inside is 14°C so bring a sweater.

Inevitably, the most remarkable stalactite and stalagmite formations have been named: there's a petrified Niagara Falls, a giant's head with a wonderfully Roman profile, a cave whose floor is covered with candles complete with holders, and a set of organ pipes. The vast Cave of the Great Wind, at 240m high, is one of the biggest in Europe – large enough to contain Milan Cathedral – and has been used for a series of experiments, ranging from sensory deprivation (as a possible treatment for drug addicts) to a subterranean version of *Big Brother* when a group of people were shut away for a month.

Sadly there is no public transport to the caves, so you need your own vehicle to get here.

The Conero Riviera

Just south of Ancona the white cliffs of **Monte Conero** plunge straight into the sea, forming the northern Adriatic's most spectacular and enjoyable stretch of coastline. It's easily accessible, with the major resorts of **Portonovo**, **Sirolo** and **Numana** all linked by bus from Ancona, either from the train station or

Piazza Cavour. Sirolo and Numana are now as crowded in July and August as the rest of the Adriatic resorts, the main difference being that their cliff-backed beaches are more picturesque. The most stunning stretch of coast, a series of tiny coves at the base of Monte Conero between Portonovo and Sirolo, is best explored by boat – they leave from both bays. You can go just for the scenery or ask to be dropped off somewhere along the way and be picked up a few hours later. The return journey should cost around €12.

This stretch of coast is the home of Rosso Conero wine, made from the same Montepulciano grape as Chianti, though less well known than its Tuscan counterpart. Rarely found outside Italy, there's a chance to sample it at the Rosso Conero **festival** at Camerano, 8km inland from Monte Conero, in the first week in September.

Portonovo

Only 11km from Ancona, **PORTONOVO**, nestling beneath Monte Conero, is a pleasant resort made up of a couple of campsites and a clutch of expensive hotels, one of which is sited in the Napoleonic fort that dominates the bay. The main attraction is the unbeatable scenery and the transparent water, and though the main pebbly pay-beach gets very busy in summer, it's easy enough to escape by walking about 1km to Mezzavalle beach (free) just north of Portonovo Bay or clambering over rocks to the few tiny beaches to the south. On the walk south, there's a lovely Romanesque church, **Santa Maria** (Tues–Sun 4.30–6.30pm; free) perched above the shore at the end of an oleander-lined path. There are lots of **trails** across Monte Conero of varying degrees of difficulty. Ask at the tourist offices or, if you understand Italian, check out ⓦwww.conero.net. The tourist office at Sirolo has maps, as do many souvenir shops in the area.

Portonovo is linked with Ancona by regular urban **buses** – from mid-June to the end of August, they run every twenty minutes. **Accommodation** is stylish rather than budget: *Emilia*, Via Collina di Portonovo (℡071.801.117, ⓦwww .hotelemilia.com; ❻), is a five-minute car journey inland – and uphill – from the beach. The walls are covered with a huge contemporary art collection, a legacy of the 1960s when artists paid for their stay with a piece of work; the filmmaker Nanni Moretti has also been a long-term guest. The hotel has a pool, rents out electric bikes for exploring the Monte Conero Park and offers a shuttle service to the beach. Down by the seashore the *Fortino Napoleonico* (℡071.801.450, ⓦwww.hotelfortino.it; ❻) was built on the orders of Napoleon to stop the English landing to take on fresh water from Monte Conero's springs. The hotel retains some military touches here and there but is generally rather chi-chi and grand. Otherwise there are two **campsites**: *Camping Club Adriatico* (℡071.801.170; May to mid-Sept) is slightly cheaper; if it's full, try the *Camping Comunale La Torre* (℡071.801.257; June to mid-Sept). As for **eating**, there's no better place to watch the sun go down than from the fashionable beach bar and restaurant *Il Clandestino* (March/April–Sept/Oct depending on the weather; to find it, follow the "Torre" signs). *Susci Italiano* is on the menu – like sushi in concept but using speciality olive oils and balsamic vinegar rather than wasabi and soy sauce.

Sirolo

Further south, **SIROLO** has an old centre of terraced cottages divided by neat cobbled streets. The main square, Piazza Veneto, is on the clifftop, with good views of the coast and Monte Conero. What used to be a quiet bolt hole is now packed-out on weekends from June to September. In season, buses run roughly every thirty minutes to the two **beaches** below: Sassi Neri, a wide, long, black-pebbled strand of beach, and San Michele, an attractive, narrow sandy stretch.

The **tourist office** is on Piazza Vittorio Veneto (daily: May–Oct 9am–1pm & 4–8pm; July & Aug same hours plus 9–11pm; ☎071.933.0611, ✉iat.sirolo @regione.marche.it). There's a good choice of **accommodation**: beach lovers should head for *Arturo*, Via Spiaggia 1 (☎071.933.0975, ⓦwww .arturoresidencesirolo.com; ❹; May–Oct), right on the white shingle strand, with four rooms and two studio apartments with cooking facilities that open out onto small balconies and the sea. It's a bus ride from Sirolo proper (or a long walk down and then back uphill), but it's one of the least expensive options in town. It has its own restaurant with live music down on the beach. At the other end of the scale is ☀ *Nove Camera* (formerly the *Rocco*), Via Torrioni 1 (☎071.933.0558, ⓦwww .novecamera.it; ❹), built into the town gate and a short walk down the main street of Corso Italia from the piazza. Once a thirteenth-century inn where St Francis is said to have slept, it's now a terribly stylish seven-room hotel. Sirolo's closest **campsite** is the *Internazionale* (☎071.933.0884, ⓦwww.campinginternazionale. com; April–Sept), set on a terraced, wooded hillside below Piazza Veneto, within sight and sound of the sea.

Eating options include *Il Grottino* (closed Mon) on Via Ospedale, just off Via Italia, a moderately priced place specializing in fish under its stone vaults. Otherwise there's *La Taverna* (☎071.9331.1382; booking advisable; closed Mon in winter), Via Italia 10, offering *enogastronomia*: local wine and several fish and pasta combinations plus the local cheese, *formaggio di Fossa*. At *Trattoria Sara* next door at number 9 (☎071.933.0716; closed Wed in winter) diners can sample robust dishes in a no-nonsense atmosphere; the seafood antipasti, risotto and tagliatelle with fish sauce are especially recommended.

Numana

NUMANA, a small port with a large pebble beach, is where you can take a boat to the offshore islets of **Due Sorelle** (June–Sept roughly hourly 9am–3pm, rest of the year twice daily; €15 return) for a spot of swimming and sunbathing. There's also the added attraction of a **museum** (daily 8.30am–7pm; €2), filled mostly with relics of the Piceni tribe, who occupied the area between Senigallia and Pescara from the seventh century BC; the extent to which they were influenced by the Greeks, who set up a trading post nearby, is clearly visible in the red-and-black pots decorated with scenes from Greek mythology. If you want **to stay**, try *Sorriso*, 50m from the beach at Via Flaminia 109 (☎071.933.0645, ⓦwww.hotelsorrisonumana.it; ❹), which has good food and a shady garden, or the *Scogliera*, Via del Golfo 21 (☎071.933.0622, ℻071.933.1403; ❸), a modern, appealing place on a small headland at the northern edge of the bay. Both are open April to October.

Loreto and around

The majority of people who visit **LORETO** are pilgrims, over four million of whom arrive every year to pay their respects at what they believe is the **House of the Virgin Mary** where Jesus spent his childhood. To find out how the house made its miraculous journey from Nazareth to Italy, see box opposite. The primitive stone building, with only three walls, sits within a

Loreto owes its existence to one of the Catholic Church's more surreal legends. The story goes that in 1292, when the Muslims kicked the Crusaders out of Palestine, a band of angels flew the **house of Mary** from Nazareth to Dalmatia, and then, a few years later, whisked it across the Adriatic to Loreto. In the face of growing scepticism, the Vatican came up with the more plausible story that the Holy House was transported to Loreto on board a Crusader ship. Not surprisingly, though, this new theory doesn't have the same hold on the Catholic imagination, and the Madonna of Loreto continues to be viewed as the **patron saint of aviators**: Lindbergh took an image of her on his landmark Atlantic flight in 1927, and a medallion inscribed with her image also accompanied the crew of *Apollo 9*. For centuries she was also credited with military victories –presumably she was thought to have power over projectiles.

grand and very-far-from-humble **basilica** (daily: April–Sept 6.15am–8pm; Oct–March 6.45am–7pm) featuring works by such Renaissance luminaries as Bramante, Antonio da Sangallo, Sansovino, Lotto and Luca Signorelli, many of which depict scenes from the life of Mary. Inside the house, pride of place is given to a copy of the famous *Black Madonna of Loreto*; the medieval original, once crazily attributed to St Luke, was destroyed in a fire in 1921. Pope Julius II contributed the cannon shell hanging on the right-hand wall, attributing his miraculous escape from it to the Madonna of Loreto's missile-deflecting powers.

As fascinating as the story is, and as magnificent the setting for the house, for the non-believer the atmosphere of devotional hard-sell here can soon become stifling. Loreto can also be a distressing or moving place, depending on your attitude to faith – between April and October so-called "white trains" bring the sick and terminally ill on three-day missions of hope, the main event being a Mass in **Piazza della Madonna**, outside the basilica. Do also note that at peak times you may not be able to look around the Holy House as a service is usually being conducted for visiting pilgrims and it is closed from 12.30pm to 2.30pm.

Over the centuries, Loreto built up a covetable collection of treasures donated by wealthy believers. One of the most costly and idiosyncratic was a golden baby bequeathed by Louis XIII of France, weighing exactly the same as his long-awaited heir, the future Louis XIV. The basilica was ransacked in 1798 by Napoleonic troops, most of the plunder ending up on the shelves of the Louvre in Paris. Following Napoleon's demise, subsequent popes managed to retrieve many of the valuables, but the majority were stolen again in 1974 in what became known as the "holy theft of the century".

The items left behind in the treasury after the 1974 burglary are now kept in the **Museo-Pinacoteca** (Tues–Sun: April–Oct 9am–1pm & 4–7pm; Nov–March 10am–1pm & 3–6pm; donations requested) housed in the west wing of the Palazzo Apostolico. It shouldn't be missed, principally for the eight paintings by Lorenzo Lotto that are held here, nearly all dated between 1549 and 1556, including his final work, *The Presentation in the Temple*. Plagued by neurosis and lack of money, Lotto finally joined the religious community at Loreto, painted some of the canvases on display, and died here in 1556. Looking at *The Presentation*, with its rotund, crumbling priest and frail, almost skeletal nun, it would appear that he never found much inner peace. *Christ and the Adulteress* is an even more powerful work, with Christ surrounded by maniacally intense men and a swooning adulteress.

Practicalities

Finding accommodation in Loreto can be difficult, particularly during the main pilgrimage seasons of December 8–12 (the anniversary of the legendary flight), August 1–20, September 5–10, Easter, and from Christmas through to January 7. In any case, it's probably best treated as a day-trip. The town is easily accessible by **train** from Ancona; the station is some way out of town but connected with the centre by regular buses. If you're determined to stay it's worth visiting Ⓦwww.le-marche.com or the **tourist office** at Via Solari 3 (Mon–Fri 9am–1pm & 4–6.30pm, Sat 9am–1pm; ⓉO71.970.276, Ⓔiat.loreto@regione.marche .it) for a complete list of the accommodation options. The one-star **hotels** are run by religious orders, among them the *Sorelle Francescane*, Via Marconi 26 (ⓉO71.970.306; ❶). For something less spartan, try the central *Hotel Giardinetto* (ⓉO71.977.135, Ⓦwww.hotelgiardinetto.it; ❶), just inside the Porta Romana in a mellow stone building on Corso Boccalini, which also has parking for €8 a night in its nearby garage. The **youth hostel** is at Via Aldo Moro 46 (ⓉO71.750.1026, Ⓦwww.ostelloloreto.it), a short walk from Piazza Basile, with beds from €16 to €25.

Your best bet for places to **eat** are the *Girarrosto* in the *Centrale* hotel on Via Solari, which serves antipasti typical of the Conero peninsula, or, for great pizza, the *Garibaldi*, further down the same street (closed Wed).

Recanati and Porto Recanati

A few kilometres along the Macerata road from Loreto is **RECANATI**, a small town that makes a comfortable living from having been the birthplace of the opera singer Beniamino Gigli and the nineteenth-century poet Giacomo Leopardi, and its coastal satellite, the little resort of **Porto Recanati**.

Recanati

On the central Piazza Leopardi, the **Museo Beniamino Gigli** (Tues–Sun 10am–1pm & 3–6pm; €2.50) housed in the nineteenth-century **Palazzo Comunale**, has costumes worn by the great tenor, presents received by him (including a dagger from D'Annunzio), and, best of all, a replica of his dressing room. It's worth dropping in, too, at the patrician house on Via Gregorio XII where the **Museo Civico Villa Colloredo Mels** (Tues–Sun 9am–noon & 3–6pm; open until 7pm in summer; €4.50) is housed, with four paintings by **Lotto** the highlight of the small collection. Among them there's a polyptych, a *Transfiguration* and a haunting *Annunciation*, better known as *The Madonna of the Cat* for the cat scuttling between the Madonna and angel – thought by some critics to represent the devil.

Left out of Piazza Leopardi, the main street leads down to the **Palazzo Leopardi** where the poet was born in 1798 and which still contains his vast library of over 25,000 volumes. You're almost certain to meet crowds of schoolkids here – Leopardi is required reading in Italian schools – but their elation tends to come from relief at finishing the tedious tour of Leopardi's gloomy house. Leopardi himself sought solace in the view from the edge of town – on a good day it extends as far as the Apennines.

Porto Recanati

PORTO RECANATI is the nearest resort to Loreto. Its main street, Corso Matteotti, is headed by the turreted tower of a medieval castle; off it is a tiny old quarter of terraced cottages surrounded by hotels and apartment buildings. Apart from the long sandy **beach**, limited attractions include a **sailing and windsurfing school** (June–Aug) – details from the **tourist office** (summer daily 9am–12.30pm & 4.30–7pm; winter Tues and Thurs only 9am–1pm; T071.979.9084, W www.portorecanatiturismo.it) on the Corso – and various beach bars and discos. If you tire of the beach, pay a visit to the art gallery inside the **castle** (Mon–Fri 4–7pm; free): among the sixteenth- and seventeenth-century works are pieces by Luca Giordano, a Baroque artist so prolific that he was known as Luca Fa-Presto ("Luca Works-Fast"). The castle itself has been completely restored and in the keep (Tues–Sun 4–8pm; free) is a collection of statuary excavated from the remains of the nearby Roman city of Potentia. Even better, the castle courtyard has an **arena** – a wonderfully atmospheric place to see films and theatre.

There are a couple of mid-range **hotels** in town: the seventeen-room *Bianchi Nicola*, Piazza Brancondi (T071.979.9016, W www.hotelbianchi.com; ❸), and the *Bianchi Vincenzo* at Via Garibaldi 15 (T071.979.9040; ❸), in a central but quiet position with one-, two- and three-room apartments overlooking the sea. In high season they're let by the week only and the price includes your own beach umbrella and sun loungers on the sand. *Enzo* at Corso Matteotti 21/23 (T071.759.0734, W www.hotelenzo.it; ❹) is a glossy four-star. The *Il Vascello* **campsite**, to the south on Viale della Repubblica (T071.759.1304), is simple and reasonably convenient.

Porto Recanati is best known for its *brodetto*, an indulgent fish soup cooked with nine varieties of fish, spiced with saffron and served with squares of toast. One of the best places to try it is the **restaurant** inside the *Bianchi Vincenzo* hotel (see above; closed to non-residents Mon) on the seafront – the chef is justifiably known as the *l'uomo del brodetto* (the "brodetto man").

Macerata and around

A little-known provincial capital surrounded by Marche's loveliest countryside, **MACERATA** is one of the region's liveliest historical towns, thanks to its ancient university. Easy-paced and unpretentious, it's an ideal place to wind down in the evenings after exploring the province. For opera and ballet fans, its annual *Stagione Lirica* (mid-July to mid-Aug; for info W www.sferisterio.it), held in Italy's best open-air venue outside Verona, is a must. And if you're the slightest bit interested in contemporary art, Macerata has a gallery that alone is reason enough for visiting the town.

Arrival and information

Old Macerata is wrapped around a hill, surrounded by modern suburbs that are home to the **train station**, a ten-minute walk south down Viale Don Bosco and connected to central Piazza della Libertà by frequent **buses**. Most stop at the Giardini Diaz, directly below the old town on the western side, across Viale Puccinotti; some continue to a more convenient stop, from where it's a five-minute climb up stepped Piaggia delle Torre to Piazza della Libertà.

The **tourist office** is on Piazza della Libertà 12 (July to mid-Sept daily 9am–1pm & 3–7pm; mid-Sept to June closed Sat pm and Sun; T0733.234.807, E iat.macerata@regione.marche.it). The website for the province is W www .provincia.mc.it.

Accommodation

There are just a handful of **hotels** in Macerata, and if you're looking for somewhere inexpensive you should book in advance, especially during the opera season (mid-July to mid-Aug).

Hotels

Arcadia Via P Matteo Ricci ☎0733.235.961, ⓦwww.harcadia.it. Aimed mainly at business travellers, so don't expect anything original decorwise, this lies on a quiet cobbled street in the historic centre. Rooms come with mini-kitchens and there's a small bar downstairs. ❸

Arena Vicolo Sreristerio ☎0733.230.931, ⓦwww.albergoarena.com. Run by the same people as the *Arcadia*, the friendly *Arena* is tucked away in a small courtyard behind the opera arena and has an interior done out in rustic style in keeping with its ancient stone structure. ❷

Claudiani Via Ulissi 8 ☎0733.261.400, ⓦwww .hotelclaudiani.it. Macerata's principal four-star option is located just off Corso Matteotti in the historic centre. Its 40 rooms are "hotel style" rather than "antique *palazzo*". ❸

Il Vecchio Granaio Località Chiaravalle, Passo di Treia ☎0733.843.488, ⓦwww.ilvecchiogranaio.it. This agriturismo complex is a pleasant out-of-town option. It's a 20min drive from Macerata along the SS361 at the km 40,500 marker (there are several buses a day to Passo di Treia from Macerata). The large guest rooms are decorated with antiques and hunting prints, and there are superlative views of the hills from the communal sun terrace, as well as a swimming pool. ❷

Hostel

Ostello Asilo Ricci Via dell'Asilo 36 ☎0733.232.515, ⓔostelloasiloricci@virgilio.it. Housed in a converted nineteenth-century *palazzo*, this is the top budget choice. It's centrally located in the old town, right next to the Sferisterio, and offers ninety beds in a choice of dorms or smaller rooms (€15 including breakfast).

The Town

Piazza della Libertà is the heart of the old town, an odd square in which the disparate buildings vie for supremacy. The Renaissance **Loggia dei Mercanti** was supplied by Alessandro Farnese, better known as Pope Paul III, the instigator of many architectural improvements to sixteenth-century Rome. It's somewhat overshadowed by the bulky Palazzo del Comune and overlooked by the looming Torre del Comune. Perhaps the square's most striking feature, however, is the mournful brick facade of **San Paolo**, a deconsecrated seventeenth-century church now used as an exhibition space.

Things pick up along the main *passeggiata* route, the boutique- and bar-lined **Corso della Repubblica**, which ends at Piazza Vittorio Veneto and the **Pinacoteca Civica** (July & Aug daily 9am–1pm & 4–7pm; Sept–June Mon 4–7pm, Tues–Sat 9am–1pm & 4–7pm Sun 9am–1pm; free). The collection here, ranging from the Renaissance perfectionist Crivelli to Ancona-born futurist Cagli, isn't bad, but you might find the twentieth-century artworks on show in the **Palazzo Ricci** (summer only daily 10am–1pm & 4–8pm; free), off the square on Via Ricci, more stimulating. There are two thrilling sculptures in the piazza by Francesco Messina – beautiful, nude of a dancer putting on her shoes, and a leaping horse, as well as a good cross section of work by the Italian futurists.

Seeing the rest of Macerata's sights doesn't take long. Via Ricci leads along towards the bleak **Piazza Mazzini**, below which is the Neoclassical **Sferisterio**, built in the early nineteenth century as an arena for *sphaera*, a traditional game that involved bashing a ball with a spiked iron glove. It was also used for bullfights, horse racing and mock jousts until 1921 when the opera festival was inaugurated and the musicians took over.

Up Via Ciccarelli from Piazza Mazzini, the town's **Duomo** on Piazza Strambi is no architectural showpiece either – a workaday chunk of Baroque, which might have looked slightly more appealing had its facade been finished. Inside there's a statue of Macerata's patron saint, Giuliano, whose path to sainthood sounds like something out of a Sunday tabloid. He arrived home to find two people in his bed and, thinking they were his wife and her lover, promptly killed them. Discovering he'd murdered his parents, he hacked one of his arms off in remorse – the severed limb is now kept in a church strongroom, encased in a sleeve of gold and silver. The relic is displayed on request, but a day's notice is required.

Eating, drinking and nightlife

Macerata's student population ensures that there's a good supply of cheap and interesting places to **eat** and **drink**, and there are some excellent, more upmarket restaurants serving the specialities of the region too. Seats for the **opera** are bookable at the Biglietteria dell'Arena Sferisterio, Piazza Mazzini 10 (Mon–Sat 9.30am–1pm & 4–8pm; ☏0733.230.735 or 0733.233.508, Ⓦwww .sferisterio.it). Ticket prices range from €15 in the balcony (not bookable) to €130 (plus 10 percent booking fee) in the front stalls.

Cafés and restaurants

Da Rosa Via Armaroli Leopoldo 17 ☏0733.260.124. Serves beautiful home-made pasta (try the ravioli with ricotta and lemon) and, in season, funghi porcini and truffles. You can eat and drink well for under €25. Closed Sun.

🏃 **Da Secondo** Via Pescheria Vecchia ☏0733.260.912. If you want to indulge yourself, head to Macerata's most famous restaurant, its walls plastered with historic photos of the town. They do a fabulous *vincisgrassi* (the rich Marche version of lasagna), along with excellent roast lamb and pigeon. Closed Mon.

Da Silvano Piazza delle Torre, just off Piazza della Libertà ☏0733.260.216. Bustling atmospheric place serving good oven-fired pizzas to the crowds heading to and from the nearby Sferisterio. Closed Mon and most of May.

Il Ghiottone Via Gramsci 30 ☏0733.234.319. No-frills, good-value self-service place near the tourist office that is usually packed with local workers at lunchtime. Closed Mon.

Trattoria da Ezio Via Crescimbeni 65 ☏0733.232.366. Reasonably priced trattoria. Gnocchi is the speciality on Thurs, fish on Fri, and *vincisgrassi* on Sat. Closed Sun.

Bars

Il Pozzo Via Costa 5, off Piazza Oberdan. A popular alternative pub-*birreria* dating back to 1984 where you can eat simple local food and listen to recorded jazz.

Roxi Bar Via Garibaldi 57. Offers live music, poetry readings and Brazilian and Cuban theme nights, as well as reasonably priced food.

Around Macerata

With its hills rising from the coast and rippling towards the Apennines, its medieval villages and scattering of Romanesque abbeys and churches, the area **around Macerata** is well worth a good chunk of time. Most villages we list below are well served by bus (approximately hourly) from Macerata's terminal on Piazza Pizzarello (☏0733.261.594). You can get to and back from most places by bus within a day, though you may be charmed into sleeping over.

The Chienti Valley

From Macerata the road and rail lines run east to the coast through the **Chienti Valley**, taking in some of the region's most characteristic hill-towns and two of its finest churches. About 10km from Macerata, close to the turn-off for Morrovalle, is the Romanesque church of **San Claudio al Chienti**, approached along a cypress-lined avenue, which has been carefully restored after years of use as a farm outbuilding.

Above San Claudio is the hill-village of **MORROVALLE**, skirted by a stepped street that disappears through arched gates. Hemmed inside the main piazza at the top of the village is the squat Palazzo del Podestà, where Italy's first pawnshop was set up by St Bernard in 1428. The building next to it is the Palazzo Lazzarini, seat of the ruling family who survived their internecine battle for the privilege of ruling Morrovalle. The *palazzo*, though built in the fourteenth century, incorporates an earlier Romanesque-Gothic portal, possibly taken from a local church.

Back in the valley, road and rail pass the ex-monastery of **Santa Maria a Piè di Chienti** (daily 8am–8pm; free) just after the fork for Montecosaro. It was built by Cluniac monks who came to the area in the tenth century, draining the flood-prone river into channels and creating fertile land out of what had been a fever-ridden marsh. Situated close to the coast, the monastery was vulnerable to Saracen invasions, so the monks encircled it with ditches, which could be flooded in the event of a raid. The monastery survived until the early nineteenth century, when it was destroyed by Napoleonic troops, and now all that remains is the church itself.

West of Macerata

Heading southwest of Macerata towards the Sibillini mountain range, you might stop off briefly at the little town of **TOLENTINO** to see the **Basilica di San Nicola** (daily 8.30am–noon & 3.30–6.30pm; free). Its west front is a real feast for the eyes – a curly Baroque facade with a grinning sun instead of a rose window and a fancily twisting Gothic portal topped by an oriental-style arch enclosing a dragon-slaying saint. Inside, the most intriguing feature is the **Cappellone di San Nicola**, a large chapel whose Gothic frescoes create a kaleidoscope of colourful scenes from the life of Christ.

Just east of Tolentino is the imposing, fourteenth-century **Castello della Rancia** (mid-March to mid-Oct Tues–Sun 10am–12.30pm & 3.30–6.30pm; mid-Oct to mid-March Sat & Sun 10am–12.30pm & 3–6.30pm; €3). This vast fort was the main grain store for the Cistercian abbey of Fiastra (see opposite) back in the twelfth century. Transformed into a castle in the fourteenth century, it became the focal point for a number of armed clashes, at one time harbouring the notorious Renaissance mercenary Sir John Hawkwood. In summer it hosts a popular music festival.

San Severino Marche

Twelve kilometres northwest of Tolentino lies the ancient town of **SAN SEVERINO MARCHE**, a pretty little place whose modern centre converges on an unusual elliptical square, **Piazza del Popolo**, surrounded by porticoes. Just above the piazza on Via Salimbeni, the town's art gallery, known as the **Pinacoteca Tacchi e Venturi** after a local historian (July & Aug Tues–Sun 9am–1pm & 4.30–6.30pm; Oct–June Tues–Sat 9am–1pm; €3), is as good a reason as any for a visit, with a memorable assembly of pieces, including works by Paolo Veneziano and Vittore Crivelli, as well as the Salimbeni brothers, the region's undervalued early Renaissance painters who were born and worked in San Severino in the fifteenth century; they are represented by delicate and expressive frescoes detached from local churches and the wooden polyptych *The Marriage of St Catherine*.

Other works by the Salimbeni brothers adorn two of San Severino's churches. One of these, the ancient **San Lorenzo in Doliolo**, at the top of Via Salimbeni, looks slightly odd thanks to a medieval brick tower standing on top of its stone portal. The Salimbeni frescoes, illustrating the story of St Andrew, are on the vault of the tenth-century crypt. The back part of the crypt is thought to be a pagan temple dating back to the time of the refugees from Septempeda (see opposite).

The other church – actually the old cathedral – is up in **CASTELLO**, the upper part of San Severino, a long and steep walk, although there are occasional buses from the main square. The **Duomo Vecchio** was founded in the tenth century but has a Romanesque-Gothic facade, simple Gothic cloisters, and a much rebuilt interior, featuring Salimbeni frescoes in the baptistry. Finds in the nearby **Museo Archeologico** on Via Castello al Monte (Tues–Sun summer 9am–1pm & 4–7pm; winter 9am–1pm; €3) were excavated from the Roman valley town of Septempeda, whose inhabitants, driven out by barbarian invasions in the sixth century, escaped up here to found San Severino.

For a congenial **place to stay** above town in the Castello, head for the *Due Torri*, Via San Francesco 21 (T0733.645.419, Wwww.duetorri.it; ❷), which is run by the third generation of the Severini family; it has spotless bedrooms in an old stone wing with tiled floors and simple furnishings. There's a popular restaurant attached, which doubles as a shop, selling local delicacies, wines and spirits.

South of Macerata: the road to Sarnano

With the Monti Sibillini on the horizon, snowcapped for most of the year, the route south from Macerata towards the spa town of Sarnano ranks as one of the Marche's most beautiful. Ten kilometres along the road, on the edge of a dense wood, is the Romanesque-Gothic complex of the **Abbazia di Fiastra** (mid-June to mid-Sept daily 10am–12.30pm & 3–7pm; mid-Sept to mid-June Sat, Sun and public hols 10am–12.30pm & 3–5.30pm; €5 for abbey and museum; Wwww.abbaziafiastramonaci.it), a Cistercian abbey with a simple, pantiled brick cloister and monastic quarters adjoining a grandiose aisled church.

The abbey complex is a popular day out with a steady stream of visitors looking round the building and its grounds, now a nature reserve. The trails through the woods are a popular Sunday stroll, and you should take time to see the **Museo della Civiltà Contadina** (open summer only same times as abbey; €2 for museum or €5 for abbey and museum), a folk museum filled with agricultural and weaving equipment laid out in the abbey's low-vaulted outhouses.

A five-minute bus ride away is the site of **Urbisaglia** (March to mid-June Sat, Sun & public hols 10am–1pm & 3–6pm; mid-June to mid-Sept daily 10am–1pm & 3–7pm; mid-Sept to Feb Sat, Sun & public hols 10am–1pm & 3–4.30pm; guided tours €2 for a single monument, €5 for three and €7 for everything). Urbs Salvia, as it was known, was one of the Marche's most important Roman towns and home to 30,000 people until it was sacked by Alaric in 409 AD. The Lourdes of its day (Urbs Salvia means "city of health"), its fame continued into the Middle Ages, when Dante invoked it as an example of a city fallen from glory in his *Paradiso*. So far an amphitheatre, theatre, baths and parts of the walls have been excavated, and frescoes of hunting scenes have been discovered in a *cryptoportico* (underpassage). The theatre was one of the largest in Italy, and could seat 12,600 spectators. Up in modern Urbisaglia, there's also a small **archeological museum** (same hours), visitable on the same ticket, containing finds from the site.

South of Urbisaglia, the hill-town health resort of **SAN GINESIO** is justifiably known as the balcony of the Sibillini: the panoramic view from the gardens of the Colle Ascarano, just outside the town walls, stretches from the Adriatic and Monte Conero to the Sibillini mountains and the highest of the Apennines, the Gran Sasso in Abruzzo. There's a fair amount to see in the town itself: its central piazza is dominated by one of the Marche's most unusual churches, the

Collegiata della Annunziata, whose late-Gothic facade is decorated with filigree-like terracotta moulding. Rising above it are two campaniles, one capped by an onion dome and the other by what looks like a manicured cactus. Gothic frescoes adorn some of the chapels, and the crypt has frescoes by the Salimbeni brothers.

Sarnano

SARNANO, south of San Ginesio, was once a poor and virtually abandoned village. In the last couple of decades or so, however, the town has woken up to the potential of its thermal springs – believed since Roman times to have wide-ranging curative properties – and has begun to develop itself into a spa resort and weekend day-trip destination. The medieval core, coiling in concentric circles around a gentle hill, has been subtly restored, and though it's now more of a showpiece than a living village, its narrow interconnecting cobbled streets and picturesque old houses make it an ideal place for an undemanding day's wandering. On the last weekend in May until mid-June every year, an arts and crafts fair draws in the crowds, with work by Italian craftsmen on sale at scores of temporary shops/exhibition spaces in and around the historic centre.

It's worth getting a map from the **tourist office** at Lago Enrico Ricciardi 1, just off Piazza della Libertà in the new town (Mon–Fri 9am–1pm & 3–6pm, Sat 9am–1pm; ☎0733.657.144, ⓦwww.sarnano.com), before heading up through **Porta Brunforte** into old Sarnano. Just inside the gate is the fourteenth-century church of **San Francesco**, decorated with Palestinian plates, thought to have been brought to Sarnano by souvenir-collecting Crusaders. On Via G. Leopardi is a fine **Pinacoteca e Museo Civici** (Sat & Sun 10am–noon & 4pm–7pm; €5), the major item being a *Madonna and Child* by Vittore Crivelli.

Continue climbing to the summit of the town and you hit **Piazza Alta**, once the political and religious centre and lined by fine medieval *palazzi*, as well as the thirteenth-century church of **Santa Maria di Piazza**, whose fifteenth-century frescoes include a figure known as the *Madonna with Angels*, for the host of celestial musicians and choristers surrounding her. The wooden statue of Christ on the altar has been saddled with one of popular tradition's strangest myths – if it's about to rain, his beard is supposed to grow. On the second Sunday in August, Santa Maria is the starting-point for Sarnano's annual medieval knees-up, or *palio* – though apart from the costumes and processions, it has more in common with a kids' sports day, featuring a tug-of-war, pole climbing, and a race in which the competitors have to balance jugs of water on their heads.

For an overnight stay, two of the most affordable **hotels** in Sarnano are *Villa*, Via Rimembranza 46 (☎0733.657.218, ⓦwww.hrlavilla.com; ❷), a shuttered villa in its own substantial garden 300m uphill from the tourist office, and *Ai Pini*, Via F. Corridoni 101 (☎0733.657.183; ❶), a small, welcoming family-run hotel between the public gardens and the town car park.

Southeast of Macerata: Fermo

Southeast of Macerata, a short distance from the coast, is the attractive old town of **FERMO**. Its web of streets is lined with graceful medieval and Renaissance buildings, erupting out of which is a wooded peak crowned with a Romanesque-Gothic cathedral. The town's most spectacular monument, however, is hidden from view – a first-century underground complex of thirty filter beds known as the **Cisterne Romane** (Tues–Sun: summer 10am–1pm & 3.30–7.30pm; winter 10am–1pm & 3.30–6pm; €3), originally designed to supply the Roman imperial fleet with fresh water when it docked at the nearby port. It's worth joining one of the guided tours (no additional charge) that leave Fermo's small museum every hour; the night tours are especially atmospheric (9pm, 10pm & 11pm every Thurs in July and daily from mid- to late Aug). Entered from Via Aceti, off the main Piazza del Popolo, the cistern is something akin to a flooded cathedral, with its well-preserved vault and arches subtly lit and reflected in the dark, still water.

Monti Sibillini National Park

With a mountain lake reddened by the blood of the devil, a narrow pass known as the gorge of hell and a cave reputed to have been the lair of an enchantress, the **Monti Sibillini** are not only the most beautiful section of the Apennines, but they teem with ancient legends too. Wolves, chamois and brown bear all have a home in the national park and even if you don't come across one of these, you may be lucky enough to see an equally rare golden eagle instead.

The best way to experience the park is by walking, cycling or horseriding, and if you're up for a challenge there's *Il Grande Anello dei Sibillini* (The Great Sibylline Ring), 120km of signposted footpaths that take nine days to walk, or four to five days to cover by mountain bike. Maps and accommodation details, including several new mountain refuges, are listed on Ⓦwww.sibillini.net. There are shorter trails too, through meadows filled with wild flowers, for which the most agreeable bases are the medieval hill-villages that crown the Sibillini foothills. Most villages are served by buses, but they're generally few and far between and it's best to have your own transport.

Amándola

The small village of **AMÁNDOLA** is fairly easy to get to on public transport, making it a good base for seeing the region. Its main sight is its **Museo Antropogeografico** (summer daily 9.30am–12.30pm & 3.30–6.30pm; winter Tues–Fri 9.30am–12.30pm, Sat & Sun 9.30am–12.30pm & 3.30–6.30pm; €5) housed in the ex-convent of the church of San Francesco and packed full of interactive exhibits about the wildlife and legends of the park. Amándola's other attraction is an excellent week-long international **theatre festival** in the first week of September. Low on pretension and high on participation, the festival overcomes language barriers with mime and movement performances and workshops – the atmosphere is irresistible, and it's well worth sticking around for the whole week.

Otherwise, Amándola is a great place to unwind after a day's hiking in the Sibillini. There's an excellent nine-room **guesthouse** in a converted eighteenth-century *palazzo*, the *Casa per Ferie Fillide*, Via Indipendenza 73 (☎0736.848.598, Ⓦwww.montesibillini.it; ❶; Oct–Easter for groups of fifteen or more only). Also recommended is the very welcoming **B&B** *Il Palazzo*, Via Indipendenza 59–61 (☎0736.847.082 or 0333.331.0878, Ⓦwww.palazzopecci.com; ❷), in a fifteenth-century mansion two-minutes' walk from the main square.

Montefortino

A few kilometres south of Amándola, the hill-village of **MONTEFORTINO** is perhaps a prettier base than Amándola though less well served by buses and touristy in season. Primarily a place to wander and admire the Sibillini views, the town also has a small **Pinacoteca** (open on request, ☎0736.859.491; free), whose chief attractions are a polyptych by Alemanno – a follower of the Crivelli who took as much delight in painting embroidery as they did – and an arresting twelfth-century portrait of a man with a pipe and candle emerging from the darkness. Appropriately, given the necromantic traditions of this area, there's also an eighteenth-century painting of Circe with her occult apparatus. A lovely place **to stay** in the historic centre is the French-owned B&B ❀ *Tabart Inn*, Via Papiri 24 (☎0736.859.054 or 339.122.6465, ⓦ www.tabart-inn.com; ❸), a sixteenth-century house with three light, spacious and elegant beamed rooms and lovely terraces overlooking the mountains. The nicest **restaurant** is *Da Benito*, Via Tenna 9 (☎0736.859.515; closed Mon), a wonderful place in autumn to eat wild mushrooms and truffles.

Montemónaco

A short way south of Montefortino, **MONTEMÓNACO**, a walled medieval village of cobbled streets and yellow stone houses, is close to some of the Sibillini's most legendary sights. One, the **cave of the sibyl**, whose occupant gave her name to the mountain group, is a two-hour walk west from the village, though periodic rockfalls can block the way. The other, through the **Gola dell'Infernaccio** (Gorge of Hell), a few kilometres southwest of the village, is an easy and spectacular hike in summer. You can take a bus from Montefortino to the Infernaccio fork, from where it's a three-hour walk to the gorge along a well-defined path. The approach through a narrow valley is atmospheric: silent, except for the distant roar of the River Tenna, with memorial plaques on the cliffs at the entrance to commemorate climbers who've died scaling the walls. The path squeezes its way under jagged rocks, accompanied by the deafening sound of raging water. Once past a second bridge it forks, the lower path leading to the tranquil source of the Tenna while the upper brings you, in about thirty minutes, to the **Hermitage of San Leonardo**, occupied by a solitary monk.

Back down in the valley, *Agriturismo La Cittadella* (☎0736.856.361, ⓦ www .cittadelladeisibillini.it; ❷), 2.5km down a dirt road from the northern end of Montemónaco, is a peaceful place for an overnight stay; their restaurant serves great local dishes such as *tagliatellini ai funghi porcini* (thin tagliatelle with ceps) and *coniglio in porchetta* (rabbit cooked with fennel), and you can buy apples and chestnuts in season. For local information call the *Comune* at Montemónaco (☎0736.856.141) or the seasonal Pro Loco office on ☎0736.856.411. If you're going to attempt a climb up Monte Sibilla, the *Rifugio Sibilla 1540* (June to mid-July & mid- to

Lago di Pilato

According to the legend surrounding the **Lago di Pilato**, Pontius Pilate's body was dispatched from Rome on a cart pulled by two wild oxen who climbed up into the Sibillini and ditched the corpse in the water here. In the Middle Ages it became a favourite haunt for **necromancers** seeking dialogues with the devil – stones inscribed with occult symbols have been found on its shores. Deciding they wanted to be rid of the magicians, one night the local lords put soldiers on guard around its shores. Nothing happened until the morning, when the soldiers discovered that the lake had turned red; assuming it was with the devil's blood, they fled. What in fact turned the water red was a mass of minuscule red *Chircephalus marchesonii*, a species of fish indigenous to Asia; a shoal was stranded here millions of years ago when the sea receded, and its descendants still thrive.

end Sept Sat & Sun; mid-July to mid-Sept daily; ☎0736.856.422, 338.429.2399 or 338.469.5073; ⓦwww.rifugiosibilla1540.com; ❶) is the best base. It lies about 6km east of Montemónaco along the path that eventually leads to the cave of the sibyl (see opposite). As the path is only barely visible you'd be advised to take the Kompass *Monti Sibillini* map which can be bought locally.

To do the best of the Sibillini treks, however, you need to drive or take a taxi 8km east from Montemónaco to the quiet village of **FOCE**. The hike up to **Lago di Pilato** (Pilate's Lake, see box, p.646) and **Pizzo di Diavolo** (Devil's Peak), is fairly tough; allow a whole day, take the Kompass map and only attempt it in good conditions during the high summer months as the snow doesn't melt until June. Here, guarding the entrance to Umbria, stands **Monte Vettore** (2476m), the highest of the Sibillini peaks.

Ascoli Piceno and the coast

Located between the Monti Sibillini and the coast, the pleasant town of **ASCOLI PICENO** is off the radar of most tourists. This seems odd considering it has plenty of grand architecture and a lovely café-lined central square that's among the most pleasant in Marche. At Mardi Gras it hosts the region's most flamboyant carnival and in August its streets are given over to the Quintana, a medieval **festival** that incorporates a spectacular joust. If that wasn't enough, Ascoli's restaurants and food stalls are the proud purveyors of *olive all'ascolana* (fried olives stuffed with veal), one of the tastiest, if not exactly healthiest, of the region's many gastronomic specialities.

The town owes its existence to a woodpecker that led a band of nomadic shepherds to the wedge of land between two rivers on which the city now stands. At least, that's one of the many legends to have grown up around the origins of Ascoli and the **Piceni tribe** for whom it is named; other versions replace the woodpecker-guide with Diomedes or the son of Saturn, and the nomadic shepherds with veterans of the Trojan War or Greek traders. Whatever the truth, the Piceni were real enough, and the relics of their civilization suggest that they were a pretty emotional and impetuous lot: writing curses on missiles, gauging grief by measuring the volume of tears, and losing a critical battle against the Romans when they interpreted an earthquake as a sign of divine wrath and abandoned the fight. Today the Ascolani seem initially to be reserved, as if in obedience to the aphorisms urging moderation, hard work and reticence that are inscribed on many of their houses.

Arrival and information

Ascoli's **train station** is just east of the town centre, ten-minutes' walk along Viale Indipendenza and Corso Vittorio Emanuele. **Buses** from other towns stop outside the train station. The **tourist office** is on the ground floor of the Palazzo del Comune (Oct–March Mon–Fri 9am–1.30pm, Tues & Thurs also 3–6pm, Sat 9am–1pm; longer hours in summer; ☎0736.253.045, Ⓔiat .ascolipiceno@regione.marche.it).

There's **internet access** at the Libreria Cattolica on Piazza Arringo (9am–11.30pm; ☎0736.259679; €2 per hr).

Accommodation

Ascoli Piceno has enough attractions to merit an overnight stay and a fair number of decent **accommodation** options, despite its relatively un-touristy status.

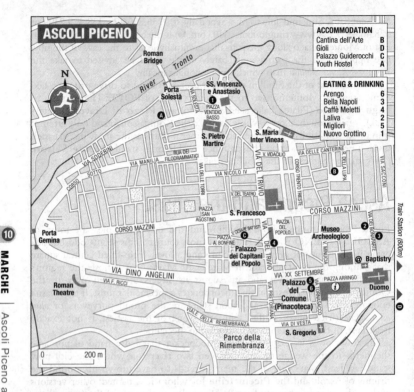

Cantina dell'Arte Rua della Lupa 8
℡0736.255.620, ⓦwww.cantinadellarte.it.
Great-value, cheerful, well-kept hotel in the centre
with eleven small rooms and five apartments in an
annexe, along with a very reasonably priced
restaurant. ❶
Gioli Viale de Gasperi 14 ℡0736.255.550,
ⓦwww.hotelgioli.it. Just outside the historic
centre, this is a smart hotel catering mostly for the
business market. ❸
Le Sorgenti Lago di Castel Trosino
℡0736.263.725, ⓦwww.agriturismolesorgenti
.org; One of several good agriturismo places within
easy reach of town, this occupies a restored
eighteenth-century villa set in rolling countryside
7km north of Ascoli. Rooms are simple and rustic,

the food is made from fresh local ingredients
(including home-pressed olive oil) and there are
plenty of local walks to enjoy.
Palazzo Guiderocchi Via Cesare Battisti 3
℡0736.244.011, ⓦwww.palazzoguiderocchi.com.
If you want to pay for a little extra comfort, this
restored palace in the old town, offers huge rooms
with high ceilings and every facility – it often has
good deals in low season. ❻
Ostello de' Longobardi Via Soderini 16
℡0736.261.862, ⓔlungbardiascoli@libero.it. The
town's most affordable option is this youth hostel
located in a spooky medieval tower bang in the
historic centre. Dorm beds cost €16. It's open all
year round.

The Town

Ascoli has a compact centre, surrounded by largely intact walls and with its areas
of interest divided into four main zones. Piazza del Popolo is the place to get
the feel of the town, while its small number of Roman remains and its churches
and museums are scattered throughout the old centre.

Piazza del Popolo

The central **Piazza del Popolo** is the stage for the evening *passeggiata*. Paved with gleaming travertine and flanked by Renaissance porticoes, it's the setting for two of the city's finest buildings, the pleasantly jumbled **Palazzo dei Capitani del Popolo** and the refined Romano-Gothic San Francesco. The former dates from the late twelfth century, when the free *Comune* of Ascoli was at its height. That anything of the building has survived is something of a miracle, for in 1535 a certain Giambattista Quieti set it on fire to incinerate a rebel barricaded inside. The interior was gutted but enough remained of the facade for a swift facelift to suffice. Rectangular windows were slotted into medieval arches, and a grand portal affixed, on top of which sits a statue to Pope Paul III, who reintroduced peace by replacing Quieti with a neutral outsider.

When they weren't slaughtering each other, at least some of Ascoli's rulers found time to collect public money in order to finance city improvements. The sixteenth-century **loggias** that enclose the piazza are one of the results – each of a slightly different width, to correspond to the size of the contribution made by the various merchants and shopkeepers who worked here.

The church of **San Francesco**, on the other hand, was financed by the sale of a Franciscan convent outside the city, after Pope Alexander IV had given the Franciscans permission to move within its walls. Construction started in 1258 but wasn't completed until 1549, when the low cupola was added. It's a somewhat restrained church, with little to seize the attention except for the intricate west portal on Via del Trivio, but a good place to take a break from the heat and bustle of Ascoli's narrow streets. Adjoining the south side of the church and overlooking Corso Mazzini is the sixteenth-century **Loggia dei Mercanti**. Formerly the scene of commercial wheeling and dealing, there are still niches cut into the back wall in which bricks could be checked for size before being purchased. The cloister to the north of the church is now also used for commerce as the site of a daily market.

▲ Piazza del Popolo, Ascoli

San Vincenzo and around

Via del Trivio continues up towards Piazza Ventidio Basso, the medieval commercial centre of town, of interest for its two churches. **San Vincenzo e San Anastasio** is Ascoli's most distinctive church, with a fifteenth-century chessboard facade that was once filled out with frescoes. Beneath the mainly eleventh-century body of the building is a primitive crypt erected over a spring that was supposed to have leprosy-curing properties. Although the plunge bath is still there, the spring was diverted elsewhere in the last century.

Across the square, **San Pietro Martire** is a far less appealing building, erected by Dominican monks in the thirteenth century in order not to be outdone by their Franciscan rivals down the road. It's as austere and intimidating as Saint Peter the Martyr himself, who, between founding Dominican communities like that at Ascoli, gained such a reputation as a persecutor of religious sects that he became the patron of inquisitors after his murder by a couple of so-called heretics.

The dark **Via Soderini**, leading west out of the square, forms the spine of Ascoli's riverside medieval quarter. Lined with buildings out of which the occasional defensive tower sprouts, it's an evocative street, giving a clear idea of how rigorously the town was defended. Tiny streets fan out from it, many of them spanned by covered passages that in times of siege served as escape routes and as stations from which to pour oil down onto the heads of attackers. Of the defensive tower houses, one of the best preserved is the **Palazzetto Longobardi**, a virtually windowless twelfth-century building, now converted into a youth hostel (see p.648).

After exploring the quarter you can cut through to the river and the thirteenth-century gate, the **Porta Solestà**, from which one of Italy's largest and most impressively preserved **Roman bridges** spans the river. An underpassage tunnels through it.

San Gregorio and around

There's little else of Roman Ascoli to see, except some sparse remains of a **Roman theatre**, on the southwest edge of town, close to the Roman **Porta Gemina**, or twin gate, at the beginning of the road to Rome. From the theatre a road leads up to the **Parco della Rimembranza**, for a great rooftop view of the town, and on to the steep and picturesque **Via Pretoriana**, whose small craft shops make it a good hunting ground for gifts. Close by, the fourteenth-century church of **San Gregorio** was ingeniously built around the remains of a Roman temple. Incorporated into the facade are two lofty Corinthian columns, originally imported by the Romans from Greece, and patches of *opus reticulatum* (diamond brickwork). In the adjoining convent is a tiny revolving door with the inscription *Qui si depositano gli innocenti* ("Here you deposit the innocent"), designed so that parents could remain anonymous when leaving unwanted children to the care of priests and nuns.

The Duomo, pinacoteca and Museo Archeologico

Ascoli's Baroque **Duomo** is situated on the east side of Piazza Arringo. The flashy interior holds chandeliers suspended on strings of illuminated beads, an apse painted with a fake Persian carpet and a cupola decorated with late nineteenth-century frescoes of obscure Ascolani saints. In the midst of this, the **polyptych** by Carlo Crivelli in the Cappella del Sacramento, is worth seeking out. The most arresting of the ten panels is the central pietà, in which the haggard expression of Mary, the torment that distorts Christ's face, and the

Magdalene's horror as she examines the wound in his hand are given heightened impact by the strict semicircular composition. Adjacent to the Duomo is the Palazzo Comunale containing the **Pinacoteca Civica** (Tues–Sun 10am–7pm; €5) containing other pieces by Crivelli.

If you want to know more about ancient Ascoli, visit the evocative **Museo Archeologico** (Tues–Sun 8.30am–7.30pm; €2), across the square. The collection includes Piceni projectiles inscribed with curses against their Roman enemies, jewellery, heavy bronze rings that were placed on the stomachs of dead women, and small test-tube-like containers used to assess the quality of grief by measuring the volume of tears.

Eating and drinking

You don't have to spend a lot to **eat** well in Ascoli. For a **drink**, there are many places to linger over a coffee or a cocktail in Piazza del Popolo. Among them is the famous Art Nouveau-style *Anisetta Meletti* that makes its own superb *amaro* and anisette and is lined with mahogany cases filled with obscure bottles.

Bella Napoli Via Bonaparte 18–20 ☎0736.257.030. The town's best pizzeria is housed inside a 16th century *palazzo*. It can get pretty lively and boisterous as the night wears on. Evenings only, closed Thurs.

Migliori Piazza Arringo 2 ☎0736.250.042. A delightful three-in-one experience comprising a sit-down restaurant, a well-stocked delicatessen and a small stall out front where you can purchase big bags of the local delicacy, *olive all'ascolana* (stuffed olives) for €2. Closed Mon.

Trattoria dell'Arengo Via Tornasacco 5 ☎333.471.3333. Just off Piazza Arringo, this serves hearty local food, such as wild boar, mushrooms and mixed grills of meats and vegetables. There's no written menu but they'll tell you (in English) the specials of the day that might include *pasta al ceppo* (shaped in the old days around a knitting needle) with tomato and ham. Closed Mon.

Trattoria Laliva Piazza della Viola 13 ☎0736.259.358. Chef Marinella Filiponia offers up Ascoli's most imaginative cooking with modern takes on Marchegiana cuisine, including dishes such as *Le Sibille*, lasagna baked with parma ham, herbs, artichokes and chilli. Closed Tues eve & Wed.

Trattoria Nuovo Grottino Piazza Ventidio Basso 2 ☎0736.251.1909. This is a popular neighbourhood place for grilled meat (*primi* €6–7 *secondi* €7–9).

The Ascoli coast

Easily accessible by bus or train from Ascoli Piceno, **SAN BENEDETTO DEL TRONTO** is the most extravagant of the Marche's resorts. Known as the "Riviera delle Palme" for the five thousand palms that shade its promenade, and with 6km of sandy white beach, it makes a nice break on a hot afternoon if you're in Ascoli and fancy a swim. There are over a hundred **hotels**, details of which are available on the searchable database at ⓦ www.le-marche.com or from the **tourist office** on Viale delle Tamerici (Mon, Wed & Fri 9am–1pm, Tues & Thurs 9am–1pm & 3–6pm, Sun 9am–noon; ☎0735.592.237, Ⓔe iat.sanbenedetto@regione .marche.it). Note that most places insist on full board in August.

GROTTAMARE, a few minutes further up the coastal train line, is a lower-key resort on the same model, but without San Benedetto's panache. If you have a car head instead the 8km inland to *La Campana*, at Contrada Menocchia 39, 6km from the hill-town of Montefiore d'Aso (☎0734.939.012, ⓦ www.lacampana.it; ❸), an agriturismo complex made up of a farm that breeds sheep and rabbits, and old stone buildings containing guest rooms. The swimming pool is on a terrace overlooking the Adriatic, while meals (bed and breakfast from May–Dec, full board from late uly to late Aug) are made from home-produced vegetables, meat, cheese and buttermilk.

Travel details

Trains

Ancona to: Bologna (37 daily; 2hr 5min); Jesi (18 daily; 20–25min); Loreto (every 30min; 15–20min); Porto San Giorgio (every hr; 30–45min); Rome (10 daily; 3–4hr); San Benedetto (every 30min; 1hr 10min); Senigallia (every 20–30min; 15–25min).
Ascoli Piceno to: San Benedetto del Tronto (16 daily; 35min–1hr).
Macerata to: San Severino Marche (every 30–40min; 25–45min); Tolentino (every hr; 20min).
Pésaro to: Ancona (every 30min–1hr; 35–50min); Fabriano (17 daily; 1hr 30min–2hr 30min).

Buses

All services are much reduced on Sundays and public holidays. Extra buses may be provided in high summer to seaside resorts.
Amándola to: Ascoli Piceno (4 daily Mon–Sat; 1hr 10min); Fermo (4 daily; 1hr); Montefortino (5 daily; 10min); Montemónaco (5 daily; 20–25min); Porto San Giorgio (4 daily; 1hr 15min); Sarnano (7 daily; 30min).
Ancona to: Jesi (25 daily; 45min); Loreto (6 daily Mon–Sat; 1hr 20min); Macerata (10 daily; 1hr 30min); Numana (16 daily, 9 on Sun; 40min); Porto Recanati (5 daily Mon–Sat; 1hr 5min); Portonovo (mid-June–Aug every 20min; 25–30min); Sirolo (16 daily, 9 on Sun; 35min).

Ascoli Piceno to: Amándola (4 daily Mon–Sat; 1hr 10min); Montefortino (5 daily Mon–Sat; 1hr 20min); Montemónaco (5 daily Mon–Sat; 1hr 30min); Rome (5 daily; 3hr); San Benedetto del Tronto (every 30min, hourly on Sun; 1hr).
Macerata to: Abbazia di Fiastra and Urbisaglia (12 daily; 10min); Amándola (6 daily; 1hr 15–20min); Ancona (10 daily; 1hr 30min); Loreto (10 daily; 50min); Naples (1 daily; 5hr 30min); Porto Recanati (11 daily; 1hr); Recanati (11 daily; 35min); Rome (5 daily; 4hr); San Severino (5 daily; 35min); Sarnano (12 daily; 55min–1hr 25min); Tolentino (12 daily; 30min); Visso (5 daily; 1hr 45min).
Pésaro to: Fabriano (3 daily; 2hr); Fano (approximately every 30min; 15min); Gradara (hourly; 55min); Sassocorvaro (5 daily; 1hr); Torrette (7 daily; 15min); Urbino (10 daily Mon–Fri, 6 Sun; 1hr).
Porto San Giorgio to: Fermo (every 30min; 15–20min).
San Leo to: Rimini (2 daily; 45min).
Urbino to: Fano (8 daily; 1hr 10–15min); Pésaro (11 daily Mon–Fri, 6 Sun; 1hr).

International ferries

Ancona to: Zadar/Bozara, Hvar/Bol and Split, Stari Gad and Korcula in Croatia (summer 4–5 weekly; winter 2 weekly; ferry from 8–9hr; catamaran from 3hr); Igoumenitsa (at least 1 daily; 15hr 30min); Patras (at least 1 daily; 21hr); Çesme, Turkey (April–Nov 1 weekly, Sat departure; 43–55hr).

11

Rome and Lazio

CHAPTER 11 **Highlights**

* **Capitoline Museums** The august and impressive home of some of Rome's finest ancient sculpture and paintings. See p.672

* **Pantheon** The most complete ancient Roman structure in the city. See p.676

* **Colosseum** One of ancient Rome's best-known and most impressive monuments. See p.693

* **Galleria Borghese** One of the city's best art galleries – and home to the cream of

the work of the city's favourite sculptor, Bernini. See p.696

* **Vatican Museums** Quite simply the largest and richest collection of art in the world. See p.706

* **Tivoli** The site of Hadrian's villa, as well as the splendid landscaped gardens of Villa d'Este. See p.719

* **Viterbo** An old medieval town well worth exploring for its Etruscan remains and museums. See p.726

▲ Classical grandeur – the Colosseum

Rome and Lazio

R**ome** is the most fascinating city in Italy, which makes it arguably the most fascinating city in the world. An ancient place packed with the relics of over two thousand years of inhabitation, you could spend a month here and still only scratch the surface. Yet it's so much more than an open-air museum: its culture, its food, its people make up a modern, vibrant city that would be worthy of a visit irrespective of its past. As a historic place, it is special enough; as a contemporary European capital, it is utterly unique.

Evenly placed between north and south, Rome is perhaps the perfect Italian capital. Former heart of the mighty Roman Empire, and still the home of the papacy, Rome is seen as a place somewhat apart from the rest of the country, spending money made elsewhere on the bloated government machine. For the traveller of course, this is much less evident than the sheer weight of history that the city supports. First are Rome's classical features, most visibly the Colosseum, and the Forum and Palatine Hill; but from here there's an almost uninterrupted sequence of monuments – from early Christian basilicas and Romanesque churches to Renaissance palaces and the fountains and churches of the Baroque period, which perhaps more than any other era has determined the look of the city today. There is the modern epoch, too, from the ponderous Neoclassical architecture of the post-Unification period to the self-publicizing edifices of the Mussolini years. These various eras crowd in on one another to an almost overwhelming degree: there are medieval churches atop ancient basilicas above Roman palaces; houses and apartment blocks that incorporate fragments of eroded Roman columns, carvings and inscriptions; roads and piazzas which follow the lines of ancient amphitheatres and stadiums.

Beyond Rome, the region of **Lazio** inevitably pales in comparison, with relatively few centres of note and a landscape that varies from the gently undulating green hills of its northern reaches to the more inhospitable mountains to the south and east. It's a relatively poor region, its lack of identity the butt of a number of Italian jokes, and it's the closest you'll get to the feel of the Italian south without catching the train to Naples. Much, however, can easily be seen on a day-trip from the capital, not least the ancient sites of **Ostia Antica** and the Roman Emperor Hadrian's villa at **Tivoli** – two of the area's most important ancient sites. Further afield, in the north of Lazio, the Etruscan sites of **Tarquinia** and **Cerveteri** provide the most obvious tourist focus, and

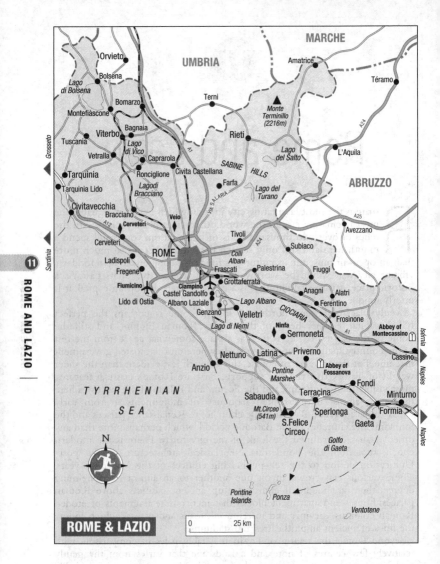

are again just about visitable on a day-trip, but you'd do better to use the pleasant provincial town of **Viterbo** as a base. Romans, meanwhile, head out at weekends to soak up the gentle beauty of lakes **Bracciano**, **Vico** and **Bolsena**. The south arguably holds Lazio's most appealing enclaves. The coast is home to unpretentious resorts like **Terracina** and **Sperlonga** – relatively unknown outside Italy; and the island of **Ponza**, accessible from Terracina and **Formia**, further down the coast, is out of season at least one of the most alluring spots on the entire western seaboard.

Roman cooking is traditionally dominated by the earthy cuisine of the working classes, with a little influence from the city's centuries-old Jewish population thrown in. Although you'll find all sorts of pasta served in Roman restaurants, spaghetti is common, as is the local speciality of *bucatini* or thick-cut hollow spaghetti (sometimes called *tonarelli*), served *cacio e pepe* (with pecorino and ground black pepper), *alla carbonara* (with beaten eggs, cubes of pan-fried bacon, and pecorino or parmesan*)*, *alla gricia* (with percorino and bacon); *all' amatriciana* (with tomato and bacon); and *alle vongole* (with baby clams). Fish is an integral, though usually pricey, part of Roman cuisine, and features most frequently in Rome as salt cod – *baccalà*; best eaten Jewish-style, deep-fried. Offal is also key, and although it has been ousted from many of the more refined city-centre restaurants, you'll still find it on the menus of more traditional places, especially those in Testaccio. Most favoured is *pajata*, the intestines of an unweaned calf. Look out, too, for *coda alla vaccinara*, oxtail stewed in a rich sauce of tomato and celery; *abbacchio*, milk-fed lamb roasted to melting tenderness with rosemary, sage and garlic; *abbachio scottadito*, grilled lamb chops eaten with the fingers; and *saltimbocca alla romana*, thin slices of veal cooked with a slice of prosciutto and sage on top. Artichokes (*carciofi*) are the quintessential Roman vegetable, served *alla romana* (stuffed with garlic and roman mint and stewed) and in all their unadulterated glory as *alla giudea* – flattened and deep-fried in olive oil. Another not-to-be-missed side dish is *fiori di zucca* – batter-fried courgette blossom, stuffed with mozzarella and a sliver of marinated anchovy. Roman pizza has a thin crust and is best when baked in a wood-fired oven (*a legna*), but you can also find lots of great pizza by the slice (*pizza al taglio*), always sold by weight. **Wine** comes mainly from the Castelli Romani (most famously Frascati) to the south, and from around Montefiascone (Est! Est! Est!) in the north. Both are basic, straightforward whites, fine for sunny lunchtimes but otherwise not all that noteworthy.

Rome

You won't enjoy Rome if you spend your time trying to tick off sights. However, there are some places that it would be a pity to leave the city without seeing. The **Vatican** is perhaps the most obvious one, most notably **St Peter's** and the amazing stock of loot in the Vatican museums; and the star attractions of the ancient city – the **Forum** and **Palatine**, the **Colosseum** – are worth a day or two in their own rights. There are also the churches, fountains and works of art from the period that can be said to most define Rome, the Baroque, and in particular the works of Borromini and Bernini, whose efforts compete for space and attention throughout the city. Bernini was responsible for the Fountain of the Four Rivers in the city's most famous square, **Piazza Navona**, among other things; but arguably his best sculptural work is in the **Galleria Borghese**, or in various churches, like his statue of St Theresa in Santa Maria in Vittoria. Borromini, his great rival at the time, built the churches of San Carlo alle Quattro Fontane and Sant'Ivo, both buildings intricately squeezed into small sites – Borromini's trademark. There are other great palaces that are themselves treasure troves of great art, like the **Doria-Pamphilj** and **Palazzo Barberini**; and unmissable museums, like the august galleries of the

Capitoline, and the main collections of the **Museo Nazionale Romano** in the Palazzo Altemps and Palazzo Massimo, all of which hold staggering and beautifully displayed collections of the cream of the city's ancient art and sculpture. And finally there's the city beneath all this: stroll through the *centro storico* in the early morning, through Trastevere at sunset, or gaze down at the roofs and domes from the Janiculum Hill on a clear day, and you'll quickly realize that there's no place in Italy like it.

Some history

Rome's early **history** is interwoven with legend. Rea Silvia, a vestal virgin and daughter of a local king, Numitor, had twin sons – the product, she alleged, of a rape by Mars. The two boys were abandoned and found by a wolf, who nursed them until their adoption by a shepherd, who named them **Romulus** and **Remus**. As they grew into manhood, under the protection of the gods, they became leaders in the small community, and later laid out the boundaries of the city on the Palatine Hill. However, it soon became apparent that there was only room for one ruler, and they quarrelled, Romulus killing Remus and becoming in 753 BC the city's first **monarch**, to be followed by six further kings.

The Roman Republic and Empire

Whatever the truth of this story, there's no doubt that Rome was an obvious spot to build a city: the Palatine and Capitoline hills provided security, and there was, of course, the river Tiber, which could easily be crossed here. Rome as a kingdom lasted until about 507 BC, when the people rose up against the tyrannical King Tarquinius and established a **Republic**. The city prospered, growing greatly in size and subduing the various tribes of the surrounding areas: the **Etruscans** to the north, the **Sabines** to the east, the **Samnites** to the south. By the time it had fought and won the third Punic War against its principal rival, **Carthage**, in 146 BC, it had become the dominant power in the Mediterranean.

The history of the Republic was, however, one of **internal strife**, marked by factional fighting among the patrician ruling classes, and the ordinary people, or plebeians, enjoying little more justice than they had under the Roman monarchs. This all came to a head in 44 BC, when **Julius Caesar**, having proclaimed himself dictator, was murdered by conspirators concerned at the growing concentration of power into one man's hands. A brief period of turmoil ensued, giving way, in 27 BC, to the founding of the **Empire** under **Augustus** – a triumph for the new democrats over the old guard. Augustus heaved Rome into the imperial era: he was determined to turn the city – as he claimed – from one of stone to one of marble, building arches, theatres and monuments of a magnificence suited to the capital of an expanding empire. Under Augustus, and his successors, the city swelled to a population of a million or more, its people housed in cramped apartment blocks or *insulae*; crime in the city was rife, and the traffic problem apparently on a par with today's, leading one contemporary writer to complain that the din on the streets made it impossible to get a good night's sleep. But it was a time of peace and prosperity too, with the empire's borders being ever more extended, reaching their maximum limits under the Emperor Trajan, who died in 117 AD. This period constitutes the heyday of the Roman Empire, a time that the historian Gibbon called "the happiest times in the history of humanity".

The **decline of Rome** is hard to date precisely, but it could be said to have started with the Emperor Diocletian, who assumed power in 284 and divided the empire into two parts, east and west. The first Christian emperor, **Constantine**, shifted the seat of power to Byzantium in 330, and Rome's period as capital of the world was over; the wealthier members of the population moved east and a series of invasions by Goths in 410 and Vandals about forty years later served only to quicken the city's ruin. By the sixth century Rome was a devastated and infection-ridden shadow of its former self.

The papal City

After the fall of the empire, the **pope** – based in Rome owing to the fact that St Peter (the Apostle and first pope) was martyred here in 64 AD – became the temporal ruler over much of Italy, and it was the papacy, under Pope **Gregory I** ("the Great") in 590, that rescued Rome from its demise. By sending missions all over Europe to spread the word of the Church and publicize its holy relics, he drew pilgrims, and their money, back to the city, in time making the papacy the natural authority in Rome. The pope took the name "Pontifex Maximus" after the title of the high priest of classical times (literally "the keeper of the bridges", which were vital to the city's well-being). The crowning a couple of centuries later of **Charlemagne** as Holy Roman Emperor, with dominions spread Europe-wide but answerable to the pope, intensified the city's revival, and the pope and city became recognized as head of the Christian world.

As time went on, power gradually became concentrated in a handful of **families**, who swapped the top jobs, including the papacy itself, between them. Under the burgeoning power of the pope, the city began to take on a new aspect: churches were built, the city's pagan monuments rediscovered and preserved, and artists began to arrive in Rome to work on commissions for the latest pope, who would invariably try to outdo his predecessor's efforts with ever more glorious buildings and works of art. This process reached a head during the Renaissance; Bramante, Raphael and Michelangelo all worked in the city throughout their careers, and the reigns of **Pope Julius II** and his successor, **Leo X**, were something of a golden age – the city was once again the centre of cultural and artistic life. However, in 1527 all this was brought abruptly to an end, when the armies of the Habsburg monarch Charles V swept into the city, occupying it for a year, while Pope **Clement VII** cowered in the Castel Sant'Angelo.

The ensuing years were ones of yet more restoration, and perhaps because of this it's the **seventeenth century** that has left the most tangible impression on Rome today, the vigour of the **Counter-Reformation** throwing up huge sensational monuments like the Gesù church that were designed to confound the scepticism of the new Protestant thinking. This period also saw the completion of St Peter's under **Paul V**, and the ascendancy of Gian Lorenzo Bernini as the city's principal architect and sculptor. The **eighteenth century** witnessed the decline of the papacy as a political force, a phenomenon marked by the seventeen-year occupation of the city in 1798 by Napoleon, after which, papal rule was restored.

The post-Unification city

Thirty-four years later a pro-Unification caucus under **Mazzini** declared the city a republic but was soon chased out, and Rome had to wait until troops stormed the walls in 1870 to join the unified country – symbolically the most important part of the Italian peninsula to do so. "Roma o morte", **Garibaldi** had cried, and he wasted no time in declaring the city the capital of the new kingdom – under **Vittorio Emanuele II** – and confining the by now quite powerless pontiff, **Pius IX**, to the Vatican until agreement was reached on a way to coexist. The Piemontese rulers of the new kingdom set about building a city fit to govern from, cutting new streets through Rome's central core (Via Nazionale, Via del Tritone) and constructing grandiose buildings like the Altar of the Nation. **Mussolini** took over in 1922, and in 1929 signed the **Lateran Pact** with Pope **Pius XI**, a compromise which forced the Vatican to accept the new Italian state and in return recognized the Vatican City as sovereign territory, independent of Italy, together with the key basilicas and papal palaces in Rome – these remain technically independent of Italy to this day.

The contemporary city

During **World War II**, Mussolini famously made Rome his centre of operations until his resignation as leader in July 1943. The city was eventually liberated by Allied forces in June 1944. The Italian republic since then has been a mixed affair, changing its government (if not its leaders) every few months until a series of scandals forced the old guard from office. Since then things have continued in much the same vein, with the city symbolizing, to the rest of the country at least, the inertia of their nation's government. In spite of this the city's growth has been phenomenal, its population soaring to getting on for four million, with a marked increase in its immigrant numbers. However, the city is looking sprucer, and more vibrant, than it has done for some time, and there are even plans afoot to deal with the city centre's chronic traffic problem, with the construction of a third metro line well under way. In short, the city is more cosmopolitan (and more expensive) than ever before, and despite the crowds, which seem to increase every year, there's never been a better time to visit.

Arrival

Rome has two **airports**: Leonardo da Vinci, better known as Fiumicino, which handles the majority of scheduled flights, and Ciampino, where you'll probably arrive if you're travelling with one of the low-cost airlines. There's a fixed price for **taxis** to the city centre from each (Fiumicino €40, Ciampino €30) and the journey time from both is thirty to forty minutes. Otherwise the public transport connections are reasonable. **Fiumicino** is linked to the centre of Rome by direct trains, which take thirty minutes to get to Termini and cost €11; services begin at 6.35am and then leave every thirty minutes until 11.35pm. There are no direct connections between the city centre and **Ciampino**, and if you're arriving here the best thing you can do is take the *Terravision* shuttle bus, timed to coincide with arrivals and departures, to Termini (€8 single, €14 return). Otherwise ATRAL buses run from the airport to the Anagnina metro station, at the end of line A, every forty minutes (€1), from where it's a twenty-minute ride into the centre (a further €1).

Travelling by **train** from most places in Italy, or indeed Europe, you arrive at **Stazione Termini**, centrally placed for all parts of the city and meeting-point of the two metro lines and many city-bus routes. There are **left-luggage** facilities here, on the lower level by platform 24 (daily 6am–midnight; €3.80 per piece for the first 5hr, then 60c per hr). As for **other train stations** in

Rome, Tiburtina is a stop for some north–south intercity trains; selected routes around Lazio are handled by the Regionali platforms of Stazione Termini (a further 5min walk beyond the end of the regular platforms); and there's also the Roma-Nord line station on Piazzale Flaminio, which runs to Viterbo.

Arriving by **bus** can leave you in any one of a number of places around the city. The main station for buses from outside the Rome region is Tiburtina. Others include Ponte Mammolo (trains from Tivoli and Subiaco); Lepanto (Cerveteri, Civitavecchia, Bracciano area); EUR Fermi (Nettuno, Anzio, southern Lazio coast); Anagnina (Castelli Romani); Saxa Rubra (Viterbo and around). All of these stations are on a metro line, except Saxa Rubra, which is on the Roma-Nord train line, connected every fifteen minutes with Piazzale Flaminio.

City transport

Like most Italian cities, even the larger ones, the best way to get around Rome is to **walk**. Rome wasn't built for motor traffic, and it shows in the congestion. Despite that, its ATAC-run **bus service** is on the whole pretty good – cheap, reliable and as quick as the clogged streets allow. There are also four **tram** lines, and Rome's **metro** operates from 5.30am to 11.30pm, although its two lines only have a handful of stops in the city centre. When the buses and the metro stop – at around midnight – a network of **nightbuses** comes into service, accessing most parts of the city and operating until about 5am.

Flat-fare **tickets** on all forms of transport currently cost €1 each and are good for any number of bus rides and one metro ride within 75 minutes of validating them – bus tickets should be stamped in machines on board the bus. You can buy tickets from *tabacchi*, newsstands and ticket machines located in all metro stations and at major bus stops, as well as from machines on the buses themselves. If you're using transport extensively it's worth getting a day pass (BIG) for €4, a three-day pass (BTI) for €11, or a seven-day pass (CIS) for €16. Ⓦ www.atac .roma.it has more information, some in English.

The easiest way to get a **taxi** is to find the nearest taxi stand (*fermata dei taxi*) – central ones include Termini, Piazza Venezia, Largo Argentina, Piazza San Silvestro, Piazza di Spagna, Piazza del Popolo and Piazza Barberini. Alternatively, you can simply call a taxi (Ⓣ06.3570, 06.4157, 06.6645, 06.8822 or 06.5551), but bear in mind that these usually cost more, as the meter starts ticking the moment the taxi is dispatched to collect you. Most cabs are white, and a journey from one side of the city centre to the other should cost no more than €10, or around €15 on Sunday or at night. Note that all taxis carry a rate card in English giving the current tariff.

Information

There are small **tourist offices** in the Fiumicino arrivals area (daily 9am–6.30pm) and at Termini by platform 24 (daily 8am–8pm), and a main **office** at Via Parigi 5 (Mon–Sat 9am–7pm; Ⓣ06.8205.9127, Ⓦ www.romaturismo.it), five-minutes' walk from Termini. They have reasonable free maps and they can help with accommodation if necessary. You'll also find information kiosks (see box, p.664) in key locations around the city centre (daily 9.30am–7.30pm).

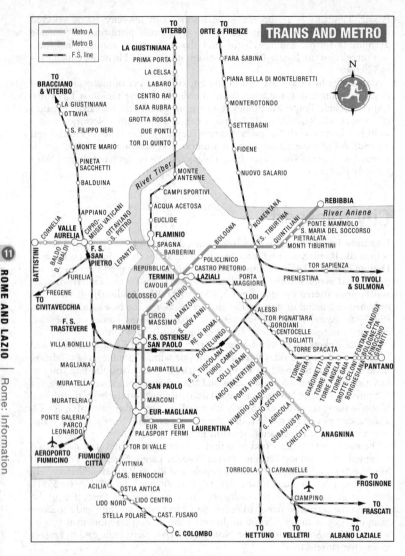

Another good source of information is the privately run **Enjoy Rome**, Via Marghera 8/A (Mon–Fri 9am–7pm, Sat 8.30am–2pm; ☎06.445.1843, ⓦwww .enjoyrome.com), whose friendly, English-speaking staff hand out lots of free information; they also operate a free room-finding service, organize tours, have a left-luggage service for customers, and run a shuttle bus to Fiumicino.

The city's best source of **listings** is the weekly *Romac'è* (€1.50), which has a helpful section in English giving information on tours, clubs, restaurants, services and weekly events, and a decent website – ⓦwww.romace.it. The twice-monthly English expat magazine, *Wanted in Rome* (€1) – ⓦwww .wantedinrome.com – is also a useful source, especially if you're looking for

Buses

#23 Piazza Clodio–Piazza Risorgimento–Ponte Vittorio Emanuele II–Ponte Garibaldi–Via Marmorata–Piazzale Ostiense–Centrale Montemartini–Basilica di S. Paolo.

#40 (Express) Termini–Via Nazionale–Piazza Venezia–Largo Argentina–Corso Vittorio Emanuele II–Piazza Pia.

#64 Termini–Piazza della Repubblica–Via Nazionale–Piazza Venezia–Largo Argentina–Corso Vittorio Emanuele II–Stazione S. Pietro.

#175 Termini–Piazza Barberini–Via del Corso–Piazza Venezia–Colosseo–Circo Massimo–Aventine–Stazione Ostiense.

#492 Stazione Tiburtina–Piazzale Verano–Termini–Piazza Barberini–Via del Corso–Piazza Venezia–Largo Argentina–Corso Rinascimento–Piazza Cavour–Piazza Risorgimento–Cipro.

#660 Largo Colli Albani–Via Appia Nuova–Via Appia Pignatelli–Via Appia Antica.

#714 Termini–Santa Maria Maggiore–Via Merulana–San Giovanni in Laterano–Viale Terme di Caracalla–EUR.

#910 Termini–Piazza della Repubblica–Via Piemonte–Via Pinciana (Villa Borghese)–Piazza Euclide–Palazzetto dello Sport–Piazza Mancini.

Minibuses

These **small buses** negotiate circular routes through the narrow streets of Rome's centre.

#116 Porta Pinciana–Via Veneto–Via del Tritone–Piazza di Spagna–Piazza San Silvestro–Corso Rinascimento–Campo de' Fiori–Piazza Farnese–Lungotevere Sangallo–Terminal Gianicolo.

#117 San Giovanni in Laterano–Piazza Celimontana–Via Due Macelli–Via del Babuino–Piazza del Popolo–Via del Corso–Piazza Venezia–Via Nazionale–Via dei Serpenti–Colosseo–Via Labicana.

#119 Piazza del Popolo–Via del Corso–Piazza Venezia–Largo Argentina–Via del Tritone–Piazza Barberini–Via Veneto–Porta Pinciana–Piazza Barberini–Piazza di Spagna–Via del Babuino–Piazza del Popolo.

Trams

#3 Stazione Trastevere–Via Marmorata-Piramide–Circo Massimo-Colosseum–San Giovanni–San Lorenzo–Via Nomentana–Parioli–Viale Belle Arti.

#8 Casaletto–Stazione Trastevere–Piazza Mastai–Viale Trastevere–Largo Argentina.

#19 Porto Maggiore–Piazzale Verano–Viale Regina Margherita–Viale Belle Arti–Via Flaminia–Ottaviano–Piazza Risorgimento.

Line #110

There are several operators offering hop-on-hop-off circuits of the city with guided commentary, but the ATAC-run **#110 bus** is still the best and most frequent. It leaves from Stazione Termini and stops at all the major sights, including Piazza di Spagna, Castel Sant'Angelo, the Vatican and Appia Antica. The whole round trip takes about two hours. In summer, departures are every fifteen minutes from 8.30am until 8.30pm daily, including holidays and Sundays. Tickets cost €16 and are valid all day.

an apartment or work. Both are available at most newsstands. Those with a bit of Italian should check the daily arts pages of the Rome **newspaper**, *Il Messaggero*, which lists movies, plays and major musical events, along with *La Repubblica*, which includes the "Trova Roma" supplement in its Thursday edition, another handy guide to current offerings.

Accommodation

There's plenty of **accommodation** in Rome, and overall the choice of hotels in the city centre has improved a lot over recent years, with plenty of new boutique hotels and comtemporary B&Bs opening up. But it's always worth booking in advance, especially when the city is at its busiest – from Easter to the end of October, and over the Christmas period. If you haven't booked, the official tourist office or the Enjoy Rome office (see p.662) are your best bets.

Hotels

Many of the city's cheapest places are located close to **Termini** station, and you could do worse than hole up in one of these, but to be honest it's not the nicest part of town and there are plenty of moderately priced places in the **centro storico** or around **Campo de'Fiori**, but they tend to fill quickly; you'll certainly need to book well in advance to be sure of a room. For more luxury surroundings, the area **east of Via del Corso**, towards Via Veneto and around the Spanish Steps is the city's prime hunting ground for beautiful, upscale accommodation – although there are a few affordable options here too. Consider also staying across the river in **Prati**, a pleasant neighbourhood, nicely distanced from the hubbub of the city centre proper, and handy for the Vatican, or in the lively streets of **Trastevere**, again on the west side of the river but an easy walk into the centre of town.

Centro Storico and Campo de' Fiori

Campo de' Fiori Via del Biscione 6 ☏ 06.6880.6865, ⓦ www.hotelcampodefiori.com. A friendly place in a nice location with 23 individually designed rooms. The sixth-floor roof terrace has some great views, and the hotel also owns a number of small apartments nearby for those keen to self-cater. ⓖ

Due Torri Vicolo del Leonetto 23 ☏ 06.6880.6956, ⓦ www .hotelduetorriroma.com. This little hotel was once a residence for cardinals, following which it served as a brothel. Completely remodelled, it retains a homely feel and some of its higher rooms have lovely rooftop views. A good location just north of Piazza Navona. ⓖ

Navona Via dei Sediari 8 ☏ 06.686.4203, ⓦ www.hotelnavona.com. Completely renovated *pensione*-turned-hotel housed in a building built on the remains of the ancient Roman baths of Agrippa. It's pretty welcoming, run by a friendly Italian-Australian, and the rooms are decent; plus it's in a good position close to Piazza Navona. ⓖ

Portoghesi Via dei Portoghesi 1 ☏ 06.686.4231, ⓦ www.hotelportoghesiroma.com. Decent, well-equipped if slightly characterless modern rooms, 5min from most *centro storico* attractions. Breakfast is served on the roof terrace upstairs. ⓖ

Santa Chiara Via Santa Chiara 21 ☏ 06.687.2979, ⓦ www.albergosantachiara .com. A friendly, family-run hotel in a great location, on a quiet piazza behind the Pantheon.

For once the rooms are nicer than the bland lobby, and some overlook the church of Santa Maria sopra Minerva. ⑧

Smeraldo Vicolo dei Chiodaroli 9 ⓣ06.687.5929, ⓦwww.smeraldoroma.com. Clean and comfortable hotel with a modern if rather bland interior and rooms with shiny new baths, televisions and a/c. The terrace and some rooms have lovely views over Rome's rooftops. Breakfast is not included in the price. ⑤

Sole Via del Biscione 76 ⓣ06.6880.6873, ⓦwww .solealbiscione.it. This place enjoys one of the best locations in the centre, and has been in the same family for generations. The rooms are simple but decent enough. The cheapest have shared bathrooms but it's worth splashing out on the ones with the spectacular view of the nearby domes from the top-floor terrace. ⑤

Zanardelli Via G. Zanardelli 7 ⓣ06.6821.1392, ⓦwww.hotelnavona.com. Run by the same people as the *Navona*, and the slightly more lavish alternative, just north of Piazza Navona, in a building which used to be a papal residence and has many original fixtures and furnishings. The rooms are quite elegant, with antique iron beds, silk-lined walls, and modern amenities, but still decently priced. ⑥

Tridente and the Quirinale

🏃 **Casa Howard** Via Capo le Case 18, Via Sistina 149 ⓣ06.69922.4555, ⓦwww .casahoward.com. Halfway between a boutique hotel and an upmarket *pensione*, the individually furnished if sometimes small rooms here are among Rome's most stylish. The location is good too, between Piazza Barberini and the Spanish Steps, but it's not cheap. ⑦

Condotti Via Mario de' Fiori 37 ⓣ06.679.4661, ⓦwww.condottigrouphotels.com. A cosy and inviting hotel with locations nearby, with comfortable rooms equipped with satellite TV and minibars. A bit devoid of personality, although this is somewhat compensated for by the welcoming staff. ⑥

Daphne Via di San Basilio 55, Via degli Avignonesi 20 ⓣ06.8745.0087, ⓦwww.daphne-rome.com. A welcoming *pensione* run by an American woman and her Roman husband. Bright, nicely renovated modern rooms in two good locations either side of Piazza Barberini, and as much advice as you need on how to spend your time in Rome. Some rooms have shared bathrooms, some are en suite. ④

De Russie Via del Babuino 9 ⓣ06.328.881, ⓦwww.hotelderussie.it. Coolly elegant and understated, this is the abode of choice for visiting movie stars in-the-know and hip travellers spending someone else's money. ⑨

Erdarelli Via due Macelli 28 ⓣ06.679.1265, ⓦwww.erdarelliromehotel.com. A rather plain hotel with no-frills rooms, but it's family-run and welcoming enough, and for its location, just around the corner from the Spanish Steps, the prices can't be beat. Most, but not all, rooms have en-suite facilities. ③

Eva's Rooms Via due 31 ⓣ06.6919.0078, ⓦwww.evasrooms.com. Large and cosily furnished rooms are the hallmark of this B&B, well located 5min walk from the Spanish Steps. Some of the rooms could do with a lick of paint, but for the price the location is great. ⑤

Firenze Palace Via due Macelli 106 ⓣ06.679.7240, ⓦwww.hotelfirenzeroma.it. Just up the street from *Erdarelli*, this three-star is a bit more expensive but has large rooms with TVs and minibars that are good value for money. ⑤

Homs Via della Vite 71–72 ⓣ06.679.2976, ⓦwww.hotelhoms.it. In the heart of the Spanish Steps neighbourhood, this small four-star hotel boasts a roof terrace with marvellous views, cosy refurbished rooms and a very friendly atmosphere – something that's not always guaranteed in the hotels of this ritzy neighbourhood. ⑦

🏃 **Modigliani** Via della Purificazione 42 ⓣ06.4281.5226, ⓦwww.hotelmodigliani .com. A young artist couple run this modern hotel on a quiet street just off Piazza Barberini. Rooms are tasteful and comfortable, and all have a/c. ⑥

Piazza di Spagna Via Mario de' Fiori 61 ⓣ06.679.3061, ⓦwww.hotelpiazzadispagna.com. This small hotel a few minutes' walk from the Spanish Steps is a good alternative to the opulent palaces that dominate the area. Rooms are comfortable and the staff friendly. ⑦

Termini and Monti

Alpi Via Castelfidardo 84 ⓣ06.444.1235, ⓦwww.hotelalpi.com. One of the more peaceful yet convenient options close to Termini, recently renovated, and within easy walking distance of the station. Pleasant, if somewhat small, rooms with bathrooms, and a great buffet breakfast – better than you would normally expect in a hotel of this category. ⑥

Artorius Via del Boschetto 13 ⓣ06.482.1196, ⓦwww.hotelartorius.com. A great choice if you want to stay in the heart of Monti, with just ten rooms decorated in a classic style. A nice courtyard for breakfast, or drinks after dark. ⑥

Des Artistes Via Villafranca 20 ⓣ06.445.4365, ⓦwww.hoteldesartistes.com. One of the better hotels in the Termini area. Exceptionally good value,

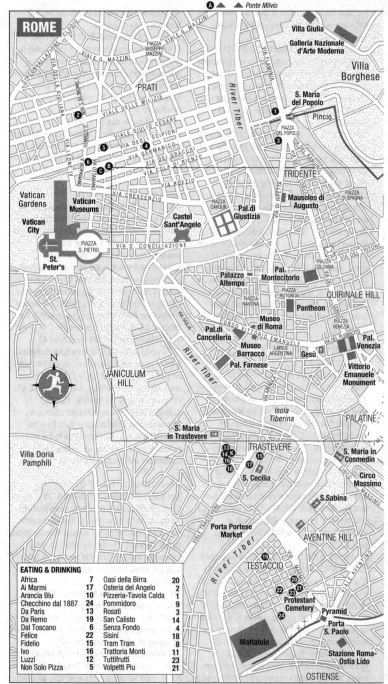

ROME

Ponte Milvio

Villa Giulia
Galleria Nazionale
d'Arte Moderna

Villa
Borghese

S. Maria
del Popolo

Pincio

PRATI

PIAZZA
GIUSEPPE
MAZZINI

VIALE G. MAZZINI

PIAZZA
DEL POPOLO

VIALE DELLE MILIZIE

VIALE GIULIO CESARE

VIA DEGLI SCIPIONI

VIA GERMANICO

VIA DEI GRACCHI

VIA COLA DI RIENZO

VIA BOEZIO

TRIDENTE

VIA CRESCENZIO

Vatican
Gardens

Vatican
Museums

Vatican
City

St.
Peter's

PIAZZA
S. PIETRO

PIAZZA
CAVOUR

Pal. di
Giustizia

Castel
Sant'Angelo

VIA D. CONCILIAZIONE

Mausoleo di
Augusto

PIAZZA
DI SPAGNA

VIA DEL TRITONE

Palazzo
Altemps

Pal.
Montecitorio

PIAZZA
COLONNA

Pantheon

PIAZZA
ROTONDA

QUIRINALE HILL

PIAZZA
NAVONA

Museo
di Roma

Pal. di
Cancelleria

Museo
Barracco

Pal. Farnese

CORSO VITTORIO EMANUELE

LARGO
ARGENTINA

Gesù

PIAZZA
VENEZIA

VIA DEL PLEBISCITO

Pal.
Venezia

Vittorio
Emanuele
Monument

VIA GIULIA

River Tiber

Isola
Tiberina

PALATINE

JANICULUM
HILL

S. Maria
in Trastevere

Villa Doria
Pamphili

TRASTEVERE

S. Cecilia

S. Maria in
Cosmedin

Circo
Massimo

S. Sabina

Porta Portese
Market

AVENTINE HILL

River Tiber

TESTACCIO

Protestant
Cemetery

Pyramid

Porta
S. Paolo

Felice

Mattatoio

Stazione Roma-
Ostia Lido

OSTIENSE

S. Paolo fuori le Mura

EATING & DRINKING

Africa	7	Oasi della Birra	20
Ai Marmi	17	Osteria del Angelo	2
Arancia Blu	10	Pizzeria-Tavola Calda	1
Checchino dal 1887	24	Pommidoro	9
Da Paris	13	Rosati	3
Da Remo	19	San Calisto	14
Dal Toscano	6	Senza Fondo	4
Felice	22	Sisini	18
Fidelio	15	Tram Tram	8
Ivo	16	Trattoria Monti	11
Luzzi	12	Tuttifrutti	23
Non Solo Pizza	5	Volpetti Piu	21

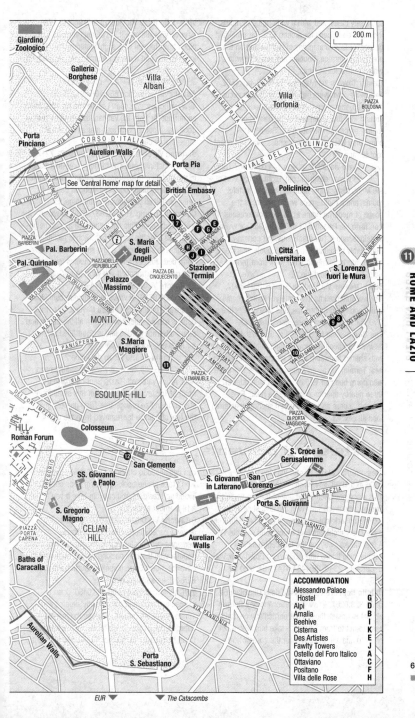

ACCOMMODATION

Alessandro Palace Hostel	G
Alpi	D
Amalia	B
Beehive	I
Cisterna	K
Des Artistes	E
Fawlty Towers	J
Ostello del Foro Italico	A
Ottaviano	C
Positano	F
Villa delle Rose	H

EUR ▼   ▼ The Catacombs

spotlessly clean, and with a wide range of rooms, including dorm beds for around €25. Eat breakfast or recover from a long day of sightseeing on the breezy roof terrace. Doubles are available with or without en-suite facilities. ⑤

Fawlty Towers Via Magenta 39 ☏06.445.4802, Ⓦwww.fawltytowers.org. Playfully named accommodation, this place has both dorm beds for around €25 and clean and comfortable hotel rooms, some with private bath. There's a communal kitchen, internet access, and a pleasant roof terrace. ②

🏃 **Grifo** Via del Boschetto 144 ☏06.487.1395, Ⓦwww.hotelgrifo.com. Right in the heart of the Monti district, this hotel has simple, tasteful rooms, and a roof terrace which overlooks the scene of medieval Rome at its most picturesque. ⑦

Positano Via Palestro 49 ☏06.490.360, Ⓦwww .hotelpositano.it. Not glamorous, but certainly reasonably priced at €100 for a double, this place has comfortable rooms 2min walk from Termini. Helpful management too. ③

Suite Dreams Via Modena 5 ☏06.4891.3907, Ⓦwww.suitedreams.it. Simple yet stylish rooms with good-sized bathrooms, and nice details like a DVD library for guests' use. Good value. ⑥

The Beehive Via Marghera 8 ☏06.4470.4553, Ⓦwww.the-beehive.com. Cheap double rooms, all with shared bathroom is this pleasant budget hotel near Termini run by an American couple. There are also dorm beds for €25 or you can self-cater in three nearby apartments for €35 a head. Free internet access and a restaurant sevring vegetarian food all day. ③

Hostels and convents

Alessandro Palace Hostel Via Vicenza 42 ☏06.446.1958, Ⓦwww.hostelsalessandro.com. This place has been voted one of the top hostels in Europe, and it sparkles with creative style. Pluses include no lock-out or curfew, a good bar with free pizza every night, internet access and satellite TV. A few blocks away, on the city centre side of Termini, you'll also find *Alessandro Downtown*, Via C. Cattaneo 23 (☏06.4434.0147). Beds go for €25–35, doubles ④

Ostello del Foro Italico Viale delle Olimpiadi 61 ☏06.323.6267, Ⓦwww.ostellionline.org. Rome's official HI hostel, though not particularly central or easy to get to from Termini – take bus #32, #224 or #280 and ask the driver for the "*ostello*". You

Villa delle Rose Via Vicenza 5 ☏06.445.1788, Ⓦwww.villadellerose.it. An aristocratic villa just a block from Termini with slightly shabby but characterful rooms and a warm wlcome from the staff. ⑤

Trastevere and Prati

Amalia Via Germanico 66 ☏06.3972.3356, Ⓦwww.hotelamalia.com. Located on an attractive corner not far from the Vatican, this is an extremely good-value option, with four-star amenities at three-star prices. ⑥

Cisterna Via della Cisterna 7–9 ☏06.581.7212, Ⓦwww.cisternahotel.it. A friendly three-star bang in the middle of Trastevere. Nineteen rooms, some with colourful tiled floors and wooden beamed ceilings, and all with private bathrooms. ⑤

Colors Via Boezio 31 ☏06.687.4030, Ⓦwww .colorshotel.com. This hostel/hotel in a quiet neighbourhood near the Vatican has kitchen facilities, a lounge with satellite TV, and a small terrace, and dorm beds for €27 and private doubles for ⑤. It also rents apartments if you want to self-cater.

La Rovere Vicolo San Onofrio 4–5 ☏06.6880.6739, Ⓦwww.hotellarovere.com. Just across the bridge from Piazza Navona, this small hotel is tucked quietly away from all the bustle and offers a terrace garden and antique-filled setting for its guests to relax in. ⑥

🏃 **Santa Maria** Vicolo dei Piede 2 ☏06.589.4626, Ⓦwww.hotelsantamaria .info. A few yards off Piazza Santa Maria in the heart of Trastevere, the rooms of this small three-star surround an orange-tree-filled garden, giving the feel of a place far removed from the city. ⑦

can call ahead to check out availability, but they won't take phone bookings. Dorm beds cost €16 including breakfast. You can join here if you're not a HI member already.

Ottaviano Via Ottaviano 6 ☏06.3973.8138, Ⓦwww.pensioneottaviano.com. A simple *pensione*-cum-hostel near to the Vatican that's very popular with the backpacking crowd; book well in advance, fluent English spoken. Dorm beds cost €25–33, en-suite doubles ②.

YWCA Via C. Balbo 4 ☏06.488.0460. Open to women and men, and conveniently situated just 10min walk from Termini, although the market outside may get you up earlier than you might want. Dorm beds cost €28, doubles ②. Curfew midnight.

Camping

All Rome's **campsites** are some way out of the city, but are easy enough to get to. The closest site is *Camping Flaminio*, 8km north of the centre at Via Flaminia Nuova 821 (℡06.333.2604, ⓦwww.campingflaminio.it; March–Oct); it also has bungalows for rent and a swimming pool, restaurant and lots of facilities. To get there from the city centre, either take the Roma-Nord service from Piazzale Flaminio to Due Ponti, or take bus #910 to Piazza Mancini and transfer to bus #200 (ask the driver to drop you at the "*fermata più vicina al campeggio*"). *Camping Tiber*, on Via Tiberina at Km1400 (℡06.3361.0733, ⓦwww.campingtiber.com; March–Oct), is another good bet – right beside the Tiber, quiet, spacious and friendly, with a bar-pizzeria, a swimming pool and hot showers; and it, too, has bungalows as well as camping spaces. It has a free shuttle service (every 30min 8am–11pm) to and from the nearby Prima Porta station, where you can catch the Roma-Nord train service to Piazzale Flaminio (about 20min).

The City

Rome's **city centre** is divided neatly into distinct blocks. The warren of streets that makes up the **centro storico** occupies the hook of land on the left bank of the River Tiber, bordered to the east by Via del Corso and to the north and south by water. From here Rome's central core spreads south and east: down towards Campo de' Fiori; across Via del Corso to the major shopping streets and alleys around the **Spanish Steps**; to the major sites of the **ancient city** to the south; and to the expanse of the **Villa Borghese** park to the north. The left bank of the river is a little more distanced from the main hum of the city centre, home to the **Vatican** and **Saint Peter's**, and, to the south of these, **Trastevere** – even in ancient times a distinct entity from the city proper, although nowadays as much of a focus for tourists as anywhere, especially at night.

Piazza Venezia

Piazza Venezia is not so much a square as a road junction, and a busy one at that. But it's a good central place to start your wanderings, close to both the medieval and Renaissance centre of Rome and the bulk of the ruins of the ancient city. Flanked on all sides by imposing buildings, it's a dignified focal point for the city in spite of the traffic, and a spot you'll find yourself returning to time and again.

Palazzo Venezia and the church of San Marco

Forming the western side of the piazza, the **Palazzo Venezia** (Tues–Sun 9am–7pm; €4) was the first large Renaissance palace in the city, built for the Venetian Pope Paul II in the mid-fifteenth century and for a long time the embassy of the Venetian Republic. More famously, Mussolini moved in here while in power, occupying the vast Sala del Mappamondo and making his declamatory speeches to the huge crowds below from the small balcony facing onto the piazza. Nowadays it's a venue for great exhibitions and home to the **Museo Nazionale di Palazzo Venezia**, a museum of Renaissance arts and crafts, with a number of fifteenth-century devotional paintings, bronzes and sculpture.

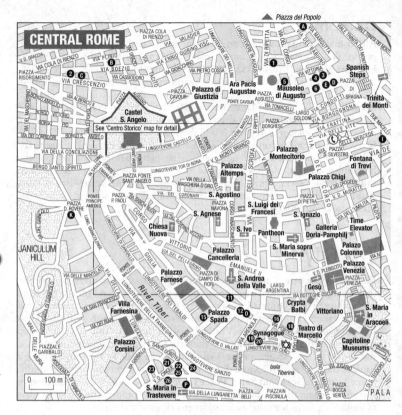

Piazza del Popolo

CENTRAL ROME

JANICULUM
HILL

0   100 m

Adjacent to the palace on its southern side, the church of **San Marco**, accessible from Piazza San Marco (Mon–Sat 8am–noon & 4–6.30pm, Sun 9am–1pm & 4–8pm, closed Mon am & third Thurs of the month), is the Venetian church in Rome – and one of its most ancient basilicas. Standing on the spot where the apostle is supposed to have lived while in the city, it was rebuilt in 833 and added to by various Renaissance and eighteenth-century popes. Look out for the apse mosaic dating from the ninth century and showing Pope Gregory offering his church to Christ.

The Vittorio Emanuele Monument (Vittoriano)

Everything pales into insignificance beside the marble monstrosity rearing up across the street – the **Vittorio Emanuele Monument** (daily 9.30–6pm; free), erected at the beginning of the twentieth century as the "Altar of the Nation" to commemorate Italian Unification. Variously likened in the past to a typewriter (because of its shape), and, by American GIs, to a wedding cake, King Vittorio Emanuele II, who it's in part supposed to honour, probably wouldn't have thought much of it – he was by all accounts a modest man. The Vittoriano, as it's known, was closed to the public for years but is now fully open, and it's great to clamber up and down the sweeping terraces and flights of steps, cutting through eventually to the Capitoline Museums behind. There are things to see inside (principally a large Unification museum), but the main interest is on the outside: the Tomb of the Unknown Soldier at the top of the first flight of steps;

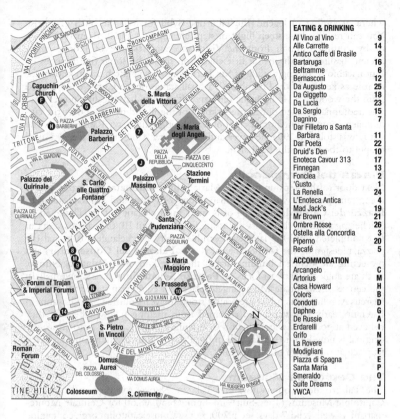

the equestrian statue of Vittorio Emanuele II, one of the world's largest, on the next level; the terraces above this; and finally the **lifts** which whisk you to the terrace at the top – not cheap, but the views are all-encompassing, and of course this is the one place from which you can't see the Vittoriano (summer Mon–Thurs 9.30am–7.30pm, Fri & Sat 9.30am–11.30pm, Sun 9.30am–8.30pm; winter Mon–Thurs 9.30am–6.30pm, Fri–Sun 9.30am–7.30pm; €7).

The Capitoline Hill

The real pity about the Vittoriano is that it obscures views of the **Capitoline Hill** behind – once the spiritual and political centre of the Roman Empire. Apart from anything else, this hill has contributed key words to the English language, including, of course, "capitol", and "money", which comes from the temple to Juno Moneta that once stood up here and housed the Roman mint. The Capitoline also played a significant role in medieval and Renaissance times: the flamboyant fourteenth-century dictator Cola di Rienzo stood here in triumph in 1347, and was murdered here by an angry mob seven years later – a humble statue marks the spot.

Santa Maria in Aracoeli

The church of **Santa Maria in Aracoeli** (daily 9am–12.30pm & 3–6.30pm) crowns the highest point on the Capitoline Hill, built on the site of a temple where, according to legend, the Tiburtine Sybil foretold the birth of Christ. You can reach it by a steep flight of steps erected by Cola di Rienzo in 1348, or by cutting through from the Vittoriano, and it's one of Rome's most ancient basilicas, with, in the first chapel on the right, some fine frescoes by Pinturicchio recording the life of San Bernardino. The church is also known for its role as keeper of the "Bambino", a small statue of the Christ child, carved from the wood of a Gethsemane olive tree. It's said to have healing powers and was traditionally called out to the sickbeds of the ill and dying all over the city, its coach commanding instant right of way through the heavy Rome traffic. The statue was stolen in 1994, however, and a copy now stands in its place, in a small chapel to the left of the high altar.

Piazza del Campidoglio

Next door to the steps up to Santa Maria is the **cordonata**, an elegant, gently rising ramp, topped with two Roman statues of Castor and Pollux, leading to **Piazza del Campidoglio**, one of Rome's most elegant squares. Designed by Michelangelo in the last years of his life for Pope Paul III, the square wasn't in fact completed until the late seventeenth century. Michelangelo balanced the piazza, redesigning the facade of what is now **Palazzo dei Conservatori** and projecting an identical building across the way, known as **Palazzo Nuovo**. Both are angled slightly to focus on **Palazzo Senatorio**, Rome's town hall. In the centre of the square Michelangelo placed an equestrian statue of Emperor Marcus Aurelius, which had previously stood for years outside San Giovanni in Laterano; early Christians had refrained from melting it down because they believed it to be of the Emperor Constantine. After careful restoration, the original is now behind a glass wall in the Palazzo Nuovo, and a copy has taken its place at the centre of the piazza.

The Capitoline Museums

The Palazzo dei Conservatori and Palazzo Nuovo together make up the Capitoline Museums (Tues–Sun 9am–8pm; €6.50, €8.50 for Centrale Montemartini as well, valid 7 days; see p.700; Ⓦ www.museicapitolini.org), containing some of the city's most important ancient sculpture and art. The **Palazzo dei Conservatori** holds the larger, more varied collection. Among its many treasures are the so-called Spinario, a Roman statue of a boy picking a thorn out of his foot; the Etruscan bronze she-wolf nursing the mythic founders of the city, and the Hannibal Room, covered in wonderfully vivid fifteenth-century paintings recording Rome's wars with Carthage, and so named for a rendering of Hannibal seated impressively on an elephant. The wonderfully airy new wing holds the original of Marcus Aurelius, formerly in the square outside, alongside a giant bronze statue of Constantine, or at least its head, hand and orb.

Museum passes

You can visit the four museums that make up the **Museo Nazionale Romano** on one ticket, valid for seven days, which costs €7 and is available from each location – Palazzo Altemps, Palazzo Massimo, Crypta Balbi and the Museo delle Terme di Diocleziano. The **Roma Pass** (Ⓣ 06.06.08, Ⓦ www.romapass.it) costs €23 and is valid for 3 days. Available from major sights and tourist information kiosks, it entitles you to travel for free on buses, trams and the metro, free admission to two and reduced entry to quite a few of the city's major sights and museums, and, perhaps most importantly, the opportunity not to queue at the first two sights you visit – quite a lifesaver at the Colosseum and one or two others.

Nearby stands the rippling bronze of Hercules, behind which are part of the foundations and a retaining wall from the original temple of Jupiter here, discovered when the work for the new wing was undertaken. And when museum fatigue sets in you can climb up to the floor above to the second-floor **café**, whose terrace commands one of the best views in Rome. The second-floor **pinacoteca** holds Renaissance painting from the fourteenth century to the late seventeenth century. Highlights include a couple of portraits by Van Dyck, a penetrating *Portrait of a Crossbowman* by Lorenzo Lotto, a pair of paintings from 1590 by Tintoretto, and a very fine early work by Lodovico Carracci, *Head of a Boy*. In one of the two large main galleries, there's a vast picture by Guercino, depicting the Burial of Santa Petronilla (an early Roman martyr who was the supposed daughter of St Peter), and two paintings by Caravaggio, one a replica of the young *John the Baptist* which hangs in the Palazzo Doria-Pamphilj, the other an early work known as *The Fortune-Teller*.

The **Palazzo Nuovo** across the square – also accessible by way of an underground walkway that takes in good views of the Roman Forum just below – is the more manageable of the two museums, with some of the best of the city's Roman sculpture crammed into half a dozen or so rooms. Among them is the remarkable, controlled statue *Dying Gaul*, as well as a *Satyr Resting* that was the inspiration for Hawthorne's book the *Marble Faun*; and the red marble *Laughing Silenus*. There are also busts and statues of Roman emperors and other famous names: a young Augustus, a cruel Caracalla, and, the centrepiece, a life-size portrait of Helena, the mother of Constantine, reclining gracefully. Don't miss the coy, delicate *Capitoline Venus*, housed in a room on its own.

The Tarpeian Rock and San Pietro in Carcere

Behind the Palazzo Senatorio, Via del Monte Tarpeio follows, as its name suggests, the brink of the old **Tarpeian Rock**, from which traitors would be thrown in ancient times – so-called after Tarpeia, who betrayed the city to the Sabines. On the left side of the Palazzo Senatorio (as you face it from the Campidoglio) steps lead down to the little church of **San Pietro in Carcere** (daily 9am–6pm; donation expected for the prison), built above the ancient Mamertine Prison, where spies, vanquished soldiers and other enemies of the Roman state were incarcerated, and where St Peter himself was held. Steps lead down into the murky depths of the jail, where you can see the bars to which he was chained, along with the spring the saint is said to have created to baptize the other prisoners down here. At the top of the staircase, hollowed out of the honeycomb of stone, is an imprint claimed to be of St Peter's head as he tumbled down the stairs (though when the prison was in use, the only access was through a hole in the ceiling). It's an unappealing place even now, and you won't be sorry to leave.

The centro storico

Immediately north of Piazza Venezia is the real heart of Rome – the **centro storico** or historic centre, which makes up most of the triangular knob of land that bulges into a bend in the Tiber. This area, known in ancient Roman times as the Campus Martius, was outside the ancient city centre, a low-lying area that was mostly given over to barracks and sporting arenas, together with several temples, including the Pantheon. Later it became the heart of the Renaissance city, and nowadays it's the part of the town that is densest in interest, an unruly knot of narrow streets and alleys that holds some of the best of Rome's classical and Baroque heritage and its most vivacious street- and nightlife. It's here that most people find the Rome they have been looking for – a city of small

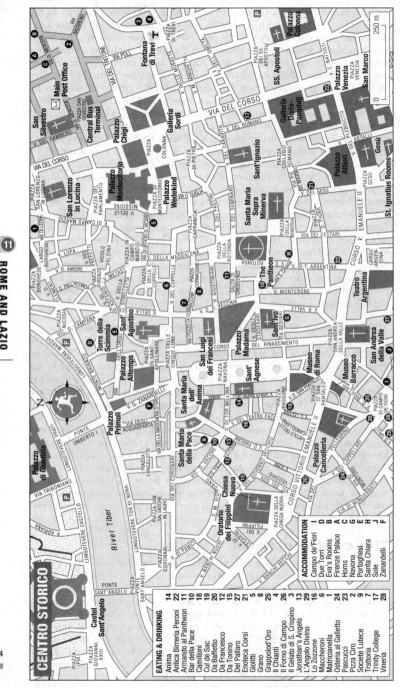

crumbling piazzas, Renaissance churches and fountains, blind alleys and streets humming with scooters and foot-traffic. Whichever direction you wander in there's something to see; indeed it's part of the appeal of the centre of Rome that even the most aimless ambling leads you past some breathlessly beautiful and historic spots.

Via del Corso

The boundary of the historic centre to the east, **Via del Corso** is Rome's main thoroughfare, leading all the way from Piazza Venezia at its southern end up to the Piazza del Popolo to the north. On its eastern side, it gives onto the swish shopping streets that lead up to Piazza di Spagna; on the western side the web of streets tangles its way right down to the Tiber. It is Rome's principal shopping street, home to a mixture of upmarket boutiques and chain stores that make it a busy stretch during the day, full of hurrying pedestrians and crammed buses, but a relatively dead one come the evening. The good news is that the top end, beyond Piazza Colonna, where the bulk of the shops are, is pedestrian-ized, so shopping and strolling is much easier and more enjoyable.

Galleria Doria Pamphilj

North of Piazza Venezia, the first building on the left of Via del Corso is the Palazzo Doria Pamphilj, one of the city's finest Rococo palaces. Inside, the **Galleria Doria Pamphilj** (daily 10am–5pm; €9, including audioguide in English; ⓦ www.doriapamphilj.it) is one of Rome's best private late-Renaissance art collections. The Doria Pamphilj family still lives in part of the building, and you're guided through the **gallery** and the **state apartments** beyond by way of a free audio tour narrated by the urbane Jonathan Pamphilj. The **picture gallery** extends around the main courtyard, the paintings displayed in old-fashioned style, crammed in frame-to-frame, floor-to-ceiling. It has perhaps Rome's best concen-tration of Dutch and Flemish paintings, with a rare Italian work by Brueghel the Elder showing a naval battle being fought outside Naples, a highly realistic portrait of two old men, by Quentin Metsys, and a Hans Memling *Deposition*, in the furthest rooms. But there is plenty of interest besides these – Caravaggio's wonderful *Rest on the Flight into Egypt*, next to his painting of *Penitent Magdelen*, *Salome with the head of St John* by Titian in the next room, and on the other side of the courtyard a series of bucolic paintings by Annibale Carracci that used to hang in the Pamphilj chapel. The gallery's most prized treasures, however, are in a small room on their own – a Bernini bust of the Pamphilj pope Innocent X and Velázquez's famous, penetrating painting of the same man. All in all it's a marvel-lous collection of work, displayed in a wonderfully appropriate setting.

Sant'Ignazio

The next left off Via del Corso after the palace leads into **Piazza Sant'Ignazio**, a lovely little square, laid out like a theatre set and dominated by the facade of the Jesuit church of **Sant'Ignazio** (daily 7.30am–12.30pm & 4–7.15pm). The saint isn't actually buried here; appropriately, for the founder of the Jesuit order, he's in the Gesù church a little way south. It's a spacious structure, built during the late seventeeth century, and worth visiting for the marvellous Baroque ceiling by Andrea del Pozzo showing the entry of St Ignatius into paradise, a spectacular work that employs sledgehammer trompe l'oeil effects, notably in the mock cupola painted into the dome of the crossing. Stand on the disc in the centre of the nave, the focal point for the ingenious rendering of perspective: figures in various states of action and repose, conversation and silence, fix you with stares from their classical pediment.

The Pantheon

Via del Seminario leads down to Piazza della Rotonda, where the main focus of interest is the **Pantheon** (Mon–Sat 8.30am–7.30pm, Sun 9am–6pm; free), easily the most complete ancient Roman structure in the city and, along with the Colosseum, visually the most impressive. Though originally a temple that formed part of Marcus Agrippa's redesign of the Campus Martius in around 27 BC – hence the inscription – it's since been proved that the building was entirely rebuilt by the Emperor Hadrian and finished around the year 125 AD. It's a formidable architectural achievement even now: the diameter is precisely equal to its height (43m), the hole in the centre of the dome – from which shafts of sunlight descend to illuminate the musty interior – a full 9m across. Most impressively, there are no visible arches or vaults to hold the whole thing up; instead they're sunk into the concrete of the walls of the building. It would have been richly decorated, the coffered ceiling heavily stuccoed and the niches filled with the statues of gods, but now, apart from its sheer size, the main things of interest are the tombs of two Italian kings, and the tomb of Raphael, between the second and third chapel on the left, with an inscription by the humanist bishop Pietro Bembo: "Living, great Nature feared he might outvie Her works, and dying, fears herself may die." The same kind of sentiments might well have been reserved for the Pantheon itself.

Santa Maria sopra Minerva

There's more artistic splendour on view behind the Pantheon, though Bernini's **Elephant Statue** doesn't really prepare you for the church of Santa Maria sopra Minerva beyond. The statue is Bernini's most endearing piece of work, if not his most characteristic: a cheery elephant trumpeting under the weight of the obelisk he carries on his back – a reference to Pope Alexander VII's reign and supposed to illustrate the fact that strength should support wisdom. **Santa Maria sopra Minerva** (Mon–Sat 7am–7pm, Sun 8am–7pm) is Rome's only

▲ The Pantheon at night

Gothic church, and worth a look just for that. Built in the late thirteenth century on the ruins of a temple to Minerva, it's also one of Rome's art-treasure churches, crammed with the tombs and self-indulgences of wealthy Roman families. Of these, the Carafa chapel, in the south transept, is the best known, holding Filippino Lippi's fresco of the *Assumption*, below which one painting shows a hopeful Carafa (the religious zealot, Pope Paul IV) being presented to the Virgin Mary by Thomas Aquinas; another depicts Aquinas confounding the heretics in the sight of two beautiful young boys – the future Medici popes Leo X and Clement VII. The lives of Leo and Clement come full circle in the church, where they are both buried and remembered by two very grand tombs either side of the high altar – Leo on the left, Clement on the right, close by which is the figure of *Christ Bearing the Cross*, a serene work that Michelangelo completed for the church in 1521.

Sant'Ivo

A few steps west of the Pantheon, on Corso del Rinascimento, the rather blank facade of the **Palazzo della Sapienza** cradles the church of **Sant'Ivo** (Sun 9am–noon) – from the outside at least, one of Rome's most impressive churches, with a playful facade designed by Borromini. Though originally built for the Barberini pope, Urban VIII, the building actually spans the reign of three pontiffs. Each of the two small towers is topped with the weird pyramidal groupings that are the symbol of the Chigi family (representing the hills of Monti di Paschi di Siena), and the central cupola spirals helter-skelter fashion to its zenith, crowned with flames that are supposed to represent the sting of the Barberini bee, their family symbol. The inside, too, is very cleverly designed, light and spacious given the small space the church is squeezed into, rising to the tall parabolic cupola.

San Luigi dei Francesi

A short walk from here, at the bottom of Via della Scrofa, the French national church of **San Luigi dei Francesi** (daily except Thurs afternoon 8.30am–12.30pm & 4–7pm) is worth a look, mainly for its works by Caravaggio. In the last chapel on the left are three paintings: *The Calling of St Matthew*, in which Christ points to Matthew, who is illuminated by a shaft of sunlight; *The Inspiration of St Matthew*, where Matthew is visited by an angel as he writes the Gospel; and *The Martyrdom of St Matthew*. Caravaggio's first public commission, these paintings were actually rejected at first, partly on grounds of indecorum, and it took considerable reworking by the artist before they were finally accepted.

Piazza Navona

Just west of San Luigi dei Francesi lies **Piazza Navona**, Rome's most famous square. Lined with cafés and restaurants, and often thronged with tourists, street artists and pigeons, it is as picturesque – and as vibrant, day and night – as any piazza in Italy. It takes its shape from the first-century AD Stadium of Domitian, the principal venue of the athletic events and later chariot races that took place in the Campus Martius. Until the mid-fifteenth century the ruins of the arena were still here, overgrown and disused, but the square was given a facelift in the mid-seventeenth century by Pope Innocent X, who built most of the grandiose palaces that surround it and commissioned Borromini to design the facade of the church of **Sant'Agnese in Agone** on the piazza's western side (daily 9.30am–12.30pm & 4–7pm). The story goes that the 13-year-old St Agnes was stripped naked before the crowds in the stadium as punishment for refusing to marry, whereupon she miraculously grew hair to cover herself. The church, typically squeezed into the tightest of spaces by Borromini, is supposedly built on the spot where it all happened.

Opposite, the **Fontana dei Quattro Fiumi**, one of three that punctuate the square, is a masterpiece by Bernini, Borromini's arch-rival. Each figure represents one of the four great rivers of the world – the Nile, Danube, Ganges and Plate – though only the horse, symbolizing the Danube, was actually carved by Bernini himself. It's said that all the figures are shielding their eyes in horror from Borromini's church facade (Bernini was disdainful of the less successful Borromini, and their rivalry is well documented), but the fountain had actually been completed before the facade was begun. The grand complexity of rock is topped with an Egyptian obelisk, brought here by Pope Innocent X from the Circus of Maxentius. Bernini also had a hand in the fountain at the southern end of the square, the so-called **Fontana del Moro**, designing the central figure of the Moor in what is another fantastically playful piece of work, surrounded by toothsome dolphins and other marine figures.

Museo di Roma

Overlooking the south side of Piazza Navona, the eighteenth-century Palazzo Braschi is the home of the **Museo di Roma** (Tues–Sun 9am–7pm; €6.50; Ⓦwww.museodiroma.comune.roma.it), which has a permanent collection relating to the history of the city from the Middle Ages to the present day. The building itself is probably the main attraction – particularly the magnificent Sala Nobile where you enter, the main staircase, and one or two of the renovated rooms – but some of the paintings are of interest, showing views of the city during different eras, and frescoes from demolished palaces provide decent enough highlights.

Museo Barracco

Across the street from the Museo di Roma, the **Museo Barracco**, housed in another palace, the so-called Piccola Farnesina (Tues–Sun 9am–Sun; €3), holds a small but high-quality collection of ancient sculpture that was donated to the city at the turn of the century by one Baron Barracco. There are some fine ancient Egyptian pieces and ceramics and statuary from classical Greece and Rome. Highlights include a head of the young Rameses II, next to a bust of an Egyptian priest, a Roman figure of an athlete from an ancient Greek original, and a highly realistic depiction of a bitch washing herself from the fourth century BC.

Piazza Pasquino and Via del Governo Vecchio

The nearby triangular space of **Piazza Pasquino** is named after the small battered torso that still stands in the corner. Pasquino is perhaps the best-known of Rome's "talking statues" of the Middle Ages and Renaissance times, on which anonymous comments on the affairs of the day would be attached – comments that had a serious as well as a humorous intent, and gave us our word "pasquinade". **Via del Governo Vecchio** leads west from here, and is home – along with the narrow streets around – to some of the *centro storico*'s liveliest restaurants and bars.

Palazzo Altemps

Just across the street from the north end of Piazza Navona, Piazza Sant'Apollinare is home to the beautifully restored **Palazzo Altemps** (Tues–Sun 9am–7pm; €7, part of the Museo Nazionale Romano; see p.672), and the cream of its collections of Roman statuary. On the ground floor at the far end of the courtyard's loggia is a statue of the Emperor Antoninus Pius, and, around the corner, a couple of heads of Zeus and Pluto, and a bust of Julia, the daughter of the Emperor Augustus. There are two almost identical statues of Apollo the Lyrist, a magnificent statue of Athena taming a serpent, pieced together from fragments found near the church of Santa Maria sopra Minerva, and, in the far corner of the courtyard, a Dionysus with a satyr and panther, found on the Quirinal Hill. Upstairs you get a slightly better sense of the original building – some of the frescoes remain and the north loggia retains its original, late-sixteenth-century decoration, simulating a vine-laden pergola. Among the objects on display there's a fine statue of Hermes, a wonderful statue of a warrior at rest, and a charmingly sensitive portrayal of Orestes and Electra, from the first century AD by a sculptor called Menelaus – his name is carved at the base of one of the figures. In a later room stands a colossal head of Hera, and – what some consider the highlight of the entire collection – the famous Ludovisi throne, embellished with a delicate relief portraying the birth of Aphrodite. Further on, the Fireplace Salon – whose huge fireplace is embellished with caryatids and lurking ibex, the symbol of the Altemps family – has the so-called *Suicide of Galatian*, apparently commissioned by Julius Caesar to adorn his Quirinal estate. At the other end of the room, an incredible sarcophagus depicts a battle between the Romans and barbarians in graphic, almost viscerally sculptural detail.

Via dei Coronari

West of Palazzo Altemps, narrow **Via dei Coronari**, and some of the streets around, are the fulcrum of Rome's antiques trade, and, although the prices are as high as you might expect in such a location, there's a huge number of shops (Via dei Coronari consists of virtually nothing else) selling a tremendous variety of stuff, and a browse along here makes for an absorbing bit of sightseeing.

Sant'Agostino

Just east of Palazzo Altemps, the Renaissance facade of the church of **Sant'Agostino** (daily 7.45am–noon & 4–7.30pm; free) takes up one side of a drab piazza of the same name. It's not much to look at from the outside, but a handful of art treasures might draw you in. Just inside the door, the serene statue of the *Madonna del Parto*, by Sansovino, is traditionally invoked during pregnancy, and is accordingly surrounded by photos of newborn babes and their blissful parents. Further into the church, take a look at Raphael's vibrant fresco of Isaiah, on the third pillar on the left, beneath which is another work by Sansovino, a craggy *St Ann, Virgin and Child*. But the biggest crowds gather around the first chapel on the left, where the *Madonna and Pilgrims* by Caravaggio – a characteristic work of what was at the time almost revolutionary realism – shows two peasants with dirty clothes praying at the feet of a sensuous Mary and Child.

Piazza Montecitorio and around

A short walk east from Sant'Agostino, **Piazza Montecitorio** takes its name from the bulky **Palazzo di Montecitorio** on its northern side, home since 1871 to the Italian parliament. Just beyond, off Via del Corso, the **Palazzo Chigi** flanks the north side of **Piazza Colonna**, official residence of the prime minister. The **Column of Marcus Aurelius** in the centre of the piazza was erected between 180 and 190 AD to commemorate military victories in northern Europe, and, like the column of Trajan that inspired it, is decorated with reliefs depicting scenes from the campaigns.

Campo de' Fiori, the Ghetto and around

Just south of the *centro storico* proper, this is Rome's old centre part two, a similar neighbourhood of cramped, wanderable streets opening out into small squares flanked by churches. However, it's less monumental and more of a working quarter as evidenced by its main focus, **Campo de' Fiori**, whose fruit and veg stalls are a marked contrast to the pavement artists of Piazza Navona. Close by are the dark alleys of the old **Jewish Ghetto**, and the busy traffic junction of Largo di Torre Argentina.

Largo di Torre Argentina and around

Largo di Torre Argentina is a large square, frantic with traffic circling around the ruins of four Republican-era temples, now home to a thriving colony of cats. On the far side of the square, the **Teatro Argentina** was in 1816 the venue for the first performance of Rossini's *Barber of Seville*, not a success at all on the night: Rossini was apparently booed into taking refuge in Bernasconi's pastry shop which used to be next door. Nearby, the **Crypta Balbi**, around the corner at Via delle Botteghe Oscure 31 (Tues–Sun 9am–7pm; €7, includes Palazzo Altemps, Palazzo Massimo, Terme Diocletian, valid 3 days), is housed on the part-excavated site of an old Roman imperial theatre and has displays covering the period from the fall of the Roman Empire to the late Middle Ages.

The Gesù and Rooms of St Ignatius

Just east of Largo Argentina, the church of **Gesù** is a huge structure (daily 6am–12.30pm & 4–7.15pm), the headquarters of the Jesuits and ideal for the large and fervent congregations the order wanted to attract – indeed, high and wide, with a single-aisled nave and short transepts edging out under a huge dome, it has since served as the model for Jesuit churches everywhere. The facade is by Giacomo della Porta, the interior the work of Vignola. The glitzy tomb of the order's founder, St Ignatius, is topped by a huge globe of lapis lazuli – the largest piece in existence. Opposite, the tomb of the sixteenth-century Jesuit missionary St Francis Xavier holds a reliquary containing the saint's arm, severed from the rest of his (incorruptible) body, which remains a focus of pilgrimage in Goa, India. Otherwise it's the staggering richness of the church's interior that you remember, especially the paintings by the Genoese painter Baciccia in the dome and the nave, the *Triumph in the Name of Jesus*, which oozes out of its frame in a tangle of writhing bodies, flowing drapery and stucco angels clinging on like limpets.

Next door, the **Rooms of St Ignatius** (Mon–Sat 4–6pm, Sun 10am–noon; free) occupy part of the first floor of the Jesuit headquarters, and are basically the rooms – recently restored – where St Ignatius lived from 1544 until his death in 1556. There are bits and pieces of furniture and memorabilia relating to the saint, but the true draw is the decorative corridor just outside, designed by Andrea Pozzo in 1680 – a superb exercise in perspective on a minimized scale, giving an illusion of a grand hall in what is a relatively small space.

Piazza Campo de' Fiori

On the other side of Largo Argentina, **Piazza Campo de' Fiori** is in many ways Rome's most appealing square, home to a lively fruit and vegetable market (Mon–Sat 8am–1pm), and flanked by restaurants and cafés. No one really knows how the square came by its name, which means "field of flowers", but one theory holds that it was derived from the Roman Campus Martius, which used to cover most of this part of town; another claims it is after Flora, the mistress of Pompey, whose theatre used to stand on what is now the northeast corner of the square – a huge complex by all accounts, which was the supposed location of Julis Caesar's assassination. Later, Campo de' Fiori was an important point on papal processions between the Vatican and the major basilicas of Rome (notably San Giovanni in Laterano) and a site of public executions. The most notorious killing was of Giordano Bruno, a late-sixteenth-century freethinker who followed the teachings of Copernicus and was denounced to the Inquisition; his trial lasted for years under a succession of different popes, and finally, when he refused to renounce his philosophical beliefs, he was burned at the stake. His death is commemorated by a statue in the middle of the square.

Palazzo Farnese and Galleria Spada

Just south of Campo de' Fiori, **Piazza Farnese** is a quite different square, with great fountains spurting out of lilies – the Farnese emblem – into marble tubs brought from the Baths of Caracalla, and the sober bulk of the **Palazzo Farnese** itself, begun in 1514 by Antonio da Sangallo the Younger and finished off after the architect's death by Michelangelo, who added the top tier of windows and cornice. The building now houses the French Embassy but is open to those organized enough to make an appointment (Mon & Thurs visits in French or Italian at 3pm, 4pm, 5pm; free; book in advance at Via Giulia 250, on ℡06.688.92818 or at ✉visitfarnese@france -italia.it; closed late July to early Sept & end Dec) – worth doing to see the amazing Baroque ceiling frescoes of Annibale Carracci in one of the rear reception rooms.

If you can't make it to the Palazzo Farnese, make do instead with the Palazzo Spada, back towards Via Arenula at Piazza Capo di Ferro 3, and the **Galleria Spada** inside (Tues–Sun 8.30am–7.30pm; €5); walk right through the courtyard to the back of the building. Its four rooms, decorated in the manner of a Roman noble family's home, have two portraits of Cardinal Bernadino Spada by Reni and Guercino, and the building itself is a treat: its facade is frilled with stucco adornments. Left off the small courtyard, there's a crafty trompe l'oeil by Borromini – a tunnel whose actual length is multiplied about four times through the architect's tricks with perspective – though to see this you have to wait for one of the guided tours.

Via Giulia

Via Giulia runs parallel to the Tiber from the Ponte Sisto, and was laid out by Julius II to connect the bridge with the Vatican. The street was conceived as the centre of papal Rome, and Julius commissioned Bramante to line it with imposing palaces. Bramante didn't get very far with the plan, as Julius was soon succeeded by Leo X, but the street quickly became a popular residence for wealthier Roman families, and is still packed full with stylish *palazzi* and antique shops.

Via Portico d'Ottavia and around

Cross over to the far side of Via Arenula and you're in what was once the city's **Jewish Ghetto**, a crumbling area of old narrow, switchback streets and alleys, easy to lose your way in. There was a Jewish population in Rome as far back as the second century BC, and although much depleted now, it still numbers 16,000 (around half Italy's total), and the quarter is thriving, with a few kosher restaurants, bakers and butchers on and around the main artery of the Jewish area, **Via Portico d'Ottavia**. This leads down to the **Portico d'Ottavia**, a not terribly well-preserved second-century BC gate, rebuilt by Augustus and dedicated to his sister in 23 BC, which was the entranceway to the adjacent amphitheatre of the **Teatro di Marcello** (daily: summer 9am–7pm; winter 9am–6pm; free). Begun by Julius Caesar, finished by Augustus, this was pillaged in the fourth century and not properly restored until the Middle Ages, after which it became a formidable fortified palace for a succession of different rulers, including the Orsini family. Crossing to the other side of Via Portico d'Ottavia, follow your nose to **Piazza Mattei**, whose **Fontana delle Tartarughe**, or "turtle fountain", is a delightful late-sixteenth-century creation, perhaps restored by Bernini.

The Synagogue
The Ghetto's principal Jewish sight is the huge **Synagogue** by the river (Sun–Thurs 10am–5pm, Fri 9am–2pm; closed Sat & Jewish holidays; €7.50), built in 1904 and very much dominating all around with its bulk – not to mention the carabinieri who stand guard 24 hours a day. The only way to see the building is on one of the short guided tours it runs in English, afterwards taking in the small two-room museum. The interior of the building is impressive, rising to a high, rainbow-hued dome, and the tours, which are included in the price and leave very regularly, are excellent, giving good background on the building and Rome's Jewish community in general.

Isola Tiberina
Almost opposite the Synagogue, the **Ponte Fabricio** crosses the river to **Isola Tiberina**. Built in 62 BC, it's the only classical bridge to remain intact without help from the restorers (the Ponte Cestio, on the other side of the island, was partially rebuilt in the nineteenth century). As for the island, it's a calm respite from the city centre proper, with its originally tenth-century church of **San Bartolomeo**, worth a peep inside for its ancient columns and an equally ancient wellhead on the altar steps, carved with figures relating to the founding of the church; the figures include St Bartholomew himself, who also features in the painting above the altar, hands tied above his head, on the point of being skinned alive – his famous and gruesome mode of martyrdom. Beyond the island, you can see the Ponte Rotto (Broken Bridge) – all that remains of the first stone bridge to span the Tiber, originally built between 179 and 142 BC.

Piazza Bocca della Verità and around
Further along the river from the Synagogue lies **Piazza Bocca della Verità**, home to two of the city's better-preserved Roman temples, the **Temple of Portunus** and the **Temple of Hercules Victor** – the oldest surviving marble structure in Rome and long known as the Temple of Vesta because, like all vestal temples, it's circular. Both date from the end of the second century BC, and although you can't get inside, they're worth a look as fine examples of republican-era places of worship.

More interesting is the church of **Santa Maria in Cosmedin** on the far side of the square (daily 10am–5pm), a typically Roman medieval basilica with a huge marble altar and a colourful and ingenious Cosmati-work marble mosaic floor – one of the city's finest. Outside in the portico, and giving the square its name, is the **Bocca della Verità** (Mouth of Truth), an ancient Roman drain cover in the shape of an enormous face that in medieval times would apparently swallow the hand of anyone who hadn't told the truth. It was particularly popular with husbands anxious to test the faithfulness of their wives; now it is one of the city's biggest tour-bus attractions.

Tridente

The northern part of Rome's centre is sometimes known as **Tridente** on account of the trident shape of the roads leading down from the apex of Piazza del Popolo – Via di Ripetta, Via del Corso and Via del Babuino. The area east of Via del Corso, focusing on Piazza di Spagna was historically the artistic quarter of the city, for which eighteenth- and nineteenth-century Grand Tourists would make in search of the colourful, exotic city. Keats and Giorgio de Chirico are just two of those who lived on Piazza di Spagna; Goethe had lodgings on Via del Corso; and institutions like *Caffè Greco* and *Babington's Tea Rooms* were the meeting-places of the local expat community for close on a couple of centuries. Today these institutions have given ground to more latter-day traps for the tourist dollar: American Express and *McDonald's* have settled in, while Via dei Condotti and around is these days strictly international designer territory, with some of Rome's fanciest stores.

Piazza del Popolo

The oval-shaped expanse of **Piazza del Popolo** is a dignified meeting of roads, now pedestrianized, that was laid out in 1538 by Pope Paul III (Alessandro Farnese) to make an impressive entrance to the city. The monumental **Porta del Popolo** went up in 1655, and was the work of Bernini, whose patron Alexander VII's Chigi family symbol – the heap of hills surmounted by a star – can clearly be seen above the main gateway. During summer, the steps around the obelisk and fountain, and the cafés on either side of the square, are popular hangouts. But the square's real attraction is the unbroken view it gives all the way down Via del Corso, to the central columns of the Vittoriano. If you get to choose your first view of the centre of Rome, make it this one.

Santa Maria del Popolo

On the far side of the piazza, hard against the city walls, **Santa Maria del Popolo** (Mon–Sat 7am–noon & 4–7pm, Sun 8am–1.30pm & 4.30–7.30pm) holds some of the best Renaissance art of any Roman church. It was originally erected here in 1099 over the supposed burial place of Nero, in order to sanctify what was believed to be an evil place. Inside, the Chigi chapel, second on the left, was designed by Raphael for Agostino Chigi in 1516. Michelangelo's protégé, Sebastiano del Piombo, was responsible for the altarpiece, and two of the sculptures in the corner niches, of Daniel and Habakkuk, are by Bernini. But it's two pictures by Caravaggio in the left-hand chapel of the north transept that attract the most attention. These are typically dramatic works – one, the *Conversion of St Paul*, showing Paul and horse bathed in a beatific radiance; the other, the *Crucifixion of St Peter*, depicting Peter as an aged but strong figure, dominated by the muscular figures hoisting him up.

Ara Pacis Augustae

Via Ripetta runs southwest from Piazza del Popolo into **Piazza del Augusta Imperatore**, an odd square of largely Mussolini-era buildings, dominated by the massive **Mausoleum of Augustus**, burial place of the emperor and his family and nowadays under restoration. On the far side of the square, the **Ara Pacis Augustae** or "Altar of Augustan Peace" is now enclosed in a controversial purpose-built structure designed by the New York-based architect Richard Meier, its angular lines and sheer white surfaces dominating the Tiber side of the square (daily 9am–7pm; €8, audioguide €3.50). The altar is a more substantially recognizable Roman remain than the mausoleum, a marble block enclosed by sculpted walls built in 13 BC, probably to celebrate Augustus's victory over Spain and Gaul and the peace it heralded. It's a superb example of Roman sculpture, with a frieze on one side showing the imperial family at the height of its power: Augustus, his great general Marcus Agrippa, and Augustus's wife Livia, followed by a victory procession containing her son – and Augustus's eventual successor – Tiberius and niece Antonia, the latter caught simply and realistically turning to her husband, Drusus. On the opposite side the veiled figure is believed to be Julia, Augustus' daughter.

Piazza di Spagna and the Keats-Shelley Memorial House

Via del Babuino leads down from Piazza del Popolo to **Piazza di Spagna**, a long straggle of a square almost entirely enclosed by buildings and centring on the distinctive boat-shaped **Barcaccia** fountain, the last work of Bernini's father. It apparently remembers the great flood of Christmas Day 1598, when a barge from the Tiber was washed up on the slopes of Pincio Hill here.

Fronting the square, opposite the fountain, is the house where the poet John Keats died in 1821. It now serves as the **Keats–Shelley Memorial House** (Mon–Fri 10am–1pm & 2–6pm, Sat 11am–2pm & 3–6pm; €4; @www .keats-shelley-house.org), an archive of English-language literary and historical works and a museum of manuscripts and literary memorabilia relating to the Keats circle of the early nineteenth century – namely the poet himself, Shelley and Mary Shelley, and Byron (who at one time lived across the square). Among many bits of manuscript, letters and the like, there's a silver scallop shell reliquary containing locks of Milton's and Elizabeth Barrett Browning's hair, while Keats's death mask, stored in the room where she died, captures a resigned grimace. Keats didn't really enjoy his time in Rome, referring to it as his "posthumous life": he was tormented by his love for Fanny Brawne, and spent months in pain before he died, confined to the rooming house with his artist friend Joseph Severn, to whom he remarked that he could already feel "the flowers growing over him".

The Spanish Steps

The only thing Spanish about the **Spanish Steps** is the fact that they lead down to the Spanish Embassy, which also gave the piazza its name. Sweeping down in a cascade of balustrades and balconies, in the nineteenth century the steps were the hangout of young hopefuls waiting to be chosen as artists' models. Nowadays the scene is not much changed, with the steps providing the venue for international posing and flirting late into the summer nights. At the top is the **Trinità dei Monti**, a largely sixteenth-century church designed by Carlo Maderno and paid for by the French king. Its rose-coloured Baroque facade overlooks the rest of Rome from its hilltop site, and it's worth clambering up just for the views, but do look inside for a couple of works by Daniele da Volterra, notably a soft, flowing fresco of the *Assumption* in the third chapel on the right, which includes a portrait of his teacher Michelangelo, and a *Deposition* across the nave.

The Trevi Fountain (Fontana di Trevi)

In the opposite direction from the Spanish Steps, across Via del Tritone, is one of Rome's more surprising sights, easy to stumble on by accident – the **Fontana di Trevi** or Trevi Fountain, a huge, very Baroque gush of water over statues and rocks built onto the backside of a Renaissance palace and fed by the same source that surfaces at the Barcaccia fountain in Piazza di Spagna. There was a previous Trevi fountain, designed by Alberti, around the corner in Via dei Crociferi, a smaller, more modest affair by all accounts, but Urban VIII decided to upgrade it in line with his other grandiose schemes of the time and employed Bernini, among others, to design an alternative. Work didn't begin, however, until 1732, when Niccolò Salvi won a competition held by Clement XII to design the fountain, and even then it took thirty years to finish the project. Salvi died in the process, his lungs destroyed by the time spent in the dank water-works of his construction. The fountain is now a popular hangout and, of course, the place you come to chuck in a coin if you want to guarantee your return to Rome. You might also remember Anita Ekberg throwing herself into it in *La Dolce Vita*, though any attempt at recreating the scene would be met with an immediate reaction buy the police here.

Galleria Colonna

A short stroll south from the Trevi Fountain brings you to the **Galleria Colonna**, at Via della Pilotta 17 (Sat 9am–1pm, free guided tours in English at 11.45am; closed Aug; €7), part of the Palazzo Colonna complex and home to one of the city's best collections of fine art still in private hands. The building itself is worth visiting for the massive chandelier-decked Great Hall, but the paintings, too, are worthy of attention, not least the two lascivious paintings of *Venus and Cupid* (one by Bronzino, the other Ghirlandaio) that eye each other across the room – once considered so risqué that clothes were painted on them and have only recently been removed. Through the Great Hall is the gallery's collection of landscapes by Dughet (Poussin's brother-in-law), and beyond that a small group of other high-quality works: Carracci's early and unusually spontaneous *Bean Eater*, Tintoretto's *Portrait of an Old* Man and a *Portrait of a Gentleman* caught in supremely confident pose by Veronese. Not a bad way to spend a Saturday morning in Rome.

Museo delle Cere and Time Elevator Roma

The **Museo delle Cere**, which occupies the other side of the Palazzo Colonna (daily 9am–8pm; €7), is a quirky first-floor museum of waxworks that hosts a diverse array of characters from history and Italian culture: not essential viewing by any means but certainly different from anything else you'll see in Rome, with wax figures of everyone from Mussolini to Francesco Totti. Close by, at Via SS. Apostoli 20, is **Time Elevator Roma** (daily 10.30am–7.30pm; €12, children €9), a multimedia film show of the history of Rome from its founding to the present day, with visitors strapped into a chair that moves around a bit like a flight simulator – a half-hour or so the kids might enjoy.

The Quirinale and around

Of the hills that rise up on the eastern side of the centre of Rome, the **Quirinale** is perhaps the most appealing, home to some of the city's greatest palaces, but also to some of Rome's greatest collections, not least in the Palazzo Massimo. It's an area that you may spend a bit of time in anyway, as it's home to Rome's main rail station, Termini, and the hotels and restaurants that surround it.

Piazza Barberini

Piazza Barberini, a frenetic traffic junction at the top end of the busy shopping street of Via del Tritone, was named after Bernini's **Fontana del Tritone**, which gushes a high jet of water in the centre of the square. Traditionally, this was the

Barberini family's quarter of the city; they were the greatest patrons of Gian Lorenzo Bernini, and the sculptor's works in their honour are thick on the ground around here. He finished the Tritone fountain in 1644, going on shortly after to design the **Fontana delle Api** ("Fountain of the Bees") at the bottom end of Via Veneto. Unlike the Tritone fountain you could walk right past this; it's a smaller, quirkier work, with a broad scallop shell studded with the bees that were the symbol of the Barberini.

Via Veneto

Via Veneto bends north from Piazza Barberini up to the southern edge of the Borghese gardens, its pricey bars and restaurants lining a street that was once the haunt of Rome's Beautiful People, made famous by Fellini's *La Dolce Vita*. They left a long time ago, however, and Via Veneto isn't really any different from other busy streets in central Rome – a pretty, tree-lined road, but with a fair share of high-class tack trying to cash in on departed glory.

The Capuchin cemetery

A little way up Via Veneto on the right, the Capuchin church of **Santa Maria della Concezione** (daily 9am–noon & 3–6pm) was another sponsored creation of the Barberini, though it's not a particularly significant building in itself and most people come to see its **Capuchin cemetery** (same times; minimum €1 donation), one of the more macabre and bizarre sights of Rome. Here, the bones of 4000 monks are set into the walls of a series of chapels, a monument to "Our Sister of Bodily Death" in the words of St Francis, which was erected in 1793. The bones appear in abstract or Christian patterns or as fully clothed skeletons, their faces peering out of their cowls in various twisted expressions of agony.

Palazzo Barberini

On the other side of Piazza Barberini, the vast **Palazzo Barberini**, at Via Barberini 18, is home to the **Galleria di Arte Antica** (Tues–Sun 8.30am–7.30pm; €5), a rich patchwork of mainly Italian art from the early Renaissance to late Baroque period that has been rearranged yet again following a recent restoration. Entry is by way of the spiral staircase on the right, the work of Borromini, which takes you up to the Gran Salone, dominated by Pietro da Cortona's manic fresco *The Triumph of Divine Providence*, which is truly one of the city's best free attractions, as the ticket office lies just beyond. In the gallery proper, Raphael's beguiling *Fornarina* is the first thing you see, a painting of the daughter of a Trasteveran baker thought to have been Raphael's mistress (Raphael's name appears clearly on the woman's bracelet); there's also Fra' Filippo Lippi's warmly maternal *Madonna and Child*, painted in 1437 and introducing background details, notably architecture, into Italian religious painting for the first time; a room full of portraits, including Bronzino's rendering of the marvellously erect *Stefano Colonna*; and portraits of both Henry VIII and St Thomas More by Hans Holbein, as well as Guido Reni's haunting depiction of Beatrice Cenci.

San Carlo, Sant'Andrea and the Palazzo del Quirinale

Heading southeast of Palazzo Barberini, along Via delle Quattro Fontane, brings you to a seventeenth-century landmark, the church of **San Carlo alle Quattro Fontane** (Mon–Fri 10am–1pm & 3–6pm, Sat noon–1pm, Sun noon–1pm). This was Borromini's first real design commission, and in it he displays all the ingenuity he later became famous for, cramming the church elegantly into a tiny and awkwardly shaped site. Outside the church are the four **fountains** that give the street and church their name, each cut into a niche in a corner of the crossroads that marks this, the highest point on the Quirinal Hill, while to the left is the featureless wall of the **Palazzo del Quirinale** (Sun 8.30am–noon; €5), a sixteenth-century structure that was the official summer residence of the popes until Unification, when it became the royal palace. It's now the home of Italy's president, and it's worth braving the security for a glimpse of the style in which popes, despots, kings and now presidents like to live, with a fine set of state rooms and works of art.

You can appreciate its exceptional siting from the **Piazza del Quirinale**, from which views stretch right across the centre of Rome. The main feature of the piazza is the huge statue of the Dioscuri, or Castor and Pollux – massive five-metre-high Roman copies of classical Greek statues, showing the two godlike twins, sons of Jupiter, who according to legend won victory for the Romans in an important battle. Nearby, there's another piece of design ingenuity on Via del Quirinale: the domed church of **Sant'Andrea al Quirinale** (Mon–Sat 8.30am–noon & 3.30–7pm, Sun 9am–noon & 4–7pm), which Bernini planned as a kind of flat oval shape to fit into its wide but shallow site. Like San Carlo, it's unusual and ingenious inside, and the upstairs rooms where the Polish saint, St Stanislaus Kostka, lived (and died) in 1568, focus on a disturbingly lifelike painted statue of Stanislaus lying on his deathbed.

Via XX Settembre and Santa Maria della Vittoria

Via XX Settembre spears out towards the Aurelian Wall from Via del Quirinale – not Rome's most appealing thoroughfare by any means, flanked by the deliberately faceless bureaucracies of the national government, erected after Unification in anticipation of Rome's ascension as a new world capital. It was, however, the route by which Italian troops entered the city on September 20, 1870, and the place where they breached the wall is marked with a column. The church of **Santa Maria della Vittoria** here (Mon–Sat 8.30am–noon & 3.30–6pm, Sun 3.30–6pm) was built by the Baroque-era architect Carlo Maderno and its interior is one of the most elaborate examples of Baroque decoration in Rome, its ceiling and walls are pitted with carving, and statues are crammed into remote corners as in an over-stuffed attic. The church's best-known feature, Bernini's carving the *Ecstasy of St Theresa*, the centrepiece of the sepulchral chapel of Cardinal Cornaro, is a deliberately melodramatic work featuring a theatrically posed St Theresa, who lays back in groaning submission beneath a mass of dishevelled garments in front of the murmuring cardinals.

Via Nazionale and Piazza della Repubblica

A couple of minutes' walk from Via XX Settembre, **Via Nazionale** connects Piazza Venezia and the centre of town with the area around Termini and the eastern districts beyond. A focus for much development after Unification, its heavy, overbearing buildings were constructed to give Rome some semblance of modern sophistication when it became capital, but most are now occupied by hotels and mainstream shops and boutiques. At the top of Via Nazionale, **Piazza della Repubblica** is typical of Rome's nineteenth-century regen-eration, a stern and dignified semicircle of buildings that was until recently rather dilapidated but is now – with the help of the very stylish *Hotel Exedra* – resurgent, centring on a fountain surrounded by languishing nymphs and sea monsters.

Santa Maria degli Angeli

Piazza della Repubblica actually follows the outlines of the exedra of the Baths of Diocletian, the remains of which lie across the piazza and are partially contained in the church of **Santa Maria degli Angeli** (Mon–Sat 7am–6.30pm, Sun 7am–7.30pm), one of Rome's least welcoming churches but giving the best impression of the size and grandeur of Diocletian's baths complex. It's a huge, open building, with an interior standardized by Vanvitelli into a rich eighteenth-century confection. The pink granite pillars, at nine feet in diameter the largest in Rome, are original, and the main transept formed the main hall of the baths. The meridian that strikes diagonally across the floor here was until 1846 the regulator of time for Romans (now a cannon shot is fired daily at noon from the Janiculum Hill).

Museo delle Terme di Diocleziano

Behind Santa Maria degli Angeli, the huge halls and courtyards of Diocletian's baths have been renovated and they and an attached Carthusian monastery now hold what is probably the least interesting part of the Museo Nazionale Romano (Tues–Sun 9am–7pm; €7, includes Palazzo Altemps, Palazzo Massimo, Crypta Balbi, valid 3 days). The museum's most evocative part is the large cloister of the church whose sides are crammed with statuary, funerary monuments and sarcophagi and fragments from all over Rome. The galleries that wrap around the cloister hold a reasonable if rather academically presented collection of pre-Roman and Roman finds: busts, terracotta statues, armour and weapons found in Roman tombs.

Palazzo Massimo

Across from Santa Maria degli Angeli, the **Palazzo Massimo**, Largo Perretti 1 (Tues–Sun 9am–7pm; €7, includes Palazzo Altemps, Terme di Diocleziano, Crypta Balbi, valid 3 days), is home to one of the two principal parts of the Museo Nazionale Romano (see p.672). As one of the great museums of Rome, there are too many highlights to do justice here, and there is something worth seeing on every floor. Start at the **basement** where there are displays of exquisite gold jewellery from the second century AD, and the mummified remains of an eight-year-old girl, along with a fantastic coin collection. The **ground floor** is devoted to statuary of the early empire, including a gallery with an unparalleled selection of unidentified busts found all over Rome – amazing pieces of portraiture, and as vivid a representation of patrician Roman life as you'll find. There are also identifiable faces – a bronze of Germanicus, a marvellous small bust of Caligula, several representations of Livia and a hooded statue of Augustus. Note the superb examples of Roman copies of Greek statuary – an altar found on Via Nomentana stands out, decorated with figures relating to the cult of Bacchus, as well as statues of Aphrodite and Melponome. The **first floor** has sculpted portraits of the various imperial dynasties in roughly chronological order, starting with the Flavian emperors – the craggy determination of Vespasian, the pinched nobility of Nerva – and leading on to Trajan, who appears with his wife Plotina as Hercules, next to a bust of his cousin Hadrian. The collection continues with the Antonine emperors – Antoninus Pius in a heroic nude pose and in several busts, flanked by likenesses of his daughter Faustina Minor. Faustina was the wife of Antoninus's successor, Marcus Aurelius, who appears in the next room. Further on are the Severans, with the fierce-looking Caracalla looking across past his father Septimius Severus to his brother Geta, whom he later murdered. Finally there's the **second floor**, which takes in some of the finest Roman frescoes and mosaics ever found. There's a stunning set of frescoes from the Villa di Livia, depicting an orchard dense with fruit and flowers and patrolled by partridges and doves, wall paintings rescued from what was perhaps the riverside villa of Augustus's daughter Julia and Marcus Agrippa, and mosaics showing four chariot drivers and their horses, so finely crafted that from a distance they look as if they've been painted.

Stazione Termini

Across the street is the low white facade of **Stazione Termini** (so named for its proximity to the Baths or "Terme" of Diocletian) and the vast, bus-crammed hubbub that is Piazza dei Cinquecento in front. The station is an ambitious piece of modern architectural design that was completed in 1950 and still entirely dominates the streets around with its low-slung, futuristic lines. As for **Piazza dei Cinquecento**, it's a good place to find buses and taxis, but otherwise it and the areas around are pretty much low-life territory and, although not especially dangerous, not a place to hang around for long either.

San Lorenzo fuori le Mura

A short walk from Termini, the studenty neighbourhood of San Lorenzo takes its name from the basilica of **San Lorenzo fuori le Mura** – one of the great pilgrimage churches of Rome, fronted by a columned portico and with a lovely twelfth-century cloister to its side (daily: summer 7am–noon & 4–7.30pm; winter closes 5.30pm). The original church here was built over the site of St Lawrence's martyrdom by Constantine – the saint was reputedly burned to death on a gridiron, halfway through his ordeal apparently uttering the immortal words, "Turn me, I am done on this side." Where the church of San Lorenzo differs is that it is actually a combination of three churches built at different periods – one a sixth-century reconstruction of Constantine's church by Pelagius II, which now forms the chancel, another a fifth-century church from the time of Sixtus III, both joined by a basilica from the thirteenth century by Honorius II. Because of its proximity to Rome's rail yards the church was bombed heavily during World War II, but it has been rebuilt with sensitivity, and inside there are features from all periods: a Cosmati floor, thirteenth-century pulpits and a Paschal candlestick, and a mosaic on the inside of the triumphal arch that is a sixth-century depiction of Pelagius offering his church to Christ; while below stairs, catacombs – where St Lawrence was apparently buried – sit among pillars from Constantine's original structure.

Ancient Rome

There are remnants of the ancient Roman era all over the city, but the most concentrated and central grouping – which for simplicity's sake we've called **Ancient Rome** – is the area that stretches southeast from the Capitoline Hill. It's a reasonably traffic-free and self-contained part of the city, but it wasn't always like this. Mussolini ploughed Via dei Fori Imperiali through here in the 1930s, with the intention of turning it into one giant archeological park, and this to some extent is what it is. You could spend a good day or so picking your way through the rubble of what was once the heart of the ancient world.

The Markets of Trajan and Imperial Forums

One of the major victims of Mussolini's plan were the **Imperial Forums**, which were built as ancient Rome grew in power and the Forum proper became too small. The ruins of forums built by Caesar, Augustus and Trajan, among others, litter either side of the Via dei Fori Imperiali, and are still being

The Forum and Palatine are now combined into one site, accessible either by the Via dei Fori Imperiali entrance to the Forum or the Palatine entrance on Via di San Gregorio. You can also exit at the Colosseum end of the Forum, or at the opposite end, where you join the path up to the Capitoline Hill. The same €12 ticket also covers you for the Colosseum. **Opening hours** of all three sites are as follows: daily: April–Aug 8.30am–6.15pm, Sept 8.30am–6pm, Oct 8.30am–5.30pm, Nov to mid-Feb 8.30am–3.30pm, mid-Feb to mid-March 8.30am–4pm, mid-March to end-March 8.30am–4.30pm.

excavated. But you can visit the largest and latest of these, the **Forum of Trajan**, which was constructed at what was probably the very pinnacle of Roman power and prestige and incorporates the crescent of shops and arcades known as the **Markets of Trajan** (Tues–Sun 9am–7pm; €6.50). Accessible from Via IV Novembre, the Great Hall here is an impressive two-storeyed space, and incorporates a number of finds from the Imperial Forums, including a colossal head of Constantine, a torso of a warrior, part of the temple of the forum of Augustus and a bit of the frieze from Casear's temple of Venus Genetriux – three columns of which still stand in the forum of Caesar across the road, and are viewable from the terrace upstairs. Afterwards descend to the Via Biberatica, whose shops and taverns wind around the bottom of the arcade before climbing to the belvedere for a better view over the forum proper, the most notable remains of which are the column stumps of the massive **Basilica Ulpia**, and the enormous **Column of Trajan** next to it – erected to celebrate the emperor's victories in Dacia (modern Romania) in 112 AD, and covered from top to bottom with reliefs commemorating the highlights of the campaign.

The Roman Forum

The five or so acres that make up the **Roman Forum** were once the heart of the Mediterranean world, and, although the glories of ancient Rome are hard to glimpse here now, there's a symbolic allure to the place, and at certain times of day a desolate drama, that make it one of the most compelling sets of ruins anywhere in the world. You need some imagination and a little history to really appreciate the place but the public spaces are easy enough to discern, especially the spinal **Via Sacra**, the best-known street of ancient Rome, along which victorious emperors and generals would ride in procession to give thanks at the Capitoline's Temple of Juno. Towards the Capitoline Hill end of the Via Sacra, the large cube-shaped building is the **Curia**, built on the orders of Julius Caesar as part of his programme for expanding the Forum, although what you see now is a 3rd-century AD reconstruction. The Senate met here, and inside three wide stairs rise left and right, on which about 300 senators could be accommodated with their folding chairs. Nearby, the **Arch of Septimius Severus** was constructed in the early third century AD by his sons Caracalla and Galba to mark their father's victories in what is now Iran. The friezes on it recall Severus and in particular Caracalla, who ruled Rome with a reign of undisciplined terror for seven years having murdered his brother. Next to the arch, the low brown wall is the **Rostra**, from which important speeches were made (it was from here that Mark Anthony most likely spoke about Caesar after his death), to the left of which are the long stairs of the **Basilica Julia**, built by Julius Caesar in the 50s BC after he returned from the Gallic wars. A bit further along,

▲ Corinthian columns in the Roman Forum

on the right, rails mark the site of the **Lacus Curtius**, the spot where, according to legend, a chasm opened during the earliest days of the city and the sooth-sayers determined that it would only be closed once Rome had sacrificed its most valuable possession into it. Marcus Curtius, a Roman soldier who declared that Rome's most valuable possession was a loyal citizen, hurled himself and his horse into the void and it duly closed. Next to the Basilica Julia, the enormous pile of rubble topped by three graceful Corinthian columns is the **Temple of Castor and Pollux**, dedicated in 484 BC to the divine twins or Dioscuri, who appeared miraculously to ensure victory for the Romans in a key battle. Beyond here, the **House of the Vestal Virgins** is a second-century AD reconstruction of a building originally built by Nero: four floors of rooms around a central courtyard, fringed by the statues or inscribed pedestals of the women themselves, with the round Temple of Vesta at the near end. Almost opposite, across the Via Sacra, a shady walkway to the left leads to the **Basilica of Maxentius**, in terms of size and ingenuity probably the Forum's most impressive remains. Begun by Maxentius, it was continued by his co-emperor and rival, Constantine, after he had defeated him at the Battle of the Milvian Bridge in 312 AD. From here the Via Sacra climbs more steeply to the **Arch of Titus**, built by Titus's brother, Domitian, after the emperor's death in 81 AD, to commemorate his victories in Judea in 70 AD, and his triumphal return from that campaign. It's a long-standing tradition that Jews don't pass under this arch.

The Palatine Hill

Rising above the Roman Forum, the **Palatine Hill** is supposedly where the city of Rome was founded, and is home to some of its most ancient remains. In a way it's a more pleasant site to tour than the Forum, and a good place to have a picnic and relax after the rigours of the ruins below. In the days of the Republic, the Palatine was the most desirable address in Rome (the word "palace" is derived from Palatine), and big names continued to colonize it during the imperial era, trying to outdo each other with ever larger and more magnificent dwellings.

Along the main path up from the Forum, the **Domus Flavia** was once one of the most splendid residences, and, to the left, the top level of the gargantuan **Domus Augustana** spreads to the far brink of the hill – not the home of Augustus as its name suggests, but the private house of any emperor (or "Augustus"). You can look down from here on its vast central courtyard with fountain and wander to the brink of the deep trench of the **Stadium**. On the far side of the stadium, the ruins of the Domus and **Baths of Septimius Severus** cling to the side of the hill, while the large grey building nearby houses the **Museo Palatino**, which contains an assortment of statuary, pottery and architectural fragments that have been excavated on the Palatine during the last 150 years. In the opposite direction from the Domus Flavia is the **Cryptoporticus**, a long passage built by Nero to link the vestibule of his Domus Aurea (see p.695) with the Palatine palaces, and decorated with well-preserved Roman stuccowork at the far end, towards the **House of Livia** – originally believed to have been the residence of Livia, the wife of Augustus, though now identified as simply part of **House of Augustus** – the set of ruins beyond. Climb up the steps by the entrance to the Cryptoporticus and you're in the bottom corner of the **Farnese Gardens**, among the first botanical gardens in Europe, laid out by Cardinal Alessandro Farnese in the mid-sixteenth century and now a tidily planted retreat from the exposed heat of the ruins. At the far end of the gardens are the traces of an **Iron Age village** that perhaps marks the real centre of Rome's ancient beginnings.

The Arch of Constantine

Outside the Colosseum exit of the Forum, the huge **Arch of Constantine** on your right was placed here in the early decades of the fourth century AD after Constantine had consolidated his power as sole emperor. The arch demonstrates the deterioration of the arts during the late stages of the Roman Empire – most of the sculptural decoration here had to be removed from other monuments, and the builders were probably quite ignorant of the significance of the pieces they borrowed: the round medallions are taken from a temple dedicated to the Emperor Hadrian's lover, Antinous, and show Antinous and Hadrian engaged in a hunt. The other pieces, taken from the Forum of Trajan, show Dacian prisoners captured in Trajan's war.

The Colosseum

The **Colosseum** is perhaps Rome's most awe-inspiring ancient monument, an enormous structure that despite the depredations of nearly 2000 years of earthquakes, fires, riots, wars and, not least, plundering for its seemingly inexhaustible supply of ready-cut travertine blocks, still stands relatively intact – a recognizable symbol not just of the city of Rome, but of the entire ancient world. It's not much more than a shell now, eaten away by pollution and cracked by the vibrations of cars and the metro, but the basic structure is easy to see, and has served as a model for stadiums around the world ever since. You'll not be alone in appreciating it and during summer the combination of people and scaffolding can make a visit more like touring a contemporary building-site than an ancient monument. But visit late in the evening or early morning before the tour buses have arrived, and the arena can seem more like the marvel it really is.

Originally known as the Flavian Amphitheatre (the name Colosseum is a much later invention), it was begun around 72 AD by the Emperor Vespasian. Inside, there was room for a total of around 60,000 people seated and 10,000 or so standing. The seating was allocated strictly, with the Emperor and his attendants naturally occupying the best seats in the house, and the social class of the spectators diminishing as you got nearer the top. There was a labyrinth below that was covered with a wooden floor and punctuated at various places for trap doors that could be opened as required, and lifts to raise and lower the animals that were to take part in the games. The floor was covered with canvas to make it waterproof and the canvas was covered with several centimetres of sand to absorb blood; in fact, our word "arena" is derived from the Latin word for sand.

The Celian Hill and San Giovanni

Some of the animals that were to die in the Colosseum were kept in a zoo up on the Celian Hill, just behind the arena, the furthest south of Rome's seven hills and probably still its most peaceful, with the **Villa Celimontana** park at its heart. At its summit, the church of **Santi Giovanni e Paolo** (daily 8.30am–noon & 3.30–6.30pm), marked by its colourful campanile, is dedicated to two government officials who were beheaded here in 316 AD after refusing military service; a railed-off tablet in mid-nave marks the shrine where the saints were martyred and buried. The remains of what is believed to be their house, the **Case Romane**, are around the corner on Clivio di Scauro (Thurs–Mon 10am–1pm & 3–6pm; €6). Around twenty rooms are open in all, patchily frescoed with pagan and Christian subjects, including the *Casa dei Genii*, with winged youths and cupids, and the courtyard or nymphaeum, which has a marvellous fresco of a goddess being attended on.

The road descends from the church and Roman house to the church of **San Gregorio Magno** on the left (daily 8.30am–12.30pm & 3–6.30pm), founded by Saint Gregory who was a monk here before becoming pope in 590 AD. Gregory was an important pope, stabilizing the city after the fall of the empire and effectively establishing the powerful papal role that would endure for the best part of the following 1500 years. Today's rather ordinary interior doesn't really do justice to the historical importance of the church, but the lovely Cosmati floor remains intact, and the chapel of the saint at the end of the south aisle has a beautifully carved bath showing scenes from St Gregory's life along with his marble throne, a beaten-up specimen that actually predates the saint by 500 years.

San Clemente

Down below the Celian Hill, five-minutes' walk from the Colosseum, the church of **San Clemente** is one of the most visited sights of Rome (church: daily 9am–7pm; free; excavations: Mon–Sat 9am–12.30pm & 3–6pm, Sun noon–6pm; €5), a cream-coloured twelfth-century basilica that's a conglomeration of three places of worship, encapsulating perhaps better than any other the continuity of history in the city. The ground-floor church is a superb example of a medieval basilica: its facade and courtyard face east in the archaic fashion, there are some fine, warm mosaics in the apse and – perhaps the highlight of the main church – a chapel with frescoes by Masolino, showing scenes from the life of St Catherine. Downstairs there's the nave of an earlier church, dating to 392 AD, and on a third level a dank Mithraic temple of the late second century where you can see a statue of Mithras slaying the bull and the seats on which the worshippers sat during their ceremonies.

San Giovanni in Laterano and the Scala Santa

At the far end of Via San Giovanni in Laterano, a ten-minute walk form the Colosseum, the basilica of **San Giovanni in Laterano** (daily 7am–6.30pm) is officially Rome's cathedral, the seat of the pope as bishop of Rome, and was for centuries the main papal residence. There has been a church on this site since the fourth century, the first established by Constantine, and the present building, reworked by Borromini in the mid-seventeenth century, evokes Rome's staggering wealth of history, with a host of features from different periods. The doors to the church were taken from the Curia of the Roman Forum, while much of what you see inside dates from 1600, when Clement VIII had the church remodelled for that Holy Year. The first pillar on the left of the right-hand aisle shows a fragment of Giotto's fresco of Boniface VIII, proclaiming the first Holy Year in 1300. Further on, a more recent monument commemorates Sylvester I – "the magician pope", Bishop of Rome during much of Constantine's reign – and incorporates part of his original tomb, said to sweat and rattle its bones when a pope is about to die. Kept secure behind the papal altar are the heads of St Peter and St Paul, the church's prize relics. Outside, the **cloisters** (daily 9am–6pm; €2) are one of the most pleasing parts of the complex, decorated with early thirteenth-century Cosmati work and with fragments of the original basilica arranged around in no particular order. Next door, the **Baptistry** (daily 7am–12.30pm & 4–7.30pm; free) is the oldest surviving baptistry in the Christian world, a mosaic-lined, octagonal structure built during the fifth century that has been the model for many such buildings since. There are more ancient remains on the other side of the church, on Piazza di Porta San Giovanni, foremost of which is the **Scala Santa** (daily: April–Sept 6.15am–noon & 3.30–6.45pm; Oct–March until 6.15pm; free), said to be the staircase from Pontius Pilate's house down which Christ walked after his trial. The 28 steps are protected by boards, and the only way you're allowed to climb them is on your knees, which pilgrims do regularly – although there is also a staircase to the side for the less penitent. At the top, the Sancta Sanctorum or chapel of **San Lorenzo** holds an ancient (sixth- or seventh-century) painting of Christ said to be the work of an angel, hence its name – *acheiropoeton*, or "not done by human hands".

Monti

Immediately north of the Colosseum, the **Esquiline Hill** is the highest and largest of the city's seven hills. Formerly one of the most fashionable residential quarters of ancient Rome, it's nowadays a mixed area that together with the

The Domus Aurea

One of the Esquiline Hill's most intriguing sights is without doubt Nero's **Domus Aurea**, though unfortunately this is currently closed due to flooding and conservation problems. Once covering a vast area between the Palatine and Esquiline, it was built by the Emperor Nero to glorify himself in typical excessive fashion. Rome was accustomed to Nero's excesses, but it had never seen anything like the Golden House before; the facade was supposed to have been coated in solid gold, there was hot and cold running water in the baths, and the grounds held vineyards and game. Nero didn't get to enjoy it for long – he died a couple of years after it was finished, and later emperors were determined to erase it from Rome's cityscape – Vespasian built the Colosseum over the lake and Trajan built his baths on top of the rest of the complex. But when it's open again you can view some of the paintings that so captivated artists when it was rediscovered during the Renaissance.

adjacent Viminale Hill make up the district known as **Monti**, an appealing and to some extent up-and-coming quarter of cobbled streets and neighbourhood bars and restaurants. It's also an area that most travellers to Rome encounter at some point – not just because of key sights like the basilica of Santa Maria Maggiore, but also because of its proximity to Termini, whose environs shelter many of Rome's budget hotels.

San Pietro in Vincoli

Recently restored, **San Pietro in Vincoli** (daily 8am–12.30pm & 3–7pm) is one of Rome's most delightfully plain churches. It was built to house an important relic, the chains (*vincoli*) that bound St Peter when imprisoned in Jerusalem and those that held him in the Mamertine Prison, which miraculously fused together when they were brought into contact with each other. The chains can still be seen in the *confessio* beneath the high altar, but most people come for the tomb of Pope Julius II at the far end of the southern aisle. The tomb occupied Michelangelo on and off for much of his career and was the cause of many a dispute with Julius and his successors. The artist eventually and reluctantly gave it up to paint the Sistine Chapel – the only statues that he managed to complete are the *Moses*, *Leah* and *Rachel*, which remain here, and two *Dying Slaves* (now in the Louvre). The figures are among the artist's most captivating works, especially *Moses*: because of a medieval mistranslation of scripture, he is depicted with satyr's horns instead of the "radiance of the Lord" that Exodus tells us shone around his head. Nonetheless this powerful statue is so lifelike that Michelangelo is alleged to have struck its knee with his hammer and shouted "Speak, damn you!"

Via Cavour and Santa Maria Maggiore

Steps lead down from San Pietro in Vincoli to **Via Cavour**, a busy central thoroughfare that carves a route between the Colosseum and Termini station. After about half a kilometre, the street widens to reveal the basilica of **Santa Maria Maggiore** (daily 7am–7pm; free), one of the city's greatest basilicas, and with one of Rome's best-preserved Byzantine interiors – a fact belied by its dull eighteenth-century exterior. Unlike the other great places of pilgrimage in Rome, Santa Maria Maggiore was not built on any special Constantinian site, but instead went up during the fifth century after the Council of Ephesus recognized the cult of the Virgin, and churches venerating Our Lady began to spring up all over the Christian world. According to legend, the Virgin Mary appeared to Pope Liberius in a dream on the night of August 4, 352 AD, telling him to build a church on the Esquiline Hill, on a spot where he would find a patch of newly fallen snow the next morning. The snow would outline exactly the plan of the church that should be built there in her honour – which of course is exactly what happened, and the first church here was called Santa Maria della Neve ("of the snow"). The present structure dates from about 420 AD, and was completed during the reign of Sixtus III, and survives remarkably intact, the broad nave fringed on both sides with strikingly well-kept mosaics. The chapel in the right transept holds the elaborate tomb of Sixtus V – another, less famous, Sistine Chapel, decorated with frescoes and stucco reliefs portraying events from his reign. Outside this is the tomb of the Bernini family, including Gian Lorenzo himself, while opposite, the Pauline Chapel is home to the tombs of the Borghese pope Paul V and his immediate predecessor Clement VIII. The high altar contains the relics of St Matthew, among other Christian martyrs, but it's the mosaics of the arch that really dazzle, a vivid representation of scenes from the life of Christ. There's a **museum** underneath the basilica that sports what even by Roman standards is a wide variety of relics (daily 9am–6.30pm; €4), and a **loggia** above the main entrance whose thirteenth-century mosaics of the legend "of the snow" are worth seeing (tours daily at 9am & 1pm, bookable in advance; €3).

Santa Prassede
South of Santa Maria Maggiore, off Via Merulana, the ninth-century church of **Santa Prassede** (daily 7am–noon & 4–6.30pm) occupies an ancient site, where it's claimed St Prassede harboured Christians on the run from the Roman persecutions. She apparently collected the blood and remains of the martyrs and placed them in a well where she herself was later buried; a red marble disc in the floor of the nave marks the spot. In the southern aisle, the Chapel of Saint Zeno was built by Pope Paschal I as a mausoleum for his mother, Theodora, and is decorated with marvellous ninth-century mosaics that make it glitter like a jewel-encrusted bowl. The chapel also contains a fragment of a column supposed to be the one to which Christ was tied when he was scourged.

The Pincio and Villa Borghese

The terrace and gardens of the **Pincio**, immediately above Piazza del Popolo, were laid out by Valadier in the early nineteenth century, and, fringed with dilapidated busts of classical and Italian heroes, give fine views over the roofs, domes and TV antennae of central Rome, right across to St Peter's and the Janiculum Hill. Beyond lies Rome's largest central open space, the **Villa Borghese**, made up of the grounds of the seventeenth-century pleasure palace of Scipione Borghese. It's a huge area, with its woods, lakes and lawns offering respite from the bustle of the city centre, and any number of attractions – including some of the city's finest museums – for those who want to do more than just stroll or sunbathe.

Galleria Borghese
Situated on the far eastern edge of the Villa Borghese park is the wonderful **Galleria Borghese** (Tues–Sun 9am–7pm; €8.50; pre-booked visits obligatory, on ☎06.32.810 or ⓦwww.ticketeria.it). Built in the early seventeenth century by Cardinal Scipione Borghese and turned over to the state when the gardens became city property in 1902, today it's one of Rome's great treasure houses and should not be missed.

The **ground floor** contains mainly sculpture: a mixture of ancient Roman items and seventeenth-century works, roughly linked together with late-eighteenth-century ceiling paintings showing scenes from the Trojan War. Highlights include, in the first room off the entrance hall, Canova's famously erotic statue *Paolina Borghese* – sister of Napoleon and married (reluctantly) to the reigning Prince Borghese – posed as Venus. Next door, there's a marvellous statue of *David* by Bernini, the face of which is a self-portrait of the sculptor, and, further on, a dramatic, poised statue of *Apollo and Daphne* that captures the split second when Daphne is transformed into a laurel tree, with her fingers becoming leaves and her legs tree trunks. Next door, the walls of the Room of the Emperors has another Bernini sculpture, *The Rape of Persephone*, dating from 1622, a coolly virtuosic work that shows in melodramatic form the story of the abduction to the underworld of the beautiful nymph Persephone. Finally, the so-called Room of Silenus contains a variety of paintings by Cardinal Scipione's protege Caravaggio, notably the *Madonna of the Grooms* from 1605, a painting that at the time was considered to have depicted Christ far too realistically to hang in a central Rome church. Look also at *St Jerome*, captured writing at a table lit only by a source of light that streams in from the upper left of the picture, and his *David holding the head of Goliath*, sent by Caravaggio to Cardinal Scipione from exile in Malta, where he had fled to escape capital punishment for various crimes, and perhaps the last painting he ever did.

The **upstairs gallery** is literally one of the richest small collections of paintings in the world. In the first room are several important paintings by Raphael, including his *Deposition*, painted in 1507 for a noble of Perugia in memory of her son. Look out also for *Lady with a Unicorn* and *Portrait of a Man* by Perugino, and a copy of the artist's tired-out *Julius II*, painted in the last year of the pope's life, 1513. In further rooms there are more early sixteenth-century paintings; prominent works include Cranach's *Venus and Cupid with a Honeycomb*, Lorenzo Lotto's touching *Portrait of a Man*, and in the opposite direction a series of self-portraits by Bernini at various stages of his long life. Next to these are a lifelike bust of Cardinal Scipione executed by Bernini in 1632, and a smaller bust of Pope Paul V, also by Bernini. Beyond here, in a further room, is a painting of *Diana* by Domechino, depicting the goddess and her attendants doing a bit of target practice, and Titian's *Sacred and Profane Love*, painted in 1514 when he was about 25 years old, to celebrate the marriage of the Venetian noble Nicolò Aurelio.

Galleria Nazionale d'Arte Moderna

The Villa Borghese's two other major museums are situated on the other side of the park, about 1km away along the Viale delle Belle Arti, and of these, the **Galleria Nazionale d'Arte Moderna**, at no. 131 (Tues–Sun 8.30am–7.30pm; €9), is probably the least compulsory; it's a lumbering, Neoclassical building housing a collection of nineteenth- and twentieth-century Italian painting and a few foreign artists. The nineteenth-century collection, on the lower floor, mostly contains the work of the Macchiaioli School of Tuscan impressionists, as well as paintings by Courbet, Cézanne and Van Gogh, while the twentieth-century collection upstairs includes work by Modigliani, De Chirico, Giacomo Balla, Boccione and the Futurists, along with the odd Mondrian and Klimt; there are also some postwar canvases by the likes of Mark Rothko, Jackson Pollock and Cy Twombly, who lived in Rome for much of his life.

Museo Nazionale Etrusco di Villa Giulia

A harmonious collection of courtyards, loggias, gardens and temples put together in a playful Mannerist style for Pope Julius III in the mid-sixteenth century, the Villa Giulia now houses the **Museo Nazionale Etrusco di Villa Giulia** (Tues–Sun 8.30am–7.30pm; €4), the world's primary collection of

Etruscan treasures (along with the Etruscan collection in the Vatican). Not much is known about the Etruscans, but they were a creative and civilized people, evidenced here by a wealth of sensual sculpture, jewellery and art. The most famous exhibit, in the octagonal room in the east wing, is the remarkable *Sarcophagus of the Married Couple* (dating from the sixth century BC) from Cerveteri – a touchingly lifelike portrayal of a husband and wife lying on a couch. Look also at the delicate and beautiful *cistae*, drum-like objects, engraved and adorned with figures, which were supposed to hold all the things needed for the care of the body after death. In the same room are marvellously intricate pieces of gold jewellery, delicately worked into tiny horses, birds, camels and other animals, as well as mirrors, candelabra, religious statues and tools used in everyday life, including a realistic bronze statuette of a ploughman at work. Further on you'll find a drinking horn in the shape of a dog's head that is so lifelike you almost expect it to bark; a *holmos*, or small table, to which the maker attached 24 little pendants around the edge; and a bronze disc breastplate from the seventh century BC decorated with a weird, almost modern abstract pattern of galloping creatures.

The Aventine and Testaccio

The area south of the Forum and Palatine has some of the city's most compelling Christian and ancient sights, from the relatively central **Circo Massimo** and **Baths of Caracalla** to the famous **catacombs** on the fringe of the city on Via Appia Antica. It also has one of Rome's leafiest and most peaceful corners in the **Aventine Hill**, along with its funkiest neighbourhoods in gentrified **Testaccio** and up-and-coming **Ostiense**.

Circo Massimo and the Aventine Hill

On its southern side, the Palatine Hill drops down to the **Circo Massimo**, a long, thin, green expanse bordered by heavily trafficked roads that was the ancient city's main venue for chariot races, and at one time this arena had a capacity of up to 400,000 spectators. On the far side of the Circo Massimo is the **Aventine Hill**, the southernmost of the city's seven hills and the heart of plebeian Rome in ancient times. These days the working-class quarters of the city are further south, and the Aventine is in fact one of the city's more upmarket residential areas, covered with villas and gardens and one of the few places in the city where you can escape the traffic. A short way up Via Santa Sabina, the church of **Santa Sabina** (daily 6.30am–12.45pm & 4–7pm) is a strong contender for Rome's most beautiful basilica: high and wide, its nave and portico were restored back to their fifth-century appearance in the 1930s. Look especially at the main doors, which boast eighteen panels carved with Christian scenes, forming a complete illustrated Bible that includes one of the oldest representations of the Crucifixion in existence. Santa Sabina is also the principal church of the Dominicans, and it's claimed that the orange trees in the garden outside, which you can glimpse on your way to the restrained cloister, are descendants of those planted by St Dominic himself. Whatever the truth of this, the views from the gardens are splendid – right across the Tiber to the centre of Rome and St Peter's.

The Baths of Caracalla

Across the far side of Piazza di Porta Capena, the **Baths of Caracalla**, Viale Terme di Caracalla 52 (Mon 9am–2pm, Tues–Sun 9am to 1hr before sunset; €6), are much better preserved and give a far better sense of the scale and monumentality of Roman architecture than most of the extant ruins in the city – so much so that Shelley was moved to write *Prometheus Unbound* here in 1819. The baths are no more than a shell now, but the walls still rise to very nearly their original height. There are many fragments of mosaics – none spectacular, but quite a few bright and well preserved – and it's easy to discern a floor plan. As for Caracalla, he was one of Rome's worst rulers, and it's no wonder there's nothing else in the city built by him. Nowadays the baths are used for occasional opera performances during the summer – one of Mussolini's better ideas.

Testaccio

Across the Aventine, on the far side of Via Marmorata, the solid working-class neighbourhood of **TESTACCIO** groups around a couple of main squares, a tight-knit community with a market and a number of bars and small trattorias that was for many years synonymous with the slaughterhouse that sprawls down to the Tiber just beyond. In recent years the area has become a trendy place to live, property prices have soared, and some uneasy contradictions have emerged, with vegetarian restaurants opening their doors in an area still known for the offal dishes served in its traditional trattorias, and gay and alternative clubs standing cheek-by-jowl with the car-repair shops gouged into Monte Testaccio.

The slaughterhouse, or **Mattatoio**, once the area's main employer, is used for concerts, raves and exhibitions now, along with stabling for the city's horse-and-carriage drivers and a branch of the **Museum of Contemporary Art of Rome**, where a couple of pavilions stage temporary exhibitions of a radical and adventurous nature. Opposite, **Monte Testaccio** gives the area its name, a 35-metre-high mound created out of the shards of Roman amphorae that were dumped here. It's an odd sight, the ceramic curls visible through the tufts of grass that crown its higher reaches, with bars and restaurants hollowed out of the slopes below.

The Protestant Cemetery

Via Zabaglia leads from Monte Testaccio to Via Caio Cestio, a left turn up which takes you to the entrance of the **Protestant Cemetery** (Mon–Sat 9am–5pm, Sun 9am–1pm; donation expected), one of the shrines to the English in Rome and a fitting conclusion to a visit to the Keats-Shelley Memorial House, since it is here that both poets are buried, along with a handful of other well-known names. In fact, the cemetery's title is a misnomer – the cemetery is reserved for non-Roman Catholics so you'll also find famous Italian atheists, Christians of the Orthodox persuasion, and the odd Jew or Muslim buried here. Most visitors come here to see the grave of Keats, who lies next to his friend, the painter Joseph Severn, in the furthest corner of the less crowded, older part of the cemetery, his stone inscribed as he wished with the words "Here lies one whose name was writ in water." Severn died much later than Keats but asked to be laid here nonetheless, together with his brushes and palette. Shelley's ashes were brought here at Mary Shelley's request and interred in the newer part of the cemetery. Among other famous internees, Edward Trelawny, friend and literary associate of Byron and Shelley, lies next to him, the political writer and activist, Gramsci, on the far right-hand side in the middle, to name just two – though if you're at all interested in star-spotting you should ask to have a look at the English booklet at the entrance.

The Piramide Cestia

The most distinctive landmark in this part of town is the mossy pyramidal tomb of one **Caius Cestius**, who died in 12 BC. Cestius had spent some time in

▲ Life and death in the Protestant Cemetery

Egypt, and part of his will decreed that all his slaves should be freed – the white pyramid you see today was thrown up by them in only 330 days of what must have been joyful building. It's open to the public on the second and fourth Saturday of each month, though you can visit the cats who live here, and the volunteers who care for them, any afternoon between 2.30pm and 4.30pm.

Centrale Montemartini

It's a ten-minute walk south down Via Ostiense to the former electricity generating station of **Centrale Montemartini** at Via Ostiense 106 (Tues–Sun 9am–7pm; €4.50, €8.50 for Capitoline Museums as well, valid 7 days), which was requisitioned to display the cream of the Capitoline Museums' sculpture while the main buildings were being renovated. It became so popular that it's now a permanent outpost, attracting visitors south to the formerly industrial area of Ostiense. The huge rooms of the power station are ideally suited to showing ancient sculpture, although checking out the massive turbines and furnaces has a fascination of its own, and more than competes for your attention. Among many compelling objects, there are the head, feet and an arm from a colossal statue, once 8m high, found in Largo Argentina; a large Roman copy of *Athena*; a fragmented mosaic of hunting scenes; and an amazingly naturalistic statue of a girl seated on a stool with her legs crossed, from the third century BC. There's also a figure of *Hercules* and next to it the soft *Muse Polymnia*, the former braced for activity, the latter leaning on a rock and staring thoughtfully into the distance.

San Paolo fuori le Mura

Two kilometres or so south of the Porta San Paolo, the basilica of **San Paolo fuori le Mura** (summer daily 7am–7pm; winter until 6pm), accessible on metro line B, is one of the four patriarchal basilicas of Rome, occupying the supposed site of St Paul's tomb, where he was laid to rest after being beheaded nearby. Of the four, this basilica has probably fared the least well over the years, and a devastating fire in 1823 means that the church you see now is largely a nineteenth-century reconstruction. For all that, it's a very successful rehash of the former church, and it's impossible not to be awed by the space of the building inside. Some parts of the building did survive the fire. In the south transept, the paschal candlestick is a remarkable piece of Romanesque carving, supported by half-human beasts and rising through entwined tendrils and strangely human limbs and bodies to scenes from Christ's life. The bronze aisle doors date from 1070 and were also rescued from the old basilica, as was the thirteenth-century tabernacle by Arnolfo di Cambio. The arch across the apse is original, too, embellished with mosaics donated by the Byzantine queen Galla Placidia in the sixth century. There's also the cloister, just behind here – probably Rome's finest piece of Cosmatesque work, its spiralling, mosaic-encrusted columns enclosing a peaceful rose garden.

Via Appia Antica: the catacombs

Starting at the Porta San Sebastiano, the **Via Appia Antica** is the most famous of Rome's consular roads that used to strike out in every direction from the ancient city. It was built by one Appio Claudio in 312 BC, and is the only Roman landmark mentioned in the Bible. During classical times it was the most important of all the Roman trade routes, carrying supplies through Campania to the port of Brindisi, and it remains an important part of early Christian Rome, its verges lined with numerous pagan and Christian sites, including most famously the underground burial cemeteries or catacombs of the first Christians. The best way to get to Via Appia Antica is by bus – take #118 from Piazzale Ostiense, #218 from Piazza Porta San Giovanni or #660 from Colli Albani metro station (on line A).

About 500m from Porta San Sebastiano, where the road forks, the church of **Domine Quo Vadis** is the first obvious sight on Via Appia. Legend has it this is where St Peter had a vision of Christ fleeing from Rome and asked "Where goest thou, Lord?" (*Domine quo vadis?*), to which Christ replied that he was going to be crucified once more, leading Peter to turn around and accept his fate. The small church is ordinary enough inside, except for its replica of a piece of marble that is said to be marked with the footprints of Christ (the original is in the church of San Sebastiano, see below).

Continuing on for 1km or so, the **Catacombs of San Callisto** (Thurs–Tues 9am–noon & 2–5pm; €5) are the largest of Rome's catacombs, founded in the second century AD; many of the early popes (of whom St Callisto was one) are buried here. The site also features some well-preserved seventh- and eighth-century frescoes, and the crypt of Santa Cecilia, who was buried here after her martyrdom, before being shifted to the church dedicated to her in Trastevere.

The **Catacombs of San Sebastiano**, 500m further on (Mon–Sat 9am–noon & 2.30–5pm; €5), are situated under a basilica that was originally built by Constantine on the spot where the bodies of the apostles Peter and Paul are said to have been laid for a time. Tours take in paintings of doves and fish, a contemporary carved oil lamp and inscriptions dating the tombs themselves. The most striking features, however, are not Christian at all, but three pagan tombs (one painted, two stuccoed) discovered when archeologists were burrowing beneath the floor of the basilica upstairs.

Trastevere

Across the river from the centre of town, on the right bank of the Tiber, the district of **TRASTEVERE** was the artisan area of the city in classical times, neatly placed for the trade that came upriver from Ostia to be unloaded nearby. Outside the city walls, Trastevere (the name means "across the Tiber") was for centuries heavily populated by immigrants, and this separation lent the neighbourhood a strong identity that lasted well into the twentieth century. Nowadays it's a long way from the working-class quarter it used to be, often thronged with tourists, lured by the charm of its narrow streets and closeted squares. However, it is among the most pleasant places to stroll in Rome, particularly peaceful in the morning, lively come the evening, as dozens of trattorias set tables out along the cobblestone streets, and still buzzing late at night when its bars and clubs provide a focus for one of Rome's most dyanamic night-time scenes.

Santa Cecilia in Trastevere

One of Trastevere's most intriguing attractions is the church of **Santa Cecilia in Trastevere** (daily 9.30am–1pm & 4–7.30pm), whose antiseptic eighteenth-century appearance belies its historical associations. A church was originally built here over the site of the second-century home of St Cecilia, whose husband Valerian was executed for refusing to worship Roman gods and who herself was subsequently persecuted for Christian beliefs. The story has it that Cecilia was locked in the caldarium of her own baths for several days but refused to die, singing her way through the ordeal (Cecilia is patron saint of music). Her head was finally half hacked off with an axe, though it took several blows before she finally succumbed. Below the high altar, Stefano Maderno's limp statue of the saint shows her incorruptible body as it was found when exhumed in 1599, with three deep cuts in her neck. Downstairs, excavations of the baths and the rest of the Roman house are on view in the crypt, but more alluring by far is the singing gallery above the nave of the church (Mon–Sat 10.15am–12.15pm, Sun 11.30am–12.30pm; ring the bell to the left of the church door to get in), where Pietro Cavallini's late-thirteenth-century fresco of the *Last Judgement* – all that remains of the decoration that once covered the entire church – is a powerful, amazingly naturalistic piece of work for its time.

Santa Maria in Trastevere

The heart of Trastevere is really **Piazza Santa Maria in Trastevere**, a large square that takes its name from the church of **Santa Maria in Trastevere** in its northwest corner (daily 7.30am–9pm). This is supposed to have been the first Christian place of worship in Rome, built on a site where a fountain of oil is said to have sprung on the day of Christ's birth, and the church's mosaics are among the city's most impressive, Byzantine-inspired works in the apse

Porta Portese flea market

Trastevere at its most disreputable but also most characteristic can be witnessed on Sunday, when the **Porta Portese flea market** stretches down from the Porta Portese gate down Via Portuense to Trastevere train station in a congested medley of antiques, old motor spares, cheap clothing, trendy clothing, cheap *and* trendy clothing, household goods, bric-a-brac and antiques and assorted junk. Come early if you want to buy, or even move – most of the bargains, not to mention the stolen goods, have gone by 10am, by which time the crush of people can be intense.

depicting a solemn yet sensitive parade of saints thronged around Christ and Mary, while underneath a series of panels shows scenes from the life of the Virgin by the painter Pietro Cavallini. Beneath the high altar on the right, an inscription – "FONS OLEI" – marks the spot where the oil is supposed to have sprung up.

Galleria Nazionale di Palazzo Corsini

Cutting north through the backstreets towards the Tiber, you'll come to the **Galleria Nazionale d'Arte di Palazzo Corsini** at Via della Lungara 10 (Tues–Sun 8.30am–7.30pm; €4), an unexpected cultural attraction on this side of the river. It's a relatively small collection, and only takes up a few rooms of the giant palace, which was a fitting final home for Queen Christina of Sweden, who renounced Protestantism and with it the Swedish throne in 1655, bringing her library and fortune to Rome, to the delight of the Chigi pope, Alexander VII. Among the highlights are works by Rubens, Van Dyck, Guido Reni and Caravaggio, and the curious Corsini Throne, thought to be a Roman copy of an Etruscan throne of the second or first century. Cut out of marble, its back is carved with warriors in armour and helmets, below which is a boar hunt, with wild boars the size of horses pursued by hunters.

Villa Farnesina

Across the road from the Palazzo Corsini is the **Villa Farnesina** (Mon–Sat 9am–1pm; €5), built during the early sixteenth century for the banker Agostino Chigi, and one of the earliest Renaissance villas, with opulent rooms decorated with frescoes by some of the masters of the period. Most people come to view the Raphael-designed painting *Cupid and Psyche* in the now glassed-in loggia, completed in 1517 by the artist's assistants. The painter and art historian Vasari claims Raphael didn't complete the work because his infatuation with his mistress – "La Fornarina", whose father's bakery was situated nearby – was making it difficult to concentrate. Nonetheless it's mightily impressive: a flowing, animated work bursting with muscular men and bare-bosomed women. He did, however, apparently manage to finish the *Galatea* in the room next door, whose bucolic country scenes are interspersed with Galatea on her scallop-shell chariot and a giant head once said to have been painted by Michelangelo in one of the lunettes. The ceiling illustrates Chigi's horoscope constellations, frescoed by the architect of the building, Peruzzi, who also decorated the upstairs Salone delle Prospettive, where trompe l'oeil balconies give views onto contemporary Rome – one of the earliest examples of the technique.

The Janiculum Hill

It's about a fifteen-minute walk up Via Garibaldi from the centre of Trastevere to the summit of the Janiculum Hill – not one of the original seven hills of Rome, but the one with the best and most accessible views of the centre. Follow Vicolo del Cedro from Via della Scala and take the steps up from the end, cross the main road, and continue on the steps that lead up the hill to the Passeggiata del Gianicolo and then to **Piazzale Garibaldi**. Just below here is the spot from which a cannon is fired at noon each day for Romans to check their watches, and spread out before you are some of the best views in Rome, taking in pretty much the whole of the city.

The Vatican

Situated on the west bank of the Tiber, just across from the city centre, the **Vatican City** was established as a sovereign state in 1929, a tiny territory surrounded by high walls on its far western side and on the near side opening its doors to the rest of the city and its pilgrims in the form of St Peter's and its colonnaded piazza. The city-state's one thousand inhabitants have their own radio station, daily newspaper, postal service, and indeed security service in the colourfully dressed Swiss Guards. It's believed that St Peter was buried in a pagan cemetery on the Vatican hill, giving rise to the building of a basilica to venerate his name and the siting of the headquarters of the Catholic Church here. St Peter's is obviously one of the highlights, but the only part of the Vatican Palace itself that you can visit independently is the Vatican Museums – quite simply, the largest, richest, most compelling and perhaps most exhausting museum complex in the world.

Castel Sant'Angelo

The great circular hulk of the **Castel Sant'Angelo** (Tues–Sun 9am–6.30pm; €8.50) marks the edge of the Vatican, designed and built by Hadrian as his own mausoleum. Renamed in the sixth century, when Pope Gregory the Great witnessed a vision of St Michael here that ended a terrible plague, the papal authorities converted the building for use as a fortress and built a passageway to link it with the Vatican as a refuge in times of siege or invasion. Inside, a spiral ramp leads up into the centre of the mausoleum, over a drawbridge, to the main level at the top, where a small palace was built to house the papal residents in appropriate splendour. Pope Paul III had some especially fine renovations made, including the beautiful Sala Paolina, whose gilded ceiling displays the Farnese family arms. You'll also notice Paul III's personal motto, *Festina Lenta* ("make haste slowly"), scattered throughout the ceilings and in various corners of all his rooms. Elsewhere, the rooms hold swords, armour, guns and the like, some lavishly decorated (don't miss the bathroom of Clement VII on the second floor, with its prototype hot and cold water taps and mildly erotic frescoes). Below are dungeons and storerooms that can be glimpsed from the spiralling ramp, testament to the castle's grisly past as the city's most notorious Renaissance prison.

Piazza San Pietro

Perhaps the most famous of Rome's many piazzas, Bernini's **Piazza San Pietro** doesn't disappoint, although its size isn't really apparent until you're right on top of it, its colonnade arms symbolically welcoming the world into the lap of the Catholic Church. The obelisk in the centre was brought to Rome by Caligula in 36 AD, and was moved here in 1586, when Sixtus V ordered that it be erected in front of the basilica, a task that took four months and was apparently done in silence, on pain of death. The matching fountains on either side are the work of Carlo Maderno (on the right) and Bernini (on the left). In between the obelisk and each fountain, a circular stone set into the pavement marks the focal points of an ellipse, from which the four rows of columns on the perimeter of the piazza line up perfectly, making the colonnade appear to be supported by a single line of columns.

Basilica di San Pietro

The Basilica di San Pietro, better known to many as **St Peter's** (daily: April–Sept 7am–7pm; Oct–March 7am–6pm), is the principal shrine of the Catholic Church, built on the site of St Peter's tomb, and worked on by the greatest Italian architects of the sixteenth and seventeenth centuries. One of the channels on the right side of the piazza funnels you into the basilica (the other two lead to the underground grottoes or the ascent to the dome – see p.706).

▲ Inside St Peter's

Bear in mind that whichever you opt for first, you need to be **properly dressed** to enter, which means no bare knees or shoulders – a rule that is very strictly enforced.

Going straight into the **church**, the first thing you see is Michelangelo's graceful pietà on the right, completed when he was just 24. Following an attack by a vandal, it sits behind glass, strangely remote from the life of the rest of the building. Further into the church, the dome is breathtakingly imposing, rising high above the supposed site of St Peter's tomb. With a diameter of 41.5 metres it is Rome's largest dome, supported by four enormous piers, decorated with reliefs depicting the basilica's so-called "major relics": St Veronica's handkerchief, which was used to wipe the face of Christ; the lance of St Longinus, which pierced Christ's side; and a piece of the True Cross. On the right side of the nave, the bronze statue of St Peter is another of the most venerated monuments in the basilica, its right foot polished smooth by the attentions of pilgrims. Bronze was also the material used in Bernini's wild spiralling baldacchino, a massive 26m high, cast out of 927 tonnes of metal removed from the Pantheon roof in 1633. Bernini's feverish sculpting decorates the apse, too, his bronze *Cattedra* enclosing the supposed chair of St Peter, though more interesting is his monument to Alexander VII in the south transept, with its winged skeleton struggling underneath the heavy marble drapes, upon which the Chigi pope is kneeling in prayer.

An entrance off the aisle leads to the **treasury** (daily: summer 9am–6.15pm; winter 9am–5.15pm; €6), which has among many riches the late-fifteenth-century bronze tomb of Pope Sixtus IV by Pollaiuolo. The **grottoes** (daily: summer 9am–6pm; winter 9am–5pm), which you can opt to visit first outside, emerging in the basilica at the central crossing, is where a good number of popes are buried, including the last one, John Paul II. Also accessible by one of three main outside entrances, the ascent to the **roof and dome** (daily: April–Sept 8am–5pm; Oct–March 8am–4pm; €7 with lift, €5 using the stairs) is well worth making. The views from the gallery around the interior of the dome give you a sense of the enormity of the church, and from there you can make the (challenging) ascent to the lantern at the top of the dome, from which the views over the city are as glorious as you'd expect.

The Vatican Museums

If you've found any of Rome's other museums disappointing, the **Vatican Museums**, on Viale Vaticano, a fifteen-minute walk from St Peter's, out of the north side of Piazza San Pietro (Mon–Sat 8.30am–4pm; closed Sun, hols & religious hols, except the last Sun of each month when admission is free; €14; Ⓦ www.vatican.va), are probably the reason why. So much booty from the city's history has ended up here, from both classical and later times, and so many of the Renaissance's finest artists were in the employ of the pope, that not surprisingly the result is a set of museums stuffed with enough exhibits to put most other European collections to shame.

As its name suggests, the complex actually holds a series of museums on very diverse subjects – displays of classical statuary, Renaissance painting, Etruscan relics, Egyptian artefacts, not to mention the furnishings and decoration of the building itself. There's no point in trying to see everything, at least not on one visit, and the only features you really shouldn't miss are the Raphael Stanze and the Sistine Chapel. Above all, decide how long you want to spend here, and what you want to see, before you start; you could spend anything from an hour to a whole day here, and it's easy to collapse from museum fatigue before you've even got to your most important target of interest. Also, bear in mind that the collections are in a constant state of restoration, and are often closed and shifted around with little or no notice – so check the website above.

Museo Pio-Clementino

To the left of the entrance, the **Museo Pio-Clementino** is home to some of the best of the Vatican's classical statuary, including two statues that influenced Renaissance artists more than any others, the serene *Apollo Belvedere*, a Roman copy of a fourth-century BC original, and the first century BC *Laocoön*, which shows a Trojan priest being crushed by serpents for warning of the danger of the Trojan horse – perhaps the most famous classical statue ever. There are also busts and statues of the Roman emperors, fantastic Roman floor mosaics, and the so-called *Venus of Cnidos*, the first known representation of the goddess.

Museo Gregoriano Egizio

The **Museo Gregoriano Egizio** isn't one of the Vatican's main highlights, but it has a distinguished collection of ancient Egyptian artefacts, including some vividly painted mummy cases (and two mummies), along with *canopi*, the alabaster vessels into which the entrails of the deceased were placed. There's also a partial reconstruction of the Temple of Serapis from Hadrian's Villa near Tivoli, along with another statue of his lover, Antinous, who drowned close to the original temple in Egypt and so inspired Hadrian to build his replica.

Museo Gregoriano Etrusco

The **Museo Gregoriano Etrusco** holds sculpture, funerary art and applied art from the sites of southern Etruria – a good complement to Rome's specialist Etruscan collection in the Villa Giulia. Especially worth seeing are the finds from the Regolini-Galassi tomb, from the seventh century BC, discovered near Cerveteri, which contained the remains of three Etruscan nobles, two men and a woman; the breastplate of the woman and her huge *fibia* (clasp) are of gold. There's also armour, a bronze bedstead, a funeral chariot and a wagon, as well as a great number of enormous storage jars, in which food, oil and wine were stored for use in the afterlife.

Galleria dei Candelabri, Galleria degli Arazzi and Galleria delle Carte Geografiche

Outside the Etruscan Museum, a large monumental staircase leads back down to the **Galleria dei Candelabri**, the niches of which are adorned with huge candelabra taken from imperial Roman villas, and the **Galleria degli Arazzi** (Gallery of Tapestries) has Belgian tapestries to designs by the school of Raphael. Next, the **Galleria delle Carte Geografiche** (Gallery of Maps), which is as long as the previous two galleries put together, was decorated in the late sixteenth century at the behest of Pope Gregory XIII to show all of Italy, the major islands in the Mediterranean, the papal possessions in France, as well as large-scale maps of the maritime republics of Venice and Genoa.

Braccio Nuovo and Museo Chiaramonti

The **Braccio Nuovo** and **Museo Chiaramonti** both hold classical sculpture, although be warned that they are the Vatican at its most overwhelming – close on a thousand statues crammed into two long galleries. The Braccio Nuovo was built in the early 1800s to display classical statuary that was particularly prized, and it contains, among other things, probably the most famous extant image of Augustus, and a bizarre-looking statue depicting the Nile, whose yearly flooding was essential to the fertility of the Egyptian soil. The 300-metre-long Chiaramonti gallery is especially unnerving, lined as it is with the chill marble busts of hundreds of nameless, blank-eyed ancient Romans, along with the odd deity. It pays to have a leisurely wander, for there are some real characters here: sour, thin-lipped matrons; kids, caught in a sulk or mid-chortle; and ancient old men with flesh sagging and wrinkling.

Raphael Stanze (Raphael Rooms)

The **Raphael Rooms** formed the private apartments of Pope Julius II, and when he moved in here he commissioned Raphael to redecorate them in a style more in tune with the times. Raphael died in 1520 before the scheme was complete, but the two rooms that were painted by him, as well as others completed by pupils, stand as one of the highlights of the Renaissance. The Stanza di Eliodoro, the first room you come to, was painted by three of Raphael's students five years after his death, and is best known for its painting the *Mass of Bolsena* which relates a miracle that occurred in the town in northern Lazio in the 1260s, and, on the window wall opposite, the *Deliverance of St Peter*, showing the saint being assisted in a jail-break by the Angel of the Lord. The other main room, the Stanza della Segnatura or pope's study, was painted in the years 1508–11, when Raphael first came to Rome, and comes close to the peak of the painter's art. The *School of Athens*, on the near wall as you come in, steals the show, a representation of the triumph of scientific truth in which all the great minds from antiquity are represented. It pairs with the *Disputation of the Sacrament* opposite, which is a reassertion of religious dogma – an allegorical mass of popes, cardinals, bishops, doctors and even the poet Dante.

The Appartamento Borgia

Outside the Raphael Stanze, the **Appartamento Borgia** was inhabited by Julius II's hated predecessor, Alexander VI, and is nowadays host to a large collection of modern religious art, although its ceiling frescoes, the work of Pinturicchio in the years 1492–95, are really the main reason to visit.

The Sistine Chapel

Steps lead from the Raphael Rooms to the **Sistine Chapel**, a huge barn-like structure that serves as the pope's official private chapel and the scene of the conclaves of cardinals for the election of each new pontiff. The ceiling frescoes here, and painting of the *Last Judgement* on the altar wall, are probably the most viewed paintings in the world: it's estimated that on an average day about 15,000 people trudge through here to take a look. It's useful to carry a pair of binoculars with you to view the ceiling, but bear in mind that photography is strictly prohibited and it's also officially forbidden to speak – a rule that is rampantly ignored.

The walls of the chapel were decorated by several prominent painters of the Renaissance – Pinturicchio, Perugino, Botticelli and Ghirlandaio. Recently restored, they would be a massive highlight anywhere else. As it is, they are

---

Julius II and the painting of the Sistine Chapel ceiling

The pope responsible for the Sistine Chapel ceiling, **Julius II**, was an avid patron of the arts, and he appointed Michelangelo to decorate the Sistine Chapel in 1508. Oddly enough, Michelangelo hadn't wanted to do the work at all: he considered himself a sculptor, not a painter, and was more eager to get on with carving Julius II's tomb (now in San Pietro in Vincoli). The pope, however, had other plans, drawing up a design of the twelve Apostles for the vault and hiring Bramante to design a scaffold for the artist from which to work. Michelangelo was apparently an awkward, solitary character: he had barely begun painting when he rejected Bramante's scaffold as unusable, fired all his staff, and dumped the pope's scheme for the ceiling in favour of his own. But the pope was easily his match, and there are tales of the two men clashing while the work was going on – Michelangelo would lock the doors at crucial points, ignoring the pope's demands to see how it was progressing – and legend has the two men at loggerheads at the top of the scaffold one day, resulting in the pope striking the artist in frustration.

Julius II lived only a few months after the ceiling was finished, but the fame of the work he had commissioned soon spread far and wide. The restorers have been able to chart the progress of Michelangelo as he moved across the vault. Images on fresco must be completed before the plaster dries, and each day a fresh layer of plaster would have been laid, on which Michelangelo would have had around eight hours or so before having to finish for the day. Comparing the different areas of plaster, it seems the figure of Adam, in the key *Creation of Adam* scene, took just four days; God, in the same fresco, took three days. You can also see the development of Michelangelo as a painter when you look at the paintings in reverse order. The first painting, over the door, the *Drunkenness of Noah*, is done in a stiff and formal style, and is vastly different from the last painting he did, over the altar, *The Creation of Light*, which shows the artist at his best, the perfect master of the technique of fresco painting.

entirely overshadowed by Michelangelo's more famous **ceiling frescoes**, commissioned by Pope Julius II in 1508. They depict scenes from the Old Testament, from the *Creation of Light* at the altar end to the *Drunkenness of Noah* over the door. Entering from behind the altar, you are supposed, as you look up, to imagine that you are looking into heaven through the arches of the fictive architecture that springs from the sides of the chapel, supported by little putti caryatids and *ignudi* or nudes. Look at the pagan sibyls and biblical prophets which Michelangelo also incorporated in his scheme – some of the most dramatic figures in the entire work, and all clearly labelled by the painter, from the sensitive figure of the Delphic Sybil, to the hag-like Cumaean Sybil. Look out, too, for the figure of the prophet Jeremiah – a brooding self-portrait of an exhausted-looking Michelangelo. The **Last Judgement**, on the altar wall of the chapel, was painted by the artist more than twenty years later. Michelangelo wasn't especially keen to work on this either, but Pope Paul III, an old acquaintance, was eager to complete the decoration of the chapel. The painting took five years, again single-handed, and is probably the most inspired and homogeneous large-scale painting you're ever likely to see, the technical virtuosity of Michelangelo taking a back seat to the sheer exuberance of the work. The centre is occupied by Christ, turning angrily as he gestures the condemned to the underworld. St Peter, carrying his gold and silver keys, looks on in astonishment, while Mary averts her eyes from the scene. Below Christ a group of angels blast their trumpets to summon the dead from their sleep. On the left, the dead awaken from graves, tombs and sarcophagi and are levitating into the heavens or being pulled by ropes and the napes of their necks by angels who take them before Christ. At the bottom right, Charon, keeper of the underworld, swings his oar at the damned souls as they fall off the boat into the waiting gates of hell.

The Pinacoteca

The **Pinacoteca** is housed in a separate building on the far side of the Vatican Museums' main spine and ranks highly among Rome's picture galleries, with works from the early to High Renaissance right up to the nineteenth century. Among early works is the stunning Simoneschi triptych by Giotto, the *Martyrdom of Sts Peter and Paul*, painted in the early 1300s for the old St Peter's, Masolino, Fra Angelico and Fra'Filippo Lippi, and Melozzo de Forlí's musical angels – fragments of a fresco commissioned for the church of Santi Apostoli. Further on are the rich backdrops and elegantly clad figures of the Umbrian School painters, Perugino and Pinturicchio. Raphael has a room to himself, where you'll find his *Transfiguration*, which he had nearly completed when he died in 1520, the *Coronation of the Virgin*, done when he was only 19 years old, and, on the left, the *Madonna of Foglino*, showing saints John the Baptist, Francis of Assisi, and Jerome. Leonardo's *St Jerome*, in the next room, is a remarkable piece of work with the saint a rake-like ascetic torn between suffering and a good meal, while Caravaggio's *Descent from the Cross*, in the next room but one, is a warts-and-all canvas that unusually shows the Virgin Mary as a middle-aged mother grieving over her dead son. Take a look also at the most gruesome painting in the collection, Poussin's *Martyrdom of St Erasmus*, which shows the saint stretched out on a table with his hands bound above his head in the process of having his small intestine wound onto a drum – basically being "drawn" prior to "quartering".

The Musei Gregoriano Profano, Pio Cristiano and Missionario Etnologico

Next door to the Pinacoteca, the **Museo Gregoriano Profano** holds more classical sculpture, mounted on scaffolds for all-round viewing, and the adjacent

Museo Pio Cristiano has intricate early Christian sarcophagi. Below these, the **Museo Missionario Etnologico** displays art and artefacts from the far east, collected by Catholic missionaries.

Eating and drinking

Rome is a great place to **eat**: its denizens know a good deal about freshness and authenticity, and can be very demanding when it comes to the quality of the dishes they are served. Consequently, eating out is a major, often hours-long, activity, and the meals you'll enjoy generally range from good to truly remarkable. Most city-centre **restaurants** offer standard Italian menus, with the emphasis on traditional Roman dishes, although a few more adventurous places have been popping up of late; plus there are numerous establishments dedicated to a variety of regional cuisines, and a reasonable number of ethnic restaurants. The city is also blessed with an abundance of good **pizzerias**, churning out thin, crispy-baked pizza from wood-fired ovens.

Coffee, snacks and lunch spots

Rome has plenty of places in which to refuel during a long day's sightseeing, and it's easy to find places that aren't just targeted at tourists. Most bars sell panini and *tramezzini*, and there are plenty of stand-up *rosticerrie* for roast chicken and the like. The following are some of our favourite places for a good-quality, unpretentious **lunch or snack**, but if you just want an ice cream or milk shake, also see box opposite.

Centro storico

Camilloni Piazza Sant'Eustachio 54
℡06.686.4995. Bus #63 or #492. The rival for Rome's best coffee with *Sant'Eustachio* across the square, and with great cakes, sandwiches and some hot food. Tues–Sun 8.30am–midnight.

Enoteca Corsi Via del Gesú 87–88. Old-fashioned trattoria and wine shop that serves up only what they happen to have cooked that morning. Lunch only, and costing around €7.50 for a main course.

Lo Zozzone Via del Teatro Pace 32. This Rome legend, just around the corner from Piazza Navona and with outside seating, serves the best *pizza bianca* in town, by general consent – as well as lots of delicious *pizza al taglio* choices. Mon–Fri 9am–9pm, Sat 10am–11pm.

Campo de' Fiori

Bernasconi Piazza Cairoli 16. Great, long-established pasticceria and café with *sfogiatelle* (flaky, custard-filled pastries) to die for and a host of other goodies.

Il Forno di Campo de' Fiori Campo de' Fiori 22. Great bakery in the corner of Campo de'Fiori that does all sorts of baked goodies, including fantastic *pizza al taglio*.

Tridente and Quirinale

Dagnino Galleria Esedra, Via E.Orlando 75
℡06.481.8660. Good for both a coffee and snack or light lunch, this long-established Sicilian bakery is a peaceful retreat in the Termini area, with tables outside on a small shopping arcade.

Pizzeria-Tavola Calda Piazzale Flaminia. Right by the #2 tram stop outside the Porta del Popolo, the *pizza al taglio*, roast chicken, roast potatoes and various *fritti* items at this long-established *tavola calda* are a godsend in a part of town lacking in good snack places. A few tables outside, too, though it's not the quietest place to eat.

Monti

Antico Caffé di Brasile Via dei Serpenti 23. Reliable old Monti stand-by that has been selling great coffee, sandwiches, snacks and cakes for over a century.

Enoteca Cavour 313 Via Cavour 313. This lovely old wine bar makes a handy retreat after seeing the ancient sites. Lots of wines and delicious (though not cheap) snacks and salads.

Testaccio

Volpetti Piu Via A. Volta 8. Testaccio *tavola calda* that's attached to the famous deli of the same name around the corner at Via Marmorata classics 47. Pizza, chicken, *supplì* – all the usual classics.

Trastevere

La Renella Via del Moro 15. Arguably the best bakery in Rome, right in the heart of Trastevere, with great focaccia and superb *pizza al taglio*. Takeaway or eat on the premises at its long counter.

Sisini Via San Francesco a Ripa 137. Hole-in-the-wall pizzeria that does great slices,

as well as roast chickens, potatoes and *suppli* and all the usual *rosticceria* fare.

Prati and the Vatican

Non Solo Pizza Via degli Scipioni 95–97. Great pizza by the slice as well as a host of hot food – *suppli, olive ascolane, fiori di zucca, crocchette* – and *porchetta* skewers.

Restaurants and pizzerias

There are lots of good restaurants in the **centro storico**, and it's surprisingly easy to find places that are not tourist traps – prices in all but the really swanky places remain pretty uniform throughout the city. The area around **Via Cavour** and **Termini** is packed with inexpensive places, although some of them are of dubious cleanliness; if you're not in a hurry, you might do better heading up to the nearby student area of **San Lorenzo**, where you can often eat far better for the same money. South of the centre, the **Testaccio** neighbourhood is also well endowed with good, inexpensive trattorias, as is **Trastevere**, across the river, Rome's traditional restaurant enclave.

Centro storico

Armando al Pantheon Salita de' Crescenzi 30 ☏06.6880.3034. Unpretentious surroundings and hearty food at good prices. Closed Sat pm & all day Sun.

Cul de Sac Piazza Pasquino 73. Busy, long-running wine bar and restaurant with an excellent wine list, a great city-centre location with outside seating, and decent wine-bar food – cold meats, cheeses, salads, soups and pasta and main courses too. One of the best *centro storico* locations for both a snack and a full meal.

Da Baffetto Via del Governo Vecchio 114 ☏06.686.1617. A tiny, highly authentic pizzeria that has long been a Rome institution. It's still good value, and has tables outside in summer, though you'll always have to queue.

Da Francesco Piazza del Fico 29 ☏06.686.4009. Not just delectable pizzas in this full-on pizzeria in the heart of trendy night-time Rome, but good

antipasti, *primi* and *secondi* too. Slapdash service, but the food is excellent and relatively inexpensive.

Da Tonino Via del Governo Vecchio 18–19 ☏06.333.587.0779. There are no menus in this unmarked *centro storico* favourite, but usually they'll just tell you what they've got that day – basic Roman food, always freshly cooked, and always delicious, although the service can be a bit slow. Closed Sun.

Grano Piazza Rondanini 53 ☏06.6819.2096. Classic Roman dishes served on this quiet piazza bang in the centre of the city. The cooking is good, the service fast, and the prices moderate.

Maccheroni Piazza delle Coppelle 44 ☏06.6830.7895. Spartan yet comfy restaurant that enjoys a perfect location on this quiet *centro storico* square. It serves good, basic Italian food at affordable prices. Closed Sun.

Matricianella Via del Leone 4 ☏06.683.2100. Handily placed just off Via del

---

Ice cream and fruit shakes

Giolitti Via Uffici del Vicario 40. An Italian institution that once had a reputation – now lost – for the country's top ice cream. Still pretty good, however, with a choice of seventy flavours.

Il Gelato di San Crispino Via della Panetteria 42. Considered by many to be the best ice cream in Rome. Wonderful flavours – all natural – will make the other *gelato* you've tasted pale by comparison.

Pascucci Via di Torre Argentina 20. The best *frullati* place in town. Your choice of fresh fruit whipped up with ice and milk – the ultimate Roman refreshment on a hot day.

Corso, this old favourite serves classic Roman food either in the bustling main dining room or on the outdoor terrace. A great city centre choice. Closed Sun.

Trattoria Via Pozzo delle Cornacchie 25 ☎06.6830.1247. The inside of this cool upstairs restaurant feels a million miles away from the streets of the *centro storico* outside, and the food makes a change too – inventive modern takes on Sicilian classics. Not cheap, but one of the better food experiences of central Rome.

Campo de' Fiori and the Ghetto

Da Giggetto Via del Portico d'Ottavia 21–22 ☎06.686.1105. Roman-Jewish fare featuring deep-fried artichokes, *baccalà*, and offal-based *rigatoni con pajata*, along with good non-offal pasta dishes, eaten outside in summer by the ruins of the Portico d'Ottavia. Not cheap, but worth it. Closed Mon.

Da Sergio Via delle Grotte 27 ☎06.686.4293. An out-of-the-way, cosy trattoria with a traditional, limited menu and the deeply authentic feel of old Rome. Outdoor seating in summer. Closed Sun.

Dar Filletaro a Santa Barbara Largo dei Librari 88. A fish-and-chip shop without the chips. Paper-covered Formica tables (outdoors in summer), cheap wine, beer and fried cod, a timeless Roman speciality. Closed in Aug.

Del Pallaro Largo del Pallaro 15 ☎06.6880.1488. An old-fashioned trattoria serving a set daily menu for €21, including wine. Located in a quiet piazza between Campo de' Fiori and Largo Argentina. No credit cards. Closed Mon.

Grappolo d'Oro Piazza della Cancelleria 80 ☎06.686.4118. This place has had a bit of a facelift but still remains relatively untouched by the hordes in nearby Campo de' Fiori, and serves imaginative Roman cuisine in traditional trattoria atmosphere at moderate prices. Closed Sun.

Osteria al Galletto Piazza Farnese 102 ☎06.686.1704. In spite of its location just off one of Rome's trendiest streets and one of its trendiest piazzas, this place retains the feel of a provincial trattoria, serving good wholesome Roman food at very decent prices. Closed Sun.

Piperno Monte de' Cenci 9 ☎06.6880.6629. This stalwart of the Ghetto is not the cheapest but is perhaps the best place for a real Roman blowout, either in its elegant dining room or on the square outside. A great place to try classics like *baccalà*, all the Roman *fritti* and some of the classic pasta dishes. Closed Mon.

Tridente and Quirinale

Antica Birreria Peroni Via San Marcello 19 ☎06.679.5310. Big bustling *birreria* with an excellent menu of moderately priced simple food that's meant to soak up lots of beer.

Beltramme Via della Croce 39. This very old-fashioned *fiaschetteria* (originally it sold only wine, by the fiasco or flask) is always packed and fairly pricey, but if you want authentic Roman food, atmosphere and service the way it used to be, this is the place. No credit cards.

'Gusto Piazza Augusto Imperatore 9 ☎06.322.6273. A slick establishment that's a restaurant, pizzeria and wine bar rolled into one. Its reasonably priced Mediterranean buffet is good value for lunch at €8 a head.

Il Chianti Via del Lavatore 81–82/A ☎06.678.7550. This Tuscan restaurant and wine bar is quite a find with good spreads of cold meats and cheeses, and full meals of pasta, pizza and beef dishes.

Otello alla Concordia Via della Croce 81 ☎06.678.1454. This place used to be one of Fellini's favourites – he lived just a few blocks away on Via Margutta – and remains an elegant, yet affordable choice in the heart of Rome. Closed Sun.

Pizza Ciro Via della Mercede 43–45 ☎06.678.6015. A big, friendly pizza place that also serves *primi*, *secondi* and desserts. Try the *linguine al cir*, which comes with seafood. Just up from Piazza San Silvestro.

Recafé Piazza Augusto Imperatore 9 ☎06.6813.4730. The entrance on Via del Corso is a Neapolitan café, while on Piazza Augusta Imperatore you can enjoy proper Neapolitan pizzas, good pasta and salad dishes and excellent grilled *secondi* for moderate prices – €11 or so for a *primo*, €15–25 for a *secondo*. Neapolitan sweets and *fritti* too.

Termini and Monti

Africa Via Gaeta 26 ☎06.494.1077. Arguably the city's most interesting (Ethiopian and Eritrean) food, testimony to its significant population from the region. No credit cards. Closed Mon.

Arancia Blu Via dei Latini 57 ☎06.445.4105. This ultra-trendy San Lorenzo vegetarian reckons itself a cut above, but in a city with very few vegetarian options it doesn't have to try too hard. Good food using fresh ingredients in an imaginative fashion.

Alle Carrette Via Madonna dei Monti 95 ☎06.679.2770. Inexpensive pizza joint that also does great desserts.

Luzzi Midway between San Giovanni in Laterano and the Colosseum, this bustling restaurant is a good choice amid the tourist joints of the neighbourhood. The food is hearty and simple, there's outside seating and it's extremely cheap – *secondi* go for €6–9. There are pizzas, too, but only in the eve. Closed Wed.

Pommidoro Piazza dei Sanniti 44 ☎06.445.2692.
This long-established family-run trattoria serves
great Roman food, with a breezy open veranda in
summer and a fireplace in winter. Closed Sun.
Tram Tram Via dei Reti 44–46 ☎06.490.416. A
grungy location but a cosy spot, this cool and
animated San Lorenzo restaurant serves good
Pugliese pasta dishes, fish and seafood and
unusual salads. Closed Mon.

🏃 Trattoria Monti Via di San Vito 13/A
☎06.446.6573. Small, family-run restaurant
that specializes in the cuisine of the Marche region
– which means great pasta, interesting cabbage-
wrapped starters and mainly meaty *secondi*. Very
much a neighbourhood place, and moderately
priced too. Closed Mon.

Testaccio

Checchino dal 1887 Via Monte Testaccio 30
☎06.574.6318. One of Rome's most classic
restaurants, and a historic symbol of Testaccio
cookery, with all the offal delights you'd expect and
an excellent wine cellar, too. Not a cheap option,
though. Closed Mon.
Da Remo Piazza Santa Maria in Liberatrice 44
☎06.574.6270. No-nonsense Testaccio pizzeria
serving some of the crispiest thin-crust Roman
pizzas you'll find. Closed Sun.
Felice Via Mastro Giorgio 29 ☎06.574.6800. Don't
be put off by the "*riservato*" signs on the tables –
the owner likes to "select" his customers. Smile
and make Felice understand that you're hungry and
fond of Roman cooking. Try *bucatini cacio e pepe*,
or lamb, and, in winter, artichokes. Closed Sun.

🏃 Tuttifrutti Via Luca della Robbia 3/A
☎06.575.7902. This Testaccio favourite is
pretty much the perfect restaurant – family-run,
with good food, decent prices and lots of
customers. The menu changes daily, and offers
interesting variations on traditional Roman dishes.
Closed Mon.

Trastevere

Ai Marmi Viale Trastevere 53–59 ☎06.580.0919.
Nicknamed "the mortuary" because of its stark
interior and marble tables, this place serves
unique "*supplì al telefono*" (deep-fried rice balls,
so named because of the string of mozzarella it
forms when you take a bite), fresh *baccalà* and the
best pizza in Trastevere. A lively slice of the real
Rome. Closed Wed.
Da Augusto Piazza de Renzi 15 ☎06.580.3798.
Diner-style neighbourhood staple serving Roman
basics in an unpretentious, bustling atmosphere.
Good pasta and soup starters and daily meat and
fish specials. Closed Wed.
Ivo Via di San Francesco a Ripa 158
☎06.581.7082. The archetypal Trastevere pizzeria,
almost in danger of becoming a caricature, but still
good. Arrive early to avoid a chaotic queue. Closed
Tues.

🏃 Da Lucia Vicolo del Mettonate 2
☎06.580.3601. Bus #23, #75, #280, #630,
#780, #H or tram #8. Outdoor Trastevere dining in
summer is at its traditional peak at this wonderful
old Roman trattoria. *Spaghetti cacio e pepe* is the
great speciality here – get here early for a table
outside. Tues–Sun noon–3pm & 7.30–11.30pm.
Da Paris Piazza San Callisto 7/A ☎06.581.5378.
Fine Roman Jewish cookery and other traditional
dishes in one of Trastevere's most atmospheric
piazzas. Closed Sun.
Dar Poeta Vicolo del Bologna 45 ☎06.588.0516.
One of the top-ten pizzerias in Rome, though don't
expect the typical crusty Roman pizza here; the
margherita (ask for it *con basilico* – with basil)
comes out of the oven soft and with plenty of good
mozzarella on top. Be prepared to wait for a table.
Closed Mon.

Prati and the Vatican

Dal Toscano, Via Germanico 58–60
☎06.3972.5717. Long-established Tuscan
restaurant that specializes in thick Tuscan steaks –
charcoal-grilled at very affordable prices.
Osteria del Angelo Via G. Bettolo 24
☎06.372.9470. Above-average and reasonably
priced Roman cooking, from a highly popular
restaurant run by an ex-rugby player. Lots of very
authentic Roman specialities. Closed Sun.

Bars

There are plenty of **bars** in Rome, and an Irish pub practically on every corner.
There's also been a recent upsurge in **wine bars** (*enoteche* or *vinerie*); the old
ones have gained new cachet, and newer ones are springing up too, often with
accompanying gourmet menus, or just plates of salami and cheese.

Bear in mind that there is sometimes considerable **crossover** between Rome's
bars, restaurants and clubs. For the most part, the places we have listed are
drinking spots, but you can eat, sometimes quite substantially, at many of them,

▲ Vineria wine bar, Campo de'Fiori

and several could be classed just as easily as nightclubs, with loud music and occasionally even an entrance charge. Although we've divided these listings into **neighbourhoods**, the areas around Campo de' Fiori, and Trastevere and Testaccio are the densest and most happening parts of town.

Centro Storico

Anima Via Santa Maria dell' Anima 57. At present one of the city's most popular bars, tricked out in postmodern-*Flintstones* chic and offering an assortment of elegant snacks to go with your cocktails. Music tends towards chill-out, lounge and softer soul stuff.

Bar della Pace Via della Pace 5. Just off Piazza Navona, this is a long-established place to dirnk in the *centro storico*, with a cosy interior and outside tables that are often thronged at night.

Jonathan's Angels Via della Fossa 18. This quirky bar, just behind Piazza Navona, certainly wins the "most decorated" award. Every inch (even the toilet, which is worth a visit on its own) is plastered, painted or tricked out in outlandish style by the artist-proprietor.

Societe Lutece Piazza di Montevecchio 17. Tucked away on a tiny piazza 5min from Piazza Navona, this is one of the city centre's coolest choices, with good cocktails and a free antipasto buffet early evening.

Trinity College Via del Collegio Romano 6. One of the better among central Rome's many Irish bars; international beers on tap and food served until 1am.

Campo de' Fiori and the Ghetto

Bartaruga Piazza Mattei 7. Wonderfully camp bar furnished with all sorts of eighteenth-century bits and pieces that, not surprisingly, make it a favourite with the thespian set.

L'Angolo Divino Via dei Balestri 12. A peaceful haven after the furore of Campo de' Fiori, this wine bar has a large selection of wine, and simple wine-bar food – bread, cheese, cold cuts, soups and the like.

Mad Jack's Via Arenula 20. One of the nicest and most authentic of Rome's army of Irish pubs. The Guinness is decent, and it's not just frequented by expats and tourists.

Vineria Campo de' Fiori 15. Long-established bar right on the Campo, patronized by devoted regulars, although it's now been refurbished, and also offers light meals.

Tridente and Quirinale

L'Enoteca Antica Via della Croce 76/B. An old Spanish Steps-area wine bar, recently refurbished, with a selection of hot and cold dishes, including soups and attractive desserts. Intriguing trompe l'oeil decorations inside, majolica-topped tables outside.

Rosati Piazza del Popolo 5. This bar hosted left-wingers, bohemians and writers in years gone by, and although that's no longer really the case its cocktails and food still draw the crowds. A nice place from which to watch the action on Piazza del Popolo.

Termini and Monti

Al Vino al Vino Via dei Serpenti 19. Seriously good wine bar situated on the Monti district's most happening street. Snacks too – generally Sicilian specialities.

Druid's Den Via San Martino ai Monti 28. Appealing Irish pub with a genuine Celtic feel (and owners) and a mixed expat/Italian clientele. Live Irish music every Mon.

Finnegan Via Madonna dei Monti 28. Decent Irish pub with live football on TV, pool, and a friendly ex-pat crowd. Seating outside as well on this bustling Monti street.

Testaccio and Trastevere

Mr Brown Vicolo del Cinque 29. This popular hangout is one of Trastevere's most charming detours, with a young, fun-loving crowd, happy hour from 9–10pm daily, cheap beers, and an assortment of salads, sandwiches and crepes. Closed Sun.

Ombre Rosse Piazza Sant'Egidio 12. A people-watching spot that has become a Trastevere institution, especially for a morning cappuccino, but also for interesting light meals.

Oasi della Birra Piazza Testaccio 41. Subterranean Testaccio bar with a beer selection that would rival anywhere in the world and plenty of wine to choose from as well. For nibbles there are generous plates of cheese and salami.

San Calisto Piazza San Calisto 4. A Trastevere bar which attracts a huge crowd on late summer nights; the booze is cheap, and you can sit at outside tables for no extra cost. During the day it's simply a great spot to sip a cappuccino and take the sun.

Prati and the Vatican

Fonclea Via Crescenzio 82A. Busy and happening bar in the Vatican area that hosts regular live music – usually jazz, soul and funk.

Senza Fondo Via Germanico 168. Convivial Prati basement pub with a good choice of beer and decent food – sandwiches, salads and plates of cold goodies mainly.

Nightlife and entertainment

Roman **nightlife** retains some of the smart-set style satirized in Fellini's film *La Dolce Vita* – designer dressing-up is still very much a part of the mainstream scene and entry-prices to the big **clubs** tend to be high. But there are a few, smaller and more alternative nightspots where your travel-crumpled clothes will be more acceptable, and a **live music scene** that is nothing if not unpretentious, although big-name acts are relatively few. The city has historically been a bit of a backwater for the **performing arts**, but this has improved in recent years and in any case, what the arts here may lack they often make up for in the charm of the setting. Rome's **summer festival** – *Estate Romana* – means that there's a good range of classical music and opera running throughout the warm months, often in picturesque locations, and both the autumn **film festival** and the *Notte Bianca* event – when music and theatre events are held all over the city all night on a Saturday in mid-September – are still going, albeit in a scaled-down form.

Clubs

Alien Via Velletri 13–19 ☏06.841.2212, ⊛www.aliendisco.it. The two halls here feature starkly contrasting decor, one redolent of maharaja plushness, the other done up in modernistic black and white. Music is a mixture of house and techno.

Black Out Via Casilina 713 ☏339.200.1029. Recently re-located but long-running club that plays punk, heavy metal and Goth music, with occasional gigs by US and UK bands.

Classico Village Via Libetta 3 ☏06.5728.8857. Industrial Ostiense location with a big dance floor, a venue for live music, and a restaurant.

Gilda Via Mario de' Fiori 97 ☏06.678.4838, ⊛www.gildabar.it. A few blocks from the Spanish Steps, this slick club is the focus for the city's minor celebs and wannabes. Their summer venue, *Gilda-on-the-Beach*, is in Fregene, at Lungomare di Ponente 11 ☏06.6656.0649, ⊛www.gildaonthebeach.it.

Gay bars, restaurants and clubs

Asinocotto Via dei Vascellari 48 ⊤06.589.8985. Gay-friendly Trastevere restaurant with a great, Proust-inspired menu of moderately priced pasta, meat and fish dishes. Worth a visit whatever your non-culinary preferences.

Coming Out Via San Giovanni in Laterano 8 ⊤06.700.9871. This small gay bar is a good place for a quiet drink.

Garbo Vicolo di Santa Margherita 1/A ⊤06.5832.0782. Friendly Trastevere bar, just behind the main piazza, with a relaxed atmosphere and a nice setting.

L'Alibi Via Monte Testaccio 44 ⊤06.574.3448. Predominantly – but by no means exclusively – male venue that's one of Rome's oldest gay clubs. Downstairs there's a multi-room cellar disco, upstairs an open-air bar, and there's a big terrace to enjoy in the warm months.

La Buca di Bacco Via San Francesco a Ripa 165 ⊤348.764.7388. This cocktail bar, wine bar and tea room is one of the new breed of openly gay establishments. Quiet during the day, lively at night.

L'Hangar Via in Selci 29 ⊤06.4881.3971. Just off Via Cavour, this is one of Rome's oldest gay spots. Saturday night it's almost impossible to get in the door it's so jammed.

Goa Via Libetta 13 ⊤06.574.8277. Long-running Ostiense club that was opened by famous local DJ Giancarlino and is still playing techno, house and jungle; *Goa* also has sofas to help you recover after high-energy dancing.

La Maison Vicolo dei Granari 4 ⊤06.683.3312. Ritzy club whose chandeliers and glossy decor attract Rome's gilded youth. Sun – gay night – is the one to go for.

Micca Club Van Pietro Micca 7/A T068744.0079. This new club has an atmospheric location in an old vaulted cellar and regular DJs playing funk and soul. It also has a vintage clothes market on Sun at 6pm.

Piper Via Tagliamento 9 ⊤06.855.5398. Established back in the 1970s, but still going strong, Piper has different nightly events and a wide variety of music.

Qube Via Portonaccio 212 ⊤06.435.5445. This Tiburtina club hosts a variety of different nights each week, including live music. Not the most original for music but its Fri gay and drag night draw a big crowd.

Live music

Alexanderplatz Via Ostia 9 ⊤06.5833.5781, ⓦwww.alexanderplatz.it. Rome's top live jazz club/restaurant with reasonable membership (€10) and free entry, except when there's star-billing. Reservations recommended. Doors open at 8pm.

Alpheus Via del Commercio 36 ⊤06.574.7826, ⓦwww.alpheus.it. Housed in an ex-factory off Via Ostiense, a little way beyond Testaccio, this has space for three simultaneous events – usually a concert, DJ, exhibition or piece of theatre.

Big Mama Vicolo San Francesco a Ripa 18 ⊤06.581.2551, ⓦwww.bigmama.it. Trastevere-based jazz/blues club of long standing, hosting nightly acts. Monthly membership costs €8, and then entry is free except for star attractions (when it's important to book ahead). Doors open 9pm.

Caffè Latino Via Monte Testaccio 96 ⊤06.5728.8556. Multi-event Testaccio club with varied live music almost every night. There's also a disco playing a selection of funky, acid jazz and R&B music. Best at weekends when it gets more crowded. Admission €6–10. Tues–Sun 10pm–3am.

Circolo degli Artisti Via Casilina Vecchia 42 ⊤06.7030.5684, ⓦwww.circoloartisti.it. A very large venue, located beyond Porta Maggiore, that was one of the first of the city's co-called *centri sociali*. A good range of bands, with frequent discos and theme nights from hip-hop to ska. Fri it hosts Omogenic – gay night. Bus #105 from Termini, or #810 from Piazza Venezia.

Gregory's Via Gregoriana 54/D ⊤06.679.6386. Just up the Spanish Steps and to the right, this elegant nightspot pulls in the crowds with its live jazz, improvised by Roman and international musicians. Tues–Sun 5.30pm–3am.

Classical music and opera

Under new directors, Rome's **orchestras** of late are approaching international standards, and although the city attracts far fewer prestigious artists than you might expect of a capital, it is becoming more and more a magnet for contemporary works – a sea change that has been inspired by the completion of the new *Auditorium*. Check the listings and keep a look-out for posters advertising little-known concerts in churches or other often spectacular venues. The city's **opera** scene has long been overshadowed by that of Milan, Parma and Naples, but it is improving. In summer, opera moves outdoors and ticket prices come down: performances are now once again held in the stunning setting at the ancient Baths of Caracalla, as well as other churches and venues all around Rome.

Auditorium/Parco della Musica Via P. de Coubertin 15 ℡199.109.783, ⊛www.auditorium .com. This landmark music complex is Rome's most prestigious venue, home to its premier orchestra, the Accademia Nazionale di Santa Cecilia, who are resident part of the year in its largest hall. Two smaller venues host chamber, choral, recital and experimental works. The complex also hosts major rock and jazz names when they come to town. Box office Mon–Sun 11am–8pm. Guided tours Mon–Sat 11am–6pm, Sun 10am–6pm.

Oratorio del Gonfalone Via del Gonfalone 32/A ℡06.687.5952. This lovely theatre, just off Campo de' Fiori, stages performances of chamber music, with an emphasis on the Baroque.

Teatro dell'Opera di Roma Piazza Beniamino Gigli 1 ℡06.4816.0255, ⊛www.operaroma.it. Nobody compares it to La Scala, but cheap tickets are a lot easier to come by at Rome's opera and ballet venue – they start at around €20 for opera, less for ballet – and important artists do sometimes perform here. Box office Tues–Sat 9am–5pm, Sun 9am–1.30pm.

Teatro Olimpico Piazza Gentile da Fabriano 17 ℡06.326.5991, ⊛www.teatroolimpico.it. Classical standards, chamber music and ballet are performed here, by resident orchestra Accademia Filarmonica Romana, as well as occasional contemporary work. Tickets are cheap and relatively easy to come by. Bus #910 from Termini.

Film

There tends to be more **English-language cinema** on offer in Rome these days, partly due to foreign demand, though if your Italian is up to it, you'll naturally also find current Italian language productions available all over town.

Alcazar Via Merry del Val 14 ℡06.588.0099. Trastevere cinema featuring mainstream American and English films, in original languages on Mon.

Metropolitan Via del Corso 7 ℡06.320.0933. The city centre's largest multi-screen cinema, with four screens showing blockbusters and all general-release films.

Nuovo Olimpia Via in Lucina 16 ℡06.686.1068. Very central, just off Via del Corso, with two

screens, and the only place in Rome to show first-run films in their original language only.

Nuovo Sacher Largo Ascianghi 1 ℡06.581.8116. Trastevere cinema set up by the Italian director Nanni Moretti, and always showing their current film – mainly foreign independent movies – in its original version on Mon.

Listings

Airport enquiries Fiumicino ℡06.65951, Ciampino ℡06.794.941; ⊛www.adr.it.

Bike and scooter rental Barberini Villa della Purificazione 84 ℡06.488.5485 rents out bikes, mopeds and scooters. Bikes cost €10 per day, mopeds €30–40, scooters €50–70. Open daily 9am–7pm.

Books All of the following are excellent English-language bookshops: Anglo-American Bookshop Via delle Vite 102 ℡06.679.5222; Almost Corner Bookshop Via del Moro 45 ℡06.583.6942; Lion Bookshop, Via dei Greci 33 ℡06.3265.4007.

Car rental All the usual suspects have desks at Fiumicino, Ciampino, Termini and elsewhere in the city. Avis ℡06.4423.0134; Europcar 06.488.2854; Hertz ℡06.321.6886; Maggiore ℡06.488.3715.

Dentist 24hr dental care is available at the George Eastman hospital, Viale Regina Elena 287.

Embassies Australia, Via Bosio 5 ℡06.852,721; Britain, Via XX Settembre 80/A ℡06.4220.0001; Canada, Via Zara 30 ℡06.445.981; Ireland, Piazza Campitelli 3 ℡06.697.9121; New Zealand, Via Zara

28 ☎06.441.7171; South Africa Via Tanaro
☎06.852.541; US, Via Veneto 119 ☎06.46.741.
Emergencies Police ☎113; carabinieri ☎112;
fire ☎115; ambulance ☎118. Both the police
and the *carabinieri* have offices in Termini.
Otherwise the most central police office is off Via
del Corso in Piazza del Collegio Romano 3
(☎06.46.86), and there's a *carabinieri* office in
Piazza Venezia.
Exchange American Express, Piazza di Spagna 38
(Mon–Fri 9.30am–5.30pm, Sat 9am–12.30pm);
Thomas Cook, Piazza Barberini 21/A (Mon–Sat 9am–
8pm, Sun 9.30am–5pm) and Via della Conciliazione
23 (Mon–Sat 8.30am–7.30pm, Sun 9.30am–5pm).
Post offices will exchange American Express
traveller's cheques and cash commission-free. The
last resort should be any of the many Ufficio Cambio,
almost always offering the worst rates.
Football Rome's two big teams, Roma and Lazio,
play on alternate Sun between Sept and May at
the Olympic Stadium, northwest of the city centre.
You can reach this by taking tram #2 from Piazzale
Flaminio to Piazza Mancini and then walking
across the river to the stadium. Lazio fans traditionally occupy the Curva Nord, the northern end
of the ground, and Roma fans the Curva Sud, and
tickets in these areas cost €15–25 (if you can get
one). It's usually easier to pick up seats in the
corner stands, or *distinti*, for €25–35; seats in the
side stands, or *tribuna*, cost €50–100. Except for
the really big games, you can get tickets at the
ground, or for Roma you can try their city centre
store at Piazza Colonna 360 (☎06.678.6514).

Hospitals In an emergency call ambulance
☎118. Otherwise the most central hospitals
with emergency facilities are: Santo Spirito,
Lungotevere in Sassia 1 (☎06.68.351), near the
Vatican, and Fatebenefratelli, Isola Tiberina
(☎06.683.7299). The Rome American Hospital,
Via E. Longoni 81 (☎06.22.551) is a private
multi-speciality hospital with bilingual staff and
has a 24hr emergency line.
Internet access Bibli, Via dei Fienaroli 28
(Tues–Sun 11am–midnight, Mon 5.30pm–
midnight); Yex Piazza Sant'Andrea delle Valle 1
(Daily 10am–11pm); internet Point Via dei Pastini
21 (daily 10am–11pm).
Lost property For property lost on a train call
☎06.4730.6682 (daily 7am–11pm); on a bus
☎06.581.6040 (Mon & Fri 8.30am–1pm, Tues–
Thurs 2.30–6pm); on the metro ☎06.487.4309.
Pharmacies The following pharmacies are open
late: Piram, Via Nazionale 228 ☎06.488.0754;
Farmacia della Stazione, Piazza dei Cinquecento 51
☎06.488.0019.
Post offices Rome's main post office is on Piazza
San Silvestro (Mon–Fri 8.30am–6.30pm, Sat
8.30am–1pm).
Train enquiries General enquiries ⊛www
.trenitalia.it; Termini ☎06.892.021, ⊛www
.romatermini.it.
Travel agents For discount tickets try the CTS
offices at Via Genova 16 ☎06.462.0431 and Corso
Vittorio Emanuele II 297 ☎06.687.2672, both
open Sat mornings, when other travel agents are
closed.

Out from the city: Ostia Antica and Tivoli

You may find there's quite enough in Rome to keep you occupied during your
stay, but it can be a hot, oppressive city and if you're around long enough you
really shouldn't feel any guilt about getting out to see something of the
countryside around. Two of the main attractions visitable on a day-trip are, it's
true, more Roman sites, but just the process of getting to them can be
energizing. **Tivoli**, about an hour by bus east of Rome, is a small town famous
for the travertine quarries nearby, the landscaped gardens and parks of its
Renaissance villas, and a fine ancient Roman villa just outside. **Ostia**, in the
opposite direction near the sea, and similarly easy to reach on public transport,
is nowadays the city's main seaside resort (though one worth avoiding; see p.739
for more attractive options just a little further south), but it was home to the
port of Rome in classical times, and the site is well preserved and worth seeing.
Bear in mind, too, that a number of **other places in Lazio** – the Etruscan sites
north of Rome, the Castelli Romani, Palestrina and Subiaco, and parts of the
southern coast – are close enough to the city to make a feasible day-trip,
especially if you have access to a car.

Ostia Antica

There are two Ostias: one a rather over-visited seaside resort, **Lido di Ostia**; the other, one of the finest ancient Roman sites – the excavations of **OSTIA ANTICA** – which are on a par with anything you'll see in Rome itself and easily merit the half-day journey out. The stop before Lido di Ostia on the train from Rome, the site of Ostia Antica marked the coastline in classical times, and the town which grew up here was the port of ancient Rome, a thriving place whose commercial activities were vital to the city further upstream. The **excavations** are relatively free of tourists (April–Oct Tues–Sun 8.30am–6pm; March 8.30am–5pm; Nov–Feb 8.30am–4pm; €6.50), and it's much easier to reconstruct a Roman town from these than from any amount of pottering around the Forum. It's also very spread out, so be prepared for a fair amount of walking.

The main street, the **Decumanus Maximus**, leads west from the entrance, past the **Baths of Neptune** on the right (where there's an interesting mosaic) to the town's commercial centre, otherwise known as the **Piazzale delle Corporazioni**, for the remains of shops and trading offices that still fringe the central square. These represented commercial enterprises from all over the ancient world, and the mosaics just in front denote their trade – grain merchants, ship-fitters, ropemakers and the like. Flanking one side of the square, the **theatre** has been much restored but is nonetheless impressive, enlarged by Septimius Severus in the second century AD to hold up to 4000 people. On the left of the square, the **House of Apulius** preserves mosaic floors and, beyond, a dark-aisled *mithraeum* has more mosaics illustrating the cult's practices. Behind here – past the substantial remains of the *horrea* or warehouses that once stood all over the city – the **Casa di Diana** is probably the best-preserved private house in Ostia, with a dark, mysterious set of rooms around a central courtyard, again with a *mithraeum* at the back. You can climb up to its roof for a fine view of the rest of the site, afterwards crossing the road to the **Thermopolium** – an ancient Roman café, complete with seats outside, a high counter, display shelves and even wall paintings of parts of the menu. North of the Casa di Diana, the **museum** (Tues–Sat 9am–4.30pm, Sun 9am–1pm; entry with ticket for the excavations) holds a variety of articles from the site, including a statue of Mithras killing a bull, wall paintings depicting domestic life in Ostia, and some fine sarcophagi and statuary from the imperial period. Left from here, the **Forum** centres on the **Capitol** building, reached by a wide flight of steps, and is fringed by the remains of baths and a basilica. Further on down the main street, more **horrea**, superbly preserved and complete with pediment and names inscribed on the marble, merit a detour off to the right; although you can't enter, you can peer into the courtyard. Beyond, the **House of Cupid and Psyche** has a courtyard you can walk into, its rooms clearly discernible on one side, a colourful marbled floor on the other.

Tivoli

Just 40km from Rome, perched high on a hill and looking back over the plain, **TIVOLI** has always been something of a retreat from the city. In classical days it was a retirement town for wealthy Romans; later, during Renaissance times, it again became the playground of the moneyed classes, attracting some of the city's most well-to-do families, who built their country villas out here. Nowadays the leisured classes have mostly gone, but Tivoli does very nicely on the fruits of its still-thriving travertine business, exporting the precious stone worldwide (the quarries line the main road into town from Rome), and supports a small airy centre that preserves a number of relics from its ritzier days.

To do justice to the gardens and villas – especially if Villa Adriana is on your list, as indeed it should be – you'll need time, so it's worth setting out early.

Villa d'Este and Villa Gregoriana

Most people head first for **Villa d'Este** (daily 8.30am to 1hr before sunset; €6.50), across the main square of Largo Garibaldi – the country retreat of Cardinal Ippolito d'Este that was transformed from a convent by Pirro Ligorio in 1550, and is now often thronged with visitors even outside peak season. They mainly come to see the fountains of the landscaped gardens, but the restored ground-floor apartments alone make the trip worthwhile, frescoed with scenes of mythology and the history of Tivoli by Girolamo Muziano and Federico Zuccari in 1555–60. Unfortunately, restoration is still going on in the gardens below, and you may find many of the famous **fountains** are temporarily closed. However, you can see the theatrical, magnificent Organ Fountain, which has been returned to its original glory and makes a most imposing sight as it gushes millions of gallons of water down the hillside. Among the other fountains you can see are the Fontana dell'Ovato, near the Organ Fountain, fringed with statues, behind which is a rather dank arcade, and the Rometta or "Little Rome", on the opposite side of the garden, which has reproductions of the city's major buildings. Finally a word of warning: be sure to drink only from those fountains marked *acqua potabile*, and don't wade or splash in the other fountains – the water is basically sewage from the town above.

Tivoli's other main attraction is **Villa Gregoriana** (daily: April–Oct 10am–6.30pm; March & Nov 10am–2.30pm; €4), a park with waterfalls created when Pope Gregory XVI diverted the flow of the river here to ease the periodic flooding of the town in 1831. Less well known and less touristed than the d'Este estate, it has none of the latter's conceits – its vegetation is lush and overgrown, descending into a gashed-out gorge over 60m deep. There are two main **waterfalls** – the larger Grande Cascata on the far side, and a small Bernini-designed one at the neck of the gorge. The path winds down to the bottom of the canyon, scaling the drop on the other side past two grottoes, where you can get up close to the pounding water, the dark, torn shapes of the rock glowering overhead. It's harder work than the Villa d'Este – if you blithely saunter down to the bottom of the gorge, you'll find that it's a long way back up the other side – but in many ways more rewarding; the path leads up on the far side to an exit and the substantial remains of a **Temple of Vesta**, which you'll have seen clinging to the side of the hill. This is now incorporated into the gardens of a restaurant, but it's all right to walk through and take a look, and the view is probably Tivoli's best – down into the chasm and across to the high green hills that ring the town.

Villa Adriana

Just outside town, at the bottom of the hill, fifteen-minutes' walk off the main Rome road (ask the Rome–Tivoli bus to drop you or take the local CAT #4 from Largo Garibaldi), the **Villa Adriana** (daily 9am to 1hr before sunset; €6.50) casts the invention of the Tivoli popes and cardinals very much into the shade. This was probably the largest and most sumptuous villa in the Roman Empire, the retirement home of the Emperor Hadrian for a short while between 135 AD and his death three years later, and it occupies an enormous site. There's no point in doing it at a gallop and, taken with the rest of Tivoli, it makes for a long day's sightseeing. Spending €3.81 on the large-scale map they sell at the bookstore near the ticket booth helps make it all manageable and comprehensive.

The site is one of the most soothing spots around Rome, its stones almost the epitome of romantic, civilized ruins. The imperial palace buildings proper are in

The Lazio transport system, run by COTRAL, is divided into seven zones, which spread out concentrically from Rome. It's possible to buy season tickets – by the day, week, or month – to travel within them. The **BIRG** (Biglietto Integrato Regionale Giornaliero) is valid all day for unlimited travel on the state railway, COTRAL buses and the Rome metro, and prices range from €2.50 to €10.50, depending on the zone. A €7 ticket, covering four zones, for example, ferries you between Rome and Viterbo. Weekly passes – the CIRS (Carta Integrata Regionale Settimanale) – cost from €9 to €41 depending on the zones you want to cover; but €41 for a week's free travel all over Lazio can't be bad. Vendors – train and bus ticket offices, newspaper stands and tobacconists – can advise you on the required zone, as can the ATAC website @www.cotralspa.it. Note that COTRAL buses often follow the school day schedule during the week and run much less frequently on weekends, especially Sundays. In smaller towns, ticket offices close in the afternoon so be sure to buy your ticket ahead of time.

fact one of the least well-preserved parts of the complex, but much else is clearly recognizable. Hadrian was a great traveller and a keen architect, and parts of the villa were inspired by buildings he had seen throughout the empire. The massive **Pecile**, for instance, through which you enter, is a reproduction of a building in Athens; and the **Canopus**, on the opposite side of the site, is a liberal copy of the sanctuary of Serapis near Alexandria, its long, elegant channel of water fringed by sporadic columns and statues leading up to a **Temple of Serapis** at the far end. Nearby, a **museum** displays the latest finds from the ongoing excavations, though most of the extensive original discoveries have found their way back to Rome. Walking back towards the entrance, make your way across the upper storey of the so-called Pretorio, a former warehouse, and down to the remains of two bath complexes. Beyond is a fishpond with a *cryptoporticus* (underground passageway) winding around underneath, and behind that the relics of the emperor's imperial apartments. The **Teatro Maríttimo**, adjacent, with its island in the middle of a circular pond, is the place to which it's believed Hadrian would retire at siesta time to be sure of being alone.

Practicalities

Buses leave Rome for Tivoli and Villa Adriana every twenty minutes from Ponte Mammolo metro station (line B) – journey-time fifty minutes. In Tivoli, the **bus station** is in Piazza Massimo near the Villa Gregoriana, though you can get off earlier, on the main square of Largo Garibaldi, where you'll find the **tourist office** (Mon & Sat 9am–3pm, Tues–Fri 9am–6.30pm; ☏0774.334.522), which has free maps and information on **accommodation**.

Northern Lazio

Northern Lazio, or "Alto Lazio", is quite a different entity from the region south of the capital and is well worth a visit. Green and wooded in the centre, its steadily more undulating hills hint at the landscapes of Tuscany and Umbria further north. Few large towns exist, however, and, with determination (and, ideally, a car), you can see much of it on day-trips from Rome. Foremost among the area's attractions is the legacy of the **Etruscans**, a sophisticated pre-Roman people swathed in mystery. To the west, some of their most important sites are readily accessible by road or rail – necropolises mainly, the only remains of a civilization that ruled this region for nearly one thousand years. To the east, the **Sabine Hills** hold picturesque olive groves, unspoilt villages and religious centres like Farfa, once the most powerful abbey in Europe. The **coastal town** of **Tarquinia Lido** further north offers an attractive escape from the hot capital in the summer months but a car is useful. Alternatively, swimmers can head by train or bus to the lakes **Vico**, **Bracciano** or **Bolsena** – playgrounds for hot and bothered Romans on summer weekends. **Viterbo**, the medieval "city of popes", can serve as a base if you're thinking of a two- or three-day visit, particularly if you're touring without a car. It's close to some fine examples of the region's **Mannerist villas and gardens** and a good source of information on Etruscan sites and local museums. Over to the east, the **lakes and mountains** of **Terminillo**, are scenically spectacular, but again difficult to reach without a vehicle.

Etruria and the coast

D.H. Lawrence had pretty much the last word on the plain, low hills stretching **north from Rome** towards the Tuscan border. "A peculiarly forlorn coast," he lamented, "the sea peculiarly flat and sunken, lifeless looking, the land as if it had given up its last gasp and was now forever inert." His *Etruscan Places*, published in 1932, is one of the best introductions to this pre-Roman civilization and their cities, which, one or two beaches excepted, are the main reasons for venturing out here.

Cerveteri

CERVETERI provides the most accessible Etruscan taster. COTRAL **buses** run from Rome's Cornelia station (line A; 65min) to Piazza Aldo Moro. The nearest train station is 7km downhill in Ladispoli.

Cerveteri dates back to the tenth century BC. Once known as *Caere*, it ranked among the top three cities in the twelve-strong Etruscan federation, its wealth derived largely from the mineral-rich **Tolfa hills** to the northeast – a gentle range that gives the plain a much-needed touch of scenic colour. In its heyday, the town spread over 150 hectares (something like thirty times its present size), controlling territory 50km up the coast. By the third century BC, *Caere* was under Roman control, leading to the decline of Etruscan culture in the region.

The present town is a thirteenth-century creation, dismissed by D.H. Lawrence – and you really can't blame him – as "forlorn beyond words". On arrival, make straight for the Etruscan **Necropolis della Banditaccia** (9am to 1hr before sunset; €6, €8 including museum; ☎0699.40.001), just 1km away from the town centre and signposted from the central piazza. From the seventh to second centuries BC, some fifty thousand Etruscans were buried in this literal city of the dead, weird and fantastically well preserved with complete streets and homes. The Etruscan elite did not practise cremation, preferring to have their remains laid on beds or in sarcophagi carved directly out of the rock. The tombs were kitted out like homes, complete with beds, furniture and wall decorations. There are twelve or so show-tombs, lying between the two main roads, the best of which are the **Tomba dei Relievi** (Tomb of the Bas-Reliefs), **Tomba delle**

Cornici (Tomb of the Frames) and the **Tomba dei Capitelli** (Tomb of the Column Capitals).

You could spend several hours wandering about, but you might be better off heading back into town to the **Museo Nazionale Cerite** (Tues–Sun 9.30am–7.30pm; €6), at the top of the old quarter in the twelfth-century Rocca. The museum has a rich, if small, collection that showcases the fine objects interred with the Etruscan dead – vases, terracottas and a run of miscellaneous day-to-day objects; most of the best stuff, though, has been whisked away to Villa Giulia in Rome. In town, quench your appetite at the traditional **trattoria** *Il Cavallino Bianco* in Piazza Risorgimento, where they serve hearty country-style food (closed Tues; ℡0699.43.693).

Civitavecchia

The only reason to break a journey in **CIVITAVECCHIA**, 30km north of Cerveteri, is to catch a **ferry** to Sardinia (see p.991 for details of crossings). The **docks** are in the city centre at the end of Viale Garibaldi beside the Forte Michelangelo, ten-minutes' walk from the **train station**. Beware of taxis (both legal and otherwise) lurking at the port and train station. They charge outrageous prices to shuttle you and your luggage around town. If you're planning on staying the night, it's best to arrange a pick up with your hotel; note also that the port has a left luggage office (Pier 18–20).

There is a **tourist office** inside the Forte Michelangelo (℡0766.20.299; Mon–Sat 9am–1pm). Heading northeast from here, Corso Centocelle is lined with cafés, restaurants and shops. Just above the fortress in Piazza Vittorio, COTRAL buses depart for Cerveteri, Tarquinia, and Viterbo. Free regular shuttles whisk passengers from the tourist office to the departure piers. Ferry tickets are sold at Piers 18-20; travel agents in town can make reservations (essential in the summer months) for a fee. Should you get stuck downtown, try the *Hotel Traiano* at Via F. Filzi 1 (℡0766.544.282, ⓦ www.hoteltraiano.com; ⑤), or, failing that, the basic and convenient *Hotel Traghetto* on Via Braccianese Claudia 4 (℡0766.25.920, ⓦ www.hoteltraghetto.it; ②), which is 300m from the port. As for **eating**, *Trattoria Sora Maria*, off Largo Plebiscito on Via Zara 14 (closed Wed; ℡0766.32.945), is known for its fish dishes; for quick sandwiches and pizzas, try *Vapoforno* around the corner on Via Regina Elena 16 (closed Sun eve).

Tarquinia

TARQUINIA, about 15km further north, is the most touted of the Etruscan necropolises, and with good reason. When not overrun with visitors, the site is quite evocative and the actual town, partial walls containing a crop of medieval towers, is a pleasant place to pass an afternoon. The museum is the region's finest outside Rome and is unmissable.

Most visitors enter the historical centre of Traquinia at the **Barriera S. Giusto**, a large parking lot just outside Piazza Cavour. The old fortified district to the north contains a twelfth-century Romanesque church, **Santa Maria di Castello**, noted for its rib vaulting, the first known example in Italy. Otherwise it's the **Museo Nazionale Tarquiniense** on the Piazza Cavour (Tues–Sun 8.30am–7.30pm; €6, €8, including necropolis; ℡0766.856.036), that draws the crowds. Though not large, the collection is choice and sensitively housed in an attractive Gothic-Renaissance *palazzo*. The ground floor exhibits superb sculpted sarcophagi, many decorated with warm and human portraits of the deceased. Upstairs are displays of exquisite Etruscan gold jewellery, painted ceramics, bronzes, candlesticks, heads and figures. The impressive top floor houses the collection's finest piece – the renowned winged horses (fourth century BC), probably from a temple frieze. The Sala delle Armi boasts panoramic views of the countryside and sea.

The site

Regular buses connect Barriera S. Giusto and the **Necropolis di Monterozzi** (summer Tues–Sun 8.30am–7.30pm; winter 8.30am–2pm; €6, €8 including museum; ☏0766.856.308), the real reason for a visit here, with its vividly painted tombs unmissable masterpieces. The walk is just twenty minutes, though: take Via Umberto I from Piazza Cavour, pass through the Porta Romana, cross Piazza Europa, follow Via IV Novembre/Via delle Croci up the hill, and the site is on the left.

Once the artistic, cultural and probably political capital of Etruria, the wooden city has now all but vanished. Founded in the tenth century BC, its population peaked around 100,000, but the Roman juggernaut triggered its decline six hundred years later and only a warren of graves remains, cut into a plateau, on the southeast edge of the modern town. Since the eighteenth century, six thousand tombs have been uncovered (900 in 1958 alone), with many more to go. Grave robbing is common (thieves are known as *i tombaroli*). Fresh air and humidity have also damaged the **wall paintings** and attempts at conservation means tombs are open on a rotating basis.

Etruscan burial places often mimicked neighbourhoods and houses (though less literally than at Cerveteri). Some frescoes may depict the inhabitants' expectations of the afterlife: scenes of banqueting, hunting and even a *ménage à trois*. The famed **Tomba dei Caronti** makes a darker prediction with demons greeting the deceased in the Underworld. The earliest paintings emphasize mythical and ritualistic scenes, but the sixth- to fourth-century works – in the dell'Orco, degli Auguri, and della Caccia e Pesca tombs – show greater social realism. This style is a mixture of Greek, indigenous Etruscan and eastern influences: the ease and fluidity points to a civilization at its peak. Later efforts grow increasingly morbid with purely necromantic drawings, enough to discourage picnic lunches on the pleasant, grassy site.

Practicalities

Tarquinia's **train station** is 2km below the town centre, connected with the central Barriera San Giusto by regular local shuttles; **buses** from Viterbo and Civitavecchia (no direct bus to/from Rome, change at Civitavecchia) also stop here. There's a **tourist office** just through the city gate at Piazza Cavour 13 (Mon–Sat 8am–2pm; ☏0766.849.282, ✉infotarquinia@apt.viterbo.it), where you can also get a list of bed-and-breakfasts – useful in a town where **accommodation** is limited. The central and gracious *B&B Ocresia* at Piazza Soderini 1 (☏0766.855.419, ✉ocresiauno@libero.it; ❷) is one of the better options. Perhaps the most atmospheric place to **eat** is *Re Tarquinio*, at Via Alberata Dante Alighieri 10, which serves meals in tufa caves tastefully made up like tombs (☏0766.842.125; closed Tues). There are many restaurants south of the Palazzo Comunale in Piazza Nazionale – try *La Cantina dell'Etrusco* on Via Menotti Garibaldi 13, which serves up rustic local fare in a converted fourteenth century cantina (☏0766.858.418; closed Tues).

Tarquinia Lido

TARQUINIA LIDO, reachable by public transport from Barriera San Giusto via the train station (see hours posted on tourist office), is home to the area's action in the summer months. The coast here is heavily developed – with restaurants, discos, sports facilities, "pubs" and even cinemas – but it might just hit the spot after sedate Tarquinia proper. The best bet, though, is to round off a day-trip with a quick dip and head back to the station. If you choose to **stay**, the *Albergo Mirmare*, Viale dei Tirreni 36 (℡0766.864.020, Ⓦwww.miramare-nautilus.it; ❷), has tidy en suites with a mishmash of antiques and 1970s plywood furnishings. The hotel is across from the free beach and its restaurant, *Nautilus*, is attached. Nearby in the Saline (salt marshes), you might find a spot at the B&B *Antica Salina* (℡0766.864.172 or 380.712.2628, Ⓔcarlotos@tiscali.it ❷). Head south for 1km along the road to the Saline and you'll see it on your left, just before you get to the salt marshes, which have been turned into a nature reserve and bird sanctuary.

Lago di Vico and Caprarola

The smallest of northern Lazio's lakes is the only one deemed worthy of nature reserve status. **LAGO DI VICO** is a former volcanic crater, ringed by mountains, the highest of which, Monte Fogliano, rises to 963m on the western shore. The **Via Cimina** traverses the summit ridges and is a popular scenic drive, dotted with restaurants, but there's a quieter road (closed to cars) near the shoreline.

Getting around this part of Lazio is difficult without private transport. But there are plenty of buses between Viterbo and the **Saxa Rubra** station in Rome which skirt the area. For the lake, pick up the bus that follows the Via Cimina from Rome to Viterbo via **Ronciglione**, and there's a stop a couple of kilometres north of the town that drops you at the lakeshore. There's also a bus service to **Caprarola** from Saxa Rubra, but the most reliable service is from Viterbo (see p.726). Don't be fooled by the rail line marked on the map that runs between Capranica and Caprarola: there are stations (a good 5km from the actual towns), but no longer any trains.

Caprarola: the Palazzo Farnese

Over and above the lake's sheer prettiness, there's not much besides the odd attractive village and a scattering of Roman and Etruscan remains – none terribly interesting in their own right, but worthwhile if you can string several together. More deserving of individual attention is the **Palazzo Farnese** at **CAPRAROLA**, which, like the villas at Bagnaia and Bomarzo, ranks among the high points of sixteenth-century Italian Mannerism.

The **palace** (Tues–Sun 8.30am–7pm with visits every 30min; €2; ℡0761.646.6052) stands huge and imposing at the top of the town's steep main street, Via Nicolai. Begun by Antonio da Sangallo the Younger for Pierluigi Farnese in the early 1520s, it was originally more a castle than a palace, situated at the centre of the Farnese family lands. Later, Cardinal Alessandro Farnese took up residence here, in 1559 hiring Vignola to modify the building while retaining its peculiar pentagonal floor-plan. Vignola was among the most accomplished architects of the late Renaissance, and his creation here exemplifies the Mannerist style at its best.

Of the palace's five floors only the *piano nobile* is open to the public, accessed by a magnificently decorated spiral staircase that opens onto a circular courtyard. The first and last rooms are perhaps the best. The former has a super-embellished grotto-like fountain and pictures of local communities like Caprarola itself (the central scene is an imaginary one). The latter, the Sala del Mappamondo, boasts huge painted maps of the known world and a wonderful ceiling fresco of the constellations.

Outside there are **gardens** (guided tours: lower gardens, see palace times above; upper gardens: winter 10am, 11am, noon, 3pm; summer 10am, 11am, noon, 3pm, 4pm, 5pm), divided into summer and winter sections. Look out for the artificial grotto and the stalactites in the lower gardens.

Practicalities

Without your own car, it's best to use Viterbo as a base and take one of the regular **buses** (daily except Sun) from here to Caprarola. This entails a very pleasant 45-minute ride through the wooded hills of the Monti Cimini that leaves you at the foot of the main street, from where it's a ten-minute walk to the palace at the top. In any case, Caprarola has few **hotels**. You could try the *La Rocca* bed and breakfast at Piazza Romeo Romei 7 (℡0761.646.411, ℮bblarocca@bblarocca .it; ❷) near the *palazzo*. For **food**, there's the *Pizzeria Bella Gioia* off to the left of *piazza* Romei in front of the palace (℡0761.646.963; closed Tues).

Bracciano

The closest of northern Lazio's lakes to Rome, **Lago di Bracciano** fills an enormous volcanic crater, a smooth, roughly circular expanse of water that's popular – but not too popular – with Romans keen to escape the summer heat of the city. It's nothing spectacular, with few real sights and a landscape of rather plain, rolling countryside, but its shores are fairly peaceful even on summer Sundays, and you can eat excellent lake fish in its restaurants.

The lake's main settlement is **BRACCIANO** on the western shore, about an hour by train from Rome Ostiense), a small town that was catapulted into the news when Tom Cruise and Katie Holmes got married here in 2006. The couple tied the knot at the imposing **Castello Odescalchi** (Tues–Sat 10am–noon & 3–6pm, Sun 9am–12.30pm & 3–6.30pm; closes 1hr earlier in winter; tours every 30min; €7; ℡0699.804.348), which dominates the town, a late-fifteenth-century structure privately owned by the Odescalchi family. The outer walls, now mostly disappeared, contained the rectangular piazza of the medieval town; the view from the ramparts is worth the admission price alone.

The best place to **swim** in the lake is from the beach at Lungolago Argenti, a ten-minute walk along the Via del Lago from Bracciano town. You can rent a boat and picnic on the beach, and the nearby trattorias are good and inexpensive – try *Da Tonino* at no. 18 right on the beach (℡0699.805.580, closed Mon), which serves good pasta and fish. The shore between Trevignano and Anguillara, both connected to Bracciano by local bus service, also boasts fine swimming spots, as well as good **restaurants** in both of the towns.

Viterbo and around

The capital of its province, and indeed of northern Lazio as a whole, **VITERBO** is easily the region's most historic centre, a medieval town that during the thirteenth century was once something of a rival to Rome. It was, for a time, the residence of popes, a succession of whom relocated here after friction in the capital. Today there are some vestiges of its vanquished prestige – a handful of grand palaces and numerous medieval churches, enclosed by an intact set of walls. The town is a well-kept place and refreshingly untouched by much tourist traffic, but only really worth staying in if you're keen to visit the surrounding area. Otherwise, buses and trains run frequently to Rome (2hr) and you can comfortably see the town in a day.

Arrival and information

Unusually for a small town, Viterbo has three **train stations**: the Porta Romana station south of the centre and Porta Fiorentina station to the north are the most convenient, being on the Roma–Viterbo line, which stops at Roma Ostiense, Trastevere and San Pietro (hourly departures throughout the day, less frequent at night; 1hr 40min). Porta Fiorentina on Viale Trento is handier for hotels. The third station is the terminus for the Roma-Nord line which originates at Rome's Piazzale Flaminia station and follows a picturesque but lengthy ride through just about every small town between Rome and Viterbo. The main **bus depot** (served by the COTRAL network) is a ten-minute walk from the centre, out past Porta Fiorentina on the Tangenziale Ovest.

There's a **tourist office** on Via Ascenzi 4 (Tues–Sun 10am–1pm & 3–6pm, ☎0761.325.992, ⓔinfotuscia@libero.it) where you can pick up the free listings guide *Tuscia: Guida all'Ospitalità*, available in both Italian and English.

Accommodation

Viterbo's best accommodation options lie in its many **B&B**s which give the opportunity to stay in atmospheric medieval buildings fitted out with modern comforts.

Al Melograno Strada S. Caterina ☎0761.250.706, ⓦwww.almelograno.net. Simple rooms located just a short walk from the Terme dei Papi and the *terme pubbliche*. ❸

B&B dei Papi Via del Ginnasio 8 ☎0761.309.039, ⓦwww.bbdeipapi.it. Modern design in a fairytale setting. The owners have filled this a vine-clad mansion with contemporary art and antiques. ❸

Rooms have themed décor and the suite comes with a canopy bed.

La Terrazza Medioevale Via San Pellegrino 1 ☎0761.307.034, ⓦwww.laterrazzamedioevale .com. A beautifully restored and classically decorated B&B situated in noble family palace. Breakfast is served on the rooftop terrace with views across town. ❸

The Town

If there is a centre to Viterbo, it's **Piazza del Plebiscito**, an appropriately named square girdled almost entirely by fifteenth- and sixteenth-century buildings. The lions and palm trees that reflect each other across the square are the city's symbols, repeated, with grandiose echoes of Venice, all over town. Peek into the fine Renaissance courtyard of the main, arcaded building of the **Palazzo dei Priori** (Mon–Sat 9am–1pm & 3.30–6.30pm, Sun 9am–noon; free). The council chamber is decorated with a series of murals depicting Viterbo's history right back to Etruscan times in a weird mixture of pagan and Christian motifs – a melange continued across the square in the church of **Sant'Angelo**.

Roads fork in many directions from the piazza. Most interesting is **Via San Lorenzo**, which sweeps past the pretty Piazza di Gesù to the macabrely named **Piazza del Morte** – the "Square of Death", after the paupers and abandoned corpses that were buried here by the monks. A left from here leads to Viterbo's oldest district, the **Quartiere San Pellegrino** – a tight mess of hilly streets, home to a number of art and antique shops. In the opposite direction, **Piazza San Lorenzo** is flanked by the town's most historic buildings, notably the **Palazzo dei Papi** itself, a thirteenth-century structure with impressive views looking over the green gorge that cuts into central Viterbo. Most of the palace is closed to the public but you can visit the Aula del Conclave, venue of the election of half a dozen or so popes; enquire at the Museo del Colle del Duomo in Piazza San Lorenzo 8/A (summer 10am–1pm & 3–8pm; winter 10am–1pm & 3–6pm; closed Mon; €5). Next, wander into the **Duomo** opposite, a plain Romanesque church that has an elegant striped floor and an understated beauty unusual among Italian churches. Northeast of Piazza del Plebiscito, Via Roma becomes **Corso Italia**, Viterbo's main shopping area and the scene of a busy *passeggiata* in the evenings. At its far end, steps lead up from Piazza Verdi to the nineteenth-century church of **Santa Rosa**, where the desiccated corpse of the town's patron saint can be seen in the second chapel on the right – a faintly grotesque, doll-like figure with a forced grin, dressed up in a nun's habit. On September 3 each year during the **festa** the icon is carried through the streets inside a huge alterpiece, to the accompaniment of much revelry and, later, fireworks.

From Piazza Verdi, follow Via Matteotti up to **Piazza della Rocca**, a large square dominated by the fierce-looking **Rocca Albornoz**, home of the small **Museo Nazionale Etrusco** (Tues–Sun 8.30am–7.30pm; €6; ☏0761.325.929), whose archeological collection includes displays of locally unearthed Roman and Etruscan artefacts. Just off the opposite side of the square, the church of **San Francesco** is also worth a quick look. The high, unusually plain Gothic church is the burial place of two of Viterbo's popes – Clement IV and Adrian V – both laid in now heavily restored, but impressive, Cosmatesque tombs on either side of the main altar.

Terme

Accessible by local bus from the station in **Piazza Martiri D'Ungheria**, Viterbo's various *terme*, or "hot baths", are a couple of kilomtres west of the city. You can take the #2 bus along the Fosso Faul gorge to the **Terme dei Papi** (☏0761.3501, ⓦwww.termedeipapi.it; €12, Sat & Sun €18; closed Tues), a spa at a four-star hotel at which you spend a very relaxing few hours lounging poolside or floating in the 40°C water. For the free public pools, stay on the bus until just before the **Strada Tuscanese**, where the parked cars and rising steam around the *pozzi* on your left hand side signal a similar hotspot called the Piscine Carletti where temperatures reach 58°C.

Eating and drinking

Viterbo has a good range of **restaurants** and a comparatively lively nightlife.

Bar Lucio Via San Pellegrino 13 ☏0761.346.6832. Open only in the eve, this bar is where Viterbo's burgeoning student population hangs out. Closed Sat & Sun.

Enopizzeria Da Lucio Via San Pellegrino 21 ☏0761.340.626. This modern wine bar-pizzeria-restaurant set in a fourteenth-century building does excellent pizzas and *fritti*. Closed Sun & Mon.

Schenardi Corso Italia 11 ☏0761.345.860. With its regilded Art Nouveau interior, this historic café is one of the nicest places for a lunchtime snack or tea. Closed Wed.

Tre Re Via M. Gattesco 3 ☏0761.304.619. This cosy place popular with locals is a good venue for trying regional specialities – the chick pea and chestnut soup is a must when in season. Closed Thurs.

Wine Bar Venezia Via Maestre 4 ☏334.165.6453, ⓦwww.wbv.it. This enoteca offers an exhaustive list of regional and national wines and a constantly changing menu made from the highest quality seasonal products. Check their website for upcoming tastings and cultural events in Viterbo. Closed Sun–Tues.

Around Viterbo

Viterbo makes by far the best base (besides Rome) for seeing much of Northern Lazio, especially the places that aren't really feasible on a day-trip from the capital. If you're without a car, don't worry. The **COTRAL** bus network (see box, p.721) is extensive, and, once you tune in to its eccentricities, virtually everywhere worth going to is accessible. The Mannerist villas of **Caprarola** and **Bagnaia** are a short distance away and easily reached on public transport, as are – from the same era – the bizarre gardens of **Bomarzo** and the shores of **Lago di Bolsena**.

Bagnaia

About 5km east of Viterbo, **BAGNAIA** isn't much of a town, but like Caprarola further south it's completely dominated by a sixteenth-century palace, the **Villa Lante**, whose small but superb estate is considered Vignola's masterpiece and a supreme creation of Mannerist garden art. Sacheverell Sitwell pronounced it "the most lovely place of the physical beauty of nature in all Italy or in all the world". The villa is easily visited from Viterbo using the hourly **bus** #6 from Piazza Martiri D'Ungheria or from the stop at the beginning of Viale Trento, or the less frequent trains of the Roma-Nord line.

A short walk uphill from the main square, the **villa** is actually two buildings, built twenty years apart for different cardinals, but symmetrically aligned as part of the same architectural plan. They are closed to the public, save for one loggia, but there's nothing much to write home about anyway; in contrast to Caprarola, it's the **gardens** (Tues–Sun 8.30am to 1hr before sunset; €2) that take pride of place – some of the period's best preserved and a summing up of Mannerist aspirations. The main group lies behind the villas, ranged over five gently sloping terraces. An attempt at a stylized interpretation of the natural world, they were an ambitious project even by the standards of the time. The route takes in various watery adventures – waterfalls, lakes and the like – and among numerous fountains and low hedges surface plenty of humorous or symbolic touches. Look for the ubiquitous shrimp motif, symbol of the villa's first patron Cardinal Gambara, allegories of the four elements, and a cascade designed as an elongated crayfish.

The adjoining **park** (hours as for the villa, free), through which you can wander at will, is a popular spot for locals who lounge and read on its ample lawns.

Outside of Bagnaia the wooded hills of Monte Cimino are part of a natural reserve where hikers, bikers and picnickers can enjoy an outing in lush pine forests.

Bomarzo

Twelve kilometres northeast of Bagnaia, the village of **BOMARZO** is home to another Mannerist creation, the **Parco dei Mostri** (daily 8.30am–1hr before sunset; €9) and a greater contrast to the former's restrained elegance would be hard to find. The "Monster Park" was built in 1552 by the hunchbacked Duke of Orsini, who set out to parody Mannerist self-glorification by deliberate vulgarity. The result was like a sixteenth-century theme park of fantasy and horror, today one of northern Lazio's primary tourist attractions.

Throughout the park, there are dank, mossy sculptures of tortoises, elephants, a whale, a mad laughing mask, dragons, nymphs, butterflies and plenty more. Highlights include a perfect octagonal temple, dedicated to Orsini's wife, and a crooked, slanting house that makes your head spin. Numerous cryptic inscriptions dot the park and add to the mystery.

Eight **buses** a day run from Viterbo and six daily from Orte to Bomarzo's Piazza Matteotti, from where the Parco dei Mostri is a signposted ten-minute walk downhill. Avoid arriving by **train.** The Attigliano-Bomarzo station is 5km away and there are no buses that run from the station to the town. The site has a self-service cafeteria, bar and ample picnic tables or else you can head back up to town to trattoria-pizzeria *Da Zena* on Via del Piano (℡0761.924.184; closed Tues).

Lago di Bolsena

North along the Via Cassia from Viterbo, **LAGO DI BOLSENA** is a popular destination, though rarely overcrowded. The western shore is better for camping rough and more picturesque into the bargain. The lake occupies the remains of a broad volcanic crater and is the largest of its kind in Europe. The immensely fertile soil and super-mild microclimate spur farmers and vintners to great heights. Dante praised the quality of its eels, though fishermen today are hampered by the so-called *sesse* – odd tide-like variations in the lake's level.

On the northern shore of the lake, **BOLSENA** is the main focus, a relaxed and likeable place that's worth a brief stop. The town itself is set 1km from the water. Medieval nooks and alleyways run off the main square, Piazza Matteotti where the deconsecrated thirteenth-century church of **San Francesco** occasionally hosts concerts and small exhibitions. The adjacent 16th century portal is the entrance to the medieval *borgo* surmounted by the well-preserved thirteenth-century Monaldeschi **castle** perched over its western end. Inside is the local **museum** (summer Tues–Sun 10am–1pm & 4–8pm; winter Tues–Fri 10am–1pm & 3–6pm; €3.50) with modest displays on underwater archeology and Villanovan and Etruscan finds, plus stunning views from the ramparts.

East of Piazza Matteotti the twelfth-century **Santa Cristina** conceals a good Romanesque interior behind a wide Renaissance facade added in 1494. Cristina, daughter of the town's third-century Roman prefect, was tortured by her father for her Christian beliefs, eventually being thrown into the lake with a stone round her neck. Miraculously the rock floated, though Cristina was martyred soon after. Adjoining the chapel is the Grotta di Santa Cristina, once part of early Christian **catacombs** (daily: summer 9.30am–noon & 3.30–6.30pm; winter 9.30–11.30am & 3–4.30pm; €4; ☎0761.799.067, Ⓦwww.basilicasantacristina.it).

There are several **bars and restaurants** around Piazza Matteotti, the best of which is *Osteria del Borgo Dentro* on Via Cavour 5 (☎0761.797.167; closed Mon) which specializes in lake fish and has an impressive selection of locally produced cheeses. In the summer, the lake shore's restaurants are abuzz with activity, most offering a full toursit menu. *La Pineta* on Viale Diaz 48 (☎0761.799.801, Ⓦwww.lapinetabolsena.it; closed Thurs and Mon–Wed at lunch) serves an exquisite 5-course lake fish menu for €25. The closest of the **campsites**, most of which are a short walk out of town, is the *Campeggio Internazionazionale Il Lago*, less than 1km away at Viale Cadorna 6 (☎0761.799.191, Ⓦwww .campingillago.it; April–Sept; ❶). The cheapest **hotel** is the *Pensione Italia*, Corso Cavour 53 (☎0761.799.193; Ⓦwww.pensioneitalia.it; ❷). For full listings of accommodation, call in at the **tourist office** at Piazza Matteotti 12 (daily: summer 9.30am–12.30pm & 4.30–7.30pm; winter 9.30am–12.30pm; ☎0761.799.923, Ⓔufficioturistico@comunebolsena.it).

Southern Lazio

The saying goes that the Italian South begins with the first petrol station below Rome, and certainly there's a radically different feel here. Green wooded hills give way to flat marshy land and harsh unyielding mountains that possess a poor, almost desperate, look in places – most travellers skate straight through en route to Naples. But the **coast** merits a more unhurried route south – its resorts, especially **Terracina** and **Sperlonga**, are fine places to take it easy after the rigours of the capital. And the **Pontine Islands**, a couple of hours offshore, are – out of high season, at least – among Italy's undiscovered treasures. **Inland**, too, the landscape can be rewarding: the day-trip towns of the **Castelli Romani** attractively encircle Lago Albano. **Subiaco** to the east and the **Ciocaria** region to the south are more remote, but hold some of Lazio's most inspiring scenery – broad tree-clad hills and valleys sheltering small, unassuming towns.

The Castelli Romani

Just free of the sprawling southern suburbs of Rome, the thirteen towns that make up the **Castelli Romani** date back to pre-Roman times. These hills – the **Colli Albani** – have long cooled rich and powerful urbanites, who also treasure the area's extraordinary white wines, inspired by the rich volcanic soil, and the spectacular views of Lago Albano. The region is now pretty heavily built-up, with most of the historic centres ringed by unprepossessing suburbs, and summer weekends see traffic jams of Romans trooping out to local trattorias. But off-peak, it's worth the journey, either as an excursion from Rome or a stop on the way south. COTRAL **buses** serve the area (every 30min; 35min) from Rome's Anagnina metro station (line A) and regular trains depart from Roma Termini for Frascati, Albano, Marino and Velletri.

▲ Lago Albano, Lazio

Frascati and around

At just 20km from Rome, **FRASCATI** is the nearest of the Castelli towns and also the most striking, dominated by the majestic **Villa Aldobrandini**, designed by Giacomo della Porta at the turn of the sixteenth century. The Baroque *palazzo* is off-limits, but the **gardens** are open (Mon–Fri: summer 9am–1pm & 3–6pm; winter 9am–1pm & 3–5pm; free). Sadly the elaborate water theatre, where statues once played flutes, no longer spouts in top form, but the view from the front terrace is superb, with Rome visible on a clear day.

Frascati's main square, **Piazza Marconi**, is right beneath the Aldobrandini villa, and home to a **tourist office** (Mon–Sat 9am–1pm, Tues & Fri 4–7pm; ☎06.942.0331). Just beyond here is the pedestrianized old centre, which revolves around the two squares of **Piazza San Pietro** and **Piazza del Mercato** just beyond. Frascati is also about the most famous of the Colli Albani wine towns: ask at the tourist office for details of winery tours and tastings, or simply indulge at one of the many enotecas in town – try the historic family enterprise *Grappolo d'Oro* in Piazza Filzi. To sample rustic, local products, head to one of the stands on **Piazza del Mercato** or one of the town's many *fraschette* (taverns) for *porchetta* (roast pork) sandwich, *coppiette* (spicy pork jerky), and pecorino (sheep) cheese. For a more formal preparation of artisanal local products, try *Signor T* just off Piazza del Mercato (☎0697.245.123, ❷www .signort.it; eve only, closed Mon). For **accommodation**, the *Pinocchio* Piazza del Mercato 21 (☎0694.17.883, ❷www.hotelpinocchio.it; ❷), has affordable, stylish rooms and its **restaurant** specializes in porcini mushrooms, grilled meats, and duck.

Tusculum (always open; free), beautifully sited 5km away on a nearby hill, was an Etruscan centre overrun by Roman patricians. The Emperor Tiberius and orator Cicero both had villas here, but Pope Celestine III destroyed the resort in 1191 and the inhabitants relocated downhill, founding modern-day Frascati. Undergrowth has submerged most of the Roman remains, but there's a small theatre, and the views, again, are fine.

Grottaferrata and Marino

Three kilometres or so south of Frascati, **GROTTAFERRATA** is also known for its wine and its eleventh-century **Abbey** – a fortified Basilian (Greek Orthodox) monastery surrounded by high defensive walls and a now empty moat (daily: 9am–12.30pm & 3.30 to 1hr before sunset; www .abbaziagreca.it; free). Within the complex, the little church of Santa Maria has Byzantine-style interior decorated with thirteenth-century mosaics and, in the chapel of St Nilo off the right aisle, frescoes by Domenichino. Through the inner courtyard there's a small museum (closed for restoration) displaying classical and medieval sculptures.

MARINO, another 4km further on, is a pleasant little town set around a pretty main square, Piazza Matteoti, where the Fontana dei Mori has mermaids and manacled Moors commemorating the Battle of Lepanto. On the first Sunday of October the town celebrates the Sagra dell'Uva festival and the foutain spouts *vino*, while at other times of years you can simply sample the local wine in the village's abundant *enotecas*, bars and pubs. For a vast selection of local wine and an artfully executed seasonal menu, try *La Credenza* restaurant on Via Cola di Rienzo 4 (☎0693.85.105, closed Sun).

Castel Gandolfo and the Via Appia

Leaving Marino, the road joins up with the ancient Roman Via Appia, which travels straight as an arrow down the west side of Lago Albano. **CASTEL GANDOLFO** is the first significant stop, best known as the pope's summer retreat–between July and September the Pope gives sporadic midday addresses on Sundays. Four hundred metres above the lake, it's a pleasantly airy place, and enjoys great views over Lago Albano from its terraces close by the main Piazza della Libertá, a pleasant oblong of cafés and papal souvenir shops, at the end of which is the imposing bulk of the Papal Palace itself. Below the town, there's a pleasant lido along the lakeshore with lots of restaurants and pizzerias and a small stretch of grey beach from where you could stroll the whole shoreline in about two hours. The road leads down from the main highway, just north of Castel Gandolfo's old centre.

From Castel Gandolfo a panoramic road leads south to **ALBANO LAZIALE**, one of the larger and in some ways more appealing of the towns along the ancient Via Appia. Its strategic position has left it with lots of Roman remnants: a crumbled old amphitheatre, once with room for 15,000 spectators, fragments of a gate right in the town centre and the foundations of the Roman garrison's baths behind the church of **San Pietro**, on the main street, Corso Matteotti. You can get the lowdown on all this in the nearby **Museo Civico**, Viale Risorgimento 3 (Mon–Sun 9am–1pm, plus Wed & Thurs 4–7pm; €2.50; ☎0693.23.490, ⓦwww.museicivicialbano.it), which has lots of information and a small but high-quality archeological collection.

There are much nicer places to stay than Albano, but if you're hungry, *Antico Forno*, a restaurant and wine bar on the main street at no. 30, is a good place for a light meal (☎0693.20.255, closed Sun). Otherwise the Via Appia continues on to **ARICCIA**, across the nineteenth-century **Ponte di Ariccia** – whose Roman viaduct arches are visible below – into the town's central piazza, a well-proportioned square that owes its appearance to Baroque master Bernini. His Pantheon-inspired church of **Santa Maria dell'Assunzione** sits across the Piazza della Repubblica from the massive **Palazzo Chigi** (Tues–Sun guided tour schedule varies; ⓦwww.palazzochigiariccia.it; €7) built for Pope Alexander VII. Locally, Bernini's fame here is eclipsed by the town's most famous food, *porchetta* – roast pork, which is served from 10am to midnight in *fraschette*, rustic taverns, clustered on Via dell'Uccelliera and Via Borgo S. Rocco.

Beyond here, **GENZANO** was once the seat of the Sforzas and is still dominated by the **Castello Sforza–Cesarini** at the top of the town, a decrepit building whose grounds now form the pleasantly bucolic **Parco Sforza** (daily 10am–1pm & 3pm to 1hr before sunset; free); its wooded paths and ponds give wonderful views over the Lago di Nemi. The town of **NEMI**, built high above the tiny crater lake, isn't much to write home about, but the local **museum** (☎069.398.04; daily 9am–7pm; €2), below the town on the lake's northern shore, contains the scant remains of two Roman pleasure boats, floating villas, built by Caligula. In ancient times they were sunk, probably to destroy traces of the emperor after his assassination. They were raised in the 1930s by Mussolini's government as part of a Fascist propaganda campaign. In the last days of the German occupation in 1944 they were set on fire so what you see today are modern models of the imperial ships. Much of the bronze fittings of these boats have been transferred to Palazzo Massimo in Rome but there are always interesting exhibitions of recent local archeological finds on display.

Palestrina to Cassino

Considering its proximity to the capital, it's a surprise that the **southeastern section of Lazio**, tucked in the foothills of the Abruzzo mountains, is so neglected and generally bypassed on the fast Autostrada del Sole heading south. For those who take the time, the area yields some real gems, from a masterpiece mosaic in **Palestrina** to the cave of St Benedict in **Subiaco** and the infamous World War II battleground at **Cassino**.

Palestrina

PALESTRINA was built on the site of the ancient Praeneste, originally an Etruscan settlement and later a favoured resort for patrician Romans. "Cool Praeneste", as Horace called it, was the site of an enormous Temple of Fortune whose foundations more or less determine the modern centre, which steps up the hillside in a series of terraces.

The bus trip from Rome takes 65 minutes (frequent departures from Ponte Mammolo-Metro B), terminating at Via degli Arcioni from where the trudge up to the town is a steep one. The main square, **Piazza Regina Margherita**, gives a chance to catch your breath and is home to the town's **Duomo**, which has a copy of Michelangelo's chunky and rather modern-looking *Pietà di Palestrina* in the left aisle – the original is now in Florence. Take a look also at the **Area Sacra** (Fri–Sun 9am to 1hr before sunset; Mon–Thurs ask at museum to visit; free), in the corner of the square, where there are a few fragments of ancient Roman floor mosaic showing sea creatures of various kinds.

The stepped streets around encourage casual strolling, but you need to save your energy for Palestrina's real attraction, right on top of the hill, the **Palazzo Barberini**, which houses the **Museo Nazionale Archeologico Prenestino** (daily 9am–7.30pm; ℡069.538.100; €3), originally built in the eleventh century and greatly modified in 1640. The palace and the terraces below were carved out of a Republican temple which previously stood on this site, and the views are magnificent from the top, surveying the countryside around as far as the eye can see. Among the collection's highlights are a number of ancient Roman pieces found locally: a torso of Fortune in slate-grey marble; the *Triade Capitolina*, showing Juno, Jupiter and Minerva, illegally excavated in the early 1990s and narrowly apprehended in the Stelvio Pass on its way out of the country; Etruscan funerary *cistae*; and, the museum's prize possession, a marvellous first-century BC *Mosaic of the Nile* housed at the very top of the building, which traces the flooding river from source to delta, chronicling everyday Egyptian life in amazing detail.

Practicalities

There's a **tourist office** on Piazzae Santa Maria degli Angeli (Mon–Sat 8am–7pm; ℡069.573.176), another in the Palazzo Barberini (hours as above). If you decide to stay, the rather basic **hotel** *Stella*, just past the cathedral at Piazzale della Liberazione 3, is good enough (℡069.538.172, Ⓦwww.hotelstella.it; ❷), and has a decent restaurant. For fresh fish and grilled meat head to the inviting *Ristorante A Modo* (℡069.531.0035; closed Wed) on Via Anicia 11.

Subiaco

Around 15km northeast of Palestrina, **SUBIACO** is beautifully set around a hill topped by the Rocca Abbazia castle, and close to Monte Liviato – one of Lazio's premier ski resorts. Purpose-built for workmen on Nero's grand villa (very meagre traces of which survive), Subiaco became the contemplative base of St Benedict in the fifth century. The hermit dwelt in a mountain cave here for three years, before leaving to found the monastery at Montecassino, but his legacy continues today in the shape of two monastic complexes just outside town.

The **Monastero di Santa Scolastica** (daily 9.30am–12.30pm & 3.30–7pm; free) is the closer (and larger) complex, where the first book to be printed in Italy came off the press in 1465. It's a pleasant three-kilometre walk along the Jenne road from the main bus stop – follow the signs left before the bridge. Dedicated to Benedict's sister, the monastery's most notable features are its three delightful cloisters, the first is from the Renaissance period; the second, one of the oldest Gothic works in Italy, lushly planted and fragrant; and the third a Cosmati work with lovely arcades of pillars.

Fifteen minutes up the same road, the landscape grows more dramatic as it approaches the craggy **Monastero di San Benedetto**, nicknamed the "swallow's nest" (hours as above; free). This is much the more interesting monastery: the church's upper part has frescoes of the fourteenth-century Sienese school and fifteenth-century Perugian school and the lower levels incorporate Benedict's cave, all raw authentic rock except for a serene statue by Raggi, a disciple of Bernini. From here a spiral staircase leads up to the chapel of San Gregorio, containing a thirteenth-century picture of St Francis that's reckoned to be the first portrait of the saint painted from life. In the other direction, stairs descend to the chapel where Benedict preached to shepherds, and a terrace that overlooks the so-called "Holy Rose Tree" – in fact, a three-forked bush allegedly created by St Francis from a bramble.

Practicalities

Subiaco and its monasteries are a comfortable **day-trip** from Rome's Ponte Mammolo station (2hr; last bus 8.30pm, Sun 7.30pm). Four daily buses also service Frosinone, a transport hub, if you're heading **south** to Campania.

The town's location may, however, make you want to linger and you can book a room at the Monastero di Santa Scolastica, which has well appointed rooms and a restaurant; it caters to pilgrms and tourists alike (℡0774.85.569, Ⓦwww .benedettini-subiaco.it; ❸). The bargain *Villino Michela B&B* at Contrada Rapello 4, 1.5km outside town towards Fiuggi, offers a warm welcome, lush garden, and free pick-up from Subiaco (℡0774.84.750, Ⓔvillino.michela@virgilo.it; ❷). The **tourist office** at Via Cadorna 59 (Mon–Sat 8am–2pm, Tues & Fri also 3–6pm; ℡0774.822.013) is eager to advise. Just downhill, towards the fourteenth-century humpbacked bridge of **San Francesco**, is a new booth promoting the **Monte Simbruini Park**, popular among climbers, kayakers, skiers and hikers.

The Ciociaria

From Subiaco the road heads south into the **Ciociaria**, a relatively remote corner of Lazio that takes its name from the bark sandals (*ciocie*) worn here in antiquity. Italic tribes – the Hernici, Equii, Volscians and Sanniti – settled this hilly land and built inaccessible, heavily fortified towns several centuries before the Romans. The extraordinary cyclopean walls, unique in Italy, can still be seen, owing to their shrewd foreign policy of allying with Rome.

FIUGGI is a spa resort, which also pumps out a popular brand of bottled mineral water. Health-conscious Italians clog the lower **Fonte** quarter – a grim modern grid – in summer. The bright and breezy **historic centre**, however, has medieval alleys, genteel cafés, panoramic views of the chestnut-clad hills and an exuberant Art Nouveau theatre. The **tourist office** is near the train station and spa below (Piazza Frascara 4; Mon–Sat 8am–2pm & 3.30–6.30pm; ℡0775.515.019, Ⓦwww.apt.frosinone.it). **Dine** just off Piazza Trento e Trieste at *La Grotta*, an appealing pizzeria, decorated with old farm tools, that serves Laziale specialities like *abbacchio scottadito* (Via Garibaldi 2; ℡0775.514.072; closed Thurs).

From Fiuggi, head west to Anagni or south to Alatri. **ANAGNI**, a former Hernici stronghold, is a well-preserved old place that produced four medieval popes including Boniface VIII. He tried to assert the papacy's absolute authority, provoking representatives of Philip IV of France to attack his **palace** (daily 9am–1pm & 3.30–6.30pm; €3) here in 1303. Visit the room where Colonna, one of Philip's henchmen, allegedly slapped Boniface – a statue of whom stands outside Anagni's **Duomo**, an imposing Romanesque basilica dating from the eleventh century. Inside there's a fine Cosmatesque pavement, a thirteenth-century baldachino, some important proto-Renaissance thirteenth-century frescoes in the crypt and a treasury containing some of Boniface's pontifical effects. Piazza Innocenzo III is home to the **tourist office** (9am–1pm & 3–7pm daily; ℡0775.727.852, www.apt.frosinone.it).

In the opposite direction, **ALATRI** – ancient Aletrium – preserves its cyclopean walls from the sixth-century BC acropolis later modified by the Romans. The best-preserved stretch is at the Porta dei Falli, with its strident fertility symbols carved on the lintel. The town's streets wind around the citadel beneath the walls, cut by two square gateways, inside of which the cathedral and Episcopal Palace stand on the site of the Hernici's ancient temples, since lost. The views, incidentally, are terrific.

FROSINONE, 10km or so further south, is the main town of the Ciociaria. This bland sprawling hub – with barely any remains of the Hernici settlement – is of little interest. From here, trains run to Rome and to Cassino and Caserta, both of which have services to Naples. COTRAL buses run north to Fiuggi, Anagni and Alatri and south to Priverno.

Cassino and the Abbey of Montecassino

The town of **CASSINO** in the southeast corner of Lazio is the site of another important monastery, the **Abbazia di Montecassino** (daily: summer 9am–12.15pm & 3.30–6.15pm; winter 9am–12.30pm & 3.30–5pm; free; Ⓦwww .montecassino.it). Three ravens guided St Benedict to this spot, after he left Subiaco in 529. He founded one of the most important and influential Christian complexes in the world. Its monks spread the word as far away as Britain and Scandinavia, while developing the tradition of culture and learning that was at the core of the Benedictine order. Ironically, its strategically vital position, perched high on a mountaintop between Rome and Naples, was the abbey's downfall. A succession of invaders coveted and fought over this vantage point, and the buildings were repeatedly destroyed.

During World War II, the abbey came to be the lynchpin of the German presence in this part of Italy. After a battle that lasted almost six months, the Allies – a mixture of Poles, New Zealanders and Indian troops – eventually bombed it to ruins in May 1944, sacrificing several thousand lives in the process. The austere medieval architecture has been faithfully recreated, but it's really more impressive for its position. Much is not open to the public, and its sterile white central courtyard is engaging only for the views of the surrounding hills and the Polish war cemetery below. The hideously ornate Baroque church has a small **museum** (€2) containing old manuscripts and suchlike. Yet you can't help but feel that Montecassino's glory days ended firmly with the war.

⑪

The **town** below was fairly comprehensively destroyed, too, and has very little appeal (except for Fiat enthusiasts, who coo over the factory). There's a **tourist office** at Via di Biasio 54 (Mon 8am–2pm, Tues–Fri 8am–2pm & 3–6pm, Sat 9am–1pm; ☎0776.21.292, ⓦwww.apt.frosinone.it). Cassino is connected by train from Rome and Frosinore buses scale the mountain to the abbey from Piazza San Benedetto twice daily, passing the train station along the route. If you need to stay, try the central *Hotel Piazza Marconi* on Via Marconi 25 (☎0776.26.025. ⓦwww.hotelpiazzamarconi.it; ❸) where the rooms are spacious and modern, each with free internet access.

The southern Lazio coast

The **Lazio coast to the south** of Rome is a more attractive proposition than the northern stretches. Its towns have a bit more charm, the water is cleaner, and in the further reaches, beyond the flats of the Pontine Marshes and Monte Circeo, the shoreline begins to pucker into cliffs and coves that hint gently at the glories of Campania – all good either for day-trips and overnight outings from the city, or for a pleasingly wayward route to Naples.

Anzio and Nettuno

Just 40 km or an hour by train, **ANZIO** is an easy day-trip from Rome. While the town itself is a resort, the water is not particularly clean and the real draw is for the town's historical monuments, both modern and ancient. Much of the town was damaged during a difficult Allied landing here on January 22, 1944, to which two military cemeteries (one British, on the road to Aprilia, and another, American, just outside nearby Nettuno, COTRAL buses pass both) bear testimony, as does a small museum (Via di Villa Adele, Tues, Thurs, Sat & Sun 10.30am–12.30pm & 4–6pm; free). North of the harbour are the seaside ruins of the Villa di Nerone (daily: summer 10.30am–12.30pm & 3.30–5.30pm; winter 10.30am–12.30pm & 2.30–4.30pm). Nero was vacationing at this sprawling beachfront estate, now a backdrop for sunbathers, when the infamous fire of 64 AD broke out in Rome.

In town, the seafood **restaurants** that crowd together along the harbour are not unreasonably priced. *La Cicala*, right by the water at Riviera Zanardelli 11 (☎06.984.6747; winter closed Wed), is as good as any; nearby at Via Porto Innocenziano 19, *Romolo al Porto* (☎06.984.4079; closed Wed & Jan), is universally recognized as Lazio's best fish restaurant. Anzio is also a possible route to Ponza; **hydrofoils** leave daily June to September from Via Porto Innocenziano (☎069.845.083, ⓦwww.vetor.it). For timings and other information, ask at the **tourist office** at Piazza Pia (Mon–Sat: winter 9.30am–1pm & 4.30–6.30pm; summer 9.30am–1pm & 5.30–7.30pm; ☎069.845.147).

NETTUNO, a couple of kilometres down the coast (walkable by the shoreline road), is more of the same, but with slightly smaller beaches; again swimming is not recommended. It's a mostly modern town, but there's a well-preserved old quarter, still walled, with a couple of decent **trattorias** on the main square – information from the **tourist office** at the port (Mon–Fri 10am–12.30pm & 5–7.30pm, Sat 10.30am–12.30pm & 5.30–7pm; ☎069.803.335).

The Pontine Marches: Sermoneta and Ninfa

Beyond Anzio and Nettuno lie the **Pontine Marshes**, until seventy-odd years ago a boggy plain prone to malaria and populated by only a few inhabitants and water buffalo. Julius Caesar hoped to drain the area, but was assassinated before he could carry out the plan. Instead Mussolini reclaimed the region in 1928 – building a series of spanking new towns and exposing fertile, fresh farmland.

At the centre of the development lies **LATINA**, the provincial capital, founded in 1932, and heart of the lively, local agricultural economy, though of little interest save for its transport connections and its numerous Fascist-era structures including the Palazzo "M", a limestone building shaped like the letter M to commemorate Mussolini. Buses zigzag up to the medieval town of **SERMONETA**, remarkable for its walls erected to safeguard against the Saracens and later struggles between the papacy and other kingdoms, which raged throughout the Middle Ages. The well-preserved **Castello Caetani** (guided tours every hour April–Oct 10am–noon & 4–6pm; Nov–March 10am–noon & 2–4pm; €5) was erected in the 1200s by the feudal Caetani family, it's a near-perfect example of the medieval system of moats, portcullises, drawbridges and tunnels designed to render the place practically impregnable. Inside, there is a huge display of arms, armour, catapults and ancient cannons, plus the vast siege cisterns and silos. To get a feel for Sermoneta, it's worth staying over, and the *Ostello San Nicola* is the place, at Via G. Matteotti 1 (℡0773.30.381, ⊛www.sannicola-hostel.com;❶), a thirteenth-century convent with Gothic church and fading frescoes, plus a mixture of dorm beds and private rooms, and communal kitchen. To **eat**, head to *Il Simposio*, Corso Garibaldi 33 (℡3392.846.905; closed Mon) specializing in hearty pastas and grilled meats. Try their pasta *al Trombolotto* a medieval sauce that combines a lemon oil and 14 herbs. From May to September, you can eat in their pergola-covered garden restaurant, *Enoteca Simposio*, Via della Condutture 2.

The ruins of **NINFA** are difficult to reach without your own transport. To get there, catch the train to Latina Scalo and take a taxi the remaining 8km, around €15. This other Caetani stronghold and its enchanting gardens (April–Oct: open first weekend and third Thurs of each month sometimes with additional opening days – check with Latina tourist office ℡0773.695.404; guided tours only, every 15min; 9am–noon & 2.30–6pm; €8) huddle at the base of the cliff. The tranquil nook inspired the poetry of Pliny the Elder: the oasis – surrounding a temple to the nymphs – later grew into a thriving fortified village in the twelfth century. Bandits, mercenaries and malaria destroyed Ninfa, dubbed the "Pompeii of the Middle Ages". The citizens fled to Sermoneta: their ruins became the backdrop of spectacular landscaping in the early twentieth century. Wild and domestic flowers, shrubs and trees flourish among charming rivulets, waterfalls and ponds: the design is spontaneous, whimsical and entirely enchanting.

Sabaudia and around

The area around **SABAUDIA**, 20km from Latina, gives some impression of the terrain's native sogginess, poised between two lagoons. Fascist propaganda claims the town was built in just 253 days. Architectural highlights include the austere rationalist-style town hall tower, the mosaiced exterior of **SS Annunziata church** and the quirky, asymmetrical post office. The **tourist office** is at Piazza del Commune 18 (open daily 9.15am–12.30pm & 4–8pm; ℡0773.515.046).

COTRAL buses stop in Piazza Oberdan from where it is just a ten-minute walk to the bridge that leads from Sabaudia across the lagoon to the coast where the beaches are unspoilt and empty most of the time except during high season. Although there are plenty of beachfront properties, there are still some places to access the sand, and parking spaces alongside. The road cuts through the dunes between the sea and the coastal lakes to the crumbling sixteenth-century **Torre Paola** above which rises the huge bulk of **Monte Circeo** to the south. Sabaudia is populated with campsites and inexpensive **hotels**. An atmospheric B&B stands 1.5km from the tower: *Bahia di Buzios* is in a verdant glade, two minutes from the sea at Via delle Querce 18 (℡0773.596.815, ⓦwww .bahiadibuzios.it; ❷).

Sabaudia's pine groves, beachfront and lake, together with Monte Circeo and the offshore Zannone island form the **Parco Nazionale del Circeo**. Created in 1934, this preserves something of the marshes' wildlife and natural beauty (information at the Sabaudia or San Felice Circeo tourist offices, ⓦwww .parcocirceo.it). It's a fine spot for appreciating flora and fauna as well as archeological ruins–there are over 100 sites in varying states of preservation. The park's office can supply information and suggest hikes.

San Felice Circeo

About 7km from the Torre Paola, the inland paved road rounds the mountain to emerge at **SAN FELICE CIRCEO**, a picturesque village of pretty stone houses bleached yellow by the sun and clinging to the side of the mountain. In summer, the lower town's marina can be unpleasantly crowded, bursting with fancy motor launches and yachts, its sandy beaches crowded with oiled bodies and roads clogged with flashy cars. To escape the overpopulated sand, rent a boat at Circeo Mare, Via Ammiraglio Bergamini 124 (℡0773.549.335, ⓦwww .circeomare.it) to visit the famous **Grotta della Maga Circe**. Or explore on foot: take a left at the lighthouse (*Faro di Torre Cervia*) for the **Grotto delle Capre** or continue straight a few kilometres to a secluded and rocky swimming spot, also great for snorkelling.

Most of San Felice's accommodation is in the lower town, but you can nab a half-board **room** with sea views in the upper town at B&B *Giardino degli Ulivi* (℡0773.548.034, ⓦwww.giardinodegliulivi.eu; ❷), Via XXIV Maggio 13. Locals crowd together here for ample dinners in the vine-covered courtyard. The smart and stylish *Claro de Lua* at Via del Sole 9 (℡0773.548.425, ⓦwww .clarodelua.it; ❹) looks across the sea to the Pontine Islands and does candlelit barbeques in a panoramic gazebo. For good seafood, try *Trattoria Il Grottino* backing onto the upper town's main Piazza Vittorio Veneto (℡0773.548.446; closed Tues); their *gnochetti alla pescatora* are delicious. Just off Piazza V. Veneto, Piazza Lanzuisi is home to a **tourist office** (daily: summer 9am–1pm, 5–8pm & 9pm–midnight; winter 8am–2pm ℡0773.549.038) that also serves as an office for the Monte Circeo park. Walk through the arch to the main road, which winds up to the summit of Monte Circeo to an ancient **temple**. The views from here are marvellous: there's a large car park at the top, with a summer bar.

Buses arrive in the lower town from Via Domenichelli and depart for Roma Laurentina, Latina, Sabaudia, Terracina, and Priverno. A local minibus service connects the lower town to the historical centre above.

Terracina

A further 15km down the coast from San Felice (buses from Rome Laurentina; stops in Sabaudia and San Felice Circeoi), **TERRACINA** is an immediately likeable little town, divided between a tumbledown old quarter high on the hill and a lively newer area by the sea. During classical times, it was an important staging-post on the Appian Way, which meets the ocean here; nowadays it's primarily a seaside resort with good, ample beaches and frequent connections with the other points of interest, including daily ferries (☎0773.790.055, ⓦwww.snapnavigazione.it) and hydrofoils (☎081.552.0763, ⓦwww.navlib.it) to Ponza.

The centre of the old quarter is **Piazza Municipio**, which occupies the site of the Roman forum – complete with the original steps and slabs – and now focuses on the colonnade of the town's **Duomo**, with its elegant campanile. An endearing church with a fine mosaic floor and a beautiful tile-studded pulpit and twisted mosaic candlestick, it was built within the shell of a Roman temple dedicated to the gods Augustus and Roma. Also on the square, the **Museo Civico Pio Capponi** (Tues–Sat 9am–1.30pm & 3–8pm, Sun 10am–1pm & 5–9pm; €1.55) has finds from the Roman town.

Terracina's main attraction, and rightly so, is the **Temple of Jupiter Anxur**, which crowns the hill. Take the steps up from Piazza Municipio onto Via Anxur and follow this for 200m, from where a road winds to the top (30min). You can also take bus line L from Via Roma or Piazzale Marconi; every hour. The temple may date back to the first century BC and was connected to Terracina by some lengthy walls, and it's these days an impressive if rather ruinous complex, with tremendous views both ways up the coast. You can walk right through the vaulted arches of the temple and scramble around among the remains of the acropolis, finishing off with a coffee in the temple's café.

Practicalities

Apart from the scrubby oval of sand fringing the centre, Terracina's **beaches** stretch west pretty much indefinitely from the main harbour and are large enough to be uncrowded. The town's **tourist office** is five-minutes' walk from the sea in the new part of town, just off Via G. Leopardi, in the park behind Piazza Mazzini (summer Mon–Sat 9am–1pm & 5–8pm, Sun 9am–1pm; winter Mon–Fri 9am–1pm, Tues & Thurs also 3–6pm; ☎0773.727.759). One of the best places to **stay** is *Lungomare 116* in the old town at Lungomare Circe 116 (☎0773.764.110, ⓦwww.lungomare116.it; ❸), minimalist rooms in a villa on the sea. Their restaurant is popular with chic locals who are attracted by a menu that constantly changes depending on the day's catch. As for **eating**, in the lower town, *La Capannina*, on Via Appia beneath Monte Giove (☎0773.702.539; closed Tues), does exquisite seafood served on a terrace overlooking the sea. At Piazza della Repubblica 41 *Da Pino* serves up superb Neapolitan-style pizzas (☎0773.702.352; closed Thurs). For a quick bite, *Il Ristoro* on Via degli Uffici is a *tavola calda*, where locals clamour for excellent – and cheap – home-made pasta dishes and second courses. They also make pizzas to order (closed Tues eve).

Sperlonga

The coast south of Terracina is probably Lazio's prettiest stretch, the cliff punctured by tiny beaches signposted enticingly from the road. **SPERLONGA**, built high on a rocky promontory, is a fashionable spot for Roman and Neapolitan families, its whitewashed houses, arched alleys and stepped narrow streets almost Moorish in feel. Both the old upper town and modern lower district are almost given over entirely to tourists during summer, but it's still a pleasant place, and cars are not allowed into the old centre. A couple of kilometres south, the remains of the **Villa of Tiberius** (daily 8.30am–7.30pm; €4) are the only real sight of note and well worth the walk along the beach – head south from the town and turn off at the stone path after Lido Le Chiuse beach club. There's a small and extremely engaging museum with finds from the villa and its attached grotto, the setting for imperial banquets. The villa is right by the beach, and you can stroll around the excavations, as well as walking into the cave where fish still dart about Tiberius's fishpond. Beyond Sperlonga the coast steepens markedly, with yet more appealing beaches and any number of handy campsites.

The **beaches** run either side of Sperlonga's headland, but a lot of space is reserved by umbrellas. The modern *Grazia* **hotel** at Via M.A. Colonna 8 (℡0771.548.223, ⓦwww.hotelgrazia.com; ❹), a block from the beach at the northern end of the beachfront strip, is a good choice with modern rooms. If you want to be up in the old town, *Corallo*, just off Piazza della Repubblica at Corso S. Leone 3 (℡0771.548.060, ⓦwww.corallohotel.net; ❺), has mod cons and some rooms have panoramic balconies. Another possibility are the many **rooms and apartments** rented during peak season; ask at the **tourist office** on Via del Porto, the road that winds round the headland to the left of the main beach (daily 8am–8pm; ℡0771.557.341) or the other at Via del Corso 25 (daily 8am–8pm). As for **food**, *Lacoonte Da Rocco* (℡0771.548.122; closed Mon) on Via Cristoforo Colombo is the best option in the lower town and serves excellent fish dishes on a patio overlooking the sea. For more down-to-earth pasta and Neapolitan style pizza, head to *L'Angolo* (℡0771.548.808; closed Tues) on the sandy southern **beach**. Back in the modern centre, *Tropical*, Via C. Colombo 19 (℡0771.549.621, ⓦwww.tropical.it; closed Mon), does pizzas and other food and has a bar.

The nearest **train station** is Fondi-Sperlonga, 8km away, where there are infrequent buses into town. Certified taxis cost €6.50 per person (illegal drivers will negotiate) wait in front of the station. COTRAL **bus services** run to/from Formia, Gaeta, and Terracina with stops along Via Cristoforo Colombo in the lower town.

Formia and Gaeta

Some 20km around the bay, hard under the glowering backdrop of the Monti Aurunci, lies **FORMIA**. This largely modern town was an important resort during Roman times. Formia is a place for a stopover rather than a stay, with plentiful train connections to Naples, Rome and Cassino, and regular ferries and hydrofoils to Ponza (see p.742). There is a **tourist office** at Viale Unità d'Italia 30–34 (summer Mon–Sat 9am–1pm & 5–8pm, Sun 9am–1pm; winter Mon–Sat 9am–1pm, Tues & Thurs 3–6pm; ℡0771.771.490) with information on ferry departures. If you are stranded here, the *Del Golfo*, Piazzale della Stazione 1 (℡0771.790.037; ❷), is the town's cheapest **hotel**, and convenient if you are coming in on the train. In the centre, a great choice for **food** is *Chinappi*, the legendary family-run restaurant that turns out creative twists on traditional *laziale* and *campano* dishes (Via Anfiteatro 8; ℡0771790.002, ⓦwww.chinappi.it; closed Thurs).

The towers, cliffs and fortifications of **GAETA**, 5km southwest, glow golden at sunset – a fine sight for motorists stuck in the inevitable A1 traffic jam here. Once a marine republic and last bastion of the Bourbons, the city now teems with American servicemen from a base here. Burgers and beer dominate the lively port, but Gaeta has an atmospheric medieval quarter too, dominated by a stocky cliff-side **castle**. Behind the gothic church, SS Annunziata, lies the chapel of the **Golden Grotto** with its shimmering gilded barrel vault and alleged handprint of the Minotaur. Another myth claims Mount Orlando trembled and split in half when Jesus died. COTRAL buses for Gaeta leave from in front of the Formia train station; others arrive from Terracina, Sperlonga and Minturno.

The Pontine Islands

Scattered across the sea between Rome and Naples, these islands are some of Italy's least known to foreign travellers. Volcanic in origin, only two are inhabited: **Ventotene** and **Ponza**. The latter bustles with Italian tourists, especially Romans, between mid-June and the end of August; at any other time, the island is yours for the asking.

As for **transport**, Formia has year-round services to Ponza, as does **Terracina**. **Anzio** has summer connections. There are also departures from **Naples**. You can reach **Ventotene** from **Formia** or **Anzio**. There are also daily departures **between the islands** of Ponza and Ventotene. For frequencies and journey times see p.744.

Ponza

The group's main island, **PONZA** is only 8km long and 2km across, at its widest point. Beautiful **Ponza town** is heaped around the bay in a series of neat, pastel-coloured pyramids, its flat-roofed houses radiate out from the pink semicircle that curls around the fishing harbour. This town makes a marvellous place to rest, having so far escaped the clutches of designer boutiques and souvenir shops. Although the island lacks specific sights, Ponza is great for aimless wanderings; locals indulge, too, in the early evening, as crowds parade along the yellow-painted **Municipio** arcade of shops and cafés. For lazing and swimming, there's a small, clean **cove** in the town and the **Chiaia di Luna** beach, a ten-minute walk away, across the island. A slender rim of sand edges the sheer sickle cliff – though be warned that the waves here are much choppier than on the sheltered side facing the mainland, and the beach is intermittently closed for safety reasons.

The only other real settlement on the island is **LE FORNA**, a wide green bay dotted with huddles of homes. The beach here is small and grubby, so instead, follow the path down from the road, around the bay to the rocks: the water of the so-called **Piscina Naturale** is lovely and clear, perfect for sheltered swimming when the fishing boats have finished for the day. The settlement straggles on from Le Forna towards the sharp northern end of the island, where the road ends abruptly and a steep stony path (to the right) leads down to more rocks where you can swim.

For really secluded sea frolicking, rent a boat for the day from **Spiaggia S. Antonio** in Ponza town (€60–100) and take your time circumnavigating the island and exploring its remote coves.

Practicalities

The **tourist office** on Via Molo Musco in Ponza town (daily 9am–1pm & 3–7pm; ☎0771.80.031) has maps and accommodation lists. You will be accosted with offers of **rooms** as you get off the ferry: a fair price is around the €40–50 mark per person, always insist on seeing the room first. There are a growing number of B&Bs on the island. A reasonable choice with tidy rooms is *Casa Simonetta* on Via Calacaparra (☎0771.808.512, ⓦwww.casasimonetta.com; ➋) in the northern part of the island. **Hotels** are pricier; the cheapest is *Pensione Silvia* on Via Marina (200m through the spooky Roman tunnel on the Santa Maria waterfront; closed Oct–April; ☎0771.80.075; ➌), a cheerful golden structure presiding over row-boat-strewn sands. *Gennarino al Mare* at Via Dante 64 (☎0771.80.071, ⓦwww.gennarinoamare.com; ➐) is next to the town beach. This sky-blue hotel – great for a splurge – nestles on a dock: all the rooms have elegant decor, private wrought-iron balconies and great seascape views. You might also try the helpful people at *TuristCasa*, Via Roma 2 (T0771.809.886, Wwww.turistcasa.it), who rent out rooms and apartments year-round.

A **bus service** connects the port with other points on the island, roughly hourly. In Le Forna, the serene and chic *Ortensia* (T0771.808.922, Wwww .hotelortensia.it; ❹) is the best and most convenient option and they also have a restaurant. **Rent scooters** along Ponza town's harbour. **Boats**, too, are a good (sometimes the only) way of seeing the most dramatic parts of the island. The Cooperativa Barcaioli Ponzesi (T0771.809.929, Wwww.barcaioliponza.it) offer trips around the island and excursions to unnhabited Palmarola and Zannone from €20 per person.

For **food**, you're spoilt for choice: Ponza town has plenty of restaurants and most are good, albeit expensive. Feast on exquisite fish dishes at the upmarket *Orestorante* overlooking the harbour at Via Dietro la Chiesa 3 (T0711.80338; dinner only; closed Nov–Easter); the more accessible *Ippocampo*, in Piazza Pisacane 7 (T0771.809852; closed Nov-Easter, does good pasta and fish – the *pappardelle con gamberi* are delicious; or check out the restaurant attached to the *Gennarino al Mare* hotel (see opposite).

Ventotene

The only other inhabited Pontine island, **VENTOTENE** is situated a fair way south: flatter, smaller and drabber than Ponza, it has reddish-brown soil dotted with cacti and shrubs. Roman politicians exiled embarrassing wives and daughters here. Later San Stefano, a half-mile offshore, housed a dramatic horseshoe-shaped prison, designed by Carpi in the eighteenth century.

Although it makes a nice stop on a leisurely route to Naples, Ventotene is unlikely to detain anyone long. However, if you decide to linger, there are a couple of places renting out rooms and an absolutely delightful family-run **hotel**, *Agave e Ginesta* on Via Calabattaglia 10/12 (T0771.187.0355, Wwww .ventotene.net; ❺), with simple, clean rooms and terrific sea views. **Eat** at *Il Giardino* on Via degli Ulivi 45 (T0771.85.020; closed Tues lunch) where the limited menu is carefully chosen based on the day's catch. The single town – village really – has a population of around five hundred, and its dusty piazza is home to a **museum** displaying finds from an imperial-era villa, remains of which blanket the headland to the left of the village. On the other side, there's a small **beach** of grey volcanic sand. At the port, you can rent a boat to take you to the small island of Santo Stefano for €10 return.

Travel details

Trains

Rome (Termini) to: Ancona (10 daily; 4hr); Anzio/ Nettuno (hourly; 1hr); Bologna (at least 2 per hr; 2hr 45min); Civitavecchia* (at least 2 per hr; 1hr 10min); Florence (at least 2 per hr; 1hr 40min); Formia (at least 2 per hr; 1hr 25min); Latina (at least 2 per hr; 35min); Milan (20 daily; 4hr 30min); Naples (at least 2 per hr; 1hr 30min–2hr); Pescara (6 daily; 4hr; also from Roma Tiburtina); Tarquinia* (12 daily; 1hr 20min).

Rome (Ostiense) to: Viterbo (hourly, 2hr)*; Bracciano (every 30min; 1hr).

Rome (Roma-Nord line from Piazzale Flaminio) to: Viterbo (5 daily; 2hr 45min).

* Trains also run from Rome Trastevere and Roma San Pietro.

Buses

Latina to: Sermoneta (Mon–Sat 9 daily, Sun 4 daily; 50min).

Rome (Anagnina) to: Palestrina (30 daily; 55min).

Rome (Laurentina) to: Sabaudia (14 daily; 1hr 40min); San Felice (14 daily; 2hr); Terracina (9 daily; 2hr 15min).

Rome (Ponte Mammolo) to: Subiaco (hourly; 1hr 15min); Tivoli (every 15min; 50min); Palestrina (30 daily; 55min).

Rome (Saxa Rubra) to: Viterbo, (every 30min; 1hr 30min).

Rome (Cornelia) to: Cerveteri (every 30min; 1hr 10min); Civitavecchia (20 daily; 1hr 35min).

Subiaco to: Frosinone (2 daily; 2hr 15min).

Terracina to: Cassino (2 daily; 2hr 10min); Formia (every 30min; 1hr); Sabaudia (9 daily; 35min); San Felice Circeo (every 40min; 15min); Sperlonga (every 30min; 40min).

Viterbo to: Bagnaia (hourly; 20min); Bomarzo (20 daily; 30min); Caprarola (12 daily; 40min); Civitavecchia (5 daily; 1hr 25min); Tarquinia (10 daily; 1hr)

Civitavecchia to: Cágliari (1 daily; 14hr 30min); Golfo Aranci (4 weekly–1 daily; 10hr); Olbia (2 daily; 5hr–7hr; 30min).

Formia to: Ponza (2 daily year round; 2hr 30min); Ventotene (2 daily; 2hr 10min); (ⓦ www.caremar.it)

Naples to: Ponza (2 daily, 2hr 55min); Ventotene (2 daily, 1hr 50min).

Terracina to: Ponza; (1–3 daily; 50min); (ⓦ www .snapnavigazione.it).

Hydrofoils

Anzio to: Ponza (2–4 daily June–Sept; 1hr 10min); Ventotene (1 daily; 1hr 10min).

Formia to: Ponza (1–3 daily; 1hr 20min); Ventotene (1–2 daily, except Tues; 55min).

Ponza to: Ventotene (1–2 daily except Tues; 55min); (ⓦ www.snav.it).

Ferries

Anzio to: Ponza (1–2 daily; 1hr 45min); (ⓦ www .vetor.it & www.caremar.it).

Abruzzo and Molise

CHAPTER 12

Highlights

* **Corno Grande** Hike in the wild and craggy Gran Sasso massif, out of which rises Italy's highest peak, the Corno Grande. See p.752

* **Parco Nazionale d'Abruzzo** Get back to nature in this lovely park, which has around one hundred indigenous species of fauna and flora. See p.758

* **Museo delle Genti d'Abruzzo, Pescara** Poetry and intricately carved objects bear witness to the industry of Abruzzo's shepherds. See p.762

* **Museo Archeologico**, **Chieti** Head here for the best and most comprehensive display of Abruzzese antiquities, including the unique Capestrano warrior. See p.764

* **Bull race at Ururi** The ordinary town of Ururi turns into a scene of frenetic activity once a year as horses, bulls and carts career through the streets. See p.766

* **Saepinum** This enchanting archeological site in rural Sepino is a throwback to the original Grand Tour, with overgrown Roman ruins dotted with inhabited dwellings. See p.769

▲ Hiking in the Gran Sasso National Park

Abruzzo and Molise

A bruzzo and Molise, one region until 1963 known simply as the Abruzzi,
together make Italy's transition from north to south. Both are sparsely
populated mountainous regions prone to earthquakes, and both have
been outside the mainstream of Italian affairs since the Middle Ages.
Bordered by the Apennines, the **Abruzzo** holds some of Italy's wildest terrain:
silent valleys, abandoned hill-villages and vast untamed mountain plains, once
roamed by wolves, bears and chamois. The Abruzzesi have done much to pull
their region out of the poverty trap, developing resorts on the long, sandy
Adriatic coastline and exploiting the tourist potential of a large, mountainous

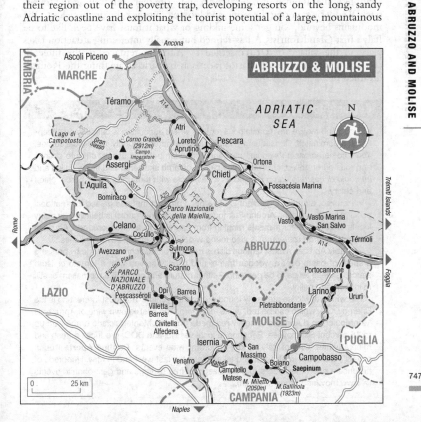

national park and some great historic towns. Most visited are **L'Aquila**, at the foot of **Gran Sasso** – the Apennines' highest peak – and **Sulmona** to the southeast; both cities are good bases. The hill-villages around L'Aquila are worth visiting, too, if you're based here for any length of time. Those below the Gran Sasso are deeply rural places, where time seems to have stopped somewhere in the fifteenth century; South of Sulmona, Abruzzo feels more traditional. In **Scanno** elderly women wear costumes that originated in Asia Minor, and make intricate lace on cylindrical cushions known as *tomboli*. Just down the road, the scruffy hill-village of **Cocullo** hosts one of Europe's most bizarre religious festivals, in which a statue of the local saint is draped with live snakes before being paraded through the streets. The main resort on the Abruzzo coast is **Pescara**, departure port for ferries to Croatia and a good base for excursions inland to **Chieti**, home to an excellent archeological museum. However the best spot for a sun-and-sand break is further south at **Vasto**, with its gently shelving sandy beach and lively old centre.

Gentler, less rugged and somewhat poorer than Abruzzo, **Molise** has more in common with southern than central Italy. Much of the region still seems to be struggling out of its past, its towns and villages victims of either economic neglect or hurried modern development. The cities, **Isernia** and **Campobasso**, are large and bland, with small historical centres but Molise has its compensations: a scattering of low-key Roman ruins – most interestingly at **Saepinum**, a quintessential Roman provincial town and a site that's still well off the tourist track. Wandering among the ruins, and looking out over the green fields to the mountains beyond, you get some inkling of what it must have been like to be Italy's first Grand Tourists. A less-refined but equally interesting attraction takes place in the village of **Ururi**, settled by Albanian refugees in the fifteenth century, where the annual chariot race is as barbaric as anything the Romans dreamed up.

Regional food and wine

Abruzzo and Molise are mountainous regions where agriculture is difficult and sheep-farming dominates. Consequently, **lamb** tends to feature strongly in the local cuisine. You'll come across *abbacchio*, unweaned baby lamb that is usually cut into chunks and roasted or grilled; *arrosticini*, tiny pieces of lamb skewered and flame grilled and *intingolo di castrato*, lamb cooked as a casserole with tomatoes, wine, herbs, onion and celery.

In Abruzzo, a crucial ingredient is **olive oil**, a product that has gained international acclaim in recent years. Around Sulmona *l'aglio rosso* (red garlic) is believed by many locals to be a cure for ailments ranging from neuralgia to arthritis; around L'Aquila in particular saffron (*zafferano*) is also found widely in sweet and savoury dishes.

Probably Abruzzo's most famous dish is *maccheroni alla chitarra*, made by pressing a sheet of pasta over a wooden frame, and usually served with a tomato or lamb sauce. Cheese tends to be *pecorino* – either mature and grainy like parmesan, or still mild, soft and milky.

The **wines** of Molise are rarely found outside the region. The most interesting is the Biferno DOC, which can be red, white, or *rosato*. The best-known wine of Abruzzo is Montepulciano d'Abruzzo, a heavy red made from the Montepulciano grape with up to 15 percent Sangiovese. Pecorino, a local varietal and DOC, produces a fresh and mineral white. One of Italy's most important wine events, **Cantine Aperte** ("open cellars") was born in Abruzzo and takes place the last weekend in May. Hundreds of producers open their doors to enthusiasts for free tastings and gastronomic events (ⓦwww.movimentoturismovino.it).

Finally there's the sheer physical aspect of the place. Forty percent of Molise is covered by **mountains**, and although they are less dramatic than Abruzzo's, there are masses of possibilities for hiking. Visitors are also starting to explore the area's ancient sheep-droving routes, known as *tratturi*, which are gaining new life as mountain-bike or horseback-riding trails, served by occasional farmhouse guesthouses and riding stables along the way.

Don't expect to rush through Abruzzo and Molise if you're relying on public transport; in both regions, **getting around** on bus and train demands patience and the careful studying of timetables (info on regional bus service in Abruzzo at Ⓦconoscere.abruzzoturismo.it; in Molise at Ⓦwww.lariverabus.it).

L'Aquila and around

The pleasant town of **L'AQUILA** is an appealing blend of ancient and modern, with a university, smart shops, bustling streets and a daily market where you can buy anything from blocks of pecorino cheese to traditional Abruzzese copper pots. It was founded in 1242 when the Holy Roman Emperor Frederick II drew together the populations from 99 Abruzzesi villages to form a new city. Each village built its own church, piazza and quarter: there's a medieval fountain with 99 spouts, and the town-hall clock still chimes 99 times every night. These days only two churches remain, albeit magnificent ones. The town is overlooked by the bulk of the **Gran Sasso** mountain range and is the main access point to the national park of the same name.

Arrival, information and accommodation

L'Aquila's **train station** is a good way downhill from the centre, connected with the main part of town by regular buses. Long-distance **buses** arrive at the new Collemaggio terminal near Porta Bazzano, which is linked to Piazza del Duomo by moving walkways that shuttle visitors through a long tunnel to the city's main square. At the **information booth** inside the terminal there are bus timetables covering the L'Aquila province and connections to Rome. The main **tourist office** is at Piazza Santa Maria Paganica 5, uphill from the Duomo (Mon–Fri 9am–1pm & 3–6pm, Sat 9am–1pm; Ⓣ0862.410.808, Ⓦwww.abruzzoturismo.it) and there is another in Piazza del Duomo (daily: summer 9am–midnight; winter 9am–9pm; Ⓣ0862.23021, Ⓦwww.centrostorico.laquila.it).

If you plan to stay the night, book ahead as L'Aquila has limited **accommodation**. Of the B&Bs, *Sweet Dreams* run by Giovanni Ranieri at Viale Duca degli Abruzzi 23 (Ⓣ0862.25.945; ❷) is a clean, well-appointed and central place with free parking. Of the hotels, the *Duomo*, Via Dragonetti 6 (Ⓣ0862.410.893, Ⓦwww.hotel-Duomo.it; ❸), is your best bet, a three-star housed in a quiet, eighteenth-century palace with great views over Piazza del Duomo, and even better views of the mountains. Otherwise try the *Castello*, Piazza Battaglione Alpini (Ⓣ0862.419.147, Ⓦwww.hotelcastelloaq.com; ❺), a swish business hotel from the 1960s that has been revamped and offers stylish, attractive rooms.

The City

L'Aquila's centre is relatively compact and easily seen on foot. The northern side of town is dominated by the formidable **Castello**, built by the Spanish in the sixteenth century. In the Fascist period the castle's surroundings were landscaped as a park, and, following the devastation wreaked by the Nazis in 1943, the

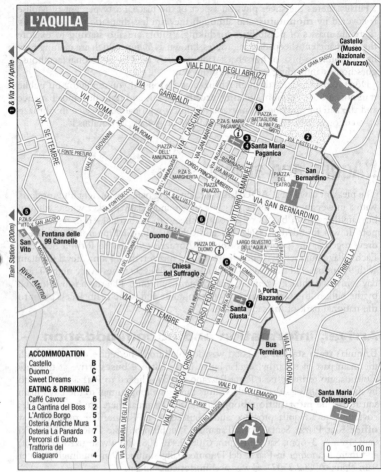

L'AQUILA

Castello
(Museo
Nazionale
d' Abruzzo)

VIALE DUCA DEGLI ABRUZZI

VIALE GRAN SASSO

VIA GARIBALDI

VIA ROMA

VIA XX SETTEMBRE

VIA ROMA

V. GIOVANNI XXIII

V. FONTE PRETURO

VIA CASCINA

VIA SAN MARTINO

PIAZZA
DELL'
ANNUNZIATA

P.ZA S
MARGHERITA

VIA ANNUNZIATA

VIA FONTESECCO

PIAZZA
DELL'
ANNUNZIATA

VIA CESURA

VIA DEL CARDINALE

VIA SASSA

Duomo

PIAZZA DEL
DUOMO

VIA DELLA INDIPENDENZA

Chiesa
del Suffragio

CORSO FEDERICO II

VIA XX SETTEMBRE

VIA S. MARIA DEGLI ANGELI

VIALE FRANCESCO CRISPI

VIALE VENTIQUATTRO MAGGIO

VIA PIAVE

VIALE DI COLLEMAGGIO

P.ZA S. MARIA
PAGANICA

CORSO PRINCIPE UMBERTO

VIA PAGANICA

VIA BOMINACO

VIA NAVELLI

P.ZA S
PALAZZO

PIAZZA
PALAZZO

VIA SALLUSTIO

CORSO VITTORIO EMANUELE

PIAZZA
BATTAGLIONE
ALPINI D'
AQUITO

VIA CASTELLO

San
Bernardino

PIAZZA
DEL
TEATRO

VIA SAN BERNARDINO

VIA FORTEBRACCIO

LARGO SILVESTRO
DELL'AQUILA

VIA CIMINO

VIA
DRAGONETTI

VIA ST GIUSTA

Porta
Bazzano

Santa
Giusta

VIA STRINELLA

VIALE CADORNA

Bus
Terminal

Santa Maria
di Collemaggio

Fontana delle
99 Cannelle

San
Vito

P.ZA S.
VITO V. SAN JACOPO

V. MADONNA DEL PONTE

River Aterno

Train Station (200m)

1 & Via XXV Aprile

Santa Maria
Paganica

N

0   100 m

ACCOMMODATION
Castello   B
Duomo   C
Sweet Dreams   A
EATING & DRINKING
Caffé Cavour   6
La Cantina del Boss   2
L'Antico Borgo   5
Osteria Antiche Mura   1
Osteria La Panarda   7
Percorsi di Gusto   3
Trattoria del
Giaguaro   4

building was renovated and the **Museo Nazionale d'Abruzzo** (Tues–Sun 8.30am–7.30pm; €4) established in the former barracks. The most interesting part of the collection is the ten-room medieval and modern section on the first floor, including works of art rescued from abandoned and earthquake-ravaged churches. The best of the paintings are the dreamy and mystical works attributed to Andrea Delitio, a fifteenth-century Abruzzese artist. The castle's eastern bastion also displays the remains of a mammoth found near L'Aquila in 1954. The castle hosts occasional concerts throughout the year; check with the tourist office for details.

From Piazza Battaglione Alpini below the castle, arcaded **Corso Vittorio Emanuele** leads into the centre of town. It's lined with upmarket clothes shops, jewellers and cafés, and liveliest in the evenings when L'Aquila's young and old turn out for the *passeggiata*. To the left down Via San Bernadino, the church of **San Bernardino** (daily 8.30am–noon & 3–6pm; free) has a sumptuous facade, with three magnificent white tiers bedecked with classical columns. Inside, the ceiling is luxuriously gilded and skilfully carved, while the glazed blue-and-white terracotta altarpiece by Andrea della Robbia – on the right as you enter – is very fine, as is San Bernardino's mausoleum, sculpted by Silvestro dell'Aquila. The Corso carries on up to the central **Piazza del Duomo** home to a **market** (Mon–Sat 8am–2pm); the numerous surrounding cafés make a pleasant spot for a coffee and a snack. The **Duomo**, having been destroyed on several occasions by earthquakes, now features a tedious Neoclassical front. The facade of the eighteenth-century **Chiesa del Suffragio**, by contrast, is a voluptuous combination of curves, topped by a flamboyant honeycombed alcove. Tumbling down the hill below the piazza, steep-stepped streets of ancient houses lead down to **Porta Bazzano**, one of the old city gates. Rather than heading straight there, take time to wander the abutting streets, lined with Renaissance and Baroque palaces.

From Porta Bazzano, head past the bus terminal where Via G. Caldora leads to the church of **Santa Maria di Collemaggio** (daily 8.30am–noon & 3–6pm; free). One of Abruzzo's most distinctive churches, its massive rectangular bulk is faced with a geometric jigsaw of pink and white stone, more redolent of a mosque than a church. It was founded in the thirteenth century by Pietro of Morrone, a hermit unwillingly dragged from his mountain retreat to be made pope by power-hungry cardinals who reckoned he would be easy to manipulate. When he turned out to be too naive even for the uses of the cardinals, he was forced to resign and was posthumously compensated for the ordeal by being canonized. Thieves stole his relics in April 1988, intending to hold them to ransom, but they were soon safely retrieved and returned to their grandiose Palladian-style sarcophagus.

Finally there's L'Aquila's best-known sight, the **Fontana delle 99 Cannelle**, outside the town centre close to the train station, tucked behind the medieval **Porta della Riviera**. Set around three sides of a sunken piazza and overlooked by abandoned houses and the tiny church of **San Vito**, each water spout is a symbol for one of the villages that formed the city. This constant supply of fresh water sustained the *Aquilani* through the plagues, earthquakes and sieges to which the city was subjected, and was used for washing clothes until after the war.

Eating, drinking and nightlife

L'Aquila has a decent selection of reasonably priced **places to eat**, ranging from restaurants serving traditional Abruzzese fare to cheap and cheerful pizzerias catering for the town's student population. Alternatively head to the western end of Piazza del Duomo where stalls sell vast *porchetta* sandwiches, local salami and pecorino.

As a university city, L'Aquila also has some good **cafés** and **pubs** in the streets and piazzas from Piazza del Duomo to Piazza S. Biagio to the northwest (eve only). A particular favourite among the young is *Caffè Cavour*, Via Cavour 16, where live music is played on some nights.

La Cantina del Boss Via Castello 3 ☎0862.413.393. Bustling wine bar with a good selection of local and national wines – 1500 lables to be exact – and great filled focaccia for €3.50. Closed Sun.
L'Antico Borgo Piazza San Vito 1 ☎0862.22.005. Tasty roasted meat dishes in a peaceful spot make this a great choice for lunch outside in summer.

Try the *grano e sapori di bosco* (wheat berries cooked as in a risotto with *funghi porcini, zafferano e tartufo*) for €8. Open daily.
Osteria Antiche Mura Via XXV Aprile 2 ☎0862.62.422. Traditional restaurant with a wide variety of local specialities – try *ceci e castagne* (chickpeas and chestnuts) or *coniglio allo zafferano* (rabbit scented with saffron). If you want to try

everything, there's a *degustazione* menu for €33. Closed Sun.

Osteria La Panarda Via G Valle 18 ☎0862.406.035. Innovative dishes drawing on local ingredients are prepared with care by Chef Gianluca Carozzi. Try the *filetto di maile allo zafferano* (pork loin in a saffron sauce). Closed Sun dinner & Mon.

Percorsi di Gusto Via Leonisi 7 ☎0862.411.429. All dishes are made from Abruzzesi ingredients and there is limited, if well-chosen, selection of pasta and meat dishes. Their creative pizzas are quite nice. Try the one with cod and potatoes for €11. Closed Tues.

Trattoria del Giaguaro Piazza Paganica 4 ☎0862.24.001. This is a well-priced trattoria with a decidedly homey feel. Their menu changes daily, according to the best produce from the market nearby; try their *ravioli di ricotta con pomodoro* for €6. Closed Mon dinner & Tues.

Parco Nazionale del Gran Sasso

Whether you approach Abruzzo from Marche in the north or Rome in the west, your arrival will be signalled by the spectacular bulk of the **Gran Sasso** massif, containing by far the highest of the Apennine peaks as well as a **national park** (ⓦwww.gransassolagapark.it) with hiking trails. If you come by autostrada from Le Marche, you'll actually travel underneath the mountains, through a ten-kilometre tunnel, passing the entrance to a particle physics research laboratory bored into the very heart of the mountain range. The massif itself consists of two parallel chains, flanking the **Campo Imperatore** plain that stretches for 27km at over 2000m above sea level. The itinerary below is an easy day's drive from L'Aquila.

Fonte Cerreto

FONTE CERRETO, just 18km from L'Aquila (buses #6 & #76 run there regularly from L'Aquila's bus terminal), is the gateway to the Gran Sasso Park. It consists of little more than a few hotels, a restaurant and a campsite clustered around a cable-car station. Most of these were built in the 1930s as part of Mussolini's scheme to keep Italians fit by encouraging them to take exercise in the mountains. Ironically, he was imprisoned here in 1943, first at the *Villetta* inn (now *Fior di Gigli*), and then at the *Ostello Campo Imperatore*, a grim hotel at the top of the cable-car route. *Il Duce* supposedly spent his days at the hotel on a diet of eggs, rice, boiled onions and grapes, contemplating suicide. Hitler came to his rescue, dispatching an ace pilot to airlift him out in a tiny plane.

The cable car runs up the mountain every thirty minutes and costs €10 (€13 on Sun) (☎0862.606.143; July to mid-Sept Mon–Sat 8.30am–5pm & Sun 8.30am–6pm; mid-Sept–June to Mon–Sat 8.30am–5pm & Sun 8am–5pm depending on snowfall). A small **tourist office** (☎0862.606.847, ⓦwww .ilgransasso.it) has details of walks and wildlife to be seen in the Gran Sasso park. They can also suggest trails for assaults on the park's highest peak, the **Corno Grande** (2912m). For accommodation, there is the *Hotel Fior di Gigli* (☎0862.606.171 & 0862.606.172, ⓦwww.fiordigigli.com; ❸), a pleasantly modernized **hotel** over a snack bar at the base of the cable car. There's cheaper accommodation in two places run by CAI (The Italian Alpine Club); one of these is the *Ostello Campo Imperatore* (☎0862.400.011 & 0862.400.000, ⓦwww.hotelcampoimperatore.com/home.htm; €30 per person for a hostel bed with breakfast or €45 for dinner, bed and breakfast), which occupies the old cable-car station; the other is the *Hotel Campo Imperatore* (phone and website as above; June to mid-Sept).

Outside the summer months, **the ascent** of Corno Grande should only be attempted by experienced climbers, and at all times includes some fairly strenuous scree-climbing and alarming descents. Perhaps the most challenging route is the tough trek from the *Ostello Campo Imperatore* right across the mountain range, taking in the Corno Grande, sleeping over at the *Rifugio Franchetti* (℡ 0861.959.634 or 333.232.4474, Ⓦ www.rifugiofranchetti.it; €20, or €40 for dinner, bed and breakfast; June–Sept), and then walking across to the Arapietra ridge. From here a ski lift will take you down to the ugly ski resort of **Prati di Tivo** – which nevertheless offers some of the best views of Gran Sasso – from where you can get a bus to the town of Téramo. If you're going to do any of the Gran Sasso trails, you'll need the CAI *Gran Sasso d'Italia* **map** (on sale in newsagents around town), and should check out **weather conditions** from either the tourist office or the CAI office at Via Sassa 34 in L'Aquila (Mon–Fri 6–8pm; ℡ 0862.24.342, Ⓦ www.cailaquila.it). West from Fonte Cerreto stretches the vast Campo Imperatore plain, long the stomping grounds of **nomadic shepherds**, who bring their flocks up to the plain for summer grazing after wintering in the south – a practice that has been going on since Roman times.

South to Sulmona: Bominaco

From L'Aquila, the SS17 follows the ancient route of the local shepherds across the saffron fields south to Sulmona. If you have your own transport, it's worth making a short detour on the way to see two of Abruzzo's most beautiful churches at **BOMINACO** (also accessible by bus from L'Aquila). The village itself is an inauspicious knot of grubby houses, but the endearingly askew and lichen-mottled facade of **San Pellegrino**, founded by Charlemagne, conceals floor-to-ceiling frescoes in vivid hues reminiscent of a peacock's plume (opened on request, see below). The brilliant thirteenth-century frescoes include pictures of the life of Christ, the Virgin and a huge St Christopher, as well as an intriguing calendar with signs of the zodiac. If you put your ear to the hole at the side of the altar, tradition says you'll hear the heartbeat of San Pellegrino buried below.

The church of **Santa Maria Assunta** (opened on request, see below), just beyond, stands on the foundations of a Roman temple to Venus. Beyond its coolly refined exterior, the creamy-white carvings are so exquisitely precise that it seems the mason has only just put down his chisel; in fact they're eight hundred years old. You can **ask for admission** to both churches from one of the volunteers at Via Ripa 4 (℡ 0862.93.756; tip expected). Bring change to illuminate the interiors (€2 for 8min).

Sulmona and around

Flanked by bleak mountains and bristling with legends about its most famous son, Ovid, **SULMONA** is a rich and comfortable provincial town owing its wealth to gold jewellery and sugared almonds. An atmospheric little place, with a dark tangle of a historical centre lined with imposing palaces, its sights can be seen in a day, but the town makes a good base for exploring the surroundings – from ancient hermitages to towns with snake-infested festivals – and you may want to stay longer.

Arrival, information and accommodation

Buses arrive in Sulmona at the Villa Comunale next to the *centro storico*. The **train station** is 1.5km outside the centre of town; bus A runs from the station to the villa. The **tourist office** (July–Sept Mon–Sat 9am–1pm & 4–7pm, Sun

9am–1pm; Oct–June Mon–Fri 9am–1pm & 3–6pm, Sat 9am–1pm; ℡0864.53.276) is at Corso Ovidio 208. There's a second information office in the old pharmacy of the Palazzo SS Annunziata with very helpful staff, maps and details of Sulmona's churches and palaces (daily 9am–12.30pm & 3.30–7pm; ℡0864.210.216, Ⓦwww.comune.sulmona.aq.it).

There's a good choice of **accommodation** and the town is well worth a stay. The most atmospheric of the affordable hotels is the *Italia*, on Piazza Salvatore Tommasi 3, just behind Piazza XX Settembre (℡0864.52.308, Ⓔgianlucadicamillo@libero.it; no credit cards; ❷). It's a little ramshackle, but has plenty of personality and a friendly owner. Another good option is the newly refurbished *Stella*, Via Mazara 18 (℡0864.52.653, Ⓦwww.hasr.it; ❷), a relaxed, family-run establishment that's deservedly popular, so book ahead. Outside of town, the friendly *B&B L'Eremo*, offers comfortable rooms with panoramic views just 1km from the Parco Nazionale della Majella (℡0864.52.749, Ⓦwww.leremo.it; ❷).

The Town

Corso Ovidio, Sulmona's main street, cuts through the centre from the park-side bus terminus, leading up to the intimate square **Piazza XX Settembre**. A couple of minutes back up Corso Ovidio stands the **Annunziata**, a Gothic-Renaissance *palazzo* adjoining a flamboyant Baroque church. It was established by a confraternity to take care of the citizens from birth until death, its steps crowded with the ill and destitute, but these days, its steps are a hangout for the town's teenagers during the evening *passeggiata*. Note the external decoration designed to remind onlookers of the cycles of life and death. The most intriguing statue, however, is just inside the entrance: Ovid, metamorphosed from pagan poet of love into an ascetic friar. Inside the Annunziata are three **museums**: one (undergoing a lengthy restoration) with exhibits on local costumes and transhumance – the practice of moving sheep to summer pastures – and examples of work by Sulmona's Renaissance goldsmiths, a trade that continues here today, as evidenced by the number of jewellers' shops along the Corso; another, the **Museo Civico** (daily 9am–1pm; €3), has local sculpture and paintings from the sixteenth to seventeenth centuries; and a third, the **Museo "in situ"** (Tues–Sun 10am–1pm; free), shows the excavations of a Roman villa inhabited from the first century BC to the second century AD, abandoned suddenly along with many other houses in the valley when a landslide or an earthquake struck. Among the fragments of fabulously coloured wall painting are depictions of Pan, Eros, Dionysus and Ariadne, and there are several floor mosaics, all well labelled.

As well as gold, the Corso's **shops** are full of Sulmona's other great product – *confetti* a confection of sugared almonds, hazlenuts or chocolate wired into elaborate flowers with the aid of coloured cellophane, crêpe paper and ribbons. Through ingenious marketing the Sulmonese *confetti* barons have made gifts of their intricate sculptures *de rigueur* at christenings, confirmations, and weddings throughout Catholic Europe.

At the end of the Corso is Piazza del Carmine, where the weighty Romanesque portal of **San Francesco della Scarpa** was the only part of the church solid enough to withstand a 1703 earthquake. The church gets its name – della Scarpa (of the shoe) – from the fact that Franciscans wore shoes instead of the sandals worn by other monastic orders. Opposite, the impressive Gothic **aqueduct**, built to supply water to the town and power to its wool mills, ends at a small fifteenth-century fountain, the **Fontana del Vecchio**, named for the bust of a chubby-cheeked old man on top. On the other side of the aqueduct is **Piazza Garibaldi**, a vast square dominated by the austere slopes of **Monte Morrone**, on which the hermit Pietro Morrone lived until he was dragged away to be made Pope Celestine V. There's a former nunnery in the corner – take a look at the courtyard, where there's a tiny door at which unmarried mothers were permitted to abandon their babies.

Eating and drinking

Sulmona has some excellent reasonably priced **restaurants**, with mains generally around the €6–7 mark. *Cesidio*, Via Solimo 25 (℡ 0864.52.724; closed Mon), is a popular local place with some great home-made pasta dishes including *pasta alla chitarra alla spazzacamino* (with capers, olives, tomato and herbs). Warmly recommended is ⚘ *Clemente*, Vico Quercia 20 (℡ 0864.52.284; closed Thurs), a bright, family-run place in an old *palazzo* that's been serving home-produced *salumi* and dishes such as *agnello con aglio, rosmarino e pecorino* (pan seared lamb with garlic, rosemary and pecorino cheese) for over fifty years. For an excellent choice of **wines** head for *La Cantina di Biffi* (℡ 0864.32.025; closed Mon, Tues at lunch), an elegantly countrified place in Via Barbato 1 off Corso Ovidio, where you can eat as well.

Parco Nazionale della Majella

The **Parco Nazionale della Majella**, 10km to the east of Sulmona, is named after the mountain – **Monte Majella** – that dominates the area. Dedicated to the goddess Maja, the mountain was held sacred by the ancient people of Abruzzo, and during the Middle Ages the region around it was named Domus Christi by Petrarch, or the "House of God", for its proliferation of hermitages and abbeys. Over a hundred **hermits** made their retreat here in the Middle Ages, some reused cave dwellings, others built churches into the rock, haunting constructions to this day. There's information at the park's visitor's centre on Via Roma in Pacentro (May–April & Sept 10.30am– 1.30pm; June–Aug 10.30am–1.30pm & 5–8.30pm; ℡ 349.153.9782, ⓦ www .parcomajella.it).

Cocullo

A tatty hill-village west of Sulmona, connected by infrequent trains and even less frequent buses, **COCULLO** is understandably neglected by outsiders for 364 days of the year. However, on the first Thursday in May it's invaded by what seems like half the population of central Italy, coming to celebrate the weird **festival of snakes**, an annual event held in memory of St Dominic, the patron saint of the village, who allegedly rid the area of venomous snakes back in the eleventh century.

The festival is an odd mixture of the modern and archaic. After Mass in the main square, a number of snake-charmers in the crowd drape a wooden statue of St Dominic with a writhing bunch of live but harmless snakes, which is then paraded through the streets in a bizarre celebration of the saint's unique powers (he was apparently good at curing snake-bites too). It's actually thought that Cocullo's preoccupation with serpents dates back to before the advent of the saint when in the pre-Christian era local tribes worshipped their goddess Angitia with offerings of snakes. For information on the festival or the village in general, contact the *Comune*'s Pro Loco (℡ 0864.490.004, ⓦ www.comune.cocullo.aq.it).

Scanno

Twenty kilometres down the road, and accessible by bus from Sulmona, **SCANNO** is another popular tourist destination, reached by passing through the narrow and rocky **Saggitario Gorge**, a spectacular drive along galleries of rock and around blind hairpin bends that widen out at the glassy green

▲ Women in traditional dress, Scanno

Lago di Scanno. Perched over the lake is a church, **Madonna del Lago**, with the cliff as its back wall, and nearby there are boats and pedaloes for rent in the summer, and a good restaurant, the *Trattoria sul Lago* (☏0864.747296; closed Thurs). If you're planning on staying there's a **campsite** *I Lupi* (☏0864.740.100, Ⓦwww.campingilupi.it; open all year), 2km away outside the town of Villalago, and on the shores of the lake, but be warned that it gets packed out in summer.

A couple of kilometres beyond, Scanno itself is a well-preserved medieval village encircled by mountains. In 1951, Henri Cartier-Bresson photographed the village, in a series of atmospheric shots focusing on the **tradional dress** worn by Scanno's women. Some elderly women can still be seen wearing the long, dark, pleated skirts and bodices with a patterned apron that suggest a possible origin in Asia Minor. Scannese jewellery also has something of the Orient about it – large, delicately filigreed earings, and a star, known as a *presuntuosa*, given to fiancées to ward off other men. If you want to see the costume and jewellery at close quarters head for the shops on Strada Roma and Corso Centrale.

It's a pleasure strolling around the **old town**, built into the steep hillside, the squares and alleyways lined with solid stone houses built by wool barons when business was good. Though shepherding as a way of life has virtually finished and the population has dwindled, it's a living village, with enough work available in Sulmona and in tourism to keep people from moving away. A **chair lift**, signposted 300m from the centre (undergoing maintenance at the time of writing, call the *Comune* at ☏0864.74.545 if you need to check), takes **skiers** up to a handful of runs on Monte Rotondo, operating also in the short summer season when it's worth going up just for the view of lake and mountains, especially at sunset.

If you're around in August, you might catch Scanno's **summer festival**, with a series of cultural events and fireworks shows held throughout the month (see Ⓦwww.scanno.org or contact the tourist office), and on January 17 there's a **lasagne festival** – more properly called the Festa di San Antonio Abate, involving the cooking of a great cauldron of lasagne and beans outside the door of the church, which is then blessed and doled out with a somewhat unholy amount of pushing and shoving.

Scanno practicalities

The **tourist office** (Mon–Fri 9am–1pm & 3–6pm, Sat 9am–1pm; ☏0864.74.317, Ⓦwww.abruzzoturismo.it) is at Piazza Santa Maria della Valle 12. **Accommodation** options include *Mille Pini*, next to the chair lift at Via Pescara 2 (☏0864.74.387, Ⓦwww.millepiniscanno.it; closed Oct–Nov; ❷), a large chalet overlooking the village and the most atmospheric place to stay. Between the lake and the village, *Hotol Nilde*, Viale del Lago 101 (☏0864.74.359, Ⓦwww.ilrifugiodellupo.it; no credit cards; ❷), is a simple family-run place with great views. They also have a slightly more upmarket place out of town towards the lake, the *Albergo Rifugio del Lupo* (☏0864.74.397, Ⓦwww.ilrifugiodellupo.it; ❹).

For **eating**, *Gli Archetti* (☏0864.74.645; closed Tues), on Via Silla 8 inside the Porta della Croce entrance to the old town, cooks up imaginative variations on traditional Abruzzese cuisine, and *Birreria La Baita* (☏0864.747.826; daily July–Oct & Dec–Feb; Fri–Sun only March–June & Nov) on the Circonvalazione, serves hearty mountain food from Abruzzo and Alto Adige, with occasional live music. It also has some cabin rooms available (Ⓦwww.labaitascanno.it; ❷).

Parco Nazionale d'Abruzzo

At four hundred square kilometres, the **PARCO NAZIONALE D'ABRUZZO** is Italy's third-largest national park and holds some of its wildest mountain land, providing great walking and a hunter-free haven for wolves, brown bears, chamois, deer, lynx, wild boar and three or four pairs of royal eagles. The central village, **PESCASSEROLI**, is the main hub for visitors, a rather commercialized spot, liberally decorated with the park's logo – a cuddly brown bear – and surrounded by campsites, holiday apartments and hotels.

The best way to strike out from Pescasseroli is to hike. The trick is to take advantage of the comprehensive information service, and get walking as quickly as possible: as soon as you get away from the vicinity of the tourist villages, the wild Apennine beauty really makes itself felt.

Arrival and information

Pescasseroli is served by **bus** (6 daily; 1hr) from Avezzano, 30km west of Sulmona and a stop on the Pescara–Rome rail line (buses to the park leave from outside Avezzano's train station). There are also bus services direct from Naples and Castel di Sangro on the border with Molise. In summer a daily service also runs from Rome.

There's a helpful **tourist office** in Pescasseroli on Via Santa Lucia (daily: summer 9am–7.30pm; winter 9.30am–1.30pm & 2–5pm; ☎0863.911.3221, ⓦwww.parcoabruzzo.it). In the same building, is the excellent **natural history museum** (hours as above; ☎0863.911.31; €6), which fills you in on the park's flora and fauna and acts as a clinic for sick animals.

There are other tourist offices in: **Opi** (Palazzo Comunale, 9.30am–12.30pm & 3.30–6.30pm; ☎0863.910.622; closed Wed), which also has a **chamois museum** (closed for restoration) and a ski museum (hours as above); inside the **Museo dell'Orso** (Bear Museum) in **Villavallelonga** (daily 10am–1pm & 3–6pm; ☎0863.949.261) and in **Villetta Barrea** (Mon–Sat 9.30am–1pm & 3–7pm, Sun 9am–1pm; ☎0864.89.333). All have leaflets outlining popular walks and hikes for all fitness levels.

Hiking routes

The tourist offices sell maps on which all **hiking routes** in the park are marked, along with an indication of the difficulty involved, the time needed, and the flora and fauna you're likely to see on the way. There are nearly 150 different routes, starting from 25 letter-coded points, so making a choice can be difficult. Note that from July 1 to September 15, some of the most popular routes are open by **reservation only** for a fee. The information offices are helpful and can arrange guided tours with park staff in English by request. During the rest of the year, these routes are open without restriction or fee, though guided tours can still be arranged.

Accommodation

In high season, there's little chance of finding a **room** on arrival; you need to book at least a month in advance and be prepared for compulsory half board in July & August. If you're coming here for a week or more, you might consider B&B accommodation in a private house or an apartment rental – the tourist office can supply you with a list.

Hotels

Al Castello Via Gabriele d'Annunzio 1, Pescasseroli
T&F 0863.910.757. Off the main piazza, this
small, stone-built guesthouse comes with squeakily
clean and pretty rooms. ❷
Degli Olmi Via Fossata 8/B, Villetta Barrea
T 0864.89.159, W www.hotel-olmi.it. Highly polished
and quiet hotel, with compulsory half board. ❹
La Torre Via Castello 3, Civitella Alfedena
T 0864.890.121, W www.albergolatorre.com.
Small, friendly hotel set in an eighteenth-century
palace near Pescasseroli. ❷

Paradiso Via Fonte Fracassi 4, Pescasseroli
T 0863.910.422, W www.albergo-paradiso.it.
Delightful hotel run by the Scottish Geraldine and
her Italian husband Marco, with warm rustic decor
and good country cooking. Ask to see Geraldine's
pub. ❺
Peppe di Sora Viale B. Croce 1, Pescasseroli
T 0863.910.693. Welcoming place, across the river
from the main town. ❷

Camping and apartments

Campers should manage to find space on one of the **campsites**, though be
warned that temperatures are low even in summer. The simplest to reach is the
Dell'Orso in Colli dell'Orso (T 0863.91995), a fairly basic affair in a lovely
location. *Sant'Andrea* (T 0863.912.173, W www.campingsantandrea.com) is
further into town off the SS83, and more built-up. Expect to pay around €6 per
tent plus €6 per person at both sites. Otherwise at nearby **Civitella Alfedena**
there's *Agenzia Wolf* (T 0864.890.360) that rents apartments year round and runs
a campsite 300m from the centre (mid-June to Sept). At **Barrea** *La Genziana*
campsite (T 0864.88.101, W www.campinglagenzianapasetta.it), which has an
on-site bar, is five-minutes' walk from the town. A camper var or tent costs €8
plus €8 per person.

Eating and drinking

Eating out in most of the park's villages means fairly cheap pizza and
pasta, and general stores that will make up sandwiches for picnics. For local

---

Park wildlife

The Abruzzo National Park is an area of exceptional biodiversity with around a
hundred indigenous species. One of the most important animals in the park is the
Marsican brown bear. Until recently an endangered species, there are now around
fifty in the park and the best time to watch for them is the crack of dawn or around
8 or 9pm – the bear should not be any danger as its first instinct on scenting
humans is to flee, but make sure you don't come between a mother and her cubs.
Another key park inhabitant is the **Apennine Wolf**, of which there are around forty.
As with the bears, it offers no danger to humans. Look out, too, for the chamois
d'Abruzzo, deer and roe deer, wildcats, martens, otters, badgers, polecats and the
edible dormouse. Wolves can also be seen at the dedicated wolf museum at
Civitella Alfedena; others can be seen close up at the fascinating clinic and natural
history museum in Pescasseroli.

Among **birds**, the park's species include the golden eagle, the peregrine hawk, the
goshawk and the rare white-backed woodpecker. Higher up are snow finches, alpine
accentors and rock partridges.

The park's **flora** includes many local orchids, among which the most important
variety is Venus's little shoe or Our Lady's slipper, which thrives on the chalky soil in
the park. There are also gentians, peonies, violets, irises and columbines, and black
pine woods at Villetta Barrea and the Camosciara.

specialities try *Plistia* at Via Principe di Napoli 28 (☏0863.910.732; closed Mon), where you can eat hearty mountain food such as soup with local vegetables and pulses, or, in spring, gnocchi with asparagus and saffron. Otherwise try *La Baita*, on Piazzale Cabinovia 20 (☏0863.910.434 or 0863.910.615; closed Tues); dishes include *spaghetti alla chitarra* and polenta. Slightly more expensive is *Il Pescatore* in Villetta Barrea on Via Roma (☏0864.89.347; ⊛www.albergoristorantepescatore.com), a large restaurant and hotel where you can feast on superlative fresh trout from the lake and home-made pasta dishes.

Festivals

Two **festivals** worth trying to coincide a trip with are the Festa della Transhumanza, (May or June, contact tourist office for exact dates) commemorating the work of local nomadic shepherds by retracing their routes on foot or on horse, followed by a tasting of local products in Pescasseroli's main square. The town's Festa della Madonna, on July 15–16, sees the black Madonna carried 9km from her sanctuary on Monte Tranquillo to Pescasseroli and back to celebrate the town's miraculous escape from being bombed during the last war after prayers were offered to the Madonna.

Northeast Abruzzo: Téramo

Rising from the Adriatic and rolling towards the eastern slopes of the Gran Sasso, the landscape of **northeast Abruzzo** is gentle, and its inland towns are usually ignored in favour of its long, sandy and highly popular coastline. **TÉRAMO**, capital of the province of the same name, is a modern town with an elegant centre and if you're heading for the sea you may well pass through.

Téramo's main attraction is the **Duomo**, (daily 7am–noon & 4–8pm; free) at the top of Corso San Giorgio, which has been recently restored. Inside is a remarkable silver **altarfront** by the fifteenth-century Abruzzese silversmith Nicolà da Guardiagrele. It has 35 panels with lively reliefs of religious scenes, starting with the *Annunciation* and moving through the New Testament, punctuating the narrative with portraits of various saints. Nicolà was famous enough to feature in a sumptuous polyptych by a Venetian artist, Jacobello del Fiore, in a Baroque chapel to the left. It features it a model of Téramo, set against a gilded sky, with Nicolà wearing a monk's habit on the left, Jacobello in the red gown on the right.

South of the Duomo, Via Irelli leads to the heart of Roman Téramo, with fragments of the **amphitheatre**, and the more substantial walls of the **theatre**, where two of the original twenty entrance arches remain. Between Piazza Garibaldi and the Villa Comunale at Viale Bovio 1 is the town's modest **Pinacoteca** (May–Sept Tues–Sun 9am–1pm & 5–8pm; Nov–April Tues–Sun 9am–1pm & 4–7pm; free). The collection of local art over the centuries is best represented by the *Madonna Enthroned with Saints* – a polyptych in which the colours are lucid and the forms almost sculpted, the work of local fifteenth-century artist Giacomo da Campli. The **Museo Archeologico** off Via Carducci on Via Delfico 30 (same hours as the Pinacoteca) is strong on Roman finds from excavations in Téramo and includes a first-century mosaic of a lion among the forum columns and marble busts.

Practicalities

Buses to Téramo stop at Piazza Garibaldi, with which the **train station** (east of the centre on Via Crispi) is linked by the regular #1 city buses. The **tourist office** (Mon–Fri 9am–1pm & 3–6pm, Sat 9am–1pm; ℡0861.244.222, ⓦ www.abruzzoturismo.it) is located on Via Oberdan 16/17, near the Museo Archeologico. Heading off Piazza Garibaldi at Via del Castello 62 there is a reasonable **hotel**, the *Castello* (℡0861.247.582; ❶), which has simple, old-fashioned rooms and its own restaurant. **Restaurants** include *Antico Cantinone* at Via Ciotti 5 (℡0861.241.774; July–Aug closed Sun; Sept–May closed Wed), which has good local fare like grilled *agnello alle erbe*, and the bustling *Enoteca Centrale*, Corso Cerulli 24 (℡0861.243.633; closed Sun), where a great wine list – 450 labels – is backed up by excellent local dishes, such as *scripelle*, thin crepes covered in broth.

The Abruzzo coast

Abruzzo's coastline stretches for 125km from the border with Marche down to the seaside resort of Vasto. Heading south, the first town of any significance is **Pescara**. Its beaches and cultural sites are enough to hold your attention for a few days and it makes an excellent base for excursions to two atmospheric medieval villages, Lorento Aprutino and Atri. Next stop along the coast is **Chieti** home to a superb archaeological museum. Further south the coast becomes less developed, though the long ribbon of sand continues, followed by the train line and punctuated with mostly small resorts. Here, hilltop **Vasto** and the seaside resort **Vasto Marina**, are attractive destinations for a beach holiday and a good jumping-off point for trips to the Trémiti islands.

Pescara and around

The main town and resort of the Abruzzo coast is **PESCARA**, a bustling, modern place that's the region's most commercial and expensive city. If you're looking for somewhere to sunbathe there are much quieter – and cleaner – places than Pescara's sixteen-kilometre beach; but if you're aiming to take a ferry over to Croatia or the islands of the Dalmatian coast, you might find yourself using the city as a departure point. It's also the nearest to the new Abruzzo airport where low-cost flights from the UK touch down.

Arrival and information

Pescara has two **train stations**, though unless you're leaving the country you only need to use one, Stazione Centrale, at Piazza della Repubblica (the other, Porta Nuova, is more convenient for ferry connections). **Buses** to Rome (quicker than the train) and Naples, as well as regional buses, leave from outside Stazione Centrale. Ryanair **flights** from London Stansted touch down at **Abruzzo Airport** (ⓦ www.abruzzo-airport.it), around 3km southwest of the city; from the airport, the #38 bus leaves for Piazza della Repubblica every fifteen minutes (€1). The **tourist office** is in Piazza della Repubblica in the ex-silos of the old station (May–Oct Mon–Sat 9am–1pm & 4.30–7.30pm, Sun 9am–1pm; Nov–April Mon–Sat 9am–1pm & 4–7pm; ℡085.421.25462, ⓦ www.abruzzoturismo.it).

Accommodation

Most **hotels** are on the beach front, north of the river and the old town. The *Alba*, Via M. Forti 14 (☎085.389.145, ⓦwww.hotelalba.pescara.it; ❸), is a fairly upmarket choice – the rooms here have a baroque touch that takes them beyond the average business hotel. The *Corso*, opposite the train station at Corso Vittorio Emanuele 292 (☎085.422.4210; no credit cards; ❷), is the oldest hotel in Pescara, offering simple rooms with high ceilings, while the *Marisa*, Via Regina Margherita 39 (☎&ⓕ085.273.45; ❷), is a friendly, family-run place two blocks in from the sea, and just a short walk from the train station. The nearest **campsite** is *Francavilla* (☎085.810.715, ⓦwww.campingfrancavilla .com; June 15–Sept 15) 10km south of Pescara at Francavilla al Mare – buses #1 and #2 stop outside.

The Town

Pescara was heavily bombed in World War II and architecturally there's little of distinction here. Opposite the Stazione Centrale, the main street, **Corso Umberto**, is lined with designer boutiques and packed with the label-conscious Pescaresi, who also hang out in the elegant cafés on **Piazza Rinascita**, known as Pescara's *salone*. In the little that remains of its historic streets, the town boasts an excellent museum, the **Museo delle Genti d'Abruzzo** at Via delle Caserme 22 (May–Oct Mon–Sat 10am–1.30pm, Thurs, Fri & Sat 9.30pm–midnight; Nov–April Mon–Sat 9am–2pm, Sun 10am–2pm; ⓦwww.gentidabruzzo.it; €5), dedicated to the life and popular traditions of the region. Perhaps the most enchanting room is one devoted to the nomadic shepherds, containing books of their poetry, carved objects and volumes of Ariosto's chivalric romance *Orlando Furioso*.

Admirers of Mussolini's poet and mentor, **Gabriele d'Annunzio**, may want to visit his birthplace at Corso Manthonè 116 (daily 9am–2pm; €2; ⓦwww .casadannunzio.beniculturali.it), while devotees of Art Nouveau and later twentieth-century art should head for the **Museo Civico Basilio Cascella** at Viale Marconi 45 (Tues–Sun 9am–1pm, Tues & Thurs 4–8pm; €2.50) home to five hundred lithographic prints, paintings, ceramics and sculptures, including a stunning set of portraits (mounted on dinner plates) by the prolific Cascella family who lived and worked here.

Eating and drinking

For meals and nightlife, head for the little that remains of the old town of Pescara near the river. Along Corso Manthonè and Via delle Caserme there are more than fifty **bars** and **restaurants**. Recommended is the *Cantina di Jozz* at Via delle Caserme 59-65 (☎085.451.8800, ⓦwww.lacantinadijozz.it; closed Mon & Sun eve), which does great Abruzzese food such as *maialino arrosto* (roast suckling pig) for €12. Otherwise, try the slow-food advocate *La Lumaca*, just down the road from the *Cantina* at no. 51 (☎085.451.0880; eve only; closed Sun) – one of their best dishes is *agnello porchettato* (lamb cooked like an aromatic hog roast) – or the 🎋 *Locanda Manthonè*, Corso Manthonè 58 (☎085.454.9034; closed Sun), loved by the Pescarese for its reasonably priced quality food, such as slow-cooked lamb with saffron.

Loreto Aprutino

LORETO APRUTINO is a quiet, medieval hilltop settlement 24km inland from Pescara. The labyrinthine old town is home to a dwindling number of artisans' workshops specializing in hand-crafted knives. There are also tiny *cantinas* in the old town selling **olive oil**, for which the area has been awarded a DOP (*denominazione di origine protetta*), the equivalent of the DOC designation for wine. Loreto heaves with people on **market day** (Thurs 7am–1pm) and in the evenings during the late-running *passeggiata*, when it's a pleasure to simply do nothing and soak up the atmosphere. At the top of the old town, on the end of a row of nineteenth-century *palazzi*, stands the church of **San Pietro Apostolo**. Its orgins are medieval and it is preceded by an elegant Renaissance portico. Inside are the relics of the town's patron saint, San Zopito, who is venerated annually on the first Monday after Pentecost with a procession led by a child riding white bull.

Regular **buses** make the trip from Pescara, dropping you on Via Roma, 150m from the **tourist office** at Piazza Garibaldi 1 (May–Oct Mon–Sat 9am–1pm & 4.30–6.30pm; Nov–April Mon–Sat 9am–1pm & 3.30–5.30pm; open the first & third Sun of the month 9am–1pm; ℡085.829.0213). It's a good day-trip from Pescara but if you decide to **stay**, the ⚹ *B&B Laurentum*, Via del Baio 3 (℡085.829.2000, ⓦwww.bedbreakfastlauretum.com; ➌), is fantastic value for money, with accommodation in a family house near the Castello. The huge frescoed rooms come with antique furniture and there's a billiards room too. For **food**, you can eat very well at *Ristorante Carmine* on Contrada Re Martello 52, just west of the *centro storico* where fresh fish from Pescara is served with care. The *coda di rospo con patate e rosmarino*, monkfish with potatoes and rosemary, is sublime.

Atri

Buses from Pescara also head to the pretty little town of **ATRI**, 30km north, well worth a visit for the fifteenth-century frescoes in its Duomo. Approaching the town is like travelling through the background of a Renaissance painting, with gently undulating hills planted with orderly olive groves.

You'll be dropped on Viale Gran Sasso from where stairs lead up to the centre and towards the main piazza, dominated by the thirteenth-century **Duomo**. Its facade is understated, pierced by a rose window and perforated by the holes in which scaffolding beams were slotted during construction. The highlight is the cycle of **frescoes** in the apse by Andrea Delitio, known for his sophisticated use of architecture and landscape and realism. *The Birth of Mary*, for example, has servants giving the newly born baby a bath. The most emotionally charged scene is the *Slaughter of the Innocents*, in which the horror is intensified by the refined Renaissance architectural setting and the fact that the massacre is coolly observed from a balcony by Herod's party of civic bigwigs.

There are plenty of cafés nearby from where you can watch the small-town life around you, or head to the *Locanda Duca d'Atri* **restaurant** at Via San Domenico 54 (℡085.879.7586; closed Mon) where you can eat reasonably priced local dishes such as *cordicelle alla pecorara*, home-made ring-shaped pasta with ricotta, vegetables and tomato sauce.

Chieti

Twenty minutes by train or bus southwest of Pescara is the relaxed and appealing town of **CHIETI**. Spread over over a curving ridge, the town offers great views of the Majella and Gran Sasso mountains and – when it's clear – out to sea. It also holds Abruzzo's best archeological museum by far.

Local buses run from the Chieti Scalo train station below the town (bus #1) and stop in Largo Cavallerizza 50m from the chunky and much-reconstructed **cathedral**, from where the main **Corso Marrucini** cuts through the town centre to Piazza Trento e Trieste. Behind the post office, off Via Spaventa, are the remains of three little **Roman temples**. However, it's the **Museo Archeologico Nazionale di Abruzzo** (Tues–Sun 9am–8pm; €2) that is of most interest, beyond Piazza Trento e Trieste and laid out in the dignified Villa Comunale. In spite of renovations the museum is still open, although most of the collection has been crowded onto the ground floor. It holds finds from Abruzzo's major sites: a massive and muscular white-marble Hercules from his temple at Alba Fucens and a miniature bronze statue of the god, one of several Roman copies of the Greek original by Lysippus. Most interesting is the *Capestrano Warrior*, a statue of a Bronze Age warrior-prince with strangely feminine hips and thighs.

Further digs in Chieti have uncovered the core of **Teate** – the main town of the Marrucini, an Italic tribe – that became a Roman colony in the first century BC. The site lies on the edge of central Chieti west of the Villa Comunale at the **Civitella archeological park** (Tues–Sun 9am–8pm; €4) which comprises the amphitheatre, thermal baths (under restoration) and a new museum with restored temple fragments and remains from Chieti and the nearby river basin.

Practicalities

Buses and **trains** drop you at Chieti Scalo down in the valley, from where it's a ten-minute journey on bus #1 up the hill to Chieti proper, 5km away. The #1 makes stops in the centre along Via Herio and at Largo Cavallerizza near the cathedral. Chieti's **tourist office** is at Via Spaventa 47, just off Corso Marrucino (Tues & Thurs 9am–1pm & 3–6pm; ☏0871.63.640, ⓦwww.abruzzoturismo.it). For **accommodation**, try *Garibaldi*, Piazza Garibaldi 26 (☏0871.345.318; ❷), which has affordable and central, if ordinary, rooms. Very good-value **meals** can also be had in central Chieti at *Trattoria Nino*, Via Principessa di Piemonte 7 (☏0871.63.781; closed Fri), near Piazza Trento e Trieste, where the service is slow but the family atmosphere and regional specialities at around €7 compensate. For a light meal, drink or dessert, head to the newly renovated *Casina dei Tigli* (☏0871.69.509; closed Mon) in the *Villa Comunale* where locals flock to see and be seen.

Vasto

VASTO, 75km southeast of Pescara and close to the border with Molise, is a fine old city, built on the site of the Roman town Histonium and overlooking the resort of **Vasto Marina**. There are boats in the summer to the Trémiti islands (see p.851), plenty of campsites, and a handful of reasonable hotels along the broad sandy **beach** – palm-lined and beach-hutted in the centre, wilder and rockier to the north (the ever shrinking free beach area is central).

Vasto is all about the beach, though if you're here for a day or so you should definitely get a bus from the train station on the seafront to the **upper town** (#4 or #1 for the Marina and Vasto Centro, roughly every 30min, more frequent in summer; 10min), whose rooftops and campaniles rise above palms and olive groves. The centre of town is **Piazza Rossetti**, its gardens dominated by the massive **Castello Caldoresco**.

Just off the piazza, next to the small Duomo, stands the Renaissance **Palazzo d'Avalos** and its enchanting Neapolitan garden, a courtyard affair with orange trees and pillars and gorgeous sea views. The *palazzo* was once the home of the poet and friend of Michelangelo, Vittoria Colonna, who was famous in her time for the bleak sonnets she wrote after her husband's death; nowadays it houses the town **museum** (July & Aug daily 10.30am–12.30pm & 6pm–midnight; Sept–June Tues–Sun 9.30am–12.30pm & 4.30–7.30pm;

€1.50 for the archeological museum, free for the art gallery's permanent collection, €1.50 for the costume museum), a somewhat sparse collection of archeological objects and beautiful old clothes, as well as some paintings by the Palizzi brothers.

Piazza del Popolo opens onto a panoramic promenade that takes you to Vasto's most memorable sight, the door of the church of **San Pietro**, surrounded by Romanesque twists and zigzags, standing isolated against a backdrop of sky, sea and trees, the rest of the church having been destroyed in a landslide in 1956.

Practicalities

The **tourist office** (June–Sept Mon–Sat 9am–1pm & 4–7pm, Sun 9am–1pm; Oct–May Mon–Fri 9am–1pm, Mon, Tues, Thurs also 3–6pm; ☏0873.367.312, ⓦwww.abruzzoturismo.it) is on Piazza del Popolo.

Pleasant as the upper town is, it doesn't offer much in the way of **accommodation**. One place to try is *Hotel San Marco*, Via Madonna dell'Asilo 4 (☏0873.60.537, ⓦwww.hotelsanmarcovasto.it; ❸), a recently renovated, friendly three-star with a bar and restaurant. Some rooms have sea views. Otherwise, most of the action is down by the beach in Vasto Marina and a bit further south in San Salvo. Note that hotels insist on half board in July and August. There are plenty of impersonal four stars to choose from. For something more intimate, choose the *Villa Vignola* (☏0873.310.050, ⓦwww.villavignola.it; ❺), a small white villa outside town with a tiny pebble beach, a garden for lounging in and a romantic terrace restaurant serving such delicacies as stuffed baby squid (around €50 a head excluding wine). If your budget won't stretch that far, *La Bitta*, Lungomare Cordella 18 (☏&ⓕ0873.801.979; no credit cards; ❷), is a spacious and welcoming hotel (open April–Sept) with good home cooking. Parking and a place on their beach included in the price. There are also numerous **campsites** along the coast. Most of them are off the SS16 towards Fóggia. *Il Piopetto* is right on the beach and has pine trees for shade (☏0873.801.466, ⓦwww.ilpiopetto.it; mid-May to mid-Sept).

For **eating and drinking**, there are loads of pizzerias and pubs in Vasto Marina, although you might consider splashing out at *Villa Vignola* (see above) or *Ristorante Castello Aragona* in the upper town on Via San Michele 105 where fresh Adriatic fish is prepared artfully and served on a panoramic terrace (☏0873.69.885; closed Mon)

Térmoli and around

Just 6km separate Vasto and the brief stretch of the **Molise coast**, which is less developed than Abruzzo's. Its only real town, **TÉRMOLI**, a fishing port and quiet, undistinguished resort, makes for a relaxing place to spend a day. The beach is long and sandy and the old town, walled and guarded by a castle, has an interesting cathedral. It's also a departure point for ferries to the Trémiti islands (see p.851) and in striking distance of the interior towns of **Portocannone**, **Ururi**, and **Larino**,

Térmoli is the place where Italian and Central European time is set – from the observatory inside the stark castle built above the beach in 1247 by Frederick II. Beyond the castle the road follows the old walls around the headland, holding what's left of the old town, focus of which is the **Duomo**. This is most notable for its Romanesque exterior, decorated all the way round with a series of blind arcades and windows – a feature introduced by Frederick II's Norman-influenced architects. Inside are the relics of St Timothy, best known for the letters he received from St Paul, who advised him on how to go about converting the Greeks. That he ended up in Térmoli is thanks to Termolese Crusaders, who brought his bones back from Constantinople as a souvenir. The Termolese hid them, fearing that if the Turks ever succeeded in penetrating the city they would seize and destroy them. In fact the relics were hidden so well they weren't discovered until 1945, during restoration work to repair bomb damage (the sacristan will show them to you).

Practicalities

Long-distance **buses** pull up in Via Martiri della Resistenza, 1km from Térmoli's centre and the **train station**. A local bus service connects the bus station with the port and historical centre. The **tourist office** (June–Sept Mon–Fri 8am–2pm & 3–6pm, Sat 8am–1pm; Oct–May Mon–Fri 8am–2pm, Mon & Wed also 3–6pm, Sat 8am–1pm; ☎0875.703.913) on Piazza M. Bega 42 near the train station. In the summer the *Comune* installs kiosks in main tourist points in the old town, which promote local crafts and Molise in general (locations subject to change).

Central **accommodation** includes *Locanda Alfieri*, Via Duomo 39 (☎0875.708.112, ⍉www.locandalfieri.com; ❸), a homey bed and breakfast 50m from the port – one of the few options in the Borgo Antico, and *Hotel Santa Lucia*, (☎0875.705.101, ⍉www.santaluciahotel.it), on Largo Pie' di Castello below the castle where each room is warmly furnished and embellished with local contemporary artwork. About 5km from town along the SS16 is the **campsite** *Campeggio Azzurra* (☎0875.52.404, ⍉www.camping.it /molise/azzurra; June–Sept), with a bar, restaurant, mini-market, and free beach. In the high season, there are buses every hour from the town centre.

While here you should certainly have a meal in one of Térmoli's seafood **restaurants**. Of these, *Ristorante Z'Bass* on Via Oberdan 8 (☎0875.706.703; closed Mon) does excellent, reasonably priced fresh fish – leave room for their home-made *pasticceria secca* (sweet pastries), booking essential in the summer. There are plenty of pizzerias and simple trattorias along Via Fratelli Brigada, the seafront and the parallel Via. Emanuele III; later on try the wine bar *Spirito di Vino* on Largo Pie di Castello 27 (☎0875.703.676; eve only, closed Tues).

The Albanian villages

PORTOCANNONE, 12km south of Térmoli, and **URURI**, another 15km beyond, are isolated villages, most easily reached by bus from Térmoli. Their isolation is such that, six hundred years after their ancestors emigrated from Albania, the locals still speak an Albanian-Italian dialect incomprehensible to outsiders. Portocannone's Romanesque church contains an icon of the Madonna of Constantinople, brought over by the original émigrés, and in Ururi, at the beginning of May, the Carresse **festival** is staged: a fierce and furious race through the village streets on gladiator-style carts, pulled by bulls and pushed by men on horseback with spiked poles. It's a ruthless business: the horses are fed beer before the race to excite them, and although the riders are supposed to push only the back of the carts, they are not averse to prodding the flanks of the bulls, who have already been given electric shocks to liven them up. The race itself is terrifying, but unforgettable, with bulls, carts and spikes hurtling past the frenzied crowds, nowadays protected by wire fences. There are almost inevitably injuries, and at least one person has been killed. If you want to go, the *Comune* website (☎0874.830.130, ⓦwww.comune.ururi.cb.it) has information and the precise dates.

Larino

Fifteen kilometres due west of Ururi, **LARINO**'s attractive medieval centre is clasped in a valley. The highlight is its cathedral, but there are also some minor Roman relics in its small museum and a neglected amphitheatre in the modern town.

To the left of the **train station**, Via Gramsci leads down to **old Larino**. The main street widens out at Piazza Vittorio Emanuele, backing onto which is the **Palazzo Ducale**, whose **museum** (Mon–Fri 8am–2pm & 3–6pm; Sat 8am–2pm; free) contains large Roman mosaics and a hoard of coins. On Via Gramsci, about halfway between the station and the *centro storico*, there's a garden that also has **Roman ruins**, including capitals and columns, and a sacrificial altar called the Ara Frentana. Close by is the **Duomo** (daily 9am–noon & 4–8pm; free), a lovely building with an intricately carved Gothic portal built in the early fourteenth century just after the town had been flattened by an earthquake and sacked by the Saracens. The oldest part of the town starts beyond the Duomo, and the streets around it offer a glimpse at centuries-old street life: women making lace and preparing vegetables outside their houses, while the kids play in the alleys with makeshift toys.

If you take the hourly bus from Piazza Vittorio Emanuele to the upper city, you'll jump a couple of centuries in five minutes. **Modern Larino** is a bustling place, built on the site of the original Samnite/Roman town. The large and overgrown **amphitheatre** off Via Viadotto Frentano is visible from the street (Mon–Fri 9am–1pm; free) and gives some idea of the importance of early second-century BC Larinum. If you want to **stay**, your only choice is the *Park Hotel Campitelli 2* (☎0874.823.541, ⓦwww.parkhotelcampitelli2.it; ❷) at Via San Benedetto 1, an air-conditioned four-star, about 1km from the station.

Isernia

ISERNIA, inland from Vasto, is a useful entry point into western Molise, with good train connections from Rome and Naples. The first settlement dates back to the Samnites, yet very little of old Isernia survives. Earthquakes, the most recent in 1984, and wars have wreaked havoc on its historical monuments; much of the centre was destroyed in a bombing raid on September 10, 1943, and a monument to the four thousand who were killed – an anguished nude, ankle-deep in fractured tiles, bricks and gutters – is the centrepiece of the square called, understandably, Piazza X Settembre. In spite of it all, the city has rebuilt its commercial centre so that it's now comparatively busy and bustling.

The city's most iconic monument is the **Fontana Fraterna** in Piazza Celestino V. The Romanequse fountain was built in the 13th century by the Rampini family from marble stripped from Roman tombs. The city's main attraction is a prehistoric site called La Pineta, an easy 1.5km from the centre, or a short bus ride on the #3 from the station. Visits are by reservation only (☎0865.413.526; Mon–Fri 9am–1pm & 3–5pm; free). In 1978 local roadbuilders unearthed traces of a Palaeolithic settlement at least 700,000 years old – the most ancient signs of human life yet found in Europe. In the southern part of Isernia near the hospital (bus #2 from the station), the **Museo Nazionale Santa Maria delle Monache** (daily 8.30am–7pm; €2), on Corso

Marcelli 48 displays finds from the site. The exhibits are backed up by a video in English, which reconstructs the settlement and puts the ancient civilization in context. Contrary to the misleading publicity, there were no human remains found, just weapons, traps, traces of pigment thought to have been used as body paint, and animal bones, laid out to create a solid platform on the marshy land for the village.

Though unbeguiling in itself, can be a good starting-point for exploring the rest of Molise: **buses** to local villages and longer-distance buses, including those to Rome and Naples, depart from outside the **train station**. The **tourist office** is at Via Farinacci 9 (Mon–Sat 8am–2pm; ☎086.53.992). You probably won't need **to stay** over, but if you do, head for *Sayonara*, a swish modern three-star at Via G. Berti 131 (☎086.550.992, Ⓦ www.sayonara.is .it; ❸) and the only central hotel. As for **eating**, try *Osteria del Paradiso*, near the cathedral on Via Occidentale 2 (☎0865.414.847; closed Sun), where you can eat good, cheap, local food such as *pasta e fagioli* (a thick soup with pasta and beans).

Campobasso and Saepinum

CAMPOBASSO, Molise's regional capital, is a modern town that makes a good base for the remarkable ruins at **Saepinum**. If you happen to be around 60 days after Easter, don't miss the town's spectacular *Corpus Domini Sagra dei Misteri* **procession**, in which citizens are dressed as saints, angels and devils, inserted into fantastic contraptions and transported, seemingly suspended in mid-air, through the streets.

At any other time of the year the most notable attraction is the **Samnite Museum** (daily 8.30am–1.30pm & 2–5.30pm; free) at Via Chiarizia 14, with statues and a scattering of archeological finds from the area, most notably the haunting contents of a Longobard tomb, a warrior buried alongside his horse. Steep alleys of the small, old **upper town** lead up to a couple of Romanesque churches – **San Bartolomeo**, which has eerily contorted figures carved around its main door, and **San Giorgio**, whose entrance displays a dragon surrounded by stylized flowers. At the top of the hill are a monastery and sixteenth-century castle. Call ahead or drop in at the city hall for a visit to the castle from which there is panorama over the environs and the historical centre's *borgo antico* below (Piazza Vittorio Emanuele 29; ☎08744.051). The **tourist office** (Mon–Sat 8am–2pm; ☎08744.15.662) at Piazza della Vittoria 14 (Staircase C, 3rd floor) in the new town has details of local events and bus routes to elsewhere in the province.

Campobasso's **hotels** are marketed to business travellers rather than tourists and most are quite dreary. One centrally located exception is the modern and functional *Centrum Palace*, Via G. Vico 2/A (☎0874.413.341, Ⓦ www .centrumpalace.it; ❷). The lobby's decor is horribly tacky but the rooms are spacious and comfortable. There are, at least, some excellent places **to eat**. Among them, *La Grotta* (also known as *Concetta*), Via Larino 7 (☎0874.311.378, closed Sat & Sun), does a full menu of solid home cooking for around €22, and if you're lucky you'll get some of the family's home-produced salami. Otherwise, *Miseria e Nobiltà*, Via Sant'Antonio Abate 16 (☎0874.94.268; closed Sun), does excellent, innovative local dishes.

Saepinum

It's **SAEPINUM**, a ruined **Roman town** to the south, close to the border with Puglia, that makes the stopover in Campobasso worthwhile. Three kilometres from the nearest village and surrounded by a lush plain fringed with the foothills of the Matese mountains, it's the best example in Italy of a provincial Roman town.

The main reason Saepinum is so intact is that it was never very important: nothing much happened here, and after the fall of the Roman Empire it carried on as the sleepy backwater it had always been – until the ninth century when it was sacked by Saracens. Over the centuries its inhabitants added only a handful of farms and cottages, incorporating the odd Roman column, and eventually moved south to the more secure hilltop site of present-day Sepino. Some have now moved back and rebuilt the farms and cottages on Saepinum's peripheries, contributing if anything to the site's appeal. Their sheep graze below an ancient mausoleum, chickens scratch around the walls, and the only sounds are the tinkling of cowbells.

Saepinum is accessible by **bus** from Campobasso – either catch one of the three services that stop at Altilia (right outside the site; no buses Sun) or take the more frequent bus to **Sepino** (12 daily except Sun; ⓦ www.lariverabus.it for schedules) and walk the remaining 3km to Saepinum. Buses return to Campobasso from the archeological site (enquire at ticket office for times). By road, look for signs to Sepino. There's agriturismo **accommodation** and a good **restaurant** at *Convivium* on Contrada Altilia, 200m from the site (ⓣ0874.790.114; ❶). There are also two bar-restaurants at the Porta Boiano and the Porta Tammaro (see below).

The site

Depending on whether you arrive by bus or by car, the entrance to Saepinum (daily 8am–7pm; free) is through the **Porta Terravecchia** or the **Porta Tammaro**, two of the town's four gates. The site is bisected by the *cardo maximus* (running north–south), still paved with the original stones and crossed by the *decumanus maximus*. In Roman city planning, this intersection marked the centre of town, home to the public buildings and trading quarters. On the left, grass spills through the cracks in the pavement of the **forum**, now used by the few local kids as a football pitch, bordered by the foundations of various municipal buildings: the *comitium* (assembly place), the *curia* (senate house), a temple, baths, and in the centre a fountain with a relief of a griffin. Beyond the forum, on the left of the *decumanus*, the **Casa Impluvio Sannitico** contains a vat to collect rainwater, a remnant from the Samnite town that stood on the site before the Romans sacked it in 293 BC.

Back down the *decumanus* on the other side of the crossroads is the well-preserved **basilica** that served as the main courthouse. Beyond is the most interesting part of the town – the octagonal *macellum* (marketplace), with its small stone stalls and central rain-collecting dish, and a series of houses fronted by workshops, with the small living quarters behind. This leads down to the best-preserved gate, the **Porta Boiano**, flanked by cylindrical towers with a relief showing two barbarians and chained prisoners. There is a small **museum** with artefacts and artwork recovered during excavation (Tues–Sun: April–Oct 9.30am–1.30pm & 3–5.30pm; Nov–March 9am–1.30pm & 3–5pm; €2).

Travel details

Trains

Campobasso to: Térmoli (8 daily; 1hr 45min); Rome (5 daily; 3hr); Naples (4 daily; 3hr).
Isernia to: Campobasso (12 daily; 1hr); Rome (5 daily; 2hr).
L'Aquila to: Sulmona (10 daily; 1hr); Terni (10 daily; 2hr).
Pescara to: Ancona (25 daily; 1hr 30min–2hr); Rome (5 daily; 4hr); Sulmona (18 daily; 1hr–1hr 10min); Térmoli (20 daily; 1hr 10min); Vasto (15 daily; 50min).
Sulmona to: Avezzano (10 daily; 1hr 15min); Celano (9 daily; 1hr).
Térmoli to: Fóggia (18 daily; 1hr).

Buses

Atri to: Pescara (6 daily; 1hr).
Avezzano to: Pescasseroli (6 daily; 1hr 30min).
Chieti to: Rome (4 daily; 2hr 30min).
Isernia to: Campobasso (4 daily; 1hr).

L'Aquila to: Bominaco (4 daily; 1hr); Rome (18 daily; 1hr 40min); Sulmona (7 daily; 1hr 30min); Téramo (9 daily; 1hr 20min).
Pescara to: Atri (12 daily; 1hr); Chieti (every 20min; 40min); L'Aquila (11 daily; 1hr 50min); Loreto Aprutino (25 daily; 35min); Rome (4 daily; 2hr 50min); Sulmona (3 daily; 1hr 30min).
Sulmona to: Cocullo (1 daily; 40min); Scanno (7 daily; 1hr).
Téramo to: Atri (4 daily; 1hr 10min).
Térmoli to: Isernia (4 daily; 1hr 25min).

Ferries

Pescara to: Stari Grad (daily; 3hr 45min); Split (daily; 5hr 45min)
Ortona via Vasto to: Trémiti islands (1 daily; 2hr).
Térmoli to: Trémiti islands (2 ferries & 2 hydrofoils daily summer, 1 ferry daily in winter; 40min–1hr 40min).
Vasto to: Stari Grad (2 weekly; 4hr).

Campania

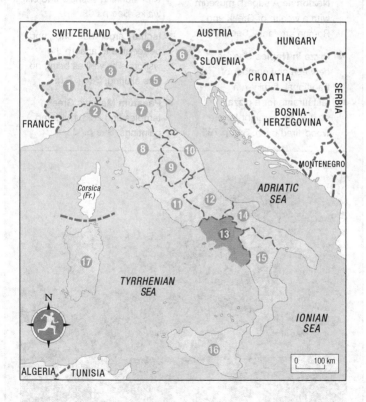

CHAPTER 13

Highlights

✴ **Miracle of San Gennaro**
The liquefaction of the saint's blood in Naples' cathedral is an occasion charged with emotion and accompanied by much festivity. **See p.784**

✴ **Museo Archeologico Nazionale** A superb museum with a wealth of Greek and Roman artefacts. **See p.790**

✴ **Pizza in Naples** Choose between any number of traditional, family-run restaurants for a pizza, sizzling hot straight from a wood-fired oven. **See p.795**

✴ **Herculaneum and Pompeii**
These sites afford an unparalleled glimpse into ancient Roman daily life and architecture. **See p.800 & p.802**

✴ **Cápri** A jewel of an island with stunning scenery and cliff walks. **See p.809**

✴ **Ischia** Larger than Cápri and better able to absorb the visitors – as well as being no less alluring. **See p.815**

✴ **Paestum** Majestic Greek temples and colourful tomb paintings. **See p.833**

▲ Sant'Angelo, Ischia

Campania

The region immediately south of Lazio, **Campania**, marks the real beginning of the Italian south or *mezzogiorno*. It's the part of the south too, perhaps inevitably, that most people see, as it's easily accessible from Rome and home to some of the area's (indeed Italy's) most notable features – Roman sites, spectacular stretches of coast, tiny islands. It's always

Regional food and wine

The flavour of Naples dominates the whole of Campania. Nowhere else in Italy is street food so much part of the culture. Most importantly, perhaps, Naples is the true home of the **pizza**, rapidly baked in searingly hot wood-fired ovens and running with olive oil. There's no such thing as "Pizza Napoletana" here; in Naples, the crucial one is the marinara – not, as you might think, anything to do with seafood, but the basic Neapolitan pizza, topped with just tomato, garlic and a leaf or two of basil, no cheese. Street food also comprises fried pizzas – *pizzette or panzarotti* – and calzone, a stuffed fried pizza with ham and cheese or vegetables. *Friggitorie* sell other fried goodies, among them heavenly *krocche* (potato croquettes), *arancini* (rice balls) and *fiorilli* (courgette flowers in batter).

Naples is also the home of pasta and tomato sauce, made with fresh tomatoes and basil, and laced with garlic. Aubergines and courgettes turn up endlessly in **pasta sauces**, as does the tomato-**mozzarella** pairing (the regions to the north and east of Naples are both big mozzarella-producing regions), the latter particularly good with *gnocchi*. **Seafood** is excellent all along the coast: clams combine with garlic and oil for superb *spaghetti alle vongole*; mussels are often prepared as *zuppa di cozze* (with hot pepper sauce and croutons); fresh squid and octopus are ubiquitous.

There are loads of great **pastries**: not to be missed is the *sfogliatella*, a flaky triangular pastry case stuffed with ricotta and candied peel, and the fragrant Easter cake, *pastiera*, made with ricotta and softened wheat grain. Further to the south, the marshy plains of the **Cilento** produce fabulous strawberries, artichokes and mozzarella cheese – much of the mozzarella that comes from here is made from pure buffalo milk, unmixed with cow's milk.

The volcanic slopes of Vesuvius are among the most ancient **wine-producing** areas in Italy, but despite that the region doesn't have a great reputation for wine. The best choices for a Campanian **white** are Greco di Tufo, Fiano di Avellino and Falanghina – all fruity yet dry alternatives. Ischia also produces good whites notably Biancolella, while Lacryma Christi, from the slopes of Mount Vesuvius, is available in red and white varieties and is enjoying a resurgence after years of being considered cheap plonk. Among pure **reds**, there's the unusual but delicious Gragnano, a red sparkling wine that's best served slightly chilled, and Taurasi – like the best wines of the region made from the local aglianico grape.

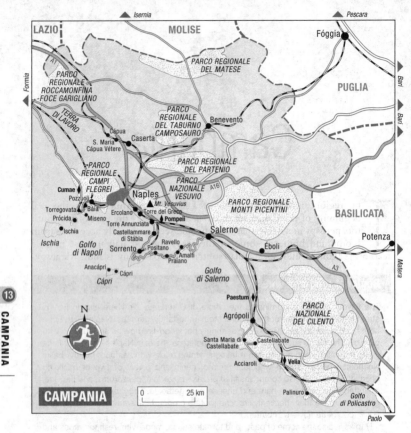

been a sought-after region, first named by the Romans, who tagged it the *campania felix*, or "happy land" (to distinguish it from the rather dull *campagna* further north), and settled down here in villas and palatial estates that stretched right around the Bay of Naples. Later, when Naples became the final stop on northerners' Grand Tours, its bay became no less fabled, the relics of its heady Roman period only adding to the charm for most travellers.

Naples is the obvious focus, an utterly compelling city and one that dominates the region in every way. Taking one of the fastest trains, you can reach it now in ninety minutes from the capital, and there's no excuse for not seeing at least this part of Campania – though of course you need three or four days to absorb the city properly, before embarking on the remarkable attractions surrounding it. The **Bay of Naples**, certainly, is dense enough in interest to occupy you for a good week: there are the ancient sites of **Pompeii** and **Herculaneum** just half an hour away – arguably Italy's best-preserved and most revealing Roman remains; there is the odd, volcanic **Campi Flegrei** area to the northwest of the city; and of course there are the islands, **Cápri**, **Ischia** and **Prócida**. Cápri swarms with visitors but is so beautiful that a day here is by no means time squandered, while Ischia, which is the largest island and absorbs tourists more readily, is a lively and attractive place in which you could while away an entire holiday.

Inland Campania is, by contrast, a poor, unknown re[gion,] though the towns just outside of Naples – **Caserta**, [...] visit; and **Benevento**, an old stop on the Roman r[oad] flavour that's quite distinct from the coastal regions. The [...] has more immediate appeal. **Sorrento**, at the far south [...] major package-holiday destination, but a cheery and li[vely...] and the **Amalfi coast**, across the peninsula, is perhaps [...] stretch of coastline, harbouring some fantastically en[...] exclusive – beach resorts. Further south, the lively port [...] to the Hellenistic site of **Paestum** and the uncrowded [...] just beyond.

Naples

Whatever your real interest in Campania, the chances are that you'll wind up in **NAPLES** (Napoli) – capital of the region and, indeed, of the whole Italian south. It's the kind of city that is laden with visitors' preconceptions, and it rarely disappoints: it is filthy, it is very large and overbearing, it is crime-infested, and it is most definitely like nowhere else in Italy – something the inhabitants will be keener than anyone to tell you. In Naples, all the pride and resentment of the Italian south, all the historical differences between the two wildly disparate halves of Italy, are sharply brought into focus. This is the true heart of the *mezzogiorno*, a lawless, petulant, yet fiercely Catholic city that has its own way of doing things. There's plenty to see – the city's **Duomo**, **Palazzo Reale** and a couple of impressive museums in the **Capidomonte** gallery and **archeological museum** – but it's not so much a city of sights as just a great place to be, particularly its dense **centro storico**. Spend a couple of days here and you're likely to be as staunch a defender of the place as its most devoted inhabitants.

Some history

There was a settlement here, **Parthenope**, as early as the ninth century BC, which was superseded by a Greek colony in 750 BC, which they gave the name Neapolis. It prospered during Greek and later Roman times, and remained independent until the **Normans** took the city in 1139. The Normans weren't here for long: like the rest of this region, the city soon came under the rule of the Hohenstaufen dynasty, who stayed rather half-heartedly until 1269, when their last king, Conradin, was beheaded in what's now Piazza del Mercato, and the **Angevins** took over the city. With one exception – Robert the Wise, who was a gentle and enlightened ruler and made the city a great centre for the arts – the Angevin kings ruled badly, in the end losing Naples to Alfonso I of Aragon in 1422, thus establishing a **Spanish** connection for the city for the next 300 years.

Following the War of the Spanish Succession, Naples was briefly ceded to the Austrians, before being taken, to general rejoicing, by **Charles of Bourbon** in 1734. Charles was a cultivated and judicious monarch, but his dissolute son

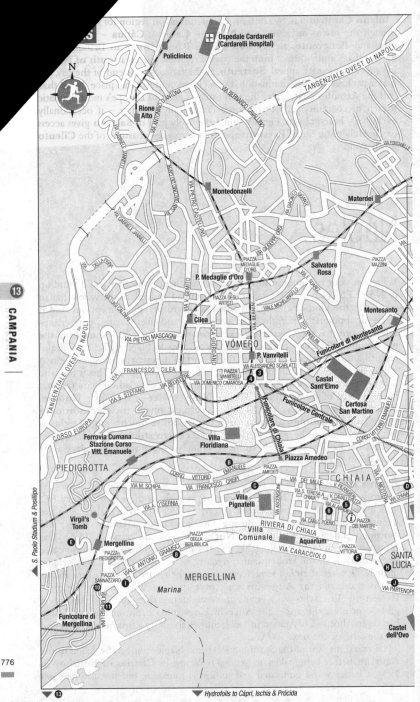

N

Ospedale Cardarelli
(Cardarelli Hospital)

Policlinico

TANGENZIALE OVEST DI NAPOLI

Rione
Alto

Montedonzelli

Materdei

PIAZZA
MAZZINI

PIAZZA
MEDAGLIE
D'ORO

P. Medaglie d'Oro

Salvatore
Rosa

Montesanto

PIAZZA DEGLI
ARTISTI

Cilea

VÓMERO

P. Vanvitelli

Funicolare di Montesanto

PIAZZA
VANVITELLI

Castel
Sant'Elmo

VIA FRANCESCO CILEA

Certosa
San Martino

Funicolare di Chiaia

Funicolare Centrale

CORSO EUROPA

Ferrovia Cumana
Stazione Corso
Vitt. Emanuele

Villa
Floridiana

Piazza Amedeo

PIEDIGROTTA

CORSO VITTORIO EMANUELE

PIAZZA
AMEDEO

CHIAIA

VIA DEL MILLE

V. FILANGIERI

VIA M. SCHIPA

VIA FRANCESCO CRISPI

VIA S. TERESA
CHIAIA

V. CAVALLERIZZA

VIA A. D'ISERNIA

Villa
Pignatelli

VIA CARLO POERIO

PIAZZA
DEI MARTIRI

Virgil's
Tomb

RIVIERA DI CHIAIA

Villa
Comunale

Aquarium

PIAZZA
VITTORIA

SANTA
LUCIA

Mergellina

PIAZZA
PIEDIGROTTA

VIALE ANTONIO GRAMSCI

PIAZZA
DELLA
REPUBBLICA

VIA CARACCIOLO

PIAZZA
SANNAZZARO

MERGELLINA

Marina

VIA PARTENOPE

Funicolare di
Mergellina

Castel
dell'Ovo

S. Paolo Stadium & Posillipo

Hydrofoils to Cápri, Ischia & Prócida

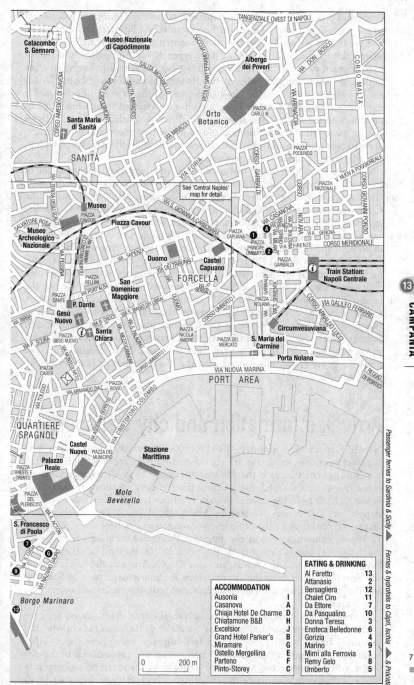

Passenger ferries to Sardinia & Sicily ▶   Ferries & hydrofoils to Capri, Ischia ▶   & Prócida

TANGENZIALE OVEST DI NAPOLI

Catacombe S. Gennaro

Museo Nazionale di Capodimonte

Albergo dei Poveri

VIA DON BOSCO

CORSO MALTA

CORSO AMEDEO DI SAVOIA

SALITA MIRADOIS

SALITA CAPODIMONTE

SALITA MOIARIELLO

VICOLO SANTERRAMO

DIOCESI SANT'EFFREMO

PIAZZA CARLO III

VIA ARENACCIA

Santa Maria di Sanità

Orto Botanico

VIA MIRACOLI

PIAZZA L. PODERICO

SANITA

VIA FORIA

VIA CARDONARA

PIAZZA NAZIONALE

CORSO GIOVANNI PORZIO

CORSO GARIBALDI

V. NUOVA POGGIOREALE

CORSO

See 'Central Naples' map for detail

VIA S. GIOVANNI A CARBONARA

NOV ARA

CORSO MERIDIONALE

VIA TERESA DEGLI SCALZI

SALVATORE ROSA

Museo

PIAZZA CAVOUR

Piazza Cavour

PIAZZA CAPUANA

VIA CASANOVA

VIA TORINO

VIA BOLOGNA

VIA GENOVA

VIA FIRENZE

A

①

②

Museo Archeologico Nazionale

VIA PESSINA

VIA S. MARIA DI COSTANTINOPOLI

VIA SAPIENZA

Duomo

VIA PORT'ALBA

PIAZZA BELLINI

Castel Capuano

PIAZZA PRINCIPE UMBERTO

VIA VENEZIA

Train Station: Napoli Centrale

ⓘ

PIAZZA DANTE

P. Dante

San Domenico Maggiore

VIA DEI TRIBUNALI

FORCELLA

VIA SERSALE

DUOMO

PIAZZA GARIBALDI

CORSO ARNALDO LUCCI

VIA GALILEO FERRARIS

Gesù Nuovo

VIA TAPIA

VIA B. CROCE

VIA S. BIAGIO DEI LIBRAI

CORSO UMBERTO I

PIAZZA NOLANA

CORSO GARIBALDI

VIA P. SCURA

ⓘ

Santa Chiara

VIA MEZZOCANNONE

PIAZZA NICOLA AMORE

PIAZZA DEL MERCATO

Circumvesuviana

VIA REGGIO DI PORTICI

PIAZZA GESU NUOVO

VIA MONTEOLIVETO

PIAZZA CARITA

CORSO UMBERTO I

S. Maria del Carmine

Porta Nolana

VIA TOLEDO

VIA ARMANDO DIAZ

PIAZZA BOVIO

VIA NUOVA MARINA

PORT AREA

VIA AGOSTINO DEPRETIS

VIA CRISTOFORO COLOMBO

QUARTIERE SPAGNOLI

Castel Nuovo

PIAZZA DEL MUNICIPIO

Stazione Marittima

Palazzo Reale

PIAZZA TRIESTE E TRENTO

PIAZZA DEL PLEBISCITO

Molo Beverello

S. Francesco di Paola

VIA A. ACTION

⑦

Ⓖ

⑨

VIA S. LUCIA

VIA NAZARIO SAURO

Borgo Marinaro

⑫

0   200 m

Ferdinand presided over a shambolic period in the city's history, abandoning it to the republican French. Their "Parthenopean Republic" here was short-lived, and the British re-installed the Bourbon monarch, carrying out vicious reprisals against the rebels. The instigator of these reprisals was Admiral Nelson – fresh from his victory at the Battle of the Nile – who was famously having an affair with Lady Hamilton, the wife of the British ambassador to Naples. Under continuing Bourbon rule, the city became one of the largest in Europe, and a requisite stop on the **Grand Tour**, a position it enjoyed not so much for its proximity to the major classical sites as for the ready availability of sex. Naples was for a long time the prostitution capital of the Continent, and its reputation drew people from far and wide, giving new meaning (in the days when syphilis was rife) to the phrase "see Naples and die".

More recently, Naples and its surrounding area have been the recipient of much of the government and EU money that has poured into the Italian South. But the real power in the area is still in the hands of organized crime or the **Camorra**, with the result that there's been little real improvement in the living standards of the average Neapolitan: a very high percentage remain unemployed, and a large number still inhabit the typically Neapolitan one-room *bassi*, letting in no light and housing many in overcrowded conditions. **Antonio Bassolino**, mayor of the city from 1993 until 2000 and currently president of Campania, has done much to promote Naples and its attractions, and scores of neglected churches, museums and palaces have been restored and are now open to the public. There's also been a burst of creative activity from local filmmakers, songwriters and artists, with a thriving contemporary **art scene** manifest in two new large galleries. However, the Camorra still cast a long shadow over modern Naples, as highlighted by Roberto Saviano's recent bestselling book and much-publicized film, *Gomorrah*, and the city's 2008 rubbish crisis. No tourist is going come into contact with the Camorra, but its hold on Naples seems to be as strong as ever.

Arrival, information and city transport

Naples' Capodichino **airport** (℡081.848.88877, ⓦwww.gesac.it) is around 7km north of the city centre. It is connected with Piazza Garibaldi (the stop is in front of the station at the *McDonald's* corner) by bus #3S approximately every thirty minutes, and the journey takes twenty to thirty minutes; buy tickets (€1.10) from the *tabacchi* in the departures hall. There is also an official airport bus, *Alibus*, also operated by ANM (℡081.763.2177), which runs to piazzas Garibaldi and Municipio every twenty minutes between 6.30am and 11.30pm (6am–midnight in the opposite direction), although it isn't very much quicker and is almost triple the price (€3). Taxis tend to take about as long as buses to reach the centre, and cost €16–20. You can also reach Salerno and Sorrento direct from the airport; there are hourly departures to Sorrento and the journey takes an hour and a half, and four departures to Salerno – an hour's journey.

By train, you're most likely to arrive at Napoli Centrale, situated on the edge of the city centre at one end of Piazza Garibaldi, at the main hub of city (and suburban) transport services; there's a **left luggage** office here (open 24hr). Some trains also pull into Stazione Mergellina, on the opposite side of the city centre, which is connected with Piazza Garibaldi by the underground *metropolitana*. For train enquiries phone ℡848.888.088, check ⓦwww.trenitalia.com or go to the information booths at Napoli Centrale (daily 7am–9pm) and be prepared to queue.

City and suburban **buses** also stop on Piazza Garibaldi, though you'll need to check the stops carefully as they are not well signed and are subject to change. CTP (℡081.700.1111) run buses to Caserta and FABN (℡800.127.157) to Benevento from here, but the main company, SITA (℡081.552.2176, ⓦwww .sitabus.it), which connects with Pompeii, Sorrento, the Amalfi coast and Salerno, leaves from Via G. Ferraris, just south of the Stazione Centrale and from their main office at Via Pisanelli 3/7, just off Piazza Municipio.

Information

There are several **tourist offices** dotted around the city: one in the Stazione Centrale (Mon–Sat 8am–8pm, Sun 9am–2pm; ℡081.268.779, ⓦwww.inaples .it), one on Piazza del Gesù Nuovo (Mon–Sat 9.30am–1.30pm & 2.30– 6.30pm, Sun 9am–1.30pm; ℡081.551.2701), and another opposite the Teatro San Carlo at Via San Carlo 9 (Mon–Sat 9.30am–1.30pm & 2.30–6.30pm, Sun 9am–1.30pm; ℡081.402.394). At each of them you can pick up a free **city map** and an English-language copy of the monthly *Qui Napoli*, a useful reference on the city and an indicator of **what's on**, as well as a decent free transport map, which details all of the many public transport options in and around the city (see below).

City transport

The only way to really **get around** central Naples and stay sane is to **walk**. Driving can be a nightmare, and to negotiate the narrow streets, hectic squares and racetrack boulevards on a moped or scooter takes years of training. In any case, *not* to walk would mean you'd miss a lot – Naples is the kind of place best appreciated from street level.

For longer journeys there are a number of alternatives, both for the city itself and the bay as a whole, and the system, most of which is run by ANM, is pretty well integrated. City **buses** will get you almost everywhere, although they are crowded and slow. The bus system is supplemented by the **metropolitana**, a small-scale underground network that crosses the city centre, stopping at about four places between Piazza Garibaldi and Mergellina, and runs eventually out to Pozzuoli in about thirty minutes; new stations – at Duomo, Piazza Municipio and Via Toledo – are in the pipeline. In addition, three **funiculars** scale the hill of the Vómero: one, the Funicolare di Chiaia, from Piazza Amedeo; another, the Funicolare Centrale, from the Augusteo station, just off the bottom end of Via Toledo; and a third, the Funicolare di Montesanto, from the station on Piazza Montesanto. A fourth, the Funicolare di Mergellina, runs up the hill above Mergellina from Via Mergellina.

Uniconapoli **tickets** for all ANM modes of transport cost a flat €1.10 for all journeys (valid 90min) and must be bought in advance from such places as *tabacchi*, newsstands, stations, or the transport booth on Piazza Garibaldi. An all-day ticket costs €3.10, or you can buy a three-day tourist ticket for €20.

If you need to take a **taxi** make sure the driver switches on the meter when you start (they often don't), or request a flat fare at the start of the journey – which you can do (there are published rates to key locations that taxi drivers have to adhere to if requested); otherwise fares start at €3 for the initial journey, €5.50 at nights or at weekends. Note that journeys to and from the airport incur an extra charge of €2.60. There are taxi ranks at the train station, on Piazza Dante, Piazza del Gesù and Piazza Trieste e Trento, among other places.

#R2 Piazza Garibaldi–Corso Umberto I–Piazza Bovio–Via Depretis–Piazza Municipio–Via San Carlo–Piazza Trieste e Trento–Piazza Municipio–Via Medina–Via Sanfelice–Corso Umberto I–Piazza Garibaldi.

#R3 Mergellina Funicolare–Via Mergellina–Via Riviera di Chiaia–Piazza Municipio–Via Medina–Via Toledo–Piazza Municipio–Via San Carlo–Piazza Trieste e Trento–Piazza Municipio–Via Riviera di Chiaia–Mergellina Funicolare.

#R4 Via Cardarelli–Via Capodimonte–Piazza Dante–Via Depretis–Piazza Dante–Via Capodimonte–Via Cardarelli.

#E1 Piazza del Gesu–Via Mezzocannone–Via Santa Chiara–Via Duomo–Via Tribunali–Via Duomo–Corso Umberto I–Via Monteoliveto–Piazza del Gesu.

#CS Via Brin–Piazza Garibaldi–Corso Umberto I–Via Duomo–Piazza Museo–Piazza Dante–Piazza Carita—Corso Umberto I–Piazza Garibaldi–Via Gianturco–Via Brin.

#140 Capo Posillipo–Via Mergellina–Piazza Vittoria–Via Riviera di Chiaia–Via Santa Lucia–Via Riviera di Chiaia–Via Mergellina–Capo Posillipo.

#401 (night bus) Piazza Garibaldi–Via Depretis–Piazza Municipio–Riviera di Chiaia–Viale Augusto–Via Diocleziano–Pozzuoli.

For details on the frequency of the rail lines, see "Travel details", on p.836.

For solely **out-of-town trips** – around the bay in either direction – or indeed to get from one side of the centre to another, there are three more rail systems. The **Circumvesuviana** runs from its own station on Corso Garibaldi, behind the main station of Napoli Centrale (and from Napoli Centrale itself), right round the Bay of Naples about every thirty minutes, stopping everywhere as far south as Sorrento, which it reaches in about an hour. In the opposite direction, the **Ferrovia Cumana** operates every ten minutes from its terminus station in Piazza Montesanto west to Pozzuoli and Baía, as does the **Circumflegrea**, which follows a different route to the same terminal at Torregevata. Uniconapoli **tickets** are valid for all these suburban lines except the Circumvesuviana, for which tickets can be bought at any train station.

Accommodation

Accommodation prices in Naples may come as a refreshing change after the north of Italy, but they're still not cheap, and you need to choose carefully from among the cheaper dives. A good many of these are situated around Piazza Garibaldi, spitting distance from the train station but rather insalubrious and noisy, and poorly placed for going out at night. A better bet is the lively and more atmospheric *centro storico*, where boutique hotels and small B&Bs are opening up all the time. If you can, try to **book in advance**, as the city gets busy in high season. Ignore the touts hanging around the station: quite apart from safety issues, you'll be charged commission.

Hotels and B&Bs

Centro storico and Piazza Garibaldi

Bella Cápri Via Melisurgo 4 ☏ 081.552.9494, ⓦ www.bellacapri.it. Cheap rooms with views over the bay, and right by the port. Plus very welcoming staff who can help you find bargains for island visits, too. They also run a hostel (see opposite). 10 percent discount on your room with this book. ❸

Casanova Via Venezia 2 ☏ 081.268.287, ⓦwww
.hotelcasanova.com. Best of the station-area budget
options, this creeper-clad hotel is quiet, run by an
affable team, and has pleasant rooms (most of
which are en suite) and a communal roof terrace. ❷
Caravaggio Piazza Riario Sforza 157
☏ 081.211.0066, ⓦwww.caravaggiohotel.it. Right in
the thick of things on the edge of Forcella, just
around the corner from the Duomo, but quiet enough,
on its own small square – which some of the nicer
rooms in this elegant old *palazzo* overlook. ❻
Correra 241 Via Correra 241 ☏ 081.1956.2842.
This well-located budget option has a deliberately
contemporary feel, with bright primary colours and
minimalist furnishings throughout. ❹
🏃 **Costantinopoli 104** Via S Maria di
Costantinopoli 104 ☏ 081.557.1035,
ⓦwww.costantinopoli104.it. A posh boutique hotel
with its own garden and swimming pool in a quiet
building just off Piazza Bellini. The rooms and
common areas are stylishly furnished with modern
design elements. ❼
Des Artistes Via Duomo 61 ☏ 081.446.155,
ⓦwww.hoteldesartistesnaples.it. A comfortable
place with simple, smallish rooms and a young,
friendly staff. Perfectly located for Spaccanapoli
and most of the major city centre sights. ❸
🏃 **Donna Regina B&B** Via L Settembrini 80
☏ 081.446.799, ⓦwww.discovernaples.net.
Inside the former Donnaregina convent, each room
of this lovely and welcoming B&B is spacious and
uniquely decorated. ❸
Duomo Via Duomo 228 ☏ 081.265.988, ⓦwww
.hotelduomonapoli.it. Newly and stylishly done up,
but with prices that are still among the lowest in
town. Most rooms face onto a tranquil internal
courtyard and all are en suite. Very welcoming. ❷
Il Convento Via Speranzella 137/A ☏ 081.403.997,
ⓦwww.hotelilconvento.com. Situated in the
Quartieri Spagnoli, just two blocks off Via Toledo,
this three-star has decent, cosy rooms, two of
which have their own roof terraces. ❻

Chiaia & Santa Lucia

Chiaja Hotel De Charme Via Chiaia 216
☏ 081.415.555, ⓦwww.hotelchiaia.it. Lovely, old

fashioned hotel near Piazza del Plebiscito. The
rooms have been fashioned from an eighteenth-
century patrician home with all the antique
furniture and old-world style to prove it. ❻
Chiatamone B&B Via Chiatamone 6
☏ 081.060.8129, ⓦwww.hotelchiatamone.it.
Between Chiaia and Santa Lucia, this warm and
welcoming family-run B&B has six spacious and
well-equipped rooms in a variety of configurations,
including a mini-apartment with kitchen. ❹
Miramare Via N. Sauro 24 ☏ 081.764.7589,
ⓦwww.hotelmiramare.com. A great location on the
waterfront a little way down from the Palazzo
Reale, this Art Nouveau gem is the less obvious –
and cheaper – alternative to the giant and more
impersonal palaces nearby, with a more homely
feel and a warmer welcome. ❽
Parteno Via Partenope 1 ☏ 081.245.2095,
ⓦwww.parteno.it. Seven individually designed and
beautifully furnished rooms in an eighteenth-
century building near Villa Communale. Great
breakfasts and wonderful attention to detail by
owners. ❺
Pinto-Storey Via Martucci 72 ☏ 081.681.260,
ⓦwww.pintostorey.it. An evocative Art Nouveau
building in Chiaia. Rooms are attractively furnished
and many have views of the bay. ❺

Mergellina

Ausonia Via Caracciolo 11 ☏ 081.682.278,
ⓦwww.hotelausonianapoli.com. A two-star
decorated to give the impression you're on a
yacht, neatly placed in Mergellina, next to the
stop for hydrofoils to the islands. Bus #R3 or
#152. ❹
Grand Hotel Parker's Corso Vittorio Emanuele
135 ☏ 081.761.2474, ⓦwww.grandhotelparkers
.it. This upmarket and extremely comfortable hotel
claims to be the oldest in Naples, and has hosted
Oscar Wilde and Virginia Woolf, as well as King
Vittorio Emanuele himself. With an exalted
vantage point over the city, the views from the
dining room over the bay and east to Vesuvius are
unparalleled. ❾

Hostels

Hostel Bella Cápri Via Melisurgo 4
☏ 081.552.9494, ⓦwww.bellacapri.it. Spanking
new upper floor hostel, with free internet access
and a large, light and airy breakfast room. Right on
the port so perfect for accessing the islands. Dorm
beds go for €20 in high season; 10 percent
discount with this book. ❷

Hostel of the Sun Via Melisurgo 15 ☏ 081.420.6393,
ⓦwww.hostelnapoli.com. Clean, colourful hostel with
kitchen, probably the best and friendliest in Naples
and next to the main ferry dock. Well placed for going
out and there's no curfew. Breakfast included. Dorm
beds €20, breakfast included; 10 percent discount on
hotel rooms with this book. ❷

Ostello Mergellina Salita della Grotta 23 ⊤081.761.2346, ⓦ www.hihostels.com. Popular HI site with a view of the bay, conveniently located not far from the Mergellina metro station, There's a 12.30am curfew, but ask for a double room and they are more flexible. Breakfast included. Three-day maximum stay in July & Aug. Dorm beds €16. ❷

Campsites

The closest **campsite** to Naples is the excellent and beautiful *Vulcano Solfatara* site in Pozzuoli at Via Solfatara 47 (⊤081.526.2341, ⓦ www.solfatara.it; April–Nov; €26 per person, ❷ for double bungalow); take the *metropolitana* to Pozzuoli and walk ten minutes up the hill. When this is closed, you're probably best off going to one of the other sites around the bay – perhaps at Pompeii, or, rather nicer, Sorrento, neither of which is more than an hour out from the city.

The City

Naples is a large, sprawling city, with a centre that has many different focuses. The area between Piazza Garibaldi and Via Toledo, roughly corresponding to the old Roman Neapolis (much of which is still unexcavated below the ground), makes up the old part of the city – the **centro storico** – the main streets still following the path of the old Roman roads. This is much the liveliest and most teeming part of town, an open-air kasbah of hawking, yelling humanity that makes up in energy what it lacks in grace. Buildings rise high on either side of the narrow, crowded streets, cobwebbed with washing; there's little light, not even much sense of the rest of the city outside – certainly not of the proximity of the sea.

But the insularity of the *centro storico* is deceptive, and in reality there's another, quite different side to Naples, one that's much more like the sunwashed Bay of Naples murals you've seen in cheap restaurants back home. **Via Toledo**, the main street of the city, edges the old centre from the **Palazzo Reale** up to the **Museo Nazionale Archeologico** and the heights of **Capodimonte**; to the west rises the **Vómero**, with its fancy housing and museums, and the slightly smug neighbourhood of **Chiaia**, beyond which lies the long green boulevard of **Riviera de Chiaia**, stretching around to the districts of **Mergellina** and **Posillipo**: all neighbourhoods that exert quite a different kind of pull – that of an airy waterfront city, with views, seafood eaten alfresco and relative peace and quiet.

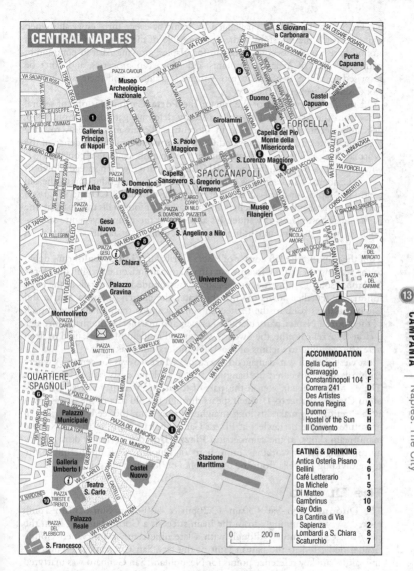

CENTRAL NAPLES

PIAZZA CAVOUR

Museo
Archeologico
Nazionale

1 Galleria
Principe
di Napoli

Port' Alba

Girolamini

Duomo

Castel
Capuano

FORCELLA

Capella del Pio
Monte della
Misericorda

S. Lorenzo Maggiore

SPACCANAPOLI

Capella
Sansevero S. Gregorio
Armeno

Museo
Filangieri

S. Domenico
Maggiore

S. Paolo
Maggiore

Gesù
Nuovo

S. Angelino a Nilo

S. Chiara

Palazzo
Gravina

University

Montecalvario

QUARTIERE
SPAGNOLI

Palazzo
Municipale

Galleria
Umberto I

Teatro
S. Carlo

Palazzo
Reale

S. Francesco

Porta
Capuana

Stazione
Marittima

Castel
Nuovo

N

CAMPANIA | Naples: The City

ACCOMMODATION

Bella Capri	I
Caravaggio	C
Constantinopoli 104	F
Correra 241	D
Des Artistes	B
Donna Regina	A
Duomo	E
Hostel of the Sun	H
Il Convento	G

EATING & DRINKING

Antica Osteria Pisano	4
Bellini	6
Café Letterario	1
Da Michele	5
Di Matteo	3
Gambrinus	10
Gay Odin	9
La Cantina di Via Sapienza	2
Lombardi a S. Chiara	8
Scaturchio	7

0   200 m

Piazza Garibaldi and around

However you get to Naples, there's a good chance that the first place you'll see is **Piazza Garibaldi**, a long, wide square crisscrossed by traffic lanes, that cuts into the city centre from the modern train station. It's the city's transport hub – most of the city buses leave from here, as do the *metropolitana* and Circumvesuviana lines – and one of its most hectic junctions; indeed it's Piazza Garibaldi, perhaps more so than any other part of the city, that puts people off Naples. The entire piazza is currently a vast construction site due to work on the new metro; pedestrians are blocked by steel walls and challenged by traffic at every turn, especially when trying to reach the bus stops at the opposite side of the piazza. Of late, the area around here has also become a centre for Naples' growing African community, with a number of African restaurants and Moroccan groceries, and don't be surprised to hear Slavic accents too – many Ukrainians find their way here to work as housekeepers in the city.

Off the far right corner of the square, the **Porta Capuana** is one of several relics from the Aragonese city walls, a sturdy defensive gate dating from 1490, delicately decorated on one side in Florentine Renaissance style. Across the road, the white and much renovated **Castel Capuano** was the residence of the Norman king William I, and later, under the Spanish, became a courthouse – which it still is. Behind here, the **FORCELLA** quarter, which spreads down to Corso Umberto I and across as far as Via Duomo, is an introduction to the old centre of Naples, an open-air **market**, stamping-ground of CD and sunglasses hawkers, contraband seafood sellers and a quantity of food stalls that make it one of the city's best places to wander. It's also one of the main city-centre strongholds of the Camorra and home to its most important families, and not an especially friendly place at night.

Off the opposite, far left corner of Piazza Garibaldi, **Via Garibaldi** runs down to the sea, past the main Circumvesuviana terminal, and, on the right, the **Porta Nolana**, a solid-looking Aragonese gateway surrounded by the stalls of the city's fish market. Further down, towards the water, the church of **Santa Maria del Carmine** dates back to the thirteenth century and is traditionally the church of the poor in Naples, particularly fishermen and mariners – the main port area is close by. Axel Munthe, the Swedish writer and resident of Cápri, used to sleep here after tending to victims of the 1884 cholera outbreak.

Just west, the still war-damaged **Piazza del Mercato** was for centuries where criminals were executed by hanging, and is a bleak, dusty square even now. There's little to detain you in this part of town, and you may as well cut back up to **Corso Umberto I**, which spears through the old part of the city. Known as the "retifilo", it makes its long straight journey from the seedy gatherings of prostitutes and kerb crawlers at Piazza Garibaldi, past many of the city's more mainstream shops, to the symmetrical **Piazza Bovio** – currently disrupted by more metro system workings. From here Via Duomo heads up the hill to the right, dividing Forcella from the *centro storico* on its left-hand side.

The Duomo

The **Duomo** (Mon–Sat 8.30am–12.30pm & 4.30–7pm, Sun 8.30am–1pm), tucked away unassumingly from the main street, is a Gothic building from the early thirteenth century (though with a late nineteenth-century neo-Gothic facade) dedicated to the patron saint of the city, San Gennaro. The church – and saint – are key reference points for Neapolitans: San Gennaro was martyred at Pozzuoli, just outside Naples, in 305 AD under the purges of Diocletian. Tradition has it that, when his body was transferred here, two phials of his blood liquefied in the bishop's hands, since which time the "miracle" has continued to repeat itself no fewer than three times a year – on the first Saturday in May (when a procession leads from the church of Santa Chiara to the cathedral) and on September 19 and December 16. There is still a great deal of superstition surrounding this event: San Gennaro is seen as the saviour and protector of Naples, and if the blood refuses to liquefy – which luckily is rare – disaster is supposed to befall the city, and many still wait with bated breath to see if the miracle has occurred. Interestingly, one of the few occasions in recent times that Gennaro's blood hasn't turned was in 1944, an event followed by Vesuvius's last eruption. The last times were in 1980, the year of the earthquake, and in 1988, the day after which Naples lost an important football match to their rivals, Milan.

The miraculous liquefaction takes place during a special Mass in full view of the congregation – a service it's perfectly possible to attend, though the church authorities have yet to allow any close scientific examination of the blood or the "miraculous" process. Whatever the truth of the miracle, there's no question it's still a significant event in the Neapolitan calendar, and one of the more bizarre of the city's institutions.

The third chapel on the right as you walk into the cathedral is dedicated to San Gennaro. It's an eye-bogglingly ornate affair, practically a church in its own right, containing the precious phials of the saint's blood and his skull in a silver bust-reliquary from 1305 (stored behind the altar except for ceremonies). On the other side of the cathedral, the basilica of **Santa Restituta** actually is a separate church, officially the oldest structure in Naples, erected by Constantine in 324 and supported by columns that were taken from a temple to Apollo on this site. Off to the right of the main altar, you pay extra to visit the **baptistry** (Mon–Sat 9am–12.30pm & 4.30–6pm, Sun 9am–1pm; €3), which also contains relics from very early Christian times, including late fifth-century mosaics and a font believed to have been taken from a temple to Dionysus. The same ticket gives you entry to the **excavations** below the church, which are open the same hours and also accessed from here – remains of a still earlier church basically, along with bits and pieces from the Roman and even Greek ancient cities. Finally be sure to also see the **crypt** of San Gennaro, founded by Cardinal Carafa and holding an altar dedicated to the saint complete with his bones.

The centro storico

The two main streets of Naples' *centro storico* are **Via Tribunali** and **Via San Biagio dei Librai** (the latter also known as "Spaccanapoli"): narrow thoroughfares, lined with old arcaded buildings, which lead due west on the path of the *decumanus maximus* and *decumanus inferiore* of Roman times, and both charged with atmosphere throughout the day, a maelstrom of hurrying pedestrians, revving cars and buzzing, dodging scooters.

Via Tribunali

On the Forcella side of Via Tribunali, just around the corner from the Duomo, the **Cappella del Pio Monte della Misericordia** (daily except Wed 9am–2.30pm; €5), is worth stopping off at before diving into the old city proper – the church of the (still-functioning but originally seventeenth-century) charity of the same name, a beautiful octagonal structure, with paintings by Caravaggio and Luca Giordano. You can also visit the organization's picture gallery upstairs, which overlooks the church.

Across Via Duomo, Via Tribunali continues on past **Piazza Girolamini**, on which a plaque marks the house where, in 1668, **Giambattista Vico** was born. Vico was a late-Renaissance Neapolitan philosopher who advanced theories of cyclical history that were far ahead of their time and still echo through twentieth-century thinking: James Joyce's *Finnegan's Wake* was based on his writings. Vico lived all his life in this district and was buried in the church of **Girolamini**, which you can't visit but which also has a small picture gallery, **Quadreria dei Girolamini** – accessed off a rather overgrown cloister from Via Duomo 142, opposite the cathedral (Mon–Fri 9.30am–12.30pm; free). Here,

▲ Via San Biagio dei Librai, Naples

half a dozen dark and dusty rooms contain paintings by the Neapolitan painters Ribera, Batistello Carcacciolo and Solimena, among others.

Further down Via Tribunali, the streets open out a little at a spot which would have been the ancient agora or forum of the ancient Greek and Roman cities at **piazza San Gaetano**. On the right the basilica of **San Paolo Maggiore** stands on the site of a Roman temple that was rebuilt as a Christian basilica, and next door is the entrance to **Sotteranea Napoli** (Mon–Wed & Fri noon, 2pm, 4pm, Thurs noon, 2pm, 4pm, 9pm, Sat & Sun 10am, noon, 2pm, 4pm, 6pm; €9.30), whose one hour thirty-minute tours, many of which are in English, take you to look at the remnants of a nearby Roman theatre and through the aqueducts and cisterns forty metres down below the old city – used from ancient times until the late nineteenth-century cholera outbreak, and then again as bomb shelters during World War II.

Almost opposite San Paolo, the church of **San Lorenzo Maggiore** is a light, spacious Gothic church, unspoiled by later additions and with a soaring Gothic ambulatory at its apse – unusual in Italy, even more so in Naples. It's a mainly thirteenth- and fourteenth-century building, though with a much later facade, built during the reign of the Angevin king Robert the Wise on the site of a Roman basilica – remains of which are in the cloisters. You can look at bits and pieces from the church in the attached **museum** or descend to the **excavations** beneath the church (both Mon–Sat 10am–5pm, Sun 10am–1.30pm; €5) to explore the remains of the Roman forum and, before that, the Greek agora – a rare chance to see exactly how the layers of the city were built up over the centuries, and to get some idea of how Naples must have looked back in the fifth century BC.

Via San Gregorio Armeno leads down to the other main axis of the old centre from here, and is one of the old city's most picturesque streets, lined with places specializing in the making of *presepi* or Christmas cribs – a Neapolitan tradition kept up to this day, although the workshops along here turn them out more or less all year round. The often-inventive creations now incorporate modern figures into the huge crib scenes, which can contain moving water features, illuminated pizza ovens and tons of moss and bark. On the right, the church of **San Gregorio Armeno** (Mon & Wed–Fri 9am–noon, Tues 9am–12.45pm, Sat & Sun 9am–12.30pm) is a sumptuous Baroque edifice with frescoes above the entrance by the late seventeenth-century Neapolitan artist Luca Giordano, not to mention two stupendously ornate gilded organs, one on each side of the nave. Up above the south aisle, you'll notice a series of grilles through which the Benedictine nuns would view the services from the **Chiostro di San Gregorio Armeno** next door – and which you can sit at yourself by walking up the street to the convent entrance on the left (Mon–Sat 9.30–noon, Sun 9.30am–1pm; free – you may have to ring the bell). It's a wonderfully peaceful haven from the noise outside, planted with limes and busy with nuns quietly going about their duties.

Spaccanapoli

Heading west down Via San Biagio leads to the **Largo di Corpo di Nilo**, where you'll find a Roman statue of a reclining old man, sculpted in Nero's time; it's a representation of the Nile and has a habit, it's claimed, of whispering to women as they walk by. The church opposite, on Piazzetta Nilo, **Sant'Angelo a Nilo**, is home to the city's earliest piece of Renaissance art – the funerary monument to Cardinal Rinaldo Brancaccio, made in Pisa in 1426 by Michelozzo and Donatello.

Further on, **Piazza San Domenico Maggiore** is marked by the **Guglia di San Domenico**, built in 1737 – one of the whimsical Baroque obelisks that were originally put up after times of plague or disease or to celebrate the Virgin. The **church** (daily 7.15am–noon & 5–7pm) of the same name flanks the north side of the square, an originally Gothic building from 1289, one of whose chapels holds a miraculous painting of the Crucifixion which is said to have spoken to St Thomas Aquinas during his time at the adjacent monastery. Look also at the Brancaccio chapel on the right; the clear, bright frescoes here by Pietro Cavallini date back to the early fourteenth century.

Off the top end of the square, Via de Sanctis leads off right to one of the city's odder monuments, the **Capella Sansevero** (Mon & Tues–Sat 10am–6pm, Sun 10am–1.30pm; €6), the tomb-chapel of the di Sangro family, decorated by the sculptor Giuseppe Sammartino in the mid-eighteenth century. The decoration is extraordinary, the centrepiece a carving of a dead Christ, laid out flat and covered with a veil of stark and remarkable realism, not least because it was carved out of a single piece of marble. Even more accomplished is the veiled figure of *Modesty* on the left, and, on the right, its twin *Disillusionment*, in the form of a woeful figure struggling with marble netting. Look, too, at the effusive *Deposition* on the high altar and the memorial above the doorway, which shows one Cecco di Sangro climbing out of his tomb, sword in hand. You might also want to venture downstairs. The man responsible for the chapel, Prince Raimondo, was a well-known eighteenth-century alchemist, and down here are the results of some of his experiments: bodies of an upright man and woman, behind glass, their capillaries and most of their organs preserved by a mysterious liquid developed by the prince – who, incidentally, was excommunicated by the pope for such practices. Even now the black entanglements make for a gruesome sight.

Continuing west, Via San Biagio becomes Via San Benedetto Croce, named after the twentieth-century philosopher who spent much of his life in this neighbourhood, living in the **Palazzo Filomarino** on the right.

Just past here on the left, the church of **Santa Chiara** (daily 8am–1pm & 4–7pm) is quite different, built in 1328 and completely destroyed by Allied bombs during the last war, after which it was rebuilt in its original bare Gothic austerity. There's not very much to see inside, but the medieval tombs of the Angevin monarchs at the far end are very fine and include that of Robert the Wise at the altar, showing the king in a monk's habit. And the attached convent has a **cloister** (entrance to the left of the church; Mon–Sat 9.30am–5.30pm, Sun 9.30am–2pm; €5) that is truly one of the gems of the city, a shady haven planted with neatly clipped box hedges, and furnished with benches and low walls covered with colourful majolica tiles depicting bucolic scenes of life outside. There's also a giant *presepe* or Christmas crib, and in the far corner a well-put-together museum showing bits from the church before the bombing as well as the excavated remains of a Roman bath complex outside.

Opposite Santa Chiara, the **Gesù Nuovo** (daily 7am–1pm & 4–7.30pm) church is most notable for its lava-stone facade, originally part of a fifteenth-century palace which stood here, prickled with pyramids that give it an impregnable, prison-like air. The inside is as over-sized and over-decorated as you might expect, and is worth a look for just that, although its most interesting feature is perhaps a quieter one: the simple chapel on the far right which is dedicated to San Guiseppe Moscati, a local doctor who died in 1927 and was reputed to perform medical miracles – as you can see from the votive plaques and thanks that plaster the walls.

Piazza del Municipio and the Museo Civico

From Piazza Bovio it's a short walk down to **Piazza del Municipio**, a busy traffic junction that stretches from the ferry terminal on the water up to the **Palazzo Municipale** at the top, dominated by the brooding hulk of the **Castel Nuovo** opposite – the "Maschio Angioino" – erected in 1282 by the Angevins and later converted as the royal residence of the Aragon monarchs. The entrance incorporates a triumphal arch from 1454 that commemorates the taking of the city by Alfonso I, the first Aragon ruler, and shows details of his triumph topped by a rousing statue of St Michael. The **Museo Civico** inside (Mon–Sat 9am–7pm; €5) incorporates the ground floor Capella Palatina, with its fourteenth- to sixteenth-century frescoes, Renaissance sculptures and fifteenth-century marble portal and rose window, and a couple of floors of paintings and sculpture – take a look at the original bronze doors from 1468 which show scenes from Ferdinand of Aragon's struggle against the local barons. The cannonball wedged in the lower left-hand panel dates from a naval battle in 1495 between the French and the Genoese that took place while the former were pillaging the doors from the castle. On the upper floor are some nice nineteenth century scenes of Naples, but it's probably the views over the port from the upper terrace that steal the show – that and the Sala dei Baroni, accessed from the courtyard, a huge room with magnificent umbrella-ribbed vaults that were once covered in frescoes by Giotto (sadly lost).

Teatro San Carlo and around

Just beyond the castle, the **Teatro San Carlo** is an oddly unimpressive building from the outside. But inside you can see why this theatre was the envy of Europe when it opened in 1737 in time for Charles of Bourbon's birthday, for whom it was built. Destroyed by fire in 1816 and quickly rebuilt, it's one of the largest opera houses in Italy and one of the most distinguished in the world. Tours take in the auditorium itself, backstage areas and the dressing rooms of the principal singers (daily 9am–7pm; €5).

Opposite, the **Galleria Umberto I** has fared less well over the years, its high arcades, erected in 1887, only now beginning to recover some of the teeming life that characterizes the rest of Naples. Outside, **Piazza Trieste e Trento** is probably as close to central Naples as you can get, though it's more a roundabout than a piazza, whose life you can watch while sipping a pricey drink on the terrace of the sleekly historic **Caffè Gambrinus**. To the left, **Piazza del Plebiscito** is a decent attempt to create a grand and symmetrical city centre space, with matching palaces on either side and a curve of columns modelled on Bernini's piazza for Saint Peter's in Rome. It's a favourite place to stroll of an evening, when its focal point, the church of **San Francesco di Paola**, is floodlit and at its most impressive. At other times its attempts at classical majesty (it's a copy of the Pantheon in Rome) only really work once you're standing under its enormous dome.

The Palazzo Reale

The **Palazzo Reale** (daily except Wed 9am–7.30pm; €4) forms the fourth side of the square, and manages better than most of the buildings around here to retain some semblance of its former glories, though it's a bland, derivative building for the most part and even a bit of a fake, thrown up hurriedly in 1602 to accommodate Philip III on a visit here and never actually occupied by a monarch long term. Indeed it's more of a monument to monarchies than monarchs, with the various dynasties that ruled Naples by proxy for so long represented in the niches of the facade, from Roger the Norman to Vittorio Emanuele II, taking in among others Alfonso I and a slightly comic Murat on the way.

Upstairs, by way of an impressive white marble double-staircase, the palace's first-floor rooms are decorated with fine Baroque excesses – gilded furniture, trompe l'oeil ceilings, great overbearing tapestries, impressive French Empire pieces and lots and lots of quite creditable seventeenth- and eighteenth-century paintings, including works by Guercino, Carraci and Titian, as well as Flemish old masters. The best bits are the little theatre – the first room on the right – which is refreshingly restrained after the rest of the palace, the vast ballroom; and the terrace, which gives good views over the port and the Castel Nuovo. Look in also on the chapel, on the far side of the central square, which has one of the city's biggest *presepi*, filled with mainly eighteenth-century figures – 210 in all.

Santa Lucia and the Castel dell'Ovo

Just south of Piazza del Plebiscito, the road curves around towards the sea. Via Santa Lucia is the main artery of the **Santa Lucia** district, home to most of the city's poshest hotels, on the streets around and along the seafront Via Partenope, and one or two decent restaurants that make it a better than average place to come and eat. Down on the waterfront, the grey mass of the **Castel dell'Ovo** or "egg-castle" (Mon–Sat 9am–6pm, Sun 9am–2pm; free) takes its name from the whimsical legend that it was built over an egg placed here by Virgil in Roman times: it is believed that if the egg breaks, Naples will fall. Actually it was built by the Hohenstaufen king Frederick II and extended by the Angevins. There's not much to see or do inside; it's just a series of terraces and views really. But the **views** are the best in town: a 360-degree panorama over the entire bay and back over Naples itself. When you're done you can go for drinks or dinner at one of the quayside restaurants in the **Borgo Marinaro** below.

Via Toledo and the Quartieri Spagnoli

Piazza Trieste e Trento marks the beginning of the city's main shopping street, **Via Toledo**, which leads north in a dead straight line, climbing the hill up to the national archeological museum and separating two very different parts of Naples. To its right, across as far as Piazza del Gesù Nuovo, the streets and buildings are modern and spacious, centring on the unmistakeable mass of the Fascist-era central **Post Office**. The streets to the left, on the other hand, scaling the footslopes of the Vómero, are some of the city's most narrow and crowded, a grid of alleys that was laid out to house Spanish troops during the seventeenth century and hence now known as the **Quartieri Spagnoli**. It's an enticing area, at least for visitors, in that it's what you expect to find when you come to Naples, with the buildings so close together as to barely admit any sunlight. But it's a poor part of town, too, home to the notorious Neapolitan *bassi* – one-room windowless dwellings that open directly onto the street – and one you might want to avoid wandering too deeply into at night.

Further up Via Toledo, off to the left, there's the equally atmospheric district of **Montesanto** on the left, focusing on the lively intersection of Piazza Pignasecca and the Montesanto funicular station just beyond; and on the right, **Piazza Dante**, designed by Luigi Vanvitelli during the eighteenth century and cutting an elegant semicircle off to the right of Via Toledo that focuses on a graffitied statue of the poet. From here you can cross the square and cut through the seventeenth-century **Port'Alba** into the very appealing **Piazza Bellini** and the old part of the city, or push straight on up the street to the archeological museum, housed in a grandiose, late-sixteenth-century army barracks on the corner of Piazza Cavour.

The Museo Archeologico Nazionale

Naples' **Museo Archeologico Nazionale** (daily except Tues 9am–7.30pm; €6.50) is home to the Farnese collection of antiquities from Lazio and Campania and the best of the finds from the nearby Roman sites of Pompeii and Herculaneum. It seems to be under almost constant reorganization, and to be honest the displays are tired and old-fashioned for the most part. But you'd be mad to miss it – it's truly one of the highlights of the city.

The ground floor of the museum has sculpture from the **Farnese collection**, displayed at its best in the mighty Great Hall, which holds imperial-era figures like the *Farnese Bull* and *Farnese Hercules* from the Baths of Caracalla in Rome – the former the largest piece of classical sculpture ever found. Don't miss *Ephesian Artemis*, an alabaster and bronze statue with rows of bulbous objects peeling off her chest – variously interpreted as breasts, eggs, bulls' scrota, dates or pollen sacs, and bees, mini-beasts and sphinxes adorning her lower half. The mezzanine floor holds the museum's collection of **mosaics** – remarkably preserved works that give a superb insight into ordinary Roman customs, beliefs and humour. All are worth looking at – images of fish, crustacea, wildlife on the banks of the Nile, a cheeky cat and quail with still-life beneath, masks and simple abstract decoration. But some highlights include a realistic *Battle Scene* (no. 10020); the *Three Musicians with Dwarf* (no. 9985); an urbane meeting of the Platonic Academy (no. 124545); and a marvellously captured scene from a comedy, *The Consultation of the Fattucchiera* (no. 9987), with a soothsayer giving a dour and doomy prediction. While at the far end the fascinating **Gabinetto Segreto** (Secret Room), contains erotic material taken from the brothels, baths, houses and taverns of Pompeii and Herculaneum – languidly sensual wall paintings, preposterously phallic lamps, and the like. Upstairs through the Salone della Meridiana, which contains a sparse but fine assortment of Roman figures, a series of rooms holds the **Campanian wall paintings**, lifted from the villas of Pompeii and Herculaneum, and rich in colour and invention. There are plenty here, and it's worth devoting some time to this section, which includes works from the Sacrarium – part of Pompeii's Egyptian temple of Isis, the most celebrated mystery cult of antiquity. In the next series of rooms, some of the smallest and most easily missed works are among the most exquisite. Among those to look out for are a paternal *Achilles and Chirone* (no. 9109); the *Sacrifice of Iphiginia* (no. 9112) in the next room, one of the best preserved of all the murals; and a group of four small pictures, the best of which is a depiction of a woman gathering flowers entitled *Allegoria della Primavera* – a fluid, impressionistic piece of work capturing both the gentleness of spring and the graceful beauty of the woman. Beyond the murals are the actual **finds from the Campanian cities** – everyday items like glass, silver, ceramics, charred pieces of rope, even foodstuffs (petrified cakes, figs, fruit and nuts), together with a model layout of Pompeii in cork. On the other side of the first floor, there are finds the **Villa dei Papiri** in Herculaneum – sculptures in bronze mainly. The *Hermes at Rest* in the centre of the second room is perhaps the most arresting item, boyishly rapt and naked except for wings on his feet, while all around are other adept statues – a languid *Resting Satyr*, the convincingly woozy *Drunken Silenus*, and a pair of youthful *Runners*.

Sanità and the catacombs

To the left of the archeological museum as you come out, **Piazza Cavour** is a busy traffic junction and from there you can stroll up through the old quarter of **Sanità**, following the tangle of streets for ten minutes or so up to the church of **Santa Maria della Sanità** on the piazza of the same name, a Dominican church from the early seventeenth century whose design was based loosely on Bramante's for Saint Peter's in Rome. There are paintings by Giordano and other Neapolitan artists inside, although perhaps of more interest are the **Catacombe di San Gaudioso** underneath (daily guided tours at 9.30am, 10.15am, 11am, 11.45am, 12.30pm; €5), an intriguing early Christian burial ground that's home to the fifth-century tomb of St Gaudioso, a bishop known as the "African", as he was from North Africa, and the final resting places of the Dominicans themselves, who were decapitated and buried sitting down.

Lifts link Sanità with Corso Amedeo up above, the main road up to Capodimonte, and you can walk up from here in ten minutes or so to another burial place, the **Catacombe di San Gennaro** (Tues–Sat guided tours hourly 9am–noon & 2–3pm, Sun 9am–noon only; €5), next door to the huge Madre del Buon Consiglio church, halfway up the hill to Capodimonte. This is a very different sort of catacomb, bigger and more open than San Gaudioso, and best known for being the final resting-place of San Gennaro, whose body was brought here in the fifth century. There are some amazing early Christian frescoes and mosaics, newly restored and amazingly bright.

The Palazzo Reale di Capodimonte

At the top of the hill, the **Palazzo Reale di Capodimonte** – and its adjoining **park** (daily 9am to 1hr before dusk; free) – was the royal residence of the Bourbon King Charles III, built in 1738 and now housing the picture gallery of the Naples museum, the superb **Museo Nazionale di Capodimonte** (Thurs–Tues 8.30am–7.30pm; €7.50), one of the best collections of art in the country. Its vast holding contains many important works by Campanian and international artists, as well as many curious *objets d'art* and fine pieces of Capodimonte porcelain.

The three-storey museum is organized, not chronologically, but by collections: between them the Borgia, Farnese and Bourbon rulers amassed some superb **Renaissance and Flemish** works. On the **first floor** there are fine portraits of the Farnese pope, Paul III, by Titian, and, in the Borgia collection, an elegant *Madonna and Child with Angels* by Botticelli, Lippi's soft, sensitive *Annunciation*, and other works by Renaissance masters – Bellini's impressively coloured and composed *Transfiguration*, Giulio Romano's dark and powerful *Madonna of the Cat* and Marcello Venusti's small-scale 1549 copy of Michelangelo's *Last Judgement* – probably the only chance you'll get to see the painting this close up. It's not just Italian work either: there's El Greco's flashy but atmospheric *Soflon*, a couple of Brueghels – *The Misanthrope* and *The Parable of the Blind* – and two triptychs by Joos van Cleve. Look out also for Titian's lascivious *Danae* and a Masaccio painting of the Crucifixion.

On the **second floor** there are some outstanding Italian paintings from the fourteenth and fifteenth centuries, of which the most famous is the *St Louis of Anjou* by Simone Martini, a fascinating Gothic painting glowing with gold leaf. An overt work of propaganda, it depicts an enthroned Louis crowning Robert of Anjou and thereby legitimizing his rule. Elsewhere there are paintings that used to hang in Naples' churches: Colantonio's *St Jerome in his Study* was painted for the altar of San Lorenzo Maggiore and there's a delicate *Annunciation* by Titian from San Domenico Maggiore – and the long series of rooms finishes off in fine style with one of Caravaggio's best-known works, *The Flagellation*. Beyond are a number of paintings by the artists of the Neapolitan Baroque – Ribera, Giordano, Stanzione – while upstairs from there is a scattering of paintings and artworks from the **twentieth century**, of which the most notable is a painting of Vesuvius in eruption by Andy Warhol.

If you have time to spare, take a walk around the **royal apartments** on the first floor, smaller and more downbeat than those at Caserta but in many ways more enjoyable. High spots are the airy, mirrored ballroom, lined with portraits of various Bourbon monarchs and other European despots, an eccentric room entirely decorated with porcelain and sprouting Chinese scenes, monkeys and fruit and flowers in 3D, and a number of rooms of beautifully decorated plates, some painted with local scenes.

Chiaia, Mergellina and Posillipo

Lined with the city's fanciest shops, **Via Chiaia** leads west from Piazza Trieste e Trento to the elegant circle of **Piazza dei Martiri** – named after the nineteenth-century revolutionary martyrs commemorated by the column in its centre. This part of town, the **Chiaia** neighbourhood, displays a sense of order and classical elegance that is quite absent from the rest of the city centre, its buildings well preserved, the people noticeably better heeled. From Piazza dei Martiri, you can stroll down to the waterfront and **Villa Comunale**, Naples' most central city park, richly adorned with Classical sculpture and the best place to appreciate the city's maritime side with views stretching right around the bay to the distinctive silhouette of Vesuvius in the east.

The road that skirts the park, **Via Caracciolo**, makes a nice way to walk around the bay to Mergellina, particularly in the early evening when the lights of the city enhance the views. On the way you might want to take in the Mediterranean marine life at the newly restored century-old **Aquarium** (March–Oct Tues–Sat 9am–6pm, Sun 9.30am–7pm; Nov–Feb Tues–Sat 9am–5pm, Sun 9am–2pm; €1.50), one large room basically, lined with tanks filled with impressive giant turtles, eels and rays as well as a couple of mock rock pools. Across the other side of Riviera di Chiaia from the aquarium, the gardens of the **Villa Pignatelli** (Wed–Mon 8.30am–1.30pm; €2) are a peaceful alternative to the Villa Comunale, and the early nineteenth-century house itself, now a museum, is kept in much the same way as when it was the home of a prominent Naples family and a meeting place for the city's elite in the 1900s. It's tastefully furnished and by Naples standards low-key, its handful of rooms holding books, porcelain, the odd painting and a set of photos signed by various aristocrats and royal personages.

Villa Comunale stretches around the bay for a good mile, at the far end of which lie the harbour and main square – **Piazza Sannazzaro** – of the **Mergellina** district, a good place to come and eat at night and a terminus for hydrofoils to the bay's islands. There's not a lot else here, though it's worth looking in on the little church of **Santa Maria in Piedigrotta** next door to the train station, home of the Madonna that gets carried through the streets every September in one of the city's most popular festivals, and the **Parco Virgiliano** just behind (daily 9am–6.30pm), where you can see the opening to a 700m-long Roman tunnel that was tunnelled through the hillside here, and the supposed burial place of the Roman poet Virgil right by it, though this has long since been discredited.

Of the other neighbourhoods nearby, the **Fuorigrotta** district, the other side of the Mergellina hill, is not really of interest unless you're going to a football match, since it's home to Napoli's **San Paolo** stadium (see box above). The same goes for **Posillipo**, further along the shore, which is an upmarket suburb of the city stacked with fat villas and pockets – though, again, you may well want to come out here to eat. See p.795 for recommendations

Vómero

Vómero – the district topping the hill immediately above the old city – is one of Naples' relatively modern additions, a light, airy and relatively peaceful quarter connected most directly with the teeming morass below by funicular railway. It's a large area but mostly residential, and you're unlikely to want to stray beyond the streets that fan out from each of the three funicular stations, centring on the grand symmetry of **Piazza Vanvitelli**.

Come up on the Montesanto funicular and you're well placed for a visit to two of the buildings that dominate Naples, way above the old city. Five-minutes' walk away, the **Castel Sant'Elmo** (Thurs–Tues 9am–6.30pm; €3) occupies Naples' highest point and is an impressive fortification, a fourteenth-century structure once used for incarcerating political prisoners and now lording it grandly over the streets below. Nowadays it houses libraries and archives and hosts exhibitions, concerts and antiques fairs, as well as boasting the very best views of Naples. You can usually go in for the view if there's nothing on, but if you're heading for the San Martino complex just beyond there's not really any point.

Beyond the castle, the fourteenth-century **Certosa San Martino** has the next-best views over the bay and is home to the **Museo Nazionale di San Martino** (Thurs–Tues 8.30am–7.30pm; €6). Indeed the views from its cunningly constructed terraced gardens are well worth the entrance fee alone but you also get to see the monastery's church, with a colourful pavement and an *Adoration of the Shepherds* by Reni above the altar, as well as works by some of the greats of Neapolitan painters in most of the chapels, as well as in the rooms off the high altar. In the museum proper, there are more paintings by Neapolitan masters – Ribera, Stanzione, Vaccaro – as well as sculpture by Pietro Bernini; the frescoed library and prior's apartments; and an unparalleled collection of *presepi* or Christmas cribs. The Baroque cloisters are lovely, too, though a little gone to seed, but they're surrounded by historical and maritime sections displaying models of ships, and documents, coins and costumes recording the era of the Kingdom of Naples. All in all one of the city's better and more diverse museums, but with very little information in English.

There's another museum up here, fifteen-minutes' walk away in the Neoclassical **Villa Floridiana**, close to the Chiaia funicular, whose lush grounds (daily 9am to 1hr before sunset) make a good place for a picnic – though the **Museo Duca di Martina** (Wed–Mon 8.30am–1.30pm; €2.50) is of fairly specialist interest, a porcelain collection varying from the beautifully simple to the outrageously kitsch – hideous teapots, ceramic asparagus sticks and the like. There are examples of Capodimonte and Meissen, and eighteenth-century English, French, German and Viennese work – as well as a handful of pieces of Qing-dynasty Chinese porcelain and Murano glass and exquisite non-ceramic items like inlaid ivory boxes and panels.

Eating, drinking and nightlife

Neapolitan cuisine consists of simple dishes cooked with fresh, healthy ingredients (see box, p.773 for more on regional specialities). As Naples is not primarily a tourist-geared city, most restaurants are family-run places used by locals and as such generally serve good food at very reasonable prices. There's no better place in Italy to eat pizza, at a solid core of almost obsessively unchanging places that still serve only the (very few) traditional varieties, and you're never far from a food stall for delectable snacks on the move at one of the city's many *friggitorie*.

Cafés, snacks and ice cream

Attanasio Vico Ferrovia 2/4, off Via Milano. Bakery that specializes in delectable *sfogliatelle* (ricotta-stuffed pastries).

Chalet Ciro Via Caracciolo 1–2. This Mergellina institution is known for its *babá* and other pastries as well as delicious ice cream. Its marathon opening hours (6.30am–2am) make it a

dependable early morning or after dinner pit stop for sweets.

Café Letterario Galleria Principe di Napoli 6–7. An elegant café inside the *galleria*, within striking distance of the Museo Nazionale. Also sells books and posters, and has internet access.

Gambrinus Via Chiaia 1–2. The oldest and best-known of Neapolitan cafés, founded in 1861. Not cheap, but its aura of chandeliered gentility – and outside seating on Piazza Trieste e Trento – makes it worth at least one visit.

Gay Odin Via Benedetto Croce 61. One of several locations around town, the Spaccanapoli branch of this long established chocolatier also sells decadent ice cream.

Remy Gelo Via F. Galiani 29/A. Off Via Caracciolo, near the hydrofoil terminal in Mergellina, this place does superb ice creams and *granite*.

Scaturchio Piazza San Domenico. Another elegant old Naples standard, it's been serving coffee and pastries in the heart of Spaccanapoli for decades.

Restaurants and pizzerias

Al Faretto Via Marechiaro 127, Posillipo ☎081.575.0407. Very atmospheric, romantic and smart restaurant, yet dinner averages only €30–40 each. Exceptionally fresh fish prepared and served with great style. Closed Mon.

Antica Osteria Pisano Piazza Crocelle ai Mannesi 1–4 ☎081.554.8325. Small and very traditional trattoria with a well-priced menu of well-loved local standards – a few pasta dishes, mainly with fish and seafood, and a short menu of meat mains for €5–8. Closed Sun & Aug.

Bellini Via Santa Maria di Constantinopoli 80 ☎081.459.774. Rife with old-world charm, this historic establishment has a convivial outside terrace screened by foliage, and several spacious inside dining rooms. Locals come for the house speciality, *linguine al cartoccio* (pasta with seafood baked in paper), but pizzas and other local dishes are always good. Closed Sun eve.

Bersagliera Borgo Marinaro 10–11 ☎081.764.6016. Fine food, especially seafood, though inevitably you pay for the location, slap next to the Castel dell'Ovo, and for the "O Sole Mio" minstrels who wander between the tables outside. The house special is *tagliatelle alla bersagliera*, with squid, shrimp, clams and mussels, and cherry tomatoes. Closed Tues.

Da Ettore Via Santa Lucia 56 ☎081.764.0498. In the heart of Santa Lucia, this casual and lively neighbourhood restaurant is famous for its *pagno-tielli* (calzoni stuffed with mozzarella, ham and mushrooms), and there is a wide selection of pizza and traditional pasta dishes too. Closed Sun.

Da Michele Via Cesare Sersale 1–3 ☎081.553.9204. Tucked away off Corso Umberto I in the Forcella district, this is the most determinedly traditional of all the Naples pizzerias, offering just two varieties (allegedly the only two worth eating) – *marinara* and *margherita* – for about €3. Don't arrive late, as they sometimes run out of dough. Closed Sun.

Da Pasqualino Piazza Sannazzaro 79 ☎081.681.524. In the business of serving local fish dishes since 1898, this old-school Mergellina ristorante-pizzeria does great and affordable seafood and pizzas, and has outside seating in the summer. Closed Tues.

Di Matteo Via dei Tribunali 94 ☎081.294.203. One of the best and most famous pizzerias in the city, a bit low on atmosphere, but the enormous and mouthwatering pizzas more than make up for it – after all, when Bill Clinton was in town, this is where he came to sample proper Neapolitan pizza. Closed Sun.

Donna Teresa Via Kerbaker 58 ☎081.556.7070. One of the few vestiges of simple dining left in Vómero, where the food and setting are simple and the prices honest. Expect to pay €12–15 for a full meal. Closed Sun.

Gorizia Via Bernini 29 ☎081.578.2248. This unpretentious Vómero restaurant is close to the Centrale and Chiaia funicular and does some of Vómero's best pizza, as well as a decent full menu. Closed Mon.

La Cantina di Via Sapienza Via Sapienza 40–41 ☎081.459.078. Proprietor Gaetano's no-nonsense food and service draws a busy lunch crowd to feast on hearty home-cooked classics like *polpette fritte* (fried meatballs) for €5 and a staggering array of seasonal vegetable side dishes. Full meals for €10–12. Closed dinner & Sun.

Lombardi a Santa Chiara Via B. Croce 59 ☎081.552.0780. Located on Spaccanapoli near the church of Santa Chiara, this well-respected ristorante-pizzeria is known for its pizzas, though there is a moderately priced menu of typical Neapolitan dishes on offer as well. Closed Mon.

Marino Via S Lucia 118 ☎081.764.0280. A warm and welcoming family-style place in Santa Lucia with good pizzas and reliable Neapolitan dishes like *scialatielli* with aubergine, tomato and mozzarella for €6. Closed Mon.

Mimi' alla Ferrovia Via Via A d'Aragona 21 ☎081.570.6883. A real old-fashioned bustling restaurant and something of a haven in the none-too-desirable streets off Piazza Garibaldi, with good traditional Neapolitan food at reasonable prices – pasta dishes for €6, and mains for €10 Closed Sun & two weeks in Aug.

Umberto Via Alabardieri 30–31 ☎081.418.555. A long-time popular choice among the professional classes of the Chiaia district, serving marvellous food in somewhat old-fashioned surroundings. Choose between a simple pizzeria and more upmarket restaurant. Closed Mon.

Nightlife

Neapolitan **nightlife** is largely concentrated in two neighbourhoods – the *centro storico* and the Chiaia district. The old part of the city centre is crammed with **bars** appealing to budget-conscious university students and a chicly bohemian crowd. The *centro storico* also has its share of disco-pubs, especially on Via G. Paladino and Via Mezzocannone near the university, where the cocktails tend to be cheap and electronic music, reggae, and rock blare till late. Bear in mind, though, that things don't really get going till at least 10pm. Most places close in the hot summer months and instead everyone congregates in the open air in Piazza del Gesù Nuovo and Piazza San Domenico Maggiore, or the gay-friendly cafés on Piazza Bellini, where tables spill out onto the square. A young professional crowd prefers the see-and-be-seen lounges and bars in the sedate Chiaia district. Here, you will find good **wine bars** with a fine selection of wines from Campania and Italy's other regions.

There are plenty of **clubs**, large and small, peppered throughout the city and its suburbs. Owing to the licensing laws, some require a *tesserino* or membership card to gain entry, which can cost upwards of €10 and can be purchased at the door. Others charge a flat cover charge, generally €15–35 and including the price of one drink. Nightclubs in Naples close down for the summer from June to September, when they move out around the bay to Posillipo, Bacoli, Fusaro, or Pozzuoli, all best reached with your own transport. Things get going around midnight or 1am. For listings of Naples nightlife, pick up *Zero* (Ⓦ www.zero.eu), or *Urban*, free monthly publications available in bars, or for big events see Ⓦ www.angelsoflove.it, Italy's answer to the Ministry of Sound.

For more highbrow **culture** there's the legendary **Teatro San Carlo** (see p.788), an opulent venue given over to classical concerts, opera, and ballet (Ⓣ 081.797.2331). You'll find tickets hard to come by, however, as they are mostly sold on subscription, but if you do manage to get hold of one, dress up. Teatro Bellini puts on theatrical performances by important playwrights but in Italian only. Smaller and more casual venues offer a variety of entertainment ranging from traditional Neapolitan comedies (Teatro Trianon) to experimental theatre (Nuovo Teatro Nuovo).

Bars and clubs

Bourbon Street Via Bellini 52/53 Ⓣ 338.825.3756, Ⓦ www.bourbonstreetjazzclub.com. A premier venue for Italian and international jazz acts, bringing a slice of American jazz culture to the heart of Naples' *centro storico*. Tues–Sun 9pm–3am. Closed June–Aug.

Enoteca Belledonne Vico Belledonne a Chiaia 18 Ⓣ 081.403.162, Ⓦ www.enotecabelledonne.com. This enoteca attracts the discerning Chiaia crowd with its convivial atmosphere and exhaustive collection of Italian wines and careful selection of cheeses and *salumi*. Daily 6pm–2am. Closed Aug.

Intra Moenia Piazza Bellini 70. A left-leaning "literary café" and one of several trendy haunts on Piazza Bellini, where tables spread across the square. A lovely place to sit and read under the wisteria on a sunny day. Substantial snacks and fancy ice creams are served, and there's internet access. Daily 10am–2am.

Jail Club Via Sedile di Porto 65 Ⓣ 347.170.3585, Ⓦ www.jailclub.it. One of the newer, larger clubs in the city, popular with students. Usually a DJ holds forth, but there are also live shows. Covers around €5.

Kinky Klub Via della Quercia 26 Ⓣ 335.547.7299, Ⓦ www.kinkyjam.com. Contrary to what the name might suggest, this popular bar just off Via Toledo is Naples' home for reggae, rocksteady, dancehall and ska. Tues–Sun 9pm–4am. Closed mid-June to mid-Sept.

Rising South Via S. Sebastiano 19 Ⓣ 335.879.428, Ⓦ www.risingrepublic.com. The coolest club in the *centro storico*, with a velvet Baroque interior. Tues Erasmus party, aimed at foreign exchange students from the nearby university; Wed reggae and Thurs–Sat electro/lounge and guest DJs. Tues–Sun 10pm–3am. Closed mid-May to Sept.

Virgilio Club Via Lucrezio Caro 6 Ⓣ 081.575.5261, Ⓦ www.virgilioclub.it. Immersed in the greenery of the Parco Virgiliano on the slopes of Posillipo, this place gets jam-packed on summer nights when they open a leafy terrace overlooking the bay. Entry

from €20. June to mid-Oct Wed–Sun 10pm–4am, opening variable in winter.

Listings

Airlines Alitalia ℡06.2222; British Airways ℡199.712.266; easyJet ℡848.887.766.
Car rental Avis ℡081.751.6052; Europcar ℡081.780.5643; Hertz ℡081.780.2971; Maggiore ℡199.151.120, SIXT ℡191.100.666.
Consulates Canada, Via Carducci 29 ℡081.401.338; UK, Via dei Mille 40 ℡081.423.8911; US, Piazza della Repubblica 2 ℡081.583.8111.
Exchange Outside normal banking hours you can change money and traveller's cheques at the booth inside Stazione Centrale (daily 8am–7.30pm).
Hospital To call an ambulance, dial ℡118; hospital numbers include ℡081.747.1111 or 081.220.5797, or go to the Guardia Medica Permanente in the Palazzo Municipio, open 24hr.
Internet As well as the hotels, cafés and bars listed in this guide, try *Internet Point* at Via de Sanctis 27, just around the corner from Piazza San Domenico, which charges €1.50 an hr.
Laundry Bolle Blu, Corso Novara 62–64, just up from the Stazione Centrale (Mon–Sat 8.30am–8pm).

Pharmacies The pharmacy at Napoli Centrale is open 24hr and there's a list of those open at night in the newspaper *Il Mattino*.
Police ℡112 or 113; you can speak to an operator in English. The main police station (*questura*) is at Via Medina 75 (℡081.794.1111); you can also report crimes at the small police station in Stazione Centrale. To report the theft of a car call ℡081.794.1435.
Post office The main post office is in the enormous building on Piazza Matteotti, just off Via Toledo (Mon–Sat 8.15am–7.20pm).
Taxis ℡081.202.020, 570.7070, 551.5151, or 556.4444.
Tours CitySightseeing Napoli operate a hop-on-hop-off service taking in the sights on several routes around town between May and Sept; tickets cost €22 and are valid for 24hr. Tours leave from just in front of the Castel Nuovo.
Travel agents CTS, Via Mezzocannone 25 (℡081.552.7975), for discount tickets, budget flights and so on. You could also try Wasteels, Stazione Centrale (℡081.201.071).

The Bay of Naples

Naples spreads right around its **bay** in an almost unbroken ribbon of docks, housing and development whose appeal is hard to discern, and only really becomes apparent the further away from the city you get. It's one of the most geologically unstable regions the world, a fact that becomes obvious west of the city, where volcanic craters, hot springs and fumaroles make up the area known as the **Campi Flegrei**, the Phlegrean Fields of classical times, a mysterious place in turn mythologized by Homer and Virgil as the entrance to Hades. These days most of the mystery is gone – like most of the bay, the presence of Naples dominates in the form of new, mostly illegal, construction – and much of the volcanic activity is extinct, or at least dormant. But parts of the area still retain some of the doomy associations that first drew the ancients here, and there are some substantial remains of their presence at **Pozzuoli**, **Baía** and **Cumae**. In the opposite direction, the coast east from Naples is even more built up, the Circumvesuviana train edging out through derelict industrial buildings and dense housing that squeezes ever closer to the track. Most people come here for the ancient sights of **Herculaneum** and **Pompeii**, or to scale **Vesuvius** – or they skip the lot for the resort town of **Sorrento**. All are easy day-trips, and

Sorrento, though overdeveloped, may be worth a little more time and makes a good springboard for seeing some of the Amalfi coast.

Pozzuoli

Heading west, the first town that can really be considered free of Naples' sprawl is **POZZUOLI**, which sits on a stout promontory jutting out from the slender crescent of volcanic hills behind. Despite achieving some glamour as the home town of Sophia Loren, it's an ordinary little place, nothing special but likeable enough, with ferry connections to the islands of Prócida and Ischia. And although you wouldn't want to stay here (unless you're a camper; see "Accommodation", p.782), it's a good first stop before travelling on to the rest of the Campi Flegrei.

Pozzuoli has suffered more than most of the towns around here from the area's volcanic activity and subsidence is still a major – and carefully monitored – problem. In town there are a number of well-preserved relics of the Romans' liking for the place. Beyond the Cumana station, between Via Roma and Via Sacchini, just east of the port, the so-called **Temple of Serapide** sits enclosed within a small park, often flooded in winter, but otherwise accessible. Its name derives from the unearthing here of a statue of the Pluto-esque Egyptian god, *Serapis Enthroned* (now in the Naples Archeological Museum), but in fact the structure has since proved to be not a temple but a richly embellished produce-market from the first–third centuries AD, one of the largest known that has been excavated. On the other side of the port, above the tourist office, the **Rione Terra** (Sat & Sun 9am–6pm; €3; booking required ℡081.741.0067 or toll-free 848.800.288) is basically the ruins of the ancient acropolis of the Greek town and the later heart of the Roman port, and you stroll through some of its ancient streets – though its opening times can be erratic. More accessible is the **Anfiteatro Flavio** on Via Domiziana just north of the centre (Mon & Wed–Sun 9am to 1hr before sunset; €4), which was at one time the third largest in Italy, holding some 20,000 spectators, and is still reasonably intact, though visitors are not allowed on the seating area. The subterranean chambers for gladiators and wild beasts are especially complete, and lying around everywhere is an abundance of beautifully carved architectural fragments.

Just north of town, ten-minutes' walk up the hill from the *metropolitana*/FS station (bus #152 and the SEPSA M1 stop outside), the **Solfatara** (April–Sept daily 8.30am–7pm, until 5.30pm out of season; €5.50) is further, and tangible, evidence of the volcanic nature of the area, the exposed crater of a semi-extinct volcano – into which you can walk – that hasn't erupted for a couple of thousand years; in fact, it was a major tourist attraction in Roman times, too. Not surprisingly, it's a weird place: sulphur fumes rise from the rocks around and the grey-yellow ground is hot to the touch (and sounds hollow underfoot), emitting eerily silent jets or fumaroles that leave the air pungent with sulphurous fumes. In the 1800s some of the fumaroles were covered with brick, creating an almost unbearably warm, sauna-like environment into which you can bend if you can stand it, while others are just left open.

Practicalities

You can get here from Naples on the Metropolitana Linea 2 from Piazza Garibaldi, or on the Ferrovia Cumana line from Montesanto station; both take about twenty minutes. Buses #152 and SEPSA M1 also run direct from Piazza

Garibaldi. There's a **tourist office** at Piazza Matteotti 1A (daily 9am–⊃ ☎081.526.6639, ⓦwww.infocampiflegrei.it). The best time to come Pozzuoli is Sunday, when the whole town turns out for the morning fis market, afterwards eating lunch in one of several waterfront **restaurants**: *Il Capitano* (☎081.526.2283), near the dock at Lungomare C. Colombo 10, is pretty good; or there's unpretentious *Don Antonio* (☎081.526.7941; closed Mon), up narrow Via Magazzini off the old port – walk around beyond the ferries and it's on the left – which does great fish fry-ups.

Baía

The next town along from Pozzuoli, reached in fifteen minutes by train from the Cumana station, by the Temple of Serapide, is **Baía**, a small port which has a set of imperial-era Roman ruins piling up on the hill above. This was one of the bay's most favoured spots in Roman times, a trendy resort at which all the most fashionable of the city's patricians had villas: the Emperor Hadrian died here in 138 AD and Nero was rumoured to have murdered his mother in Baía.

Steps lead up to the entrance of Baía's extensive **Parco Archeologico** (Tues–Sun 9am–1hr before sunset; €4) – excavations of a very important Roman palace of the first century BC to the fourth century AD, with an enormous network of baths which served the imperial fat cats of the era. It's an evocative location, structured across several levels. Follow the steps down from the entrance level to the first terrace of the palace: the rooms on the right contain patches of Roman stuccowork depicting birds and mythical creatures and a statue of Mercury, beheaded by vandals. In the centre are the remains of a small theatre and an open space – thought to be a *piscina* – with a pretty garden portico on one side.

Many of the finds from Baía and around are in the **Museo Archeologico** (Tues–Sun 9am–3.45pm; €4), housed in part of the town's mammoth fifteenth-century Aragon castle, a fifteen-minute walk up the main road towards Bacoli. Among the finds on display here is a *sacellum* – a shrine dedicated to the imperial cult – from the forum of ancient *Misenum* on Capo Miseno, rebuilt here on the ground floor, and a *nymphaeum* or monumental fountain, partially reconstructed on the top floor.

Cumae

Further up the coast, the town of **CUMAE** was the first Greek colony on the Italian mainland, a source of settlers for other colonies (Naples was originally settled by Greeks from Cumae) and a centre of Hellenistic civilization. Later it was home to the so-called Cumaean Sibyl, from whom Tarquinius purchased the Sibylline Books that laid down the laws for the Republic. The **site** (daily 9am to 1hr before sunset; €4 combined ticket with Anfiteatro Flavio and Báia), a short walk from the bus stop, is spread over a large area and not at all comprehensively excavated. But the only part you're likely to want to see forms a tight nucleus close to the entrance. The best-known feature is the Grotto of the Sibyl, a long, dark corridor that was home to the most famous of the ancient oracles. The cave is rectangular in shape, with light admitted from a series of openings in the western wall; the Sibyl used to dispense her wisdom from the three large

far end of the forty-foot passageway, the most famous occasion
...eas came here to consult her – an event recorded by the lines
...up either side of the entrance.

...Cumae is still to come. Climb up the steps to the right of the
...d follow the winding Via Sacra past a constructed belvedere on
...fairly scanty remains of a temple on the right to the Acropolis.

...the remains of a temple to Jupiter, but it's the **views** that you
...really come for: from the far side of the temple way south across the shellfish-
filled **Lago Fusaro** and the bottom corner of the coast; and, if you clamber
down from the other side of the temple, north up the curving coast to the Gulf
of Gaeta.

Herculaneum

East of Naples the first real point of any interest is the town of **Ercolano**, the
modern offshoot of the ancient site of **HERCULANEUM**, which was
destroyed by the eruption of Vesuvius on August 24, 79 AD and is situated at
the seaward end of the town's main street (daily: March–Sept 8.30am–7.30pm;
Oct–Feb 8.30am–6pm; €11 or combined ticket with Pompeii and the Villa
Oplontis, valid 3 days, €20; ⓦ www.pompeiisites.org). The site was discovered in
1709, when a well-digger accidentally struck the stage of the buried theatre.
Excavations were undertaken throughout the eighteenth and nineteenth
centuries, during which period much of the marble and bronze from the site
was carted off to Naples to decorate the city's palaces, and it wasn't until 1927
that digging and preservation began in earnest. Herculaneum was a residential
town, much smaller than Pompeii, and as such it makes a more manageable site,
less architecturally impressive but better preserved and more easily taken in on
a single visit. Archeologists held for a long time that unlike in Pompeii, on the
other side of the volcano, most of the inhabitants of Herculaneum managed to
escape. However, recent discoveries of entangled skeletons found at what was
the shoreline of the town suggest otherwise, and it's now believed that most of
the population was buried by huge avalanches of volcanic mud, which later
hardened into the tufa-type rock that preserved much of the town so well. In
early 2000 the remains of another 48 people were found; they were carrying
coins, which suggests they were attempting to flee the disaster.

The site

Because Herculaneum wasn't a commercial town, there was no central open
space or forum, just streets of villas and shops, cut as usual by two very straight
main thoroughfares that cross in the centre. Start your tour just inside the
entrance at the bottom end of Cardo III, where you'll see the **House of the
Argus** (Casa d'Argo) on the left, a very grand building judging by its once-
impressive courtyard – although upstaged by the the so-called **Hotel** (Casa
del Albergo) across the street, which covers a huge area, though you can only
really get a true impression of its size from the rectangle of stumpy columns
that made up its atrium. Further up, Cardo III joins the Decumanus Inferiore,
just beyond which it's the large **Thermae** or bath complex which dominates
– the domed frigidarium of its men's section decorated with a floor mosaic
of dolphins, its caldarium containing a plunge bath and a scallop-shell apse.
Still intact are the benches where people sat and the wooden, partitioned
shelves for clothing.

On the far side of the baths, the **House of Neptune and Amphitrite** (Casa di Nettuno ed Anfitrite) holds sparklingly preserved and richly ornamental wall mosaics. Adjacent is the **House of the Beautiful Courtyard** (Casa del Bel Cortile) where skeletons of bodies still lie in the positions they fell. Turning right at the top of Cardo IV takes you around to Cardo V and most of the rest of the town's **shops** – a variety of places including a baker's, complete with ovens and grinding mills, a weaver's, with loom and bones, and a dyer's, with a huge pot for dyes. Behind the ones on the left you can see the **Palestra**, where public games were held, opposite which there's a well-preserved **Taverna** with counters and, further down Cardo V on the right, another the **Taverna del Priapo**, with a Priapic painting behind its counter.

Further down Cardo V, the **House of the Deer** (Casa dei Cervi) was another luxury villa, its two storeys built around a central courtyard and containing corridors decorated with richly coloured still-lifes. A covered passageway leads down from here to another **baths** building on the left – in fact one of the most impressive – and intact – structures in Herculaneum, complete with extremely well-preserved stuccowork and a pretty much intact set of baths; it also has a complete original Roman door, the only one in Herculaneum that wasn't charred by fire. If you find it open, the damp mustiness makes it certainly the most evocative stop on a tour of the site.

Cut back from Cardo V to Cardo IV and the **House of the Wooden Partition** (Casa del Tramezzo di Legno) with its original partition doors (now under glass). Nearby, the **House of the Mosaic Atrium** (Casa del Atrio Mosaico) was a grand villa in its day and retains its mosaic-laid courtyard, corrugated by the force of the tufa.

Mount Vesuvius

Since its first eruption in 79 AD, when it buried the towns and inhabitants of Pompeii and Herculaneum, **Mount Vesuvius** (1281m), has dominated the lives of those who live on the Bay of Naples, its brooding bulk forming a stately backdrop to the ever-growing settlements that group around its lower slopes. It's still an active volcano, the only one on mainland Europe. There have been more than a hundred eruptions over the years, but only two others of real significance – one in December 1631 that engulfed many nearby towns and killed 3000 people; and the last, in March 1944, which caused widespread devastation in the towns around, though no one was actually killed. The people who live here still fear the reawakening of the volcano, and with good cause – scientists calculate it should erupt every thirty years or so, and it hasn't since 1944. It's carefully monitored, of course, and there is apparently no reason to expect any movement for some time. But the subsidence in towns like Ercolano below is a continuing reminder of the instability of the area, one of southern Italy's most densely populated: around half a million people would be immediately threatened by another eruption.

There are several ways of **getting to Vesuvius**, or at least the car park and huddle of souvenir shops and cafés which sits just above the greenery among the bare cinders of the main summit and crater. You can drive here, and pay for parking. Or there are roughly hourly **buses from Pompeii** – the CS station and Piazza Antifeatro – between 8.05am and 3.35pm; the journey takes just over an hour and the last bus back is at 4.40pm. Tickets cost €9 return. Two of the buses go **via Ercolano** CS station, leaving there at 8.25am and 12.45pm; tickets from there cost €7.60. You can also rent minibus taxis from Ercolano which charge €15 per person and wait while you see the crater – but you have to wait until they're full at both ends. There are also services **from Naples**, Piazza Garibaldi (Hotel Terminus) – two in the morning, at 9.25am and 10.40am, taking an hour thirty minutes and returning at 12.30pm and 2pm respectively.

The ascent

Making the **ascent** to the crater (daily: Jan & Feb, Nov & Dec 9am–3pm; March & Oct 9am–4pm; April & May, June & Sept 9am–5pm; July & Aug 9am–6pm; €6.50) from the car park takes between twenty and thirty minutes depending how fit you are. It's a stony and mildly strenuous stroll across reddened, barren gravel and rock along a marked-out path that nowadays is roped off to minimize the chance of stumbling and falling down the sheer drop to the right. At the top is a deep, wide, jagged ashtray of red rock swirled over by midges and emitting the odd plume of smoke, though since the last eruption effectively sealed up the main crevice this is much less evident than it once was. There's also a small kiosk selling drinks and trinkets, and the path continues halfway around the crater so you can get a view from the other side – a further fifteen minutes or so on foot.

Pompeii

The other Roman town to be destroyed by Vesuvius – **POMPEII** – was a much larger affair than Herculaneum and one of Campania's most important commercial centres – a moneyed resort for wealthy patricians and a trading town that exported wine and fish. In effect the eruption froze the town's way of life as it stood at the time; indeed the excavations have probably yielded more information about the ordinary life of Roman citizens during the imperial era than anywhere else: their social conventions, class structure, domestic arrangements and (very high) standard of living. Some of the buildings are even covered with ancient graffiti, either referring to contemporary political events or simply to the romantic entanglements of the inhabitants; and the full horror of their way of death is apparent in plaster casts made from the shapes their bodies left in the volcanic ash – with faces tortured with agony, or shielding themselves from the dust and ashes.

The first parts of ancient Pompeii were discovered in 1600, but it wasn't until 1748 that **excavations** began, continuing more or less without interruption until the present day. Indeed, exciting discoveries are still being made. A privately funded excavation some years ago revealed a covered heated swimming pool, whose erotic wall paintings have been deemed by the Vatican to be unsuitable for children. And, in a further development, a luxury "hotel" complex was uncovered in 2000 during the widening of a motorway, slabs of stacked cut marble suggesting it was still under construction when Vesuvius erupted. Recently, a flood of new funds is being used to excavate a further twenty hectares of the site; it is hoped to resolve whether or not the survivors attempted, vainly, to resettle Pompeii after the eruption

Arrival, information and accommodation

To **reach Pompeii from Naples**, take the Circumvesuviana east to Pompeii-Villa dei Misteri – about 35 minutes; this leaves you right outside the western,

Vesuvius had been spouting smoke and ash for several days before the eruption on 24 August. Fortunately most of Pompeii had already been evacuated when disaster struck: out of a total population of 20,000 it's thought that only 2000 actually perished, asphyxiated by the toxic fumes of the volcanic debris, their homes buried in several metres of volcanic ash and pumice. **Pliny**, the Roman naturalist, was one of the casualties – he died at nearby Stabiae (now Castellammare) of a heart attack. But his nephew, Pliny the Younger, described the full horror of the scene in two vivid letters to the historian Tacitus, who was compiling a history of the disaster, writing that the sky turned dark like "a room when it is shut up, and the lamp put out".

Porta Marina entrance to the site. The **site** (daily: April–Oct 8.30am–7.30pm, last entry 6pm; Nov–March 8.30am–5pm, last entry 3.30pm; €11, combined ticket with Herculaneum and Villa Oplontis, valid 3 days, €20; Ⓦwww .pompeisites.org) covers a wide area, and seeing it properly takes half a day at the very least; really you should devote most of a day to it and take plenty of breaks – unlike Herculaneum there's little shade, and the distances involved are quite large: flat, comfortable shoes are a must.

All of this makes Pompeii sound a bit of a chore – which it certainly isn't. But there is a lot to see, and you should be reasonably selective: many of the streets aren't lined by much more than foundations, and after a while one ruin begins to look much like another. Again, many of the most interesting structures are kept locked and only opened when a large group forms or a tip is handed over to one of the many custodians. It's worth studying the **site map**, which you'll find at every entrance – pins on the map indicate which areas are currently closed, as the site is in continuous restoration. To be sure of seeing as much as possible you could take a tour, although one of the pleasures of Pompeii is to escape the hordes and absorb the strangely still quality of the town, which, despite the large number of visitors, it is quite possible to do.

If you want to make Pompeii an overnight stop, there are plenty of **hotels** and an excellent **youth hostel**, *Casa del Pellegrino*, Via Duca d'Aosta 4 (Ⓣ081.850.8644, Ⓦwww.hostelbookers.com; dorms €14–16.50), situated 300m from the Stazione Pompei-Santuario. There are also a couple of handy **campsites** including *Camping Pompei* at Via Plinio 113, south of the main entrance (Ⓣ081.862.2882, Ⓦwww.campingpompei.com; from €4 per person, ❶ for a bungalow). Modern Pompeii's **tourist office** at Via Sacra 1, just off the main square (Mon–Sat 9am–6pm; Ⓣ081.850.7255), has plans of the site, town plans and details of other accommodation.

The site

Entering the site from the Pompeii–Villa dei Misteri side, through the Porta Marina, the **Forum** is the first real feature of significance, a long, slim open space surrounded by the ruins of what would have been some of the town's most important official buildings – a basilica, temples to Apollo and Jupiter, and a market hall. Walking north from here, up the so-called Via di Mercurio, takes you towards some of the town's more luxurious houses. On the left, the **House of the Tragic Poet** (Casa del Poetica Tragico) is named for its mosaics of a theatrical production and a poet inside, though the "Cave Canem" (Beware of the Dog) mosaic by the main entrance is more eye-catching. Close by, the residents of the **House of the Faun** (Casa del Fauno) must have been a friendlier lot, its "Ave" (Welcome) mosaic outside beckoning you in to view the atrium and the copy of a tiny, bronze, dancing faun (the original is in Naples) that gives the villa its name.

On the street behind, the **House of the Vettii** (Casa dei Vettii) is one of the most delightful houses in Pompeii and one of the best maintained, a merchant villa ranged around a lovely central peristyle that gives the best possible impression of the domestic environment of the city's upper middle classes. The first room on the right off the peristyle holds some of the best of Pompeii's murals: the one on the left shows the young Hercules struggling with serpents. There are more paintings beyond here, through the villa's kitchen in a small room that's normally kept locked – erotic works showing various techniques of lovemaking together with an absurdly potent-looking statue of Priapus from which women were supposed to drink to be fertile.

Cross over to the other side of the site for the so-called **new excavations**, which began in 1911 and actually uncovered some of the town's most important quarters. The **Grand Theatre**, for one, is very well preserved and is still used for performances, overlooking the small, grassy, column-fringed square of the **Samnite Palestra** – a refectory and meeting-place for spectators from the theatre. Walk around to the far left side of the Grand Theatre, down the steps and up again, and you're in front of the **Little Theatre** – a smaller, more intimate venue also still used for summer performances and with a better-kept corridor behind the stage space.

Walk up from here to rejoin the Via dell' Abbondanza, where there's lots of interest – the Lararium has a niche with a delicate relief showing scenes from the Trojan war; the **Fullonica Stephani** is a well-preserved laundry, with a large tiered tub for washing; the **House of the Venus in the Shell** is named after the excellently preserved painting on its back wall; while next door, the **House of Octavius Quartio** is a gracious villa fronted by great bronze doors, with paintings of Narcissus gazing rapt at his reflection in the villa's lovely garden, which has been replanted with vines and shrubs. Just beyond here is the town's **Amphitheatre** – one of Italy's most intact and accessible, and also its

▲ Pompeii's amphitheatre

If you want to look down across the whole Bay of Naples but don't fancy sweating your way up Vesuvius, head a few kilometres further around the bay to Castellammare Di Stabia. Here you can take a **funivia** or cable car up to the top of **Monte Faito** (1100m; daily every 20–30min: mid-June to Aug 7.25am–7.15pm; rest of year 9.35am–4.25pm; €6.71 return, children €2.58; July, Aug & Sun €7.23), an eight-minute journey but even so definitely not for those of a delicate disposition, giving increasingly stupendous views of the bay and of the deepening gulf between you and the tree-filled hillside below. At the top, there are a couple of bars selling drinks and sandwiches, and if you really can't face the trip down it's comforting to know that several roads meet here and there's a Circumvesuviana bus stop nearby.

oldest, dating from 80 BC; it once had room for a crowd of some 12,000 – well over half the town's population. Next door, the **Palestra** is a vast parade ground that was used by Pompeii's youth for sport and exercise – still with its square of swimming pool in the centre. It must have been in use when the eruption struck Pompeii, since its southeast corner was found littered with the skeletons of young men trying to flee the disaster.

One last place you shouldn't miss at Pompeii is the **Villa dei Misteri**. This is probably the best-preserved of all Pompeii's palatial houses, an originally third-century BC structure with a warren of rooms and courtyards that derives its name from a series of paintings in one of its larger chambers: depictions of the initiation rites of a young woman into the Dionysiac Mysteries, an outlawed cult of the early imperial era. Not much is known about the cult itself, but the paintings are marvellously clear, remarkable for the surety of their execution and the brightness of their tones and colours.

Sorrento

Topping the rocky cliffs close to the end of its peninsula, 25km south of Pompeii, the last town of significance on this side of the bay, **SORRENTO** is solely and unashamedly a resort, its inspired location and mild climate drawing foreigners from all over Europe for close on 200 years. Ibsen wrote part of *Peer Gynt* in Sorrento, Wagner and Nietzsche had a well-publicized row here, and Maxim Gorky lived for over a decade in the town. Nowadays it's strictly package-tour territory, but not too much the worse for it, with little of the brashness of its Spanish and Greek equivalents but all of their vigour, a bright, lively place that retains its southern Italian roots. Cheap restaurants aren't too hard to find, nor – if you know where to look – is reasonably priced accommodation; and it's a handy place outside Naples itself from which to explore the rugged peninsula (even parts of the Amalfi coast) and the islands of the bay.

Arrival and information

Sorrento's **train station** is located in the centre of town, five minutes from the main Piazza Tasso along busy Corso Italia; the **bus station** is just in front. There's a **tourist office** in the large yellow Circolo dei Forestieri building at Via Luigi de Maio 35, just off Piazza San Antonino (Mon–Sat 8.45am–6.15pm; ☎081.807.4033, ⓦwww.sorrentotourism.com), which has free maps and bus and ferry timetables, and information about excursions. You can walk pretty much everywhere in

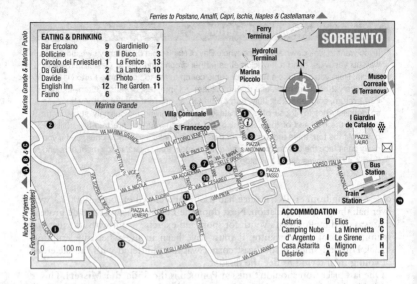

EATING & DRINKING

Bar Ercolano	9	Giardiniello	7
Bollicine	8	Il Buco	3
Circolo dei Foriestieri	1	La Fenice	13
Da Giulia	2	La Lanterna	10
Davide	4	Photo	5
English Inn	12	The Garden	11
Fauno	6		

SORRENTO

Ferries to Positano, Amalfi, Capri, Ischia, Naples & Castellamare

Ferry Terminal

Hydrofoil Terminal

Marina Piccolo

Museo Correale di Terranova

Marina Grande

Villa Comunale

S. Francesco

I Giardini de Cataldo

PIAZZA LAURO

PIAZZA S. ANTONINO

PIAZZA TASSO

Bus Station

CORSO ITALIA

Train Station

PIAZZA A. VENIERO

VIA DEGLI ARANCI

0   100 m

ACCOMMODATION

Astoria	D	Elios	B
Camping Nube		La Minervetta	C
d' Argento	I	Le Sirene	F
Casa Astarita	G	Mignon	H
Désirée	A	Nice	E

Sorrento, but if you want a bit of easy orientation, there are **mini train tours** that leave every 35 minutes from Piazza Tasso (daily 9am–midnight; €6 adults, €3 children); tours last about thirty minutes. If you don't want to rely on public transport, you can rent scooters at Jolly Service & Rent, just off the eastern end of Corso Italia at Via degli Aranci 180 (℡081 877 3450), and at the other end of town at Corso Italia 3 (℡081.878.2403); rates start at €27 a day, €150 a week.

Accommodation

Hotels

Astoria Via Santa Maria delle Grazie 24 ℡081.807.4030, ⓦwww .hotelastoriasorrento.com. It's unusual to find a hotel right in the heart of old Sorrento, and this place, only open since May 2008, is quite special, with reasonably sized doubles that have been nicely furnished and equipped (breakfast included). ④

Casa Astarita Corso Italia 69 ℡081.877.3991, ⓦwww.casastarita.com. More of a *pensione* than a hotel, this has six nice rooms overlooking the street, all with bathroom, flatscreen TVs and fridges, and charges €95–100 a night, including internet access and a good breakfast round a communal table each morning. Cosy, friendly, and in a good position, it's one of Sorrento's best options at this price. ③

Désirée Via Capo 31/B ℡081.878.1563, ⓦwww .desireehotelsorrento.com. About 700m from the end of Corso Italia, this is a nice small hotel with good-sized doubles with balconies overlooking the sea, for around €95 a night (triples and quads also available) – though they vary a bit in size. Breakfast is included. ④

Elios Via del Capo 33 ℡081.878.1812, ⓦwww .hotelelios.it. About 300m from the end of Corso Italia, this very friendly one-star enjoys a good location next door to the slightly sprucier Désirée. The rooms are nothing special, but they enjoy lovely views, and you get a very warm welcome. Prices don't include breakfast other than coffee but there's a kitchen for rustling up your own which you can enjoy on the large seaward-facing terrace. ④

Mignon Via Sersale 9 ℡081.807.3824, ⓦwww .sorrentohotelmignon.com. A really nice and well-located two-star with 24 very well-appointed rooms, all with satellite TV, a/c and free internet access. ③

La Minervetta Via Capo 25 ℡081.877.4455, ⓦwww.laminervetta.com. Sorrento's only boutique hotel perches on the cliff overlooking Marina Grande. There's a lovely lounge terrace overlooking the sea, and below that a plunge pool and steps leading down to Marina Grande's beaches and restaurants. And the rooms are gorgeous – prices start at around €300 for one of their deluxe rooms. ⑨

Nice Corso Italia 257 ☎081.878.1650, ⓦwww
.hotelnice.it. Bang on the corner of Corso Italia, this
couldn't be more convenient for the station, and it's
a friendly place, with good-sized if blandly
furnished doubles with TV, telephone, a/c and
breakfast. The front rooms can be a bit noisy; the
back ones are more peaceful and overlook an
orange and lemon grove. ❹

Hostels and campsites

There's a private **youth hostel**, *Le Sirene*, Via degli Aranci 160 (☎081.807.2925,
ⓦwww.hostellesirene.com; dorm beds €20–25, doubles ❷, including breakfast),
which is a bit spartan but decent enough. To get there from the train station, turn
right on the main road and Via degli Aranci is 200m down on the left. The closest
of the **campsites** is the scenic but handy *Nube d'Argento* site, right on the other
side of the town centre, 100m from the end of Corso Italia at Via del Capo 21
(☎081.878.1344, ⓦwww.nubedargento.com; prices start at €11 per person). If
that's full, try the slightly cheaper *Santa Fortunata*, just over a kilometre further
on at Via del Capo 41 (☎081.807.3579, ⓦwww.santafortunata.com; April–Oct),
which has a private beach and superb sea views.

The Town

Sorrento's centre is **Piazza Tasso**, built astride the gorge that runs through the
centre of town; it was named after the wayward sixteenth-century Italian poet
to whom the town was home and has a statue of him in the far corner. There's
nothing much to see in the town itself, but it's nice to wander through the
streets that feed into the square, some of which are pedestrianized for the lively
evening *passeggiata*. **Via San Cesareo** forms a backbone to the small grid of
streets, most of them lined with shops selling tourist gear and *limoncello*. It's
worth strolling down from here to linger in the shady gardens of the **Villa
Comunale**, whose terrace has lovely views out to sea. Off to the right, you can
also peek into the small thirteenth-century cloister of the church of **San
Francesco** just outside, planted with vines and bright bougainvillea – a
peaceful escape from the bustle of the rest of Sorrento.

Skirting the northern edge of the old town, Sorrento's main artery is **Corso
Italia**, and this is also pedestrianized every evening after 7pm for the lively
evening *passeggiata*. A little way down on the left, Sorrento's **Cattedrale** has been
much rebuilt, and the real challenge of its gaudy interior is how to tell the fake
marble from the real marble. The nearby **Museo Bottega della Tarsialignea**
at Via San Nicola 28 (June–Sept Tues–Sun 10am–1pm & 4–7.30pm; Oct–May
Tues–Sun 10am–1pm & 3–6.30pm; €8), housed in an ancient mansion in the
artisanal quarter of the old town, is a shrine to Sorrento's craft speciality of inlaid
woodwork – cheap and pretty awful examples of which you see all over town.
Don't let the tourist tat put you off: the ground floor here has some clever and
stylish examples of contemporary *intarsio* work (it's for sale, but not at all cheap),
while upstairs displays the work of Sorrento's late-nineteenth-century *intarsio*
greats. At the other end of town, the local **Museo Correale di Terranova**,
housed in the airy former palace of a family of local counts at the far end of Via
Correale (daily except Tues 9am–2pm; €6), has more examples of *intarsio*, various
Roman finds, along with a lot of badly lit paintings by local artists upstairs, best
of which by far is the late eighteenth-century roulette game, *Il Biri Bisso*, painted
on wood by one Francesco Celebrano.

The beaches

Strange as it may seem, Sorrento isn't particularly well provided with **beaches**,
and in the town itself you either have to make do with the small strips of sand

of the **Marina San Francesco** lido, right below the Villa Comunale gardens and accessible by a lift or steps, or the rocks and tiny, crowded strip of sand at **Marina Grande** – fifteen-minutes' walk or a short bus ride (roughly every 30min) west of Piazza Tasso. Both places charge for beds and parasols, although there is a small patch of sand, immediately right of the lift exit at Marina San Francesco, that is free. There are several ways to get down to Marina Grande on foot: the nicest are either following the city walls from the end of Via S. Nicola or by following the road that edges past the *Hotel Bellevue Syrene* off Villa Communale; both end up at the same flights of steps that lead down to the east end of Marina Grande's bay, just above the *Da Giulia* restaurant.

If you don't fancy the crowds in Sorrento, you can try the beaches further west. Twenty-minutes' walk from the centre of Sorrento along Via del Capo (which is the continuation of Corso Italia), or a short bus ride from Piazza Tasso, there are a couple of options. The first is the **Ruderi Villa Romana Pollio**, ten-minutes' walk from the bus stop at Capo di Sorrento on the main road, where the ruins of a Roman villa lie on and around the seashore rocks. The other is reachable by strolling 100m further along the main road and taking a path off to the right just before the *Hotel Dania*, which shortcuts in ten minutes or so to the **Marina di Puolo**, a short stretch of mainly sandy beach lined by fishing boats and a handful of trattorias that is perhaps the best place to swim just outside Sorrento.

In the opposite direction, the adjacent-but-one town of **Meta** is home to **Alimuri** beach – two decent-sized stretches of grey sand that face away from each other on a small spit that sticks out from the high-sided cliffs of the bay here. A lift can deliver you there from the road above, or you can drive down to a small car park.

Eating and drinking

Cafés and gelaterie

Bar Ercolano Piazza Tasso. The friendlier and less self-important of the two main bar terraces on Piazza Tasso. A good place to start the day with a pastry.

Circolo dei Foriestieri Via Luigi di Maio 35. Fancy old-world charm, decently priced if basic food, and wonderful views. A good place for a pre-dinner aperitif so you can pretend you're staying in one of the swanky hotels with seaview lounges.

Davide Via PR Giuliani 41. A decent long-established family-owned and run gelateria bang in the centre of Sorrento.

Fauno Piazza Tasso 13/15. The place to watch the crowds drift by during the evening *passeggiata*.

Restaurants

Il Buco Rampa Marina Piccola 11, Piazza San Antonino ☎ 081.878.2354. Housed in the wine cellar of a former monastery, this is Sorrento at its gastronomic best, with a real variety of antipasti and *primi* that focus on local ingredients and a *secondi* menu that is mainly about fish. You can order à la carte and pay around €18 for a pasta dish, €25 for a main course, or choose from menus

that start at €50 for three courses to €85 for six. Closed Wed.

La Fenice Via degli Aranci 11 ☎ 081.878.1652. A great place with a covered patio and lively atmosphere, specializing in fish; mains around €18. Closed Mon.

Giardiniello Via Accademia 7 ☎ 081.878.4616. Just off Corso Italia, between Piazza Sant'Antonio and Via Tasso, this pizzeria-*ristorante* with a small garden specializes in fish, shellfish and barbecued meats, and is a touch cheaper than the other places in the centre of town – try the *gnocchi alla sorrentina* at €5. Closed Thurs.

Da Giulia Via Marina Grande 67 ☎ 081.807.2720. With a menu as short as the menus in the upper town are long, this restaurant serves simple food in perhaps Sorrento's best location – on the waterfront of Marina Grande. Very good for simple pasta dishes, with half a dozen great seafood and tomato-based *primi*, and the same number of principally fish *secondi*. No credit cards.

La Lanterna Via San Cesareo 23 ☎ 081.878.1355. Down a dead end just off Piazza Tasso, this has long been one of the better restaurants in the centre of town, with tables outside and consistently good food – great fish, but much else besides. It's moderately priced, and there's also a *Lanterna Due*, around the corner on Santa Maria delle Grazie.

Bars

Bollicine Via Accademia 7. In the heart of the old town, this is a small, wood-panelled wine bar with a wide range of good Campanian wines.

English Inn Corso Italia 55. Capacious English-style pub with an outside dance floor.

Photo Via Correale 19/21. Just beyond Piazza Tasso, this is a deliberately cool bar-restaurant, though its studied boutiquey ambience means you could be pretty much anywhere.

The Garden Corso Italia 50/52. A wine shop and wine bar with a few outside tables that is a great place to take the weight off.

The islands

Guarding each prong of the Bay of Naples, the islands of Cápri, Ischia and Prócida between them make up the best-known group of Italian islands. Each is a very different creature, though. **Cápri** is a place of legend, home to the mythical Sirens and a much-eulogized playground of the super-rich in the years since – though now settled down to a lucrative existence as a target for day-trippers from the mainland. Visit by all means, but bear in mind that you have to hunt hard these days to detect the origins of much of the purple prose. **Ischia** is a target for package tours (predominantly from Germany) and weekenders from Naples, but its size means that it doesn't feel as crowded as Cápri, and plentiful hot springs, sandy beaches and a green volcanic interior make the island well worth a few days' visit. Pretty **Prócida**, the smallest of the islands and the least interesting – though the best venue for fairly peaceful lazing – remains reasonably untouched by the high season.

Cápri

Sheering out of the sea just off the far end of the Sorrentine peninsula, the island of **Cápri** has long been the most sought-after part of the Bay of Naples. During Roman times Augustus retreated to the island's gorgeous cliffbound scenery to escape the cares of office; later Tiberius moved the imperial capital here, indulging himself in legendarily debauched antics until his death in 37 AD. After the Romans left, Cápri was rather neglected until the early nineteenth century, when the discovery of the Blue Grotto and the island's remarkable natural landscape coincided nicely with the rise of tourism. The English especially have always flocked here: D.H. Lawrence and George Bernard Shaw were among more illustrious visitors; Graham Greene and Gracie Fields had houses here; and even Lenin visited for a time after the failure of the 1905 uprising.

Cápri tends to get a mixed press these days, the consensus being that while it might have been an attractive place once, it's been pretty much ruined by the crowds and the prices. And Cápri *is* crowded, to the degree that in July and August, and on *all* summer weekends, it would be sensible to give it a miss. But reports that the island has been irreparably spoilt are overstated. Ischia is busy too, Prócida isn't nearly as interesting – or beautiful – and it would be hard to find a place with more inspiring views. It's expensive, though prices aren't

Getting to the islands

Ferries and hydrofoils from the mainland to the islands operate from Naples, Pozzuoli and Sorrento, with some connections from Salerno, Amalfi and Positano. There are two departure points in Naples: the main harbour (Molo Beverello), at the bottom of Piazza Municipio, and the quayside at Mergellina. Whichever route you take, day-trips are quite feasible; usually the last connection delivers you back on the mainland in time for dinner. On foot, you can simply buy tickets when you turn up at the offices at the port; in general it's better to buy a single rather than a return ticket since it doesn't work out to be more expensive and you retain more flexibility on the time you come back. Having said that, on summer Sundays (especially on Cápri and Prócida, and especially by hydrofoil), it's a good idea to buy your return ticket as soon as you arrive, to avoid the risk of finding the last boat or hydrofoil fully booked. If you're looking at price, the state-run ferry Caremar is usually the cheapest. If you're **driving**, you should probably book, or at least turn up well in advance – though there's no real point in taking a car to any of the islands apart from Ischia.

The following gives a rough idea of frequencies during the summer (they're greatly reduced off-season). For specific timings you can look in *Il Mattino*, check with the local tourist offices or look up the companies online: Caremar (☎892.123, ⓦwww .caremar.it), Alilauro (☎081.497.2238, ⓦwww.alilauro.it), SNAV (☎081.428.5555, ⓦwww.snav.it), NLG (☎081.552.0763, ⓦwww.navlib.it), Med March (☎081.333.4411, ⓦwww.medmargroup.it), and Prócida Lines (☎081.896.0328). In any case, always double check times, since they are far from set in stone. There is also a public transport option, the **Metro del Mare** (☎199.600.700, ⓦwww.metrodelmare.com) that links Naples to Cápri and around twenty towns around the Bay of Naples and the Gulf of Salerno. The service runs with greater frequency in the summer months.

Hydrofoils and fast ferries

Naples (Molo Beverello)–Cápri (20 daily; 45–50min).
Naples (Molo Beverello)–Casamícciola, Ischia (6 daily; 1hr).
Naples (Molo Beverello)–Forío, Ischia (6 daily; 50min).
Naples (Molo Beverello)–Ischia Porto, Ischia (20 daily; 45–60min).
Naples (Molo Beverello)–Prócida (9 daily; 35–40min).
Naples (Mergellina)–Cápri (6 daily; 35min).
Naples (Mergellina)–Casamícciola, Ischia (6 daily; 45min).
Naples (Mergellina)–Forío (via Ischia Porto: 3 daily; 1hr).
Naples (Mergellina)–Ischia Porto, Ischia (10 daily; 40min).
Naples (Mergellina)–Prócida (2 daily; 20min).
Casamícciola, Ischia–Prócida (6 daily; 20min).
Ischia Porto, Ischia–Prócida (3 daily; 15min).
Ischia Porto, Ischia–Cápri (1 daily; 50min).
Prócida–Ischia Porto, Ischia (3 daily; 20min).
Salerno–Cápri (2 daily; 1hr).
Sorrento–Ischia Porto, Ischia (1 daily direct, and 1 daily via Cápri).
Sorrento–Cápri (16 daily; 20–25min).

Ferries

Naples (Molo Beverello)–Cápri (3 daily; 1hr 20min).
Naples (Molo Beverello)–Casamícciola, Ischia (4 daily; 2hr).
Naples (Molo Beverello)–Ischia Porto, Ischia (8 daily; 1hr 30min).
Naples (Molo Beverello)–Prócida (6 daily; 1hr).
Pozzuoli–Ischia Porto, Ischia (7 daily; 1hr).
Pozzuoli–Casamícciola, Ischia (6 daily; 1hr 30min).
Pozzuoli–Prócida (6 daily; 35min).
Ischia Porto, Ischia–Prócida (6 daily; 25min).
Sorrento–Cápri (2 daily; 50min).
Salerno–Cápri (2 daily; 2hr 10min).
Salerno–Ischia Porto, Ischia (1 daily; 2hr 30min).

⓭

CAMPANIA

really any higher than at other major Italian resorts, and you can find very reasonably priced and attractive accommodation in Anacápri; alternatively, just visit on a day-trip, which should give you time enough to see the major sights of the island.

Arrival and information

There are three **tourist offices** on the island (ⓦ www.capritourism.com). The tourist booth at Marina Grande is just on the left at the beginning of the quay (April–Oct Mon–Sat 9am–1pm & 3.30–6.45pm, Sun 9am–1pm; Nov–March Mon–Sat 9am–3pm; ⓣ 081.837.0634) and sells a handy map (€1); in Cápri town there is an office at Piazza Umberto I April–Oct Mon–Sat 8.30am–8.30pm, Sun 9am–3pm; Nov–March Mon–Sat 9am–1pm & 3.30–6.45pm; ⓣ 081.837.0686); and there's another in Anacápri, at Via G. Orlandi 59 (Mon–Sat 9am–3pm; ⓣ 081.837.1524).

All hydrofoils and ferries arrive at **Marina Grande**, roughly in the middle of Cápri's northern coast, with the island's main town perched up the hill. It's a busy quayside but there's nothing much to see, and you may as well head straight on to Cápri town. You could walk it, but with 300 steps to climb most people take the **funicular** (daily 6.30am–10pm; till midnight April–Sept; €1.40 one-way) or, if there are queues, a **bus**. The island's bus service connects all the main centres – Marina Grande, Cápri, Marina Piccola, Anacápri – every fifteen minutes; they also run regularly down to the Blue Grotto from Anacápri, and also to Punta Carena. Tickets cost €1.40 for a single trip, €2.20 for an hour and €6.90 for a day. An alternative is one of Cápri's stylish convertible taxis, but these are very expensive; there's a taxi stand out of the port and up to the right (ⓣ 081.837.0543).

Accommodation

If you're contemplating **staying overnight** on Cápri in peak season – and the island is a lot quieter after the day-tripping crowds have gone home – book well ahead as space is extremely limited.

▲ Marina Grande, Cápri

Cápri Town and Marina Grande

🏃 **A Paziella** Via Fuorlovado 36
ⓣ081.837.0044, ⓦwww.apaziella.com.
Cool and breezy even on the hottest day, this place has a palpable serenity, yet it's located in the middle of town, just seconds away from all the shopping, smart restaurants and nightlife. Closed mid-Oct to March. ❽

Da Giorgio Via Roma 34 ⓣ081.837.5777,
ⓦwww.dagiorgiocapri.com. Gracious rooms with views of the bay, this is an excellent choice, not least because the same property also boasts one of the island's most appealing restaurants. Closed Jan–Feb. ❺

Italia Via Marina Grande 204 ⓣ081.837.0602,
ⓦwww.hotelitaliacapri.com. This elegant old mansion, surrounded by flower gardens and occupying its own corner on the road up to Cápri Town is full of charm. All of the airy rooms have private balconies and half of them sea-views; the others look out over the gardens. Breakfast €10 extra. Open year-round.

Quattro Stagioni Via Marina Piccola 1,
Cápri Town ⓣ081.837.0041, ⓦwww
.hotel4stagionicapri.com. In a pretty location, a little way out of Cápri Town at the fork of the roads to Marina Piccola and Anacápri, this place offers a 10 percent discount to carriers of this book from mid-March to Oct. ❹

🏃 **Weber Ambassador** Via Marina Piccola,
Marina Piccola ⓣ081.837.0141, ⓦwww
.hotelweber.com. Comfortable choice with great views from its multi-levelled terrace. Cosy and elegant inside, and steps leading directly down to the Marina Piccola beach. ❻

Anacápri and around

Alla Bussola di Hermes Traversa La Vigna 14
ⓣ081.838.2010, ⓦwww.bussolahermes.com. A former dorm for backpackers re-incarnated as a luxurious boutique hotel, and still good value though obviously very different. Closed Nov–Feb. ❺

La Bougainville Viale Tommaso de Tommaso 6
ⓣ081.837.3641, ⓦwww.hlb.it. A comfortable choice, set in a lush flower garden, which some rooms overlook, and situated on the main bus line from Anacápri to the rest of the island. Amenities include a good restaurant, a solarium and guest pick-up/drop-off at Marina Grande. Closed mid-Nov to mid-March. ❻

🏃 **Villa Eva** Via La Fabbrica 8
ⓣ081.837.1549, ⓦwww.villaeva.com. For a long time now, *Villa Eva* has been the cult budget option of the island, and the legend only gets better. A wide choice of individually styled rooms to choose from, most of them spacious and light, as well as a grand-piano-shaped pool and a welcoming poolhouse/snack-bar, where breakfast is served. Closed Nov–March. ❹

Cápri Town and Marina Piccola

CÁPRI is the main town of the island, nestled between two mountains. Its houses are connected by winding, hilly alleyways that give onto the dinky main square of **Piazza Umberto I**, or "La Piazzetta", crowded with café tables and lit by twinkling fairy lights in the evenings. Don't neglect the maze of charming streets behind La Piazzetta, or the covered walkways up the steps to the right as you enter the square, past the Baroque dome of the seventeenth-century parish church of **Santo Stefano**, itself also worth a look for its marble floor originally from the ancient Roman Villa Jovis and the ruins of other Tiberian villas. Also just up the steps, directly across from the church, is a modest local museum, the **Museo del Centro Caprense "Ignazio Cerio"** at Piazzetta Cerio 5 (Tues–Sat 10am–1pm, Thurs 3–7pm; €2.60), which houses archeological remains, artefacts of the island's prehistory, and various zoological and botanical finds.

On the far side of town is the **Certosa San Giacomo** on Viale Certosa 11 (Tues–Sat 9am–2pm, Sun 9am–1pm; free) a run-down old monastery with a multilingual lending library and a small collection of metaphysical paintings by Karl Diefenbach, a German painter who lived on the island until his death in 1913. On past the monastery, at the other side of the island, the **Giardini di Augusto** give tremendous views of the coast below and the towering jagged cliffs above. The zigzag pathway down, Via Krupp, was reopened in 2008 after being closed for 32 years due to the danger of falling rocks, and you can wind down to either the beach (rocks really), or, beyond, to

Marina Piccola – a small huddle of houses and restaurants around patches of pebble beach: reasonably uncrowded out of season, though in July or August you might as well forget it. Marina Piccola is also accessible by bus from the Cápri town bus terminus.

Walks around Cápri Town

Up above the Certosa, and a further pleasant walk fifteen minutes through Cápri town, the **Belvedere del Cannone** has marvellous views, especially over the **Faraglioni** rocks to the left and Marina Piccola to the right. Further out of Cápri town, there are two walks worth doing to the eastern edge of the island. One, up to the ruins of Tiberius's villa, the **Villa Jovis** (daily 9am to 1hr before sunset; €2), is a steep forty-minute hike from Piazza Umberto following Via Botteghe out of the square and Via Tiberio up the hill. It was here that Tiberius retired in 27 AD, reportedly to lead a life of vice and debauchery and to take revenge on his enemies, many of whom he apparently had thrown off the cliff face. You can see why he chose the site: it's among Cápri's most exhilarating, with incredible vistas of the Sorrentine Peninsula, including the Amalfi Coast, and the bay; on a clear day you can even see Salerno and beyond. There's not much left of the villa, but you can get a good sense of the shape and design of its various parts from the arched halls and narrow passageways that remain. Below, there's another villa, the more recent **Villa Lysis** (April–Oct Mon–Sat 9am–1.30pm, 2.30–6.30pm; free), known to locals as Villa Fersen after Count Fersen-Adelsward, a gay Swedish millionaire writer who built the house in the early 1900s apparently to entertain his young Italian lovers, as well as his heroin and cocaine habits. The house is interesting enough from the outside but there's nothing left of the original outlandish furnishings inside.

The other walk is to the **Arco Naturale**, an impressive natural rock formation at the end of a high, lush valley, a 25-minute stroll from Cápri town, again following Via Botteghe out of the square but branching off up Via Matermania after ten minutes or so; just follow the signs. You can get quite close to the arch owing to the specially constructed viewing platforms. Just before the path descends towards the arch, steps lead down to the **Grotta di Matermania**, ten minutes away down quite a few steps – a dusty cutaway out of the rock that was converted to house a shrine to the goddess Cybele by the Romans. Steps lead on down from the cave, sheer through the trees, before flattening into a fine path that you can follow to the **Tragara Belvedere**, affording some of the island's best views along the way, and, eventually, back to Cápri town – reachable in about an hour.

Anacápri

The island's other main settlement, **ANACÁPRI**, is more sprawling than Cápri itself and less obviously picturesque, its main square, **Piazza Vittoria**, flanked by souvenir shops, bland fashion boutiques and restaurants decked with tourist menus – Cápri without the chic.

A short walk away from Piazza Vittoria down Via G. Orlandi, the church of **San Michele** (daily: April–Oct 9am–7pm; Nov–March 9.30am–3pm; €2) is one of two principal sights, its tiled floor painted with an eighteenth-century depiction of the Fall that you view from an upstairs balcony – a lush work after a drawing by the Neapolitan painter **Solimena**, in rich blues and yellows, showing cats, unicorns and other creatures. The other is a walk in the opposite direction from Piazza Vittoria, past a long gauntlet of souvenir stalls to Axel

Munthe's **Villa San Michele** (daily: March 9am–4.30pm; April & Oct 9am–5pm; May–Sept 9am–6pm; Nov–Feb 9am–3.30pm; €5; Ⓦ www.villasanmichele.org), a light, airy house with lush and fragrant gardens that is one of the real highlights of the island. A nineteenth-century Swedish writer and physician to the elite, Munthe lived here for a number of years, and the place is filled with his furniture and knick-knacks, as well as Roman artefacts and columns plundered from a ruined villa on the site. Busts and bronzes abound, Corinthian capitals are converted as coffee tables, other surfaces topped with intricate Cosmati mosaic-work. His book *The Story of San Michele* – more the story of his life – is well worth reading. There's also an attractive, small natural history exhibition in the gardens, which fills you in on local flora and fauna.

Monte Salaro and the Blue Grotto

A chair lift operates from Piazza Vittoria up to **Monte Solaro** (daily: March–Oct 9.30am to 6.30pm; Nov–Feb 10.30am–3pm; return €8, one-way €6), the island's highest point (596m). The trip only takes twelve minutes. There's not much at the top – a ruined castle and a café – but the ride and the location are very tranquil and the 360-degree views are marvellous – perhaps the bay's very best.

Continuing in the same direction, a good 45-minute hike starting off down Via Lo Pozzo (or reachable by bus every twenty minutes from Piazza Vittoria), you come to the **Blue Grotto** or Grotta Azzurra, probably the island's best-known feature – though also its most exploitative, the boatmen here whisking visitors onto boats and in and out of the grotto in about five minutes flat (daily 9am to 1hr before sunset, but not in case of adverse weather; rowboat into the grotto €6, plus admission €4). The grotto is quietly impressive, the blue of its innards caused by sunlight entering the cave through the water, but it's rather overrated. Technically, you can swim into the cave – it's not the exclusive preserve of the boatmen, though they'll try to persuade you otherwise – but the route through is so busy that unless you're a strong swimmer it's only advisable to try at the end of the day after the tours have finished. You can also get here direct from Marina Grande for €11 per person.

Eating

The island is overloaded with places to eat, but only a few of them are anywhere near good-value, so you can always knock yourself up a picnic lunch if you prefer: in Cápri town there are a supermarket and bakery a little way down Via le Botteghe, off La Piazzetta, and a well-stocked *salumerie* at Via Roma 13 and 30. Tucked away just a few metres back down towards Marina Grande from the island's little roundabout, there's also a sizeable supermarket that carries just about every sort of food and more.

Cápri Town and Marina Grande

Aurora Via Fuorlovado 18–22 ☎081.837.0181. This attractive place is the longest-established restaurant; on the island, with tables outside and a crunchy speciality called *pizza all'acqua* (€6–10 depending on topping). Closed Nov–March.

Buca di Bacco "da Serafina" Via Longano 25 ☎081.837.0723. Just behind La Piazzetta, this old favourite is rated by locals and visitors alike as one of the best of the best; try the *spaghetti alla pescatora* for €15, or fresh fish mains start around €10. Closed Mon & Jan.

Da Gemma Via Madre Serafina 6 ☎081.837.0461. Graham Greene's favourite restaurant, and still good, up the steps from La Piazzetta in a white-washed arcade. The buffet spread is generally good. Or go for their wood-fired pizzas. Closed Nov–April and Thurs May, June & Oct.

Da Giorgio Via Roma 34 ☎081.837.0898. Popular and surprisingly inexpensive (for Cápri) and yet in a picturesque location. Try the *linguine ai frutti di* *mare* at €12. The place also offers good-value hotel rooms (see "Accommodation"). Closed Tues & Jan–Feb.

La Capannina Via le Botteghe 12bis ☏081.837.0732. Up to the left from La Piazzetta, this place is considered by many as the island's top restaurant; fish main courses such as *pezzogna* (local red snapper) go for around €28. Closed Wed and Nov to mid-March.

Anacápri

🏃 **Il Solitario** Via G. Orlandi 96 ☏081.837.1382. Take the little walkway back from the street and discover an arboured garden patio setting decorated with appealingly kitsch painted statues and coloured fairy lights. The food is excellent, the prices moderate, and the service very friendly. Closed Tues & Nov and two weeks in Feb.

Materita Via G. Orlandi 140/Piazza Diaz ☏081.837.3375. Attractive and well located, with cosy seating inside and terrace tables, too. The signature dish is the Neapolitan-style wood-fired pizza, served both lunch and dinner, but there's also a full menu. Closed Tues & Nov to mid-Dec.

Ischia

Largest of the islands in the Bay of Naples, **Ischia** (pronounced Iss-kee-ah) rises out of the sea in a cone-shaped series of pointy green hummocks. German, Scandinavian and British tourists flock here in large numbers during peak season, attracted by its charming beach resorts and thermal springs. Although its reputation has always been poorer than Cápri's – it is perhaps not so dramatically beautiful – you can at least be sure of being alone in exploring parts of the mountainous interior, and **La Mortella**, the exotic garden cultivated by the British composer William Walton and his widow Susana, is an unmissable attraction. Indeed, if you're after some beach lounging, good walking and lively nightlife within striking distance of Naples and the rest of the bay, it might be just the place.

Ischia Porto and Ponte

The main town of Ischia is **ISCHIA PORTO**, where the ferries dock, an appealing stretch of hotels, ritzy boutiques and beach shops planted with lemon trees and Indian figs fronted by golden sands: **Spiaggia San Pietro** is to the right of the port, accessible by following Via Buonocore off Via Roma. The inexplicably named **Spiaggia degli Inglesi**, on the other side is reachable by way of the narrow path that leads over the headland from the end of Via Jasolino. Apart from the sunbathing the main thing to do is to window-shop and stroll along the main Corso Vittoria Colonna, either branching off to a further beach, the Spiaggia **dei Pescatori**, or following it all the way down to the other part of Ischia's main town, **ISCHIA PONTE**, also reachable by bus #7, a quieter and less commercialized centre. Ischia Ponte is home to the island's **Museo del Mare** (daily: April–June, Sept & Oct 10.30am–12.30pm & 3–7pm; July & Aug 10.30am–12.30pm & 6.30–10pm; Nov–March 10.30am–12.30; closed Feb; €3), which traces the community's seafaring roots with ancient, barnacle-encrusted pottery retrieved from the sea and samples of marine fauna, as well as the full range of navigation instruments from sextants to sonar. But the main focus of this area is the **Castello Aragonese** (daily 9am to 1hr before sunset; €10, includes the lift to the top; allow at least an hour for a visit), accessible via a short causeway, whose stunningly distinctive pyramid was one of the backdrops in the film *The Talented Mr Ripley*. The citadel itself is rather tumble-down now and closed to the public, but below is a complex of buildings, almost a separate village really, around which you can stroll. There's the weird open shell of a cathedral destroyed by the British in 1806, a prison that once held political prisoners during the Unification struggle, and the macabre remnants of a convent, in which a couple of dark rooms ringed with a set of commode-like seats served as a cemetery for the dead sisters – placed here to putrefy in front of the living members of the community. The rest of the convent has been converted to a rather nice hotel (see below).

Arrival, information and accommodation

Ischia Porto's helpful **tourist office** is right by the quayside ferry ticket offices (Mon–Sat 9am–2pm & 3–8pm; ☎081.507.4231, ⊛www.infoischiaprocida.it). The **bus terminus** is just behind here: buses CS (clockwise) and CD (counter-clockwise) circle the island every thirty minutes, stopping just about everywhere. Tickets cost €1.20 and are valid for one hour thirty minutes, day tickets are €4, two-day tickets €6.

There is plenty of **accommodation** in Ischia Ponte and Ischia Porto, though bear in mind that many places close from November to Easter, opening only for a short time between Christmas and New Year. Due to its role as the arrivals harbour, Ischia Porto is a more lively place to stay, but Ponte is decidedly more charming, and preferable for long-term stays.

Hotels

Continental Mare Via B. Cossa 25, Porto ☎081.982.577, ⊛www.continentalmare.it. A breezily elegant hotel in a splendid location west of the port with its own stretch of beach. Rooms are spacious and contemporary in style, the best ones enjoying balconies with sea views. ❼

Eurocamping dei Pini Via delle Ginestre 28, Porto ☎081.982.069, ⊛www.ischia.it/camping. A pleasant campsite with nice stands of trees a short walk from the port. To get there, follow Via Mazzella away from the sea and turn right several roads after the football fields. Bungalows too. ❶

🏃 **Il Monastero** Castello Aragonese, Ponte ☎081.992.433, ⊛www.locandasulmare.it. Located on the upper floors of the Castello

Aragonese, this is the place to stay in Ischia Ponte, with twenty guestrooms in former nuns' cells, which are suitably spare but coolly comfortable in style. The hotel has a broad, sunny terrace overlooking the sea and a picturesque café and restaurant, *Il Terrazzo.* ❹

Locanda Sul Mare Via Jasolino 80, Porto ☎081.981.470, ⊛www.locandasulmare.it. Near to the port, this tiny, idiosyncratically decorated and very pleasant hotel is a great bargain and has a decent restaurant. ❸

Macrí Via Jasolino 96, Porto ☎&℻081.992.603. Just steps from the ferry port, this prettily furnished and simple budget option boasts its own bar, parking and garden. Breakfast is an additional €6 per person. ❷

Eating and drinking

There's no shortage of **café** and **restaurant** options in Ischia. The port is full of places catering to tourists just off the ferry and is dense with tourist traps serving mediocre food at inflated prices.

Al Pontile Via Luigi Mazzella 15, Lungomare Aragonese 6, Ponte ☎081.983.492. On the water-front directly opposite the Castello, this café and unassuming little restaurant serves anything from just drinks and light snacks and salads.

Calise Caffe Concerto Piazza degli Eroi 69, Porto ☎081.991.270. An island institution with many locations, this branch is set in the midst of a veritable jungle oasis. It's a truly all-purpose gastronomic venue, and you'll find everything from excellent ice cream to scrumptious cakes and full meals and snacks. After hours, *Calise* turns into a lounge bar and music venue and is open until 4am in the summer. Closed Wed Nov–March.

Da Coco' Piazzale Aragonese, Ponte ☎081.981.823. In an enviable position just below the Castello Aragonese, this bar-restaurant boasts lovely sea views and great seafood for around €10. Closed Wed Sept–April.

Gennaro Via Porto 59, Porto ☎081.992.917. Established in 1965, this seafood specialist in the harbour serves traditional Ischitana fare like *zuppa di cozze* (mussels in broth), *spaghetti alle vongole* (with clams), and a grilled fish and prawns. Pair with the local Ischia DOC wine made with white biancolella grapes. Full meals from €40. Closed Nov to mid-March.

Casamicciola Terme and Lacco Ameno

The island is at its most developed along its northern and western shores – heading west from Ischia Porto. The first village you reach, **CASAMICCIOLA TERME**, is a spa centre with many hotels and a crowded central beach – though you can find a quieter one on the far side of the village. Ibsen spent a summer here, and the waters are said to be full of iodine (apparently beneficial for the skin and the nervous system), but otherwise you may as well push on to **LACCO AMENO**, a brighter little town, again with a beach and with spa waters that are said to be the most radioactive in Italy. It's known for the ten-metre-tall offshore tufa rock, affectionately nicknamed **Il Fungo**, and the **Museo Archeologico di Pithecusa** (Tues–Sun: May–Oct 9.30am–1pm & 4–8pm; Nov–April 9.30am–1pm & 3–7pm; €5), housed in the eighteenth-century Villa Arbusto, whose most celebrated piece is the Coppa di Nestore, engraved with a light-hearted challenge to the cup mentioned in Homer's *Iliad*, while a shipwreck scene on a locally made bowl is thought to be the oldest example of figurative painting in Italy.

La Mortella

Between Lacco Ameno and Forío, at Via F. Calise 39 (ask the bus driver to drop you off), the stunning garden of **La Mortella** (Easter–Nov Tues, Thurs, Sat & Sun 9am–7pm; ⓦwww.ischia.it/mortella; €10, or €15 with concert) is one of Ischia's highlights, created by the English composer William Walton and his Argentinian widow Susana, who still lives here. The Waltons moved to Ischia, then sparsely populated and little known to tourists, in 1949, forerunners of a coterie of writers and artists including Auden and Terence Rattigan. With the garden designer Russell Page, they created La Mortella from an unpromising volcanic stone quarry.

Paths wind up through the abundant site, which has some three hundred rare and exotic plants. Near the entrance is a glasshouse sheltering the world's largest water lily, while above the glasshouse is a charming terraced **tearoom**, where the strains of Walton's music can be heard and there's a **museum** which shows a video about the composer and features portraits by Cecil Beaton, a bust by Elizabeth Frink, and paintings and set-designs by John Piper. Paths loop through luxuriant foliage to the pyramid-shaped rock that holds Walton's ashes, a cascade guarded by a sculpted crocodile and a pretty **Thai pavilion** surrounded by heavy-headed purple agapanthus. At the garden's summit, a belvedere provides superb views across the island.

Forío

FORÍO sprawls around its bay, another growing resort that is quite pretty behind its seafront of bars and pizzerias, focusing around the busy main street of Corso Umberto. Out on the point on the far side of the old centre (turn right at the far end of Corso Umberto), the simple **Chiesa Soccorso** is a bold, whitewashed landmark from which to survey the town. There are good **beaches** either side of Forío: the **Spiaggia di Chiaia**, a short walk to the north; to the south **Cava del Isola**, which is popular with a young crowd; and the **Spiaggia di Citara**, a somewhat longer walk to the south along Via G. Mazzella. Here you'll find the **Giardini Poseidon**, an extensive complex of blissfully relaxing thermal baths on the seafront (April–Oct daily 9am–7pm; €28 per day, €23 for a half-day, beginning at 1pm; prices increase in Aug; credit cards accepted for treatments only; ⓦwww.giardiniposeidonterme.com).

If you decide **to stay**, try the charming and central *Punta del Sole* on Piazza Maltese (℡081.989.156, ⒲www.casthotels.com; ❸), with balconied rooms set in a beautiful garden; or, in the centre of Forío, there's friendly and fun *Ring Hostel*, Via Gaetano Morgera 66 (℡081.987.546, ⒲www.ringhostel .com; dorm beds from €18, doubles from ❷), cheerfully run by three local brothers who all speak English and provide transport shuttles around the island. There are some good **eating** options here too: head for the delightful *Umberto a Mare*, tucked under the Chiesa Soccorso at Via Soccorso 2 (℡081.997.171; closed lunch & Jan–March), whose pretty whitewashed interior looks out onto the sea and offers seasonal cuisine with lots of seafood. In the town centre, along Via Marina on the port, there are several good-value places that specialize in fish. One of the best, *La Bussola* at no. 36 (℡081.997.645; closed Mon Oct–April), serves wood-fired pizzas for both lunch and dinner, fresh fish at about €10, and has ample terrace seating for good people-watching.

Sant'Angelo and around

Ischia is most pleasant on its southern side, the landscape steeper and greener, with fewer people to enjoy it. **SANT'ANGELO** is probably its loveliest spot, a tiny fishing village crowded around a narrow isthmus linking with a humpy islet that's out of bounds to buses, which drop you right outside. It's inevitably quite developed, centring on a harbour and square crowded with café tables and surrounded by pricey boutiques, but if all you want to do is laze in the sun it's perhaps the island's most appealing spot to do so. There's a reasonable **beach** lining one side of the isthmus that connects Sant'Angelo to its islet, as well as the nearby stretch of the **Spiaggia dei Maronti**, 1km east, which is accessible by plentiful taxi boats from Sant'Angelo's harbour (around €5), or on foot in about 25 minutes – take the path from the top of the village.

Taxi boats will drop you at one of a number of specific features: one, the **Fumarole**, is where steam emerges from under the rocks in a kind of outdoor sauna, popular on moonlit nights; further along close by a couple of hotels is a path that cuts inland through a mini-gorge to the **Terme Cavascura**, the most historic hot springs on the island, used since Roman times (mid-April to Oct, daily 9.30am–6pm; €10 for swim and sauna; ⒲www.cavascura.it).

There are plenty of places to **stay** in and around Sant'Angelo. The very central *La Conchiglia* Via Chiaia delle Rose 1 (℡081.999.270, ⒲www .conchigliahotel.com; April–Oct; ❸,) is primarily a good family-run restaurant with has upstairs rooms with lovely views to rent. Also very central is *La Palma* Via Conte Maddalena 15 (℡081.999.215, ⒲www.lapalmatropical .it; mid-March to Oct; half-board only ❼), a recently renovated Moorish-style villa that offers great views of Sant'Angelo and the bay and has plushly furnished rooms and an inviting garden terrace restaurant. Right on Maronti Beach itself, one of the best bargains is the *Villa Casa Bianca*, towards the eastern end of the beach (℡081.905.212, ⒲www.casabiancaischia.it; March–Oct; half-board only ❺) – a gleaming Mediterranean villa with a pool and a sweeping terrace that affords views of Cápri. Finally, up in the village of Succhivo, ten-minutes' walk back in the direction of Forío (the bus passes right by), *Casa Giuseppina*, at Via Gaetano D'Iorio 11 (℡081.907.771, ⒲www.casagiuseppina.it; April–Oct; minimum stay 3 nights at the weekend; half-board only ❹), is a family-run, pleasantly rustic garden villa with a swimming pool and hot tub.

Fontana and Monte Epomeo

Up above Sant'Angelo looms the craggy summit of Ischia's now dormant volcano, **Monte Epomeo**. Both CD and CS buses regularly stop at **FONTANA**, a superb ride up, with wonderful views back over the coast, from where you can climb up to the summit of the volcano. Follow the signposted road off to the left from the centre of Fontana: after about five minutes it joins a larger road; after another ten to fifteen minutes take the left fork, a stony track off the road, and follow this up to the summit – when in doubt, always fork left and you can't go wrong. It's a steep hour or so's climb, especially at the end when the path becomes no more than a channel cut out of the soft rock. However, there are a couple of scenically placed cafés in which to gather your energies at the top, where the views are stunning. Bear in mind, too, that you can drive to within about twenty minutes of the summit, leaving your vehicle by the signs for the military exclusion zone.

Prócida

A serrated hunk of volcanic rock that's the smallest (population 10,000) and nearest island to Naples, **Prócida** has managed to fend off the kind of tourist numbers that have flooded into Cápri and Ischia. It lacks the spectacle, or variety, of both islands, though it compensates with extra room and extra peace.

The island's main town, **MARINA GRANDE**, where you arrive by ferry, is a slightly run-down but picturesque conglomeration of tall pastel-painted houses rising from the waterfront to a network of steep streets winding up to the fortified tip of the island – the so-called **Terra Murata**. Part of this was once given over to a rather forbidding prison, now abandoned, but it's worth walking up anyway to see the abbey church of **San Michele** (Mon–Sat 9.45am–12.45pm & 3–6pm, Sun 9.45am–12.45; €2 donation requested), whose domes are decorated with a stirring painting by Giordano of St Michael beating back the Turks from Prócida's shore. The views, too, from the nearby belvedere are among the region's best, taking in the whole of the Bay of Naples, from Capo Miseno bang in front of you right around to the end of the Sorrentine peninsula and Cápri on the far left. Look out for handwritten notes by the custodian lamenting thefts from the church.

For the rest, Prócida's appeal lies in its opportunities to swim and eat in relative peace. There are **beaches** in Marina Grande itself, on the far side of the jetty, and, in the opposite direction, beyond the fishing harbour, though both are fairly grubby. Similarly, **Spiaggia Chiaia**, just beyond the fishing harbour of nearby Coricella, is a reasonable bathing beach but isn't very large and can get crowded. You can walk there, or the Chiaiolella bus stops nearby.

On the whole if you want to swim you're better off making the fifteen-minute bus journey from Marina Grande to **CHIAIOLELLA**, where there's a handful of bars and **restaurants** around a pleasant, almost circular bay and a long stretch of sandy beach that is the island's best. By taking the road up from behind the beach you can cross the (officially closed) bridge onto the islet of **Vivara**, a nature reserve, very peaceful and overgrown. It's a refreshingly bucolic affair after the rest of the island, where the settlement is pretty much continuous, the narrow roads and constant traffic making walking uncomfortable.

Practicalities

The **tourist office** is at the port at Via V.Emanuele 173 (daily 9.30am–1pm & 3–6pm; ☎081.810.1968, ⓦwww.procida.it). For **getting around**, buses L1 and L2 connect Marina Grande with Chiaiolella roughly every twenty minutes and coincide with all ferry and hydrofoil arrivals; tickets cost €1.10 one-way and are sold on board. There's not much choice if you want to **stay** on the island: there are only a handful of hotels, together with a couple of *pensioni*. Note that at all places you *must* book in advance. Perhaps the nicest option, if your budget stretches to it, is *La Casa Sul Mare* at Via Salita Castello 13 (☎081.896.8799, ⓦwww.lacasasulmare.it; ⑥), in Terra Murata on the way to San Michele – rooms are simple, fresh and elegant and all have a seaview terrace. Alternatively, overlooking Chiaiolella, there is the *Riviera* hotel, ten-minutes' walk from the beach at Via G. de Procida 36 (☎081.896.7197, ⓦwww.hotelrivieraprocida.it; closed Oct–March; ❷) – the bus goes right by. The *Crescenzo*, at Via Marina Chiaiolella 33 (☎081.896.7255, ⓦwww.hotelcrescenzo.it; ❸), is a three-star with a fine *ristorante*-pizzeria. Or there's the *La Tonnara*, Via Marina Chiaiolella 51 ☎081.810.1052, ⓦwww.latonnarahotel.it; ⑥), which enjoys an enviable position right on the marina, as well as just metres away from the bridge crossing to the Vivara nature reserve, and whose fourteen luxury guestrooms all have panoramic sea views. For **camping**, the best bet is *Vivara* at Via IV Novembre 2 (☎081.896.9242; mid-June to mid-Sept), 30m from the sea, with caravans for rent and a bar; to get there, take the Marina Grande–Chiaiolella bus L1 and get off at Piazza Olmo. As regards **eating**, in Marina Grande, restaurants line the waterfront Via Roma: *La Medusa*, opposite the ferry terminal at no. 116 (☎081.896.7481; closed Tues), is not cheap but is very good, with great seafood house specialities of *pepata di cozze* and spaghetti with sea urchins. In Chiaiolella, there's *Il Galeone* (☎081.896.9622), right by the bus stop between the bay and the beach, with excellent pizzas and good fresh fish and seafood.

Inland Campania

As most people head to the coast, few visitors reach **inland Campania**. Indeed the territory immediately north of Naples, mostly a sprawl of unenticing suburbs is irredeemably grim. Almost entirely dominated by the Camorra it's offputtingly sometimes known as the "**Triangle of Death**". It's not an area to linger, and you'd do well to pass right through and not stop until you reach **Caserta** just beyond, where the vast royal palace and its gardens is an obvious draw. Further inland, **Benevento** has a historic centre well worth exploring.

Caserta and around

A short train or bus ride direct from Naples, **CASERTA**, incongruously surrounded by a sprawl of industrial complexes and warehouses that stretches all the way back to Naples, is known as the "Versailles of Naples" for its vast eighteenth-century **Palazzo Reale**, the only attraction in this otherwise completely nondescript modern town. Begun in 1752 for the Bourbon King Charles III to plans drawn up by Vanvitelli, and completed a little over twenty years later, it's an awesomely large complex, built around four courtyards, with a facade 245m long. However, it's a dull structure that generally substitutes size for inspiration. Only the majestic central staircases up to the **royal apartments** (Mon & Wed–Sun 8.30am–7.30pm; €4.20, €6 for apartments and gardens combined, ⓦwww.reggiadicastera.org) hit exactly the right note. The apartments themselves are a grand parade of heavily painted and stuccoed rooms, sparsely furnished in French Empire style, with great, overbearing classical statues and smug portraits of the Bourbon dynasty – look out for the one of the podgy Francis I with his brat-like children.

Behind the palace, the **gardens** (Mon & Wed–Sun: Jan, Feb, Nov & Dec 8.30am–2.30pm; March 8.30am–4pm; April 8.30am–5pm; May & Sept 8.30am–5.30pm; June, July & Aug 8.30am–6pm; Oct 8.30am–4.30pm; €2) are on no less huge a scale, stretching out behind along one central three-kilometre-long axis and punctured by myth-inspired fountains. The main promenade is longer than it looks from the palace (it's a good 30min walk or a short bicycle ride), and regular buses make the round trip, dropping you off at selected intervals along the way and turning round by the main cascade at the top, completed in 1779, which depicts Diana turning Actaeon into a stag. Walk to the top, look back at the palace, hop on a bus … and depart.

Santa Maria Cápua Vetere and Cápua

Regular buses run from Caserta, either from the bus/train station or the stop just to the left as you exit the palace, for the 7km to **SANTA MARIA CÁPUA VETERE** – a not especially pleasant journey past signs, petrol stations and run-down housing, but worth the trip to see this historic town. In its day this originally Etruscan, later Samnite, city, then known as Cápua, was the second city of Italy, centre of the rich and important region of Campania and famous for its skill in working bronze. Its first-century AD **amphitheatre** (Tues–Sun 9am to sunset; combined ticket with Mithraeum and Museo €2.50) was once the largest in Italy after the Colosseum, and a few very minimal parts of it remain on the far side of town, a right turn shortly after Piazza San Francesco d'Assisi. It held a reputed Roman gladiator school and barracks, and it was here that the gladiators' revolt, led by Spartacus, broke out in 73 BC – a revolt that was only put down after two years and four lost battles. The amphitheatre now is much less well preserved than the one in Pozzuoli, having lost almost all of its marble and its surrounding tiers – with many of the remaining ones having been concreted over. But the network of tunnels underneath survives reasonably intact, and is partly accessible. The **Mithraeum** – about twenty minutes on foot, down Via Anfiteatro and then left hidden away down Via Morelli – is one of the best preserved in the country and redolent with the bizarre bloodletting rites that accompanied the cult of Mithraism. It boasts a well-preserved fresco of Mithras himself in action. Ask for access at the **Museo Archeologico dell'Antica Cápua** at Via Roberto D'Angio 48 (Tues–Sun 9am–7pm; same ticket; to get here from the amphitheatre, cross the road, head left, then take the first right), most of whose rich collection of painted tombs survived bombing in the last war and are on display.

There are heaps of rubble and a handful of artefacts dotted around the amphitheatre, not least a large piece of mosaic, but most of the finds have made their way to nearby **CÁPUA**, to the excellent **Museo Provinciale Campano di Cápua** at Via Roma 68 (Tues–Sat 9am–1.30pm, Sun 9am–1pm; €5), sited on the broad curve of the Volturno River and a more attractive place than Santa Maria. The museum holds a fascinating collection of **Madri Dei** or **Matres Matutae** – formidable votive figures of women holding children, found in a nearby shrine to the Mater Matuta, an ancient Italic divinity. Early effigies have two or three children in their arms, while later Roman-era statues have twelve, deemed by the Romans to be the ideal number. The museum also contains remnants of statuary from the original Porta Federiciana, the "Gateway to the South" constructed in 1234 during the reign of Federico II, two towers of which can still be seen outside the town.

Benevento

Appealing **BENEVENTO**, reachable in about an hour and thirty minutes from Naples by bus or train (the private FBN line is quickest), was another important Roman settlement, a key point on the Via Appia between Rome and Bríndisi and as such a thriving trading town. Founded in 278 BC, it was at the time the farthest point from Rome to be colonized, and even now it has a remote air about it, circled by hills and with a centre that was (pointlessly) bombed to smithereens in the last war and even now seems only half rebuilt. Its climate also ranks among southern Italy's most extreme.

Buses from Naples drop you in a large parking lot, where you'll also find the **tourist office** on the corner of Via Sandro Bertini (daily 9am–1pm & 3.30–7.30pm; ☎0824.28.180), and from where Via Rettori heads to the principal Piazza IV Novembre. From here the main street, **Corso Garibaldi**, is pedestrian-only and leads off to the right. The first significant sight is the excellent **Museo Sannio** (Tues–Sun 9am–1pm; €4), in the cloister behind the eighth-century church of Santa Sofia, which holds a good selection of Roman finds from the local area, including a number of artefacts from a temple of Isis – various sphinxes, bulls and a headless statue of Isis herself. There are also terracotta votive figurines from the fifth century BC, and the cloister itself has capitals carved with energetic scenes of animals, humans and strange beasts, hunting, riding and attacking. Further along Corso Garibaldi, off to the right, the **Arch of Trajan** is the major remnant of the Roman era, a marvellously preserved triumphal arch boasting much more distinct images than Rome's arches, and you can get close enough to study its friezes. Built to guard the entrance to Benevento from the Appian Way, it's actually as heavy-handed a piece of self-acclaim as there ever was, showing the Emperor Trajan in various scenes of triumph, power and generosity. Farther down, the city's **Duomo** is an almost total reconstruction of its thirteenth-century Romanesque original; what's left of its famous bronze doors, believed to be Byzantine, is now stashed inside.

There are more bits and pieces from Roman times scattered around the rather battered but picturesque old quarter of town, the **Triggio** – reached by following Via Carlo Torre off to the left of the main road beyond the cathedral. The **Bue Apis**, at the far end of Corso Dante, is another relic from the temple of Isis, a first-century BC sculpture of a bull. And in the heart of the old quarter there are the substantial remains of a **Teatro Romano** (daily 9am to sunset; €2), built during the reign of Hadrian. In Hadrian's time it seated 20,000 people; it seats rather fewer today, but it's still an atmospheric sight – looking out over the green rolling countryside of the province beyond and Benevento, relatively unvisited by tourists.

The Amalfi Coast

Occupying the southern side of Sorrento's peninsula, the **Amalfi Coast** (Costiera Amalfitana) lays claim to being Europe's most beautiful stretch of coast, its corniche road winding around the towering cliffs that slip almost sheer into the sea. By car or bus it's an incredible ride (though it can get mighty congested in summer), with some of the most spectacular stretches between Salerno and Amalfi. If you're staying in Sorrento especially it shouldn't be missed on any account; in any case the towns along here hold the beaches that Sorrento lacks. The coast as a whole has become rather developed, and these days it's in fact one of Italy's ritzier bits of shoreline, villas atop its precarious slopes fetching a bomb in both cash and kudos. While it's home to some stunning hotels, budget travellers should be aware that you certainly get what you pay for here.

Coming **from Sorrento**, buses normally join the coast road a little way **west of Positano**. If the coast road is closed, however, which it is from time to time due to landslides and forest fires, the bus from Sorrento will take the alternative route, via Castellammare and Agerola, right over the backbone of the Sorrentine peninsula, which is itself a journey worth making – the bus zigzagging down the other side in a crazy helter-skelter of hairpin bends to join the road a few kilometres **west of Amalfi**.

Positano

There's not much to **POSITANO**, only a couple of decent beaches and a great many boutiques; the town has long specialized in clothes made from linen, georgette and cotton, as well as handmade shoes and sandals. But its location, heaped up in a pyramid high above the water, has inspired a thousand postcards and helped to make it a moneyed resort that runs a close second to Cápri in the celebrity stakes. Since John Steinbeck wrote up the place in glowing terms back in 1953, the town has enjoyed a fame quite out of proportion to its size. Franco Zefferelli is just one of many famous names who have villas nearby, and the people who come here to lie on the beach consider themselves a cut above your average sun-worshipper.

Arrival and information

Buses stop at various points along the main coastal road – Viale G.Marconi – which skirts the top of the Old Town of Positano: there's a stop on the Amalfi side of town, from where it's a steep walk down or a short bus ride to the little square at the bottom end of Via Cristoforo Colombo, five-minutes' walk from the seafront; or you could get off on the other side of the centre by the

Internazionale, from where Viale Pasitea winds down to the Fornillo part of own. **Ferries** and **hydrofoils** from Cápri, Naples, Amalfi and Salerno pull in at the jetty just to the right of the main beach where there are also plenty of ticket booths. Arriving by car you'll shell out a lot on garage space – up to €4 an hour – as parking is very limited. There's a busy **tourist office** just back from the beach by the church steps at Via del Saracino 4 (June–Oct Mon–Sat 8.30am–8pm; Nov–May Mon–Fri 8.30am–3pm; ℡089.875.067, ⓦwww .aziendaturismopositano.it).

Accommodation

Hostel Brikette Via G. Marconi 358 ℡089.875.857, ⓦwww.brikette.com. A couple of minutes' walk from the bus stop at the *Bar Internazionale* on the main coastal road, this is by far the cheapest accommodation option in Positano. It's friendly and clean, with stunning Mediterranean views, bar and internet access, but the dorms are a bit spartan and airless – you"ll pay €22 for a bed in a twenty-bed dorm, €25 in an eight-bed dorm.
Il San Pietro di Positano Via Laurito 2 ℡089.875.455, ⓦwww.ilsanpietro.it. If money is truly no object, head a bit south of town on the corniche road. This is the area's most luxurious hotel, built down a rocky cliff face with plush, individually designed rooms and suites, fresh flowers, private beach and tennis court, and its own kitchen garden. Not to mention the breath-taking views. ❾
Maria Luisa Via Fornillo 42 ℡089.875.023, ⓦwww.pensionemarialuisa.com. Very friendly, and great value though of course it's quite a climb down to the beach and back. Closed Jan & Dec. ❸

🏃 **Palazzo Murat** Via dei Mulini 23 ℡089.875.177, ⓦwww.palazzomurat.it. Perhaps the nicest place to stay if you want to be right in the heart of things, just 2min from the main beach, and with thirty good-sized and well-equipped rooms – though most of them are not in the old *palazzo* itself but in the newer extension. ❽
Pupetto Via Fornillo 37 ℡089.875.087, ⓦwww .hotelpupetto.it. Right on Fornillo beach and with access for guests, this bright spot offers a huge terrace and pastel rooms with sea views. Full-range restaurant, from wood-fired pizza to catch of the day. ❻
🏃 **Villa Verde** Viale Pasitea 338 ℡089.875.506, ⓦwww.pensionevillaverde .it. Just below the main road through town, this place is friendly, very relaxed, and its fourteen good-sized rooms all have a/c and TV, and their balconies overlook central Positano from a wonderfully peaceful vantage point. Excellent value. ❸

The Town

Positano is, of course, expensive, but its beaches are nice enough and don't get too crowded. The main beach, the **Spiaggia Grande** right in front of the village, is reasonable, although you'll be sunbathing among the fishing boats unless you want to pay over the odds for the pleasanter bit on the far left. There's also another, larger stretch of beach, **Spiaggia del Fornillo**, around the headland to the west, accessible in five minutes by a pretty path that winds around from above the hydrofoil jetty – although its main section is also a pay area. Nonetheless the bar-terrace of the *Pupetto* hotel (see above), which runs along much of its length, is a cheaper place to eat and drink than anywhere in Positano proper.

Eating and drinking

Bruno Via C. Colombo 157 ℡089.875.392. A little bit distanced from the more touristy places near the beach, both in distance and in price, but the food is good, and well-priced.
La Cambusa Piazza Vespucci 4 ℡089.875.432. One of the fanciest options near the seafront just

back from the Spiagia Grande on the left, It's unashamedly a tourist hangout but its fish and seafood options are pretty good, and it's a fine place to watch the self-regarding Positano world go by. Closed Tues.

Lo Guarracino Via Positanesi d'America 12
⊤089.875.794. Great food, relatively reasonably priced, and wonderful views from a bright, flower-fringed terrace overlooking the sea and Fornillo beach.

O Capurale Via Regina Giovanna 12 ⊤081.811. Just around the corner from *La Cambusa*, this place has been around for over a century and feels like it, with a nicely painted fish-themed ceiling and really good fish-dominated menu.

Praiano and the Grotta dello Smeraldo

Around 6km east of Positano, **PRAIANO** is much smaller and very much quieter than its more renowned neighbour, and as such you might be tempted to stay here instead. It consists of two tiny centres: Véttica Maggiore, which is Praiano proper, scattered along the main road from Positano high above the sea; and Marina di Praiano squeezed into a cleft in the rock down at shore level, a couple of kilometres further along towards Amalfi.

There's not much to either bit of the village, but it does make a more peaceful and quite frankly more authentic place to stay than Positano. There's nothing whatsoever to see, but there are a few decent places to swim. The closest are the swimming spots off rocks down immediately below the village, most notably **Spiaggia Gavitella** which you can reach from the main road by taking the path from the *San Gennaro* restaurant or from the Smeraldo hotel; there's also the small patch of shingly beach at **Marina di Praia**, surrounded by a couple of restaurants and places offering rooms. And there are some decent, properly sandy spots beyond Marina di Praia on the way to Amalfi (see below for more on these).

Accommodation

Casa Angelina Via Caprigilione 147
⊤089.813.1333, ⓦwww.casangelina.com. Newish boutique hotel that is the cool person's choice in Praiano, with a lobby full of contemporary art and a selection of rooms decorated with stark modern white minimalism. ❾

Continental Via Roma 21 ⊤089.874.084, ⓦwww.continental.praiano.it. Right by the bus stop on the main road above Marina di Praia, this is one of the best choices along this stretch of coast, a converted old *palazzo* plus a series of chalet rooms and even a campsite, *La Tranquillità* (⊤089.874.084; closed Nov–April). ❸

Costa Diva Via Roma 12 ⊤089.813.076, ⓦwww.locandacostadiva.it. Up above

Marina di Praia, this hotel spills down a lovely, leafy series of terraces from the road; all rooms have sea views and balconies. ❹, ❺ in July & Aug.

Il Pino Via Caprigilione 13 ⊤089.874.389, ⓦwww.hotelpino.it. This hotel's neat, modern and well-equipped rooms are bang on the main road in the centre of Praiano and has double rooms – all with balcony and sea view. ❹, ❺ in July & Aug.

Onda Verde Via Terramare 3 ⊤089.874.143, ⓦwww.ondaverde.it. Extremely well placed, perched on the cliff edge at Marina di Praiano, this lovely hotel has a great location, very nice rooms and even does cooking classes. ❻

Eating and drinking

La Brace opposite the *Tramonto d'Oro* hotel
⊤089.874.226. Excellent pizzas straight from the wood-fired oven and great, very fresh fish which you can eat on the covered terrace. Closed Tues Oct–March.

Trattoria San Gennaro next to the church
⊤089.874.293. As central as you get in Praiano,

and serving huge portions of *antipasto di mare* and *primi* like *scialatilli con zucchine e gamberetti* (home-made pasta with courgettes and prawns) for €8. Closed Thurs.

dello Smeraldo

out of Praiano, the **Grotta dello Smeraldo** (daily: March–Oct Nov–Feb 10am–4pm; €5) is one of the most highly touted local es around here, a flooded cavern in which the sunlight turns the shade of green. You can reach it by taxi boat from either Praiano or Amalfi (tickets cost about €10 return, plus the entrance fee), but more cheaply there's a bus stop nearby and car parking, too, if you have your own vehicle. Arriving by boat leaves you at grotto level, whereas by road you have to take the lift down to the grotto, which you then tour by boat. It's not unimpressive, but is basically one huge chamber and it doesn't take long for the boatman to whisk you around the main features, best of which is the intense colour of the water, and the stalagmites and stalactites that puncture and drip from every surface.

Amalfi

Set in a wide cleft in the cliffs, **AMALFI**, a mere 4km or so further east, is the largest town and perhaps the highlight of the coast, and a good place to base yourself. It has been an established seaside resort since Edwardian times, when the British upper classes found the town a pleasant spot to spend their winters. Actually Amalfi's credentials go back much further: it was an independent republic during Byzantine times and one of the great naval powers, with a population of some 70,000; Webster's *Duchess of Malfi* was set here, and the city's traders established outposts all over the Mediterranean, setting up the Order of the Knights of St John of Jerusalem. Amalfi was finally vanquished by the Normans in 1131, and the town was devastated by an earthquake in 1343, but there is still the odd remnant of Amalfi's past glories around today, and the town has a crumbly attractiveness to its whitewashed courtyards and alleys that makes it fun to wander through.

Arrival and information

Amalfi's most immediate focus is the seafront, a humming, cheerfully vigorous strand given over to street stalls, a car park for the town's considerable tourist traffic, and an acceptably crowded **beach**, although once again the best bits are pay areas only. The **tourist office**, at Corso Roma 19 (Mon–Fri 8am–1.30pm & 3–5pm, Sat 8am–1pm; ☎089.871.107, ⓦwww.amalfitouristoffice.it), is situated in the courtyard next to the **post office** in Corso Repubblica Marinara, the road that runs along the waterfront. **Ferries** and **hydrofoils** to Salerno, Positano, Cápri and Ischia leave from the landing stages in the tiny harbour, buses from just in front.

Accommodation

Centrale Largo Piccolomini 1 ☎089.872.608, ⓦwww.amalfihotelcentrale.it. An excellent location, and a better choice than the dowdier *Sant'Andrea* – see below – with good-sized and pleasantly furnished rooms, including TV, telephone, a/c and breakfast, eaten from the hotel's lovely roof terrace. ❸

Lidomare Via Piccolomini 9 ☎089.871.332, ⓦwww.lidomare.it. Tucked away off to the left of Piazza Duomo, this is perhaps the most characterful of Amalfi's central cheapies, a beautiful, family-run ex-Ducal palace, nicely old-fashioned and full of antiques. Most of the rooms are lovely and large, and over half of them face the sea. ❹

If you're on a tight budget you could either stay in the adjacent village of **Atrani** – see p.829 – or opt for the cosy **youth hostel** *Beata Solitudo*, located at Piazza Avitabile 4 in Agerola, 16km north of Amalfi (℡081.802.5048, ⓦwww.beatasolitudo.it; dorm beds €11.50, 2–5-person bungalows €50–90; double rooms ❷), which has really nice private rooms with TVs and en-suite facilities as well as a small **campsite** with a few bungalows. Regular buses run between Agerola and Amalfi.

Luna Convento Via Pantaleone Comite 33 ℡089.871.002, ⓦwww.lunahotel.it. On the main road running east out of Amalfi, this is a lovely five-star hotel housed in a former convent dating from 1200, with individual rooms, some of which have been fashioned from cells. The rooms vary quite a bit, but the cloister, where you can sip your aperitif, or just while away the hours wondering how the other half of Amalfi lives, is delightful. ❾

Residenza della Duca Via Mastalo del Duca 3 ℡089.873.6365, ⓦwww .residenzadelduca.it. Tiny *pensione* tucked away at the top of a building amongst the alleys and tiny courtyards off to the left of Amalfi's main street – take a left just past *Trattoria Gemma* and then a right and you're there. All rooms have bathrooms with Jacuzzi-style showers and flat-screen TVs,

telephone and a/c, and breakfast is included in the price. ❹

Sant'Andrea Via San Camera 1 ℡089.871.145. This small hotel, stuffed full of pictures and ornaments, couldn't be more centrally placed, and its plain but decent rooms are well priced, with private bath, and including TV, telephone and a/c. Breakfast, though, is extra. ❷

Santa Caterina Via Maura Comite 9 ℡089.871.012, ⓦwww.hotelsantacaterina.it. A kilometre west of town right on the coast road, this elegant villa with period furnishings is probably Amalfi's best hotel, and very much the celebrity choice, but also still family-owned and run. There's a seawater pool and small spa and fitness centre, and rocks to swim from, all accessible by a lift which plummets down from the bougainvillea-wreathed terrace. Rooms in high season start at around €400. ❾

The Town

The **Duomo** (daily: summer 9am–9pm; winter 10am–5pm; €5 for cloister & museum), at the top of a steep flight of steps, utterly dominates the town's main piazza, its tiered, almost gaudy facade topped by a glazed tiled cupola that's typical of the area. The bronze doors of the church came from Constantinople and date from 1066. Inside it's a mixture of Saracen and Romanesque styles, though now heavily restored, and the cloister – the so-called **Chiostro del Paradiso** – is the most appealing part of the building, oddly Arabic in feel with its whitewashed arches and palms. The adjacent **museum**, housed in an ancient bare basilica, dates back to the sixth century and has various medieval and episcopal treasures, most intriguingly an eighteenth-century sedan chair from Macau, used by the bishop of Amalfi, a thirteenth-century mitre sewn with myriad seed pearls and a lovely fourteenth-century bone and ebony inlaid box, made by the renowned Embriarchi studio in Venice. Steps lead down from the museum to the heavily decorated **crypt**, where the remains of the apostle St Andrew lie under the altar, brought here (minus head) from Constantinople by the Knights of Malta in 1204.

Turn left at the bottom of the cathedral steps and then left again up some steps just before the Pansa bakery, and a narrow, partly covered passage takes you through to Piazza Municipio, where the small **Museo Civico** (Mon–Fri 8.30am–1.30pm, Tues–Thurs also 4.30–6.30pm; free), part of the Municipio, has the original paintings of the 12 apostles that you can view in mosaic on the cathedral's facade and the *Tavoliere Amalfitana*, the book of maritime laws that governed the republic, and the rest of the Mediterranean until 1570. Further along the waterfront, the old **Arsenale** is a reminder of the military might of the Amalfi republic, and its ancient vaulted interior now hosts art exhibitions and suchlike.

▲ The beach at Amalfi

In the opposite direction from the cathedral you can follow the main street of **Via Genova** up through the heart of Amalfi and out the other side, to where the town peters out and the gorge narrows into the **Valle dei Mulini** (Valley of Mills), once the centre of Amalfi's high-quality paper industry. The **Museo delle Carte** (daily 10am–6.30pm; €3.50; ⓦ www.museodellacarta.it) is not an essential stop by any means but it is the only dynamic remnant of the industry, housed in a mill that dates back to 1350 and claims to be the oldest in Europe. If you're feeling energetic you can do a walk that takes you right up into the heart of the valley, past some of the remains of the mills which sit by the river in charming dereliction,

Eating and drinking

Da Meme Salita Marino Sebaste 8 ☎089.830.4549. Decent pasta dishes from €6, pizzas for €4 and good-vaiue fish priced at €8 upwards, and you get to eat dinner in the vaulted interior of this former monastery, or outside among the white vaulted passageways of old Amalfi.

Il Mulino Via della Cartiere 36 ☎089.872.223. At the top of the main street, 10min walk from the Duomo, this is a cheery family-run place that does good home-made *pasta alla pescatora* for around €8. Closed Mon.

La Caravella Via Mateo Camera 12
℡089.871.029. One of the town's posher options for a night out, or when you're tired of same old offerings everywhere else. They serve great, individual takes on traditional dishes, all put together with fresh local ingredients – a cut above the rest in price as well as tone. Open daily noon–2.30pm & 7.15–10.30pm; closed Tues.

Maccus Largo S. Maria Maggiore 13
℡089.873.6385. Good, reasonably priced food that maks the most of this atmospheric little square. Daily noon–3pm & 7–10.30pm.

San Guiseppe Via Ruggiero 4, no phone. Left off the main street by *Trattoria Gemma* and then right, this very simple restaurant puts a few tables out on a tiny courtyard and serves excellent pizzas and pretty much everything else at low prices – great value.

Taverna degli Apostoli Supportivo Sant' Andrea 6 ℡089.872.991. Because of its location bang next to the cathedral steps, most people assume this is just another tourist joint. But its relatively small menu chalked on the blackboard outside is a good indication that it's not. Good food and a warm welcome.

Trattoria da Gemma Via Frá Gerardo Sasso 11
℡089.871.345. A stalwart of the Amalfi restaurant scene, and still one of the best and most atmospheric places to eat in town, with a small, carefully considered menu, strong on fish and seafood with mains at around €25, and a lovely terrace overlooking the main street. Closed Wed.

Atrani

A short walk around the headland (take the path off to the right just before the tunnel through the *Zaccaria* restaurant), **ATRANI** is an extension of Amalfi really, and was indeed another part of the maritime republic, with a similarly styled church sporting another set of bronze doors from Constantinople, manufactured in 1086. It's a quiet place, which benefits from all the attention bestowed on its neighbour, with a pretty, almost entirely enclosed little square, Piazza Umberto, giving onto a usually gloriously peaceful (and free) patch of sandy **beach** – hard to believe the bustle of Amalfi is just around the corner.

Another good reason for coming here is that it has a great **place to stay** in the *A'Scalinatella*, Piazza Umberto 1 (℡089.871.492, ⑩www.hostelscalinatella .com), hostel and hotel – a friendly, family-run establishment that offers dorm beds for €21–25 per person and private rooms with bath for around €40 per person in various different buildings around town. The two principal **bars** on Atrani's main square, *Birecto* and *Risacca*, host quite a scene, vying for the custom of young travellers from the *Scalinatella* hostel. Our favourite is Luigi's *Birecto*, which has reasonably priced drinks, decent pizzas and other food, and free internet access on their tabletop laptops, but *Risacca* offers much the same. For more formal **eating**, try *A'Paranza*, on the road that leads inland from the main square at Traversa Dragone 2 (℡089.811.840; closed Tues), a friendly seafood trattoria with fabulous home-made pasta and a speciality of *zuppa di pesce*. Le Arcate (℡089.871.367; closed Mon) right by the beach, hogs the best location in Atrani (or indeed Amalfi), and serves pizza and a good range of seafood pasta dishes.

Ravello

The best views of the coast can be had inland, high above Amalfi in **RAVELLO**: another renowned spot "closer to the sky than the seashore", wrote André Gide – with some justification. Ravello was also an independent republic for a while, and for a time an outpost of the Amalfi city-state. Now it's not much more than a large village, but its unrivalled location, spread across the top of one of the coast's mountains, makes it more than worth the thirty-minute bus ride through the steeply cultivated terraces up from Amalfi – although, like most of this coast, the charms of Ravello haven't been recently discovered. Wagner set part of *Parsifal*, one of his last operas, in the place; D.H. Lawrence wrote some of *Lady Chatterley's Lover* here; John Huston filmed his languid movie *Beat the Devil* in town; and more recently the writer and political polemicist Gore Vidal lived here for many years.

Arrival and information

Small orange SITA buses run up to Ravello from Amalfi roughly hourly from Piazza Flavio Gioià. If you can't tear yourself away, the **tourist office** is two minutes from the main square, off Via Roma (Mon–Sat: May–Sept 9am–8pm; Oct–April 9am–7pm; ☎089.857.096, ⊛www.ravello.it/aziendaturismo) and has information on **rooms**. There's a useful **car park** that often has space just below the main square.

Accommodation

Garden Via Boccaccio 4 ☎089.857.226, ⊛www .hotelgardenravello.it. Just the other side of the tunnel from central Ravello this small hotel and restaurant occupies a prime spot looking up the coast, and makes the most of it with a large airy lobby and ten rooms that all have sea views. The rooms aren't huge but they have small terraces and are well kept and well-equipped, and the views are great. ❹

Palazzo della Marra Via della Marra 3 ☎089.858.302, ⊛www.palazzodellamarra.com. Very central, and with a nice restaurant (see opposite), this is perhaps the cheapest place to stay in Ravello though they only have four rooms. ❸

Toro Via Roma 16 ☎089.857.211, ⊛www .hoteltoro.it. In about as central a location as you can get in Ravello, just off the main piazza, the ten good-sized rooms here vary quite a bit in size but are tastefully furnished and in any case feel cool and peaceful compared to the touristy hubbub outside. Rooms include breakfast, and have TV and telephone but no a/c. ❹

Villa Amore Via dei Fusco 5 ☎089.857.135, ⊛www.villaamore.it. Down a short path off the main route between the centre of Ravello and the Villa Cimbrone, the rooms here are nothing special but some of them enjoy the best views in town – quite something by Ravello standards. There's a small and peaceful garden, and a restaurant that uses organic ingredients from the hotel's own garden. The drawback is that you have carry your luggage from the nearest parking 10min walk away back on the main piazza – or pay €5 per piece for the hotel to do it for you. ❸

Villa Maria Via Santa Chiara 2 ☎089.857.255, ⊛www.villamaria.it. A lovely old-fashioned hotel situated 5min from the centre of Ravello on the way to Villa Cimbrone. It's not especially cheap, but the rooms have all facilities, including a/c and satellite TV, and rates include free parking and a pool at the nearby co-owned Giordano as well as the all-important trafficking of your luggage. ❼

The Town

Everything in Ravello revolves around the main **Piazza Duomo**, where the **Duomo**, a bright eleventh-century church, renovated in 1786, is dedicated to St Pantaleone, a fourth-century saint whose blood – kept in a chapel on the left-hand side – is supposed to liquefy (like Naples' San Gennaro and others) once a year on July 27. It's a richly decorated church, with a pair of twelfth-century bronze doors, cast with 54 scenes of the Passion; inside, there are two monumental thirteenth-century ambones (pulpits), both wonderfully adorned with intricate and glittering mosaics. The more elaborate one to the right of the altar, dated 1272, sports dragons and birds on spiral columns supported by six roaring lions, while the one on the left illustrates the story of Jonah and the whale. Downstairs in the crypt the **museo** (daily 9am–7pm; €2) holds the superb bust of Sigilgaita Rufolo and the silver reliquary of Saint Barbara, alongside a collection of highly decorative, fluid mosaic and marble reliefs from the same era.

The Rufolos figure again on the other side of the square, where various left-overs of their **Villa Rufolo** (daily: June–Sept 9am–9pm; Oct–May 9am–6pm; €6)

lie scattered among rich gardens overlooking the precipitous co
the spectacular main venue for the prestigious open-air chamber
from March to October. The programme is widely advertised ar
€20 (details from the Ravello Concert Society ⊤089.858
.ravelloarts.org). If the crowds (best avoided by coming early in
put you off, turn left by the entrance and walk up the steps over
the best (free) view over the shore, from where it's a pleasant stroll through the
back end of Ravello to the main square. Alternatively, walk in the opposite
direction for ten minutes to the **Villa Cimbrone** (daily 9am to sunset; €6),
whose formal gardens spread across the furthest tip of Ravello's ridge. Most of
the villa itself is now a luxury hotel but you can peep into the flower-hung
cloister and crypt as you go in, and the gardens are dotted with statues and little
temples and lead down to what must be the most gorgeous spot in Ravello – a
belvedere that looks over Atrani below and the sea beyond.

Eating and drinking

Cumpa Cosimo Via Roma 48
⊤089.857.988. Great local food, home-made pasta and wine at moderate prices in the heart of Ravello – though there are no views or outside seating.

Da Salvatore Via della Repubblica 2
⊤089.857.227. In business for just over fifty years, *Salvatore* has fantastic views from both the interior restaurant and outside terrace, and a refreshingly different menu from many of the other places in town. It's not Ravello's cheapest choice,

but not horrendous either; plus, if you want to spend less money and still enjoy the view you can eat in their simpler downstairs pizzeria which does starters and pizzas only in the eve.

Figli di Papa Via della Marra 7 ⊤089.858.302. Housed in the small *Palazzo Marra pensione*, just off the main square, the menu here is varied and well-priced, with a reasonable selection of non-fish options. You can eat outside on their terrace (no views) or in the high vaulted rooms inside. Closed Tues Nov–March.

Salerno

Capital of Campania's southernmost province, the lively port of **SALERNO**
is much less chaotic than Naples and is well off most travellers' itineraries,
giving it a pleasant, relaxed air. It has a good supply of cheap accommodation,
which makes it a reasonable base for some of the closer resorts of the Amalfi
coast and for the ancient site of Paestum to the south. During medieval times
the town's medical school was the most eminent in Europe; more recently, it
was the site of the Allied landing of September 9, 1943 – a landing that reduced
much of the centre to rubble. The subsequent rebuilding has restored neither
charm nor efficiency to the town centre, which is an odd mixture of wide,
rather characterless boulevards and a small medieval core full of intriguingly
dark corners and alleys. It is, however, a lively, sociable place, with a busy
seafront boulevard and plenty of nightlife and shops.

Arrival, information and accommodation

Salerno's **train station** lies at the southern end of the town centre on Piazza
Vittorio Veneto. City and local **buses** pull up here; those from Paestum and
further south arrive and leave from Piazza della Concordia, down by the waterside
nearby; buses from Naples use the SITA bus station at Corso Garibaldi 119.
Ferries and **hydrofoils** from Amalfi, Cápri and Positano arrive in the harbour.
 For information, there are two **tourist offices**: one right in front of the station
on the corner of Piazza Vittorio Veneto and Corso Garibaldi (Mon–Fri 9am–2pm

–8pm, Sat 9am–1pm & 3.30–7.30pm; ☎089.230.411); and another, slightly
more helpful one on the seafront at Lungomare Trieste 7/9 (Mon–Fri 9am–2pm
& 3–8pm, Sat & Sun 9am–noon; ☎089.224.744). The town isn't chock-full of
hotels: the comfortable *Plaza*, Piazza Vittorio Veneto 42 (☎089.224.477, ⓦwww
.plazasalerno.it;❸), is a decent choice and handy for transport and the town centre;
and, a few yards away, the friendly if fairly basic *Santa Rosa pensione* on the second
floor at Corso V. Emanuele 16 (☎&ⓕ089.225.346;❷), provides a cheaper alternative. There's also the *Ave Gratia Plena* official HI **youth hostel**, the other side of
the centre on Via dei Canali (☎089.234.776, ⓦwww.ostellodisalerno.it), a clean
and welcoming place with both dorm beds (€15) and doubles (❶) in a former
church and cloister complex – follow Via Mercanti to its end, continue under the
arch onto Via Dogana and Via dei Canali is on the right.

The Town

There isn't a great deal to see in Salerno, but it's pleasant to wander through the
vibrant streets of the centre, especially the ramshackle old medieval quarter,
which starts at the far end of the pedestrianized main shopping drag of **Corso
V. Emanuele**. The old quarter's main street is **Via Mercanti**, and it's been
spruced up quite a lot over recent years. Part of the makeover is the **Pinacoteca
Provinciale di Salerno**, housed in the seventeenth-century Palazzo Pinto at
Via Mercanti 63 (Tues–Sun 9am–7.45pm; free) – half a dozen rooms, basically,
displaying one or two nice fifteenth-century altarpieces and a couple of works
by Carlo Rosa and other Neapolitan Baroque artists. Off to the right of
Via dei Mercanti, up Via Duomo, the **Duomo** (Mon–Sat 10am–6.30pm, Sun
1–6.30pm) is Salerno's highlight, an enormous church built in 1076 by Robert
Guiscard and dedicated to St Matthew. Entrance is through a cool and shady
courtyard, built with columns plundered from Paestum, and centring on a
gently gurgling fountain set in an equally ancient bowl. In the heavily restored
interior, the two elegant mosaic pulpits are the highlight, the one on the left
dating from 1173, the other, with its matching paschal candlesticks, a century
later. Immediately behind there's more sumptuous mosaic work in the screens
of the choir, as well as the quietly expressive fifteenth-century tomb of Margaret
of Anjou, wife of Charles III of Durazzo, in the left aisle. To the left of the tomb,
steps lead down to the polychrome marble crypt, which holds the body of
St Matthew himself, brought here in the tenth century.

From the cathedral, turn right at the bottom of the steps for the **Museo
Diocesano** (daily 9.30am–12.30pm & 3–6.30pm; free), where there's only one
thing to see – a large eleventh-century altar-front, embellished with ivory panels,
69 in all, depicting Biblical scenes, which claims to be the largest work of its kind
in the world. Failing that, turn left out of the church, left at the bottom of the steps,
left again and then first right, and 100m or so further on is the **Museo Provinciale** (Tues–Sun 9am–7.45pm; free), which occupies two floors of an restored
Romanesque palace. It's full of local archeological finds, and has an array of terracotta heads and votive figurines, lots of jewellery and lamps and household objects,
from Etruscan as well as Roman times, but its most alluring piece is a sensual *Head
of Apollo* upstairs, a Roman bronze fished from the Gulf of Salerno in the 1930s.

After the cathedral, Salerno's most interesting attraction is the **Giardini della
Minerva** on Via Ferrante Sanseverino (Tues–Sun; summer 9am–1pm & 5–9pm;
winter 9am–1.30pm, Mon 3–6pm; free), a medicinal garden laid out according
medieval medical principles and traversed by channels of tinkling water. It's a gloriously fragrant place, its shady terraces wonderfully soothing in summer, and there's
even a café serving herbal tea to ensure you leave healthier than you arrived.

Eating and drinking

Salerno is a sociable place, and while it's not a tourist town there are plenty of good places to **eat and drink**. The *Hostaria Il Brigante*, just above the cathedral at Via Fratelli Linguiti 4 (℡089.226.592), is a great, old-fashioned *osteria* near the Duomo with mains at around €10 – try its *zuppa dell'aglio* and *calamarata* pasta dishes. The *Antica Pizzeria Vicolo delle Neve*, a left turn off Via Mercanti about 50m past the Duomo, is a deliciously downbeat place serving pizzas and local specialities, with a particularly good *calzone* (℡089.225.705; closed Wed & lunchtimes), while a block further on *Trattoria Peppe 'A Seccia*, Via Antica Corte 5 (℡089.220.518; closed Mon), has tables outside on its small square and serves decent local food at reasonable prices – good fish and seafood, including *zuppa di cozze*.

Paestum

About an hour's bus ride south of Salerno, the ancient site of **Paestum** (daily 9am to 1hr before sunset; €4, €6.50 for site plus museum) spreads across a large area at the bottom end of the **Piana del Sele** – a wide, flat plain grazed by the buffalo that produce a good quantity of southern Italy's mozzarella cheese. Paestum, or Poseidonia as it was known, was founded by Greeks from Sybaris in the sixth century BC, and later, in 273 BC, colonized by the Romans, who Latinized the name. But by the ninth century a combination of malaria and Saracen raids had decimated the population and left the buildings deserted and gradually overtaken by thick forest – the site wasn't rediscovered until the eighteenth century during the building of a road through here. It's a desolate, open place even now ("inexpressibly grand", Shelley called it), mostly unrecognizable ruin but with three golden-stoned **temples** that are among the best-preserved Doric temples in Europe. Of these, the Temple of Neptune, dating from about 450 BC, is the most complete, with only its roof and parts of the inner walls missing. The Basilica of Hera, built a century or so earlier, retains its double rows of columns, while the Temple of Ceres at the northern end of the site was used as a Christian church for a time. In between, the forum is little more than an open space, and the buildings around are mere foundations.

The splendid **museum** (daily 9am–7pm; closed first and third Mon every month; €4, €6.50 including site), across the road, holds Greek and Roman finds from the site and around. Straight ahead of you as you enter are some stunning sixth-century bronze vases (*hydriae*), decorated with rams, lions and sphinxes; behind them more bronze – gleaming helmets, breastplates and greaves. Make a point of seeing the rare Greek tomb paintings, the best of which are from the Tomb of the Diver, graceful and expressively naturalistic pieces of work, including a diver in mid-plunge, said to represent the passage from life to death, and male lovers banqueting. Attractive fourth-century terracotta plates depict all sorts of comestibles – fruit, sweets, fruit and cheese, and a set of weathered archaic period Greek metopes from another temple at the mouth of the Sele River, a few kilometres north, shows scenes of fighting and hunting. On the first floor, which is devoted to Roman finds, highlights are a statue of an abstracted-looking Pan with his pipes, a third-century relief showing a baby in pointed hat and amulets, and a sarcophagus cover of a tenderly embracing couple.

Practicalities

It's perfectly feasible to see Paestum on a day-trip from either Salerno or Agrópoli. CSTP bus #34 runs between Salerno train station and Agropoli, stopping off at Paestum on the way; it takes 55 minutes from Salerno, and fifteen minutes from Agrópoli, to reach Paestum.

You can also stay in one of the many hotels or campsites that are strewn along the sandy shore beyond the site. The **tourist office** tucked away on a side street to the left of the museum at Via Magna Grecia 887 (Mon–Sat 9am–1pm & 3–7pm, closes 5pm in winter, Sun 9am–1pm; ☎0828.811.016, ⓦwww.infopaestum .it) has details. For **hotels** just walk down to the beach (about 15min) and take your pick: close to the site to the left of where the main road hits the beach is *Calypso*, Via Mantegna 63 (☎0828.811.031, ⓦwww.calypsohotel.com; ❹), one of the few hotels around that can cope with vegan, macrobiotic and organic diets (with traditional food as well). The cheerful and very good-value *Baia del Sole*, Via Torre di Mare 48 (☎0828.811.119, ⓦwww.baiadelsolepaestum.it; ❷), is also a rarity in that it does not require half board in high season and has a nice garden. If you prefer to be a little more secluded try *Villa Rita* at Via Nettuno 9 (☎0828.811.081, ⓦwww.hotelvillarita.it; ❸), which is pleasantly situated in relaxing gardens with a pool just south of the archeological site.

There's some excellent **food** in the area, with the locally produced buffalo mozzarella featuring heavily on menus of most of the **restaurants**. Try the excellent *Nettuno* on Via Principe di Piemonte (☎0828.811.028) in an old building right by the temples, where the house speciality is crepes with buffalo mozzarella, or the more intimate and upmarket *Enoteca Tavernelle*, Via Tavernelle 14 (☎0828.722.440), about 1km out on the Salerno road.

The Cilento coast

Immediately south of Paestum, the coastline bulges out into a broad mountainous hump of territory known as the **Cilento** – one of the remotest parts of Campania. **AGRÓPOLI**, the first town you reach, fifteen minutes out from Paestum and on the main Salerno–Reggio railway line, is a good base for the ruins (buses every hour), and its blend of the peaceful old quarter, heaped on a headland, and the new modern centre down below makes for a nice place to spend a few days, with a vivacious main-street *passeggiata*. The beaches aren't great, but you can swim from the flat rocks in the harbour and the water's perfectly clean. For accommodation, the *Hotel Carola* in the harbour at Via Carlo Pisacane 1 (☎0974.826.422, ⓦwww.hotelcarola.it; ❸), has attractive, freshly done-up double rooms with balconies, or there's the *Serenella*, Lungomare San Marco 150 (☎0974.823.333, ⓦwww.hotelserenella.it; usually full board in Aug, ❹), which has a private beach. Agrópoli also has an HI **youth hostel**, *La Lanterna*, Via Lanterna 8 (☎0974.838.364, ⓦwww.hihostels.com; closed Nov to mid-March), about 1km from the station and conveniently close to the bus stop for Paestum; as well as dorm beds it also offers family rooms (€11.50–17 per person) and does full dinners for €10.

Santa Maria di Castellebate

The next town, **SANTA MARIA DI CASTELLEBATE**, is a pleasant and lively seaside town, with an animated waterfront which forms the start of a lovely crescent of sand that runs right round to the next town along, the less alluring **San Marco**. There's also the old town of Santa Maria which is also worth getting up to if you can, high on a hill a couple of kilometres inland, and with an intriguing little enclosed square, almost Moorish with its arches and passageways and tremendous views. In seaside Santa Maria the first stretches of beach are given over to beach bars and an excellent waterside hotel (see below), but there are other, free stretches beyond (and there's nothing wrong with the town patch). The town's best **hotel**, the lovely *Palazzo Belmonte*, set in its own terraced gardens (℡0974.960.211, Ⓦwww.palazzobelrionte.com; ❺), which has well-equipped rooms either inside the original *palazzo* or in chalets in the gardens themselves, and a nice pool – and the food – served in the gardens each evening – is something special. Otherwise there is no shortage of places to **eat** in Santa Maria. Try the *Taverna del Mare*, right on the beach, which is busy and reasonably priced.

Acciaroli, Marina d'Ascea and Velia

Buses run down to **ACCIAROLI**, about 25km south of Agrópoli, one of the Cilento's larger resorts and a port for the hydrofoils plying the coast during summer. The railway joins the shoreline again at **MARINA D'ASCEA**, a fairly indifferent resort but surrounded by hotels and campsites, especially along the lengthy sand beach that stretches north to Marina del Casalvelino.

Some 20km further on, **MARINA DI VELIA** gives access to the site of **Velia** (daily 9am to 1hr before sunset; €2.50) – comprising the ruins of the Hellenistic town of Elea, founded around 540 BC and an important port and cultural centre, home to its own school of philosophy. Later it became a favourite holiday resort for wealthy Romans, Horace being just one of many who came here on the advice of his doctor. The decline of Velia parallels that of Paestum – malarial swamp rendering much of the area uninhabitable – though the upper reaches were lived in until the fifteenth century. There, however, the comparison ends: the remains of Velia are considerably more decimated than those of Paestum and the town was never as crucial a centre, with nothing like as many temples. At the top of the site the "**Porta Rosa**", named after the wife of the archeologist who conducted the first investigations, is one of the earliest arches ever found – and the first indication to experts that the Greeks knew how to construct such things. Across from here, the **Acropolis** on the next peak has relics of an amphitheatre and a temple, together with a massive Norman tower – visible for some distance around.

Palinuro

Cheerful **PALINURO**, further south, is worth a stop, named after the legendary pilot of the *Aeneid*, who is supposed to have drowned here. It's a much livelier place than anywhere else on the Cilento coast, and so can be packed out. But it's a relatively sprawling place, and a good alternative to Agrópoli and Santa Maria, both as a base for the site of Velia and a beach-bumming spot – the sea here is one of the cleanest spots on the coast, and the sandy beach and harbour are lovely, if busy, with boats and people. From the harbour, you can explore the stunning craggy coast of the Capo Palinuro, studded with a series of caves, either by taking a guided **boat tour** (€8) or – more fun – by renting a **motorboat** (€25 for 2hr, plus around €10 for petrol).

The best **hotel** option is *Hotel Residence La Torre* (Via Porto 3; ℡0974.931.107, Ⓦwww.latorrepalinuro.it; ❹), just 10m from the harbour; its rooms are comfortable and well-kept and there's a sociable bar – a great place for a sundowner. In town, the attractive central **campsite** provides shade and has a rudimentary restaurant, with access to a sandy beach where steps from a series of rock pools take you straight into the sea. There's a good beachfront restaurant, the *Taverna del Porto*, which does great pizzas and excellent pasta and seafood. Otherwise a number of good, unpretentious **eating** options line Via Indipendenza, the best of which is friendly *L'Ancora* at no. 115 (℡0974.931.373); its speciality is *zuppa di pesce* and the wood-fired oven turns out large and delicious pizzas. Alternatively, blow your last few euros at the *Da Carmelo* restaurant (☏0974.931.138), 2km south of town at Località Isca, whose fish and seafood are said to be the best for miles around.

Travel details

Naples and the bay

Metropolitana/FS

City centre stops include Piazza Garibaldi, Piazza cavour, Montesanto, Piazza Amedeo, Vanvitelli, Mergellina, Museo, Dante – with stops at Duomo, Municipio and Toledo to come. Trains every 8min.
Circumvesuviana (information ☏081.772.2444). This line runs between Naples and Sorrento, with many stops around the southern part of the bay, including Ercolano and Pompeii, every 30min, up to 40 daily from 5.09am to 10.42pm.
Circumflegrea and **Ferrovia Cumana** (information ☏800.001.616). These two lines connect Naples Montesanto to Fuorigrotta, Agnano, Bagnoli, Pozzuoli, Baía, Fusaro, Cumae and Torregaveta. Departures every 20min.

Funiculars

(information ☏800.568.866).
Funicolare Centrale Piazza Augusteo–Piazza Fuga Daily 6.30am–10pm; every 10min.
Funicolare di Montesanto Montesanto FS–Via Morghen Daily 7am–1pm; every 10min.
Funicolare di Chiaia Parco Margherita Via Cimarosa Daily 6.30am–10pm; every 12min.
Funicolare di Mergellina Temporarily closed.

Trains

Benevento to: Fóggia (9 daily; 1hr 15min); Naples (18 daily; 1hr 5min–2hr 20min).
Naples to: Agrópoli (20 daily; 1hr 40min); Benevento (18 daily; 1hr 5min–2hr 20min); Caserta (every 30min; 35–45min); Fóggia (9 daily; via Caserta or Benevento 2hr 20min–5hr); Formia (every 30min; 1hr 20min); Rome (every 30min; 1hr 30min–2hr 30min); Salerno (every 30min; 50min); Santa Maria Cápua Vetere (every 30min; 50min); Sapri (hourly; 2hr 50min).
Salerno to: Paestum/Agrópoli (hourly; 35min); Sapri (every 30min; 2hr).

Buses

Agrópoli to: Acciaroli (6 daily; 1hr); Paestum (hourly; 10min); Salerno (hourly; 1hr 20min); Sapri (1 daily; 3hr 30min).

Naples to: Amalfi (4 daily; 1hr 55min); Bari (3 daily; 3hr); Benevento (6 daily; 1hr 30min); Cápua (hourly; 1hr 15min); Caserta (every 20min; 45min); Salerno (every 15–30min; 1hr 10min); Sorrento (2 daily Mon–Sat at 8.45am and 9.10am; 1hr 20min); Pompeii (every 30min; 35min); Positano (2 daily Mon–Sat at 8.45am and 9.10am; 2hr 10min).
Naples Capodichino airport to: Sorrento (6 daily; 1hr 30min).
Ravello to: Amalfi (15 daily; 30min).
Salerno to: Agrópoli (hourly; 1hr 20min); Amalfi (hourly; 1hr 10min); Naples (every 15–30min; 1hr 5min); Padula (2 daily; 1hr 50min–2hr); Paestum (hourly; 1hr); Positano (every 1–2hr; 2hr); Sorrento (every 1–2hr; 2hr 45min).
Sorrento to: Amalfi (18 daily; 1hr 30min); Naples (1 daily at 6.40pm; 1hr 15min); Naples Capodichino Airport (6 daily; 1hr); Positano (18 daily; 1hr 5min); Salerno (12 daily; 2hr 45min).

Ferries and hydrofoils

For details of ferry and hydrofoil connections to the islands from Naples, the Amalfi Coast and Salerno, see p.810.
Metro del Mare ☏199.600.700, ⊛www
.metrodelmare.com The Metro del Mare services connect up Pozzuoli, Naples, Sorrento, Positano, Amalfi, Minori, Salerno and several points in between. During high season they run down to the main towns of the Cilento too. Fares are cheap, and about the most you'll pay is for the trip from Naples to Salerno, which takes the best part of 3hr.
Naples to: Aeolian Islands/Milazzo (June–Sept twice weekly at 8pm; 9hr 30min/18hr 50min); Aeolian Islands (hydrofoil: June–Sept twice daily 4–6hr); Cágliari (ferry: weekly/twice weekly in high season at 7.15pm; 16hr 15min); Palermo (twice daily; 10hr); Sorrento (6 daily hydrofoils; 35min).
Salerno to: Amalfi (April–Sept 6 daily hydrofoils; 35min); Positano (5 daily hydrofoils; 1hr 10min).

Puglia

CHAPTER 14

Highlights

* **Vieste and Péschici** For sun and sea, head for these resorts, with the option of travelling onwards to the Trémiti Islands. See p.848 & 850

* **Trani** The eleventh-century cathedral here is a gem, its interior restored to its original Norman state and the building itself impressively located on the waterfront of what was one of Italy's most important medieval ports. See p.853

* **Castel del Monte** Puglia's greatest Swabian castle is a testament to thirteenth-century engineering. See p.858

* **Martina Franca** This lively town with its Moorish feel makes a good base for exploring the surrounding area's *trulli* – Puglia's traditional conical whitewashed buildings. See p.862

* **Ostuni** One of the most stunning hill-top towns in southern Italy, with a sun-bleached old quarter and a sandy coastline 7km away. See p.870

* **Lecce** In the southern tip of Italy, Lecce is an exuberant city of Baroque architecture and opulent churches. See p.872

▲ The coastline at Vieste

14

Puglia

Puglia is the long strip of land, 400km from north to south, that makes up the heel of Italy. For centuries it was a strategic province, colonized, invaded and conquered (like its neighbours, Calabria and Sicily) by just about every major power of the day – from the Greeks through to the Spanish. These days clean seas and reliable sunshine are the draw for holiday-makers both Italian and foreign, and acres of campsite-and-bungalow-type tourist villages stud the shoreline, though there are still quiet spots to be found. Low-cost flights to Bari and Bríndisi have opened up the area to British tourists, many of whom have been buying and doing up *trulli* (ancient store houses, see p.862) and *masserie* (farm estates) as holiday accommodation. There's a brisk air of investment in many resorts, from the new top-of-the-range spa hotels in converted *masserie* to agriturismo places, where you can holiday among olive groves and orchards and go horseriding or mountain biking. B&Bs have been springing up everywhere, often in the historic centres of towns, so a stay of a day or two is much more affordable than it used to be.

There's plenty of architectural interest throughout Puglia, as each ruling dynasty left its own distinctive mark on the landscape – the Romans their agricultural schemes and feudal lords their fortified medieval towns. Perhaps most distinctive are the kasbah-like quarters of many towns and cities, a vestige of the Saracen conquest of the ninth century – the one at **Bari** is the biggest and most atmospheric. The Normans endowed Puglia with splendidly ornate cathedrals, while the Baroque exuberance of towns like **Lecce** and **Martina Franca** are testament to the Spanish legacy. But if there's one symbol of Puglia that stands out, it's the imposing castles built by the Swabian Frederick II all over the province – foremost of which are the **Castel del Monte** (immortalized on the Italian five-cent euro coin) and the remnants of the palace at **Lucera**.

Puglia's cities, generally visited only as transport hubs, merit some exploration nevertheless. **Táranto** and its surroundings have fought a losing battle with the local steel industry, but **Lecce** is worth a visit of a day or two for its crazed confection of Baroque churches and laid-back café life. Though **Bari** is not a traditional tourist destination, reinvestment in its maze-like old city is drawing visitors in-the-know for its ambiance and excellent restaurants, while **Bríndisi**, best-known for its ferry connections with Greece, lies just 15km away from the beautiful **Torre Guaceto** nature reserve, a long stretch of uncontaminated sand dunes, *macchia* and clear water where you can cycle, walk or scuba dive.

The geographical diversity of Puglia is very attractive. The **Tavoliere** (table-land) of the north boasts mile after mile of wheatfields, while there's plenty of barren mountain scenery in the undulating plateau of **Le Murge**, in the centre of the province. The hilly, forested **Gargano promontory** juts out to the east,

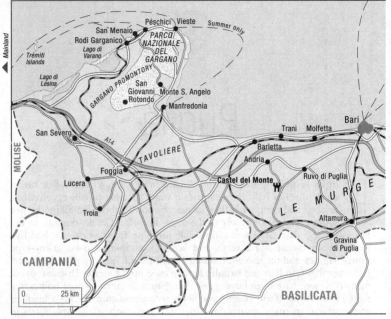

and is fringed by gently shelving, sandy beaches, seaside hotels and campsite villages that make good places for a family holiday – though you'll need to catch a ferry to the **Trémiti Islands** for the clearest sea. The best escape is to the southernmost tip, the **Salentine peninsula** where the terrain is rocky and dry, more Greek than Italian, and there are some beautiful coves and sea caves to swim in.

Getting around Puglia by public transport is fairly easy, at least as far as the main towns and cities go. FS **trains** connect nearly all the major places, while small, private lines head into previously remote areas – in the Gargano and on the edges of Le Murge. Most other places can be reached by **bus**, although isolated village services can be infrequent or inconveniently early – a problem that can only really be solved by taking, or renting, your own **car**. In July and August buses connect coastal towns. It's a thoroughly pleasant area to travel around: old-fashioned courtesy towards the traveller means that if you ask someone for information and they don't know the answer, they invariably make it their business to find out. It helps to speak a bit of Italian in these circumstances but you don't have to be fluent – people will respond if you make the effort.

Fóggia and around

The province of Foggia, known also as the **Tavoliere** (table lands), occupies a broad **plain** stretching from the foothills of the Apennines in the west and the Gargano massif in the east. The Romans exploited the flat, fertile land, to feed the hungry mouths of an expanding empire although by the Middle Ages, the area was largely abandoned as it was difficult to defend against the impromptu raids of the Lombards and Saracens. The few settlements that did survive were unhealthy

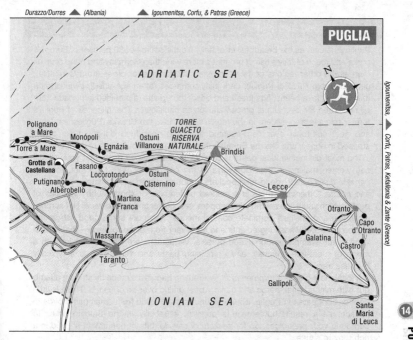

places, earthquake-prone swamplands rife with malarial mosquitoes. It wasn't until the 1920s that the Tavoliere became "the breadbasket of Italy" as it was dubbed by Fascist rhetoric, outfitted with modern irrigation and drainage that transformed the formerly malarial swamps into the rich agricultural lands they are today. As the capital and transport hub of the province, Fóggia is somewhere you will probably pass through rather than linger – for more of an idea of what the Tavoliere is like, head for the walled town of **Lucera** or the little village of **Tróia**.

Fóggia

The Tavoliere's main town, **FÓGGIA**, looms out of the plain unexpectedly, a fine starting point for exploring northern Puglia and the Gargano promontory, though not an encouraging stop in itself. Although Fóggia flourished under Frederick II, who declared it an imperial residence and built a palace here, the town was devastated in turn by the French in 1528, an earthquake in 1731 and Allied bombs during World War II. Today the city's streets are all reassuringly earthquake-proof, wide and low-built, a modern layout that is handsome enough, but you're going to have to search hard in between the tree-lined boulevards for what is left of the old town.

Arrival and information

Fóggia is an important rail junction on the main Bolzano–Lecce and Rome–Lecce lines. FS services arrive here from Rome and Milan and head south to Bari and Lecce, also running to Manfredonia; Ferrovie del Gargano (FG; ☎0881.587.211, ⊛www.ferroviedelgargano.com) trains go to Bari and San Severo (change for service to Péschici Calanelle). The **train station** is on Piazzale Vittorio Veneto, on the northern edge of town, a short walk from Piazza

Puglia is known as the breadbasket of Italy. It's the source of 80 percent of Europe's pasta and much of Italy's fish; it produces more wine than Germany and more olive oil than all the other regions of Italy combined. It's famous for olives (from Cerignola), almonds (from Ruvo di Puglia), dark juicy tomatoes (often sun-dried), *cime di rapa* (turnip tops) fava beans, figs (fresh and dried), *cotognata* (a moulded jam made from quinces) and for its melons, grapes and green cauliflower. The influence of Puglia's former rulers is also evident in the region's food. Like the **Greeks**, Pugliesi eat lamb and goat spit-roast over herb-scented fires and deep-fried doughnut-like cakes steeped in honey; and like the **Spanish** they drink almond milk, *latte di mandorla*.

The most distinctive local **pasta** is *orecchiette*, ear-shaped pasta that you will still see women making in their doorways in the old part of Bari. Look out, too, for *panzarotti alla barese*, deep-fried pockets of dough stuffed with tomato or *prosciutto* and *ricotta*. Otherwise, there is a marked preference for short, stubby varieties of pasta, which you'll find served with peppers, cauliflower and *cime di rapa*. Not surprisingly, fish and shellfish dominate coastal menus. There are some good fish soups (*zuppe di pesce*) whose ingredients and style vary from place to place – the Bríndisi version, for example, is dominated by eels. Vegetarians are well catered for with a range of meat-free antipasti, and combining pasta and vegetables is a typically Pugliese trait.

A local meat dish is *gnummerieddi*, resembling haggis it's made by stuffing a lamb gut with minced offal, herbs and garlic – best grilled over an open fire. There is little beef or pork eaten in Puglia, poultry is uncommon, aside from small game birds in season; as a result, horsemeat is popular, especially in the Salento area. To confound your prejudices, go for *pezzetti di cavallo*, bits of horsemeat stewed in a rich tomato sauce.

Cheeses are a strong point, including ricotta, *cacioricotta*, *canestrato*, (sheep's milk cheese formed in baskets) and *burrata* (cream encased in mozzarella, a specialty of Andria). Pair these products with the local durum wheat breads, the most famous of which, *pane di Altamura*, carries the DOP seal of quality.

There have recently been immense improvements in Puglia's **wines**. While historically the inclination was towards mass production, yields have been reduced and grapes are now picked at precisely the right moment. Look for the formidable reds Primitivo di Manduria (aka red Zinfandel), Salice Salentino, and Negroamaro. Locorotondo is a straightforward, fresh white from Salento, a region known also for its *rosati* (rosé) called Salento Rosato, and dessert wine called Aleatico.

Cavour and the centre. SITA **buses**, which serve the whole region, arrive at and depart from just outside the train station; buy tickets inside the train station or at the *Kiwi Bar* (open 4am–11pm daily), on the corner of Viale XXIV Maggio. The **tourist office** (Mon–Fri 8am–2pm, Tues & Thurs also 3.30–6pm; ⊤0881.725.536, Ⓦwww.viaggiareinpuglia.it) is a twenty-minute walk into town, on the first floor at Via E. Perrone 17, off Piazzale Puglia and has a lot of good information on the whole province. If you are headed for the Gargano, it's worth picking up *Tutto Gargano* (Ⓦwww.tuttogargano.com) from a newsstand, a great resource for accommodation and information on festivals and events.

Accommodation

Staying in Fóggia may be necessary if you arrive late or need to leave early: *Hotel Venezia*, Via Piave 40 (⊤0881.770.903, Ⓦwww.hotelvenezia.it; ❷), is a good, three-star hotel; head down Viale XXIV Maggio from the station, then third right. *Hotel Europa*, Via Monfalcone 52 (⊤0881.721.057, Ⓦwww.hoteleuropafoggia.com; ❺), is more upmarket, with helpful staff – again it's down Viale XXIV Maggio from the station, then second right. Finally, *Cacciatore*, in the historic centre near the cathedral at Via Arrigotti 4 (℡0881.771.839; ❸), is a good, friendly, family-run one-star with restaurant. The only time that bed space will be short is at the beginning of May, during the Fiera Internazionale dell'Agricultura (𝕎www .fieradifoggia.it), a huge agricultural **festival** held on the outskirts of the town.

The Town

The old town lies scattered around the **Duomo**, which is to the left off Corso Vittorio Emanuele, the main drag that runs down from the central, fountained Piazza Cavour. The cathedral is an odd Romanesque–Baroque sandwich, the top part tacked on in the eighteenth century after the earthquake.

While you're here, take a look at the recently renovated **Museo Cívico** on Piazza Nigri (Tues–Sun 9am–1pm; €2), reached by walking down the Corso to Via Arpi. Incorporated into the side of the building are three portals, one of which – the Porta Grande, with the pensive-looking eagles – is all that remains of Frederick II's imperial palace. Duck inside and there are the usual regional archeological finds, a small picture gallery, and a more interesting section on local life and folklore.

That really is it as far as Fóggia's sights go, though there are enough green spaces and shopping streets in the new town to occupy any remaining time – something you might well have if you stopped in Fóggia to change trains.

Eating and drinking

Good **food** options include *Chacaito-L'osteria di Zio Aldo*, near the Museo Civico at Via Arpi 62 (℡0881.708.104; closed Sun & Aug), a gourmet's delight offering seasonal dishes that might include *orecchie di ciuccio* (donkey ear-shaped pasta) with baby courgette or salt-cod on a bed of bean purée flavoured with saffron, plus delicious desserts and an extensive wine list; expect to spend around €35 per head excluding wine. *Giordano da Pompeo*, Vico al Piano 14 (℡0881.724.640; closed Sun & last two weeks in Aug), down Corso Vittorio Emanuele II and right at the Palazzo Vescovile, is another fine place to indulge in Pugliese specialities in a similar price bracket. For a more economical meal, try *Il Rugantino*, Via Don Luigi Sturzo 23 (closed Mon) – head down Corso Roma and turn left at the sanatorium – which offers great pizzas and other dishes. For a **drink**, *Gran Caffè Duetto* (closed Sun) on Corso Vittorio Emanuele 64 does a great happy hour.

Lucera

Just 18km west, within easy reach of Fóggia (regular buses), **LUCERA** (pronounced Loosh-airer) makes a wonderful and charming introduction to Puglia. A small town with a bright, bustling centre and a lively *passeggiata* on summer evenings, it was once the capital of the Tavoliere – a thriving Saracen (North African Arab colonizer) hub. Frederick II, having forced the Arabs out of Sicily, resettled 20,000 of them here, on the site of an abandoned Roman town, allowing them complete freedom in religious worship – an almost unheard of act of liberalism for the early thirteenth century.

The **cathedral** (daily 8am–noon & 4–7pm; free) was built in the early fourteenth century after Frederick II's death, when the Angevins arrived and a conflict with the Saracens began. The Angevins won and built the cathedral on the site of a mosque; by the end of their rule, few of the town's original Arab-influenced buildings were left. However, the Arabic layout of Lucera survived and there's a powerful atmosphere here – best appreciated by wandering the narrow streets of the old town, peering into the courtyards and alleyways.

The main sights are outside the old centre, most notably the vast **Castello** (Tues–Sun: summer 9am–2pm & 3–6pm; winter 9am–2pm; free), built by Frederick and designed to house a lavish court that included a collection of exotic wild beasts. To get there from Piazza Duomo follow Via Bovio and Via Federico II to Piazza Matteotti and look for the signs. The castle commands spectacular views over the Tavoliere, stretching across to the Apennines to the west and the mountains of Gargano to the east. Contained within the kilometre-long walls are the remains of Frederick's great palace, evocative fragments of mosaic work and fallen columns now surrounded by wild flowers. At the Roman **amphitheatre** (closed for restoration at time of writing) on the western edge of town, audiences of 18,000 once watched gladiatorial battles.

Practicalities

Buses arrive from Foggia every 30min at the train station (currently closed) and in Piazza del Popolo, from where it's only a short walk up Via Gramsci to the Duomo, which marks the centre of the medieval walled town. Close to the cathedral is the **tourist office** in Piazza Nocelli 6 (year-round Tues–Sun 9am–2pm; March–Oct also Tues–Fri 3–6pm; ☎0881.522.762, ⓦwww .comune.lucera.fg.it).

You can **stay** in town at the businesslike *Hotel Villa Imperiale* at Viale Ferrovia 15 (☎0881.520.998, ⓦwww.labalconata.it; ❸), just outside the gate into the old town. For **eating**, *Il Cortiletto*, just behind the cathedral at Via de Nicastri 26 (☎0881.542.554; closed Sun and Mon at lunch), prepares excellent local food and a vast array of Pugliese wine, while the pub-like *Lupus in Fabula*, Via Mazzacarra 4 (☎0881.530.593; closed Sun lunch and 30 July–10 Aug), also in the old town, is a restaurant/wine bar/jazz club serving a menu of typically Luceran dishes at moderate prices.

Tróia

Frequent buses also make the short ride (from either Lucera or Fóggia) to **TRÓIA**, 18km due south of Lucera. The locals seem curiously blasé as to the origin of their village's name; it means "slut" in Italian, but no one is able to offer a logical connection with the village. Whatever the reason, the Tróiani atone for the name by having three patron saints, whose relics are paraded around town in a procession during the Gesta dei Santi Patroni every July 17.

At all other times of the year Tróia is a quiet, dusty village, its only sight the fine **Duomo** (daily 8.30am–noon & 3–7pm; free), an intriguing eleventh-century blend of Byzantine and Apulian–Romanesque styles, with a generous hint of Saracen influence. The great bronze doors are covered with reliefs of animals and biblical figures, while above, surrounded by a frenzy of carved lions frozen in stone, is an extraordinary rose window. Distinctly Saracen, the window resembles a finely worked piece of oriental ivory, being composed of eleven stone panels, each one delicately carved. There's more exact detail inside, too, including a curiously decorated pulpit and some ornate capitals.

Manfredonia

By Puglian standards, **MANFREDONIA** is a new town, a mere 600 years old, founded – as the name suggests – by Manfred, illegitimate son of Frederick II. The Austrians struck the first blow of World War I on Italian soil here by bombing the town's station in 1915, but this is really Manfredonia's only claim to fame. Heavy industry on the northern outskirts and the flat, featureless landscape ensure that for most visitors it's little more than a gateway to the Gargano promontory, and most people pass through quickly. Still, what the town lacks in ambience and historical sights is more than made up for by its sandy beaches, which stretch for miles down the coast.

The **Castello**, on Corso Manfredi, was begun by Manfred and later extended by the Angevins. The Spanish added huge bastions in 1607 to stave off a Turkish attack: they failed to do so, with the Turks landing in 1620, ravaging the hapless inhabitants and destroying much of the town – though most of the protective walls still survive. The castle now houses the **Museo Nazionale** (daily except first and last Mon of the month: 8.30am–7pm; €2.50), largely devoted to funeral art from the seventh and sixth centuries BC. The prize exhibits are several stone tombstones, richly carved with images of armoured warriors, female figures and scenes from daily life.

Practicalities

The easiest way to reach Manfredonia is by train from Fóggia: from the **station** turn right and it's a short walk along Viale A. Moro to Piazza Marconi. Just across the square, Corso Manfredi leads up to the small **tourist office** in the *Comune* building at Piazza del Popolo 10 (Mon–Fri 9am–1pm; ☎0884.587.838), which has some information on the Gargano area. A **ferry** service runs to Vieste and to the Trémiti Islands (see p.851) from Molo Ponente pier; **tickets** can be bought from Ditta A. Galli e Figlio, Corso Manfredi 4/6 in town or the harbourside Tirrenia office (☎892.123, ⓦ www.tirrenia.it). If you need to catch the hydrofoil, check schedules in advance as, at the time of print, there were only early morning departures; if you miss the departure and need to stay overnight note that most accommodation is strung out along the gulf. *Albergo Gabbiano*, Viale Eunostides 20 (☎0884.542.554, ⓦ www.albergogabbiano.it; ➌), 200m from the seafront at the nearby resort of **Siponto** is a good option.

There are plenty of **restaurants** in Manfredonia, one of the best of which is *Coppola Rossa*, Via dei Celestini 13 (☎0884.582.522; closed all day Mon & Sun eve), where you can feast on grilled antipasti, *troccoli alla scoglio* (tiny pasta in a sauce of clams, eels, tomatoes and oil), *orecchiette* with scampi, or *ciambotta* (fish soup).

The Gargano promontory

The **Gargano promontory** rises like an island from the flat plains of the Tavoliere. It has a remarkably diverse landscape: beaches and lagoons to the north, a rocky, indented eastern coast and a mountainous, green heartland of oaks and beech trees – reminiscent of a Germanic forest rather than a corner of southern Italy. For centuries the promontory was extremely isolated, visited only by pilgrims making their way along the valley to Monte Sant'Angelo and its shrine. Tourism has taken off in a big way, especially around the seaside resort of Vieste, but in 1991 the whole peninsula became a national park, helping to protect the Gargano from overbearing development and ensuring that much of the interior remains supremely unspoiled and quiet.

It may seem as though the promontory is one long strip of private beach, but bear in mind that by Italian law everyone has access to the actual seashore, as well as the 50m length between the reserved areas. Check with your hotel – often the price of a sunbed and umbrella at the nearest beach is included in the cost of an overnight stay.

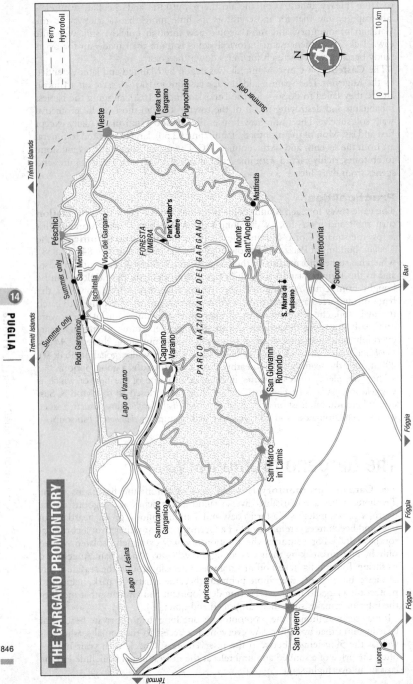

THE GARGANO PROMONTORY

Ferry
Hydrofoil

0   10 km

Trémiti Islands

Trémiti Islands

Termoli

Vieste

Testa del Gargano

Pugnochiuso

Péschici

San Menaio

Vico del Gargano

Ischitella

Rodi Garganico

Summer only

Summer only

FORESTA UMBRA

Park Visitor's Centre

Mattinata

Monte Sant'Angelo

Manfredonia

Siponto

S. Maria di Pulsano

Lago di Varano

Cagnano Varano

PARCO NAZIONALE DEL GARGANO

San Giovanni Rotondo

Lago di Lésina

Sannicandro Garganico

San Marco in Lamis

Apricena

San Severo

Lucera

Fóggia

Fóggia

Fóggia

Bari

Summer only

Arrival and transport

Approaches to the promontory are pretty straightforward. **FS trains** run from Fóggia to Manfredonia on the southeast side of Gargano, from where it's only 16km by **bus** to Monte Sant'Angelo. Alternatively, in the north of the region, **Ferrovie del Gargano** (℡0881.587.211, ⓦwww.ferroviedelgargano.com) operates trains between Fóggia and San Severo. You then change here for onward travel to Péschici-Calanelle, from where a bus connects with Péschici. Note that most FG stations are quite a distance from the towns and villages they serve, so always go for the connecting bus if there is one.

Getting around the interior can be a little more tortuous. **Buses** are run by two companies: SITA (℡0881.773.117, ⓦwww.sitabus.it) serves the inland towns and operates the inland route to Vieste; and FG, which runs the trains and connecting buses in northern Gargano, including a coastal bus route to Vieste, via Manfredonia, Mattinata and Pugnochiuso. There is also a regular **ferry service** connecting Manfredonia, Vieste, and Péschici, and seasonal service linking some coastal towns (connections vary dramatically from season to season).

Monte Sant'Angelo

Just north of Manfredonia, perched almost 800m up in the hills, **MONTE SANT'ANGELO** is the highest – and coldest – settlement in the Gargano. Pilgrims have trudged up the switchback paths and roads for centuries to visit the spot where the archangel Michael is said to have made four separate appearances, mostly at the end of the fifth century – making the sanctuary here one of the earliest Christian shrines in Europe and one of the most important in Italy. Today, the pilgrims come by bus, and the village is a bit of a tourist trap. But the annual major festivals on May 8 and September 28, 29 and 30 attract locals from miles around, some of whom turn up in traditional dress.

SITA **buses** (every hour from Manfredonia) drop you in Piazza Duca d'Aosta, from where you should follow the road uphill to the edge of the old town and the Via Reale Basilica; here you'll find the famous **Santuario di San Michele Arcangelo** (July–Sept Mon–Sat 7.30am–7.30pm, Sun 6.30am–7.30pm; Oct–June Mon–Sat 7.30am–noon, 2.30–6pm, Sun 6.30am–7pm; free). From the small courtyard on the right a flight of stone steps leads down to the crypts that form the entrance to the church built on the site of the cave in which the archangel first appeared (in 490). Opposite, another set of steps leads down to the nearby ruins of the **Complesso di San Pietro**, behind which is the so-called **Tomba di Rotari** (8.30am–12.30pm, 2.30–dusk; free) – an imposing domed tower that contained a baptistry; the large baptismal font is just on the right as you enter the tower. Little remains of the church itself, wrecked by an earthquake, but look out for the rose window – a Catherine wheel of entwined mermaids. Back on Via Reale Basilica, it's an easy clamber up to the ruined Norman **Castello** (daily: July & Aug 8am–7pm; Sept–June 9am–1pm & 2.30–6pm; €1.80) for good views over the town and valley.

Practicalities

For overnight stays (though don't count on available beds at the main festival times) there is a three-star hotel run by a religious institution but open to everybody next to the Santuario: *Casa del Pellegrino* (℡0884.561.150, ⓦwww .santuariosanmichele.it; ❷). The rooms are modern and well looked after, and there's a set lunch and dinner menu for €14, but you must be in by midnight. Facing the sanctuary is the family-run *Michael*, on Via Reale Basilica 86 (℡0884.565.519, ⓦwww.hotelmichael.com; ❹) About 1km outside of town along the road to Pulsano, the *Rotary Hotel* occupies a panoramic position (℡0884.562.146, ⓦwww.hotelsantangelo.com; ❹); the same owners operate the nearby *Hotel Sant'Angelo* (℡0884.565.536; same website; ❹).

For snacks, ignore the touristy places in the lower town and head instead for the bakery outside the castle, where they'll make you up a tasty sandwich and sell you a cold beer. One of the best **restaurants** in town is *Medioevo*, Via Castello 21 (℡0884.565.356; closed Mon), serving excellent seasonal dishes and delectable home-made desserts. Another culinary highlight is *Taverna Li Jalantuúmene* (℡0884.565.484; closed Tues in winter & Jan), on the tiny whitewashed Piazza De Galganis in the maze of streets opposite the Santuario. The menu is constantly changing to reflect the seasonal produce and features both traditional and innovative recpies. The *orecchiette con zucca, mandorle, e pecorino* (with pumpkin, almonds, and cheese) and *filetto di mucca podolica* (free-range steak) are superb.

The pilgrim route: San Giovanni Rotondo

The ancient **pilgrim route** weaved its way along the Stignano Valley between San Severo in the west and Monte Sant'Angelo, and until comparatively recently was the only road that linked the villages of the Gargano interior. With your own transport, it's still a good route for exploring a couple of the region's most important religious centres. If you want to follow any part of the pilgrim route by bus, you'll have to plan your itinerary carefully and be prepared to travel in leisurely fashion.

Direct bus services between Monte Sant'Angelo and the first village on the route, **SAN GIOVANNI ROTONDO**, run every couple of hours, although the SITA bus from Manfredonia or Fóggia is much more frequent (see p.842). Nestling under Monte Calvo, the highest peak hereabouts, San Giovanni Rotondo is a modern centre for pilgrimage on a massive scale: it's the burial place of Padre Pio, a local priest who died in 1968 and was canonized in 2002. Pio received the stigmata and won an immense following – especially among Italian Catholics – for his model piety and legendary ability to heal the sick. Proof of his divinity was announced in 2008 when his body was exhumed and pronounced to be in good condition and without signs of the stigmata 40 years after his burial.

A whole industry has grown up in San Giovanni Rotondo, fuelled by the seven million and more pilgrims who pass through every year, making it the most visited pilgrimage site in the world after Lourdes. In 2004, renowned architect Renzo Piano completed a striking new church, the shape of which resembles a large snail – its "shell" forming the roof and enveloping the pilgrims below. The town takes its name from the **Rotonda di San Giovanni**, a building of indeterminate origin on the edge of the old town – like the Tomba di Rotari (see p.847), it's thought to have been a baptistry, built on the site of an earlier pagan temple.

Vieste and around

VIESTE juts out into the Adriatic on two promontories, the easternmost point of the Gargano peninsula. Fifty years ago there wasn't even a proper road here, but today Vieste, with its excellent beaches, is the holiday capital of Gargano, and the streets and sands are packed in August. Despite the crowds, it has managed to survive as a lively and inviting town, with an interesting historic core and active nightlife that warrant a stop of a day or two – particularly if you're planning to take the ferry from here to the Trémiti Islands.

Arrival, information and accommodation

You **arrive** by bus at Piazzale Manzoni, to the west of the town centre; bear right from here along Viale XXIV Maggio, which becomes Corso Lorenzo Fazzini – the main street. At no. 8 is the main **tourist office** (Jun–Aug Mon–Fri 8am–2pm & 3–9pm; Sept–May Mon–Fri 8am–2pm & 4–8pm; ☎0884.707.495, ⓦwww .viaggiareinpuglia.it).

There's no shortage of **accommodation** in Vieste but the dwindling number of budget options and rooms are hard to come by if you want just one night's stay (try to call a day in advance). For help finding **self-catering** accommodation (minimum stay of a week), ask at SOL (see p.850).

Hotels

Albergo Torrente Lungomare Mattei
☎0884.700.945, ⓦwww.altorrente.it. Located 2.5km from the old town, this is an economic and atmospheric seaside choice. Easter–Oct. ❸
Albergo Vela Velo Lungomare Europa 55
☎0884.706.303, ⓦwww.velovela.it. This small, friendly two-star is a good-value option, 1.5km north of the castle along the shore. Room rates include the use of a sunbed and umbrella at the San Lorenzo beach (except in high season) and it's an easy cycle into town on one of their mountain bikes (free to guests). April–Oct. ❸

Punta San Francesco Via S Francesco 2
☎0884.701.422, ⓦwww.hotelpuntasanfrancesco .it. Though it's starting to show its age, this hotel enjoys a quiet position in the old town with lovely views over the promontory. All rooms are en suite. ❹
Seggio Via Veste 7 ☎0884.708.123, ⓦwww .hotelseggio.it. An upmarket option in the old town with vertiginous views down to its swimming pool, and with its own private sandy beach and lagoon. April–Oct. ❺

The Town

The **old town** sits on the easternmost of the two promontories, at the tip of which stands the **Chiesa di San Francesco**, once a thriving monastery, and a *trabucco* – used by fishermen to catch mullet. Probably Phoenician in origin, these cantilevered arrangements of wooden beams, winches and ropes are peculiar to the rocky Gargano coast.

From the church, climb up Via Mafrolla, walking through the old town to Piazza Seggio. Straight ahead, Via Duomo is the site of the so-called **Chianca Amara**, the "bitter stone", where as many as 5000 local people were beheaded when the Turks sacked the town in 1554. Further down, past the stone, the **Cattedrale**, eleventh century in origin but tampered with in the nineteenth century, provides a cool retreat from the fierce glare of the sun in the white-washed streets.

Eating and drinking

There are plenty of fish restaurants to choose in and around the old town. If you're on a budget, try the pair of cheerful pizzerias in Piazza Vittorio Emanuele II. The terrace **bar** at *Seggio* (see above) is a perfect place to chill before dinner.

Dragone Via Duomo 8 ☎0884.701.212. Located in a natural cave, *Dragone* is good for local fish dishes, such as smoked eel from nearby Lesina, and unusual desserts. It offers a four-course menu for €35, including drinks, or if you prefer something lighter, there are platters of Gargano cheeses and vegetables and regional wine by the glass. Closed Nov–March and Tues in April, May, Sept & Oct.
Osteria degli Archi Via Ripe 2 ☎0884.705.199. Occupying a restored stone building in the sea wall

at the Punta di San Francesco end of the old town, it specializes in locally caught grilled seafood. Closed Mon Oct–April and all of Dec–Feb.
Piazzetta Petrone Via Mons. Palma 41
☎0884.706.453. Located on the edge of the old town above the cathedral, this pizzeria has a lovely terrace, wood-fired oven and uses the best of local ingredients such as *caciocavallo* (a local cheese) and sausage.

Around Vieste

There are a number of day-trips worth making **around Vieste**. The most obvious move is to the **beaches**: head for the small one between the promontories or to the north, San Lorenzo, with fine, soft, gently shelving sand, or finally, just south of town, Pizzomunno, which is also sandy. They all go in for the grill-pan variety of sunbathing with rows and rows of sunbeds. Slightly less crowded, if you're lucky, is the marvellous Scialmarino beach, 4.5km up the coast towards Péschici. Nicest of all is the small Baía di San Felice, squeezed between two headlands and backed by pine trees, just before you get to the Testa del Gargano, several kilometres south of town.

If you want to swim away from the crowds, consider an organized boat trip to the grotto-ridden **coastline** around the "head" or Testa del Gargano. Boats leave for the three-hour grotto excursion from next to San Francesco church at around 8.30am and 2.30pm; tickets cost €15 and are available from Gargáno Viaggi (see box, p.852) and SOL (daily: June–Aug 9.30am–1.15pm & 5pm–1am; mid-March to May, Sept to mid-Nov 9am–1pm & 4–8pm; closed mid-Nov to mid-March; ☎340.906.2046, ⓦ www.solvieste.it) at Via Trepiccioni 5. If you really want to get away from it you could rent your own boat for the day, from SOL.

The **interior** of the Gargano promontory can make a cool break from its busy coast, and though there's not much public transport, apart from the odd bus from Vieste, San Menaio and Rodi Garganico, you can rent mountain bikes or fix up jeep safaris or pony trekking. The main tourist office is in Monte Sant'Angelo on Via Sant'Antonio Abate 121 (☎0884.568.911, ⓦ www.parcogargano.it). The SOL agency (see above) also arranges tours and rent out cars and mountain bikes.

Péschici and northern Gargano

Atop its rocky vantage point overlooking a beautiful sandy bay, **PÉSCHICI** is a little smaller than Vieste and one of the most attractive village resorts in the Gargano. Though originally built in 970 AD as a buffer against Saracen incursions, its labyrinth of tiny streets and houses sporting domed roofs has a distinctly Arabic flavour. Beach-lazing is the focus, although the town also makes a good base for exploring some of the caves and defensive medieval towers of the nearby coastline. The easiest trips are to the grotto at **San Nicola**, 3km east of town (some buses), or 5km west to the **Torre di Monte Pucci** for fine coastal views (and where there's a *trabucco* restaurant for refreshments in the summer months).

Arrival and information

The FG **train** line ends at Calanelle, a few kilometres west of Péschici, but there's a connection to the town by a **bus**. This, and other buses, drops you in the newer, beach resort part of Péschici, from where it's a short walk down to the main street – Corso Garibaldi – and the sea.

Ferries to the Trémiti Islands from Péschici (calling at Rodi Garganico on the way) leave at around 9am from the port, take one hour and cost €5 for the return trip (the ferry brings everyone back at around 4.30pm). You can buy tickets onshore next to the boat right up until departure.

Accommodation

Most **hotels** are the newer part of town. Many are on the beach or have sunbeds reserved at a private beach club at a reduced price.

Baia San Nicola Località San Nicola
ⓣ0884.964.231, ⓦwww.baiasannicola.it. Along
the coast at Punta San Nicola, 2km east of
Péschici, this campsite features sandy beaches and
shady pine groves. Pitches from €7 plus €9 per
person in high season. Closed mid-Oct to mid-May.
Hotel d'Amato Località Spiaggia ⓣ0884.963.415,
ⓦwww.hoteldamato.it. Off the SS89 next to the
beach, this hotel offers modern rooms, a restaurant,
a bar and two swimming pools. April to mid-Oct. ❺

Locanda Al Castello Via Castello 29
ⓣ0884.964.038. Up in the old town, down a
narrow lane of whitewashed houses, *Al Castello*
has a few simple rooms and a restaurant offering
five or six daily specials. ❸
Villa a Mare Località Marina di Peschici, Via
Marina 1 ⓣ0884.963.414, ⓦwww.villaamare.it.
Newly renovated and well kept hotel next to the
sea with a shady patio garden next to the car park.
April to mid Oct. ❻

Eating and drinking

There are scores of **restaurants**, pizzerias, *gelaterie* and **bars** in the old town,
scene of a lively *passeggiata* that goes on all evening.

Fra Stefano Via Forno 8 ⓣ0884.964.141. An
informal place serving inexpensive delicious fish
grilled over a wood fire, *ruoto* (baby goat with little
onions and potatoes) and *capistrelli* (home-made
pasta with seafood and white beans). Closed
Feb–March and Mon–Thurs Nov–Jan.
Grotta delle Rondini Via al Porto 64
ⓣ0884.964.007. Built in a natural cave near the

port outside the old town, fish is the specialty and
the antipasti are especially good. Closed Nov–Feb.
La Collinetta Località Madonna di Loreto
ⓣ0884.964.151. This hotel-restaurant, on the
coast road to Vieste serves reasonably priced fish
dishes such as seafood gratin and red mullet
baked in foil. Its hotel's half-board options are
worth looking into. Closed Oct to mid-March.

West along the coast and onwards

A string of white sandy beaches stretch from San Menaio to **RODI
GARGANICO** – originally a Greek settlement ("Rodi" is derived from
Rhodes) and nowadays, with its beaches and fast hydrofoil links with the
Trémiti Islands, a highly popular resort in summer. It's busy and expensive in
August, but go a couple of months either side and it can be delightful. **SAN
MENAIO** is much quieter than Rodi – more compact and with fewer villas –
and even in high season it's easy to get away from it all by walking a few
hundred metres south along the strand.

From Rodi Gargánico, both road and rail skirt the large **Lago di Varano**, a
once-malarial swamp that swallowed the ancient Athenian town of Uria in the
fourth century BC. The preserve of eel fishermen, it's the least-visited region
on the Gargano promontory, and consequently attracts a great variety of birdlife,
particularly curlews and warblers. Further west, the thin **Lago di Lésina** is a
highly saline shallow lagoon, cut off from the sea by a 27-kilometre stretch of
sand dunes. It's still mercifully free from development – unlike the northern spit
of Varano, which is slowly beginning to fill with campsites.

The Trémiti Islands

A small group of islands 40km off the Gargano coast, the **Trémiti Islands** –
Isole Trémiti – are almost entirely given over to tourism in the summer, when
the tiny population is swamped by visitors. Despite this, they remain relatively
unspoilt and the sea crystal clear. The main Trémiti group consists of three
islands: **San Nicola**, **San Domino** – the biggest – and **Capraia**, of which only
the first two are inhabited.

The islands were traditionally a place of exile and punishment. Augustus
banished his granddaughter Julia to the islands, while Charlemagne packed his

There are year-round catamaran and hydrofoil connections to the **Trémiti Islands** from Vieste (Aug 3 daily, rest of year 1 daily; 1hr); tickets are available online, at the port, and from a number of agencies around town, including Gargáno Viaggi at Piazza Roma 7 (☎0884.708.501, ⓦwww.garganoviaggi.it). Companies providing connections from Vieste include NavLib (☎081.552.0763, ⓦwww.navlib.it), Tirrenia (☎892.123, ⓦwww.tirrenia.it). There's also a summer service from Manfredonia (see p.845), Vasto (see p.764) and Ortona (see p.770). **Ferries** and **monostabs** (fast ferries) for foot passengers run throughout the year from Térmoli (see p.765). **Tourist motor cruisers** from Péschici and Rodi Gargánico also offer day-trips to the islands during the holiday season.

father-in-law off here (minus eyes and limbs) in the eighth century. Monks from Montecassino, on the mainland, first set about building a formidable fortress-abbey on one of the islands in the eleventh century, which managed to withstand frequent assault by the Turks. Later, during the eighteenth century, the islands returned to their old role as a place of confinement for political prisoners, though the Bourbons, concerned at the decline in the local population, shipped in two hundred single women from Naples to encourage a recovery.

Most **ferries** arrive at **SAN NICOLA**, where you can wander around the monastic fortress and the tiny church of **Santa Maria a Mare**, built by the monks in the eleventh century on the site of an earlier ninth-century hermitage. San Nicola is rugged and rocky with no beaches, although there is nude bathing on its east side and good swimming off the whole island.

Ignore the offers of pricey boat trips to the other islands and instead jump on the regular ferry that takes about a minute to cross to **SAN DOMINO**. It's a greener island than its neighbour, its pines offering welcome shade from the heat. Although there's a sandy **beach** – Cala delle Arene – right where the ferry lands on the northeast side of the island, it's packed in the summer. Your best bet is to follow the signs for the *Villaggio TCI* (see below) and make for the west of the island and the quieter coves, such as Cala dello Spido. For **walking**, head for the Punta di Diamante; maps are pinned up in some of the bars or can be bought from souvenir shops.

Practicalities

Accommodation on the islands is limited to San Domino and is largely full board in high season: count on paying €50–60 a night per person. The *municipio* on San Domino holds a list of private rooms, or you could try the most appealing of the small hotels, *Albergo Pineta* (☎0882.463.202; ⓦwww.albergolapineta.info; closed Nov–March; ❹), a whitewashed villa surrounded by pine trees, near some peaceful rocky coves just outside the tiny village centre on Via della Cantina Sperimentale 3. Alternatively, there are two places in the village: *Al Faro* at Via Aldo Moro 22 (☎0882.463.424; March–Oct; ❹), with purple bougainvillaea clambering over the outside and a brightly painted interior, and *Albergo Gabbiano* in Piazza Belvedere (☎0882.463.410, ⓦwww.hotel-gabbiano.com; closed Dec; ❻) ensconced in greenery at Piazza Belvedere; it's essential to book ahead for all three. Camping is now forbidden on the islands so the former *Villaggio TCI* (☎0882.463.402, ⓦwww.touringclub.it; April–Sept) campsite now rents out **cabins** by the week; for a stay of less than seven nights, call a couple of days beforehand to ask about vacancies. Bear in mind that mosquitoes tend to be a serious problem in the summer months and that, as provisions have to be ferried across from the mainland, eating out can be a costly exercise – buy some picnic food before you get on the boat.

Trani and Molfetta

The initial part of the coastal route south from Manfredonia is unremarkable, with flat lands given up to saline extraction. The first town of note down the coast is **TRANI**, a place with an unusually cosmopolitan air. One of the most important medieval Italian ports, it was a prosperous trading centre with a large mercantile and Jewish community; during the Middle Ages it rivalled Bari as a commercial port, and in the fourteenth century was powerful enough to take on the domineering Venetians.

Centrepiece of the town is the cream-coloured, eleventh-century **Duomo** (daily 8am–12.30pm & 3–7.30pm; free), right on the sea at the edge of the Old Town. Dedicated to San Nicola Pellegrino, it consists of no fewer than three churches, stacked on top of each other like an inverted wedding cake – the facade austere but lightened by a pretty rose window. The interior has been restored to its original Norman state, the stark nave displaying a timbered ceiling. A wander through the adjacent streets gives an impression of the medieval city, not least in the names that echo the town's mercantile and Jewish origins – Via Sinagoga, Via Doge Vecchia and Via Cambio (Street of the Money-changers). The city centre bursts with activity in the evenings when locals pour into the town's excellent **restaurants** and wine bars, most of which are concentrated around the port. Among these is *Conteinfiore* on Via Ognissanti 18 (T0883.508.402; closed Sun & Mon at lunch), serving outstanding fish dishes that change according to the day's catch – try the *taglioni alle vongole con carciofi* – in a tree-filled patio (heated in winter).

The rail line continues south to **MOLFETTA**, a working port, unashamedly non-touristy and all the better for it; the waterfront is active with visiting ships and thronged by an evening *passeggiata* that sweeps down to the docks to watch the sunset.

Bari

The commercial and administrative capital of Puglia, a university town and southern Italy's second city, **BARI** has its fair share of interest. But although it's an economically vibrant place, the town harbours no pretensions to being a major tourist attraction. People come here primarily for work or to leave for Croatia and Albania on its many ferries.

Bari was already a thriving centre when the Romans arrived. Later, the city was the seat of the Byzantine governor of southern Italy, while, under the Normans, Bari rivalled Venice both as a maritime centre and, following the seizure of the remains of St Nicholas, as a place of pilgrimage. Since those heady days, Bari has declined considerably. Its fortunes revived briefly in 1813 when the king of Naples foisted a planned expansion on the city – giving the centre its contemporary gridded street pattern, wide avenues and piazzas. And Mussolini instituted a university and left a legacy of strident Fascist architecture. However, the city was heavily bombed during the last war, and today its compact and dynamic centre is a symbol of the south's zeal for commercial growth. Fortunately, heavy investment in redeveloping the old centre has given Bari a new lease on life.

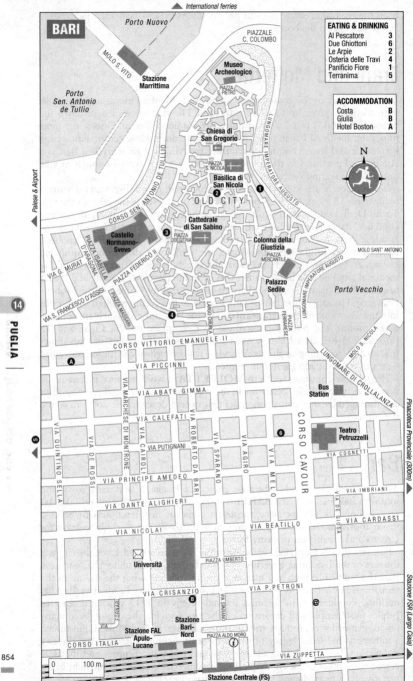

Arrival and information

Bari's **airport** (℡0805.800.200, Ⓦwww.seap-puglia.it) is 25km northwest from the city centre and is served by low-cost airlines from the UK. The #16 AMTAB bus connects the airport with the central station every forty minutes to an hour (5am–11pm; 40min; €0.80); there's also an hourly shuttle bus run by Autobus Tempesta (daily 5.10am–10.40pm; 30min; €4.15 one-way; ℡0805.219.172, Ⓦwww.autoservizitempesta.it).

There are three train stations. **Stazione Centrale** in Piazza Aldo Moro is on the southern edge of the modern centre and serves regular FS trains and those of the private Ferrovia del Sud-Est line (℡0805.462.111, Ⓦwww.fseonline.it), which run down to Táranto via Alberobello, Locorotondo and Martina Franca (see p.861 for more on this route). Just to the west, also on Piazza Aldo Moro, the separate **Stazione Bari-Nord** is for trains run by the private FerroTram-Viaria company (℡0805.299.342, Ⓦwww.ferrovienordbarese.it), connecting Bari with Andria, Barletta, Bitonto and Ruvo di Puglia. Adjacent to this, on Corso Italia, is the **Stazione FAL Apulo-Lucane**; trains and buses from here are run by Ferrovia Appulo-Lucane (℡0805.725.211, Ⓦwww.fal-srl.it) and go to Altamura, Gravina, and Matera and Potenza in Basilicata.

Buses complicate things further: from the coastal towns north of Bari you'll arrive at Piazza Eroi del Mare; SITA buses from inland and southern towns pull up in Largo Sorrentino (behind the train station); Miccolis buses from Rome arrive either here or on Piazza Aldo Moro. Buses belonging to the private rail line FAL, from Basilicata, arrive at the station on Corso Italia, while FSE buses from Bríndisi pull in at their station on Largo Ciaia.

Ferries from Albania, Croatia, Montenegro and Greece (Igoumenitsa, Corfu and Patras) all use the Stazione Maríttima, next to the old city, which is connected with the main FS train station by bus #20.

Getting around, your best bet is to walk – not a bad option in such a small city. The **tourist office** is at Piazza Aldo Moro 33/A, in a small cul-de-sac to the right as you come out of the main train station (Mon–Sat 10am–1pm & 3–6pm; Sun 10am–1pm; ℡0809.909.341, Ⓦwww.viaggiareinpuglia.it).

Accommodation

The majority of **accommodation** is found in the modern part of Bari although some small B&Bs are sprouting up in the old city (see the tourist office for a list). The most affordable hotels are found around the train station, though the area takes a turn for the worse after dark.

Costa Via Crisanzio 12 ℡0805.219.015, Ⓦwww .hotelcostabari.com. Simple but attractive rooms in an apartment building one block from the station. ❸
Giulia Via Crisanzio 12 ℡080.521.6630, Ⓦwww .hotelpensionegiulia.it. In the same building as *Costa*, this *pensione* is run by a pleasant couple, has internet access and some en-suite rooms. ❷

Hotel Boston Via Piccinni 115 ℡080.521.6633, Ⓦwww.bostonbari.it. A stone's throw from the old city, this business traveller's hotel has comfortable, if characterless, rooms and is in safe area convenient for an evening *passeggiata*. ❺

Baresi bag snatchers

A word of warning: the Baresi take positive delight in portraying the old city as a den of thieves, and certainly strolling through the narrow alleys with your camera in full view isn't particularly wise. **Bag snatching** by young kids on mopeds (the *topini*, or "little mice") isn't as rife as it once was, but neither is it extinct, so it's best to keep your wits about you.

The City

Even if you're only in Bari to catch a ferry, try to make time for a wander around the **old city**, an entrancing jumble of streets that's possibly the most perplexing place to walk around in southern Italy. Situated at the far end of Corso Cavour, its labyrinth of seemingly endless passages weaving through courtyards and under arches was originally designed to spare the inhabitants from the wind and throw invaders into a state of confusion. This it still does admirably, and even with the best of maps you're going to get lost. Life is lived very much outdoors, and on summer evenings it's full of people sitting outside their kitchen doors.

The **Basilica di San Nicola** (daily 7.30am–1pm & 4–7pm; museum Tues–Fri 10am–noon; free), in the heart of the old city, was, as an inscription at the side of the main door testifies, consecrated in 1197 to house the relics of the saint plundered a century earlier from southern Turkey. The real beauty of the church lies in its stonework, with the twelfth-century altar canopy one of the finest in Italy. The motifs around the capitals are the work of stonemasons from Como, whilst the lovely twelfth-century carved doorway and simple, striking mosaic floor behind the altar are heavily influenced by the Saracens. Best of all is the twelfth-century episcopal throne behind the altar, a superb piece of work supported by small figures wheezing beneath its weight. Down in the crypt are the remains of the saint – patron of Bari, many surrounding towns, orphans, pawnbrokers, thieves, sailors, and of Russians.

It's not far from the basilica to Bari's other important church, the **Cattedrale di San Sabino** (Mon–Sat 8.30am–12.30pm & 4–7.30pm, Sun 8am–12.30pm & 5–8.30pm; free), off Piazza Odegitria, dedicated to the original patron saint of Bari, before he was usurped by Nicholas, and built at the end of the twelfth century. Come just for the contrast: uncluttered by arches, it retains its original medieval atmosphere and – unlike the basilica – a timbered roof. The cathedral houses an eighth-century icon known as the *Madonna Odegitria*, brought here for safety from Constantinople by Byzantine monks. It's said to be the most authentic likeness of the Madonna in existence, having been taken from an original sketch by Luke the Apostle, and it's paraded around the city at religious festivals.

Due west of the piazza Odegitria, the **Castello Normanno-Svevo** (Thurs–Tues 9am–7pm; €2) sits on the site of an earlier Roman fort. Built by Frederick II, much of it is closed to the public, but it has a vaulted hall that provides a cool escape from the afternoon sun. You can also see a gathering of some of the best of past Puglian artistry in a display of plaster-cast reproductions from churches and buildings throughout the region – particularly from the Castel del Monte, the cathedral at Altamura, and an animated frieze of griffins devouring serpents, from the church of San Leonardo at Siponto.

At the time of writing the collection for the **Museo Archeologico** was closed and in the process of being transferred from the new city to the old town's ex-monastery of Santa Scolastica. It holds a good selection of Greek and Puglian ceramics and a solid collection of artefacts from the Daunic, Messapian and Peucetic peoples – Puglia's earliest inhabitants.

The new town

There's not a lot to the "**new town**" of Bari: straight streets are lined with shops and offices, relieved occasionally by the odd bit of greenery. **Corso Cavour**, Bari's main commercial street, bordered with trees, leads down to the waterfront. Along Lungomare in Palazzo della Provincia, the **Pinacoteca Provinciale**

Ferries from Bari

International ferry services run from Bari to Greece, Albania and Croatia; for information and timetables call ⓣ800.573.738 or visit ⓦwww.porto.bari.it. Travel agents often have special offers on **tickets**; as a general rule, you will save 20 percent if you buy a return ticket. Once you've got your ticket, you must report to the relevant desk at the Stazione Maríttima at least two hours before departure. Prices given below are for travel in high season.

Albania

Tirrenia (ⓣ892.123, ⓦwww.tirrenia.it), Ventouris (ⓣ0805.217.609, ⓦwww.ventouris.gr), Azzura (ⓣ0805.928.400, ⓦwww.azzuralines.com), and Agemar (ⓣ0805.211.069, ⓦwww.agemar.it) run car ferries to Durazzo/Durres in Albania daily all year round; the journey takes eight hours overnight (from €60 one-way, €83 for a reclining seat).

Croatia

Jadrolinija operates services to Rijeka, Stari Grad, Dubrovnik, Korcula, and Split in **Croatia**, departing late evening for a night crossing of the Adriatic. For the full timetable visit ⓦwww.jadrolinija.hr or contact Agenzia P. Lorusso (ⓣ0805.217.619, ⓦwww.agenzialorusso.it) in the Stazione Marittima. (tickets start at €50 for deck passage one-way).

Greece

Ferry services to **Greece** are operated by Ventouris, Superfast (ⓦwww.superfast.com) and Agoudimos (ⓦwww.agoudimos-lines.com). All three companies offer online booking. Ventouris runs two to four services daily to Corfu and Igoumenitsa; one-way prices start at €65 per person, €76 extra for a car, plus port fees. The service to Igoumenitsa takes eleven hours and thirty minutes and the service to Corfu takes eleven hours. Superfast runs a daily overnight sailing to Corfu (8hr), Igoumenitsa (9.5hr), and Patras (15hr) year-round and the seats cost from €71 (cars €49).

(Tues–Sat 9am–1pm & 4–7pm, Sun 9am–1pm; €2.58) contains mostly southern Italian art ranging from the twelfth to nineteenth centuries, but there are also works by Tintoretto and Paolo Veronese that were moved from the cathedral, and a small collection of paintings by the twentieth-century Bolognese painter, Giorgio Morandi.

Eating and drinking

There are lots of colorful choices of **places to eat** in and around the old town of Bari. Most offer traditional Pugliese dishes and seafood, along with the Bari speciality of *orecchiette*, ear-shaped pasta. In the evenings stalls sell *panzerotti* and *sgagliozze* (fried polenta cubes) around Piazza Mercantile and Piazza del Ferrarese.

Al Pescatore Piazza Federico II di Svevia 8 ⓣ0805.237.039. A couple of blocks east of the castle (watch your bag in this area), this no-nonsense choice serves fine fish for around €25 a head. Closed Mon

Due Ghiottoni Via Putignani 11 ⓣ0805.232.240. One of the town's top restaurants serves good shellfish and a refined version of Pugliese cuisine in attractive surroundings just outside the old city. Count on €60 for a full meal. Closed Aug & Sun, except in summer.

Le Arpie Vico Arco Carmine 1/3 ⓣ0805.217.988. Rustic and moderately priced serving generous antipasti and classic local specialities like *tiella di riso, patate, e cozze* (rice casserole with potatoes and mussels). Closed Wed and two weeks in July.

Panificio Fiore Strada Palazzo di Cittá 38. Locals queue for their delicious *focaccia barese*, simply garnished with tomatoes, olives, salt and olive oil (€1.50). Closed Thurs eve and Sun.

Osteria delle Travi Largo Chiurlia 12 ⓣ0805.617.150. This inexpensive old-town trattoria

serves authentic local food in pleasing surroundings – don't miss the antipasti buffet. Reservations recommended. Closed Sun eve and Mon.
Terranima Via Putignani 213–215 ☎ 0805.219.725. Informal café-restaurant serving a daily changing menu of regional specialities for around €20 without drinks. There's often live music in the eve. Closed Sun & Aug.

Listings

Airport information Bari Palese ☎ 0805.800.200, ⓦ www.seap-puglia.it.
Exchange Outside banking hours in Piazza Aldo Moro, inside Stazione Centrale and at the Stazione Marittima.
Police Via G. Murat ☎ 0805.491.331.

Post office The main office is near the university in Piazza Umberto I 33/A (Mon–Fri 8am–6.30pm, Sat 8.30am–12.30pm).
Taxis Radio Taxi ☎ 0805.543.333, ⓦ www.taxibari .it. (24hr).

Le Murge

Rising gently from the Adriatic coast, **Le Murge** – a low limestone plateau – dominates the landscape to the south and west of Bari. The towns in the region are not natural holiday destinations: the area is sparsely populated and the small settlements that exist are rural backwaters with a slow pace of life. But they do make an interesting day out or a good stopover if you're heading for the region of Basilicata. There are some buses and trains from Bari, but, as always, in Puglia without your own car travelling very extensively can be difficult.

The Low Murge

Easily reached from Barletta or Bari, the main town of the Low Murge is **ANDRIA**, a large agricultural centre at its best during its Monday morning market – otherwise it has little to hold you. It was, though, a favourite haunt of Frederick II, who was responsible for the major local attraction these days, the **Castel del Monte**, 17km south – the most extraordinary of all Puglia's castles and one of the finest surviving examples of Swabian architecture (daily: March–Sept 10.15am–7.15pm; Oct–Feb 9am–6pm; ticket office closes 30min earlier; €3). Unfortunately, there is only an infrequent bus service from Andria (2 daily April–Oct). Contact the Pro Loco office in Andria at Via Vespucci 14 (Mon–Fri 9.30am–12.30pm & 4–8pm, Sat 9.30am–12.30pm; ☎ 0883.592.283, ⓦ www .proloco.andria.ba.it) for timetables.

Begun by Frederick in the 1240s, the castle is a high, isolated fortress built around an octagonal courtyard in two storeys of eight rooms. A mystery surrounds its intended purpose. Although there was once an iron gate that could be lowered over the main entrance, there are no other visible signs of fortification, and the castle may have served as merely a hunting lodge. Nonetheless, the mathematical precision involved in its construction, and the preoccupation with the number eight, have excited writers for centuries. It's argued the castle is in fact an enormous astrological calendar, or that Frederick may have had the octagonal Omar mosque in Jerusalem in mind when he designed it; yet, despite his recorded fascination with the sciences, no one really knows the truth. There is only one record of its use. The defeat of Manfred, Frederick's illegitimate son, at the battle of Benevento in 1266 signalled the end of Swabian power in Puglia; and Manfred's sons and heirs were imprisoned in the castle for over thirty years – a lonely place to be incarcerated.

Southeast of Andria (but best reached by hourly bus from Molfetta), the old centre of **RUVO DI PUGLIA** is an attractive stop, with a quiet, timeless atmosphere. In the autumn, the pavements of the Old Town are traditionally strewn with almonds, spread out to dry in the sun. Just across from the **tourist office** on Via Vittorio Veneto 48 (Mon–Sat 9.30am–12.30pm & 4.30–7.30pm, Sun 9.30am–12.30pm; ☎080.361.5419), the **Museo Jatta** in Piazza Bovio (Mon–Wed 8.30am–1.30pm, Thurs–Sat 8.30am–7.30pm; ⓦwww.palazzojatta.org; free but €1.50 charge for tours in English) houses a dusty collection of local copies of ancient Greek pottery as well as some beautiful originals, including a fifth-century-BC crater depicting the death of Talos. Ruvo's thirteenth-century **Duomo**, tucked into the tightly packed streets of the town's old quarter, is also well worth a look. Its beautiful portal is guarded by animated griffins balancing on fragile columns, with a staggering amount of decoration on the outer walls, a fine rose window and arches that taper off into human and animal heads.

The High Murge

Around 45km south of Bari (and reachable by FAL train), **ALTAMURA** is the largest town in the High Murge, originally a fifth-century-BC Peucetian settlement – you can still see some parts of the old town. Given its many historical layers, it's perhaps appropriate that Altamura is home to one of southern Italy's best **archeological museums** (Mon–Fri 8.30am–7.30pm, Sat & Sun 8.30am–1.30pm; €2) on Via Santeramo 88. The collection here traces the history of the people of the Murge from prehistory to late medieval times, with plenty of exciting finds from all over the peninsula.

Altamura's most striking feature is its **Duomo**, a mixture of styles varying from Apulian-Romanesque to Gothic and Baroque. Take a look, too, at the tiny church of **San Niccolò dei Greci** on Corso Federico di Svevia; built by the Greek colonists in the thirteenth century, it housed their Orthodox religious ceremonies for more than 400 years.

Some 12km west, not far from the border with Basilicata, lies **GRAVINA DI PUGLIA** – a fortified town clinging to the edge of a deep ravine. During the early Barbarian invasions the locals took refuge in the caves along the sides of the gully, a move that seems to have paid off until the arrival of the Saracens, who promptly massacred every cave-dwelling inhabitant. Under the Normans, the shattered town settled down to a quieter life as a fiefdom of the wealthy pope-producing Orsini family, whose emblem – an enormous spread eagle – is all over town. In the dilapidated old quarter, the cave-church of **San Michele delle Grotte** (closed to the public), a dark, dank affair hewn out of the rock, holds bones that are said to be the remains of victims of the last Saracen attack, almost a thousand years old. The **Museo Ettore Pomarici Santomasi** (Mon–Sat 9am–1pm & 4–7pm, Sun 9.30am–12.30pm; ⓦwww.fondazionesantomasi.it; €3) at Via Museo 20 contains archeological finds including Roman coins, Bourbon arms and uniforms as well as sixteenth- and seventeenth-century paintings, but more engaging is the reconstruction of San Vito Vecchio, another cave-church, set up on the ground floor with some remarkable thirteenth- to fourteenth-century frescoes.

Down the coast from Bari

The coast south of Bari is a craggy stretch, with rock-hewn villages towering above tiny sandy coves. Just ten minutes by FS train from Bari (or bus #12 from Piazza Aldo Moro), **TORRE A MARE** is one of the easiest escapes from the city, situated on a rocky ledge high above two large caves. Being so close to Bari, the village can become quite crowded, but there will be fewer people around another twenty minutes on, at **POLIGNANO A MARE**, which, despite a newfound popularity, remains fairly low-key. It's a small port with a whitewashed medieval centre sprinkled with bars, souvenir and *focacciarie* shops, perched on the edge of the limestone cliffs, and where people head for on a Sunday to watch the waves crashing against the rocks or to sunbathe on the clifftops. If you don't have a car, it is best reached by train, although there is a bus service, run by FSE, from Largo Ciaia in Bari. If you'd like to **stay**, head for the appealing *Covo dei Saraceni*, Via Conversano 1/A (℡080.424.1177, ⑩www.covodeisaraceni.com; ❼), which sits right above the rocks and has comfortable rooms – some with large balconies and private terraces – and a restaurant with panoramic views. If you're feeling flush, don't miss a meal at *A Da Tuccino* a few kilometres north along the coast at Via Santa Caterina 69/F (℡080.424.1560, ⑩www.tuccino.it; closed Mon). The region's best seafood restaurant, it is know for its *crudi* (raw fish); the menu varies according to the catch of the day; booking is essential and a full meal with wine will cost around €50, not much more than its competitors.

Egnázia and Fasano

Some 8km beyond Polignano a Mare lies the commercial port of **MONÓPOLI**, with a nice old town and a charming **Duomo**, but not much else to see. There's more interest south, at the site of the ancient city of **Egnázia** (daily 8am to 1hr before sunset; ⑩xoomer.alice.it/egnazia; €3 including museum). If you don't have your own transport, it's best reached by bus from **Fasano** train station (call or visit Fasano's tourist office for timetable; Piazza Ciaia 10; ℡080.441.3086; Mon–Sat 9am–1pm & 4–7pm). Right next to the seafront excavations, the water is tempting and clear, so bring swimming stuff and a picnic. Egnázia (also known as Gnathia) was an important Messapian centre during the fifth century BC, fortified with over 2km of walls, large parts of which still stand in the northern corner of the ruined town – up to 7m high. It was later colonized by the Greeks and then the Romans (in 244 BC), who built a forum, amphitheatre, a colonnaded public hall and temples: one was dedicated to Syria, a popular early Roman goddess, who, according to Lucian, was worshipped by men dressed as women. Horace is known to have dropped by here to see the city's famous altar, which ignited wood without a flame.

With the collapse of the Roman Empire, the city fell to subsequent barbarian invasions, and was almost completely destroyed by the Gothic king Totila in 545 AD. A community struggled on here, seeking refuge in the Messapian tombs, until the tenth century when the settlement was finally abandoned. There's an on-site **museum** (same hours and ticket as above) housing an array of artefacts, including examples of the distinctive earthenware for which the ancient town was prized.

Places to stay in nearby **Selva di Fasano** include a hill station of villas in lush gardens above the town of Fasano. Try *La Silvana*, Viale dei Pini 87 (℡080.433.1161, ⑩www.lasilvanahotel.it; ❸), an unpretentious hotel with large, simply decorated rooms, balconies and plenty of terrace space. Alternatively, there's the luxurious *La Peschiera*, on Contrada Losciale in Monopoli's Localitá Capitolo (℡080.801.066, ⑩www.peschierahotel.com; ❾), a Bourbon-era fish hatchery converted into a fine resort. Rooms have enchanting sea views and private beaches.

The FSE line: Castellana Grotte to Martina Franca

Meandering lazily down towards the **Valle d'Itria**, the Ferrovia Sud-Est train passes through some of the prettiest of Puglia's landscapes. Olives gradually lose ground to vineyards and cherry and peach orchards, neatly partitioned by dry-stone walls. The barren limestone terrain of Le Murge swallows rivers whole producing a landscape cut by deep ravines and pitted with caverns and grottoes. About 40km out of Bari are the **Grotte di Castellana**, a spectacular set of underground caves (mid-March to early Nov, Dec 26–Jan 6 & Feb carnival time tours hourly 8.30am–1pm & 2.30–7pm; rest of year tours 9.30am–12.30pm; €15 for a full 3km/2hr tour, €10 for 1km/50min tour excluding Grotta Bianca; ℡0804.998.211, 𝕎www.grottedicastellana.it). A lift takes you down to the largest of the caverns, La Grave, 60m below ground. From here, there's over 1km of strangely formed caves to explore, ending in the most impressive of them all, the Grotta Bianca – a shimmering sea of white stalagmites and stalactites. To **get to the caves**, simply follow the signs from the Castellana-Grotte station, from where it's about 500m to the grotto.

Alberobello

Beyond Putignano, traditional *trulli* (see box, p.862) buildings dominate the landscape. If you want to take a closer look, head for **ALBEROBELLO**. Around 1500 *trulli* pack the narrow streets; most are south of Largo Martellotta in the Rione Monti zone, the rest to the north in Rione Aia Piccola. You can pick up a town map from the **tourist office** in the central Piazza Ferdinando IV

▲ Trulli houses in Alberobello

Curious-looking **trulli** are dotted throughout the Murge area of Puglia. Cylindrical, white-washed buildings with grey conical roofs tapering out to a point or sphere, they are often adorned with painted symbols. Unique to Puglia, their ancient origins are obscure, but are probably connected to feudal lords who made people working their land build their houses without mortar so they could easily be pulled down if tax inspectors came round. The thick walls insulate equally against the cold in winter and the summer heat, while local limestone is used to make the two-layered roofs water-tight. Most *trulli* have just one room but when more space was needed, a hole was simply knocked in the wall and an identical structure built next door. Although originally they were both dwellings and store houses, these days they're being snapped up by Italians and foreigners as holiday homes, and some are rented out as self-catering or B&B accommodation.

(Mon–Fri 9am–1pm & 3–6pm; ☎0804.325.171; about a 10min walk from the station). Inevitably, a rampant tourist industry has grown up around the cute conical stone huts, and the proprietors of *trulli* given over to displays of woolly shawls, liqueurs and other souvenirs practically drag in passers-by and don't let them go until they've bought something.

If you want to complete the *trulli* experience by **staying** in one, check in at *B&B Pietradimora* (☎0804.324.370, ⓦ www.pietradimora.it; ●), a beautifully restored set of *trulli* on Via Monte San Marco 28. Breakfast is served on a panoramic terrace. Another central choice is the spick-and-span *Lanzillotta* at Piazza Ferdinando IV 33 (☎0804.321.511, ⓦ www.hotellanzillotta.it; ❷). *Trullidea* rents basic *trulli* in town and in the countryside for short and long-term stays (☎0804.323.860, ⓦ www.trullidea.it; ❸). They can also arrange cooking courses and excursions.

For **food** in Alberobello, *L'Aratro* (☎0804.322.789; closed Mon & Jan), set inside a *trullo*, is a stellar option serving a dizzying number of antipasti and local specialities including *purè di fave e cicoria* (blended broad beans and chicory) and *cavatelli con cime di rapa* (pasta with turnip tops and fried breadcrumbs). Excellent pizzas and *crostini* can be washed down with cold beer at *Pizzeria Pozzo Contino* on Via Brigida Regina.

Just a few kilometres south, **LOCOROTONDO**, which owes its name to its circular layout, has good views over the whole area, speckled with red- and grey-roofed *trulli* in a sea of vines and olive and almond trees. It's a great place to wander for an hour or so.

Finally, on the road between Locorotondo and Ostuni, **CISTERNINO** rejoices in the nickname "La Vera" (the Real Thing) and is a marvellous antidote to touristy Alberobello: it's a pleasure to wander around the tiny, whitewashed alleyways of its old town. A series of **open-air concerts** are held in the main square, Piazza Vittorio Emanuele, between late June and September: among them is *Pietre che Cantano* ("The Stones that Sing"; ⓦ www.pietrechecantano.com).

Martina Franca

The *trulli* are still plentiful by the time you reach **MARTINA FRANCA**, a surprising town with a jubilant Baroque sensibility and a lively *passeggiata* at weekends. It is reputed to have been founded by settlers from Táranto fed up with constant Saracen attacks during the tenth century, but it was the Angevin prince of Táranto who bolstered the community in the early fourteenth century by granting it certain tax privileges. The town derives its name from this – *franca* meaning duty or stamp. Today its medieval core is adorned with some of the most subtle and least overbearing examples of architecture from the Baroque period you'll find.

Through the **Porta di Santo Stefano**, which marks the entrance to the old town, Piazza Roma is dominated by the hulking **Palazzo Ducale**, which dates from 1688, and is now the town hall. A handful of rooms are open to the public most mornings (Mon–Fri) – most of them smothered in classical eighteenth-century Arcadian murals. Just across the square, the narrow Via Vittorio Emanuele leads right into the old town and Piazza Plebiscito, fronted by undulating Baroque facade of the **Chiesa di San Martino**, an eighteenth-century church built on the site of an earlier Romanesque structure, of which only the campanile survives. From adjacent Piazza Immacolata you can either bear left down Via Cavour, with its Baroque *palazzi* and balconied streets, or wander further into the old town; the roads running around the edge of the surviving fourteenth-century town walls offer an excellent panorama of the Valle d'Itria, with its neatly ordered fields dotted with *trulli*.

Southern Italy's top performing arts festival, the **Festival della Valle d'Itria** (℡0804.805.100, ⓦwww.festivaldellavalleditria.it), takes place in Martina Franca in late July/early August every year. On a par with the *Maggio Musicale* in Florence, the festival is mainly operatic, with performances in the appropriately grand Palazzo Ducale. It's a congenial and unpretentious event, though tickets aren't cheap, they're available from the festival office in the Palazzo Ducale.

Practicalities

There's a spasmodic bus service from the **FSE train station** up to the centre of town; otherwise you'll have to walk for fifteen minutes – go left out of the station and up Viale della Libertà to Corso Italia, which leads to the old town centre. The **tourist office** on Piazza Roma 35 (Mon–Fri 9am–1pm & 5–7.30pm, Sat 9am–12.30pm; ℡0804.805.702) has good maps of the town. The cheapest **hotel** is the *Hotel da Luigi* on Via Táranto, Zona G25 (℡0804.856.066; ❶), though this is 2km out of town and at festival time you won't get a room here. Pricier, but in town, is the comfortable *Dell'Erba*, Via Taranto 68 (℡0804.301.055, ⓦwww.hoteldellerba .com; ❸), with a swimming pool, restaurant and plenty of sun terraces. For more atmospheric and cost-effective accommodation, consider renting a traditional apartment in the old town. Studio apartments work out at €37.50 per person per night for two sharing, plus linen charge (no minimum stay); contact *Villaggio In* at Via Arco Grassi 8 (℡080.480.5911, ⓦwww.villaggioin.it; ❷).

An excellent **restaurant** is *La Cantina*, Vico 1 Lanucara 12 (℡0804.808.031; closed Mon), signposted off Piazza XX Settembre, the main gate to the old town – try the *bucatini con fagioli* (pasta with beans) or *agnello con fave e cicoria* (lamb with broad beans and wild chicory). Or head straight for the town's best pizzas at *La Panca* (℡0804.801.629; closed Mon), Via Principe Umberto 51, just off Piazza M. Immacolata in the old town. For refined, upscale Pugliese cooking, don't miss *Ritrovo degli Amici* on Corso Messapia 8 (℡0804.839.249; closed Sun eve & Mon), just off Piazza XX Settembre on a little, flower-filled patio. If you're after **snacks** or picnic food, try *Fratelli Ricci*, the *rosticceria* at Via Cavour 19 (closed Mon). They sell the wonderful hot foods and sandwiches.

Táranto

Straddling two harbours and set beside the deep blue waters of the Ionian, **TÁRANTO** is an unpretentious city with a thriving fish market, fabulous restaurants and a top-notch archeological museum. Known as **Taras** to the

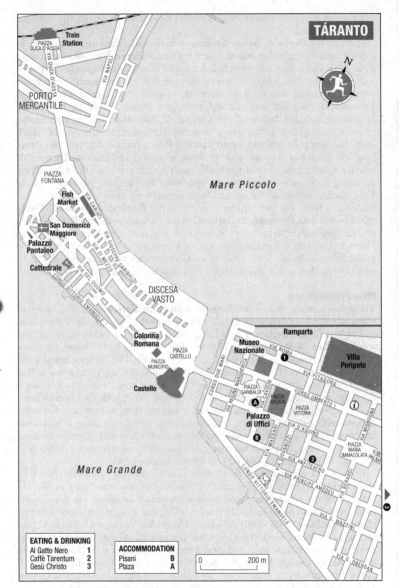

TÁRANTO

Mare Piccolo

Mare Grande

PIAZZA DUCA D'AOSTA
Train Station
VIA NAPOLI
VIA DUCA D'AOSTA
PORTO MERCANTILE
PIAZZA FONTANA
Fish Market
VIA CARIATI
San Domenico Maggiore
Palazzo Pantaleo
VIA GIUSEPPE GARIBALDI
VIA DI MEZZO
Cattedrale
VIA DEL DUOMO
CORSO VITTORIO EMANUELE
DISCESA VASTO
Colonna Romana
PIAZZA CASTELLO
PIAZZA MUNICIPIO
Castello
Ramparts
Museo Nazionale
VIA ROMA
1
Villa Peripato
VIA PITAGORA
CORSO DUE MARI
VIA REGINA MARGHERITA
PIAZZA GARIBALDI
VIA CAVOUR
PIAZZA ARCHITA
CORSO UMBERTO I
A
PIAZZA VITTORIA
i
Palazzo di Uffici
B
VIA D'AQUINO
VIA MIGNOGNA
VIA MASSARI
VIA GIOVANIZZI
VIA ANFITEATRO
2
PIAZZA MARIA IMMACOLATA
V. DI PALMA
VIA BERARDI
LUNGO VITTORIO EMANUELE
VIA PRINCIPE AMEDEO
VIA G. MAZZINI
VIA G. OBERDAN

EATING & DRINKING
Al Gatto Nero 1
Caffè Tarentum 2
Gesù Christo 3

ACCOMMODATION
Pisani B
Plaza A

0   200 m

ancient Greeks, the port became the first city of Magna Graecia (the area of southern Italy colonized by the Greeks) and was renowned for its oysters, mussels and dyes – the imperial purple was the product of decayed Tarentine molluscs. Resplendent with temples, its acropolis harboured a vast bronze of Poseidon that was one of the wonders of the ancient world. Sadly, little remains of ancient Taras or even of later Roman Tarentum, although their monuments and relics are on display in the city's museum. After being destroyed by the

Romans, Táranto was for years little more than a small fishing port, its strategic position on the sea only being recognized in Napoleonic times. It was home to the Italian fleet after Unification, and consequently heavily bombed during World War II; attempts to rejuvenate the town have left its medieval heart girdled by heavy industry, including the vast Italsider steel plant that throws its flames and lights into the skies above.

Finding your way around is easy. The city divides neatly into three distinct parts: the northern spur is the industrial area, home of the steel works and train station. Cross the Ponte di Porta Napoli and you're on the central island containing the old town. The southern spur holds the modern city centre (Borgo Nuovo), the administrative and commercial hub of Táranto, linked to the old town by a swing-bridge.

Arrival, information and accommodation

Buses generally arrive at and depart from Porto Mercantile Castello, except FS connections with Metaponto and Potenza, which arrive at Piazza Duca d'Aosta, just outside the **train station**. National and regional bus services, run by Miccolis (℡0994.704.451, ⓦwww.miccolis-spa.it) and Marino (℡199.800.100, ⓦwww .marinobus.it), stop at Porto Mercantile and Discesa Vasto in the old town. The old town is a 400m walk from the train station; buses #1 or #3 run to Corso Umberto I in the modern city. Get off just after Palazzo di Uffici and you're close to the **tourist office** on Corso Umberto I 121 (Mon–Fri 9am–1pm & 4.30– 6.30pm, Sat 9am–noon; ℡0994.532.392, ⓦwww.viaggiareinpuglia.it). Timetables for **city buses** are posted in the AMAT office just around the corner on Via D'Aquino 21(℡0994.526.785; ⓦwww.amat.taranto.it).

Finding **accommodation** can be a headache, as Táranto isn't really geared up for tourism: a central, inexpensive hotel is *Plaza*, Via d'Aquino 46 (℡0994.590.775, ⓦwww.hotelplazataranto.com; ❸), while just around the corner, at the end of an alleyway with potted plants, the basic *Pisani*, Via Cavour 43 (℡0994.534.087, no site or email ❶), has clean en-suite rooms.

The City

In Greek times the island holding the **old town** wasn't an island at all but part of the southern peninsula, connected by an isthmus to the southern spur. The Greeks raised temples and the acropolis here, while further south lay the residential districts. There's one extant fragment of ancient Táranto – the Doric **columns**, re-erected in a corner of **Piazza Castello**, which once adorned a temple of Poseidon. The rest of the tiny island is a mass of poky streets and alleyways, buttressed by scaffolding seemingly to prevent the whole place from falling down. The Aragonese **Castello** (now owned by the navy) at the southern end surveys the comings and goings of warships and fishing boats. The narrow canal they slide through, between the city's two inland "seas", was built in the late nineteenth century, on the site of the castle's old moat. "Seas" is a bit of a misnomer: the Mare Piccolo is really a large lagoon, home to Táranto's famous oysters and the Italian navy; and the Mare Grande is actually a vast bay, protected by sea walls and the offshore fortified island of San Pietro.

At the heart of the old town lies the eleventh-century **Duomo**, which once did duty as a mosque – dedicated to Táranto's patron saint, Cataldo (Cathal), a seventh-century Irish monk who on returning from a pilgrimage to the Holy Land was so shocked by the licentiousness of the town's inhabitants that he decided to stay and clean the place up. His remains lie under the altar of a small chapel. As for the rest of the church, restoration has stripped away most of the Baroque alterations, and fragments of a Byzantine mosaic floor have been revealed.

A few blocks away, check out the city's **fish market**, on Via Cariati, a lively affair where the best of the local catch is displayed at the crack of dawn: octopuses lie dazed, clams spit defiantly at you, while other less definable creatures seem preoccupied with making a last dash for freedom before the restaurateurs arrive – some of the city's finest restaurants are just across the road.

The Borgo Nuovo

It's a short walk across the swing-bridge to Táranto's modern centre or **Borgo Nuovo** – though this, like Bari's, has limited charms, its wide streets laid out on a grid pattern that forms the focus of the city's *passeggiata*, around piazzas Vittoria and Archita. Nearby, the **Villa Peripato** was *the* place for the Tarentini to take their early-evening stroll at the beginning of the last century, but today the city's gardeners seem to be fighting a losing battle with the ponds and undergrowth.

The only real attraction in this part of town – and it's a gem – is the **Museo Archeologico Nazionale** Piazza Cavour (daily 8.30am–7.15pm; ⓦwww .museotaranto.it; €5), which offers a fascinating insight into the splendour of ancient Taras. Its pottery collection is one of the world's largest with over 50,000 pieces. The work of the goldsmiths of Taras is a particular highlight, all delicately patterned and finely worked in gold filigree. Several finds from Greek tombs are also worth a look, including a tiny terracotta model of Aphrodite emerging from the sea (dated end of fourth, early third century BC).

Eating and drinking

For **meals**, *Gesu' Christo* on Via C Battisti 10 in the new city is a popular, convivial place for seafood at moderate prices – the fish comes fresh from the market just around the corner (☎0997.353.663; closed Sun eve & Mon). One of the city's historic trattorias *Al Gatto Nero*, Via Cavour 2 (☎0994.529.875; closed Mon), delivers friendly service, excellent antipasti and inventive pasta dishes such as linguine with tuna, mint and lemon. *Caffe Tarentum* on Via Anfiteatro 97 serves excellent coffee and typical almond-based sweets like *mustazzueli* as well as savory snacks (closed Tues).

Northwest of Táranto

Inland and **northwest** of Táranto, the scenery changes dramatically, with gorges and ravines marking a landscape that's closer to that of Basilicata than Puglia. **MASSAFRA**, about 15km from Táranto (regular trains and FSE buses from Porto Mercantile), is split in two by a ravine, the Gravina di San Marco, lined with grottoes dating mainly from the ninth to the fourteenth centuries. Many contain cave-churches, hewn out of the rock by Greek monks and decorated with lavish frescoes. All such sites in Massafra are visitable only by guided tours arranged with the **tourist office** at Piazza Garibaldi (winter Mon–Fri 9.30am–noon; summer 9.30am–noon & 4–7pm; ☎0998.804.695 or 338.565.9601). The **Santuario della Madonna della Scala** is built onto an earlier cave-church; a Baroque staircase runs down to the eighteenth-century church, which features a beautiful fresco of a *Madonna and Child*, dating from the twelfth to the thirteenth centuries; more steps lead down to an eighth-century crypt. The nearby **Cripta della Buona Nuova** houses a thirteenth-century fresco of the Madonna and a striking painting of *Christ Pantocrator*. About 200m away, at the bottom of the ravine, is a mass of interconnected caves known as the **Farmacia del Mago Greguro**, now in a pretty pitiful state but once used by the medieval monks as a herbalist's workshop.

Bríndisi

Across the peninsula, 60km east of Táranto on the opposite coast, lies **BRÍNDISI**, once a bridging point for crusading knights and still a town that makes its living from people passing through. The natural harbour here, the safest on the Adriatic coast, made Bríndisi an ideal choice for early settlers. In Roman times, the port became the main crossing point between the eastern and western empires, and later, under the Normans, there came a steady stream of pilgrims heading east towards the Holy Land. The route is still open, and now Bríndisi – primarily – is where you come if you're **heading for Greece** from Italy. On arrival, you may well think that the entire town is full of shipping agents: this, when all is said and done, is the town's main business. But even if you're leaving the same night you'll almost certainly end up with time on your hands. You could just while away time in a bar or restaurant in the old town – it is pretty compact and, although it isn't brimming with ancient monuments, has a pleasant, almost oriental flavour about it, and a few hidden gems tucked down its narrow streets. If you decide to stay, you will find that Bríndisi's youth hostel is a fun place to base yourself for day-trips to the beach, Ostuni or the Torre Guaceto, a lovely nature reserve for biking and swimming.

Arrival and information

Bríndisi's **airport** (☎0805.800.200, ⓦwww.seap-puglia.it), served by Ryanair from Stansted, is 7km from the city centre; an airport bus run by STP heads into town, stopping at the the the Stazione Maríttima, the train station, Viale A. Moro (for hotel *Mediterraneo*), Via Indipendenza (for hotels *Torino* and *Barsotti*), Via del Mare (for hotel *Approdo*) and Via de Simone (for the youth hostel); buy the €3 ticket on board. There are also regular buses from the airport direct to Lecce (see p.872); the service is run by COTRAP – tickets cost €5 (sold onboard) and the trip takes forty mintes. Arriving by **ferry** from Greece leaves you at **Costa Morena**, a couple of kilometres southeast of town; a shuttle bus run by the port authority links this with the town centre, dropping off and picking up at the intersection of Corso Garibaldi and Lungomare Regina Margherita, in front of the maritime station.

Marozzi **buses** link the town with Rome (4 daily) and Miccolis buses connect it with Naples (3 daily); these buses arrive at, and depart from, Viale P. Togliatti, a continuation of Viale A. Moro in the new part of town. There are other daily departures to Siena, Florence, and Pisa.

Central Bríndisi is small enough to walk around, but for **transport** around town, lots of buses run down Corso Umberto and Corso Garibaldi. The **tourist office** is at Lungomare R. Margherita 43/44 (Apirl–Oct daily 9am–1pm & 3–11pm; Nov–March Mon–Fri 9am–1pm & 3–8pm, Sat 9am–1.30pm; ☎0831.523.072 ⓦwww.viaggiareinpuglia.it). The website ⓦwww.brindisiweb .com, has some useful tourism links.

Accommodation

Probably the best choice is the friendly 🛏 **youth hostel**, 2km out of town in Casale at Via Brandi 2 (☎338.323.5545, ⓦwww.hostelcarpediem.it; €13), with

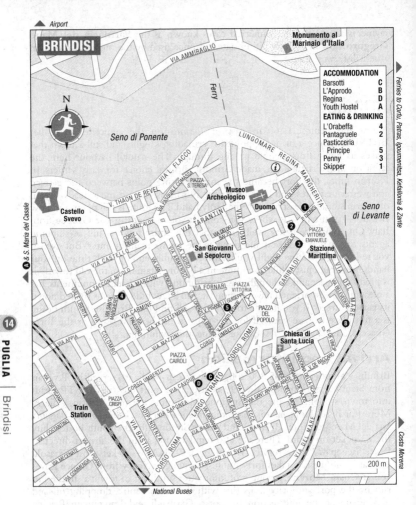

no lock-out, a lively atmosphere, and free shuttles to the port and airport. You can rent a bed for the day (€8) if you've got a night departure, with full use of the facilities, including hot power-showers, laundry, bike rental, book exchange, bar and pool table. Alternatively try the *Hotel Regina*, Via Cavour 5 (℡0831.562.001, ⓦwww.hotelreginaweb.com; ❸), down a quiet side street 150m from the station or *L'Approdo*, Via del Mare 50 (℡0831.529.667, ⓦwww.lapprodohotel.it; ❸), several minutes' walk from the and next to a popular pizza restaurant; it offers special deals on triple and quadruple rooms. Both hotels have air conditioning.

The Town

The top of **Scalinata Virgiliana** (Virgil's Steps) marks the end of the ancient Via Appia, which ran all the way from the Porta Capena in Rome. Two columns stood here for years – useful navigation points for ships coming into harbour. The single column that remains has been restored, as has the area around it; the other column was carried off to Lecce. A marble tablet in the corner of the piazza marks the supposed site of the house in which Virgil died, in 19 BC. Via Colonne, with its seventeenth- and eighteenth-century *palazzi*, runs up to the **Duomo** – a remarkable building, if only for the fact that it's survived seven earthquakes since its construction in the eleventh century. Just outside is the **Museo Archeologico Provinciale** (daily 9am–1pm, Tues, Thurs & Sat 4–6.30pm; free). In addition to ornaments and statues from the necropolises that lined the Via Appia in Roman times, several rooms accommodate bronzes recovered in underwater exploration nearby, as well as finds from the excavations at Egnázia (see p.860). Follow Via Tarentini from here and bear left for the tiny round church of **San Giovanni al Sepolcro**, an eleventh-century baptistry. It's a little dark and decrepit inside, but you can just make out some of the original thirteenth-century frescoes. And there are more frescoes, this time a century older, in the **Chiesa di Santa Lucia**, just off Piazza del Popolo.

Bríndisi's most important medieval monument is further afield: the **Chiesa di Santa Maria del Casale** (check with the tourist office for hours and ring for entrance at the gate; free) – a 3km bus ride towards the airport from town; take bus #4, from the train station, and ask the driver when to get off. Built by Philip of Anjou at the end of the thirteenth century, it's an odd mixture of styles: the facade is adorned with an Arabic mass of geometric patterns, worked in two shades of sandstone, and the portal has an almost Art Deco touch to it. The stark interior is rescued from gloom by some fourteenth-century frescoes depicting frightening allegorical scenes relating to the Last Judgement, a vision of hell designed to scare the living daylights out of the less devout.

Eating and drinking

It's not difficult to **eat and drink** cheaply in Bríndisi: *Pasticceria Principe* on Via De Cesare has delicious pastries as well as a excellent savoury snacks and there are plenty of *alimentari* and *pizza al taglio* shops in town. You can have a memorable meal at the popular *Trattoria Pantagruele*, Via Salita di Ripalta 1 (℡0831.560.605; closed Sat lunch, Sun & two weeks in Aug), which serves excellent local dishes, especially seafood. If you fancy a night out try *L'Orabeffa*, (℡340.260.8301; closed Tues) towards the castle at Via Marconi 33, a pub with live music, open till 3am.

Listings

Around Bríndisi: Torre Guaceto

Just 15km northwest of Bríndisi is a beautiful nature reserve and protected marine area known as **Torre Guaceto**. You'll need a car to get here, but it's a lovely spot for biking through maquis and olive groves, scuba diving over small reefs of coral and sea grass, or chilling out on the sandy beach; to visit, book at the Serranova visitor's centre (℡0831.989.885, ⓦwww.riservaditorreguaceto.it).

14

PUGLIA | Bríndisi

A staggering array of **agents** sell ferry tickets to Albania and Greece, and you should take care to avoid getting ripped off. Ignore the touts clustered around the train station in high season, who specialize in selling imaginary places on non-existent boats, and *always* buy your ticket direct from the company's office or an approved agent. Among the **reliable general agencies** are Adriatic Mediterranean Lines, Via B.S. Giorgio 6 (℡0831.528.554, ⓦwww.adriaticmediterraneanlines.com), opposite the station; and Utac Viaggi, Bastione San Giacomo 70 (℡0831.524.921, ⓦwww.utacviaggi.it), near the harbour. Discovery, Via Provinciale per Lecce 27 (℡0831.573.800, ⓦwww.discoveryto .it), also sells onward ferry tickets to the Cyclades and Crete.

Routes
A variety of **routes** operate most of the year, although service is reduced outside the peak season – roughly defined as between mid-July and mid-August. **Services** – including some high-speed catamarans – sail to Vlore in Albania and Corfu, Igoumenitsa, Patras, Cephallonia and Zante in Greece. Visit ⓦwww.adriaticmediterraneanlines .com for **timetables** and **prices**. As a rule (though there are exceptions), nearly all the reliable companies sail in the evening.

Prices and boarding
Prices vary considerably according to season but there's not much difference between the companies: you'll be looking at a one-way, high-season fare to Corfu/ Igoumenitsa for around €60 per person on deck or €66 for a reclining seat (cabins are available for a higher charge); from €60 extra for a car. High-speed links are more expensive. There are reductions of around 10–20 percent on the return fare if you book with the same company you travel out with and discounts if you have an InterRail, EuroRail, or Italian rail pass (high-season supplements apply). Check on purchase whether your ticket includes **embarkation tax** – currently €5 per person or per car.

Leaving Italy, you should arrive at least one hour – preferably two in high season – before your ship's departure. Allow enough time to get there by the free shuttle bus from Stazione Maríttima (the journey takes around 20min but find out beforehand when the shuttles depart) and make sure that any stopover you are making on the way to Patras is clearly marked on your ticket. It's advisable to **stock up on food and drink** in Bríndisi's supermarkets, as there are the inevitable mark-ups once on board.

Ostuni

OSTUNI, 40km northwest of Bríndisi (35min by train), is known as "the white city" and is one of southern Italy's most stunning small towns. Situated on three hills at the southernmost edge of Le Murge, it was an important Greco-Roman city in the first century AD. The old centre spreads across the highest of the hills, a gleaming white splash of sun-bleached streets and cobbled alleyways, dominating the plains below. Seven kilometres away, the popular sandy coastline has Blue Flag beaches.

Arrival, information and accommodation

The **train station** is some way out of town, though there's a connecting bus service. Pullman **buses** to and from Bríndisi terminate outside the sports centre, from where there are buses into the town centre, or it's around a twenty-minute walk. You'll find the **tourist office** at Corso Mazzini 8 just off Piazza della Libertá (July & Aug daily 8am–2pm & 5.30–8.30pm; rest of the year Mon–Fri 8am–2pm & 3.30–5.30pm, Sat 8am–2pm; ℡0831.301.268).

Ostuni's proximity to the coast makes budget **accommodation** tricky to find in July and August. The best budget option is the B&B *Nonna Isa*, next to the public gardens at Via Alfieri 9 (℡0831.332.515, ⓦwww.nonnaisa.it; ❷). *Tre Torri* is a cheap, central **hotel** at Corso Vittorio Emanuele 298 (℡0831.331.114, ⓦwww.paginegialle.it/hoteltretorri-br; ❷). An alternative is to stay in one of the many excellent **agriturismo** places out of town: *Il Frantoio* (℡0831.330.276, ⓦwww.masseriailfrantoio.it; ❻) on the SS16 towards Fasano at the km874 milestone is a traditional white farmhouse in 72 hectares of olive grove, with eight rooms furnished with family furniture and heirlooms. The estate produces organic olive oil, fruits and vegetables. Horseriding is available and rates include access to a private beach.

The Town

The maze of well-preserved winding streets provides a fascinating amble, and there are some exceptional views – particularly from Largo Castello over the woods to the north. Bits of cavorting Baroque twist out of unexpected places, including an ornamented eighteenth-century obelisk, 21 metres high, dedicated to Saint Oronzo, which stands in Piazza della Libertà (or Piazza Saint Oronzo) on the southern edge of the old town. This is the focal point on summer Saturday nights for hordes of people who drive in from the country-side, meet their friends and pack out the bars and cafés. From there, follow the Via Cattedrale uphill towards the Duomo, taking note of the monumental palaces and churches that trim the ascent. One of these, the **Chiesa di San Vito**, houses an ethnography museum (closed for restoration at time of writing) which has displays on prehistory, the highlight of which is "Delia", the skeleton of a young pregnant woman found in a crouched position, her bones decorated before burial. At the top of the hill, the fifteenth-century church is

▲ The beautiful old centre of Ostuni

nestled into a charming piazza dominated by the Palazzo Vescovile and the Palazzo del Seminario.

Eating and drinking

Ostuni has some excellent **restaurants**, but they are comparatively expensive: try the wonderful local food, at the much-feted ⚜ *Osteria del Tempo Perso*, signposted up in the old town at Via G. Tanzarella Vitale 47 (☎0831.304.819; closed all day Mon & lunchtimes except Sat & Sun). *Vecchia Ostuni* at Largo Lanza 9, just off Piazza della Libertá (☎0831.303.308; closed Tues), has a vast array of antipasti including deep-fried courgette flowers, snails in a piquant tomato sauce, twists of mozzarella, and pickled peppers. *Porta Nova*, Via G. Petrarolo 38 (☎0831.338.983; closed Wed; signposted from near the cathedral), set in a fifteenth-century stone city gate overlooking olive groves and the sea, serves very good shellfish and some elaborate fish, pasta and vegetable combinations. The old town is full of **pubs and bars** and you can get pizza by the slice in Piazza della Libertá; *Sax*, on Via Cattedrale 17 (closed Tues) serves drinks and snacks including pizza and panini.

Lecce and Salento

Some 40km south from Bríndisi, Baroque **Lecce** is a place to linger, with a few diverting Roman remains and a wealth of fine architecture scattered about an appealing old town. It's also a good starting point for excursions around **Salento**, the name given to the very tip of Italy's heel extending from just south of Ostuni to Santa Maria di Leuca. Here the landscape begins to take on a distinctive Greek flavour, a mildly undulating region planted with carob, prickly pear and tobacco. The Adriatic coast is pitted with cliffs topped with ruined watchtowers, and rugged coves and caves trail right the way down to the **southern cape**. The hinterland, by comparison, is more barren, although again there's a Greek feel to it, with tiny, sun-blasted villages growing out of the dry, stony, red earth and flat-roofed houses painted in bright pastel colours.

Lecce

The exuberant building styles on display in **LECCE** are the legacy of religious orders (Jesuits, the Teatini and Franciscans) who came to the region at the end of the sixteenth century, bringing an influx of wealth which paid for the opulent churches and *palazzi* that still pervade today's city. The flowery style of "Leccese Baroque" owed as much to the materials to hand as to the skills of the architects: the soft local sandstone could be intricately carved and then became hard with age. Unfortunately, modern pollution is in danger of ruining many of the buildings, keeping the mass of Lecce's stonemasons and carpenters well occupied.

Arrival and information

Regional **buses** arrive at the Porta Napoli, and the train station. FSE and FS **trains** use the same station, 1km south of the centre at the end of Via Oronzo Quarta. Between mid-June and late September, **Salento in Treno e Bus** (☎0833.541.025, ⊕www.salentointrenoebus.it) services depart from several places in town – including the City Terminal (near the *Tiziano* hotel), Viale dell'Universitá and the FS station – and head to Otranto, Santa Maria di Leuca (via Gallipoli) and the seaside resort of Porto Cesareo, among other destinations.

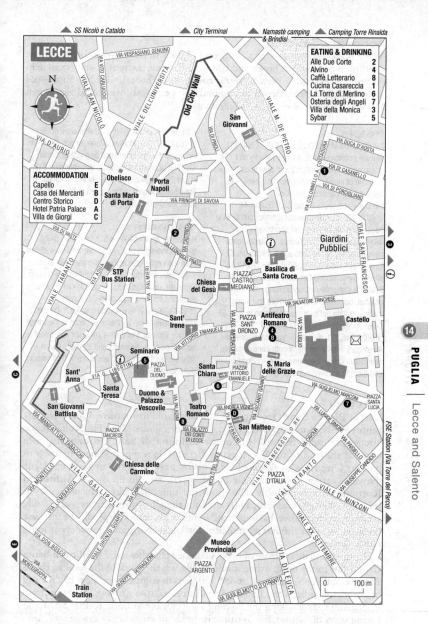

For transfers from Bríndisi **airport** see p.867. The website has timetables or ask for more information from the **tourist office** in Palazzo dei Celestini, Via Principe Umberto I 13 (daily 9am–1pm & 4.30–7pm; ☎0832.683.398, ⓦ www.turismo.provincia.le.it), right next to the church of Santa Croce. There is also a small office on Via Libertini 76 (daily 9am–1pm & 4–7pm; ☎0832245.497, ⓦ www.salento4you.it) near the Duomo.

Accommodation

There is accommodation for all budgets in Lecce. In recent years there has been a diffusion of boutique hotels and B&Bs. Otherwise, the tourist offices can help you find a reasonably priced private **room** in an historic building in the old town and on the outskirts (from around €60 per night); you could also search ⓦ www.abitalecce.it or www.caffelletto.it.

Hotels

Cappello Via Monte Grappa 4 ☎ 0832.308.881, ⓦ www.hotelcappello.it. A large, friendly and efficiently run hotel with a/c and private bathrooms a couple of minutes' walk from the station – for once, a fairly salubrious area. ❷

Casa dei Mercanti Piazza Sant'Oronzo 44 ☎ 0832.277.299, ⓦ www.casadeimercanti.it. Nine newly renovated rooms and apartments overlooking Piazza Sant'Oronzo. All apartments have flatscreen televisions and full kitchens. ❸

Centro Storico Via Vignes 2/B ☎ 0832.242.727, ⓦ www.bedandbreakfast.lecce.it. An appealing B&B in a sixteenth-century building with vaulted ceilings, balconies, a reading room and a sun terrace looking out over the city's monuments. ❷

Hotel Patria Palace Piazza Riccardi ☎ 0832.245.111, ⓦ www.patriapalacelecce.com. An elegant hotel in an eighteenth-century palace near Santa Croce, the rooms have Art Deco accents and there is a swimming pool. ❺

Villa de Giorgi Via S. Fili 110, Monteroni di Lecce ☎ 0832.327.065, ⓦ www.villadegiorgi.it. Set in an old manor house surrounded by gardens dotted with fountains and sculptures, this charming B&B is just 7km southwest of the city in a quiet suburb. Breakfast is served in the garden in the summertime. March–Dec. ❸

Campsites

Namastè Via Novoli km 4.5 ☎ 0832.329.647, ⓦ www.ostellolecce.it. Accessible with the #26 bus from the Lecce train station, this campsite is open year round and starts at €7 a night for a tent pitch.

Torre Rinalda Camping Village Localitá Torre Rinalda, Litoranea S. Cataldo-Casalabate ☎ 0832.382.077, ⓦ www.torrerinalda.it. On the coastal road 15km northeast of Lecce in the village of Torre Rinalda, this deluxe campsite has a pool, tennis courts, and a *discoteca*, and a private beach. Tent pitches from €31.50 per group in high season. June to mid-Sept.

The City

Start at **Piazza Sant'Oronzo**, the hub of the old town, named after the first-century bishop of Lecce who went to the lions under Nero. His bronze statue lurches unsteadily from the top of the **Colonna di Sant'Oronzo** that once stood at the end of the Via Appia in Bríndisi. It reappeared here in 1666 to honour Oronzo, who was credited with having spared the town from plague ten years earlier. The south side of the piazza is taken up by the **Anfiteatro Romano**, which probably dates from the time of Hadrian. In its heyday it seated 20,000 spectators; today it's used for the Christmas nativity scene. Sadly, most of its decorative bas-reliefs of fighting gladiators and wild beasts have been removed to the town's museum for safekeeping, and nowadays it looks rather depleted.

The finest and most ornate of Lecce's Baroque churches is the **Basilica di Santa Croce**, just to the north, whose florid facade was the work of the local architects Zimbalo and Penna and took around 150 years to complete; its upper half is a riot of decorative garlands and flowers around a central rose window. Head west from Piazza Sant'Oronzo along the bustling Via Vittorio Emanuele to Piazza Duomo. Facing onto the square, the **Seminario** holds an impressively ornate well, with carved stone resembling delicately wrought iron. The balconied **Palazzo Vescovile** adjoins the **Duomo** itself, twelfth-century in origin but rebuilt entirely in the mid-seventeenth century by Zimbalo. He tacked on two complex facades and an enormous five-storeyed campanile that towers 70m above the square.

There is further work by Zimbalo in the **Church of San Giovanni Battista** (or del Rosario), by the Porta Rudiae in the southwest corner of town. The ornate facade and twisting columns front some extremely odd altars, while dumpy cherubim dive for cover amid scenes resembling an exploding fruit bowl. But if the Baroque trappings of the town are beginning to pall, you might want to check out the odd relic from other eras, too, not least a well-preserved **Teatro Romano** near Piazza Sant'Oronzo, the only one of its kind to be found in Puglia, with rows of seats and orchestra floor still remarkably intact. There's also the fine Romanesque church of **SS Nicolò e Cataldo** (generally open mornings; free), a ten-minute walk north along Viale San Nicola from Porta Napoli. Built by the Normans in 1190, its cool interior reveals a generous hint of Saracen in the arches and the octagonal rounded dome. Little remains of the frescoes that once covered its walls, though an image of St Nicolò can be found on the south side, together with a delicately carved portal.

Eating and drinking

Lecce's **bar and café scene** is flourishing, and evenings are especially busy as *leccesi*, eager to see and be seen, make the rounds of the city's most popular watering holes and pastry shops during the ritual *passeggiata*. **Eating out** is a serious business. To rival mamma's home cooking, restaurants have to offer flawless local dishes made from traditional recipes. The cuisine is firmly seasonal, so look for artichoke dishes in the spring, *cime di rapa* (turnip tops) and other leafy greens in the winter, and recipes rich with eggplants and peppers in the summer.

Cafés and bars

Alvino Piazza Sant'Oronzo. In spite of a fancy new restoration that wiped away its old-world charm, *Alvino* still serves some of the city's most reliable sweet and savoury snacks. Sample their vast array of *paste di mandorle* (almond paste cookies).
Caffè Letterario Via G. Paladini 46. An arty little bookshop-café serving tasty snacks and drinks from 7.30pm–2am, with a DJ or live music usually on Wed or Fri nights.
La Torre di Merlino Vico del Tufo 10. A well-stocked wine bar offering a spectacular selection of wines and cheese, as well as full meals, near Santa Croce. Closed Mon.
Sybar Piazza Duomo. A laid-back café and eatery open from breakfast till late evening serving *pasticciotti* (cream-filled pastries typical of Lecce) and *rustici* (puff pastry filled with tomato sauce and béchamel) all day. Closed Mon.

Restaurants

Alle Due Corte Corte dei Giugni 1 ☎0832.242.223. Simple dishes and mouthwatering antipasti draw locals and tourists alike. Try the *taieddha* (oven baked potatoes, tomatoes, onions and mussels). Closed Sun.
Cucina Casareccia Via Col. A. Costadura 19 ☎0832.245.178. Be sure to call ahead for one of the dozen tables at this Leccese favorite known for its home-style cooking and atmosphere. The pasta is made on site and condiments change according to the season. The *pezzetti di cavallo* (horse stew), a Leccese specialty, is one of the city's best. Closed all day Mon & Sun eve.
Osteria degli Angeli Via Cavour 4 ☎0832.244.250 Just across from the Castello, this *osteria*-pizzeria is a good choice for antipasti and a pizza (around €15). Closed Sun in summer and Tues in winter.
Villa della Monica Via SS. Giacomo e Filippo 40 ☎0832.409.556 An elegant fish restaurant in the new city renowned for its huge range of *antipasti di mare*. In summer you can sit in the gleaming, fountain-studded marble courtyard. Closed Tues.

Otranto and the southern cape

OTRANTO, a kasbah-like town nestling around a harbour, is only an hour by train from Lecce, set in an arid, rocky and windblown landscape, with translucent seas to swim in. The port overflows with tourists in August, when Otranto's nightlife is at its peak, and the town is most entertaining, but the picturesque location, charming whitewashed lanes, and slow pace will reward visitors year-round.

Otranto's **history** is decidedly grim. One of the last Byzantine towns to fall to the Normans in 1070, it remained a thriving port for Crusaders, pilgrims and traders. But in 1480 a Turkish fleet laid siege to the town, which held out for fifteen days before capitulating. It's said that as a punishment the archbishop, on capture, suffered the indignity of being sawn in half, a popular Turkish spectacle at that time. Nearly 12,000 people lost their lives and the 800 survivors, refusing to convert, were taken up a nearby hill and beheaded. Otranto never really recovered, though the town does feature one glorious survivor of the Turkish attack inside its cathedral: an extraordinary **mosaic floor**.

Arrival, information and accommodation

Note that the **train station** is a fifteen-minute walk north of the centre, so you may want to arrange a pick-up with your hotel. The **tourist office** on Piazza Castello (July & Aug daily 9am–1.30pm & 4–8.30pm; Sept–June Mon–Sat 9am–1.30pm, Tues & Thurs also 4–6pm; ℡0836.801.436, Ⓦwww.comune .otranto.le.it) has all the usual information, including where to rent **bicycles** and scooters. A variety of musical and theatrical events are held in Otranto throughout the summer, usually centred around the castle, along with an annual **festival** commemorating the "800 Martyrs" on August 13–15.

For **accommodation**, your best bet is the light, modern *Bellavista*, Via Vittorio Emanuele 18 (℡0836.801.058, Ⓦwww.hotelbellavistaotranto.it; ❷), right in the centre of things near the beach just outside the old town. Alternatively, the **B&B** *Palazzo d' Mori* on the Bastione dei Pelasgi with pleasant whitewashed rooms overlooking the bay (℡0836.801.088, Ⓦwww .palazzodemori.it; April–Oct; ❹) is another good choice in the historical centre. A bit further out, the *Masseria Bandino* on the road to Uggiano La Chiesa is a charming rural hotel set in an eighteenth-century farmhouse (℡0836.804.647, Ⓦwww.masseriabandino.it; ❸) .

The Town

Down a small alleyway just to the left of the castle is the town's Romanesque **Cattedrale di Santa Maria Annunziata** (daily 7.30am–noon & 3–5pm; free). The marble-columned nave is adorned by an incredible multicoloured mosaic in stone. The central theme is the "Tree of Life". Historical and animal figures are shown as a mix of myth and reality – Alexander the Great, King Arthur, the Queen of Sheba, crabs, fish, serpents and mermaids. The work of a twelfth-century monk, its rough simplicity provides a captivating picture, empowered by a delightful child-like innocence. The rose window was added in the fifteenth century.

Not far from the cathedral, the town's Aragonese **Castello** (daily 9am–1pm, summer also 4–9pm; €2) juts out into the bay, defending the harbour. Its walls incorporate fragments of Roman and medieval inscriptions, while Charles V's coat of arms looms from its portal. Out on the southern edge of town is the cypress-tree-covered hill, where the survivors of the Turkish siege were beheaded. At the top of the hill, the sixteenth-century **Chiesa di San Francesco di Paola** holds the names of the victims, together with a vivid description of the terrible events of July 1480.

On the Bastione dei Pelasgi, the newly restored **Basilica di San Pietro e Paolo** (same hours as cathedral; free) is one of the most important Byzantine monuments in the Salento. This tiny chapel has frescoes, some with Greek inscriptions dating from the tenth to the thirteenth centuries, including a *Last Supper*.

Eating and drinking

The crush of tourism has left Otranto with few excellent **restaurants**. *Da Sergio* on Corso Garibaldi 9 is an exception specializing in honest, local cuisine (℡0836.801.408; closed Wed in winter & mid-Nov to late Dec & Feb), where an average meal costs €40. The air-conditioned self-service restaurant *Boomerang*, at 13/14 Via Vittorio Emanuele II, by the park next to the beach, serves delicious, low-priced, simple meals, as well as fresh antipasti and pasta. Alternatively, in nearby Tenuta Frassanito, along the road to San Cataldo, *Da Umberto* (℡0836.803.473; closed Wed & Jan) does great fish dishes and pizzas – its speciality is *tagliolini all'aragosta* (pasta with lobster) at around €35 per head.

To the southern cape

From Otranto, all the way down to the cape at Santa Maria di Leuca, the coastline is steep and rugged. The unmissable journey along the winding road takes you past one spectacular view of sheer cliffs and blue sea after another. **CAPO D'OTRANTO**, 5km south of Otranto, is the easternmost point on the Italian peninsula, topped by a lighthouse and the rather desolate ruins of a seventh-century abbey. This is the first place in Italy to see the sun rise, and is a popular place to welcome in the New Year. On clear mornings there's a commanding view across the straits – the mountains of Albania are visible about 80km away – and on seriously clear days they say you can even see Corfu, 100km away.

Places to stay along this route include *Camping Porto Miggiano* (℡0836.944.303, ⓦwww.campingportomiggiano.it; March–Oct) a small, simple but beautiful campsite set among olive trees with steps leading down to a beach; it's situated 16km from Otranto, just south of Santa Cesarea Terme; small bungalows are also available, and there's a restaurant on site. In Castro Marina, the *Hotel degli Ulivi* (℡0836.943.037, ⓦwww.hoteldegliulivi .net; ❸), has pleasant rooms with big balconies, and a restaurant with a view over the sea. If all this is giving you vertigo, head for Castro town itself and the B&B *Il Giardino*, Via Sant'Antoino 207 (℡340.603.5400, ⓦwww .ilgiardinonelsalento.it; ❷), which has a large garden for breakfast or relaxing. For truly transcendent accommodation, splurge at the *Convento di Santa Maria in Costantinopoli B&B* on Via Convento in nearby Marittima di Diso just a few kilometres west (UK number only: ℡+44 773.636.2328, ⓔathenamalpas@yahoo.com; ❼). The sixteenth-century converted monastery and its four guest rooms are filled to the brim with proprietor Lord Alastair McAlpine's museum-worthy collection of African art and textiles.

There isn't really much to draw you down as far as **SANTA MARIA DI LEUCA**, a somewhat barren spot, with a scattering of Neolithic remains and an uninspiring marina. There are stunning views, however, from the belvedere at this once-supposed "end of the world" marked by the tiny **church** of Santa Maria Finibus Terrae. In fact, the cape isn't really Puglia's southernmost point: that distinction goes to the Punta Ristola, a little to the west. Nonetheless, this is a lovely place to rent a boat for the afternoon and swim in the sea caves along the coast: try Colaci Mare, Via Q Ennio (℡0833.758.936, ⓦwww.colacimare.com), at the harbour. They arrange excursions of the area's grottoes starting at €11 and rent boats starting at €40 for a half day. You can get down this far, or at least as far as **Gagliano del Capo**, by train: it's at the end of the FSE rail line, just 5km from the cape; the Salento in Treno e Bus service runs to the cape from Otranto (and from Lecce via Gallipoli or inland via Maglie).

The western peninsula: Galatina and Gallipoli

About half an hour down the rail line from Lecce, **GALATINA** is an intriguing Salentine town on the edge of an area known as Grecia Salentina, a key Greek colony in medieval times which has retained Greek customs and language up until the present. It's an important centre of the Italian tobacco industry today, with much of the weed grown in the fields around. It's also famed for its excellent local **wine**; stop by at *Enoteca Bellone* on Via Soleto 2 (☎0836.564.072; closed Thurs afternoon & all day Sun) for good pasta and wine, including hard-to-find local pasta shapes that are produced in-house. In the old part of town, the church of **Santa Caterina di Alessandria** (daily 9am–noon & 4.30–7pm; free) is also well worth a look for the stunning fourteenth-century frescoes that cover its interior.

The **tourist office** at Via V. Emanuele II (Mon–Fri 9.30am–6.30pm; ☎0836.569.984, ⓦwww.comune.galatina.le.it) will give the low-down on events surrounding the *festa*, which is gaining a higher profile these days after years of discouragement by both the Church and the municipality; it also offers free bike rental (you'll need to leave ID). The plush, elegant *Palazzo Baldi*, in a courtyard a few steps from the cathedral at Corte Baldi (☎0836.568.345, ⓦwww.hotelpalazzobaldi.com; ❺), is the only central **hotel**, but there are a couple of agreeable, central **B&Bs**: *Safi*,Via Ottavio Scalfo 70/74 (☎0836.569.401, ⓦwww.safibedbreakfast.it; ❸), a Baroque townhouse 200m from the tourist office; and *Grand*, up a slightly uninviting alleyway at Vico del Monte 21 (☎0836.563.950; ❷), round the corner from the tourist office. As for eating and drinking, *Il Covo della Taranta*, Corso Garibaldi 13, four doors down from the chapel of St Paul is a pub-trattoria that serves lunch and dinner accompanied by occasional world-music jam sessions. At *Il Borgo Antico*, Via Siciliani 80, you can eat a good home-cooked meal for under €15, excluding drinks (☎0836.566.521; closed Wed).

The dance of the spider

The inland towns around Galatina are where the phenomenon of **tarantism** grew in the sixteenth century and is still remembered today. This strange affliction was commonly attributed to a spider bite, with the tarantula-sized wolf spider thought to be the culprit. Symptoms ranged from restlessness to paranoia and victims were believed to be cured by gyrating and dancing in a trance-like state, sometimes for days, in a style that would later be called the *tarantella* (locally, *pizzica*). While there is no medical explanation for the affliction (wolf spiders rarely come into contact with humans and are not particularly venomous), various theories have been put forward. One suggests tarantism is a form of dancing mania, similar to the outbreaks recorded in medieval Europe, while others believe it's simply a form of ritualized dancing. Whatever the truth, a whole subculture has been born around the dance which is is always accompanied by the beat of tambourines and singing.

Galatina is the prime place in Salento to see tarantism in the flesh. Once a year, on the feast day of Saints Peter and Paul (June 29), musicians, dancers, academics, photographers and curious bystanders gather at the chapel of St Paul near the cathedral for performances. You should get to Galatina by 4.30am or 5am to see the dancing before the crowds arrive for the official early morning Mass. Also worth timing your visit for is the all-night music festival "the night of the tarantula" (*la notte della taranta;* ⓦwww.lanottedellataranta.it) held in late August at Melpignano (between Galatina and Otranto).

Gallipoli

First impressions of **GALLIPOLI** (not the World War I battlefield in Turkey) are fairly uninspiring. The new town sprouted on the mainland once the population outgrew its original island site in the eighteenth century, and all that remains of the once-beautiful Greek city (the Kale' polis) is a rather weather-beaten fountain, which sits in the new town near the bridge. Over the bridge, things are more interesting: the old town itself is a maze of meandering and twisting whitewashed streets, with tiny tomatoes hanging on the walls to dry, providing a sudden blaze of colour alongside the fishing nets. Only the Aragonese castle, which squats in one corner of the island, still retains an Italian air in the town.

For **accommodation**, try *Al Pescatore* on Riviera C. Colombo 39 (T 0833.263.656, W www.al-pescatore.it; ❹), an attractive hotel in the old quarter with some rooms overlooking the sea and a good restaurant (closed Mon in winter) serving home-cooked seafood at low-to-moderate prices. Decent B&Bs include *Palazzo de Tomasi*, in the historic centre at Riviera A. Diaz 99 (T 380.505.3335, W www.salanitro.it; ❺), and *Salanitro*, Strada Vicinale Patitari (T 347.600.8262, W www.salanitro.it; ❺), at the town entrance when coming by autostrada from Lecce, just 350m from the sea. There's a good **campsite** 5km to the north: *La Vecchia Torre* (T 0833.209.083, W www.lavecchiatorre.it; June–Oct) at Rivabella on the coast road to Santa Maria al Bagno. Other than *Al Pescatore*, a fine place to **eat** in Gallipoli's old quarter is *Il Bastione*, Riviera N. Sauro 28 (T 0833.263.836; closed Nov and Mon Oct-April), where you can sample fresh fish in every way imaginable – raw, grilled, fried, baked, or cooked in salt – on a seafront terrace. Don't miss the *gamberi rossi crudi* (raw red shrimp) fished off the coast of Gallipoli and simply seasoned with olive oil and pepper.

Travel details

Trains (FS unless otherwise stated)

Altamura to: Gravina (FAL, hourly; 10min).
Bari to: Alberobello (FSE, hourly; 1hr 30min); Altamura (FAL, 14 daily; 1hr); Andria (Ferrovia del Nord Barese, hourly; 1hr); Barletta (hourly; 55min); Bríndisi (hourly; 1hr 20min); Fasano (10 daily; 40min); Grotte di Castellana (FSE, hourly; 55min); Lecce (hourly; 1hr 30min–2hr); Locorotondo (11 daily; 1hr 40min); Martina Franca (11 daily; 1hr 50min); Matera (FAL, 14 daily; 85min); Molfetta (hourly; 30min); Ostuni (hourly; 1hr); Péschici (1 daily; 4hr); Polignano a Mare (hourly; 30min); Putignano (hourly; 1hr); Rome (6 daily; 4hr 40min); Ruvo di Puglia (Ferrovia del Nord Barese, hourly; 40min); Táranto (19 daily; 1hr 30min); Trani (hourly; 30min).
Bríndisi to: Fasano (hourly; 35min); Lecce (25 daily; 30min); Ostuni (24 daily; 25min); Taranto (15 daily; 1hr).
Fóggia to: Bari (hourly; 1hr 30min); Barletta (hourly; 40min); Bríndisi (13 daily; 2hr 40min);

Fasano (10 daily; 2hr 15min); Manfredonia (23 daily; 30–40min); Molfetta (hourly; 1hr 5min); Ostuni (10 daily; 2hr); Péschici (5 daily; 2hr 20min); San Severo (23 daily; 25min); Trani (hourly; 50min).
Lecce to: Gallipoli (11 daily; 1hr); Gagliano del Capo (FSE, 10 daily; 1hr 30min; FS 1 daily; 2hr); Otranto (FSE, 8 daily; 1hr 10min); FS 2 daily; 50min); Rome (5 daily; 6hr 15min–10hr).
San Severo to: Péschici (8 daily; 1hr 30min).
Táranto Grottaglie (14 daily; 15min); Martina Franca (8 daily; 40min); Massafra (12 daily; 15min); Metaponto (19 daily; 35min); Naples (3 direct trains daily; 4hr 35min).

Buses

NB: Bus services on Sun are drastically reduced.
Bari to: Andria (11 daily; 1hr 45min); Barletta (3 daily; 1hr); Canosa di Puglia (3 daily; 75min); Molfetta (hourly; 40min); Naples (3 daily; 3hr); Rome (4 daily; 5hr); Trani (3–4 hourly; 1hr 5min).

Fasano to: Martina Franca (12 daily; 20min); Egnázia (6 daily, more in summer; 20min); Selva Fasano (6 daily; 10min).

Fóggia to: Lucera (hourly; 30min); Manfredonia (12 daily; 50min); Monte S. Angelo (8 daily; 1hr 35min); San Severo (6 daily; 45min); Troia (hourly; 40min); Vieste (5 daily; 2hr 45min).

Lecce to: Salento-in-Treno-e-Bus services (mid-June to late Sept only); Gallipoli (14 daily; 1–2hr); Otranto (8 daily; 1hr); Porto Cesareo (6 daily; 1hr); San Cataldo (8 daily; 30min); Santa Maria di Leuca (13 daily; 1hr 45min).

Manfredonia to: Bari (5 daily; 2hr 15min); Monte Sant'Angelo (hourly; 45min); San Giovanni Rotondo (12 daily; 40min); Vieste (5 daily; 2hr).

Molfetta to: Ruvo di Puglia (hourly; 30min).

Péschici to: Rome (2 daily; 6hr 40min); Vieste (12 daily; 45min).

Vieste to: Fóggia (5 daily; 2hr 45min); Rome (2 daily; 7hr 15min).

Ferries and hydrofoils

Manfredonia to: Vieste (June–Sept 1 daily; 45min).

Péschici to: Trémiti via Rodi Gargánico (June–Sept 1 daily; 1hr 15min).

Trémiti Islands to: Manfredonia (June, July & Sept 1 daily; 2hr); Ortona (end June to early Sept 1 daily; 2hr); Térmoli (June–Sept 2–3 daily; 50min; ferries rest of year 2–3 weekly; 1hr 40min); Vasto (end June to early Sept 1 daily; 1hr); Vieste (June, July & Sept 1 daily, Aug 3 daily; 1hr); Monostabs (April & May 1 daily; 1hr 10min; ferries rest of year).

Vieste to: Trémiti (Jan–March & Oct–Dec 1 weekly; 2hr 15min).

International ferries

Bari to: Corfu (2 daily; 11hr); Durres/Durazzo, Albania (at least 1 daily; 9hr); Igoumenitsa (2 daily; from 9hr 30min); Patras (daily; from 15hr 30min); Rijeka via Dubrovnik, Korcula, Stari Grad and Split in Croatia (July & Aug 2 weekly; 32hr).

Brindisi to: Corfu (6 weekly; from 7hr); Igoumenitsa (6 weekly; 8hr); Cephallonia (13 sailings through July & Aug; 16hr); Patras (at least 1 daily in summer; 13hr).

Basilicata and Calabria

CHAPTER 15

Highlights

* **Matera** Sliced by a ravine containing thousands of *Sassi* – cave dwellings gouged out of rock – Matera's unique landscape never ceases to astonish. See p.867

* **Cripta del Peccato Originale, Contrada Petrapenta** The best example of the region's distinctive rock-hewn churches with vibrant eighth-century frescoes inside. See p.889

* **Tropea promontory** This region has it all – white sandy beaches, turquoise water, hills tumbling down to the coast and – in Tropea town and Pizzo – two of the most beautiful old centres in Calabria. See p.895

* **Bronzi di Riace** Two extraordinary seven-foot-high, bronze statues of Greek athletes housed in Reggio's Museo Nazionale. See p.899

* **Purple Codex, Rossano** An illustrated manuscript from the sixth century with early depictions of the life of Christ. See p.905

* **Capo Colonna** A solitary Doric column marks the spot of what was the most important Greek temple on the Ionian coast. See p.907

▲ Matera

Basilicata and Calabria

M ore than any other regions of the Italian South, **Basilicata** and **Calabria** represent the quintessence of the *mezzogiorno*, the southern regions of Italy that are traditionally poor. After Unification in 1861, the area was largely neglected and sank into abject poverty that was worsened by emigration. Conditions here were immortalized in Carlo Levi's *Christ stopped at Eboli* – a vivid account of his time in exile during the Fascist era in which he describes a south characterized by apathy where malaria is endemic and the peasants' way of life is deeply rooted in superstition. Things have improved, particularly in Basilicata, although tourism is yet to bring the riches found to the north in Puglia and Campania.

In Basilicata, the greatest draw is **Matera**, whose distinctive *Sassi* – cavelike dwellings in the heart of the town – give it a uniquely dramatic setting. In the northern part of the region, near the uninspiring city of Potenza, **Melfi** and **Venosa** are bastions of medieval charm with important relics from the Byzantine and Norman eras. Of the region's two coasts, it is the **Tyrrhenian** that is most engaging, with spots like **Maratea** offering crystal clear water, a bustling harbour, and opportunities to discover remote sea grottoes. The **Ionian** coast, on the other hand, is less charming, though worth a visit for its ancient sites in **Metaponto** and **Policoro** – ruins of the once mighty states that comprised Magna Graecia.

While conditions in Basilicata have improved, **Calabria** remains arguably more marginalized than it was before Unification. Since the war, a massive channelling of funds to finance huge irrigation and land-reclamation schemes, industrial development and a modern system of communications has brought built-up sprawl to previously isolated towns such as **Crotone** – often hand in hand with the forces of organized crime. The **'Ndrangheta** Mafia maintains a stranglehold across much of the region. Having moved on from kidnappings and localized extortion to become an international network that deals in heroin and supposedly even nuclear waste, these days it's thought to be far more powerful and dangerous than the Neapolitan Camorra.

Although unchecked development financed by the 'Ndrangheta has marred parts of the coastline, resorts such as **Scilla**, **Tropea** and **Capo Vaticano** are still charming, and have become favourite hideaway resorts for discerning Italian and foreign visitors. The interior parts of the region are dominated by

The cuisine of **Basilicata**, also known as the **cucina lucana** (Lucanian cuisine), derives from a poor tradition that depended heavily on preserving food, especially pork and fruit, which are dried, and vegetables, which are preserved in oil. **Arab influence** still pervades in the form of aubergines and desserts incorporating figs, almonds and honey. **Basilicata** is an important producer of durum wheat, which is used to make fresh pasta, rustic breads prepared in wood-fired ovens, and *frieslle*, stale bread softened with water, oil and tomatoes. **Strong cheeses**, like matured or smoked ricotta and aged *caciocavallo* are favoured. A rare breed of cows, the *mucca podolica*, grazes around Matera and the milk and meat they produce are wonderfully flavourful.

Calabria shares many culinary traditions with its neighbour Basilicata. The trademark of Calabrian cuisine, however, is *peperoncino*, spicy chilli pepper, used liberally in many dishes, and thought to ward off illness and misfortune. Try the spicy *sorpressata* salami, **'Nduia**, a hot *peperoncino* and pork fat spread. As in all southern cuisine, cheeses such as *caciocavallo*, mature *provola* and *pecorino* are ubiquitous. The *cipolla rossa di Tropea* is a sweet red onion used in rustic pies, meat dishes, and in sweet preserves called **composte**. For desserts, try *mostazzolo*, an almond cookie sweetend with honey or wine must, or anything containing *bergamotto*, a citrus fruit that grows along the south coast. Dried figs are a staple and can be found stuffed, dipped in chocolate, or simply arranged in braids or wheels.

Cirò is the success story of Calabrian wine making. Made from the ancient **gaglioppo** grape, it has been given some modern touches and now shifts bottles outside its home territory. Not surprisingly, given its far-south position, Calabria also turns out sweet whites such as Greco di Bianco. The **aglianico** grape makes a star appearance in Basilicata: Aglianico del Vulture is the region's only DOC; it's been dubbed "the Barolo of the south" for its complexity and penchant for ageing. Other wines worth trying are the sweet, sparkling Malvasia and Moscato.

the mountain grandeur of the **Sila** and **Aspromonte** ranges, each offering excellent hiking and rustic local cuisine.

Good **transport** services exist in Basilicata, but in hilly and coastal areas, a car is useful. Be warned that if you're planning on driving, the roads tend to be narrow and provincial and you should allow more time than you think you'll need. There's a mine of information on transport and the region in general at Ⓦ www.aptbasilicata.it. In Calabria there are reliable train services connecting the coastal towns, supplemented by buses in summer. Again your own transport is critical for reaching the more remote mountainous interior.

Potenza and around

Way up in the northwest of Basilicata, the regional capital, **POTENZA**, has suffered badly from the effects of earthquakes and war, which have robbed it of much of its historical heritage. However, there are three **train stations** and a bus terminal, and should you find yourself obliged to stop here for a connection, a trip to the town's only attraction, the **Museo Archeologico Nazionale** (summer Mon & Sun 2–8pm, Tues–Sat 4–7pm; winter Tues–Sun 9am–1pm; free), next to the cathedral, is a good enough way to pass the time; it is home to the region's most important collection of finds from the prehistory of Lucania (the Roman name for Basilicata), plus some well-preserved ceramics, terracottas and statuettes from Greek Metapontum.

North of Potenza lie several towns from the Norman era with some good examples of their brand of hybrid architecture. All are connected by bus with Potenza, and most are on the main Potenza–Fóggia rail line.

Melfi

North of Potenza on the SS93, on the far side of the imposing Monte Vulture (1326m), is the historic town of **MELFI**, long a centre of strategic importance, taken by the Normans in 1041 and their first capital in the south of Italy. Repeatedly damaged by earthquakes, the town's formidable castle now contains a **museum** (Mon 2–8pm, Tues–Sun 9am–8pm; ⓦ www.archeobasi .it; €2.50) housing prehistoric finds and objects from the Greek, Roman and Byzantine eras. A separate door from the courtyard gives access to the museum's most celebrated item, an exquisitely carved Roman sarcophagus from the second century, showing the image of the dead girl for whom it was made, reclining on cushions, with five statuettes of gods and heroes on the sides.

In the centre of town off Via Vittorio Emanuele II is the **Duomo**, originally twelfth-century but almost entirely rebuilt in 1700. After the 1930 earthquake, a Byzantine-style *Madonna and Child* fresco was brought to light, which you can see to the left of the altar; a chapel on the right also has a Madonna, in her role as protector of the city – a copy of the original statue stolen from here in 1982. The cathedral's campanile has miraculously survived the various cataclysms: the two black stone griffins symbolized the Norman hegemony in the region and are visible everywhere in Melfi, having been adopted as the town's emblem.

Melfi has a basic, clean **hotel**, *Il Tetto* on Piazza IV Novembre (☎0972.236.837, ⓦ www.albergoiltetto.com). You'll find an excellent **restaurant-pizzeria** a little way down from the cathedral at Via Vittorio Emanuele 29, the *Delle Rose* (☎0972.21.682; closed Thurs), with outdoor seating in summer. The *baccala alla trainera*, salt cod with *peperoncino* is particularly delicious. This and other local specialities feature on two *degustazione* menus (€20 & €30), while for those on a tight budget there's a *menu turistica* (€15). No pizza at lunch.

Venosa

If Melfi preserves the appearance of a dark medieval town, nearby **VENOSA** has an attractive airiness; a harmonious place surrounded by green rolling hills and neatly divided parcels of farmland, it is rich with historical associations. Known in antiquity as Venusia, it was in its time the largest colony in the Roman world, and much is made of the fact that it was the birthplace of Quintus Horatius Flaccus, known to English speakers as **Horace** (65–8 BC); his supposed house lies past Venosa's cathedral on the right (by appointment ☎339.480.7431; free). Inside are the remains of a bathing complex and a bas-relief. The town's chief attraction is the **Area Archeologica** (Mon–Wed 9am to 1hr before sunset, Tues 2pm to 1hr before sunset; €2.50) located just outside of the *centro storico* on Via Olfantina in Localitá San Rocco. The complex consists of ruins from the Roman era including housing, shops, and a church. More interesting is the adjacent **Abbazia della Trinità**, a sprawling church and abbey begun in the eleventh century and used as the resting place of various Norman bigwigs including Robert Guiscard, it is now in a state of partial ruin but the perimeter walls and some decorations survive.

Matera and around

The town of **MATERA**, in the interior of Basilicata, dates from the Middle Ages when Byzantine and Benedictine monks built rock-hewn churches and monasteries into what are now called the **Sassi** – literally "stones" – an intricate series of terraced caves. Later, farmers, seeking safety from invasions, also settled in the *Sassi*, fashioning their homes, stables, and shops out of the rock, creating one of Italy's oddest townscapes and its most significant troglodyte settlement. During the Spanish Bourbon era wealthy *Sassi* dwellers were able to move out of the cave dwellings to the plain above, while the masses were left in abject squalor below. The unhealthy living conditions were recorded in Carlo Levi's 1945 memoir *Christ Stopped at Eboli*, in which the author's sister compared the *Sassi* to Dante's *Inferno*, so horrified was she by their disease-ridden inhabitants. During the 1950s twenty thousand people were forcibly removed from the *Sassi* and rehoused in modern districts in the new town. Nowadays it's hard to picture the conditions that previously existed here; EU funds and private investments have poured in, and now the area has been cleaned up and repopulated with homes, B&Bs, hotels, restaurants and workshops. In 1993, the city and its grotto-filled outskirts were declared a UNESCO World Heritage Site, and in 2003 Mel Gibson filmed his controversial *The Passion of the Christ* here.

Arrival and information

Matera's **train station** is on Piazza Matteotti and is served by the FAL line, linked to Altamura and Bari in Puglia and to Potenza and Ferrandina in Basilicata. SITA **buses** also stop here, connecting Matera to Miglionico, Montescaglioso, Policoro and Metaponto. Nearby on Via Spine Bianche is the town's helpful **tourist office** (Mon–Sat 8.30am–1pm & 4–7.30pm, Sun 8.30am–1pm; ℡0835.331.817, ⓦwww.aptbasilicata.it).

Accommodation

Apart from Maratea, Matera is the only place in Basilicata where you might have difficulty finding **a room** for the night – booking a week or so in advance is highly recommended. There are a lot of new B&Bs and some beautiful hotels recently opened in the *Sassi* themselves, which are probably the most atmospheric places to stay – although of course the swish furniture, modern plumbing and decor would be unrecognizable to any former *sasso* dweller.

Capriotti Piazza Duomo ℡0835.333.997, ⓦwww .capriotti-bed-breakfast.it. Three tastefully decorated, light-flooded rooms, each with its private entrance and own outdoor space, in the vaulted rooms of a restored sixteenth-century *sasso* close to the Duomo. ❷

Italia Via Ridola 5 ℡0835.333.561, ⓦwww .albergoitalia,com. Piano's most modern hotel, catering mostly to business travellers, where Mel Gibson and his cast stayed, and the best option if you don't fancy sleeping in a cave. ❸

Le Monacelle Via Riscatto 9/10 ℡0835.344.097, ⓦwww.lemonacelle.it. Built into a former monastery and conservatory,

this small hotel near the Duomo also has hostel accommodation from €17 per person. ❸

Locanda di San Martino Via Fiorentini 71 ℡0835.256.600, ⓦwww.locandadisanmartino.it. A lovely hotel in the *Sassi* built into a former carpenter's workshop and a deconsecrated chapel. The rooms are beautifully furnished, fragrant and cool. ❹

Sant'Angelo Piazza S. Pietro Caveoso ℡0835.314.010, ⓦwww .hotelsantangelosassi.it. A beautifully styled four-star in the *Sassi* with enormous rooms gouged out of the living rock and affording marvellous views over the Parco della Murgia. Service is wonderfully attentive. ❺

The Town

Most visitors to Matera head straight for the atmospheric *Sassi* and understandably so, but Matera Piano – the "new" town above begun in the seventeenth century is worthy of exploration, too, with a host of churches and a livelier feel.

The Sassi

Divided into two sections – Sasso Caveoso and Sasso Barisano – the **Sassi** district can be entered from a number of different points around the centre of town, some signposted, some not. Via Buozzi weaves through both zones and is a useful reference point although you will need to leave it in order to penetrate the warren of *chiese rupestri*, or **cave churches** (all open daily: April–Oct 9am–1pm & 3–7pm; Nov–March 9.30am–1.30pm & 2.30–4.30pm; €2.50 each or €6 for all). Note that there's no sun cover, flights of steps are unavoidable, and you'd do well to take some water. To get the most out of the whole area equip yourself with an *itinerario turistico* and a map, both available from the tourist office, or take a tour (see box below).

The most spectacularly sited church, **Santa Maria de Idris**, is perched on the conical Monte Errone that rises in the midst of the *Sassi*. Inside are frescoes dating from the fourteenth century. The most interesting interior is found in the **Convincinio di Sant'Antonio**. This former monastery complex of four interlinking thirteenth-century churches was turned into wine cellars in 1700 – look for the spouts for wine emerging from what appears to be an altar – and later into houses. Of particular interest are tombs in the floor converted into water tanks that demonstrate considerable ingenuity: the porous stone had to be waterproofed, and rainwater channelled into the tanks.

Built on a rocky spur rising above the *Sassi*, the thirteenth-century **Duomo** (closed for restoration) retains a strong Apulian-Romanesque flavor. Between the figures of Peter and Paul on the facade is a sculpture of the patron of Matera, the Madonna della Bruna. Every July 2, a painting of the saint is carried through the streets on a papier-mâché float. At the end of the day-long festivities, onlookers storm the float and break it apart, believing the pieces offer protection and blessings.

Just below the Duomo in the Palazzo Pomarici, **MUSMA** (Tues–Sun: April–Oct 10am–2pm & 4–8pm; Nov–March 10am–2pm; €5) is a new contemporary sculpture museum appropriately set in rooms carved from the rock. Its permanent collection features works by Picasso, Pompodoro and Gio' and there are regular temporary exhibits.

For a fascinating glimpse of what life was like for the *Sassi*-dwellers, head for the **Casa Grotta**, just before the Convivcno di S. Antonio (daily: April–Oct 9.30am–7.30pm; Nov–March 10am–5pm; ⓦwww.casagrottamatera.com; €2). Reconstructed inside a *grotto* and using original furniture, utensils and clothes, it gives an insight into how families with several children and livestock managed

Sassi tours

For access to parts of the *Sassi* you might otherwise miss on your own, you can join a guided **tour** – 🎋 Ferula Viaggi, on Via Cappelluti 34 in the old town (ⓣ0835.336.572, ⓦwww.ferulaviaggi.it), charges around €10 per person for groups of five or more in English. Alternatively, you can arrange tours of six of the *chiese rupestri* through Sassi Tourism at Via Lucana 238 (ⓣ0835.319.458, ⓦwww.sassitourism.it). La Scaletta, the local cultural association, oversees two other churches: Madonna dell Virtú and San Nicola dei Greci (ⓣ0835.336.726, ⓦwww.lascaletta.net; €2).

to live together in one-room cave dwellings. If you want to explore the **caves** and more *chiese rupestri* in the Parco della Murgia (☎0835.336.166; ⓦwww .parcomurgia.it) on the far side of the ravine, there are several entrances from SS7 northwest of Matera. The park is best seen with a guide – Ferula Viaggi (see box opposite) organizes excursions-who can lead you to some of the hundreds of hypogeums and rock-hewn churches in the park's 8000 hectares.

The new town

The centre of "new" Matera, built in the seventeenth century, is **Piazza Vittorio Veneto**, a large and stately square, which in the evening is given over to a long procession of shuffling promenaders. The *materani* take their evening stroll seriously, and the din of the crowds rising up out of this square can be like the noise from a stadium. Matera's modern quarters stretch out to the north and west of here, but most of the things worth seeing are along the Via Ridola, and Via del Corso.

Winding off from the bottom end of the piazza, the narrow Via del Corso leads down to the seventeenth-century church of **San Francesco d'Assisi** (daily 7.30am–noon & 4–7pm; free), whose ornate Baroque style was superimposed on two older churches, traces of which, including some eleventh-century frescoes, can be visited through a passage in the third chapel on the left. In the main church are eight panels of a polyptych by Bartolomeo Vivarini, set above the altar. From San Francesco, you can head to the endearing Piazza del Sedile just above the *Sassi* or onto Via Ridola to admire the elliptical facade of the **Chiesa del Purgatorio** (daily 8.30am–12.30pm & 4–7pm; free), gruesomely decorated with skulls.

Eating and drinking

Thanks to the surge in tourism, there's plenty of choice for **eating** in Matera. In spite of its close proximity to the sea, traditional Materan food is dominated by meat dishes. You'll find lots of cafés and bars around Piazza San Pietro Caveoso and along Via Buozzi in the *Sassi* or near Piazza Vittorio in *Piano*.

Camera Club Via S. Biagio 13 ☎335.109.9603. In a set of caves on the edge of the *Sassi* near Piazza Vittorio this watering hole prepares delicious sandwiches and light meals with cold beer. There is an outdoor seating area in the eve. Open late.

Don Matteo Via S. Biagio 12 ☎0835.334.145. Chef Donato Malacarne's elegant restaurant serves *lucana* dishes with an innovative flair. The *maialino al moscato di Trani* (suckling pig in *moscato* wine sauce) is magnificent. There are tasting menus from €25, expect to pay from €50 à la carte. Closed Wed and lunch except Sun.

Il Borghese Via Lucana 198 ☎0835.314.223. A good place frequented by locals with great antipasti and typical *lucana* dishes such as *cavatelli con peperoni cruschi* (pasta with sundried peppers) and *agnello grigliato* (grilled lamb). Expect to pay around €30 for dinner, less at lunch. Closed Wed.

Il Terrazzino Vico San Giuseppe 7 ☎0835.334.119. Enjoy the view over the *Sassi* at this atmospheric spot. Try the oven-baked *orecchiette al tegamino* (with local sausage, tomatoes and mozzarella), or *la pignata*, a dish of oven-roasted lamb with vegetables and cheese. There's a tourist menu priced at €15; eating à la carte should cost €20–25. Closed Tues and first two weeks of July.

Lucanerie Via S. Stefano 61 ☎0835.332.133. This cheerfully decorated trattoria offers some of the best and most abundant *antipasti misti* in town, but save room for specialities like *cavatelli con peperoni cruschi* (home-made pasta with flakes of fried sundried peppers) or *tortino di formaggio di capra* (a creamy goat cheese dessert). Meals from around €25 a head. Closed Sun dinner & Mon.

The Cripta del Peccato Originale and Montescaglioso

Fourteen kilomtres south of Matera in **CONTRADA PETRAPENTA**, the **Cripta del Peccato Originale** (Crypt of Original Sin; Tues–Sun 10am–2pm;

☎320.535.0910, ⓦwww.artezeta.it; €8 includes guided tour), is lauded as the "Sistine Chapel of cave churches". Inside, late eighth-century frescoes depict surprisingly dynamic Old Testament scenes, saints, and angels on a white background embellished with tendrils of red flowers. Note that you need to **book** in order to visit.

Twenty kilometres southeast of Matera and served by buses from the town, the hilltop village of **MONTESCAGLIOSO** was once a Greek settlement and is now the site of a magnificent eleventh-century Benedictine abbey of **San Michele** (daily 10am–1pm & 3–5pm; €4 includes guided tour; closed Mon afternoon). The abbey has been recently restored and commands good views over the Bradano Valley. You could easily spend a few hours here exploring the town's winding back streets. For **food**, head to *Caveosus* on Via Chiesa Maggiore 1 (☎0835.201.912; closed Tues) where a delicious home-cooked meal will cost around €15. To **stay**, *L'Orto di Lucania* on SP175, 3km west of Montescaglioso (☎0835.202.195, ⓦwww.ortodilucania.it; ❷) is an agriturismo with a wonderful restaurant (booking essential). The rooms and apartments are well kitted out and there's a pool and lovely grounds with fruit trees.

Basilicata's Ionian coast

A leisurely thirty-minute drive from Matera, **Basilicata's Ionian coast** from **Metaponto** to **Policoro** consists of a mountainous interior backing onto a seaboard punctuated only by holiday resorts, a plethora of campsites – overflowing in the summer months with legions of Italians – and some notable historical sites. Of these, the most significant are connected with the periods of Greek occupation, the most recent of which was that of the Byzantines, who administered the area on and off for five hundred years.

Metaponto

The most extensively excavated of the Greek sites, and one of the few places of any real significance on the Ionian coast of Basilicata, is at **METAPONTO**, an important road and rail junction connecting the coastal routes between Táranto and Reggio with the interior of Basilicata – to Potenza by train and Matera by bus. Metapontum was settled in the eighth century BC and owed its subsequent prosperity to the fertility of the surrounding land – perfect for cereal production (symbolized by the ear of corn stamped on its coinage). Pythagoras, banished from Kroton, established a school here in about 510 BC that contributed to an enduring philosophical tradition. The city's downfall came as a result of a series of catastrophes: absorbed by Rome, embroiled in the Punic Wars, sacked by the slave-rebel Spartacus, and later desolated by a combination of malaria and Saracen raids.

Metaponto today is a straggling, amorphous place, comprising train station, museum, ruins, and modern apartment buildings. Arriving at the station, you're in Metaponto Borgo. The **Museo Archeologico Nazionale** (Tues–Sun 9am–8pm, Mon 2–8pm; €2.50) located at Via Aristea 21, is a short walk north. The exhibits are mainly fifth- and fourth-century BC statuary, ceramics and jewellery, and there's a fascinating section on the new insights revealed by the study of fingerprints on shards found in the artisans' quarter. Nearby in Piazza

Giovanni XXIII, the **tourist office** (June–Sept daily 9am–1pm & 4–7pm; ☎0835.745.606, ⊛www.prolocodimetaponto.it) has lots of maps and information to help navigate the area but is open only in the summer. From the Borgo, follow Via di Apollo 500m east to the entrance of the **Zona Archeologica** (Tues–Sun 9am to 1hr before sunset; Mon opens at 2pm; free) which has the the remains of a theatre and a Temple of Apollo Licius. The latter is a sixth-century BC construction that once possessed 32 columns, but you need some imagination to picture its original appearance. In a better state of preservation, the **Tavole Palatine** (same times), or Temple of Hera, is a few kilometres northwest where the main SS106 crosses the River Bradano. With fifteen of its columns remaining, it is the most suggestive remnant of this once mighty state. Buses leave from the train station and head to the Zona Archeologica and Tavole Palatine; enquire at the tourist office for schedules.

Lido di Metaponto

Three kilometres south of Borgo, **LIDO DI METAPONTO** has sandy, well-equipped **beaches**, numerous **campsites** and a handful of hotels. Of the campsites, the *Camping Internazionale* on Viale delle Nereidi Grecia (☎0835.741.916, ⊛www.villageinternazionale.com) is clean, very near the beach and has bungalows as well as places for tents and campers. The best-value **hotel** is the *Kennedy* at Via Ionio 1, about 1km from the station, off the Lido road (☎0835.741.960, ⊛www.hrkennedy.it; ❸). It has some apartments as well as rooms, and may be half-board only in high season.

Policoro

There's a fabulous collection of antiquities at the newly renovated **Museo Nazionale della Siritide**, 25km down the coast, just behind the village of **POLICORO** on Via Colombo 8. The museum (Mon–Wed 9am–8pm also Tues 2–8pm; €2.50) contains clay figurines and jewel-bedecked skeletons among other material taken from the zone between the Sinni and Agri rivers, in its time one of the richest areas on this coast and site of the two Greek colonies of **Siris** and **Heraclea**. The latter was where Pyrrhus, king of Epirus, first introduced elephants to the Romans, and, although winning the first of two battles in 280 BC, suffered such high losses that he declared another such victory would cost him the war – so bequeathing to posterity the term "Pyrrhic victory". The ruins of Heraclea are just behind the museum and although they are in a poor state, it is worth taking a wander. The museum and archeological site are a twenty-minute walk from the bus station in the centre of Policoro. Local buses link the terminal to the museum between 10am and 4pm. For **food**, ⅍ *Pitty* is a terrific, if oddly named, fish restaurant in Piazza Dante near the bus terminal (closed Mon Oct–May).

Basilicata's Tyrrhenian coast

The northern stretch of **Basilicata's Tyrrhenian coast** is the most visited part of the entire region (Matera is a close second), its sheer cliffs and rocky coves refreshingly unspoilt by the holiday industry. The obvious stop here is **Maratea**, hemmed in by the mountains and offering some first-rate beaches that get overcrowded in summer.

Maratea

MARATEA's chief allure is its coastal villages – Acquafreedda, Cersuta, Fiumi-cello, Porto, Marina and Castrocucco – which stretch for 35km along a beautiful rocky **coastline**. Most of the action – and accommodation – is in or around the little seaside area of **Fiumicello**, 5km north of **Maratea Paese** (the inland part of Maratea), though the chic elite who have colonized much of the area prefer to be seen in the bars and restaurants of **Marina di Maratea**, directly below Maratea Paese – if nothing else, a pleasant place to stroll around and gawp at the yachts. The whole area is well endowed with sandy **beaches**, including those at Fiumicello and Acquafredda; most are well signposted, but don't hesitate to explore the less obvious ones. The coast is also home to fifty or so grottoes, most accessible only by boat; enquire at the tourist office (see below) for boat rental agencies.

If you fancy some exercise, try climbing up to **Monte San Biagio** (624m) the highest point above Maratea. The peak is dominated by the **Redentore**, an enormous marble Christ symbolically positioned with its back to the sea, looking towards the mountains of the interior. Opposite the statue, and looking as if it were about to be crushed under the giant's feet, is an eighteenth-century church, the **Santuario di San Biagio**, dedicated to the town's patron saint. On the second Sunday of May, a statue of the patron saint is carried up the hill in a large procession.

Practicalities

Most **trains** stop at the main Maratea station, at the bottom of Maratea Paese, from where it's a five-minute minibus or taxi ride (or a 20min walk) to Fiumicello. There are also stations at Acquafredda and Marina di Maratea. SITA (Ⓦwww.sitabus.it) runs **buses** along the coast and to other towns in Basilicata year-round and there is a July and August-only minibus service (up to four a day, tickets bought on board) that connects Marina di Maratea, Fiumicello and Maratea Paese in that order. The **tourist office** is on Piazza del Gesu' in Fiumicello (July & Aug daily 8am–2pm & 4–8pm; Sept–June Mon–Sat 8am–2pm, Mon & Thurs 3–6pm; Ⓣ0973.876.908, Ⓦwww.apt.basilicata.it).

Accommodation can be hard to come by at any time, and in high season is often expensive, with many hotels requiring half board during the peak period. To avoid this, you may do better to rent rooms – ask for a list from the tourist office. The most distinctive hotel in Maratea Paese is *La Locanda Delle Donne Monache*, Via C. Mazzei 4, sited in an elegantly renovated eighteenth-century convent (Ⓣ0973.876.139, Ⓦwww.locandamonache.com; April–Oct; ❸). More functional and cheaper is *Fiorella*, Via Santa Venere 21 (Ⓣ0973.876.921; ❸), a spacious and basic hotel, open all year round, just outside Fiumicello near the petrol station. On the edge of Fiumicello at Via Rasi 4/C, *B&B Laino* (Ⓣ0973.876.506 or 329.240.4320; Ⓦwww.beblaino.it; ❷) has six rooms, two apartments and a swimming pool.

There are dozens of **restaurants** in the area; most along the coast serve fish and or pizza and are open April to October and weekends only the rest of the year. Some of the best are in Fiumicello, where, on the main Via Santa Venere, *El Sol's* pizzas and seafood dishes such as mussels and swordfish, generally pull in a big local crowd (Ⓣ0973.876.928). *Il Sacello* at *La Locanda Delle Donne Monache* (see above) prepares the best in local cusine, both land and sea based – try the *linguine con baccala e peperoni cruschi* (linguine with cod and fried pepper flakes).

Calabria's Tyrrhenian coast

The northern stretch of the Tyrrhenian coast in Calabria is peppered with holiday complexes that crowd the flat littoral. There are some absorbing places to break the journey, notably the towns of **Diamante**, **Belvedere** and, further south, **Paola**. Following the coast down, the main SS18 runs alongside the railway line, though the frequent trains don't always stop at smaller places.

The province of Catanzaro begins at the Savuto River, and from here down to Reggio the SS18, autostrada and main rail line all run parallel along the coast, apart from the stretch of the Tropea promontory. The plain that stretches east from here, the **Piana di Sant'Eufemia**, is the narrowest part of the Calabrian peninsula, much of it reclaimed only in the last hundred years from malarial swamp: the mosquitoes remain but they no longer carry the disease. **Lamezia** has Calabria's main **airport** (☎0968.414.333, ⊛www.sacal.it) served by budget airlines including Ryanair, while **Sant'Eufemia-Lamezia** is the **rail and road junction** for Catanzaro and the Ionian coast. Heading south on the highway you begin a slow ascent on the long viaduct that is one of the engineering feats of the Autostrada del Sole, the views growing more inspiring as it rises above the coast to the high tableland of the Tropea promontory.

Diamante

DIAMANTE glistens on its small promontory jutting into the Tyrrhenian. The town's narrow whitewashed lanes have been adorned with striking modern murals, making it a fascinating place for a wander, and there are a couple of good, moderately priced fish **restaurants** with outside seating down by the seafront at Spiaggia Piccola (beyond the jetty). Most relaxed is the *Taverna del Pescatore* (☎0985.81.482; closed Tues), with views over the small port – expect to pay around €40 for a full meal, excluding drinks. If you want **to stay**, try the 🏛 *Ferretti Hotel* on the seafront at Via Poseidone 1 (☎0985.81.428, ⊛www .ferrettihotel.it; June-Sept; ❼), a luxurious modern place with its own swimming pool, restaurant, tennis court, private beach and excellent service.

Belvedere Marittimo, some 10km further down the coast, overlooks its unexceptional marina from a spur a little way inland. It's an imposing and elegant town, full of greenery and having little of the air of neglect typical of Calabria's older centres. At the top, an impressive **castle** stands guard, originally a Norman construction but rebuilt under the Aragonese, whose coat of arms can be seen above the main gate. The inside has been gutted, however, and it's closed to the public. Down in **Belvedere Marina**, the best place to eat is the *Milleluci* on Via Grossi (☎0985.82.229; closed Tues from mid-Sept to mid-June), which serves pizzas baked in a wood-fired oven alongside such specialities as *gnocchi di patata alla pescatora* (potato gnocchi with seafood) for around €7.

Paola

About 40km further down the coast, the sizeable town of **PAOLA** is an important rail and road junction for Calabria's interior, and the site of the **Santuario di San Francesco di Paola**, in a ravine above the town. Not to be confused with Francis of Assisi, this St Francis spent most of his life here in Paola and, as Calabria's principal saint, is venerated throughout the south. People visit the shrine at all times of year, but particularly during the week leading up to the May 4 festa.

There are several reasonably priced **hotels** and **trattorias** around the station by the sea, but Paola's bargain is the hotel *Casa del Pellegrino San Francesco di Paola*, a neat two-star at Via Valle della Timpa, aimed at pilgrims but open to all (℡0982.611.457, ✉info@hotelsanfrancescodipaola.it; ❶). There are also a couple of good **places to eat** near the central piazza above the *Casa del Pellegrino*: the *Eureka*, in Via del Cannone (℡0982.587.356; closed Tues), which does good fish from around €10 and has outdoor seating in summer, and pizzeria *Le Arcate* (℡0982.585.377; closed Mon in winter), through the arch at Via Valitutti 5, where a margherita costs €4.

Pizzo

Following the railway or the SS18, you might want to spend some time in the picturesque little town of **PIZZO**, neatly placed for the **beaches** around Tropea and site of a small **castle** (daily: summer 9am–9pm; winter 9am–7pm; €2; ⓦwww.murat.it) overlooking the sea just off the main Piazza della Repubblica. Built in 1486 by Ferdinand I of Aragon, it holds the room in which the French general **Murat** was imprisoned, with some of his personal effects and copies of the last letters he wrote, and the terrace where he was shot in October 1815. Murat, Napoleon's brother-in-law and one of his ablest generals, met his ignominious end here after attempting to rouse the people against the Bourbons to reclaim the throne of Naples given to him by Napoleon; the people of Pizzo ignored his haughty entreaties, and he was arrested and court-martialled.

A couple of kilometres north of the centre, you might drop in on the **Chiesetta di Piedigrotta** (daily 9am–1pm & 3–7.30pm; ⓦwww.chiesettadipiedigrotta.it; tickets €3 from *Bar Aquarium* near the entrance), a curious rock-hewn church next to a sandy beach, signposted off the coastal SS22. Created in the seventeenth century by Neapolitan sailors rescued from a shipwreck, the church was later enlarged and its interior festooned with eccentric statuary depicting episodes from the Bible. Most of this was the work of a local father-and-son team, and it was augmented by another scion of the family in 1969, who restored the works and contributed a scene of his own, a double portrait of Pope John XXIII and President Kennedy.

Practicalities

Pizzo has a **tourist office** located over the arches at the bottom of Piazza della Repubblica (summer daily 10am–1pm & 4.30–7.30; winter Mon–Sat 10am–1pm & 4–7pm; ℡0963.531.310). There are good **places to stay** though as it's a beach resort booking is essential in the summer. On Via Armonia in the *centro storico* is the clean little B&B *Casa Armonia* (℡0963.533.337, ⓦwww.casaarmonia.com; ❸). Another good option is *A Casa Janca* (℡0963.264.364 or 349.574.7135; ❺), a first-rate agriturismo on the main road out of town heading north (200m before the Agip station.) Furnished in traditional rustic style, the place is locally renowned for its **restaurant**, where non-guests can also dine for around €35 on Calabrian specialities such as *zuppa di cipolla* (onion soup); half board here costs €140 for two.

There's a good choice of **places to eat** in the centre of Pizzo clustered under the arcade in Piazza della Repubblica. On the Piazza is *Pizzeria La Ruota* (℡0963.532.427, closed Wed) where pizzas cost between €4 and €8 – try the house speciality, *La Ruota*, with tuna, olives and peppers. Alternatively, walk down to the port area for a range of seafood restaurants, one of them, *La Nave* (℡0963.532.211; closed Wed), in the form of a ship. Between April and July sample the tuna or swordfish, for which Pizzo is a fishing centre. Make sure you also try the famous local ice cream, *tartufo di Pizzo* – a portion is a bit like eating a whole box of chocolate truffles.

Tropea and around

Southwest of Pizzo, **TROPEA** can claim to be the prettiest town on the whole of the southern Tyrrhenian coast, built right on the edge of steep cliffs, towering high over its beach. It is also (after Maratea in Basilicata) the most fashionable, with a seaside charm missing from many of the other Calabrian resorts, and not yet entirely eroded by the annual influx of tourists. There are

▲ The coastline at Tropea

numerous beaches around the town, all within easy walking distance of the town centre, and the buildings have character without being twee – see particularly the lovely Norman **cathedral** at the bottom of Via Roma, whose interior harbours a couple of unexploded American bombs from the last war (one accompanied by a grateful prayer to the Madonna), a Renaissance ciborium and a statue of the *Madonna and Child* from the same period. The views from the upper town over the sea and the church of **Santa Maria dell'Isola** on its rock (closed for restoration) are superb, and on a clear day you can see the cone of Strómboli and sometimes other Aeolian Islands looming on the horizon.

Arrival and information

Trains from Lamezia, Reggio Calabria, and surrounding coastal villages arrive at Tropea's station located on the outskirts of the *centro storico*, 1km from the beach. In summer, regular bus services link the coastal resorts to Tropea, but transport is more infrequent out of season. Check with the tourist office for schedules.

The **tourist office** is in Piazza Ercole (daily: summer 9am–1pm & 3–9pm; winter 9am–1pm & 3–7pm; ℡0963.61.475). For **internet** access try *Quellila della Bottega Artigiana*, in the historic centre on Largo Ruffa 5/6 (Mon–Sat 10am–1pm & 5pm–midnight, Sun 5pm–midnight; April–Oct).

Accommodation

In August it is vital to book **accommodation** ahead; Tropea is the best-known resort on the Calabrian coast and consequently expensive, too.

Camping Marina del Convento Via Marina del Convento ℡0963.62.501, ⓦwww .marinadelconvento.it. On the beach at the base of the centre of Tropea, this campsite also has small simple apartments for €500 a week in mid-season rising to €900 a week in Aug. May–Oct.

Camping Marina dell'Isola Via Marina dell'Isola ℡0963.61.970, ⓦwww.maregrande.it. Right on the beach in the centre of town, this campsite charges around €12 to pitch a tent plus €10 per person.

Gurnella Contrada Grunella ℡0963.61.427, ⓦwww.gurnella.it. Clean and modern self catering apartments just outside the centre with lovely views over the town an out to sea. Prices for a two-room apartment range from €270 a week mid-season to €750 in high season.

Virgilio Viale Tondo ℡0963.61.978, ⓦwww .hotel-virgilio.com. A blandly furnished but welcoming family-run three-star that requires half or full board in high season. ⓥ

Eating and drinking

Tropea has more **trattorias** per square metre than any other town in Calabria, often with budget-priced tourist menus. **Nightlife**, meanwhile, is tranquil, with good wine bars and ice-cream parlours in which to while away the evening.

La Cantina del Principe Largo Galluppi 18 ℡0963.61.400. Authentic, moderately priced Calabrese food served in a beautifully converted cellar; mains from about €10, though prices rise for the month of Aug. Closed Nov–March.

La Munizione Largo Duomo 12. Enoteca behind the cathedral, with a roof terrace boasting excellent views. It serves around 130 wines and cocktails from €5.

Le Volpi e L'Uva Via Pelliccia 2/4, signed off Corso Vittorio Emanuele II. Around 300 wines and good

snacks, around the €5 mark, in an intimate enoteca.

Osteria del Pescatore Via del Monte 7 ℡0963.603.018. Excellent, good-value fish served up in a vaulted cellar around the corner from the cathedral; a big plate of *spaghetti alla tropeana* is around €5. Closed Nov–Easter.

Vecchio Forno Via Caivano, off Corso Vittorio Emanuele II. The most historic place to eat in town, serving crisp, fresh pizza for around €4 – the smell of *peperoncino* is heavenly.

Capo Vaticano

Further around the promontory, **CAPO VATICANO** holds some of the area's most popular beaches, including **Grotticelle** and **Tonicello**, both spacious enough to allow you to get away from the bustle. Grotticelle has a **campsite** immediately above it, *Quattro Scoglie* (☎0963.663.126, ⓦwww.grotticelle.it; April–Oct), where pitching a tent will cost you €13 plus €13 per person. They also rent self-contained **apartments** (from €1000 a week in high season for a two-room place) and run a **hotel** (half board obligatory in Aug; ❸) a few minutes' walk further up the road. If you have transport the agriturismo *Tenuta U' Locu* (☎348.343.0389, ⓦwww.romasrl.org; ❶) 4km up the coast has apartments and rooms for rent and friendly owners who will happily suggest the best beach excursions.

Scilla and Villa San Giovanni

Heading south, looking out to sea, the proximity of Sicily becomes the dominant feature, and the stretch of the autostrada that dives down to the town of Villa San Giovanni can claim to be one of the most panoramic in Italy, burrowing high up through mountains with the Straits of Messina glittering below. Travelling by train or following the old coastal road, you skirt the so-called Costa Viola (Violet Coast), passing through **SCILLA**, ancient Scylla, with a fine sandy **beach** and lots of action in the summer. This was the legendary location of a six-headed cave monster, one of two hazards to mariners mentioned in the **Odyssey**, the other being the whirlpool Charybdis, corresponding to the modern Cariddi located 6km away on the other side of the Strait. Crowning a hefty rock, a **castle** separates the main beach from the fishing village of Scilla to the north. The most popular **place to stay** in town is the newly renovated *Albergo Le Sirene* on Via Nazionale 57 (booking advisable in summer, ☎0965.754.019; ❸): try to get one of the two front rooms facing the sea. There are several good fish **restaurants** along the seafront, including *Il Pirata* at Via Grotte 22 (☎0965.704.292; closed Wed Oct–May), which does excellent *maccheroncini con pesce spada* (pasta with swordfish). There's also a fixed-price menu at €30.

From Scilla it's just 9km to **VILLA SAN GIOVANNI**, worth stopping at only as a point of embarkation for Sicily. State-run FS **ferries** (☎892.021, ⓦwww.trenitalia.it) leave from directly behind the train station about every thirty minutes (less frequently Sun and hols) and arrive at the train station in Messina in about forty minutes; if you're travelling by **car** it's more convenient to catch one of the private Caronte ferries, (☎800.627.414, ⓦwww.carontetourist.it), under the train tracks to the right of the station, which leave approximately every twenty minutes and pull in closer to the entrance of the autostrada. Both companies charge around €1 for foot passengers and €30 for cars. If you're heading for Reggio, take a train or one of the city buses #106 or #108 from outside the station.

Reggio Calabria and around

As you approach **REGGIO CALABRIA**, the provincial capital, you travel through some of the most extreme landscapes in the south. Dilapidated villages lie stranded among mountains, which are themselves torn apart by wide *fiumare*, or riverbeds – empty or reduced to a trickle for most of the year, but swelling with the melting of the winter snows to destructive torrents. Reggio itself was one of the first ancient Greek settlements on the Italian mainland; today, it's

REGGIO CALABRIA

Straits of Messina

ACCOMMODATION
B&B Delfina   B
Lido   A
EATING & DRINKING
Baylik   1
La Forchetta D'Oro 2

Calabria's biggest town by some distance, with a population of over 180,000 – but also one that's been synonymous for years with urban decline and the influence of the '**Ndrangheta Mafia**. Although efforts to regenerate the city are evident wherever you look, there's little to detain you here for more than a day and most travellers use it merely as a gateway to Sicily or the Aeolian Islands.

Arrival, information and accommodation

There is a small **airport** (℡899.282.829; Ⓦwww.sogas .it) outside Reggio, serving primarily Italian destinations and there are frequent bus shuttles to the centre and Villa San Giovanni. If you're **arriving by train**, get off at **Reggio Lido** for the port or museum. Buses end up at the **Reggio Centrale** station, 1km or so down the long Corso Garibaldi. You may want to make use of **city buses** for getting from one end of town to the other (Line A and #108, #123, #124, and #127 stop at both the museum and the station); tickets cost €0.80 from kiosks and *tabacchi*. There are several **internet** points around the station and along Corso Garibaldi. There is a **tourist office** at Via Venezia 1/A (Mon–Fri 9am–12.30 & 3–5pm; ℡0965. 21.010, Ⓦwww.prolocoreggiocalabria.it).

Accommodation options are reasonable with the clean, central *B&B Delfina* at Via Crocefisso 58 (℡334.161.3905; Ⓦwww.bb-delfina.com; ②), near the Duomo. Otherwise try the *Hotel Lido* at Via Tre Settembre 6 (℡0965.25.001, Ⓦwww.hotellido.rc.it; ③), a three-star with cheerful rooms at the other end of the Corso, near the Lido station.

The Town

The **Museo Nazionale** at the northern end of Corso Garibaldi (Tues–Sun 9am–7pm; €6) is Reggio's main draw. It holds the most important collection of archeological finds in Calabria, full of items dating from the Hellenic period, with examples from all the major Greek sites in Calabria, including the famous *pinakes* or carved tablets from the sanctuary of Persephone at Locri. The most renowned exhibits in the museum are the **Bronzi di Riace**: two bronze statues dragged out of the Ionian Sea in 1972 near the village of Riace. They are shapely examples of the highest period of Greek art (fifth century BC), and especially prized because there are so few finds from this period in such a good state of repair. Upstairs, you can see examples of Byzantine and Renaissance art, including two works by Antonello da Messina.

The other must-see attraction in Reggio Calabria is the **Piccolo Museo di San Paolo** at Via Reggio Campi 4 (Wed, Sat & Sun 9.30am–noon; free; ☎0965.892.426), an impressive private collection of religious art including some 160 Russian icons and a *St Michael* attributed to Antonello da Messina. A stroll along the **lungomare** seaside esplanade along the sandy beach is pleasant, affording wonderful views of the Sicilian coastline and Mount Etna. There are remains of sixth-century BC city walls and a Roman bathing complex at the southern end before the Villa Comunale. Just west of the ancient baths stands the **Duomo** (daily 8am–noon & 4–8pm; free), heavily restored after an earthquake.

Eating and drinking

There are a handful of **eating** places around Corso Garibaldi, including the very good *La Forchetta D'Oro* near the main train station at Via Bixio 5 (☎0965.896.048; closed Wed except in Aug), where you could eat a fish dinner for under €25 a head, or meat dishes such as *maccheroncini* with spicy local *salsiccia* (sausage). Worthy of the hike 1.5km north of the Museo Nazionale to Vico Leone, *Baylik* serves up the city's best fish (☎0965.48.624; closed Mon), including spaghetti with *fiori di zucca e pesce spada* (courgette flowers and scampi) and excellent grilled prawns for around €35 for a full meal. The best **gelateria** in town is *Cesare*, a kiosk on Piazza Indipendenza between the Lido train station and the Museo Nazionale.

Aspromonte

Most visitors to Reggio leave without having ventured into the great massif of **Aspromonte**, the last spur of the Apennines on the tip of Italy's boot. Here you can be on a beach and a ski slope within the same hour, passing from the brilliant, almost tropical vegetation of the coast to dense forests of beech and pine that rise to nearly 2000m. Although it recently became a national park (ⓦwww.parcoaspromonte.it), the thickly forested mountain has not yet shown any sign of becoming a tourist destination. This is mostly due to its reputation as the stronghold of the '**Ndrangheta**, the Calabrian mafia, and as such most Italians would think you mad for going there. On top of this, the area remains virtually unsigned, and the oppressive tree cover rarely breaks to provide views. If you're in a car take notice of the *Strada Interotta* ("Road interrupted") signs that you'll find at the entrances: you should not even think about attempting the rocky dirt tracks across the range unless you are driving an off-road vehicle.

If the walking and hiking still draws you, will find access to the Aspromonte range is easiest from the Tyrrhenian side, with several buses a day leaving Reggio's Piazza Garibaldi for Gambarie and winding their way up the highly scenic SS184 from Gallico, through profusely terraced groves of vine and citrus to the village of **SANTO STEFANO**, famous as the birthplace and final resting place of the last of the great brigands who roamed these parts, **Giuseppe Musolino** (1875–1956). Occupying a sort of Robin Hood role in the popular imagination, Musolino was a legend in his own lifetime, the last thirty years of which he spent in jail and, finally, a lunatic asylum – the penalty for having led the *Carabinieri* on a long and humiliating dance up and down the slopes of Aspromonte during his profitable career. Just above the village, in the cemetery, you can see Musolino's grave, now renovated but until recently daubed with the signatures of people come to pay their respects.

If you're in the region in late summer it's worth timing your visit to see the large **fair** that takes place every year on the first two days of September at the **Santuario della Madonna di Polsi**, a 10km hike from the park entrance: an unashamedly pagan event that involves the sale and slaughter of large numbers of goats. Its popularity has a darker side, however: the fair is well known to provide a convenient cover for the annual meeting of 'Ndrangheta cells from all over the world.

Cosenza and around

In Calabria's interior, **COSENZA** is a burgeoning city with a small and clean historic centre surrounded by rings of featureless modern construction. The one thing worth seeing in town is the stately **Duomo** (daily 8.30am–noon & 4–7pm) in the historic town centre on the main street, Corso Telesio. Consecrated on the occasion of Frederick II's visit to the city in 1222, it contains the lovely tomb of Isabella of Aragon, who died in Cosenza in 1271 while returning with her husband Philip III – seen kneeling beside her – from an abortive Crusade in Tunisia, and a copy of a thirteenth-century Byzantine icon, the *Madonna del Pilerio*, which was once carried around the country during times of plague.

Tradition has it that under the Busento River in Cosenza is the burial place of **Alaric the Goth**, the barbarian who gave the Western world a jolt when he prised open the gates of Rome in 410 AD. Struck down for his sins by malaria while journeying south, he was interred here along with his booty, and the course of the river deviated to cover the traces, lending Cosenza a place in history and giving rise to countless, fruitless projects to discover the tomb's whereabouts.

Practicalities

The **bus station** is below Piazza Fera, from where it's a twenty-minute walk down the length of Corso Mazzini to the hotels and the *centro storico*. Arriving by train, you have to take a bus (every 20min) from the **train station** a little way outside town – buy your ticket from the bar inside the station. The main **tourist office** is in Piazzetta Toscano behind the Duomo (Mon–Fri 9am–12.30pm, Mon & Thurs 4–6pm).

Hotels are mostly expensive, business-traveller places, but there are one or two nicer alternatives. The *Excelsior* on Piazza Matteotti (℡0984.74.383, Ⓦwww.italiaabc.it/a/excelsior; ❷) is a spacious, comfortable and well-furnished hotel, close to the historic centre and offering great value for money, or try the more business-like *Home Club*, Via G. Mancini, on the edge of the *centro storico* (℡0984.76.833, Ⓦwww.homeclub.it; ❸). For **eating** try *Calabria Bella*, (℡0984.793.531) in the old town on Piazza Duomo, which has outside seating in summer and serves traditional local dishes; a generous mixed plate of antipasti can be had for about €8. There are numerous cafés and pubs, but the best aperitif is to be found at the old-fashioned *Gran Caffè Renzelli*, up past the Duomo on Corso Umberto.

Around Cosenza

People spending any time in Cosenza will probably be mostly interested in excursions into the **Sila highlands** (see below), but some of the villages dotted around the surrounding hills shouldn't be ignored. In summer, the streets are lively until late, and at night the views over the bowl of the valley are magnificent, with glittering threads and clusters of light. It's also in the summer that the village **festas** normally take place, with each *Comune* vying to outdo the others in terms of spectacle and expense.

The hilltop village of **RENDE** holds the prize for the tidiest village in the region: it has good views and an absorbing little **museum** (daily 9am–1pm & 4–7pm; free) in the Palazzo Zagarese, on Via de Bartolo, devoted to local folk art, costumes, cuisine, music, the Albanian community and emigration. Rende also boasts a decent choice of places to **eat** and drink, including the good-value pizzeria, *L'Arco*, at Via Costa 4/B (℡0984.443.230; eve only, closed Tues Sept–May), with a panoramic terrace, where pizzas start at €4. Northeast of Cosenza, above the village of **LUZZI**, stands the **Abbazia di Sambucina**. A Cistercian abbey founded in the twelfth century and long the centre of this order of monks throughout the south, it has a beautiful, lightly pointed portal (rebuilt in the fifteenth century) and the original presbytery. Buses for the villages depart from the **bus station** in Cosenza, below Piazza Fera, but to get the most out of these places you ideally need your own transport, as services normally stop at nightfall.

The Sila

Covering the widest part of the Calabrian peninsula, the **Sila** massif, east of Cosenza, is more of an extensive plateau than a mountain range, though the peaks on its western flank reach heights of nearly 2000m. Protected by the Parco Nazionale della Sila (Ⓦwww.parcosila.it), it's divided into three main groups, the Sila Greca, Sila Grande and Sila Piccola, of which the Sila Grande is of most interest to tourists.

At one time the Sila was one huge forest and was exploited from earliest times to provide fuel and material for the construction of fleets, fortresses and even for church-building in Rome, resulting in a deforestation that helped bring about the malarial conditions that for centuries laid much of Calabria low. The cutting of trees is now strictly controlled, and **ancient pines** (the so-called **Giganti della Sila**), which can live for several hundred years, are among the region's chief attractions. There's plenty here, too, for the outdoors enthusiast: in summer the area provides relief from the heat of the towns; and in winter there's downhill and cross-country skiing.

The Sila Grande

Densely forested, and the highest, most extensive part of the Sila range, the **Sila Grande** is home to Calabria's main **ski slopes** as well as the region's three principal **lakes** – all artificial (for hydroelectric purposes) and much loved by fishing enthusiasts, who come out in force at weekends. If you want to spend any time up here, the **campsites** enjoy good lakeside locations, while the hotels are mainly in the towns and villages, and many close out of season.

Camigliatello

The town of **CAMIGLIATELLO** is the best-known of the resorts, a functional place that's well connected by bus with Cosenza, though it lacks any intrinsic charm. Centred on Via Roma, the town has three ski slopes of its own, and another in Contrada Moccone (a *frazione* of Campigliatello 3km west), plus a confusion of hotels, restaurants, and souvenir shops. If you fancy **skiing**, day passes are available from €15 and you will find the slopes have facilities for renting equipment (from €20 per day). Several ski clubs offer tuition (group lessons from €20 per person per hr). For information call Ski Club Camigliatello (℡0984.929.755) or Scuola Sci (℡333.256.6588). The Sila terrain also makes ideal **riding** country, though most stables are open in summer only; the Pro Loco can arrange outings. If you want to **stay**, try the plain but inexpensive *Miramonti* on Via Forgitelle (℡0984.579.067, ⓦwww.miramontisila.it; ❶) which also has a restaurant preparing simple local cuisine, or the comfortable and just slightly pricier *Meranda*, Via Roma, Camigliatello (℡0984.578.022; ❷), which also has a restaurant.

For a **snack** in Camigliatello, *Bar Centrale* on Via del Turismo, just north of Via Roma, has pastries, panini and other fast food, while Contrada Moccone has a great-value **trattoria**, *Da Fulvio* (℡0984.578.790; closed Mon), which has a well-deserved reputation for good-value, simple local cooking, using lots of wild mushrooms and wild boar (set menu €15). The Pro Loco **tourist office** at the top of Via Roma keeps slightly erratic opening hours (in theory Tues–Sun 9.30am–12.30pm & 3.30–7pm; ℡0984.578.159), and has maps of the area and suggestions for **walking routes** in the park.

The Strada delle Vette

Camigliatello is a useful starting-point for a tough hike that takes in the area's highest peaks, following the **Strada delle Vette** ("road of the peaks") for 13km through pine and beech woods before forking off and up to the three **peaks** of Monte Scuro, Monte Curcio and, highest of all, Monte Botte Donato (1928m). The trail, which is often snowbound between December and May, continues on down to **Lago Arvo** and the resort of **LORICA**, from where it's a shorter distance than following the *strada delle vette* to reach Botte Donato. Or you can save the sweat and take the chair lift from the Località Cavaliere, just outside town. Lorica, like Camigliatello, is dedicated to tourism in the height of the winter and summer seasons, but its lakeside location makes it a more relaxed spot, with lots of places for picnicking under the pines and observing the antics of the black squirrels that inhabit them. Lorica also boasts a comfortable four-star hotel, *Park 108* at Via Nazionale 86 (℡0984.537.077, ⓦwww.hotelpark108.it; ❸), that doesn't ask for half board in high season and has a sauna and fitness centre.

The town is connected with Cosenza by **bus**, arriving in the morning and returning in the afternoon.

Parco Nazionale Pollino

Straddling Basilicata and Calabria, the **Parco Nazionale Pollino** (Pollino National Park) is Italy's largest, covering an area of nearly two thousand square kilometres. It is named for the *Massiccio del Pollino*, a massif in the southern Apennines that reaches a height of 2248m, offering spectacular views over pine forests, plains, limestone slopes, and beyond, to both the Tyrrhenian and Ionian seas. That, and its other major peaks such as the **Serra Dolcedorme** (2267m), are best explored on organized hiking excursions (see below) aimed at seeking out the park's rare flora and fauna which include the cuirassed pine (the park's symbol), the roe deer and the golden eagle.

The park's lower slopes are home to nearly sixty villages, best seen by car, as public transport connections are irregular. From Calabria, one logical gateway is **LAINO BORGO**, just off the A3 autostrada, known for its **Santuario delle Cappelle**, fifteen chapels frescoed with scenes from the life of Christ. From here, it is a short drive to **Laino Castello**, an eerie medieval hamlet abandoned after an earthquake in the 1980s that holds commanding views over the Lao River Valley. The park's limestone terrain is particularly susceptible to erosion, which gives rise to its many grottoes including the **Grotta del Romito** in **PAPASIDERO**, just across the border in Basilicata. Many guided excursions depart to the Pollino massif from Papasidero though the town itself is worth a stroll for its elaborately carved portals that precede churches and *palazzi nobili*. Near the park's eastern boundary are several towns – Acquaformosa, Civita, S. Basile, S. Costantino Albanese and S. Paolo Albanese among them – founded between1470 and 1540 by Albanian refugees fleeing persecution by the Turks. Here language, costume and religious customs have a decidedly eastern flavour.

Activities

From horseriding to hiking there are plenty of **activities** on offer in the park. Try the following operators:

CAI (Club Alpino Italiano) Via C.Pepe 74, Castrovillari ☎334.100.5054, ✉www.caicastrovillari.it. The Italian Alpine Club can arrange hikes and nature trails with English-speaking guides.
Ente Parco Complesso Monumentale Santa Maria della Consolazione, Rotonda ☎0973.669.311, ✉www.parcopollino.it. The official national park office.

Ferula Viaggi Via Cappelluti 34, Matera ☎0835.336.572, ✉www.ferulaviaggi.it. Multi-day hiking or biking excursions with guides and lodging.
Viaggiare nel Pollino ☎0973.669.290, ✉www .viaggiarenelpollino.com. Thematic tours, hiking, biking, and rafting excursions. The website has a mine of information on the park.

Calabria's Ionian coast

Calabria's Ionian coast is a mainly flat sandy strip, sometimes monotonous but less developed than the Tyrrhenian side of the peninsula, and with cleaner water. At the border with Basilicata, mountainous slopes soon give way to the wide **Piana di Sibari**, the most extensive of the Calabrian coastal plains, bounded by Pollino to the north, the Sila Greca to the west and the Sila Grande in the south. The rivers flowing off these mountains, which for centuries kept the land well watered and rich, also helped to transform it into a stagnant and malarial mire,

The wealth of Sybaris was only one factor in its fame. The inhabitants of the city – said to number 100,000 – were so fond of luxury and their excesses so legendary that we derive the modern word **sybarite** from their reputation. The city's laws and institutions were apparently made to ensure the greatest comfort and well-being of its citizens, including the banning from the city of all noisy traders, such as metalworkers, and the planting of trees along every street for shade. Cooks were so highly prized that they were apparently bought and sold in the marketplace for great sums and were allowed to patent their recipes, while inventions ascribed to the Sybarites include pasta and the chamberpot. This was all too much for the Crotonians, who, under their general Milo destroyed the city in 510 BC, diverting the waters of the river over the site to complete the job.

and although land reclamation has restored the area's fertility, without visiting the museum and excavations at **Sybaris** you could pass through the area with no inkling of the civilization that once flourished on these shores. Southeast of here, two monastery complexes and **Crotone**, another ancient Greek city, provide a trio of points of interest as you travel along the coastline.

The southern part of Calabria's Ionian seaboard is less developed than the rest of the region, perhaps because it's less interesting scenically and most of the seaside towns and villages strung along it are unappealing. If you like sandy **beaches**, though, this is where to find them – either wild and unpopulated or, if you prefer, glitzy and brochure-style, as at **Soverato**. At **Locri** there's the region's best collection of Greek ruins and, overlooking the coast a short way inland, the craggy medieval strongholds of **Squillace** and **Gerace**.

Sybaris

Long one of the great archeological mysteries tantalizing generations of scholars, the site of ancient **SYBARIS** (Sibari) was only definitely identified in the late 1960s, when aerial and X-ray photography confirmed that the site previously known to be that of Roman Thurium was also that of Sybaris. There are in fact three separate levels of construction that have been unearthed here, one Greek and two Roman, one on top of the other. Together these make up one of the world's largest archeological sites, covering a thousand hectares (compared with Pompeii's fifty), though only ten hectares have so far been dug up.

The **excavations** lie across the rail lines, some 4km south down the SS106, on the right-hand side (daily 9am to 1hr before sunset; free; ☎0981.79.166). Most of them belong to the Roman period, but something of the earlier site might still be turned up – the silt and sand of the river bed have yet to be explored properly, work having been effectively halted for much of the last twenty years owing to shortage of funds. Of the Roman city, the remains are at least impressively displayed and maintained, including baths, a patrician's house with mosaics, and a *decumanus* – main street – claimed to be the widest in existence. There's more to be seen, from here and other local sites, at the **Museo della Sibarite** (Tues–Sun 9am–7.30pm; €2; ☎0981.79.391), down a left turn about 1km before the excavations, on the banks of the River Crati.

Rossano

Down the coast, the resort of **ROSSANO SCALO** has far outstripped its parent-town of **ROSSANO** in terms of size and bustle, and most of the holiday-makers who frequent its beaches never even get round to visiting the hilltop town, 7km up an awkward winding road – something that has helped to preserve the old centre from excessive development. The foremost Byzantine centre in the south, Rossano was the focus of a veritable renaissance of literature, theology and art between the eighth and eleventh centuries, a period to which the town's greatest treasures belong. Its majolica-tiled **Cattedrale** is an Angevin construction largely rebuilt after an 1836 earthquake, but it does have a much-venerated ninth-century Byzantine fresco, *Madonna Achiropita*, whose Greek epithet, meaning "not painted by hand", refers to its divine authorship. Next to the cathedral, the **Museo Diocesano** (summer daily 9am–1pm and 4.30–8pm; Sept–June Tues–Sat 9.30am–12.30pm & 4–7pm; Sun 10am–noon & 4.30–6.30pm; €2.50) contains the famed **codex purpureus Rossanensis**, or Purple Codex, a unique sixth-century manuscript on reddish-purple parchment illustrating the life of Christ. The book, which was brought from Palestine by monks fleeing the Muslim invasions, is open at one page, but you can leaf through a copy and see, among other things, how the Last Supper was originally depicted, with Christ and his disciples not seated but reclining on cushions round the table, and all eating from the same plate.

In contrast to the cathedral's grandiosity, the diminutive church of **San Marco** (daily 9am to 1hr before sunset; free), at the end of Corso Garibaldi on the edge of town, retains a primitive spirituality. The five cupolas of the tenth- or eleventh-century construction, surrounded by palms on a terrace that looks out over the gorge below, impart an almost Middle Eastern flavour.

Practicalities

Hotels are all in the modern lower town and most are neither especially cheap nor lovely. *Murano* at Via Mediterraneo 2 in Lido Sant'Angelo (☎0983.511.788, ⓦwww.hotelmurano.it; ❹) is an attractive modern exception, with great sea views and a maritime feel, while *Scigliano* (☎0983.511.846, ⓦwww.hotelscigliano.it; ❸), at Viale Margherita 257, 50m up from the level crossing from Lido Sant'Angelo, is a family-run place with an award-winning restaurant. For **camping**, *Oriental Park* (☎0983.290.266, ⓦwww.orientalpark.altervista.org) is 1km north of Rossano Scalo and has chalets for rent (❶).

Up in the old town, just off Piazza Anargiri in Via San Bartolomeo, you'll find the best **trattoria**, *La Villa*, offering alfresco eating in summer (☎0983.522.214; eve only, closed Tues Sept–June). It serves typical Calabrese food, with lots of local sausage and tomatoes; prices range from about €15 to €30 a head. There's another, slightly cheaper, more casual evenings-only place, *La Bizantina* (☎0983.525.340; closed Mon Sept–June), right outside San Marco, which has great antipasti (try *peperoni e patate*, roast red peppers and potatoes).

Crotone and around

South of Rossano lies an empty stretch of beaches, with, inland, the vineyards of Cirò, the source of Calabria's best-known **wine**. Crossing the River Neto into the fertile **Marchesato** region, you'll have your approach to **Crotone** (the ancient Greek city of Kroton) blighted by a smoky industrial zone – not the most alluring entry into a city, but a rare thing in Calabria, and a reminder of the false hopes once vested in the industrialization of the region.

The site of ancient **Kroton** has been entirely lost, but in its day this was among the most important colonial settlements of Magna Graecia, overshadowed by its more powerful neighbour Sybaris, but with a school of medicine that was famous throughout the classical world and closely linked with the prowess of the city's athletes, who regularly scooped all the honours at the Olympic Games back in Greece. In 530 BC the mathematician and metaphysician Pythagoras took up residence in Kroton and it later went on to be the first of the Greek cities in Calabria. However, increasingly destabilized by internal conflicts the city was eventually destroyed by the Romans. A resurgence of sorts occurred in the thirteenth century when it was made the main town of the Marchesato region, a vast feudal domain held by the powerful Ruffo family of Catanzaro. But its prosperity was always hindered by the scourge of malaria provoking the author George Gissing – himself a victim of malaria during his visit in 1897 – to condemn Crotone as "a squalid little town".

In spite of it all, Crotone today has an agreeable, unspoiled old centre, and makes a good base for the **beaches** that spread to the south and for the Greek ruins at Capo Colonna. The town's new **Museo Archeologico Nazionale** (Tues–Sun 9am–7pm; €2) on Via Risorgimento holds the best collection of finds from Magna Graecia on the Ionian coast. Most noteworthy is the so-called **Treasure of Hera**, a beautifully restored group of bronze statuettes – including a sphinx, a gorgon, a horse, a winged siren and a very rare nuraghic boat from Sardinia dating from the seventh to the fifth centuries BC. The most dazzling item is a gold diadem, expertly worked with garlands of leaves and sprigs of myrtle.

Practicalities

Arriving by **train** you may want to take a taxi or bus to cover the 1.5km to the centre of town, Piazza Pitagora, and most of the hotels. There's a **tourist office** at Via Torino 148, obscurely sited halfway between the station and the old town (Mon & Wed 9am–1pm & 3–5pm, Tues, Thurs & Fri 7.30am–1pm; ☎0962.23.185). The **bus** station is on Via Ruffo, a couple of streets east of Piazza Pitagora, where most provincial and regional buses arrive.

Nearby, the rather cramped *Pace*, Via Cutro 56 (☎0962.22.584; ●), is central Crotone's cheapest **accommodation** choice. Better are the *Concordia* on Piazza Vittoria, just off Corso Vittorio Emanuele (☎0962.23.910, Ⓦwww .hotelconcordiakr.com; ●), whose dingy entrance hall belies this eighteenth-century building's attractive rooms, and – for a bit of luxury – *Residence Casarossa*, Via per Capocolonna (☎0962.934.201, Ⓦwww.casarossa.it; ●), which boasts a private beach and all mod cons.

As for **eating**, Crotone is one of the best places in the region to eat fish, being blessed with some of the least over-fished waters in the Mediterranean and a couple of talented chefs. Head for the excellent ⚜ *Da Ercole* (☎0962.901.425, closed Sun Sept–June) along the seafront at Viale Gramsci 122, owned by chef Ercole Villirillo, who runs cookery classes all over the world. It's one of the few places anywhere that you can sample such dishes as *linguine a pitagora* (which feature *prine*, a kind of sea anemone) or *ricciola* with wild artichokes (*ricciola con carciofi selvatici*) – a meal here will probably weigh in at about €50. Also on the seafront on Via Bartolo, highly rated ⚜ *Sosta da Marcello* (☎0962.23.821; closed Sun except Aug and dinner in winter). In the centre, *Caffè Italia* on Piazza Vittoria is one of Crotone's most historic cafés, good for a refreshing *latte di mandorla* (almond milk) or the local speciality of rose-shaped pastries.

Inland to Santa Severina

From Crotone's bus office on Via Ruffo there are a couple of departures daily to **SANTA SEVERINA**, on the eastern fringes of the Sila Piccola. A Byzantine fortified town built on a hilltop, it's well worth a detour, principally for the Norman castle that dominates it. Rebuilt by Robert Guiscard on the ruins of a

Byzantine stronghold and remodelled by the Swabians and Angevins, the renovated castle holds a first-rate **museum** (Tues–Sun 9am–1pm & 3–7pm; €5 including entrance to Museo Diocesano), taking in all parts of the construction from the foundations to the first-floor rooms. From the stout battlemented walls long views extend over the hilly surroundings towards the mountains of the Sila. On the other side of the piazza, whose flagstones are studded with symbols of the zodiac, the **Duomo** lies adjacent to an eighth-century Byzantine **baptistry** (ask the cathedral's nuns to open it for you), which preserves traces of frescoes of the saints, Greek inscriptions on the capitals and its original font. On the other side of the Duomo, the **Museo Diocesano** also repays a visit (Tues–Sun 9am–1pm & 3–7pm; €5 including entrance to Castello), containing a painfully graphic fifteenth-century Christ on the cross, an early printed edition of the Bible, and – its greatest treasure – the *Spilla Angioina*, a brooch from about 1300, studded with gold, pearls and rubies. If you're looking for a full **meal** in Santa Severina, try the *Locanda del Re* (☎0962.51.662) on the steps below the castle which, thanks to serving as the *mensa* for the town police, is open every day. Food is rooted in the medieval traditions of the area, so expect handmade pasta, lots of wild mushroom, wild pig, ricotta and pecorino. The owners also have little **apartments to rent** (✉lalocandadelre@hotmail.com; ❶) in a pretty old house in the *centro storico*.

A nice alternative, 3km outside town at Cerzeto off the SS107, is the 🍴*Agriturismo Il Querceto* (☎0962.51.467, ⓦwww.agriturismoilquerceto.kr.it), a fifty-hectare organic farm which raises beef and grows citrus fruit and olives. They have rooms and apartments, a swimming pool, and mountain bikes to rent. You can stay on a B&B basis (❶) or half board (€45 per person).

Capo Colonna to Le Castella
Another worthwhile excursion from Crotone is to the famed column at **Capo Colonna** on Calabria's extreme eastern point, for which you have to drive or walk 11km along the coast. The column is a solitary remnant of a vast structure that served as the temple for all the Greeks in Calabria. Dedicated to Hera

▲ Olive grove, inland Calabria

Lacinia, the temple originally possessed 48 of these Doric columns and was the repository of immense wealth before being repeatedly sacked as Magna Graecia and Hellenism itself declined.

There are some excellent **bathing spots** not far south of here. The so-called **ISOLA CAPO RIZZUTO** is a spit of land, not an island, with a choice of sandy or rocky inlets to swim from. During the winter the resort is dead, but it can get quite congested in the height of summer and difficult to find a place to stay. Nearby **LE CASTELLA** is another busy holiday spot, but not yet strangled by tourism. It would be hard to spoil the beautifully sited Aragonese **fortress** (Tues–Sun 9am to 1hr before sunset; €3) on an islet just off the main town. You could wander round the outside of the castle and swim off the rocks, though you'll probably be more tempted by the arc of beach to the south. For **food**, you can't do better than *L'Aragonese* (☏0962.795.013), right opposite the castle, serving lots of fresh fish and pizzas in the evening.

Catanzaro and Squillace

Despite its fine position, set high up in the foothills of the Sila and with good views out to sea, Calabria's regional capital, **CATANZARO**, has little innate charm. It's a crowded, overdeveloped, traffic-ridden city, within a short ride of some five-star beaches, but otherwise best avoided. There's more interest further on down the coast at the ruined basilica of Santa Maria della Roccella, or **La Roccelletta**, 100m down the road that branches off the SS106, signposted towards San Floro and Borgia. Half-hidden in an olive grove, this partly restored redbrick shell is all that remains of what was once the second-largest church in Calabria (after Gerace). Of uncertain date, though probably Norman in origin and founded by Basilian monks, it still has a mighty impact on the unsuspecting viewer. The church is part of a larger **Zona Archeologica** (daily 9am to 1hr before sunset; free) of the Roman town of Scolacium. The best-preserved item here is a **theatre**, once able to hold some 3500 spectators, and thought to have been abandoned following a fire some time after 350 AD.

Five kilometres further south along the coast, at Lido di Squillace, is the turn-off for the old town of **SQUILLACE**, 8km up in the hills, once an important centre but now just a mountain village, isolated on its high crag. There are lofty views to be enjoyed over the Gulf and beyond Catanzaro as far as the Sila Piccola mountain range, and the **Castle** (usually someone there Mon–Sat 9am–1pm, but if closed ask at the *Comune* on Piazza Municipio; ☏0961.914.020) is one of the most romantic collections of ruins in Calabria. The place is probably most renowned for its associations with **Cassiodorus**, whose monastery was located in the vicinity – though all trace of it has long since disappeared. Cassiodorus (480–570), scholar and secretary to the Ostrogoth Theodoric, used his position to preserve much of Italy's classical heritage against the onset of the Dark Ages and the book-burning propensities of the Christians. Retiring to spend the last thirty years of his life in seclusion here, Cassiodorus composed histories and collections of documents – of invaluable use to historians.

Soverato

South of Squillace, the golden sands of **SOVERATO** beckon, a resort that is increasingly attracting the international market. The private lidos hold sway here, charging up to €15 for a day under a parasol on a clean **beach** with access to a bar, but it's easy to find free beaches by following the coast away from town in either direction if you fancy more seclusion. **Accommodation** options in

Soverato include a couple of two-stars: *San Vincenzo*, Corso Umberto I 296 (T0967.21.106; ❷), in the centre of town; and the *Riviera* on Via Regina Elena (T0967.25.738; ❷), with sea views. Slightly more upmarket are the well-equipped *Gli Ulivi*, Via A Moro 1 (T0967.521.194, W www.hotelgliulivi.it; ❺), which has its own strip of beach and requires half board in peak season. The *Campeggio Glauco* **campsite** at Località San Nicola (T0967.25.533, W www .campeggioglauco.it; open June–Sept) is 1km north of Soverato and faces onto the beach; it costs €8 to pitch a tent plus €6.50 per person.

Locri and Gerace

Continuing south, you soon come to the most famous classical site on this coast, **Locri Epizefiri** (daily 9am until one hour before sunset; free), some 5km beyond the resort town of **LOCRI**. Founded sometime in the seventh century BC, the city of Locri was responsible for the first written code of law throughout the Hellenic world. Its moment of glory came in the second half of the sixth century when, supposedly assisted by Castor and Pollux, ten thousand Locrians defeated 130,000 Crotonians on the banks of the River Sagra, 25km north. The walls of the city, traces of which can still be seen, measured some 8km in circumference, and the excavations within are now interspersed over a wide area among farms and orchards. Your own transport would be useful to reach some of the more far-flung features, though the most interesting can be visited on foot without too much effort, including a fifth-century BC Ionic temple, a Roman necropolis and a well-preserved Graeco-Roman theatre. In any case make a stop at the **museum** (Tues–Sun 9am–7pm; €2) to consult the plan of the site, and examine the most recent finds, including a good collection of **pinakes**, or votive ceramics – though most of the best items have been appropriated by the Museo Nazionale in Reggio.

After the Saracens devastated Locris in the seventh century AD, the survivors fled inland to found **GERACE**, on an impregnable site that was later occupied and strengthened by the Normans. At the end of a steep and tortuous road 10km up from modern Locri, its ruined **castle** stands at one end of the town on a sheer cliff; it's usually accessible, though officially the site is out of bounds due to the very precarious state of the paths and walls. Easier to visit is the **Duomo** (daily 8am–noon & 4–6pm; free), founded in 1045 by Robert Guiscard, enlarged by Frederick II in 1222 and today still the biggest church in Calabria. Its simple and well-preserved interior has twenty columns of granite and marble, each different and with various capitals; the one on the right nearest the altar in *verde antico* marble that changes tone according to the weather. There's an attractive **hotel-restaurant** in Gerace, the *Casa di Gianna* (T0964.355.024, W www.lacasadigianna.it; ❹) on Via Paolo Frascá 4, a gem of a four-star with just ten rooms and a terrace restaurant.

Travel details

Trains

Cosenza to: Naples (5 direct daily; 4–5hr; 6 daily via Paola; 3–6hr); Paola (27 daily; 25min); Rome (1 direct daily; 6hr 35min; 10 daily via Paola or Naples; 5hr–7hr 45min).

Matera to: Bari (Ferrovia Appulo–Lucane) (14 daily; 1hr 25min).

Metaponto to: Bari (4 direct daily; 2–3hr; 10 daily via Táranto; 2hr 20min–3hr 40min); Cosenza (1 direct daily; 2hr 30min; 7 daily via Sibari; 2hr 25min–4hr 50min); Reggio (1 daily; 5hr); Sibari

(14 daily; 1hr–1hr 30min); Táranto (20 daily; 40min–1hr 10min).

Paola to: Naples (21 daily; 2hr 30min–4hr 15min); Reggio (21 daily; 2hr–4hr 30min); Rome (11 daily; 4hr 30min–5hr 30min).

Potenza to: Fóggia (14 daily; 2hr); Metaponto (10 daily; 1hr 30min); Salerno (11 daily; 1hr 40min); Táranto (8 daily; 2hr 15min).

Reggio to: Catanzaro (3 direct daily; 3hr 30min; 12 daily via Lamezia; 3hr 30 min); Naples (10 daily; 4hr 20min–9hr 10min); Rome (10 daily; 6hr 20min–12hr).

Tropea to: Rome (1 daily; 7hr 15min); Lamezia Terme (hourly; 1hr); Reggio Calabria (2 daily; 2hr).

Buses

Cosenza to: Catanzaro (Mon–Sat 8 daily; 2hr); Naples (1 daily; 4hr); Rome (2 daily; 6hr).

Matera to: Metaponto (Mon–Sat 4 daily; 50min).

Potenza to: Matera (Mon–Sat 4 daily; 1hr 30min); Naples (Mon–Sat 2 daily; 2hr); Rome (Mon–Sat 2 daily; 4hr 35min).

Reggio to: Florence (2 daily; 12hr); Rome (3 daily; 8hr).

Tropea to: Capo Vaticano (mid-June to mid-Sept 4 daily; 20min).

Ferries and hydrofoils

Reggio to: Aeolian Islands (summer up to 4 daily to each island; winter 1 daily; from 2hr to Lípari to 3hr 30min to Alicudi); Messina (12 daily; 1hr 20min).

Villa San Giovanni to: Messina (every 20min; 40min).

Sicily

CHAPTER 16

Highlights

* **Monreale** The magnificently mosaiced cathedral is a testament to Sicily's eclectic Arab, Norman and Byzantine heritage. See p.929

* **The Aeolian Islands** An archipelago of seven islands with active volanoes, lava beaches, fractured coastlines and whitewashed villages. See p.933

* **Mount Etna** It's an eerie climb up the blackened lunar landscape of this smoking volcano, dominating the landscape of eastern Sicily. See p.946

* **Teatro Greco, Siracusa** Choose between classical dramas or more modern productions, staged every summer in the city's spectacular Ancient Greek theatre. See p.959

* **Noto** The apotheosis of Baroque town planning, with glorious golden vistas of extravagant balconied *palazzi* and soaring church facades. See p.961

* **Valley of the Temples, Agrigento** A spectacular sight, especially at night when the towering Doric columns are artfully floodlit. See p.965

* **Villa Romana del Casale, Piazza Armerina** The vitality, colour and diversity of the mosaics at this Roman villa are not to be missed. See p.970

▲ Lipari, Aeolian Islands

Sicily

I like Sicily extremely – a good on-the-brink feeling – one hop and you're out of Europe ...

D. H. Lawrence in a letter to Lady Cynthia Asquith, 1920

The Sicilians aren't the only people to consider themselves, and their island, a separate entity. Coming from the Italian mainland, it's very noticeable that **Sicily** (Sicilia) has a different feel, that socially and culturally you *are* all but out of Europe. The largest island in the Mediterranean, and with a strategically vital position, Sicily has a history and outlook derived not from its modern parent but from its erstwhile foreign rulers – from the Greeks who first settled the east coast in the eighth century BC, through a dazzling array of Romans, Arabs, Normans, French and Spanish, to the Bourbons seen off by Garibaldi in 1860. Substantial **relics** of these ages remain: temples, theatres and churches are scattered about the whole island. But there are other, more immediate hints of Sicily's unique past. A hybrid Sicilian language, for a start, is still widely spoken in the countryside; the food is noticeably different, spicier and with more emphasis on fish and vegetables; even the flora echoes the change of temperament – oranges, lemons, olives and palms are ubiquitous.

A visit here still induces a real sense of **arrival**. The standard approach for those heading south from the mainland is to cross the Straits of Messina, from Villa San Giovanni or Reggio di Calabria: this way, the train-ferry pilots a course between *Scylla* and *Charybdis*, the twin hazards of rock and whirlpool that were a legendary threat to sailors. Coming in by plane, too, there are spectacular approaches to both the coastal airports at Palermo and Catania.

Once you're on land, deciding **where to go** is largely a matter of time. Inevitably, most points of interest are on the coast: the interior of the island is often mountainous, sparsely populated and relatively inaccessible. The capital, **Palermo**, is a memorable first stop, a bustling, noisy city with an unrivalled display of Norman art and architecture and Baroque churches, combined with a warren of medieval streets and markets. Heading east, there's no better place in Sicily for a traditional sea, sun and sand holiday than **Cefalù**, with a magnificent golden sandy beach and a mellow medieval core overlooked by a beetling castle-topped crag. An hour or so further east is the workaday port of Milazzo, departure point for the **Aeolian Islands**, an archipelago of seven islands. Here you can climb two active volcanoes, laze on lava beaches, snorkel over bubbling underwater fumaroles, and wallow in warm, reeking sulphurous mud baths.

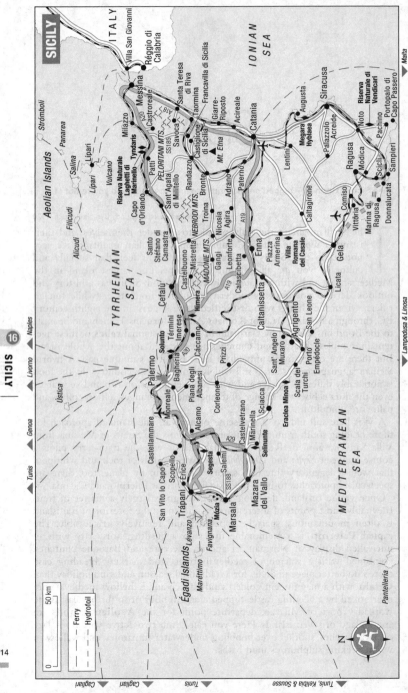

SICILY

ITALY

Villa San Giovanni

Réggio di Calabria

Aeolian Islands

Stromboli

Panarea

Salina

Filicudi

Lipari

Alicudi

Vulcano

Lipari

IONIAN SEA

Messina

Milazzo

Castroreale

Santa Teresa di Riva

Tyndaris

Riserva Naturale Laghetti di Marinello

Patti

Savoca

Francavilla di Sicilia

Taormina

Giarre-Riposto

Acireale

Capo d'Orlando

Sant'Agata di Militello

Castiglione di Sicilia

Catania

PELORITANI MTS.

SS185

Mt. Etna

Randazzo

Bronte

Adrano

Paternò

Riserva Naturale di Vendicari

Santo Stefano di Camastra

NEBRODI MTS.

Troina

Nicosia

Agira

Siracusa

Augusta

Mistretta

Gangi

Leonforte

Paternò

Megara Hyblaea

Palazzolo Acreide

Noto

Pachino

Portopalo di Capo Passero

Castelbuono

MADONIE MTS.

Calascibetta

Enna

Piazza Armerina

Villa Romana del Casale

Ragusa

Módica

Scicli

Sampieri

Cefalù

Himera

Calanissetta

Caltagirone

Comiso

Vittória

Marina di Ragusa

Donnalucata

TYRRHENIAN SEA

Términi Imerese

Solunto

San Leone

Agrigento

Licata

Gela

Ústica

Naples

Livorno

Genoa

Bagheria

Palermo

Monreale

Piana degli Albanesi

Caccamo

Prizzi

Sant'Angelo Muxaro

Porto Empédocle

Scala dei Turchi

Eraclea Minoa

Castellammare

Corleone

Castelvetrano

Sciacca

MEDITERRANEAN SEA

Alcamo

Marinella

Selinunte

San Vito lo Capo

Scopello

Segesta

Salemi

SS188

Érice

Trápani

Mozia

Mazara del Vallo

Marsala

Égadi Islands

Levanzo

Favignana

Maréttimo

Pantelleria

Tunis

Malta

Lampedusa & Linosa

Cagliari

Tunis

Tunis, Kelibia & Sousse

SICILY

N

50 km

0

Ferry

Hydrofoil

Sicily's food has been influenced by the island's endless list of invaders, including Greeks, Arabs, Normans and Spanish, even the English. Sicily is famous for its **sweets**, like the rich *cassata* ice cream dish, and *cannoli* – fried pastries stuffed with sweet ricotta and rolled in chocolate. Dishes like orange salads evoke North Africa; **couscous** is a more obvious pointer. Just as in Naples, street food is all over, with rice balls, potato croquettes, fritters and dinky-sized pizzas. Naturally, fish such as anchovies, sardines, tuna and swordfish are abundant, teamed often with the ever-popular pasta in dishes like *spaghetti con le sarde*. **Cheeses** are *pecorino, provolone, caciocavallo* and, of course, the sheep's-milk ricotta which goes into so many of the sweet dishes.

Wine-making in Sicily is associated mainly with the fortified **Marsala**, but the island has also made a name for itself as a producer of quality everyday wines such as Corvo (red and white) and Regaleali (white). These names have no DOC designation, but Corvo in particular is found all over Italy – a tribute to its quality.

The islands are also linked by hydrofoil with the major port of **Messina**, separated from mainlaind Italy by the Straits of Messina. If you are travelling to Sicily overland from Italy, Messina will unavoidably be your point of arrival. Devasted by an earthquake and tidal wave in 1908, it is a modern city of little charm and unlikely to hold your interest for long. The most obvious target from here is the almost too charming hill-town of **Taormina**, spectacularly located on a rocky bluff between the Ionian sea and the soaring peak of Mount Etna. For a gutsier taste of Sicily, head to Catania, the island's second city, intellectual and cultured, with a compact Baroque core of black and white stone, and two exuberant markets. From Taormina or Catania, a skirt around the foothills, and even better, up to the craters of **Mount Etna**, is a must.

In the south of the island is **Siracusa**, once the most important city of the Greek world, and a Baroque group of towns centring on **Ragusa**. The south coast's greatest draw are the Greek temples at **Agrigento**, while inland, **Enna** is typical of the mountain towns that provided defence for a succession of the island's rulers. Close by is **Piazza Armerina** and its Roman mosaics, while to the west, most of Sicily's fishing industry – and much of the continuing Mafia activity (see box, p.916) – focuses on the area around **Trápani**. To see all these places, you'll need at least a couple of weeks – more like a month if you want to travel extensively inland, a slower and more traditional experience altogether.

Getting around

Getting around Sicily can be a protracted business. **Trains** along the northern and eastern coasts (Messina–Palermo and Messina–Siracusa) are extensions of – or connect with – trains from Rome and Naples, and delays of at least an hour are frequent. **Buses** are generally quicker. There's no single bus company – Interbus, SAIS and AST are the main three, and each has a website (see p.928). Expect little (if any) service anywhere on a Sunday.

Palermo and around

Palermo is fast, brash, loud and exciting. Exotic Arabic cupolas float above exuberant Baroque facades, high-fashion shops compete with raffish street markets, and walls of graffitied municipal cement abut the crumbling shells of collapsing *palazzi* sprouting clusters of prickly pear. Add to this a constant soundtrack of sputtering, swirling traffic, and some of the most anarchic driving in Europe, and you'll quickly see that this is not a city for the faint-hearted. With Sicily's greatest concentration of sights, and the biggest historic centre in Italy bar Rome, Palermo is a complex, multilayered city that can easily feel overwhelming if you try to do or see too much. The best thing to do here is just to wander as the fancy takes you, sifting through the city's jumbled layers of crumbling architecture, along deserted back alleys, then suddenly emerging in the midst of an ebullient street market. If you only have a day, select an area (La Kalsa, with its two museums, for example, of the sprawling markets of Ballaro or Capo), and explore: have a couple of target sights in mind by all means, but don't neglect to wander up any particular alley or street that takes your interest. If, on the other hand, you want to see all the major sights and leave time to explore the labyrinthine historical centre at random, allow at least four days in cool weather. In summer, Palermo is far too hot to be comfortable between noon and around 5pm, so schedule in a leisurely lunch and siesta.

The essential sights are pretty central and easy to cover on foot. Paramount are the hybrid **Cattedrale** and nearby **Palazzo dei Normanni** (Royal Palace); the glorious Norman churches of **La Martorana** and **San Giovanni degli Eremiti**; the Baroque **San Giuseppe dei Teatini** and **Santa Caterina**; and first-class **museums** of art and archeology.

If the urban grit and grime become overwhelming, head to the fine beach at **Mondello** (see p.929), to the famous medieval cathedral of **Monreale** (see p.929),

(see p.929)

The Mafia

Whatever else the **Mafia** is, it isn't an organization that impinges upon the lives of tourists. For most Sicilians, mafia with a small m is so much a way of life and habit of mind that they don't even think about it. If a Sicilian lends a neighbour a bag of sugar, for example, both will immediately be aware of a favour owed, and the debtor uncomfortable until the favour has been returned, and balance restored. As for allegience to friends, it would be very rare indeed for a Sicilian, asked to recommend a hotel or restaurant, to suggest that you go to one that does not belong to a friend, relative, or someone who forms part of his personal network of favours.

The Mafia, with a capital M, is an **early medieval conspiracy**, created to protect the family from oppressive intrusions of the state. Existing to this day, Sicily continues to endure this system of allegiance, preferment and patronage of massive self-perpetuating proportions, from which few local people profit. In many parts of the region, owners of shops and businesses are expected to give **pizzo** (protection money) to the local Mafia. Recently, in an effort to counter extortion, the mayor of Vittoria, in the province of Ragusa, announced that any business that had paid *pizzo*, but was willing to denounce the Mafia, would be exempted from local taxes, while in Siracusa, local businesses clubbed together to refuse to pay *pizzo*. Nevertheless, the Mafia continues to have real clout: it is not for nothing that international businesses such as IKEA have found it impossible to open in Sicily.

or take a ferry or hydrofoil to the tiny volcanic island of **Ústica** (see p.930), 60km northwest.

Some history

Occupying a superb position in a wide bay beneath the limestone bulk of Monte Pellegrino, Palermo was originally a Phoenician, then a Carthaginian colony. Its mercantile and strategic attractions were obvious, and under Saracen and Norman rule in the ninth to twelfth centuries it became the greatest city in Europe – famed both for the wealth of its court, and as a centre of learning, that brought together the best of Western and Arabic thought. There are plenty of relics from this era, but it's the rebuilding of the sixteenth and seventeenth centuries that really shaped the city centre. In the nineteenth century, wealthy Palermitani began to shun the centre for the elegant suburbs of new "European" boulevards and avenues to the north of Piazza Politeama.

During World War II Allied bombs destroyed much of the port area and the medieval centre (including seventy churches), and for decades much of central Palermo remained a ramshackle bombsite. It is only recently that funds from Rome and the EU have united with political willpower to kickstart the regeneration of the historic centre.

Arrival, information and transport

Palermo's Falcone Borsellino **airport** (☎800.541.880, ⓦwww.gesap.it) is at Punta Raisi, 31km west of the city. Buses (Prestia & Comandè ☎091.580.457) run into the city every thirty minutes from 6.30am until midnight, taking forty-five minutes, and stop outside Politeama theatre, Stazione Marittima, and at Stazione Centrale; tickets (€5) on board. For the return, departures are at 4am, 5am and then every thirty minutes until 11pm. **Trains** (€5) run from the airport to Stazione Centrale every thirty minutes between 6.30am and midnight (the last two trains wait for any delayed flights) and between 5am and 11pm from Stazione Centrale.

All trains arrive at the Stazione Centrale (enquiries ☎091.603.3121) at the southern end of Via Roma, and the majority of the country- and island-wide **buses** (see p.928 for details) operate out of Via Paolo Balsamo alongside. Buses #101 and #102 run from the station along Via Roma to Via della Libertà and the *linea gialla* and *linea rossa*, little buses that run through the *centro storico*, can also be picked up at the station.

All **ferry** and **hydrofoil** services (see p.928) dock at the Stazione Marittima, just off Via Francesco Crispi, from where it's a ten-minute walk up Via E. Amari to Piazza Castelnuovo. Or take bus #101 or #102, which run up to Via Roma and the train station.

Driving in the city is best avoided. Overtaking on both sides is the norm, and indicating virtually unheard of. Blackmarket parking attendants will guide you to a space and charge you a small amount (50 cents or so per hr), and meters are installed over some parts of the centre. Renting a **bike** (see p.928) is an alternative for the steely nerved.

Information

Palermo's main **tourist office** is at Piazza Castelnuovo 34 (Mon–Fri 8.30am–2pm & 3–7pm, Sat 9am–1pm; ☎091 605.8531, ⓦwww.palermotourism.com); it has excellent free maps of the city and province, free booklets containing

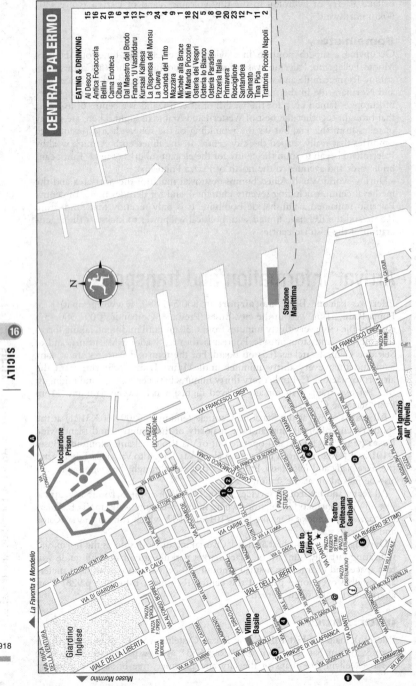

CENTRAL PALERMO

EATING & DRINKING

Al Desco	15
Antica Focacceria	16
Bellini	21
Cama Enoteca	19
Cibus	6
Dal Maestro del Brodo	14
Franco 'U Vastiddaru	13
Kursaal Kalhesa	17
La Dispensa del Monsù	3
La Cueva	24
Locanda del Tinto	9
Mazzara	1
Michele alla Brace	18
Mi Manda Piccone	22
Osteria dei Vespri	5
Osteria lo Bianco	8
Osteria Paradiso	10
Pizzeria Italia	20
Primavera	23
Roscioglione	12
Santandrea	7
Spinnato	11
Tina Pica	2
Trattoria Piccolo Napoli	

Stazione Marittima

Ucciardone Prison

Sant Ignazio All' Olivella

Teatro Politeama Garibaldi

Bus to Airport

Villino Basile

Giardino Inglese

La Favorita & Mondello

Museo Mormino

918

16

SICILY

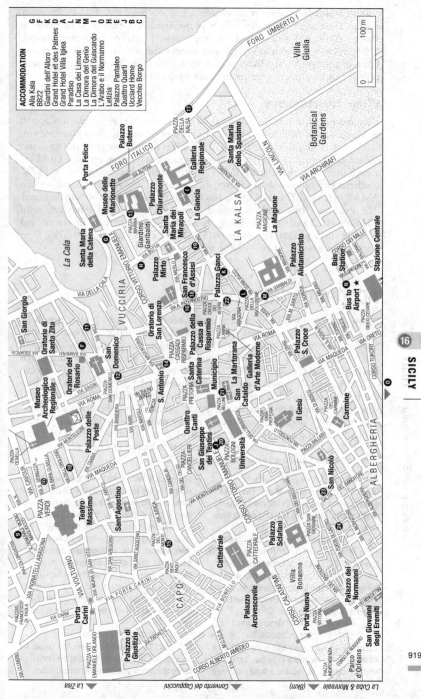

ACCOMMODATION

Alla Kala	G
BB22	F
Giardini dell'Alloro	K
Grand Hotel et des Palmes	D
Grand Hotel Villa Igiea	A
Paradiso	L
La Casa dei Limoni	N
La Dimora del Genio	M
La Dimora del Guiscardo	I
L'Arabo e il Normanno	O
Letizia	H
Palazzo Pantaleo	E
Quattro Quarti	J
Ucciardi Home	B
Vecchio Borgo	C

FORO UMBERTO I

Villa Giulia

Botanical Gardens

0   100 m

Porta Felice

Palazzo Butera

PIAZZA DELLA KALSA

Museo delle Marionette

Palazzo Chiaramonte

Galleria Regionale

Santa Maria dello Spasimo

La Gancia

LA KALSA

La Magione

PIAZZA MAGIONE

Palazzo Aiutamicristo

Bus Station

Stazione Centrale

Bus to Airport ★

Palazzo S. Croce

Il Gesù

Carmine

ALBERGHERIA

16

SICILY

919

◀ La Zisa   ◀ Convento dei Cappuccini   ◀ La Cuba & Monreale (8km)   ◀ Palazzo dei Normanni current events and transport information, and also provides a list of accommodation. There are two smaller offices at the Stazione Centrale (same hours as above; ☎091.616.5914) and at the airport (daily 8.30am–midnight; ☎091.591.698), as well as several information kiosks dotted about the centre. For more complete **city listings** pick up a copy of the local paper, *Il Giornale di Sicilia*, or look out for the more youth-oriented *Lapis* (free).

City transport

City buses (AMAT ⓦwww.amat.pa.it) cover every corner of Palermo as well as Monreale and Mondello. There's a flat fare of €1 valid for two hours, or you can buy an all-day ticket for €3.50, while tickets for the *linea gialla* and *rossa*, and the *circolare* (which covers the *centro storico*) minibus services, cost just €0.52 for a day's use – buy them from AMAT booths outside Stazione Centrale, at the southern end of Viale della Libertà, in *tabacchi* and anywhere else you see the AMAT sign. Validate tickets in the machine at the back of the bus as you board. The main city **bus rank** is outside Stazione Centrale and buses run until midnight (11.30pm on Sun). There are **taxi** ranks outside the train station and in other main piazzas, or call ☎091.513.311, 255.455 or 339.408.5713). The minimum fare is €4.50; be sure the meter is switched on.

Accommodation

If you arrive late and need a place on spec, most of Palermo's budget **hotels** lie on and around the southern ends of Via Maqueda and Via Roma, close to Stazione Centrale. However, you will get far more for your money staying in one of the new wave of **B&Bs**, known for their good service. The **youth hostel**, *Baia del Corallo* (☎091.679.7807, ⓦwww.ostellopalermo.it, €17, double or family room ❶) is by the sea 12km northwest of the city. Take bus #101 from the train station to Piazza de Gaspari, and then bus #628 to Punta Matese. If you prefer to stay in an **apartment**, try the Palazzo Conte Federico, a magnificent (if chilly) palace built over the Punic city walls, close to the Ballarò market, which has several apartments for rent for €150 per night, or Orizzonte Rosso (☎333.663.8666, ⓦwww.orizzonterosso.com) which also organizes upmarket boat trips and tailormade excursions all over Sicily.

Alla Kala Corso Vittorio Emanuele 71 ☎091.743.4763, ⓦwww.allakala.it. Five stylish designer rooms with magnificent views of the sailing marina, and a keen following among those in the know. ❹

BB22 *Palazzo* Pantelleria, Largo Cavalieri di Malta 22 ☎091.611.1610 or 335.790.8733, ⓦwww.bb22.it. Faultless Milanese designer-chic (resinated cement floors, perspex chairs, walls painted in matt hues of stone) in a historic *palazzo* a few steps from the Vucciria market. Breakfast is served on a small roof terrace. ❹–❺

Giardini dell'Alloro Vicolo S.Carlo 8 ☎091.617.6904 or 338.224.3541, ⓦwww .giardinodellalloro.it. Lovely B&B in the heart of La Kalsa with books for guests to borrow, a courtyard where breakfast is served, and a living room used

as a space for exhibitions by contemporary Sicilian artists. The five rooms each feature several original works of art. All rooms have kettles and mugs, and there is a small kitchen for the use of guests. ❸

Grand Hotel et des Palmes Via Roma 398 ☎091.602.811, ⓦwww.grandhoteletdespalmes .com. Although it may no longer have the cachet it had in the days when guests included Wagner, the *Des Palmes* remains a comfortable four-star chain hotel conveniently located on the main Via Roma. Some of the rooms are huge, and there are often discounts (❹) via internet bookings in low season. ❻

Grand Hotel Villa Igiea Via Belmonte 43 ☎091.543.744, ⓦwww.hilton.com. This classic Art Nouveau building, originally a villa of the Florio family (the people who pioneered tuna canning), was designed by Ernesto Basile in 1900, and stands outside the city centre above the marina of Acquasanta. Sumptuous, popular with tour groups and often full, so book ahead. ❼

La Casa dei Limoni Piazza Giulio Cesare 9 ☎334. 834.3888/338.967.8907, ⓦwww.lacasadeilimoni.it Clean, friendly B&B right opposite the train station. Great value for money. ❶

🏃 **La Dimora del Genio** Via Garibaldi 58 ☎347.658.7664, ⓦwww.ladimoradelgenio .it. Five cosy rooms in a centrally heated seventeenth-century *palazzetto*, furnished with a tasteful blend of antiques, modern furniture, and original paintings by Palermo artist Maurizio Muscolino. Not all rooms have en-suite bathrooms, so avoid those if you don't like padding around at night in your pyjamas. The friendly owner is a talented cook, and offers cooking courses for guests, as well as a splendid Sun dinner for €30 a head. ❸–❹

La Dimora del Guiscardo Via Vetriera 83–5 ☎328.662.6074, ⓦwww.ladimoradelguiscardo.it. Funky little B&B in the heart of La Kalsa, close to the areas bars and restaurants. Clean, simple rooms, and shared bathroom. ❷

L'Arabo e il Normanno Piazza d'Orleans 10 ☎091.652.3417 or 339.336.5607, ⓦwww .laraboeilnormannobb.com. Little B&B run by a charming gay couple. It is right opposite the Orleans metro stop, so ideal if you are arriving late from the airport. 5 percent of profits go to a Third World charity. ❸

Letizia Via dei Bottai 30 ☎091.589.110, ⓦwww .hotelletizia.com. Each room in this delightful hotel, just off Piazza Marina, has its own colour scheme and furnishings. There's an enclosed courtyard for breakfast, a restaurant and free internet access for guests. ❸

Palazzo Pantaleo Via Ruggero Settimo 74/H ☎091.325.471 or 335.700.6091,

ⓦwww.palazzopantaleo.it Seven large, light, airy rooms in an eighteenth-century *palazzo* on a quiet *piazzetta* off this major shopping street, a short walk from Piazza Politeama. A safe location. Internet access in all rooms. ❸–❹

Paradiso Via Schiavuzzo 65 ☎091.617.2825. The windows of this basic, old-fashioned first-floor *pensione* overlook the Piazza della Rivoluzione. It's good and central, the couple who run it are a delight, and the ten rooms without bath are among the cheapest in town. No credit cards. ❶

Quattro Quarti Palazzo Arone di Valentino, Corso Vittorio Emanuele 376 ☎091.583.687, or 347.854.7209. ⓦwww.quattroquarti.it. A superior B&B with four smart elegant rooms and a suite in part of a huge *palazzo* owned by the Arone di Valentino family. Guests are very well looked after, making this a great place to consider if you are a little nervous about finding your feet in Palermo. In the main part of the palace, there is a plush suite of rooms furnished with antiques, whose guests have included Camilla Parker Bowles. ❹, Camilla suite ❻

🏃 **Ucciard Home** Via Enrico Albanese 34–36 ☎091.348.426, ⓦwww.hotelucciardhome .com. Trendy designer hotel opposite the prison, with fourteen comfortable, stylish rooms and lovely, luxurious bathrooms. The warm, and extremely obliging, staff are a world away from most you'll encounter in the city's hotels. A true oasis. ❻

Vecchio Borgo Via Quintino Sella 1–7 ☎091.611.1446, ⓦwww.classicahotels.com. A smart and appealing hotel between the Piazza Politeama and one of Palermo's best weekend markets. Comfortable rooms with bold printed fabrics and all amenities (including internet points). Excellent breakfast, including home-made cakes. Garage €15 a night, outdoor car park €7 a night. ❺

The City

Historical Palermo sits around a crossroads, the **Quattro Canti**, a gleaming Baroque crossroads that divides old Palermo into its quadrants. **Albergheria** and **Capo** quarter lie roughly west of Via Maqueda; the **Vucciria** and **La Kalsa** lie to the east, closest to the water. You'll find virtually all the surviving ancient monuments and buildings of the city in these four areas.

Around the Quattro Canti

On the southwest corner of Quattro Canti (entrance on Corso Vittorio Emanuele), **San Giuseppe dei Teatini** (Mon–Sat 7.30–11am & 6–8pm, Sun 8.30am–12.30pm & 6–8pm), begun in 1612, is the most harmonious of the city's Baroque churches. Outside, across Via Maqueda, is **Piazza Pretoria**, floodlit at night to highlight the nude figures of its great central fountain, a racy sixteenth-century Florentine design. The piazza also holds the restored **Municipio**, while towering above both square and fountain is the massive flank of **Santa Caterina** (daily 9.30am–1pm; April–Oct also afternoons), Sicilian Baroque at its most exuberant, every inch of the enormous interior covered in a wildly decorative, pustular relief-work.

Piazza Bellini, just around the corner, is the site of two more wildly contrasting churches. The little Saracenic red domes belong to **San Cataldo**, a perfectly proportioned twelfth-century Byzantine chapel flooded with light (daily 9.30am–1pm; summer also afternoons 3.30–6pm; €1). Never decorated, it retains a good mosaic floor. San Cataldo's understatement is more than offset by the splendid intricacy of the adjacent **La Martorana** (Mon–Sat 8am–1pm & winter 3.30–5pm, summer 3.30–7pm, Sun 8.30am–1pm; free) – one of the finest survivors of the medieval city. With a Norman foundation, the church received a Baroque going-over in 1588. Happily, the alterations don't detract from the power of the interior, entered through the slim twelfth-century campanile, which retains its ribbed arches and slender columns. A series of spectacular **mosaics**, animated twelfth-century Greek works, are laid on and around the columns supporting the main cupola. Two original mosaic panels have been set in frames on the walls just inside the entrance to the church: a kneeling George of Antioch (the church's founder) dedicating La Martorana to the Virgin, and King Roger being crowned by Christ.

The Albergheria

The Albergheria district just to the northwest of the train station hasn't changed substantially for several hundred years. A maze of tiny streets and tall leaning buildings, it's an engaging place to wander, much of the central area taken up by a street market that all but conceals several fine churches. Via Ponticello leads down past the Baroque church of **Il Gesù**, or **Casa Professa** (Mon–Sat 7–11.30am & 5–6.30pm, Sun 7am–12.30pm & 5–6.30pm), the first Jesuit foundation in Sicily and gloriously decorated inside, to **Piazza Ballarò** – along with adjacent **Piazza del Carmine** the focus of a raucous daily **market**, with bulging vegetable stalls, unmarked drinking dens and some good snack stalls.

At the westernmost edge of the quarter, over Via Benedettini, is the Albergheria's quietest haven, the deconsecrated church of **San Giovanni degli Eremiti** (Mon–Sat 9am–7pm, Sun & hols 9am–1pm; €6) – St John of the Hermits. Built in 1132, it's the most obviously Arabic of the city's Norman relics, with five ochre domes topping a small church that was built upon the remains of a mosque.

Palazzo dei Normanni

From San Giovanni it's a few paces to the main road, where, if you turn right and then veer left up the steps, you'll climb out of the fast traffic to gaze on the vast length of the **Palazzo dei Normanni**, or Palazzo Reale (entrance on Piazza Indipendenza). Originally built by the Saracens, the palace was enlarged considerably by the Normans, under whom it housed the most magnificent of medieval European courts – a noted centre of poetic and artistic achievement. Sadly, there's little left from those times. The long front was added by the Spanish in the seventeenth century and most of the interior is now taken up by the Sicilian Regional Parliament (which explains the security guards and the limited opening hours). Be prepared to queue.

Of the Royal Apartments (Mon, Tues & Thurs–Sat 8.30am–noon & 2–5pm, Sun 8.30am–12.30pm; €6, including Cappella Palatina) the showpiece is undoubtedly the Sala di Ruggero, one of the earliest parts of the palace and richly covered with a twelfth-century mosaic of hunting scenes. The highlight of the visit, however, is the beautiful **Cappella Palatina** (Mon–Sat 8.30am–noon & 2–5pm, Sun 8.30–9.45am & 11.45am–12.30pm), the private royal chapel of Roger II, built between 1132 and 1143. This is the undisputed artistic gem of central Palermo, its cupola, three apses and nave entirely covered in mosaics of outstanding quality. The oldest are those in the cupola and apses, probably completed in 1150 by Byzantine artists; those in the nave are from the hands of local craftsmen, finished twenty-odd years later and depicting Old and New Testament scenes. The colours are vivid and, as usual in Byzantine art, the powerful image of *Christ as Pantocrator* (creator of everything) dominates. Aside from the mosaics, the chapel has a delightful Arabic ceiling with richly carved wooden stalactites, a patterned marble floor and an impressive marble Norman candlestick (by the pulpit), 4m high and contorted by manic carvings.

The Cattedrale

Spanning Corso Vittorio Emanuele, the early sixteenth-century **Porta Nuova** commemorates Charles V's Tunisian exploits, with grim, turbaned prisoners adorning the western entrance. This gate marked the extent of the late medieval city, and the long road beyond heads to Monreale.

The Corso runs back towards the centre, past the huge bulk of the Norman **Cattedrale** (daily 9.30am–5.30pm; free). The triple-apsed eastern end and graceful matching towers date from 1185, and despite the Catalan-Gothic facade and arches, there's enough Norman carving and detail to rescue the exterior from mere curiosity value. The same is not true, however, of the sterile Neoclassical interior. The only items of interest are the fine fifteenth-century portal and wooden doors and **royal tombs**, containing the remains of Sicilian monarchs – including Frederick II and his wife, Constance of Aragon. There's also a **treasury** (€2.50) to the right of the choir, the highlights of which are a jewel- and pearl-encrusted skullcap and three simple, precious rings, all enterprisingly removed from the tomb of Constance in the eighteenth century.

The Capo

From the cathedral you can bear left, around the apses, and up into the **Capo** quarter, whose tight web of impoverished streets are home to yet another market. Just around the corner from Piazza del Monte is the fine church of **Sant'Agostino** (Mon–Sat 7am–noon & 4–6pm, Sun 7am–noon; free), built in the thirteenth century. Above its main door (on Via Raimondo) there's a latticework rose window, and inside, some calming sixteenth-century cloisters. The stalls of the **clothes market** (daily 8am to around 8pm) along **Via Sant'Agostino** run all the way down to Via Maqueda and beyond, the streets off to the left gradually becoming wider and more nondescript as they broach the area around the monumental Neoclassic **Teatro Massimo**, supposedly the largest theatre in Italy. To appreciate the interior fully take a **tour** (Tues–Sun every 30min 10.30am–3.30pm, except during rehearsals; €5), or attend one of the classical concerts or operas held here between October and June.

The theatre marks the dividing line between old and new Palermo. Via Maqueda becomes **Via Ruggero Settimo**, which cuts up through the gridded shopping streets to the huge double square made up of **Piazza Castelnuovo** and **Piazza Ruggero Settimo** (commonly referred to as Piazza Politeama). Dominating the whole lot is Palermo's other massive theatre, the **Politeama Garibaldi**, topped by a flamboyant statue group of sword-brandishing figures on leaping horses.

The Vucciria

Via Roma, running from Stazione Centrale, is a fairly modern addition to the city, all clothes and shoe shops. It's nothing like as interesting as the parallel **Via Maqueda**, but stick with it as far as the church of Sant'Antonio on the corner of Via Roma and Corso Vittorio Emanuele. Behind here – down the steps – is the **Vucciria market** (daily 8am to around 8pm), once the most famous market in Palermo, but now a shadow of its former self, though it still has several basic bars and fish trattorias.

The northern limit of the market is marked by the distinctive church of **San Domenico** (Tues–Sun 9am–11.30pm, Sat & Sun also 5–7pm; free), with a fine eighteenth-century facade and tombs inside containing a host of famous Sicilians. The **oratory** behind the church (Oratorio del Rosario; Mon–Fri 9am–1pm & 2–5.30pm, Sat 9am–1pm; free but tipping is usual) contains fine stuccowork by Serpotta and a masterful van Dyck altarpiece, painted in 1628 before the artist fled Palermo for Genoa to escape the plague.

From Piazza San Domenico, Via Roma continues north, passing (on the left) Palermo's main post office. Behind this surreal Fascist-era bulk is a sixteenth-century convent housing the **Museo Archeologico Regionale** (Tues–Sat 8.30am–1.45pm, Sun & Mon 8.30am–6.45pm; €6), a magnificent collection of finds, mainly from western Sicily, displayed on three floors. Two cloisters hold anchors and other retrieved hardware from the sea off the Sicilian coast, while there are also Egyptian and Punic remains and Roman sculpture – notably a giant enthroned Zeus. The highlight however are the finds from the temples of Selinunte (see p.979), notably the vivid fifth-century BC sculpted panels from Temples C and F – such as Perseus beheading the Medusa with a short sword. Upstairs is a glistening, muscular study of Hercules subduing a

▲ Palermo street scene

stag, found at Pompeii while on the top floor are beautifully preserved Roman mosaics.

Heading towards the water from Via Roma, you'll come to the church of **Santa Zita** (also known as Santa Cita or San Mamiliano), on quiet Via Squarcialupo, whose marvellous **oratory** (Mon–Fri 9am–1pm; ring the bell if closed, or ask in the church in front; €2) holds one of Serpotta's finest works – the *Battle of Lepanto*. From here streets spread back to the thumb-shaped inlet of **La Cala**, Palermo's **old harbour**. This was once the main port of Palermo, stretching as far inland as Via Roma, but during the sixteenth century silting caused the water to recede to its current position, and La Cala now does duty as a yachting marina.

La Kalsa

This southeastern quarter of old Palermo was worst hit during the war, but, after years of decay, it's sloughing off its desolate image, as the numerous cranes and tiers of scaffolding testify. It's here that you'll find some of Palermo's most remarkable buildings and churches, as well as its only central park, **Villa Giulia**, just a few minutes' walk along Via Lincoln from the train station and home to an extensive botanical garden (Mon–Fri 9am–5pm, Sat & Sun 8.30am–1.30pm; €4).

Head back up Via Lincoln, turn right down *palazzo*-lined Via Garibaldi, then turn right down Via Magione to the church of **La Magione** (daily 9.30am–6.30pm; free), approached through a palm-lined drive. Built in 1151, the simple, sparse Norman church has beautiful cloisters (undergoing a lengthy restoration) and a chapel, a rare plaster preparation of a crucifixion fresco and a lovely small Arab-Norman column carved with a Koranic inscription. The church marks the edge of **La Kalsa** (its name is from the Arabic *khalisa*, meaning "pure"), an area subjected to saturation bombing during World War II, because of its proximity to the port. The worst of the bombsite is now greened over and a popular spot for football practice. Across the square, set back off Via Spasimo, is the complex of **Santa Maria dello Spasimo** (daily 8am–midnight; free), a former church, now roofless except for its Gothic apse, that holds atmospheric night-time jazz concerts. It is also one of the venues for the annual **KalsArt festival** (Ⓦ www.kalsart.it; mid-June to mid-Sept), a huge cultural extravaganza of live music, theatre and cinema that takes place at a number of venues around this part of town.

From Via Alloro, which runs on the north side of the square, turn down Via A Paternostro, and then down Via Merlo to the late eighteenth-century **Palazzo Mirto** (daily 9am–6.30pm; €3), one of the few *palazzi* in the city to have retained its imposing original fixtures and fittings. Passing through the Giardino Garibaldi and Piazza Marina brings you to Corso Vittorio Emanuele, which runs down to the water and ends in the Baroque **Porta Felice**. The whole area beyond the gate was flattened in 1943, and has since been rebuilt as the ugly **Foro Italico** promenade. Back beyond the Porta Felice, around the corner from the vast **Palazzo Chiaramonte**, onetime headquarters of the Inquisition, is the engaging **Museo delle Marionette** off Via Butera at Novolo Niscemi 5 (Mon–Sat 9am–1pm; Ⓦ www.museomarionettepalermo.it; €5), a definitive collection of traditional Sicilian puppets, screens and painted scenery. In summer the museum puts on free shows (*Spettacolo dei pupi*; Ⓣ 091.328.060, or ask the tourist office for the current schedule).

Galleria Regionale and the Galleria d'Arte Moderne

Situated at Via Alloro 4 is the Palazzo Abatellis, a fifteenth-century palace housing Sicily's **Galleria Regionale** (Tues–Fri 9am–1pm & 2–7pm, Sat–Mon

9am–1pm; €6), a stunning medieval art collection. Inside, there's a simple split: sculpture downstairs, and paintings upstairs, the one exception being a magnificent fifteenth-century fresco, the *Triumph of Death*, displayed in the former chapel, coating an entire wall. The other masterpiece on the ground floor is a calm, perfectly studied, white marble bust of Eleanora of Aragon by the fifteenth-century artist Francesco Laurana. Upstairs there are thirteenth- and fourteenth-century Sicilian works, Byzantine in style, and a fine collection of works by Antonello da Messina (1430–79), including three small portraits of *Sts Gregory, Jerome and Augustine* and a celebrated *Annunciation*.

Continuing up Via Alloro, you pass the mighty ruins of Palazzo Bonagia, used in the summer for concerts and theatre, and, on Piazza Sant'Anna, the Convento di Sant'Anna, stunningly restored and now opened as the seat of the **Galleria d'Arte Moderne** (Tues–Sun 9.30am–6.30pm; €7) its collection of nineteenth- and twentieth-century Sicilian works displayed thematically (portraits, nudes, mythology, seascapes, landscapes etc) to great effect. The **café**, spilling into the courtyard in summer, is one of the loveliest places in the city for lunch or an aperitif.

The outskirts

If you are interested in seeing more of Palermo's **Norman relics**, bus #124 runs west from the Politeama to **La Zisa** (from the Arabic, *el aziz*, "magnificent"), a huge palace begun by William I in 1160, with a fine exterior and a rich, well-crafted Islamic interior, housing a collection of Islamic art and artefacts (Mon–Sat 9am–7pm, Sun & hols 9am–1pm; €3). Closer to the centre, about 1km beyond Porta Nuova at Corso Calatafimi 100, is **La Cuba**, the remains of a slightly later Norman pavilion that formed part of the same royal park as La Zisa, now tucked inside an army barracks, but well restored and open to the public (daily 9am–6.30pm; €2).

But for real horror-movie stuff, take bus #327 from Piazza Indipendenza southwest along Via dei Cappuccini as far as Via Pindemonte. Close by, in Piazza Cappuccini, the catacombs of the **Convento dei Cappuccini** (daily 9am–noon & 3–5.30pm; €1.50) is home to some 8000 mummified bodies, preserved by various chemical and drying processes – including the use of vinegar and arsenic baths, dressed in suits of clothes, then placed in niches along rough-cut stone corridors. Descending into the catacombs is quite unnerving, especially if you arrive in a lull between coach parties. Different caverns are reserved for men, women, the clergy, doctors, lawyers and surgeons. Suspended in individual niches, hand-written notes about their necks, the bodies have become vile, contorted, grinning figures – some decomposed beyond recognition, others complete with skin, hair and eyes.

Eating and drinking

Vendors in the markets and on numerous street corners sell classic Palermitani street food such as *pane e panelli*, chickpea-flour fritters served in bread, *crocchè* (potato croquettes with anchovy and *caciocavallo* cheese), and *pane con la milza* (bread with spleen).

Cafés and street food

Cibus Via E Amari 64. High-class grocery store with a great deli counter, and a wood-fired oven where you can get light blistered pizzas and other savoury pastries to eat in or take away. It is 5min walk from the hydrofoil port, so an ideal place to stock up if you are sailing to Ústica or the Aeolian Islands. Mon–Sat 8.30am–11.30pm, Sun 8.30am–2pm & 6–11pm.

Franco 'U Vastiddaru Piazza Marina. Palermitani street food such as *pane e panelli pane con la milza* (*pane ca meusa* in Sicilian) – which you can eat at tables under the trees of Piazza Marina's central garden.

Mazzara Via Magliocco 15 (off Via Ruggero Settimo alongside Rinascente). Long-established bar-pasticceria where Tomasi di Lampedusa is reputed to have penned some of *The Leopard*. These days it serves light brunch and lunches alongside a dangerous selection of pastries and ice creams: try the roast beef with rocket and shaved parmesan. Closed Mon.

Michele alla Brace Piazza Borgo Vecchio. At the tiny market of Piazza Borgo Vecchio, you can't miss this huge grill with a couple of plastic tables and a steaming cauldron of vegetables. Buy your fish from one of the nearby stalls and bring it to Michele, who will grill it, and provide you with veg, drinks and a table. Closed Wed.

Rosciglione Via Gian Luca Barbieri 5. Watch *cannoli* being made as you eat them at this bakery (which exports worldwide) on the edge of the Ballarò market. Mon–Sat 7am–1pm & 1.30–6.30pm, Sun 7am–1pm.

Spinnato Via Principe di Belmonte 107–115. With tables outside on one of Palermo's pedestrianized streets, this the perfect place for breakfast, delicious cakes and ice creams.

Restaurants

Al Desco Via Judica 23 ℡ 091.609.0587. Little restaurant run by a couple who retired from their jobs to follow their passion for food. Ingredients are bought fresh each day at the market, cooked by the wife, and served by the husband. Booking recommended. Eve only, closed Sun.

Antica Focacceria San Francesco Via A. Paternostro 58 ℡ 091.320264. This old-fashioned place has been in the same family for five generations. Downstairs they serve traditional Palermitani street food, such as *focaccia schietta* (focaccia with offal and *caciocavallo*), *sfincione* (pizza with onion, tomato, *caciocavallo* and breadcrumbs), *cazzilli* (potato croquettes) and *panelle* (chick pea flour fritters). Upstairs you can eat full meals (try the *pasta con le sarde*, pasta with sardines). In summer you can eat outside. Closed Tues & mid-Jan.

Bellini Piazza Bellini ℡ 091.615.5691. The best bet for alfresco pizzas (starting at €3); outdoor tables are in the shadow of La Martorana church. Closed Mon & Dec.

Dal Maestro del Brodo Via Pannieri 7 ℡ 091.329.523. Exuberant family-run place in the heart of the Vuccirìa market, named for its *bollito di carne con patate e zaffarano*, meat broth with potatoes and saffron. Fresh fish as well. Closed Sun in summer, Mon in winter.

La Dispensa del Monsu Via Principe di Villafranca 59 ℡ 091.609.0465. Wonderful delicatessen specializing in cheese, that has developed into a fine, but relaxed, restaurant on a safe street in the new town. The menu is by no means limited to deli produce, but all ingredients are carefully sourced, whether it be a local ricotta, or an Irish Angus steak.

Locanda del Tinto Via XX Settembre 56/A ℡ 091.582.137. Urbane place on one of the nineteenth-century boulevards beyond Piazza Politeama, with a constantly changing menu and a lunchtime buffet (€8) or sushi (€18), popular with shoppers and people on lunchbreaks. Deftly made pizza and focaccia in the evenings.

Mi Manda Piccone Via A Paternostro 59 ℡ 091.616.0660. Enoteca in the old town with a fine choice of mostly Sicilian wines, and a menu that changes with the seasons. Come at around 7.30pm for an aperitif, or from 8.30pm for dinner. Popular dishes include a frittata of fave beans, artichokes and peas served with fresh ricotta, and *spaghetti alla bottarga*. Eve only, closed Sun.

Osteria lo Bianco Via E Amari 104 ℡ 091.251.4900. Decorated with Juventus souvenirs and religious bric-a-brac, this is one of the cheapest places to eat in town. Traditional Palermitano food, such as *pasta con sarde*, *polpette* (meatballs) in tomato sauce, or a stew of beef, peas and carrots, two courses with wine and fruit for less than €15. Closed Sun.

Osteria Paradiso Via Serradifalco 23. No phone. Typical family-run trattoria, to the north of La Zisa, open only at lunchtime and specializing in fish. There is no written menu – the owner just tells you what's available that day. Specialities include fish cooked in seawater, raw prawns dressed with olive oil and lemon juice, and deep-fried *cicirello*, a long skinny silver fish. Arrive early to get a table. Closed Sun.

Osteria dei Vespri Piazza Croce dei Vespri ℡ 091.617.1631. An *osteria* that began as a hobby nine years ago, and has now become one of Palermo's best restaurants. Dishes are complex, but not unnecessarily so, and there is a loyal use of local Sicilian ingredients. The *degustazione* menu is usually around €60 per person, excluding wine. Closed Sun.

Pizzeria Italia Via Orologio 54 (opposite Teatro Massimo) ℡ 091.589.885. Attracting large queues, this is the best place in town for light, oven-blistered pizzas (€3–10). Try the "Palermitana" with tomato, anchovies, onion, artichokes, *caciocavallo* cheese and breadcrumbs. Eve only; closed Mon.

Primavera Piazza Bologni 4 ☎091.329.408. Not far from the cathedral, off Via Vittorio Emanuele, with outdoor seating in a lovely little piazza, this popular, reasonably priced trattoria serves home-style cooking such as *pasta con le sarde* and *bucatini con broccoli*. Bottles of good, inexpensive local wine as well. Closed Mon.

Santandrea Piazza Sant'Andrea ☎091.334.999 or 328.131.4595. Chic, buzzy but relaxed family-run place a stone's throw from Piazza San Domenico

and the Vucciria market, considered to be one of Palermo's best restaurants. Dishes are seasonal and inventive, with a strong emphasis on local ingredients. Book early to eat alfresco. Closed Sun.

Trattoria Piccolo Napoli Piazzetta Mulino di Vento 4 ☎091.320.431. Lively trattoria off the Vecchio Borgo market founded in 1951 and run by three generations of the same family. They have two boats at Terrasini: fish is brought in daily, and anything not eaten that day is sold on to the local market stalls. Try raw prawns, pasta with *neonati* (new-born fish) or what may prove to be the best *caponata* you will ever taste. Open Mon–Sat for lunch only, Fri & Sat eve also.

Bars and nightlife

The main focus of **nightlife** is the **Kalsa** area, in particular the streets between Piazza Garibaldi and Piazza Magione, which are packed with stylish bars and pubs. Two places to head for are ⅔ *Kursaal Kalhesa*, Foro Umberto I 24 (closed Sun eve & Mon) a trendy wine-bar-cum-bookshop set within the ancient fortifications of Arabic Palermo, where they do a great Sunday brunch for €23; and the hip restaurant-club *Tina Pica*, Via Giovanni Meli 13 (closed Mon). For great wines and nibbles, you won't do better than the cosy, candle-lit *Cama Enoteca* (7pm–2am; closed Mon), Via Alloro 105; the bar staff are welcoming and knowledgeable, and the variety of wines almost overwhelming. Latin-American *La Cueva*, Via delle Balate 15, on the edge of the Ballarò market, is a great, relaxed nightspot. In summer, most young people go to **Mondello** (see opposite), and buses run there and back till late.

Listings

Bike rental Rent Bike, Via Giardinaccio 66 (off Via Maqueda) ☎331.750.7886. €10 per day.
Buses AST ☎091.620.8111, ⓦwww .aziendasicilianatrasporti.it (Castelbuono, Monreale, Módica, Comiso and Ragusa); Cuffaro ☎091.616.1510, ⓦwww.cuffaro.info (Agrigento); Interbus ☎091.304.0900 or 091.616.7919, ⓦwww.interbus.it (Siracusa, Trapani, Erice); SAIS ☎091.616.6028, ⓦwww.saisautolinee.it (Catania, Enna, Piazza Armerina and Messina); Salemi ☎091.617.5411 or 0923.981.120, ⓦwww .autoservizisalemi.it (Marsala and Mazara del Vallo); Segesta ☎091.616.9039, ⓦwww.segesta .it (Trápani).
Car rental Avis, Via Francesco Crispi 115 ☎091.586.940; Hertz, Via Messina 7/C ☎091.323.439; Maggiore, Stazione Notarbartolo 79 ☎091.591.681; Sicily By Car, Via Mariano Stabile 6/A ☎091.581.045. All of these also have desks at Punta Raisi airport.

Consulates Netherlands, Via Roma 489 ☎091.581.521; UK (part-time only), Via Cavour 117 ☎091.326.412; US, Via Vaccarini 1 ☎091.305.857. For nationals of most other countries, the nearest consulates are in Naples or Rome.
Exchange There are exchange offices at Punta Raisi airport (Mon–Fri 9am–4pm) and the central post office's BancoPosta at Via Roma 322 (bank hours).
Ferry and hydrofoils Grandi Navi Veloci (Grimaldi), services to Livorno, Rome and Tunis (at the port ☎091.587.404, ⓦwww.gnv.it); NGI to Ustica (caravan inside port ☎091.7437393, ⓦwww .ngi-spa.it); Siremar, to Ústica (by the port at Via F. Crispi 120 ☎091.749.3111, ⓦwww .siremar.it); Ústica Lines, to the Aeolian Islands, Cefalù and Naples (ticket office in port or at Agenzia Pietro Barbaro, Via Principe di Belmonte 51/55 ☎091.333333, ⓦwww.usticalines.it);

Tirrenia, to Naples, Genoa and Cágliari (at the port on Via Molo ℡091.602.1111, ⊛www.tirrenia.it).
Gay and lesbian information ARCI Gay, Via Genova 7 ℡338.669.7407, ⊛www.arcigay.it. ARCI Donna ℡091.345.799, ⊛www.arcidonna.it.
Hospital Policlinica, Via Carmelo Lazzaro ℡091.655.1111. For an ambulance call ℡118.
Internet access Along Via Maqueda near the train station, or *Aboriginal Café*, Via Spinuzza 51, opposite the Teatro Massimo ℡091.662.2229 or 328.933.0660, ⊛www.aboriginalcafe.com (Mon–Sat 6pm–3am).
Left luggage Stazione Centrale by track 8 ℡091.603.3040 (daily 7am–11pm); Stazione Marittima ℡091.611.3257 (daily 7am–8pm).

Pharmacist All-night service at Via Roma 1, Via Roma 207, and Via Mariano Stabile 177. There's also a list in the daily newspaper *Il Giornale di Sicilia.*
Police Central city station at Piazza Vittoria ℡112.
Post office Main post office is the Palazzo delle Poste on Via Roma (Mon–Sat 8am–6.30pm). Poste restante closes at 1.30pm daily.
Travel agents Compagnia Siciliana Turismo, Via E Amari 124 ℡091.743.9611 (for excursions in Sicily); Travel Cafe, Via Carducci 18 ℡091.336.900; CTS Viaggi Via Garzilli 28/G ℡091.332.209 (Mon–Fri 9am–1pm & 3.30–7pm, Sat 9am–1pm); Pietro Barbaro, Via Principe di Belmonte 51/55 ℡091.333.333 (Mon–Fri 9am–1pm & 4–6pm, Sat 9am–1pm).

Mondello

The most obvious trip from central Palermo is the 11km run to **MONDELLO**, a small seaside resort tucked under the northern bluff of Monte Pellegrino. It has a two-kilometre sandy **beach** curving round to a tiny working harbour, dominated by the Liberty-style *Charleston*, Viale Regina Elena (℡091.450.171), Palermo's most celebrated restaurant, and the ruins of a medieval tower. There's a line of simpler **restaurants** overlooking the water that dish up fresh fish (try *Calogero*, where you stand up and eat freshly caught and cooked octopus. Although crowded, summer nights at Mondello are a lot of fun. In winter it's more laid-back, and rarely very busy, but some of the restaurants and snack stalls are still open. To get to Mondello, take bus #806 or #833 from the Politeama theatre or Viale della Libertà – a thirty-minute ride.

Monreale

The marvellous Monreale cloister ... conjures up an impression of such grace as to make one want to stay there forever ...

Guy de Maupassant

The Norman cathedral at **MONREALE** (Royal Mountain) holds the most impressive and extensive area of Christian medieval mosaic work in the world, the undisputed apex of Sicilian-Norman art. This small hill-town, 8km southwest of Palermo, commands unsurpassed views down the Conca d'Oro Valley, to the capital in the distant bay. Bus #389 runs frequently from Piazza dell'Indipendenza, and the journey takes twenty minutes.

The severe, square-towered exterior of the **Duomo** (daily 8am–6.30pm, Sun 8am–12.30pm & 3–7pm; free) is no preparation for what's inside. The **mosaics** were almost certainly executed by Greek and Byzantine craftsmen, and they reveal a unitary plan and inspiration. What immediately draws your attention is the all-embracing half-figure of Christ in the central apse, the head and shoulders alone almost twenty metres high. Beneath sit an enthroned Madonna and Child, attendant angels and, below, ranks of saints, each individually and subtly coloured and identified by name. Worth singling out here is the figure of **Thomas à Becket** (marked *SCS Thomas Cantb*), canonized in 1173, just before the mosaics were begun. The nave mosaics are no less remarkable, an animated series that starts with the Creation (to the right of the altar) and runs around the whole church. Most scenes are instantly recognizable: Adam and Eve, Abraham on the point of sacrificing his son, a jaunty Noah's Ark; even the Creation, shown in a set of glorious, simplistic panels portraying God filling his world with animals, water, light … and people.

Ask at the desk by the entrance to climb the **terraces** (daily 9.30am–5.30pm, Sun 8am–12.30pm & 3.30–7pm; €1.50) in the southwest corner of the cathedral. The steps give access to the roof and leave you standing right above the central apse – an unusual and precarious vantage point. It's also worth visiting the **cloisters** (same hours as Duomo; €6), part of the original Benedictine monastery established here in 1174. The formal garden is surrounded by an elegant arcaded quadrangle, 216 twin columns supporting slightly pointed arches – a legacy of the Arab influence. No two capitals are the same, each a riot of detail and imagination: armed hunters doing battle with winged beasts, flowers, birds, snakes and foliage. Entrance to the cloisters is from Piazza Guglielmo, in the corner by the right-hand tower of the cathedral.

If you want **to stay** over, try the *Carrubella Park Hotel*, Via Umberto I 233 (℡091.640.2187, ⓦwww.sicilyhotelsnet.it; ❹), a pleasant family-run place with great views over the valley of the Conca d'Oro

Ústica

A volcanic, turtle-shaped island 60km northwest of Palermo, **ÚSTICA** is somewhere you could spend an entire holiday, though it is close enough to Palermo for a day-trip – however, travel doesn't come cheap; expect to pay around €30 return by ferry, €40 by hydrofoil. Ústica's fertile uplands are just right for a day's ambling, while the rough coastline is touted a skin-diver's paradise, the clear water bursting with fish, sponges, weed and coral. Less adventurous types can easily take a boat trip through Ústica's rugged grottoes and lava outcrops.

The small port of **Ústica town**, where the boats dock, has a few bars, a bank, a dozen restaurants and a handful of places to stay. All these sit around a sloping double piazza, just five-minutes' walk uphill from the harbour. Ústica town has a couple of good **hotel** choices: *Clelia*, at Via Magazzino 7 (℡091.844.9039, ⓦwww.hotelclelia.it; ❸), with a roof terrace overlooking the sea, and the friendly but basic *Ariston*, Via della Vittoria 5 (℡091.844.9042; ❸), which has rooms with views and can arrange diving and boat trips. Alternatively, look out for signs advertising *camere* (rooms). For a **meal** with a view, dine at *La Luna sul Porto* (℡091.844.9799), below the piazza and above the port, on Via Vittorio Emanuele (closed Sun in winter) or try local fare such as fish soup with tomatoes, garlic and capers at the *Clelia's* restaurant.

The Tyrrhenian coast

From Palermo, the whole of the rugged **Tyrrhenian coast** is hugged by rail, road and motorway, and for the most part, pretty built up. The first attraction is **Cefalù**, a beach resort and cathedral town. Beyond Cefalù, there are several resorts tucked along the narrow strip of land between the **Nebrodi mountains** and the sea, most of them not worth going out of your way for. The lovely **Riserva Naturale Laghetti di Marinello**, however, is definitely worth making a beeline for, although most people tend to head straight for the port of **Milazzo** – Sicily's second-largest port – the main departure point for ferries and hydrofoils to the seven fascinating islands of the **Aeolian archipelago**.

Cefalù

Despite being one of Sicily's busiest international beach resorts, **CEFALÙ** remains a fairly small-scale fishing port, tucked onto every available inch of a shelf of land beneath a fearsome crag, **La Rocca**. Roger II founded a mighty cathedral here in 1131 and his church dominates the skyline, the great twin towers of the facade rearing up above the flat roofs of the medieval quarter. Naturally, the fine curving sands are the major attraction but Cefalù is a pleasant town, and nothing like as developed as Sicily's other package resort of Taormina.

Halfway along **Corso Ruggero**, the main pedestrianized road through the old town, stands the **Duomo** (daily: summer 8am–7pm; winter 8am–5.30pm; free) built – partly at least – as Roger's gratitude for fetching up at Cefalù's safe beach in a violent storm. Inside, covering the apse and presbytery, are the earliest and best preserved of the church **mosaics** in Sicily, dating from 1148. Forty years earlier than those in the cathedral at Monreale, they are thoroughly Byzantine in concept. In high season, when Cefalù's tangibly Arabic central grid of streets is crowded with tourists, you'd do best to visit the cathedral early in the morning, before succumbing to the lure of the long sandy **beach** beyond the harbour. There are a couple of other places also worth venturing to: the **Museo Mandralisca** (daily 9am–7pm; €5), at Via Mandralisca 13 (across from Piazza Duomo), has a wry *Portrait of an Unknown Man* by Antonello da Messina, and a huge shell collection; and **La Rocca** (daily 8am–8pm; €3.50), which holds the megalithic Tempio di Diana, from where paths continue right around the crag, inside medieval walls, to the sketchy fortifications at the very top.

Practicalities

The **tourist office** is at Corso Ruggero 77 (Mon–Sat 8am–8pm; summer also Sun 9am–1pm; ☎0921.421.050, ⓦwww.cefalu-tour.pa.it; also check out ⓦwww.palermotourism.com for information on Cefalù), with free maps and accommodation lists. If you want to **stay over**, try the clean, basic and small *Locanda Cangelosi*, centrally placed at Via Umberto I 26 (☎0921.421.591, ⓦwww.locandacangelosi.it; no credit cards; ❶); it also has a handful of two-, three- and four-bed apartments with kitchens to rent. Alternatively, the pleasant *B&B delle Rose* (☎&ⓕ0921.421.885; half board in July & Aug; ❷), at Via Gibil-manna, twenty-minutes' walk out of town along Umberto I, has rooms with private terraces. Otherwise, for a selection of B&B rooms and apartments right on the seafront, try *Villa Cerniglio*, Lungomare G. Giardina ☎320.119.5311 or 0921.923.877, ⓦwww.villacerniglia.com; ❷–❹). There are no outstanding **restaurants**, but you'll eat adequately at *Al Porticciolo*, Via Carlo Ortolani Bordonaro 66 and 92 (☎091.921.981; closed Wed in winter), with a terrace built right onto the rocky shore.

Marinello and the Nebrodi mountains

If you fancy a lingering journey along the Tyrrhenian coast, head for the superb and unspoilt **Riserva Naturale Laghetti di Marinello** 10km east of Patti, where saltwater lagoons, sand dunes and dramatic rocky cliffs provide an important sanctuary for migratory birds, and where there are some great walks. The cliffs above the reserve are dominated by the lavishly kitsch **Sanctuario di Tindari** (daily 6.45am–12.30pm & 2.30–7pm) built in the 1960s to celebrate numerous miracles attributed to a Byzantine icon of a Black Madonna. It's a hugely popular pilgrimage spot (indeed Tindaro and Tindara are extremely common Christian names in these parts) so Sundays are best avoided. From the front of the sanctuary a path leads to what is left of ancient **Tyndaris** (daily 9am–7pm; €2) including an overrestored Roman basilica and a well-preserved Roman house with mosaic floors.

To really get off the beaten track, there are a number of routes into the **Nebrodi mountains**, taking you through isolated hill-towns and villages that have changed little in centuries. Autumn weekends are a great time to visit, as virtually every village holds some kind of *sagra*, a festival celebrating a single foodstuff, such as mushrooms, olive oil or bread. See Ⓦwww.parcodeinebrodi .it for more information. If it's spectacular scenery you are after, take the SS118 to Etna via the welcoming hill-town of **NOVARA DI SICILIA**, best known for *maiorchina*, a sheep cheese so strong you could swear the Novara flocks are grazed on chilli. For somewhere to **stay**, *Sganga Kondé* (☏0941.650.526), on the main road through town, is a very pleasant B&B in a huge *palazzo*, run by ex Rai journalist, Minni Stancanelli; Mussolini spent a night here in 1927. For **food**, there are a couple of traditional trattorias.

Milazzo

At the foot of a hilly sickle-shaped castle-topped cape, and dominated by a giant oil refinery, **MILAZZO** is the main port of departure for the **Aeolian Islands** (see box opposite), which means, at best, a couple of hours in town waiting for a ferry or hydrofoil – at worst, a night in one of the hotels.

If there's time to kill, you might like to poke around the streets of the **Borgo**, the Old Town on the top of the hill, where the restored **castle** (guided tours Tues–Sat 9.30, 10.30 & 11.30am, March–May also 3, 4 & 5pm; June–Aug 5, 6 & 7pm; Sept 4, 5 & 6pm; Oct to end-Feb 2.30 & 3.30pm; €3.10) sits inside a much larger and older walled city, complete with its own cathedral. Dotted around the Borgo are plenty of pubs, open every evening in summer, at weekends in winter. The steps that run down the far side of the castle walls lead to the Spiaggia di Ponente, a long **beach** of grey gravel with crystal-clear waters.

Practicalites

Buses (including the Giuntabus service from Messina, whose timings are pretty much organized to tie in with hydrofoil arrivals and departures) stop on the port-side car park (turn right as you disembark from the hydrofoil). The **train station** is 3km south of the centre, but local buses run into town every thirty minutes during the day, dropping you on the quayside or further up in Piazza della Repubblica. Milazzo's helpful **tourist office** is at Piazza Duilio 20

(Mon–Sat 8am–2pm and possibly some afternoons; ☎090.922.2865, ⓦwww
.aastmilazzo.it), just back from the harbour.

The nicest places **to stay** are Italy's only eco-hotel, the friendly ⚘ *Petit
Hotel*, Via dei Mille 37 (☎090.928.6784, ⓦwww.petithotel.it; ❸), in a
nineteenth-century building on the seafront overlooking the hydrofoil dock,
where breakfasts include organic yogurt, eggs and jams; and the elegant,
minimalist, family-run *Cassisi*, Via Cassisi 5 (☎090.922.9099, ⓦwww
.cassisihotel.com; ❸). For something cheap, try the *California* at Via del Sole 9
(☎090.922.1389; no credit cards; ❶), or *Jack's*, a couple of blocks back from
the port at Via Colonnello Magistri 47 (☎090.928.3300, ⓦwww.jackshotel
.it; ❷), both have clean functional rooms with bathrooms. There are plenty of
places to **eat** along the seafront, or head to *Al Bagatto*, Via M Regis 11
(☎090.922.4212; closed Wed) a wine bar where you can sample local salami
and cheeses with a glass of wine, as well as more substantial dishes.

The Aeolian Islands

Volcanic in origin, the **Aeolian Islands** are named after Aeolus, the Greek god
who kept the winds he controlled shut tight in one of the islands' many caves.
According to Homer, Odysseus put into the Aeolians and was given a bag of
wind to help him home, but his sailors opened it too soon and the ship was
blown straight back to port. More verifiably, the islands were coveted for their
mineral wealth, the mining of obsidian (hard, glass-like lava) providing the basis
for early prosperity. Later their strategic importance attracted the Greeks, who
settled on Lípari in 580 BC, but they later became a haven for pirates and a
place of exile, a state of affairs that continued right into the twentieth century
with the Fascists exiling their political opponents to Lípari.

The twentieth century saw mass emigration, and even now islands such as
Panarea and Alicudi have just a hundred or so year-round inhabitants. It's only
recently that the islanders stopped scratching a subsistence living and started
welcoming tourists, so you won't be alone if you come during the summer
months, when the population of the islands leaps from 10,000 to 200,000.
Every island is **expensive**, with prices in shops as well as restaurants reflecting
the fact that most food is imported. But get out to the minor isles or come in
blustery winter for a taste of what life was like on the islands twenty – or a
hundred – years ago: unsophisticated, rough and beautiful.

Getting to the Aeolian Islands

Sailings **from Milazzo** operate daily and are frequent enough to make it unnecessary
to book except in the high season (unless you're taking a car), although bear in mind
that there is a severely reduced service between October and May – and that even
moderately rough weather can disrupt the schedules. The **shipping agencies** are
down by the harbour and open usual working hours in summer and just before
departures in the low season – Siremar (Via dei Mille 19 ☎090.928.3242, ⓦwww
.siremar.it) for ferries and hydrofoils, Ústica Lines (Via dei Mille 32 ☎090.928.7821,
ⓦwww.usticalines.it) for hydrofoils only, and NGI (Via dei Mille 26 ☎090.928.3415) for
ferries only. **Hydrofoils** are more frequent and twice as quick, but almost twice the
price of the ferries. The islands can also be reached from Palermo, Naples, Cefalù,
Messina and Reggio di Calabria (see "Travel details", p.982).

Getting around in summer is easy, as ferries (*traghetti*) and hydrofoils (*aliscafi*) link all the islands. In winter, services are reduced and in rough weather cancelled altogether, particularly on the routes out to Stromboli, Alicudi and Filicudi. A car might be worth taking to Lípari and Salina, but bikes are better and you can rent them on the spot.

In high season (Easter & July–Aug), **accommodation** is scarce, many places insist on half-board, and you'd be wise to book in advance. From October to March prices can drop by up to 50 per cent. There are **campsites** on Vulcano, Salina and Lípari – but camping rough is illegal.

There are **ATMs** on all the islands but Alicudi. Power cuts are commonplace, caused by storms in winter, and in August by over-demand, so if you're spending any time on Alicudi, Filicudi or Strómboli, a torch is a good investment. Don't be surprised if hotels ask you to go sparingly with the **water** as it is imported by tanker.

Vulcano

Closest to the Sicilian mainland, **VULCANO** is the first port of call for ferries and hydrofoils – 45 minutes by hydrofoil, around an hour and a half by ferry. From the harbour of **Porto di Levante** you can walk up to the main crater of the volcano in around an hour; the last volcanic explosion here was in 1890. A second hike is to **Vulcanello**, the volcanic pimple just to the north of the port, spewed out of the sea in 183 BC. Just fifteen-minutes' walk from the port, across the neck of land separating it from Porto di Ponente, there's an excellent black-sand **beach**. On the way you'll pass Vulcano's sulphurous **mud baths** and **hot springs** bubbling into (and warming) the sea. If you opt for a wallow in the mud, you'll reek of it for days afterwards, and don't wear any jewellery, because it will be stained and corroded.

High prices and mass-tourism make Vulcano best seen in a day-trip. If you do want to stay, the summer-only **tourist office** at the port (June–Sept daily 8am–2pm; ℡090.985.2028) has information on rooms. The cost of food on the island is exorbitant, and you have to choose carefully from the battery of **restaurants** (most of which close between Nov and Easter) along the road that bends around from the port.

Lípari

LÍPARI is the biggest and most heavily populated of the islands. Development has not been carefully controlled, and although parts of the island are beautiful and unspoilt, getting there inevitably means passing through villages cluttered with brassy holiday houses. The main port and capital, **Lípari Town** is a busy little place bunched between two harbours.

Arrival, information and accommodation

Hydrofoils and ferries dock at the deep **Marina Lunga**, which curves around to the north, while the smaller **Marina Corta**, formed by a church-topped mole and dwarfed by the castle that crowns the hill above, is used by excursion boats.

The **tourist office** at Corso Vittorio Emanuele 202 (Mon–Fri 8.30am–1.30pm & 4.30–7.30pm; July & Aug also Sat 8.30am–1.30pm; ℡090.988.0095, Ⓦwww.aasteolie.191.it) has a list of hotels and information for all the Aeolian Islands. In July and August it's a good idea to listen to the offers of **rooms** as you step off the boat. Expect to pay around €25–40 per person in August, €20 at other times of the year, for something with a shower, kitchen and balcony or terrace. There are also two pleasant rooms to rent from Christine Berart, the islands' veterinarian, at Vico Montebello 19 (☎090.9880.783 or 338.886.1297, ℮christine@eolnet.it; ❷). The nearest **campsite** is *Baia Unci Campsite* (☎090.981.1909; open mid-March to mid-Oct), 3km away from the port at the busy resort of Canneto; the bus from Lípari stops outside.

Carasco Porto delle Genti ☎090.981.1605, ⓦwww.carasco.it. Best choice in town if you have children, as this 1960s hotel, fused to a cliff on the edge of town, has a vast pool. All the rooms have terraces, and virtually all have sea views. Facilities include a decent restaurant and a poolside bar. ❷

🏃 **Diana Brown** Vico Himera 3 ☎090.981.2584, ⓦwww.dianabrown.it. Spotless place on a quiet alley off the main Corso, run by a charming South African lady who has lived on the island for thirty years, and so can give good advice on anything you need to know. Rooms come with fridges and kettles; breakfast is served on a sunny roof garden; and there is a wonderfully well-stocked book-exchange. ❷

Enza Marturano Via Maurolico 35 ☎368.322.4997, ⓦwww.enzamarturano.it. Four bright rooms ranged around a communal lounge/ kitchen close to the Marina Corta; breakfast included. It is worth checking the website for special off-season deals. No credit cards. ❷

Hotel Tritone Via Mendolita ☎090.981.1595, ⓦwww.bernardigroup.it. Comfortable hotel in a quiet part of town, but just a 5min walk from the centre, built around a swimming pool with thermally-heated spring water. There is also a well-equipped spa centre, with a wide range of massage therapies and beauty treatments. It is owned by the same people as the excellent *Filippino* restaurant (see below). ❻

Villa Meligunis Via Marte 7 ☎090.981.2426, ⓦwww.villameligunis.it. If you fancy staying in the lap of luxury, push the boat out at this gorgeous converted *palazzo* with excellent views of the citadel and sea from its rooftop restaurant, and a pool alongside; it offers great discounts off-season. ❻

Island transport

From Lípari Town, the rest of the island is easy to reach on a network of **buses**, which leave regularly from a stop by Marina Lunga, opposite the Esso service station. Around here, too, are a couple of **scooter and bike rental** outfits. Roberto (☎340.548.4396) rents out *motorinos* (€18 per day, rising to €25 in July and €35 in Aug) and also organizes **boat trips** on his little fishing boat; for lunch, you can opt for fresh fish, cooked on a single ring in the tiny galley. Typically, you'll pay around €35 for an all-day trip, which takes you swimming off the island of Panarea and then see the evening explosions off Strómboli; day-trips to Panarea or Vulcano, allowing plenty of swimming, are around half that price.

Lípari Town

The upper town within the fortress walls, the **Castello**, has been continuously occupied since Neolithic times. Alongside the well-marked **excavations**, there's a tangle of churches flanking the main cobbled street, and several buildings that make up the separate arms of the **Museo Eoliano** (Mon–Sat 9am–1pm & 3–6pm, Sun 9am–1pm; €6) – a lavish collection of Neolithic pottery, late Bronze Age artefacts, and decorated Greek and Roman vases and statues. Highlights are the towering pyramids of amphorae rescued from ancient shipwrecks, a stunning array of miniature Greek theatrical masks found in tombs, and unique polychrome painted pottery ascribed to an artist known as the Lipari painter.

Eating and drinking

The town's numerous **restaurants and pizzerias** have (often poor, and inevitably over-priced) tourist menus at around €15–20, and even the cheaper places impose hefty 15 or 20 percent service charges. Two great places are the expensive *Filippino* on Piazza Municipio (☎090.9811.002, ⓦwww.filippino.it)

where the food is creative and delicious, and *Kasbah* (℡090.9811.075), off the Corso on Via Maurolico, a relaxed and elegant place, serving reasonably priced food in a garden planted with citrus trees.

There's a SISA **supermarket** and various *alimentari* and bakeries on the main Corso – if you're self-catering, head for the deli counter and fruit and veg section at the SISA, and buy your bread from the bakery opposite.

Canneto

CANNETO, a resort with a long pebble beach to the **east** of the island, is a good place to take the kids. Otherwise, the island's east coast has been marred by extensive pumice mining. Although this has now been banned, and there are plans to create nature reserves, for the time being it is the **west coast** that has most to offer. If you are after beaches and a walk, take the bus west out of Lípari town (direction Pianoconte) and ask to get down at Localitá Monte, from where it's a thirty-minute walk to the pebbly beach at Valle Muria (if you don't want to walk you can get there and back by boat from Marina Corta in summer: look out for Barney in the green and yellow boat; €4 each way). Continuing beyond Localitá Monte, the road climbs up to **Quattrocchi** ("Four Eyes"), with much-photographed views over spiky *faraglioni* rocks to Volcano. Just after the village of **Pianoconte**, a side road slinks off down to the ancient thermal baths at **San Calogero** hidden behind a long-disused spa hotel: there's usually an unofficial guide to show you around and allow you a dip in the 57°C Roman pool. For a great coastal hike, stay on the bus from Lípari asking the driver to drop you at the **Cave Caolina**, a quarry of multi-coloured clays used as pigments by the Lípari painter (whose work can be seen in the Museo Archeologico) from where an easy-to-follow path leads down through the quarry, and back to San Calogero, passing sulphurous fumaroles, a hot spring, and a couple of places where you can scramble down the cliffs for a swim. If you feel happier with a map, there are large-scale Isole Eolie maps on sale in many shops along the main *corso*.

Salina

North of Lípari, **SALINA**'s two extinct volcanic cones rise out of a fertile land that produces capers and white malvasia. It's excellent **walking** country with marvellous vantage points over the other islands. Tourism came to Salina far later than Lípari and Vulcano, with the happy result that development and building have always been strictly controlled. Although you could bring a car, there is really little need as there are bus services between all the main villages.

Walking trails cut right across Salina, in particular linking Santa Marina and Lingua with the peak of **Monte Fossa delle Felci** (962m). There are trail heads signed from the road between Santa Marina and Lingua, and also from the Circonvalazione that cuts behind Santa Marina. If you want an easier time of it, take a **bus** to the sanctuary of Madonna del Terzito at Valdichiesa – in the saddle between the two mountains – from where there's a broad easy-to-follow jeep track; this is about 10km to the top, and should take a couple of hours.

Santa Marina di Salina

The principal island port is **SANTA MARINA DI SALINA** on the east coast – a relaxed village ranged along a single, pedestrianized main street, with good swimming from a beach of large stones. You may be able to find private **rooms** here, or try the *B&B Da Sabina*, at the far end of the village from the port at Via Risorgimento 5/C (℡090.984.3134 or 333.272.6025, ⓦwww.bbsalina.it; ❸, rising to ❹ in Aug). *Mamma Santina*, Via Sanità 40 (℡090.984.3054, ⓦwww.mammasantina.it; ❺; open end March to Nov), signposted to the left up the hill off the main street of Via Risorgimento, has a great pool, though service is not always up to scratch. Down on the seafront is the *Mercanti di Mare* (☏090.9843.536, ⊛www.hotelmercantidimare.it; ❹), whose owner, Alberto, is author of a book of the same name, about the seafaring history of the islands. He has nine white, airy rooms and a terrace with views over the sea to Strómboli, Panarea and Lípari.

Nni Lausto (☏090.9843.486, open May–Oct) on Via Risorgimento, is a cool wine bar and **restaurant** whose New York-trained owner-chef brings an adventurous new twist to local dishes. Try the *tartare di tonno*, raw tuna dressed with wild fennel and capers, or spaghetti with raw sea urchin. The *Porto Bello* restaurant above the port (closed Wed in winter, & all Nov) serves excellent local antipasto, and beautifully prepared pasta and fish dishes.

Lingua

LINGUA, sitting by a pretty lagoon 3km south, is a pleasant alternative base to Santa Marina. There's a small ethnographic **museum** in front of the lagoon (July & Aug daily 9am–1pm & 5–8pm; Sept–June variable; free), though the main draw is the seafront piazza, hub of Salina summer-life, where the tiny **bar** ♣ *Da Alfredo* is famous throughout Italy for its fresh fruit and nut granitas. They also do *pane cunzato*, a huge round of grilled bread piled with various combinations of home-cured tuna, capers, tomatoes, baked ricotta and olives. For more formal meals or pizza, they have a restaurant behind.

The smart *La Salina* has lovely **rooms**, many with private terraces, set in the buildings of the former salt works by the lagoon (☏090.9843.441, ⊛www .lasalinahotel.com; ❺). If you're on a tight budget, best value on the island is the assembly of half a dozen funky **apartments** known as the *Villagio* (☏335.666.0777 or 329.796.6120; ❶) on the main road through the village, overlooking the lagoon. You'll also find rooms at the **restaurant** *'A Cannata* (☏090.984.3161, ⊛www.acannata.it; ❷–❸) and *Il Delfino*, right on the seafront at Via Garibaldi 19 (☏090.984.3024, ⊛www.ildelfinosalina.com; ❷–❸). Half board is compulsory at both in August (a hefty €120 or so per person) and both have minibuses to ferry guests between the port and Lingua.

Malfa and around

Salina's largest village, **MALFA**, set back from the sea, is home to the island's most charismatic hotel, the family-run *Signum* (☏090.984.4222, ⊛www .hotelsignum.it), which has elegant rooms set around an infinity pool, and an excellent restaurant. Malfa, itself, though quite heavily trafficked in the centre, has an appealing little fishing port tucked away at the foot of beetling cliffs, and reached by either road or paved stepped footpaths. If you are around in late afternoon, don't miss watching the sunset from the chic cliff-top bar of the *Santa Isabel* hotel (open Easter to Oct).

From Malfa, several buses a day take the windy side road to **Pollara**, where the film *Il Postino* was shot. You can rent the very house used in the film, though it is pretty basic and quite expensive. Call Pippo Cafarella (☏339.425.3684).

Rinella

Most ferries and hydrofoils also call at the little port of **RINELLA**, on the island's south coast, with a black-sand beach; buses meet most boat arrivals on the quayside (and call here several times a day). There's a little **hotel**, *L'Ariana* (☏090.980.9075, ⊛www.hotelariana.it; half board in Aug; closed mid-Nov & Dec; ❷), occupying a nineteenth-century villa with a frill of terracotta busts around its roof, just above the port. There is great home-cooked food at the amiable *Bar Papero*, tucked behind the main road on Piazzetta Anna Magnani, and two excellent **pizzerias**, *Da Marco* above the port, or *Le Tre Pietre*, on the main road out of the village. The village is also the site of the island's **campsite**, *Tre Pini* (☏090.980.9155, ⊛www.trepini.com; April–Oct), right on the shore under pines.

Panarea

Only 3km by 1.5km, **PANAREA** is the smallest, loveliest, most painfully stylish and ridiculously expensive of the Aeolians, and in summer its harbours, hotels and villas overflow with an international crowd of designers, models, pop stars, film stars, royalty and their lackeys. In low season, however, the island is an utter delight, accommodation prices relatively sane, and the three-hour walk, up the peak of Pizzo Corvo, and hugging the fractured coastline, one of the most stunning anywhere in Italy.

Cars are banned, and the only transport is by Vespa or electric golf car. Panarea's couple of hundred year-round inhabitants live in three linked hamlets on the eastern side of the island, Ditella, San Pietro and Drauto, with the boats docking at **San Pietro**. One of the least expensive places to stay are the **rooms** owned by Pippo and Maria Soldino in Iditella beyond the Carabinieri barracks. They are spotlessly clean, have their own terraces, are set in a garden, and out of season Pippo and Maria will cook for you (☏090.983.061 or 334.703.5010; ❷–❹). Good value, in low season at least, is the *Albergo Girasole* (☏090.983018 or 328.861.8595, ⊛www.hotelgirasole-panarea.it), also family-run, at Drauto, out on the way to the sandy beach at Zimmari. Or you could try the gorgeous *A Quartara* Via S. Pietro 15 (☏090 983027, ⊛www.quartarahotel.com; closed Nov–March; ❻–❾) an intimate boutique hotel where the staff make everyone feel special. The *Raya* on Via S. Pietro is the hotel that put Panarea on the party map, but unless you're a member of the in-crowd, it's really not worth considering, as how you are treated depends very much on who you are. However, if it happens not to be a guest-list only night, you could go for an aperitif or after-dinner **drink** on the fine terrace of the lovely bar.

The **food** is usually good at the *Trattoria da Francesco*, just above the port, and almost inevitably so at the charming, harbourside *Trattoria da Adelina*, Via Comunale del Porto 28 (☏090.983.246). thirty-minutes' walk south of San Pietro, and clearly signposted, is Zimmari, the island's one sandy **beach** and, high above here on the other side, **Punta Milazzese**, where you can see the foundations of 23 Bronze Age huts, and, below it, the glorious cove of Cala Junco. Just before you reach the Bronze Age village is the beginning of the well-marked track up Pizzo Corvo, circling the entire island and ending up at **Calcara** to the north of town, where there are steaming fumaroles on the beach.

Strómboli

Despite the regularity of the volcanic explosions, people have always lived on **STRÓMBOLI**. It is in a constant state of activity, throwing up fountains of fire and glowing rock every twenty minutes or so. A full eruption happens on average every 10 years. A flow of lava is often visible from afar, slowly sliding down the northwest side of the volcano into the sea. In January 2003 there was a colossal landslide, triggering a ten-metre-high tsunami that inundated the coasts of Sicily and Calabria.

Most of the many hotels and rooms to let on the island are on the eastern side, in the adjacent parishes of San Vincenzo, San Bartolo and Piscità, often grouped together as **Strómboli Town** and something of a chic resort since Rossellini and Ingrid Bergman immortalized the place in the 1949 film *Strómboli*. From the quayside, the lower coastal road runs around to the beach of **Ficogrande** and, further on, **Piscità**, with a series of tiny lava coves with ashy sand. It's around 25 minutes on foot from the port to here. The other road from the dock cuts up to the Piazza di **San Vincenzo**, whose square offers glorious views of the offshore islet of Strombolicchio.

On the other side of the island, accessible by hydrofoil, the hamlet of **Ginostra** is a laid-back place of steeply terraced white Aeolian houses, where the only way of getting about is on foot or donkey. **Hydrofoils** run back to Strómboli Town twice a day in summer (once daily in winter), but these are susceptible to cancellation because of rough waters.

Guides for the **ascent of the volcano** (depending on the level of activity) cost around €20 per person; try Magmatrek on Via Vittorio Emanuele (☎090.986.5768 or 333.906.6053, ⓦwww.magmatrek.it), where the staff are well informed and in constant radio contact with the volcanologists at the control centre. The climb up takes three hours, and you are expected to go at a fair whack; at first, it is no different from climbing any mountain, then suddenly all vegetation stops, giving way to black ash strewn with small jagged boulders spewed out by the volcano. Once on the top, all you can see at first are clouds of white steam – then suddenly there will be a resounding clash, the clouds glow red, and spouts of fire shoot up into the air, the glowing boulders drawing tracks of red light across the night sky. You should not attempt the climb alone. Be equipped for a tough-ish hike, and for a night climb bring warm clothes and a torch.

The best **boat trips** are the tours around the island, calling at Ginostra and Strombolicchio (3hr; €15), and trips out at night to see the Sciara del Fuoco (2hr 20min; €15). Try Pippo (☎090.986.135 or 338.985.7883) – who has a stand in front of the *Beach Bar*, or Paola and Giovanni (☎338.431.2803) who work from opposite the *Sirenetta* hotel in Ficogrande.

Practicalities

In summer, the quayside is thick with three-wheelers and touts offering **rooms**; prices start at around €25 per person. If you want to book a room in advance, first choice is the lovely *Casa del Mulino* (☎090.986.701 or 338.540.8931, michele.wegner@gmail.com) in Piscità with four simple rooms in an old windmill perched right on the lava-cliff edge above a black sandy cove. Another good bet is *Villa Petrusa*, Via Soldato Panettieri 4 (☎090.986.045, ⓕ090.986.126; closed Nov–March; ❸), with an attractive garden. If you want to stay in Ginostra, try one of the rooms at the *B&B Luna Rosa* (☎090.981.2305; ❶–❸) or contact Magmatrek guide Mario Priuti about houses to rent (☎339.787.8465).

The most convivial **restaurant** in Strómboli town is *Zurro*, down by the port at Via Marina (☎090 986 283) named for its piratical-looking owner-chef, an ex-fisherman whose food is both flamboyant and delicious. Summer nights often see impromptu parties on the beach at Petrazze, to the south of the port, while the best spot to hang out in town is *Bar Ingrid*, in the square by San Vincenzo church.

Filicudi

FILICUDI, the larger of the two most westerly islands, is a fascinating place, the contours of its sheer slopes traced with steep stone terraces and crisscrossed by stone mule tracks. It is an island best explored by foot, which may be just as well, as there is no public transport. The tarmac road that connects the several small settlements gives a false impression of the island, making villages seem far apart, that are in fact just a few minutes walk away, at least if you are fit: most of the tracks are pretty steep, occasionally following, but mostly cutting between, the ancient terraces carved into the slopes of maquis and prickly pear.

The main settlement is **Filicudi Porto**, which has a couple of shops, bars, hotels and a pharmacy. Inland, accessible by road or mule track are three white-washed villages, **Valdichiesa**, **Rocche Ciauli** and **Pecorini**. And down on the west coast, about 3km by road from the port, is the lovely little seaside village of **Pecorini Mare**. If you are not up to walking to your destination, a red minivan taxi meets most boat arrivals (€12 per person to Pecorini Mare). If it's not there call D&G Servizio Navetta (☏347.757.5916).

There are plenty of good **walks** along the ancient mule tracks of Filicudi: one of the nicest is out to the abandoned village of **Zucco Grande**. Walk up to *La Canna* hotel (see p.940) from the port – follow the well-kept stone mule track that begins from a point almost opposite the hydrofoil and ferry dock – then continue until you meet the tarmacked road. The path continues on the other side of the road, heading towards the settlement of Valdichiesa. After about twenty minutes, the path forks, and there is the first of several signs to Zucco Grande. The path is well-marked, following the contours through a prickly terrain of gorse, lentisk, prickly pear and euphorbia. Another twenty minutes brings you to the village, abandoned forty years ago when its last inhabitants left for Australia. A couple of pioneering souls have bought ruins here, which are being renovated, but at the moment there is just one inhabitant, Giovanni, who has a couple of rooms and can provide a basic dinner (☏347.813.2579 or 368.407.544).

Practicalities

As long as you don't mind a steep ten-minute haul up a stone-stepped alley, you could do no better than *La Canna* (☏090.988.9956, ⒲www.lacannahotel.it; ⓪), a family-run hotel in the hilltop village of Rocche Ciauli, above the port. Fourteen pleasant rooms open onto a huge whitewashed terrace with views of five other islands. There is a decent-sized swimming pool, and the restaurant serves typical Aeolian food often with fish caught by the owner. They also have several houses to rent around the island.

If you want a beachside base, head for Pecorini a Mare, where there is little to do except eat good food, hunt for seashells (Filicudi has some of the best shells in the archipelago) and walk slowly up the hill out to the clifftop viewpoint above at Punta Stimpagnato (allow about 30min) to watch the sun set over the mid-sea rock known as La Canna. The nicest place to stay here is *La Sirena* (☏090.988.9997 or 349.869.3320, ⒲www.pensionelasirena.it; ⓪) run by an Englishwoman and her Sicilian husband (who is also a great cook). They have several rooms (most with cooking facilities) and houses around the traffic-free village. The food is among the best you'll find anywhere on the islands.

Alicudi

End of the line Europe doesn't come much more remote than **Alicudi**, a stark cone rising from the sea two and a half hours from Milazzo by hydrofoil. Electricity arrived only in the 1990s, and the sole way of getting about is on foot, though the six donkeys are used to carry heavy loads. There are just eighty year-round inhabitants, while superstitions and sightings of ghosts abound – as does the conviction that some Alicudari are blessed with the power to control the weather and divert cyclones. Up the sheer slope behind the tiny port, terraced smallholdings and whitewashed flat-roofed houses linked by lava-paved paths cling on for dear life, among bursts of bougainvillea.

Most of the **hiking** here is up stepped tracks that seem to have been designed with giants in mind, so be prepared for a good deal of calf-work. If you don't fancy hauling yourself to the top (675m; 2hr), you'll still get plenty of exercise climbing up to the church of San Bartolomeo, where controversy rages over the removal of the statue of the saint to a more easily accessible church lower down the hill (it is said that since the statue was moved, the island has had bad luck). Otherwise, follow the path north out of the port behind the church of the Carmine from where it's a easy walk to the narrow stony beach of Bazzina, with a couple of smallholdings behind it.

Practicalities

There is one **hotel** in the port, the modern twelve-room *Ericusa* (℡090.988.9902, Ⓦwww.alicudihotel.it; ⑤) with sea-views and a restaurant. Otherwise contact Silvio Taranto, Via Regina Elena, 98050 Alicudi (℡090.988.9922) who can put you in touch with people who have rooms to rent. For twenty years Silvio and his wife have been cooking dinner at their house above the port for whoever needs a place to eat. There's no menu and no choice, and everyone eats the same, sitting at long tables on the family's terrace, drinking locally produced red wine. Another good place to **eat** is *Da Rosina Alla Mimosa* higher up in the village (℡090.988.9937 or 368.361.6511, Ⓦwww.rosina-barbuto.it) named after a huge mimosa tree that was uprooted by a recent tornado. Virtually everything is produced or (in the case of rabbit, goat and fish) caught by the family. In autumn there are wild mushrooms and from autumn to spring wild greens such as fennel and borage. There are also a handful of simple rooms to rent.

The Ionian coast

Sicily's eastern **Ionian coast** draws the largest number of visitors, attracted by **Taormina**, most chic of the island's resorts and famed for its remarkable Graeco-Roman theatre, and **Mount Etna**, Europe's highest volcano. Further south, out of the lee of Etna, lie traces of the **ancient Greek cities** that once lined the southeastern coast, notably Megara Hyblaea. The route concludes in **Siracusa** – formerly the most important and beautiful city in the Hellenistic world.

Messina and south

MESSINA may well be your first sight of Sicily, and – from the ferry – it's a fine one, the glittering town spread up the hillside beyond the sickle-shaped harbour. Sadly, the image is shattered almost as soon as you step into the city, bombed and shaken to a shadow of its former self by plague, cholera and earthquakes; the great earthquake of 1908 killed 84,000 people, levelled the city and made the shore sink by half a metre overnight. Allied bombing raids in 1943 didn't help, undoing much of the post-earthquake restoration.

Today, the remodelled city guards against future natural disasters, with wide streets and low, reinforced concrete buildings marching off in all directions. Not surprisingly, it's a pretty dull spectacle, and there's little point in hanging around for longer than you need to. If you've time on your hands, wander up to Via XX Settembre from the port to the **Duomo** (Mon–Sat 7am–7pm, Sun 7.30am–1pm & 4–7.30pm; free) a faithful reconstruction of the medieval cathedral built by Roger II. The facade retains its grand doorways and some original sculpture, and the detached **campanile** reputedly contains the largest astronomical clock in the world, a panoply of moving gilt figures including a crowing cock, roaring lion and a succession of doves and angels accompanying the Madonna. You can climb the campanile if you want a closer look (mid-April to mid-Sept daily 9am–1pm & 4.30–6.30pm; mid-Sept to Oct daily 9am–1pm; Nov to mid-April open Mon–Sat for groups, by appointment only; ☎090.675.175).

Much of what was salvaged from the various disasters resides in the **Museo Regionale** (Mon & Fri 9am–1.30pm, Tues, Thurs & Sat 9am–1.30pm & 3–5.30pm, Sun 9am–12.30pm, closed Wed; last entry 30min before closing; €4.50), 3km north of the centre – a 45-minute walk along Via della Libertà, or tram #28 to the terminus, Annunziata. This beautifully laid-out museum includes a couple of **Caravaggio**s, commissioned by the city in 1604, damaged works by Antonello da Messina, and the city's rescued archeological remains. Messina is the place to be only on the feast of the Assumption, or **ferragosto** (Aug 15), when a towering carriage, the Vara – an elaborate column supporting dozens of papier-mâché putti and angels, topped by the figure of Christ – is hauled through the city centre, followed by a firework display on the seafront.

Practicalities

Trains use the Stazione Centrale by the harbour, adjacent to the **Stazione Maríttima**, where train-ferries from Calabria dock. Other **ferries** and **hydrofoils** (to and from Villa San Giovanni, Reggio di Calabria and the Aeolian Islands) dock at quays further to the north, on Via Vittorio Emanuele and Via della Libertà. Interbus and SAIS **buses** for Palermo, Rome and Catania leave from Piazza della Repubblica by the train station, while those for Milazzo (for connections to the Aeolian Islands) depart from the Giuntabus office at Via Terranova 8 (at the corner of Viale San Martino), a five-minute walk away. There are two **tourist offices** just outside the train station: one on Piazza della Repubblica (Mon–Thurs 9am–1.30pm & 3–5pm, Fri 9am–1.30pm; sometimes also open Sat mornings; ☎090.672. 944), where good English is spoken, the other just beyond on Via Calabria (Mon–Sat 8am–6.30pm; ☎090.674.236, ⓦwww.aziendaturismomessina.it); both can supply you with Aeolian Islands ferry timetables and accommodation lists.

Unless you arrive late in the day, it's unnecessary to stay in Messina. Still, there are a couple of basic **hotels** on Via N. Scotto, an alley on the south side of Piazza della Repubblica, beyond the SAIS office, the better one being *Touring*, at no. 17 (☎&ⓕ090.293.8851; ❶–❷), which also has rooms with or without bathroom. A slicker option is the modern *Excelsior* (☎090.293.1431; ❸), near Piazza Cairoli at Via Maddalena 32. Messina has some good **restaurants**, many serving freshly caught swordfish from the straits; May and June are the height of the swordfish season. *Lungomare da Mario*, opposite the hydrofoil dock at Via Vittorio Emanuele 108 (☎090.42.477; closed Wed except Aug) has good fresh fish and an exceptional antipasto buffet, perfect for a quick lunch before catching the hydrofoil to the Aeolian Islands; otherwise tasty panini and other cold **snacks** are on offer at *Salumeria Nucita*, an *alimentari* at Via Garibaldi 125 (closed Wed eve & Sun). If it's breakfast you're after, head to Piazza Cairoli, where there are two good long-established café-*pasticcerie*: *Billé* at no. 7 (closed Tues) and *Irrera* at no. 12.

The coastal route south

South of Messina, the coast is not particularly attractive, the long grey gritty sands backed with a raggle-taggle of holiday houses. The undistinguished ribbon resort of **Santa Teresa Di Riva** is the jumping-off point for the foothills of the **Monti Peloritani**, the long mountain range that cuts south from Messina. Buses from Santa Teresa twist the 4km up to **SAVOCA**, a peaceful hill-village, where houses and churches perch precariously on the cliffsides in clumps, topped by a tattered castle. Signs point you to the **Cappuccini monastery** whose catacombs (Tues–Sun: April–Sept 9am–1pm & 4–7pm; Oct–March 9am–noon & 3–5pm; donation requested) maintain a selection of mummified bodies, two to three hundred years old, dressed in their eighteenth-century finery. Have a drink afterwards at the *Bar Vitelli*, used as the scene of Michael Corleone's betrothal in Coppola's film *The Godfather*.

Taormina

TAORMINA, perched high on Monte Tauro, with Mount Etna as backdrop, looks down on two grand sweeping bays and is Sicily's best-known resort. D.H. Lawrence was so enraptured that he lived here from 1920–23, in a house at the top of the valley cleft, behind the remains of the Greek theatre. Although international tourism has taken its toll, Taormina is still a very charming town, peppered with small, intimate piazzas. The single traffic-free main street is an unbroken line of fifteenth- to nineteenth-century *palazzi* decked out with flower-filled balconies, and there is an agreeably crumbly castle. The downside is that between June and August it's virtually impossible to find anywhere to stay, and the narrow alleys are shoulder-to-shoulder with tourists. April, May or September are slightly better, but to avoid the crowds completely come between October and March, when it's often still warm enough to swim in the sea.

Arrival and information

Trains pull up at the handsome Taormina-Giardini station on the water's edge, below town. It's a very steep thirty-minute walk up to Taormina (turn right out of the station and then, after 200m, left through a gap in the buildings, marked "Centro") and the road is extremely busy. Much better to take one of the fairly frequent local buses that pick up outside the train station, or else arrive by **bus** at the bus terminal, on Via Luigi Pirandello in Taormina itself: bear left up the road from the terminal, turn through the Porta Messina, and the main street, Corso Umberto I, lies before you. If you're arriving by **car**, make for the Porta Catania multi-storey car park, situated below Piazza S. Antonio. The **tourist office** (Mon–Thurs 8.30am–2pm & 4–7pm, Fri 8.30am–2pm; ☎0942.23.243, ⓦwww.gate2taormina.com) is in the fourteenth-century Palazzo Corvaja, off Piazza Vittorio Emanuele, the first square you come to.

Accommodation

Finding **accommodation** in summer is a time-consuming business, so it's well worth booking ahead. There's also a small **youth hostel**, *Taormina's*

Odyssey (☎0942.24.533, ⊛www.taorminaodyssey.com; €17–18), just outside the centre at Traversa G. Martino 2 off Via Fontana Vecchia; book well ahead to secure a bed.

Leone Via Bagnoli Croce 126 ☎&℗0942.23.878. Simple place close to the public gardens, which also has one of the few no-frills bars in town (you can get a glass of wine for €1.30). No credit cards. **❶**

Pensione Svizzera Via Pirandello 26 ☎0942.23.790, ⊛www.hotelpensionesvizzera .com. Just up from the bus terminal and cable car station this comfortable hotel has excellent views from its spacious rooms (with varying prices depending on size and view), a 24hr bar-service, wi-fi throughout and a shuttle to a private beach. **❸–❺**

🏃 **San Domenico Palace** Piazza San Domenico 5 ☎0942.613.111, ⊛www.thi.it. The last word in luxury. One of the most celebrated hotels in Italy, housed in a fifteenth-century convent, with gorgeous formal gardens, unsurpassable views, a Michelin-starred restaurant, and stratospheric prices. Staff are refreshingly both relaxed and gracious. Spend a night in one of the suites, and you feel you've died and gone to heaven. **❾**

Villa Belvedere Via Bagnoli Croce 79 ☎0942.23.791, ⊛www.villabelvedere.it. Decent, if unexciting rooms; there's a great pool in a lavish garden, and fantastic views. **❼**

Villa Floresta Via Damiano Rosso 1 ☎0942.620.184, ⊛www.villafloresta.it. Pleasant, family-run B&B in a nineteenth-century *palazzo* tucked into a courtyard with a crumbling fifteenth-century staircase behind Piazza del Duomo. **❷**

Villa Greta Via Leonardo da Vinci 41 ☎0942.28.286, ⊛www.villagreta.it. Family-run place 15min walk out of town on the road up to Castelmola, with superb balcony views, as well as a dining room with good home cooking. In winter, there's tea with complimentary home-made cakes and biscuits. **❸**

🏃 **Villa Sara** Via Leonardo da Vinci 55 ☎0942.28.138, ⊛www.villasara.net. Exceptional B&B a 15min walk (or a brief bus ride) up the road to Castelmola. It doesn't look much from the outside, but behind the bare walls is a gracious two-storey apartment where a friendly family rent out their spacious rooms, each with its own bathroom and its own large terrace commanding great views over Taormina, Etna and the sea. **❷**

Villa Schuler Piazzetta Bastione ☎0942.23.481, ⊛www.villaschuler.com. This lovely old hotel has been in the same family of German émigrés for a century, and retains the feel of an elegant family-run *pensione* (they take no tour groups). There are great views from its rooms and terrace, and a beautiful garden behind. Worth checking the website for special offers. **❺–❻**

The Town

The **Teatro Greco** (daily 9am to 1hr before sunset; €6) is a great starting point, its panoramic views encompassing southern Calabria, the Sicilian coastline and snowcapped Etna. It was founded by Greeks in the third century BC but the visible remains are almost entirely Roman, dating from the end of the first century AD, when Taormina thrived under imperial Roman rule. The theatre was converted to stage gladiatorial combat and deep trench was dug in the orchestra to accommodate animals and fighters. Between July and August the theatre hosts an international **arts festival** including film, theatre and music (tickets and information from the tourist office).

There are a few other Roman vestiges around town, including a much smaller **Odeon** (used for musical recitations) next to the tourist office. Really, though, Taormina's attractions are all to do with strolling and window-shopping along the Corso. Centre of town is **Piazza IX Aprile**, with its restored twelfth-century **Torre dell'Orologio** and fabulous views of Etna and the bay from the terraces of its pricey cafés. Fused to a crag five kilometres above Taormina, and reached by regular bus, is the small, and often claustrophobically touristy village of **Castelmola**. To escape the crowds, take the path behind the cemetery up to the heights of **Monte Venere** (885m, about 2hr) – for marvellous local vistas.

Eating, drinking and nightlife

Eating in Taormina can be an expensive business. For snacks, or picnic ingredients head for the indoor **market** off Via Cappuccini (mornings only, Mon–Sat). **Nightlife** in Taormina is none too exciting, with most of the action focused on the **gay bars** around gorgeous Piazza Paladini, just off the Corso. For unpretentious after dinner boozing head for the boho *Re di Bastoni* Corso Umberto I (closed Mon in winter) or the Irish pub *O'Seven*, Largo La Farina 6. For an aperitif or after dinner drink, *the* place to go is the *Wunderbar Café*, Piazza IX Aprile, once the haunt of Garbo and Fassbinder.

Al Grappola d'Uva Via Bagnoli Croce 6–8. Friendly, unpretentious wine bar – a good place to sample Etna wines and local cheeses. They can also organize tours of Etna's vineyards.
A'Zammara Via Fratelli Bandiera 15 ☏0942.24.408. Romantic place where you sit in a garden of orange trees eating the likes of home-made *tagliolini* with prawns and pistachios.
Trattoria da Nino Via Luigi Pirandello 37 ☏0942.21.265. Welcoming place, that despite its touristy appearance, is popular with locals for its fresh food: the mixed vegetable or mixed fish antipasto are particularly good.
Vecchia Taormina Vico Ebrei 3 ☏0942.24.359. Popular pizzeria in an alley across from the Duomo serving light, blistered pizzas from its wood-fired oven.

Taormina's beaches

The **coastline** below the town is a tantalizing combination of grottoes and rocky coves but many of its **beaches** are either private lidos or simply too packed in summer to be much fun. The closest beach to town is **Mazzarò** with its much-photographed offshore islet. There's a **cable car** service down to the beach (€1.80 one-way, €3 return) that runs every fifteen minutes from Via Pirandello (the road that encircles old Taormina) as well as a steep path that starts just below the cable car station. The huge resort of Giardini-Naxos, a favourite with international package companies, is best avoided: there are far better places in Sicily for a sun and sand holiday. If you do fancy staying along the coast here, the best target is **ACIREALE**, superbly sited high above the rocky shore, and surrounded by lemon groves. It's been a spa town since Roman times, but was destroyed by the devastating 1693 eruption of Etna, and rebuilt over the solidified streams of lava. Today, the town is known for hosting some of the best Carnevale celebrations in the country, with extraordinarily elaborate flower-decked floats and fancy dress parades taking over the city for five noisy days.

It is easier to arrive in Acireale by bus than by train, as the bus stops in the centre; the train stops to the south of town near a complex of thermal baths. Having wandered the town, be sure to head down to the little seaside settlement of **Santa Maria La Scala**, huddled around a miniscule harbour full of painted fishing boats, with three or four little trattorias. To get here on foot, go down Via Romeo (to the side of the Municipio), cross the busy main road, and then take the steep little path that runs down to the water.

Mount Etna and the Gole di Alcantara

The bleak lava wilderness around the summit of **Etna** is one of the most memorable landscapes Italy has to offer. Its height is constantly shifting, depending on whether eruptions are constructive or destructive, and over the last century it has ranged from 3263m to the present estimate of 3340m.

Whatever its exact height, Etna is a substantial mountain, one of the world's biggest active volcanoes, and on a clear day it can be seen from well over half of Sicily. Some of its eruptions have been disastrous: in 1169, 1329 and 1381 the lava reached the sea and in 1669 Catania was wrecked and its castle surrounded by molten rock. The Circumetnea railway line has been repeatedly ruptured by lava flows: nine people were killed on the edge of the main crater in 1979 and in 2001 military helicopters were called in to water-bomb blazing fires. This unpredictability means that it is no longer possible to get close to the main crater. An eruption in 1971 destroyed the observatory supposed to give warning of just such an event, and the volcano has been in an almost continual **state of eruption** since 1998, the most recent being in late 2002 when the resort of Piano Provenzana on the northern side was engulfed with lava. If you do attempt the summit, be sure to heed the warnings.

While in the area, try to make time, too, for the dramatic riverscapes of the **Gole di Alcantara**, between the northern slopes of Etna and the foothills of the Peloritani mountains.

Mount Etna: the ascent

There are several **approaches** to the volcano. If you have a car, you can enjoy some of the best scenery on the north side of the volcano by taking the circular road that leads up from **Linguaglossa** to Piano Provenzano, a good place to bring the kids to learn to ski or toboggan. There are a couple of **rifugi** here – the comfortable, warm *Rifugio Ragabo* (☏095.647.841, ⓦwww.ragabo .it; €50 per person, half pension), and the more basic *Rifugio Citelli* (☏095.930.000, ⓦwww.caipedara.it; ❶), from where the views on a clear day stretch over the Ionian sea to the Aspromonte mountains of Calabria. Both organize excursions.

▲ Approaching the barren summit of Mount Etna

On public transport, you'll just see Etna from the southern side, though this does at least get you pretty near the summit. Although there are frequent **buses** to Nicolosi from Catania, only one (around 8am from outside Catania train station) continues to the **Hotel/Rifugio Sapienza** at the end of the negotiable road up the south side of Etna. In summer 2001 and winter 2002 this was a scene of frenetic activity, when dams and channels were cut to contain the molten lava that threatened to engulf the whole area. However, the row of souvenir shops, the couple of restaurants, and the totally refurbished *Hotel/Rifugio Sapienza* (℡095.915.321; ❸) are still standing, surrounded by rills of lava. Arriving on the early-morning bus, you should have enough time to make it to the top and get back for the return bus to Catania – it leaves around 4.30pm from the hotel.

There are two ways **up the volcano** from the refuge, by foot or cable car. Now open again after being destroyed in the last eruption, **cable cars** run between 9am and sunset, weather permitting (€49.50 return). The price includes a minibus from the top cable car station to just below the main crater, though many people prefer to walk. **Walking up** from *Rifugio Sapienza* will take around four hours. However you go, at whatever time of year, take warm clothes, good shoes or boots and glasses to keep the flying grit out of your eyes. You can rent boots and jackets cheaply from the cable-car station. Food up the mountain is poor and overpriced.

The Circumetnea railway

A private line, 114km long, the **Circumetnea railway** (℡095.541.250, ⓦwww.circumetnea.it) runs around the base of the volcano passing lava-strewn slopes. The line runs between Catania and Giarre-Risposto, taking about three hours and thirty minutes, and you could start either at Catania (Borgo Stazione, see p.949) or, if approaching from Taormina, at Giarre. There are usually about five services daily in winter and four in summer. Returning to Catania by regular train from Giarre will take twenty minutes; and the journey between Giarre and Taormina also twenty minutes.

Getting off the train to visit some of the towns en route is possible, but not always easy: at **Bronte** for example, which produces 80 percent of Italy's pistachios, the town centre is a long, steep climb up from the station, though the pistachio ice creams and other sweet goodies on offer in its cafés might persuade you it is worth it. You might want to make a beeline for the little village of **Maletto** in June, when it hosts a strawberry festival, the Sagra di Fragola, while for anyone interested in wine, a stop at **Passopisciaro** and **Solicchiata** is a must: a rare chance to visit pre-phylloxera vineyards, and avante garde producers such as Frank Cornellisen (℡0942.986.315), who shuns the use of sulphates, and Andrea Franchetti (℡338.130.0778), producer of the internationally renowned and prize-winning *Passopisciaro*.

Most people, however, choose to break the journey at dark, medieval **Randazzo**, the town closest to the summit of Etna, and built entirely of lava. Although dangerously near Etna, Randazzo has never been engulfed, although the lava-flow came so close in 1981 that the town was evacuated: you can see the lava fields clearly on the fringes of town. Poke around the dour streets – meticulously restored after being bombed to bits in 1943, when it figured as the last Sicilian stronghold of the Axis forces – and stop for lunch at *San Giorgio e Il Drago*, Piazza San Giorgio 28 (℡095.923.972; closed Tues & Jan) a trattoria in a nineteenth-century wine cellar. If you decide you want to stay close to Etna, the nicest place to stay, especially if you have children, is the *Turismo Rurale Parco Statella* (℡095.924.036, ⓦwww.parcostatella.com; ❸) an eighteenth-century villa with a vast park, horseriding and its own restaurant, 2km outside town on the way to Linguaglossa.

The **visitor centre** (8am to 1hr hour before sunset; ℡0942.985010, Ⓦwww
.terralcantara.it; €4 entry, more in summer, plus extra for excursions) at Motta
Camastra (see below) arranges excursions in the Etna region. You can go on guided
walks, take on whitewater rafting, or rent waders and salopettes to waddle and
splash down the river when the water level is deemed low enough to be safe. There
are also guided quad excursions in the Alcantara Valley or up Mount Etna
(℡0942.980338 or 339.879.2940, Ⓦwww.siciliaquad.com).

The Gole di Alcantara

Around 2400 BC, the volcano of Monte Moia, at the head of the Alcantara
valley, erupted smothering the river and filling the valley with lava. Over four
millennia, the river has carved its way through the deposits of slick grey basalt,
scooping it into all manner of strange, sculptural rock formations. Heading
along the SS185 from the coast just south of Taormina, the most theatrical
(and touristy) part of the gorge is at **Motta Camastra**. There's a **visitor
centre** (see box above), a restaurant and souvenir shops. A couple of hundred
metres after the visitor centre, there is free public access to the gorge, down a
flight of steps.

If you want to escape the crowds, continue another 4km to the largely
modern town of **Francavilla di Sicilia**. Here, following brown signs to *Le
Gurne*, you twist up to the ancient, and largely abandoned, centre of town, from
where a well-marked path winds down to the river, through groves of citrus and
nut trees overlooked by a toothy old castle. Here you'll find a series of waterfalls
and natural round ponds where you can swim.

The nicest place to stay in the Alcantara valley is **Castiglione di Sicilia**.
Fused to a hilltop high above the valley, the town's lovely weather-eroded
houses with pantiled roofs cluster below the remains of a castle founded in the
fifth century BC by Greek exiles from nearby Naxos. There are plenty of old
churches to poke around, though the most remarkable of these is a perfectly
restored Byzantine chapel in the valley below, known as "La Cuba" for its
perfect symmetry. Behind "La Cuba" a path leads to the river, where there are
more little waterfalls and pools. Castiglione's real pleasures are gastronomic: at
Alcantara Formaggi, Via Federico II (℡0942.984.268) the Camiglia family
produce a range of traditional and inventive cheeses, mostly made of local
sheep's milk; while the *Dispensa dell'Etna*, Piazza Sant'Antonio 2 (℡339.713.9000)
is a wine bar and restaurant showcasing an exuberant range of local wines,
preserves and other produce. If you want to **stay**, try the smart little hotel with
a great restaurant off the main piazza: *Hotel Federico II*, Via Maggiore Baracca 2
(℡0942.980.368, Ⓦwww.hotelfedericosecondo.it; ❸–❹).

Catania

Bang in the middle of the Ionian coast, **CATANIA** is Sicily's second-largest
city, a major transport hub, a thriving commercial centre, and a lively, energetic
place with a more international outlook than Palermo. Defined by Etna – even
the city's main street is named after the volcano – and the ubiquitous black-grey
volcanic stone in pavements and buildings, there's more openness and space
than in Palermo, but far less to see, as the ancient and medieval city was engulfed

by lava in 1669, and then devastated by an earthquake in 1693. Spearheaded by architect Giovanni Vaccarini, Catania was rebuilt swiftly and on a grand scale, making full use of the lava that had been the old city's nemesis.

Arrival and information

The **airport**, Fontanarossa (℡095.340.505, Ⓦwww.aeroporto.catania.it), is 5km south of the centre. The Alibus #457 (5am–midnight; every 20min; €0.80) runs from right outside to the central Piazza Stesicoro (on Via Etnea) and to Stazione Centrale in around twenty minutes. A taxi from the rank outside the airport costs around €20 for the same. If you're heading straight to the **Aeolian Islands**, there is one direct bus daily from May to September from the airport to the port of Milazzo at around 4pm.

The **Stazione Centrale** (℡892.021), where all mainline trains arrive, is in Piazza Giovanni XXIII, northeast of the centre. To get into the centre, take one of the AMT (℡095.751.9111, Ⓦwww.amt.ct.it) city buses from the ranks outside the station: #1/4, #4/7, #432 and #448 run along Via VI Aprile and Via Vittorio Emanuele to Piazza del Duomo. For the round-Etna train, head to the **Stazione Circumetnea** (℡095.541.250, Ⓦwww.circumetnea.it; see box, p.947) at Via Caronda, at the northern end of Via Etnea, by the Borgo metro station.

There's a **tourist office** (Mon–Sat 8am–8pm; ℡095.730.6255) inside Stazione Centrale, but the main office (same times; ℡095.730.6211 or 095.730.6233, Ⓦwww.apt.catania.it) is signposted off Via Etnea, at Via Cimarosa 10. There's also a branch at the airport (Mon–Sat 8am–8pm, Sun 10am–4pm; ℡095.730.6266). For **what's on** check out Catania's daily newspaper, *La Sicilia*, and the free fortnightly arts and entertainment guide, *Lapis*.

City transport

Catania is served by a network of AMT **city buses**, whose main ranks are outside the Stazione Centrale. Other central pick-up points are Piazza del Duomo, Piazza Stesicoro, and Piazza Borsellino (below Piazza del Duomo), where there's a stop for the airport. Tickets (€0.80) are valid for any number of journeys within ninety minutes and are available from *tabacchi*, the newsagents inside Stazione Centrale or the booth outside the station. The same outlets also sell a *biglietto giornaliero* (€2), valid for one-day's unlimited travel on all local AMT bus routes.

The city has a **metro** system (℡095.534.323), which operates every fifteen minutes (7am–8.20pm) on a limited route running from the main Stazione Centrale (beyond Platform 11) south to Catania Porto and north and northwest to Catania Borgo, the terminal for the Stazione Circumetnea on Via Caronda. Tickets cost €0.80 for any number of journeys within ninety minutes, and are available from *tabacchi* at the train station. All tickets must be punched at machines before boarding the train. There are **taxi ranks** at Stazione Centrale, Piazza del Duomo and Via Etnea (Piazza Stesicoro); call ℡095.330.966 or 095.338.282 for 24-hour service. **Driving** and parking in Catania is a stressful experience: ask at your hotel where to park.

Accommodation

Catania has a wide choice of **places to stay**. As well as the places listed below, there's a private **hostel**, the ⚹ *Agora*, on Piazza Currò (℡095.723.3010, Ⓦwww.agorahostel.com), offering dorm bunks (€18) and a couple of doubles (❶), with internet access and laundry facilities. It also owns one of Catania's most popular and atmospheric pubs, the *Agora*, where you can eat and drink from morning till the early hours outside or in an underground grotto, which has a river running through it.

B&B 5 Balconi Via del Plebiscito 133 ☏338.727.2701, ⓦwww.5balconi.it. Stylish B&B run by a friendly young Italo-English couple in an old-fashioned, neighbourly quarter behind Castello Ursino. The three rooms are furnished with elegant flea-market finds. As the name implies, it has five balconies. Breakfast includes traditional Catanese pastries. ②

Mount Etna ▲　▲ Stazione Circumetnea

CATANIA

N

Orto Botánico

Villa Bellini

Teatro ⓘ Metropolitan

Anfiteatro Romano

Sant'Agata al Cárcere

San Nicolò

San Giuliano

Collegiata

San Benedetto

University

Municipio

Museo Belliniano

Teatro Romano

Odeon

Sant' Agata

Teatro Bellini

Duomo

Porta Ujeda

Castello Ursino

Palazzo di Giustizia

Stazione Metropolitana

Collegio Cutelli

Stazione Centrale

Molo Vecchio

Taormina & Messina ▲　Piazza Giovanni XXIII

EATING & DRINKING	
Antica Marina	8
De Fiore	2
Camelot	9
La Collegiata	3
Nievski	4
Savia	1
Sicilia in Bocca	6 & 7
The Other Place	5
Pub	5

ACCOMMODATION	
Agorá	G
B&B 5 Balconi	J
B&B BaD	H
B&B Bianca	B
B&B Casa Barbero	A
Holland International	F
Hotel Gresi	C
La Vetreria	I
Liberty Hotel	E
Una Hotel	D

0   100 m

▼ Airport, Beaches & Campsites

B&B BaD Via C Colombo 24 ☎ 095.346.903. Four rooms and an apartment in a funky self-styled designer B&B owned by a couple of graphic designers, and conveniently located behind the Pescheria and Piazza del Duomo. **②**

B&B Bianca Via S Tomaselli 43 ☎ 095.989.0989, ⓦ www.bianca-bb.it Young, friendly B&B behind the Giardino Bellini, where the owners will make sure you are well-informed about what's going on in Catania. There are two rooms, at present with shared bathroom. The communal area is a cheerful place to hang out and chat, with white walls and fittings, scarlet chairs, and an orange sofa where you can flop and watch a DVD. **②**

B&B Casa Barbero Via Caronda 209 ☎ 095.820.6301, ⓦ www.casabarbero.it. Deft use of contemporary colours and design in a beautifully restored Liberty-era *palazzo* with six quiet rooms set around a courtyard. Breakfast is served either in the courtyard, or in the elaborately stuccoed and frescoed dining room, at tables elegantly laid with Japanese-style ceramics and modern pewter. Bikes for guest use (free but €100 deposit). **②–③**

Holland International Via Vittorio Emanuele 8 ☎ 095.533.605, ⓦ www.hollandintrooms.it. Old-fashioned *pensione*, convenient for the station, and competitive prices for rooms on the first floor of an old *palazzo* with vaulted frescoed ceilings. There are rooms with and without bathroom (**①** for the latter). The friendly Dutch owner speaks good English. **②**

Hotel Gresi Via Pacini 28 ☎ 095.322.709, ⓦ www .gresihotel.com. Newly refurbished traditional hotel, with a pleasantly old-fashioned atmosphere, where the spacious rooms have frescoed ceilings. Good location between Via Etnea and the bustling Piazza Carlo Alberto market. **③**

La Vetreria Via Grimaldi 8 ☎ 095.281.537, ⓦ www.residencelavetreria.com. The breakfast room with toy cupboard and little table and chairs signals straight away that this is a place where kids are genuinely welcomed. Occupying a 1920s mirror factory, this popular hotel has tastefully furnished, spacious rooms and apartments with cooking facilities. **③**

Liberty Hotel Via San Vito 40 ☎ 095.311.651, ⓦ www.libertyhotel.it. Intimate and romantic hotel in an early twentieth-century *palazzo*, a 10min walk from Via Etnea. Wonderfully refurbished in carefully researched Liberty style, the hotel has a calm atmosphere and a trellis-shaded courtyard, making this an idea place to recuperate after a long journey. There's no restaurant, but a local pizzeria will deliver to the hotel. **④–⑤**

Una Hotel Via Etnea 218 ☎ 095.250.5111, ⓦ www.unahotels.it. Chic designer hotel whose decor reflects the dominant black and cream tones of the city's Baroque architecture: floors of Etna lava and Comiso limestone; beds laid with cream cotton and black velvet; and Baroque-style chairs sprayed gold and upholstered in black velvet. Facilities include roof terrace and restaurant-bar with spectacular views of Etna; and a gym with steam bath. Check website for offers, especially for weekend stays. **⑥**

The City

Catania's main square, **Piazza del Duomo**, is a handy orientation point and a stop for most city buses: **Via Etnea** heads north, lined with the city's most fashionable shops and cafés; the fish market and port lie behind to the south; the train station to the east; and the best of the Baroque quarter to the west. It's also one of Sicily's most attractive city squares, rebuilt completely in the first half of the eighteenth century by Vaccarini. Most striking of the buildings is the **Municipio** on the northern side, best seen from the central reserve of the piazza beside the **elephant fountain**, the city's symbol, an eighteenth-century lava elephant supporting an Egyptian obelisk on its back.

The **Duomo** (daily 9.30am–12.30pm & 4–6.30pm; free) on the piazza's eastern flank, retains marvellous volcanic-rock medieval apses (seen through the gate at Via Vittorio Emanuele 159), though the rest was remodelled by Vaccarini, who incorporated granite columns from Catania's Roman amphitheatre (see p.952) onto the facade. The interior has a series of richly adorned chapels, notably the Cappella di Sant'Agata to the right of the choir, which holds the relics of the saint paraded through the city on her feast day.

Nearby is Catania's **market**, with slabs and buckets full of twitching fish, endless lanes of vegetable and fruit stalls, and a couple of excellent lunchtime trattorias. From here you can wind through an atmospheric, if dilapidated, neighbourhood to an open space punctured by the **Castello Ursino**, once the proud fortress of Frederick II. Originally the castle stood on a rocky cliff, over the beach, but following the 1669 eruption, which reclaimed this entire area from the sea, all that remains is the blackened keep. The **Museo Civico** inside is undergoing an interminable restoration, though occasionally some of its exhibits are dusted off and displayed elsewhere (ask at the tourist office, see p.949 for details).

Back towards the centre, **Via Crociferi** is lined with some of the most arresting religious and secular Baroque buildings in the city, best seen on a slow amble, peering in the eighteenth-century courtyards and churches. At the bottom of the street, the house where composer Vincenzo Bellini was born in 1801 now houses the **Museo Belliniano** (Mon–Sat 9am–1pm, ☏095.715.0535; €2), a collection of photographs, original scores, his death mask and other memorabilia. West from here, the **Teatro Romano** (Mon–Sat 9am–1pm & 3–7pm, Sun 9am–1pm; free) was built of lava in the second century AD on the site of an earlier Greek theatre, and much of the seating and the underground passageways are preserved. Further west, down Via Teatro Greco, the pretty crescent of Piazza Dante stares out over the unfinished facade of **San Nicolò** (daily 9am–1pm; free), the biggest church in Sicily, stark and empty of detail both outside and in – save for a meridian line drawn across the floor of the transept.

Nearby, a few minutes' walk north, the little twelfth-century church of **Sant'Agata al Carcere** was built on the site of the prison where St Agatha was confined before her martyrdom. From here, you drop down into **Piazza Stesicoro**, the enormous square that marks the modern centre of Catania, one half of which is almost entirely occupied by the closed-off, sunken, black remains of the **Anfiteatro Romano**, dating back to the second or third century AD. In its heyday, the amphitheatre could hold around sixteen thousand spectators, and from the church steps above you can see the seating quite clearly.

Eating

They take food seriously in Catania, as the city centre's bustling markets testify. For the best **snacks**, try the markets in Piazza Carlo Alberto and the stall-heavy streets through the Porta Uzeda, to the south of the Duomo. Another popular area for food is lively Piazza Federico di Svevia outside the Castello Ursino. Don't miss the chance to sample the Catanese speciality *selz* – fruit and nut syrups with soda water – served at kiosks throughout the city, most famously on Piazza Vittorio Emanuele (corner of Corso Umberto and Via Oberdan).

Antica Marina Via Pardo 29 ☏095.348.197. Trattoria bang in the heart of the fish market where you can eat fresh fish on tables laid with paper cloths. Closed Wed.

Camelot Piazza Federico di Svevia 75 ☏095.723.2103. Lively place where you can feast for a song on Sicilian antipasti and barbequed meat and drink local wine from plastic cups. Open eve, Sun lunchtime, closed Mon.

De Fiore Via Coppola 24 ☏095.316.283. Cosy, family-run trattoria, serving good, traditional Sicilian food at moderate prices. Closed Mon.

Savia Via Etnea 302. Located opposite the main entrance to the Villa Bellini, this is one of the town's finest stand-up café-bars, and has a fine choice of sweet pastries and savouries. Closed Mon.

Sicilia in Bocca Piazza Pietro Lupo 16–18 ☏095.7461361 and an old warehouse on Via Dusmet ☏095.315472. Two branches of a popular and fairly expensive restaurant. A good option for Sicilian specialities such as *pennette alla norma* and swordfish *involtini*. Piazza Pietro branch closed Wed; Via Dusmet branch closed Mon.

Bars and nightlife

Catania's city council operates **café-concerto** periods during the summer, when the streets and squares of the old town, between Piazza Università and Piazza Bellini, are closed to traffic between 9pm and 2am. The bars here all spill tables out onto the squares and alleys, and live bands keep things swinging until late. Catania's student population ensures a fair choice of youthful **bars and pubs** – some with live music – that stay open late. Three good choices are *La Collegiata*, Via Collegiata 3, a studeny place with a pleasant terrace for a night-time drink; *Nievski*, on Via Alessi 15, a funky, alternative joint occupying several floors of a ramshackle building (closed Sun lunch & Mon); and finally, *The Other Place Pub*, Via E Reina 18, which is always lively.

Listings

Buses The bus station is at Piazza Giovanni XXIII, opposite the train station. AST (℡ 095.723, ⓦ www.aziendasicilianatrasporti.it; Rifugio Sapienza, Nicolosi, Módica, Scicli, Piazza Armerina and Siracusa); Interbus/Etna Trasporti (℡ 095.532.716, ⓦ www.interbus.it; Enna, Noto, Piazza Armerina, Ragusa, Siracusa and Taormina); SAIS (℡ 095.536.201, ⓦ www.saisautolinee.it; Agrigento, Enna, Messina, Palermo).

Car rental Avis at the airport and Via V Cágliari 1, central booking line ℡ 0645.2108.391, ⓦ www .avis.co.uk or www.avisautonoleggio.it; SIXT at airport ℡ 095.340.252 and Via Umberto 294/B ℡ 095.538.831, ⓦ www.e-sixt.co.uk or www .sixt.it; Hertz at airport ℡ 095.341.595 and Via Toselli ℡ 095.322.560, ⓦ www.hertz.co.uk or www.hertz.it; Holiday Car Rental at airport ℡ 095.346.769, ⓦ www.holidaycarrental.it; Maggiore at airport ℡ 095.340.594 and Piazza G. Verga ℡ 095.536.927, ⓦ www.maggiore.com or www.maggiore.it.

Emergencies ℡ 113 for all emergency services.

Hospital Ospedale Garibaldi, Piazza Maria di Gesù 7, Pronto Soccorso ℡ 095.759.4368.

Internet access Internetteria, Via Penninello 44, just off Via Etnea ℡ 095.310.139. Open Mon–Sat 10am–11pm, Sun (winter only) 5–10pm.

Pharmacies Croce Rossa, Via Etnea 274 ℡ 095.317.053; Cutelli, Via Vittorio Emanuele II 54 ℡ 095.531.400; Europa, Corso Italia 111 ℡ 095.383.536. Open all night.

Police Emergencies ℡ 112; Carabinieri, Piazza Giovanni Verga 8, or Vigili Urbani, Via Veniero 7 ℡ 095.531.333. The Questura (police station) is in Piazza S. Nicolella 8 ℡ 095.736.7111.

Post office Main post office and poste restante at Via Etnea 215, close to the Villa Bellini (Mon–Sat 8.15am–6.30pm).

Travel agents La Duca Viaggi, Piazza Europa 2 ℡ 095.722.2295.

Siracusa

Under Ancient Greek rule, **SIRACUSA** was the most important city in the Western world. Today it is one of Sicily's main draws, thanks to an extensive archeological park, and a charming historic centre occupying an offshore island where Greek, Roman, medieval and Baroque buildings of mellow golden limestone tangle along a labyrinth of cobbled streets. In between the two, is modern Siracusa, a busy and functional city of undistinguished apartment-lined boulevards.

Some history

It's hardly surprising that Siracusa attracted the **Greek** colonists who settled the site in 733 BC. An easily defendable offshore island with fertile plains across on the mainland and two natural harbours, it was the perfect site for a city, and within a hundred years, ancient Syracuse was so powerful that it was sending out its own colonists to the south and west, and soon became the power base of ancient Sicily's most famous and effective rulers.

It's worth buying a **combined ticket** (valid two days) if you're planning to see Siracusa's major sights: a ticket for the Parco Archeologico and the Museo Archeologico costs €9.

Syracuse assumed an almost mythic eminence under **Gelon**, the tyrant of Gela, who began work on the city's Temple of Athena. It was an unparalleled period of Greek prosperity and power in Sicily, though this troubled Athens, and in 415 BC a fleet of 134 triremes was dispatched to take Syracuse – only to be destroyed. Those who survived were imprisoned in the city's stone quarries.

In the fourth century BC, under **Dionysius the Elder**, the city became a great military base, the tyrant building Euryalus forts and erecting strong city walls. Syracuse more or less remained the leading power in Europe for two hundred years until it was attacked by the **Romans** in 215 BC. The subsequent **two-year siege** was made long and hazardous for the attackers by the mechanical devices contrived by Archimedes – who was killed by a foot soldier as the Romans finally triumphed.

From this time, Syracuse withered in importance. It became, briefly, a major religious centre in the early **Christian period**, but for the most part its days of power were done: it was sacked by the Saracens and most of its later Norman buildings fell in the 1693 earthquake. Passed by until the twentieth century, the city suffered a double blow in World War II when it was **bombed** by the Allies and then, after its capture, by the Luftwaffe in 1943. Luckily, the extensive ancient remains were little damaged, and although decay and new development have reduced the attractions of the modern city, Siracusa remains one of the most fascinating cities on the island.

Orientation

The original Greek settlement was on the fortified island of **Ortygia**, compact enough to see in a good half-day's stroll and almost completely late-medieval in character. The Greek city spread onto the mainland in four distinct areas: **Achradina**, over the water from Ortygia, was the city's commercial and administrative centre and today encompasses the new streets that radiate out from the train station; **Tyche**, to the northeast, was residential and now holds the archeological museum and the city's extensive catacombs; **Neapolis**, to the west, is the site of the fascinating archeological park based on ancient Syracuse's public and social amenities; while **Epipolae** stretches way to the northwest, to the city's outer defensive walls and the Euryalus fort.

Arrival and information

The **train station** is on the mainland, a twenty-minute walk from either Ortygia or Neapolis. AST city and regional **buses** (℡0931.462.711) stop here, and the Interbus office (℡0931.66.710) is also located here.

The main **city bus stops** are in Piazza Archimede and Largo XXV Luglio on Ortygia, and along Corso Umberto on the mainland; tickets cost €0.90, valid for two hours. **Drivers** will find the city a breeze after Palermo and Catania, and parking places relatively easy to come by. For maps, accommodation listings, details of performances in the Greek theatre, and other information, visit the **tourist office** at Via Maestranza 33 in Ortygia (summer Mon–Sat 8.30am–1.45pm & 4.30–7pm; winter Mon–Thurs 8.30am–1.45pm & 2.45–5.30pm, Fri & Sat 8.30am–1.45pm; ℡0931.464.255) or at Via San Sebastiano 43, near the catacombs in Tyche (Mon–Thurs 8.30am–1.30pm & 3–6pm, Fri & Sat

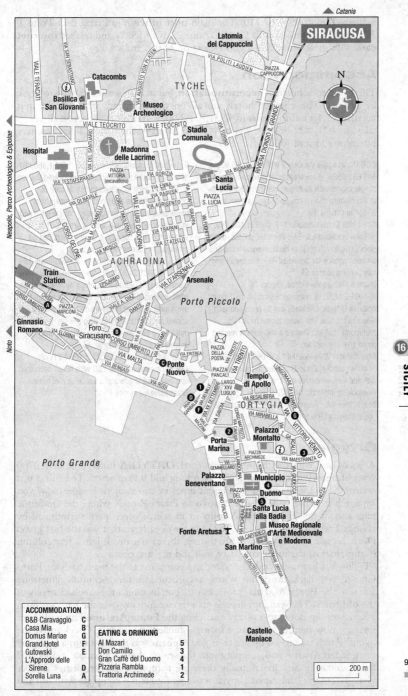

SIRACUSA

▲ Catania

Latomia
dei Cappucci

PIAZZA
CAPPUCCINI

VIA POLITI LAUDIEN

Catacombs

TYCHE

VIA AUGUSTO VON PLATEN

VIA SAN SEBASTIANO

VIALE TERACATI

Basilica di
San Giovanni

Museo
Archeologico

VIALE TEÓCRITO

VIA DEL SANTUARIO

VIALE TEÓCRITO

Stadio
Comunale

VIA TORINO

RIVIERA DIONISIO IL GRANDE

N

Hospital

Madonna
delle Lacrime

PIAZZA
VITTORIA
(excavations)

VIA GORIZIA

VIA BIGNAMI

Santa
Lucia

VIA TESTAFERRATA

VIA ENNA

VIA DI NATALE

CORSO TIMOLEONTE

VIALE LUIGI CADORNA

VIA M. CARABELLI

VIA RAGUSA

VIA AGRIGENTO

PIAZZA
S. LUCIA

VIA TRAPANI

VIA MONTE GRAPPA

VIA RESETTARA

VIA MOSCO

VIA STATELLO

CORSO GELONE

ACHRADINA

VIA EPICARMO

VIA D'ARSENALE

Train
Station

Arsenale

V. DIAZ

VIALE A. DIAZ

Porto Piccolo

Ginnasio
Romano

Foro
Siracusano

CORSO UMBERTO I

PIAZZA
MARCONI

VIA CRISPI

VIA FLORINA

VIA R. MARGHERITA

VIA DANTE

CORSO UMBERTO I

VIA PALERMO

PIAZZA
DELLA
POSTA

VIA ERITREA

VIA TRIESTE

VIA MALTA

Ponte
Nuovo

PIAZZA
PANCALI

VIA TRENTO

VIA BENGASI

LARGO
XXV
LUGLIO

Tempio
di Apollo

VIA RODI

VIA XX SETTEMBRE

VIA RESALIBERA

LUNGOMARE DI LEVANTE

RIO GARIBALDI

VIA SAVOIA

ORTYGIA

VIA MIRABELLA

VIA G. PICALO

VITTORIO VENETO

VIALE MAZZINI

CORSO MATTEOTTI

Porta
Marina

Palazzo
Montalto

VIA DELL'APOLLO

PIAZZA
ARCHIMEDE

VIA MAESTRANZA

Porto Grande

VIA LANDOLINA

VIA
GEMMELLARO

VIA RESINA

VIA GIUDECCA

Palazzo
Beneventano

Municipio

Duomo

PIAZZA
DEL
DUOMO

VIA LARGA

VIA NIZZA

Santa Lucia
alla Badia

FORO ITALICO

Fonte Aretusa

Museo Regionale
d'Arte Medioevale
e Moderna

VIA PICHERALE

VIA CAPODIECI

San Martino

LUNGOMARE ORTIGIA

VIA CASTELLO MANIACE

Castello
Maniace

ACCOMMODATION
B&B Caravaggio	C
Casa Mia	B
Domus Mariae	G
Grand Hotel	F
Gutowski	E
L'Approdo delle	
Sirene	D
Sorella Luna	A

EATING & DRINKING
Al Mazari	5
Don Camillo	3
Gran Caffè del Duomo	4
Pizzeria Rambla	1
Trattoria Archimede	2

0   200 m

◀ Neapolis, Parco Archeologico & Epipolae

◀ Noto

8.30am–1pm; ℡0931.67.710). The main **post office** is in Piazza delle Poste. *Il Paradiso degli Orchi*, Via della Conciliazione 22, is a friendly and relaxed **internet café** with great music and a good selection of teas and wine.

Accommodation

There's a good choice of **accommodation**, but in high season it's wise to book in advance. The cheaper hotels are all on the mainland, while the nearest **campsite**, *Agriturist Rinaura* (℡0931.721.224), is 4km away and open all year – take bus #21, #22 or #23, #24 or #25 from outside the station. They also have bungalows to rent (**②**).

B&B Caravaggio Via Cairoli 8 ℡0931.465.932 or 349.652.8803, ⓦwww.bbcaravaggio.com. Clean, simple rooms with bathroom and good breakfasts, in the modern town a couple of blocks from the bridge to Ortygia. **②**

Casa Mia Corso Umberto 112 ℡0931.463.349, ⓦwww.bbcasamia.it. B&B in an old *palazzo* not far from Ortygia with antique beds, eleven rooms and an inner terrace for breakfast. Bikes, internet and two parking spaces. **②**

Domus Mariae Via Vittorio Veneto 76 ℡0931.24.858, ⓦwww.domusmariae.eu. Elegant hotel on Ortygia, efficiently run by nuns and with views to the sea. The swish rooms have TVs, bathrooms and a/c. There's a solarium, a reading room and a chapel too. **⑤–⑥**

Grand Hotel Viale Mazzini 12 ℡0931.464.600, ⓦwww.grandhotelsr.it. This veteran haunt of the rich and famous enjoys a prime position in Ortygia overlooking the Porto Grand. Access to a private beach, lavish furnishings and all the refinements you'd expect at the price. **⑦**

Gutowski Lungomare Vittorini 26 ℡0931.465.861, ⓦwww.guthotel.it. Lovely hotel overlooking the sea on Ortygia's east side, with tastefully bare but comfortable rooms and good bathrooms. Great breakfasts, with freshly squeezed orange juice and, in summer, home-made almond granita. There is also a little wine bar, and private dinners can be arranged for four or more guests. **④**

L'Approdo delle Sirene Riva Garibaldi 15 ℡0931.24.857, ⓦwww.apprododellesirene .com. Pleasant B&B in a tastefully renovated waterfront building in Ortygia, just across the bridge from the mainland. Great home-made breakfasts are served on a terrace overlooking the sea, and the hotel has a boat for excursions. You can also borrow bikes, free of charge. **③–④**

Sorella Luna Via F Crispi 23 ℡0931.21178, ⓦwww.sorellalunasrl.it. B&B with nicely decorated and furnished rooms and a spacious roof terrace. Great value for money. **②**

Ortygia

A fist of land with the thumb downturned, **ORTYGIA** stuffs more than 2700 years of history into a space barely 1km long and 0.5km across. The island was connected to the mainland at different times by causeway or bridge: today you approach over the wide **Ponte Nuovo** to Piazza Pancali, where the sandstone remnants of the **Tempio di Apollo** sit in a little green park surrounded by railings. Erected around 570 BC in the colony's early years, it was the first grand Doric temple to be built in Sicily, though there's not much left: a few column stumps, part of the inner sanctuary wall and the stereobate.

Follow Via Savoia towards the water and you come to the main harbour, Porto Grande. Set back from the water, a curlicued fifteenth-century limestone gateway, the **Porta Marina**, provides one entrance into the webbed streets of the **old town**. The walk uphill ends on a terrace looking over the harbour, from where you slip down to a piazza encircling the **Fonte Aretusa**. The freshwater spring – now neither fresh nor a spring – fuelled an attractive Greek myth: the nymph Arethusa, chased by the river god Alpheus, was changed into a spring by the goddess Artemis and, jumping into the sea off the Peloponnese, reappeared as a fountain in Siracusa. Actually, there are natural freshwater springs all over Ortygia, but the landscaped, papyrus-covered fountain – complete with fish and

▲ Piazza del Duomo, Ortygia, Siracusa

ducks – is undeniably pretty. Admiral Nelson took on water supplies here before the Battle of the Nile.

The old town's roads lead on, down the "thumb" of Ortygia, as far as the **Castello Maniace** on the island's southern tip. Built by Frederick II in 1239, the solid square keep is now a barracks and off-limits. Back on the main chunk of Ortygia, the severe thirteenth-century Palazzo Bellomo houses the **Museo Regionale d'Arte Medioevale e Moderna**, an outstanding collection of medieval art, which has been closed for another of Sicily's interminable restorations. Parts of the collection occasionally see the light of day in exhibitions, so do keep an eye out as there are some wonderful pieces in here, including an exquisite, damaged fifteenth-century *Annunciation* by Antonello da Messina.

Ortygia's highlight is the splendid **Piazza del Duomo**, an elongated space from which impressive buildings radiate out up either flank, including the seventeenth-century **Municipio** with the remains of an early Ionic temple in its basement. This was abandoned when work began on the most ambitious of all Siracusa's temples, the **Tempio di Atena**, in the fifth century BC. In the normal run of things it might be expected to have suffered the eventual ruination that befell most of the Greek temples in Sicily. Yet much of it survives, thanks to the foundation in the seventh century AD of a Christian church, which incorporated the temple in its structure – thus keeping the masonry scavengers at bay. The **Duomo** itself (daily 8am–noon & 4–8pm; free) makes the grandest statement about Ortygia's continuous settlement, with twelve of the temple's fluted columns, and their architrave, embedded in its battlemented Norman wall. Inside, the nave of the Christian church was formed by hacking eight arches in the cella walls.

Achradina

Buses run from Largo XXV Luglio over Ponte Nuovo and into **ACHRADINA**, the commercial centre of ancient Syracuse. The **Foro Siracusano** was the site of the *agora*, the market place and public square, and there are a few remains still to be seen – though the dominant feature is the Fascist-era war memorial in its garden. Behind the train station, off Via Elorina, is the **Ginnasio Romano**, not a gymnasium at all, but a small first-century AD Roman theatre – partly sunken under moss-covered water – and a few pieces of a temple and altar.

Tyche

TYCHE, north of the train station, and home to the Museo Archeologico, is connected to Ortygia's Largo XXV Luglio by buses #3, #5, #12 and #15. Get off at Viale Teocrito and follow signs east for the archeological museum and west for Neapolis.

The well-organized **Museo Archeologico** (Tues–Sat 9am–7pm, Sun 9am–2pm; last entry 1hr before closing; €6 or combined ticket with Parco Archeologico €9) starts with geological and prehistoric finds, then moves through rooms devoted to the colonies of Naxos, Lentini, Zancle and Megara Hyblaea, and to the main body of the collection: an immensely detailed catalogue of life in ancient Syracuse. The most famous exhibit is a headless **Venus** arising from the sea, the clear white marble almost palpably dripping. Look out, too, for the section dealing with the temples of Syracuse; fragments from each (like the seven lion-gargoyles from the Tempio di Atena) are displayed alongside model and video reconstructions.

Tyche is riddled with **catacombs**, since the Romans forbade burial within the walls of a city. All are now inaccessible apart from those beneath the **Basilica di San Giovanni**, a stone's throw from the archeological museum off Viale Teocrito (Tues–Sun 9.30am–12.30pm & winter 2.30–4.30pm, summer 2.30–5.30pm; tour of catacombs €3.50), built over the burial site of Roman martyr St Marcian. The presence of the saint made this a hugely popular burial place, and there are thousands of niches hollowed into the walls to contain the remains of Roman Syracuse's Christians.

Opposite the museum, across Viale Teocrito, the monolithic **Santuario della Madonna delle Lacrime** (daily 7am–12.30pm & 4–7pm; free) is the newest and least harmonious addition to the city's skyline. Completed in 1994 to house a statue of the Madonna that allegedly wept for five days in 1953, it was designed to resemble a giant teardrop.

Neapolis

NEAPOLIS, to the west of Tyche, is now contained within the **Parco Arche-ologico** (daily 9am to 1hr before sunset) an extensive area that's worth at least half a day, so bring water and a picnic. Although you don't pay to see the initial excavations, visiting the Greek theatre and quarries – easily the most interesting parts – costs €6, paid at a separate entrance (€9 with entrance to Museo Archeo-logico). The **Ara di Ierone II**, an enormous third-century BC altar on a solid white plinth, is the first thing you see, across the way from which is the entrance to the theatre and quarries. The **Teatro Greco** is prettily sited, cut out of the rock and looking down into trees below. It's much bigger than the one at Taormina, capable of holding around fifteen thousand people. Around the top of the middle gangway are a set of carved names which marked the various seat blocks occupied by the royal family. Greek dramas are still played here in May and June.

Walk back through the theatre and another path leads down into a leafy **quarry**, the **Latomia del Paradiso**, best known for an unusually shaped cavern that Dionysius is supposed to have used as a prison. This, the **Orecchio di Dionigi** (or "Ear of Dionysius"), is a high, S-shaped cave 65m long: Carav-aggio, a visitor in 1586, coined the name after the shape of the entrance, but the acoustic properties are such that it's thought that Dionysius may have used it to eavesdrop on his prisoners from above.

The ticket for theatre and Latomia del Paradiso also gives access to the ellip-tical **Anfiteatro Romano**. A late building, dating from the third century AD, it's a substantial relic with the tunnels for animals and gladiators clearly visible. Again, some of the seats are inscribed with the owners' names.

Castello Eurialo

For terrific views over the city head a few kilometres west of Siracusa to the military and defensive works begun under Dionysius the Elder to defend the port from land attack. They basically consisted of a **great wall**, which defended the ridge of Epipolae (the city's western limit), and the massive **Castello Eurialo** (daily until 1hr before sunset; €2) – the most important surviving Greek fortification in the Mediterranean. There are three defensive trenches, the innermost leading off into a system of tunnels and passages. Climb up to the castle proper for hearty **views** down to the oil refineries and tankers of the coast north of the city, and over Siracusa itself.

Bars and **pizzerias** share the view, and make this a great place for an evening out. **Buses** #9, #11, #25 and #26 make the fifteen-minute ride from the Corso Gelone, outside the archeological park, to the village of Belvedere; the site is just before the village, on the right.

Eating, drinking and nightlife

Many of Siracusa's **restaurants** are overpriced, but there are a few good-value places. Good **bars** and **cafés** are easy to find. In the daytime, the *Gran Caffè del Duomo*, right in front of the cathedral, is the place to sit and sup, while in the evening, Ortygia's tiny **Piazzetta San Rocco**, and the streets around it, are the focus of Siracusa's **night scene**.

Al Mazari Via G Torres 7 ☏ 0931.483.690. Sophisticated, yet cosy restaurant, run by a family from Mazara del Vallo. Dishes, such as couscous, are typical of western Sicily.

Don Camillo Via Maestranza 96 ☏ 0931.67.133. Siracusa's finest fish restaurant, with a showy client list including biorgio Armani, Steve Martin, Bono and Gerard Depardieu.

Pizzeria Rambla Via Riva Garibaldi 4
℡ 0931.66.638. This place may look touristy, but they make a great, light, crisp pizza and the staff are friendly and professional.

Trattoria Archimede Via Gemmellaro 8. Fish restaurant popular with locals; they do a great *cavatelli* (home-made pasta) with swordfish, sea urchins, tomatoes and zucchini. Closed Sun.

The southern coast and the interior

The **southern coast** and hinterland marks a welcome break from the volcanic fixation of the blacker lands to the north: here the towns are largely spacious and bright, strung across a gentler, unscarred landscape that rolls down to the sea, and endless long sandy beaches. Sicily's southeastern bulge was devastated by a calamitous seventeenth-century earthquake and the inland rebuilding, over the next century, was almost entirely Baroque in concept and execution. **Noto**, closest to Siracusa, is the undisputed gem, but there are Baroque treasures aplenty both at **Modica** and **Ragusa**. The coast, too, has some jewels: 10km south of Noto is the magical **Riserva Naturale di Vendicari**, and though certain stretches of the coast are marred by industrial development and pollution, there are some magnificent sands further west. Further west still, is **Agrigento**, sitting on a rise overlooking the sea above its famed series of Greek temples.

Slow cross-country trains and limited-exit motorways do little to encourage stopping in the island's **interior**, but it's only here that you really begin to get off the tourist trail. Much of the land is burned dry during the long summer months, sometimes a dreary picture, but in compensation the region boasts some of Sicily's most curious towns. **Enna** is the obvious target, as central as you can get, the blustery mountain town a pace apart from the dry hills below. There are easy trips to be made from here, north into the hills and south to **Piazza Armerina** and the fabulous Roman mosaics.

Riserva Naturale di Vendicari and the coast

A line of small-town resorts stretch from Siracusa to Vittoria, and in between there are several sweeps of pristine sands: most notably at the **Riserva Naturale di Vendicari**, 10km south of Noto (daily: summer 7am–8pm; winter 7am–6.30pm; parking €3; free entry) a lovely coastal nature reserve. Paths lead to unspoilt beaches of white gold sand and salt lakes, that, between October and March, attract flamingoes, herons, cranes, black storks and pelicans. Until recently turtles would nest on the beaches, but local appetite for turtle soup led to their disappearance. There are now projects under way to encourage the turtles back to Vendicari. For **accommodation** and **food**, try the *Agriturismo Calamosche* (℡ 3478.587.319; April–Oct; ➊) inside the reserve at the Cala Mosche entrance: look out for a hand-painted sign off the main road. They have seven simple rooms and produce their own vegetables, almonds, lemons and oil, which are served along with local hams and cheeses, fish and game in the reasonably priced restaurant.

To the southeast of the reserve is **Capo Passero**, where the Ionian Sea meets the Sicilian Channel. If you have your own transport, follow signs from the little resort of *Portopalo di Capo Passero* along tiny roads between huge polytunnels of tomatoes, to the **Isola dei Correnti**. If the sea is not too wild, you can wade out to this little island. Continuing west, there is a stunning two-kilometre sweep of sand at **SAMPIERI**, a small fishing village and resort. If you want to **stay** you couldn't do better than ⚓*Poggio Bellavista*, (☎0932.939.068, ⓦwww.poggio-bellavista.com; ❷) a welcoming and comfortable B&B, with five pretty rooms, perched on the hillside a kilometre outside town. The English-speaking owners go out of their way to make guests feel at home. There are good **beaches** further west as well, most notably Kamarina, with evocative, if incomprehensible, relics of a Hellenistic-Roman city. Beyond here, the coast gets too close to Sicily's ugliest and most polluted town, the industrial port of **Gela**, for comfort.

The Baroque towns

The **earthquake of 1693**, which destroyed utterly the towns and villages of southeastern Sicily, had one positive and lasting effect. Where there were ruins, a new generation of confident architects raised new planned towns in an opulent Baroque style. All were harmonious creations, and in 2001 eight of them were selected by UNESCO as World Heritage Sites. Funding has poured into the area, and in recent years there has been an explosion of new hotels and B&Bs. **Noto**, recently restored to perfection, is the most eagerly promoted by the tourist board, while **Ragusa Ibla**, a Baroque town built on a medieval plan, has become a destination for the stylish international set, with a handful of bijou B&Bs and a couple of Michelin-starred restaurants. Liveliest of the lot is **Módica**, a vibrant town famous for the production of chocolate.

Noto

NOTO, half an hour by train or bus from Siracusa, is easily the most harmonious town of those rebuilt after the earthquake, and during the mid-nineteenth century, it replaced Siracusa as provincial capital. Planned and laid out by Giovanni Battista Landolina and adorned by Gagliardi, there's not a town to touch Noto for uniform excellence in design and execution. Each year more monuments are restored, regaining their original honey-coloured facades, and each year more tour groups visit.

The pedestrianized main Corso is lined with some of Sicily's most captivating buildings, from the flat-fronted church of **San Francesco**, on the right, along as far as Piazza XVI Maggio and the graceful, curving church of **San Domenico**. And **Piazza Municipio** is arguably Sicily's finest piazza with its perfectly proportioned, tree-planted expanses. The **Duomo**, a fine example of Baroque at its most muscular and finished in 1770, has reopened following the collapse of its dome in 1996. Opposite, the **Municipio** (or Palazzo Ducezio) is flanked by its own green spaces, the arcaded building presenting a lovely, simple facade of columns and long stone balconies. Head up the steep Via Corrado Nicolaci, an eighteenth-century street that contains the extraordinary

At the time of writing, a **new airport** for low-cost flights was due to open at Comiso. Airlines likely to use the airport include Ryanair, easyJet and Meridiana.

Palazzo Villadorata at no. 18, its six balconies supported by a panoply of griffins, galloping horses and fat-cheeked cherubs.

Practicalities

If you want to stay in Noto you'll need to book ahead in high season. The **tourist office** in Piazza XVI Maggio (Mon–Sat 9am–1.30pm; ℡0931.836.744, Ⓦwww.apt-siracusa.it) has details of numerous **rented rooms** and **B&B** places. Among them are *B&B Gulliver*, Via Tasca 2 (℡0931.894.119, Ⓦwww .bbgulliver.it; ❶–❷), which has four comfortable rooms, three with bathrooms, and a kitchen for the use of guests; otherwise there's the friendly *B&B Centro Storico*, Corso Vittorio Emanuele 54 (℡0931.812.063, Ⓦwww.centro-storico .com; no credit cards; ❷–❸). There's also a **youth hostel**, *Il Castello*, housed in a converted *palazzo* on Via Fratelli Bandiera in the upper part of town (℡392.415.7899, Ⓦwww.notobarocca.com/ostello; €16). If you prefer a **hotel**, try the charming *Albergo della Fontanella*, Via Pilo Rosolino 3 (℡0931.894.735, Ⓦwww.albergolafontanella.it; ❸), in a restored nineteenth-century *palazzo* in the *centro storico*. A good alternative in summer is to stay on the coast at **Noto Marina**, 8km southeast, so you can spend days on the beach and evenings sightseeing. There's a cluster of holiday hotels here.

You can **eat** at the bustling, straightforward *Trattoria Giglio*, just to the side of the town hall at Piazza Municipio 8–10 (℡0931.838.640) and at the small *Trattoria del Carmine*, Via Ducezio 9 (℡0931.838.705), which serves *cucina casalinga* at low prices. Don't leave town without sampling the ice creams and granitas at *Caffè Sicilia*, near the Duomo at Corso Vittorio Emanuele 125, made in traditional flavours such as jasmine and rose.

Módica

Linked by both train and bus with Siracusa and Ragusa, **MÓDICA**, is another Baroque town well worth a visit. A powerful medieval base of the Chiaramonte, Módica's upper town is watched over by the magnificent eighteenth-century facade of **San Giorgio**, at the head of a vast flight of steps. It's thought that Gagliardi was responsible for this: the elliptical facade is topped by a belfry, the church approached by a symmetrical double staircase which switchbacks up across the upper roads of the town. Today, Módica is a vibrant town, famous for the production of **chocolate**. It is powerful, gritty stuff, made as the Mayans did, a technique introduced to Sicily by the Spanish, without cocoa butter, and without heat, so that the sugar doesn't melt, and the texture remains crunchy. Traditional flavours are vanilla and cinnamon, innovations include sea salt and chilli. Sample it at *Caffè dell'Arte*, Corso Umberto 1, 114 or *Bonajuto*, in a little alleyway across the street.

Accommodation includes *L'Orangerie*, a tranquil, refined B&B tucked off Corso Umberto 1 at Vico de Naro 5 (℡0932.754.703, Ⓦwww.lorangerie .it; ❸–❹) with three suites and four rooms in a *palazzo* with frescoed ceilings and flower-filled terraces. For somewhere to **eat** in Módica, try *Osteria dei Sapori Perduti*, Corso Umberto 1 228-30, which serves reasonably priced traditional dishes with a strong emphasis on beans and pulses. The menu is in Sicilian, but translations are available.

Ragusa

RAGUSA is a town with two identities, literally split in two by the earthquake: the old town of **Ragusa Ibla**, on a jut of land above its valley, was flattened, and within a few years a new town, **Ragusa Superiore** was built on a grand planned grid, on a higher ridge to the west. Meanwhile, Ibla was rebuilt – in Baroque style – along its old medieval streetplan.

In the second half of the last century people began to move out of Ibla for the modern comforts of life in the apartment buildings rapidly sprouting up in Ragusa Superiore. All commercial and social activity shifted to here, and until ten years ago Ibla was all but abandoned. Since then, thanks to generous European and government funding, Ibla has been painstakingly restored, and scores of B&Bs and stylish second homes now occupy its lovely limestone Baroque houses and palaces. However, with a population of just 2000 (out of a total of 70,000), and little in the way of ordinary shops or bars, Ibla is very much a museum town, virtually pedestrianized and dedicated only to tourism. Ragusa Superiore, on the other hand, is a busy and likeable provincial capital, mostly modern, but with a good slice of Baroque on the edge of the cleft between the two cities, where you may well want to spend a little time.

Arrival, information and accommodation

The **train station**, which is also where **buses** arrive, is in Ragusa Superiore. A left turn takes you along the main road and over the exposed **Ponte Nuovo**, one of three bridges spanning a huge gully in the ridge. The **tourist office** is in Ragusa Ibla at Via Capitano Bocchieri 33 (Mon–Fri 9am–1.30pm, Tues also 4.30–6.30pm; ☏0932.221.529 or 800.015.477. The best accommodation is in Ragusa Ibla.

Caelum Hyblae Salita Specula 11, Ragusa Ibla ☏0932.220.402 or 329.072.6015, ⊛www .bbcaelumhyblae.it. Tucked behind the apse of the Duomo, this refined B&B has five cool, minimalist rooms with linen sheets, magnificent views, and terraces on its roof and on the ground floor. The name of the hotel originates from when the sixteenth-century astrologist Giovanni Battista Hodierna observed the night sky from here. The owner organizes occasional chamber music evenings. ❸
Eremo della Giubiliana 7.5km out of Ragusa, along the road to Marina di Ragusa ☏0932.669.119, ⊛www.eremodellagiubiliana.it. An upmarket agriturismo (with its own 700m private airstrip no less) housed in the restored buildings of a feudal estate dating back to the twelfth century. The grounds are gorgeous, and you can dine on their own organically grown food. ❼
Le Chicce Salita Specula 7, Ragusa Ibla ☏0932.239.180 or 330.849.862,

⊛www.bblechicche.com. Wonderful roof terrace and five rooms furnished with a stylish mix of antique and contemporary furniture, including hand-painted wardrobes, Philippe Starck chairs and mirrors that reproduce the shapes of the columns in the Duomo. ❷
Locanda Don Serafino Via XI Febbraio 15, Ragusa Ibla ☏0932.222.0065, ⊛www.locandadonserafino .it. A small, exclusive hotel, beautifully set within the hefty stone walls of a nineteenth-century mansion. Two of the rooms, occupying the former stables, are carved straight into the bare rock, and one of them (room 8) has a bathroom inside a cave. ❻
L'Orto sul Tetto Via Ten. Distefano 56, Ragusa Ibla ☏0932.247.785 or 338.478.0484, ⊛www .lortosultetto.it. A warm, friendly place a short walk from the Duomo with three serene bedrooms, run by a mother and son. Breakfasts are served on a roof terrace full of plants and include pastries fresh from the bakery. ❷

Ragusa Superiore

Ragusa Superiore is essentially a gridded Baroque town, slipping off to right and left on either side of the steeply sloping **Corso Italia**. To the right, down the Corso on a wide terrace above Piazza San Giovanni, stands the **Duomo**, conceived on a grand, symmetrical scale. Finished in 1774, its tapered columns and fine doorways are a fairly sombre background to the vigorous small-town atmosphere around. Back towards the train station, underneath the Ponte Nuovo, there's an important **Museo Archeologico** (daily 9am–1.30pm & 4–7.30pm; €2) dealing mainly with finds from the archeological site of Kamarina (sixth century BC) on the coast to the southwest.

Rasuga Ibla

It's Ragusa Ibla, the original **lower town**, where most people head, its weather-beaten roofs straddling the outcrop of rock about twenty-minutes' walk away. The main attraction, situated in the gleaming central core of the town, is Ibla's Duomo, **San Giorgio**. Stridently placed at the top of Piazza Duomo, it's one of the masterpieces of Sicilian Baroque, built by Rosario Gagliardi and finished in 1784. The glorious three-tiered facade, sets of triple columns climbing up the wedding cake exterior to a balconied belfry, is an imaginative work, though typically not much enhanced by venturing inside. As with Gagliardi's other important church in Módica (see p.962), all the beauty is in the immediacy of the powerful exterior.

The whole town – often deathly quiet – is ripe for aimless wandering. Gagliardi gets another credit for the elegant rounded facade of the church of **San Giuseppe** in Piazza Pola, a few steps below the Duomo, while Corso XXV Aprile continues down past abandoned *palazzi* to the **Giardino Ibleo** (daily 8am–8pm), gardens occupying the very edge of the spur on which the town is built. If you can't face the walk back to the upper town, the **bus navetta** from Largo Kamerina plies between the upper and lower towns every thirty minutes or so.

Eating and drinking

Ibla has two rival Michelin-starred **restaurants**, each of them well worth splashing out on. However, if you are on a budget, a good alternative is a picnic; wander down narrow, curving Corso 25 Aprile, lined with fancy shops selling local produce. Try *Salumeria Barocco*, which has a superb range of carefully sourced local cheeses. There is also a bakery at number 84 where you can get bread, pizza and *impanata* (*calzone*-like pastries filled with vegetables, ham or cheese). Another good place for a simple snack is the *Forno San Paolo*, opposite the car park at the entrance to Ibla. It bakes traditional *scacce*, scorched bread-dough pastries filled with aubergine, spinach, cauliflower or the like.

Pasticceria di Pasquale Corso Vittorio Veneto 104, Ragusa Superiore. The best ice cream and pastries in either town. Just downhill from the Duomo of San Giovanni.

Ristorante Duomo Via Capitano Bocchieri 31 Ragusa Ibla ☎0932.651.265. Meticulously sourced Sicilian ingredients reworked to stunning effect, in what is arguably Sicily's greatest restaurant. Put yourself in the hands of chef Ciccio Sultano, and opt for one of the tasting menus with wines, selected from the copious cellar, to match each course. Expensive but worth it. Closed Sun & Mon in summer, Sun eve & Mon in winter.

Ristorante Locanda Don Serafino Via Orfanotrofio 39, Ragusa Ibla ☎0932.248.778. In a vaulted medieval wine cellar, lit by candles, this is a place to feast on artisan cheeses, Ragusana beef and lamb, Nebrodi mountain pork and fresh fish. Try the fillet beef with tobacco and salt-baked potatoes and don't miss the selection of puddings made with local carob. Closed Tues.

Trattoria la Bettola Largo Kamarina, Ibla ☎0932.653.377. A rarity in Ibla: a simple, inexpensive family-run trattoria with red-and-white tablecloths that has been around for 30 years, serving local dishes such as *maiale ubriaco*, pork braised in wine and wild herbs.

Agrigento

Though handsome, well-sited and awash with medieval atmosphere, **AGRIGENTO** is rarely visited for the town itself. The interest instead focuses on the substantial **remains** of Pindar's "most beautiful city of mortals", a couple of kilometres below. Here, strung out along a ridge facing the sea, is a series of **Doric temples** – the most captivating of Sicilian Greek remains and a grouping unique outside Greece.

In 581 BC colonists from nearby Gela and from Rhodes founded the city of **Akragas** between the rivers of Hypsas and Akragas. They surrounded it with a mighty wall, formed in part by a higher ridge on which stood the acropolis (and, today, the modern town). The southern limit of the ancient city was a second, lower ridge and it was here, in the "**Valle dei Templi**", that the city architects erected their sacred buildings during the fifth century BC.

Valle dei Templi

A road winds down from the modern city to the Valle dei Templi, with buses stopping at a car park between the two separate sections of **archeological remains** (the eastern and western zones), and the museum (see below). Entrance to both the eastern and western temple sites costs €8, or €10 including the museum (daily 8.30am–5pm in winter, 8.30am–7pm in summer, usually also 8pm–midnight in July and August; ☏0922.621.611). Guided tours are sometimes offered in English – ask at the information kiosk in the car park for details.

The eastern zone

The **eastern zone** is unenclosed and is at its crowd-free best in early morning or late evening. A path climbs up to the oldest of Akragas's temples, the **Tempio di Ercole** (Hercules). Probably begun in the last decades of the sixth century BC, nine of the original 38 columns have been re-erected, everything else scattered around like a waiting jigsaw puzzle. Retrace your steps back to the path which leads to the glorious **Tempio della Concordia**, dated to around 430 BC: perfectly preserved and beautifully sited, with fine views to the city and the sea, the tawny stone lending the structure warmth and strength. That it's still so complete is explained by its conversion (in the sixth century AD) to a Christian church. Restored to its (more or less) original layout in the eighteenth century, it's kept its lines and slightly tapering columns, although it's fenced off to keep the crowds at bay. The path continues, following the line of the ancient city walls, to the **Tempio di Giunone** (or Hera), an engaging half-ruin standing at the very edge of the ridge. The patches of red visible here and there on the masonry denote fire damage, probably from the sack of Akragas by the Carthaginians in 406 BC.

The western zone

The **western zone**, back along the path and beyond the car park, is less impressive, a vast tangle of stone and fallen masonry from a variety of temples. Most notable is the mammoth construction that was the **Tempio di Giove**, or Temple of Olympian Zeus. The largest Doric temple ever known, it was never completed, left in ruins by the Carthaginians and further damaged by earthquakes. Still, the stereobate remains, while on the ground, face to the sky, lies an eight-metre-high *telamone*: a supporting column sculpted as a male figure, arms raised and bent to bear the temple's weight. Other scattered remains litter the area, including the so-called **Tempio dei Dioscuri** (Castor and Pollux), rebuilt in 1832 and actually made up of unrelated pieces from the confused rubble on the ground.

Museo Nazionale Archeologico

Via dei Templi leads back to the town from the car park via the excellent **Museo Nazionale Archeologico** (Tues–Sat 9am–7pm, Mon & Sun 9am–1pm; €6). The extraordinarily rich collection is devoted to finds from the city and the surrounding area; the best displays are the cases of vases (sixth to third century BC) and a reassembled *telamone* stacked against one wall. Nip over the road on the way out for the **Hellenistic–Roman quarter** (daily 9am until 1hr before sunset; free), which contains lines of houses, inhabited intermittently until the fifth century AD, many with mosaic designs still discernible.

Agrigento

It would be a mistake not to scout round the town of **Agrigento**. Thoroughly medieval at its heart, its tiny stepped streets and fine churches look down over the Valle dei Templi (dramatically floodlit at night) and beyond to the sea. The main street, **Via Atenea**, starts at the eastern edge of the old town, above the train station, the streets off to the right harbouring ramshackle *palazzi* and the church of **Santa Maria dei Greci**. Built over a fifth-century BC Greek temple, of which the flattened columns are visible in the nave, while an underground tunnel reveals the stylobate and column stumps, all part of the church's foundations.

When you're done with the ruins and the old town, you could always head out to the local beach resort of **SAN LEONE**, a pleasant, low-key place 6km away, served by half-hourly buses from outside the train station. Even better, drive or take a bus (run by Lumia ℡0922.20.414) to **REALMONTE**, 15km to the west. A couple of kilometres from here, a bank of curving white cliffs sculpted by wind and waves into a wildly tilting natural staircase – the **Scala dei Turchi** – descend to the sea: from Realmonte, follow the signs to Scala dei Turchi, and leave your car in the car park, from where it's a ten-minute walk. There's a pleasant **B&B**, *Scala dei Turchi* in the piazza at Realmonte (℡0922.816.238, ⓦwww.scaladeiturchi.net).

Practicalities

Trains arrive at Agrigento Centrale station at the edge of the old town; don't get out at Agrigento Bassa 3km north of town. **Regional** buses and **city buses** to the temples and the beach at San Leone use the terminal in Piazza Roselli, near the post office. Buy city bus tickets (€1) from kiosks or *tabacchi*. The old town stretches west of the three main interlocking squares, piazzas Marconi, Aldo Moro and Vittorio Emanuele. Via Atenea is Agrigento's principal artery, running west from Piazza Aldo Moro, off which runs Via Empedocle with the **tourist office** at no. 73 (Mon–Fri 8am–2pm plus Wed 3.30–6pm; ℡800.236.837).

Finding **accommodation** in Agrigento shouldn't be a problem, except perhaps in peak season. To find a B&B on spec, wander along Via Atenea, though if you want to stay at the very special *Camere a Sud*, Via Ficani 6 off Via Atenea (℡349.638.4424, ⓦwww.camereasud.it; ❷) book ahead; it's quiet, comfortable and sunny, with white-walled rooms, vivid soft furnishings, paintings by Catanese artist Antonio Recca and a roof terrace where you can while away the hours. Another good option is B&B *Portatenea*, Via Atenea, on the corner with Via C. Battisti (℡349.093.7492, ⓦwww.portatenea.com; ❷) with colour-drenched rooms, a roof terrace and friendly owners. For full-on luxury, stay at the *Villa Athena*, Via dei Templi (℡0922.596.288, ⓦwww.athenahotels.com; ❻), right in the archeological zone, with a pool, garden, restaurant and big windows soaking up the views. You can **camp** 6km away at the coastal resort of San Leone, at *Internazionale San Leone* (℡0922.416.121); bus #2 from outside the train station (every 30min until 9pm).

As for **eating**, there's the budget *Atenea* (☎0922.20.247), a friendly, family-run trattoria at Via Ficani 32, in a quiet courtyard just off the Via Atenea (no credit cards; closed Sun). In the same neighbourhood, at Via Giambertoni 2, the folksy *Ambasciata di Sicilia* (☎0922.20.526; closed Mon) is small but has a view-laden terrace and serves good *antipasto rustico* and fresh fish. The best ice creams in town (try the fresh ricotta, pistachio, or almond) are at *Le Cuspidi*, Piazza Cavour 19. There is also a branch at San Leone by the Agrigento bus stop.

Eraclea Minoa

From Agrigento you're well positioned for moving on into western Sicily, and frequent buses get you to Sciacca in around two and a half hours. If you can, though, first drop in on the other important local Greek site, **ERACLEA MINOA** – originally named Minoa after the Cretan king Minos, who chased Daedalus from Crete to Sicily and founded a city where he landed. The Greeks settled here in the sixth century, later adding the tag Heraklea. A buffer between the two great cities at Akragas, 40km to the east, and Selinus, 60km west, Eraclea Minoa was dragged into endless border disputes, but in spite of this it flourished. Most of the remains date from the fourth century BC, Eraclea Minoa's most important period, three hundred years or so before the town declined.

The **site** (daily 9am to 1hr before sunset; free) is finely situated right on the coast, at the mouth of the River Platani. Apart from the good **walls**, once 6km long, which survive in interrupted sections, the main attraction is the sandstone **theatre**; some of the finds are held in a small on-site **museum**. While you're here, you'll be hard put to resist a trip down to the **beach**, one of the best on Sicily's southern coast, backed by pine trees and chalky cliffs.

Practicalities

Without your own transport, you can get here between June and September by **buses** from Cattolica Eraclea or from the SS115, both accessible from Agrigento, but outside the summer months you're going to have to do some tough walking: take any bus running between Agrigento and Sciacca and ask the driver to let you off at the turning; it's 5km west of Montallegro, on the SS115, and the site is another 3.5km from there.

At the foot of the road from the site, a couple of **bar-restaurants** sit right on the beach with **rooms** advertised – *Rido Gabbiano* is a good option here, with rooms and apartments (☎0922.846.061 or 339.813.7907).

Heading on, walk west from the site turning and you should be able to flag down a bus going to Sciacca.

Inland to Enna

The most scenically rewarding parts of Sicily's **interior** are in the east, primarily the hill-towns and villages that lie in a wide half-circle to the north of Enna.

From Agrigento, however, there are several worthwhile routes – most only practicable for travellers with transport. One route goes by way of **Sant'Angelo Muxaro** (daily buses from Agrigento), beyond which begins the most convoluted approach to Palermo, the twisting road climbing up to 1000m at Prizzi, from where there are occasional bus services down to **Corleone**. A fairly large town for these parts, it lent Mario Puzo's fictional Godfather, Don Corleone, his adopted family name – and it's the name of one of Sicily's most notorious real-life Mafia clans. There's a bus from Corleone to Palermo, another 60km.

The other option from Agrigento, better if you want to head on to the most appealing parts of the interior, is the **route to Enna**. There's a local bus service that connects up the nearer places, while trains make the journey, too, up through gentle, tree-planted slopes and then across the hilltops. At Canicatti the line splits, trains running south to Licata, on the coast.

Enna and around

From a bulging V-shaped ridge almost 1000m up, **ENNA** lords it over the surrounding hills of central Sicily. The approach to this doughty mountain stronghold is formidable, the bus climbing slowly out of the valley and looping across the solid crag to the summit and the town. For obvious strategic reasons, Enna was a magnet for successive hostile armies, who in turn besieged and fortified the town, each doing their damnedest to disprove Livy's description of Enna as *inexpugnabilis*.

Despite the destructive attention, most of Enna's remains are medieval and in good shape, with the prize exhibit the thirteenth-century **Castello di Lombardia** (Easter–Oct daily 8am–8pm; free), dominating the easternmost spur of town. A mighty construction with its strong walls complete, it guards the steep slopes on either side of Enna, its six surviving towers (out of an original twenty) providing lookouts. From the tallest, the **Torre Pisana**, the magnificent **views** take in Enna itself, some rugged countryside in all directions and, if you're lucky, Mount Etna.

In the centre of town virtually all the accredited sights lie stretched out along and around **Via Roma**, which descends from the castle. It's a narrow street, broken by small piazzas – one of which fronts the hemmed-in **Duomo**, dating in part from 1307. The spacious sixteenth-century interior (9am–noon & 4–7pm; free) features huge supporting alabaster columns, the bases of which are covered with an amorphous writhing mass of carved figures. There's a museum worth seeing as well – the **Museo Varisano** – if it has reopened, which is just over the way in Piazza Mazzini; it covers Neolithic to Roman times and includes a fine series of painted Greek vases.

Via Roma slopes down to the rectangular **Piazza Vittorio Emanuele**, focal point of the evening *passeggiata*. Off here, there's a long cliff-edge belvedere, while the bottom of the piazza is marked by the plain, high wall of the **Chiesa di San Francesco**, whose massive sixteenth-century tower previously formed part of the town's system of watchtowers. This linked the castle with the **Torre di Federico**, which stands in isolation in its little park in the largely modern south of the town. An octagonal tower, 24m high, it's a survivor of the alterations to the city made by Frederick of Aragon who added a (now hidden) underground passage linking it to the *castello*.

Practicalities

All long-distance and most local **buses** use the bus terminal on Viale Diaz in the new town – turn right out of the terminal, right again down Corso Sicilia and it's around a ten-minute walk to Piazza Vittorio Emanuele. Enna's

Italian football

Calcio – football, or soccer – is Italy's national sport, and enjoys a fanatical following across the country. It's usually possible to get tickets to see one of the big sides – as long as they're not playing each other – and it's one of the best introductions to modern Italian culture you'll find.

Pretty in pink – Palermo players celebrate ▲

AC Milan fans light up the San Siro ▼

The history, the teams

Italy's first football club, Genoa, was created by a group of English expats who also set up the country's first league with three clubs from Turin in 1898. Genoa regularly won the championship in the early years of the twentieth century, although the first national league, formed in 1929, was won by Internazionale of Milan. Since World War II, Italian football has been dominated by Internazionale, AC Milan and Juventus (Turin), who have between them won the *scudetto* (championship) 54 times. It's a testament to the English origins of the game that AC Milan, as well as Genoa, continue to use anglicized names, and to sport the cross of St George in their insignia. Unfortunately, the other thing that has been copied from the English is hooliganism, which is rife in Italian football. It led to the death of a policeman at a Catania game in February 2007 – following which the entire league programme was cancelled. The previous year, 2006, was also full of drama. While the Italian national team triumphed at the World Cup in Germany, domestic football was rocked by a match-fixing scandal with Juventus and a number of other top clubs (Lazio, Fiorentina and AC Milan among them) all implicated and given stiff penalties.

Despite the bad publicity, Juventus and AC Milan, along with Internazionale, continue to take turns at the top of Serie A (Italy's premier division), while AS Roma and SS Lazio of Rome are also regular contenders, although Lazio's star has faded after their fans became perceived as one of the worst examples of Italy's right-wing lunatic fringe. Elsewhere in the country, Venice's hometown club, Venezia, was once a contender but has been consigned to the lower divisions after falling foul of one of the first match-fixing scandals. In the same region, **Chievo Verona** and **Udinese** remain unfashionable but strong and stable clubs. In Tuscany, **Fiorentina** reckon themselves among the big teams, while Emilia-Romagna's big club is **Parma**, who have declined since their heyday in the 1990s and now reside in Serie B. Further south, **Napoli** are beginning to relive their Eighties "glory days", when they were led by Diego Maradona, though they still struggle to fill their giant 80,000 capacity stadium. Conversely, the other big southern clubs, **Palermo** and **Catania** of Sicily, and **Cagliari** of Sardinia, currently thrive in Serie A.

We've given details of the big city clubs in the Guide, but wherever you are, grab a paper and see what's on. There are companies that put together packages to see Serie A games: try their websites at Ⓦ www.fanfare-events.com or www.footballencounters.co.uk.

▲ Appealing to the great referee in the sky

▼ Italian football press

▼ David Trezeguet of Juventus

Talking football

Italy's newspapers are relatively light on sports coverage, but if you speak a little bit of Italian and are a keen football fan it can be worth getting hold of a copy of one of the three big Italian daily sports papers: the pink *Gazzeto dell Sport*, *Tuttosport* or the *Corriere dello Sport*. Here are some of the words you'll need to know for a proper appreciation of the Italian national game.

▶▶ **corner**   angolo
▶▶ **foul**   fallo
▶▶ **goalkeeper**   portiere
▶▶ **manager**   allenatore
▶▶ **match**   partita
▶▶ **midfielder**   centrocampista
▶▶ **offside**   fuorigioco
▶▶ **pitch**   campo
▶▶ **referee**   arbitro

Football shirts on sale in Florence ▲

Paolo Maldini – still playing for AC Milan aged 40 ▼

Going to a game

Going to see one of the top teams, especially AC or Inter Milan at the San Siro, or Juventus (currently playing at Turin's Stadio Olimpico while their ground is rebuilt), may be one of the highlights of your trip. And because of the number of teams – both professional and semi-pro – there's always likely to be a game on close to where you're staying. Serie A games are played on Sunday afternoons, though there are also evening kick-offs on Saturday and Sunday, while most Serie B games take place on Saturday afternoons, with evening games on Friday and Monday. Serie A **tickets** cost €15–20 for seats in the *curva* (end) stands, although these are usually snapped up by diehard fans or *tifosi*. The corner seats, in the so-called *distinti* stands, may be easier to find and cost €25 or so, while seats in the *tribuna* (side stands) start at around €50 and go up to €100 for the very best seats. Most clubs sell tickets online, but many also have club shops in city centres; alternatively, tickets are sold direct from the stadium. For sustenance during the match, you should try *borghetti* – little vials of cold coffee "corrected" with a stiff spirit.

An Italian dream team

Italy has produced some of the world's finest footballers. Here's our ultimate selection of masters past and present:
▶▶ **goalkeeper** Dino Zoff (Juventus)
▶▶ **defenders** Claudio Gentile (Juventus), Fabio Cannavaro (Real Madrid), Giacinto Facchetti (Inter), Paolo Maldini (Milan), Franco Baresi (Milan)
▶▶ **midfielders** Gianni Rivera (Milan), Marco Tardelli (Juventus)
▶▶ **forwards** Roberto Baggio (Juventus), Luigi Riva (Cagliari), Sandro Mazzola (Inter)

train station is 5km below town – a local bus runs roughly hourly to the centre (less frequently on Sun), while a taxi will cost €8. You can reach everywhere in Enna itself very easily on foot, though should you need to take a local bus (to nearby Pergusa, for example – see below), tickets (€1) can be bought from *tabacchi* and are valid for one hour. The **tourist office** is at Piazza Colajanni 6 in the upper town next to *Hotel Sicilia* (Mon–Fri 7.45am–2.15pm, Wed 2.45–6.15pm; ☏0935.500.875).

Accommodation includes a pleasant B&B, *Proserpina*, centrally located on Piazza Scelfo (☏333.299.1957, Ⓦwww.bbenna.it; ❶). For **meals**, *La Fontana*, Via Vulturo 6 (☏0935.25.465; closed Fri in winter), is friendly and does homemade pasta; or there's fresh fish at the pricier, more refined *Ristorante Ariston*, Via Roma 353 (☏0935.26.038; closed Sun). The **market** in Enna is held on Tuesday mornings in Piazza Europa, below the Torre di Federico II.

Pergusa

From Enna, you can head out to the nearby Lago di **PERGUSA**, supposedly the site of Hades' abduction of Persephone to the underworld; buses (#5; roughly hourly) leave from outside San Francesco church. These days the famed Lago di Pergusa is encircled by a motor-racing track, alongside which are several places to **stay**. The most original of these is *La Casa del Poeta*, Contrada Parasporino (☏0935.541.578, Ⓦwww.lacasadelpoeta.it; ❸) about a kilometre from the lake, the rooms are serene and minimalist, and the grounds include a swimming pool.

Piazza Armerina and around

To the south of Enna, less than an hour away by bus, **PIAZZA ARMERINA** lies amid thick tree-planted hills; it's a quiet, unassuming place mainly seventeenth and eighteenth century in appearance, with a skyline pierced by towers and houses huddled together under the joint protection of castle and cathedral. All in all, it's a thoroughly pleasant place to idle around, though the real local draw is an imperial **Roman villa** that stands in rugged countryside at Casale, 5km southwest of Piazza Armerina. Hidden under mud for seven hundred years, the excavated remains reveal a lavish villa, probably a hunting lodge and summer home, decorated with polychromatic mosaic floors that are unique in the Roman world for their quality and extent.

Practicalities

Buses drop you in Piazza Sen. Marescalchi, in the lower town. The old town is up the hill, centred around Piazza Garibaldi, off which is the **tourist office**, at Via Generale Muscara 47 (Mon–Fri 8am–2pm, plus Wed 3–6.30pm; ☏0935.680.201, Ⓦwww.comune.piazzaarmerina.it). Just opened on Piazza Duomo is the sleek, designer hotel *Suite d'Autore*, (☏0935.688.553, Ⓦwww.suitedautore.it; ❹–❺). If that's too extravagant for your taste, try one of the B&Bs, such as *Il Giardino delle Zagare*, Via Favara 15 (☏0935.680.388, Ⓦwww.ilgiardinodellezagare.com; ❷) which has a double room, a couple of mini apartments and a garden. Another option is the *Ostello del Borgo*, Largo San Giovanni 6 (☏0935.687.019, Ⓦwww.ostellodelborgo.it; ❷, €16.50 in dormitory with AIG card, available here for €3), which has triples, doubles and dorm beds, in a refurbished fifteenth-century monastery.

Eating options include *La Tavernetta*, in town at Via Cavour 14 (℡0935.685.883; closed Sun), which has reasonably priced fish, while *Da Pepito*, Via Roma 140 (℡0935.685.737; closed Tues in winter), opposite the park, serves tasty Sicilian dishes. Three kilometres outside town in Contrada Bellia, *Al Fogher* (℡0935.684.123; closed Sun eve & Mon) serves up delights such as risotto with goose liver, ricotta and pumpkin.

The Villa Romana del Casale

A regular **bus service** runs to the villa between May and September from Piazza Sen. Marescalchi in Piazza Armerina, leaving at 9am, 10am, 11am, noon, 3pm, 4pm, 5pm and 6pm, returning from the villa half an hour later. Otherwise you'll have to take a **taxi** (around €25 there and back, including waiting time) or **walk** the 6km: head down Via Matteotti or Via Principato and follow the signs; it takes around an hour on foot and is an attractive walk. It's also feasible to visit on a day-trip **from Enna**, but check the bus schedules before setting out.

There are major restoration works in progress at the **Villa Romana** but on most days you should still be able to see just about everything. For as long as the work lasts, ticket prices have been halved and entrance hours reduced (currently daily 10am–5pm; €3; when work is finished daily 8am to 1hr before sunset; €6). The villa dates from the early fourth century BC and was used right up until the twelfth century when a mudslide left it largely covered until comprehensive excavations in the 1950s. It's been covered again since to protect the mosaics, while walkways lead visitors through the rooms in as logical an order as possible. The **mosaics** themselves are identifiable as fourth-century Roman-African school, which explains many of the more exotic scenes and animals portrayed; they also point to the villa having had an important owner, possibly Maximianus Herculeus, co-emperor with Diocletian.

The **main entrance** leads into a wide courtyard with fountains, where the **thermae** (baths) group around an octagonal *frigidarium* and a central mosaic showing a lively marine scene. A walkway leads out of the baths and into the villa proper, to the massive central court or **peristyle**, whose surrounding corridors are decorated with animal-head mosaics. From here, a balcony looks down on one of the villa's most interesting pictures, a boisterous circus scene showing a chariot race. Small rooms beyond, on either side of the peristyle, reveal only fragmentary geometric patterns, although one contains probably the villa's most famous image, a two-tiered scene of ten realistically muscular **Roman girls in "bikinis"**, taking part in various gymnastic and athletic activities.

Beyond the peristyle, a long, covered corridor contains the most extraordinary of the mosaics: the **great hunting scene**, which sets armed and shield-bearing hunters against a panoply of wild animals. Along the entire sixty-metre length of the mosaic are tigers, ostriches, elephants, even a rhino, being trapped, bundled up and down gangplanks and into cages, destined for the Games back in Rome. The square-hatted figure overseeing the operation is probably Maximianus himself: his personal area of responsibility in the imperial Tetrarchy was North Africa, where much of the scene is set.

Other rooms beyond are nearly all on a grand scale. The **triclinium**, a dining room with three apses, features the labours of Hercules, and a path leads around the back to the **private apartments**, based around a large basilica. The best mosaics here are a children's circus, where tiny chariots are drawn by colourful birds, and a children's hunt, the kids chased and pecked by the hares and peacocks they're supposed to snare.

Trápani and the west

The **west** of Sicily is a land apart. Skirting around the coast from **Trápani** – easily the largest town in the region – the cubic whitewashed houses, palm trees, active fishing harbours and sunburned lowlands seem more akin to Africa than Europe; and historically, the west of the island has always looked south. The earliest of all Sicilian sites, the mountain haunt of **Érice** was dominated by Punic influence, the Carthaginians themselves entrenched in **Marsala**, at Sicily's westernmost point, for several hundred years, while the Saracen invaders took their first steps on the island at **Mazara del Vallo**, a town still strongly Arabic at heart. The Greeks never secured the same foothold in Sicily's west as elsewhere, although the remains at **Segesta** and **Selinunte** count among the island's best. Also worth seeing are the three islands of the **Égadi** archipelago, and the stunning stretch of coastline protected by the **Riserva Naturale dello Zingaro**.

Trápani and around

Out on something of a limb, **TRÁPANI** is an attractive enough town, though with little to keep you long – more a stopover, perhaps, en route to the offshore Égadi Islands (see p.975) or inland to Érice (see p.973). A rich trading centre throughout the early Middle Ages, halfway point for Tunis and Africa, Trápani has suffered years of decline since then, and today ails from its remote position on Sicily's western tip, despite the revitalization of the huge salt pans to the south of town.

Arrival and information

Approaching by land from the east of the island, you'll arrive in the modern part of town: most **buses** (including those to and from Érice) pull up at the terminal in Piazza Malta; **trains** stop just around the corner in Piazza Umberto I. If you're heading straight off to the Égadi Islands, note that the fast buses from Palermo, Palermo airport and Agrigento stop at the ferry and hydrofoil terminals, as well as the bus station. **Ferries** for the Égadi Islands, Pantelleria, Cágliari and Tunis dock at the Molo di Sanità, while **hydrofoils** for the Égadi Islands, Ústica and Naples dock to the east of the Molo, on Via A. Stati. Trápani's **airport**, 15km south of the centre at Birgi, has flights from Italian cities and Pantelleria.

The **tourist office** is in the Casina delle Palme behind the waterfront (Mon–Sat 8am–2pm; ℡0923.29.000, ⓦwww.apt.trapani.it), and there's **internet** access at Piazza Garibaldi 28 (on the seafront not far from the port), and at *M Point*, Corso Vittorio Emanuele II 17 in the old town.

Accommodation

Finding somewhere to stay at Easter will be tricky, unless you book well in advance, but at other times rooms are easy to come by. The best campsite here is *Lido Valderice* (summer ℡0923.573.477, winter ℡0923.573.086, ⓦwww.campinglidovalderice.com; open all year) on the beach at Bonagía, a twenty-minute bus ride away. There are around eight buses daily (except Sun in winter) from Trápani bus station (direction Bonagía) to the turn-off, from where it's a fifteen-minute walk.

B&B Ai Lumi Corso Vittorio Emanuele 71
☏0923.872.418, ⓦwww.ailumi.it. Five small, but pristine rooms entered through a flower-filled courtyard. They also own the trattoria of the same name down the street. ❸
B&B Almaran Via San Cristoforo 8
☏349.611.0211, ⓦwww.almaran.it. Clean and pretty place, tucked behind the waterfront. ❸

Messina Corso Vittorio Emanuele 71
☏0923.21.198, ⓔalbergo-messina@libero.it. Cheapest hotel in town: friendly, old-fashioned and clean but a bit dingy and often booked up. ❶
Nuovo Russo Via Tintori 4, just off the Corso
☏0923.22.166, ⓦwww.nuovoalbergorusso.it. Bright, airy rooms with a nice old-fashioned feel overlooking the main Corso. ❷

The Town

Trápani's **old town**, broadly speaking the area west of the train station, sports a mix of often incongruous architectural styles, something that harks back to Trápani's past as a complex medieval Mediterranean trading centre. It's particularly true of the medieval **Jewish quarter**, a wedge of hairline streets and alleys that holds one of the city's most characteristic buildings, the **Palazzo della Giudecca** on Via Giudecca – sixteenth-century, with a stone-studded tower and finely wrought Spanish-style Plateresque windows. Just up from here, Trápani is at its most engaging, Corso Italia preceding a confused set of three piazzas, enlivened by their surrounding churches: one doorway of the sixteenth-century **Chiesa di Santa Maria di Gesù** (Via San Pietro) is defiantly Renaissance in execution, and further up, on Piazzetta Saturno, the fourteenth-century church of **Sant'Agostino** retains a Gothic portal and delicate rose window.

Off Piazzetta Saturno, pedestrianized Via Torrearsa neatly splits the old town. West of here Trápani's layout becomes more regularly planned, while the main drag and shopping street, the elegant, pedestrianized **Corso Vittorio Emanuele**, changes name to Via Carolina and then Via Torre di Ligny as it runs towards the **Torre di Ligny** – utmost point of the scimitar of land that holds the old town. Finish off your circuit at the daily **market**, at the northern end of Via Torrearsa, where fish, fruit and veg is sold from the arcaded Piazza Mercato di Pesce; there are several lively bars in the area.

Celebrations and processions at Easter in Trápani are given added piquancy by the carriage around town on Good Friday of the **Misteri**, a group of life-sized eighteenth-century wooden figures representing scenes from the Passion. At other times they are on display in the exuberantly sculpted **Chiesa del Purgatorio** (call ☏347.4063 for access; free), on Via Domenico Giglio, near the junction with Via Francesco d'Assisi.

Except on arrival, you hardly need to set foot in the newer parts of the city. The only incentive is the interesting **Museo Regionale Pepoli** (daily 8.30am–1.30pm; €4), a good three-kilometre bus ride away in the drab heart of modern Trápani: take bus #25 from Piazza Vittorio Emanuele, Via Libertà or Via Garibaldi, and get off at the park, Villa Pepoli, outside the Santuario dell'Annunziata, the fourteenth-century convent whose cloisters house the museum. The convent's Cappella della Madonna contains the city's sacred statue, the **Madonna di Trápani**, attributed to Nino Pisano, which stands under a grandiose marble canopy by Antonello Gagini. Approached through bird-filled cloisters, the museum includes a bit of everything, from local archeological finds to delicate seventeenth-century coral craftwork and a good medieval art section. Look out for the grim wooden guillotine of 1789 downstairs and the eighteenth-century majolica-tiled scene of *La Mattanza* (the annual tuna-fish kill).

Eating and drinking

Eating is particularly enjoyable in Trápani. For good, quite reasonably priced fish head to the *Trattoria del Porto*, Via A. Stati 45 (☎0923.547.842). More refined meals are on offer at *P&G*, Via Spalti 1, near the station (☎0923.547.701; closed Sun & Aug), a semi-formal place with local *busiate* pasta. The best ice creams in town are at *Sebastiano*, Via Roma 15, and for a quiet **drink** outside, head to one of the many little bars or cafés along the newly pedestrianized streets of the historic centre.

Érice

The nearest and most exhilarating ride from Trápani is to **ÉRICE**, fifteen minutes away by a new **cable car** (*funivia*). It's a mountain town with creeping hillside alleys, stone buildings, silent charm and powerful associations. Founded by Elymnians, who claimed descent from the Trojans, the original city was known to the ancient world as Eryx, and a magnificent temple, dedicated to Venus Erycina, Mediterranean goddess of fertility, once topped the mountain. Though the city was considered impregnable, Carthaginian, Roman, Arab and Norman invaders all forced entry over the centuries. But all respected the sanctity of Érice: the Romans rebuilt the temple and set two hundred soldiers to serve as guardians of the shrine, while the Arabs renamed the town Gebel-Hamed, or Mohammed's mountain.

Arrival, information and accommodation

To **get to** Érice from Trápani, take bus #23 (direction Ospedale S. Antonio Abbate) and get off at the stop before the hospital, from where it's a short walk to the **funivia station** (if you're driving, there's a car park). The return trip costs €5 and you arrive at the Porta Trápani in Érice. The cable car operates Mon–Sat 2–8.30pm, Sun 9.30am–midnight, longer hours in summer. Nearby on Via Guarrasi 1, Érice's helpful **tourist office** (Mon–Fri 8am–2pm; ☎0923.869.388) can help with **accommodation**.

Elimo Via Vittorio Emanuele 75 ☎0923.869.377, ⊛www.hotelelimo.it. Luxurious rooms in a beautifully restored hotel with a small courtyard garden. ❺–❻

Il Carmine Piazza del Carmine 23 ☎0923.869.089, ⊛www.ilcarmine.com. Several simple, bright rooms in a former Carmelite convent in the heart of town. ❷

Moderno Via Vittorio Emanuele 63 ☎0923.869.300, ⊛www.hotelmodernoerice.it. The best aspect of the *Moderno* is it's panoramic roof terrace, where there's a bar and where breakfast can be taken. The rooms aren't so terrific, at least not for the price, though rates are more reasonable in low season. ❺

Ulisse Camere Via Santa Lucia 2 ☎0923.860.155, ⊛www.sitodiulisse.it. Nicely furnished rooms with and without bathroom dispersed over two buildings. The best are grouped around a tranquil central courtyard. They also have a restaurant serving local dishes, such as couscous. ❷

The Town

Scout around the town at random: the most convoluted of routes is only going to take you a couple of hours and every street and piazza is a delight. You enter through the Norman **Porta Trápani**, just inside which the battlemented fourteenth-century campanile of the **Duomo** did service as a lookout tower for Frederick III of Aragon. From here there's no set route, though passing through pretty **Piazza Umberto** with its couple of outdoor bars is a good idea;

and a natural start or finish is at the ivy-clad **Norman Castello** at the far end of town; it was built on the site of the famed ancient temple, chunks of which are incorporated in the walls. When it's fine, the **views** from the terraces of Érice are phenomenal – over Trápani, the slumbering whales of the Égadi Islands and on very clear days as far as Cape Bon in Tunisia.

Eating and drinking

If you're coming for the day you may want to bring a picnic since **restaurant** prices in Érice are vastly inflated – the gardens near the Torretta Pepoli make a lovely picnic spot, with great views of the Égadi Islands, especially at sunset.

Caffè Maria Corso Vittorio Emanuele 4. Don't leave town without a visit to the café or its sister pasticceria a few doors down, for marzipan goodies and exquisite *cannoli*. The café's founder, Maria Grammatico, learned her trade as a girl in a convent, and has co-written a recipe book with writer Mary Taylor Simeti.
Monte San Giuliano Vicolo San Rocco 7 ☎0923.869.595. Really excellent food in a

restaurant entered through a medieval stone archway. Closed Mon & two weeks in Nov & Jan.
La Pentolaccia Via Guarnotti 17 ☎0923.869.099. Atmospherically housed in an old monastery this moderately priced place serves good, home-made pasta and couscous. Closed Tues.
La Vetta Via G. Fontana. Standard trattoria serving pizza in the evenings, with tables outside in summer. Closed Thurs.

The Temple of Segesta

If time is limited, it's hard to know which to recommend most: the heights of Érice or Trápani's other local attraction, the temple at **SEGESTA** (daily 8am to 1hr before sunset; €6), 35km southeast of Trápani. Although unfinished, this Greek construction of 424 BC is one of the most inspiring of Doric temples anywhere and, along with the theatre, virtually the only relic of an ancient city whose roots – like those of Érice – go back to the twelfth century BC. Unlike Érice, though, ancient Segesta was eventually Hellenized and spent most of the

▲ Temple of Segesta

later period disputing its borders with Selinus to the south. The temple dates from a time of prosperous alliance with Athens, the building abandoned when a new dispute broke out with Selinus in 416 BC.

The **temple** itself crowns a low hill, beyond a café and car park. From a distance you could be forgiven for thinking that it's complete: the 36 regular white stone columns, entablature and pediment are all intact, and all it lacks is a roof. However, get closer and you see just how unfinished the building is: stone studs, always removed on completion, still line the stylobate, the tall columns are unfluted and the cella walls are missing. Below the car park, a road winds up through slopes of wild fennel to the small **theatre** on a higher hill beyond; there's a **minibus** service every thirty minutes if you don't fancy the twenty-minute climb. The view from the top is justly lauded, across green slopes and the plain to the sea, the deep blue of the bay a lovely contrast to the theatre's white stone – not much damaged by the stilted motorway snaking away below.

Without your own transport, **getting to Segesta** involves a twenty-minute uphill walk from Segesta-Tempio town, to which there are at least four **buses** (Mon–Sat 8am, noon, 2pm & 5pm) from Piazza Malta in Trápani, the last one returning at around 6.30pm; there is no service on Sundays. **Trains** to Segesta-Tempio, a twenty-minute walk from the site, are infrequent, but there are more regular trains connecting Trápani and Palermo with the station of **CALATAFIMI**, about a two-kilometre walk from the temple.

The Égadi Islands

Of the various islands, islets and rock stacks that fan out from the west coast of Sicily, the three **Égadi Islands** (Isole Égadi) are best for a quick jaunt – connected by ferry and hydrofoil with Trápani. Saved from depopulation by tourism, in season at least you're not going to be alone, certainly on the main island, **Favignana**, where in August every scrap of flat rock and sand is filled. But a tour of the islands is worthwhile, not least for the caves that perforate the splintered coastlines. Out of season things are noticeably quieter, and in May or June you may witness the bloody **Mattanza**, an age-old slaughter in this noted centre of tuna fishing: its future, however, is unsure, due to bureaucratic wrangling and in-fighting between two factions of *tonnaroti* (tuna fishermen).

Ferries to the islands depart from Trápani's Molo di Sanità; **hydrofoils** from further east along Via Ammiraglio Staiti. Though less frequent, ferries are, as always, much cheaper.

Favignana

FAVIGNANA, island and port town, is first stop for the boats from Trápani, and makes a good base since it has virtually all the accommodation and the Égadi's only campsites. Only 25 minutes by hydrofoil from the mainland, the island attracts a lot of day-trippers, keen to get onto its few rocky beaches. But get out of the main port and it's easy enough to escape the crowds, even easier with a bike (which can be rented for from Isidoro, at Via Mazzini 40). **Caves** all over the island bear prehistoric traces and many are accessible if you're determined enough. Otherwise, the two wings of the island invite separate **walks**; best is the circuit around the eastern part, past the bizarre ancient quarries at

Cala Rossa, over the cliffs to Cala Azzura and then following the coast past the ugly tourist village at Punta Fanfalo to Lido Burrone, the island's best beach, only 1km from the port.

The most unusual **accommodation** on the island is at the striking *Hotel delle Cave*, a designer hotel with just fourteen rooms built on the lip of an abandoned quarry out at Zona Cavallo (℡0923.925.423, Ⓦwww.hoteldellecave.it; ❺), with two mini hydromassage pools and gardens inside the quarry itself. You might also like to try its sister hotel, *Cave Bianche* (℡0923.925.451, Ⓦwww .hoteldellecave.it; ❼) inside a quarry near the sandy beach of Cala Azzurra. There's a pool, hydromassage, and a restaurant, while rooms are chic and minimalist. Top choices in town include the nice *Aegusa*, at Via Garibaldi 11 (℡0923.922.430, Ⓦwww.aegusahotel.it; ❹), and, just on the fringe of town, the pleasant *Hotel Favignana*, Contrada Badia 8 (℡0923.925.449, Ⓦwww .favignanahotel.com; ❸–❹). There are two **campsites** outside town, both an easy walk and both well signposted.

Levanzo

LEVANZO, to the north, looks immediately inviting, its white houses against the turquoise sea reminiscent of the Greek islands. The steep coast is full of inlets and is riddled with caves. One, the **Grotta del Genovese**, was discovered in 1949 and contains some remarkable Paleolithic incised drawings, six thousand years old, as well as later Neolithic pictures. To arrange to see the cave you'll have to contact the guardian, Natale Castiglione, who lives at Via Calvario 11 (℡0923.924.032, Ⓦwww.grottadelgenovese.it; daily in summer; weekends only in winter; tours €16, by jeep in winter, by boat in summer), near the hydrofoil quay. The island's **interior** has some great **walks** along old cart tracks, and there's a paved (and virtually traffic-free) cornice road leading to a lovely white pebble **beach** by the jagged rocks of the Faraglioni.

The nicest place to **stay** is the Lisola Residence (℡320.180.9090, Ⓦwww .lisola.eu; ❷), seven apartments sleeping between two and four, occupying simple tufa cottages originally built by nineteenth-century tuna-canning magnate Florio for his workers 400m outside the port. There's a large pool, canvas sun umbrellas and loungers, and free transport to the port whenever you need it.

Maréttimo

MARÉTTIMO, furthest out of the Égadi Islands, is the place to come for solitude. Very much off the beaten track, it's reached by only a few tourists. White houses are scattered across the rocky island, and there's a bar in the main piazza, along with two restaurants. The spectacular fragmented coastline is pitted with rocky coves sheltering hideaway **beaches**, and there are numerous gentle **walks**, which will take you all over the island.

To organize **rooms**, call *Rosa dei Venti* (℡0923.923.249 or 333.675.8893, Ⓦwww.isoladimarettimo.it; ❶), which has half a dozen with bathrooms, as well as apartments with cooking facilities, and can arrange **boat trips**. Alternatively, try the *Maréttimo Residence* (℡0923.923.202, Ⓦwww.marettimoresidence.it; ❷), a little cluster of resort cottages, usually rented weekly, above a stony beach south of the main port, or ask at the café in the main square.

North of Trápani

Frequent buses run north from Trápani, cutting away from the coast until reaching the popular seaside resort of **SAN VITO LO CAPO** at the very nib of the northwestern headland. There are some good sands nearby, while the cape itself is only a stride away. From San Vito, you have to return to Trápani for onward transport. **Buses** or, more frequently, trains cut across the headland to **CASTELLAMMARE DEL GOLFO**, another popular resort built on and around a hefty rocky promontory, which is guarded by the squat remains of an Aragonese **castle**. The local **train station** is 4km east of town; a bus meets arrivals and shuttles you into Castellammare.

If you're looking for an atmospheric place to **stay** you could do much better by moving the 10km west up the coast to hamlet of **SCOPELLO**; there are four buses a day (Mon–Sat) from Castellammare's bus station on Via della Repubblica off the main Via Segesta.

The road to Scopello from Castellammare forks just before the village, with one strand running the few hundred metres down to the **Tonnara do Scopello**, set in its own tiny cove. This old tuna fishery is where the writer Gavin Maxwell lived and worked in the 1950s, basing his *Ten Pains of Death* on his experiences here. It's almost too picturesque to be true – not least the row of abandoned buildings on the quayside and the ruined old watchtowers tottering on jagged pinnacles of rock above the sea. The actual village of Scopello perches on a ridge a couple of hundred metres above the coastline, comprising little more than a paved square and a fountain, off which run a couple of alleys. In summer, particularly, book in advance if you want **to stay** here. *La Tranchina*, at Via A. Diaz 7 (☎&℡0924.541.099; ❸), has comfortable rooms with a friendly English-speaking owner, though you'll need to book ahead. You eat well here too – fresh fish, and interesting pasta dishes such as pasta with peppers and home-cured *bottarga* (tuna fish egg roe). *La Tavernetta*, next door at no. 3 (☎0924.541.129, ⓦwww.scopelloonline .com/latavernetta; ❸), has similarly pleasant rooms, some with distant sea views, and it also has a restaurant. The nearest **campsite** is *Baia di Guidaloca* (☎0924.541.262; April–Sept), 3km south of Scopello and a stone's throw from the lovely bay of **Cala Bianca**, where there's good swimming; the bus from Castellammare passes right by.

Just 2km from Scopello (no buses but it's a nice, easy walk) is the southern entrance to the **Riserva Naturale dello Zingaro**, Sicily's first nature reserve, comprising a completely unspoiled seven-kilometre stretch of **coastline** backed by steep mountains. At the entrance, there's an **information hut**, where you can pick up a plan showing the **trails** through the reserve. It's less than twenty minutes to the first beach, Punta della Capreria, and 3km to the successive coves of Disa, Berretta and Marinella, which should be a little more secluded.

South of Trápani

The coast south of Trapani may lack the drama of that to the north, but there are nevertheless several places you may wish to visit. The major attraction is the **ancient Greek site Selinunte**, with its massive ruined temples, though anyone at all interested in Sicily's past should take care not miss the

Phoenician island colony of **Mózia**. There are also three historic port towns you might want to see: **Marsala**, famous for sweet wine, Mazara del Vallo, the most Arabic town in Sicily, and the vibrant and attractive fishing port of **Sciacca**.

There's little else to stop for around the western coast; even less inland, which is crossed by one major road, the SS188, running from Marsala to **Salemi**, centre of a prosperous wine-making region.

Mózia

Around 15km south of Trápani, the unique Phoenician settlement of **MÓZIA** (also known as Mothia or Motya) lies just offshore from the crystalline patchwork of saltpans, which line this part of the coast. Situated on one of the islands in the shallow **Stagnone lagoon**, it was excavated in the late nineteenth century by an Englishman, Joseph Whitaker. You can explore the **ruins** (summer daily 9am to 1hr before sunset; €6) and visit the **museum** he established, which is worth a visit for its magnificent and sensual sculpture alone, *Il Giovinetto di Mózia*. If you're reliant on public transport, the island is more easily reached from Marsala: regular **buses** run from Piazza del Popolo to the ferry landing. And should you want **to stay** in the area, the peaceful agriturismo *Baglio Vajarassa* (☎0923.968.628, Ⓦwww.bagliovajarassa.com; no credit cards; ❸, half board €60 per person) on Contrada Spagnola 176, a couple of kilometres south of the ferry landing, offers rooms furnished with antiques, and typical local dishes for dinner around a communal table.

⑯ Marsala

Bypassing Mózia, and pretty much keeping within sight of the sea all the way, the western rail loop runs down the coast from Trápani to **MARSALA**, a distance of around 25km. The city, which takes its name from the Arabic Marsah-el-Allah, the port of Allah, was once the main Saracenic base in Sicily, but since the late eighteenth century it has been better known for the dessert wine that carries its name, something every bar and restaurant will sell you.

The centre of Marsala is extremely attractive, a clean sixteenth-century layout that's free of traffic and littered with high, ageing buildings and arcaded courtyards. But, pleasant as the town is, save your energy for two excellent museums. The most central, behind the cathedral at Via Garraffa 57, is the **Museo degli Arazzi** (Tues–Sat 9.30am–1pm & 4.30–6pm, Sun 9.30am–1pm; €2.50), whose sole display is a series of eight enormous hand-stitched wool and silk **tapestries** depicting the capture of Jerusalem – sixteenth-century and beautifully rich, in burnished red, gold and green. Afterwards, walk out to the cape (follow the main Via XI Maggio to Piazza della Vittoria and bear left towards the water); one of the stone-vaulted warehouses that line the promenade holds the equally impressive **Museo Archeologico e della Nave Punica** (daily 9am–6pm; €3). Its major exhibit is a reconstructed Punic war ship once rowed by 68 oarsmen, probably sunk during the First Punic War, and rediscovered in 1971. Other bits and pieces on display are from the excavated site (mostly Roman) of Lilybaeum. If you want a **meal** in Marsala, head for *Il Gallo e l'Innamorata*, Via S Bilardello 18 (☎329.291.8503) a small *osteria* with great food, including bruschetta with *bottarga* and *busiati con ragu di tonno*.

Mazara del Vallo

Half an hour's driving further on from Marsala, **MAZARA DEL VALLO** is Sicily's most important fishing port and a place of equal distinction for the Arabs and Normans who dominated the island a thousand years ago. The first Saracen gain in Sicily, Mazara was Arabic for 250 years until captured by Count Roger in 1075: the island's first Norman parliament met in the town 22 years later, and a relic of that period is the tiny pink-domed Norman chapel of **San Nicolò**, on the edge of the harbour. North Africans crew the colourful fishing boats that block the harbour and river, the old city kasbah once more houses a Tunisian community. Wandering around the **harbour** area is the most rewarding thing to do in Mazara, although you can also spend an enjoyable hour or so pottering around the town. There's a remodelled Norman **Duomo**, which shelters some Roman and Byzantine remains, and in nearby Piazza del Plebiscito, the fifteenth-century church of Sant'Egido has recently been transformed into the **Museo del Satiro** (daily 9am–6pm; €6), home of a somewhat risqué fourth-century BC bronze satyr captured in the ecstatic throes of an orgiastic Dionysian dance. It was hauled up by a Mazara fishing boat, the *Captain Ciccio*, in the waters between Pantelleria and Cape Bon, Tunisia, in 1998. Sadly, as the fishermen brought the catch aboard, one of the arms broke off and has so far not been recovered. Across the square is the **Museo Civico**, which has been closed for restoration for several years, though it is hoped it will re-open soon (call the *director* for information; ☎0923.949.593).

Selinunte (Selinus)

The westernmost of the Hellenic colonies, the Greek city of Selinus – **SELINUNTE** in modern Italian – reached its peak in the fifth century BC when a series of mighty temples was erected. A bitter rival of Segesta, whose lands lay adjacent to the north, the powerful city and its fertile plain attracted enemies hand over fist, and it was only a matter of time before Selinus caught the eye of Segesta's ally, Carthage. Geographically vulnerable, the city was sacked by Carthaginians, any recovery forestalled by earthquakes that later razed the city. Despite the destruction, which left the site completely abandoned until it was rediscovered in the sixteenth century, the ruins of Selinus have exerted a romantic hold ever since.

The **site of Selinus** is set back behind the village of Marinella (see p.980). It's split into two parts with **temples** in each, known only as Temples A–G. The two parts are enclosed within the same site, with the car park and entrance (summer daily 9am to 1hr before sunset; €6) lying through the landscaped earthbanks that preclude views of the east group of temples from the road. The first stop is at the **East Group**. Shrouded in the wild celery which gave the ancient city its name, the temples are in various stages of ruin: the most complete is the one nearest the sea (Temple E), while the northernmost (Temple G) is a tangle of columned wreckage six metres high in places. The road leads down from here, across the (now buried) site of the old harbour to the second part of excavated Selinus, the **acropolis** (where there is another car park), a site containing what remains of the other temples (five in all), as well as the well-preserved city streets and massive, stepped walls which rise above the duned beach below. Temple C stands on the highest point of the acropolis, and there are glorious views from its stones out over the sparkling sea: from this temple were removed some of the best metopes, now on show in Palermo's archeological museum. To get there you'll need to take a **bus** from Piazza Reina Margherita (5 daily; 25min) in **Castelvetrano**, itself thirty minutes by bus from Mazara del Vallo.

Marinella

Marinella, right next to the Greek ruins of Selinunte, is no longer the isolated place it once was, with new buildings in the centre and the seafront slightly top-heavy with trattorias and *pensioni* these days. But it remains an attractive place, certainly if you're planning to make use of the fine sand **beach** that stretches west from the village to the ruins. **Buses** pull up on the road that leads down to the seafront, where the main **hotels** and restaurants are situated. First choice here is the *Lido Azzurro*, Via Marco Polo 98 (📞&🖨0924.46.256; half board in July & Aug; ❷), a charming villa with sea-facing balconies and an owner who speaks good English. Opposite the temple car park, the sign pointing to "Chiesa" leads to the old abandoned train station, just before which you'll find *Il Pescatore*, at Via Castore e Polluce 31 (📞0924.46.303; no credit cards; ❶), with a very genial host, fruit breakfasts on the terrace and rooftop camping. There are also two **campsites** virtually next to each other on the main road, 1500m north of the village: the *Athena* (📞0924.46.132) and *Il Maggiolino* (📞0924.46.044, 🌐www.campingmaggiolino.it); the bus from Castelvetrano passes right by them. Via Marco Polo, the road above the west beach, is where all the best **eating and drinking** places are, starting down at the little harbour where a couple of bars put out tables from where you can watch the sun set – *Cala Nnino*, here, is worth a visit for its sea urchin (*ricci*). Alternatively, if you're feeling energetic, walk the 3km to the restaurant *La Pineta* on the east beach, **Mare Pineta**, for its great location, fish dishes and speciality bread.

Sciacca

FS buses leave from outside Castelvetrano train station three times daily (1 on Sun) for the atmospheric port of **SCIACCA**, picking up at the abandoned Selinunte station in Marinella village. Sciacca's **upper town** is skirted by medieval walls, which form high sides to the steep streets, rising to a ruined Spanish **castle**. Below, the **lower town** sits on a clifftop terrace overlooking the harbour, where it's easy to while away time drinking in the coastal views. There are also some wonderful **Roman hot springs**, still in operation next to the *Grand Hotel delle Terme* (Mon–Fri 8am–1pm as long as there are no patients; 📞0925.23.133, 🌐www.grandhoteldelleterme.com), and a helpful **tourist office** at Corso Vittorio Emanuele 84 (Mon–Sat 9am–2pm; 📞0925.22.744).

With an active harbour and some good beaches close by, Sciacca makes a nice place to stay over, and there are a few bed and breakfasts, notably the central *Locanda al Moro*, Via Liguori 44 (📞0925.86756, 🌐www.almoro.com; ❸) which has ten minimalist rooms with stylish bathrooms in a restored thirteenth-century house. The nearest **campsite**, *Makauda Beach* (📞0925.997.001, 🌐www.makaudabeach.it), 9km east of town at località San Giorgio Tranchina, also has bungalows and is best reached by taxi if you don't have your own transport.

Pantelleria

Forty kilometres nearer to Tunisia than to Sicily, **PANTELLERIA** is the most singular of Sicily's outlying volcanic islands. Madly trendy (Armani has a *dammuso* here, Madonna rents one) its strategic position kept it in the mainstream of Sicilian history for years. Nowadays the most visible sign of its past is the gloomy black **Castello Barabacane**, whose origins are Roman, but whose present appearance owes most to the Spanish. The island was used as one of the main Mediterranean bases by the Fascists during World War II, and was bombed without mercy by the Allies in May 1943 as they advanced from North Africa. In part, this explains the morose appearance of the island's main town (also called Pantelleria) – thrown up in unedifying concrete.

There are no beaches of any kind in Pantelleria, its rough **black coastline** mainly jagged rocks, but the **swimming** is still pretty good in some exceptionally scenic spots. Inland, the largely mountainous country offers plenty of rambling opportunities, all an easy moped- or bus-ride from the port. If you're spending any length of time on Pantelleria, you may want to stay in one of the local **dammuso** houses: a throwback to the buildings of Neolithic times, their strong walls and domed roofs keep the temperature down indoors. Many are available on Ⓦ www.pantelleriatravel.com.

The island's main drawback is the cost of living: there are only a few hotels, where there may be a minimum three-day stay in July and August, while food (and water) is mostly imported and therefore relatively expensive. The best times to visit are May/June or September/October, to avoid the summer's ferocious heat.

Getting to Pantelleria

Siremar (Ⓦ www.siremar.it) runs **ferries** to Pantelleria from Trápani (June–Sept 1 daily; Oct–May Sun–Fri 1 daily, returning Mon–Sat 1 daily; 5hr 45min; July, Aug €27.90, June, Sept €25.90, low season €24 each way).

Pantelleria is a thirty-minute **flight** from Trápani (1–3 daily), and a fifty-minute flight from Palermo (1–2 daily); the normal one-way fare from either is around €80, but with special offers on the web, you can end up paying less than half that (try Ⓦ www.expedia.it and www.edreams.it).

Pantelleria Town

PANTELLERIA TOWN is the site of most of the island's accommodation and facilities. For online information, consult Ⓦ www.pantelleria.it. The **airport** is 5km southeast of town; a bus connects with flight arrivals and drops you in the central Piazza Cavour. **Arriving by sea**, you'll disembark right in the centre of town, unless bad weather forces a landing at Scauri, a smaller port on the island's southwestern side, from where a bus takes foot passengers into town.

The few **hotels** in town include the *Miryam*, Corso Umberto I, at the far end of the port, near the castle (☏ 0923.911.374, Ⓦ www.miryamhotel.it; ❸), which is bright and pleasant inside despite rather glum external appearances; and the *Mediterraneo Hotel* (☏ 0923.911.299, Ⓦ www.pantelleriahotel.it; ❹), nearer the dock at Via Borgo Italia 6, with harbour-facing rooms. Prices soar, however, in high season.

The best places **to eat** are *La Pergola*, Via Contrada Suvaki (℡0923.918.420; closed Tues), which has extremely good, fresh local food, and is open all year, and *Acqua Marina*, Via Borgo Italia (near the Miryam), a trendy spot with large windows opening right onto the harbour.

Around the island

Local buses leave from Piazza Cavour, with regular departures to all the main villages on the island – but note that there are no services on Sundays. There are seven daily buses along the **southwest coast** to the village of **Scauri**, passing on the way the first of the island's strange **sesi**, massive black Neolithic funeral mounds of piled rock, with low passages leading inside. On foot, it's just over an hour from the sesi to **Sataria**, where concrete steps lead down to a tiny square-cut **sea pool**. In the cave behind are more pools where warm water bubbles through, reputed to be good for curing rheumatism and skin diseases.

Along the **northeast coast** to the villages of Kamma and Tracino (4 daily buses), get the bus to drop you at the top of the route down into **Gadir**, a small anchorage with just a few houses hemmed in by volcanic pricks of rock. From here it's an easy, fairly flat hour's stroll to the charming **Cala Levante**, a huddle of houses around another tiny fishing harbour. Where the road peters out, bear right along the path at the second anchorage and keep along the coast for another five minutes until the **Arco dell'Elefante**, or "Elephant Arch", hoves into view, named after the hooped formation of rock that resembles an elephant stooping to drink.

The principal inland destination is Pantelleria's main volcano, the **Montagna Grande**, whose summit is the island's most distinctive feature seen from out at sea. Buses (3 daily) run from the port for the crumbly old village of **Siba**, perched on a ridge below the volcano. To climb the peak of Montagna Grande (836m), keep left at the telephone sign by the *tabacchi* here, and strike off the main road. From Siba, another (signposted) path – on the left as you follow the road through the village – brings you in around twenty minutes to the **Sauna Naturale** (or Bagno Asciutto). It's little more than a slit in the rock-face, where you can crouch in absolute darkness, breaking out into a heavy sweat as soon as you enter.

Travel details

Trains

Services are drastically reduced on Sun and hols.
Agrigento to: Palermo (11 daily; 2hr).
Catania to: Enna (Mon–Sat 7 daily; 1hr 20min); Messina (1–2 hourly; 1hr 30min); Palermo (3 daily; 3hr 45min); Siracusa (hourly; 1hr 30min); Taormina (at least 1 hourly; 40min).
Enna to: Catania (6 daily; 1hr 20min); Palermo (2 daily; 2hr 20min).
Messina to: Catania (1–2 hourly; 1hr 30min–2hr); Cefalù (12 daily; 2–3hr); Milan (10 daily; 13hr); Milazzo (1–2 hourly; 25min–45min); Naples (10 daily; 5hr 50min–6hr 30min);

Palermo (12 daily; 3hr 15min–4hr 30min); Rome (18 daily; 7–9hr); Taormina (1–2 hourly; 40min–1hr 10min).
Palermo to: Agrigento (11 daily; 2hr); Catania (3 daily; 3hr 45min); Cefalù (hourly; 45min–1hr); Enna via Caltanisetta (3 daily; 2hr 10min–3hr 15min); Marsala via Trapani (5–6 daily; 2hr 50min–3hr 40min); Mazara del Vallo via Alcamo (5 daily; 2hr 30min–3hr); Messina (13 daily; 3hr–4hr); Milazzo (13 daily; 2hr 30min–3hr); Trápani (7 daily; 2hr 15min–3hr 40min).
Ragusa to: Módica (8 daily; 20min); Noto (5 daily; 1hr 30min).
Segesta Tempio to: Trápani (3–4 daily; 20min).

Siracusa to: Catania (10 daily; 1hr 30min); Messina (9 daily; 3hr); Noto (9 daily; 30min); Ragusa (4 daily; 2hr 10min); Taormina (10 daily; 2hr).

Trápani to: Marsala (13 daily; 30min); Mazara del Vallo (13 daily; 45min–1hr); Palermo (8 daily; 2hr 15min–3hr 45min); Segesta–Tempio (3–4 daily; 20min).

Circumetnea trains

Catania to: Paternò/Adrano/Bronte/Maletto/Randazzo (9 daily in summer, 16 daily in winter; 35min/1hr/1hr 35min/1hr 50min/2hr).
Randazzo to: Linguaglossa/Giarre–Riposto (7 daily in summer, 10 daily in winter; 30min/1hr).

Buses

Schedules below are for Mon–Sat services; on Sun and holidays services are either drastically reduced or non-existent.
Agrigento to: Catania (hourly; 2hr 50min); Palermo (hourly; 2hr 15min); Trápani (3 daily; 3hr 20min–4hr).
Catania to: Agrigento (hourly; 2hr 50min); Enna (12 daily; 1hr 30min–2hr 25min); Messina (1–2 hourly; 1hr 35min); Nicolosi (hourly; 40min); Noto (7 daily; 2hr 25min–2hr 15min); Palermo (hourly; 2hr 40min); Piazza Armerina (3–6 daily; 1hr 50min); Ragusa (12 daily; 2hr); Rifugio Sapienza (1 daily; 2hr); Rome (2–3 daily; 11hr); Siracusa (approx hourly; 1hr 20min); Taormina (16 daily; 1hr 40min).
Enna to: Catania (8–10 daily; 1hr 15min); Piazza Armerina (4–6 daily; 30min).
Messina to: Catania (1–2 hourly; 1hr 35min); Catania airport (16 daily; 1hr 50min); Giardini-Naxos (7 daily; 55min); Milazzo (approx hourly; 50min); Palermo (6 daily; 2hr 40min); Randazzo (2 daily; 1hr 50min); Taormina (9 daily; 1hr–1hr50min).
Milazzo to: Messina (approx hourly; 50min).
Palermo to: Agrigento (hourly; 2hr 15); Catania (hourly; 2hr 40min); Cefalù (3 daily; 1hr); Marsala (hourly; 2hr 30min); Messina (6 daily Mon–Sat; 2hr 40min); Siracusa (3 daily; 3hr 15min); Trápani (hourly; 2hr).
Piazza Armerina to: Enna (6 daily; 30min); Palermo (5 daily Mon–Sat; 2hr 15min).
Siracusa to: Catania (approx hourly; 1hr 20min); Catania airport (7 daily; 1hr 10min); Noto (12 daily; 55min); Piazza Armerina (1 daily; 2hr 30min); Ragusa (5 daily Mon–Sat; 2hr 15min); Rome (1 daily; 13hr).
Taormina to: Catania (16 daily; 1hr 40min); Catania airport (6 daily Mon–Sat; 1hr 25min).

Trápani to: Agrigento (3 daily Mon–Sat; 3hr 20min–4hr); Érice (10 daily; 50min); San Vito Lo Capo (8 daily; 1hr 20min).

Ferries

The services detailed here refer to the period from June to Sept; you should expect frequencies to be greatly reduced or suspended outside these months, especially to the Aeolian Islands.
Lípari to: Alicudi (5 weekly; 3hr 10min–3hr 50min); Filicudi (5 weekly; 2hr–2hr 45min); Milazzo (7 daily; 2hr); Naples (5 weekly; 14hr); Panarea (1–2 daily; 1hr 45min–2hr); Salina (2 daily; 50min); Strómboli (1–2 daily; 3hr–4hr 15min); Vulcano (3 daily; 25min).
Messina to: Lípari (4 daily; 1hr 40min–3hr); Villa San Giovanni (every 20min; 40min).
Milazzo to: Alicudi (2 daily; 6hr); Filicudi (2 daily; 4hr 55min); Ginostra (5–8 weekly; 6hr); Lípari (6–9 daily; 2hr); Naples (2 weekly; 16hr 30min); Panarea (6–10 weekly; 4–5hr); Rinella (6–8 weekly; 3hr 40min); Santa Marina (4 daily; 3hr–3hr 40min); Strómboli (6–10 weekly; 5hr 10min–7hr); Vulcano (3–6 daily; 1hr 30min).
Palermo to: Cágliari (1 weekly; 14hr 30min); Genoa (1 daily; 20hr); Livorno (3 weekly; 17hr); Naples (1 daily; 11hr); Ústica (1 daily; 2hr 20min).
Trápani to: Cágliari (1 weekly; 11hr); Favignana (3 daily; 55min–1hr 25min); Levanzo (3 daily; 50min–1hr 30min); Maréttimo (1 daily; 2hr 35min); Pantelleria (1 daily; 5hr 45min).

Hydrofoils and fast ferries

Most of the services listed are greatly reduced or suspended outside the summer season.
At the time of publication, it was uncertain whether the customary daily summer hydrofoil service between the Aeolian Islands and Palermo will function in the future. There is also some doubt as to whether regional government subsidies to the hydrofoil companies will continue, which could result in services being even further reduced.
Lípari to: Alicudi (2 daily; 1hr–2hr 45min); Filicudi (2 daily; 1hr); Ginostra (3 daily; 1hr–1hr 25min); Messina (3 daily; 1hr 50min–2hr 10min); Milazzo (16 daily; 1hr); Panarea (5 daily; 1hr); Reggio di Calabria (3 daily; 1hr 55min); Salina (12 daily; 20min); Strómboli (5 daily; 1hr 15min–1hr 45min); Vulcano (17 daily; 10min).
Messina to: Lípari (3 daily June–Sept; 1 daily Oct–May; 1hr 40min); Reggio di Calabria (3 daily June–Sept, 1 daily Oct–May; 15–25min); Vulcano (3 daily June–Sept, 1 daily Oct–May; 1hr 20min–3hr 10min).

Milazzo to: Alicudi (2 daily; 2hr 55min); Filicudi
(2 daily; 2hr 20min); Ginostra (3 daily; 1hr 45min–
2hr 30min); Lípari (10 daily; 45min–1hr); Panarea
(5 daily; 1hr 45min–2hr 10min); Rinella (2 daily;
1hr 40min); Santa Marina (8 daily; 1hr 20min–2hr);
Strómboli (5 daily; 1hr 25min–2hr 20min); Vulcano
(approx hourly; 45min).
Trápani to: Favignana (14 daily; 25min); Levanzo
(10 daily; 35min); Maréttimo (3 daily; 1hr);
Pantelleria (1 daily in summer; 2hr 30min); Ústica
(3 weekly; 2hr 30min).
Ústica to: Palermo 2–3 daily; 1hr 15min).

Palermo to: Pantelleria (1–2 daily; 50min).
Trápani to: Pantelleria (1–3 daily; 30min).

Catania to: Malta (3–6 weekly July & Aug, 1–2
weekly March–June & Sept to early Oct; 3hr).
Palermo to: Tunis (1 weekly; 9hr).
Trápani to: Tunis (1 weekly; 8hr 15min).

Sardinia

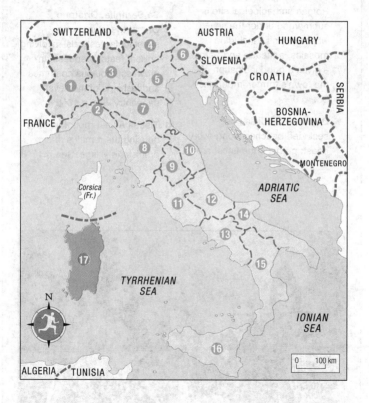

CHAPTER 17

Highlights

* **Cágliari's old town** Cágliari's Castello quarter is the most atmospheric part of town, a dense warren of alleys girded by thick walls. See p.994

* **Nora** Although much of this Carthaginian and Roman archeological site is submerged under the sea, what remains – including mosaics, a theatre and baths – gives a good indication of the town's former importance. See p.998

* **Beaches** Sardinia has secluded beaches along every coast; perhaps the finest are at Chia and La Pelosa. See p.998 & p.1020

* **Nuraghe Su Nuraxi** Sardinia's mysterious prehistoric *nuraghi* are strewn throughout the island, and this is one of the most impressive. See p.1000

* **Sa Sartiglia, Oristano** One of the island's most spectacular festivals, involving brilliant feats of equestrian prowess, fabulous costumes and lashings of medieval pageantry. See p.1002

* **Tiscali** A vast mountain cave housing the remains of a prehistoric village. See p.1008

▲ Masked riders at the Sa Sartiglia festival

17

Sardinia

loser to the North African coast at Tunisia than the Italian mainland and with a fierce sense of independence, **Sardinia** (Sardegna) can feel distinctly un-Italian. D.H. Lawrence found it exotically different when he passed through here in 1921 – "lost", as he put it, "between Europe and Africa and belonging to nowhere." The island may seem less remote nowadays – and it's certainly more accessible, with frequent flights serving Cágliari, Olbia and Alghero – but large tracts remain remarkably untouched by tourism, particularly the interior. The island's main draw, however, is its dazzling coastline, with some of the cleanest beaches in Italy, which can be packed in peak season (particularly August), when ferries bring in a steady stream of sun-worshippers from what the islanders call *il continente*, or mainland Italy. The weather is generally warm enough for a swim as early as May, however, and October is bright and sunny – reason enough to avoid the summer crowds.

Although not famed for its cultural riches, the island does hold some surprises, not least the remains of the various civilizations that passed through here. Its central Mediterranean position ensured that it was never left alone for long, and from the Carthaginians onwards the island was ravaged by a succession of invaders, each of them leaving some imprint behind: Roman and Carthaginian ruins, Genoan fortresses and a string of elegant Pisan churches, not to mention some impressive Gothic and Spanish Baroque architecture. Perhaps most striking of all, however, are the remnants of Sardinia's only significant native culture, known as the **nuraghic** civilization after the 7000-odd *nuraghi* that litter the landscape (see p.989).

On the whole, Sardinia's smaller centres are the most attractive, but the lively capital, **Cágliari** – for many the arrival point – shouldn't be written off. With good accommodation and restaurants, it makes a useful base for exploring the southern third of the island. The other main ferry port is **Olbia** in the north, little more than a transit town but conveniently close to the pristine beaches of the jagged northern coast. The Costa Smeralda, a few kilometres distant, is Sardinia's best-known resort area and lives up to its reputation for glitzy opulence.

Both Olbia and Cágliari have airports, as does the vibrant resort of **Alghero** – a fishing port with a distinctive Catalan flavour in the northwest of the island that retains a friendly, unspoiled air despite its healthy tourist industry. Sardinia's biggest interior town, **Nuoro**, makes a useful stopover for visiting some of the remoter mountain areas. Of these, the **Gennargentu** range, covering the heart of the island, holds the highest peaks and provides rich evidence of the island's traditional culture, in particular the numerous village **festivals**.

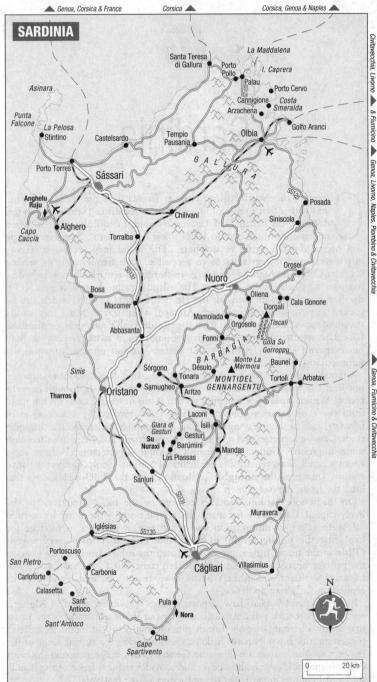

SARDINIA

Asinara

Punta Falcone

La Pelosa
Stintino

Castelsardo

Santa Teresa di Gallura

Porto Pollo

La Maddalena

I. Caprera

Palau

Cannigione

Porto Cervo

Arzachena

Costa Smeralda

Golfo Aranci

Olbia

Porto Torres

Sássari

Anghelu Ruju

Capo Caccia

Alghero

Chilivani

Tempio Pausania

G A L L U R A

SS125

Posada

Siniscola

Torralba

Orosei

Nuoro

Bosa

Macomer

Oliena

Cala Gonone

Dorgali

Tiscali

Mamoiada

Orgósolo

Abbasanta

Fonni

Gola Su Gorroppu

B A R B A G I A

Baunei

Monte La Mármora

Sinis

Sórgono

Désulo

Tonara

MONTI DEL GENNARGENTU

Tortolì

Arbatax

Oristano

Samugheo

Aritzo

Tharros

Laconi

Ísili

Gestúri

Mandas

Giara di Gestúri

Su Nuraxi

Barúmini

Las Plassas

Sanluri

Muravera

Iglésias

SS130

San Pietro

Portoscuso

Carloforte

Carbonia

Calasetta

Sant' Antioco

Sant'Antioco

Villasimius

Cágliari

Pula

Nora

Chia

Capo Spartivento

N

0   20 km

Sardinian cooking revolves around the freshest of ingredients simply prepared: seafood – especially **lobster** – is grilled over open fires scented with myrtle and juniper, as is meltingly tender **suckling pig**. A few wild boar escape the fire long enough to be made into *prosciutto di cinghiale*, a ham with a strong flavour of game. Being surrounded by sparkling seas, Sardinians also make rich, Spanish-inspired **fish stews** and produce **bottarga**, a version of caviar made with mullet eggs. **Pasta** is substantial here, taking the form of *culurgiones* (massive ravioli filled with cheese and egg) or *malloreddus* (saffron-flavoured, *gnocchi*-like shapes), while cheeses tend to be made from ewe's milk and are either fresh and herby or pungent and salty – like the famous **pecorino sardo**. The island is also famous for the quality and variety of its bread, ranging from parchment-thin *pane carasau* to chunky rustic loaves intended to sustain shepherds on the hills. As in Sicily, there is an abundance of light and airy **pastries**, frequently flavoured with lemon, almonds or orange flower water.

Vernaccia is the most famous Sardinian wine: a hefty drink reminiscent of sherry and treated in a similar way – the bone-dry version as an **aperitif** and the sweet variant as a **dessert wine**. The stand-out **red** is the Cannonau di Sardegna, a heady number much favoured by locals. Among the **whites**, look out for dry Torbato or the full-flavoured Trebbiano Sardo, both perfect accompaniments to local fish and seafood.

Some history

Of all the phases in Sardinia's chequered history, the prehistoric **Nuraghic era** is perhaps the most intriguing. Although little is known about the society, plenty of traces survive, most conspicuous of which are the mysterious, stone-built constructions known as *nuraghi*, mainly built between 1500 and 500 BC both for defensive purposes and as dwellings, and unique to Sardinia. The Nuraghic culture peaked between the tenth and eighth centuries BC, trading with the **Phoenicians**, among others, from the eastern Mediterranean. But from the sixth century BC, the more warlike **Carthaginians** settled on the island, with their capital less than 200km away near present-day Tunis and their occupation continued gradually until it was challenged by the emergence of **Rome**. Caught in the middle, the Sards fought on both sides until their decisive defeat by the Romans in 177–6 BC, during which some 27,000 islanders were slaughtered. A core of survivors fled into the impenetrable central and eastern mountains, where they retained their independence in an area called Barbaria by the Romans, known today as the **Barbágia**.

The most impressive remains left by the Romans can be seen in **Cágliari**, on the coast south of the capital at **Nora**, and at **Tharros**, west of Oristano – all Carthaginian sites later enlarged by Roman settlers – and strong Latin traces still survive in the Sard dialect today. After the Roman withdrawal around the fifth century, the destructive effects of malaria and corsair raids from North Africa prompted the abandonment of the island's coasts in favour of more secure inland settlements. The numerous coastal watchtowers which can still be seen today testify to the constant threat of piracy and invasion.

In the eleventh century ecclesiastical rights over Sardinia were granted to the rising city-state of **Pisa**, with its influence mainly concentrated in the south, based in **Cágliari**, and Pisan churches can be found throughout Sardinia. By the end of the thirteenth century, however, Pisa's rival **Genoa** had established itself in the north of the island, with power-bases in Sássari and on the coast,

17

SARDINIA

while the situation was further complicated in 1297, when Pope Boniface VIII gave James II of Aragon exclusive rights over both Sardinia and Corsica in exchange for surrendering his claims to Sicily. Local resistance to the Aragonese was led by **Arborea**, the area around present-day Oristano, and championed in particular by **Eleanor of Arborea**, a warrior whose forces succeeded in stemming the Spanish advance. Following her death in 1404, however, Sardinian opposition crumbled, beginning three centuries of **Spanish occupation** of the island. Traces of Spain's long dominion survive in Sardinia's dialects and in the sprinkling of Gothic and Baroque churches and palaces, with **Alghero**, in particular, still boasting a strong Catalan dialect and the air of a Spanish enclave.

In the wake of the War of the Spanish Succession (1701–20), Victor Amadeus, Duke of Savoy, took possession of the island, which became the new **Kingdom of Sardinia**. The years that followed saw a new emphasis on reconstruction, with the opening of schools, investment in industry and agriculture, and the building of roads. But Savoy's quarrels became Sardinia's, and the island found itself threatened by **Napoleon**, who led an unsuccessful attempt at invasion in 1793.

Garibaldi embarked on both his major expeditions from his farm on one of Sardinia's outlying islands, **Caprera**, and the Kingdom of Sardinia ended with the **Unification of Italy** in 1861. Since then, Sardinia's integration into the modern nation-state has not always been easy. Outbreaks of **banditry**, for example, associated with the hinterland and the Gennargentu mountains in particular, were ruthlessly suppressed, but there was little money available to address the root causes of the problem, nor much interest in doing so. The island benefited from the **land reforms** of Mussolini, however, which included the harnessing and damming of rivers, the draining of land, and the introduction of agricultural colonies from the mainland.

After **World War II**, Sardinia was granted semi-autonomous status, and the island was saturated with enough DDT to rid it of malaria forever. Such improvements, together with the increasing revenues from tourism, have helped marginalize local opposition towards the central government, eroding the support of separatist groups to the more remote inland mountain areas.

Getting to Sardinia

If you're coming direct from the UK, you'll find the regular **flights** operated by Ryanair to **Alghero and Olbia** and by easyJet to **Cágliari** and **Olbia** hard to beat for price. From the Italian mainland there are frequent daily flights to all three of the island's airports from Rome, Milan and Bologna, with less frequent connections from smaller centres. Most routes are served by Alitalia, Air One and Meridiana; prices start at around €75 for a one-way Rome–Olbia ticket, and there are plenty of deals and weekend discounts available.

A cheaper option is to take a **ferry** from mainland Italy, as well as from Sicily, Corsica and France (see box opposite). You should make bookings several months in advance for summer crossings, even if you're on foot; August sailings can be fully booked up by May. Basic prices range from about €15 to €100 per person, depending on the season and the route taken: pricier tickets include use of a reclining armchair, while the cheapest tickets ("*Ponte*") involve sleeping on deck. A **berth** provides a better night's sleep, but adds another €20 or so. The charge for a vehicle starts at around €35 for a small **car** in low season. Fares on the **high-speed ferries** (*mezzi veloci*) are €30–90 travelling second-class (up to 50 percent more in the peak season), plus €50–120 for a small car. Look out for

Ferries to Sardinia

From	To	Line	No. per week	Duration
Ajaccio	Porto Torres	SNCM	1	4hr
Bonifacio	S. Teresa di Gallura	Saremar & Moby Lines	2–49	1hr
Civitavécchia	Arbatax	Tirrenia	2	10hr 30min
Civitavécchia	Cágliari	Tirrenia	7	14hr 30min–16hr 30min
Civitavécchia	Golfo Aranci	Sardinia	6–21	3hr 45min–7hr
Civitavécchia	Olbia	Tirrenia, Moby Lines & SNAV	12–56	5–10hr
Fiumicino	Arbatax	Tirrenia	2 (late July to Aug)	4–5hr
Fiumicino	Golfo Aranci	Tirrenia	7 (late July to mid-Sept)	4hr 30min
Genoa	Arbatax	Tirrenia	2	15hr 30min–20hr
Genoa	Olbia	Tirrenia, Grandi Navi Veloci & Moby Lines	3–22	8hr–13hr 30min
Genoa	Palau	Enermar	3–5 (June–Sept)	12–13hr
Genoa	Porto Torres	Tirrenia & Grandi Navi Veloci	7–21	8–11hr
Livorno	Golfo Aranci	Sardinia	7–21	6–10hr
Livorno	Olbia	Moby Lines	12–27	6–11hr
Marseille	Porto Torres	SNCM & La Meridionale	2–4 (April–Oct)	16hr 15min
Naples	Olbia	DiMaio Lines	1 (mid-June to Aug)	14hr 30min
Naples	Palau	Linee Lauro & DiMaio Lines	1 (mid-June to mid-Sept)	14hr 30min
Palermo	Cágliari	Tirrenia	1	14hr 30min
Piombino	Olbia	Linee dei Golfi	10–14	4hr 30min–7hr
Porto Vecchio	Palau	Linee Lauro	1 (mid-June to mid-Sept)	2hr
Propriano	Porto Torres	SNCM & La Meridionale	1–5	3–4hr
Trápani	Cágliari	Tirrenia	1	10–11hr

discounts applying to return tickets bought in advance within certain periods, and for special deals for a car plus two or three passengers.

Getting around the island

Much the most convenient way of getting around the island is by **car**; there are rental offices in all the major towns (see p.998 for those in Cágliari), though a decent network of public transport covers most localities. There is an island-wide **bus** service run by ARST, while FdS and FMS are concentrated in specific areas and FdS additionally covers the longer hauls between towns. **Trains** connect the major towns of Cágliari, Oristano, Sássari and Olbia, while smaller narrow-gauge FdS lines link Nuoro and Alghero with the main network. From mid-June to mid-September, the FdS-run Trenino Verde steam trains (ⓦwww.treninoverde.com) take scenic routes to various destinations around the island, including Bosa, Palau and Arbatax.

Cágliari and around

Viewing **CÁGLIARI**, **Sardinia's capital**, from the sea at the start of his Sardinian sojourn in 1921, D.H. Lawrence compared it to Jerusalem: "strange and rather wonderful, not a bit like Italy", and the city still makes a striking impression today. Crowned by its historic nucleus squeezed within a protective ring of Pisan fortifications, its setting is enhanced by the calm lagoons (*stagni*) west of the city and along the airport road, a habitat for cranes, cormorants and flamingos. In the centre, the evening promenades along Via Manno are the smartest you'll see in Sardinia, dropping down to the noisier Piazza Yenne and Largo Carlo Felice, around which most of the shops, restaurants, banks and hotels are located. At the bottom of the town, the porticoes of portside Via Roma shelter more shops and bars.

Cágliari's main attractions are the **archeological museum** with its unique collection of nuraghic statuettes, the city walls with their two **Pisan towers** looking down over the port, and the **cathedral** – all within easy distance of each other. There is also a sprinkling of Roman remains, including an impressive **amphitheatre** while nearby excursions include **Nora**, the most complete ancient site on Sardinia and the **islands** of Sant'Antíoco and San Pietro.

Arrival, information and transport

Cágliari's **airport** (Ⓦ www.sogaer.it) sits beside the city's largest *stagno* (lagoon). An ARST bus service runs to Piazza Matteotti in town at least every thirty minutes from 8.45am until the last flight arrival – about 11.30pm – and takes ten minutes (tickets €2 from the airport shop); otherwise a taxi ride costs around €15, more after 10pm.

Cágliari's **port** is a short walk from Piazza Matteotti, which holds the **tourist office** (Mon–Fri 8.30am–1.30pm & 2–8pm, Sat & Sun 8am–8pm; ☏070.669.255, toll-free ☏800.203.541), as well as the **train** and **bus stations**. The square is also the terminus for most **local buses**, tickets for which are sold at a booth in the piazza (€1 for 90min, €1.50 for 2hr or €2.30 for a day's travel); useful routes include #7 and #8 running up to the museums and cathedral; the latter carries on to the Roman amphitheatre. The **FdS station**, for slow trains to Arbatax (see p.1010), is in Monserrato, northeast of Cágliari; you can get there by tram from Piazza Repubblica (bus #30 or #31 from Piazza Matteotti).

Accommodation

Cágliari has a good selection of **hotels and B&Bs**, though availability may be restricted in high season, and single rooms are at a premium at all times. The biggest concentration of places is on or around the narrow Via Sardegna, running parallel to Via Roma. The nearest **campsite** is beyond **Quartu Sant'Elena**, a 45-minute bus ride east along the coast, where *Pini e Mare* (☏070.803.103, Ⓦ www.piniemare.com; Easter–Oct) has bungalows (❸) as well as tent pitches in woods close to the sea.

AeR Bundes Jack Via Roma 75 ☏070.657.970, Ⓔ hotel.aerbundesjack @libero.it. Right across from the port, on the third floor (there's a lift), this hotel's spotless, a/c rooms, mostly en suite, have solid wood furnishings and antique tiled floors. Breakfast (€6) is available May–Sept. The friendly host family also runs the adjacent *B&B Vittoria* (❷). No credit cards. ❷

Arcobaleno Via Sardegna 38 ☏070.684.8325, Ⓦ www.soggiornoarcobaleno.com. Clean and modern en-suite rooms with a/c, and some with exposed brickwork and wi-fi. ❸

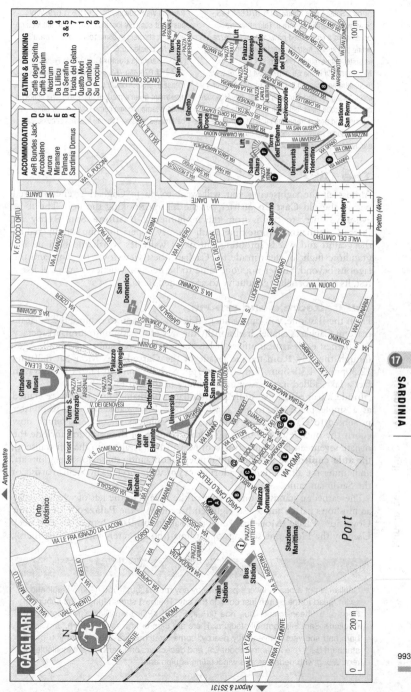

CÁGLIARI

▲ Amphitheatre

▲ Orto Botánico

Cittadella dei Musei

San Michele

San Domenico

Palazzo Viceregio

Cattedrale

Università

Bastione San Remy

Palazzo Comunale

S. Saturnio

Cemetery

Port

Train Station

Bus Station

Stazione Marittima

▲ Airport & SS131

▲ Poetto (4km)

ACCOMMODATION

AeR Bundes Jack	D
Arcobaleno	C
Aurora	F
Miramare	E
Palmas	B
Sardinia Domus	A

EATING & DRINKING

Caffè degli Spiritu	8
Caffè Libarium	6
Nostrum	4
Da Lilicu	7
Da Serafino	3 & 5
L'Isola del Gelato	1
Quatto Mori	2
Su Cumbidu	9
Su Procciu	

Il Ghetto

Santa Croce

Torre San Pancrazio

Palazzo Viceregio

Cattedrale

Museo del Duomo

Palazzo Arcivescovile

Torre dell'Elefante

Santa Chiara

Università

Seminario Tridentino

Bastione San Remy

Aurora Salita Santa Chiara 19 ☎070.658.625, Ⓦwww.hotelcagliariaurora.it. This attractive *pensione* in a dilapidated *palazzo* behind Piazza Yenne has sunny, tastefully restored rooms, mostly en suite, with exposed brickwork. ❷

Miramare Via Roma 59 ☎070.664.021, Ⓦwww .hotelmiramarecagliari.it. On the second floor of a block facing the port (but with no lift), the *Miramare* has a boutique hotel feel, with a mix of designer touches and period trappings such as four-poster beds in some rooms. All rooms are en suite, with a/c. Rooms with views cost extra. ❹

Palmas Via Sardegna 14 ☎070.651.679. Very basic but centrally located on the main tourist strip, with box showers in some rooms but no private WCs. No breakfast. ❶

Sardinia Domus Largo Carlo Felice 26 ☎070.659.783, Ⓦwww.sardiniadomus.it. Pleasant, professionally run B&B in an old apartment given a modern makeover. The spacious, wood-beamed rooms come with a/c, en-suite bathrooms, plasma TVs and internet access. ❸

The City

Almost all the sightseeing you will want to do in Cágliari is encompassed within the old **Castello** quarter, on the hill overlooking the port. The most evocative entry to this is from the monumental **Bastione San Remy** on Piazza Costituzione, whose nineteenth-century imperialist tone is tempered by the graffiti and weeds sprouting out of its walls. It's worth the haul up the grandiose flight of steps inside for Cágliari's best views over the port and the lagoons beyond. Sunset is a good time to be here, or whenever you feel like a rest, its shady benches conducive to a snatched siesta.

The Cattedrale and around

From the Bastione, you can wander off in any direction to explore the intricate maze of Cágliari's citadel, traditionally the seat of the administration, aristocracy and highest ecclesiastical offices. It has been little altered since the Middle Ages, though the tidy Romanesque facade of the **Cattedrale** (Mon–Sat 8.30am–12.30pm & 4.30–8pm, Sun 8.30am–1pm & 4.30–8pm) in Piazza Palazzo is in fact a fake, added in the twentieth century in the old Pisan style.

Inside, a pair of massive stone **pulpits** flank the main doors: they were crafted as a single piece in around 1160 to grace Pisa's cathedral, but were later presented to Cágliari along with the same sculptor's set of lions, which now adorn the outside of the building. Other features of the cathedral include the ornate seventeenth-century **tomb** of Martin II of Aragon (in the left transept), the **aula capitolare** (off the right transept), containing some good religious art, and, under the altar, a densely adorned **crypt** with carvings by Sicilian artists of the Sardinian saints.

The cathedral stands in one corner of the square, to the left of which are the archbishop's palace and – also eighteenth-century – the **Palazzo Viceregio** or Governor's Palace (Mon–Fri 8am–8pm, Sat & Sun 9am–2pm & 4–8pm; free). Used by the Piedmontese kings of Sardinia (though rarely inhabited by them),

Poetto

Cágliari is not a beach-lover's paradise by any means, but if you need a break and a swim, head to the **beach** just outside the city. The best stretch fringes the suburb of **Poetto**, a fifteen-minute bus ride (#P, #PF and #PQ) from Piazza Matteotti past Cágliari's Sant'Elia football stadium. There are 6km of fine sandy **beach**, and small bars and showers conveniently nearby; some stretches are lidos where you pay a standard daily rate for entry (about €5), and deckchairs and parasols are available for rent, along with pedaloes and windsurfing equipment.

▲ Via Roma arcade, Cágliari

its stately rooms today hold meetings of the provincial assembly and occasional exhibitions. Behind the cathedral on Via Fossario, the **Museo del Duomo** (daily: April–Oct 9am–noon & 5–7pm; Nov–March 9am–12.30pm & 4–6pm; €2) is primarily worth seeing for two items: the fifteenth-century *Tríttico di Clemente VII*, a painting of unknown authorship, but possibly a copy of a lost painting by Rogier van der Weyden, and the powerful *Retablo della Crocefissione*, a six-panelled polyptych attributed to Michele Cavaro (1517–84).

At the far end of Piazza Palazzo a road leads into the smaller Piazza Indipendenza, location of the **Torre di San Pancrazio**, one of the main bulwarks of the city's defences erected by Pisa after it had wrested the city from the Genoans in 1305 (though these did not prevent the Aragonese from walking in just fifteen years later). It's worth ascending the tower (Tues–Sun: May–Oct 9am–1pm & 3.30–7.30pm; Nov–April 9am–4.30pm; €4) for the magnificent views seawards over the old town and port. From here it's a short walk southwest to the city's second watchtower, the **Torre dell'Elefante** (same hours and price), named after a small carving of an elephant on one side. Like the other tower, it has a half-finished look, with the side facing the old town completely open.

The Cittadella dei Musei

Through the arch at the top of Piazza Indipendenza, Piazza dell'Arsenale holds a plaque recording the visit made by Cervantes to Cágliari in 1573, shortly before his capture and imprisonment by Moorish pirates. Across the square, the **Cittadella dei Musei** stands on the site of the former royal arsenal, housing the city's principal museums. The main attraction is the **Museo Archeologico** (Tues–Sun 9am–8pm; €4, or €5 with Pinacoteca), a must for anyone interested in Sardinia's past. The island's most important Phoenician, Carthaginian and Roman finds are gathered here, including busts and statues of muses and gods, jewellery and coins, and funerary items from the sites of Nora and Tharros. But the museum's greatest pieces are from Sardinia's **nuraghic** culture, including a series of bronze statuettes, ranging from about thirty to ninety centimetres in height, spindly and highly stylized but packed with invention and quirky humour.

The Cittadella's other museums are also worth exploring. The smallest and most surprising is the **Mostra di Cere Anatomiche** (Tues–Sat 9am–1pm & 4–7pm, Sun 9am–1pm; €1.50), which displays 23 nineteenth-century wax models of anatomical sections, gruesome reproductions of works made by the Florentine Clemente Susini. Further up, the **Museo d'Arte Siamese** (Tues–Sun 9am–1pm & 4–8pm; mid-Sept to mid-June also 3.30–7.30pm; €4) holds a fascinating array of items from Southeast Asia – the collection of a local engineer who spent twenty years in the region – including Siamese paintings of Hindu and Buddhist legends, Chinese bowls and boxes, Japanese statuettes and a fearsome array of weaponry. Lastly, the excellent **Pinacoteca** (Tues–Sun 9am–8pm; €2, or €5 with Museo Archeologico) contains mostly Catalan and Italian religious art from the fifteenth and sixteenth centuries. Look out in particular for the trio of panel paintings next to each other on the top level: the *Retablo di San Bernardino* by Joan Figuera and Rafael Thomas, *Annunciation* by Joan Mates, and *Visitation* by Joan Barcelo.

The Roman amphitheatre and botanic gardens

From Piazza dell'Arsenale, Viale Buon Cammino leads to Viale Fra Ignazio and the entrance to the **Anfiteatro Romano** (Tues–Sat: 9.30am–1.30pm, Sun April–Oct 9.30am–1.30pm, Nov–March 10am–1pm; €4.30). Cut out of solid rock in the second century AD, the amphitheatre could hold the entire city's population of about 20,000. Despite the decay, with much of the site cannibalized to build churches in the Middle Ages, you can still see the trenches for the animals, the underground passages and several rows of seats. Music, dance and theatre performances take place here in the summer months (tickets from the booth at the entrance). Turn left out of the amphitheatre and walk a few minutes down Viale Fra Ignazio da Laconi to the **Orto Botánico** (daily 8am–1.30pm, April–Oct also 3–7pm; €2), one of Italy's most famous botanical gardens, with over five hundred species of Mediterranean and tropical plants – a shady spot on a sizzling afternoon.

East of the centre, there's little to see in Cágliari's traffic-thronged new town beyond the banks and businesses, the one exception being the fifth-century church of **San Saturno**, Sardinia's oldest and one of the most important surviving examples of early Christian architecture in the Mediterranean. Set in its own piazza off busy Via Dante, looking Middle Eastern with its palm trees and cupola, the basilica was erected on the spot where the Christian martyr Saturninus met his fate during the reign of Diocletian. Around the sturdy walls, which withstood severe bombardment during World War II, lie various pieces of flotsam from the past: four cannonballs, fragments of Roman sarcophagi and slabs of stone carved with Latin inscriptions. The interior – closed for restoration at time of writing – is bare of decoration, though it does hold an excavated necropolis.

Eating, drinking and nightlife

Cágliari has a great range of **restaurants**, often with competitively priced tourist menus. For a morning **coffee**, afternoon tea or evening drink, Piazza Yenne makes a pleasant, relatively traffic-free alternative to the bustling cafés along Via Roma. In the summer months, the city's **nightlife** shifts outside the centre to Poetto (see box, p.994; last bus back around 1am), with its blitz of bars, fairgrounds and ice-cream kiosks.

Caffè degli Spiritu Bastione San Remy. This chic, loungey bar, with great views over the city, is a popular hangout on summer evenings, and there are DJs and live music until late at weekends.

Caffè Libarium Nostrum Via Santa Croce 33. With tables outside right on the old city walls, affording marvellous views, this is a great place for a snack and a drink from early morning to late at night. Closed Mon in winter.

L'Isola del Gelato Piazza Yenne 35. Cágliari's top gelateria offers a staggering variety of ice-cream flavours, as well as yoghurt with fresh fruit, making this a great breakfast stop too. Closed Nov–Feb.

Da Lillicu Via Sardegna 78 ☏070.652.970. This Cágliari institution serves sensational antipasti followed by a small menu of fishy Sard specialities (€8–15) on plain marble tables. It's popular with locals, so you'll need to book. Closed Sun lunch.

Da Serafino at Via Sardegna 109 and Via Lepanto 6 ☏070.651.795. Honest, local dishes, informally served, are extremely good value, with mains at €4–9. Closed Thurs.

Quattro Mori Via Angioy 93 ☏070.650.269. One of Cágliari's best restaurants, with a solid reputation for its endless courses of delectable Sard dishes, especially seafood. Despite relatively high prices, there's usually a full house and the atmosphere gets quite merry. Booking essential. Closed Sun eve & Mon.

Su Cumbidu Via Napoli 11 ☏070.660.017. This cosy wood-beamed restaurant serves heaving plates of antipasti and mainly meaty Sardinian specialities, while its sister restaurant *Su Procciu* (closed Mon), up the hill under Portico Sant'Antonio, off Via Manno, specializes in fish.

Listings

Airlines Air One ☏199.207.080, ⊛www.flyairone.it; Alitalia ☏06.2222, ⊛www.alitalia.it; easyJet ☏899.678.990, ⊛www.easyjet.com; Meridiana ☏892.928, ⊛www.meridiana.it; Ryanair ☏899.678.910, ⊛www.ryanair.com.
Bus operators ARST, for places within the province excluding the southwest (☏070.40.981,

⊛www.arst.sardegna.it); FdS, for Oristano, Sássari and Nuoro (☏800.460.220, ⊛www.ferroviesardegna.it); FMS, for the southwest (☏800.044.553, ⊛www.ferroviemeridionalisarde.it); Turmo for Olbia and Santa Teresa di Gallura (☏0789.21.487, ⊛www.turmotravel.it).

17

SARDINIA | Cágliari and around

Car rental Hertz, Piazza Matteotti 8
☎070.651.078 and airport ☎070.240.037,
🌐www.hertz.it; Ruvioli, Via dei Mille 9
☎070.658.955 and airport ☎070.240.323,
🌐www.ruvioli.it; SIXT, airport ☎070.212.045,
🌐www.e-sixt.it.
Consulates Britain, Viale Colombo 160, Quartu
Sant'Elena ☎070.828.628; Denmark, Via Roma
127 ☎070.668.208; Germany, Via R. Garzia 9
☎070.307.229; Holland, Viale Diaz 76
☎070.303.873.
Ferries Tirrenia, Stazione Maríttima
☎810.171.998, 🌐www.tirrenia.it.
Festivals Sant'Efisio: May 1–4, including a
procession to the saint's church at Nora.
Hospital Via Peretti 21 ☎070.543.266.
Internet access Bips, Via Sicilia 23 (daily 8am–
9pm) and World Link Center, Via Cavour 49

(daily 9am–11pm) both have internet access and
phones with reasonable long-distance rates.
Laundry Coin-operated *lavanderia* at Via Sicilia
20/A (daily 8am–10pm, last wash at 9pm;
€4 for 6kg).
Left-luggage Office inside *McDonald*'s in Piazza
Matteotti (daily 5am–9pm; €1 per bag per hr).
Post office Piazza del Cármine (Mon–Fri 8am–
6.50pm, Sat 8am–1.15pm).
Taxis Rank at Piazza Matteotti; Coop Radio Taxi
(☎070.400.101) operates 24hr.
Train information FS ☎892.021, 🌐www
.ferroviedellostato.it; FdS ☎800.460.220, 🌐www
.ferroviesardegna.it.
Travel agents CTS, Via Balbo 12 ☎070.488.260;
Viaggi Orrù, Via Baylle 111 ☎070.659.858.

Nora and the southwest coast

The easiest excursion you can make from Cágliari is to the waterside archeological site at **NORA**, 40km south of the city. In summer there's a bus service
direct to the site; the rest of the year the nearest stop is the village of **PULA**,
3km away and served by hourly ARST buses (6 on Sun). It's worth going to
Pula anyway, as the village **museum** (daily 9am–8pm; €5.50 including site at
Nora) gives a good explanation of the Nora finds.

Founded by the Phoenicians and settled later by Carthaginians and Romans,
Nora (daily 9am–dusk; €5.50 including museum) was abandoned around the
third century AD, possibly as a result of a natural disaster. Now partly submerged
under the sea, the remains on land include houses, Carthaginian warehouses, a
temple, baths with some well-preserved mosaics, and a theatre which hosts
summer performances. The rest is rubble, though its position on the tip of a
peninsula gives it plenty of atmosphere.

Outside the site stands the rather ordinary-looking eleventh-century church
of Sant'Efisio, site of the saint's martyrdom and the ultimate destination of
Cágliari's four-day May Day procession. Behind the church is a lovely sandy bay,
lapped by crystal-clear water, but packed with day-trippers in season. There's a
fine **hotel** 1km away on the road back to Pula, *Su Gunventeddu* (☎070.920.9092,
🌐www.sugunventeddu.com; ❹), just 100m from a good beach, with spacious,
quiet rooms and a good restaurant (closed Tues & Wed lunch). In Pula itself
there's the good-value, flower-bedecked *Quattro Mori* at Via Cágliari 10
(☎070.920.9124; ❶; no credit cards). Off the central Piazza del Pópolo, you can
eat well at *Sa Macinera* (closed Mon in winter), a ristorante-pizzeria with
outside tables.

The coast south holds some of Sardinia's most exclusive hotels, biggest and
flashiest of which is the *Forte Village* (☎070.92.171, 🌐www.fortevillageresort
.com; late March to Oct; half board; ❾). Nearby are two **campsites**, sheltered
by pinewoods and right by the sea: *Flumendosa* (☎070.920.8364, 🌐www
.campingflumendosa.it) and *Cala d'Ostia* (April–Oct; ☎070.921.470,
🌐campingcaladostia.com). There are spectacular **beaches** all down this coast,
especially around **Chia**, while beyond **Capo Spartivento**, the coastal road
offers terrific views over a deserted cliff-hung coastline, sheltering a few small
sand beaches which are accessible on an infrequent bus service in summer.

Sant'Antíoco

Measuring about 15km in length by 10km at its widest, the wedge-shaped **SANT'ANTÍOCO** is the larger of Sardinia's southwest islands, served by four daily FMS buses from Cágliari, about a two-hour ride. The port area of the island's main town (also called Sant'Antíoco) is just the other side of the causeway. The sheltered harbour made this an important base for the Carthaginians and the Romans, allowing them to command the whole of Sardinia's southwest coast.

In the upper part of the town, on Piazza Parrochia, the twelfth-century **Basilica of Sant'Antíoco** was built over Christian **catacombs**, which were in turn enlarged from an existing Carthaginian burial place; you can visit these dingy corridors, with authentic skeletons and reproductions of ceramic objects unearthed during excavation, on a guided tour (Mon–Sat 9am–noon & 3–6pm, Sun 10–11am & 3–6pm; €2.50).

Sant'Antíoco's archeological zone is signposted up a side road outside the church, less than a kilometre's walk towards the sea. The most impressive site is that of an extensive **Punic tophet**, or burial site (daily 9am–7pm; €4), dedicated to the Carthaginian goddess Tanit and once covering the entire hill where the old city now stands. The numerous urns scattered about here (mostly modern reproductions) were long believed to contain the ashes of sacrificed first-born children, but this is now thought to have been Roman propaganda. Finds from here and from the Phoenician, Carthaginian and Roman cities are collected in the **Museo Archeologico** (same times as tophet; €6), at the bottom of the hill.

Returning into the town on Via Necrópoli, you can use your ticket for the museum and archeological zone for the small but engrossing **Museo Etnográfico** (daily: April–Sept 9am–8pm; Oct–March 9.30am–1pm & 3–6pm; €3): one capacious room crammed to the rafters with examples of rural culture – tools, agricultural implements, crafts, bread- and pasta-making equipment – all enthusiastically explained (in Italian) by a guide. A little further down the same road, the **villaggio ipogeo** or Punic necropolis (same times as ethnographic museum; €2.50) is also worth a glance, consisting of restored *hypogea*, or underground chambers that once held Carthaginian tombs and were later converted into plain dwellings by the local people. Nearby, the **Forte Su Pisu** (same times and price as ethnographic museum), dating from 1812, was stormed by corsairs three years later, resulting in the massacre of the entire garrison. There's not much to see here, but it's been tidily restored and is a panoramic spot. Various combinations of **ticket** are available; one that includes all the sites above costs €13.

Practicalities

The **tourist office** is in the lower part of town, on Piazza Repubblica (March–Oct Mon–Fri 10am–1pm & 4–6pm; Nov–Feb Mon–Fri 10am–1pm & 5–9pm, Sat 10am–noon; ☎0781.82.031). **Bikes and scooters** can be rented nearby at Euromoto, Via Nazionale 57 (☎0781.840.907 or 347.880.3875), and there's **internet** access at *Semantica*, Via Eleonora d'Arborea 38 (Mon–Sat 5–9pm). Accommodation is on the scarce side, and if you're thinking of staying, be sure to book ahead. The best hotels are on the main road through town: the *Hotel del Corso*, above a pleasant bar at Corso Vittorio Emanuele 32 (☎0781.800.265, ⓦwww.hoteldelcorso.it; ❸), with a panoramic roof-terrace, and the *Moderno* at Via Nazionale 82 (☎0781.83.105, ⓦwww.albergoristorantemoderno.com; ❸), more modest but with a very good restaurant specializing in fish dishes. The small port and resort of **Calasetta**, 10km north of town and the terminus for the FMS bus from Cágliari, has *Cala di Seta*, Via Regina Margherita 61 (☎0781.88.304, ⓦwww.hotelcaladiseta.it; ❺), with cosy, wood-beamed rooms, while Sant'Antíoco's sole **campsite**, *Tonnara* (☎0781.809.058, ⓦwww .camping.it/italy/sardegna/tonnara; April–Sept), is on the western side of the island at the sheltered inlet of Cala Sapone, with caravans and chalets (❺).

San Pietro

Ferries from Calasetta make the five-kilometre crossing to the approximately ten-by-seven-kilometre island of **SAN PIETRO** roughly every hour (30min; around €18 for two people in an average-sized car). In summer, drivers should join the queue in good time – and be sure to get a return ticket. San Pietro's dialect is pure Piedmontese, two and a half centuries after the Savoyan king Carlo Emanuele III invited a colony of Genoans to settle here after their eviction from the island of Tabarca, near Tunisia. The settlers were later abducted and taken back to Tunisia in one of the last great pirate raids, but were returned once the ransom demands had been met. The island's only town, elegant **CARLOFORTE** (named after the king), is prettier than Sant'Antíoco, with pastel seafront houses overlooking a palm-fringed port, and narrow balconied alleys beyond. It's lively in summer, particularly during May and June's La Mattanza tuna festival, and the island's panoramic beauty spots and secluded coves are within easy reach.

The few **places to stay** are concentrated in Carloforte. Family-run B&B *Il Ghiro* (☎338.205.0553, ⓦwww.carlofortebedandbreakfast.it; ❸) at Piazza Repubblica 7, the town's liveliest square, has wood-beamed rooms and arty decor; alternatively, the *Hieracon* at Corso Cavour 62 (☎0781.854.028, ⓦwww .hotelhieracon.com; ❺) – right from the port as you leave the ferry – has a

⑰

SARDINIA | Cágliari and around

Visiting Su Nuraxi

If you only have time to see one of Sardinia's *nuraghi* (see p.989) you should make it the biggest and most famous of them: **Su Nuraxi**, between Cágliari and Oristano. The majestic UNESCO-protected complex (daily 9am–dusk; €7) is a compelling sight, surrounded by the brown hills of the interior, and a good taste of the primitive grandeur of the island's only indigenous civilization. The snag is access: the site lies fifteen-minutes' walk west of the village of **Barúmini**, 50km north of Cágliari, to which there are only two to three daily ARST buses.

Su Nuraxi's dialect name means simply "the nuragh", and not only is it the largest nuraghic complex on the island, but it's also thought to be the oldest, dating probably from around 1500 BC. Comprising a bulky fortress surrounded by the remains of a village, Su Nuraxi was a palace complex at the very least – possibly even a capital city. The central tower once reached 21m (now shrunk to less than 15m), and its outer defences and inner chambers are connected by passageways and stairs. The whole complex is thought to have been covered with earth by Sards and Carthaginians at the time of the Roman conquest, which may account for its excellent state of preservation: if it weren't for a torrential rainstorm that washed away the slopes in 1949, the site may never have been revealed at all.

There are several **accommodation** possibilities in the village, the most appealing of which is ⚵ *Sa Lolla* (☎070.936.8419, ⓦwww.wels.it/salolla; ❷), a rustic-style hotel on Via Cavour with a fantastic **restaurant** attached – worth the journey in itself. Barúmini also offers a choice of B&Bs, with a cluster near the post office on Viale Umberto, all of a similar standard and similarly priced (❶): try *Casa del Rio* at Via IV Novembre 24 (☎070.936.8141 or 340.686.2858), or *Casa Piras*, Traversa Principessa Maria 15 (☎070.936.8372 or 349.883.7015; closed Nov, Jan & Feb).

stylish, old-world ambience. Availability is extremely limited in the holiday season, and it's worth asking about **rooms for rent** at the **tourist office**, opposite the port on Piazza Carlo Alberto III (Mon–Sat 10am–1pm & 5–8pm, Sun 10am–1pm; ℡0781.854.009, ⓦwww.prolococarloforte.it).

The island is renowned for its seafood, with tuna a speciality, and there are many good **restaurants**, particularly around the port: chichi *Da Nicolo* (℡0781.854.048; closed Mon), on the seafront at Corso Cavour 32, is good for a splurge, while ⅋ *Al Tonno di Corsa*, at Via Marconi 47 (℡0781.855.106; closed Mon Sept–June), is a friendly trattoria with sea views and outstanding fish dishes made to local recipes.

Oristano and around

The province of Oristano roughly corresponds to the much older entity of **Arborea**, the medieval *giudicato* which championed the Sardinian cause in the struggle against the Spaniards. Then as now, **ORISTANO** was the region's main town, and today it retains more than a hint of medieval atmosphere. The historic centre has a relaxed and elegant feel, and although it is 4km from the sea, the town is attractively surrounded by water, its lagoons and irrigation canals helping to make this a richly productive agricultural zone (the southern lagoon, the Stagno di Santa Giusta, is home to a local colony of Sardinia's flamingo population). Many people, however, come to Oristano simply to visit the nearby Sinis peninsula, home to the impressive Punic and Roman ruins of **Tharros** and a string of wild beaches.

Arrival and information

Oristano's **train station** is at the eastern end of town, a twenty-minute walk from the centre, also linked by local buses running every 20–35 minutes – buy tickets from the bar outside the station. The ARST **bus station** is on Via Cágliari, while long-distance FdS buses pull in at Via Lombardia, ten minutes from Piazza Roma down Via Tirso (tickets from *Blu Bar*). The local **tourist office** is between Piazza Eleonora and the Duomo at Via Ciutadella di Menorca 14 (Mon–Fri 9am–noon & 4.30–7.30pm Sat 9am–noon; ℡0783.70.621, ⓦwww.comune.oristano.it), while information for the whole province is available from the **EPT** at Piazza Eleonora 19 (Mon–Thurs 9am–1pm & 4–6.30pm, Fri 9am–1pm; ℡0783.36.831).

Accommodation

You'll need to book way ahead if you want to stay in Oristano during the Sa Sartiglia festivities (see box, p.1002), and in fact accommodation can be hard to come by at any time, with most of the **hotels** geared towards business travellers, and a clutch of excellent **B&Bs** (none of which accepts credit cards). The nearest **campsites** lie 6km away at Marina di Torre Grande, Oristano's lido, accessible on frequent buses from Oristano's bus and train stations. The best-equipped is *Spinnaker* (℡0783.22.074, ⓦwww.campingspinnaker.com; Easter–Oct), which is near the beach and has bungalows (❸).

L'Arco Vico Ammirato 12, off Piazza Martiri ℡0783.72.849 or 335.690.4240, ⓦwww .arcobedandbreakfast.it. This spotless B&B has wood-beamed rooms with terracotta floors,

and a warm welcome. There's a small terrace, too. ❷
Duomo Via Vittorio Emanuele 34 ℡0783.778.061, ⓦwww.hotelduomo.net. Just across from the

Duomo, this hotel is a modern refurbishment of a seventeenth-century building, with comfortable rooms set around a central courtyard. ⑤

Eleonora Piazza Eleonora d'Arborea 12 ☎0783.704.35 or 347.481.7976, ⓦwww .eleonora-bed-and-breakfast.com. A cosy home-from-home in an atmospheric *palazzo*, parts of which date from medieval times. Rooms have en-suite bathrooms, and there's wi-fi access. ②

Palazzo Corrias Piazza Eleonora d'Arborea 4 ☎0783.781.94 or 349.568.1703, ⓦwww.palazzocorrias.com. This friendly B&B is set in one of Oristano's most historic old *palazzi*, in the family for generations. The B&B's interior is all faded grandeur, with frescoed ceilings, marble floors and antique beds. Bathrooms are shared. ②

The Town

In the heart of the town is Oristano's central symbol, the marble statue of **Eleonora d'Arborea**, presiding over the piazza named after her. Eleonora was the *giudice* of the Arborea region from 1384 to 1404 and is the best loved of Sardinia's medieval rulers, having been the only one who enjoyed any success against the island's aggressors, most notably the Aragonese. She died from plague in 1404, though her most enduring legacy survived her by several centuries: the formulation of a **Code of Laws**, which was eventually extended throughout the island. Eleonora statue, carved in 1881, shows her bearing the scroll on which the laws were written, while inset panels depict her various victories.

Although it's called the **Casa di Eleonora**, the fine house – now semi-derelict – at Via Parpaglia 6–12 (off Piazza Roma) could not in fact have been her home, as it was built over a century after her death. She is, however, unequivocally buried in the fourteenth-century church of **Santa Chiara**, in the parallel Via Garibaldi.

Off Via Parpaglia, Piazzetta Corrias holds Oristano's **Antiquarium Arborense** (daily 9am–2pm & 3–8pm; €3), one of Sardinia's most absorbing museums, housed in a sixteenth-century merchant's house. As well as rotating exhibitions of its extensive collection of nuraghic, Phoenician, Roman and Greek artefacts, there's a collection of medieval and Renaissance art and scaled-down reconstructions of Oristano in 1290 and Roman Tharros.

At one end of Via Parpaglia, linked to Piazza Eleonora by the narrow pedestrianized Corso Umberto, is Piazza Roma, where pavement bars are clustered around the base of the **San Cristóforo** bastion, erected by the *giudice* Mariano II in 1291, once the fulcrum of Oristano's fortifications. The only other survivor of the city's ancient defences is the smaller **Portixedda** ("little gate") tower, at the bottom of Via Mazzini, off Via Roma (Tues–Sun

Sa Sartiglia

The rituals of Oristano's flamboyant **Sa Sartiglia** festival perhaps originated with knights on the Second Crusade, who in the eleventh century may well have imported the trappings of Saracen tournaments to Sardinia. In the period of the Spanish domination, similarly lavish feasts were held for the ruling knights. In time, these celebrations took on a more theatrical aspect and merged with the annual Carnival – the Sa Sartiglia is now a three-day festival that closes the Carnival period, ending on **Shrove Tuesday**. With all the participants masked and costumed, the whole affair exudes a drama unrivalled by Sardinia's other festivals. The climax of proceedings, in Piazza Eleonora, is the joust after which the festival is named, when the mounted contestants attempt to lance a ring, or *sartiglia*, suspended in the air, charging towards it at full gallop.

10am–noon, also 5–7pm in summer, 4–6pm in winter; free), once the entrance to the city.

Oristano's **Duomo** stands in a spacious square up Via Duomo, which is behind Piazza Eleonora. Though started in the thirteenth century, most of the present building is a Baroque reworking, retaining only parts of the apses from its original construction. With the fourteenth-century bell tower topped by a multicoloured tiled cupola and seminary next door, it forms an atmospheric ensemble.

Eating and drinking

Most of Oristano's **restaurants** are scattered on or around Piazza Roma, including the reliable *Trattoria Gino*, Via Tirso 13 (closed Sun), which features traditional Sardinian dishes such as *ravioli sardi* (made with butter and sage) and *sebadas* (warm, cheese-filled pastries topped with honey). A few doors further up the street, the stylish *Cocco & Dessi* has quality meat and seafood dishes, with mains at €12–20, pizza and good lunchtime deals (closed Tues). For cheap pizza and pasta try *La Torre* on Piazza Roma (closed Mon); their speciality is *pizza ai funghi porcini*. You might like to finish your meal with a glass of Oristano's celebrated Vernaccia dessert wine. For daytime snacks or an evening **drink**, the hip *Lolamundo Café* has tables in the quiet Piazzetta Corrias (closed Sun).

Tharros

About 20km west of Oristano, the Punic and Roman ruins at **Tharros** are served by four ARST buses daily (summer only). Like Nora (see p.998), Tharros is pitched on a limb of land surrounded by water, though in this case it's a clenched fist, dominated by a sturdy Spanish watchtower. The peninsula, which forms the northern tip of the mouth of the Golfo di Oristano, was settled by Phoenicians as early as 800 BC. The **site** (daily 9am to 1hr before sunset; €5, including museum at Cabras, see below) consists mostly of Punic and Roman houses arranged on a grid of streets, of which the broad-slabbed Decumanus Maximus is the most impressive. But the things you'll notice immediately on entering the site are the solitary remnants of a first-century BC Roman temple, with only two of its four Corinthian columns still upright. Like Nora, there is much more submerged underwater, as a result of subsidence.

Near the site stands the fifth-century church of **San Giovanni di Sinis**, which vies with Cágliari's San Saturno for the title of oldest Christian church in Sardinia. Further back up the road towards Oristano (signposted off the Tharros road) is the sanctuary of **San Salvatore**, whose main interest is in a subterranean fourth-century chamber dedicated to Mars and Venus, complete with faded frescoes of Venus, Cupid and Hercules – ask the custodian to let you see it. The sanctuary forms the focus of a wild **festival** on the first weekend of September, the main feature of which is a race run at dawn to the village of **Cabras**, 8km away, by the town's boys. Barefoot and clad in white shirts and shorts, they bear aloft the statue of San Salvatore in a re-enactment of a frantic rescue mission undertaken four centuries ago to save the saint from Moorish attackers. There are regular ARST buses from Oristano to Cabras, where the **Museo Civico** at Via Tharros 121 (daily 9am–1pm & 4–8pm, 3–7pm in winter; €3, or €5 including Tharros), on the banks of the lagoon near the southwest entrance to town, has shelves full of finds from Tharros.

Bosa

BOSA is a picture-perfect town of pastel houses huddled around a hilltop castle on the banks of the Temo river, 62km north of Oristano (2hr by bus). Its attractions are low-key – wandering the mazy cobbled lanes of the medieval **Sa Costa** district up to the **castle** is probably the best way to spend your time – but it makes a pleasant, if sleepy place to hole up for a few days. Most of the tourist activity is concentrated in the less attractive but livelier **Bosa Marina** a few kilometres west, where a crescent of sandy beach is backed by hotels, restaurants and bars.

Arrival, information and accommodation

Buses stop at Piazza Zanetti, a short walk from Bosa's **tourist office** at Via Azuni 5 (Mon–Sat 10am–1pm; ☎0785.376.107, ⓦwww.infobosa.it). There's another tourist office in Bosa Marina, on the main Via C. Colombo (mid-June to mid-Sept daily 8.30am–12.30pm & 3.30–11pm; mid-Sept to mid-June Mon–Fri 8.30am–12.30pm & 3.30–7.30pm; ☎0785.377.108); the office is also the agent for the Trenino Verde, a narrow-track tourist train to Macomer, 30km inland, which leaves from here in the summer months. In Bosa, **bikes and kayaks** are available for rent from Pischedda Noleggio, in a hut at the northern end of the old bridge, and there's an **internet point** at Via Gioberti 12 (Mon–Sat 9am–1pm & 5–8.30pm, closes at 7.30pm in winter).

Most of Bosa's **hotels** require full- or half-board in season. There's more choice – though far less character – in Bosa Marina, including, at Via Sardegna 1, one of Sardinia's rare **youth hostels**, (☎0785.375.009, ⓦwww .valevacanze.com; €16 per dorm bed, private doubles ❶), a quiet, modern place which also serves cheap meals. Ask at the tourist office for details of **apartments** to rent. The nearest **campsite**, *Turas* (☎0785.359.270; June–Sept), lies a couple of kilometres south down the coast from Bosa Marina, connected by summer buses.

Hotels

Bainas *On the road to San Pietro* ☎339.209.0967 or 338.306.0004; ⓔagriturbainas@tiscali.it. A 10min walk from Bosa, this attractive agriturismo is a peaceful spot surrounded by fields and orchards, with en-suite rooms giving onto a veranda, and an excellent restaurant (see opposite). ❷

B&B Belvedere Via Belvedere 21 ☎349.594.7875, ⓔbelvedere@bosa.it. Up several flights of steps from the Corso, this B&B is worth the trek, with four cosy en-suite rooms, and panoramic views over the rooftops. ❸

Corte Fiorita Via Lungo Temo De Gasperi 45 ☎0785.377.058, ⓦwww.albergo-diffuso.it. Divided between three buildings, the main part of this hotel overlooks the river. It has plenty of atmosphere, with opulent trimmings and bedrooms with balconies, internet connection and riverside views (for a supplement). ❹

Sa Pischedda Via Roma 8 ☎0785.373.065, ⓦwww.hotelsapischedda .it. At the southern end of the old bridge, this fine old *palazzo* has a grand staircase leading up to attractive, a/c rooms, some with balcony. There's an excellent restaurant, too. ❹

Stella Maris Via C. Colombo 11 ☎0785.375.162, ⓦwww.stellamarisbosa.com. The best of Bosa Marina's fairly uninspiring hotels Is a friendly place on the riverside. All rooms have en-suite bathrooms. ❸

The Town

Bosa's low-key attractions can easily be explored on foot, and it's a pleasant place for a wander. **Sa Piana**, the lower town, is cut through by cobbled Corso Vittorio Emanuele, Bosa's main drag, which runs parallel to the river. North of here, the medieval lanes of **Sa Costa**, or upper town, struggle up the hill towards the castle; take any road leading up from the **cathedral**, at the northern end of Bosa's old bridge. Keep climbing for about twenty minutes to reach the **Castello Malaspina** (May, June, Sept & Oct daily 10am–1pm & 3.30–6pm; July daily 10am–1pm & 4–7.30pm; Aug daily 10am–7.30pm; Nov–April usually Sat 10am–1pm & 3.30–6pm, Sun 3.30–6pm, but check first at ☏333.544.5675; €2), erected by the Malaspina family in 1122 – there's also a road that skirts round the back of town, leading to the castle gate. Within the ramparts, take a look inside the church to see some rare Catalan frescoes dating from around 1300. From the ramparts themselves, the panoramic view takes in town, river and sea, and you can pick out Bosa's former cathedral of **San Pietro**, Sardinia's oldest Romanesque church, built in the eleventh century, with a Gothic facade added by Cistercian monks a couple of hundred years later. For a closer look, follow the country road running parallel to the south bank of the river from the old bridge eastwards for about 2km (May, June, Sept & Oct Tues–Sun 10am–1pm & 3.30–6pm; July daily 10am–1pm & 4–7.30pm; Aug daily 10am–7.30pm; during rest of year, call ☏333.544.5675; €1).

Bosa Marina

In the opposite direction, **BOSA MARINA** lies 5km downstream of the old bridge, on what was the town's original site before its inhabitants shifted to a more defensible position. Today it is a conventional minor resort with a small choice of hotels and bars and a broad swathe of sandy beach. Across the river, you can also swim from the rocks at the mouth of the Temo, or further north off the beautiful rocky coast accessible from the Alghero road. This undeveloped, highly panoramic stretch of coast is one of the last habitats in Sardinia of the griffon vulture.

Eating and drinking

In Bosa, the *Sa Pischedda* hotel (see opposite) has a renowned **restaurant** with outdoor seating in summer, and also runs the riverside *Ponte Vecchio* restaurant nearby (mid-June to mid-Sept), both reasonably priced. The *Bainas* agriturismo (see opposite) serves wholesome organic and vegetarian dishes, using its own homegrown produce, but you'll need to call ahead. Alternatively, the rustic but elegant *Borgo Sant'Ignazio*, in an alley above the Corso, Via Sant'Ignazio 33 (☏0785.374.129), offers delicious local specialities of a meatier nature, with main courses at €10–15. For lunchtime **snacks** and refreshments, avoid the pricey bars on the main Corso in favour of the *Taverna*, on Piazza Cármine (closed Thurs in winter).

Nuoro and around

"There is nothing to see in Nuoro: which to tell the truth, is always a relief. Sights are an irritating bore," wrote D.H. Lawrence of the town he visited in 1921, though he was impressed by its appearance to him "as if at the end of the world, mountains rising sombre behind". **NUORO**'s superb backdrop – beneath the soaring peak of Monte Ortobene and opposite the sheer and stark heights of Monte Corrasi – is still its main draw, and it makes a useful transport junction and base for excursions. The last century has witnessed few changes, bar an unsightly accretion of apartment blocks and administrative buildings. Nuoro can lay claim to a distinguished literary heritage, however: Sardinia's best-known poet, **Sebastiano Satta** (1867–1914), was Nuorese, as was the author **Grazia Deledda** (1871–1936), who won the Nobel Prize for Literature in 1926 in recognition of a writing career devoted to recounting the day-to-day trials and passions of local villagers.

Nuoro's biggest annual **festival**, the **Festa del Redentore**, is one of the most vibrant events on the island's calendar, taking place over the last ten days of August, when enthusiastic dancing and singing in dialect culminate with a costumed procession to Mount Ortobene (see opposite).

Arrival, information and accommodation

You can reach Nuoro in an hour and a quarter on the narrow-gauge FdS line from Macomer, a stop on the main train line from Cágliari, or on an FdS bus from Cágliari or Sássari. Nuoro's **train station** is a twenty-minute walk from the centre of town along Via La Mármora, where frequent **city buses** stop (buy tickets from the shop inside the station). ARST and FdS **buses** stop at Via Sardegna, ten-minutes' walk south of the station. The main **tourist office** is at Piazza Italia 19, on the edge of the old quarter (June–Sept daily 9am–7pm; Oct–May Mon–Fri 8.30am–1.30pm & 3–5.30pm; ☏0784.238.878). There's also a private information office at Corso Garibaldi 155 (Mon–Fri 9am–1pm & 3.30–7pm, Sat 9am–1pm; ☏0784.38.777), which can arrange excursions around Nuoro.

Nuoro has few **accommodation** options; consider staying outside town on Monte Ortobene or even further afield in Oliena (see opposite for both). In town, the *Grillo*, near the ethnographic museum at Via Monsignor Melas 14 (☏0784.38.678, ⓦwww.grillohotel.it; ❸), is one of the cheaper hotels – a rather charmless business-class place. You may prefer one of the town's B&Bs (no credit cards): *Silvia e Paolo*, right in the centre of town at Corso Garibaldi 58 (☏0784.31.280 or 328.921.2199, ⓦwww.silviaepaolo.it; ❶), has spotless, comfortable rooms, while no-frills *Giada*, near the tourist office at Via Ballero 32 (☏338.853.5759; ❷), has plain rooms and kitchen facilities.

The Town

Nuoro's **old quarter** is the most appealing part of town, spread around pedestrianized **Corso Garibaldi**, along which a buzzing *passeggiata* injects a bit of life into the place. Just off here, on Via Satta, is **MAN** (Museo d'Arte Nuoro; Tues–Sun 10am–1pm & 4.30–8.30pm; €3; ⓦwww.museoman.it), a superb collection of twentieth-century and contemporary art from the whole island, with a preponderance of local artists. Displayed on four floors, the works are refreshingly diverse, and there are also temporary exhibitions of modern Italian art. At the top of the Corso, turn right past the Duomo and along Via Mereu to reach the impressive **Museo della Vita e delle Tradizioni Popolari Sarde** (daily: mid-June to Sept 9am–8pm; Oct to mid-June 9am–1pm & 3–7pm; €3), which holds Sardinia's most comprehensive range of local costumes, jewellery, masks, carpets and other handicrafts, as well as traditional musical instruments from around the island. Turn left at the eastern end of the Corso and up Via Deledda for the **Casa di Grazia Deledda** (same hours as ethnographic museum; €2.50), the restored home of Nuoro's literary star, displaying various photos and mementoes. Turn south down Via Deledda to find the **Museo Archeologico** (Tues & Thurs 9am–1pm & 3–5pm, Wed, Fri & Sat 9am–1pm; free), accessed from Via Manno or Via Asproni, which takes in everything from rocks and skulls to carved vases, neolithic jewelry and nuraghic art.

Eating and drinking

Many of the town's **restaurants** feature regional specialities: the best is *Il Rifugio* at Via Mereu 28 (℡0784.232.355; closed Wed), where main courses are €9–15 and the pizzas are delicious. Other places include the arty *Tascusi*, Via Aspromonte 13 (closed Sun), with good fixed-priced deals, and *Su Nugoresu*, Piazza San Giovanni 9, a pleasant trattoria in a pretty piazza with tables outside in summer (closed Mon in winter), both off the top end of the Corso. For breakfast or a lunchtime snack, *Bar Nuovo* at the top of Corso Garibaldi has outdoor tables; for evening **drinks**, *Café San Juan* on Piazza San Giovanni has cosy nooks in various rooms.

Monte Ortobene

Between mid-June and mid-September bus #8 runs every twenty minutes or so (with a much reduced service in winter) from Nuoro's Piazza Vittorio Emanuele up to the summit of **Monte Ortobene**, 8km away, from where there are striking views over the gorge separating Nuoro from the Supramonte massif. This is the venue for Nuoro's **Festa del Redentore** at the end of August, when a procession from town weaves up the mountain to the bronze **statue** of the Redeemer at the top (955m). The statue makes an excellent vantage point, with dizzying views down to the valley floor. The woods are perfect for walks and picnics, and there are possibilities for horse riding at Farcana, signposted left near the top, where there's also a grand open-air public swimming pool open in summer. There's an excellent **B&B** on the mountain, the friendly 🜨 *Casa Solotti* (℡0784.33.954 or 328.602.8975, ⓦwww.casasolotti.it; ❷; no credit cards), just after the Farcana turn-off, offering wonderful mountain views and great breakfasts; ring ahead for directions or a pick-up from Nuoro.

The interior and the east coast

Though little travelled by tourists, Sardinia's **interior** is in many ways the most interesting part of the island, dominated by thick forests and rugged peaks. The local inhabitants have retained a fierce sense of independence and loyalty to their traditions, and this is especially true in the ring of the once almost impenetrable Monti del **Gennargentu**, centred on the island's highest peak, La Mármora (1834m). The range forms the core of the **Barbágia** region, called Barbaria by the Romans who, like their successors, were never able to subdue it, foiled by the guerrilla warfare for which its hidden recesses proved ideal. The Barbágia has huge appeal to outdoors enthusiasts; mountain hiking in particular is increasingly popular – ask at Oliena's tourist office for routes and lists of guides (see p.1008).

Sardinia's long **eastern seaboard** is highly developed around the resorts of Siniscola and Posada, but further south it preserves its desolate beauty, virtually untouched apart from a couple of isolated spots around **Cala Golone**, and, further down, **Tortolì** and the small port of **Arbatax**.

Oliena and Tiscali

The multicoloured rooftops of **OLIENA**, 12km southeast of Nuoro, are visible across the valley (buses roughly every two hours). Though famed as the haunt of bandits until relatively recent times, the village prefers its reputation as the producer of one of the island's best **wines**, the Nepente – a variety of the prized

The Barbágia's villages evolved primarily as shepherds' settlements, whose isolated circumstances and economic difficulties in the postwar years led to widescale emigration and, among those who stayed behind, a crime wave. Sheep-rustling and internecine feuding came to be replaced by the infinitely more lucrative practice of the **kidnapping** and ransoming of wealthy industrialists or their families; during 1966–68, scores of carabinieri were drafted into the area to comb the mountains for the hideouts, rarely with any success. Recent years, however, have seen a lull in the kidnaps, since the high-profile case of Farouk Kassam, an eight-year-old boy, who was abducted on the Costa Smeralda and held for seven months in 1992, having part of his ear cut off by his kidnappers to accelerate the ransom payment.

Some 18km south of Oliena, **Orgósolo** is stuck with its label of bandit capital of the island. Perhaps the village's most infamous son is **Graziano Mesina**, the so-called "Scarlet Rose", who won local hearts in the 1960s by robbing from the rich to give to the poor and only killing for revenge against those who had betrayed him. Roaming at will through the mountains, even granting interviews to reporters and television journalists, he was eventually captured and incarcerated in Sássari prison. Escaping in 1968, he was recaptured near Nuoro and flown by helicopter the same day to appear on television in Cágliari. He was finally freed in 2004 after forty years behind bars, and returned to live in Orgósolo.

Today, the only traces of the area's violent past are in its vivid, graffiti-style **murals**, with a concentration in Orgósolo, some covering whole buildings. Portraying village culture and history, many of the paintings are peopled with gun-toting locals and illustrate the oppression of the landless by the landowners.

Cannonau – a dry, almost black concoction that turns lighter and stronger over time. The best place to sample it is the Cantina Oliena winery, at Via Nuoro 112 (Mon–Fri 8.30am–1pm & 3.30–5.30pm, Sat 8.30am–noon).

Oliena lies on the slopes of **Monte Corrasi**, a dramatically rugged limestone elevation which forms part of the Supramonte massif and rises to 1363m. There are numerous organized **excursions** you can make around its various caves and crags, the most famous of which is to the remote Valle Lanaittu and the nuraghic village of **TISCALI** (daily: May–Sept 9am–7pm; Oct–April 9am–5pm; €5), spectacularly sited within a vast mountain-top cavern, a half-day trip from Oliena. All hikes should be accompanied by a guide, which can be arranged through Oliena's helpful **tourist office** on the main Corso Deledda (Mon–Sat 9.30am–1pm & 4–7pm; ☎0784.286.078). There's internet access here too, and bilingual staff can also book **accommodation** in the area: the best options are *B&B Santa Maria* at Via Grazia Deledda 76 (☎0784.287.278 or 328.117.8551; ⓦwww.bbsantamaria.it; ❷), with comfortable rooms and friendly staff; *CiKappa*, Via M. Luther King (☎0784.288.721, ⓦwww.cikappa.it; ❷), a functional hotel further up the hill, with a lively pizzeria below; and *Cooperativa Turistica Enis*, up a steep hill 3km south in località Maccione (☎0784.288.363, ⓦwww.coopenis .it; ❷), where there are also pitches for **camping** and a superb **restaurant** (closed Nov–March) with lofty views over the valley.

Dorgali

Centre of the renowned **Cannonau** wine-growing region, **DORGALI** attracts a lot of tourists in summer, both for its craftwork and as a starting point for excursions into the mountains, to places such as Tiscali (see above). Local information is handled at the **tourist office** at Via Lamarmora 108 (Mon–Fri 9am–1pm & 4–8pm, 3.30–7.30pm in winter, July & Aug also Sat 9am–1pm &

4–8pm; ☎0784.96.243, ⓦwww.dorgali.it), and there's a good **hotel** signposted off the SS125 a couple of kilometres south of town, the *Sant'Elene* (☎0784.94.572, ⓦwww.hotelsantelene.it; ❸).

Cala Gonone

Ten kilometres east of Dorgali, the small port of **CALA GONONE** is reached by heading south on the SS125 and turning left into the long tunnel through the rock wall, from which the road plunges down to the bay. Beautifully sited at the base of the 900-metre-high mountains, this once tiny settlement was until recently accessible only by boat. Now hotels and villas dominate the scene, though these have not spoilt the sense of isolation, and it is worth a visit if only to take advantage of the numerous boat tours to the secluded beaches up and down the coast. Among the best are **Cala Luna** and **Cala Sisine**, though if you are here for a short time you would do well to choose a tour that combines pauses at these swimming stops with exploration of the deep grottoes that pit the shore.

Most famous of these is the **Grotta del Bue Marino**, formerly home to a colony of Mediterranean monk seals, or "sea ox". It's among Sardinia's most spectacular caves, a luminescent gallery filled with remarkable natural sculptures, resembling organ pipes, wedding cakes and even human heads – one of them is known as *Dante*, after a fondly imagined resemblance to the poet. Boat trips from Cala Gonone cost around €16.50 including entry to the grotto.

Tickets for the various excursions are sold at the port, and there's a **tourist office** on Via Bue Marino (daily: March–June 9am–noon & 3–7pm; July & Aug 9am–10pm; ☎0784.93.696, ⓦwww.calagonone.com). Best of the **hotels** here are the bougainvillea-covered *Cala Luna*, on Lungomare Palmasera (☎0784.93.133, ⓦwww.hotelcalaluna.com; Easter–Nov; ❺), with direct access to the beach, and lively *Pop* (☎0784.93.185; ❷), by the harbour, also with sea views and an excellent restaurant. There's also an excellent, well-equipped **campsite**, a brief walk up from the beach and near the tourist office (☎0784.93.165, ⓦwww.campingcalagonone.it; mid-March to Oct).

There's a good range of **places to eat** in town, including a few pricey gourmet seafood parlours along the waterfront (most close in winter). The trattoria attached to the *San Francisco* hotel on Via Magellano cooks up wonderful ravioli and gnocchi as well as fish and pizzas (closed Tues in winter), while the *Roadhouse Blues* birreria on Lungomare Palmasera serves snacks and beers till late (closed Tues in winter & all Dec–Feb). On the seafront at Piazza

---

Hikes from Cala Gonone and Dorgali

South of Cala Gonone lies one of Sardinia's last truly untouched tracts, a majestic mountain landscape, largely devoid of human life, cut through by the Flumineddu valley and, high above it, the highly panoramic SS125. There are several half- or full-day **hikes** which can be made here, for example following the coast south **from Cala Gonone** to the beaches at Cala Luna and Cala Sisine. From Cala Sisine, the route wanders inland up the Sisine canyon, as far as the solitary church of San Pietro, from where a track leads down to Baunei. Dorgali's tourist office can supply a list of guides for the Sisine canyon, for Tiscali (see opposite), and for the **Gorroppu gorge**, one of southern Europe's deepest canyons. Even for shorter hikes, you'll need hardy footwear with a secure grip and ankle support, and preferably some protection for your head against bumps and falls: the boulders can be extremely slippery, especially when wet.

Andrea Doria, *Su Recreu* serves the town's best ice cream, as well as meals, sandwiches and snacks.

The Gennargentu massif

The central region of the Barbágia holds the **Gennargentu** chain of mountains – the name means "silver gate", referring to the snow that covers them every winter. Here, you'll find the island's only skiing facilities on **Monte Bruncu Spina**, Sardinia's second-highest peak (1829m). In spring and summer, you can explore this and other areas on **mountain treks**, best undertaken in the company of guides for which the tourist office at Nuoro can supply a list.

The nearby settlements make useful bases for both skiers and trekkers, for example **FONNI**, 13km due south of Mamoiada and at 1000m the island's highest village. Try to coincide your visit with one of Fonni's costumed **festivals**, principally the Madonna dei Mártiri, on the Monday following the first Sunday in June, and on San Giovanni's day on June 24. Of the **hotels** here, try the modern and clean *Cualbu* on Via del Lavoro (☎0784.57.054, ⓦwww .hotelcualbu.com; ❸), or *Sa Orte*, Via Roma 14 (☎0784.58.020, ⓦwww .hotelsaorte.it; ❸), an elegantly restored granite building with period trappings; both have their own restaurants.

Other feasible bases for the area include **TONARA**, about 30km southwest of Fonni, where the family-run **hotel** *Locanda del Muggianeddu* (☎0784.63.885; ❶; no credit cards) has a restaurant. *Il Castagneto* is an independent **hostel** (☎0784.610.005; Easter to mid-Nov; €14), signposted on the northern edge of the village, with ample dormitory space as well as en-suite doubles (❶). Hostellers and others can enjoy wonderful views over wooded slopes from the outdoor tables at the **pizzeria** here (closed Tues in winter). Finally, **ARITZO**, 15km south, has several **hotels**: try the old-fashioned but comfortable *Moderno*, at the top of the village on Viale Kennedy (☎0784.629.229, ⓦwww .hotelmodernoaritzo.it; ❷), with a small garden and restaurant.

Tortolì and Arbatax

South of Cala Gonone and the majestic Gorroppu gorge the SS125 descends steeply to **TORTOLÌ**, 5km inland from the port of **ARBATAX**, a fairly nonde-script port from which ferries ply twice weekly to Genoa, Civitavécchia and (summer only) Fiumicino. The small beach here is famous for its red rocks, but there are better beaches outside town – north around **Santa Maria Navarrese** and south at **Lido Orrì**. There's a seasonal **tourist office** at Arbatax station (Wed–Mon June to mid-Sept 9.30am–12.30pm & 6.30–8.30pm) that has infor-mation on sea **excursions**, including to the Grotta del Bue Marino (see p.1009) for €35–50, while Tortolì's Pro Loco on Via Mazzini is open year-round (June to mid-Sept Mon–Sat 9am–12.30pm & 4.30–8pm; mid-Sept to May Mon–Fri 9am–12.30pm; ☎0782.622.824). **Ferry tickets** are available from the Tirrenia office near the port, on your right as you walk towards the station (Mon–Fri 9am–1pm & 4–7pm, Sat 9am–1pm, Sun 10pm–midnight; ☎0782.667.067).

Frequent daily **buses** connect Cágliari and Nuoro with Tortolì, which, along with Arbatax, is also on the FdS narrow-gauge Trenino Verde **railway**. The train follows an inland route to Cágliari, with a change at Mandas; the full journey from the coast to Cágliari takes around seven dawdling hours (Wed–Mon mid-June to mid-Sept only). A frequent summer shuttle **bus** (#2) connects Tortolì, Arbatax, Lido Orrì and Porto Frailis.

There's little to detain you here, but if you need to **stay**, try the small *Gabbiano* (June–Sept; ☎0782.667.622; ❷; no credit cards), a couple of kilometres south of the port in the Porto Frailis district and near a good beach. Otherwise, head towards Tortolì, where there is a small selection, including the *Splendor* on Viale Arbatax (⊤0782.623.037; ❷) – opposite the Esso station on the other side of the rail tracks. Best of the local **campsites** is *Telis* at Porto Frailis (⊤0782.667.140, ⓦwww.campingtelis.com), which has bungalows to rent (❷). As for **restaurants**, there are few places in Arbatax itself, but Porto Frailis district is a better choice, where *Il Faro*, overlooking the beach, has a good choice of fish (⊤0782.667.499; closed Mon in winter).

Olbia

The largest town in Sardinia's northeastern wedge, **OLBIA** owes its recent phenomenal growth to the huge influx of tourists bound for one of the Mediterranean's loveliest stretches of coast, the **Costa Smeralda** (see p.1013). Awash with traffic and ugly apartment blocks, **Olbia** is the least Sardinian of all the island's towns. Its port and airport, however, make it an inevitable stop for some and its numerous bars and restaurants are usually a-buzz with tourists, sailors from the port and US service personnel from the nearby NATO base.

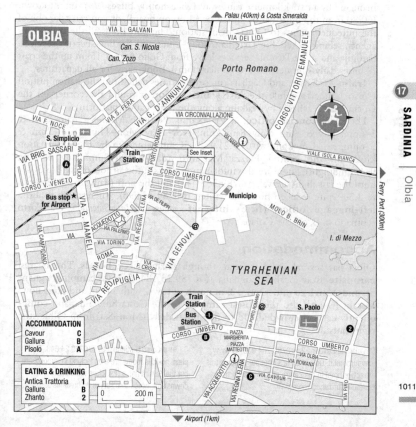

If you're stuck for an afternoon here, you might as well visit the town's only item of historical interest, the little basilica of **San Símplicio** (daily 9am–1pm & 3.30–8pm), on the street of the same name. Part of the great Pisan reconstruction programme of the eleventh and twelfth centuries, the simple granite structure has three aisles separated by pillars and columns recycled from Roman constructions – even the stoup for the holy water was formerly an urn that held cremated ashes. The church is the venue for Olbia's biggest **festa**, six days of processions, costumed dancing and fireworks around May 15, commemorating San Símplicio's martyrdom in the fourth century.

Arrival and information

Olbia's **airport** (ⓦwww.olbiairport.it) is connected by **buses** #2 and #10 every twenty minutes (hourly on Sun) until 8pm, which take just ten minutes to reach the central Piazza Regina Margherita (tickets €0.80 from the bar or ticket machine in the terminal, €1.30 on board). **Taxis** cost about €15. There is a summer-only bus service (5–12 daily) from the airport to the **resorts** of Arzachena, Palau and Santa Teresa di Gallura (see pp.1014–1016), so you can avoid Olbia completely if you're bound for the beach-chequered coast or for Corsica.

Ferries (see box, p.991) dock at the island of Isola Bianca, connected to the mainland by a two-kilometre causeway; twice-hourly **buses** (#9) run into town (€0.80 from the information office, or €1.30 on board), or you can take one of the infrequent trains to Olbia's main station. The port holds all the main ferry agents, selling tickets for Tirrenia, Moby Lines and Sardinia Ferries services. Sardinia and some Tirrenia services leave from Golfo Aranci, 15km up the coast (8 buses daily summer only, or regular trains). Book early for all departures.

Trains for Sássari and Cágliari run several times daily from the station just off Corso Umberto, while the ARST **bus station** is round the corner on the Corso (also reachable by walking along the train station platform).

The main **tourist office**, at Via Nanni 39 (June Mon–Sat 8am–2pm & 3–6pm; July & Aug daily 8am–2pm; Nov–May Mon–Thurs 8am–2pm & 3–6pm, Fri 8am–2pm; ☎0789.21.453), is supplemented by the information kiosk on the central Piazza Matteotti (daily: 9am–9pm; July & Aug 9am–midnight). There are also information desks at the airport (daily 8/8.30am until the last flight arrival; ☎0789.563.444) and the port (daily: 6am–12.40pm & 2.30–9pm; reduced hours in winter; ☎0789.24.696), where there is also a **left-luggage office**. There's **internet** access at *InterSmeraldo*, Via Porto Romano 6/B, off the Corso.

Accommodation

Olbia has several good, central, though fairly pricey, **hotels**. The nearest **campsite** is at località Cugnana (☎0789.33.184, ⓦwww.campingcugnana .it; mid-March to mid-Oct), 12km north of town, with a pool and bungalows to rent (❸): it's also the closest campsite to the Costa Smeralda, and consequently can get crowded. Up to five buses daily (Mon–Sat) from Olbia stop right outside.

Cavour Via Cavour 22 ☎0789.204.033, ⓦwww .cavourhotel.it. One of Olbia's cheaper options, this attractive hotel in the centre of town has simple, tastefully furnished rooms. ❸

Gallura Corso Umberto 145 ☎0789.24.648. The plain, no-frills rooms are a bit lacking in atmosphere, but the *Gallura* has a first-class restaurant downstairs, which also serves up breakfasts. ❸

Li Licci Località Valentino Stazzo La Gruci
☎079.665.114, ⓦwww.lilicci.com. There are a
number of *agriturismi* within easy reach of Olbia,
and this is the best of them: a 20min drive away,
with simple rooms and an outstanding restaurant –
worth a trip in its own right. ❸

Pisolo Via Fiume d'Italia 6 ☎0789.209.115 or
340.243.0845, ⓔpisolo32@aliceposta.it. This
friendly B&B, just off Olbia's main street, has two
brightly coloured rooms with en-suite bathroom. No
credit cards. ❸

Eating and drinking

Olbia has plenty of **restaurants**, catering to the huge numbers of tourists that
pass through here. The **cafés** and **bars** on Piazza Margherita are good for
coffees, fresh *cornetti* and **drinks**, with seating both inside and out.

Antica Trattoria Via Pala 6 ☎0789.25.725. A
popular place, with lower prices for its pastas,
pizzas and seafood than the classier *Gallura*.
Closed Sun.

🏃 **Gallura** (see opposite). Top-quality food and
smart surroundings attract plenty of locals
to this restaurant, lauded by many Italian foodie
guides. Excellent wine list too.

🏃 **Li Licci** (see above). A meal at this
atmospheric agriturismo is quite an

experience. There are panoramic views across the
surrounding woodland, and the food is superb: the
place to come for Sardinian specialities such as
porcheddu (roast suckling pig) and the teardrop-
shaped *malloreddus* pasta. Booking essential.
Zhanto Via delle Terme 1, just off the Corso
☎0789.25.674. This restaurant serves pizzas as
well as a regular restaurant menu (mains are
€8–15) in elegant surroundings. There's a small
garden, too. Closed Sun.

The Costa Smeralda and around

Long a magnet for Italy's glitziest celebrities, the five-star development of the
Costa Smeralda, built in the 1960s, helped to transform the economy of the
entire island. A coastline this beautiful inevitably comes at a price, however:
budget accommodation is virtually non-existent, and the high-end hotels that
cram this corner of the island are disappointingly soulless. **Arzachena** or
Cannigione are both cheaper bases from which to explore the area.

The Costa Smeralda begins about 12km north of Olbia and is is defined as
the ten-kilometre strip between the gulfs of Cugnana and Arzachena. Although
strict rules were imposed to prevent overzealous development – you won't see
any multistorey hotels, advertising hoardings or fast-food restaurants – the Costa
lacks any genuine fishing villages and the luxurious holiday villages have a
bland, almost suburban feel. This hasn't stopped the mega-rich from coming in
droves – Silvio Berlusconi owns six properties here.

You can judge for yourself by taking a look at the "capital" of the Costa
Smeralda, **PORTO CERVO**, connected to Olbia and Arzachena by ARST
buses (3–7 daily Mon–Sat). The "local"-style rustic-red architecture here
embodies the dream of an idyllic Mediterranean village without any of the
irritations of real life. Graffiti- and litter-free, Porto Cervo exults in its exclu-
sivity, with a glittering yachting marina as its centrepiece.

You'll need your own transport to reach the sandy **beaches** dotted down
the coast south of Porto Cervo. None is clearly marked; just follow any dirt
track down to the sea – the rougher it is, the more promising. Try **Cappric-
cioli** and **Liscia Ruia**, 6km south of Porto Cervo and near the Costa
Smeralda's most exclusive hotel, the *Cala di Volpe* (☎0789.976.111, ⓦwww
.starwoodhotels.com; ❾) – but free to all.

▲ The Costa Smeralda

Arzachena

ARZACHENA is a not particularly inspiring inland town, though it has banks, stores, restaurants and a handful of pricey but characterless **hotels**. Most affordable of these, the *Citti*, lies on the edge of town on the main road to Palau at Viale Costa Smeralda 197 (℡0789.82.662, Ⓦwww.hotelcitti.com; ❹), with a small pool, while *Casa Mia*, on the other side of town on the Olbia–Palau road, Viale Costa Smeralda (℡0789.82.790, Ⓦwww.hotelcasamia.it; ❻), has a garden and restaurant; both have significantly lower rates outside peak season. At least five buses daily leave Olbia on the northward-bound SS125 that takes in Arzachena, Palau and Santa Teresa di Gallura.

Sharing many of the Costa Smeralda's natural features, the **Golfo di Arzachena** is a deep narrow bay with facilities concentrated in and around **CANNIGIONE**, a small fishing port and yachting resort linked to Arzachena by bus (Mon–Sat 5–8 daily). The region's main **tourist office** is here, on Lungomare Andrea Doria (June–Sept Mon & Sat 9am–1pm, Fri 9am–2pm, Tues–Thurs 9am–2pm & 3–7pm; Oct–May daily 9am–1pm; ℡0789.892.019), and there's also a private tourist office at Via Nazionale 47 (April–Oct Mon–Sat 9am–12.30pm & 6–8pm; July & Aug also Sun 9am–11.30pm; ℡0789.88.510). Virtually all Cannigione's hotels are ❻ and above; the cheapest one is *Hotel del Porto*, opposite the marina at Via Nazionale 94 (℡0789.88.011, Ⓦwww .hoteldelporto.com; ❹), which has rooms with balconies and a good seafood restaurant. The *Villaggio Isuledda* **campsite** (℡0789.86.003, Ⓦwww.isuledda.it;

mid-April to mid-Oct), a couple of kilometres north of Cannigione in **LA CONIA**, is right on the shore and has a range of mobile homes and bungalows to rent (③—⑤).

The Maddalena Islands

The profusion of minor **islands** off this stretch of coast, over sixty in all, can be explored on various boat tours. From **PALAU**, 10km up the coast from Cannigione, ferries leave every fifteen minutes in peak season (around €10 return per person, €42 return for two people in a medium-sized car; book ahead in high season) for the main island of the Maddalena archipelago, **La Maddalena**. An upbeat, attractive town, it has few sights as such, but is full of life in the summer months. From here, you can drive, bike or hike across to neighboring **Caprera**, the island on which Garibaldi spent his last years.

La Maddalena

It takes twenty minutes to cross what Nelson called "Agincourt Sound" from Palau to the port and sole town on **LA MADDALENA**, classified as a national park. The town, bearing the same name as the island, is a cheerful place with a population of about 15,000, swollen by a large number of Italian and US sailors. Their headquarters are on the eastern side of town, a drab area of barracks, though the main military installations and submarine base are situated on the neighbouring island of Santo Stéfano, briefly captured by Napoleon in 1793 in an abortive attempt to take Sardinia.

Most of the town's action takes place in the narrow lanes between Piazza Umberto I and Cala Gavetta (the marina for small boats), a five-minute walk from the ferry port (heading left) and site of the **tourist office** (Mon & Wed 9am–1pm & 3.30–5.30pm, Tues, Thurs & Fri 9am–1pm; ☎0789.736.321). The town is not particularly well off for **hotels**. Cheapest are the *Arcipélago* at Via Indipendenza Traversa 2 (☎0789.727.328; ③), a signposted fifteen-minute walk east from the ferry port, offering modern, quiet rooms, and, in the opposite direction, the recently revamped *Gabbiano* at Via Giulio Césare 20 (☎0789.722.507, ⓦwww.hotel-ilgabbiano.it; ⑥; closed Jan to mid-Feb), panoramically sited on the shore beyond Cala Gavetta. There are also three **campsites**, all outside town and all closed outside the summer months: *Il Sole*, on Via Indipendenza (☎0789.727.727), *Maddalena*, in the Moneta district (☎0789.728.051, ⓦwww.campingmaddalena.it), and *Abbatoggia* (☎0789.739.173, ⓔcamping.abbatoggia@tiscali.it), close to some good beaches in the north of the island. The last two sites also have caravans and bungalows to rent (③—⑥).

The island invites aimless wandering and offers a variety of sandy and rocky beaches in mostly undeveloped coves. **Buses** run to various parts of the island (and to Caprera) from Piazza Umberto I near the port (every 30min–1hr in summer; every 1–2hr in winter). **Bikes** and **mopeds** can be rented from any of the outlets on the seafront towards Cala Gavetta for about €10 a day for a bike, or €40 for a scooter (prices drop outside peak season). The **beaches** on the northern and western coasts are most attractive, particularly those around the tiny port of Madonetta, 5km west of La Maddalena, and at Cala Lunga, 5km north of town.

Caprera

Though partly used for military purposes, **CAPRERA**'s protected wooded parkland is open to all, and is undeveloped apart from Garibaldi's house in the centre and a couple of secluded, self-contained tourist complexes.

Giuseppe Garibaldi (1807–82) came to live in Caprera in 1855, after a twenty-year exile from Italy. It was from here that he embarked on his spectacular conquest of Sicily and Naples in 1861, accompanied by his thousand Red-Shirts, and it was here that he returned after his campaigns to resume a simple farming life. Having bought the northern part of the island for £360, he spent much of his time writing his memoirs and some bad novels. In 1864 a group of English admirers provided the money for Garibaldi to buy the rest of Caprera from local landowners.

The **museum** (Tues–Sat 9am–1.30pm; €4) is in Garibaldi's old house, the elegant South American-style **Casa Bianca**, which has been preserved pretty much as he left it. Visitors are escorted past the bed where he slept, a smaller one where he died, various scrolls, manifestoes and pronouncements, as well as an array of personal memorabilia. A stopped clock and a wall-calendar indicate the precise time and date of his death. The tour ends with Garibaldi's **tomb** in the garden, its rough granite contrasting with the more pompous tombs of his last wife and five of his children. Garibaldi had requested to be cremated, but following the wishes of his son Menotti his corpse was embalmed. In 1932, fifty years after his death, his tomb was opened to reveal the body perfectly intact.

Santa Teresa di Gallura and around

The road from Olbia and Palau passes a succession of lovely bays, some dramatic rocky coastline, and a handful of campsites. Six kilometres west of Palau, the slender isthmus of **Porto Pollo** is Sardinia's busiest watersports centre, with ideal conditions for **windsurfing** and **kitesurfing**. There are numerous surf schools and rental outfits, while the sheltered, dune-backed beaches will equally appeal to non-surfers. Some 15km further west, **SANTA TERESA DI GALLURA** is Sardinia's northernmost port, served by regular buses from Arzachena and Palau (5–12 daily). The town gets extremely lively in summer, with a buzzing nightlife, but the main draw is the **beaches**, many enjoying superb views over to Corsica, just 11km away. There's one stretch of sand right at the edge of town, but some of the finest beaches on the whole island are a short bus ride away (up to 5 daily June–Sept), with **Punta Falcone** and **La Marmorata** to the east, and **Capo Testa**, with its wind-sculpted granite rock formations, 3km west of Santa Teresa.

Practicalities

Santa Teresa's **tourist office** is on the main Piazza Vittorio Emanuele (June & Sept daily 9am–1pm & 4.30–7.30pm; July & Aug 9.30am–midnight; Oct–May Mon, Thurs & Fri 9am–1pm, Tues & Wed 9am–1pm & 3.30–6.30pm; ☎0789.754.127, ⊛www.comunesantateresagallura.it). You can rent **bikes** (€10 a day) and **scooters** (€26 a day) nearby at Piazza San Vittorio 7. From the port on the eastern side of town, Moby Lines and Saremar operate sailings to Bonifacio in Corsica (2–7 daily; 1hr; from €18 return per person, €44 return per car). The town's plentiful **hotels** – most of which demand at least half-board in July and August – include the comfortable, family-run *Scano* at Via Lazio 4 (☎0789.754.447, ⓦwww.albergoscano.it; ❸), but the town's **B&Bs** offer better value (no credit cards accepted). *La Chicca di Francesca* at Via Basilicata 4 (☎0789.754.691 and 347.335.079, ⓦwww.lachiccadifrancesca.com; closed Dec & Jan; ❸), is set in lush gardens and has three rooms with wood furnishings and air-conditioning, while nearby ✴*Le Ortensie* at Via Campania 15 (☎0789.755.469 and 328.255.6559, ⓦwww.bbleortensie.com; ❸) is spotless and welcoming, with delicious breakfasts. The nearest **campsite** is *La Liccia* (☎0789.755.190, ⓦwww.campinglaliccia.com; May–Sept), 6km west, signposted off the Castel-sardo road, near a beach and with bungalows (❸). Santa Teresa has no shortage of bars and **restaurants**: for a good meal try *Pepè Satan*, at Via Lamarmora 20 (closed mid-Oct to mid-April), a backstreet pizzeria with courtyard, or *Il Grottino* at Via del Mare 14 (closed Thurs Nov–May), another good pizzeria, which also serves fish and meat dishes.

Sássari and around

Sardinia's second city, **SÁSSARI**, combines an insular, traditional feel, as embodied in its well-preserved tangle of lanes in the old quarter, with a forward-looking, confident air that is most evident in its modern centre. As a holiday destination, however, this inland town has limited appeal, lacking enough entertainment to fill more than a couple of afternoons or evenings. Historically, while Cágliari was Pisa's base of operations during the Middle Ages, Sássari was the Genoan capital, ruled by the Doria family, whose power reached throughout the Mediterranean. Under the Aragonese it became an important centre of Spanish hegemony, and the Spanish stamp is still strong, not least in its churches. In the sixteenth century the Jesuits founded Sardinia's first **university** here, which continues to excel in the spheres of law, medicine and politics.

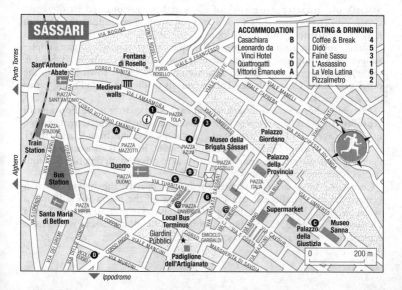

If lively Sássari leaves you longing for some peace and quiet, the undeveloped coastline around **Stintino**, at Sardinia's northwestern tip, makes a worthwhile excursion.

Arrival, information and accommodation

If you're coming to Sássari by **train**, you'll probably have to change at Ozieri-Chilivani station to arrive at Sássari **station**, at the bottom of the old town's Corso Vittorio Emanuele. There's a **left-luggage** office here (daily 8am–2.20pm), and also one at the **bus station** on Via XXV Aprile, a right turn out of the train station, where all long-distance buses arrive and depart, as well as the regular service linking the city with **Alghero airport** (ⓦwww.algheroairport.com). Sássari's **tourist office** is at Via Sebastiano Satta (Mon–Thurs 9am–1.30pm & 4–6pm, Fri 9am–1.30pm; ☏079.231.777). There's **internet access** at Net Gate, Piazza Università 4.

Accommodation in Sássari can be a problem: phone ahead to ensure availability.

Hotels

Casachiara Vicolo Bertolinis 12 ☏079.200.5052 or 333.695.7118, ⓦwww.casachiara.net. This B&B on the second floor of an eighteenth-century *palazzo* in the old quarter has been given a colourful makeover. Bathrooms are shared. No credit cards. ❷

Leonardo da Vinci *Via Roma 79* ☏079.280.744, ⓦwww.leonardodavincihotel.it. A smart three-star geared mainly towards conference groups, but it's comfortable enough, and there's private parking. ❹

Quattrogatti Vicolo Sant'Eligio 5 ☏079.237.819 or 349.406.0481, ⓦwww.quattrogattibnb.it. A modern B&B with three individually decorated, spacious rooms, which come with DVD players and private bathrooms. No credit cards. ❷

Vittorio Emanuele Corso Vittorio Emanuele 100 ☏079.235.538, ⓦwww.hotelvittorioemanuele.ss.it. An old-town *palazzo* flashily renovated to appeal to business folk. Comfortable and good value, if a little bland. ❷

The City

Sássari's **old quarter**, a network of alleys and piazzas bisected by the main Corso Vittorio Emanuele, is a good area for strolling around. At the heart of it is the **Duomo** (daily 8.30–noon & 4–7.30pm), whose florid facade is Sardinia's most imposing example of Baroque architecture, added to a simpler Aragonese-Gothic base from the fifteenth and sixteenth centuries. Behind it, the eighteenth-century **Palazzo Ducale** now houses the town hall. On the other side of the Corso, **Piazza Tola** retains its medieval feel and is the venue of a daily market.

The only other sight worth seeking out in the old quarter is the **Fontana di Rosello** (Tues–Sat 9am–1pm & 5–8pm; reduced hours in winter; free), symbol of the city, at the bottom of a flight of grassy steps accessible from Corso Trinità, at the northern end of the old town. Built in 1606 in late Renaissance style by Genoese stonemasons, the fountain is elaborately carved with dolphins and four statues representing the seasons.

Connected by a series of squares to the old quarter, the **newer town** is centred on the grandiose Piazza Italia. Leading off the piazza is Via Roma, a wide, café-lined boulevard, at the top of which is the impressive **Museo Sanna** (Tues–Sun 9am–8pm; €2), Sardinia's second archeological museum whose most interesting exhibits are nuraghic sculptures.

Eating and drinking

Sássari has some great **restaurants**: the quality is generally superb and prices are among the lowest in Sardinia. The town also has a lively **bar** scene, with those along Via Roma and on Piazza Castello packed out and open late in summer.

Coffee & Break Piazza Azuni 19. For breakfast, a refreshing frappé or an aperitif, this cosy bar with outside tables also serves panini, *pizzette* and pastas. Closed Sun.

Didò Via Largo Pazzola 8 ⊤079.200.6089. A range of pastas and good-value set menus on weekday lunchtimes, otherwise mains are €6–10. Try the house special, spaghetti Didò, with sausage, olives and parsley. Closed Sun.

Fainè Sassu Via Usai 17, off Piazza Castello. The menu here is confined to a *sassarese* speciality, *fainè*, a sort of pancake made of chickpea flour, either plain or cooked with onions, sausage or anchovies – great for a snack. Closed Wed & June–Sept.

L'Assassino Vicolo Ospizio Cappuccini 1, off Via Rosello ⊤079.235.041. Among the old town's cheaper choices, a casual trattoria with good fixed-price deals. Photos and paintings of Sássari line the walls. Closed Sun.

Pizzalmetro Via Usai 10. Delicious pizzas are served by the metre to eat in or take away – just point out how much you want. Even only. Closed Mon.

La Vela Latina Largo Sisini 3 ⊤079.233.737. A smart, modern trattoria specializing in traditional Sard dishes, hidden away in the old town. Tables outside in summer. Closed Sun.

Stintino and around

The port and resort of **STINTINO**, on Sardinia's northwestern tip, was until recently nothing more than a remote jumble of fishermen's cottages jammed between two narrow harbours. Fortunately its discovery by the tourist industry has not resulted in any drastic alterations, and Stintino remains a small, laid-back village, the only one in the tongue of land forming the western arm of the **Golfo di Asinara**. Between two and eight **buses** a day head here from Sássari, and there are buses from Alghero in the summer months.

Most of the peninsula's sunning and swimming takes place further up the coast at La Pelosa (see p.1020), but the only reasonably priced **accommodation** in the area is in Stintino itself. The cheapest choice is the B&B *Il Porto Vecchio*, Via Tonnara 69 (⊤079.523.212 or 339.435.3582, ⓦwww.bbstintino.com; ❸; no credit cards). If you want a touch more luxury, consider *Silvestrino* at Via Sássari 4 (⊤079.523.007, ⓦwww.silvestrino.it; obligatory full- or half-board in high season; March–Oct; ❹), whose excellent restaurant specializes in lobster soup, or *Geranio Rosso*, Via XXI Aprile 8 (⊤079.523.293; ❹), which has a pizzeria on site. There are also **apartments** to rent in the area (up to €1300 per week for four): Stintours on Lungomare Colombo (⊤079.523.160, ⓦwww.stintours.com) can make bookings, and also rents out **cars**, **bikes and scooters**, and has **internet**

The Cavalcata

One of Sardinia's showiest festivals – the **Cavalcata** – takes place in Sássari on the penultimate Sunday of May, the highlight of a month of cultural activities. Northern Sardinia's equivalent to Cágliari's Sant'Efisio festival and originally staged for the benefit of visiting Spanish kings or other dignitaries, it attracts hundreds of richly costumed participants from villages throughout the province and beyond. The festival is divided into three stages: the morning features a horseback parade and a display of the embroidered and decorated costumes unique to each village, after which there is a show of stirring feats of horsemanship at the local race course. The day ends with traditional songs and dances back in Piazza Italia.

access. The **tourist office** is on Via Sássari (June to mid-Sept 9.30am–8.30pm; mid-Sept to Oct, April & May Mon–Sat 9.30–1pm & 3–5.30pm; Jan–March, Nov & Dec Mon, Wed & Fri 9.30am–12.30pm, Tues, Thurs & Sat 9.30am–12.30pm & 3.30–5.30pm; ☎079.520.081).

Four kilometres up the road from Stintino a collection of tourist villages clutter up the otherwise idyllic promontory of **La Pelosa**, served by bus from Stintino (2–8 daily). Hotels and self-catering apartments back some of Sardinia's most deluxe **beaches**, with views out to the isles of Piana and the larger, elongated **Asinara**, the only known habitat of a miniature white ass from which the island takes its name, and previously a prison island. Between Easter and September, you can explore it on daily boat excursions from Stintino, leaving at 9/10am, returning at 5/6pm; the full visit including swimming stops and guide costs around €55–70; book tickets at Stintours (see p.1019).

Alghero

ALGHERO, 40km southwest of Sássari, is a very rare Italian phenomenon: a tourist town that is also a flourishing fishing port, giving it an economic base entirely independent of tourists. The predominant flavour here is Catalan, owing to a wholesale Hispanicization that followed the overthrow of the Doria family by Pedro IV of Aragon in 1354, a process so thorough that it became known as "Barcelonetta". The traces are still strong in the old town today, with its flamboyant churches and narrow cobbled streets named in both Italian and Catalan, all sheltered within a stout girdle of walls.

Arrival and information

Visitors arriving at **Alghero airport** (ⓦwww.algheroairport.com) can catch local buses into the centre of town (tickets €0.70 from the shop at one end of the terminal), or direct services to Cágliari, Oristano, Santa Teresa di Gallura and Sássari. Taxis into Alghero cost around €23. Bus timetables and other information can be obtained from the airport's **tourist office** (daily 8.30am–1pm & 3.30–10pm; ☎079.935.150), or Alghero's main **tourist office** (Mon–Sat 8am–8pm; also Sun April–Sept 10am–1pm; ☎079.979.054), at the top end of the Giardino Público. **Trains** arrive some way out of the centre, but regular city buses (#AP and #AF) connect the station to the port. **Buses** from the airport arrive on Via Cagliari; out-of-town **buses** from other destinations arrive on Via Catalogna, both next to the Giardino Público. A good way to get around the town and its environs is by **bike**: Cicloexpress, off Via Garibaldi at the northern end of the port, charges €30–50 per day for a scooter, €9–13 for a bicycle. There's **internet** access at *Bar Miramare* on Via Gramsci (daily 8am–noon & 3pm–2am).

Accommodation

The choice of **accommodation** in Alghero is extensive, though much of it closes down in winter; in July and August, booking ahead is essential. There's a useful **hostel** 6km along the coast at Fertilia, reachable by local bus on Via Parenzo, off Via Zara (☎079.930.478; €17). It's modern and clean with some private rooms (❶); call first to check availability. just 2km north of Alghero, there's a well-equipped **campsite**, *La Mariposa* (☎079.950.360, ⓦwww .lamariposa.it; Easter–Oct), with private rooms and bungalows (❶–❸), and direct access to the beach.

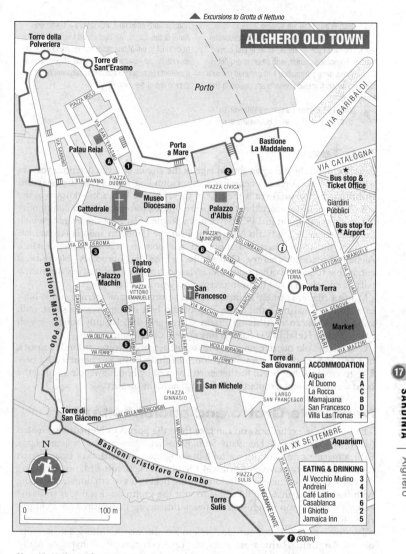

Excursions to Grotta di Nettuno

ALGHERO OLD TOWN

Torre della Polveriera

Torre di Sant'Erasmo

Porto

VIA GARIBALDI

PIAZZA MOLO

VIA SANT'ERASMO

VIA SANNINO

Palau Reial

Porta a Mare

Bastione La Maddalena

VIA CATALOGNA

★ Bus stop & Ticket Office

PIAZZA DUOMO

VIA MANNO

PIAZZA CÍVICA

Giardini Púbblici

★ Bus stop for Airport

Cattedrale

Museo Diocesano

VIA ROMA

Palazzo d'Albis

VIA MINERVA

PIAZZA MUNICIPIO

VIA COLUMBANO

i

VIA DON DEROMA

VICOLO ADAMI

VIA ROMA

PORTA TERRA

VIA VITTORIO EMANUELE

VIA CAGLIARI

Palazzo Machin

Teatro Cívico

PIAZZA VITTORIO EMANUELE

San Francesco

VIA BARCELONETA

Porta Terra

VIA CAVOUR

VIA DORIA

VIA PRINCIPE UMBERTO

VIA ARDUINO

VIA MAIORCA

VIA CARLO ALBERTO

VIA MACHIN

VIA SIMON

VIA GENOVA

VIA SASSARI

Market

VIA GIOBERTI

VIA DELITALA

VICOLO BURAGNA

VIA MAZZINI

VIA FERRET

VIA LACCU

VIA FERRET

Torre di San Giovanni

ACCOMMODATION

Aigua	E
Al Duomo	A
La Rocca	C
Mamajuana	B
San Francesco	D
Villa Las Tronas	F

San Michele

LARGO SAN FRANCESCO

PIAZZA GINNASIO

Torre di San Giácomo

VIA DELLA MISERICORDIA

VIA MAIORCA

VIA XX SETTEMBRE

Aquarium

Bastioni Cristóforo Colombo

PIAZZA SULIS

EATING & DRINKING

Al Vecchio Mulino	3
Andreini	4
Café Latino	1
Casablanca	6
Il Ghiotto	2
Jamaica Inn	5

Bastioni Marco Polo

N

Torre Sulis

0   100 m

▼ ● (500m)

Aigua Via Machin 22 ☎ 340.077.7688, ⓦ www
.aigua.it. Three mini-apartments in the same
building, with vaulted wood ceilings, exposed
brickwork and tiled floors, and each equipped with
kitchen facilities. No credit cards. ❸

B&B Al Duomo Via Sant'Erasmo 12
☎ 03.209.448.743. Conveniently located close to
the cathedral and port, this B&B has three spacious
rooms (one en suite). The friendly owner puts on a
good, cake-laden breakfast and is happy to advise
on sightseeing, though she speaks little English. ❹

Mamajuana Vicolo Adami 12 ☎ 339.136.9791,
ⓦ www.mamajuana.it. This very central B&B is in a
smartly renovated building in the heart of the old
town, with wood-beamed, en-suite rooms; guests
are given their own keys to come and go as they
please. No credit cards. ❸

La Rocca Via Roma 75 ☎ 079.979.062, ⓦ www
.bblarocca.com. In a restored sixteenth-century
palazzo in the heart of the old town, this B&B has
just one room, but it's spacious and charmingly
old-fashioned. No credit cards. ❺

San Francesco Via Machin 2
   ⊤079.980.330, ⓦwww.sanfrancescohotel
.com. The only hotel in the old town is just behind
the San Francesco church, with clean and quiet en-
suite rooms, simply furnished and grouped round a
cloister. Classical music concerts are put on in the
summer. ❸

Villa Las Tronas Lungomare Valencia 1
   ⊤079.981.818, ⓦwww.hotelvillalastronas.it.

Spectacularly sited on a promontory a 10min walk
south of the centre, this castellated former residence
from 1884 is full of character, still retaining a baronial
air with its old-fashioned furnishings. There's also an
excellent restaurant, a spa and a saltwater pool
carved out of the rock. ❾

The Town

A walk around the old town should take in the circuit of seven defensive **towers** which dominate Alghero's centre and its surrounding walls. From the **Giardini Púbblici** the **Porta Terra** is the first of these massive bulwarks – known as the Jewish Tower, it was erected at the expense of the prosperous Jewish community before their expulsion in 1492. Beyond is a puzzle of lanes, at the heart of which the pedestrianized Via Carlo Alberto, Via Principe Umberto and Via Roma have most of the town's bars and shops. At the bottom of Via Umberto stands Alghero's sixteenth-century **Cattedrale**, whose incongruously Neoclassical entrance is round the other side on Via Manno; inside, the lofty nave's alternating pillars and columns rise to an impressive octagonal dome.

Most of Alghero's finest architecture dates from the same period and is built in a similar Catalan-Gothic style. Two of the best examples are a short walk away: the **Palazzo d'Albis** on Piazza Cívica and the elegantly austere Jewish palace **Palau Reial** in Via Sant'Erasmo (now a restaurant).

Outside the old quarter, most of the tourist activity revolves around the **port**, its wide quay nudged by rows of colourful fishing boats and bordered by bars. The town's **beaches** begin further north, backed by hotels, sweeping round the coast virtually uninterrupted until Fertilia, near the airport.

Neptune's Grotto and ancient sites

The best of the excursions you can take from the port is to **Neptune's Grotto** (daily: Jan–May, Nov & Dec 9am–5pm; June–Sept 9am–8pm; Oct 10am–6pm; €10), a marine cave with dramatically lit stalagmites and stalactites. Boats depart several times daily between April and October: tickets cost €14, not including the entry charge to the grotto. Before buying tickets, it's worth double-checking with the operator that you'll be able to visit the grotto on that day, as you can't enter if the sea is too rough – and if the winds are up, be prepared for a choppy ride (40min).

Two ancient sites 10km outside Alghero are also worth visiting. The necropolis of **Anghelu Ruju**, a pre-nuraghic cave complex of 38 hypogea (daily: March 9.30am–4pm; April 9am–6pm; May–Oct 9am–7pm; Nov–Feb 10am–2pm; €3, or €5 with tour; including Nuraghe Palmavera €5, or €9 with tour), is on the road to Porto Torres, near the airport, and reached by several daily buses from Alghero. On the road to Porto Conte (1 bus daily Mon–Sat) are the **nuraghe di Palmavera** (same hours and prices as Anghelu Ruju), comprising a ruined palace dating from around 1100 BC and surrounded by fifty or so circular huts.

Eating and drinking

Alghero's **restaurants** are renowned for their seafood, always fresh, inventively prepared and tastefully presented; spring and winter are the best seasons.

Remember when ordering that most places price fish by weight: two-to-three *etti* (an *etto* is 100g) usually gets you a healthy portion.

Al Vecchio Mulino Via Don Deroma 3 ☎079.977.254; In the heart of the old town, this serves up tasty, well-priced sea- and land-based dishes and pizzas in low-vaulted cellars and has a good selection of white wines. Closed Nov & two weeks in Jan, also lunchtime & all day Tues in winter and lunchtimes, except July & Aug.

Andreini Via Ardoino 45 ☎079.982.098; The place to come for a first-rate – if pricey – fishy feast (though they also offer creative meat dishes), in an atmospheric, grotto-like dining room, or outside in summer. Closed Mon in winter.

Café Latino Piazza Duomo 6. A great place for an evening aperitif, with parasols on the walls overlooking the port. Snacks and ice creams are also served. Closed Tues Oct–May.

Casablanca Via Principe Umberto 76. The best place in town for a straightforward pizza or pasta dish in a convivial atmosphere; mains are around €10–16. Closed Wed in winter.

Il Ghiotto Piazza Cívica 23. A great range of takeaway snacks, as well as hot meals – pastas, seafood and meat – and fine Sardinian wines. Closed Nov.

Jamaica Inn Via Principe Umberto 57. This pub – right in the thick of things – is a lively spot for cocktails, and it serves snacks too. Open late. Closed Mon.

Travel details

Trains

Alghero to: Sássari (6–11 daily; 35min).

Arbatax to: Cágliari (mid-June to early Sept Wed–Mon 2 daily via Mandas; 6hr 45min).

Cágliari to: Arbatax (mid-June to early Sept Wed–Mon 2 daily via Mandas; 6hr 45min); Macomer** (7 daily; 1hr 45min–2hr 45min); Olbia** (5 daily; 3hr 30min–4hr 15min); Oristano (12–17 daily; 1hr–1hr 45 min); Sássari** (5 daily; 3hr 20min–4hr25min).

Macomer to: Cágliari** (7–9 daily; 1hr 50min–2hr 30min); Nuoro (Mon–Sat 6 daily; 1hr 15min).

Nuoro to: Macomer (2–7 daily; 1hr 15min).

Olbia to: Cágliari** (5 daily; 3hr 45min–4hr 20min); Golfo Aranci (5–7 daily; 25min); Oristano* (5 daily; 2hr 35min–3hr); Sássari* (6–7 daily; 2hr).

Oristano to: Cágliari (hourly; 1hr–1hr 40min); Macomer (7–8 daily; 45min–1hr 10min); Olbia* (5 daily; 2hr 30min–3hr); Sássari* (5 daily; 2hr 20min–2hr 45min).

Sássari to: Alghero (6–11 daily; 35min); Cágliari** (5–6 daily; 3hr–3hr 40min); Macomer (5–6 daily; 1hr 15min–1hr 35min); Olbia* (6–7 daily; 1hr 45min–2hr); Oristano* (5–6 daily; 2hr–2hr 35min).

*may involve changing trains at Ozieri-Chilivani

**may involve changing trains at Oristano and/or Ozieri-Chilivani

Buses

Alghero to: Bosa (2–6 daily; 1hr–1hr 40min); Nuoro (2 daily; 3hr 30min); Sássari (hourly; 1hr).

Cágliari to: Barúmini (2–3 daily; 1hr 30min); Nuoro (1 daily; 2hr 50min); Olbia (1–3 daily; 4hr 20min); Oristano (Mon–Sat 2 daily; 2hr); Sant'Antíoco (1–2 daily; 2hr–2hr 35min); Sássari (2–4 daily; 3hr 15min).

Nuoro to: Alghero (2 daily; 2hr); Aritzo (1 daily; 2hr); Cágliari (2 daily; 2hr 30min–4hr 50min); Désulo (Mon–Sat 1 daily; 1hr 20min); Fonni (2–6 daily; 40min–1hr 30min); Olbia (4–8 daily; 2hr 30min–3hr 20min); Orgósolo (4–9 daily; 35min); Oristano (1 daily; 1hr); Santa Teresa di Gallura (1 daily; 3hr 10min); Sássari (3–7 daily; 1hr 45min–2hr 45min); Tonara (1 daily; 1hr 30min).

Olbia to: Arzachena (5–12 daily; 50min); Nuoro (6–8 daily; 2hr 30min); Palau (5–12 daily; 1hr–1hr 10min); Porto Cervo (Mon–Sat 3–5 daily; 1hr 10min); Santa Teresa di Gallura (5–6 daily; 2hr); Sássari (Mon–Sat 2 daily; 1hr 30min–2hr).

Oristano to: Bosa (Mon–Sat 4 daily; 2hr); Cágliari (Mon–Fri 2 daily; 2hr); Santa Teresa di Gallura (1 daily; 4hr 50min); Sássari (1 daily; 2hr).

Sássari to: Alghero (8–9 daily; 30min); Bosa (3–7 daily; 1hr 50min–2hr 20min); Cágliari (4–5 daily; 2hr 30min–3hr 15min); Nuoro (2–6 daily; 1hr 50min–2hr 25min); Olbia (1 daily; 1hr 30min); Oristano (2–3 daily; 1hr 45min–2hr); Santa Teresa di Gallura (3–5 daily; 2hr 35min); Stintino (2–8 daily; 1hr 15min).

Ferries

Arbatax to: Civitavécchia (2 weekly; 10hr 30min); Fiumicino (late July to early Sept 2 weekly; 4hr–5hr 30min); Genoa (2 weekly; 15hr 30min–20hr).

Cágliari to: Civitavécchia (1–2 daily; 14hr 30min–16hr 30min); Naples (1–2 weekly; 16hr); Palermo (1 weekly; 14hr 30min); Trápani (1 weekly; 10–11hr).

Golfo Aranci to: Civitavécchia (early April to late Sept 1–3 daily; 3hr 45min–7hr); Fiumicino (late July to early Sept 1–3 daily; 4hr 30min); Livorno (2–5 daily; 5–10hr).

Olbia to: Civitavécchia (1–7 daily; 5–10hr); Genoa (3–21 weekly; 8hr–13hr 30min); Livorno (1–4 daily; 6–11hr); Piombino (1–2 daily; 4hr 30min–7hr).

Palau to: Genoa (June–Sept 3–5 weekly; 12–13hr); La Maddalena (1–4 hourly; 20min); Naples (mid-June to mid-Sept 1 weekly; 14hr 30min).

Porto Torres to: Genoa (1–4 daily; 8–11hr).

International ferries

Palau to: Porto Vecchio, Corsica (mid-June to mid-Sept 1 weekly; 2hr).

Porto Torres to: Ajaccio, Corsica (1 weekly; 4hr); Marseille, France (April–Oct 2–4 weekly; 10–17hr); Propriano, Corsica (1–5 weekly; 3–4hr).

Santa Teresa di Gallura to: Bonifacio, Corsica (2–14 daily; 1hr).

Contexts

Contexts

History

A specific Italian history is hard to identify. Italy wasn't formally a united country until 1861, and the history of the peninsula after the Romans is more one of warring city states, colonization and annexation by foreign powers. It's almost inconceivable now that Italy should fragment once again, but the regional differences remain strong and have, in recent years, become a major factor in Italian politics.

Early times

A smattering of remains exist from the Neanderthals who occupied the Italian peninsula half a million years ago, but the main period of colonization began after the last Ice Age, with evidence of **Paleolithic** and **Neolithic** settlements dating from around 20,000 BC and 4000 BC respectively. More sophisticated tribes developed towards the end of the prehistoric period, between 2400 and 1800 BC; those who left the most visible traces were the **Ligurians** (who inhabited a much greater area than modern Liguria), the **Siculi** of southern Italy and Latium, and the **Sards**, who farmed and raised livestock on Sardinia. More advanced still were migrant groups from the eastern Mediterranean, who introduced the techniques of working copper. Later, various **Bronze Age** societies (1600–1000 BC) built a network of farms and villages in the Apennines, and on the Sicilian and southern coasts, the latter population trading with Mycenaeans in Greece.

Other tribes brought Indo-European languages into Italy. The Veneti, Latins and Umbrii moved down the peninsula from the north, while the Piceni and the Messapians in Puglia crossed the Adriatic from what is now Croatia. The artificial line between prehistory and history is drawn around the eighth century BC with the arrival of the **Phoenicians** and their trade links between Carthage and southern Italy. This soon encouraged the arrival of the **Carthaginians** in Sicily, Sardinia and the Latium coast – just when **Greeks** and **Etruscans** were gaining influence.

Etruscans and Greeks

Greek settlers colonized parts of the Tuscan coast and the Bay of Naples in the eighth century BC, moving on to **Naxos** on Sicily's Ionian coast, and founding the city of Syracuse in the year 736 BC. The colonies they established in Sicily and southern Italy came to be known as **Magna Graecia**. Along with Etruscan cities to the north they were the earliest Italian civilizations to leave substantial buildings and written records.

The Greek settlements were hugely successful, introducing the vine and the olive to Italy, and establishing a high-yielding agricultural system. Cities like **Syracuse** and **Tarentum** were wealthier and more sophisticated than those on mainland Greece, dominating trade in the central Mediterranean, despite competition from Carthage. Ruins such as the temples of **Agrigento** and **Selinunte**, the fortified walls around Gela, and the theatres at Syracuse and

Taormina on Sicily attest to a great prosperity, and Magna Graecia became an enriching influence on the culture of the Greek homeland – Archimedes, Aeschylus and Empedocles were all from Sicily. Yet these colonies suffered from the same factionalism as the Greek states, and the cities of Tarentum, Metapontum, Sybaris and Croton were united only when faced with the threat of outside invasion. From 400 BC, after Sybaris was razed to the ground, the other colonies went into irreversible economic decline, to become satellite states of Rome.

The **Etruscans** were the other major civilization of the period, mostly living in the area between the **Tiber** and **Arno** rivers. Their language, known mostly from funerary texts, is one of the last relics of an ancient language common to the Mediterranean. Some say they arrived in Italy around the ninth century BC from western Anatolia, others that they came from the north, and a third hypothesis places their origins in Etruria. Whatever the case, they set up a cluster of **twelve city states** in northern Italy, traded with Greek colonies to the south and were the most powerful people in northern Italy by the sixth century BC, edging out the indigenous population of Ligurians, Latins and Sabines. Tomb frescoes in Umbria and Lazio depict a refined and luxurious culture with highly developed systems of divination, based on the reading of animal entrails and the flight of birds. Herodotus wrote that the Etruscans recorded their ancestry along the female line, and tomb excavations in the nineteenth century revealed that women were buried in special sarcophagi carved with their names. Well-preserved chamber tombs with wall paintings exist at **Cerveteri** and **Tarquinia**, the two major sites in Italy. The Etruscans were technically advanced, creating new agricultural land through irrigation and building their cities on ramparted hilltops – a pattern of settlement that has left a permanent mark on central Italy. Their kingdom contracted, however, after invasions by the **Cumans**, **Syracusans** and **Gauls**, and was eventually forced into alliance with the embryonic Roman state. Almost none of their towns have survived the archeological record – the only exception being modern-day Marzabotto or Misa, a fine example of Etruscan urban planning.

Roman Italy

The growth of **Rome**, a border town between the Etruscans and the Latins, gained impetus around 600 BC from a coalition of Latin and Sabine communities. The **Tarquins**, an Etruscan dynasty, oversaw the early expansion, but in 509 BC the Romans ejected the Etruscan royal family and became a **republic**, with power shared jointly between two consuls, both elected for one year. Further changes came half a century later, after a protracted class struggle that resulted in the **Law of the Twelve Tables**, which made patricians and plebeians equal. Thus stabilized, the Romans set out to systematically conquer the northern peninsula and, after the fall of Veii in 396 BC, succeeded in capturing **Sutri** and **Nepi**, towns which Livy considered the "barriers and gateways of Etruria". Various wars and truces with other cities brought about agreements to pay harsh tributes.

The **Gauls** captured Rome in 390, refusing to leave until they had received a vast payment, but this proved a temporary reversal. The Romans took **Campania** and the fertile land of Puglia after defeating the **Samnites** in battles over a period of 35 years. They then set their sights on the wealthy Greek colonies to the south, including Tarentum, whose inhabitants turned to the

Greek king, **Pyrrhus of Epirus**, for military support. He initially repelled the Roman invaders, but lost his advantage and was defeated at **Beneventum** in 275 BC. The Romans had by then established their rule in most of southern Italy, and now became a threat to Carthage. In 264 they had the chance of obtaining **Sicily**, when the Mamertines, a mercenary army in control of Messina, appealed to them for help against the Carthaginians. The Romans obliged – sparking off the **First Punic War** – and took most of the island, together with Sardinia and Corsica. With their victory in 222 BC over the Gauls in the Po Valley, all Italy was now under Roman control.

They also turned a subsequent military threat to their advantage, in what came to be known as the **Second Punic War**. The Carthaginians had watched the spread of Roman power across the Mediterranean with some alarm, and at the end of the third century BC they allowed **Hannibal** to make an Alpine crossing into Italy with his army of infantry, horsemen and elephants. Hannibal crushed the Roman legions at Lago Trasimeno and Cannae (216 BC), and then halted at Cápua. With remarkable cool, considering Hannibal's proximity, **Scipio** set sail on a retaliatory mission to the Carthaginian territory of **Spain**, taking Cartagena, and continuing his journey into **Africa**. It was another fifty years before Carthage was taken, closely followed by all of Spain, but the Romans were busy in the meantime adding **Macedonian Greece** to their territory.

These conquests gave Roman citizens a tax-free existence subsidized by captured treasure, but society was sharply divided between those enjoying the benefits, and those who were not. The former belonged mostly to the **senatorial party**, who ignored demands for reform by their opposition, the popular party. The radical reforms sponsored by the tribune **Gaius Gracchus** came too close to democracy for the senatorial party, whose declaration of martial law was followed by the assassination of Gracchus. The majority of people realized that the only hope of gaining influence was through the army, but **General Gaius Marius**, when put into power, was ineffective against the senatorial clique, who systematically picked off the new regime.

The first century BC saw civil strife on an unprecedented scale. Although Marius was still in power, another general, **Sulla**, was in the ascendancy, leading military campaigns against northern invaders and rebellious subjects in the south. Sulla subsequently took power and established his dictatorship in Rome, throwing out a populist government which had formed while he was away on a campaign in the east. Murder and exile were common, and cities which had sided with Marius during their struggle for power were punished with massacres and destruction. Thousands of Sulla's war veterans were given confiscated land, but much of it was laid to waste. In 73 BC a gladiator named **Spartacus** led 70,000 dispossessed farmers and escaped slaves in a revolt, which lasted for two years before they were defeated by the legions.

Julius Caesar and Augustus

Rome became calmer only after Sulla's death, when **Pompey**, another general, and **Licinus Crassus**, a rich builder, became masters of Rome. Pompey's interest lay in lucrative wars elsewhere, so his absence from the capital gave **Julius Caesar** the chance to make a name for himself as an orator and raiser of finance. When Pompey returned in 60 BC, he made himself, Crassus and Caesar rulers of the **first Triumvirate**.

Caesar bought himself the post of consul in 59 BC, then spent the next eight years on campaigns against the **Gauls**. His military success needled Pompey, and he eventually turned against his colleague, giving Caesar the chance to hit back.

In 49 BC he crossed the river **Rubicon**, committing the offence of entering Roman territory with an army without first informing the Senate, but when he reached the city there was no resistance – everyone had fled, and Caesar became absolute ruler of Rome. He spent the next four years on civil reforms, writing his history of the Gallic wars, and chasing Pompey and his followers through Spain, Greece and Egypt. A group of enemies within the Senate, including his adopted son **Brutus**, conspired to murder him in 44 BC, a few months after he had been appointed ruler for life. **Octavian**, Caesar's nephew and heir, Lepidus and Marcus Antonius (**Mark Antony**) formed the **second Triumvirate** the following year. Again, the arrangement was fraught with tensions, the battle for power this time being between Antony and Octavian. While Antony was with **Cleopatra**, Octavian spent his time developing his military strength and the final, decisive battle took place at **Actium** in 31 BC, where Antony committed suicide.

As sole ruler of the new regime, Octavian, renaming himself **Augustus Caesar**, embarked on a series of reforms and public works, giving himself complete powers despite his unassuming official title of "First Citizen".

The emperors

Tiberius (14–37 AD), the successor to Augustus, ruled wisely, but thereafter began a period of decadence. During the psychopathic reign of **Caligula** (37–41) the civil service kept the empire running; **Claudius** (41–54) conquered southern Britain, and was succeeded by his stepson **Nero** (54–68), who violently persecuted the **Christians**. Nero committed suicide when threatened by a coup, leading to a rapid succession of four emperors in the year 68. The period of prosperity during the rule of the **Flavian** emperors (Vespasian and his sons Titus and Domitian) was a forerunner for the **Century of the Antonines**, a period named after the successful reigns of Nerva, Trajan, Hadrian, Antonius and **Marcus Aurelius**. These generals consolidated the empire's infrastructure, and created an encouraging environment for artistic achievement. A prime example is the formidable bronze equestrian statue of Marcus Aurelius in Rome – a work not equalled in sophistication until the Renaissance.

A troubled period followed under the rule of Marcus Aurelius' son **Commodus** (180–193) and his successors, none of whom were wholly in control of the legions. Artistic, intellectual and religious life stagnated, and the balance of economic development tilted in favour of the north, while the agricultural south grew ever more impoverished.

Barbarians and Byzantines

In the middle of the third century, incursions by **Goths** in Greece, the Balkans and Asia, and the **Franks** and **Alamanni** in Gaul foreshadowed the collapse of the empire. **Aurelian** (270–275) re-established some order after terrible civil wars, to be followed by **Diocletian** (284–305), whose persecution of Christians produced many of the Church's present-day saints. **Plagues** had decimated the population, but problems of a huge but static economy were compounded by the doubling in size of the army at this time to about half a million men. To ease administration, Diocletian **divided the empire** into two halves, east and west, basing himself as ruler of the western empire in Mediolanum (Milan). This measure brought about a relative recovery, coinciding with the rise of **Christianity**, which was declared the state religion during the reign of **Constantine** (306–337). **Constantinople**, capital of the eastern empire, became a thriving trading and manufacturing city, while Rome itself went into decline, as the enlargement of the senatorial estates and the impoverishment of the lower classes gave rise to something comparable to a primitive feudal system.

Barbarians (meaning outsiders, or foreigners) had been crossing the border into the empire since 376 AD, when the **Ostrogoths** were driven from their kingdom in southern Russia by the **Huns**, a tribe of ferocious horsemen. The Huns went on to attack the **Visigoths**, 70,000 of whom crossed the border and settled inside the empire. When the Roman aristocracy saw that the empire was no longer a shield against barbarian raids, they were less inclined to pay for its support, seeing that a more comfortable future lay in being on good terms with the barbarian successor states.

By the fifth century, many legions were made up of troops from conquered territories, and several posts of high command were held by outsiders. With little will or loyalty behind it, the **empire floundered**, and on New Year's Eve of 406, Vandals, Alans and Sueves crossed the frozen Rhine into Gaul, chased by the Huns from their kingdoms in what are now Hungary and Austria. By 408, the imperial government in Ravenna could no longer hold off **Alaric** (commander of Illyricum – now Croatia) who went on to **sack Rome** in 410, causing a crisis of morale in the west. "When the whole world perished in one city," wrote Saint Jerome, "then I was dumb with silence."

The bitter **end of the Roman Empire** in the west came after **Valentinian III**'s assassination in 455. His eight successors over the next twenty years were finally ignored by the Germanic troops in the army, who elected their general **Odoacer** as king. The remaining Roman aristocracy hated him, and the eastern emperor, **Zeno**, who in theory now ruled the whole empire, refused to recognize him. In 487, Zeno rid himself of the Ostrogoth leader **Theodoric** by persuading him to march on Odoacer in Italy. By 493, Theodoric had succeeded, becoming ruler of the western territories.

A lull followed. The Senate in Rome and the civil service continued to function, and the remains of the empire were still administered under Roman law. Ostrogothic rule of the west continued after Theodoric's death, but in the 530s the eastern emperor, **Justinian**, began to plan the reunification of the Roman Empire "up to the two oceans". In 536 his general **Belisarius** landed in Sicily and moved north through Rome to Ravenna; complete reconquest of the Italian peninsula was achieved in 552, after which the Byzantines retained a presence in the south and in Sardinia for five hundred years.

During this time the **Christian Church** developed as a more or less independent authority, since the emperor was at a safe distance in Constantinople. Continual invasions had led to an uncertain political scene in which the **bishops of Rome** emerged with the strongest voice – justification of their primacy having already been given by Pope Leo I (440–461), who spoke of his right to "rule all who are ruled in the first instance by Christ". A confused period of rule followed, as armies from northern Europe tried to take more territory from the old empire.

Lombards and Franks

During the chaotic sixth century, the **Lombards**, a Germanic tribe, were driven southwest into Italy, and by the eighth century, when the **Franks** arrived from Gaul, they were extending their power throughout the peninsula. The Franks were orthodox Christians, and therefore acceptable to Gallo-Roman nobility, integrating quickly and taking over much of the provincial administration. They were ruled by the Merovingian royal family, but the mayors of the palace – the Carolingians – began to take power in real terms. Led by **Pepin the Short**, they saw an advantage in supporting the papacy, giving Rome large endowments and forcibly converting pagans in areas they conquered. When Pepin wanted to oust the Merovingians, and become King of the Franks, he appealed to the pope in Rome for his blessing, who was happy to agree, anointing the new Frankish king with holy oil.

This alliance was useful to both parties. In 755 the pope called on the Frankish army to confront the Lombards. The Franks forced them to hand over treasure and 22 cities and castles, which then became the northern part of the **Papal States**. Pepin died in 768, with the Church indebted to him. According to custom, he divided the kingdom between his two sons, one of whom died within three years. The other was Charles the Great, or **Charlemagne**.

An intelligent and innovative leader, Charlemagne was proclaimed King of the Franks and of the Lombards, and patrician of the Romans, after a decisive war against the Lombards in 774. On Christmas Day of the year 800, Pope Leo III expressed his gratitude for Charlemagne's political support by crowning him **Emperor of the Holy Roman Empire**, an investiture that forged an enduring link between the fortunes of Italy and those of northern Europe. By the time Charlemagne died, all of Italy from south of Rome to Lombardy, including Sardinia, was part of the huge **Carolingian Empire**. The parts that didn't come under his domain were Sicily and the southern coast, which were gradually being reconquered by Arabs from Tunisia; and Puglia and Calabria, colonized by Byzantines and Greeks.

The task of holding these gains was beyond Charlemagne's successors, and by the beginning of the tenth century the family was extinct and the rival Italian states had become prizes for which the western (French) and eastern (German) Frankish kingdoms competed. Power switched in 936 to **Otto**, king of the eastern Franks. Political disunity in Italy invited him to intervene, and in 962 he was crowned emperor; Otto's son and grandson (Ottos II and III) set the seal on the renewal of the Holy Roman Empire.

Popes and emperors

On the death of **Otto III** in 1002, Italy was again without a recognized ruler. In the north, noblemen jockeyed for power, and the papacy was manipulated by rival Roman families. The most decisive events were in the south, where Sicily, Calabria and Puglia were captured by the **Normans**, who proved effective administrators and synthesized their own culture with the existing half-Arabic, half-Italian south. In **Palermo** in the eleventh century they created the most dynamic culture of the Mediterranean world.

Meanwhile in Rome, a series of reforming popes began to strengthen the Church. **Gregory VII**, elected in 1073, was the most radical, demanding the right to depose emperors if he so wished. **Emperor Henry IV** was equally determined for this not to happen. The inevitable quarrel broke out, over a key appointment to the archbishopric of Milan. Henry denounced Gregory as "now not pope, but false monk"; the pope responded by excommunicating him, thereby freeing his subjects from their allegiance. By 1077 Henry was aware of his tactical error and tried to make amends by visiting the pope at **Canossa**, where the emperor, barefoot and penitent, was kept waiting outside for three days. The formal reconciliation did nothing to heal the rift, and Henry's son, **Henry V**, continued the feud, eventually coming to a compromise in which the emperor kept control of bishops' land ownership, while giving up rights over their investiture.

After this symbolic victory, the papacy developed into the most comprehensive and advanced centralized government in Europe in the realms of law and finance, but it wasn't long before unity again came under attack. This time, the threat came from **Emperor Frederick I** (Barbarossa), who besieged many northern Italian cities from his base in Germany from 1154. **Pope Alexander III** responded with ambiguous pronouncements about the imperial crown being a "benefice" which the pope conferred, implying that the emperor was the pope's vassal. The issue of papal or imperial supremacy was to polarize the country for the next two hundred years, almost every part of Italy being torn by struggles between **Guelphs** (supporting the pope) and **Ghibellines** (supporting the emperor).

Henry VI's son, **Frederick II**, assumed the imperial throne at the age of three and a half, inheriting the Norman **Kingdom of Sicily**. Later linked by marriage to the great **Hohenstaufen** dynasty in Germany, he inevitably turned his attentions to northern Italy. However, his power base was small, and opposition from the Italian commune and the papacy snowballed into civil war. His sudden death in 1250 marked a major downturn in imperial fortunes.

The emergence of city states

Charles of Anjou, brother of King Louis IX of France, defeated Frederick II's heirs in southern Italy, and received **Naples** and **Sicily** as a reward from the pope. His oppressive government finally provoked an uprising on Easter Monday 1282, a revolt that came to be known as the **Sicilian Vespers**, as some two thousand occupying soldiers were murdered in Palermo at the sound of the bell for vespers. For the next twenty years the French were at war with **Peter of Aragon**, who took Sicily and then tried for the southern mainland.

If imperial power was on the defensive, the papacy was in even worse shape. Knowing that the pontiff had little military backing or financial strength left, **Philip of France** sent his men to the pope's summer residence in 1303, subjecting the old man to a degrading attack. Boniface died within a few weeks; his French successor, Clement V, promptly moved the papacy to **Avignon** in southern France.

The declining political power of the major rulers was countered by the growing autonomy of the cities. By 1300, a broad belt of some three hundred virtually **independent city states** stretched from central Italy to the northernmost edge of the peninsula. In the middle of the century the population of Europe was savagely depleted by the **Black Death** – brought into Europe by a Genoese ship returning from the Black Sea – but the city states survived, developing a concept of citizenship quite different from the feudal lord-and-vassal relationship. By the end of the fourteenth century the richer and more influential states had swallowed up the smaller **comune**, leaving four as clear political front runners. These were **Genoa** (controlling the Ligurian coast), **Florence** (ruling Tuscany), **Milan**, whose sphere of influence included Lombardy and much of central Italy, and **Venice**. Smaller principalities, such as Mantua and Ferrara, supported armies of mercenaries, ensuring their security by building impregnable fortress-palaces.

Perpetual vendettas between the propertied classes often induced the citizens to accept the overall rule of one **signore** in preference to the bloodshed of warring clans. A despotic form of government evolved, sanctioned by official titles from the emperor or pope, and by the fifteenth century most city states were under princely rather than republican rule. In the south of the fragmented peninsula was the **Kingdom of Naples**; the **States of the Church** stretched up from Rome through modern-day Marche, Umbria and the Romagna; **Siena**, **Florence**, **Modena**, **Mantua** and **Ferrara** were independent states, as were the **Duchy of Milan**, and the maritime republics of **Venice** and **Genoa**, with a few odd pockets of independence like Lucca, for example, and Rimini.

The commercial and secular city states of late medieval times were the seedbed for the **Renaissance**, when urban entrepreneurs (such as the Medici) and autocratic rulers (such as Federico da Montefeltro) enhanced their status through the financing of architectural projects, paintings and sculpture. It was also at this time that the Tuscan dialect – the language of Dante, Petrarch and Boccaccio – became established as Italy's literary language; it later became the nation's official spoken language.

By the mid-fifteenth century the five most powerful states – Naples, the papacy, Milan, and the republics of Venice and Florence – reached a tacit agreement to maintain the new balance of power. Yet though there was a balance of power at home, the history of each of the independent Italian states became inextricably bound up with the power politics of other European countries.

French and Spanish intervention

The inevitable finally happened when an Italian state invited a larger power in to defeat one of its rivals. In 1494, at the request of the Duke of Milan, **Charles** VIII of France marched south to renew the Angevin claim to the Kingdom of Naples. After the accomplishment of his mission, Charles stayed for three months in Naples, before heading back to France; the kingdom was then acquired by **Ferdinand II of Aragon**, subsequently ruler of all Spain.

The person who really established the Spanish in Italy was the Habsburg Charles V (1500–58), who within three years of inheriting both the Austrian and Spanish thrones bribed his way to being elected Holy Roman Emperor. In 1527 the imperial troops sacked **Rome**, a calamity widely interpreted at the time as God's punishment of the disorganized and dissolute Italians. The French remained troublesome opposition, but they were defeated at Pavia in 1526 and Naples in 1529. With the treaty of Cateau-Cambrésis in 1559, Spain held Sicily, Naples, Sardinia, the Duchy of Milan and some Tuscan fortresses, and they were to exert a stranglehold on Italian political life for the next 150 years. The remaining smaller states became satellites of either Spanish or French rule; only the papacy and Venice remained independent.

Social and economic troubles were as severe as the political upheavals. While the papacy combated the spread of the **Reformation** in northern Europe, the major manufacturing and trading centres were coming to terms with the opening up of the Atlantic and Indian Ocean trade routes – discoveries which meant that northern Italy would increasingly be bypassed. Mid-sixteenth-century **economic recession** prompted wealthy Venetian and Florentine merchants to invest in land rather than business, while in the south high taxes and repressive feudal regimes produced an upsurge of banditry and even the raising of peasant militias – resistance that was ultimately suppressed brutally by the Spanish.

The seventeenth century was a low point in Italian political life, with little room for manoeuvre between the papacy and colonial powers. The Spanish eventually lost control of Italy at the start of the eighteenth century when, as a result of the War of the Spanish Succession, Lombardy, Mantua, Naples and Sardinia all came under Austrian control. The machinations of the major powers led to **frequent realignments** in the first half of the century. Piemonte, ruled by the Duke of Savoy, Victor Amadeus II, was forced in 1720 to surrender Sicily to the Austrians in return for Sardinia. In 1734 Naples and Sicily passed to the Spanish Bourbons, and three years later the House of Lorraine acquired Tuscany on the extinction of the Medici.

Relatively enlightened Bourbon rule in the south did little to arrest the economic polarization of society, but the northern states advanced under the intelligent if autocratic rule of Austria's **Maria Theresa** (1740–80) and her son **Joseph II** (1780–90), who prepared the way for early industrialization. Lightning changes came in April 1796, when the French armies of **Napoleon** invaded northern Italy. Within a few years the French had been driven out again, but by 1810 Napoleon was in command of the whole peninsula, and his puppet regimes remained in charge until Waterloo. Napoleonic rule had profound effects, reducing the power of the papacy, reforming feudal land rights and introducing representative government to Italy. Elected assemblies were provided on the French model, giving the emerging middle class a chance for political discussion and action.

Unification

The fall of Napoleon led to the Vienna Settlement of 1815, by which the Austrians effectively restored the old ruling class. **Metternich**, the Austrian Chancellor, did all he could to foster any local loyalties that might weaken the appeal of unity, yet the years between 1820 and 1849 became years of revolution. Uprisings began in Sicily, Naples and Piemonte, when **King Ferdinand** introduced measures that restricted personal freedom and destroyed many farmers' livelihoods. A makeshift army quickly gained popular support in Sicily, and forced some concessions, before Ferdinand invited the Austrians in to help him crush the revolution. In the north, the oppressive laws enacted by **Vittorio Emanuele I** in the Kingdom of Piemonte sparked off student protests and army mutinies in Turin. Vittorio Emanuele abdicated in favour of his brother, Carlo Felice, and his son, **Carlo Alberto**; the latter initially gave some support to the radicals, but Carlo Felice then called in the Austrians, and thousands of revolutionaries were forced into exile. Carlo Alberto became King of Sardinia in 1831. A secretive, excessively devout and devious character, he did a major volte-face when he assumed the throne by forming an alliance with the Austrians.

In 1831 further uprisings occurred in Parma, Modena, the Papal States, Sicily and Naples. Their lack of coordination, and the readiness with which Austrian and papal troops intervened, ensured that revolution was short-lived. But even if these actions were unsustained, their influence grew.

One person profoundly influenced by these insurgencies was **Giuseppe Mazzini**. Arrested as Secretary of the Genoese branch of the Carbonari (a secret radical society) in 1827 and jailed for three months in 1830, he formulated his political ideology and set up "**Young Italy**" on his release. Among the many to whom the ideals of "Young Italy" appealed was **Giuseppe Garibaldi**, soon to play a central role in the **Risorgimento**, as the movement to reform and unite the country was known.

Crop failures in 1846 and 1847 produced widespread **famine** and **cholera outbreaks**. In Sicily an army of peasants marched on the capital, burning debt collection records, destroying property and freeing prisoners. Middle- and upper-class moderates were worried, and formed a government to control the uprising, but Sicilian **separatist** aims were realized in 1848. Fighting spread to Naples, where **Ferdinand II** made some temporary concessions, but nonetheless he retook Sicily the following year. At the same time as the southern revolution, serious disturbances took place in Tuscany, Piemonte and the Papal States. Rulers fled their duchies, and Carlo Alberto altered course again, prompted by Metternich's fall from power in Vienna: he granted his subjects a constitution and declared war on Austria. In Rome, the pope fled from rioting and Mazzini became a member of the city's republican triumvirate in 1849, with Garibaldi organizing the defences.

None of the uprisings lasted long. Twenty thousand revolutionaries were expelled from Rome, Carlo Alberto abdicated in favour of his son Vittorio Emanuele II after military defeats at the hands of the Austrians, and the dukes returned to Tuscany, Modena and Parma. One thing that survived was Piemonte's constitution, which throughout the 1850s attracted political refugees to the cosmopolitan state.

Cavour and Garibaldi

Nine years of radical change began when **Count Camillo Cavour** became Prime Minister of Piemonte in 1852. The involvement of Piemontese troops in the Crimean War brought Cavour into contact with Napoleon III at the Congress of Paris, at which the hostilities were ended, and in July 1858 the two men had secret talks on the "Italian question". Napoleon III had decided to support Italy in its fight against the Austrians – the only realistic way of achieving unification – as long as resistance was non-revolutionary. Having bargained over the division of territory, they waited for a chance to provoke Austria into war. This came in 1859, when Cavour wrote an emotive anti-Austrian speech for Vittorio Emanuele at the opening of parliament. His battle cry for an end to the **grido di dolore** (cry of pain) was taken up over Italy. The Austrians ordered demobilization by the Piemontese, who did the reverse.

The war was disastrous from the start, and thousands died at Magenta and Solferino. In July 1859, Napoleon III made a truce with the Austrians without consulting Cavour, who resigned in fury. Provisional governments remained in power in Tuscany, Modena and the Romagna. Cavour returned to government in 1860, and soon France, Piemonte and the papacy agreed to a series of plebiscites, a move that ensured that by mid-March of 1860, **Tuscany** and the new state of **Emilia** (duchies of Modena and Parma plus the Romagna) had voted for **union with Piemonte**. A secret treaty between Vittorio

Emanuele and Napoleon III ceded Savoy and Nice to France, subject to plebiscites. The result was as planned, no doubt due in part to the presence of the French Army during voting.

Garibaldi promptly set off for Nice with the aim of blowing up the ballot boxes, only to be diverted when he reached Genoa, where he heard of an **uprising in Sicily**. Commandeering two old paddle steamers and obtaining just enough rifles for his thousand Red Shirts, he headed south. More support came when they landed in Sicily, and Garibaldi's army outflanked the 12,000 Neapolitan troops to take the island. After that, they crossed to the mainland, easily occupied Naples, then struck out for Rome. Cavour, anxious that he might lose the initiative, hastily dispatched a Piemontese army to **annexe the Papal States**, except for the Patrimony around Rome. Worried by the possibility that the anti-Church revolutionaries who made up the Red Shirt army might stir up trouble, Cavour and Vittorio Emanuele travelled south to Rome, accompanied by their army, and arranged plebiscites in Sicily, Naples, Umbria and the Papal Marches that offered little alternative but to vote for annexation by Piemonte. After their triumphal parade through Naples, they thanked Garibaldi for his trouble, took command of all territories and held elections to a new parliament. In February 1861, the members formally announced the **Kingdom of Italy**.

Cavour died the same year, before the country was completely unified, since Rome and Venice were still outside the kingdom. Garibaldi marched unsuccessfully on Rome in 1862, and again five years later, by which time Venice had been subsumed. It wasn't until Napoleon III was defeated by Prussia in 1870 that the French troops were ousted from Rome. Thus by 1871 **Unification** was complete.

The world wars

After the Risorgimento, some things still hadn't changed. The ruling class were slow to move towards a broader based political system, while living standards actually worsened in some areas, particularly in Sicily. When Sicilian peasant farmers organized into **fasci** – forerunners of trade unions – the prime minister sent in 30,000 soldiers, closed down newspapers and interned suspected troublemakers without trial. In the 1890s capitalist methods and modern machinery in the Po Valley created a new social structure, with rich **agrari** at the top of the pile, a mass of farm labourers at the bottom, and an intervening layer of estate managers.

In the 1880s Italy's **colonial expansion** began, initially concentrated in bloody – and ultimately disastrous – campaigns in Abyssinia and Eritrea in 1886. In 1912 Italy wrested the Dodecanese islands and Libya from Turkey, a development deplored by many, including **Benito Mussolini**, who during this war was the radical secretary of the PSI (Partito Socialista Italiano) in Forlì.

World War I and the rise of Mussolini

Italy entered **World War I** in 1915 with the chief aims of settling old scores with Austria and furthering its colonial ambitions through French and British support. A badly equipped, poorly commanded army took three years to force Austria into defeat, finally achieved in the last month of the war at Vittorio Veneto. Some territory was gained – Trieste, Gorizia, and what became

Trentino-Alto Adige – but at the cost of over half a million dead, many more wounded, and a mountainous war debt.

The middle classes, disillusioned with the war's outcome and alarmed by inflation and social unrest, turned to Mussolini, now a figurehead of the Right. In 1921, recently elected to parliament, Mussolini formed the Partito Nazionale Fascista, whose **squadre** terrorized their opponents by direct personal attacks and the destruction of newspaper offices, printing shops, and socialist and trade union premises. By 1922 the party was in a position to carry out an insurrectionary "**March on Rome**". Plans for the march were leaked to Prime Minister Facta, who needed the king's signature on a martial law decree if the army were to meet the march. Fears of civil war led to the king's refusal. Facta resigned, Mussolini made it clear that he would not join any government he did not lead, and on October 29 **was awarded the premiership**. Only then did the march take place.

Zealous **squadristi** now urged Mussolini towards **dictatorship**, which he announced early in 1925. Political opposition and trade unions were outlawed, the free press disintegrated under censorship and Fascist takeovers, elected local governments were replaced by appointed officials, powers of arrest and detention were increased, and special courts were established for political crimes. In 1929, Mussolini ended a sixty-year feud between Church and State by reorganizing the **Vatican** as an autonomous Church state within the Kingdom of Italy. (As late as 1904, anyone involved in the new regime, even as a voter, had been automatically excommunicated.) By 1939, the motto "Everything within the State; nothing outside the State; nothing against the State" had become fact, with the government controlling the larger part of Italy's steel, iron and ship-building industries, as well as every aspect of political life.

World War II

Mussolini's involvement in the **Spanish Civil War** in 1936 brought about the formation of the "**Axis**" with Nazi Germany. Italy entered **World War II** totally unprepared and with outdated equipment, but in 1941 invaded Yugoslavia to gain control of the Adriatic coast. Before long, though, Mussolini was on the defensive. Tens of thousands of Italian troops were killed on the Russian front in the winter of 1942, and in July 1943 the Allied forces gained a first foothold in Europe, when Patton's American Seventh Army and the British Eighth Army under Montgomery landed in Sicily. A month later they controlled the island.

In the face of these and other reversals Mussolini was overthrown by his own Grand Council, who bundled him away to the isolated mountain resort of Gran Sasso, and replaced him with the perplexed **Marshal Badoglio**. The Allies wanted Italy's surrender, for which they secretly offered amnesty to the king, Vittorio Emanuele III, who had coexisted with the Fascist regime for 21 years. On September 8 a radio broadcast announced that an **armistice** had been signed, and on the following day the Allies crossed onto the mainland. As the Anglo-American army moved up through the peninsula, German divisions moved south to meet them, springing Mussolini from jail to set up the **republic of Salò** on Lago di Garda. It was a total failure, and increasing numbers of men and women from Communist, Socialist or Catholic parties swelled the opposing partisan forces to 450,000. In April 1945 Mussolini fled for his life, but was caught by partisans before reaching Switzerland. He and his lover, Claretta Petacci, were shot and strung upside down from a filling station roof in Milan's Piazzale Loreto.

The postwar years

A popular mandate declared Italy a republic in 1946, and Alcide de Gasperi's **Democrazia Cristiana** (DC) party formed a government. During the 1950s Italy became a front-rank industrial nation, massive firms such as Fiat and Olivetti helping to double the GDP and triple industrial production. American financial aid – the Marshall Plan – was an important factor in this expansion, as was the availability of a large and compliant workforce, a substantial proportion of which was drawn from the villages of the south.

The DC at first operated in alliance with other right-wing parties, but in 1963, in a move precipitated by the increased politicization of the blue-collar workers, they were obliged to share power for the first time with the **Partito Socialista Italiano** (PSI). The DC politician who was largely responsible for sounding out the socialists was **Aldo Moro**, the dominant figure of Italian politics in the 1960s. Moro was prime minister from 1963 to 1968, a period in which the economy was disturbed by inflation and the removal of vast sums of money by wealthy citizens alarmed by the arrival in power of the PSI. The decade ended with the "**autunno caldo**" ("hot autumn") of 1969, when strikes, occupations and demonstrations paralysed the country.

The 1970s and 1980s

In the 1970s the situation continued to worsen. More extreme forms of unrest broke out, instigated in the first instance by the far right, who were almost certainly behind a bomb which killed sixteen people in Piazza Fontana, Milan, in 1969, and the Piazza della Loggia bombing in Brescia five years later. **Neo-fascist terrorism** continued throughout the next decade, reaching its hideous climax in 1980, when 84 people were killed and 200 wounded in a bomb blast at Bologna train station. At the same time, a plethora of left-wing terrorist groups sprang up, many of them led by disaffected intellectuals at the northern universities. The most active of these were the **Brigate Rosse** (Red Brigades). They reached the peak of their notoriety in 1978, when a Red Brigade group kidnapped and killed Aldo Moro himself. A major police offensive in the early 1980s nullified most of the Brigate Rosse, but a number of hardline splinter groups from the various terrorist organizations are still in existence.

Inconsistencies and secrecy beset those trying to discover who was really responsible for the terrorist activity of the 1970s. One Red Brigade member who served eighteen years in jail for his part in the assassination of Aldo Moro recently asserted that it was spies working for the **Italian secret services** who masterminded the operation. A report prepared by the PDS (Italy's party of the democratic left) in 2000 stirred up further controversy: it alleged that in the 1970s and 1980s the Establishment pursued a "**strategy of tension**" and that indiscriminate bombing of the public and the threat of a right-wing coup were devices to stabilize centre-right political control of the country. The perpetrators of bombing campaigns were rarely caught, said the report, because "those massacres, those bombs, those military actions had been organized or promoted or supported by men inside Italian state institutions and, as has been discovered more recently, by men linked to the structures of United States intelligence". "Other bombing campaigns were attributed to the left to prevent the

Communist Party from achieving power by democratic means," said Valter Bielli, PDS MP, and one of the report's authors. The report drew furious rebuttals from centre-right groups and the US embassy in Rome.

By whatever means, the DC government certainly clung to power. It was partly sustained by the so-called "historic compromise" negotiated in 1976 with **Enrico Berlinguer**, leader of the **Partito Comunista Italiano** (PCI). By this arrangement the PCI – polling 34 percent of the national vote, just three points less than the DC – agreed to abstain from voting in parliament in order to maintain a government of national unity. The pact was rescinded in 1979, and after Berlinguer's death in 1984 the PCI's share of the vote dropped to around 27 percent. The combination of this withdrawal of popular support and the collapse of the Communist bloc led to a realignment of the PCI under the leadership of **Achille Occhetto**, who turned the party into a democratic socialist grouping along the lines of left-leaning parties in Germany or Sweden – a transformation encapsulated by the party's new name – the **Partito Democratico della Sinistra** ("Democratic Party of the Left").

In its efforts to exclude the left wing from power, the DC had been obliged to accede to demands from minor parties such as the **Radical Party**, which gained eighteen seats in the 1987 election, one of them going to the porn star Ilona Staller, better known as **La Cicciolina**. Furthermore, the DC's reputation was severely damaged in the early 1980s by a series of scandals, notably the furore surrounding the activities of the P2 Masonic Lodge, when links were discovered between corrupt bankers, senior DC members, and fanatical right-wing groups. As its popularity fell, the DC was forced to offer the premiership to politicians from other parties. In 1981 Giovanni Spadolini of the Republicans became the first non-DC prime minister since the war, and in 1983 **Bettino Craxi** was installed as the first premier from the PSI, a position he held for four years.

Even through the upheavals of the 1970s the national income of Italy continued to grow, and there developed a national obsession with **Il Sorpasso**, a term signifying the country's overtaking of France and Britain in the economic league table. Experts disagreed as to whether *Il Sorpasso* actually happened (most thought it hadn't), and calculations were complicated by the huge scale of tax evasion and other illicit financial dealings in Italy. All strata of society were involved in the withholding of money from central government, but the ruling power in this **economia sommersa** (submerged economy) was, and to a certain extent still is, the **Mafia**, whose contacts penetrate to the highest levels in Rome. The most traumatic proof of the Mafia's infiltration of the political hierarchy came in May 1992, with the murders of anti-Mafia judges **Giovanni Falcone** and **Paolo Borsellino**, whose killers could only have penetrated the judges' security with the help of inside information.

Italy today: Mani Pulite and the Berlusconi effect

The murders of the immensely respected Falcone and Borsellino marked a fault-line in the political history of modern Italy, and the late 1980s and early 1990s saw the rise of a number of new political parties, as people became disillusioned with the old DC-led consensus. One was the right-wing **Lega Nord** (Northern League), whose autocratic leader, **Umberto Bossi**, capitalized on concerns that the hard-working, law-abiding north was supporting the corrupt south, while the Fascist MSI, renamed the **Alleanza Nazionale** (AN), or National Alliance, and now a wide coalition of right-wingers led by the persuasive Gianfranco Fini, has gained ground in recent years.

In 1992 the new government of **Giuliano Amato** – a politician untainted by any hint of corruption – instigated the biggest round-up of Mafia members in nearly a decade, leading to the arrest of Salvatore "Toto" Riina, the Mafia **capo di tutti capi** (boss of bosses) and the man widely believed to have been behind the Falcone and Borsellino killings. The arrest of Riina followed the testimony of numerous supergrasses, who also implicated key members of the establishment in Mafia activities, including the former prime minister **Giulio Andreotti**, who was brought to trial.

Bettino Craxi once called Andreotti a fox, adding "sooner or later all foxes end up as fur coats", but it was **Craxi** himself who was one of the first to fall from grace. Craxi was at the centre of the powerful Socialist establishment that ran the key city of Milan, when in February 1992 a minor party official was arrested on corruption charges. This represented just the tip of a long-established culture of kickbacks and bribes that went right to the top of the Italian political establishment, not just in Milan but across the entire country, and was nicknamed **tangentopoli** ("bribesville"). By the end of that year thousands were under arrest and what came to be known as the **Mani Pulite** or "Clean Hands" investigation, led by the crusading Milan judge, Antonio di Pietro, was under way.

The established Italian parties, most notably the Christian Democrats and the Socialists, were almost entirely wiped out in the municipal elections of 1993, and, the national **elections of 1994** saw yet another political force emerge to fill the power vacuum: the centre-right **Forza Italia** or "Come on Italy", led by the media mogul **Silvio Berlusconi**, who used the power of his TV stations to build support, and swept to power as prime minister in a populist alliance with Bossi's Lega Nord and the fascist National Alliance. The fact that Berlusconi was not a politician was perhaps his greatest asset, and most Italians, albeit briefly, saw this as a new beginning – the end of the old, corrupt regime, and the birth of a truly modern Italian state. However, as one of the country's top northern industrialists, and a former crony of Craxi, Berlusconi was as bound up with the old ways as anyone. Not only did he resist all attempts to reduce the scope of his media business, with which, as prime minister, there was a clear conflict of interest, but in time he himself came under investigation concerning the tax dealings of his Fininvest group.

At the end of 1994 Berlusconi was himself forced to resign after the withdrawal of Bossi's Lega Nord from the coalition, and various factions took turns at governing until the formation of a broad centre-left alliance in 1996, known as the **ulivo** ("olive tree"), led by **Romano Prodi**, head of the small

Partito Popolare Italiano, which in order to gain a majority in the Chamber of Deputies formed alliances with most of the other parties, including the Lega Nord.

In January 1999, Craxi was convicted with twenty others of corruption and sentenced to five years in prison, dying a year later in exile in Tunisia. The most influential public figure to be tried in the late 1990s, however, was **Berlusconi**, who was **convicted** and sentenced in August 1998 to two years and nine months in jail. Perhaps not surprisingly, Berlusconi has since been acquitted of a number of the charges against him, and, although further offences have come to light (bribing the judiciary among them), the ongoing proceedings have served more as a background to his resurgent political career than anything else.

Compared with the turmoil of the early 1990s, the political situation had reached a fairly even plateau. The Christian Democratic party had dissolved; the shift from proportional representation to a first-past-the-post system had begun; and a trend towards two large coalitions – one on the centre-left and the other on the centre-right – indicated a major break from the fragmented, multiparty political landscape of the postwar era. In October 1998, the relatively prolonged period of stability ended when the Prodi government was ousted, but the left coalition carried on for another three years under a succession of leaders – **Massimo D'Alema**, Giuliano Amato and the slick and successful ex-mayor of Rome **Francesco Rutelli** – until the April 2001 elections saw them crushingly defeated by Berlusconi's Forza Italia.

In a televised interview Berlusconi made an unofficial agreement with the Italian people (*"contratto con gli italiani"*) whereby he promised to accomplish various economic reforms including lowering taxes and increasing employment. However, with the Italian economy at zero growth, high inflation and the highest debts in the EU, he failed to fulfil any of his electoral promises – though a number of bills were passed that conveniently protected his own business interests and thwarted any attempts by the judiciary to pursue charges of corruption. Berlusconi was also condemned by many Italians for his mismanagement of events at the G8 Summit in Genoa in 2001, during which demonstrator Carlo Giuliani was shot dead by a *carabiniere*. His support for the 2003 invasion of Iraq and his participation in the so-called "Coalition of the Willing", along with the deployment of Italian troops in Iraq, fuelled further disquiet; in 2006 Berlusconi was forced to call early elections and on April 9 he was narrowly defeated by **Romano Prodi**, who immediately pledged to withdraw troops from Iraq, to further links with Europe and to boost the economy by cutting both labour costs and the budget deficit. However, Prodi 's centre-left government was a disaster, lasting less than two years and beset by crisis after crisis (not least the rubbish piling up on the streets of Naples because the city's mafia-run waste disposal set-up couldn't deal with it), and Berlusconi swept back to power in April 2008, easily beating his main rival, the ex-mayor of Rome Walter Veltroni. Whether Berlusconi will deliver at the third time of asking is debatable, and there are no signs of contrition over his previous shady dealings. But he has hit the ground running, promising to sort out the problems of organized crime, the huge national debt and bloated government machine, and even the country's beleaguered national airline, Alitalia. Perhaps the most remarkable thing, though, is that he has been given the chance at all.

Italian art

Pick up any history of Western art and you'll find the biggest chapter by far will be on Italy. The country's contribution to the pantheon of creativity through the past three thousand years is immense, whether it's the legacy of the Romans and the early Christian era or the enormous and unprecedented achievements of the Renaissance in Florence and Rome. It's the reason many people visit Italy in the first place, and this short history is designed to give you the most basic of backgrounds to enhance your trip.

The Etruscans

A sensible way to begin any account of Italian art is with the **Etruscans**, who lived in central Italy – in Etruria – from around 900 BC until their incorporation into the Roman world in 88 BC. The Romans borrowed heavily from their civilization, and thus in many ways the influence of the Etruscans is still felt today: our alphabet, for example, is based on the Etruscan system; and bishops' crooks and the "fasces" symbol, of a bundle of rods with an axe – found, among other places, behind the speaker's rostrum in the US House of Representatives – are just two other Etruscan symbols that endure. The Etruscans were also master craftsmen, working in terracotta, gold and bronze, and accomplished carvers in stone, and it is these skills – together with their obvious sensuality and the ease with which they enjoyed life – that make their civilization so beguiling. A lot of Etruscan objects have survived from tombs, particularly those found in the sites of Tarquinia and Cerveteri – terracotta sculptures such as the sculpture of the married couple or Apollo and Hercules in the Villa Giulia museum in Rome, or bronzes like the Orator and the Chimera in the archeological museum in Florence.

The Romans

The militaristic **Romans**, who wrested control of the region from the Etruscans, are not usually known as great artists. There were great builders, certainly, and the wall paintings and mosaics of Pompeii and Herculaneum demonstrate that there were gifted artists around. But the fact is that a great deal of Roman art and sculpture is in fact copied from ancient Greek originals – most famously the Laocoön and Apollo Belvedere in the Vatican or any number of sculptures in the Palazzo Nuovo of the Capitoline Museums in Rome. There's no doubting the skill of Roman sculptors who recreated these works, though, and the Romans as a whole were prolific creators of sculptural art. Above all they were good portraitists, and there are lots of likenesses of both ordinary people and most of the great emperors still with us today, including a huge hoard in the Vatican Museums, as well as fantastic sarcophagi portraying battle scenes in relief – a medium which was also used to adorn triumphal arches and other architectural features.

Early Christian and Byzantine art

The **early Christians** borrowed the tendency to decorate sarcophagi with relief sculptures from the Romans, though by now these depicted fundamental Christian themes like the shepherd and the lamb, Christ enthroned or the alpha and omega symbols. Early Christian paintings were done in the catacombs and other burial places, mainly depictions of saints but again often borrowing colour and other styles from the Romans. However, mosaics were the more commonly used medium as the decoration in churches, especially during the reign of the Emperor Justinian, whose period in power during the middle of the sixth century marks the high point of early **Byzantine** art. These usually depicted a group of saints lined up with the church's donor, centring on a figure of Christ enthroned in glory, for example in the basilica of Santa Maria Maggiore in Rome, whose mosaics are a fifth-century comic strip of the Old Testament, or, a little later, in the new Christian Roman capital of Ravenna, where the sixth-century basilicas of San Vitale and Sant'Apollinaire Nuovo hold stupendous cycles of mosaics.

The Middle Ages

The medium of mosaic stayed in use for hundreds of years, and indeed was the principal method used to decorate the basilica of San Marco in Venice (see p.289) in the thirteenth century. However, mosaic was an inevitably monumental and static medium, and before long frescoes became preferred in churches, albeit following the rather stiff and formal styles of the mosaicists, along with panel paintings depicting Christ or the Madonna and a group of saints.

    Nicola Pisano (1220–1285) was the first great sculptor of the Middle Ages in what we now call Italy, a native of Pisa and famous for his work on the pulpit in Pisa's baptistry, whose sculptural complexity bears comparison with the best pre-Christian sarcophagi. He passed on his talent to his son, **Giovanni Pisano** (1250–1315), who continued to work in the same Gothic tradition but with more fluidity and skill, creating pulpits in both Pistoia and Pisa cathedrals as well as a series of statues for the facade of Siena's cathedral and another pulpit inside. One of Nicola Pisano's assistants on this, **Arnolfo di Cambio** (1240–1310) was also very active at this time. He produced the famous statue of St Peter in St Peter's in Rome, whose foot is worn smooth by worshippers, and developed the design for funerary tombs which was followed for the next couple of centuries, but he's perhaps best-known as the architect responsible for the construction of the cathedral in Florence in the late 1200s.

    At about the same time, **Pietro Cavallini** (1250–1330) introduced a new level of realism into the mosaics he designed and the frescoes he painted, moving away somewhat from the stiff Byzantine figures people were used to – as evidenced by the frescoes in the basilica of St Francis in Assisi, in the church of Santa Cecilia in Rome, and some fragmentary frescoes in Naples. **Cimabue**, too (1240–1302), was a pioneer of his time, name-checked by Dante in his *Purgatorio* as being eclipsed in talent only by his pupil, **Giotto di Bondone** (1267–1337) – no disgrace as Giotto, as he is now known, was certainly the greatest artist of this time, widely regarded as the link between Gothic art and everything else that followed. This is due to the fact that he was the first to truly break away from the heavily stylized forms of the Byzantine and Gothic era and give his figures proper, human form. His frescoes in the Scrovegni Chapel in Padua are justifiably famous, and have a humane power that makes them one of the great unmissable sights of Italy, although most other works by him are lost or disputed – apart from his frescoes in the basilica of St Francis in Assisi, an altarpiece in the Uffizi, a crucifix in Rimini and one or two other small-scale works.

Despite the influence of Giotto, the dominant school of painting at the time was in fact in Siena, headed up by **Duccio di Buoninsegna** (1255–1318) and **Simone Martini** (1284–1344), both of whom followed a more traditional path, engaging with the more formal Byzantine style to some extent but making it into a more refined and elegant style of their own. Duccio's masterpiece is probably his *Maesta*, currently in the museum of Siena's cathedral, which was so admired on its completion that it was carried around the town in a procession. Simone Martini was a pupil of Duccio and painted the same subject in the town hall of Siena; he is also known for his frescoes in the church of St Francis in Assisi and a high-grade *Annunciation* in the Uffizi.

The fifteenth century: the Renaissance

The fifteenth century in Italy really belongs to what we now call the **Renaissance**, a remarkable time, centred on Florence and Tuscany in particular, when in architecture at least there was an attempt to get back to classical ideas coupled with ingenious new building methods and techniques, while in the visual arts there was a move away from a more iconic style of painting towards an approach that placed man centre stage in as realistic a fashion as possible, with perspective, elements of portraiture and landscape. At the same time artists in general began to gain a new respect, moving gradually away from being considered as mere artisans to take their place as members of the professional classes.

If the Renaissance begins anywhere it's with **Lorenzo Ghiberti** (1378–1455), whose victory in a competition sponsored by the Florentine authorities to design the doors of the city's baptistry arguably kickstarted the century, and occupied the artist for the best part of the next fifty years, with a design that exhibited more drama, naturalism and perspective than had been previously seen, and spawning a legacy of Florentine sculptors who would blaze a trail through the rest of the fifteenth century. The runner-up in the competition, **Filippo Brunelleschi** (1377–1446), went on to specialize in architecture, and added a dome to the city's cathedral that would prove to be one of the engineering wonders of the century (see p.455), while Ghiberti's pupil **Donatello** (1386–1466) became arguably the greatest sculptor of his age, with an appreciation of nature and an ability to render it in marble that upstaged everyone who had gone before. His skill is manifest in numerous examples around the country, but most notably in his early sculptures of the evangelists in Orsanmichele in Florence, now split between the church and the Bargello, where his iconic figure of David also resides. In 1425 Donatello began to work with another sculptor, **Michelozzo** (1396–1472), producing the tomb of Cardinal Brancacci in Naples, among other things; Michelozzo also worked on

Ghiberti's bronze doors. Another sculptor who went in for the baptistry doors competition was **Jacopo della Quercia** (1374–1438), a Sienese artist who was influenced by the work of Nicola Pisano and Arnolfo di Cambio. He is responsible for the Fonte Gaia in Siena's main square, and work in the churches of San Frediano and San Petronio, in Lucca and Bologna respectively.

The invention of perspective is sometimes credited to **Paolo Uccello** (1397–1475), whose most famous work, in the National Gallery in London, shows the foreshortened body of the "soldier who died for perspective" in his *Battle Scene* there. But Uccello was more interested in perspective for its own sake (hence a painting like this) rather than using it to create more realistic pictures, and it was **Masaccio** (1401–1428), who in fact developed it properly – most potently in his fresco of the Trinity in the church of Santa Maria Novella, whose extraordinary depth and realism were revolutionary at the time. His contemporary **Masolino da Panicale** (1383–1447) was another veteran of Ghiberti's doors, but he painted in a more traditional style that harkened back to his Gothic predecessors.

Masaccio's only pupil, **Fra' Flippo Lippi** (1406–1469), was a clear follower of his master, but he was influenced by the Flemish masters too, as we can see in his dramatic and naturalistic frescoes in Prato's cathedral. At the same time, **Fra Angelico** (1395–1455) painted more monumental and in some ways more staid creations, though with a greater emphasis on colour – as you can see if you visit the home of his greatest works, painted in the monastery at which he was a Dominican monk – San Marco in Florence. Meanwhile, in Verona, Fra Angelico's contemporary **Antonio Pisanello** (1395–1455) was decorating some of the principal churches of his home town in a well-developed Gothic style, along with a series of frescoes in the Palazzo Ducale in Mantua.

One of the painters closest in style to Masaccio was **Domenico Ghirlandaio** (1449–94), whose frescoes adorn the church of Santa Maria Novella among other churches in Florence. However, perhaps the greatest of the next generation of Renaissance artists was **Luca Signorelli** (1445–1523), who in fact painted Fra Angelico's portrait (as well as his own) into his amazing *Last Judgement*, in a chapel in Orvieto cathedral – a work which is said to have influenced Michelangelo's later work on the same subject in the Sistine Chapel.

To the south of Florence, in Arezzo, another contemporary of Mantegna, **Piero della Francesca** (1410–1492), was experimenting with perspective in the same way, but his work today looks less archaic, almost modern, in its outlook compared to others of the time, with calm, understated colours and cool sense of form – best seen in his series of paintings depicting the *Legend of the True Cross* in Arezzo's church of San Francesco.

Piero della Francesca was a big influence on the Umbrian painter, **Melozzo da Forli** (1438–1494), who worked in Rome in the last two decades of the fifteenth century, decorating a number of churches, including Santi Apostoli and San Marco – the latter including a famous picture showing his patron pope Sixtus IV that's now in the Vatican Pinacoteca. Among fellow Umbrians, **Pietro Perugino** (1446–1524) was known for his harmoniously composed paintings – less full of drama than some of his contemporaries, but theatrically staged nonetheless, as serene, beautifully coloured tableaux, that almost epitomize the symmetical beauty of much of Renaissance art. His assistant, **Pinturrichio** (1454–1513) also produced beautifully composed works of great form and colour, but made no attempt at any sort of profound vision; some of his best-known and most accessible work is in the church of Santa Maria del Popolo in Rome.

Andrea Mantegna (1431–1506), who worked in the north of Italy, in Padua and then Mantua, was one of the most inventive practitioners of the new

Renaissance techniques, peopling his paintings with living, breathing human beings and setting them against backdrops that had realism and perspective – much more so, say, than his contemporary **Benozzo Gozzoli** (1421–1497), whose frescoes in the chapel in Florence's Palazzo Medici-Ricciardi are more decorative than naturalistic. Some of Mantegna's best work is in the Palazzo Ducale in Mantua, where he painted a series of marvellous family frescoes for the Gonzagas.

Towards the end of the fifteenth century, **Sandro Botticelli** (1445–1510), too, developed a style of his own, apprenticed at a young age to Fra' Filippo Lippi but increasingly creating pictures which married naturalism with elegance. He also worked as much for wealthy merchants as the Church, painting canvases rather than frescoes, and as such his work is smaller-scale and less concerned with monumental religious themes than others, and overall more decorative, using ancient Greek and Roman stories as his subject matter instead.

Botticelli's best-known contemporary was **Leonardo da Vinci**, (1452–1519), a Florentine who died in France and is now known as the ultimate "Renaissance Man", as comfortable designing weaponry or writing a learned thesis as with drawing or painting. Precious little work has survived from Leonardo, partly because he was so busy with other projects, and partly because he insisted on deciding when something was completed himself, and so works were often left unfinished or never delivered. The *Last Supper* in Milan's Santa Maria delle Grazie is probably his most famous piece of work in Italy, and is an incredibly naturalistic for its time, not only realistically depicting the characters in the story, but actually telling the story, too.

The sixteenth century: the High Renaissance and Mannerism

At the end of the fifteenth century the emphasis shifted from Florence, to Rome and to Venice. The **High Renaissance** is generally used to describe a period of time during the first half of the sixteenth century, when all the ideas of the Renaissance were in tune, and there was a group of artists – led by Michelangelo and Raphael in Rome, and Titian in Venice – who were at the height of their powers, interpreting the humanist principles of the time with an almost divine virtuosity and skill, until the mid-century backlash started with the more empty showiness of **Mannerism**.

At the turn of the sixteenth century Ghirlandaio's studio took on a young and hungry Florentine painter called **Michelangelo Buonarotti** (1475–1564), who from the outset was something special, studying anatomy so as to get the draughtsmanship of his figures exactly right, as can be seen in his early – and renowned – figure of *David* in the Uffizi. Michelangelo preferred sculpture to painting, but his fame quickly spread, and he was still a relatively young man when he was called to Rome to decorate the Sistine Chapel for Pope Julius II in 1506 – a feat which took four years, and to this day is perhaps the most heroic and accomplished single piece of work that any painter has achieved. He was an artist who never let up, and it's possible to follow the development of his style around Italy, taking in early works like the figure of Bacchus in Florence's Bargello and his pietà in St Peter's in Rome right up to the Sistine Chapel's dark *Last Judgement*, which he painted over thirty years after the ceiling. It's perhaps testament to Michelangelo's originality and uncompromising approach that both Sistine Chapel works caused an equal level of outcry at the time.

His contemporary **Raphael** (1483–1520), a native of Perugia, with Michelangelo represents the high point of the Renaissance, the point at which the era's ideas and inventions with regards to form, light, naturalism and composition all converged. Unlike Michelangelo, Raphael was an out-and-out painter, and naturally he was called to work for the pope as well, his best work probably being the suite of rooms he decorated for the same Pope Julius II in the Vatican Palace. It seems almost incredible that these two great artists were for a period working in the same building at the same time, creating arguably the two greatest pieces of Renaissance painting ever within a few yards of each other. Yet that is what happened, although Raphael enjoyed a much shorter life than Michelangelo, and works by him are scarce by comparison. However, his later work in the nearby Villa Farnesina in Rome is also among his best, and there are paintings by him in a number of different Italian galleries.

Venice was a booming city at this time, and it first embraced the Renaissance in the elderly figure of **Giovanni Bellini** (1430–1516). He had been influenced by Andrea Mantegna, who had married his sister, and became known for introducing naturalistic details into his religious paintings. He also headed up a large workshop, one that was responsible for turning out the next generation of Venetian painters, including Sebastiano del Piombo, Giorgione and Titian. **Giorgione** (1476–1510) died young and there's hardly any work by him in existence now, but what there is marks him out as one of the greatest Venetian painters, in particular a mysterious painting that has been named *The Tempest* due to the fact that no one really know what it depicts or what it is about. It was a revolutionary painting for its time, principally in the way it incorporates nature into the composition, almost as a character in its own right. The second great Venetian painter of this time was **Titian** (1487–1576), a talent so revered that it was said that even the Holy Roman Emperor Charles V had stopped to pick up one of his brushes – a story which perhaps says as much about the evolving status of artists during the Renaissance as it does about Titian. Titian was a colourist, and brilliant, too, at composition, and he re-wrote the rules of both in his great painting of *The Assumption* in the Frari church in Venice. He was also a great portraitist, as can be seen in his depiction of the Farnese pope, Paul III which hangs in the Capodimonte Museum in Naples, as well as many other great portraits he painted during his long careeer. **Sebastian del Piombo** (1485–1547) is thought to have perhaps finished some of Giorgione's paintings after he died, and he also worked with Raphael on the Villa Farnesina, but he became closest of all to Michelangelo, whose influence can be seen in his later works, for example the two that hang in the Trinita dei Monti church in Rome.

Of the Venetians that followed this group, **Lorenzo Lotto** (1480–1556) followed in the footsteps of Giorgione, as did his friend **Palma il Vecchio** (1480–1528), although it's **Tintoretto** who stands out. His distinctive, dramatic style prefigured the Baroque with its theatrical lighting and dashing, almost unfinished style – all a far cry from the cool delivery of Titian, but typical of the time in his determination to break free of the dominant Renaissance approach and forge a style of his own. A prolific artist, his work can be found everywhere, all over Italy, but the four paintings he did for the Scuola di San Marco in Venice are among his best, as are those in the Scuola di San Rocco, also in Venice.

The third great sixteenth-century Venetian painter was arguably **Paolo Veronese**, who was also a great stylist, painting big narrative works that decorated the Palladian Villa Barbaro in Maser and the church of San Giovanni e Paolo in Venice. Meanwhile in Parma, **Correggio** (1489–1534) was busily decorating the churches and the cathedral in a soft flowing style in which he perfected his *sotto in su* technique, in which figures are depicted on domes and ceiling as if floating in the sky – an effect which was to be take up with a vengeance in the decades to come.

Mannerism

Veronese and Correggio worked towards the end of the sixteenth century, and in some way their styles anticipate what has become known as **Mannerism**, a somewhat derogatory term derived from the Italian word *maniera* or "style". This alluded to the fact that the artists that followed on from the Renaissance greats had to find a way of distinguishing themselves, which they did by using increasingly flashy techniques of perspective and draughtsmanship – all style and no substance, if you like. Mannerist paintings tended to go for cheap and immediate effects – in colour, subject matter and delivery – and as such they prefigure the equally dramatic Baroque era that was to follow. Perhaps the ultimate Mannerist painter is **Giulio Romano** (1499–1546), whose frescoes in Mantua's Palazzo del Te are the last word in shocking even now. But other painters fall into this post-Renaissance category, for example **Francesco Parmigianino** (1503–1540), who worked alongside Correggio in Parma and is probably best-known for a painting that has become known as the *Madonna with the Long Neck*, in the Uffizi in Florence, a very elegant painting that typifies the Mannerist approach to the human form.

Other so-called Mannerist painters include **Giorgio Vasari** (1511–1574), whose work is common in Italy – he was quite prolific – although he is probably best-known for his biographies of the various Renaissance artists, from which we know a great deal about these men and their time. **Agnolo Bronzino** (1503–72) was another gifted Mannerist painter who worked mainly in Florence and concentrated on portraiture. His contemporary, **Benvenuto Cellini** (1500–71) was an artist turned writer who made beautiful pieces in bronze and gold that still survive today but who is more renowned for his racy autobiography which describes his life in Rome during the sixteenth century. Giovanni da Bologna or **Giambologna** (1529–1608), as he's better known, was a Florentine sculptor who also worked in bronze and marble, and whose aim to produce a piece that could be viewed form all angles was Mannerist to its core, and can be seen at its best in Florence's Bargello.

The Baroque

The end of the sixteenth century saw upheaval in Europe, with the Reformation gaining pace in northern Europe and the Catholic Church forced to retrench in its southern heartlands, giving way to a another new style that got stuck with a derogatory name, the **Baroque**, a term which literally meant grotesque, and was coined to describe the grand and theatrical style in paintings and architecture that swept Europe at the beginning of the seventeenth century.

The first artist of the Baroque age was perhaps **Annibale Carracci** (1560–1609), of Bologna, whose work in the Palazzo Farnese, depicting a series of mythological scenes, prefigures the style with its overtones of fantasy, illusion and mild titillation. **Guido Reni** (1575–1642), also from Bologna, focused more on religious themes, but with a sentimentality that made his pictures popular everywhere and his work much in demand. Less sentimental but equally dramatic, the works of **Michelangelo Merisi da Caravaggio** (d.1610) have stood the test of time better, as has his reputation, perhaps because his story fits the archetype of artist-as-outlaw that's very much in tune with modern tastes. Nonetheless his pictures were strikingly original at the time, using models from the streets for religious figures and making street life, clothes, and the nitty-gritty of the human form, warts and all, a fit subject for religious art – as can be seen in his paintings in the church of Santa Maria del Popolo and other churches in Rome, where he worked for much of his life. Caravaggio was a great dramatist, composing his pictures in a theatrical manner that was increasingly typical of the times. He was also a superb technician, particularly with regard to light, and perhaps the greatest exponent of a technique known as chiaroscuro – basically the interplay of light and dark on the canvas. This style was taken up with relish by the artists of the Baroque era, and done to death by some of them, not least a group of painters from Naples – **Luca Giordano** (1632–1705), **Massimo Stanzione** (1585–1656) and **Battistello Caracciolo** (d.1637) – who raised the city's status in the art world at a time when it was becoming one of the most populous and important cities in Europe. Giordano in particular was a massively prolific painter, and you can't move for his work in Naples, though perhaps the best place to see it is the Cappella del Pio Monte della Misericordia, where one of his finest paintings hangs alongside a great work by Caravaggio, both done for the same church. Hot on the heels of these artists in Naples was **Francesco Solimena** (1657–1747), a Neapolitan late Baroque painter who was hugely successful, and whose work is also ubiquitous, but which is at its best in the city's Gesu Nuovo.

A pupil of Carracci, **Domenichino** (1581–1641) also worked on the Farnese Palace, and decorated the church of Sant'Andrea delle Valle in Rome with another student of Carracci, **Giovanni Lanfranco** (1582–1647), though the two fell out shortly after this, after which Domenichino went to Naples and relative obscurity. Lanfranco meanwhile went on to bigger and better things, becoming an expert in *sotto in su* technique and as such landing commissions for all kinds of domes and ceilings, both in Rome and in Naples. Another follower of Carracci, and also from Bologna, Giovanni Francesco Barbieri, known as **Guercino** or "the squinter" because he was cross-eyed (1591–1666), fell out with Reni, who accused him of stealing all his ideas, but who still managed to produce a fair body of work, most famous of which is his *St Petronilla* altarpiece which he painted for St Peter's but which now hangs in Rome's Capitoline Museums.

Working alongside Lanfranco in Rome, **Pietro da Cortona** (1596–1669) was another great illusionist, whose ceiling in the Palazzo Barberini in Rome is perhaps the ultimate in Baroque *sotto in su* trickery – a mass of writhing figures, clouds and drapery that are at once in the room with you and at the same time escaping to into the sky beyond. The Barberini pope, Urban VIII, was the greatest pope of the Baroque age, not least because he was the patron of **Gianlorenzo Bernini** (1598–1680), who was without question the greatest Baroque artist of all, producing a lifetime's work of sculpture and architecture that more than any other defines what Baroque really means. The best of his small-scale statues – in Rome's Galleria Borghese – are virtuosic pieces of dynamic sculpture, intensely theatrical, that invite you to study them from all angles, while Bernini's work for Rome's church of Santa Maria in Vitorria, depicting the *Ecstasy of St Theresa*, is the very essence of Baroque drama.

All those who came into contact with Bernini were influenced by him, and **Giovanni Baciccia** (1639–1709) was no exception, taking on the illusionistic challenge of the age and decorating the Gesu church in Rome with a vigour and invention that rivalled even Cortona's Palazzo Barberini work.

Andrea Pozzo (1642–1709), too, took the style's illusionism to an extreme, decorating another Jesuit Rome church, Sant'Ignazio, with one of the biggest fakes of the era – painting in a trompe l'oeil dome which from one point in the nave looks exactly like the real thing.

The eighteenth century

The late Baroque style became what is known as the **Rococo** in the early eighteenth century – basically an ornate style of interior decoration that is a toned-down and more domestic version of the Baroque. By comparison to what had gone before, the period, and indeed the eighteenth century in general, was not a great era for Italian art, partly because interior decoration was indeed what artists increasingly came to specialize in, working for the aristocracy and the wealthy merchant classes rather than their traditional patron, the Church. Landscape painting became popular, as seen in the Venetian scenes of **Francesco Guardi** (1712–93) and **Antonio Canaletto** (1697–1768), the latter of whom churned out views of Venice that were extremely popular, though he never reproduced the same quality when painting other cities. Guardi, too, painted only Venice, though with a more impressionistic style that is maybe more suited to modern tastes. Perhaps the greatest Italian Rococo artist, however, was **Giambattista Tiepolo** (1696–1770), whose flamboyant frescoes were sought after in palaces and castles all over Italy, although they were essentially fantasy works, used as decoration rather than for any deeper meaning – an approach that was ably continued by his son **Giandomenico Tiepolo** (1727–1804).

Later eighteenth century Italian art took many forms – the architectural fantasies and complex etchings of **Giambattista Piranesi** (1720–78), for example, or the Venetian genre scenes of **Pietro Longhi** (1702–85). But ultimately the style that caught on was the one that prevailed over the rest of Europe, **Neoclassicism** – a movement inspired by the art and architecture of the ancient world, which at the time was being excavated in sites around Rome and in Pompeii and Herculaneum, and which for most people mean a return to truly civilized artistic ideals. **Antonio Canova** (1757–1822) was the best-known and most prolific Italian Neoclassical artist; he produced a huge body of work and there are lots of examples across the country, although he is perhaps most famous for his renderings of Napoleon at the beginning of the nineteenth century, and in particular of his famously sluttish sister, Pauline, in the Galleria Borghese.

The nineteenth century to the modern day

The nineteenth century, too, was not an especially auspicious time for Italian art, and the international focus was by now firmly in France and elsewhere. After Canova, the mantle of Neoclassical sculpture had been taken up by **Pietro Canonica** (1869–1959), a Rome-based sculptor who specialized in civic and public sculpture as well as busts of the rich and famous, and **Vincenzo Gemito**

(1859–1929), known for his genre studies of Naples lowlife. Another Neapolitan artist, **Domenico Morelli** (1823–1901), also specialized in historical and religious themes, passing on his penchant for drama to his student **Antonio Mancini** (1852–1930). Mancini quickly developed a style of his own which had more in common with the realist movement that by this time was sweeping through France and other parts of Europe. Shortly after, around the middle of the nineteenth century, a group of painters based in Tuscany, the **Macchiaioli** movement, also tried to get away from a more traditional approach, prefiguring to some extent the French Impressionists, though they were much less influential. They saw their brief as loosening the chains of figurative painting while also depicting real-life themes, and one of their best-known figures, **Giovannia Fattori** (1825–1908), while initially concentrating on historical scenes and portraits, eventually became a painter of landscapes in a style that was influenced by the French Barbizon school.

Giovanni Fattori taught the young **Amedeo Modigliani** (1884–1920), a painter from Livorno who lived fast and died young after he decided to ditch the relatively wholesome landscapes of the Macchiaioli to concentrate on idiosyncratic depictions of the lowlife of Paris, where he died at the age of 35. The big homegrown Italian movement of the twentieth century, however, was the **Futurists**, a quasi-fascist group of abstract painters led by the poet Filippo Marinetti who believed in the purity of the modern world and all that went with it, including war, weaponry and in particular World War I, which unfortunately claimed their most talented painter **Umberto Boccioni** (1882–1916) as a victim. Other Futurists included **Giacomo Balla** (1871–1958) and **Carlo Carra** (1881–1966), and you can see much of their work in Rome's Galleria Nazionale d'Arte Moderna, along with selected works by perhaps the greatest and most influential Italian artists of the twentieth century, **Giorgio de Chirico** (1888–1978), who with Carra set up the **Metafisicamovement** after World War I – a reaction against Cubism and abstraction and a precursor of Dadaism and the Surrealist movement and work of Magritte. De Chirico is known for his strange dreamlike landscapes – figurative and yet unreal – which display an almost dysfunctional vision of the modern world, although the artist did go back to a more traditional approach later in life. You can see his work in various venues in Rome, but best of all in his studio on Piazza di Spagna.

Italian architecture

The architecture of Italy perhaps doesn't dominate the Western world in the same way the country's art does, but the fact remains that tracing the history of Italy's buildings is akin to tracing that of Europe in general. The Renaissance and Baroque periods are the most distinctive architectural periods, but the fact is that buildings and architecture from all eras make up the very fabric of the Italian landscape – more, perhaps, than any other European country.

The Greeks and Etruscans

The first great Italian builders were the **Greeks**, who during the Hellenistic age – between the third and first century BC – left an indelible mark on the Italian regions they occupied. Greek architecture followed a very rigid system, one that has been subsequently followed on and off by just about every architectural era at some point, so it's hard to overstate their importance, which was based on the three classical orders: the Doric, the oldest and lowest, Ionic, the middle order, and Corinthian, the highest and most florid. You can find examples, of each in the various **temples** the Greeks left in the south – at Paestum, just south of Naples, and at Agrigento and Siracusa in Sicily, the latter of which has been incorporated into the city's cathedral. The Greeks left small **theatres** too, two examples of which are again in Sicily, in Taormina and Siracusa.

At the same time as the Greeks were leaving their mark on the south, the **Etruscans** occupied parts of central Italy, though they didn't leave much in the way of architecture apart from a series of necropolises, at Cerveteri and Tarquinia in Lazio, and a third-century-BC gateway in Volterra in Tuscany, part of a set of walls that once encircled this ancient Etruscan city.

The Romans

The **Romans** were great and ingenious builders, and they moved architectural forms on from the Greeks, still using columns and pediments but often making these more decorative than supportive. That they could do this was down to the invention of concrete, which allowed the Romans more flexibility in what they built, and their use of the arch, the innate strength of which allowed them to build more solid yet more diverse structures. As with the everything else, the Romans were less interested in aesthetics than the Greeks, and favoured function above form at all times; they also liked to build on a large scale, preferring big, grandiose, imperial structures that showed off the power of their system and empire. The Pantheon and Colosseum in Rome are just two examples of this love of size for its own sake, but really any Roman site demonstrates it.

The Roman love of order is also evident in the planned nature of their **towns**, which had their random, poor quarters but whose commercial heart, around the main forum, had a uniform style across the empire. You can see this in Rome itself, and in the ruins at nearby Ostia Antica, while settlements like

Pompeii and Herculaneum demonstrate how rigid the Roman street grid could be, with three horizontal main streets – the *decumanus inferior, major* and *superior* – crossed at right angles by other main streets or *cardos*. The forums were surrounded by shops and businesses, law courts usually in the form of a basilica – a long building with aisles either side and at least one temple – usually a rectangular colonnaded building topped with a triangular pediment with steps leading up to the main entrance.

The Romans also built for their leisure time, constructing theatres and more usually **amphitheatres** for the staging of gladiatorial games and other spectacles. The Colosseum in Rome is the best-known and largest example of this kind of building, but there are other impressive amphitheatres dotted all over in Italy – in Pompeii and Pozzuoli near Naples, and in Verona, to name just the most intact examples.

Roman militarism led to the building of some structures that had no more purpose than to celebrate a famous victory or conquest of a new territory, the **triumphal arch** – a form which interestingly stayed with us right up to the nineteenth century (for example in Paris and New York). Usually they would be decorated with frieze sculptures illustrating the heroic battles. There are three intact triumphal arches in and around the forum in Rome, and others in Benevento near Naples, in Aosta, and in Rimini and Ancona on the Adriatic coast. Another way of celebrating imperial triumphs was to decorate a **column** with sculpted friezes, but far fewer of these survive – only two in fact, in Rome, dedicated by and to the emperors Trajan and Marcus Aurelius.

Finally there was are the **mausoleums** that were raised by emperors to hold the remains of them and their families – planned as large and fitting tributes to their imperial dynasties. As you might expect the best of these are in Rome, and most impressive is probably the mausoleum of Hadrian, which has been adapted as the Castel Sant'Angelo and is as much a medieval and Renaissance monument as a Roman one.

The early Christian and Byzantine era

The first Christian structures in Italy were probably the **catacombs**. A series of artificial underground tunnels and caverns, they're not strictly architecture as such, but some of the features – altars, arches, etc, used in underground places of worship – were later adopted when Christianity became the dominant religion and Christian buildings were erected above ground, too.

The first Christian buildings adopted the Roman **basilica** as their model, for example in Santa Sabina or Santa Maria Maggiore in Rome, with one main and two side aisles, and were often built on the site of a saint's martyrdom or final resting-place, for example St Peter's on the Vatican Hill. Often they incorporated ancient columns from previous Roman buildings, and were quite bare. Later, the capital of the Church moved to Ravenna and early Christian architecture moved to a **Byzantine** style, with round churches, mosaics rather than paintings, and often a dome – a style which caught on quickly, and, as you can tell from looking at the skyline of Rome today, never really went away.

The Middle Ages

The first style of the Middle Ages, predominant during the tenth and eleventh centuries, was the **Romanesque**, identifiable by its round arches and a return to the basic basilical plan, often with transepts added – not only to add extra space but also so that the footprint of the church made the shape of a cross. There was also a tendency to build campaniles or bell towers separate from the church, and sometimes a separate baptistry too – as can be seen in Pisa, where the Duomo, baptistry and famous leaning bell tower form a perfect Romanesque ensemble. There are other superb examples of the Romanesque style in Parma and Modena, and in the south at Monreale in Sicily, whose Norman cathedral still bears a large Byzantine strain in its impressive mosaics – a bit like another Romanesque-Byzantine hybrid, the basilica of San Marco in Venice. Another fine Romanesque Italian church, and one which formed something of a blueprint for many that followed, is the church of Sant'Ambrogio in Milan.

By the twelfth century, the **Gothic** style began to dominate across Europe, characterized by its use of pointed arches, vaulting, and an emphasis on verticality, space and light. However, it never took hold in Italy to the extent it did in France or England, and as a result there are relatively few Gothic buildings here, and those that exist have often been dulled by the heavier lines of the Renaissance style that succeeded it. The style was adopted most successfully in Venice, where a particular form of florid Gothic architecture took root and is in evidence throughout the city – in the Palazzo Ducale most prominently, but also in some of the buildings on the Grand Canal, the Ca' Foscari and Palazzi Giustinian for example. Otherwise there are isolated examples of the Gothic style throughout the country: Cistercian abbeys like that of Fossanova in Lazio; some of the French-looking churches of the Angevin monarchs of Naples, in particular the monastic complex of Santa Chiara; and the cathedral in Siena, which exhibits a peculiarly Italian form of the Gothic style – very ornate on the outside, much like the nearby cathedral of Orvieto in Umbria. Perhaps the most impressive Gothic building in Italy, at least from a purists' point of view, is the cathedral of Milan, a vast building which took five hundred years to build but exhibits all the classic features of the style, with a facade and roof that is a forest of pinnacles.

The Renaissance

Spreading through Italy from the fifteenth century onwards, the Renaissance was perhaps the high point of Italian architecture, as it was in the arts and most other disciplines, and its influence on building methods and styles remains to this day. Essentially, the Renaissance ushered in the period of the professional architect rather than a collection of masons, whose vision of a building was paramount; it also led to a spread of architectural ideas and techniques to domestic as well as religious and royal buildings.

Florence was at the heart of the Renaissance and the architect who led its revival was **Filippo Brunelleschi** (1377–1446), who became famous for designing an elegant dome to top the city's Gothic cathedral – a dome which was not only a magnificent engineering feat at the time but today is still the most enduring symbol of the city. Brunelleschi was familiar with and keen to emulate the building methods and feats of ancient Rome and Greece but was also successful in creating his own style, which incorporated the methods of the past but in an increasingly modern way. As such, he more than anyone is responsible for the fact that so many modern buildings still incorporate the columns and capitals, pediments and frames of ancient Greece and Rome.

Another Florentine, **Michelozzo di Bartolomeo** (1396–1471), succeeded Brunelleschi as chief architect of the cathedral, and built the seminal Medici-Ricciardi palace – a prototype for the classic Renaissance palace, with its rustic basement and more refined first floor. He worked on a number of other Florentine buildings at the time including the "tribune" of the Annunziata church, which he designed as an ancient Roman temple – a design which was finished off by **Leone Battista Alberti** (1404–72). Alberti was like Leonardo da Vinci in that he was the complete Renaissance man, skilled in all disciplines but perhaps excelling at architecture, although unlike his contemporaries he had nothing to do with the actual building of any of his designs. His focus was on the aesthetic of a building rather than what made it stand up, and as such he could let his imagination run riot, which he did in buildings like the Palazzo Rucellai in Florence, the Tempio Malatestiano in Rimini and the church of Sant'Andrea in Mantua.

Domestic architecture

Italian architecture isn't just about palaces and churches: **domestic architecture** is also a source of interest and the layout of small towns and farming settlements have had as much impact on Italy's landscape as the country's better-known monuments and buildings.

Hill-towns

Throughout the Middle Ages, the countryside was unsafe, unhealthy and, in many places, uncultivated, but its topography, with an abundance of hills and mountains rising steeply from fertile plains, provided natural sites for **fortified settlements** which could both remove the population from malarial swamps and bandits and preserve the limited fertile land for cultivation.

In the period of their greatest expansion – between the twelfth and fourteenth centuries – **hill-towns** sprang up all over the peninsula. Many were superimposed on early Etruscan cities – Chiusi and Cortona – or were cave dwellings, such as Matera, in Basilicata. Most hill-towns were built within high and sometimes battlemented walls, the sheer drop afforded by these sites (often extended by the use of towers) enabled inhabitants to make good use of gravity by dropping a crushing blow onto the heads of enemies attempting to scale the walls. It was also a good way of dispatching the dead, as well as a simple form of rubbish disposal. Houses were densely packed together and constructed with materials found on or near their site, which adds to the impression that they arise naturally from their geological foundations. Most day-to-day activities were carried out in the streets, traces of which are still visible in the surviving evidence of public fountains and washhouses, wells and communal ovens.

Although many hill-towns were genuinely self-contained communities, they were often under the political and economic control of the cities, particularly in north and central Italy. Each city-state set up **satellite towns** of its own, to protect trade routes or to operate as garrisons for soldiers, weaponry and food in case of war. For example, Siena established the fortified hill-town of Monteriggioni in the early thirteenth century along an important route from Rome into France, which also passed through **San Gimignano**. At roughly the same time, Florence founded similar frontier outposts, including San Giovanni Valdarno, Scarperia and Firenzuola.

The building of the Palazzo Rucellai was overseen by **Bernardo Rossellino** (1409–64), another architect who had a big influence both in Florence and beyond. He also competed the work on Brunelleschi's cathedral dome and is perhaps best known for the design and creation of the Renaissance 'new town' of Pienza for pope Pius II.

The High Renaissance

Arguably the greatest architect of the High Renaissance was **Donato Bramante** (1443–1514), who learned a lot from his Florentine predecessors but spun it into a style of his own, in the ingenious rebuildings of the churches of San Satiro and Santa Marie delle Grazie in Milan, and most famously in his little Tempietto in Rome, which faithfully turned back to the classical orders of the past but with a small-scale sensibility that was very much of its time. Bramante's best years were in Rome, and he was commissioned to develop the buildings of the Vatican Palace as well as rebuilding St Peter's itself. The Greek

Villas and farmhouses

If you're travelling through Tuscany, Umbria or Marche, you're likely to see another classic Italian structure – the **country villa** or *Casa della Mezzadria*, which became widespread during the Rennaisance. Usually square in plan, it was built using a combination of brick, stone and terracotta under a tent-like roof with a dove tower (*la torre colombaia*) at its apex – doves and pigeons were adept at killing snakes and consuming weeds and also provided valuable meat for the table. The house derives its name from the system of sharecropping or *mezzadria* (based on the word *mezza* – "half"), under which the peasant farmer yielded up half his produce to the landowner. Used only occasionally by the landlord, these houses were the primary residence of the estate manager (il *fattore*), who oversaw the landlord's interests.

In contrast, the architecture of the **farming complex** (*la cascina*) was stark, with high rectangular porticoes supported by square columns. The estate accommodated four architecturally distinct elements: the owner-manager's house, which was more elaborate in design and often taller than the other buildings; housing for workers, tenement-like in character, with external balconies running along the upper floors used to dry and store crops; cow barns; and stables for horses with hay lofts above. Today, many farmhouses have been converted into tourist accommodation or agriturismos.

In southern Italy the **masseria** is a more common type of farming settlement – massive, complex structures that dominate vast tracts of countryside. Consisting of a dense cluster of separate buildings, *masserie* were sometimes enclosed by a high-perimeter wall with defence towers built into it. At its largest a *masseria* virtually operated as a self-contained village incorporating church, school, medical clinic and shop, in addition to accommodating the full range of agricultural requirements for stabling, housing (of day labourers called *braccianti*) and storage. In their purest, least-altered form, village *masserie* are still visible in parts of Sicily. **Trulli**, found along the coast of Puglia and inland, form one of the most remote, curious and ancient types of farm settlement in Italy. Of uncertain origin, they consist of clusters of single circular rooms, each covered by a conical roof (see p.862).

cross plan he came up with for the latter never saw the light of day, but the building was started while he was alive and as such he must take credit for at least part of it.

The St Peter's project spanned more than a century, and Bramante's place was taken by **Michelangelo** (1475–1564), who added the dome but died before he could achieve very much. In Rome, the other great artist of the High Renaissance, **Raphael** (1483–1520), undertook architectural commissions too, designing the Chigi chapel in the church of Santa Maria del Popolo and encouraging his pupil **Giulio Romano** (1499–1546) to take on vast projects such as the Palazzo del Te in Mantua. Raphael decorated another building for the Chigi family in Rome, the Villa Farnesina, which was built to the designs of **Baldassare Peruzzi** (1481–1536), an important architect who designed much in his native Siena, and who worked on the Villa Farnese in Caprarola in Lazio with **Antonio Sangallo the Younger** (1483–1546) – the most talented member of a family of architects. Sangallo was very much the successor of Bramante and Raphael in Rome, and was responsible – again along with a very aged Michelangelo – for perhaps the city's finest Renaissance palace, the supremely elegant and dignified Palazzo Farnese, in 1514.

Meanwhile **Jacopo Sansovino** (1486–1570) was the principal architect at the time in Venice, and was responsible for many of the large public buildings around Piazza San Marco, most notably the Library and Loggetta, as well as several churches, all of which display an inventiveness that plays well with the fripperies of the existing Venetian Gothic buildings there. Not far from Venice, in Vicenza, **Andrea Palladio** (1508–80) achieved an influence that stretched far and wide, with his refined take on Renaissance principles, building a number of palaces and villas between 1540 and 1580 that became the apotheosis of the refined country house – a symmetrical central block, with a columned portico and a central dome. Palladio rigorously followed classical rules and while this means his buildings sometimes appear dull it is also perhaps the reason why his principles are still alive today.

In Rome **Giacomo Vignola** (1507–73) took over as the latest architect to oversee the progress of St Peter's and at the same time built the influential church of the Gesu in the city, to a striking new design that dispensed with aisles and focused everything on the enormous cupola and the high altar. The church, or at least its facade, was finished by **Giacomo della Porta** (1533–1602), who unwittingly came up with a design that more or less every Roman church would follow for a century or more – one which used all the columns and pediments of the classical orders, but mixed them up in a new and freer way than before, with scrollwork and other features that heralded the new, flashier age of the Baroque.

The Baroque era

As in painting and sculpture, the **Baroque era** was one of massive change, with the Church defiant in the face of the Reformation sweeping across the rest of Europe, and looking for new ways to keep the faithful on message. The theatrical and dramatic nature of the painting and sculpture at the time seeped into architecture, too, and nowhere more so than in Rome, where the Baroque became the dominant architectural style – and the one that most defines the city today (much as Florence is above all defined by the Renaissance).

The chief architect of this time was **Carlo Maderno** (1556–1629), and it was he who took over and at long last finished St Peter's, some would say by ruining its original design and converting it to a Latin cross that undermined the original dome-focused plan. It's the St Peter's of Maderno that you see today, and the church is in many ways a Baroque church inside and out – much like the piazza outside, whose columned arms are the brainchild of the greatest sculptor and architect of the Baroque age, **Gianlorenzo Bernini** (1598–1680). Bernini was a prodigy of the most amazing kind, the son of a sculptor and extremely successful – as a sculptor – while still very young. He was enormously talented and incredibly prolific, which means that he more than anyone else maybe shaped the Rome you see today. Patronized as he was by the pope at the time, Urban VIII, it's Bernini's features that define the interior of St Peter's, not least his vast and flashy baldachino under the dome, and although he only gravitated towards architecture later in life he is responsible for a variety of buildings and architectural features around the rest of the city. He restored Piazza Navona and added the massive Fountain of the Four Rivers as its centrepiece; he built the small oval church of Sant'Andrea delle Quirinale, and he worked on the enormous Palazzo Barberini, the seat of his benefactor Urban VIII, as well as the Montecitorio and Chigi palaces.

It's said that the figure in Bernini's fountain of the Four Rivers in Rome is shielding its eyes from the horrors of the nearby church of Sant'Agnese in Agone, because it was built by **Francesco Borromini** (1599–1667), his greatest rival, and the only one who came close to Bernini in talent at the time. As well as being more of an architect, Borromini was a very different sort of man to Bernini: more troubled, and much less of a man about town, but he, too, left his mark on Rome, becoming known as an architect who could could come up with ingenious solutions to thorny architectural problems, often shoehorning grand buildings into sites that they were ill-suited for – for example the churches of San Carlo alle Quattro Fontane and Sant'Ivo alla Sapienza, both of which are clever and unique designs. He also worked with Bernini on the Palazzo Barberini, adding a lovely circular staircase as a counterpart to Bernini's more traditional rectangular one.

The other great Baroque architect active in Rome was **Pietro da Cortona** (1596–1669), whose contribution to the Palazzo Barberini is mentioned on p.686, but who also designed the clever and very theatrical church of Santa Maria della Pace and its small piazza.

Outside of Rome, the big centres for the Baroque were in southern Italy – in **Naples**, where architects like **Cosimo Fanzago** (1591–1678) and **Fernando Sanfelice** (1675–1748) were active, and in **Lecce**, whose central core is a Baroque extravaganza, with an array of exuberant buildings fashioned from the soft local sandstone.

Neoclassicism

Like much of the rest of Europe, Italy entered a relatively bland era after the Baroque – deliberately so, for the spirit of the **Neoclassical** movement that followed was essentially a revolt against the excesses of the Baroque style, and at heart a return to the solid principles of Classicism. **Luigi Vanvitelli** (1700–73) was probably the foremost eighteenth-century Italian architect. The son of a Dutch landscape painter living in Naples, he worked with **Nicola Salvi** (1697–1751) on the Rococo fantasy, Rome's Trevi Fountain, and later, after a handful of small commissions in Rome, designed and built the humungous Royal Palace at Caserta in 1752, a massive Versailles-like blend of both perfect symmetry and ludicrous grandiloquence, as well as remodelling the more restrained Palazzo Reale in nearby Naples. His successor as most prominent Italian architect was **Giuseppe Valadier** (1762–1839), a purer exponent of Neoclassical principles, who taught architecture at Rome's Accademia San Luca and laid out many key parts of the city centre, including the great open space of the Piazza del Popolo, the Pincio and the streets leading off it.

The nineteenth century saw the construction of a series of **shopping arcades** in the big Italian cities – the Galleria Umberto in Naples, what is now the Galleria Sordi in Rome and perhaps most successfully the Galleria Vittorio Emanuele II in Milan, built in 1865 by **Giuseppe Mengoni** (1829–77), who unfortunately died when he fell from the roof a few days before it opened. Around this time, the era of the Unification of Italy, Rome was remodelled as a capital fit for the new country, and it saw a huge amount of construction, most of it a mixture of the functional nineteenth-century apartment buildings that you find in most European capitals and the odd piece of faux-grandeur like the semi-circular Piazza della Repubblica at the top of Via Nazionale, or, most strikingly, the hideous Vittoriano monument overlooking Piazza Venezia, the work of one **Giuseppe Sacconi** (1854–1905) in 1895 – though even this monstrosity has become accepted over the years.

The modern era

The early **twentieth century** saw several international styles touch Italy in some way, for example Art Nouveau, but none really caught on and there wasn't a new indigenous architectural movement until the **Futurists**, and their chief architect, **Antonio Sant'Elia** (1888–1916), who never really built anything but who had far-reaching ideas about the modern city that at the time were more science fiction than anything else. **Giuseppe Terragni** (1904–43) was his true heir, an arch-rationalist who built the Casa del Fascio in Como in 1936, and was the designer of an unrealized project in Rome based on Dante's *Divine Comedy* as a tribute to the Italian poet. Terragni worked under Mussolini but died young, after which Mussolini's preferred architect became **Marcello Piacentini** (1881–1960), who was responsible for some of the most celebrated of the Duce's architecture – the Stadio dei Marmi, the housing complex of Garbatella and EUR, all in Rome, as well as the chilling open space of Brescia's Piazza della Vittoria. Piacentini worked on EUR's Palazzo dello Sport with **Pier Luigi Nervi** (1891–1979), a celebrated Italian architect who specialized in buildings based around prefabricated and reinforced concrete and who later became known for enormous works such as aircraft hangars, the trade fair halls in Turin and the Olympic Stadium and the Papal Audience Chamber in Rome. Nervi worked with another Italian architect, **Gio Ponti** (1891–1979), on the prestigious and at the time – 1950 – audacious Pirelli Tower in Milan, until recently still the tallest building in Italy. Ponti was a great Italian designer as well as architect and set up the bilingual design magazine *Domus*, which is still in circulation today.

Perhaps the most famous Italian architect of the current era is **Renzo Piano** (b.1937), though more for his work outside Italy than in his home country. Famous initially for his Paris Beaubourg collaboration with Richard Rogers, he has since worked on numerous prestige projects around the world – Hong Kong's airport, the redesign of Potsdamer Platz in Berlin, and a lot of big museum projects and extensions. But he recently returned to his roots, designing the hugely successful Auditorium Parco della Musica in Rome.

Italian cinema

From the earliest days of **cinema**, the Italians have always been passionate movie-lovers and movie-makers. But Italy's films really came to the forefront of world cinema in the postwar period; this was partly due to the location shift from studio-based films to the country's towns and landscape. Their style and technique were ground-breaking, and the use of real sites added a dimension, a mood, which made Italian cinema linger in the memory. The endless expanse of the Po Valley plain in *Obsession*, the steaming sulphur springs outside Naples in *Voyage to Italy*, the deserted, off-season seaside resort of Rimini in *I Vitelloni*, created an atmosphere that could never have been achieved in a studio.

The background

The Italians were once famous for their silent costume epics, pre-World War I dramas that had monumental backdrops and crowd scenes – a leftover from the Italian grand opera tradition. They were often set in the period of the Roman Empire, anticipating the Fascist nostalgia for ancient Rome by at least a decade. **Giovanni Pastrone**'s **Cabiria** (1914), set in ancient Carthage, was the most sophisticated and innovative of these, with spectacular sets and lighting effects that the American director D.W. Griffiths imitated in his masterpiece **Intolerance** (1916). This borrowing of Italian expertise by Hollywood gave the Taviani brothers the story for their **Good Morning Babylon** (1987).

Even in its early stages Italian cinema was handicapped by the economic problems that were destined to keep it lagging behind the American industry. The reason for this was not simply lack of funds, but also an inability on the part of the government to realize what a moneyspinner the indigenous film-making talent could be, and what the unregulated influx of foreign films into Italy would mean for the home market. In addition to this, the Americans themselves began making films in Italy, attracted by the cheap labour, the locations, and the quality of the light, thereby devastating the already fragile home-grown industry. An American film crew arrived in 1923 to make an epic version of **Ben Hur**. Three years prior to this, 220 films were made in Italy; by 1927 the number had dropped to around a dozen a year.

The **Fascist regime** (1922–43) was surprisingly slow to recognize the potential, in both economic and propaganda terms, of the cinema. But in 1934 Mussolini did begin to mete out financial support. He also limited the number of foreign imports, had film added to the arts festival in Venice, and in 1937 inaugurated "Cinecittà", the film studio complex just outside Rome. From 1938 to 1944 the proportion of Italian productions to imports rose rapidly, though home-produced films would never account for more than a third of the total number of films distributed in the country.

Films made during the Fascist period featured glorious victories from the past (the Romans again), and from the present – the war in Ethiopia, for example. During this time, although not all movies were vehicles for propaganda, no films could be made that were overtly critical of the regime. Most popular at the time were the escapist, sentimental, "white telephone" films, so-called because the heroine would have a gleaming white telephone in her boudoir, Hollywood-style – a touch of the exotic for the average Italian at the time, who rarely even saw such a thing, let alone owned one.

Italians were not, however, cut off from what was going on in world cinema between the wars, and the ideas and techniques of Eisenstein and, even more so, of **French directors**, particularly Renoir, Pagnol and Carné, began to filter through. As with literature, probably the biggest single influence on the emerging generation of Italian film-makers was the American novel. Hemingway, Faulkner and Steinbeck spoke directly to the young generation: their subjects were realistic, their stylistic approach was fresh, even raw, and the emotion seemed genuine.

It was not surprising, then, that the late 1930s and early 1940s saw an element of **documentary-style realism** creep into film-making. Contemporary social themes were addressed; non-professional actors were sometimes used. Directors – even those with the official stamp of approval – made the occasional realistic documentary, with none of the bombast or gloss of the typical Fascist film. It was on films such as these that future Neorealist directors such as Visconti, Rossellini and De Sica, and the writer Zavattini, worked their apprenticeships, learning techniques that they would draw on a few years later when they were allowed to unleash their creative imaginations.

A film made in 1943 caused a considerable stir. When it was first shown, Mussolini's son Vittorio walked out, exclaiming "This is not Italy!" But Mussolini allowed it to be distributed anyway, probably because there was nothing politically controversial in it. The film was **Luchino Visconti**'s **Obsession**, an unauthorized adaptation of the American novel **The Postman Always Rings Twice** by James M. Cain. Visconti transposed this lowlife story of adultery and murder to northern Italy, the characters playing out their seedy tragedy in the relentlessly flat landscape of the Po Valley and among the surreal carnival floats in Ferrara. It showed two ordinary people in the grip of a violent passion, so obsessed with each other that they bring about their own destruction. The original negative was deliberately destroyed when the official film industry was moved north to Mussolini's Saló Republic on Lake Garda. *Obsession* was something new in the Italian cinema: it had an honesty and intensity, a lack of glamour, that pointed the way to the Neorealist films of the immediate postwar period.

The Neorealists

The end of the war meant the end of Fascist domination of everything, including the film industry; but Italy was left emotionally as well as physically shattered. It now seemed important to film-makers to make sense of the intense experience the Italian people had undergone, to rebuild in some way what had been destroyed.

As the tanks were rolling out of Rome in 1945, **Roberto Rossellini** cobbled together the bare minimum of finances, crew and equipment and started shooting **Rome, Open City**. He used real locations, documentary footage, and low-grade film, and came up with a grainy, idiosyncratic style that influenced not only his Italian contemporaries, but also the American film noir of the late 1940s, and the grittily realistic films of the early 1950s – as well as the French New Wave of the 1960s.

Neorealism had no manifesto, but its main exponents – Rossellini, De Sica and Visconti – developed the following aims, even if they didn't always stick to them: to show real people rather than conventional heroes (using non-actors), real time, real light, real places (shooting on location, not in studios). Their intention was to present the everyday stuff of life and not romantic dreams.

Unusually for an "art" film, *Rome, Open City* was a box office hit. It had a good emotional, even melodramatic story, with touches of humour, and packed a terrific moral punch. Set in a downbeat quarter of occupied Rome, it is about a partisan priest and a communist who join forces to help the Resistance. The Nazis are depicted as effeminate and depraved, while the partisans – including a band of children – are the true heroes, though Rossellini seems to pursue immediacy at the expense of making political statements.

This was the first in Rossellini's so-called "war trilogy". It was followed by **Paisà** (1946), which traced the Allied occupation north from Sicily to the Po Valley, in six self-contained episodes; and the desolate **Germany, Year Zero** (1947), set in the ruins of postwar Berlin, about a child whom circumstances push to suicide.

In these, as in other Neorealist films, children are seen as the innocent victims of adult corruption. **Vittorio De Sica's Shoeshine** (1946) is an anatomy of a friendship between two Roman boys, destroyed first by black-marketeers, then by the police. A young boy is the witness to his father's humiliation in De Sica's **Bicycle Thieves** (1948) – also set in the poorer quarters of Rome – when he sees him steal a bicycle out of desperation (a bicycle will enable him to get his job back) and immediately get caught. The child's illusions are dashed, and the blame is laid on society for not providing the basic human requirements. At the time *Bicycle Thieves* was called the only truly communist film of the postwar decade, but in retrospect the message, as in *Rome, Open City*, seems politically ambiguous. Crowds are seen as hostile and claustrophobic, and the only hope seems to lie in the family unit, which the hero falls thankfully back on at the end.

The conflict between Catholic and Marxist ideology is a recurrent theme in Italian cinema, from Rossellini through to Pasolini, and the Taviani brothers in the 1980s, and it's often this that gives their films the necessary tension. More than anyone, Visconti exemplifies this dichotomy. Born an aristocrat in the famous Milanese family, and sentenced to death (though not executed) for being anti-Fascist in 1944, he was influenced by the writings of Antonio Gramsci, and right up until his death in 1976 veered between two milieux for his films – the honest, suffering sub-proletariat, and the decadent, suffering upper classes.

In 1948 Visconti made a version of the nineteenth-century Sicilian author Giovanni Verga's novel **The House by the Medlar Tree**, about a family of fishermen destroyed by circumstance, which he filmed as **The Earth Trembles**. It was shot on location on the stark Sicilian coast, using an entire village as cast, speaking in their native Sicilian (with an Italian voice-over and subtitles). He adapted the story to incorporate a Marxist perspective, but this fades from view in the pervading atmosphere of stoic fatalism, closer to Greek tragedy than to the party line. Something else that detracted from the intended message was the sophisticated visual style: stunning tableaux such as the one where the wives, dressed in black, stand waiting for their husbands on the skyline, looking out to sea, prompted Orson Welles to remark that Visconti shot fishermen as if they were Vogue models. Indeed, style constantly threatened to overtake content in Visconti's work, culminating in the emotionally slick **Death In Venice** (1971).

The end of Neorealism

By the **early 1950s**, Neorealism was on the way out. Social problems no longer occupied centre stage, and film-makers now concentrated on the psychological, the historical, even the magical side of life. There were several reasons for this, not least that the trauma of World War II had receded, and cities (and lives) were being rebuilt. As Rossellini said in 1954, "you can't go on making films about heroism among the rubble for ever". Directors wanted to move on to new themes. Another reason for the break was government intervention. The cinema industry was in the doldrums, and the Christian Democrat minister Giulio Andreotti had banned any more Neorealist films from being made on the grounds that social criticism equalled communism. The Cold War was just beginning.

Neorealist films had in any case, with one or two exceptions, rarely been good box office. Of the Italian-made films, the general public tended to prefer farces, historical dramas or comedies. The Neapolitan comic actor Totò – who had a colossal career spanning scores of films and several decades – was a particular favourite. In **Totò looks for a Home** (1949), he and his family search for somewhere to live in the postwar ruins of Rome, in a comic variation on a Neorealist theme. It was a sign of the times that people preferred to laugh at their problems rather than confront them.

De Sica meanwhile had moved on from the unremitting pessimism of *Bicycle Thieves* to a fantastic fable set in Milan, **Miracle in Milan** (1951), about a young man who is given a white dove which possesses the power to grant the wishes of everyone living in his slummy suburb. Surreal special effects are used to create a startling impact, for example in a shot of the hero and heroine flying high above the pinnacles of Milan cathedral on a broomstick. The moral is still a Neorealist one, but with a change of emphasis: art and imagination can help your problems disappear for a while, but won't solve them.

In 1954 **Visconti** made **Senso**, another adaptation of a nineteenth-century novel but worlds away from **The Earth Trembles**. It opens to the strains of Verdi in the Venice opera house, La Fenice, one night in 1866, and is Visconti's view of the politically controversial Unification, portrayed through the lives of a few aristocratic individuals. It was a theme he would return to in **The Leopard** (1963). **Senso** was the first of Visconti's historical spectaculars, and the first major Italian film to be made in colour.

The Fifties and the next generation of directors

Neorealism was dead, but the next generation of film-makers – Fellini, Pasolini, Bertolucci, Antonioni, Rosi – could not help but be influenced at first by its ideals and techniques, though the style each of them went on to evolve was highly personal.

Federico Fellini, for one, saw Neorealism as more a world-view than a "school". His early films, such as **La Strada** (1954), follow a recognizably realistic storyline (unlike his later movies), but the whole feeling is different from the films of the 1940s. His characters are motivated by human values rather than social ones – searching for love rather than solidarity. All through his long career Fellini used films as a kind of personal notebook in which to hark back to his youth. **I Vitelloni** (1953) is set in an unrecognizable Rimini, his birthplace, before the days of mass tourism; **Amarcord** (1973) is again set in Rimini, this time under Fascism. He also explores his own personal sexual fantasies and insecurities, as in **Casanova** (1976) and **The City of Women** (1980).

But Fellini isn't all nostalgia and sex. There are philosophical themes that run through his work, not least the gap between reality and illusion. The heroine of **The White Sheikh** (1952) falls in love with the Valentino-type actor playing the romantic lead for "photo romance" comics (being shot on the coast outside Rome), and has her illusions dashed when reality intervenes and he makes a bungling attempt to seduce her. *Casanova* too is an oddly (and deliberately) artificial-looking film. It wasn't actually shot in Venice, and the water in the lagoon is in fact a shaken plastic sheet – an odd backlash against the real landscapes of the Neorealists.

Religion is also a theme in Fellini's work, and he's at his best when satirizing the Roman Catholic Church, as in the grotesque clerical fashion parade in **Roma** (1972), or the malicious episode in **La Dolce Vita** (1960) where a couple of children claim to have had a vision of the Virgin Mary, and create the press event of the month.

Pier Paolo Pasolini, murdered in mysterious circumstances in 1975, was a practising Catholic, a homosexual and a Marxist, as well as a poet and novelist. His films reflected this cocktail of ideological and sexual tendencies, though in a less autobiographical way than Fellini's. They're also far more disturbing and challenging: **Theorem** (1968) intercuts shots of a spiritually empty middle-class Milanese family, into which a mysterious young stranger insinuates himself, with desolate scenes of a volcanic wasteland. **The Gospel According to Matthew** (1964) is a radical interpretation of a familiar story (and an excellent antidote to Zeffirelli's syrupy late-1970s **Jesus of Nazareth**) in which Jesus is not a man of peace but the champion of the sub-proletariat and the enemy of hypocrisy. It was filmed in the surprisingly biblical-looking landscape of the poorer regions of southern Italy – Puglia and Calabria – and used the peasants of the area in the cast. Pasolini's **Decameron** (1971) was a record hit at the box office because of its explicit sex scenes, though the director's intention had been political rather than salacious, with Boccaccio's fourteenth-century tales transposed from their original middle-class Florentine setting to the dispossessed of Naples.

Otherwise, the real box-office earners in the 1960s and 1970s were the so-called "spaghetti westerns", shot in the Arizona-look-alike interior of Sardinia, the best of which were directed by **Sergio Leone**.

Bernardo Bertolucci started out as Pasolini's assistant, and shared his politics, though his own films are more straightforward and accessible. **The Spider's Strategem** (1970), filmed in the strange, star-shaped Renaissance town of Sabbioneta near Mantua, was the first of many feature films sponsored by RAI, the Italian state TV network, and is about the anatomy of a destructive father-son relationship with constant flashbacks to the Fascist era. Another early film, **The Conformist** (1970), adapted from the novel by Alberto Moravia, had the spiritually empty hero (or rather, anti-hero) search for father-substitutes in Fascist Rome – again a dream-like jumble of flashbacks. **The Conformist** was Bertolucci's first step on the path to world recognition; subsequent projects, from **Last Tango in Paris** (1972), through **1900** (1976), **La Luna** (1979), the Oscar-winning **The Last Emperor** (1987) and the ill-judged **The Sheltering Sky** (1990), have made him one of the country's most commercially successful directors.

Michelangelo Antonioni again had a Neorealist background, but in the films he made in the 1960s and 1970s he shifted the emphasis from outward action and social realism to internal and psychological anguish. The locations he chose – the volcanic landscape of Sicily for **L'Avventura** (1960), the bleak townscape of industrial Milan in **La Notta** (1961), the impersonal Stock Exchange building in Rome for **The Eclipse** (1962), the alienating oil refineries and power plants at Ravenna for **The Red Desert** (1964) – made perfect settings for what were almost cinematic equivalents of existential novels.

The Neapolitan director **Francesco Rosi** made a series of semi-documentary "enquiry" films attacking various aspects of the Italian establishment: the Sicilian Mafia in **Salvatore Giuliano** (1962), the construction industry in Naples in **Hands Over the City** (1963), the army in **Many Wars Ago** (1970), and vested interests of all kinds in **The Mattei Affair** (1972). Not that these are dry analyses of Italian society: the viewer has to sort through the pieces of evidence – the newsreel footage, the half-heard comments, the absence of comment – to come to his or her own conclusions about the truth, in kind of do-it-yourself mystery stories.

Later on, in the late 1970s and 1980s, Rosi went in a more personal direction. **Christ Stopped at Eboli** (1979) is a surprisingly unincisive critique of "the problem of the south", set in a poverty-stricken mountain village in Basilicata. **Three Brothers** (1981) looks at three different political attitudes, as the brothers of the title, reunited for their mother's funeral back home in Puglia, argue, reminisce and dream. Oddly enough, in 1984 Rosi made a completely apolitical film of the opera **Carmen**.

Nostalgia... to the present

Italian cinema of the Seventies and Eighties was dominated by foreign co-productions and TV-sponsored films, which, like elsewhere, led to a loss of national identity. Audiences were steadily eroded by the successive onslaughts of television, video and TV deregulation. Some directors tried to address this problem by focusing on purely Italian themes, others by looking to the past.

Ermanno Olmi's **The Tree of Wooden Clogs** (1978) has a cast from Bergamo speaking dialect with Italian subtitles, and did well at the box office worldwide. Also prominent among Italian directors of the time were the **Taviani brothers**, whose **Padre Padrone** (1977), a mini-epic set in Sardinia that details the showdown between an overbearing father and his rebellious son, and **Kaos** (1984), an adapation of Pirandello stories shot in scenic Sicily, are both loving of the Italian landscape and redolent of a time past. Together with **Good Morning Babylon** (1987), these films put the brothers' work centre-stage internationally.

Nostalgia was a keynote of the time. **Giuseppe Tornatore**'s Oscar-winning **Cinema Paradiso** (1988) was shot in the director's native village near Palermo, and tells its story through a series of flashbacks. The central figure, a successful film director named Salvatore, returns to the village for a funeral, only to find that the magical Cinema Paradiso of his childhood is about to be razed to make way for a car park. Similarly, in **Ettore Scola**'s **Splendor** (1989), the owner of the cinema in a small provincial town is forced to sell up to a property developer because of declining audiences and debt. In equally poignant vein, **Michael Radford**'s **Il Postino** (1994) is a humorous tale set in 1930s Italy, which follows the artistic and political awakening of the central character, played by Italian comic Massimo Troisi (who sadly died soon after the film's completion).

In this rather soul-searching period of Italian film-making, the films of **Gabriele Salvatores** dealt with groups of Italians abroad, often cut adrift, or seeking escape. His **Mediterraneo** (1991) shows eight reluctant Italian sailors stranded on a Greek island in 1941, and recounts their gradual integration into local life, while **Marrakech Express** (1989) has a group of seven setting off for Morocco in search of their friend, and **Puerto Escondido** (1992) explores life for an Italian in a commune in Mexico.

If the films best known outside Italy were rather escapist in their subject matter, it was a different story at home. During the late 1980s and early 1990s, film-makers began to address the major preoccupation of the time, namely the corruption at the heart of Italian society. The nicely titled **The Brownnose** (**Il Portaborse**; 1991) by **Daniele Luchetti** satirizes the favoured Italian way of outwitting the system and getting things done – the oiling of the wheels of bureaucracy by means of gifts and bribery involves the anti-hero in all manner of scrapes.

Gianni Amelio's political drama **Open Doors** (**Porte Aperte**; 1990), from Leonardo Sciascia's novel of the same name, is set in Fascist Palermo just before World War II, but its subject matter – a liberal judge being obstructed in his investigations of all-pervasive corruption – was particularly apposite at the time. The same director's **Stolen Children** (**Il Ladro di Bambini**; 1992) is a better-known film outside Italy, and deals with corrupt society as seen through the eyes of a child. Amelio made no new work for five years until **The Way We Laughed** (**Così Ridevamo**; 1998), the story of two brothers leaving rural Sicily for Turin in the late 1950s, a film which suggests that the present-day malaises that Italy is experiencing have their roots in the betrayals and violence in the late 1950s and early 1960s.

Films with a much more hard-hitting, realistic edge also began to emerge, among them **Mario Martone**'s **Rehearsal for War** (**Teatro di Guerra**; 1998), which examines the Yugoslav conflict and the power of the imagination in our perception of evil. Meanwhile, such directors as **Marco Risi** dealt with specific social problems – his **Mery per Sempre** (1989) follows the lives of half a dozen youngsters in prison, and its sequel, **Ragazzi Fuori** (1990), shows them fresh out of the clink.

More provocative still, **Daniele Cipri** and **Franco Maresco**'s **Toto Che Visse Due Volte** (**Totò And His Two Lives**; 1998), set in Sicily, ruffled a few feathers with its violation of religious and sexual taboos (including a depiction of a statue of the Virgin Mary being assaulted). Critics disliked the film's clumsiness, but this iconoclastic work didn't trouble the establishment. When the film censors banned its release, the deputy prime minister – a film buff – stepped in and disbanded their board.

A sea change

In the 1990s a sea change took place in Italian film as screenplay writers, cinematographers and directors began to shake free of nostalgia and corruption themes and explore contemporary life in an idiosyncratic, amusing and penetrating way. Director, actor and screenwriter **Nanni Moretti** achieved great acclaim with his **Dear Diary** (**Caro Diario**; 1993). In three parts, the film covers such diverse subjects as twentieth-century architecture, children and telephones, Pasolini's unsolved murder, the myth of rural idyll, as well as Moretti's own fight against cancer. Much of the film is spent following Moretti on his scooter through Rome, or travelling by ferry from one island to another. His latest film **The Son's Room (La Stanza del Figlio**; 2001), however, is a much darker work exploring a family's grief; the film won a Palme d'Or at Cannes and much critical attention.

In his films, Moretti appears to be continually questioning the worth of everything, including his own work; indeed, he went too far for some critics in **Aprile** (1998), which focuses on his inability to decide how to finish his films – or even whether to finish them. Although it wasn't as well received as his other works, it's still a very funny film; in it, Moretti feels obliged to make a film about Italian politics, but is continually sidetracked by his real passions, including the birth of his first child.

An Oscar-winning work by **Roberto Benigni**, known for such slapstick-style movies as **Johnny Stecchino** (1991) and **The Monster** (1994), marks another brave foray into new territory. Benigni's **Life is Beautiful (La Vita è Bella**; 1997) addresses the Holocaust and dares to combine comedy with genocide. A parent's desire to protect the innocence of their child, rather than the Holocaust itself, is the theme of the film, and Benigni (who also plays the lead role with his wife, Nicoletta Braschi, as his co-star) distinguishes between laughing *at* the Holocaust and laughing *in* the Holocaust; visual gags, dramatic tension and a poignancy that's almost unbearable at times permeate the film. In answer to critics who accuse him of treating a painful subject with too much levity, Benigni claims that Italian Holocaust survivors are only just beginning to talk about the events of more than fifty years ago and that a film like *La Vita è Bella* is justified if it opens up debate.

Film-makers have found a new assurance, and cinema audiences are flocking to the box office, not least because of the mediocrity (at best) of what's on TV. Benigni's **Pinocchio** (2002) grossed US$7m in its first weekend, a new record at the Italian box office. The story is adapted from the Italian writer Carlo Collodi's 1880 fable and, as he did in **Life is Beautiful**, Benigni doubles as star and director, playing opposite his wife, Braschi, who is the blue-haired fairy. True to the original story, the film is a moral tale in which the puppet who dreams of becoming a real boy has to learn honesty first through a series of adventures. Benigni's film represents a reclaiming of cultural property: Disney reportedly tried to trademark the character Pinocchio, claiming that it was their animation that everyone thought of first when they heard the name, but they lost their claim.

Other directors to have enjoyed success both at home and abroad include **Gabriele Muccino**, whose coming-of-age story **Come te nessuno mai (But Forever in My Mind**; 1999) is an interesting take on the US high-school comedy genre; his very Italian students are highly politicized youngsters, planning strikes and taking part in a 24-hour sit-in, both of which provide a backdrop for the inevitable angsting and first love. Muccino's romantic comedy **The Last Kiss (L'Ultimo Baccio**; 2001), a film dealing with panic at parenthood and the chasing of vanishing youth, won a flurry of awards and universal approval. He has recently directed a Hollywood movie, **The Pursuit of Happyness** (2006) starring Will Smith. **Ferzan Ozpetek**, a Turk who has lived in Rome for more than twenty years, made a name for himself with **Turkish Bath** (1997) and **Harem Sauré** (1999). His more mainstream film, **Ignorant Fairies (Le Fate Ignoranti**; 2001), deals with the themes of love, loss and deception wrapped up in a soundtrack of Middle Eastern and Latin music. Commenting on the current changes in Italian film, Ozpetek says, "The public is more demanding now. At the same time, people have become more willing to experiment, to go to see quality Italian films with fully developed stories and interesting characters. Before they would have looked to foreign films for that type of cinema."

An example of one such quality film is **Giuseppe Piccioni**'s **Light of My Eyes** (**Luce Dei Miei Occhi**; 2001). Set in Rome, it's a haunting exploration of the alienation that many feel in their lives and their romantic relationships. The story is particularly strong thanks to the character of Maria, the female lead, free of the usual stereotypes and beautifully acted. **La Sconosciuta** (2006) by Tornature has an equally strong female lead; the story involves an East European prostitute forced to abandon her children as she tries to earn a living in an Italian town.

Many have been looking to Naples and Sicily as the most vibrant sector of the film industry, part of a general resurgence in artistic activity in southern Italy that's connected with a new pride in regional identity. **Vincenzo Marra**'s **Sailing Home** (**Tornando a Casa**; 2001) was made on a shoestring budget: it uses fishermen rather than professional actors, is spoken in Neapolitan dialect (at home it was released with Italian subtitles) and was shot in semi-documentary style. His follow up, **Vento to Terra** (2004), was also shot in Naples, as was **The Session is Open**, a startling documentary about the trial of a notorious member of the Camorra.

More accessible to an international audience perhaps is Neapolitan director **Antonio Capuano**'s **Luna Rossa** (2001), a mesmerizing portrayal of a Camorra family from the inside, borrowing from Greek tragedy for its structure and with a soundtrack by indie-rockers Almamegretta. Visually rich, brooding, confusing and violent, the film is artistically assured in a way that few others have been in recent years. Another gritty film directed by Capuano's is **Mario's War** (2005), which looks at a well-to-do Neapolitan family who foster a disturbed boy, although the most notorious Italian film to emerge in recent year is definitely Matteo Garrone's **Gomorrah** (2008), based on Roberto Saviano's best-selling book about the Neapolitan Camorra. It's a tough affair, portraying a Naples you're not likely to see on any visit – it's shot in the housing projects and wastelands north of the city and uses locals as actors.

Books

A comprehensive background reading list for Italy would run on for dozens of pages, and would include a vast number of out-of-print titles (OP). Most of our recommendations are in print, but those that aren't shouldn't be too difficult to track down. The book symbol 🕮 marks titles that are particularly recommended.

Travel classics

Vincent Cronin *The Golden Honeycomb*. Disguised as a quest for the mythical golden honeycomb of Daedalus, this is a searching account of a sojourn in Sicily in the 1950s. Although overwritten in parts, it has colourful descriptions of Sicily's art, architecture and folklore.

Charles Dickens *Pictures from Italy*. The classic mid-nineteenth-century Grand Tour, taking in the sights of Emilia, Tuscany, Rome and Naples, in elegant, measured and incisive prose.

Norman Douglas *Old Calabria*. A brilliant travel chronicle based on the author's wanderings around Calabria in the early twentieth century. Wide-ranging and digressive, it's a classic of the genre. See also *Siren Land* (OP) and the novel, *South Wind*, which focus on Cápri and the Bay of Naples.

Johann Wolfgang Von Goethe *Italian Journey*. Surprisingly readable account of a journey all through the peninsula at the end of the eight-eenth century, a classic of travel writing and a decisive point in Goethe's own transition from Sturm und Drang to classicism.

Henry James *Italian Hours*. Urbane travel pieces from the young James; perceptive about particular monuments and works of art, superb on the different atmospheres of Italy.

Jonathan Keates *Italian Journeys*. Frank yet affectionate journey through the Italian social, cultural and historical landscape. Full of

engaging anecdotes, its witty portraits get under the surface of Italy and its people.

🕮 **D.H. Lawrence** *D.H. Lawrence and Italy*. Lawrence's three Italian travelogues collected into one volume. *Sea and Sardinia* and *Twilight in Italy* combine the author's seemingly natural ill-temper when travelling with a genuine sense of regret for a way of life almost visibly passing away. *Etruscan Places*, published posthumously, consists of his more philosophical musings on Etruscan art and civilization, and remains one of the most illuminating books written on the period.

David Leavitt *Florence, a Delicate Case*. Though a book largely about Florence's expat community over the last 150 years may sound insular and antique, Leavitt injects a good deal of wit and sensitivity into this quirky portrait of Florence. Refreshingly free of cultural overload, the account focuses on the city's more shadowy side – its role as a destination for suicides and taboo-breakers – and there's a flamboyant cast of characters.

🕮 **Norman Lewis** *Naples '44*. Lewis was among the first Allied troops to move into Naples following the Italian surrender in World War II, and this is his diary of his experi-ences there. Part travelogue, part journalism, this is without question the finest thing you can read on World War II in Italy – and, despite its often bleak subject matter, among the most entertaining. Lewis's more recent *In Sicily* is a broad contemporary portrait of the island he has married into and returns to frequently. Subjects range from reflections on Palermo's ruined *palazzi* to the impact of immigration, and there's plenty on the Mafia.

Charles Lister *Heel to Toe*. Firmly in the tradition of such English travelwriters as Douglas and Gissing, the author sets off on a bicycle, soon transferring to a moped, for a journey along the Ionian coast from Bríndisi to Reggio. Mixing history and culture with strong opinions and copious digression, it's chatty and accessible, if somewhat over-written. In a similar style, Lister's *Between Two Seas* (OP) charts his walk along the Appian Way.

Mary McCarthy *The Stones of Florence/Venice Observed*. A mixture of high-class reporting on the contemporary cities and anecdotal detail on their histories; one of the few accounts of these two cities that doesn't read as if it's been written in a library.

Jan Morris *Venice* (titled *The World of Venice* in US). Some people think this is the most acute modern book written about any Italian city, while others find it unbearably fey. At least give it a look. The author has more recently published what she claims is her final book, *Trieste and the Meaning of Nowhere*, an aptly elegiac salute to this curious frontier city.

H.V. Morton *A Traveller in Italy*; *A Traveller in Rome* and *A Traveller in Southern Italy*. Morton's leisurely and amiable books were written in the 1930s, long before modern tourism got into its stride, and their nostalgic charm has a lot to do with their enduring popularity. But they are also packed with learned details and vivid descriptions.

William Murray *Italy: the Fatal Gift* (OP). Murray spent several years in Italy shortly after the last war, and this is a collection of essays inspired by his time there, and many return visits since. Skilfully combining personal anecdote and contemporary Italian history and politics, it's one of the most insightful introductions to the country and its people you can buy.

Eric Newby *Love and War in the Apennines*. An anecdotal, oddly nostalgic account of the sheltering of the author by local people in the mountains of Emilia-Romagna in the closing months of World War II. Newby's *A Small Place in Italy*, recounting his life in a small farmhouse at the foot of the Alps, is equally evocative, and reads much more "authentically" than other expatriates-in-Italy tales.

Contemporary travel and impressions

Anne Calcagno, Matthew Spender (ed) *Travelers' Tales: Italy*. Crammed with evocative period detail by the likes of H.V. Morton as well as contemporary writing specifically commissioned for this volume by Tim Parks, Lisa St Aubin de Terán and others, this makes a perfect introduction to the richness and variety of the country. See also *Tuscany: True Stories*, edited by

Calcagno and Tara Austen Weaver, a similar collection.

Matthew Fort *Eating up Italy*. Foodwriter Fort's voyage around Italy on a Vespa, discovering the mainland by eating its food from region to region, and painting an eloquent picture of the contemporary country. See also his more recent *Sweet Honey, Bitter Lemons*, which focuses on Sicily.

Annie Hawes *Extra Virgin*.
Belonging to the Mayes/Mayle
school of expats setting up in sunny
rural climes, but superior to most of
the genre in every way, this relates
how two sisters overcome various
adversities and much local incompre-
hension to find their idyll on a
Ligurian mountain. It's funny and
smart, interspersed with plenty of
culinary culture and peasant lore.

Frances Mayes *Under the Tuscan Sun*,
Bella Tuscany. Follow the trials and
triumphs of American author and
boyfriend as they renovate a
farmhouse near Cortona, interspersed
with recipes. The echoes of Peter
Mayle in Provence will put many off.

Peter Moore *Vroom with a View*.
Moore is an entertaining and honest
travel companion on this Bryson-like
tour of Italy on a battered scooter,
sharing all the highs and lows along
the way. A fun and light-hearted
holiday read.

Tim Parks *Italian Neighbours*,
An Italian Education, *Europa* and
A Season with Verona. Novelist Tim
Parks has lived in Italy since 1981.
Through deftly told tales of family
life, his books examine what it means
to be Italian, and how national
identity is absorbed. *Europa* is a
bawdy, savage tale of love gone
wrong, set among a group of
academics travelling to lobby the
European Parliament in Strasbourg,
while *A Season with Verona* relates his
passion for his local football team,
but drawing in much more besides.

History

The Longman History of Italy
This eight-volume series covers the
history of Italy from the end of the
Roman Empire to the present, each
instalment comprising a range of
essays on all aspects of political,
social, economic and cultural
history. Invaluable if you've
developed a special interest in a
particular period.

R.J.B. Bosworth *Mussolini*. This
gripping account of modern Italy's
most traumatic period paints a
vivid picture of *Il Duce*, and warns
of the strong fascination for
him that still exists in Italy today.
The same author's more recent
Mussolini's Italy brings to life the
realities for the Italian people
during the same period.

Jerome Carcopino *Daily Life in
Ancient Rome*. Detailed but never
dull, this is a seminal work of
Roman social history, with
background on everything from
education and religion to domestic
daily rituals.

Christopher Duggan *The Force
of Destiny*. Recently published
history of the Italy since Unification which explores just how much
of a unified nation Italy is, particularly since the political crises of the
last twenty years.

Edward Gibbon *The History of the
Decline and Fall of the Roman Empire*.
Awe-inspiring in its erudition,
Gibbon's masterpiece is one of the
greatest histories ever written, and
one of the finest compositions of
English prose. Penguin publish an
abridged version for those without
the time to tackle the entire work.

Paul Ginsborg *A History of
Contemporary Italy*. A very
scholarly but readable account of
postwar Italian history, illustrating the
complexity of contending economic,
social and political currents. Bringing
the story up to date, Ginsborg's
Italy and its Discontents unravels the
knotty background to Berlusconi's
rise to power and his tussles with
the judiciary.

Michael Grant *A History of Rome*. A straightforward and reliable summary of an impossibly complicated story.

Tom Holland *Rubicon*. An introduction to the Roman Republic from its founding to its demise (and that of Augustus). Its vivid descriptions put the flesh on the bones of this period of history.

Christopher Hibbert *Rome: The Biography of a City*. The history of Italy's capital made easy, this is by far the most comprehensive, yet concise, account of the city through the ages. The companion volumes, *Venice: The Biography of a City* (OP) and *Florence: The Biography of a City*, are particularly good on those cities, and have more coverage of the twentieth-century than most.

Valerio Lintner *A Traveller's History of Italy*. A brief history of the country, from the Etruscans right up to the present day. Well written and sensibly concise, it's just the thing for the dilettante historian of the country.

John Julius Norwich *The Normans in Sicily*. Accessible, well-researched story of the Normans' explosive entry into the south of Italy and their creation in Sicily of one of the most brilliant medieval European civilizations. Just as stimulating is his *A History of Venice*, the most engrossing treatment of the subject available.

Giuliano Procacci *History of the Italian People*. A comprehensive history of the peninsula, charting the development of Italy as a nation-state.

Denis Mack Smith *The Making of Italy 1796–1866; Italy and its Monarchy*. The former is an admirably lucid explanation of the various forces at work in the Unification of Italy, while the latter deals with Italy's short-lived monarchy, whose kings ruled the country for less than a century. The same author has also written a couple of excellent biographies, *Mazzini* and *Mussolini*.

Mark Thompson *The White War*. Italy's role in World War I is just a sideshow in many non-Italian histories of the conflict, and is often misrepresented within the country. Thompson's book is a a magisterial account of the catastrophes and triumphs of the Italian campaign, and a brilliant explication of the part the war has played in forming the nation's self-image.

Crime and society

Luigi Barzini *The Italians*. Long out of print but still a highly readable and respected work on the Italian nation. And not as out of date as you might think.

Tobias Jones *The Dark Heart of Italy*. Written during a three-year period in Parma, this is an interconnected sequence of essays dealing with various aspects of modern Italian society, from the legal and political systems to the media and football. Bewildered and fascinated at every turn, Jones reveals a culture in which evasiveness and ethical malleability are as significant as the much-celebrated virtues of vivacity, charm and sophistication.

Norman Lewis *The Honoured Society*. Lewis's classic account of the Mafia, originally written in the 1960s, is still the most enjoyable introduction to the subject available.

Douglas Preston with Mario Spezi *The Monster of Florence*. Between 1974 and 1985 the area around Florence was terrorized by Italy's most notorious serial killer. The crimes were truly monstrous, but Preston describes them without undue prurience, in a gripping book which develops into a hard-hitting indictment of the (still unfinished) investigation. Essentially a modern Italian tale of incompetent officials, deranged conspiracy theorists and unbelievable "witnesses".

Robert Saviano *Gomorrah*. Saviano's expose of the Neapolitan Camorra is the first to have dished the dirt on the most violent grouping of Italy's various organized criminal gangs, and he is currently in hiding because of it. At heart it's a passionate protest against a problem which only seems to get worse, and has been made into a well-received movie.

Alexander Stille *Excellent Cadavers*. Stille traces the rise, successes,

failures and eventual assassinations of anti-Mafia magistrates Giovanni Falcone and Paolo Borsellino, as well as blowing the cover of Andreotti and Craxi.

Peter Robb *Midnight in Sicily*. The Australian Robb spent fifteen years in the Italian south tracing the contorted relations between organized crime and politics. Here, he focuses on the structure of the Mafia, the trials of the bosses in the 1980s, the high-profile assassinations that ensued, and the trial of Andreotti. It's a thorough, fast-paced study, providing deep insights into the dynamics of Sicilian society and an authentic portrait of Palermo.

Art, architecture and archeology

Michael Baxandall *Painting and Experience in Fifteenth-Century Italy*. An invaluable analysis, concentrating on the way in which the art of the period would have been perceived at the time.

Jacob Burckhardt *The Civilization of the Renaissance in Italy*. A nineteenth-century classic of Renaissance scholarship.

Frederick Hartt *History of Italian Renaissance Art: Painting, Sculpture and Architecture*. If one book on this vast subject can be said to be indispensable, this is it. In view of its comprehensiveness and acuity, and the range of its illustrations, it's something of a bargain.

Anthony Hughes *Michelangelo*. Part of the acclaimed Phaidon Art and Ideas series, this is an ideal single-volume introduction to arguably the greatest artist of the Renaissance. Setting Michelangelo within his historical and political context,

Hughes examines his work not only as the expression of an individual sensibility but also in the light of the often fraught relations between artist and patron. An accessible and stimulating read.

Ross King *Brunelleschi's Dome*. An intriguing account of the architectural innovations and intense rivalries behind the construction of Florence's Duomo. It also paints an engaging picture of life in the medieval city.

Peter Murray *The Architecture of the Italian Renaissance*. Begins with Romanesque buildings and finishes with Palladio – valuable both as a gazetteer of the main monuments and as a synopsis of the underlying concepts.

Catherine Puglisi *Caravaggio*. An intelligent and engaging study of one of the most innovative artists of the Renaissance, enhanced with sumptuous colour plates throughout.

Nigel Spivey *Etruscan Art*. An in-depth look at the art of the elusive Etruscans, whose history and lives are told through their tomb art. Sumptuously illustrated throughout, this is an intriguing story of a long lost race.

Giorgio Vasari *Lives of the Artists*. The sixteenth-century artist's classic work on his predecessors and contemporaries, with essays on Giotto, Brunelleschi, Mantegna, Leonardo, Michelangelo, Raphael and more. The first real work of art history and still among the most penetrating books you can read on Italian Renaissance art, published in an abridged version by OUP.

Specific guides

Helena Attlee and Alex Ramsay *Italian Gardens*. Evocatively photographed, this is a guide to more than sixty of the peninsula's most beautiful gardens. Both practical and up to date, the guide provides histories and descriptions, as well as detailed information on locations, facilities, opening times and accessibility.

Tim Jepson, Simon Rigge, Syd Lewis *Wild Italy*. Guide to the flora and fauna of the Italian peninsula by a *Rough Guide* contributor.

Gillian Price *Walking in the Dolomites*. A lively and informative specialized guide to the best walks in the Dolomites. Cicerone also publishes guides to Alta Via 1 & 2 and to various *Vie Ferrate* for more on these peculiarly Italian phenomena.

Victoria Pybus *Live and Work in Italy*. Accessible and informative handbook on all aspects of living and working in Italy, including regional differences.

Ancient literature

Catullus *The Poems of Catullus*. Although his name is associated primarily with the tortured love poems addressed to Lesbia, Catullus also produced some acerbic satirical verse; this collection does full justice to his range.

Cicero *Selected Works*. The rhetorical prose of Cicero was for many Renaissance scholars the paragon of literary style, and his political ideas provided similarly fertile material for discussion.

Juvenal *The Sixteen Satires*. Savage attacks on the follies and excesses of Rome at the end of the first century and start of the second.

Livy *The Early History of Rome*. Lively chronicle of the city's evolution from the days of Romulus and Remus; Penguin also publishes later instalments of those parts of Livy's history that have survived, including the gripping *War with Hannibal*.

Marcus Aurelius *Meditations*. The classic text of Stoic thought, written by one of the few Roman emperors it's easy to admire.

Ovid *Metamorphoses* and *Erotic Poems*. The mythical tales of the *Metamorphoses* have been so frequently quarried by artists that they can be enjoyed both as literature and as a key to some of the masterworks of Renaissance and later art. His elegiac love poems have a sexual candour that makes them seem almost modern.

Petronius *Satyricon*. A fragmentary, spicy narrative written by one of Nero's inner circle; Fellini's film of the same name gives a pretty accurate idea of the tone.

Plautus *Pot of Gold, and other plays.* The most popular playwright of his time, whose complicated plots provided a model for Renaissance comedies such as *The Comedy of Errors.*

Seneca *Four Tragedies and Octavia.* Violent, fast-paced drama from Nero's one-time tutor. The only plays to have survived from the Roman Empire.

Italian classics

Dante Alighieri *The Divine Comedy.* No work in any other language bears comparison with Dante's poetic exegesis of the moral scheme of God's Creation; in late medieval Italy it was venerated both as a book of almost scriptural authority and as the ultimate refinement of the vernacular Tuscan language.

Ludovico Ariosto *Orlando Furioso.* Italy's chivalrous epic, set in Charlemagne's Europe; has its exciting moments, but most readers would be grateful for an abridged version. Penguin's verse translation is pacier and more accessible than Oxford's prose version.

Giovanni Boccaccio *The Decameron.* Set in the plague-racked Florence of 1348, this assembly of one hundred short stories is a fascinating social record as well as a constantly diverting comic sequence.

Baldassare Castiglione *The Book of the Courtier.* Written in the form of a series of dialogues held in the court of Urbino, this subtle, entertaining book defines all the qualities essential in the perfect gentleman.

Benvenuto Cellini *Autobiography.* Shamelessly egocentric record of the travails and triumphs of the sculptor and goldsmith's career; one of the

Suetonius *The Twelve Caesars.* The inside story of Caligula, Nero, Domitian & others – elegantly written.

Tacitus *Annals of Imperial Rome.* Covers much of the terrain dealt with by Suetonius, but from the stance of the diligent historian and serious moralist.

Virgil *The Aeneid.* The central work of Latin literature, depicting the adventures of Aeneas after the fall of Troy, and thus celebrating Rome's heroic lineage.

freshest literary productions of its time.

Giacomo Leopardi *Leopardi*, tr. Eamon Grennan. Generally considered the greatest Italian poet since Dante, and a formative influence on the poets who followed.

Niccolò Machiavelli *The Prince.* A treatise on statecraft which actually did less to form the political thought of Italy than it did to form foreigners' perceptions of the country.

Alessandro Manzoni *The Betrothed.* No poolside thriller, but a skilful melding of the romance of two young lovers and a sweeping historical drama, all suffused with an almost religious sense of human destiny. First published in 1823, but reissued in 1840 after Manzoni had improved the novel's diction through study of the Tuscan dialect – a landmark in the transition towards linguistic nationalism.

Petrarch *Selections from the Canzoniere.* Often described as the first modern poet, by virtue of his preoccupation with worldly fame and secular love, Petrarch wrote some of the Italian language's greatest lyrics. This slim selection at least hints at what is lost in translation.

Leonardo da Vinci *Notebooks*. Miscellany of speculation and observation from the universal genius of Renaissance Italy – essential to any understanding of the man.

Modern Italian literature

Giorgio Bassani *The Garden of the Finzi-Continis*. Gentle, elegiac novel, set in the Jewish community of Ferrara during the Fascist period, on the eve of the mass deportations to Germany. Infused with a sense of regret for a Europe that died with the war.

Gesualdo Bufalino *A Plague Spreader's Tale*. One of Sicily's most esteemed twentieth-century writers, Bufalino arrived late on the literary scene, publishing this first novel when he was into his 60s. Most of his output has now been translated.

Italo Calvino *If on a Winter's Night a Traveller*. Calvino's fiction became increasingly concerned with the nature of fiction itself, and this involuted, witty novel marks the culmination of the process. Other titles include *The Castle of Crossed Destinies*, *Invisible Cities*, *Difficult Loves* and *Mr Palomar*.

Umberto Eco *The Name of the Rose*. An allusive, tightly plotted monastic detective story. Check out also his equally hyped, though rather more impenetrable, *Foucault's Pendulum* and *Baudolino*, another medieval fable, this time interspersed with reflections on the postmodern age.

Dario Fo *Plays I*. This collection includes a trio of Fo's most famous plays – *Mistero Buffo*, *Accidental Death of an Anarchist* and *Trumpets and Raspberries* – along with two previously unpublished short works. The Nobel Prize winner fabulously weaves together contemporary politics, surreal farce and the traditions of commedia dell'arte.

Carlo Emilio Gadda *That Awful Mess on Via Merulana* (OP).

Superficially a detective story, this celebrated modernist novel is so dense a weave of physical reality and literary diversions that the reader is led away from a solution rather than towards it; it enjoys the sort of status in Italian fiction that *Ulysses* has in English.

Natalia Ginzburg *The Things We Used to Say*. The constraints of family life are a dominant theme in Ginzburg's writing, and her own upbringing is the source material for this characteristically rigorous yet lyrical work.

Giuseppe di Lampedusa *The Leopard*. The most famous Sicilian novel, written after the war but recounting the dramatic nineteenth-century transition from Bourbon to Piemontese rule from an aristocrat's point of view. A good character-study and rich with incidental detail, including some nice description of the Sicilian landscape.

Carlo Levi *Christ Stopped at Eboli*. First published in 1945, this memoir, describing Levi's exile to a remote region of Basilicata by the Fascists, was the first to awaken modern Italy to the plight of its southern regions.

Primo Levi *If This is a Man / The Truce*; *The Periodic Table*. Levi's experiences in Auschwitz are the main subject of *If This is a Man*, while *The Truce* records his journey back to Turin after his liberation. Levi's training as a chemist forms the background of *Periodic Table*, a mixture of autobiographical reflections and practical observations. All show an unwavering exactitude of recollection and judgement.

Elsa Morante *History*. Capturing daily Roman life during the last war, this is probably the most vivid fictional picture of the conflict as seen from the city.

Alberto Moravia *The Conformist*. A psychological novel about a man sucked into the abyss of Fascism by his desperation to conform; *The Woman of Rome* is an earlier work, a teeming and sensual novel, centred on the activities of a Roman prostitute.

Pier Paolo Pasolini *A Violent Life*. This super-naturalistic evocation of life in the slum areas of Rome caused a scandal when it was published in 1959, but is now considered one of the classics of Italian postwar fiction.

Cesare Pavese *Moon and the Bonfire; Devil in the Hills*. Exploring the difficulties of achieving an acceptance of one's past, *Moon and the Bonfire* was written shortly before Pavese's suicide at the age of 42; *Devil in the Hills* is an early collection of tales of adolescence in and around Turin.

Leonardo Sciascia *Sicilian Uncles; The Wine Dark Sea; The Day of the Owl*. Writing again and again about his native Sicily, Sciascia has made of that island "a metaphor of the modern world". Economically written, Sciascia's short stories are packed with incisive insights, and infused with the author's humane and sympathetic views of its people. *The Moro Affair* is an illuminating account of the kidnapping of the ex-prime minister Aldo Moro by the Brigate Rosse in 1978.

Ignazio Silone *Fontamara; Bread and Wine*. From his exile in Switzerland, Silone wrote about his native Abruzzo, and about the struggle for social justice. *Fontamara* tells the tale of a small village driven to revolt against its landlords and the Fascist thugs sent to enforce their rule; *Bread and Wine*, a more introspective work, examines the parallels between Silone's political commitment and religious belief. The two works, together with *The Seed Beneath the Snow*, are published in one volume by Steerforth Press, titled *The Abruzzo Trilogy*.

Italo Svevo *Zeno's Conscience*. Complete critical indifference to his early efforts so discouraged Svevo that he gave up writing altogether, until encouraged by James Joyce, who taught him English in Trieste. The resultant novel is a unique creation, a comic portrait of a character at once wistful, helpless and irrepressible.

Giovanni Verga *Cavalleria Rusticana; Sparrow; The House by the Medlar Tree*. Verga, born in the nineteenth century in Catania, spent several years in various European salons before coming home to write his best work. Much of it is a reaction against the pseudo-sophistication of society circles, stressing the simple lives of ordinary people, accompanied by a heavy smattering of emotion, wounded honour and feuds to the death.

Elio Vittorini *Conversations in Sicily*. A Sicilian emigrant returns from the north of Italy after fifteen years to see his mother on her birthday. The conversations of the title are with the people he meets on the way, local villagers and his mother, and reveal a poverty- and disease-ridden Sicily, though the scenes are affectionately drawn.

William Weaver (ed) *Open City: Seven Writers in Postwar Rome*. A nicely produced anthology of pieces by the cream of Italy's twentieth-century novelists – Bassani, Silone, Ginzburg, Moravia, among others – selected and with an introduction by one of the most eminent Italian translators of recent years.

Literature set in Italy

Michael Dibdin *Ratking, Vendetta, Cabal, Dead Lagoon.* The late Michael Dibdin's Aurelio Zen is a classically eccentric loner detective, and this is a classic series of well-plotted detective yarns. However, Dibdin is as interested in the country as he is in his characters, and these novels tell us plenty about the way Italian society operates, as well as touring an array of locations, from Rome to Naples to Venice and Sardinia.

E.M. Forster *A Room with a View.* Set in and around Florence, this is the ultimate novel about how the nature of the Italian light, temperament and soul can make the English upper classes lose their heads.

Nathaniel Hawthorne *The Marble Faun.* A nineteenth-century take on the lives of Anglo-American expats in the Eternal City – sculptors, passionate lovers, devotees of Classical Purity – the usual mad mix and excessive goings-on that you'll still find today.

Ernest Hemingway *A Farewell To Arms.* Hemingway's first novel is partly based on his experiences as a teenage ambulance driver on Italy's northeast front during World War I –

a terse account of the futility of this particular corner of the conflict.

David Hewson *A Season for the Dead; The Sacred Cut; Villa of Mysteries;* and others. Hewson's Nic Costa is the idealistic young Italian detective with an ex-commie father and a hard-bitten partner in these preposterous police procedurals set in Rome. Good local colour and detail and fast-moving, if sometimes unbelievable plots – the ideal Italian holiday read.

Patricia Highsmith *The Talented Mr Ripley.* The novel follows the fortunes of the eponymous hero through Italy as he exchanges his own identity for that of the man he has murdered. Good locations in its movie, starring Matt Damon and directed by Anthony Minghella.

Donna Leon *Death at La Fenice, A Venetian Reckoning, Fatal Remedies* and others. Venice-based crime thrillers featuring Guido Brunetti, the honest police commissario in a world of high-level intrigue and corruption. Public scandals and Brunetti's private life are absorbingly interwoven, and these atmospheric tales usually work on several different levels.

Ancient Rome

Lindsey Davis *Venus in Copper, The Jupiter Myth* and others. These crime novels set in the age of the Emperor Vespasian follow super-sleuth Marcus Didius Falco as he unpicks mysteries and dastardly doings.

Allan Massie *Augustus, Tiberius, Caesar.* A trilogy of novels that tells the stories of the three emperors as if they were recently discovered autobiographies. Massie's historical precision and careful dramatization hold up well.

Robert Graves *I Claudius* and *Claudius the God.* Having translated Suetonius' *Twelve Caesars*, Graves used the madness and corruption of the Imperial Age to create a gripping, if not necessarily historically accurate, tale. The classic book on the imperial Caesars,

Thornton Wilder *The Ides of March* (OP). A suppositional reconstruction of the last year of the life of Julius Caesar through his letters, writings and reports. A brilliant portrayal of the burdens and isolation of leadership.

Thomas Mann *Death in Venice.*
Irascible and ultra-traditional old
novelist visits Venice to recover after
a breakdown and becomes obsessed
with a beautiful young boy,
awakening an internal debate about
the nature of beauty and art to
which the city is a fitting and
resonant backdrop.

Ian McEwan *The Comfort of
Strangers.* An ordinary young English
couple fall foul of a sexually
ambiguous predator in a Venice
which is never named, but evoked by
means of arch little devices such as
quotes from Ruskin.

John Mortimer *Summer's Lease.*
The chattering classes revel in
Chiantishire. Not exactly profound,
but hugely entertaining.

Magdalen Nabb *Death of an
Englishman; The Innocent; The Monster
of Florence;* and many other titles.
These thrillers make the most of
their settings in lowlife Florence, and
their lead character, police marshall
Salvatore Guarnaccia.

Michael Ondaatje *The English
Patient.* The novel that inspired the
Anthony Minghella film starring
Juliette Binoche and Ralph Fiennes.
A nurse cares for her patient, burnt
beyond recognition, in an abandoned
Italian monastery during World War II
as his true identity, and the story of
the passionate but doomed affair he
has survived, are uncovered.

Susan Sontag *The Volcano Lover.*
A profound and surprising novel,
based on the notorious affair
between Nelson and Lady Hamilton,
wife of the volcano-fixated English

ambassador to Naples. An absolute
must-read for visitors to Naples.

Stendhal *The Charterhouse of Parma.*
A panoramic nineteenth-century
French novel that dramatizes the
struggles and intrigues of the Italian
Papal States before Unification. A
wonderful read, and a good insight
into the era to boot.

Irving Stone *The Agony and the
Ecstasy.* Stone's dramatized life of
Michelangelo, popular "faction" that
is entertaining even if it doesn't
exactly get to the root of the artist's
work and times.

Barry Unsworth *After Hannibal* and
Stone Virgin. After Hannibal is a black
comedy of expat life, set in Umbria,
where the author lives. The earlier
Stone Virgin, set in Venice, is about a
conservation expert who falls under
the spell of a statue of the Madonna
he is working on – and of a member
of the family who owns it.

Roger Vailland *The Law.* This
evocation of life in a small Pugliese
town, of its people, etiquette and
harsh tradition, is tight, considered
and utterly convincing.

Salley Vickers *Miss Garnet's Angel.*
The unique atmosphere of Venice is
captured in this tale of a desiccated
spinster awakened by the city to the
finer things in life. The author's
sound knowledge of the place and its
art triumphs over a potentially
hackneyed tale.

Edith Wharton *Roman Fever and
Other Stories.* The title story of this
collection recounts two old women's
stingingly bitchy reminiscences about
their adolescence in Rome.

Food and drink

Antonio Carluccio *Carluccio's Complete Italian Food*. This isn't the last word in Italian cookery, and isn't the right book if you're looking for something comprehensive. But Carluccio's passion for food is infectious, as is his back to basics message that a meal – however humble or grand – is only as good as the land or sea from which its ingredients come.

Elizabeth David *Italian Food*. The writer who introduced Italian cuisine – and ingredients – to Britain. Ahead of its time when it was published in the Fifties, and imbued with all the enthusiasm and diversity of Italian cookery. An inspirational book.

🏃 **Marcella Hazan** *The Classic Italian Cookbook*. A step-by-step guide that never compromises the spirit or authenticity of the recipes, Hazan draws her recipes from all over the peninsula, emphasizing the intrinsically regional nature of Italian food. The best Italian cookbook for the novice in the kitchen,

Fred Plotkin *Italy for the Gourmet Traveller*. Comprehensive, region-by-region guide to the best of Italian cuisine, with a foodie's guide to major towns and cities, a gazetteer of restaurants and specialist food and wine shops, and descriptions of local dishes, with recipes.

Claudia Roden *The Food of Italy*. A culinary classic, this regional guide takes in local recipes from the people for whom they are second nature. Authentic and accessible.

Michele Shah *Wines of Italy*. An excellent pocket guide to the regional wines and winemaking techniques of Italy, with up-to-date information on the best current producers and labels.

🏃 **Various** *The Silver Spoon*. Quite simply the most successful cookbook sold in Italy, and now available in translation, this is the biggest collection of authentic Italian recipes you can find.

Language

Language

Language

Italian

The ability to speak English confers prestige in Italy, and there's often no shortage of people willing to show off their knowledge. But using at least some Italian, however tentatively, can mark you out from the masses in a country used to hordes of tourists. The words and phrases below should help you master the basics, and the *Rough Guide Italian Phrasebook* – which packs a huge amount of vocabulary into a handy dictionary format – is a useful back-up. There are lots of good pocket dictionaries – the Collins range represents the best all-round choice.

Pronunciation

Italian is one of the easiest European languages to learn, especially if you already have a smattering of French or Spanish. **Pronunciation** is straightforward: all Italian words are stressed on the penultimate syllable unless an accent (´ or `) denotes otherwise, and words are usually enunciated with exaggerated, open-mouthed clarity.

The only difficulties you're likely to encounter are the few consonants that are different from English:

c before e or i is pronounced as in church, while **ch** before the same vowels is hard, as in cat.

sci or **sce** are pronounced as in sheet and shelter respectively.

The same goes with **g** – soft before e or i, as in geranium; hard before h, as in garlic.

gn has the ni sound of onion.

gl in Italian is softened to something like li in English, as in stallion.

h is not aspirated, as in honour.

When speaking to strangers, the third person is the polite form (ie *lei* instead of *tu* for "you"). It's also worth remembering that Italians don't use "please" and "thank you" half as much as English speakers: it's all implied in the tone, though, if in doubt, err on the polite side.

Words and phrases

Basics

good morning	buongiorno	no	no
good afternoon/ evening	buonasera	please	per favore
goodnight	buonanotte	thank you (very much)	(molte/mille) grázie
hello/goodbye	ciao (informal; to strangers use phrases above)	you're welcome	prego
		all right/that's ok	va bene
goodbye	arrivederci	how are you?	come stai/sta? (informal/formal)
yes	si	I'm fine	bene

do you speak english?	parla inglese?	What's your name?	Come ti chiami/si chiama? (informal/formal)
I don't understand	non ho capito		
I don't know	non lo so	wait a minute!	aspetta!
excuse me	mi scusi	let's go!	andiamo!
excuse me (in a crowd)	permesso	here/there	qui/là
		good/bad	buono/cattivo
I'm sorry	mi dispiace	big/small	grande/píccolo
I'm here on holiday	Sono qui in vacanza	cheap/expensive	economico/caro
I'm English/Irish/	Sono Inglese/irlandese	early/late	presto/tardi
Welsh/Scottish/	Gallese/Scozzese	hot/cold	caldo/freddo
American	Americano/a (m/f)	near/far	vicino/lontano
Australian	Australiano/a (m/f)	quickly/slowly	velocemente/lentamente
Canadian	Canadese		
a New Zealander	Neozelandese		

Questions

where?	dove?	why?	perché?
where is/are ...?	dov'è/dove sono ...?	is it/is there ...?	c'è ...?
when?	quando?	What time does it open/close?	A che ora apre/chiude?
what?	cosa?		
what is it?	cos'è?	What's it called in italian?	Come si chiama in italiano?
how much/many?	quanto/quanti?		

Travel and directions

Where is ...?	Dov'è ...?	hydrofoil	l'aliscafo
How do I get to ...?	Per arrivare a ...?	plane	l'aereo
the centre	il centro	train	il treno
the (main) square	la piazza (principale)	Do I have to change?	Devo cambiare?
the station	la stazione	Which platform does it leave from?	Da quale binario parte?
the bus station	l'autostazione		
the port	il porto	How long does it take?	Quanto ci vuole?
Turn left/right	giri a sinistra/destra		
Go straight on	vai sempre diritto	Can you tell me when to get off?	Mi può dire dove scendere?
How far is it to ...?	Quant'è lontano a ...?		
What time does the ... arrive/leave?	A che ora arriva/parte ...?	I'd like a ticket to ...	Vorrei un biglietto per ...
bus	l'autobus	one-way	solo andata
coach	il pullman	return	andata e ritorno
ferry	il traghetto		

Signs

entrance/exit	entrata/uscita	gentlemen/ladies	signori/signore
arrivals/departures	arrivi/partenze	wc	gabinetto/bagno
free entrance	ingresso líbero	vacant/engaged	libero/occupato

no smoking	vietato fumare	pull/push	tirare/spingere
open/closed	aperto/chiuso	cash desk	cassa
closed for restoration	chiuso per restauro	out of order	guasto
closed for holidays	chiuso per ferie	ring the bell	suonare il campanello

Accommodation

I'd like to book a room	Vorrei prenotare una cámera	with a balcony	con balcone
I have a booking	Ho una prenotazione	hot/cold water	acqua calda/fredda
Is there a hotel nearby?	C'è un albergo qui vicino?	How much is it?	Quanto costa?
Do you have ...?	Ha ...?	Is breakfast included?	È compresa la prima colazione?
a single/double/triple	una cámera singola/doppia/tripla	Do you have anything cheaper?	Ha qualcosa che costa di meno?
a bed	un letto	Can I see the room?	Posso vedere la cámera?
for one/two/three night/s	per una/due/tre notti	I'll take it	Lo/La prendo (m/f)
for one/two week/s	per una/due settimana/e	hotel	albergo
		hostel	ostello
with a double bed	con un letto matrimoniale	campsite	campeggio
		lift	ascensore
with twin beds	con due letti	key	chiave
with a shower/bath	con doccia/bagno	full/half board	pensione completa/mezza pensione

Restaurants

I'd like to reserve a table (for two)	Vorrei riservare una tavola (per due)	The bill, please	Il conto, per favore
Can we sit outside?	Possiamo sederci fuori?	Is service included?	Il servizio è incluso?
		(set) menu	menù (fisso)
Can I order?	Posso ordinare?	waiter/waitress	cameriere/a
I'm a vegetarian	Sono vegetariano/a (m/f)	knife	coltello
Does it contain meat?	C'è carne dentro?	fork	forchetta
		spoon	cucchiaio
It's good	È buono	plate	piatto
		bicchiere	glass

Shopping and services

I'd like to buy ...	Vorrei comprare ...	bank	banca
How much does it cost/do they cost?	Quanto costa/cóstano?	money exchange	cambio
		post office	posta
It's too expensive	È troppo caro	tourist office	ufficio di turismo
with/without	con/senza	shop	negozio
more/less	più/meno	supermarket	supermercato
enough, no more	basta	market	mercato
I'll take it	Lo/la prendo (m/f)	ATM	Bancomat
Do you take credit cards?	Accettate carte di credito?		

Days, times and months

What time is it?	Che ore sono?	Friday	venerdì
It's four o'clock	Sono (le quattro)	Saturday	sabato
today	oggi	Sunday	domenica
tomorrow	domani	January	gennaio
day after tomorrow	dopodomani	February	febbraio
yesterday	ieri	March	marzo
now	adesso	April	aprile
later	più tardi	May	maggio
in the morning	di mattina	June	giugno
in the afternoon	nel pomeriggio	July	luglio
in the evening	di sera	August	agosto
Monday	lunedì	September	settembre
Tuesday	martedì	October	ottobre
Wednesday	mercoledì	November	novembre
Thursday	giovedì	December	dicembre

Numbers

1	uno	19	diciannove
2	due	20	venti
3	tre	21	ventuno
4	quattro	22	ventidue
5	cinque	30	trenta
6	sei	40	quaranta
7	sette	50	cinquanta
8	otto	60	sessanta
9	nove	70	settanta
10	dieci	80	ottanta
11	undici	90	novanta
12	dodici	100	cento
13	tredici	101	centuno
14	quattordici	110	centodieci
15	quindici	200	duecento
16	sedici	500	cinquecento
17	diciassette	1000	mille
18	diciotto	5000	cinquemila

Italian menu reader

Basics and snacks

aceto	vinegar	burro	butter
aglio	garlic	caramelle	sweets
biscotti	biscuits	cioccolato	chocolate

formaggio	cheese	riso	rice
frittata	omelette	sale	salt
marmellata	jam	uova	eggs
olio	oil	yogurt	yoghurt
olive	olives	zucchero	sugar
pane	bread	zuppa	soup
pepe	pepper		

The first course (il primo)

brodo	clear broth
minestrina	clear broth with small pasta shapes
minestrone	thick vegetable soup
pasta al forno	baked pasta, usually with minced meat, tomato and cheese
pasta e fagioli	soup with pasta and beans
pastina in brodo	pasta in clear broth
stracciatella	broth with egg

Pasta

bucatini thick, hollow spaghetti-type pasta common in Rome and Lazio

cannelloni thick pasta tubes usually filled with veal

capellini thin noodles of pasta, thicker than *capelli d'angeli*

conchiglie seashell-shaped pasta shapes, good for capturing thick sauces

farfalle literally "butterflies", or bow ties

fettucini flat, ribbon-like egg noodles

fusilli tight spirals of pasta

gnocchi potato and pasta dumplings, often served "*alla sorrentina*", or with tomato and basil sauce

lasagne big squares of egg noodles, most commonly baked in the oven with white sauce and beef *ragú*

linguini thin, flat noodles, often served with seafood

macaroni small tubes of pasta

maltagliati flat triangles of pasta, often used in soup

orecchiette small ear-shaped pieces of pasta

paccheri large tubes of pasta

panzarotti filled pasta shapes from puglia

pappardelle thick flat egg noodles

penne the most common tubes of pasta

pici thick tuscan spaghetti

ravioli literally "little turnips" – flat, square parcels of filled pasta

rigatoni large, curved and ridged tubes of pasta – larger than *penne* but smaller than *paccheri*

spaghetti the most common pasta shape of all – long, thin, non-egg noodles

tagliatelle flat ribbon egg noodles, slightly thinner than *fettucini*

tonnarelli another name for *bucatini*

tortellini/tortolloni triangles of filled pasta folded into rounded shapes.

tortiglioni narrow *rigatoni*

Pasta sauce (salsa)

amatriciana cubed bacon and tomato

arrabbiata ("angry") spicy tomato with chillies

bolognese meat

burro butter

carbonara cream, ham and beaten egg

funghi mushroom

panna cream

parmigiano parmesan cheese

peperoncino olive oil, garlic and fresh chillies

pesto ground basil, garlic and pine nuts

pomodoro tomato

puttanesca ("whorish") tomato, anchovy, olive oil and oregano

ragù meat

vongole clams

The second course (il secondo)

Meat (carne)

agnello	lamb
bistecca	steak
carpaccio	slices of raw beef
cervello	brain, usually calves'
cinghiale	wild boar
coniglio	rabbit
costolette	cutlet, chop
fegato	liver
maiale	pork
manzo	beef
ossobuco	shin of veal
pancetta	bacon
pollo	chicken
polpette	meatballs
rognoni	kidneys
salsiccia	sausage
saltimbocca	veal with ham
spezzatino	stew
trippa	tripe
vitello	veal

Fish (pesce) and shellfish (crostacei)

acciughe	anchovies
anguilla	eel
aragosta	lobster
baccalà	dried salted cod
calamari	squid
cefalo	grey mullet
cozze	mussels
dentice	sea bream
gamberetti	shrimps
gamberi	prawns
granchio	crab
merluzzo	cod
ostriche	oysters
pesce spada	swordfish
polpo	octopus
rospo	monkfish
sampiero	John Dory
sarde	sardines
sogliola	sole
tonno	tuna
trota	trout
vongole	clams

Vegetables (contorni) and salad (insalata)

asparagi	asparagus
carciofi	artichokes
carciofini	artichoke hearts
cavolfiori	cauliflower
cavolo	cabbage
cipolla	onion
erbe aromatiche	herbs
fagioli	beans
fagiolini	green beans
finocchio	fennel

funghi	mushrooms
insalata verde/mista	green salad/mixed salad
lenticchie	lentils
melanzane	aubergine
patate	potatoes
peperoni	peppers
piselli	peas
pomodori	tomatoes
radicchio	red salad leaves
spinaci	spinach

Cooking terms

al dente	firm, not overcooked
al ferri	grilled without oil
al forno	baked
al sangue	rare
alla brace	barbecued
alla griglia	grilled

alla milanese	fried in egg and breadcrumbs
allo spiedo	on the spit
arrosto	roast
ben cotto	well done
bollito/lesso	boiled

cotto	cooked
crudo	raw
fritto	fried
in umido	stewed

pizzaiola	cooked with tomato sauce
ripieno	stuffed
stracotto	braised, stewed

Cheese (formaggio)

dolcelatte creamy blue cheese

fontina northern Italian cheese, often used in cooking

gorgonzola soft, strong, blue-veined cheese

mozzarella soft white cheese, traditionally made from buffalo's milk

pecorino strong, hard sheep's cheese

provola/provolone smooth, round mild cheese, made from buffalo or sheep's milk; sometimes smoked

ricotta soft, white sheep's cheese

Desserts (dolci), fruit (frutta) and nuts (noci)

amaretti	macaroons
ananas	pineapple
anguria/coccomero	watermelon
arachidi	peanuts
arance	oranges
banane	bananas
cacchi	persimmons
ciliegie	cherries
crostata	pastry tart with jam or chocolate topping
fichi	figs
fichi d'india	prickly pears
frágole	strawberries
gelato	ice cream
limone	lemon

macedonia	fruit salad
mandorle	almonds
mele	apples
melone	melon
pere	pears
pesche	peaches
pinoli	pine nuts
pistacchio	pistachio nut
sorbetto	sorbet
torta	cake, tart
uva	grapes
zabaglione	dessert made with eggs, sugar and marsala wine
zuppa inglese	trifle

Drinks

acqua minerale (con gas/senza gas)	mineral water (fizzy/still)
aranciata	orangeade
birra	beer
bottiglia	bottle
caffè	coffee
cioccolato caldo	hot chocolate
ghiaccio	ice
granita	iced drink with coffee or fruit
latte	milk
limonata	lemonade
spremuta	fresh fruit juice
spumante	sparkling wine

succo	concentrated fruit juice with sugar
tè	tea
tonica	tonic water
vino	wine
rosso	red
bianco	white
rosato	rosé
secco	dry
dolce	sweet
litro	litre
mezzo	half
quarto	quarter
caraffa	carafe
salute!	cheers!

Glossary of artistic and architectural terms

agora square or marketplace in an ancient Greek city

ambo a kind of simple pulpit, popular in Italian medieval churches

apse semicircular recess at the altar (usually eastern) end of a church

architrave the lowest part of the entablature

atrium inner courtyard

baldachino a canopy on columns, usually placed over the altar in a church

basilica originally a Roman administrative building, adapted for early churches; distinguished by lack of transepts

belvedere a terrace or lookout point

caldarium the steam room of a Roman bath

campanile bell tower, sometimes detached, usually of a church

capital top of a column

Catalan-Gothic hybrid form of architecture, mixing elements of fifteenth-century Spanish and northern European styles

cella sanctuary of a temple

chancel part of a church containing the altar

chiaroscuro the balance of light and shade in a painting, and the skill of the artist in depicting the contrast between the two

ciborium another word for *baldachino*, see above

cornice the top section of a classical facade

cortile galleried courtyard or cloisters

cosmati work decorative mosaic work on marble, usually highly coloured, found in early Christian Italian churches, especially in Rome; derives from the name Cosma, a common name among families of marble workers at the time

cryptoporticus underground passageway

cyclopean walls fortifications built of huge, rough stone blocks, common in the pre-Roman settlements of Lazio

Decumanus Maximus the main street of a Roman town – the second cross-street was known as the Decumanus Inferiore

entablature the section above the capital on a classical building, below the cornice

ex voto artefact designed in thanksgiving to a saint

fresco wall-painting technique in which the artist applies paint to wet plaster for a more permanent finish

loggia roofed gallery or balcony

metope a panel on the frieze of a Greek temple

Mithraism pre-Christian cult associated with the Persian god of light, who slew a bull and fertilized the world with its blood

nave central space in a church, usually flanked by aisles

pantocrator usually refers to an image of Christ, portrayed with outstretched arms

piano nobile main floor of a *palazzo*, usually the first

polyptych painting on several joined wooden panels

portico covered entrance to a building, or porch

presepio/presepe Christmas crib

putti cherubs

reliquary receptacle for a saint's relics, usually bones; often highly decorated

sgraffito decorative technique whereby one layer of plaster is scratched to form a pattern

stereobate visible base of any building, usually a Greek temple

stucco plaster made from water, lime, sand and powdered marble, used for decorative work

thermae baths, usually elaborate buildings in Roman villas

triptych painting on three joined wooden panels

trompe l'oeil work of art that deceives the viewer by means of tricks with perspective

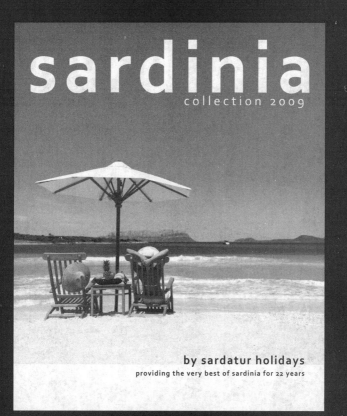

sardatur holidays is the UK's foremost specialist to Sardinia. We offer a selection of hand-picked apartments and villas, luxury hotels and resorts, we can provide traditional packages and tailor-made itineraries. Whether you are looking for a charming boutique hotel, spa retreat, beachside property, rural hideaway or family friendly resort, you only have to ask.

Call for a brochure on 020 8940 8399
or e-mail us at info@sardinia-holidays.co.uk

Our first Italia Collection brochure is out in February 2009
call to reserve a copy

sardatur holidays

1 Castle Yard, Richmond, Surrey TW10 6TF
Email: info@sardinia-holidays.co.uk
Website: www.sardinia-holidays.co.uk

SARDEGNA

Stay In Touch!

Subscribe to Rough Guides' **FREE** newsletter

Small print and
Index

A Rough Guide to Rough Guides

Published in 1982, the first Rough Guide – to Greece – was a student scheme that became a publishing phenomenon. Mark Ellingham, a recent graduate in English from Bristol University, had been travelling in Greece the previous summer and couldn't find the right guidebook. With a small group of friends he wrote his own guide, combining a highly contemporary, journalistic style with a thoroughly practical approach to travellers' needs.

The immediate success of the book spawned a series that rapidly covered dozens of destinations. And, in addition to impecunious backpackers, Rough Guides soon acquired a much broader and older readership that relished the guides' wit and inquisitiveness as much as their enthusiastic, critical approach and value-for-money ethos.

These days, Rough Guides include recommendations from shoestring to luxury and cover more than 200 destinations around the globe, including almost every country in the Americas and Europe, more than half of Africa and most of Asia and Australasia. Our ever-growing team of authors and photographers is spread all over the world, particularly in Europe, the USA and Australia.

In the early 1990s, Rough Guides branched out of travel, with the publication of Rough Guides to World Music, Classical Music and the Internet. All three have become benchmark titles in their fields, spearheading the publication of a wide range of books under the Rough Guide name.

Including the travel series, Rough Guides now number more than 350 titles, covering: phrasebooks, waterproof maps, music guides from Opera to Heavy Metal, reference works as diverse as Conspiracy Theories and Shakespeare, and popular culture books from iPods to Poker. Rough Guides also produce a series of more than 120 World Music CDs in partnership with World Music Network.

Visit www.roughguides.com to see our latest publications.

Rough Guide travel images are available for commercial licensing at www.roughguidespictures.com

Rough Guide credits

Text editor: Andy Turner
Layout: Ajay Verma
Cartography: Deshpal Dabas
Picture editor: Sarah Cummins
Production: Rebecca Short
Proofreader: Elaine Pollard
Cover design: Chloë Roberts
Photographer: Jon Cunningham, Michelle Grant, Chris Hutty, Roger d'Olivere Mapp, James McConnachie, Dylan Reisenberger, Helena Smith, Natascha Sturny and Karen Trist
Editorial: Ruth Blackmore, Keith Drew, Edward Aves, Alice Park, Lucy White, Jo Kirby, Jo Kirby, Natasha Foges, Róisín Cameron, Emma Traynor, Emma Gibbs, Kathryn Lane, Christina Valhouli, Monica Woods, Mani Ramaswamy, Harry Wilson, Lucy Cowie, Helen Ochyra, Alison Roberts, Joe Staines, Peter Buckley, Matthew Milton, Tracy Hopkins, Ruth Tidball; **Delhi** Madhavi Singh, Karen D'Souza, Lubna Shaheen
Design & Pictures: **London** Scott Stickland, Dan May, Diana Jarvis, Mark Thomas, Nicole Newman, Emily Taylor; **Delhi** Umesh Aggarwal, Jessica Subramanian, Ankur Guha, Pradeep Thapliyal, Sachin Tanwar, Anita Singh, Nikhil Agarwal

Production: Vicky Baldwin
Cartography: **London** Maxine Repath, Ed Wright, Katie Lloyd-Jones; **Delhi** Rajesh Chhibber, Ashutosh Bharti, Rajesh Mishra, Animesh Pathak, Jasbir Sandhu, Karobi Gogoi, Alakananda Bhattacharya, Swati Handoo
Online: **London** George Atwell, Faye Hellon, Jeanette Angell, Fergus Day, Justine Bright, Clare Bryson, Aine Fearon, Adrian Low, Ezgi Celebi, Amber Bloomfield; **Delhi** Amit Verma, Rahul Kumar, Narender Kumar, Ravi Yadav, Debojit Borah, Rakesh Kumar, Ganesh Sharma, Shisir Basumatari
Marketing & Publicity: **London** Liz Statham, Niki Hanmer, Louise Maher, Jess Carter, Vanessa Godden, Vivienne Watton, Anna Paynton, Rachel Sprackett, Libby Jellie, Laura Vipond, Vanessa McDonald; **New York** Katy Ball, Judi Powers, Nancy Lambert; **Delhi** Ragini Govind
Manager India: Punita Singh
Reference Director: Andrew Lockett
Operations Manager: Helen Phillips
PA to Publishing Director: Nicola Henderson
Publishing Director: Martin Dunford
Commercial Manager: Gino Magnotta
Managing Director: John Duhigg

Publishing information

This ninth edition published May 2009 by
Rough Guides Ltd,
80 Strand, London WC2R 0RL
14 Local Shopping Centre, Panchsheel Park, New Delhi 110017, India
Distributed by the Penguin Group
Penguin Books Ltd,
80 Strand, London WC2R 0RL
Penguin Group (USA)
375 Hudson Street, NY 10014, USA
Penguin Group (Australia)
250 Camberwell Road, Camberwell,
Victoria 3124, Australia
Penguin Group (Canada)
195 Harry Walker Parkway N, Newmarket, ON, L3Y 7B3 Canada
Penguin Group (NZ)
67 Apollo Drive, Mairangi Bay, Auckland 1310, New Zealand
Cover concept by Peter Dyer.
Typeset in Bembo and Helvetica to an original design by Henry Iles.

Printed in Italy by L.E.G.O. S.p.A, Lavis (TN)

1112pp includes index

A catalogue record for this book is available from the British Library

ISBN: 978-1-84836-031-0

1 3 5 7 9 8 6 4 2

Help us update

We've gone to a lot of effort to ensure that the ninth edition of **The Rough Guide to Italy** is accurate and up-to-date. However, things change – places get "discovered", opening hours are notoriously fickle, restaurants and rooms raise prices or lower standards. If you feel we've got it wrong or left something out, we'd like to know, and if you can remember the address, the price, the hours, the phone number, so much the better.

Please send your comments with the subject line "**Rough Guide Italy Update**" to ⓒ mail@roughguides.com. We'll credit all contributions and send a copy of the next edition (or any other Rough Guide if you prefer) for the very best emails.

Have your questions answered and tell others about your trip at
ⓦ community.roughguides.com

Acknowledgements

Martin Dunford would like to thank Massimiliano at *Casa Howard* and Cory at the *Hotel Navona* in Rome, Katie Parla for drinks, pizza and wisdom on Rome and Naples and some great Naples listings – and, as ever, the gang: Caroline, Daisy and Lucy.

Celia Woolfrey would like to thank Roberto Peretta and Orietta Olivetti for their great company and their help and guidance; Sabina de Lorenzo in Bolzano, Beate Mitterstieler at Vigiljoch and Renate Ortner in Merano for their kind hospitality; Amanda Monroe at Rail Europe Ltd; Alessandro and Paola Brenna for their apartment and car in Bormio, and finally a big thank you to Martin Gee for his patience, support and good humour – even after long days on the road and unexpected hikes at 3000m.

Charles Hebbert would like to thank Caroline, Craigie, Maria Teresa and Leonardo.

Jeffrey Kennedy would like to thank Jean-François Martin, Hanna & Aldo Parodi, Marla Gulley & Fabrizio Roncaglia, Clark Lawrence, Bruno Rota, and a special thanks to Erika Carpaneto

Natasha Foges would like to thank Will for his good humour, careful driving and *nuraghi*-spotting skills.

Joe Fullman: a very big thank you to everyone in Italy who took the time to help me out – in particular Marco in Bologna, Carlo in Rimini and Giulia in Parma. Biggest thanks go to my parents for letting me use their house and for providing cheerful accompaniment on several of my trips, to Charles and Cynthia for the kind loan of their Marche home – don't worry, the secret of Montevecchio will remain safe with me – and to Nicola for remaining ever-lovely.

Matthew Teller would like to thank Alessandra Smith, Adriana Vacca and Stefania Gatta of ENIT, London; Miria Sanzone and Irene Lilla, Distretto dei Laghi, Stresa; Jennifer at Orta San Giulio tourist office; Giuseppe Pisilli, Provincia di Como; Laura Maglia and Francesca Zuccoli, Provincia di Lecco; Alessandra Pitocchi, Turismo Bergamo; Armando Pederzoli and colleagues, Comune di Brescia; Francesca Fiorilli at "Lago di Garda è…"; Patricia, Associazione Albergatori Sirmione; Marta Cobelli, Consorzio Riviera dei Limoni, Gargnano; and Lucy Ratcliffe for impeccable Milan material.

Readers' letters

Thanks to all the readers who have taken the time to write in with comments and suggestions (and apologies if we've inadvertently omitted or misspelt anyone's name):

Clare Argent, John Banfield, Ellen Baurichter, Julia Blackburn, Geoffrey Boyfield, Elise Bruhl, Kay Burtenshaw, Joost den Butter, Pauline Chambers, Rob Clements, Will Cyphers, Anna Dalton, VIctoria Fu, Alexandra Goulding, Judith Hale, Jeff Hennessey, Margaret Hughes, John Hunt, Kate and Bryn Jones, Sheila and Milo Kane, Cluadia Lopez, Dr Amruta Lotlikar, Catherine Mason, Jack Nowicki, Karen Palmer, Maureen Rees, Giulia Savini, Zoe Schoenfeld, Maureen Sheldon, Nina Skaya, Alan Smith, Dr Julia Speht, HP & G Stoffel, Susan Stonard, Kirsty Stone, Bill and Carolyn Thomas, Martin Thomas, Susan Whitby, Emily Van Evera, Stefanie van der Gracht, Susan Whitby, Peter Wilkes

Photo credits

All photos © Rough Guides except the following:

SMALL PRINT

Index

Map entries are in colour

INDEX

O

Map symbols

----	International boundary	(i)	Tourist office
---	Chapter division boundary	$\mathbb{C}$	Phone office
---	Provincial boundary	★	Bus stop
	Motorway	♦	Place of interest
	Major road	∴	Ruin
	Minor road	♟	Castle
	Steps	♚	Vineyard
	Pedestrianized street	✉	Post office
	Gate	✈	Airport
	Railway line	⊞	Hospital
	Funicular railway	🅿	Parking
--Ⓜ--	Metro line and station	⊤	Fountain
•---•	Cable car	✡	Synagogue
-----	Path		Swimming pool
	River	♠	Monastery
-----	Canal route	⋒	Abbey
— —	Ferry route	⚓	Campsite
	Wall	⚑	Church (regional maps)
≍	Bridge		Church (town maps)
𝖳𝖳𝖳𝖳	Rocks		Building
𝆏	Mountain range	⬯	Stadium
⁘	Gorge/cutting		Christian cemetery
▲	Peak		Park
⌂	Cave		Beach
@	Internet		

I

INDEX

1111